Private Letter from Count Metternich to Sir Edward Grey,
March 14, 1912.
(Grey MSS., Vol. 23.)

British Documents on the Origins of the War

1898–1914

Edited by G. P. GOOCH, D.Litt., F.B.A., and HAROLD TEMPERLEY, Litt.D., F.B.A.

Vol. VI

ANGLO-GERMAN TENSION
Armaments and Negotiation, 1907–12

LONDON:

1930

59—2—6

(Crown Copyright Reserved)

Reprinted with the permission of
the Controller of Her Britannic Majesty's Stationery Office

JOHNSON REPRINT CORPORATION
111 Fifth Avenue, New York, N.Y. 10003

JOHNSON REPRINT COMPANY LTD.
Berkeley Square House, London, W.1

First reprinting, 1967, Johnson Reprint Corporation
Printed in the United States of America

VOLUME VI

ANGLO-GERMAN
TENSION
Armaments and Negotiation, 1907-12

Edited by

G. P. GOOCH, D.Litt., and HAROLD TEMPERLEY, Litt.D.,
with the assistance of
LILLIAN M. PENSON, Ph.D.

Table of Contents.

Foreword to Volume VI.

THE decision to publish a selection from the British Documents dealing with the origins of the War was taken by Mr. Ramsay MacDonald, Prime Minister and Secretary of State for Foreign Affairs, in the summer of 1924. It was confirmed and announced by Mr. (now Sir) Austen Chamberlain in a letter of the 28th November, 1924 (published in "The Times" on the 3rd December), addressed to Dr. R. W. Seton-Watson. Some extracts from this letter were published by the Editors in the Foreword to Volume XI, and it need only be said here that the Secretary of State for Foreign Affairs referred to "impartiality and accuracy" as being the necessary qualifications for any work which the Editors were to publish.

The sixth volume deals mainly with Anglo-German relations between 1907 and 1912, and occasionally with British relations with France and Russia as affected thereby. It thus covers the years during which tension increased, and deals with the most important efforts made by negotiation to relax that tension. The main topics of discussion were the question of naval armaments, the possibility of limiting their increase by mutual agreement between Great Britain and Germany, and the German proposal for a political formula as a preliminary to such limitation. The Bagdad railway and the question of Persia were important subsidiary topics. The most serious and definite attempts to solve these problems are to be found in the Bethmann Hollweg proposals of August to December 1909 (Chapter XLV), the Gwinner–Cassel negotiations of 1909–10 (Chapter XLVI, part II), and the long drawn out discussions culminating in the Haldane Mission of 1912 (Chapters XLVIII–XLIX).

During the year 1911 the important question of Morocco brought Great Britain and Germany to the verge of war over the crisis of Agadir. But this very serious incident did not in fact terminate the discussions on limitation of armaments, and is reserved for full separate treatment in the seventh volume.

Apart from Agadir, Anglo-German relations from 1907–12 are given with unusual fulness. The reason for this is that the negotiations at all points were affected by popular and press comment in both countries. Representative extracts from the newspapers have been given, and special care has been taken to reproduce the summaries of the German press provided by Sir Fairfax Cartwright and the impression produced on English statesmen by these opinions. At the same time the reports of British naval experts have been reproduced to show the information on the actual facts of shipbuilding possessed by the British Foreign Office.

Many of the incidents related have been the subject of lively discussion in the press in the past, but the corresponding negotiations have not been equally revealed. It will be found instructive to read the British reply to the German Emperor's letter to Lord Tweedmouth, which took the form of a Memorandum by Sir Edward Grey (pp. 134–5), and to see the diplomatists' view of the German Emperor's interview in the *Daily Telegraph* in 1908 (pp. 201–226).

An authorised text is given of the speech made by Sir Edward Grey on May 26, 1911, before the Committee of Imperial Defence (pp. 781–90). Extracts from this "exposition . . . . of the international situation" were given by Lord Oxford and Asquith in his book on *The Genesis of the War*, but the full text is now reproduced except for a few passages of little importance whose subject matter is indicated. The text has been submitted to Lord Grey, who has added two explanatory footnotes on pp. 786 and 788.

The visits of King Edward VII to Wilhelmshöhe (pp. 43–6), to Cronberg (pp. 173–200), and to Berlin (pp. 227–237) are fully described in Sir Charles Hardinge's important reports, special interest attaching to the discussions at Cronberg.

The German Emperor's views during this period are reported very fully in many conversations with diplomatic and other representatives (*e.g.*, pp. 12, 20–1, 92–4, 96–8, 111–2, 137–8, 175–8, 181–90, 233–6, 281, 434–5, 437–8, 441, 530–3, 543). One of the rare conversations with the Emperor Nicholas II is reported on pp. 465–6. There are important conversations with Admiral von Tirpitz (pp. 1–3, 255–6, 515–7). Those with the two German Chancellors of the period are too numerous to particularize; but special attention may be called to those between Herr von Bethmann Hollweg and Lord Haldane during the Haldane Mission which are now for the first time described in full from the British side.

The British version of the well-known conversation between Sir Henry Campbell-Bannerman and M. Clemenceau on April 9, 1907, is here given (pp. 22–7), and the other conversations with the French statesman in August (pp. 157–8) and December 1908 (pp. 168–9) are also printed.

Some important minutes of Sir Eyre Crowe will be found on pp. 11, 13, 109–10, 533–6.

A most valuable addition to the sources previously used by the Editors is provided by the private papers of Sir Charles (now Baron) Hardinge, which have now been kindly placed at the disposal of the Editors. They were not available until after the preparation of this volume was nearly complete, and it was possible therefore to reproduce only a few of the documents. Among those printed in the present volume there is an important memorandum by Sir Edward Grey given to His Majesty King Edward VII before the interview with the Emperor William at Cronberg (p. 779), from which an extract was quoted by Sir Sidney Lee in his *Life of King Edward VII*, a private letter from Sir E. Goschen upon the Bethmann Hollweg negotiations which is printed on p. 287, and an interesting statement by Lord Salisbury in 1896 on British Foreign Policy which was sent to Sir C. Hardinge in September 1908 (p. 780). The collection is valuable for the whole period 1906–10 and further documents of this time will ultimately be published. Since the publication of Lord Newton's *Life of Lord Lansdowne*, the present Marquis of Lansdowne has kindly given the Editors access to his father's private correspondence. They have been thus enabled to discover that the official report by Sir Edmund Monson on King Edward's reception in Paris in May 1903 is the only important piece of information on the subject, and that the private correspondence reveals nothing further on this subject (pp. 762–8). These private papers, added to those of Sir Edward (Viscount) Grey, and of Sir Arthur Nicolson (Lord Carnock), for the first time enable a full record of British diplomacy of the period to be given. It is hoped in a concluding volume to publish selections from the papers of the late Lord Lansdowne and Lord Hardinge in so far as they deal with periods covered by the volumes already published, with other information discovered since the publication of the earlier volumes.

It may perhaps be necessary for the Editors to explain here the character of the private correspondence of the Secretary of State with the diplomats or Foreign Office subordinates. Lord Salisbury appears to have been an exception to the rule both of his predecessors and his successors in the fact that in some cases he recorded official conversations in correspondence which was treated as private. All the evidence shows that Lord Lansdowne and Sir Edward Grey did nothing of the kind. Their private correspondence is not, as in some other countries, of semi-official or demi-official kind. It is familiar in character and intended merely to supplement or colour the dryness of official communications. The whole tenour of the correspondence shows that the letters were not intended for publication. The purport of the private letters of Lord Carnock and Lord Hardinge appears to be exactly stated in a letter written by Lord Grey to Dr. Gooch on February 5, 1929: " I did not see Carnock's papers when I was writing [*i.e., Twenty-Five Years*], but he and Hardinge used to show me private letters that they received at the time when I was S[ecretary] of S[tate]. I did not, however, regard anything except my own letters and official papers as deciding policy."

It may be added, as was stated with regard to interviews with Russian diplomats in Volume IV, that there do not seem to have been any conversations of importance with German diplomats during the period covered by this volume of which some written evidence is not here published.

In accordance with the practice of the Foreign Office already observed in the case of Volumes I, II, III, IV, V and XI of the series, the documents in the present volume containing information supplied or opinions expressed by certain Foreign Governments have been communicated to them for their agreement. The response in this volume has been quite satisfactory.

The Editors have inserted asterisks to indicate gaps or omissions in documents. As a rule these gaps are due to the unimportance of the matter omitted, in which case an indication of subject is usually given. In a few instances they are due to a desire to consult the susceptibilities of the persons or the Governments concerned. The Editors have, however, omitted nothing which they consider essential to the understanding of the history of the period. They think it well here to repeat their statements made in the preface to previous volumes, that they would feel compelled to resign if any attempt were made to insist on the omission of any document which is in their view vital or essential. In addition to despatches and telegrams, there are memoranda and minutes which are properly official documents. No objection has been raised by His Majesty's Secretary of State for Foreign Affairs to the publication in this volume of any documents of the above kind, nor to the publication of certain similar papers or of private letters, which are not properly official documents, but which are preserved in the Foreign Office.

His Majesty the King has graciously consented to the publication of Minutes and other papers by King Edward. The Editors have also to acknowledge assistance given to them in several ways by the late Lord Carnock, by Lord Grey in connexion with the reproduction of his speech of May 26, 1911, by Lord Newton, whose biography of Lord Lansdowne has now been published, and by Mr. Marcus Dawkins in connexion with Lord Lansdowne's private papers. In conclusion, the Editors desire to acknowledge the friendly assistance and advice of various officials at the Foreign Office, among whom they would like to mention the Librarian, Mr. Stephen Gaselee, C.B.E., the late Sir J. W. Headlam-Morley, formerly Historical Adviser, and Mr. J. W. Field. They are also indebted to Captain G. Alliston for his work in the preparation of the map illustrating the Bagdad Railway negotiations. They wish also to thank Sir Maurice Hankey and others at the Committee of Imperial Defence for their assistance, Sir Robert Holland of the India Office, the officials of the Record Office in London, Mr. Wright, who is in charge of the Diplomatic and Embassy Archives formerly at Cambridge and now at Canterbury, and Miss Priscilla BoysSmith, B.A., who assisted in the preparation of the volume for press.

G. P. GOOCH.

HAROLD TEMPERLEY.

Note on the Technical Arrangements of Documents, &c.

THE technical arrangement and details of the volume are very similar in principle to those of Volumes III and IV. The material deals mainly with one subject, Anglo-German relations in 1907–12. The amount of detail, however, is greater than in those volumes, no part of the subject having been already treated in Parliamentary Papers.

Within the chapters and their sub-sections, the papers are placed in chronological order as in previous volumes; and, as before, chronological order means the date of despatch, whether to or from London, not the date of receipt. The latter is added wherever possible, and readers should be careful to note it.

Most of the documents are taken from the official series of Foreign Office papers in the Public Record Office. The classification of these papers for the period 1898–1905 was thus described in the note prefaced to Volumes I and II (p. ix) :—

"They are classified mainly by country (F.O. France, etc.) and within countries by years. For each year the diplomatic documents are separated from the commercial and other classes. Within the diplomatic class there are volumes of outgoing and incoming despatches, outgoing and incoming telegrams, communications with the Foreign Ambassador ('Domestic') and with other Government Departments ('Various'). Papers relating to certain subjects have been specially treated. Some have been placed together in a miscellaneous series (F.O. General), as in the case of The Hague Peace Conference. In other instances all papers relating to a certain geographical area have been placed together, as with African affairs (after 1899) and the affairs of Morocco. Correspondence with the British representative of Paris or elsewhere appears in these cases under F.O. Africa or F.O. Morocco. A third method was to separate the correspondence relating to a special aspect of affairs from the other papers of the country concerned, thus removing them from chronological sequence. This was the case with despatches on African affairs down to 1899, which appear in special series of F.O. France (Africa), F.O. Germany (Africa), etc."

The Note prefaced to Volume III (pp. ix–x) described further the arrangement inuagurated at the beginning of 1906 :—

"A new system was inaugurated at the beginning of the year 1906. From that date all papers, irrespective of country, are first divided into certain general categories, 'Political' (the former 'Diplomatic'), Commercial, Consular, Treaty, etc. The papers are, however, not removed from their original files, the contents of each file being treated as one document. The files of papers are classified within the general categories according to the country to which their subject most properly belongs. The volumes containing papers relating to any country are therefore in a sub-section of the main series, and these sub-sections are arranged in alphabetical order, (e.g., Political, Abyssinia, etc.). Previously the correspondence with, say, the British Ambassador at Paris was kept distinct from the communications of the French Ambassador in London, the latter being termed 'Domestic.' This distinction is now abolished, and all papers relating to a subject are placed together in one file or in a series of files. The historian finds many difficulties in this arrangement, as the files are not arranged in the volumes in chronological or alphabetical sequence. The Foreign Office overcomes these difficulties by compiling a manuscript register of the contents, but this method cannot be used so satisfactorily by the historian. It is to be feared that the new arrangement makes it more difficult for the historian to be sure he has found all the papers relating to a given incident."

The Editors are informed that the system or arrangement started in 1906 will be continued for the remainder of the period down to the outbreak of the War; but at present this process or arrangement in bound volumes has only reached the year 1908. Beyond this date the documents are still at the Foreign Office in the original loose files, and have not been sorted into any regular sequence. The task of surveying the available material is thus one of great difficulty. The Editors hope that it has been fulfilled adequately by the combination of three methods. A large proportion of the more important papers are printed in the bound volumes of the many series of the "Confidential Print," and from the references given in these access to the originals in the Foreign Office files is easy. The printed texts can then be checked and the notes and minutes reproduced from the originals. For the subject of the present volume the "Confidential Print" has been particularly valuable, as most of the papers relating to Anglo-German negotiations in 1910–12 were printed together in two volumes termed "Limitation of Armaments." Secondly, application has been made to the Foreign Office library staff for papers to which accidental reference has been found. Thirdly, the Foreign Office registers of despatches and telegrams sent to or received from every British Embassy or Legation have been at the disposal of the Editors for the purpose of searching for documents not otherwise to be found. It is hoped that by the use of these means the danger of material omissions has been overcome; but the position is not nearly so satisfactory as in the period for which strict chronological series exist.

The use of the Embassy archives to supplement the documents found in the Foreign Office series has not been possible for the period and subjects with which this volume is concerned. With the exception of Japan (to 1910) and Russia, the Embassies and Legations have not yet sent to England papers of any date after 1905. The Editors have already recorded in previous volumes their regret for this serious handicap to their work. It is especially to be regretted since in collecting the material used for this volume a few documents have been found in the " Confidential Print " for which no original is traceable in the Foreign Office archives. In each case a note is attached stating that the text has been taken from the "Confidential Print." This was not the case in Volumes IV and V, and its rarity in the present volume makes it unnecessary for the Editors to alter their judgment that the records are more exact and complete after 1906.

The private collections available at the Foreign Office have again been found of great value. Many letters have been printed from the private correspondence of Sir Edward (Lord) Grey and from that of Sir Arthur Nicolson (Lord Carnock). The papers of Sir Charles (Lord) Hardinge have now been made available for future use, as have those of Lord Lansdowne. Sir Charles Hardinge's memoranda upon King Edward's visits have once more been quoted in full, and his private collection of papers has made possible the tracing of some documents which would not otherwise have been available.

The value of minutes continues to increase as a later period is reached, and the present volume contains many of great interest by King Edward, Sir Edward Grey, Sir Charles Hardinge, Sir Arthur Nicolson, Mr. Eyre Crowe, and others.

Plan of Volume VI.

Chapter XLII deals with Anglo-German Relations during 1907. The larger portion is devoted to the reports of Captain Dumas, the British Naval Attaché at Berlin, on naval propaganda and shipbuilding; the visits of King Edward to Gaeta and Wilhelmshöhe; and summaries of the abundant comment in the German press. The second part of the Chapter (pp. 78–107) describes the German Emperor's visit to England, and includes some important memoranda by Sir Edward Grey and Mr. Haldane on the Bagdad Railway (pp. 91–9).

The year 1908 is the subject of *Chapter XLIII.* The principal topics are the German Emperor's letter to Lord Tweedmouth; the visit of King Edward to Cronberg, where an important conversation on the naval rivalry took place between the Emperor and Sir Charles Hardinge (pp. 173–200); and the *Daily Telegraph* interview (pp. 201–226).

King Edward's visit to Berlin opens *Chapter XLIV*, which is concerned with England and Germany during the larger part of the year 1909. The subject of British and German Naval Programmes is dealt with in the second section of the chapter, and the important question of the building of Austro-Hungarian Dreadnoughts is also discussed (pp. 269–70).

Chapter XLV contains a full discussion of the naval and neutrality proposals initiated by the new German Chancellor Herr von Bethmann Hollweg in August 1909 in the hope of restoring friendly relations with Great Britain.

The negotiations concerned with the Bagdad Railway between 1905 and 1910 fill the whole of *Chapter XLVI.* The discussions of 1909–10 between Dr. Gwinner and Sir Ernest Cassel are the theme of the second and concluding section.

Chapter XLVII relates to Anglo-German negotiations during the year 1910. The chief topics of discussion are the Bagdad Railway and the Persian question, in which Russia as well as Germany was interested. In the autumn the naval negotiations again became of importance, and consideration of a naval and political agreement was resumed, but no progress towards a solution was made.

Chapter XLVIII continues the naval and neutrality negotiations from January 1911 to February 1912. A summary of the discussions from April 1909 to May 1911 is provided in a Memorandum by Sir Eyre Crowe (pp. 631–6). These negotiations, though interrupted by the Agadir crisis, were not terminated by that incident, which is reserved for treatment in Volume VII; for the problems were once more discussed during the Haldane Mission of 1912, which forms the subject of *Chapter XLIX.* Lord Haldane's Diary of his visit to Berlin is reproduced in full together with all relevant papers, and the attempt to reach agreement on naval strength and neutrality is traced up to the summer of 1912 when it was finally abandoned.

The *Appendices* deal with various subjects. *Appendix I* contains two despatches describing King Edward's visit to Paris in 1903 which was not found until after Volume II had been published. *Appendix II* gives the despatch of Captain Dumas of February 1, 1907, to which a reference is made on pp. 13–4. *Appendix III* supplies an additional Memorandum from the Hardinge MSS. prepared for the Cronberg interview in 1908. *Appendix IV* provides an interesting extract from a letter of Lord Salisbury of August 31, 1896, explaining his general views on foreign policy. *Appendix V* reports Sir Edward Grey's speech to the Dominion Delegates at the Imperial Conference at the Committee of Imperial Defence on May 26, 1911. The sixth *Appendix* contains a memorandum communicated to Tewfik Pasha on September 23, 1909, describing the conditions on which Great Britain would consent to the raising of the Turkish customs duties. The seventh gives a memorandum sent to Sir E. Cassel by Sir H. Babington Smith setting forth Dr. Gwinner's proposals with reference to British participation in the Bagdad Railway. The last *Appendix* contains the text of a despatch to Count de Salis of November 26, 1907, describing a conversation between Sir Edward Grey and Count Metternich upon the Bagdad Railway question.

Erratum.

Page 101, *Note* (¹) to *Ed. note*, line 2. For " M. Sevastropoulo " read " M. Sevastopoulo."

List of Principal Editorial Notes.

List of Abbreviations.

A. & P.... ... ... British Parliamentary Papers, *Accounts and Papers.*

B. F. S. P. ... ... *British and Foreign State Papers.*

D. D. F.... ... ... *Documents Diplomatiques Français.*

G. P. ... ... *Die Grosse Politik der Europäischen Kabinette.*

Ö-U. A. ... ... *Österreich-Ungarns Aussenpolitik, 1908–14.*

Siebert ... ... B. de Siebert: *Entente Diplomacy and the World,* edited, arranged and annotated by G. A. Schreiner (New York and London, 1921).

[This is an English translation,([1]) with the addition of a chronological list of documents by the American Editor of *Diplomatische Aktenstücke zur Geschichte der Ententepolitik der Vorkriegsjahre* (Berlin and Leipzig, 1921).

Siebert-Benckendorff.. This refers to a new German edition of the above by Herr von Siebert, containing a number of additions. It is entitled *Graf Benckendorffs Diplomatischer Schriftwechsel* (Berlin and Leipzig, 1928).

([1]) [The Editors have followed the rule in this and other cases of citing an English edition where possible. Thus they have given references to the Emperor William II's *My Memoirs* (1922) and not to *Ereignisse und Gestalten* (1922.)]

Names of Writers of Minutes.

F. D. A. = Mr. F. D. Acland ... ... Parliamentary Under-Secretary of State for Foreign Affairs, 1911-5.

H. H. A. = Mr. H. H. (later Earl of Oxford and) Asquith — Prime Minister and First Lord of the Treasury, 1908-16.

E. B. = Sir Eric Barrington ... ... Private Secretary to the Marquess of Lansdowne, 1900-5; Assistant Under-Secretary of State for Foreign Affairs, 1906-7.

F. A. C. = Mr. (later Sir F.) Campbell ... ... Assistant Under-Secretary of State for Foreign Affairs, 1902-11.

R. H. C. = Mr. R. H. Campbell ... ... Clerk in the Foreign Office, 1907; Acting 3rd Secretary in the Diplomatic Service, 1910; Private Secretary to Sir A. Nicolson, 1913-6.

E. A. C. = Mr. (later Sir E.) Crowe ... ... Senior Clerk, Foreign Office, 1906-12; Assistant Under-Secretary of State for Foreign Affairs, 1912-20; Permanent Under-Secretary of State for Foreign Affairs, 1920-5.

F. = Baron Fitzmaurice of Leigh ... ... Parliamentary Under-Secretary of State for Foreign Affairs, 1905-8.

E. G[orst] = Sir Eldon Gorst ... ... Assistant Under-Secretary of State for Foreign Affairs, 1904-7; Agent and Consul-General in Egypt, 1907-11.

E. G. = Sir Edward (later Viscount) Grey (of Fallodon) — Secretary of State for Foreign Affairs December 11, 1905-December 11, 1916.

C. H. = Sir Charles (later Baron) Hardinge (of Penshurst) — Assistant Under-Secretary of State for Foreign Affairs, 1903-4; Ambassador at St. Petersburgh, 1904-6; Permanent Under-Secretary of State for Foreign Affairs, 1906-10; Viceroy and Governor-General of India, 1910-6.

W. L. = Mr. (later Sir) W. Langley ... ... Senior Clerk, Foreign Office, 1902-7; Assistant Under-Secretary of State for Foreign Affairs, 1907-18.

L. = The Marquess of Lansdowne ... ... Secretary of State for Foreign Affairs, November 12, 1900-December 11, 1905.

R. C. L. = Mr. (later Sir) R. Lindsay ... ... 2nd Secretary of British Embassy at Washington, 1905-7; at Paris, 1907-8; Assistant Private Secretary to Sir E. Grey, 1908-9; 2nd Secretary at The Hague; 1st Secretary, 1911-2.

L. M. = Mr. (later Sir) Louis Mallet ... ... Private Secretary to Sir E. Grey, 1905-6; Senior Clerk, 1906-7; Assistant Under-Secretary of State for Foreign Affairs, 1907-13.

R. P. M. = Mr. R. P. Maxwell ... ... Senior Clerk, Foreign Office, 1902–13.

M. = Mr. (later Viscount) Morley (of Black- Secretary of State for India, 1905–10, and
burn) March–May, 1911; Lord President of the
Council, 1910–4.

H. N. = Mr. H. C. Norman ... ... 2nd Secretary at St. Petersburgh, 1903–6;
employed in Foreign Office, 1906–14; Coun-
cillor at Buenos Aires, 1914.

A. P. = Mr. A. Parker ... ... Junior Clerk, Foreign Office, 1906–12; Assistant
Clerk, 1912–7; Librarian, 1918–9.

G. S. S. = Mr. G. S. Spicer ... ... Private Secretary to Sir T. Sanderson,
1903–6; and to Sir C. Hardinge, 1906;
Assistant Clerk, 1906–12; Senior Clerk,
1912–9.

W. T. = Mr. W. G. (later Baron) Tyrrell ... Senior Clerk, 1907–18; Private Secretary to
Sir E. Grey, 1907–15; Assistant Under-
Secretary of State for Foreign Affairs,
1918–25; Permanent Under-Secretary,
1925–8; Ambassador at Paris, 1928–

G. H. V. = Mr. G. H. Villiers ... ... Clerk in Foreign Office, 1903–13

List of King Edward's Minutes.

[Attached to the following documents.]

LIST OF DOCUMENTS.

Chapter XLII.
Anglo-German Relations, 1907.

I.—GENERAL.

b 2

II.—THE VISIT OF THE EMPEROR WILLIAM II TO WINDSOR, NOVEMBER 1907.

Chapter XLIII.
Great Britain, France and Germany, 1908.

I.—GENERAL RELATIONS.

III.—THE "DAILY TELEGRAPH" INTERVIEW.

Chapter XLIV.

Great Britain and Germany, January–July 1909.

I.—KING EDWARD'S VISIT TO BERLIN.

II.—NAVAL PROGRAMMES, JANUARY–JULY 1909.

Chapter XLV.

Herr von Bethmann Hollweg's Proposals, August–December 1909.

Chapter XLVI.

The Bagdad Railway, 1905–10.

I.—INTERNATIONAL POURPARLERS, 1905–9.

     c

II.—THE GWINNER–CASSEL NEGOTIATIONS, 1909–10.

c 3

Chapter XLVII.

Anglo-German Negotiations, 1910.

Chapter XLVIII.

Naval Negotiations, January 1911–February 1912.

Chapter XLIX.

The Haldane Mission, 1912.

Appendix I.

No.	Name.	Date.	Main Subject.	Page
—	(a) *From* Sir E. Monson...	1903. 5 May (*Recd. 5 May*)	King Edward's visit to Paris	762
—	(b) ,, ,, ...	8 May (*Recd. 9 May*)	Same subject	763

Appendix II.

—	*From* Sir F. Lascelles	1907. 1 Feb. (*Recd. 4 Feb.*)	Enclosing naval report from Captain Dumas	769

Appendix III.

—	Memorandum by Sir E. Grey	1908. 31 July	Notes given to King Edward VII in view of Cronberg interview	779

Appendix IV.

—	Communication from Mr. Iwan-Müller	1908. 29 Sept.	Extract from a letter from Lord Salisbury of August 31, 1896	780

Appendix V.

—	Extract from Minutes of the Committee of Impe- rial Defence	1911. 26 May	Speech by Sir E. Grey	781

Appendix VI.

—	Memorandum communi- cated to Tewfik Pasha	1909. 23 Sept.	British position as regards the 4 per cent. increase of the customs dues	791

Appendix VII.

No.	Name.	Date.	Main Subject.	Page
—	The Gwinner proposals as regards Bagdad Railway	1909. Nov.	Memorandum by Sir H. Babington Smith of his conversation with Dr. Gwinner...	793

Appendix VIII.

| — | *To* Count de Salis | 1907. 26 Nov. | *Conversation* with Count Metternich: interests of the Powers in Bagdad Railway ... ... | 795 |

CHAPTER XLII.

ANGLO-GERMAN RELATIONS, 1907.

I.—GENERAL.

No. 1.

Sir F. Lascelles to Sir Edward Grey.

F.O. 371/257.

(No. 15.)   Confidential.   *Berlin, D. January* 10, 1907.

Sir,   R. *January* 14, 1907.

I have the honour to enclose a very interesting report by Captain Dumas of a conversation he has had with Admiral von Tirpitz,(¹) who, I understand, is suspected in certain quarters in England of a desire to take a favourable opportunity of attacking England, and is believed here to share the apprehensions which I hope are less generally entertained than they were a year ago, that England intended to attack Germany. I had myself a short conversation with Admiral von Tirpitz a few days ago, in which I told him that there were people in England who really believed that the German fleet were being constructed solely with the view of an attack upon England. His Excellency scouted the idea as ridiculous and impossible and was at a loss to understand how anyone in England could really believe it. I can only hope that Captain Dumas' plain and straightforward language to Admiral von Tirpitz may have the effect of making His Excellency understand that the fear entertained in Germany of an attack by England is as baseless as the fear entertained in England of an attack by Germany.

I may add that, before calling upon Admiral von Tirpitz, Captain Dumas asked whether I saw any objection to his broaching this subject, as well as the question of disarmament at the forthcoming Hague Conference, and that I had expressed the opinion that he would do well to do so.

I have, &c.

FRANK C. LASCELLES.

Enclosure in. No. 1.

Captain Dumas to Sir F. Lascelles.

F.O. 371/257.

Confidential.

Your Excellency,   *Berlin, January* 9, 1907.

I have the honour to submit the following Report of a conversation I had this morning with his Excellency Admiral von Tirpitz, on whom I was paying the customary New Year's visit. I commenced by thanking his Excellency for the courtesy with which I had been treated by his officers during the year and then expressed—which I had been directed to do, on the part of my Lords Commissioners of the Admiralty—the regret and total lack of sympathy they felt at and with the publication of such tasteless and mischief-making cartoons as had lately appeared in "Punch" and which, I am told, has caused much offence in Germany. His Excellency expressed himself as very sensible of this courtesy, and deplored the stupidity of the press, who did not really reflect the state of feeling existing between the two countries, although he could not deny that the withdrawal of our ships from

---

(¹) [The account of this conversation by Admiral von Tirpitz is given in Admiral von Tirpitz : *Politische Dokumente. Der Aufbau der deutschen Weltmacht* (Stuttgart and Berlin, 1924), pp. 53–5.]

the Mediterranean and the posting of a fleet at Sheerness had given rise to a feeling here that the British Admiralty was preparing for a war with Germany. He acknowledged that we had a perfect right to do so, especially in view of a possible alliance with France; but the public were not able to grasp that, and so looked upon the arrangement of our fleets as a sort of a menace.

I said, of course we were preparing for a war with everyone, but that was the duty of an Admiralty—to which his Excellency assented—and did not mean at all that we wanted one, in fact I was quite sure that we did not.

I also pointed out that if that was the feeling here, very much the same sort of thing regarding his Excellency existed in England, and, to speak plainly, if sinister designs on the part of England were suspected here, I believed that exactly the same sort of feeling regarding Germany existed in England; and that, if I was correct, every effort should be made, by bringing naval officers on both sides together, to remove it.

His Excellency became very excited, and said, "Good Heavens, whatever have I said or done to give rise to such an opinion? If I had wished for or harboured such designs, I could have doubled our navy last year; whereas, in fact, I have done nothing of the sort. Besides, how could I dream of attacking England with a navy less than a quarter the size? I have much too high a respect for your officials to believe that such an opinion can be seriously entertained."

I ventured to point out that I had not said that it was an official opinion, but probably just as ill-founded as those he had mentioned to me as existing in Germany and held by just the same class.

He also pointed out that any such attack could but result in "the temporary commercial ruin of Germany and would be a crime and a bad blunder."

He went on to say that he loved England, his wife and daughters were educated there, and he had numberless friends in the country, and that it was impossible to imagine that Germany, and he more than any of his countrymen, could be suspected.

He said, further, that it was simpler to understand that Germany might fear the designs of England, who, he knew, had offered to lend France 200,000 men last spring, but that assistance would have been helpless against the 4,000,000 men Germany could put into the field; to which I assented; and said his Excellency must therefore acknowledge that we, knowing that, could never really have made such a useless offer, which, I think, rather astonished his Excellency.

He spoke, further, of the newspapers, and said that while in his own country they were like private-owned tramp steamers who went wherever it paid them most, in England they were like a well-organized private-owned line of steamers, who altered their route and destination *en masse* at the orders of the political clubs, and it was through them that much might be done to improve the tone of the press.

However, he went on, naval officers are the best of friends, and plain speaking is of enormous value, and I am therefore greatly obliged to you for telling me what you have so straightforwardly.

He then spoke of disarmament, and I in my turn called his Excellency's attention to the very strong remarks made in the German papers last summer regarding England's honesty of purpose in the matter, and expressed my belief that the British Government were perfectly serious in bringing this matter forward at the forthcoming Hague Conference.

He said, "Yes, perhaps it is true; but our people do not and will never understand such a scheme. I myself realize the Puritan form of thought such as is possessed by Sir Henry Campbell-Bannerman, and that he is perfectly honest and feels it a religious duty; but look at the facts. Here is England, already more than four times as strong as Germany, in alliance with Japan, and probably so with France, and you, the colossus, come and ask Germany, the pigmy, to disarm. From the point of view of the public it is laughable and Machiavellian, and we shall never agree to anything of the sort.

Also, look at the past year. What have you done? Why, you have built faster than you have ever done before; and we, why, we have gone quietly on with our programme of old construction, and laid down nothing new at all. Which country has done anything? Yours or mine? I am prepared to acknowledge that it is a correct religious aspiration, but not practical for people who live in the world. We have decided to possess a fleet, and that fleet I propose to build and keep strictly to my programme."

We had some further conversation, but of no particular interest, and I left; but I would remark that his Excellency was far more cordial in his manner than he has ever been before.

I also called to-day on Admiral von Müller, Chief of the Kaiser's Marine Cabinet, to whom I expressed the same sentiments on behalf of our Admiralty regarding the objectionable cartoon, and he also expressed his great obligations for this courtesy. He also spoke of The Hague Conference, and said it was futile to expect Germany to consider disarming.

He further expressed a hope that our fleets might meet this year, and spoke of the pleasure with which he himself renewed his old acquaintanceships in the British navy.

Lastly, he mentioned Captain-Lieutenant Widenmann, the proposed new German Naval Attaché in London, and said he had selected an officer with every English sympathy, and who, having served under Admiral Koerper, would more easily take his place.

They were sending a young officer because it was thought that those so senior as Admiral Koerper caused some social difficulties in the Diplomatic world, but Captain-Lieutenant Widenmann would be promoted within the next year.

I have, &c.
PHILIP DUMAS,
Captain and Naval Attaché.

MINUTES.

It was no doubt quite proper in the present instance for the Admiralty to disclaim any sympathy with the recent cartoon in *Punch*—which was neither very judicious nor very funny. But I am not sure that the procedure adopted is quite correct; it might if taken as a precedent, conceivably lead to difficulties. I should say that any apology for or disclaimer of a publication in the English press to a foreign sovereign should not be made without the Secretary of State for F[oreign] A[ffairs] being previously informed. Circumstances could easily be imagined where such an apology would be quite inopportune—though this was not the case in the present instance. Captain Dumas is not only a naval officer speaking for the Admiralty, but also the naval attaché to the embassy, which represents the King and H[is] M[ajesty's] G[overnment]; and these two characters cannot be kept altogether distinct.

E. A. C.
Jan. 14.

In the present case no harm has been done.

E. B.
C. H.

I do not altogether like this conversation. The part about the absurdity of our intending to attack Germany is all right; and also the reference to feeling here as to Germany's designs against us. It was also right to say that we are in earnest in wishing to discuss, not " disarmament," but a reduction of expenditure or anything to arrest further increase of expenditure. This was mooted here last year especially at a time, when it was said that Germany meditated a new and increased programme of naval construction and as a matter of fact our original programme of new construction was cut down partly because Germany was not laying down ships so quickly as had been anticipated, when our programme was drawn up originally. Our programme of new construction will depend greatly upon Germany and it rests with her to force or slacken the pace so far as we are concerned (and indeed so far as France is concerned too). This might have been a comment to meet Admiral von Tirpitz' point that we are doing more than Germany in shipbuilding.

The Admiral's view that the English Press is more organized politically than the German is quite wrong so far as foreign politics are concerned.

None of our officers or diplomatists should discuss with Germans what assistance we may offer or may have offered to France at any time past or future. This should be pointed out to our Embassy at Berlin with a view to possible future conversations.

E. G.

Done privately.

[C. H.]
Jan. 16.

No. 2.

Mr. Cartwright to Sir Edward Grey.

F.O. 371/257.

(No. 2.) Confidential.   *Munich,* D. *January* 12, 1907.

Sir,   R. *January* 21, 1907.

The press of South Germany summarises, as it usually does at the beginning of the year, the more important events of the preceding one. The views expressed by the newspapers are greatly influenced by the colour of their politics and it almost seems as if they could be divided, as to their general views into two groups : the Government organs and the papers of all other shades of politics put together. The organs influenced by the Government see everything *couleur de rose,* except the recent action of the late Reichstag, and for them the past year is one full of success for the Imperial Authorities who found Germany at the beginning of the year in danger of a conflict with foreign Powers over Morocco which peril was conjured away by the ability displayed by them at the Algeciras Conference. For these organs of the press the present new year dawns more brightly than the preceding one for Germany; it cannot be said that any foreign complications are threatening at present and the relations between Great Britain and Germany have been materially improved by the meeting of the Kaiser and King Edward at Cronberg.([1]) The commerce of the country is in a flourishing condition and were it not for the inconsiderate action of the Centre party in the Reichstag, there would be no black spot on the horizon to disturb all good Germans from heartily rejoicing round their Christmas-trees. The more independent newspapers, however, judge matters more critically. As far as I am able to form an opinion the general impression is that it is quite true that the new year opens with a less stormy outlook than the preceding one. The Morocco question is no longer prominent, but if it is not so, it is not due to any remarkable ability shown by the Imperial Government who, in a heedless manner brought Germany into a very difficult position from which she escaped without the horrors of a general war only through the steadfast determination of the Great Powers to compel her to come to a reasonable understanding with regard to the question at issue. For the independent press the peaceful termination of the Algeciras Conference was a blessing to the German people whose interests were not seriously involved in Morocco. Another point over which they rejoice is that, to the great advantage of the country, the Kaiser, since that event, has been somewhat more cautious in handling foreign affairs.

It is noteworthy that as a general rule throughout the press there seems to be a feeling of satisfaction that the past year marked a distinct progress as regards the relations between Great Britain and the Empire and generally speaking allusions to the United Kingdom assume a friendly character.

The most notable point to remember in the foreign policy of Germany during the last few years is the absence of businesslike qualities on which it is conducted. No definite aim appears to have been laid down which is steadfastly pursued in a practical and sensible manner. "Weltpolitik," as understood at Berlin, would appear to be more and more a desire to gain merely notoriety among nations. The Kaiser has dreamed of empire in South Africa and China and his eyes now turn towards South America and perhaps already he may be aspiring to obtain the Crown

---

([1]) [Sir C. Hardinge's account of the Cronberg meeting of August 15–16, 1906, is given in *Gooch & Temperley,* Vol. III, pp. 366–70, No. 425. *cp.* Sir Sidney Lee : *King Edward VII* (1927), Vol. II, pp. 529–31.]

of Jerusalem and the domination over Asia Minor. While the Kaiser is haunted by this idea of worldly grandeur the mass of the population ask only for peace and quiet and to be allowed to acquire wealth by industrial labour.

One of the most serious evils which affect Germany at present is the absence of men of character at the helm of affairs. Little by little Ministers have effaced themselves before the Kaiser and have been reduced to the position of senior Clerks of Departments. Even the Secretary of State for Foreign Affairs is now but an Under-Secretary to the Chancellor who himself has been gradually losing prestige and has become little more than a first Secretary to the Kaiser. His Majesty's personality is more and more dominating every branch of public life. The effect of this on German diplomacy is very marked and should not be lost sight of. Loss of authority in the German Foreign Office leads to demoralisation in the German diplomatic service. The Representatives of Germany abroad try to emancipate themselves from control and are too apt to act on their own initiative. What occupies their thoughts when writing their despatches is the desire of favourably attracting on themselves the notice of the Kaiser and they pay little heed to the correctness of the information they send home or whether their Reports will be useful to the Chancellor. Hence German Diplomatists often sin from excess of zeal and their actions lead the Imperial Government into positions from which retreat is sometimes difficult. Two years ago at Lisbon the German Chargé d'Affaires probably exceeded his instructions in sending to the Portuguese Government what amounted practically to an ultimatum on the Madeira Syndicate Question. At Madrid in the days immediately preceding the fall of Monsieur Delcassé—a period when German Diplomacy was almost in an hysterical state—the German Ambassador, Herr von Radowitz, perfectly terrorised the Spanish Minister of State, the Marquis de Casa Urrutia, probably without the knowledge of Berlin, but all he obtained by his dictatorial attitude was to gain the cordial hatred of the Spanish officials. And yet a few months later Herr von Radowitz complained to a colleague that he was blamed at Berlin for his want of vigour. Many other instances of the brutality of German methods might be cited which would tend to show that the principle upon which German diplomacy seems to act at present is to alternately bully to persuade and flatter to win over, but this Imperial method can hardly be said to have met with much success as regards the relations of the Empire with her neighbour France or with the more distant United States. The belief that German diplomacy is uncertain in its action and is too much influenced by the Kaiser and that it is rather inclined to neglect the real interests of the country in the pursuit of a policy of adventure has a disquieting effect upon foreign public opinion and tends to group foreign countries together against Germany.

This is one of the causes why so little confidence is now held in the efficacy of the Triple Alliance, both in Germany and Austria, the parties most interested in its maintenance at present. Officially every opportunity is taken to remind the world that such a political combination still exists, but the German public, although it is in many questions influenced by the official press, will not allow itself to be deluded by such assertions. That somewhat coarse newspaper " Simplicissimus " which, however, often represents the opinion of the man in the street, recently issued a cartoon which perhaps gives as correct an idea as possible of the general views held there with regard to the Triple Alliance. The cartoon represented this Alliance as a porcelain group in a glass case and underneath was written : " This artistic group is of so delicate a nature that to prevent it from being broken it must be protected by a glass-shade." This general want of confidence in the stability of that Alliance which for so long has been as it were the corner-stone of European Diplomacy, produces a feeling of despondency in this country and uncertainty as to her future—a future moreover seriously threatened by the growing friendship amongst themselves of the other Powers which surround Germany. Although every pretence is made that Germany is so strong that she can stand by herself and that no one can do her harm, yet even in Pan-Germanic circles a want of confidence is expressed in the wisdom of the foreign policy of the Imperial Government who have brought things to this pass and the opinion has been expressed that the nation should be further protected by an increase of armaments : in these the German public have confidence, in their Foreign Office they have none.

With regard to this point I will quote a passage from an article of the Stuttgart "Schwäbische Merkur" of December 29th last, to the effect that the year closes with the international situation in a very critical and uncertain condition and that therefore the words of Cromwell had better be borne in mind by all Germans : "Trust in God and keep your powder dry."

It is greatly to be regretted that a rooted opinion exists in Germany which is largely fostered by the official press that the isolation which the German public dread is due to the manœuvres of the British Government and that it is now a fundamental principle of British policy to labour to bring about a grouping of the Powers which will hold Germany at bay and prevent her from taking a leading part in world policy to which by her size and importance she has a right to aspire. In fact it is one of the unfortunate aspects of the situation here that the Imperial Government through its organs does so much to instil a mistrust in the actions of the British Government and in so many insidious ways labours to keep up a lurking hatred in the public mind against Great Britain. The public is also taught to believe that the liberal Government in England could easily come to terms over every question in dispute between the two countries and pacify definitely any animosities which still continue to exist between the two nations, were it not that in the British Cabinet, as at present constituted, there are Ministers who are inspired by a rooted hatred of Germany and who help to render any genuine and lasting *entente* between the two countries impossible.

As year succeeds year the fact which is most noticeable in German politics is the ever increasing immediate interference of the Kaiser in the direction of home and foreign questions and no attempt is now made to disguise this fact. If I may be allowed to form an opinion it would be that, in South Germany at least, the tendency of the Kaiser to ever increase his autocratic power in the State is not appreciated by the mass of the people, neither has His Majesty gained in prestige by doing so during the past year, nor has the confidence of the public in his judgment been augmented. The uncertainty as to what His Majesty will do next cannot help having a depressing influence on the industrial classes and the business world. The sudden dissolution of the Reichstag seems to be the latest *coup de théâtre* of the Kaiser who at that moment must have been in one of his optimistic moods as to his personal influence on public opinion. Of late, however, the semi-official press shows less confidence as to a satisfactory result from an appeal to the polls and gives expression to querulous complaints as to the attitude assumed by many liberal newspapers in England—who, it is assumed, represent the views of the British Government—in expressing their sympathy with the opposition party in the Reichstag. It would appear, however, that in official circles in Berlin they are still somewhat sanguine as to the results of the elections, at least so I was informed the other day by the Prime Minister of Würtemberg who had just returned from the Imperial capital, but His Excellency said to me that he feared that the new Reichstag would be composed very much like the previous one.

With reference to the sudden dissolution of the Reichstag, it may be of some interest to report that I learn on good authority that two or three days before it took place, Count Lerchenfeld, the Bavarian Representative on the Federal Council at Berlin, came to Munich and reported to Baron von Podewils, the Prime Minister here, that in his opinion the parliamentary difficulty would be solved satisfactorily. The Bavarian Government, and I presume therefore the Governments of the other States of the Empire, were kept entirely in the dark as to the Emperor's resolution and the news of the dissolution came as a perfect surprise to the Bavarian Prime Minister, the Federal Council being only informed of the intentions of the Imperial Government at the last moment. In fact Baron von Podewils did not hide his annoyance at the cavalier manner in which the second largest State in the Empire had been treated by the Imperial Government in the matter of such importance in domestic politics and his annoyance was increased by the vigorous attack made by the Chancellor on the Centre party, a party which is now in power in Bavaria and likely to remain so for a considerable time.

To understand the situation in Germany as it is at the present moment and to be able to forecast the immediate future, too much attention cannot be paid to the character of the Emperor. His moods and thoughts are the pivot on which German home and foreign policy turn. It may be thought perhaps presumptuous on my part if at this distance from Berlin I venture to give you any information on this very delicate matter, but it appears to me that those who live under the shadow of the Emperor, see him day by day and are personally influenced by his charm when he wishes to exert it, are perhaps less capable of forming a true estimate of the total effect of the Kaiser's personality in German politics than those who live a little further away from him. In South Germany the newspapers are more emancipated from control than in Prussia, they are daily becoming more free and outspoken in their criticisms of high persons and high questions and therefore one can learn a great deal by perusing them carefully, for it must be remembered that in this part of the country there is loyalty to the Empire but no affection for Prussia. As an example of this I will mention that on the recent visit of the Emperor to Munich in October last the Regent strongly expressed the hope that the Empress should accompany His Majesty, not, I am told, in order that this might produce a better effect on the population, but because His Royal Highness felt reluctant to engage for forty-eight hours in the exchange of civilities with the Emperor alone. The Empress being present, the Regent could turn all his attentions to her, which he did in a very marked manner.

For the reasons I have just mentioned I venture to make a few observations with regard to the Emperor which are the result of a study of the press and of conversations with persons here.([2]) There seems to be a conviction among well-informed people that the strain to which His Majesty's nervous system has been exposed during recent years has brought about a physical condition in the Kaiser which is much to be deplored and to which must be attributed in great part the ups and downs of his moods, passing from exultant optimism to deep depression. "I am not understood" is what His Majesty is often reported to say when, after he has met with the approval by the men surrounding him for any action he has suddenly resolved to take, he finds to his astonishment a public opinion opposing a passive resistance to his desires; by his habit of selecting for his *entourage* men of colourless opinions, he has put himself into the unfortunate position of being unable to probe seriously below the surface of questions and to learn the reality of things by encouraging contradiction. At moments, however, he begins to realize that there is danger ahead and he feels disheartened, though his confidence in himself is so great that he cannot bring himself to believe that he has really engaged on a wrong path; then, in despair, he makes speeches like the one he delivered at Breslau at the late autumn manœuvres, where in vigorous terms he denounced all those who were opposed to him as pessimists and enemies of the nation.

It is this uncertainty of his moods and humours—hidden in great part from the public—which render it so difficult to follow all the turns and twists of German politics and in this respect I would draw attention to a matter of a somewhat delicate nature, but which I think it will be as well not to lose sight of as it may throw a curious light upon certain actions of His Majesty. I allude to the rumours which many may think puerile and unfounded but which nevertheless appear to me to have some foundation in fact, namely, that the Kaiser at times, in his moments of despondency, has recourse to the society of persons who are either addicted to the

([2]) [Marginal comment by Sir C. Hardinge: "About 20 years ago Mr. Cartwright knew the Emperor, then Prince William, extremely well."]

cult of spiritualism or at least have no antipathy to approach the outskirts of that faith. The Kaiser's love of ideas, his versatility, his buoyancy of spirits, now probably less than in his earlier days, his real generosity of temperament and vivid imagination, tend to make him feel sympathetic towards a state of mind which may be described as that of a mystic. It is well known that the Emperor entertains an old friendship for Prince Philip of Eulenburg who is notorious for the interest he has always shown in the study of spiritualism, and although that nobleman has no direct influence upon politics, still when the Emperor pays him a visit it is not likely that in their conversations they avoid discussing the questions of the day, and it is therefore more than probable that the Prince may then sow ideas in the Emperor's mind which—though they may not blossom at the moment—may do so at a later date. The Prince, however, does not stand alone in the interest he shows in spiritualism : if the talk in society here be correct there are a number of high-born ladies and gentlemen near the Court who follow the same tendencies and who are doing their best to influence the Emperor. Men in such high position as Count Moltke, head of the General Staff, have more than once been mentioned to me as looking with favour on this cult. It is all very well to ridicule the attempts of these people to win the Kaiser over to themselves but they come in contact with him, they flatter him at every opportunity, they wish to make of him an "illuminated" and inspired Emperor, and all these efforts are brought to bear upon a character which always seeks for excitement. The moment may come when their efforts will prove to a certain extent successful and for that reason their manœuvres should be watched as they might have political results in a moment of moral crisis in the Emperor's mind. Many begin with music and epicureanism and end by wishing to consult the spirits; when the latter stage is reached there is no question so foolish that it may not be put to them, nor any action so incomprehensible that it may not be undertaken under their advice. In great people who lead an agitated life there is often the craving to pry into the future; they are not all Wallensteins in military circles at Berlin but like that political soldier of fortune they are apt to be credulous and to desire to seek for information from the modern astrologer, the spiritualistic medium.

If we take into consideration the points which I have attempted to lay before you, especially the last mentioned, the importance of the direct influence of the Emperor in public affairs, the question which we are apt to ask ourselves is what under these circumstances should be the best policy for His Majesty's Government to pursue in dealing with Germany. In trying to find an answer to this question I would venture to suggest that two points should be borne in mind, namely the attitude which should be assumed by His Majesty's Government towards the Imperial Authorities at Berlin, and the attitude they should assume towards the German nation as a whole. The first should be governed by business considerations alone : no concession should be given without an equivalent. Great Britain should act fairly and straightforwardly towards Germany but nothing is to be gained from the Berlin Authorities by servility or show of fear. As regards the second point it seems to me that it would be a wise policy for the British Government to do all that lies in their power to conciliate and to pacify German public opinion and to encourage the development of that natural sympathy which exists between an Englishman and a German, when not of the official class.

It is not unusual for persons who seek to be humorous rather than serious to make light of Royal interviews and visits. But for the masses who occupy themselves but superficially with foreign affairs and scarcely read official or semi-official communications, a Royal interview attracts their attention and they become for them an outward and visible sign that strained relations do not exist between the two countries whose Sovereigns meet in a friendly way. When relations have been strained and animosities have been encouraged and allowed to accumulate, a public meeting between two Sovereigns, though it may not appreciably alter the main line of the policy of their respective Governments, helps nevertheless to produce a *détente* in the public mind and this gives valuable assistance to the efforts of diplomacy to maintain peace.

In connection with this matter I think it only right to say that could it be found possible to confer the Garter upon the aged Prince Regent of Bavaria, it would be not only an honour highly gratifying to His Royal Highness personally but one which would be appreciated throughout this part of Germany. I feel sure that the arrival of a Garter Mission here would be one of those incidents which attract universal attention and would be taken generally in Bavaria as a sign of the friendly disposition felt by King Edward for their Ruler and also, what is perhaps more important, as a token of His Majesty's sincere desire to encourage the development of a kindlier feeling between the two nations.

It is a common fault of foreign diplomatists who live in Berlin to assume that because the German Government is not really a Parliamentary one, therefore little heed need be paid to public opinion which in their view has no appreciable effect on the actions of the Imperial Authorities. This mistake comes from living in the atmosphere of dominant militarism which prevails in Berlin. The Prussian Excellencies are too often engaged in the unfortunate attempt to look down upon Germany from their Pomeranian flats. The heart and nervous centre of the country is not to be found in the north but in the central and southern portions of the Empire; from them—now as in the middle ages—come the artists, the poets and the thinkers of Germany, who exert a vibrating influence on Teutonic life. Prussia is but the fist of the Empire and the evolution which it appears to me is at present going on in Germany, perhaps slowly but surely, is a revolt of the brains of the country against their long subjection to the highly organized material forces of the north. I cannot help observing that public opinion in Germany, and especially in South Germany, is beginning to pronounce itself with much more freedom as the Emperor seeks to assume greater personal authority in the management of public affairs; this awakening of the forces of democracy should not be lost sight of even in a State like the German Empire which is crushed by militarism. The foreign country which has succeeded in calming down irritation against herself in Germany will find that her task is easier in dealing with the Authorities in Berlin, who cannot help taking into some consideration the passive resistance of public opinion in moments of crises. It will become daily more difficult for the Emperor to rush the nation into an adventure when he is made to feel that the public do not approve of his schemes, and for this reason it is wise for every foreign Power to try and conciliate public opinion in Germany and to endeavour in every way to avoid newspaper controversies on trifling matters in an irritating spirit. But although it would certainly be to our advantage in a moment of crisis to have German public opinion not unfavourably disposed towards ourselves as it might exert a restraining influence at Berlin, still it would be a weak reed to rely on the efficacy of such public opinion alone. It was efficacious in the Morocco episode, for the Kaiser then discovered that the public mind was not sympathetic to his schemes. But this success cannot be expected to occur every time. It will be necessary therefore for Great Britain to seek some further protection for herself: where is she to find it?

Here it is necessary for me to make allusion to the colonial question. As already often reported to you the feeling in favour of these Colonies has been at no time very favourable to them and this feeling has grown still more hostile during the past year. The long war in South West Africa and the heavy burdens it has placed upon the nation have disheartened the country with regard to African possessions, and the colonial scandals, revealed in the past year as existing at head-quarters and in the distant Colonies, have produced a profound feeling of despondency among large masses of the population, if not among the upper classes who seem to treat the matter with considerable levity. It is unfortunate for the Kaiser's Government that they should have left the impression on the public mind that they were more intent upon protecting the reputation of their colonial officials than to seek out for the truth with regard to them. It does not render the Kaiser more sympathetic to the electors for the new Reichstag at this moment that he should have assumed the attitude not of a knight struggling against vice but rather of an evil spirit protecting other evildoers. For these reasons it seems to me probable that whatever the results of the coming elections may be, the Imperial Government will find it exceedingly difficult to obtain any large sums of money for carrying out what they are pleased to call their colonial policy.

I cannot, however, too strongly draw your attention to the difference of opinion which exists throughout Germany with regard to the Kaiser's policy as to the Fleet. The Reichstag may be reluctant to spend money on the Colonies but when the Imperial Government comes before it with an urgent appeal for funds for strengthening the Fleet, although no enthusiasm may be shown in the matter, yet I feel sure that the money will be voted. Whatever may be the intentions of the Emperor and his advisers as to the ultimate purpose for which the Navy will be employed, I feel sure that in the minds of the great mass of the population it is not intended primarily for the purpose of aggression against England. To many here the great cost of the ship-building programme is recognized as a misfortune for the country, but Germany instinctively feels that with isolation in prospect—with weak statesmen at the helm of affairs—with danger and uncertainty ahead as daily inculcated on the nation by the official press—with the sentiment that foreign Powers are grouping themselves together with the ultimate intention of barring the way to Germany's eventual access to the Mediterranean and to the Near East—a powerful Navy is always an increase of strength to the Empire should she suddenly find herself drawn into a contest with foreign nations for her very existence. To the man in the street the uses to which the German Navy may be put are vague, but he feels more confidence in the effect such a Fleet may have on foreign Powers than in the capacity of the present diplomacy of the Wilhelmstrasse to protect the country. The feeling against England is to a great extent artificial but is unfortunately encouraged by the Imperial Government for the purpose of frightening the public into granting subsidies for the construction of big ships. If the Emperor asks for money for ship-building he will get it. It is therefore useless for the British press to sound a note of alarm every time Germany lays down a new vessel of war: the German naval programme will be carried through however much we may dislike the fact and not improbably will be even increased beyond its present scale.

Count Reventlow, a noted Pan-German writer on naval matters, addressed a letter last autumn to a Hanoverian newspaper which had been agitating actively for an increase in the German Navy. The Count, while sympathising with the views of the Editor, advised him to moderate his zeal; he pointed out that to attract so much attention to the increase of the German Navy would only alarm foreign nations and would drive them into a union to protect themselves which might have serious results for the Empire. Count Reventlow said: "Let us build ships and as many as we possibly can, but do not let us talk about them; we have the right to build them, we threaten no one but we wish to be strong."

It would be well for Great Britain to ponder seriously on the advice given by Count Reventlow to his compatriots and also to abstain from continual recriminations against Germany, because she is engaged in carrying out an extensive naval programme. However much we dislike it, the programme will be carried out in its entirety. As I have already said it is not intended as an immediate threat to England but the day may come when the Kaiser might be persuaded to believe that Great Britain has weakened her position at sea and in that case he might be inclined to estimate that the balance of chances for a successful naval war are not so completely against him as at present. When that day dawns it is only too likely that he will try the use of threats against England to attain his purposes, but should they fail—what then? Will he not be driven to have recourse to the decision of arms to save his prestige? Such being the case it seems to me that every shilling we spend in maintaining the efficacy of the British Fleet is a shilling spent in the direction of the maintenance of the peace of Europe, for the Imperial Authorities, who have no regard for weakness, will only bow before those who can convince them that they possess power and strength.

I have, &c.

FAIRFAX L. CARTWRIGHT.

NOTES.(³)

This is an excellent and valuable report in all respects. It gives interesting information which appears to be generally reliable, and there are some minor points which seem to call for a few words of criticism.

1. Mr. Cartwright probably underrates the nature of the influence wielded by Prussia in the German Empire. A wrong impression is conveyed by his suggestion that whilst Prussia supplies the material force, Central and South Germany contribute the brain. Most impartial Germans will agree that, except perhaps in the province of art and literature, Prussia is in every department of national life the leading element making for efficiency. Germany is what it is, in virtue of having become Prussianized.

2. When Germany is described as a state crushed by militarism, it should have been made clear that this description represents merely the opinion of a certain school of foreign (not— German) critics. No German, except perhaps an extreme socialist, would admit that his country is crushed by militarism. The whole nation is genuinely proud of its army (not to speak of the navy) and feels convinced that its possession and maintenance confer the greatest possible advantages from an economical as well as from a political point of view. The " burden of militarism " which according to a large section of the British press is weighing Germany down, is, there, regarded as a laughable myth. This was explained in a speech of great force and eloquence by one of the German delegates at the last Hague conference, which was at the time received with unanimous approval and praise in Germany.

3. Mr. Cartwright does well to deprecate newspaper polemics, but he appears very much to overrate the " restraining influence " exercised by German public opinion. If the Emperor was forced to make concessions at Algeciras, this was due to very different forces than his consideration for German public opinion. In fact a large part of the present discontent in Germany is caused by the unprovoked interference of the emperor in foreign affairs where human interests are predominant and the humiliation felt by German public opinion at the rebuff inflicted upon the foreign policy of the emperor. Mr. Cartwright himself admits that the anti-English feeling in Germany and particularly in the German press is largely due to the direct influence of the government. It is not however accurate to say that the feeling so promoted is entirely artificial, because there is in the minds of most German people an innate predisposition to that feeling, due to historical causes. These causes, which cannot be elaborated within the compass of the present minute, reach back in practically unbroken connection to the rivalry between Prussia and Hanover and particularly to the attitude of Frederick the Great after the lapse of the treaty [convention] of Westminster in 1762.

4. The suggestion that the British government should adopt a separate policy towards " the German nation as a whole " apart from its government, would, if practicable, involve very serious dangers. The British gov[ernmen]t cannot properly have relations with anybody in Germany except the Emperor and his government. If H[is] M[ajesty's] G[overnment] were to embark on the perilous course of " influencing," or " pacifying " as Mr. Cartwright says, German public opinion, they would almost inevitably lay themselves open to the reproach of carrying on intrigues with Germans not in agreement with the policy of their own government. We should and do resent any such proceedings on the part of foreign governments in this country, and we should be careful not to fall into the same error ourselves.

5. The information in possession of this office shows undisputably that the whole German navy is inspired by the conviction that the object of its existence is ultimately to fight England, and that this feeling has from the beginning been deliberately fostered by the German government not only in the navy but throughout Germany with the object of obtaining parliamentary sanction for the construction of a powerful battle fleet.

[E. A. C.]

Foreign Office, Jan. 21/07.

(³) [These notes were based upon a minute by Mr. Crowe which was attached to Mr. Cartwright's despatch before circulation.]

No. 3.

Sir F. Lascelles to Sir Edward Grey.

F.O. 371/257.
(No. 37.)   Most Confidential.   *Berlin, D. January* 31, 1907.
Sir,   R. *February* 4, 1907.

The night before last I had an opportunity of having a short conversation with the Emperor at a Ball given by Prince and Princess Eitel Friedrich. I told His Majesty that Herr von Tschirschky had mentioned to me that afternoon that His Majesty had shown him the very friendly letter which the King had addressed to him on the occasion of his Birthday, and I added that the King would appreciate His Majesty's kindness in receiving Mr. Farquharson, whom His Majesty had sent with the letter and present. His Majesty expressed his satisfaction at the King's friendly letter, which was some comfort when the English Press was again beginning its attacks upon him. On my expressing astonishment, His Majesty said that the whole of the foreign press had been completely wrong about the elections, but the worst offenders had been the "Standard" and the "Illustrated London News." Perhaps people in foreign countries would eventually grasp the meaning of the recent elections, which by diminishing the power of the Social Democrats would increase the power of the German Empire and thus furnish an extra guarantee for the maintenance of peace, as any power who wished to attack Germany would now hesitate before doing so. What was even worse than the opinions of the Press was the fact that not only the Press but the governments of Foreign countries seemed to have received a false impression as to the elections, and he really did not know what the Ambassadors in Berlin had been about. I replied that I could only answer for myself, and that during the period preceding the elections, I had carefully avoided anything in the nature of a prophecy. At that moment the conversation was interrupted by Prince Eitel Friedrich who came to announce that supper was served.

I have had no opportunity of renewing this conversation, but I have been informed by my Austro-Hungarian colleague that the Emperor called upon him yesterday, in accordance with His Majesty's invariable habit of visiting him on the anniversary of the death of the Archduke Rodolphe [*sic*]. His Majesty had used very similar language to him, had made the same complaint with regard to the foreign press in general and the English press in particular, and had also made the same remarks about the Ambassadors in Berlin. M. de Szogyenyi had asked to which Ambassadors His Majesty referred and eventually elicited that His Majesty's remarks did not apply either to him or to me, of whom His Majesty spoke in flattering terms, but rather, if not exclusively, to the Russian Ambassador, who for a considerable time had led a very secluded life on account of the illness of his wife, and has recently suffered himself from a somewhat severe attack of influenza. The Emperor said that Count Osten-Sacken saw very few people and it seemed that the information he received was often inaccurate.

I have, &c.
FRANK C. LASCELLES.

MINUTES.

The emperor seems to have the English press on the brain. It is evidently impossible for an ambassador to make the "retort courteous" to H[is] I[mperial] M[ajesty]. If he were to read the press of his own country he would find that English papers only echo in a faint whisper what the German people shout from the housetops.

The only interesting thing about this incident is that it is clearly thought worth the while of the emperor's advisers to cut out and mark passages from English papers which may be calculated to displease him.

E. A. C.
Feb. 4.

Surely the Emperor cannot believe that either the " Standard " or the Illustrated represent the views of H[is] M[ajesty's] G[overnment].

E. B.
C. H.
E. G.

[ED. NOTE.—The following minutes are attached to Captain Dumas' report of January 29, 1907, F.O. 371/257. The text of the report is printed *infra*, pp. 769–78, *App.* II.

MINUTES.

Captain Dumas' Secret Report on the probable uses of the German fleet in a war with England.

This report, although it deals with problems of naval strategy and tactics from the professional and technical point of view, deserves, and will repay, careful study on the part of the layman.

Admirably as I think Captain Dumas sets out his facts, calculations, and conclusions, there are certain points on which I venture seriously to differ from him, and on which, if his judgment were to be unquestionably accepted by the Admiralty, the Lords Commissioners would, I consider, be misled. (The opinions expressed in the report respecting certain aspects of the German character in general, and of the present younger generation in particular, would not in themselves be so important as to make it necessary to question them. But if, on the strength of those opinions, the Admiralty were to build up certain theories that should materially influence their decisions as regards meeting Germany in war, it is possible that any initial error may have unfortunate consequences.

The statements which I do not believe to be justified are those concerning

(i.) the alleged lack of stability of character; want of organising power beyond a facility for imitation; deficiency of initiative or independent thought; immersion in detail, tending to obscure final aims; and

(ii.) the alleged decadence of the martial or military spirit amongst the German people.

It would be difficult to controvert these statements by detailed argument; I can only say that they appear to me to be a serious and fundamental misreading of the German character. The history of the extraordinary recovery and rise of Prussia after her disastrous defeat of 1806, the tremendous energy and adaptability shown in the great struggles of 1813 1814 and 1815 speak volumes against the theory that the German collapses hopelessly under failure, or lacks all power of rapid reorganization.

It is possible that the German navy may betray the faults of a system admittedly built up in imitation of the British fleet. But to ascribe to the inventors and perfectors of modern armies; the producers of *the* classical works on strategy and tactics; the leaders in scientific thought; and the creators of modern German commerce and industries, lack of initiative and independent thought, seems a strange paradox, for which much weighty evidence would have to be adduced to make it readily credible.—Nor is it easy to believe in the decay of the military spirit of a country in which the armed forces are among all classes looked upon as the special pride of the nation.)(1)

The question arises whether this despatch should be passed on to the Admiralty without comment, or whether something should be said on the above points in order to prevent Captain Dumas' opinions from being accepted unchallenged. In ordinary circumstances it would have been for the ambassador to express his views of the general statements contained in the naval attaché's report. I am afraid we must conclude from Sir F. Lascelles' silence that he either agrees with Captain Dumas, or does not consider it necessary or important to record his dissent, and I doubt whether much would be gained by referring the matter back to him.

Perhaps Sir E. Grey would consider the propriety of our saying to the Admiralty, when forwarding the report, that the general criticisms of German character pronounced by Captain Dumas are not borne out by the information in this department and that especially in the absence of any endorsement on the part of H[is] M[ajesty's] embassy at Berlin, it would be well to receive them with caution. At the same time something appreciative might be said respecting Captain Dumas' otherwise excellent report and generally about his energy and efficient assistance to the embassy, of which I know Sir F. Lascelles thinks very highly.

E. A. C.
Feb. 4.

(1) [The brackets were inserted by Sir Edward Grey. *cp.* his minute, *infra*, p. 14.]

Write to Adm[iral]ty as proposed in the last par[agraph] and send a copy of Mr. Crowe's minute with the exception of the last 2 paragraphs to the First Lord privately.

E. B.

I think it would be a mistake to address the Admiralty officially as suggested by Mr. Crowe, since Sir F. Lascelles has made no observations but I see no harm in sending a copy of Mr. Crowe's mem[orandu]m privately to the Admiralty and if Sir E. Grey approves I will send it to the First Sea Lord.

C. H.
Feb. 18.

I will send to Lord Tweedmouth privately an extract from Mr. Crowe's minute. I have marked the part, which might be typed for me to send.

But this is a most interesting report, full of thought and observation and seeing Capt[ain] Dumas himself warns us on the first page against relying too much on its conclusions, he is fully justified in putting his opinions forward. It is a valuable contribution to the study of the question.

E. G.]

No. 4.

Sir F. Lascelles to Sir Edward Grey.

F.O. 371/258.
(No. 51.) Confidential.   *Berlin, D. February* 6, 1907.
Sir,   R. *February* 11, 1907.

With reference to my despatch No. 37 most confidential of the 31st ultimo,([1]) I have the honour to report that I mentioned to Herr von Tschirschky yesterday the short conversation which I had with the Emperor on the night of the 26th. I said that I hoped that His Majesty's remark that he did not know what the Ambassadors at Berlin were about did not apply to me, and that, judging by the English papers which I had read myself, I did not see that His Majesty's remarks about the English press were justified. Herr von Tschirschky replied that I might feel relieved with regard to the first point, but that the Emperor had felt annoyed at the tone taken generally by the foreign press with regard to the probable result of the elections, and there had been some articles in the English papers which certainly had been hostile to Germany. He had however not thought it worth while to mention the matter to me. He could however tell me quite confidentially that the King had expressed to Prince Radolin, in the interview which he had granted him on the previous day in Paris, his strong disapproval of an article he had just read in the "Observer." Herr von Tschirschky went on to say that the relations between the two countries had certainly improved but that a good deal of mutual suspicion still existed, and that many people in England seemed to think that the German fleet had been built solely for the purpose of attacking England. Count Metternich, in reporting conversations he had had with leading English statesmen —Herr von Tschirschky mentioned the names of Mr. Balfour, Mr. Haldane and Mr. John Morley—had pointed out that each of these, while repudiating such a belief for himself individually had admitted that it was held in England by a considerable number of people. The usual form was "I do not believe it myself but they" without specifying who the "they" were—"tell me, &c."

I replied that I was aware of this belief which I had done my best to combat, but it really did not appear to me to be more unreasonable than the fear which had certainly been entertained in Germany that England intended to attack Germany. To such an extent had this fear been entertained that the Emperor two years ago had summoned Count Metternich to Berlin to learn his views on the subject, and Count Metternich had been able to assure His Majesty that no serious man in England had ever entertained the idea of an attack by England on Germany.

([1]) [*v. supra*, p. 12, No. 3.]

Things had no doubt improved since then, but the mutual suspicion although diminished still existed and it was probable that some considerable time would elapse, during which it was to be hoped that no untoward incident would occur, before it entirely disappeared. Herr von Tschirschky said he also thought that some time would elapse before the mutual suspicion disappeared. He did not anticipate any untoward incident. Things had certainly improved but might be better and he hoped they would soon become so. In conclusion Herr von Tschirschky called my attention to the reticence of the German Press on the subject of the King's visit to Paris, which a year ago would have given rise to much comment and conjecture and he would assure me that this reticence had been entirely spontaneous and that it had not been necessary for him to give any instructions to the Press Bureau on the subject.

I have, &c.
FRANK C. LASCELLES.

MINUTES.

The usual empty talk!

E. A. C.
Feb. 11.
E. B.

If Germany would place some limit on her naval construction scheme suspicion of Germany's intention would soon evaporate on this side of the Channel.

C. H.
E. G.

No. 5.

Mr. Cartwright to Sir Edward Grey.

F.O. 371/259.
(No. 27.)   *Munich, D. March 13, 1907.*
Sir,   R. *March 15, 1907.*

The smallest incident which in any way affects Great Britain's position in the world at once gives rise to comments and criticisms in the German Press, generally of a character unfriendly to ourselves. The latest example of the kind is a discussion which is going on in the Press of this country with regard to the political meaning of the visit paid by the Empress Dowager of Russia to Queen Alexandra; this visit is evidently giving rise to a certain feeling of discontent that a real understanding will soon be arrived at between Russia and England. In fact everything which in any way redounds to the credit of Great Britain arouses in this country what must appear to most persons a somewhat puerile manifestation of jealousy and envy. Even so sensible a newspaper as the " Frankfort Gazette " cannot help venting in a recent article its little grievances against Great Britain.

The Frankfort organ begins by asserting that Sir Henry Campbell-Bannerman's recent article in the " Nation " on disarmament([1]) has met with little favour in political circles both in France and other countries, and this clearly proves that the blame for opposing general disarmament must not be laid on the shoulders of Germany alone. The Right Honourable gentleman's intentions are no doubt excellent, but the world is not prepared as yet to take up his ideas in a serious manner. Although he may be right in theory, yet theory alone is of little value, and the capacity of a statesman must be judged by what he can accomplish practically. If all he has to show is that in her new naval programme Great Britain proposes to lay down two gigantic battleships and threatens immediately to construct a third of these giant ships if the Powers do not accept her proposal for the limitation of armaments—that is really not much to bring as a peace offering to the Conference

([1]) [" The Hague Conference and the Limitation of Armaments," the *Nation*, March 2, 1907.]

at The Hague. If the British Premier is in earnest in this matter, he must come forward at the Conference with something more genuine than the above proposal. The whole situation as regards this subject is unreal, and British statesmen are perfectly well aware that no scheme for the limitation of disarmament[2] will be accepted by any of the Powers at the Conference; they, therefore, keep a very sharp look-out at the political condition of affairs in foreign countries and in the world in general. The " Frankfort Gazette " then states that it is a good thing, now and then, to explain to the public the actual state of relations which exist between the Great Powers in Europe, and it then passes in review the chief questions which affect Great Britain's position in various parts of the world.

It begins with the visit of the Dowager Empress to England and it makes merry over the amiable things which are being said at the present moment about Russia —England's traditional enemy. Even the liberal newspapers which recently became jubilant over the cry of " vive la Douma! ", are now full of pleasant compliments to the Dowager Empress whose late Consort was the very representative of autocratic Czardom. All this is intended to help to bring Russia into the arms of England. It cannot, however, be forgotten that the liberal Press committed themselves to encourage the development of a liberal and constitutional régime in Russia, but as this has not yet been accomplished, innocent people would imagine that the party at present in office in England would abstain as far as possible from having any relations with a Czar who is still autocratic. This would certainly be the case if Sir Henry Campbell-Bannerman was able to have his own way, but it is well known that Sir Henry's views do not represent those of the mass of the public in England, and that he does not even entirely represent the views of his own party. If one is to judge of public opinion in England as expressed in her newspapers, it must be evident to every one that the British public are determined to arrive at an understanding with Russia, and they will in no way be influenced by the manner in which the internal affairs of Russia may be eventually settled.

Turning to the statements of the " Times " with regard to the approaching conclusion of an Asiatic arrangement between Russia and England, the " Frankfort Gazette " observes that this arrangement probably alludes to the settlement of differences between those Powers in Persia and Afghanistan. In its opinion, as regards Persia, there will be many difficulties to overcome before an understanding can be arrived at, as there is nothing to show that Russia is prepared to allow South Persia to fall under exclusive British influence. That something is brewing, however, is certain, and the presence of so many English newspaper correspondents at Tehran is evidence that trouble is in the air. The article repudiates then the statements published by the " Daily Mail " that Germany is trying to obtain possession of certain coalfields on the Turco-Persian frontier in the direction of Bagdad. The only interesting point for Germans in those " Daily Mail " rumours is that they are an indication of the senseless jealousy of Germany which exists in England, and of the light it throws on the secret desire harboured by many Englishmen that Great Britain should herself acquire possession of these very coalfields. As regards Afghanistan, the " Frankfort Gazette " acknowledges that England has apparently secured a real success in the Ameer's visit to India, and it would appear as if that sovereign were going to introduce all manners of reforms in his own country, of course under British direction. It is therefore to be assumed that Russia has for the moment renounced all further pretensions to influence in that quarter.

Coming to European affairs, the Frankfort paper asserts that the Great Powers appear at present to be fairly peacefully disposed; there are, however, envious persons who imagine that certain small States exist who are in danger of being drawn into the German net. The " Times " correspondent in Paris—whose anti-German sentiments are well known—thinks it is his duty to draw attention to the

[2] [Thus in original.]

excellent relations which luckily exist between Berlin and Copenhagen, insinuating that the recent Treaty touching the nationality of children in Schleswig, and the exchange of friendly visits between the Kaiser and the Danish Sovereign, are proofs of the intentions of Germany to draw Denmark under her influence. In Norway, it is stated, the popularity of the Kaiser is such that British influence is on the decline, and so intriguing Germany has succeeded in bringing about an understanding between the Powers who hold the entrance to the Baltic Sea with a view to closing that Sea to foreigners. This terribly alarms the British public who, knowing that Russia will have a word to say to this arrangement, seek to arouse her fears, and the "Times" therefore serves up the above information as a breakfast dish for the Empress Dowager on the morning of her arrival in London. This is all either mischief making, or pure Midsummer Night's madness.

Not satisfied with pointing to the Scandinavian danger, the "Times," on the occasion of King Edward conferring the G.C.B. on Prince Henry of the Netherlands, indulges in a panegyric on the virtues of the Dutch and the historic necessity of their standing well with Great Britain, taking care, of course, not to allude to the injuries inflicted by her on the Dutch race in South Africa, but concluding its article with the insidious remark that Great Britain would never allow Belgium and Holland to be absorbed by a Great European Power. By that Power of course Germany is meant and the only answer to such absurd suggestions is that neither Belgium nor Holland are or ever will be threatened in their existence by Germany.

In conclusion I think it well to report to you that I have noticed complaints in the Press about the paucity of British newspapers which are represented by their own correspondents in Berlin, and that it would be a good thing for the creation of better relations between the two countries if men of intelligence and impartial views represented the more important British newspapers in that city. It is asserted that at present the only English correspondent of some standing in Berlin is the correspondent of the "Times" there, and it is stated that unfortunately he takes every opportunity of representing things in a manner unfavourable to the Imperial Government; as the other newspapers in England receive their foreign information in great part from the "Times," the wrong views which the correspondent of that paper expresses with regard to German affairs, filters little by little right down through the whole British Press. A recent example of the bias of the "Times" correspondent which has been brought to my notice is the long telegraphic account which he sent home of a speech delivered in a recent colonial debate in the Reichstag by one of the Deputies of the opposition, in which that gentleman violently attacked the Imperial Government. The reply of the Chancellor however, was reported in a very few words.

It is very unfortunate that a rooted idea exists in this country among the general public, which the Imperial Government do nothing to correct, that the "Times" is a British Government organ and can be influenced by them, and the fact that its general tone is anti-German is often adduced by the German Press as a proof of the real sentiments of His Majesty's Government towards Germany.

I have, &c.

FAIRFAX L. CARTWRIGHT.

No. 6.

Sir F. Lascelles to Sir Edward Grey.

F.O. 371/259.
(No. 114.)   Berlin, D. March 21, 1907.
Sir,   R. March 25, 1907.

I have the honour to forward, herewith, a despatch, as marked in the margin, which I have received from Captain Dumas, Naval Attaché to this Embassy, relating to an article in the "Berliner Tageblatt" relative to the development of navies.

I have, &c.
FRANK C. LASCELLES.

Enclosure in No. 6.

Captain Dumas to Sir F. Lascelles.

(No. 12.) Confidential.
Your Excellency,   Berlin, March 21, 1907.

I have the honour to submit the subjoined translation of an article which appeared in the "Berliner Tageblatt" of the 16th March, and which is signed "Ragna." It is so interesting that one would have expected to see it copied in every German paper, and the fact that it has not been so leads me to believe that orders have been given to repress it.

The Development of Navies.

That the present composition of the Reichstag being, as it is, so favourable to the Government will lead to new and extensive demands in connection with the fleet must be clear even to the uninitiated. Under these circumstances it is of interest to give a graphic description of the latest advances in the navies of the Great Powers as far as definite information on the subject can be relied on.

Since the British navy began the "Dreadnought," the endeavour to increase the size of ships has been noticeable everywhere, and that to such a degree that the building cost of a single type of ships now is double what it was five years ago.

The proceedings of the German Admiralty will certainly cause the greatest sensation, especially in the naval circles of the other Maritime Powers, as soon as the particulars as to the measurements of the new German armoured cruiser "F" are made public, the designs for which are now complete, and the building will be commenced within a very short time.

According to our information, it appears that the ship will exceed in size all the armoured cruisers at present in course of construction or projected in or by any other navy in the world, and in the German navy will assume the enormous advance of from 11,600 tons—that of the latest armoured cruisers, "Gneisenau" and "Scharnhorst," now in course of construction—to 19,200 tons displacement.

This mighty ship will also be superior in speed to any other vessel in our navy, with, of course, the exception of the torpedo-boats. for, by using Parsons turbines of from 40,000 to 50,000 i.h.p., a speed of at least 25 knots per hour will be attained. That the cost of construction of such an engine of war is equally enormous is plain, and will amount in the case of the armoured cruiser "F" to 36,500,000 marks.

The two new Japanese armoured cruisers which it is intended to build, each of 18,650 tons, will be the nearest in size to the new German ship; they also will have Parsons turbines and a speed of 25 knots. The latest English armoured cruisers of the "Invincible" class, on the contrary, are already, with their 17,527 tons, considerably behind that of Germany.

With regard to battle-ships, Japan stands at the present time in the first place in the matter of size, if we take into consideration those ships in course of construction and designed. The two ships "Satsuma" and "Aki," now being built, are of 19,500 tons; while the two newer battle-ships, for which the money has been voted, are to be of 21,000 tons. Then comes France with six uniform battle-ships of 18,350 tons, of which two are already in hand; and England with the "Dreadnought" of 18,000 tons, completed, and three similar ships of 18,300 tons, the keels of which are already laid.

With regard to the new German battle-ships, the "Ersatz Bayern" and "Ersatz Sachsen," which have been already allocated to the Imperial Yard at Wilhelmshaven and the Weser Yard in Bremen, nothing authentic has been made public, but we can judge pretty well that here also special surprises are at hand now that the, up to the present, limited policy for building new ships has been broken in the matter of the armoured cruiser "F."

The United States' navy has also of late been considering the designs of various naval architects, and seems to think that one of 20,000 tons is the best.

After the battle-ships and armoured cruisers the use of torpedo-boats in a future naval war comes under consideration, and these are in favour in every navy, as, after costly experiments, a range of 2,000 metres has been obtained, whereas formerly not one-half of this could be counted on.

The torpedo charge has also been greatly increased, the cause being traceable to the last great war, where, for example, although a Japanese merchant-ship was hit at close quarters by several Russian torpedoes, and the Russians made so sure that they had accomplished their object that they withdrew, yet the Japanese succeeded in bringing the steamer into harbour, where, after a short time of repair, she was able to proceed.

The size of the newer torpedo-boats increases steadily, which is necessary in view of the strength of the armament and the use of light nickel steel armour plating. England has already built torpedo-boats of 800 tons displacement, and the new German boats of this kind, such as the turbine-boat "G 137," lately launched at the Germania Yard, have a displacement of 600 tons. And gradually the opinion that in a torpedo-boat one possesses a very effective weapon for a comparatively small outlay is under-going a considerable change. The English experiment, at present but lightly touched upon, with a view to using small motor torpedo-boats worked by methylated spirit or petroleum, shows another side of the picture, but it is noteworthy that for the price of one "Dreadnought" one could build about 350 of this type of vessel.

It is very encouraging that meanwhile the German navy is by no means idle in this connection—a very important question as regards the purse of the taxpayer—of using a cheaper and yet not less effective weapon. It is due, moreover, to a very special order of the Emperor that extensive and thorough trials are taking place with motor-boats in our navy, though not at present with a view to using them as torpedo-boats.

In the matter of submarines the German navy has entered the experimental stage with, at the present moment, two such boats. The great number of submarines in the French navy need not be too highly valued, as they represent far too many experimental types. Those of the British navy, however, are of a uniform type of construction, and already form a stately fleet.

A comprehensive survey of the strength of the various fleets of to-day by no means places that of Germany at a disadvantage in the matter of battle-ships, which represent the fighting ships, for here, among all navies, we take the second place.

We do not come off so well in the matter of armoured cruisers, but still, taking into consideration the unfavourable local conditions which obtain in the case of the two navies—those of France and the United States—which are about equal to ours, it is, after all, but a matter of the defence of coast lines that are far distant from each other, and the superiority of the navy of Germany over those of each of the two Powers mentioned no longer to-day admits of any doubt.

Therefore the efforts of those in authority should be in the direction of preserving this position for the German navy, but the idea of wresting the first place must be designated as quite hopeless, in view of the enormous superiority of the fleets of England and the present political situation, and, indeed, it might also be designated as purposeless.

I have, &c.
PHILIP DUMAS, *Captain.*

No. 7.

Sir F. Lascelles to Sir Edward Grey.

F.O. 371/259.
(No. 122.)   *Berlin,* D. *March* 28, 1907.
Sir,   R. *April* 2, 1907.
I have the honour to forward, herewith, a despatch, as marked in the margin, which I have received from Colonel Trench, Military Attaché to this Embassy, relating to his conversation with the Emperor.

I have, &c.
FRANK C. LASCELLES.

Enclosure in No. 7.

Colonel Trench to Sir F. Lascelles.

(No. 43.)
Sir,   *Berlin, March* 24, 1907.
On the occasion of their Majesties the Emperor and Empress dining yesterday with your Excellency at the British Embassy, I had the honour of several conversations with the Emperor, one of them lasting about twenty minutes.

The topics were, as usual, very varied, and included spring inspections at Potsdam, this year's Imperial manœuvres, the units formerly belonging to the Hanoverian army —an illustrated history of which the Emperor presented me with a fortnight ago—the recent election for the Reichstag and the comments on German politics in the English and French press. His Majesty seemed disappointed with the remarks in the English papers, and said that the only article which had given an account that was at all correct was one by " Dicey " (Sir E.?) in the " Review " (of Reviews?),(1) which was so accurate that it might have come from the office of the Imperial Chancellor. The Emperor said that he was so pleased with this paper that he had had it translated and widely distributed.

The Emperor seemed to have taken a good deal of interest in the all-night sitting of the House of Commons, and discussed it at length, referring especially to Mr. Haldane, of whom he spoke in high praise, and whose plan for the organization of the territorial army he again spoke about, as also the great benefit he believed Mr. Haldane had derived from his Berlin visit.

His Majesty referred, apparently with some feeling, to the omission of the British Ministers generally to come to Berlin. " Why don't they do the same as Haldane has done? Why didn't Lansdowne come? Why doesn't Sir Edward Grey come over and discuss things with the Imperial Chancellor? Instead of coming here, off they go to France! " I referred to the great charm (especially after a winter in the north) of the sunny south, of which the Emperor himself had spoken with so much appreciation and kindly memories to me three weeks ago, and the conversation turned to the Emperor's many visits to the Mediterranean and the various places and persons, mainly British, with whom he had become acquainted. The way His Majesty remembered their names, and seemed to have followed their subsequent careers, was remarkable.

After taking leave, the Emperor called me to accompany him to his carriage, and said he had learnt that the monument to His late Royal Highness the Duke of Cambridge was to be unveiled in the summer, and that he wished me to say that he

(1) [It seems probable that the article to which the Emperor referred is one by Mr. Edward Dicey in the *Empire Review* of March 1907, entitled " The German Elections, and After."]

would much like, not only as his relation, but also as a Field Marshal of the British army, to send a Representative to the ceremony. He also much hoped that the German regiment with which the late Duke was connected would be permitted (I think His Majesty meant invited) to send a deputation to be present at the ceremony.

I understand that the Emperor expressed himself somewhat to the same effect to His Serene Highness Prince Francis of Teck, who is also writing, doubtless, to His Majesty the King on the subject.

I have, &c.
F. TRENCH,
Colonel and Military Attaché.

MINUTES.

It is curious how the Emperor has it on his brain that British Ministers do not go to Berlin for their pleasure trips. He made the same complaint to me at Friedrichshof and one could hardly explain to him that Berlin is not at all an attractive town!

C. H.

There is no ground for a reproach against me of partiality in foreign visits for I make none.

E. G.

No. 8.

Mr. Cartwright to Sir Edward Grey.

F.O. 371/259.
(No. 32.)   *Munich,* D. *March* 28, 1907.
Sir,   R. *March* 30, 1907.

When it was first announced that Prince Bülow would go to the Riviera during the Easter holidays, the German public were informed that he was going there merely on account of his health and that if a meeting should take place between himself and Signor Tittoni, it would only be to enable the leading statesmen of the two countries to exchange courtesies with each other, and that there were no serious political questions to discuss, as the relations between Berlin and Rome were entirely satisfactory. To those who have been observing what has been going on between Germany and Italy of late doubts must have arisen as to the correctness of these semi-official communications to the Press. For a long time past articles have been appearing in the German news-papers showing that all is not going on smoothly between the two countries and that a profound dissatisfaction exists at Berlin ever since the Algeciras Conference at the uncertainty of public opinion in Italy with regard to the Triple Alliance and the influence that opinion may eventually have on the Italian Government. Moreover, it is no secret to those who have any connection with the official world in Germany that Count Monts, the German Ambassador at Rome, is not in a position to exert much personal influence with the Italian Foreign Office in a manner likely to prove beneficial to the views of his Government.

Under these circumstances I think it may be of interest to report to you the substance of a curiously worded article, evidently written in Berlin, which appeared in the last number of the Stuttgart "Schwäbischer Merkur." The article in question states that it is not to be wondered at that the meeting at the present moment of the two leading statesmen of Germany and Italy should give rise to comments as to the real relations which exist between the most powerful member of the Triple Alliance and the Kingdom of Italy. The moment is an important one as the time is approaching for convoking the new Hague Conference. It then draws attention to the fact that the "Giornale d'Italia" recently gave the information that in the Imperial Chancellerie in Berlin the opinion was held that the attitude of Italy with regard to the Peace Conference was unsatisfactory and unreliable. Even if, says the "Schwäbische Merkur," the Imperial Chancellor were convinced from the reports which had reached him that such was the attitude of Italy, he certainly would not have given vent to his feelings in so crude a form. The Wurtemberg paper asserts, however, that the intelligent public will understand that the statement made in the "Giornale d'Italia," as coming from Berlin, was merely a ballon d'essai launched by the Imperial authorities to give an opportunity to Signor Tittoni to clearly explain the attitude of his country, which it would have been difficult for the German Chancellor to demand of him directly as it would not be possible for Prince Bülow to appear to have any doubts as to the fidelity of Germany's ally. Italy's explanations have now been given indirectly without delay. At least a German newspaper correspondent has been informed by the Private Secretary's Department of the Italian Consulta that Italy would scrupulously fulfil her duties as a member of the Triple Alliance, and that, as regards her attitude at The Hague Conference, she would give her support to any measures which contributed to the maintenance of peace, but that she would do nothing at that Meeting which would render Germany's relations with other Powers more difficult. The "Schwäbische Merkur" states that a prelude of this kind was to be expected on the part of Italy before the interview at Rapallo could take place, because it is not easy to loyally receive an ally unless you are convinced that he will be faithful to his engagements. It must, however, be remembered that the exchange of civilities which may take place at the Rapallo meeting will be carefully hedged in by diplomatic precautions. An alliance, properly understood, entails the common action of the allies in matters of great importance with regard to foreign affairs. A case in point would be the attitude they would assume towards a question of such importance as that of general disarmament, a proposal which at present Great Britain alone supports with great tenacity in a truculent manner. England's attitude on this point gives the impression that the purpose of that Power is not to maintain peace but to fish in troubled waters. Regret is expressed by the Stuttgart organ that Italy seems inclined just now to resort again to her habitual policy of duplicity, as so far the only point which is certain is that she undertakes not to do anything which might render Germany's position with regard to other Powers more difficult than it is. This indeed is a very reserved attitude for an ally to assume. However, this much is satisfactory that Italy's position on this point is at least clear. In conclusion it may be asserted that the meeting at Rapallo will take place on the following terms, namely, that it will be understood on both sides that the Triple Alliance does not bind Italy to give positive support to Germany under all circumstances, and that Germany in return is also in a position not to subordinate her clear and well understood interests to the mere requirements of the other members of the Triple Alliance.

I have, &c.
FAIRFAX L. CARTWRIGHT.

No. 9.

Sir F. Bertie to Sir Edward Grey.

Private and Secret.([1])

My dear Grey, *Paris, April* 11, 1907.

After I had made my communication to Clemenceau this morning about the proposed notes to be exchanged with Spain([2]) he said that he must speak to me very frankly but seriously with regard to one subject referred to during his conversation with Sir Henry Campbell Bannerman here on Tuesday last (9th). They had he said been talking about Germany and he had expressed the sincere desire of France to maintain peace but he had pointed out the possibility of the ambition and proceedings of Germany bringing about such a state of things as must result in war. It seemed as if Germany was gradually assuming the attitude of France under Napoleon and that

([1]) [Grey MSS., Vol. 11.]

([2]) [A telegram reporting this communication and other documents upon this subject will be printed in *Gooch & Temperley*, Vol. VII.]

everybody would be expected to give way to German pretensions. There might come a moment when Europe would have to resist. Germany was making her influence very predominant in Denmark and what would happen if she adopted a policy towards Holland that would make that Country subservient to her aims. In the present circumstances and state of affairs he regretted the reductions in the British Army and he had expressed this feeling to Sir Henry Campbell Bannerman and had been quite taken aback by the Prime Minister having said (lui ayant jeté à la figure) that he did not think that English public opinion would allow of British Troops being employed on the Continent of Europe. Clemenceau thought that the Prime Minister could not be aware of the communications which had passed between the General Staff French and the General Staff British during the acute stages of the Morocco crisis when it had been contemplated that in certain eventualities 115,000 British Troops would be employed in Belgium or elsewhere in support of France.([3]) Was there now to be a change of attitude on the part of England? France ardently desired to maintain peace and nothing save dire necessity would make her resort to war. She had not detached Italy from the Triplice. It was sufficient for France to feel sure that no attack would come from that quarter. Her right would be safe, but how about her left if she had to face Germany? Could she only rely on Naval support? This would be very very serious. He must inform the President of the Republic and the Minister for Foreign Affairs of what the Prime Minister had said, but he would not inform his other colleagues in the Cabinet for he hoped that the Prime Minister had spoken without full consideration of the effect of what he said. The effect on his Colleagues of such an exposition of British policy would be disastrous. He said that he would instruct Cambon to speak to you on the subject. He sincerely trusted that his anxiety would be relieved by you. It was not that he had raised the question of the employment of British Troops. The Prime Minister "m'a jeté ça en pleine figure."

Yours sincerely,
FRANCIS BERTIE.

([3]) [cp. *Gooch & Temperley*, Vol. III, pp. 169–203 *passim*, and pp. 438–40, *App.* D.]

No. 10.

Sir Edward Grey to Sir F. Bertie.

Private.([1])

My dear Bertie, *Foreign Office, April 13*, 1907.

The Prime Minister tells me that he dwelt upon the reluctance of the British people to undertake obligations, which would commit them to a Continental war, but that he made no statement to the effect that under no circumstances should we allow British troops to be employed on the Continent of Europe.

As regards the Algeciras Conference our view was that had Germany then attacked France and in effect made our agreement with France the ground of a quarrel with her the feeling of the British people would have been strongly roused.

This is in substance contained in the records of my conversations with Cambon at the time, all of which were seen by the Prime Minister.

It was then urged by the French that even if no obligations were undertaken by us, we should allow our military and naval experts to confer with the French experts so that each should know how much the other could do and by what methods help could best be given in an emergency. This could be done without committing either of us, but was essential to make prompt co-operation possible, if a crisis arose in connection with the Algeciras Conference.

To this we agreed and the Prime Minister knew at the time that such consultation was taking place.

([1]) [Grey MSS., Vol. 11.]

The whole thing is really in a sentence : public opinion here would be very reluctant to go to war, but it would not place limits upon the use of our forces, if we were engaged in war, and all our forces naval and military would then be used in the way in which they would be most effective.

It is not a matter to be made the subject of any written communication, but you should take any opportunity of correcting M. Clemenceau's impression, and I shall give the same explanation to M. Cambon, if he asks me as you say he will do.

I have shown this letter to the Prime Minister, who confirms its accuracy.

Y[ou]rs,
E. G[REY].

MINUTE.

Sent to the Prime Minister, who returned it to me at the Cabinet saying it was all right.

E. G.
13.4.07.

No. 11.

Sir F. Bertie to Sir Edward Grey.

Private and Secret.([1])

My dear Grey,   *British Embassy, Paris, April* 17, 1907.

I made to Clemenceau this morning the communication desired by your letter of the 13th instant.([2]) He begged me to thank you for it. He said that he did not attribute to Sir Henry Campbell Bannerman a statement to the effect that under no circumstances would H[is] M[ajesty's] Government allow British troops to be employed on the continent of Europe. He understood Sir Henry in referring to the reductions in the British Army, which Clemenceau had deprecated in the interest of the peace of Europe, to say that he thought that English public opinion would be very reluctant to allow British Troops to be employed on the Continent. He was afraid that this might indicate a change of attitude on the part of H[is] M[ajesty's] Gov[ernmen]t.

As to the communications between the British and French Naval and Military Experts Clemenceau said that the proposal had come from H[is] M[ajesty's] Gov[ernmen]t. To this I replied that if so it was in the stead of something more definite which had been suggested by Cambon. He admitted that this might be the case.

As to public opinion in England being very reluctant to go to war Clemenceau remarked that it could not be more so than public opinion in France. The Public and the Government would regard the possibility of war with the greatest aversion and there would be no war unless it were forced upon them.

What Sir Henry Campbell Bannerman said to Clemenceau([3]) was I suppose intended as a douche to cool any martial ardour that he might feel in reliance on military support from us. The French Government are however anything but bellicose. They are terribly afraid lest Germany should place France in a position in which war would become unavoidable. As Pichon told me this evening that Clemenceau had been pleased with your explanations and assurances I think that the latter must be more satisfied than he chose to admit to me, and that possibly Cambon will not say anything to you on the subject.

Yours sincerely,
FRANCIS BERTIE.

([1]) [Grey MSS., Vol. 11.]
([2]) [*v.* immediately preceding document.]
([3]) [*cp. supra*, pp. 22–3, No. 9.]

No. 12.

Sir F. Bertie to Mr. Mallet.

F.O. 371/254.

My dear Mallet,   *British Embassy, Paris, April* 17, 1907.

In order to comply with recent F[oreign] O[ffice] instructions I have converted into a despatch the private communications April 11 to 17([1]) concerning Sir Henry Campbell Bannerman's observations to Clemenceau. I send the despatch herewith for you to hand over to Crowe if the matter is to be kept on official record.

Yours ever,
FRANCIS BERTIE.

([1]) [*v. supra*, pp. 22–4, Nos. 9 and 11.]

No. 13.

Sir F. Bertie to Sir Edward Grey.

F.O. 371/254.
(No. 196.)   *Paris*, D. *April* 17, 1907.

Sir,   R. *April* 19, 1907.

I had occasion to call on the President of the Council on the 11th instant in order to make to His Excellency, in the absence from Paris of the Minister for Foreign Affairs, a communication in your name on the question of the proposed exchange of notes with the Spanish Government regarding the maintenance of the *Status Quo* in the Mediterranean and in that part of the Atlantic which washes the shores of Europe and Africa.([1])

On the termination of our conversation on that question Monsieur Clemenceau said that he must speak to me very frankly but seriously with regard to one subject which had been referred to during his interview with Sir Henry Campbell-Bannerman at this Embassy on the 9th instant.([2]) They had, His Excellency said, been talking about Germany and he had expressed the sincere desire of France to maintain peace, but he had pointed out the possibility of the ambition and proceedings of Germany bringing about such a state of things as must result in war. It seemed as if Germany was gradually assuming the attitude of France under Napoleon, and that everybody would be expected to give way to German pretensions. There might come a moment when Europe would have to resist. Germany was making her influence very predominant in Denmark, and what would happen if she adopted a policy towards Holland that would make that country subservient to her aims? In the present circumstances and state of affairs he regretted the reductions in the British Army and he had expressed this feeling to Sir Henry Campbell Bannerman and had been quite taken aback by the Prime Minister having said ("lui ayant jeté à la figure") that he did not think that English public opinion would allow of British Troops being employed on the Continent of Europe. Monsieur Clemenceau thought that the Prime Minister could not be aware of the communications which had passed between the French General Staff and the British General Staff during the acute stages of the Morocco crisis, when it had been contemplated that in certain eventualities 115,000 British Troops would be employed in Belgium or elsewhere in support of France. Was there now to be a change of attitude on the part of England? France ardently desired to maintain peace and nothing save dire necessity would make her resort to war. She had not detached Italy from the Triple Alliance. It was sufficient for France to feel sure that no attack

([1]) [A telegram reporting this communication and other documents upon this subject will be printed in *Gooch & Temperley*, Vol. VII.]

([2]) [*v. supra*, pp. 22–3, No. 9.]

would come from that quarter. Her right would be safe, but how about her left if she had to face Germany? Could she only rely on Naval support from England? This would be very very serious. He must inform the President of the Republic and the Minister for Foreign Affairs of what the Prime Minister had said, but he would not inform his other colleagues in the Cabinet, for he hoped that the Prime Minister had spoken without full consideration of the effect of what he said. The effect on the French Cabinet of such an exposition of British Policy would be disastrous. His Excellency stated that the French Ambassador in London would be instructed to speak to you on the subject. He sincerely trusted, he said, that his anxiety would be relieved by you. It was not that he had raised the question of the employment of British Troops. Sir Henry Campbell-Bannerman "m'a jeté ça en pleine figure."

Having reported to you the observations which had been made to me by Monsieur Clemenceau I received authority from you to remove from his mind certain impressions which he had derived from Sir Henry Campbell-Bannerman's language and to give to His Excellency explanations in regard to the communications which had passed between the British and French Military Authorities during the acute stages of the Morocco crisis. For this purpose I called on the President of the Council this morning. I told him that I had reported to you the observations which he had made to me on the 11th instant, that you had communicated on the subject with the Prime Minister and that you had authorized me to say that though Sir Henry Campbell-Bannerman had in conversation with His Excellency dwelt upon the reluctance of the British people to undertake obligations which would commit them to a continental war, he made no statement to the effect that under no circumstances would His Majesty's Government allow British Troops to be employed on the Continent of Europe. Monsieur Clemenceau at once admitted that Sir Henry had not gone so far as to say that under no circumstances would British Troops be allowed by His Majesty's Government to be employed on the Continent. What he had understood Sir Henry to intimate in referring to the reductions in the British Army was that he thought that English public opinion would be very reluctant to allow British Troops to be employed on the Continent.

I then explained to M. Clemenceau that as regarded the Morocco question the view of His Majesty's Government had been that had Germany attacked France during the Algeciras Conference and in effect made the Anglo-French Agreement the ground of quarrel the feeling of the British people would have been strongly roused. The Prime Minister had been kept informed of the conversations which you had had with the French Ambassador in London on this point. Monsieur Cambon had urged that even if no obligations were to be undertaken by His Majesty's Government they should allow the British and French Military and Naval Experts to confer together so that each party should know how much the other could do and by what methods help could best be given in an emergency, as such consultations would not commit either party and were essential to make prompt co-operation possible if a crisis should arise in connection with the Algeciras Conference. His Majesty's Government had agreed to such consultations and Sir Henry Campbell-Bannerman was cognizant of the fact that they were taking place.

Monsieur Clemenceau made the observation that he thought that the proposal for conferences between the Military and Naval Experts of the two countries came from His Majesty's Government. I replied that if so it was, to the best of my recollection, in the stead of something more definite suggested by Monsieur Cambon; and M. Clemenceau said he thought that I was right in my recollection.

I told the President of the Council that in your instructions to me you had said that the whole matter might be summed up to the effect that public opinion in England would be very reluctant to go to war, but that it would not place limits on the use of British Forces if the country were engaged in war, and both the Naval and Military Forces would be used in the way in which they would be most effective.

Monsieur Clemenceau said that naturally public opinion in England would be very reluctant to go to war, but it could not be more unwilling to go to war than public opinion in France. It would be a great mistake to suppose that France or the French Government would regard the possibility of war with any other feeling than the greatest aversion. There would be no war unless it were forced on them. His Excellency requested me to transmit to you his thanks for the communication which I had made to him on your behalf.

I have, &c.
FRANCIS BERTIE.

MINUTES.

See Sir F. Bertie's letter herewith.(³)
I presume no further action is at present required or contemplated.

E. A. C.
Ap. 19.

See Sir E. Grey's conversation with M. Cambon.(⁴)

E. B.
E. G.

Q[ue]ry. Has the French Government through their general Staff, or otherwise, got in their possession any record justifying, or which might seem to justify, M. Clemenceau's assertion about the employment of 115,000 British troops in Belgium under certain eventualities in agreement with them.(⁵)

F.

Sir E[dward] Grey has verbally answered Lord Fitzmaurice's question.

E. A. C.
Ap. 23.

(³) [v. immediately preceding document.]
(⁴) [v. immediately succeeding document.]
(⁵) [cp. Gooch & Temperley, Vol. III, ch. XX, pp. 169–203, passim.]

No. 14.

Sir Edward Grey to Sir F. Bertie.

F.O. 371/254.
(No. 237.) Secret.
Sir,
Foreign Office, April 19, 1907.

M. Cambon referred to-day to the feeling which had been aroused against England in Holland by the Boer War, and in Belgium by the Congo Agitation.

He said these had been serious factors, and Germany had been very active in both countries. No one wished to have war, but it was necessary to have full information, and he referred to a conversation which M. Clemenceau had had with Sir Henry Campbell-Bannerman and which had given rise to the impression that under no circumstances would British troops be used on the Continent.(¹)

I told him this was a quite mistaken impression of the conversation. What Sir Henry Campbell-Bannerman desired to convey was that we should be very reluctant to go to war. But he never intended to imply that, if we were engaged in a war, there would be any limitation of the use of our troops. On the contrary, our naval and military forces would be used without limitation in the way in which they would be most effective. I said this had already been explained to M. Clemenceau.

With regard to Holland, I thought feeling there was being softened by the grant of self-government to the Transvaal, and by the fact that General Botha was now here as one of the Colonial Premiers, and was engaged among other things with the question of imperial defence. The way in which he was received must, I thought, have its effect in Holland.

[I am, &c.]
E[DWARD] G[REY].

(¹) [v. *supra*, pp. 22–7, Nos. 9–13.]

No. 15.

Sir F. Lascelles to Sir Edward Grey.

Private.([1])

My dear Grey,   *Berlin, April* 19, 1907.

The day before yesterday, Berlin went stark staring raving mad. There was a fall of six points in German securities on the Bourse and a general impression that war was about to break out between England and Germany. Prince Albert of Schleswig-Holstein who was dining with me said that every one he had met had been in a state of great excitement and fear, and seemed to think that war was imminent. All this about two Articles which had appeared, one in the "Neue Freie Presse" the other in the Cologne Gazette about the King's visit to Gaeta,([2]) and his intention to isolate and humiliate Germany. It is possible that the fact that the Cologne Gazette is in touch with the German Foreign Office may have occasioned this panic, and an article which appeared in that paper yesterday, to the effect that there was nothing in the King's visit which could cause uneasiness to Germany, has calmed people's minds and brought them back to a state approaching sanity. There is however great suspicion of England generally and of the King in particular. The demand that the question of the limitation of expenditure on armaments shall be discussed at the Hague Conference is looked upon as a deep laid plot to put Germany in a false position, and to cast upon her the odium of refusing to entertain so humanitarian a proposal and the King's visits to Spain and Italy are supposed to have had the sole object of forming an alliance against Germany. This of course is absolutely ridiculous and could not signify if there were a statesman at the head of affairs here who was capable of guiding or even checking public opinion, but Bülow lets things slide and I am told does absolutely nothing but prepare the brilliant speeches which he makes to the Reichstag. It would be a pity if this anti-English feeling were to develop still further, although I do not think it will ever become really dangerous.

There is no doubt that there is a great feeling of "nervosity" in Germany just now, to be explained perhaps by the fact that the Germans have an uneasy feeling that their Country does not occupy the position in Europe which it used to and ought to hold, and this is quite true. But the Germans, as a rule cannot admit that this can be possibly due to any fault of their own, but can only be the consequence of the machinations of some wicked man. Formerly this man was Delcassé, now it is the King. This nervosity seems not to be confined to the public, but to have spread to the official classes, and I was told yesterday by a newspaper correspondent that the language held to him at the Foreign Office was perfectly correct as regards the King, whose visits could not be of any concern to the German Gov[ernmen]t, but that there was one thing which they were determined to guard against, and that was being left in the lurch by Italy at the Hague as they had been at Algeciras. . . . .([3])

Yours sincerely,

FRANK C. LASCELLES.

([1]) [Grey MSS., Vol. 22.]

([2]) [For King Edward's visit to Gaeta and Press comments upon it, *v.* Sir Sidney Lee: *King Edward VII*, (1927), Vol. II, pp. 541–4.]

([3]) [The rest of this letter refers to Franco-German relations in general terms.]

No. 16.

Mr. Cartwright to Sir Edward Grey.

F.O. 371/259.
(No. 45.)
Sir,

Munich, D. *April* 23, 1907.
R. *April* 26, 1907.

The meeting of King Edward with the King of Italy at Gaeta, although it had attracted a fair amount of attention in the German press, had not in any special degree alarmed the public of this country, to the majority of whom there seemed in itself nothing very extraordinary that the King of England, while cruising in the Mediterranean, should pay a visit of courtesy to the King of Italy who was likewise cruising about in those waters. It would have been fortunate had the German public been able to continue to remain in that state of mind, but unhappily Herr Bassermann thought proper to select the very moment when the Royal meeting was about to take place to deliver himself of an oration of the most pessimistic kind with regard to Germany's present position in the world, and which was full of utterances of alarm with regard to her future. Simultaneously with this speech there appeared in the Vienna "Neue Freie Presse" an article written in a similar tone and the arguments used in it were reinforced by another article in the Cologne Gazette, and the contents of the latter—as if by design—were immediately telegraphed all over Germany. The effect produced was immediate. The public who had been advised by their newspapers to view with calmness the meeting at Gaeta, as its political importance was said to have been effaced by the previous exchange of views between Prince Bülow and Signor Tittoni at Rapallo, pricked up their ears and asked each other what had so suddenly happened to disturb the serenity of the political atmosphere. As here it was taken for granted that the Vienna article and the one in the Cologne Gazette had been inspired from headquarters at Berlin, nearly every editor in Germany thought it his duty to immediately turn on the limelight of publicity on the Gaeta meeting for the benefit of his readers and to take advantage of the incident to give vent to all the pent up spleen accumulated within himself against Great Britain and her perfidious policy. The result was a whirlwind of wrath in the press against England and the most absurd accusations were made against her. The present Liberal Cabinet were denounced as being more treacherous in their methods towards Germany than that of Mr. Balfour, and some newspapers insinuated that the meetings at Cartagena and Gaeta were merely intended to make Great Britain's position in the Mediterranean so secure that it would allow her to withdraw many of her war vessels from those waters to the North Sea, so that the British Government, while desiring to limit their naval forces, were by their Diplomacy enabled to increase the strength of their Fleet in that part of the world where it would be most efficient as against Germany. The harm that this anti-British campaign would do if allowed to continue, became so apparent to the Imperial authorities, that they took immediate steps to repudiate the Vienna newspaper and the Cologne Gazette and to issue reassuring messages to the public asserting that the Imperial Government had been for a long time past perfectly well aware that the King of England had the intention of visiting the King of Italy; they also announced that the exchange of such courtesies in no way affected German interests and that Germany was no more isolated after the meeting at Gaeta than she was before. To further reassure the public, rumours were started that Signor Tittoni had expressed a desire to visit Baron von Aehrentahl [*sic*] before the meeting of The Hague Conference, and here and there allusions were made in the press to a possible visit of the Kaiser to Spain with insinuations that while King Edward only went to Cartagena unofficially "pour tâter le terrain," the German Emperor would pay an official visit to Madrid to show the world the excellent relations which at present exist between Spain and his own country.

The sudden curb put by the Imperial Government on the outbursts of the press has no doubt produced an apparent calm among the public, but it cannot be said that they really feel reassured with regard to foreign affairs. A great confusion seems to exist in the public mind, and it can only have been increased by the sudden note of alarm which has been sounded by what are generally considered inspired organs, and then suddenly silenced. To whatever foreign country the German public turn their gaze at the present moment, they seem to meet there with little sympathy for themselves. This state of things is clearly recognised by the more serious newspapers here, and they point out that if Germany looks towards Russia—a country of which she has a remarkable dread—she cannot help noting with dissatisfaction that the revolution there, whose triumph she does not wish to see too complete on account of the possible moral reflex influence it might have upon her, yet does not seem to impede as much as she would like the marked recovery of the Russian Government from the effects of the Japanese war. Russia may become strong again in less time than it would suit the German Government; therefore she must be very careful to do nothing which would [be] likely to cause any friction between the two neighbouring Empires. Without being able to call Russia an enemy, Germany can hardly call her a friend at a moment when she is already allied with France and may be so to-morrow with Great Britain.

If the press turn their attention towards Austria, one would imagine that they would feel some satisfaction in contemplating that sturdy ally of Germany, but even here there is a skeleton in the cupboard. The Emperor Franz Joseph is old and in indifferent health; on his death the unforeseen may occur, for should Hungary assert herself as decidedly with regard to foreign affairs as she has so far done with the internal affairs of the Dual Empire, it is recognised here that a coolness might very quickly arise between Germany and Austria-Hungary, and the strong pro-British feeling which exists among the Magyars is anything but a pleasant prospect to thoughtful Germans.

As regards Italy it is evident to everybody that the breach between Rome and Berlin is widening; every attempt is made in the press to hide this fact, but even the newspapers most submissive to official influence cannot always accept the assurances that all is well in that direction. As a sample of the strange efforts made by the Imperial authorities to deceive the public with a view to calming them, I will quote the statement recently made in so sensible a newspaper as the Frankfort Gazette, namely that the Gaeta meeting in no way concerns Germany, and that King Edward went out to meet King Victor Emmanuel not with a view to isolate Germany, but because Great Britain, having aggressive schemes on portions of Arabia, wished to divert the attention of the Sultan from that part of his dominions by occupying him in Europe, and to do so perfidious Albion found it convenient to encourage Italy to enter upon an adventurous policy in the Balkans to satisfy her vanity.

The German reader when he finds in his newspapers allusions to Spain and Portugal, cannot help realising that Germany encounters little sympathy in those quarters, and it is no consolation to him to be fed with abuse and contempt of the two Kingdoms in the Iberian peninsula.

But to turn to France. If at the present moment the German allows himself to be guided by the press, he would seem to see a bright spot on his political horizon. Every effort is at present being made to persuade the public here to believe that Germany's relations with France and the United States are not only correct, but are bordering on the most cordial friendship. Professor Schiemann asserted the other day in the "Kreuz Zeitung" that Monsieur Cambon brings with him an atmosphere of peace which will be welcome by the German official world, as it represents the views of intellectual France which sooner or later will become the views of the masses in that country. For the Professor all that Monsieur Cambon has to do is to pursue in Berlin a truly French policy which Germany will appreciate and respect. This she has not done for some time past, hence all the trouble and misunderstandings between the two countries. If I grasp the Professor's ideas correctly, he means that ever since the entente cordiale Great Britain has moulded the foreign policy of France not in the interests of that country but in those of herself.

In spite of the attempts made to depict the relations between Germany and France in bright colours, it is impossible not to be struck when one reads the press or talks to anyone here on foreign affairs, how deep the pessimism has grown on the subject of Germany's present position in the world. As an instance of this I would mention a letter published in the Berlin "Reichsbote," the so-called organ of the Court Chaplains (Hofprediger), to the effect that the mass of Germans are inspired more by the desire to avoid a war which they feel convinced will prove disastrous, than by the idea of defending the national prestige. They are ready to put up with every uncalled-for and intolerable national indignity rather than to assume a spirit of resistance to foreign outrage and to run the risk of a war, whether fortunate or unfortunate. The Democratic newspapers make fun of such sentiments which are those of the reactionary party, who stand up for the Kaiser and all he does, whether right or wrong, and they suggest that as in the opinion of the Conservatives the Kaiser is without blame, while they recognise that his policy is unfortunate, they ought, if they were logical, to ask for the head of Prince Bülow, as the person responsible for the misfortunes of Germany.

If we wish to know what the Centre party think on such matters, I cannot do better than give you in a few words the views expressed on foreign affairs by the leading Catholic paper in Bavaria, the Munich " Bayerische Kurier." It asserts that when the higher military circles in the country talk of hostilities being in sight, the public remain indifferent, for military men are always on the look-out for war. The same is the case when the Diplomatists talk of the maintenance of peace, for they will go on doing so to the very eve of the outbreak of war. Therefore what military men or Diplomatists say about a situation often signifies little. It is different, however, when we find in the higher official circles in Berlin serious talk being entertained of the possibility of an impending war, and it is no use hiding the fact from the public that during the last few weeks the political situation has decidedly changed for the worse. After severe criticism of the manner in which German foreign policy has been conducted of late, the " Bayerische Kurier " declares that the Centre Party will stand up for peace, while defending Germany's prestige and her right of expanding her trade in any direction without hindrance in peaceful rivalry side by side with that of other countries. Germany must be strong, but the Imperial Government must clearly make it understood that she seeks for no conquests abroad to the detriment of other nations, and that she desires no further acquisitions of Colonies beyond those which she already possesses.

The nervousness and confusion of mind which is shown by the press in Germany since King Edward's journey to Spain and Italy is very remarkable, and it reveals itself in violent articles complaining of the course pursued by German foreign policy and attacking sometimes in veiled terms the Kaiser himself, and more often in open language the Chancellor and his agents who are held responsible for it. At a moment when the German public require more than ever to have confidence in their Foreign Office, rumours are current throughout the press that friction exists in the Wilhelmstrasse between the Chancellor and Herr von Tschirschky, and although the accuracy of these rumours is denied by the semi-official press, they are generally believed to have a substantial foundation of truth in them. As far as I am able to understand the matter, the causes of the trouble appear to be of two kinds : firstly, jealousy of Herr von Tschirschky on the part of Prince Bülow because of the favour shown to the former by the Kaiser; secondly, the telegram sent to the London " Tribune " by Herr von Tschirschky during the absence of the Chancellor in Italy, in which it was stated that Germany had no intention of keeping away from the discussion at The Hague Conference of the British proposal for the limitation of armaments. The Berlin " Deutsche Tageszeitung," which is generally reputed to be one of Prince Bülow's organs, criticises Herr von Tschirschky very severely for having sent the above telegram, as it interfered with the Chancellor's plans for pursuing a dilatory policy with regard to Germany's attitude at The Hague Conference until he had ascertained how the Powers would finally group themselves respecting the question of the limitation of armaments. Moreover, according to the "Deutsche Tageszeitung" the Chancellor did not approve of the words in Herr von Tschirschky's telegram that Anglo-German relations would continue to improve steadily at the very moment when King Edward by his visits to Cartagena and Gaeta was giving German Diplomacy rude blows.

But it is not only the Chancellor and the Secretary of State and the intriguers in the Wilhelmstrasse who are being attacked in the press just now for the failure of German foreign policy, but the German Diplomatic Agents abroad are also meeting with severe criticism and are accused sometimes of incapacity and sometimes of not keeping their Government informed as to the real drift of public opinion abroad with regard to Germany. A few days ago the Frankfort Gazette laid the blame for the want of sympathy enjoyed by Germany in Spain on the hectoring methods employed by Herr von Radowitz in his attempts to coerce the Spanish Government. The Berlin "Deutsche Tageszeitung" three days ago tried to screen the Chancellor from the charge of ignorance as to Italy's real policy by attacking Count Monts, the German Ambassador in Rome, for not having informed the Imperial Government accurately as to the currents of opinion which were running in high political circles in that capital. Finally, the Munich "Bayerische Kurier" quotes with approval a series of charges brought forward by a Berlin "Freisinnige" newspaper against the leading officials of the Wilhelmstrasse of late years, such as Prince Bülow, Herr von Holstein and Baron von Richthofen, and laying the chief blame on Count Metternich, German Ambassador in London, for his failure to understand British policy with the consequent result of totally misleading the Imperial Government with regard to it. This unfavourable view of the present Representative of the German Empire in Great Britain is indorsed by Herr Müller, Deputy to the Reichstag for Meiningen, who the other day informed a reporter of the Vienna newspaper "Die Zeit" that the unfortunate position in which Germany found herself to-day was in great part due to the incapacity of Count Metternich; the latter had allowed himself to be surprised by the conclusion of the Anglo-French entente, from which time date serious international complications, and in short Herr Müller described the Count as an inefficient Ambassador ("ein sehr unfähiger Botschafter").

In the midst of the nervousness which is being created in Germany by the present international situation in Europe, and the hysterical outbursts of wrath against England which it produces in this country from time to time, it is pleasant to turn to a few soberly written articles in the press and to the expressions of views held by public men who seem to understand the real causes which have led Germany into the unsatisfactory situation in which she now finds herself. The opinions they express are that the blame lies with Germany herself: instead of following a well defined foreign policy and trying to make friends abroad, she follows an undefined and restless one which creates for herself enemies in every quarter. Moreover, the country suffers from the fact that the officials of the Wilhelmstrasse, instead of giving their whole attention to obtain good and correct information with regard to foreign countries for the guidance of the Kaiser, are too much engaged in merely trying to find out what is in His Majesty's mind. The Frankfort Gazette of the eighteenth instant brings the indictment against the German Foreign Office home to its readers in very lucid language, and I may sum up its drift in one phrase: It is not King Edward who isolates Germany by his visits to foreign Courts; if Germany is isolated, it is that she isolates herself.

I have, &c.

FAIRFAX L. CARTWRIGHT

MINUTE.

The whole despatch is most interesting and well worth reading.

C. H.
E. G.

No. 17.

Sir F. Lascelles to Sir Edward Grey.

F.O. 371/260.
(No. 198.)   *Berlin, D. May 9,* 1907.
Sir,   R. *May* 13, 1907.
In a conversation which I had with Herr von Tschirschky on the 7th instant,
His Excellency expressed the gratification with which he had received a despatch from
the German Chargé d'Affaires in London, reporting a conversation which he had had
with you on the subject of Prince Bülow's speech in the Reichstag. Herr von
Tschirschky was glad that the speech had been so well received in London, and he
confidently hoped that the good impression which the speech had produced would lead
to a further improvement in the relations between our two countries. He thought,
however, that it would be advisable to proceed very gradually and with great caution so
as to avoid a revival of the mutual suspicion which he trusted was now subsiding.
I said that I entirely shared the hope which His Excellency had expressed, and
felt all the more justified in doing so as I had recently had a long conversation with
Count Metternich who seemed inclined to take a less gloomy view of the relations
between the two countries than usual.

I have, &c.
FRANK C. LASCELLES.

MINUTES.

It is a curious illusion that Prince Bülow need only make a courteous speech in order to
effect " improved relations." We remember his exuberantly friendly speeches and press-interviews
on the subject of France. They bore no relation whatever to the proceedings of the German
gov[ernmen]t before, during, and after, Algeciras. A little caution is justified.

E. A. C.
May 13.

It is something to hear that the gloomy C[oun]t Metternich is less gloomy than usual.
E. B.
C. H.

My recollection is that I contrasted Prince Bülow's speech favourably with Herr Basserman[n]'s
and said it would now be easy for me to speak in the same tone as Prince Bülow, but I think
there is a record of the conversation.([1])

E. G.

([1]) [Sir Edward Grey wrote a short account of the conversation to Sir F. Lascelles in his
despatch No. 133 of May 3, 1907. The tenour of it is sufficiently indicated in his minute.]

•

No. 18.

Sir F. Lascelles to Sir Edward Grey.

F.O. 371/260.
(No. 199.) Confidential.   *Berlin, D. May 9,* 1907.
Sir,   R. *May* 13, 1907.
My French Colleague has been good enough to inform me that in a recent
conversation which he had with Herr von Tschirschky, the conversation turned on

the understanding which had been arrived at between France and Japan.([1]) It was not to be expected that such an understanding would be agreeable to the German Government who had taken no part in bringing it about, and had not even been consulted on the subject, but Herr von Tschirschky had stated that he regarded it as a further guarantee of the maintenance of Peace in the Far East, and therefore satisfactory to Germany.

Mr. Cambon added that he had reported the conversation to his Government, not because he attached any great importance to it, but because he regarded it as an act of politeness on the part of Herr von Tschirschky, which he hoped might meet with some recognition in Paris.

I have, &c.
FRANK C. LASCELLES.

MINUTE.

Herr von Tschirschky's language on this occasion closely resembles Prince Bülow's speech in the Reichstag which welcomed the Anglo-French understanding of 1904.([2]) Prince Bülow, it will be remembered, quite cynically declared, a year afterwards that the circumstances in 1904 were such as did not make it prudent for him then to express the real view of the German government, such as he could do in 1905 (after Mukden).([3])

E. A. C.
May 13.
E. B.
C. H.
E. G.

([1]) [The Franco-Japanese agreements were signed on June 10, 1907, v. B.F.S.P., Vol. 100, pp. 913–4. A reference to the negotiations is given in Gooch & Temperley, Vol. IV, pp. 285–6, Ed. note.]

([2]) [Speech of April 12, 1904. cp. Gooch & Temperley, Vol. III, p. 69, No. 86, p. 154, No. 194, encl., pp. 348–9, Ed. note, p. 399, App. A, p. 421, App. B, and p. 431, App. B, encl. 2. An extract from the speech is quoted on pp. 348 and 431.]

([3]) [cp. speech of March 29, 1905, ib. p. 348, Ed. note, and p. 431, App. B, encl. 2. An extract from the speech is quoted on p. 348.]

No. 19.

Sir F. Lascelles to Sir Edward Grey.

F.O. 371/260.
(No. 213.)
Sir,

Berlin, D. *May* 15, 1907.
R. *May* 21, 1907.

I have the honour to transmit, herewith a despatch by Captain Dumas, Naval Attaché to H[is] M[ajesty]'s Embassy on the subject of the Annual Meeting of the German Navy League which took place last week at Cologne.

Captain Dumas has touched on all the points of interest in the Meeting, but should a fuller précis of the speeches of the various members be desired, I have the honour to refer you to the summary and short account of the press views which appeared in the Times of the 14th instant.

The Meeting passed two resolutions, one, to the effect that in view of the ceaseless activity of other Powers in increasing their fighting strength, it was absolutely necessary to hasten on the ship-building programme laid down in the Fleet laws of 1900 and 1906; the other declaring that the meeting takes act of the President's declaration that the League as a national and non-political league, refrains from any agitation for or against any political party and declares the motion of the Bavarian section, with their own consent, to be thus dealt with. Finally a vote of confidence and heartfelt thanks was conveyed to the President for his zeal and energy in the interests of the League.

I have, &c.
FRANK C. LASCELLES.

Enclosure in No. 19.

Captain Dumas to Sir F. Lascelles.

Confidential.
Your Excellency,   *Berlin, May* 15, 1907.

I have the honour to submit the following notes and remarks concerning the annual meeting of the German Navy League which took place last week at Cologne :—

The interest taken in this meeting was great, because of the use made by General Keim, the Managing Director, of the propaganda of the League for political purposes against the Centrum and Socialistic parties in the late general election. This gave great offence to the members in Bavaria, who were, it was said, bringing forward a Resolution condemning this interference with politics, and threatening to resign their membership *en masse* unless their Resolution was agreed to, which fact would probably have spelt ruin for the League. The danger was apparently considered so great that His Majesty the Kaiser sent Field-Marshal von Hahnke to represent him at, and convey a special message to, the meeting, and owing to this fact and, as it would appear, a general conciliatory spirit that prevailed, the representatives of Bavaria seem to have finally withdrawn their Resolutions.

At the same time, General Keim seems to have stated that he proposed to continue to use their propaganda—as a factor above party politics—against any party that was inimical to the rapid development of the fleet, and, I need hardly say, made use of the bogey of the overwhelming sea power of England as a menace to German development to enforce his other remarks.

This last, of course, brought all parties momentarily together, but whether the South German branches will continue their support to the movement on reflection time alone can show. The greater part of the business was done in secret conclave, but at the banquet held in the evening various speeches were made, from which the following extracts are interesting :—

The President called attention to the dangers of a superior fleet cutting off from Germany her supplies of raw materials and ruining her sea trade. To obviate that the rate of naval construction must be increased, and every effort made by the Navy League to insure that a fleet of 18,000-ton battle-ships should be in the hands of the Emperor as soon as possible. In view of the peace-threatening dangers to Germany which obtained on every side, and which the comedy at The Hague Peace Conference could do nothing to remove, heavy armaments at sea were all important to Germany.

In the course of his remarks Field-Marshal von Hahnke said that His Majesty prized the League very highly, and saw in their efforts the embodiment of the ideal of arousing, strengthening, and fostering in the German peoples a desire for and interest in sea power and a strong fleet. On account of this the Kaiser had commissioned him to convey to the League his greeting and especial heartfelt Imperial thanks for the self-sacrifice and discretion with which they had carried out their laborious and comprehensive work, and which had filled His Majesty with pride and joy. He was also to call their attention to the fact that union is strength.

During the meeting it was stated that the present number of members was 911,293, so that it is plain how immense is the strength of this wide-spread League if its propaganda is to be made use of for political purposes.

In any case, in view of their perpetual efforts to increase the rate of construction of the fleet, there can be little doubt that their efforts will shortly be crowned with success. I venture to call attention to this probability because I so often see the German Fleet Bill spoken of as a sort of fixed basis for the future construction of other countries, that it is well to recognize that Germany not only can, but is very likely to, complete its provisions long before the year 1920, when its fulfilment is expected, and should that be so, the monetary cost to Great Britain would of necessity be very considerable.

I have, &c.

PHILIP DUMAS,

Captain and Naval Attaché.

No. 20.

Sir E. Goschen to Sir Edward Grey.

F.O. 371/195.
(No. 62.) Very Confidential.   *Vienna,* D. *May* 17, 1907.
Sir,   R. *May* 21, 1907.

There was a very full attendance of diplomatists at Baron d'Aehrenthal's first official reception after his return from Berlin, every one being anxious to hear the impressions left upon him by his visit to that capital. As far as I could learn he held more or less the same language to everyone, laying great stress upon the fact that perfect calm reigned in Berlin official circles, and that he could not discern amongst them the slightest trace of nervousness with regard to the European situation.

His Excellency told me that before Prince Bülow's speech the atmosphere had not been quite so clear and that there had been some rather wild talk both in the Press and in subordinate military circles. As regards the Press, the Government had done everything possible to imbue it with their own pacific feelings, and had succeeded except in the case of a few minor newspapers whose opinions carried no weight. With respect to the bellicose feeling in junior military circles His Excellency said that it was only natural that men whose profession was arms should talk about war more than other people, and it was equally natural that superior officers should not go out of their way to quench a military spirit amongst their juniors as long as it was not carried too far. This was very different from encouraging a bellicose spirit, and he was sure that nothing of the sort was taking place.

All Baron d'Aehrenthal's language on this subject, to which he recurred time after time, appeared to denote a feeling of relief of so pronounced a nature that it gave me the impression that he had found the situation at Berlin very different from that which he had expected, and that he himself had gone there with feelings of the greatest uneasiness with regard to the immediate future. I now know for a fact that this uneasiness existed, as I have since learnt from a prominent member of the Austrian Government that, with the exception of himself, the whole Cabinet had been, after the Royal meetings at Cartagena and Gaeta, in a state of absolute panic, and that at one moment they had thought that war would be a question of days! According to his own account my informant had finally succeeded in arguing his colleagues into a calmer frame of mind, but only with the greatest difficulty. This would certainly explain Baron d'Aehrenthal's relief and satisfaction.

Baron d'Aehrenthal also told me that he had found both the Emperor of Germany and Prince Bülow amicably disposed towards England, that, in fact, the Emperor had lost no opportunity of expressing His great admiration for Great Britain and her people and His earnest desire that Germany should be on the best of terms with her.

Mutatis mutandis His Excellency held exactly the same language to the French Ambassador, M. Crozier.

To all of us he said that his visit to Berlin had strengthened him in the opinion that any clouds which might have recently existed on the European political horizon had cleared away, and that he completely shared the confidence of the German Emperor and His Government that there was nothing in the present European situation to cause the slightest anxiety or uneasiness.

I have, &c.
W. E. GOSCHEN.

No. 21.

Mr. Cartwright to Sir Edward Grey.

F.O. 371/351.
(No. 54.)   *Munich*, D. *May* 22, 1907.
Sir,   R. *May* 24, 1907.

I have the honour to report that signs are appearing now and then in the German press which show that ever since the " Daily Mail " published an interview between Mr. Sidney Whitman and the Sultan, apprehensions have been growing in this country with regard to the possible diminution of Germany's influence at the Porte. As I have reported in my despatch No. 48 of this series of the 6th instant,(¹) the speech delivered by Prince Bülow in the Chambers has not really reassured the German public with regard to Germany's present position in the world, and a great deal of nervousness continues to exist here although the newspapers have been quieter in their tone and are doing their best to minimise the prospect of the growing isolation of Germany in Europe. If there was one country in Europe besides Austria on whose friendship the public here had been taught to believe Germany could thoroughly rely, it was Turkey, and that faith in the continuance of this friendship has been considerably shaken, is shown by the appearance of an article in so serious a newspaper as the Stuttgart " Schwäbische Merkur " and to which I venture to draw your attention.

The article opens by putting the question whether Germany's influence is really beginning to diminish at Constantinople. It quotes Mr. Whitman's interview with the Sultan and then states that Germany's friend, the Grand Vizier, has recently transacted a financial Loan with the Anglo-French Ottoman Bank, giving as securities revenues which ought to have been employed for the purpose of facilitating the construction of the Bagdad Railway. This fact, taken into consideration with certain other disagreeable ones of recent date, leads one to the conclusion that even in Constantinople a campaign has been begun which has for its subject the isolation of Germany. When a friendship like that between Turkey and Germany, which had become as it were a fundamental principle of European politics, and the durability of which seemed beyond doubt, suddenly has the continuity of its existence questioned, then it is time for Germany to put aside mere rumours and to look the matter straight in the face, without unnecessary nervousness and without any attempt to deceive herself.

The article then reviews in detail the Macedonian Reform schemes and asserts that the credit for them in the East is generally given to Germany. The difficulties

(¹) [Not reproduced. It describes Prince Bülow's speech of April 30, in which he referred to Germany's attitude to the discussion of limitation of armaments at the Hague Conference, and spoke hopefully on Germany's foreign relations.]

which certain of the Powers are raising now before they will sign the Protocol allowing the increase in the Customs dues,([2]) will very possibly result in the whole Macedonian Reform scheme breaking down from want of funds, and the blame for this will of course be laid upon Germany. This, to a certain degree, will affect her prestige in the near East. If the Protocol is signed and the Customs duties are increased, Germany, nevertheless, will be the sufferer, for the "Schwäbische Merkur" states that the Sultan, with the approval of the Grand Vizier, Germany's supposed friend, by a secret arrangement made on the 1st instant, has contracted a Loan with the Ottoman Bank at 7 per cent., of which the Turkish Government received £T. 200,000 on account, the guarantee given being the surplus revenue expected to be derived from the increase of Customs dues after providing for the expenses of the Macedonian Reform scheme. Germany had a right to expect from the promises which had been repeatedly made by the Sultan and by the Grand Vizier that a portion of this excess revenue from the increased Customs duties would be used for augmenting the security of the interest on Loans contracted for the construction of the Bagdad Railway. Now all of a sudden the Porte is in want of money and appears to be very urgently so, not only on account of having to meet unpaid salaries in Macedonia, but the expenses of the Yemen campaign and also a dowry has to be provided for the Sultan's daughter on her marriage. The "Schwäbische Merkur" looks upon these explanations as unsatisfactory; in any case in its opinion it seems strange that just those excess revenues which in a way were pledged to assist Germany in the construction of the Bagdad Railway, should at the first opportunity have been seized upon on frivolous pretexts for other purposes.

There can be no doubt that Great Britain and France availed themselves of the difficult position in which the Sultan found himself to induce him to act in a manner which is unfair to Germany. It is true that the Grand Vizier has tried to set matters right by giving Germany a concession for draining the marshes at Konia and Eski-Sher, by which land will be recovered which, it is asserted, may prove of value for agricultural purposes. Such questionable compensations ("solche Zukunftsmusik") cannot be considered as an equivalent for the political and economic harm done by delaying the construction of the Bagdad Railway to its final end, which is not Bagdad but the Persian Gulf. Even if the Grand Vizier were to offer all the marshes of Asia Minor to Germany to drain, there would be no money value in such concessions, for in all similar enterprises there always remains to be faced the bottomless marsh of Turkish official corruption, and there are unfortunately Powers who are alternately ready to make use of this corruption to prevent the successful carrying out of any undertakings they object to.

If in any sense of the word one can talk of a political influence exercised by Germany in Turkey, this influence is merely due to the confidence which the Sultan has in the personality of the Kaiser, and to the prestige which the German army generally enjoys among the governing classes in Turkey, a prestige which is so great that it overcomes even the intrigues which are rampant at Yildiz Kiosk. The best proof of the esteem in which Germany is held in Turkey is shown by the number of German officers in the service of the Sultan; it will be time enough to talk of Germany's diminished influence there when one of these officers has been dismissed and replaced by an official of another foreign nationality. When that occurs it will be a conclusive proof that the Sultan is beginning to believe in the overwhelming power by land and sea of the Anglo-French Entente. So far there is nothing to show that the Sultan holds such views.

Nevertheless it may be asked whether Germany is approaching the moment when in the near East the erroneous idea will begin to gain ground that her political weight in the world has diminished. One thing is clear and that is that the Powers of the *Entente Cordiale* are working all they can to persuade the Sultan to believe that Germany need no longer be feared in Europe, and it is regrettable to note that the

([2]) [cp. *Gooch & Temperley*, Vol. **V**, pp. 196–9, *passim.*]

campaign which they have carried on against the Bagdad Railway Scheme is meeting with some success at the Porte, at the very moment when the German Ambassador is leaving Constantinople for the Peace Conference. This Diplomatist could do no more than he did, that is to protest personally to the Sultan in the most energetic manner against this breach of good faith, confidence and friendship; it is to be hoped that this decided action on the part of the German Representative will have dispelled from the Sultan's mind any doubts he may momentarily have held as to Germany's power. May this be the last misunderstanding between Germany and the Porte which has been brought about on the Bosphorus by the *Entente Cordiale* between Great Britain and France, for as far as regards the Bagdad Railway it is certain that its construction will not be prevented by any such misunderstandings. By wavering in her friendship with Germany, Turkey cuts her own throat, for the construction of the Bagdad Railway is a necessity for the welfare of the Ottoman Empire, and as Germany has been granted the concession for the entire construction of the line, and holds the majority of the shares, it must follow that before long—if Germany is impeded in every way from completing the line—Turkey will be driven to come and beg Germany to do so. Of course this will depend upon Germany being able to hold her own in Europe against the ring of Powers which it is attempted to create around her. No one can tell what will happen on the world's stage in the next ten years, the time required for the completion of the Bagdad Railway, and what may happen in Europe will react on the near East. Constantinople has always been considered as the key to the trade of the near and far East, but now its importance is that it has become a political point of observation: it is there that the first signs may be expected to appear of a diminution of Germany's prestige in the world and belief in her power in the West of Europe.

I have, &c.

FAIRFAX L. CARTWRIGHT.

No. 22.

Mr. Cartwright to Sir Edward Grey.

F.O. 371/253.
(No. 59.)   *Munich, D. June 10, 1907.*
Sir,   R. *June 12, 1907.*

The Paris "Temps" quite recently published a statement to the effect that the Kaiser had the intention of cruising about next spring in the Mediterranean and that he would seize the occasion to visit Monaco to inspect the Institute for Deep Sea Researches which has been established there by the Prince. The "Temps" added that rumours were in circulation that in certain circles attempts would be made to bring about a meeting on that occasion between President Fallières and the Kaiser.

The Munich "Neueste Nachrichten" commenting upon this statement observes that it is quite true that next spring the Emperor will cruise in the Mediterranean and that he will visit the new villa he has purchased in Corfu, the "Achilleion," but that all reports regarding an interview between His Majesty and President Fallières are premature, though such a meeting is not without the range of possibility.

The "Süddeutsche Reichskorrespondenz" in its last issue publishes a communiqué dated from Berlin and called "Hopes for the spring 1908." It says that it can only be with the most laudable intentions that the French press is now beginning to talk of the possibility of a meeting taking place between the President and the Kaiser during the latter's intended cruise in the Mediterranean and visit to the "Achilleion" next spring. It is far from Germany's desire to allow a blight to fall upon such Spring Hopes ("Frü[h]lingsgedanken") but she thinks it better to warn all friends of a closer understanding between herself and France to beware of exaggerated expectations. Well informed circles in Germany feel convinced that a friendly meeting between the Heads of the French Republic and the German Empire would not be distasteful to a large section of the public on either side of the Vosges. But this meeting can only be the last word and not the first in the accomplishment of a most desirable *rapprochement* which is more likely to be brought about the less one talks and writes about it.

I have, &c.

FAIRFAX L. CARTWRIGHT.

MINUTES.

This is an interesting report which reaches us now for the first time. There can be little doubt that those who are working for a Franco-German rapprochement will leave no stone unturned to bring about such a meeting, tho' so far it is scarcely within the horizon.

It is noteworthy that Germany appears to be showing a real desire to conciliate French opinion over the Morocco question, *e.g.*, by giving way about the Engineer question, and now, according to today's *Times* by giving up their Public Works Contract at Tangier.

G. S. S.
E. B.
C. H.
E. G.

No. 23.

Mr. Cartwright to Sir Edward Grey.

F.O. 371/261.
(No. 73.) Confidential.

Munich. D. August 7, 1907.
R. *August 9, 1907.*

Sir,

The Royal meeting off Swinemünde has attracted the attention of every newspaper in Germany but the more they write about it the less clearly one can understand the object of the meeting. The semi-official press, inspired by the "Süddeutsche Reichskorrespondenz," take the view that the meeting is purely an act of friendship and as such is interesting as showing that Germany is not isolated but has friends among the nations, but that it has no political significance in the proper sense of the word. To talk of the Kaiser having gone to meet the Tsar to negotiate an understanding with him is—in the opinion of the German newspapers— an absurdity. It is contrary to German policy and to the Bismarckian traditions to go in search of fantastic ententes inspired by impulse and founded on no solid basis. Germany's political position in Europe is secured by the Triple Alliance whose duration proves that it efficaciously serves the interests of the central European Powers. As regards Germany's relations to Russia in their normal condition they should be good and it has been the tradition of the House of Prussia to hold out the hand of friendship to the Tsar. It is but a proof of neighbourly good conduct to do so at a moment when his authority is threatened by a revolution. It would be futile, however, to pretend—say the German newspapers—that the two Emperors spent their time in idle conversation. Like two experts who take pleasure in closely examining a picture they have no intention of buying, so the two Sovereigns must have passed in review the political events of the moment although they may have no direct interest in their solution. Germany is satisfied with her position—she fears no one—she seeks for no new ententes—she remains firmly attached to the Triple Alliance. Such is the general tone of the German press.

In spite of the attempts made by the majority of German newspapers to persuade their readers that the meeting off Swinemünde had no real political significance, serious people here are of opinion that the meeting was not so entirely of a non-political character but that the important questions discussed there must be sought for in other directions than those looked to by the general public.

At the present moment there are two questions which principally occupy the attention of the Austrian Government: the first is that on the death of the Emperor Franz Joseph the Austro-Hungarian Empire shall pass as a whole to the Heir-Apparent and that Hungary shall not be allowed to separate herself from Austria with the same facility that Norway did from Sweden. The second is that Bulgaria shall not be allowed to take advantage of any difficulties arising in Austria at the death of the Emperor or in Turkey on the death of the Sultan to upset the present state of things in the Balkans. The members of the Triple Alliance view these two questions in not exactly the same manner. In spite of all the Kaiser's professions of friendship towards the Tsar, Germany desires to see the maintenance of a strong Austria as an eventual bulwark against Russia which it may be expected will some day recover her natural influence in European affairs. Italy views the question in a somewhat different light. For many Italians it would be an advantage to their country to see a weakened Austria on the frontier but to many—and perhaps to the more far sighted—a strong Austria is in reality the greatest security against Pan-Germanic attempts to get down to the Mediterranean, the greatest peril for Italy. It may not unreasonably be expected that at Swinemünde Germany has been able to render Austria a service by obtaining assurances from Russia that she in common with some other Powers will use all her moral influence to prevent Hungary from acting in a manner inimical to the dynastic interests of the House of Habsburg. The three Emperors are all the more inclined to act in common defence of their personal interests at a moment when Social Democracy is gaining such force in their respective dominions.

As regards the second question—the future of the Balkans—it interests Russia and Italy to an almost equal degree. Italy desires the maintenance of the status quo in the Balkans from fear that should it be disturbed her interests would suffer and she would not be strong enough by herself to safeguard them; Russia on her side is particularly anxious to prevent Constantinople from falling into Bulgarian hands while through internal disturbances she is too weak to prevent it. Should the Kaiser have been in a position at Swinemünde to assure the Tsar that in an emergency Austria would paralyse a Bulgarian advance on the Bosphorus, Germany would have done Russia a really good turn which may help not a little to weaken the bonds which unite the Tsar to France and so prepare the way for a close understanding between the three Emperors.

The dream of reconstituting the Alliance between the three Emperors undoubtedly exists in some quarters, perhaps more so in Austria than in this country, and hints are thrown out in the press here and there that the sympathy so openly shown by certain influential Parties in England for the Constitutional movement in Russia will tend to drive the Tsar and his Government into the arms of Germany and Austria which are wide open to receive him. The part that Monsieur Iswolsky may play in bringing this about is still uncertain but he is generally credited with not being adverse to Russia following such a course. This gentleman is well known here where he was for a short time Russian Minister and where he returns every year to visit his family who usually spend part of the summer at Tegernsee. If one is to believe what one hears Monsieur Iswolsky's sympathies lean more towards Germany than towards France. It is said that his desire is to be some day Russian Ambassador in Berlin and that he is preparing the way to be received there as *persona gratissima*. Should he be appointed to that post it may be safely assumed that he will labour with a freer hand there than he can in his present position to bring about a close understanding between his country and Germany.

The German newspapers are all agreed that the internal state of Russia must have been one of the chief objects which occupied the attention of the two Sovereigns but they do not throw much light upon this matter and limit their observations to the statement that under no circumstances Germany will interfere in Russian affairs. The German public are really quite in the dark as to what is going on in the neighbouring Empire and the truest thing which can perhaps be said with regard to it is what Count Witte stated the other day to an inquiring German journalist who wished to know all about the actual state of Russian affairs. The Count humorously remarked:—"Behind us lies a swamp—the Revolutionary movement—and there is no bridge which leads back to the mainland—the ancien régime; before us lies the open sea and we have no ships—political leaders—who can safely take us across it."

I have, &c.

FAIRFAX L. CARTWRIGHT.

MINUTE.

An interesting and suggestive despatch.

E. G.

MINUTE BY KING EDWARD.

A most able dispatch and I entirely agree (especially from what I have recently heard) that his statement about M. Iswolsky is quite correct.

E.R.

No. 24.

Mr. Cartwright to Sir Edward Grey.

F.O. 371/261.
(No. 77.)   *Munich, D. August 17, 1907.*
Sir,   R. *August 19, 1907.*

In continuation of my despatch No. 76 of yesterday's date([1]) I have the honour to report that articles appear in the inspired press this morning expressing the greatest satisfaction at the meeting which took place on the 14th instant between the King and the Kaiser at Wilhelmshöhe.([2]) They declare that this meeting is a proof that by pursuing a loyal and straightforward policy and by avoiding to beg for the friendship of any Power Germany has recovered by her own weight her proper position in the Council of the Nations.

The "Münchner Post," the chief Munich Democratic newspaper, published this morning an interesting article in which it expresses a very different appreciation of the Royal meeting than does the inspired press.

The "Münchner Post" begins by making a comparison between the visit of the Tsar to Swinemünde and that of King Edward to Wilhelmshöhe. It says that the Tsar came to Germany pursued by terror and was only protected from peril by the combined German fleets; the King, on the other hand, cheerful and uncrushed by cares, free and unhindered in his movements, can travel through Europe and is sure of meeting everywhere friendly faces and respect. The Tsar was received coolly by the German nation, and if one reads between the lines of the inspired press one is convinced that he met with but little consideration even in official circles. King Edward, however, was received not only as an unquestioned equal but almost as an Over-Lord. The Constitutional Monarch came here, surrounded by the prestige which is due partly to personal intelligence and partly to the power, wealth, and energy of the British nation which he represented, a prestige which has had no equal in history, for as matters stand no Empire in the world can compare in majesty with that of Great

([1]) [Not reproduced. It reports similar comments on King Edward's visit and references to the general situation.]
([2]) [King Edward arrived at Wilhelmshöhe on August 14, and left the same evening for Ischl. Sir C. Hardinge's account of the meeting at Wilhelmshöhe is given, *infra*, pp. 43–6. For the visit to Ischl, *v. Gooch & Temperley*, Vol. V, pp. 208–11, No. 165; *cp.* Sir Sidney Lee: *King Edward VII*, (1927), Vol. II, pp. 547–9.]

Britain. For a long time Germany has not fully recognised this fact. During the last fifteen years German foreign policy has been based on a senseless attempt to rival Great Britain. At times Germany has indulged in dreams of a maritime combination, consisting of herself, Russia and France, directed against British sea power. To attain this she initiated a policy of feverish shipbuilding. Then came the South African war which was hastily considered in this country as the first step in the downfall of the British Empire and Germany therefore strained every nerve to prepare herself to be ready to acquire a share of that Empire when the critical moment should come; it was beyond the comprehension of a Prussian that the conquered South African Republics would in a few years receive Constitutional Self-Government and fall into the ranks of British Colonies. Whilst the South African struggle continued German Diplomacy was very loud in its talk, boasting that no great question in "Weltpolitik" could in future be settled without Germany having the last word to say in the matter. It was even thought that the day might possibly come when sea power would be divided between Germany and Russia. Since the Conference at Algeciras, since the collapse of Russia, since the conclusion by England of "ententes" with France, Italy, Spain and Japan, in short since it has been unquestionably shown that in every direction British Diplomacy is far more clear-sighted and obtains better results than that of Germany, politicians in this country have become considerably more modest in their talk. Finally, the German people—if not their Government—have learnt to understand what no sensible person attempts now to contradict that in the event of an international dispute England would prove more powerful than Germany, and for this reason no man here wishes to see the Empire launched into a struggle with Great Britain.

I have, &c.

FAIRFAX L. CARTWRIGHT.

No. 25.

Memorandum by Sir C. Hardinge, August 19, 1907.[1]

Secret.

(13146*)

Owing to bad weather in the North Sea the King arrived at Cassel three hours later than was intended. His Majesty was met at the station by the German Emperor, attended by Prince Bülow and a large staff, and was received with full military honours. The reception of the King by enormous crowds who lined the road from the railway station to the Palace of Wilhelmshöhe was most enthusiastic and very gratifying to His Majesty. On arrival at the Palace the Cassel Army Corps, under the command of the Duke of Würtemberg, marched past the King and the German Emperor.

At the request of Prince Bülow, whom I used to know very well at Bucharest in 1893–94, when his Excellency was German Minister and I was in charge of His Majesty's Legation, I called upon him in the evening in his apartments in the Palace and had a long conversation with him lasting for more than an hour.

I should preface my report of his conversation by stating that although I was well aware that he had suffered from serious illness about a year ago I could detect no change in him from his former self, his charm of manner and vigour of expression being as remarkable as when I knew him fourteen years ago.

Prince Bülow had evidently carefully prepared what he intended to say to me, and he held forth to me almost without interruption for about half an hour.

He said that when he met M. Isvolsky at Swinemünde he had heard from him that the Anglo-Russian Agreement was practically concluded, the points remaining under

---

[1] [For Prince Bülow's brief account of his conversation with Sir C. Hardinge, *v. G.P.* XXIV, pp. 5–7.]

discussion being practically only questions of detail. He also understood that the interests of Germany would be in no way affected by the Agreement. In Thibet Germany had no interests, while the same might be said as regards Afghanistan. In Persia Germany had no political interests and did not desire them, but she did not wish her commercial interests to be on an inferior footing to those of other Powers, and he had received with satisfaction an assurance that this would not be the case. Under these circumstances he could warmly welcome the conclusion of an Agreement between Great Britain and Russia as likely to remove all causes of friction and conflict between the two Powers in Asia, and as tending to consolidate the interests of peace in Europe.

It was with similar feelings that he had received the news of the conclusion of the Russo-Japanese Convention, which he trusted would finally terminate the hostility which had prevailed between Russia and Japan in the Far East during so many years.

Turning to Morocco, Prince Bülow said that he was most anxious for an improvement in the relations between France and Germany, and expressed his conviction that with the display of tact on both sides, and particularly by the local Representatives of each Power, this desirable result could be obtained. He was fully convinced that France had not the slightest intention or desire to attack Germany, and he gave me the most formal assurances that Germany had no desire to attack France, nor to "brutaliser" France, nor to create difficulties for France in Morocco or elsewhere. He had given stringent instructions in this sense to the German Legation at Tangier, and especially to make the Moorish authorities understand that they could expect no support from the German Government or German Representatives in opposition to France and Spain in Morocco, so long as the actions of the two latter Powers remained in conformity with, and within the limits prescribed by, the Act of Algeciras. He fully realized the difficulties of France in Morocco, and he would do nothing to increase them. All he wanted was that German traders and merchants should not be treated unfairly by the French authorities in Morocco, and that German commerce should not be excluded from fair competition in that country. He contrasted unfavourably to France the treatment accorded to German trade in British and French Colonies, but he trusted that the French Government would abstain from any similar treatment of German trade in a country where they were carrying out the mandate of Europe. He was glad to say that there was already a visible *détente* in the relations of France and Germany, which he hoped might be still further accentuated in the near future, and although he believed that public opinion in Germany entertained no feelings of animosity towards France or the French people he fully realized that it was an easier task for Germans to maintain that frame of mind than for Frenchmen, who still felt the effect of events which occurred nearly forty years ago. He repeated with emphasis the assurances given above, of which, I told him, I was very pleased to be able to take note.

I mentioned to Prince Bülow that I had recently received a visit at the Foreign Office from Dr. Rosen, the German Minister at Tangier, who had wished, at Count Metternich's suggestion, to explain to me the German point of view on the many incidents which had occurred during the past year in Morocco, and which had been the cause of friction between the Powers. I said that I had not been at all convinced by Dr. Rosen, and that, from the manner in which all friction had subsided as soon as Dr. Rosen had gone on leave, I could not help having the conviction, as I had already told Count Metternich, that Dr. Rosen wished to make a name for himself at Tangier, and had thought to do so by raising endless difficulties with the French Legation. Prince Bülow remarked that he had shared the same impression that Dr. Rosen was a "carriériste," but that in any case he had given such strict instructions that there could be no further question of such difficulties as had arisen over the appointment of an engineer and of the construction of a drain—matters of really very secondary importance.

When Prince Bülow alluded to the state of affairs in the Balkan Peninsula, I told him of Sir E. Grey's proposal, which I had been instructed to submit to Baron Aehrenthal, for simultaneous representations at Sophia, Belgrade, and Athens for the suppression of the bands in Macedonia.(²) He said that he thought the proposal a good one, and that the German Government would always support a policy which met with the general approval of the Powers, and more particularly with that of Austria and Russia in the Balkans.

Prince Bülow further alluded to the friction which has recently arisen between the United States and Japan, and said that, from the information which he had received from Washington and Tôkiô, it was very improbable that there would be hostilities between these two Powers, since the Americans realized that war would inevitably entail the loss of the Philippines to the United States, while the Japanese were still suffering severely from their losses in men and money during the past war, and had not yet made good the wear and tear of the Japanese fleet and of their naval armaments. He hoped and believed that the American fleet would not proceed to the Pacific, since such a step would only play into the hands of the Chauvinists of the two countries, but that the surest means to insure this undesirable result would be to tell the American Government that their fleet ought not to go.

He asked me whether our delegation at The Hague Conference intended to propose the reassembly of the Conference every seven years on the invitation of the Dutch Government. I replied that the matter was a delicate one, that we had no desire to wound the susceptibilities of the Russian Government or of the Emperor by proposing the withdrawal of the right of invitation from them, and that I thought it more probable that the American delegation would take the initiative in making this proposal, which we would be ready to support. He said that M. Isvolsky had spoken to him on this subject and had expressed his personal view that he would be very glad if the responsibility for the convocation of future Peace Conferences were removed from the shoulders of the Russian Government, but that he had not submitted the matter to the Emperor Nicholas and did not know how His Majesty would regard the proposal.

Prince Bülow, referring to the German Ambassador in London, said that, though Count Metternich was dull and sleepy, he loved England and thoroughly understood English life and thought. He had also been always perfectly loyal both to Germany and England, and when he had been summoned two or three years ago to come to Berlin to explain the attitude of the British Government, who were accused by the German press of seeking a pretext to attack Germany, he had in his presence spoken out so plainly to the Emperor as to convince His Majesty that the fears conjured up by the German press were baseless. I confined my remarks on this subject to saying that, although Count Metternich was a pessimist and not of a lively disposition, His Majesty's Government had reason to be thankful that during the years when relations between the British and German Governments were somewhat strained he had always carefully avoided making unnecessary difficulties and fanning the flame of the irritation existing between the two countries, and for this His Majesty's Government had every reason to be thankful. Prince Bülow thanked me warmly for this remark, with which he entirely concurred.

He further alluded to the necessity for the display of mutual tact by the press of England and Germany, and expressed his regret that Prince Albert of Schleswig-Holstein and Lord Lonsdale were such personal friends of the Emperor, since he was convinced that their influence over His Majesty was bad and not conducive to friendly relations between the British and German Royal families. He expressed himself as hopeful for the future, and confident that the improvement in the relations between Great Britain and Germany would continue, and thus become a safeguard and guarantee of the peace of the world. I assured Prince Bülow that it was the most earnest desire of His Majesty's Government to have the most friendly relations with Germany, which they would do all in their power to maintain, and I pointed out to his Excellency as examples our consistent action at The Hague in co-operating as much as possible with the German delegation at the Peace

(²) [v. Gooch & Temperley, Vol. V, pp. 207–8, No. 164, and p. 210, No. 165.]

Conference, and the immediate action taken by Sir E. Grey to obtain the internment of Morenga by the Cape Government as soon as news had been received from Count Metternich of his intended raid across the German frontier. For this action Prince Bülow expressed his warm gratitude, and said that it would be much appreciated by the Emperor.

I have compressed as much as possible the views expressed to me by Prince Bülow during a conversation lasting considerably more than an hour, and I should mention that the King had two long interviews with Prince Bülow, and I understand from His Majesty that the tenor of what passed was practically the same as I have reported above.

Although the Emperor was pleased to talk to me a good deal during the course of the King's stay at Wilhelmshöhe, His Majesty studiously avoided all reference to political questions in which Great Britain and Germany are interested, and I therefore refrained from making any allusions to them. The King also told me that the Emperor had not discussed politics with His Majesty.

I may mention, however, that the Emperor told me that when he saw the Emperor Nicholas at Swinemünde he found him in the best of spirits, full of optimism for the future, and determined to dissolve every Duma that should venture to act in opposition to the Government. M. Isvolsky was not, however, in an equally hopeful frame of mind. . . . .(³)

(³) [The rest of this memorandum deals with the visit to Ischl, and is printed in *Gooch & Temperley*, Vol. V, pp. 208–11, No. 165.]

No. 26.

Sir C. Hardinge to Sir Edward Grey.

Private.(¹)
Very Confidential.
My dear Grey, *Kimbolton, August* 21, 1907.

I enclose to you a printed memorandum(²) containing an account of the interviews which I had with Prince Bülow and Baron Aehrenthal at Wilhelmshöhe and Ischl on the occasion of the King's visits to those places last week, and I hope that you will entirely approve of all that I said to them.

If I may make a suggestion it might perhaps be of use if you communicated to M. Cambon part of what Bülow said to me of the attitude of Germany in Morocco. The impression he made on me was that he wishes to be friendly, but I confess that I have never felt much confidence in anything that he said to me. He has always struck me as very cunning and clever.

No allusion was made by Bülow to the Bagdad Railway, and I therefore did not mention it, but Aehrenthal made inquiries as to our attitude towards the scheme, and I explained to him your views. He seemed to consider our position perfectly legitimate, and I have little doubt that what I said to him will get round to Bülow.

The only other point of interest worth mentioning is my impression of the personal relations between the King and the two Emperors. Although the King was outwardly on the best of terms with the German Emperor, and laughed and joked with him, I could not help noticing that there was no real intimacy between them, and no "empressement" on the part of either of them to monopolise each other's company. I think this was more marked on the part of the Emperor than on the part of the King, who with the desire to show his friendliness towards the Kaiser extended his invitation to Windsor from five days to a week.

(¹) [Grey MSS., Vol. 53.]
(²) [*v.* immediately preceding document.]

On the other hand the relations between the King and the Emperor of Austria appeared to me to be of the most friendly and intimate character. They seemed to delight in each other's company and were practically inseparable. I confess I am not surprised at our King's affection for the Emperor, as he is so quiet and dignified, and with an extraordinary charm of manner.

Yours very sincerely,
CHARLES HARDINGE.

No. 27.

Sir F. Lascelles to Sir Edward Grey.

F.O. 371/261.
(No. 371.)
Sir,

Berlin, D. August 21, 1907.
R. *August* 23, 1907.

With reference to my Despatch No. 361 of the 15th instant,([1]) I have the honour to report that the German Papers have continued to devote considerable space to the King's visit to Wilhelmshöhe. It is universally remarked that the speeches of the two Sovereigns were couched in unusually warm terms and it is pointed out with particular pleasure that, while the Emperor only spoke of " good " relations between the two countries, evidently referring to these now existing, the King thought of the future and expressed his wish for " the best and pleasantest " relations. Most of the Articles admit that a meeting between two Sovereigns that lasts only a few hours and a couple of speeches cannot in themselves introduce a new era, but they can be taken as a sign of the times, and also as a good example, and one is justified in hoping that the days of strained relations between England and Germany are at last over.

I have the honour to transmit a translation of an extract from the leading Article of the *North German Gazette* of the 18th instant.([2])

I have, &c.
(For Sir Frank Lascelles),
GRANVILLE.

MINUTE BY KING EDWARD.

This is satisfactory.

E.R.

([1]) [Not reproduced. It summarises press comments upon King Edward's visit to Wilhelmshöhe.]
([2]) [Not reproduced.]

No. 28.

Sir Edward Grey to Sir F. Bertie.

F.O. 371/354.
(No. 472.) Confidential.
Sir,

Foreign Office, August 22, 1907.

I told M. Geoffray to-day that, though I had not yet seen Sir Charles Hardinge, he had sent me a written account of his interview with Prince Bülow.([1])

It had been very favourable and friendly in tone.

The only subjects which it had been arranged that Sir Charles Hardinge should initiate with Prince Bülow were the trouble caused by Morenga, who had made an incursion from British territory into German South-West Africa, and The Hague

([1]) [*v. supra*, pp. 43–6, No. 25.]

Conference, with regard to which it was to be pointed out that the German Government must now feel quite sure that whatever differences of opinion might have arisen the whole conduct of the British Delegation, had no political motive.

Prince Bülow volunteered the statement that he was satisfied from M. Isvolsky that the interests of Germany would in no way be affected by the pending Anglo-Russian Agreement, and he had said that he would welcome the conclusion of such an Agreement, as likely to make for peace.

With regard to Morocco, Prince Bülow had said that he was most anxious for an improvement in the relations between France and Germany. He thought this could be effected by a display of tact on both sides, especially on the part of the local representatives of the two Powers. He was convinced that France had no intention of attacking Germany. And he gave most formal assurances that Germany had no intention of attacking France, nor of creating difficulties for her in Morocco. He realised the difficulties which France already had in Morocco, and he did not desire to increase them. He had sent instructions that the Moorish authorities were to be made to understand that, as long as France and Spain acted in conformity with, and within the limits of, the Algeciras Act, the Moorish authorities would have no support from the German Government or German representatives in opposition to France and Spain. All Prince Bülow wanted was that German traders and merchants should not be unfairly treated by the French authorities, and should not be excluded from fair competition.

M. Geoffray said all that France desired was to act in conformity with the Algeciras Act—he further observed that during the last few weeks there had been a favourable change in the attitude of the German Legation in Morocco.

I said it was very likely that, when Prince Bülow spoke of the need for tact on the part of local representatives, he had Dr. Rosen in his mind.

It had been arranged that Sir Charles Hardinge was not to say anything about the Bagdad Railway unless the Germans mentioned it to him.

Prince Bülow had made no mention of it. But at Ischl Baron d'Aehrenthal had asked what our attitude towards the Bagdad Railway was. Sir Charles Hardinge had told him, and Baron d'Aehrenthal said this seemed a very natural view for us to take.(²)

I had, of course, no doubt that the Germans had instigated Baron d'Aerenthal's question. And I reminded M. Geoffray of what I had already said to M. Cambon about the Railway(³): that the Memorandum(⁴) we had put forward was not final, but intended to prepare the way for discussion, and that though we did not press for discussion we expected the subject would be discussed with us whenever it came up.

At Ischl, Sir Charles Hardinge had spoken to Baron d'Aerenthal of the urgent need for the Powers to do something to discourage and repress the action of the bands in Macedonia. Baron d'Aerenthal had received the idea favourably, and I understood was discussing it with Russia.

The reports from Macedonia about the Greek and Bulgarian bands were very bad, and it was more than ever necessary that the Powers should take this seriously into their consideration. I understood that the Austrian and Russian Ambassadors at Constantinople were communicating to their Colleagues proposals about judicial reform.

[I am etc.]
E[DWARD] G[REY].

(²) [v. supra, p. 46, No. 26. No reference is made to this subject in the account of the meeting at Ischl in Sir C. Hardinge's memorandum. The subjects mentioned, in the last two paragraphs of Sir E. Grey's despatch are discussed there. v. Gooch & Temperley, Vol. V, pp. 208–11, No. 165.]

(³) [v. infra, pp. 357–8, No. 252.]

(⁴) [v. infra, pp. 355–6, No. 250.]

No. 29.

Sir Edward Grey to Sir N. O'Conor.

F.O. 371/380.
(No. 348.)
Sir,
Foreign Office, August 22, 1907.

The Turkish Ambassador told me to-day that he was being pressed by the Palace for information as to what had passed at the various interviews which had taken place lately, such as that between Signor Tittoni and Baron d'Aerenthal, and those of Sir Charles Hardinge at Wilhelmshöhe and Ischl.(¹)

I told him I could say nothing about these interviews except that, as far as we were concerned, they had been of a very friendly character.

The Ambassador said he assumed the subject of Morocco was discussed, and I said that that at any rate was not a subject in which I thought the Turkish Government had any interest.

The Ambassador said he supposed some subjects had been discussed in which the Turkish Government had an interest, such for instance as Macedonia, and he observed in the papers an impression that some new scheme of reforms was being elaborated.(²)

I said judicial reforms were under discussion, as he knew, but we had not been discussing other reforms. We had discussed the urgency of using our influence to stop the outrages of the bands in Macedonia. The Turkish Government had lately asked us to support representations at Athens, and further action of that kind, they must feel, would be entirely in their own interest.

The Ambassador asked me whether we were contemplating internal measures in Macedonia itself for the repression of the bands, and I replied that the step required for repression was the extension and free use of the Gendarmerie against the bands. But that had been put forward at Constantinople, and the Sultan already knew about it.

[I am, &c.]
E. G[REY].

(¹) [v. supra, pp. 43–6, No. 25 and note (³).]
(²) [v. Gooch & Temperley, Vol. V, ch. XXXVI, pp. 196–231.]

No. 30.

Sir F. Lascelles to Sir Edward Grey.

F.O. 371/262.
(No. 379.)
Sir,
Berlin, D. August 27, 1907.
R. August 31, 1907.

Considerable interest has been evinced in the Press with regard to a visit which the French Ambassador paid to Prince Bülow at Norderney on Saturday last. Some attempts were made, especially before the visit came off, to impute to it all sorts of far-reaching motives, some papers even going so far as to suggest that a Franco-German Commercial Treaty or Intercolonial Arrangement was to be arranged. The semi-official papers have now announced in a few words that it was merely a friendly and polite visit during which the two Statesmen were able to assure themselves of the peaceful development of Franco-German relations, and the rest of the papers repeat the same at somewhat greater length. It is pointed out that this interview, the visit of M. Clemenceau to the King at Marienbad, and the conversations of Baron von Aehrenthal and Mr. Tittoni on the Semmering and at Ischl are further links in the chain of political meetings which all have the same beneficial tendency of ensuring the peace of the world. The King's name is seldom omitted in such Articles, and His Majesty is apparently believed to have been more or less instrumental in them all. The various official and semi-official communiqués stating that Baron von Aehrenthal's interviews with Sir Charles Hardinge and Mr. Tittoni have resulted in complete agreement on the question of the reform of justice in Macedonia are quoted in full with satisfaction, and great pleasure is expressed at the renewal of cordial relations between Austria-Hungary and Italy and the assurance that both countries firmly base their policy on the Triple Alliance.

The situation in Morocco naturally occupies much space in the columns of the Press. The North German Gazette, in its weekly review, assures its readers that France is quite determined to abide by the Algesiras Act, and observes that a conclusive proof of the absurdity of supposing that she intends to conquer Morocco is afforded by the small number of troops sent out which would be quite insufficient for such an operation. Some of the other Papers are less convinced on this point and the Liberal "Frankfurter Zeitung" published a leading Article on Saturday, expressing not only the belief that France would probably be forced to go further, but the conviction that the other Powers ought to allow and request her to do so.

There is on the whole in fact a most unusually peaceful and amicable tone in German journalism—even the subject of Morenga's reappearance on the borders of German South-West Africa is treated with moderation—but one or two slightly jarring notes have made themselves heard. The "Hamburger Nachrichten," for instance has published an Article warning its readers against attaching too much importance to all these meetings of Monarchs and statesmen, throwing doubts on the honesty of the King's friendly utterances, and urging the Germans to keep their weather eye open and their powder dry.

I have, &c.
(For Sir Frank Lascelles),
GRANVILLE.

No. 31.

Sir F. Bertie to Sir Edward Grey.

F.O. 371/354.

(No. 417.) Confidential.

Sir,

Paris, D. August 28, 1907.
R. August 30, 1907.

I had occasion to see the Minister for Foreign Affairs yesterday and I showed to him your despatch No. 472, Confidential, (28631), of the 22nd instant[1] which l had just received, as I thought that M. Geoffray might not have reported so fully as your despatch records the information which you gave to him in regard to the interviews which Sir Charles Hardinge had at Wilhelmshöhe with Prince Bülow and at Ischl with Baron d'Aehrenthal.

M. Pichon expressed himself as much pleased with the information which your despatch contained, and at the evidence which it afforded of the relations of mutual confidence established between His Majesty's Government and the Government of the French Republic. His Excellency said that there certainly was a relaxation of the tension between Germany and France and that the German Government were not making difficulties in regard to the French treatment of the Morocco question.

I have, &c.
FRANCIS BERTIE.

[1] [*v. supra*, pp. 47–8, No. 28.]

No. 32.

Mr. Cartwright to Sir Edward Grey.

F.O. 371/262.
(No. 83.) Very Confidential. *Munich,* D. *August* 30, 1907.
Sir, R. *September* 2, 1907.

A few days ago Count Seckendorff passing through Munich came to see me and during a long conversation I had with him he made some observations which it may be worth while to report to you.

He began by saying that he was pleased to see the present *détente* between Germany, France, and England, he thought, however, that the change had come too suddenly to make educated people in Germany believe that it was anything else but an illusion. Until five months ago the German press under inspiration from headquarters had done its utmost to arouse alarm in the public and to draw its attention to the perfidy of Great Britain who was trying to isolate Germany; taking this into consideration it was not to be wondered at, that belief in the real friendship of England did not exist here to any appreciable extent. The change of scene which has taken place is looked upon as diplomatic, serving some purpose, but not as genuine. For several years past sixty millions of Germans have been daily taught to believe that King Edward was bent upon humiliating Germany; now they are suddenly asked to receive him as a friend. Is it then to be wondered at that they should remain silent and incredulous at the present moment? Time alone can bring about a change in the feelings now entertained in Germany towards England and the press of both countries can render a real service in the interests of peace if they abstain as much as possible from discussing controversial questions. Count Seckendorff fully recognised the harm done by the German newspapers and he could only wish that press-writers in this country would for a time forget the existence of England and abstain from exciting the German public to be on the *qui vive* to discover some new perfidy of Great Britain.

Unfortunately, according to Count Seckendorff, the ruling classes in Berlin have a rooted dislike of England. This is partly due to their education and partly to the traditions they have inherited. A generation ago Prince Bismarck had thrown the whole weight of his authority in fostering the spread of the misrepresentation that the interference in politics of the late Empress Frederick must end by having mischievous consequences for the Empire. Her influence was English influence and it was all the more resented by the Prussian aristocracy because it was exerted by a woman in Germany who had remained at heart a British Princess. As the *entourage* of the Kaiser is mainly drawn from the anti-English Prussian aristocracy it follows that there are always influences at head-quarters which will do their utmost to keep up strained relations between Germany and England. What these intriguers will work for is to prevent a lasting *rapprochement* between the Kaiser and King Edward. When the atmosphere is serene between the two Sovereigns they will know how to raise clouds by seizing some opportunity when the Kaiser is in an irritable mood to repeat to him some unfounded remark attributed to the King which they know will cause annoyance to the Emperor. In this way mischief is created and attempts made to keep up friction between the two Courts. The Kaiser for instance is naturally fond of Englishmen and likes to show them kindness. This displeases the "influential people" at Berlin who do their best to prevent the Kaiser from coming into contact with such foreigners. They will even go further than this. Count Seckendorff declared to me that on the occasion of the Kaiser's visit to Lisbon on his way to Tangier the *entourage* induced His Majesty to show but scant courtesy to the Marquis de Soveral simply because the latter was a friend of King Edward. Such is the dread lest any British influence should approach the Kaiser.

I asked Count Seckendorff how he could explain that the German nation, so powerful and so weighty in the world, should show alarm and take umbrage at any diplomatic move which other nations, however remote, might engage in. His reply struck me as rather strange; he said : "The majority of us Germans cannot shake off the feeling that we belong to a parvenu nation and therefore we are always on the look out to see if any other country is offering us some slight." He cited as an example of the correctness of his statement that when the late Count Waldersee was in London, I believe for the King's Coronation, he was all the time occupied in observing whether the Field-Marshal who had acted as Commander-in-Chief of the international forces in China met with due regard and proper respect. The idea that he should not be taken very seriously worried him profoundly. Another instance of this exaggerated sensitiveness on the part of Germans, according to Count Seckendorff, was that the "influential people" the other day opposed King Edward's visit to Wilhelmshöhe until the Kaiser had been invited to pay a formal visit to England. Should the King go to Berlin these people will proclaim that England has bent the knee to Germany and that it is England who has sought for the friendship of this country and not Germany for that of England. That ideas of this kind exist also beyond the *entourage* of the Kaiser may be gathered by a perusal of the German press just now. It is not demonstrative; it has received the word to be discreet but it cannot hide its satisfaction at the amiabilities paid by England to Germany and at the sight of the French Ambassador travelling to Norderney there to consult the German Chancellor on Moroccan affairs. It is needless to say that this latter incident is interpreted as the greatest possible triumph of German policy over that of Monsieur Delcassé.

I pointed out to Count Seckendorff that the German press was somewhat difficult to please for at the present moment when relations were better between our two countries it merely recognised that the British Liberal press spoke amiably of Germany by orders from the Government but that in reality the majority of Englishmen remained Imperialists and therefore they were suspicious of if not hostile to Germany.

Count Seckendorff said that this attitude was in great part due to the force of the Bismarckian tradition and that time alone could bring about a change in this respect. He was of opinion that the mass of Germans were unreasonably alarmed at England's diplomacy and that they were equally suspicious of King Edward. I replied it was a regrettable state of things that Germans through prejudice should have no confidence in the friendly advances of Great Britain; but on the other hand there were good reasons why foreign diplomacy should be suspicious of German policy : of late years it had shown itself uncertain in its aims and wanting in directness. This was generally attributed to the fact that the foreign policy of the Empire depended on the Kaiser's will or on the influence exerted by those who were near him. Now it was easier to understand the wish of a nation than the motives which prompted a man or a handful of men to act.

The answer of Count Seckendorff was that foreign Governments were making a mistake in imagining that it was the Kaiser who alone directed German foreign policy. No doubt he sometimes rushed in impetuously and entangled the threads of German diplomacy but the "influential people" in Berlin were determined to gradually exclude the Kaiser from interfering spasmodically in foreign affairs and their intention was to return to the Bismarckian principles which were that the foreign policy of the Empire should be produced in the Wilhelmstrasse and not at the Palace.

I observed that this might come in the course of time but that for the present it would be very difficult to persuade foreign Governments to believe that the Kaiser had not the last word to say to any question and as long as this belief lasted it must necessarily follow that what the Powers wished to ascertain were the Kaiser's views and not those of Prince Bülow.

Count Seckendorff asserted that the Ambassadors in Berlin were making a great mistake in ignoring Prince Bülow and always trying to run after the Kaiser. The Chancellor was far more the Master than he was generally credited with being and this was especially the case since he had removed every rival out of his way. He was touchy on the matter of his position and his ambition was, now that he seemed all-powerful, to imitate Prince Bismarck and to make Germany understand that he had left his stamp on the direction of German foreign policy. Unfortunately, Count Seckendorff asserted, the Prince, like most Germans of his class, in reality entertained a dislike of England.

On my enquiring whether the Chancellor's position was secure Count Seckendorff declared that at no time had his favour with the Kaiser been so great as at present but he confessed that physically "il avait du plomb dans les ailes."

Turning to another subject Count Seckendorff said that the position of an Ambassador in Berlin was a very difficult one for the "influential people" there were determined to prevent a German Emperor from contamination by too frequent intercourse with foreign representatives. Should the Ambassador become too popular at Court these people would not rest until they had driven him from his post and the means they have recourse to for this purpose would not be above criticism. On the other hand, if the Ambassador enjoyed no Court favour, he would be held of little account. Another observation of Count Seckendorff was that if the foreign representative was timid and insignificant, as Monsieur Bihourd had been, he met with little consideration at the German Foreign Office, where respect was only shown for determination and decision. Monsieur Cambon had undoubtedly improved the relations between France and Germany but then he had come to Berlin with the prestige of intelligence and of past successes, but as regards Court Circles his position was still uncertain and the "influential people" among themselves nicknamed him from his appearance the "country doctor."

At the conclusion of our conversation I happened to mention that I had seen Madame Iswolsky the previous week and that she had told me that her husband intended, if possible, to come to Munich next month by way of Vienna. I then asked Count Seckendorff whether he had heard the report that Monsieur Iswolsky desired very much to become Russian Ambassador at Berlin. He replied that this gentleman and especially his wife desired that post, but he thought that it would be very difficult for the Czar to replace him at St. Petersburg just now.([1])

I have, &c.

FAIRFAX L. CARTWRIGHT.

([1]) [In despatch No. 39 of September 10 Sir Edward Grey conveyed his thanks to Mr. Cartwright for this despatch, which he had "read with interest."]

No. 33.

Mr. Cartwright to Sir Edward Grey.

F.O. 371/262.
(No. 85.)   *Munich, D. September 3, 1907.*
Sir,   R. *September 6, 1907.*

If a barometer were wanted which could show the state of the political weather in Germany it would be found in the way in which the anniversary of the battle of Sedan is celebrated in this country. For the week preceding this anniversary last year the German press had been indefatigable in drawing attention to the importance of keeping alive in the memory of the younger generation the remembrance of that historic victory. Much care was taken to explain to the public the significance of the great efforts which had preceded the creation of the Empire, and as a result last year Munich and other towns in this country were hung with banners on Sedan Day and meetings were held to commemorate it. When about a month later occurred the centenary of the battle of Jena the German press took the opportunity of showing another display of fine martial spirit, pointing out the duty of every German to buckle on his sword, as his forefathers had done, to meet the dangers which were threatening the Empire. This year not a word is to be found in the press on the subject of Sedan; not a banner was hung yesterday from the public buildings in Munich; only a few meetings of veterans took place but they were of little importance. Sedan Day resembled any other day of the week.

What is the meaning of this sudden change of front since last year? The explanation may be found in an article which appeared yesterday—Sedan Day—in the Munich "Neueste Nachrichten" on the subject of a possible meeting between the Kaiser and Monsieur Fallières. It cannot be said that the hopes held out that such a meeting may take place are very sanguine but the fact that such articles issue from Berlin is interesting as showing what is in the mind of the governing classes in that city. The article in question—which is not the only one of its kind which has lately appeared in the press—begins by stating that the rumours with regard to a meeting between the Kaiser and the French President emanate from Belgium and have aroused a great interest in the French press where the idea has been received on the whole very favourably. According to these reports the Kaiser intends to visit Monaco and would meet the President at some spot in the vicinity of that Principality while the German fleet would anchor in the Bay of Villefranche. The Munich "Neueste Nachrichten" declares that however pleasing such a meeting would be to the Imperial Government it must be reserved as the crowning effort of a policy which is at present still in a state of evolution. Referring to an article in the "Temps" the Munich organ observes that that French newspaper appears to be satisfied with the present attitude of Germany towards France but is unable to understand the policy pursued by Germany from 1905 onwards until a quite recent date. The Munich "Neueste Nachrichten" explains that if Germany was unfriendly to France at that period it was due to the aggressive policy pursued by the Republic towards an independent State—Morocco—in which Germany had considerable commercial interests and aspirations. The Conference at Algeciras wiped out the affront to which Germany had been exposed and now so long as France keeps within the limits of the International Act she will find that Germany will raise no opposition to French action in Morocco. What France, however, must remember is that her interference there must partake of a policing character only and be carried on in the interests of public order and security and must not degenerate into a policy of annexation. The sooner General Drude's expedition comes to an end the better it will be for the maintenance of the peace of Europe and the quicker France settles up the damage done by her military forces to the private property of German subjects the better it will be for the development of friendly relations between the two countries—but, concludes the Munich newspaper, in politics one must always be prepared for the unforeseen.

The Stuttgart "Schwäbische Merkur" in its number published on Sedan Day makes no allusions to the German victory but takes the opportunity of drawing attention to an article in the review "L'Europe Nouvelle" in which General Grandin argues that there can be no lasting understanding between Germany and France so long as Alsace–Lorraine remain in their present condition. In his opinion the only way out of the difficulty is either to neutralise the two Provinces, or to sell them to France, or to exchange them for some French Colony. The "Schwäbische Merkur" has no other observation to make except that this idea cannot possibly be entertained on this side of the Rhine, and as one has to take into consideration that the majority of the French people holds such views a *rapprochement* between Germany and France must appear to be still a long way off.

I have, &c.

FAIRFAX L. CARTWRIGHT.

No. 34.

Sir F. Lascelles to Sir Edward Grey.

F.O. 371/261.
(No. 393.)
Sir,

Berlin, D. September 4, 1907.
R. September 9, 1907.

Publicity has been given during the past week in nearly all the papers to the fact that at the Wilhelmshöhe meeting between the Emperor and the King, the former refused admittance to any German journalists and only allowed four English pressmen access to the castle.

This report not having been officially denied, the press are displaying considerable irritation at what they conceive to be such unfair treatment, and the " Börsen Courier" of yesterday publishes a leading article, in which it expresses its regret that the Emperor has never been able to overcome his antipathy to the class of German pressmen in general, and has steadily refused to regard the press as a serious and worthy profession. But the matter has a graver aspect, in the paper's eyes : it is not a question of personal preferences, but an acknowledged right which in this case has been infringed. The press is the natural mouthpiece of the Government in every state, and the leader and instructor of the nation; and the German people have an indisputable right to know what the Government are doing and arranging; by the Constitution the German nation is entrusted with the Government of the State; all the more then have the press, who are the nation's informant, the right to take part in and be present at any events which concern the country's welfare. The whole article is couched in very bitter terms, and it comes as a rather curious commentary upon the Emperor's recently delivered speech of conciliation, charity and general peace, on which I reported in my despatch No. 392 of today's date.(¹)

I have, &c.
(For Sir F. Lascelles),
GRANVILLE.

(¹) [Not reproduced. The speech referred to is that given by the Emperor William II at a Banquet in the Museum of Münster on August 31, 1907.]

No. 35.

Sir F. Bertie to Sir Edward Grey.

F.O. 371/255.
(No. 442.)
Sir,

Paris, D. September 12, 1907.
R. September 13, 1907.

Owing to an oversight an article which was published in the " Dépêche Coloniale" of the 28th of August was not brought to your notice. It is written by Monsieur Etienne and deals with Anglo-German relations, its object being to prove that England and Germany should not be regarded as irreconcilable enemies, and that the Anglo-French Entente is not dependent on their hostility.

Copies of the article are enclosed herein.(¹)

I have, &c.
FRANCIS BERTIE.

(¹) [It has not been thought worth while to print M. Étienne's article as Sir F. Bertie's covering letter describes its subject. Nor has it been thought necessary to quote despatch No. 460 of September 21, 1907, from Sir F. Bertie, which encloses an article in the *Temps* of the same date by " English Subscriber " which is a rejoinder to M. Étienne.]

MINUTES.

The writer of this Article, Monsieur Etienne, ex-Minister of the Interior and of War, is a Deputy, and was for some time head of a very active Colonial group in Paris, and, until the time of the Entente Cordiale, a pronounced Anglophobe. No great weight is however attached in France to his opinions, while the purity of his motives, is, I believe, not always beyond question.

There exists in France at the present time a small but mischievous party who are endeavouring to undermine the Anglo French entente, and to promote a similar French understanding with Germany, and it is the policy of this set to point to the present difficulties which France is experiencing in Morocco to prove that the Anglo French entente never possessed, and was never intended by England to possess, any real advantage for France; and this article is typical of the views held in those circles.

Monsieur Etienne's object appears to be to demonstrate that the interests of England and Germany are not essentially divergent and that the relations between the two Governments have never been characterized by any real hostility, consequently that it would be wise for France to realize this, and to understand that should she ever become embroiled with Germany she could not rely on receiving the support of this country, while in the event of an Anglo German war she would be forced to play the role of a hostage : he deduces therefore in a somewhat subtle way that France should detach herself from her present intimate relations with Great Britain.

Passing to a closer consideration of Monsieur Etienne's article : attention is arrested by his statement that in spite of the polemics of the Press on both sides, the actual defined policy of England and Germany towards one another fails to lend any confirmation to the alarmist prophecies of those who believe in real anglo-German antagonism.

But German policy for more than 20 years, ever since the time when Bismarck preached the necessity of Germany becoming a colonial—and world—power, can be shown to have followed a line consistently unfriendly to the interests of Great Britain. From 1884 onward there have been numerous quarrels between the two countries in all of which Germany adopted a deliberately hostile and aggressive attitude towards Great Britain, which was deeply resented by successive British Foreign Secretaries. In proof of this I should like to quote from Mr. Crowe's memorandum of January 1st last, and to draw attention to the peculiar methods employed by Bismarck in connection with the first German annexation in South West Africa, the persistent way in which he deceived Lord Ampthill up to the last moment as to Germany's colonial ambitions, and then turned round to complain of the want of sympathy shown for Germany's " well-known " policy : the sudden seizure of the Cameroons by a German doctor armed with British letters of recommendation to the local people officially obtained at a time when England had proclaimed her intention to accede to the natives' petition for a British Protectorate : the deliberate deception practised on the Reichstag and upon the German public by the publication of pretended communications to Lord Granville, which were never actually made by the German Ambassador in London : the abortive German raids on Sta. Lucia Bay in South East Africa : the dubious proceedings by which German claims were established over a large portion of the dominions of the Sultan of Zanzibar : the hoisting of the German flag over large parts of New Guinea immediately after inducing England to postpone her already announced intention to occupy some of those very parts by representing that the line of rival territorial claims might first be settled in a friendly manner—all these proceedings show a distinctly hostile attitude.

Monsieur Etienne proceeds to point out- that it was a cardinal axiom of Bismarck's policy to maintain good relations between London and Berlin, which is only true in so far that the late Chancellor of the Empire did not desire a war between the two countries, and felt that Germany could aggrandize herself more effectually at the expense of this country without actually engaging in hostilities—he proceeded therefore to entangle England with France in Egypt, and with Russia in Asia, posing meantime as the friend of all parties. The threatening attitude of both France and Russia towards this country reached such a pitch that Great Britain was induced to conclude in 1887 the two Secret Mediterranean agreements which marked the nearest approach ever made by the Government of this country to joining the Triple Alliance. This was followed up by the efforts of Germany, through the notorious Karl Peters and other German Agents, in defiance of existing Treaties, to establish German Power in Uganda across the line of communication running from Egypt to the head waters of the Nile.

We come next to the famous Kruger telegram which Monsieur Etienne makes out to have been inspired by the Emperor's ardent and chivalrous nature, as also by the wish to render necessary the due observance in London of the agreement between the two countries, and to have been innocent of any unfriendly character. But it is well known that the Emperor's Government was thoroughly alive to the hostile character of that demonstration as is proved by the fact that preparations were made at Berlin for safeguarding the German fleet in the contingency of a British attack, which would not have been anticipated had the telegram been merely the outcome of the chivalrous feelings of the Emperor's heart.

Monsieur Etienne continues to point to further proofs of German friendliness towards England by instancing the acquiescence of Germany in England's advance to Dongola, but Germany had no interests there and was not in position to thwart it. He quotes English support of German policy in China—probably referring to the latter's forward policy in Shantung and later to the "Yangtse Agreement." In Shantung Germany began by the seizure of Kiaochau after obtaining the acquiescence of Russia and then planned the absorption of the whole of this large and fertile Province. The concession of the privileged rights which she wrung from the Chinese Government was obtained in great measure through her official assurance that her claims were supported by England, which is totally untrue, England never having been consulted on this project, which in deference to her own interests she would inevitably have opposed.

As to the Yangtse Agreement, Germany first secretly approached Russia with a view to conclude an agreement by which Germany would have obtained a foothold on the Yangtse, then considered to be practically a British preserve. These overtures being rejected Germany, wishing to prevent us from obtaining that which she had failed to secure, proposed to His Majesty's Government a self-denying agreement stipulating that neither Power should endeavour to obtain any territorial advantages in China. His Majesty's Government did not conceal their great reluctance to enter into such an arrangement but nevertheless again yielded to the policy of conciliating Germany by meeting her expressed wishes and signed the agreement, which the German Government proceeded to interpret in a most peculiar manner laying down that Russian aggression in Manchuria did not come within the scope of the Yangtze Agreement, and continuing themselves meanwhile to prosecute vigorously their designs on Shantung.(²)

Monsieur Etienne tries to show that at the outbreak of the Boer war when the continental press (he does not say whether he means to include that of Germany) was lavishing the vilest invective upon this country, the relations between England and Germany continued in their normal excellent path as is evidenced by the agreements regarding Samoa, and the Neutral Zone in West Africa.

But in both these cases British rights were sacrificed in the hope of conciliating Germany and with the desire of putting the relations of the two countries on to a friendly footing. We consented to these sacrifices with the sole object of improving our relations with Germany and it is consequently hardly fair to instance these agreements as a proof of the excellent terms on which the two countries stood.

It is unnecessary to pause to call attention to the extraordinary campaign of calumny directed against this country from Germany during the Boer war, for it is still fresh in everybody's mind : it was undoubtedly fostered and encouraged in every way by the German Government and directly by Prince Bülow himself in the Reichstag.

We have also very good evidence to show that the Emperor made several attempts during the war to form a coalition to force Great Britain to bring the hostilities to an end.

Monsieur Etienne points to the fact that the Emperor refused to receive Kruger in Berlin, which he interprets as indicative of a special friendliness towards England—he forgets however that by that time the ex-President was a discredited fugitive, and that to have received him in Berlin would have been a tactical blunder of the first order.

Monsieur Etienne remarks that both during and after the South African war Germany continued her naval armaments as a matter of course and thereby caused considerable excitement in the British Press which had scarcely recovered from its recent shocks. He omits however to mention that this excitement and suspicion were more than justified by the German Navy Bill of 1900 which aims at placing Germany in a position to challenge British Maritime supremacy. By this Bill the provisions of which will now probably be carried into effect long before the time stipulated Germany was to possess in 1917 a homogeneous active fleet of 38 first class battle-ships, based on excellent naval ports fully equipped with every appliance, the most advanced of these being at Borkum only 10 hours' steaming from the mouth of the Thames. Small wonder then that British public opinion is stirred by the German Navy Bill and refuses to believe that this vast fleet is being prepared with the sole object of protecting German commerce. From the German Emperor downwards all Germans unite in requiring that the command of the sea shall at no distant date be in German hands.

Monsieur Etienne points to Germany's prompt adhesion to the Khedivial decrees in 1906[4](³) as a further instance of German goodwill. Although the Foreign Office received plentiful professions of German goodwill and of her anxiety to be the first to adhere to the decrees in question, yet in point of fact she was by no means the first and only ended in yielding after protracted negotiations had been carried on between the two Governments.

The Anglo-German Arbitration Treaty instanced by Monsieur Etienne cannot be regarded as serious evidence that friendly sentiments animate the two Governments, as these Treaties were reciprocally exchanged by most of the Powers and do not possess any special signification.

(²) [Marginal comment by Mr. Campbell : " What Germany did actually was to induce us to sign a self-denying ordinance for China, and then to call it the Yangtze Agreement, as giving Germany equal rights in the Yangtze Valley with G[rea]t Britain.—F. A. C. 17.9." For the Anglo-German Agreement of October 16, 1900, and its interpretation, v. Gooch & Temperley, Vol. II, ch. IX, pp. 1–31, and Vol. III, pp. 412–3, App. A, and pp. 426–8, App. B.]

(³) [v. Gooch & Temperley, Vol. III, p. 23, No. 22.]

The visit of King Edward to Kiel to which Monsieur Etienne draws attention was rendered necessary by the fact that His Majesty had not up till then paid to Germany the official visit which he owed according to custom upon his accession to the throne and it is to be noted that His Majesty expressly paid his visit to Kiel and not to Berlin.

Monsieur Etienne comes next to the Morocco crisis of 1905 and observes that although the German press was not sparing of its attacks on France and other Powers that supported her at Algeciras it is specially noteworthy that England was exempted from these diatribes. But during all that time Germany was occupied in trying hard to detach England from France and was doing her best to persuade the British Representative at Algeciras that he should throw over France and go in for a policy of co-operation with Germany : it was not likely therefore that at that moment the German press would adopt towards us the same attitude as it did towards France, and France's other friends.

Monsieur Etienne next observes that the advent to power of the Liberal Party in England coincided with an exchange of amenities of various kinds between London and Berlin. English journalists and municipalities were certainly invited over to Germany, and the invitations accepted : to have declined them would have been churlish and this country has always been ready to move as far as possible in the path of conciliation with Germany.

The Tabah incident is quoted by Monsieur Etienne as having given German diplomacy the opportunity of showing itself " English as regards Egypt " but there is plenty of evidence to show that German agents were all the time intriguing hard against the British Agency, Monsieur Oppenheim in particular earning great notoriety in this respect.

Finally both the Royal meetings at Kronberg and Wilhelmshöhe were devoid of political results : the former was purely private in every way, the Sovereigns meeting so to say on " neutral " ground and while the latter was of a more official character, it has no greater signification than the fact that the relations between the two Courts are no longer on the strained footing of a few years ago.

Monsieur Etienne would be more accurate if he described the present state of Anglo-German relations as correct rather than cordial; it is difficult to see how, with the continual growth of the German fleet the ultimate object of which can only be to try conclusions with that of Great Britain, the relations can become very much closer than they are at present.

G. S. S.
Sep. 16.

Mr. Spicer has drawn up a severe indictment of Germany but it is in my opinion correct.

F. A. C.
17.9.
C. H.

A very valuable analysis of and comment upon the article.

E. G.

No. 36.

Sir F. Bertie to Sir Edward Grey.

F.O. 371/255.
(No. 444.)
Sir,

Paris, D. September 12, 1907.
R. *September 14, 1907.*

By a despatch of the 19th of June (No. 311 Confidential)([1]) I had the honour to report to you a conversation which I had with Monsieur Etienne regarding an invitation which he had received from the Prince of Monaco to join him on his yacht at Kiel during the Regatta there.

As you know, Monsieur Etienne did go to Kiel and was received by the German Emperor, and what passed at the interview and whether Monsieur Etienne had a sort of mission or not from the French Government was a matter of discussion in the French Press.

With reference to this matter I beg leave to call your attention to an article published in the " Indépendance Belge " of the 1st instant which article was, I have reason to believe, inspired from French Official Quarters. It is as follows :

> " Il faut croire qu'il est des hommes politiques qui n'ont pas le loisir de relire les fables de La Fontaine. A propos de la récente rencontre de M. Cambon

([1]) [Not reproduced, as its tenour is indicated.]

et du Chancelier de Bülow, des gens bien intentionnés et empressés ont apporté de petits papiers dans certains journaux pour insinuer que le commencement de la détente, dont cette rencontre préméditée est la manifestation, était une des conséquences de l'entrevue de Monsieur Etienne et de l'Empereur Guillaume ce printemps à Kiel.

" C'est ennuyeux de répéter toujours la même chose mais on ne saurait se lasser de répéter pour ceux qui ne veulent pas entendre.

" Nous n'avons assez dit ici pour n'avoir pas à insister que M. Etienne était allé à Kiel de son mouvement particulier sans avoir reçu un mandat ou une mission quelconque du Gouvernement. Monsieur Pichon a dû affirmer ceci du haut de la tribune et la continuation de cette petite campagne de petits communiqués présentés sous forme de petits entre-filets prouve que la précaution n'était pas inutile.

" On comprend mal la persistance des amis de Monsieur Etienne à vouloir créer cette légende quand même ; d'autant que nous savons maintenant à peu de choses près le sujet de la conversation qui fut échangée à Kiel entre le Député français et l'Empereur allemand ; nous connaissons même certaines phrases textuelles du colloque dont M. Etienne fut un moment troublé au point d'en perdre l'assurance, ce qui n'est guère ni dans son tempérament ni dans ses habitudes.

" Il est inutile de dire que nous tenons nos renseignements de bonne source et qu'on ne pourra leur opposer aucun démenti sérieux ; nous ne pourrions en accepter du reste que de M. Etienne lui-même, et s'il s'en produisait nous savons quoi répondre.

" M. Etienne était allé à Kiel avec l'idée d'amorcer quelques arrangements à côté favorables à des entreprises financières caressées par de grosses banques dirigées par de puissants personnages ayant occupé de hautes situations et qui croyaient pouvoir compter sur une sorte de reconnaissance de Guillaume II.

" Mais l'Empereur d'Allemagne fit comprendre d'un mot net que toutes ces considérations secondaires ne l'intéressaient nullement.

" Voyez-vous, mon cher M. Etienne," dit-il en excellent français, " il ne peut être question entre vous et nous pour arriver à un résultat sérieux qu'à une alliance ferme, complète de l'Allemagne et de la France, alliance contre l'Angleterre la Chine et le Japon qui sont nos adversaires naturels.

" M. Etienne ne put dissimuler un mouvement de profonde surprise et il perdit pied un moment devant cette botte inattendue, puis se ressaisissant il essaya un :

" Mais alors, une France arrondie de son territoire naturel.

" Ce mot coupa net à toute conversation sur ce point, car l'Empereur ne répondit que par un haussement d'épaules qu'il tempéra par un sourire amical.

" Ce simple trait que nous garantissons, prouve bien combien M. Pichon avait été bien avisé, quand M. Etienne était venu le prévenir de son désir de se rendre à Kiel, de se borner à lui souhaiter bon voyage.

" Pourquoi dans ces conditions s'obstine-t-on à ressusciter de temps en temps la légende de la mission occulte confiée au député d'Oran?

" Continuera-t-on encore?
" Nous ne le souhaitons pas."

One of the persons referred to as " de puissants personnages ayant occupé de hautes situations " is undoubtedly Monsieur Rouvier with whom Monsieur Etienne is associated in various commercial speculations.

Monsieur Etienne has not so far as I am aware made any statement in contradiction of the Article in the Belgian Newspaper.

I have, &c.
F. BERTIE.

No. 37.

Sir F. Lascelles to Sir Edward Grey.

F.O. 371/262.
(No. 434.) Confidential.

Berlin, D. October 3, 1907.
R. October 7, 1907.

Sir,

I have the honour to forward, herewith, a despatch, as marked in the margin, which I have received from Captain Dumas, Naval Attaché to this Embassy, relating to the rumoured new Navy Bill to be introduced in the next Reichstag.

I have, &c.
FRANK C. LASCELLES.

Enclosure in No. 37.

Captain Dumas to Sir F. Lascelles.

(No. 53.) Confidential.

Your Excellency,

Berlin, October 3, 1907.

I have the honour to call your attention to the frequent statements in the German newspapers of late as to the introduction, during the forthcoming session of the Reichstag, of either a new Navy Bill or of an amendment to the existing one.

I may say here that while calling at the Admiralty a short time ago I asked if anything of the sort was projected and was told by my usual informant, one of Admiral von Tirpitz' Naval secretaries, that he personally knew nothing about it. However as now papers of such widely differing political views as the Berliner Tageblatt, Berliner Neueste Nachrichten, Der Vorwärts, Kölnische Zeitung, Münchener Zeitung and the Kieler Neueste Nachrichten (the last being the semi-official Naval organ of the Government) are all agreed that such a bill must come it would seem really probable that an amendment, at least, is projected.

Thus the Münchener Zeitung says that Prince Bülow seems to have come to an understanding with his parliamentary guests as to how a new Navy Bill is to be got through and what new taxes will be accepted by the Reichstag.

The Berliner Neueste Nachrichten speaks of an ultimatum having been sent to the Government by the armour plate makers and that a new Navy Bill must come this winter also that the Centrum Party has stated its willingness to grant the extra forty millions in view.

The Kölnische Zeitung while deprecating attacks on Admiral von Tirpitz says that anyway everyone must be prepared for a new Navy Bill.

The Kieler Neueste Nachrichten says that it hears from a reliable source that if alterations are made in the fleet bill they will refer to Par. 2, which states that with the exception of loss battleships are to be replaced after 25 and cruisers after 20 years and it is believed that in future battleships will be replaced after 20 years' service.

I need hardly say that the above is a very attenuated resumé of the articles on this subject confirmatory remarks having appeared in almost every paper of note in Germany.

Summing it up the least that would appear likely is the shortening of the official life of the battleships to 20 years while personally I have an idea that a further increase in the number of the armoured cruisers will be put forward by the supporters of the Navy League who I need hardly say are at the bottom of the whole agitation.

If only the first however is carried through it would mean that Germany in 1920 would possess 38 battle-ships of 20 or less years old and, even if the whole of the Coast defence battleships are broken up which I doubt, nine more of a greater age all of which however would have been modernized within the past 24 years.

Of course I am by no means suggesting that these ships would be the equal of those of England but the public will probably fail to realise this as they only judge by numbers.

Hence I deem it my duty to submit these facts to your attention as broadly speaking, if a bill is brought in in the above sense, we shall probably see statements in the press that by that time (1920) Germany will possess 47 battleships and Great Britain some 56 or a margin of superiority which allows of no force of these vessels being kept in foreign waters at all. I would further point out what is seldom recognized at home that the manning of these ships would cause but little trouble in Germany where as I hear constantly said by those most qualified to know they already possess some 60,000 more reservists than they could possibly require in time of war.

I have, &c.
[PHILIP DUMAS,]
Naval Attaché.

No. 38.

Sir F. Lascelles to Sir Edward Grey.

F.O. 371/262.
(No. 440.) Confidential.
Sir,

Berlin, D. *October* 7, 1907.
R. *October* 14, 1907.

The North German Gazette published this evening, contains an official announcement stating that the Imperial Statthalter in Alsace Lorraine is desirous of vacating his post on account of age, and has handed in his resignation. Count von Wedel, Ambassador at Vienna, has been appointed successor to Prince Hohenlohe Langenburg, and the vacant post at Vienna will be filled by Herr von Tschirschky. The direction of the Foreign Office will devolve upon Herr von Schoen, German Ambassador at St. Petersburg. The retirement of Prince Hohenlohe Langenburg, who has now reached his 75th year, is not likely to occasion much surprise. He was the third holder of the post and succeeded his relative Prince Chlodwig Hohenlohe Schillingsfürst, afterwards Chancellor of the Empire, in 1894. The thirteen years of his rule at Strassburg have not been characterised by any events of importance. He steadily and successfully pursued the policy of conciliation adopted by his predecessors, and the news of his resignation will be received with regret in the Reichsland. Prince Hohenlohe was related to the Emperor by marriage, being the uncle of the Empress. Before his appointment to Strassburg he had a distinguished military and civil career. He served in the Franco-Prussian war on the staff of General von Werder, and afterwards became a Conservative member of the Reichstag of which he was for some time Vice President. He took great interest in colonial questions and was the first President of the German Colonial League.

Count von Wedel's resignation of the post of German Ambassador at Vienna has also been expected for some time, but it was not known whether he would retire altogether or whether he would be appointed to a different post. It appears that his conduct of affairs at Vienna has not given entire satisfaction to the authorities in Berlin and his appointment to Strassburg is looked upon as "the kick upstairs."

Herr von Tschirschky was appointed to the post of Secretary of State for Foreign Affairs on the death of Baron Richthofen in January 1906, and it was generally supposed that Prince Bülow was anxious to appoint Dr. von Mühlberg to the vacant post; but that the Emperor would not agree and insisted on the appointment of Herr von Tschirschky. The latter had impressed His Majesty favourably while Prussian Minister at Hamburg, during which time he frequently accompanied the Emperor on his journeys abroad as representative of the Foreign Office. It is said that Herr von Tschirschky had been reluctant to accept the post and only did so at the urgent request of the Emperor, and on the last occasion that I saw him he informed me that he found that his health, and especially his eyes, was not equal to the heavy strain involved by the work of the Foreign Office and that he shortly would be offered an Embassy abroad.

I am informed that Prince Bülow had never liked the appointment of Herr von Tschirschky whom he had always been jealous of as a possible successor in the

Chancellorship; and that he made up his mind to get rid of him before the session of the Reichstag, and to secure the appointment of Herr von Mühlberg as his successor. I learn however on good authority that the Emperor has again interfered and insisted on the appointment of Herr von Schoen, who like his predecessor, recommended himself to the Emperor while accompanying His Majesty on his journeys abroad; and it was after the Tangier visit that he was transferred from Copenhagen to St. Petersburg in succession to Count Alvensleben. His previous career has been varied and he has not had so much diplomatic service as his predecessor. He began life in the army and for some time occupied the post of Court Marshal at Coburg. It is worthy of remark that he is a South German by birth and not of an aristocratic family.

The resignation of Herr von Tschirschky is the third incident which has occurred since May whereby Prince Bülow has been relieved of persons whose influence was displeasing to him. By the scandals connected with the disclosures in the Zukunft he got rid of the powerful backstairs influence of Prince Eulenburg and his friends, and he utilised this opportunity to secure the retirement of Count Posadowsky whose influential position rendered him a possible candidate for the Chancellorship. By the transference to Vienna of the Secretary of State for Foreign Affairs, it would seem that Prince Bülow has removed from Berlin every member of the Government who might pose as a rival for his post, and he will meet the Reichstag with a subservient Government behind him. It is said that he has never been so high in the favour of the Emperor as now and he therefore will have every support in his endeavour to keep the "bloc" majority together.

I have, &c.

FRANK C. LASCELLES.

MINUTES.

Prince Bülow would have preferred Dr. von Mühlberg to Herr von Schoen as a successor to Herr von Tschirschky, but his position will nevertheless be strengthened by the removal of the latter to Vienna.

R. H. C.

This despatch offers a further proof of how important it is for officials who wish to get on in Germany to become personal friends of the Emperor : and this is also the reason—to a certain extent—of the constant intriguing in German official circles.

G. S. S.

Prince Bülow was never in higher favour but cannot choose his own Lieutenants.

W. L.

According to a private letter from Sir F. Lascelles, P[rin]ce Hohenlohe did not at all want to resign and did not know that there was any idea of moving him from his post until he met the Emperor at Carlsruhe at the funeral of the Grand Duke of Baden. The Emperor then spoke of a change at Stra[s]sburg and the same evening Wedel's appointment appeared in the press. Prince Ernst Hohenlohe was dismissed from the Col[onial] Office in precisely the same manner.

C. H.
E. G.

No. 39.

Sir F. Lascelles to Sir Edward Grey.

F.O. 371/262.

(No. 473.) Confidential. *Berlin.* D. *October* 24, 1907.

Sir, R. *October* 28, 1907.

I have the honour to forward, herewith, a despatch, as marked in the margin, which I have received from Captain Dumas R.N. Naval Attaché to this Embassy, relating to the new German Shipbuilding programme.

I have, &c.

FRANK LASCELLES.

Enclosure in No. 39.

Captain Dumas to Sir F. Lascelles.

Germany. N.A. Report 59/07.

Confidential,   *British Embassy,*

Your Excellency,   *Berlin, October 23, 1907.*

I have the honour to submit the following considerations which arise from the reported provisions of the expected amendment to the Fleet Bill, and which, we may now, I think, be certain, will enact that the replacement of battle-ships shall in future take place after a life of 20 years.

The present shipbuilding programme is as follows :—

Year.	Ship to be replaced or built.
1906–1907	Sachson, Bayern, Cruiser E.
1907–1908	Wurttemburg, Baden, Cruiser F.
1908–1909	Oldenburg, Siegfried, Cruiser G.
1909–1910	Frithjof, Beowulf, Cruiser H.
1910–1911	Heimdal, Additional ship. Cruiser Kaiserin Augusta.
1911–1912	Hildebrand, Cruisers J and Freya.
1912–1913	Hagen, Cruisers K and Victoria Luise.
1913–1914	Odin, Cruiser Hertha.
1914–1915	Aegir, Cruiser Vineta.
1915–1916	Brandenburg, Cruiser Hansa.
1916–1917	Kurfurst Fried Wilhelm, Cruiser Furst Bismarck.
1917–1918	Weissenburg & Worth.

This programme is roughly based on the replacement of the battleships at 25 years' life and the recognition that as soon as possible the ships of the Frithjof class, which in reality are coast defence vessels of some 4,000 tons, should be wiped off a list supposed to contain only modern battleships.

Lastly an additional battleship to complete the agreed upon number of 38 in all is to be constructed.

But it by no means allows for the replacement of the ships at 20 years' service and this we can deduce from the following table :—

Ship.	Completion.	Year of Replacement.	Commencement.
Sachsen	1878	1898	1899
Wurttemburg	1881	1901	1898
Bayern	1882	1902	1899
Baden	1884	1904	1901
Oldenburg	1887	1907	1904
Siegfried	1890	1910	1907
Frithjof	1892	1912	1909
Beowulf	1892	1912	1909
Kurf Fried Wilh	1893	1913	1910
Brandenburg	1893	1913	1910
Weissenburg	1893	1913	1910
Heimdall	1894	1914	1911
Hildebrand	1894	1914	1911
Worth	1894	1914	1911
Hagen	1895	1915	1912
Odin	1896	1916	1913
Aegir	1897	1917	1914
Kaiser Fried III	1898	1918	1915
Kaiser Wilhelm II ...	1900	1920	1917
Kais Wilh der Grosse ...	1901	1921	1918
Kais Karl der Grosse ...	1901	1921	1918
Kais Barbarossa	1901	1921	1918

which gives us that if the programme was strictly carried out the following would
be the necessary construction :—

1908–1909	Oldenburg & Siegfried,
1909–1910	Frithjof & Beowulf,
1910–1911	Kurf Fried Wilhelm, Brandenburg & Weissenburg,
1911–1912	Heimdall, Hildebrand & Worth,
1912–1913	Hagen,
1913–1914	Odin,
1914–1915	Aegir,
1915–1916	Kaiser Friedrich III,
1916–1917	Nil,
1917–1918	Kaiser Wilhelm II,
1918–1919	Kaisers Wilh der Grosse, Karl der Grosse & Barbarossa,

which with the Shipbuilding resources of the German Empire could easily be
accomplished.

But in view of the fact that by the Fleet Bills of 1900 and 1906 an armoured
cruiser fleet and replacements for the existing vessels has to take place as they reach
the age of 20 years and further that an additional battleship has to be built the
resulting combination is as follows :—

1908–1909	Oldenburg, Siegfried, Cruiser G,
1909–1910	Frithjof, Beowulf, Cruiser H,
1910–1911	Kurf Fried Wilh, Brandenburg, Weissenburg. An additional ship & Cruiser Kaiserin Augusta,
1911–1912	Heimdall, Hildebrand, Worth, Cruisers J & Freya,
1912–1913	Hagen, Cruisers K & Victoria Luise,
1913–1914	Odin, Cruiser Hertha,
1914–1915	Aegir, Cruiser Vineta,
1915–1916	Kaiser Friedrich III & Cruiser Hansa,
1916–1917	Cruiser Furst Bismarck,
1917–1918	Kaiser Wilhelm II & Cruiser Prinz Heinrich,
1918–1919	Kaisers Wilhelm der Grosse, Karl der Grosse & Barbarossa,

a programme which would be for the years 1910–1911–1912 excessive in cost as
well as beyond the shipbuilding capacity of the Empire to carry through.

Now it seems certain that we shall not find any change whatever in the building
programme for next year proposed in the forthcoming estimates (though I imagine
that the new Siegfried will be of greater displacement than the new Oldenburg) but
that very fact will enormously increase the ever-growing discontent of the Navy
League and I might almost add the nation at large with the comparative size and
armament of the earlier German ships with those of England and to speak plainly
I believe that unless a well-considered programme is formulated during the coming
year a very serious state of affairs will arise in Germany.

Also as regards classification while the Frithjof class are considered as
battleships it must be recollected that they are only of some 4,000 tons and possess
a very poor and badly protected armament even as compared with the Worth class
and this fact having already struck the Navy League there is likely to be an outcry
for their speedy replacement which I believe would be met by constructing these
reliefs before the vessels of that class.

A further point worth noticing in this connection is that in any case the vessels
of the Worth class would be relieved before ten years' time which would probably
satisfy the agitators. Again I do not believe that any programme will satisfy the
people at large which does not include the replacement of the Kaiser class.
Whatever they may appear on paper I have never met any German, whether Naval
Officer or civilian, who has any opinion of them as fighting ships while I fancy that
the Naval Officers think much the same of the Wittelsbach class.

Lastly there is the question of the additional battleship but as that need not be finished till 1920 when the tale of 38 battleships must be completed it can of course be constructed in any convenient year up to 1917.

Now from constant consideration of the subject I am of opinion that the shipbuilding capacity of Germany could cope for a short time with, the construction of four large armoured ships in one year and in view of this and the possible outcry spoken of above I am inclined to believe that it is more likely, if for two or three years a very heavy programme was proposed, that the Admiralty would prefer to replace the smaller vessels during those years because they could then point out how impossible and unfair it is in these days for anyone to look upon such craft as practical battleships and so to some extent disarm criticism and still more an outcry from England which they fear and dislike above all.

Summing up then some programme such as the following may fairly be expected, indeed as regards numbers it is certain if the 20 years life is agreed to, though I would deprecate its acceptance as anything but very problematical after 1914–1915.

1908–1909	Oldenburg, Siegfried & Cruiser G.
1909–1910	Frithjof, Beowulf & Cruiser H.
1910–1911	Hildebrand, Odin, Kurfurst Friedrich Wilhelm and Cruiser Kaiserin Augusta.
1911–1912	Aegir, Brandenburg, Cruisers J and Freya.
1912–1913	Weissenburg, Worth, Cruisers K & Victoria Luise.
1913–1914	Hagen, additional battleship, Cruiser Hertha.
1914–1915	Kaiser Friedrich III, Cruiser Vineta.
1915–1916	Kaisers Wilhelm II, Wilhelm der Grosse, & Cruiser Hansa.
1916–1917	Kaisers Karl der Grosse & Barbarossa & Cruiser Furst Bismarck.

The first and most showy result of such a programme is that by the year 1915 at latest the whole of the battleships would be replaced at 20 years official life while after the financial year 1910–1911 the expenses as shown now would tend to fall. In reality of course with the size of battleships, speed and armament constantly increasing, the cost, at the most moderate computation, of a battleship in the near future will rise to some £2,500,000 and the true prospect is rather the reverse. I would here like to point out that much of the frightful cost to be foreseen is due to the absolute secrecy preserved by Germany with regard to the armament of her new vessels thus inducing other countries to enter into ruinous competition with a view to possessing something certainly better.

Against this prospect of the increase in the cost of battleships it is probable that large armoured cruisers are now at their maximum size at all events until the battleships rise to some 30,000 tons and I should therefore compute that for the future we may take their cost roughly at two-thirds of that of a battleship.

Anyhow taking the above figures as an approximate guide the cost of this programme would be some 65 million pounds instead of the equally roughly computed sum, which the programme of 1900 allowed for, of 24 million pounds : or, if they fail to rebuild the Kaiser class till their proper date, of 55 million to 24. Broadly speaking therefore we see an increase of cost during the next ten years of at least 30 million pounds or 3 millions a year and this be it remembered is to be incurred on the sole ground of the replacement of the battleships at 20 years service even if that be only completed within ten years.

This increase does not by any means complete the extra costs to be foreseen. It is certain now, I think, that an extensive fleet of submarines will be built which were not allowed for in either of the Navy Bills, and, taking the number to be built during the next few years at six only, we here again find an addition to the required budget of about £500,000 annually. All this extra expenditure I need hardly say is already causing some uneasiness in financial circles in Germany where

F

it is realised that even now the Exchequer is practically at the end of its resources as regards financial contributions towards the Imperial requirements and only this morning I see suggestions that the Government should in consequence assume the monopoly of the manufacture and sale of spirits.

This I believe would prove almost as great a failure as the other taxes which have lately been raised for similar purposes for drinking is undoubtedly falling in Germany and moreover, as a matter of personal observation, I believe that it is extra food rather than an extra drink that is looked upon as a treat by the public at large and therefore it is the drink which would first be given up.

Under any circumstances this question of a greater Naval budget must be a very anxious one for Germany.

The second result is that Germany will or may possess nine battleships of Dreadnought or later types in 1912 and certainly 17 in 1916 beyond which date it is probably foolish to reckon and especially as even such a prospect will far from satisfy the Navy League.

As regards numbers I am of opinion that the Frithjof class at least may be discounted as soon as their reliefs are commenced and consequently even the British public should show no anxiety on their account.

The Brandenburg class however come under a different heading and broadly speaking the temptation to retain them as coast defence vessels after their replacement is not I think likely to be withstood.

If that should prove the case I would beg to point out that it is probable that it will be largely said in England that Germany possesses or will possess 42 battleships and I note this because such numbers are responsible for such foolish outcry in a still more foolish press.

In conclusion I would submit that although much of the above is based on probabilities yet in their broadest aspects those probabilities are what might be called minimum certainties and as such I have ventured to develop them in the hope that my remarks may be of use in settling our future programme.

Lastly it is a matter of not infrequent comment here that in its benevolent behaviour towards the somewhat embarrassing propaganda of the Navy League the German Government has had in view the turning of the eyes of the people away from other grievances. If that is so I am of opinion that they have done more than they suspected for now all political parties are convinced of the necessity of a great and strong Navy and judging by their speeches are ready to pay the price.

Whether that price would not remove the grievance is so doubtful that even now it is a question if, when that price is realised, we may not see every effort made to end the agitation a result which, I am convinced, would be welcomed by none more than the German Admiralty who see with horror in the other and adventurous policy a dreadful and devastating war with Great Britain.

I have, &c.
PHILIP DUMAS,
Captain and Naval Attaché.

MINUTE.

The views of the German Admiralty as stated in the concluding sentence are of great interest, and it seems that a persistent policy on the part of our Admiralty in regulating our building programme by the double of that of Germany may in the end induce the German public to cry out " Enough."

C. H.
E. G.

No. 40.

Sir F. Bertie to Sir Edward Grey.

F.O. 371/256.
(No. 521.) Confidential.   Paris, D. October 30, 1907.
Sir,   R. November 1, 1907.

Monsieur Eugène Lautier, the Foreign Editor of the "Figaro," has published an article in this morning's issue of that paper with the object of refuting the statement made in the course of the Moltke–Harden trial in Berlin that an interview between the German Emperor and Monsieur Loubet in April 1904 in the Mediterranean fell through owing to the "mauvaises dispositions" of the French Government.

Monsieur Lautier states that such is not the case. According to him, Monsieur Loubet first mentioned the matter to the German Ambassador in Paris before his visit by sea to Italy, and said "J'ai vingt ans de plus que l'Empereur. Néanmoins, si nous rencontrons le Hohenzollern je n'hésiterai pas à faire la première visite."

Monsieur Lautier comments on this initiative and gives it as his opinion that France could not have shown in a better or clearer manner that her "rapprochement" with England and the renewal of friendship with Italy was not directed against Germany.

Monsieur Lautier states that the President of the Republic and his "entourage" really believed that a meeting with the German Emperor would take place: Monsieur Delcassé, who had meant to return from Rome to Paris by land embarked at Naples with the President on account of the possibility of this meeting Uniforms and a new Imperial flag were taken on board and the Band practised the German National Anthem.

The German Emperor, however, returned to Germany without meeting the President, and shortly afterwards showed his dissatisfaction with the turn things had taken by a speech at Carlsruhe as to the necessity for keeping "the powder dry and the sword sharpened."

Monsieur Eugène Lautier is a conscientious journalist and had personal relations both with Monsieur Loubet and Monsieur Delcassé.

I showed the Article to-day to Monsieur Louis and I asked him what he knew of the circumstances referred to by Monsieur Lautier. Monsieur Louis after reading it said that it was possible that Monsieur Loubet may have spoken to Prince Radolin to the effect stated by Monsieur Lautier, but there had never been any official or unofficial discussions between the French and German Foreign Offices on the question of a meeting between Monsieur Loubet and the German Emperor.

My recollection of what the French Ambassador at Rome told me is that the German Ambassador meddled in the settlement of the arrangements for the visit of the President of the French Republic by constant inquiries at the Consulta and objections to anything being done in excess of the arrangements on the occasion of the German Emperor's visit to Rome; and, as stated in the "Figaro," pressed the Italian Government not to give opportunities for popular demonstrations in favour of French friendship. Monsieur Barrère's account of the question of a meeting between the President of the Republic and the German Emperor was that it was His Majesty who wished for a meeting, but would not take the first step; that he was furious at the tone of the speeches at Naples on the occasion of the departure of Monsieur Loubet from Naples, and that His Majesty, after waiting about in the Mediterranean in the hope of a request from Monsieur Loubet for a meeting, which never came, went off in a huff to the Adriatic and travelled home viâ Venice.

I have, &c.
FRANCIS BERTIE.

MINUTE.

M. Louis denies that any communications either official or unofficial passed between the French and German Foreign Offices as to a meeting between M. Loubet and the Emperor.

G. S. S.

M. Loubet was ready to call first if they did meet, but apparently did not go out of his way to arrange a meeting.

W. L.
C. H.

Each probably desired a meeting, if the other would take the initiative : each was probably afraid that political capital would be made of his having taken the initiative.

E. G.

No. 41.

Count de Salis to Sir Edward Grey.

F.O. 371/262.
(No. 511.)
Sir,

Berlin, D. November 19, 1907.
R. November 21, 1907.

I have the honour to transmit, herewith, a translation of the new German Navy Bill, as published last night in the semi-official North German Gazette.

This morning's papers express universal surprise and almost unanimous disappointment at the extreme insufficiency, as they term it, of the proposals.

I have, &c.
J. DE SALIS.

Enclosure in No. 41.

Translation of Extract from the North German Gazette of November 19, 1907.

The proposal for the change to be made in the present navy bill, was accepted by the Federal Council on November 14th. It is worded as follows :—

Draft

of a bill for changing § 2 of the law of June 14, 1900 concerning the German fleet. (Reichs-Gesetzbl. p. 255.)

We, William, by the grace of God, German Emperor, King of Prussia, &c., with the agreement of the Federal Council and of the Reichstag, order the following :—

Single Paragraph.

Instead of § 2 of the law of June 14, 1900 concerning the German fleet (Reichs-Gesetzblatt, p. 255), the following is inserted :—

§ 2.

Except in cases of ships lost, battle-ships and cruisers shall be replaced after 20 years.

The time is counted from the year in which the first instalments were granted for the ship to be replaced until the granting of the first instalments for the ship intended to replace it.

For the time between 1908 and 1917 the building of ships shall be governed according to Annex B.

In witness whereof, &c.

Annex B.

Distribution of the new ships to be built between 1908 and 1917, according
to each year :—

Year.				Battle-ships.	Big Cruisers.	Small Cruisers.
1908	...	...	...	3	...	2
1909	...	...	...	3	...	2
1910	...	...	...	3	...	2
1911	...	...	...	2	...	2
1912	...	...	...	1	1	2
1913	...	...	...	1	1	2
1914	...	...	...	1	1	2
1915	...	...	...	1	1	2
1916	...	...	...	1	1	2
1917	...	...	...	1	1	1
Total	...	...		17	6	19

Reasons.

During the discussion of the first navy bill in 1898, it was pointed out by the representative of the Federal Governments that 25 years is perhaps too long to allow for the life of a ship (*Cf.* Report of the Budget Commission of March 17, 1898).

The 25 years allowed are reckoned according to the bill from the granting of the first instalment for the ships to be replaced till the granting of the first instalment of the ships intended to replace them. However the life of a ship must be considered much longer from a military and technical point of view.

The military-technical birthday of a ship is not the day when the first instalment was granted, but the time when the military and technical requirements regulating the construction are finally settled. Further a ship is not put out of commission when the first instalment for the new ship is granted, but only when the new ship is finished and has been commissioned. Consequently when the battle-ships are put out of commission they are really not 25 but 30 years old. As the experience of all navies has shown they are then quite out of date and in the last few years quite unserviceable for warfare.

This is justified by the swift progress that is continually being made in all departments of the construction of ships, machines and arms, and which must be taken into account by every navy. It has been proved by experience since the first Navy Bill that the life of battle-ships must be shortened, if the ships are to remain fit for warfare until they are put out of commission.

Distinguished experts of foreign navies are of opinion that the life of a battle-ship should not exceed 15 to 20 years. According to the proposal of the Federal Governments, by which the life of a battle-ship is fixed at 20 years calculated in the same manner as hitherto, the real life from the beginning of the construction till rejection is still about 25 years. This time is so long, in consideration of the continuous technical progress, that towards the end a battle-ship would be of scarcely any use in the first line of battle.

By the shortening of the life of battle-ships, three additional substitutes will be required in the time from 1908 till 1917.

In order to include these 3 ships in the present substitution table,—Annex B of the Bill, see p. 7—a new Annex B is required.

There is also a second reason for this new Annex B. If it were required to substitute the battle-ships and big cruisers between 1908 and 1917 in the years in which they must be replaced according to § 2, Section 1, in consideration of the shortened life during that period, the following plan for the construction of new ships would result :—

Year.				Battle-ships.	Big Cruisers.	Total.
1908	...	...	...	2	1	3
1909	...	...	...	6	...	6
1910	...	...	...	1	...	1
1911	...	...	...	2	...	2
1912	...	...	...	2	...	2
1913	...	...	...	...	...	...
1914	...	...	...	1	...	1
1915	...	...	...	...	4	4
1916	...	...	...	1	2	3
1917	...	...	...	1	...	1
Total		...	...	16	7	23

Such a plan of construction is irrational. Therefore in the new Annex B the new battle-ships falling due for construction from 1908 till 1911 are distributed as regularly as possible over the first 4 years; the big cruisers and battle-ships falling due for construction between 1912 and 1917 are distributed over the six years; in the interest of regularity one new battle-ship falling due after 1917 is included in the period from 1912 to 1917. To adjust this, the construction of one big cruiser is postponed till after 1917.

The entire costs incurred by the change in the Law equal approximately the cost of three battle-ships.

No. 42.

Count de Salis to Sir Edward Grey.

F.O. 371/262.
(No. 529.) Confidential.   Berlin, D. December 4, 1907.
Sir,   R. December 9, 1907.
     I have the honour to forward, herewith, a despatch, as marked in the margin, which I have received from Captain Dumas Naval Attaché to this Embassy, relating to the amendment of the Fleet Bill, with observations on the consequent programme.

I have, &c.
J. DE SALIS.

Enclosure in No. 42.

Captain Dumas to Count de Salis.

Confidential.
Sir,   British Embassy, Berlin, December 2, 1907.
     I have the honour to submit the following translation of the Amendment to the fleet Bill which has now been published on acceptance by the Bundesrat.

I also append some remarks in elucidation of the consequent programme of shipbuilding and proceed with the Memo[randum] printed in connection with the Naval Estimates and the considerations that arise therefrom.

We, William, by the grace of God German Emperor, King of Prussia enact in the name of the Empire, subject to the assent of the Bundesrat and Reichstag, as follows.—

The following is to be substituted for section 2 of the law of the 14th June 1900 concerning the German Fleet.

Section 2.

Losses of ships excepted Battle-ships and Cruisers are to be replaced after 20 years.

This period will be reckoned from the granting of the first instalment for the ship to be replaced to the granting of the first instalment for the replacing ship.

For the period from 1900 [*sic.* 1908] to 1917 the replacing construction *i.e.*, building of substitute ships, will be in accordance with Appendix B.

APPENDIX B.

Distribution over the individual years of the replacing construction—*i.e.*, building of substitute ships—to be taken in hand during the years 1908 to 1917 inclusive.

Year.				Battleships	Large Cruisers.	Small Cruisers.
1908	...	...	...	3	...	2
1909	...	...	...	3	...	2
1910	...	...	...	3	...	2
1911	...	...	...	2	...	2
1912	...	...	...	1	1	2
1913	...	...	...	1	1	2
1914	...	...	...	1	1	2
1915	...	...	...	1	1	2
1916	...	...	...	1	1	2
1917	...	...	...	1	1	1
				17	6	19

Argument.

In 1896 [*sic.* 1898] during the discussions over the first fleet Bill it was pointed out by the representative of the allied Govern[men]ts that with a period of 25 years the duration of life of a battleship was possibly made too long.

The 25 years replacing period was reckoned in accordance with the law, from the granting of the first instalment for the ship to be replaced to the granting of the first instalment for the replacing ship. In reckoning the life of the ship in a military and technical sense a considerably longer period has, however, to be considered.

The technical military birthday of a ship is not the day of the granting of the first instalment but the time of finally deciding on the plan of construction based on military and technical requirements. Moreover the replacing of a ship does not take place when the first instalment for the replacing of the ship is granted but when the replacing ship is completed and commissioned.

As a result of this battleships on being replaced are not 25 but about 30 years old and they are then, as the experience of all Navies teaches, completely obsolete and during the later years of this period are no longer of any use in a battle. This is caused by the rapid progress which is continually being made in all branches of ship-building in engine construction and in gunnery. This has to be taken into account by every Navy.

From the experience which has been gained since the first fleet Bill was passed it is established that the duration of life of battleships must be shortened if ships are to remain suitable for employment in the battle line until they are so replaced.

Distinguished Officers of foreign Navies are of the opinion that the duration of life of a battleship should not exceed 15 to 20 years. With the demand of the allied Governments to fix the life of battleships at 20 years, reckoned in the same way as in the past, the actual life from the commencement until the ship is replaced will always be about 25 years. This period having regard to the continuous progress of science, is still so long that at the end of it a battle-ship can scarcely be considered fit for the first line of battle.

Through the shortening of the life of battleships, in the period from 1908 to 1917, three additional battleships will be required as substitutes. In order to include those 3 ships in the table of replacing ships—Appendix B of the law for which see above—a new Appendix B is necessary.

There is a second reason for such an appendix. If it is desired, having regard to the shortened duration of life during the period 1908–1917, to replace the ships and large cruisers in the years in which they should be replaced in accordance with § 2, para. 1 then, in consequence of the want of uniformity in the grants of former years, the following programme of replacements would obtain—

Year.				Battleships.	Large Cruisers.	Total.
1908	...	...	...	2	1	3
1909	...	...	...	6	...	6
1910	...	...	...	1	...	1
1911	...	...	...	2	...	2
1912	...	...	...	2	...	2
1913	...	...	...	...	...	...
1914	...	...	...	1	...	1
1915	...	...	...	...	4	4
1916	...	...	...	1	2	3
1917	...	...	...	1	...	1
				16	7	23

such a plan of construction is irrational. In the new Appendix B therefore the 11 battleships to be constructed as *replacing* ships from 1908 to 1911 are as far as possible divided equally between the first four years and the replacing construction falling due from 1912 to 1917 both in battleships and large cruisers, is spread uniformly over the following 6 years in which, in the interests of uniformity, is included 1 replacing battleship from the period after 1917.

In compensation 1 *replacing large cruiser is postponed* to the years after 1917.

The total cost of the alteration is approximately equal to the cost of three battleships.

Amendment ends.

From the above it will be seen that the whole increase in numbers which this new programme entails is really three more battle-ships and one less cruiser.

It is quite otherwise however with time.

Now it will have been observed in the foregoing that only replacement ships are spoken of but reference to the original fleet Bill of 1900 shows that the following *new construction* also was approved.

1908	...	...	...	...	...	1 Large cruiser.
1909	...	...	...	...	...	1 ,, ,,
1910	...	...	...	...	...	1 Battleship.
1911	...	...	...	...	...	1 Large cruiser.
1912	...	...	...	...	...	1 ,, ,,
1917	...	...	...	...	...	1 Small cruiser.

Therefore taking the new Appendix B in conjunction with this *new or additional construction programme* we arrive at the following which is Germany's actual building programme for the next ten years—

Year.				Battleships.	Large Cruisers.	Small Cruisers.	T.Bs.
1908	...	...	...	3	1	2	12
1909	...	...	...	3	1	2	12
1910	...	...	...	4	...	2	12
1911	...	...	...	2	1	2	12
1912	...	...	...	1	2	2	12
1913	...	...	...	1	1	2	12
1914	...	...	...	1	1	2	12
1915	...	...	...	1	1	2	12
1916	...	...	...	1	1	2	12
1917	...	...	...	1	1	2	12
				18	10	20	120

which shortly indicates that in the next four years Germany will lay down 12 battleships instead of 8 as the former programme provided for.

Now by the lists of the ships of the German Navy as published in the estimates of this year and 1906 the order of replacement can be decided and substituting for these we can see at a glance what ships Germany will possess in any given year by the following table.

I do not take it beyond 1914 because I am of opinion that in 1911 the Navy League will force on the Government a wholly new programme which I believe will increase the permanent number of battleships to forty.

I am allowing three years for the completion in every way of a battleship or large cruiser and I would like here to record my conviction that there will be absolutely no delay in carrying out the whole programme to the letter.

On the 1st July in each year, then, Germany will possess.

	1908.	1909.	1910.	1911.	1912.	1913.	1914.
Battleships							
Earlier types ...	37	37	33	30	27	24	22
Dreadnoughts ...	...	...	4	7	10	14	16
Large cruisers							
Earlier types ...	14	14	14	14	14	14	14
Invincibles ..	..	...	1	3	4	4	5

of the number of Battleships of earlier types shown as existing those of the Frithjof and Wörth types are even now of very little fighting value and a revised list showing only battleships of a first-class fighting value would read.

	1908.	1909.	1910.	1911.	1912.	1913.	1914.
Battleships—							
Earlier types ...	20	20	20	20	20	20	20
Dreadnoughts ...	...	...	4	7	10	14	16
	20	20	24	27	30	34	36

thus showing the enormously rapid growth of the fighting value of the German fleet.

I should perhaps also remark that in the last two years of this period the Kaiser class also may be partly discounted.

In view of these tables which undoubtedly represent the opinions as held by the most able Officers in this country I think it can clearly be realised why the German

Admiralty are proposing such enormous sacrifices to bring the fleet up to some sort of a standard fit to cope with the Sea power of England, who, they literally and truly believe, may attack them on the smallest pretext thus only forestalling, while Germany is still weak, that war which they also—whether rightly or wrongly time alone can show—believe must ensue between the two countries. And this, I submit, is borne out fully by the Memo[randum] which is published in connection with the Naval Estimates of this year and which reads as follows.—

Memorandum.

The necessary strengthening of the coast defences, the construction of a dock on the lower Elbe, extra costs for shipbuilding and armaments, a further increase of crews for the ships, the substitution of modern vessels for the out of date training ships and finally the increase of pay and wages as well as the table money make a new further estimate of costs imperative.

1. Shipbuilding and Armaments.

a. Increased costs of ships and torpedo boats.

In all great Navies unceasing efforts are made to perfect more and more the gunnery and torpedo armaments of ships and torp[edo] boats. If the German ships and torpedo boats are not to lag behind those of other Nations then it is impossible for us not to recognize possible technical improvements. This entails an increase in the costs of ships and torpedo boats which is further increased by the general rise in prices.

b. Increase of the Shipbuilding Reserve funds.

The demands on the shipbuilding reserve funds have become very considerable. Also the experience of the Russo-Japanese war have [sic] shown the necessity for special vessels such as mining-ships, Workshop repair vessels, fleet colliers and so on.

Further in all great Navies the advantage of giving modern ships a thorough re-construction once during their period of existence in order to preserve their fighting value has shown itself to be urgently necessary.

By this means the ships receive technical improvements which have, in the course of their existence, shown themselves to be desirable and capable of being carried out. To this end the present reserve funds now 12·4 million marks yearly are insufficient and in future will amount to some 20 millions.

c. Increase in the funds for Submarines.

The necessity for applying more money for this purpose will very soon now occur.

Firstly it has transpired that only submarines of greater displacement than those hitherto constructed can answer all requirements.

Secondly the number to be laid down yearly must be increased as soon as the trial period is concluded, and this may very shortly be expected.

For the year 1909 ten millions and from 1910 onwards fifteen millions marks may be expected to be demanded.

d. Reduction of the life of Battle-ships.

Already dealt with in the Amendment to par 2 of the Fleet Bill.

2. Increase in the Personnel.

In order to profit by the technical improvements in gunnery and ships an increase in the crews becomes necessary.

Further the substitution of large cruisers for sailing ships in the training service as well as their increased numbers makes an addition to the personnel imperative.

The increase on these grounds amounts to.—

Naval officers	10
Engineer officers	9
Seamen, &c.	575

3. Permanent Expenses.

Owing to numerous unforeseen but necessary measures a considerable increase has here developed.

In consequence of the rise in price in all provisions an increase in the table and victualling costs at home must be allowed for entailing an additional yearly sum of nearly two million marks.

Also the change of type of training ships has given rise to considerable extra expenses. and lastly it has been made clear that an increase in the costs of keeping ships and their armaments in good repair also the expenses of gunnery practice justify the great demands which will be made for them.

In consequence of this in the estimates for 1908 the recurring expenses are increased by 13 million marks.

Further of late, owing to the uncertainty as to the working expenses of modern ships and, even when not considerable, the extra cost of an increased personnel, a much greater increase of the recurring expenses must be reckoned with than had up to the present been allowed for.

4. Other Non-Recurring Expenses.

It has been shown necessary to improve the Coast Defences of the Baltic and North Sea.

Besides this a dry docking establishment must be installed on the Lower Elbe.

Therefore in this portion of the Estimates provision has been made with this end in view.

5. New Table of Costs.

The following table gives a summary of the probable financial requirements up to the year 1917.

The division of the costs into those raised from income and loan is carried out according to the plan in the Memo[randum] of the Imperial Budget for 1907. Pages 45–51.

Year.			Recurring Expenses.	Formation of Estimates. Ship-building and Armts.	Non-Recurring Expenses.	Total.	Paid for by— Income.	Loan.	Yearly Increase.
1908	...	...	6·78	8·56	1·72	16·96	12·46	4·5	1·4
1909	...	...	7·18	11·34	1·75	20·27	14·38	5·9	1·98
1910	...	...	7·68	12·60	1·75	22·04	15·69	6·35	1·30
1911	...	...	8·26	13·05	1·75	23·08	16·86	6·22	1·17
1912	...	...	8·88	12·20	1·50	22·45	17·48	4·97	·32
1913	...	...	9·48	10·53	1·50	21·51	17·93	3·58	·45
1914	...	...	10·58	9·25	1·5	20·83	18·42	2·41	·48
1915	...	...	10·48	8·35	1·25	20·08	18·72	1·36	·30
1916	...	...	10·88	8·35	1·25	20·45	19·37	1·11	·65
1917	...	...	11·28	6·35	1·25	20·88	19·97	·91	·60

Comparing the estimated costs as now put forward with those in the Naval Estimates for 1906 we obtain the following table of increases.

Year Estimates.	08	09	10	11	12	13	14	15	16	17
1906	11·24	12·54	13·13	13·72	14·31	14·83	15·25	15·63	15·7	16
1908	12·45	14·38	15·69	16·86	17·48	17·93	18·42	18·72	19·4	20
More ..	1·22	1·84	2·56	3·14	3·17	3·10	3·17	3·09	3·7	4

N.B. I have turned the figures which are given in Marks into Millions sterling.

Memo[randum] ends.

Considering the above two facts stand out very clearly.

1. The serious incapacity shown by the German Admiralty, despite their love of detail, to reckon on future requirements and which of itself causes one to view these estimates for the future with doubt.

2. That the Admiralty, or rather I should perhaps say the German Government, are carrying out the behests of the Navy League, a large body of whom are permeated with fear of the designs of England, and that therefore we by no means see here the end of this alarming increase.

However as things are what the whole amounts to is that their Naval Estimates are to rise year by year as follows.

1908	...	...	...	£16,500,000 and paid by loan £4,500,000
1909	...	...	...	20,250,000 5,890,000
1910	...	...	...	22,000,000 6,350,000
1911	...	...	...	23,000,000 6,225,000
1912	...	...	...	22,500,000 4,970,000
1913	...	...	...	21,500,000 3,580,000
1914	...	...	...	20,800,000 2,415,000
1915	...	...	...	20,000,000 1,365,000
1916	...	...	...	20,400,000 1,115,000
1917	...	...	...	20,800,000 915,000

£37,325,000

and although with the present wave of prosperity passing over the country there can be little doubt that for the next three or four years the money can and will be found yet, should lean years come, it is by no means unlikely that a demand for economy may arise when it is possible that this ever increasing expense on the Fleet may come to an end. I would also beg to call attention to the huge amounts which will have to be raised by loan during the construction of the programme of which no less than some £23,000,000 must be obtained during the next four years.

Here again we might find cause for a cry of halt especially as the announcement of the finance Minister in the past few days that Germany has raised £80,000,000 by loan during the past six years is even now causing much comment in the press. But I confess that I do not believe that in practice any such economies will occur. The Navy League has been preaching danger in every village within the Empire for the past few years and the people at large have come to believe that in a Fleet is their only safety. Under these circumstances I am of opinion that they are prepared for even greater sacrifices should they be called for.

I have, &c.

PHILIP DUMAS,
Captain and Naval Attaché.

No. 43.

Count de Salis·to Sir Edward Grey.

F.O. 371/262.
(No. 538.)   Confidential.   *Berlin,* D. *December* 10, 1907.
Sir,   R. *December* 16, 1907.

I have the honour to forward, herewith, a despatch, as marked in the margin, which I have received from Captain Dumas, Naval Attaché to this Embassy, relating to the Reichstag debate on the subject of the new Fleet Bill.

I have, &c.
J. DE SALIS.

Enclosure in No. 43.

Captain Dumas to Count de Salis.

Sir,   *Berlin, December* 9, 1907.

I have the honour to submit the following translations of Admiral von Tirpitz' and other leading Deputies' speeches in the Reichstag on the occasion of the general Budget debate commencing on the 28th November.([1])

Admiral von Tirpitz said.   The bill laid before you has in the first place a military object.   By its means we wish to bring the present condition of our ships up to the highest standard of efficiency and to maintain them always at the same point of efficiency as those of the other great powers.

A considerable number of our ships, owing to the rapid advance of technical improvements, are no longer at that point and require speedy replacement.   In accordance with the terms of our present fleet bill that replacement would be too slow.   We hear every day drastic expressions of opinion on the part of the Navy League as to their condition but our ships are not so bad as these expressions would imply or as the Navy League would wish to make them appear.

The Secretary of state then gave reasons for the reduction of the life of the battle ships to 20 years (I cannot find these are anywhere published) and also referred in the most friendly way to the services on behalf of the fleet of Doctor Lieber—at one time the leader of the Centrum party—who would not have allowed this defect in the fleet bill to persist : the fleet bill which he at that time helped so largely to bring safely into port through so many parliamentary quick sands.

Now there exist two possibilities.

First the proposition of the Navy League, which condemns the arrangement whereby the substitution age must be arrived at before replacement.   But in that case every ship must go from time to time under the microscope to examine whether it fulfils the latest requirements.

That is ideal but radical and has moreover the disadvantage of enormous cost.

The other way, as proposed by the federated states, is to reduce the actual age of the ships and the moment has now come for so regulating them.

I have spoken during many years with parliamentarians on the subject and it seems clear to us that we must come into line with other Nations as to the lowest limit in this matter.   To that limit we adhere in the present bill.

Technique goes steadily forward and ships built to-day are wholly out of date in 25 years.

No one need fear that we are asking too much in the present bill and I would urgently advise the House to maintain the Bill, so much envied us by other Nations, at its highest level.   It is for the consequent and systematic development of the fleet the safest if not the only guarantee.

Dr. Spahn, the leader of the Centrum, in support remarked that the Reichstag had already mortgaged its voice in the matter by its adherence to the proposition for the widening and deepening of the Kiel Canal.

([1]) [Not reproduced.]

Herr Bassermann, the leader of the National Liberal party, said that without a strong fleet Germany would be only a second rate power. My friends will therefore vote for the fleet bill and will also vote the four millions asked for submarines in the fleet bill. . . . .([1])

Prince Bülow said nothing directly about the Bill only calling on the deputies to consider ways and means for the provision of the funds required.

Herr Bebel, the leader of the Social-democrats, remarked as follows. "We are in a perpetual danger of war. The Official press complains bitterly that Germany stands alone and that all the alliances are made without her. It was hoped that healing would once come from Windsor but it does not appear so—as on the very day that the two Monarchs parted the fleet Bill was introduced. No one thinks of peace. We are all warlike in our behaviour.

Has the majority considered against whom the increase of the fleet is actually directed?

The Navy League declares it openly. England and once more and again England.

That this feeling exists also among widespread ranks of the people is shown by a poem, written ostensibly by a cadet but in reality by a Pastor, which is handed to every cadet on entering the school in which the words occur. "And if England, jealous, gets in our way we trust to our Emperor."—

Broadly speaking the press has been extraordinarily silent up to date as regards any pros and cons for this Fleet Bill and no one so far as I have seen, has ever published the appalling mass of debt which its carrying out must entail on the country.

Against that I have seen no single word of doubt as to its advisability and I do not think that any will arise the only question being as to the method of the financial provision for its effective realisation.

I have, &c.

PHILIP DUMAS,
Captain and Naval Attaché.

([1]) [Thus in original.]

II.—THE VISIT OF THE EMPEROR WILLIAM II TO WINDSOR, NOVEMBER 1907.

No. 44.

Sir C. Hardinge to Sir Edward Grey.

Private.([1])

My dear Grey,

H.M. *Yacht Victoria and Albert,*
April 7, 1907.

The King spoke to me yesterday and again today on the subject of a possible visit by the German Emperor to England this year, and His Majesty asked me to write to you to ascertain your views.

The King wishes me to remind you that the Emperor has not returned the official visit paid by the King to Kiel in 1904 and that he has not been to England since His Majesty's accession with the exception of a private visit paid to the King at Sandringham in November 1902. Last year owing to the Moroccan conflict, the King, in accordance with your advice, renounced all idea of inviting the Emperor to Windsor, but he thinks that it would be neither polite not politic to delay the return visit which the Emperor has yet to pay, and which all the other Sovereigns

([1]) [Grey MSS., Vol. 53.]

whom the King has visited have already returned. The King would therefore like to invite the German Emperor to come to Windsor in November, and he thinks that this invitation would be greatly appreciated by the Emperor William and the German people, and would tend to improve the relations between the two countries, without giving our friends any real cause for suspicion or alarm as to the motives of the invitation on the part of the King.

It seems to me that this visit has to be paid some time or other, and that there is the possibility that with the visit in view German policy abroad might assume a less aggressive attitude than at present, while the invitation to the Emperor might help to mitigate any ill-feeling that he will probably have towards us when we have negotiated our agreement with Russia, or that may be created by our attitude towards the question of the limitation of expenditure on armaments at the Hague Conference. For these reasons I think it would be advisable that the return visit should take place at Windsor this autumn, unless something quite unforeseen should occur to prevent it, and it is possible that an invitation to Windsor might be the best means of preventing any such incident arising. It should certainly improve the relations between the two Sovereigns which, to judge from the Emperor's language to the French Chargé d'Affaires at Berlin, must be very bitter on his side, and I do not think it need cause alarm to the French Gov[ernmen]t who know what their mutual feelings are to each other.

Perhaps you will think over this and let me hear your views some time or other. There is no great hurry.

It blew very hard when we left Toulon yesterday, but it has been a delightful day to-day and I hope this will continue tomorrow when we arrive at Carthagena.

Y[ou]rs very sincerely,
CHARLES HARDINGE.

No. 45.

Sir Edward Grey to Sir F. Bertie.

Private.([1])

My dear Bertie, *Foreign Office, June 19, 1907.*

I do not think a visit from the President is necessary this year, and it seems hardly possible.

Parliament will probably sit till September: after that we shall all be exhausted, and away for some weeks.

For some time, I have been much preoccupied as to how the visit of the German Emperor in return for the King's visit to Kiel was to be arranged. It ought to have taken place before now, but the political atmosphere has not been favourable. The longer it is deferred, the greater will be the discourtesy and soreness, and unless things are to get worse the visit must take place some time. It is now proposed that it should be in November, and I believe an invitation has actually been sent.

The moment for doing so is opportune. One or two difficulties in Morocco have been settled amicably, and the exchange of Notes with Spain([2]) has just given a new evidence of a sympathetic policy between France and England. France has also made her agreement with Japan. All these signs as to the strength of the position are so marked that it should be not only innocuous, but salutary, to take the opportunity of arranging the German Emperor's visit.

If that visit is exploited in any way which is undesirable from a political point of view, it might be well to consider whether it should not be followed by a visit

([1]) [Grey MSS., Vol. 71.]
([2]) [This subject will be dealt with in a later volume.]

from President Fallières some time next year. So far as I am concerned, I should be all in favour of that, if it became necessary to show that there was no change in our foreign policy.

The King of Denmark and his Government have been lavish of assurances similar to those which he gave to M. Clémenceau. I doubt whether there was ever any thing much in the rumour that Denmark contemplated a Treaty with Germany.

Yours sincerely,

E. GREY.

No. 46.

Mr. Lister to Sir Edward Grey.

F.O. 371/255.
(No. 333.)   *Paris,* D. *July* 4, 1907.
Sir,   R. *July* 5, 1907.

I have the honour to transmit to you herewith an article([1]) from the pen of M. Arthur Meyer, the Editor of the "Gaulois," dealing with the international situation and the respective attitudes to one another of England, France and Germany.

M. Meyer's views are not unlike those habitually expressed by M. Ernest Judet, namely, that British Policy is now exclusively occupied in preparing for a struggle with Germany, and that the "Entente" with France has been negotiated by British Statesmen chiefly with the intention of using the French Army in the great war which it is supposed will sooner or later break out.

M. Arthur Meyer alludes to the forthcoming visit of the German Emperor to England, and hints that the invitation addressed to His Majesty by the King is an indication of the view prevalent in England that the state of France and the French Army is so bad that it would not be safe to count upon them at the present moment. A tendency has hence manifested itself to show a conciliatory disposition towards Germany and to postpone the tragic dénouement, which has been the hidden aim of British Policy.

This is the significance of the heading "Partie Remise."

M. Meyer in this article gives himself the double satisfaction of a hit at the hated present régime and also at the "Entente" with England, which he and the great majority of Nationalists and clericals have only very grudgingly accepted.

I have, &c.

REGINALD LISTER.

([1]) [Not reproduced.]

No. 47.

Sir Edward Grey to Lord Knollys.

Private.([1])
My dear Knollys,   *August* 28, 1907.

I think it will be most serious, if the German Emperor brings two Ministers, especially if Bülow comes.([2])

I believe when the King went to Kiel that Selborne was the only Minister with him, and for the German Emperor to come and to stay for a week with two Ministers

([1]) [Grey MSS., Vol. 64.]
([2]) [Prince Bülow had been invited by the Duke of Connaught in Karlsruhe to accompany the Emperor, *v. G.P.* XXIV, p. 15, *n.*]

will turn the visit into a demonstration, for which no precedent can be found. I earnestly hope that this may be avoided.

I fear a troublesome time is ahead of us in Morocco, and even if the German Government continues to observe its present favourable attitude, the strain which the troubles in Morocco are placing upon the French is not favourable to the popularity of our Entente.

> Yours sincerely,
> E. GREY.

No. 48.

Sir Edward Grey to 'Sir F. Lascelles.

Private.([1])

My dear Lascelles,   *September* 18, 1907.

Hardinge has shown me your letter about the Emperor's visit.([2]) What you say about the probability of his being accompanied by Bülow as well as Von Einem appears to me so serious that I must beg you to do everything that you possibly can to prevent the visit assuming these proportions.

I have no doubt that, as you say, whether the Emperor is accompanied by two Ministers or by one, whether he comes with a large suite or a small one, the German press will make all possible political capital out of the visit. But so long as it is confined to its proper proportions as a purely private affair, whatever the German press may make of it can probably be discounted, though even this may not be quite easy. If, however, it assumes the form of a regular demonstration which, if two Ministers come, it will undoubtedly do, the matter becomes much more serious, and gives some excuse for tongues which are only too ready to wag to say that the visit has great political significance.

The present moment is a critical one in our relations with France: her position in Morocco is just now not enviable, and the enemies of our entente with her are only too ready to point to her difficulties in that country as evidence of what they have always endeavoured to make the world believe: namely that we wittingly gave France what we knew was valueless in return for important concessions in Egypt and elsewhere.

If those who hold these views in France and those who make use of them in Germany (it was the Emperor who said France had got a hornet's nest out of the Entente) can fix on any thing just at this moment which has the appearance of a cooling off towards France on our part and a definite rapprochement with Germany, their case will be strengthened.

They will represent that, now that we have got all that there was to get out of France, and put her in a thoroughly unsatisfactory position, we intend to leave her in the lurch, and draw towards Germany to see what we can get in that quarter.

It is manifestly in the interests of Germany to make this view prevail, since by so doing she would alienate France from us and draw her closer to herself. It will be said that it is entirely consistent with the reputation for fickleness which we enjoyed in Europe until quite recent times. And so we shall run the risk of returning to our position of isolation in Europe, and of losing much of the strong position which our recent policy has won for us.

Nobody is more anxious than I am that our relations with Germany should be friendly. But they can only be so, as I have said more than once, on the distinct understanding that our friendship with Germany is not at the expense of our friendship with France. And, just at this time, when the political situation is such as to make France not unnaturally nervous, I am particularly anxious that nothing should occur

([1]) [Grey MSS., Vol. 22.].

([2]) [A private telegram in the Hardinge MSS. indicates that a letter was sent by the bag leaving Berlin on September 11. Its text has not been traced.]

which would lend any colour to the idea that we are wavering by a hair's breadth from our loyalty to the entente, and are contemplating a new departure in policy.

I cannot, therefore, too earnestly impress upon you the necessity of taking every possible opportunity of letting the Germans understand the necessity of preserving the entirely private character of this visit. There should be no difficulty in conveying this to them, and also the fact that this character would at once disappear if the Emperor were to come here accompanied by two of his Ministers, whose inevitable meetings with Ministers here would almost certainly give the impression that some sort of negotiations were on foot.

Apart from these more general considerations, it is far from desirable that Bülow as an individual should come to this country. It is not forgotten that during the worst period of the South African war he never raised a finger to check the campaign of calumny which was rampant in Germany, and some not very pleasant utterances of his in connection with this may be raked up by our press. It should not be hard to drop a hint that his coming might lead to some unpleasant comments and reminiscences which, however much we regretted them, we should be powerless to prevent, and which might spoil the friendly reception of the German visit.

I may sum up my views by saying that I shall welcome the visit and be glad of it, if it appears to be the natural consequence of the personal relationship between the King and the Emperor, and simple evidence of the fact that there is no quarrel between England and Germany. If, on the other hand, it is made to assume the character of a political demonstration, I shall deplore it, and dread the consequences, which may be beyond our control.

Yours, &c.
E. GREY.

Of course, there would be no objection to Von Jenisch, who constantly travels with the Emperor, coming if he wishes to bring someone from the Foreign Office; that could not occasion any comment.

E. G.

No. 49.

Sir F. Lascelles to Sir Edward Grey.

Private.([1])
My dear Grey,   Berlin, September 20, 1907.

Many thanks for your very interesting letter of the 18th.([2]) I quite understand that recent events in Morocco should have made the French nervous, and that you should be anxious that nothing should occur which would lend colour to the idea that we are wavering by a hair's breadth from our loyalty to the entente. I hope therefore that it will be a satisfaction to you to hear that to the best of my knowledge and belief, Bülow will not accompany the Emperor to England in November. I went to the German Foreign Office on Tuesday, the usual day for the reception of the Ambassadors, and in the absence of Tschirschky had a conversation with Pourtales. He told me that although nothing had yet been definitely settled as to the persons who were to accompany the Emperor, it had been decided that the following categories should form His Majesty's suite. The Ober Hof Marschall, the three Cabinets, Military, Naval and Civil, probably a General Aide de Camp, two A.D.C.'s and a doctor. In addition to these the Minister of War would accompany the Emperor, having been personally invited

([1]) [Grey MSS., Vol. 22.]
([2]) [v. immediately preceding document.]

by the King. He believed that Bülow would not be of the party and that the
Foreign Office would probably be represented by Jenisch, as he did not think that
Tschirschky would go. Pourtales is such a cautious man that I do not think he
would have told me that Bülow was not likely to go unless he were quite certain.
Then the Empress' suite would probably consist of two gentlemen and three ladies.
I said that I should be glad to know when definite arrangements had been made,
but that I hoped that the Emperor might be persuaded to reduce his suite as much
as possible. Windsor Castle was no doubt a big place, but there were limits to the
accommodation it could afford, and I had no doubt that the King would desire to
invite other guests to have the honour of meeting Their Majesties.

Admiral Müller the head of the Naval Cabinet told Dumas a couple of days
ago that the Emperor had decided to go from Brünsbüttel to Portsmouth escorted
by a fleet of cruisers. Müller suggested that the North Sea and the Channel were
perhaps not quite comfortable places to be in during November, as Fog and bad
weather might be expected at that time of year, but the Emperor said that he had
known very fine weather in the North Sea in November, and in any case that
was the way he was going. It is evident from the fact that the Emperor
means to have an escort of cruisers, and from the number of persons he proposes
to bring with him that he considers the visit as a State visit and not as a private
one. I certainly understood that it was to be regarded as a return visit to the
State visit which the King paid to the Emperor at Kiel in 1904, and I gathered
from what the King told me, before I left England at the end of July that this
was His Majesty's view. He commanded me to be at Windsor in time
for luncheon on the 11th of November, in order to be present at the
official reception which would take place later in the afternoon in full
uniform. Then again the presentation of an address in the Guildhall would
not be compatible with a private visit. If however, as I believe, Bülow is not to
come, I would suggest that it might be better to emphasize the official and State
character of the visit, and to dwell upon the absence of the Chancellor as a proof
of the slight political importance which the Emperor himself attached to it. It has
struck me that this would probably be quite as agreeable to French sentiment as
the idea of the private character of the visit, and I do not see how it could afford
any justification even to the most determined enemy of the Entente to suggest
that it indicated " a cooling off towards France on our part and a definite
rapprochement with Germany." Personally I should like to see such a rapprochement if it could be brought about without any diminution of our friendship with
France, and I believe the thing is possible. I have, so frequently, under your
instructions, explained both in public speeches and in conversation that we do not
intend to leave France in the lurch, and that Friendship with Germany does not
imply hostility to any other country that I think the German Government have
realised that the Entente is the keystone of our policy and that we do not intend
to abandon it. At the same time there are indications that the German Government
wish to be on better terms both with us and with France, and I believe that
Jules Cambon, who is shortly expected back in Berlin has great hopes of bringing
this about as regards France. I presume that you will agree that so laudable a
desire should not be discouraged, and it seems to me that the Emperor's visit might
furnish an opportunity of conveying to him our hope of seeing the Peace of Europe
secured, by the establishment of friendly relations between the three countries.

Yours sincerely,
FRANK C. LASCELLES.

No. 50.

Sir C. Hardinge to Sir F. Lascelles.

Private.([1])

My dear Lascelles,   *Foreign Office, October 2, 1907.*

I expect you will have noticed that there has been in the last few days a recrudescence of press rumours to the effect that Bülow is coming here with the Emperor. These rumours may or may not be true; they may conceivably be "bal[l]ons d'essai" sent up to see how the news of his coming would be taken in England. But, however that may be, I think we should be careful to be on the safe side.

Sir Edward has shown me his correspondence with you with regard to this question, and he has discussed it with me in all its aspects; I therefore know exactly what his feelings are.

Though in other respects he welcomes the Emperor's visit, he sees in it two possible sources of danger. One is the possibility of its assuming proportions which would give it the appearance of a political demonstration and cause misgiving in France as to our good faith. The other is that, instead of leading to more friendly relations between this Country and Germany, the visit may, through some untoward event, have the opposite effect. There is no circumstance so likely to lead to either of these results as the fact of Bülow accompanying the Emperor.

With regard to the first, Sir Edward has in his letter to you of the 18th([2]) fully entered into the danger of the situation as regards France. I can only add that there are already signs of nervousness in the French press, as you will see from an article in the "Débats" of a day or two ago, which we are sending to you officially.

As to the second, I need add nothing. Sir Edward has explained his fears that allusions may be made in the press here to Bülow's passive attitude towards the campaign of calumny which raged in Germany during the South African War, and to some of his most inexcusable utterances at that time, and there are already signs that his fears on this score are fully warranted.

You say in your letter of the 20th([3]) that you had gathered from Pourtalès that, though nothing had yet been definitely settled, Bülow was not to be included in the Emperor's Suite. But you do not say whether you dropped any hint, such as Sir Edward wished (see the last paragraph but one of his letter of the 18th), warning Pourtalès against a change of plans in the direction of including Bülow. I think this should undoubtedly be done.

You could easily use the recent rumours in the press as a peg on which to hang a very distinct hint in this sense. If you put it on the ground of the risk which the visit would run of being spoiled through an outburst of press polemics, just at the critical moment, it could not possibly be a legitimate cause of offence. In any case it is very essential that a hint should be given without delay, for it is of the utmost importance that Bülow shall not come, and to give it after a public announcement had been made that he was coming would be a much less simple matter.

I think that you will see the need for prompt action when I tell you that the Editor of a very important paper has already mentioned to me that, in view of these persistent rumours, he proposed to publish a leading article in which it would be made abundantly clear that Bülow's presence would not be welcome. I begged him not to do so at any rate at present, as I consider that it will be far better if the visit can be prevented without anything of this nature appearing in the press.

([1]) [Grey MSS., Vol. 22.]
([2]) [*v. supra*, pp. 81–2, No. 48.]
([3]) [*v.* immediately preceding document.]

But, as you know, we cannot really control the newspapers in any way, and if Bülow's coming is definitely announced, articles of this sort, which can only lead to unpleasantness, will inevitably follow.

[Yours sincerely,]
CHARLES HARDINGE.

No. 51.

Sir F. Lascelles to Sir Edward Grey.

Private.([1])
My dear Grey,   Berlin, October 4, 1907.
. . . .([2]) I asked Schwabach whether he knew anything about the probability or otherwise of Bülow's going to England with the Emperor. He thought that the probability was that Bülow would not go. He would find it difficult to leave Berlin at the time and moreover he might think that his presence would give undue political importance to the visit. I said that I believed it would be better on the whole that Bülow should not come. He was not popular in England and his presence might recall certain unfortunate utterances which it would be advisable to pass over in silence during the Emperor's visit. I am in hopes that Schwabach may find means of having a hint conveyed to Bülow to this effect, but I am afraid of taking any more direct steps which I think might do more harm than good. I will develop my reasons more fully in a letter which I will write to Hardinge in answer to one which I received from him last night.

There is at all events one Frenchman who does not share the apprehensions of his countrymen as to the effect of the Emperor's visit and that is Jules Cambon, who is looking forward to it with great interest and feels sure that it will be the means of improving the relations between France and Germany. He hopes indeed that Bülow will accompany the Emperor, as then he would be convinced that nothing definite would be said and he believes that Bülow's agreeable but vague generalities would do more good than harm.

Please excuse the inordinate length to which this letter has grown.

Yours sincerely,
FRANK C. LASCELLES.

([1]) [Grey MSS., Vol. 22.]
([2]) [The opening paragraphs of this letter refer to current rumours on the likelihood of Prince Bülow's visiting England, and to possible changes in the German Foreign Office.]

No. 52.

Sir F. Lascelles to Sir Edward Grey.

F.O. 371/262.
(No. 439.)   Berlin, D. October 7, 1907.
Sir,   R. October 14, 1907.
It is semi-officially announced that the Emperor and Empress will visit Queen Wilhelmina of the Netherlands on their return to Berlin from London in November. The North German Gazette in a leading article on the subject states that the inhabitants of the Netherlands will see in Their Majesties' visit a new proof of the sympathy entertained for them and they can only regard with astonishment the attempts of the French Press in Belgium to utilise the occasion of the Imperial visit to accuse Germany of fresh schemes and dark designs on the Netherlands.

Such attacks, says the organ of the Government, even when Paris papers of the stamp of the Figaro participate in them can scarcely be expected to find credit anywhere and least of all in Holland. The inhabitants of that country live too close to Germany to believe that she ever needed the suppression of smaller States to attain her development. For the whole of the last generation the Minor Powers have recognised that their development during the. 36 years of peace has been curtailed in no way by Germany.

I have, &c.
FRANK C. LASCELLES.

No. 53.

Sir Edward Grey to Sir F. Lascelles.

Private.([1])

My dear Lascelles,   *October* 10, 1907.

Metternich spoke to me to-day([2]) about the article in " The Times " on the subject of the Emperor's visit.

I told him that I was very sorry that this article had been written. As he had already heard from Hardinge, we had deprecated articles of this kind, because we knew that some papers were sure to publish them if Bülow came with the Emperor. I had heard in fact that if he did come other papers besides " The Times " would write in the same strain.

The article had, no doubt, been produced by statements in the Press to the effect that Bülow was coming.

It was not in our power to control such articles, and as a matter of fact, in one instance where we had known of the intention to publish such an article now, we had advised against publication.

I am really very sorry that this campaign has been started in advance. I knew it was inevitable if Bülow did come. If the articles to the effect that he intended to come were inspired, it is unfortunate that this should have been done.

As Metternich has referred to the matter, and as you may probably hear of the article from other sources, I think it well to let you know what has passed.

Yours sincerely,
E. GREY.

I certainly hope that Bülow is not coming, but what I regret is that something unpleasant should have been published, when we were giving the Germans to understand that if Bülow did not come nothing of the kind would happen.

([1]) [Grey MSS., Vol. 22.]
([2]) [For Count Metternich's report of this conversation, *v. G.P.* XXIV, p. 15.]

[*ED. NOTE.*—The *Times* article of October 10 is not here reproduced in view of its length. The general line of criticism was that the Anglo-Russian Agreement and the difficulties of carrying out the German Fleet Bill made it difficult for Prince Bülow to maintain the anti-British attitude shown during the crisis of South Africa. It expressed the hope however that Prince Bülow had come to see that this attitude had not been " very worthy of himself or of his position." The *Times* leader was due to the announcement that Prince Bülow would accompany the Emperor William II on his state visit. It was announced, in any case, on October 22 that he would not do so.]

No. 54.

Sir F. Lascelles to Sir Edward Grey.

F.O. 371/262.

(No. 450.)   *Berlin, D. October* 14, 1907.

Sir,   R. *October* 16, 1907.

In my despatch No. 446 of the 10th instant,([1]) I had the honour to report that since the official announcement was made that the Emperor and Empress intended to pay a visit to His Majesty the King in November, a marked improvement had taken

([1]) [Not reproduced, as its tenour is indicated.]

place in the tone of the German press towards England. On the day on which that despatch was written an article appeared in the "Times" bitterly attacking Prince Bülow and deprecating in somewhat unmeasured terms his rumoured intention to accompany the Emperor to England. Some months ago an article of this kind would have been the signal for an outburst of anti-English sentiments in the German Press, but I am glad to be able to report that but very little notice has been taken of the views expressed by the "Times." A good effect has been caused by the articles which appeared in the Westminster Gazette and the Tribune sharply criticising the "Times" article, and the German papers appear quite satisfied at the attitude assumed by the English press on the question.

The Cologne Gazette, which is in close touch with the German Foreign Office, points out to its readers that on the Continent the "Times" is regarded as being the leading newspaper in Great Britain and a true mirror for the reflexion of British public opinion, but in England the "Times" is by no means regarded in this manner. There it is known that the "Times" represents the views of but a small group of unimportant persons, whose opinions have no weight in current politics. The object of the article was to extract a hostile reply from the German press and thus to arouse public opinion against the Imperial visit; but, as it appears that the weight of public opinion in England is strongly opposed to the views expressed in the "Times," public opinion in Germany can well afford to ignore its foolish and spiteful attacks.

I have, &c.

FRANK C. LASCELLES.

No. 55.

Sir F. Lascelles to Sir Edward Grey.

Private.(¹)
My dear Grey,   *Berlin, October* 17, 1907.

Very many thanks for your account of your conversation with Metternich about the article in "The Times" on the subject of the Emperor's visit.(²) It was certainly a mischievous one—I am afraid intentionally so—but I am in hopes it will not have done much harm. You will see by my despatches that the line which the German Press has taken, is that as other influential English papers, and more especially those that support the government, such as "The Tribune" and "Westminster Gazette" have strongly condemned the language of the "The Times" it is unnecessary for the German Press to take any notice of it.

Prince Albert of Schleswig Holstein tells me that his military friends here are greatly exercised about General French's visit to St. Petersburg where he was to meet a French General. This could only mean the conclusion of a military Convention between the three countries which must be directed against Germany and therefore war was imminent. This of course is absolute nonsense, but it is perhaps not unsatisfactory to know that there are certain people in Germany who have a salutary dread of us. . . . .(³)

Yours sincerely,
FRANK C. LASCELLES.

(¹) [Grey MSS., Vol. 22.]
(²) [*v. supra*, p. 86, No. 53.]
(³) [The rest of this despatch refers to Franco-Spanish relations.]

No. 56.

Sir Edward Grey to Sir F. Lascelles.

F.O. 371/257.   *Foreign Office, November* 1, 1907.
Tel. (No. 73.)   D. 1 P.M.

The King received last night a tel[egram] from the Emperor stating that he had been suffering since a week from bronchitis and acute cough and that he felt quite unable to meet the strain of the visit to Windsor. The Emperor has suggested that Crown Prince should take his place and accompany the Empress or that visit should be postponed till next spring or summer.

The King has replied pointing out what a disappointment the relinquishment of the visit would be to H[is] M[ajesty], the Royal Family and the British Nation, and has urged the Emperor to reconsider his decision, offering at the same time to modify the programme of the visit in any manner that the Emperor may desire.

You should see Prince Bülow at once and strongly urge upon him the unfortunate result upon public opinion in this country which a postponement of the visit would entail. There is little doubt that this decision would be attributed to the recent scandals in Berlin and nothing that we could say or do would alter the impression. The action of the Emperor in relation to these incidents has been favourably commented on here.

Everything connected with the visit is now on such a footing that we are confident that it will be well received by the press and public opinion, and that the Emperor will receive personally a cordial and friendly welcome. In view of this a postponement at the eleventh hour would produce general disappointment and might check the improvement in Anglo-German relations which has hitherto been evident.

Unless the Emperor is really seriously ill you should do all you can to urge that the visit should take place.

No. 57.

Sir F. Lascelles to Sir Edward Grey.

F.O. 371/257.   *Berlin, D. November* 1, 1907, 11·20 P.M.
Tel. (No. 37.) Secret.   R. *November* 2, 1907, 8 A.M.

I saw Prince Bülow this evening. He told me half an hour before I arrived he had received a telegram from C[oun]t Metternich giving an account of his conversation with Lord Knollys. This was the first he had heard of there being any question of postponement of the visit and he had at once written to the Emperor that he presumed either that the King had misunderstood the Emperor's telegram or that Lord Knollys had misunderstood what the King had said. He respectfully requested that this mystery might be explained.

I then read him your tel[egram] No. 73.([1]) He at once telephoned to the palace to ask for an immediate audience as I had just made a most important communication to him. At his urgent request I made a paraphrase of the three last paragraphs of your tel[egram], and while I was doing so he received the Emperor's answer to his letter which he read to me. It was to the effect that H[is] M[ajesty] had been unwell for several days and that yesterday he had been seized by a fainting fit and that he felt in such a state of collapse partly owing to illness and partly to mental anxiety that he had suggested Crown Prince should accompany the Empress to England instead of himself. Since he had received the King's telegram he would do his best to become strong enough to undertake the

([1]) [*v.* immediately preceding document.]

journey to England, and with this object in view he had gone out riding today and would see (? no) more people. It was his earnest wish to go to England and he would certainly do so if he could, but he was in such a miserable state yesterday that he felt bound to indicate possibility of his being unable to do so.

Prince Bülow read to me the whole of the Emperor's letter to him which was written on the fly leaf of Count Metternich's telegram, and said that it was impossible to doubt sincerity of the Emperor's desire to go to England. His Majesty had certainly been unwell. He had been confined to his room eight days ago, three of which he had passed in bed, and it was probably under the impression of a fainting fit that he had telegraphed to the King.

Prince Bülow added that he would certainly do all in his power to induce the Emperor to go to England. He had always been strongly in favour of visit, and had been greatly disconcerted by Count Metternich's telegram.

No. 58.

Sir Edward Grey to Sir F. Lascelles.

F.O. 371/263.
(No. 304.)
Sir,
Foreign Office, November 1, 1907.

I expressed to Count Metternich to-day my urgent hope that the Emperor's visit would not be abandoned or delayed.

I said it would be a very great pity if the visit did not take place at present. Some trouble had been taken to ascertain what the Emperor's reception was likely to be, and I was sure that it would now be most cordial. The fact was that the pain to which the public knew he must have been put by the recent trial had created great sympathy for him, and admiration had been aroused by the public belief that it was his determination, however painful things might be, that nothing should be hushed up.

If the visit did not take place, it was sure to be supposed that there was some reason not stated which had interfered with it, and in some quarters it might be thought that there was some political difficulty which had arisen between Germany and England.

Count Metternich entirely agreed as to the desirability of the visit taking place, but said that he was bound to believe the reason of health might be a serious one.

I told him I quite understood that the Emperor would probably be feeling the strain of recent events. But it might be that this would pass in a few days; and, if so, the knowledge that his good reception here was assured would be of value.

We then had a good deal of informal conversation of a more general kind.

Count Metternich asked me why it was that I had thought that a visit from Prince Bülow might not be desirable.

I said I had ascertained that in commercial circles there was still some soreness arising from memories of the war in South Africa. During that time, commercial men from this Country had had to visit Germany in the usual course of business, and had been made to feel very severely the ill-will felt by Germany towards us then. It was also remembered that on one or two occasions connected with the war Prince Bülow's utterances had been exceedingly cold.

His presence here might have provoked some of these reminiscences to find expression in some quarters. And as our King, when he went abroad, was accompanied by one Minister only, and never by the Prime Minister, if the Emperor had come here accompanied by two Ministers, including the Chancellor who corresponded to the Prime Minister here, some people might have felt it necessary to correct the impression that great political significance was to be attached to the visit.

Count Metternich observed that the article in " The Times " had been repudiated by all other papers.

I answered that no doubt it was felt on all sides that that article was premature, trying in tone, and unnecessary. But it did not follow that if Prince Bülow had actually come to England nothing would have been said.

Count Metternich told me that he had himself received a letter from Prince Bülow, stating much the same consideration as I had urged except as respects the Press whose utterances would not influence him. Having regard to the political importance which might be attached to his presence here, and in view of the fact that no British Minister had visited Berlin in this way for some thirty years, Prince Bülow felt that a visit from him might have seemed a little out of proportion. He had also felt there was truth in what I had said some time ago to the effect that, if the relations between the two Countries were to improve, they should be allowed to do so quietly, and should not be hurried.

I said I thought the course of events had shown the truth of this remark : our relations had continued to improve recently.

Count Metternich admitted this was so. But he wished the leaders of public opinion, including important Members of the Government, would do something to make public opinion more warmly disposed towards Germany. He was sure this would not be objected to in France, because the last thing France desired was to see trouble between England and Germany, for fear the brunt of the trouble should fall upon France. It seemed to him that we desired our relations with Germany to be correct, and that we were willing to remove difficulties if need be, but that we still wished to keep Germany at arm's length. Personally, he thought that if Prince Bülow, holding the great position of influence in Germany that he did, had come here and met important Members of the Government the result would have been good.

I said that, with regard to influencing public opinion here, it must be borne in mind that the warmth of feeling which grew up between France and ourselves was not forced by the leaders of public opinion, whose only part in the first instance had been to remove difficulties. When this was done, the growth of good feeling was spontaneous.

I thought that the attitude of our Press and of public opinion generally towards Germany was progressing satisfactorily. And it was often a good rule in public life, certainly in Parliamentary life, to say as little as possible when things were of themselves moving in the right direction.

Count Metternich said there were no difficulties left between England and Germany. He thought that in the case of France the King and Members of the Government had helped materially to encourage good feeling. He would like to see something of the same kind done with regard to Germany.

I observed that public opinion here had been favourably impressed by the restraint of the German Press when Morenga re-organised, on British territory, his attack upon the German Colony ; by the recognition of the efforts of the Cape Government to co-operate against Morenga afterwards ; and also by a work recently published by the General Staff recognising the difficulties against which we had had to contend in the South African war. If the Emperor's visit took place and was well received, as I was sure it would be, this also would help in the same direction.

I suggested that, should reasons of health be really so serious as to prevent the Emperor from coming, a visit from the Crown Prince would certainly be well received, and would avoid any impression that there was a set back in our political relations.

[I am, &c.]

E. G[REY].

No. 59.

Memorandum by Sir Edward Grey.

*Views of the Foreign Office on subjects which the German Emperor may possibly
raise during the visit of H[is] M[ajesty] to Windsor.*

F.O. 371/263.   *November,* 1907.

Bagdad Railway.

As regards the Bagdad Railway, the attitude of H[is] M[ajesty's] G[overnment]
is by no means one of determined opposition, provided that Great Britain and France
are allowed a fair share in the control of the Railway, and that any arrangement
which may be come to does not conflict with the views of the Russian Government.

H[is] M[ajesty's] G[overnment] feel,, however, that if other nations are to
take part in the enterprise the German Gov[ernmen]t should make proposals to other
Powers with whom she wishes to cooperate including ourselves.

On political grounds, British interests are clearly affected by a Railway which
would form the most direct mail route to India.

Moreover, Great Britain holds a preponderant position in the Persian Gulf which
has been steadily built up during the last two centuries. At the present time nearly
all the shipping is British, and the greater part of the trade is in the hands of British
and Indian merchants. Also a very large number of Indian pilgrims visit the shrines
in Mesopotamia every year.

For these reasons H[is] M[ajesty's] G[overnment] could not welcome a Railway
to the Persian Gulf if they were excluded from a fair share in its permanent control.
But they fully realise that the proposed Railway is the result of German effort; and
they are quite willing to consider favourably any practical suggestion for preserving
the German character of the Company, if the management of the line were
international.

Persia.

If any reference is made to the recent Anglo-Russian Convention it can be
pointed out that care was taken during the negotiations that nothing should be
inserted in the Convention which might be regarded as an infringement of the
commercial interests in Persia of Germany and other Powers. The German
Gov[ernmen]t have themselves admitted that they have no political interests in
Persia.

Morocco.

The attitude of His Majesty's Government as regards Morocco is governed by
the Anglo-French Agreement of 1904, in which His Majesty's Government undertook
not to obstruct the action of France in Morocco and also promised diplomatic support,
as well as by the Algeciras Act, which, in common with France, Germany and the
other signatory Powers, they are determined loyally to uphold. In fulfilling their
obligations to France, His Majesty's Government are actuated by no unfriendly
feelings towards Germany.

His Majesty's Government have been able to note with pleasure that, by the
acquiescence of Germany in the French occupation of Ujda, as well as in the Franco-
Spanish occupation of Casablanca and in the operations to be conducted jointly by
France and Spain for the suppression of the contraband trade in arms, the relations
between France and Germany in regard to Morocco have of late pursued a more
normal course. .

Royal Visits.

The King paid a State visit to the German Emperor at Kiel in 1903 [*sic*].([1]) A
meeting between the King and Emperor took place at Friedrichshof in 1906,([2]) and

([1]) [*v. Gooch & Temperley,* Vol. IV, pp. 1–2, No. 1, and *note* ([1]), and No. 2.]
([2]) [*v. ib.,* Vol. III, pp. 365–72, Nos. 423–6.]

His Majesty paid a private visit to the German Emperor at Wilhelmshöhe in 1907.(³) The visit of the German Emperor to the King at Windsor is the return State visit to the State visit paid by the King at Kiel. There is therefore no further question of a State visit to be paid by the King to the German Emperor at Berlin or elsewhere. If the King paid a visit next year to Berlin it would entail a further visit from the Emperor to London at a later date. It would also make it difficult for the King to avoid a visit to Madrid. In the event of an invitation to Berlin being offered by the Emperor, the proposed visit of the French President to London, the suggested visit of the King of Roumania and the possibility of an interview with the Emperor of Russia, would leave but little time available for which such an invitation could be accepted during next summer. It is not suggested that other visits to Berlin or London should not take place in future years, but a sufficient interval should be allowed to leave room for visits and return visits with Sovereigns of other countries, and this would not be the case if official visits to Berlin and return visits of the Emperor to London took place at such short intervals as one year.

Sir F. Lascelles.

Sir Frank Lascelles' appointment as His Majesty's Ambassador in Berlin expired in Oct[ober] 1906. The appointment was renewed for two years and he was informed by the Secretary of State that this decision was to be regarded as final. Sir F. Lascelles' term of service will therefore expire in Oct[ober] 1908 and no further prolongation is contemplated.

E[DWARD] G[REY].

(³) [*v. supra*, pp. 42–7, Nos. 24–6.]

[*ED. NOTE.*—The Emperor William II and the Empress arrived at Windsor on November 11. The official visit ended on November 18, when the Empress returned to Germany and the Emperor went to Highcliffe Castle where he remained until December 11. The visit is described from the English side in Lord Haldane : *Before the War* (1920), ch. 2, *Autobiography* (1929), pp. 220–3; Sir Sidney Lee : *King Edward VII* (1927), Vol. II, pp. 551–63; Viscount Morley : *Recollections* (1917), Vol. II, pp. 237–8. For the German side, *v. G.P.* XXIV, pp. 17–22; *The Kaiser's Letters to the Tsar* (1920), pp. 235–9; Emperor William II : *My Memoirs* (1922), pp. 114–5; Baron von Schoen : *The Memoirs of an Ambassador* (1922), pp. 59–63.]

No. 60.

Memorandum by Sir Edward Grey.

Most Secret.

(9178.) *Foreign Office, November 13, 1907.*

In the course of my conversation with the German Emperor yesterday the subject of Macedonia was mentioned.

The Emperor spoke with emphasis of the way in which the different nationalities treated each other. He said that Italy always had her eye on Albania, which was her *vis-à-vis*, and that he was quite sure that Austria would never tolerate any attempts by Italy to get a footing across the water. He dwelt upon the intense ecclesiastical rivalry between Patriarchists and Exarchists, and said it was the ambition of Prince Ferdinand to make himself King of the Balkans, with Constantinople as his capital.

The Emperor said that the Turkish Government was more fit to rule than any of these other nationalities. It was tolerant as between different religions to an extent which they were not.

I told him I feared the Turkish Government made it impossible for the country to develop. It did not pay its officials or soldiers, and the Palace clique at Constantinople made it impossible to secure good Governors or for good Governors to have a chance of ruling their district well. The Financial Commission had improved Macedonia by securing that the Turkish troops were paid, as otherwise they committed great excesses.

The Emperor spoke with great appreciation of the qualities of the Turkish population. He said the development of the country in which the Anatolian railways were had been extraordinary. Since the railways had been made they grew a great deal of corn, and the country had progressed generally. When the last extension of the railway southwards was made the people had travelled hundreds of miles to see it, and had expressed their thanks most enthusiastically for the building of the railway.

Germany desired to go on with this work of development, and to continue the railways.

The Sultan had a great deal of property in the Mosul district. Considerable development had already taken place there; and owing to the efforts of the Sultan there were now 15,000 Arabs who, instead of fighting with each other as they used to do, had laid aside their spears and taken to ploughing and cultivating the land.

It would be necessary for irrigation to go hand in hand with the progress of the railways. Germany had engineers who were specially suited for this work, and the Emperor's view was that Germany should do in Mesopotamia what we had done in Egypt. German capital had gone into our work in Egypt, and when his opinion had been asked on this point he had always said it was quite right that German capital should go there.

He told me of an incident which had impressed him very much when he saw Mr. Rhodes.

Mr. Rhodes had told him that he took a map to bed with him every night, and studied what parts of the world there were waiting for European development. He had perceived Mesopotamia to be one of these; and that was the place which Germany ought to take in hand. Mr. Rhodes had said this spontaneously to the Emperor at the very moment that the latter had conceived the idea of the Bagdad Railway, and when there were only four persons—himself, the Sultan, the German Chancellor, and the German Ambassador at Constantinople—who knew of the project.

The Emperor had said to Mr. Rhodes: "You are perfectly right, and that is what we intend to do."

Mr. Rhodes had replied that the Emperor would have his support with British public opinion, and that he would do all he could at the Foreign Office in London to encourage the project.

The Emperor had equally encouraged Mr. Rhodes' railway and telegraph projects in southern Africa, and had given him at once the right to make his railway through German territory, on the condition that the materials for making that part of the line should be purchased in Germany.

The Emperor spoke with the greatest appreciation of the help he had had from Mr. Rhodes. For instance, when there were difficulties about Samoa, Mr. Rhodes had gone to the Foreign Office in London, and the whole thing had been settled in a very short time.

Germany's view with regard to the Bagdad Railway was entirely commercial. Germany desired no further territory. Her own Colonies were ample for her needs. And besides that, there were large German places of business flourishing in British Colonies.

I observed that this was because we practised the policy of the open door.

The Emperor said that of course this was so. He was all in favour of the open door, and very much of a free trader himself.

I observed that, with regard to the Bagdad Railway, there must necessarily be a strategical as well as a commercial side.

The Emperor said this was no doubt the case, and the Railway would shorten the way for us to India.

I said that, as the railway had a strategical value, public opinion here would be very suspicious if the undertaking was entirely under the control of a Foreign Power.

The Emperor said that there would be no ground for any suspicion. Germany was not going to acquire any territory in Mesopotamia, and the Turks would not be able to use the railway against us.

I told him that, when the Bagdad Railway was last discussed in this country,(1) it was the political rather than the commercial side which had been emphasized, and it might be so again.

The Emperor said he knew that France and Russia had put a political construction upon the project, and Germany had offered some time ago that there should be English and French co-operation. This offer had been refused, and now, though the Germans would be quite willing to have English and French capital, they felt that they must certainly carry through the undertaking themselves.

E. GREY.

(1) [v. Gooch & Temperley, Vol. II, pp. 174–96, and infra, pp. 325–7, Ed. note.]

No. 61.

Sir F. Bertie to Sir Edward Grey.

F.O. 371/256.
(No. 545.)
Sir,

Paris, D. November 14, 1907.
R. November 15, 1907.

I had the honour to transmit to you in my despatches Nos. 532 and 541 of the 6th and 12th instant(1) respectively articles from the "Temps" and the "Aurore," both of them organs in touch with the French Government, expressing the opinion that the visit of the German Emperor to England would be advantageous to French interests.

The "Journal des Débats" which represents the Moderate Republicans in opposition, publishes in its issue of yesterday evening an article on the same subject by its Foreign Editor, Monsieur Robert de Caix, who as also Monsieur Tardieu of the "Temps" and Monsieur Lautier of the "Figaro" is of great authority on foreign and colonial affairs in the French Press.

M. de Caix refers to the toasts exchanged at Windsor between the King and the German Emperor, which reflect a situation now thoroughly understood. Anglo-German relations, without being exactly cordial, are no longer strained and are again in that normal state which is shewn by the interchange of speeches by Heads of State containing expressions of friendliness and peaceful intentions. Frenchmen would even be glad if matters went further, and if the words of the Emperor William, so well calculated to touch the hearts of Englishmen by their reference to Queen Victoria and to Windsor as a home, were to produce the effect desired by His Majesty. French opinion understands too well what would be the nature of an Anglo-German "rapprochement" to be at all anxious on the subject. The "Entente" with England has been too well proved during the last three and a half years to allow any doubts to exist lest a "rapprochement" between England and Germany would affect it. On the contrary it is recognised that so far from splitting up the "Entente" it would have to be grafted on to it.

M. de Caix then points out that British policy was not actuated by any aggressive design towards another Power in seeking closer relations with France. It was rather inspired by its old idea of maintaining the balance of power in Europe. German Diplomacy has itself aided during the last two years in consolidating the "Entente Cordiale" and showing the good reasons which existed for its conclusion. It is its task now to remove from the edifice, which it was unable to shake, the appearance of a rampart erected as a defence against the tendencies of German Policy. France is so sure of England that she can willingly join in the wish expressed by M. de Schoen in an interview with Reuter's correspondent that the

(1) [Not reproduced.]

visit of the German Sovereigns may serve to renew the relations of friendship formerly existing between the two countries. There is no longer any danger that these relations will assume the form of a co-operation on the part of England with the Triple Alliance which was in former times designed to hold France in check in the Mediterranean and on the Continent. Anglo-German friendship is now-a-days only possible on condition that the general state of things be accepted which is the result of all that has happened since the Agreement of April 8th, 1904.

Monsieur de Caix concludes by stating " C'est pourquoi, si le voyage de Guillaume II en Angleterre peut nous inspirer un sentiment quelconque, ce ne saurait être que le regret de voir nos amis d'Angleterre si unanimes à lui refuser toute importance politique." Editorial articles on the subject of the Emperor's visit to England are also published by the " Radical" and the " Petite République," both organs of the " Bloc" majority. The former comments on the toasts exchanged at Windsor and states that the Emperor's reference[s] to his desire for peace are reassuring. The visit is more of a family nature than one with political purposes, but it is likely that Morocco will form the subject of conversation. The " Petite République" (Moderate Socialist) speaks of the cordial reception of the Emperor in London, and declares that no umbrage will be taken on this side of the Channel at the visit, which will be regarded with entire calm. The article concludes " Nous n'avons jamais cherché à envenimer les haines et nous savons que les relations correctes entre la Grande Bretagne et l'Allemagne n'affectent nullement la cordiale entente qui nous unit à nos voisins d'Outre-Manche."

I have, &c.
FRANCIS BERTIE.

MINUTES.

The French press appears fully to recognize that the visit will exercise no prejudicial effect on the " Entente."

G. S. S.
W. L.

It is satisfactory to note that our loyal support of French policy is generously recognised by the French press.

C. H.
E. G.

MINUTE BY KING EDWARD.

The article in Journal des Débats is very satisfactory.

E.R.

No. 62.

Note of a Private Conversation between Sir Edward Grey and Mr. Haldane on November 14, 1907.(¹)

F.O. 371/340.

We recognize that the object of the commercial development of Mesopotamia is one, which should not be opposed.

What we desire is to insure that the quickest route between West and East should not be under the exclusive control of a virtually foreign Company, which would be in a position to affect seriously commercial relations between England and India or to sanction its use for strategic purposes in hostility to British Interests, which have existed in Southern Mesopotamia and the Persian Gulf for more than 200 years.

(¹) [This note was sent to Count de Salis as an enclosure in Sir E. Grey's despatch No. 335 of November 15, v. infra, p. 98, No. 64.]

We could not however discuss the question *à deux*, but only *à quatre*, for the various interests, strategical, political and commercial affect France and Russia as well as ourselves.

It does not seem impossible to reconcile all these with the commercial object of what we recognize to be a German enterprize.

If the German government can accept this point of view there would probably be no difficulty in arranging for a preliminary discussion by the Gov[ernmen]ts interested if the German Gov[ernmen]t take the initiative, and the question of how these interests might be adjusted is a business matter, which could be discussed by experts at Berlin.

It is important however that if discussions are to take place on a business footing the matter should be kept secret.

MINUTE.

A copy of this document in Mr. Haldane's handwriting was given by Mr. Haldane to the German Emperor at 7 P.M. on Nov[ember] 14, and at a further interview H[is] M[ajesty] accepted this document as one with which he was in complete agreement. This statement was made in the presence of Herr von Schön and C[oun]t Metternich.

[C. H.]

No. 63.

Memorandum dictated by Mr. Haldane.

Most Secret.

(9178.) *November 15, 1907.*

I left Sir Edward Grey and Sir Charles Hardinge soon after 12 on Thursday the 14th and went to Windsor.

I made a copy in my own handwriting of the document we had discussed,([1]) and headed it as a note of a private conversation between Sir Edward Grey and myself.

I received a communication from the Emperor's Secretary saying that the Emperor wished to see me at 7 that evening.

I also heard that the Emperor had spoken to the King upon the subject of the Bagdad Railway when they were out shooting. I thought it best to see the King, and I explained to him exactly what had happened, and how it came that I had been the bearer of a communication to the Foreign Office, and of information from that Office in return. The King approved, and wished that the German Emperor should be informed of his approval.

At 7 I saw the Emperor.

I found him very enthusiastic about the possibility of an agreement, and eager to say that, about the strategic question of the gate, Germany would make no difficulty of any sort.

I said to him that there was another part which would require attention. The footing on which we stood with Russia and France was now so friendly that it was impossible that we should discuss matters without keeping them informed, and that it was really essential that the discussion should go on *à quatre* instead of *à deux*.

The Emperor expressed himself in a quite friendly spirit on this, but with considerable vehemence. He said he knew that Russia was opposed to the whole project, and would at once make difficulties. Also he felt confident that France would at once proceed to make claims for further recognition about Morocco, in exchange for what she was asked to do about the railway. He said, further, that the Concession was really a German affair, and that it was all very well for Germany to discuss the matter freely with a Power with which she was on as good terms as she was with

([1]) [*v.* immediately preceding document.]

England, but that her people would certainly object to her having *pourparlers* with France and Russia.

I observed that difficulties, which seemed serious if they were taken in the abstract, sometimes became much less so when the men of business had come in and discussed matters; and this might be the case when the business men had come in and ascertained what it was that France and Germany wanted. I had ascertained quite definitely that our view was that the question was a commercial one, in which Germany had special rights by virtue of her Concession; and that, therefore, it was open to His Majesty, if he chose to proceed upon that footing, to say how much he would give up of his commercial advantages.

The Emperor did not seem altogether happy, but he said he would examine this matter, and he would communicate with me after dinner.

Immediately before dinner Herr von Schön came up to me and said that there had been a mistake. The Emperor had not known that he, Herr von Schön, had discussed the whole question of the Bagdad Railway with M. Isvolsky before he himself had left St. Petersburgh, and that they were entirely at one and would have negotiated and signed an Agreement had M. Isvolsky not been taken ill. He added that the Emperor considered that this altered the whole features of the difficulty, and made matters much more easy, and that, after the theatrical performance which was to follow the dinner party that night, the Emperor wished to see me in his private room.

I went to the Emperor's private room at 1 o'clock in the morning and the conversation lasted till 2.

Herr von Schön and Count Metternich were present.

The Emperor said that he had not known of M. Isvolsky's conversations with Herr von Schön, and that he was now of opinion that there would not be the smallest difficulty with Russia. As regards France, he said there would be no difficulty either, because he had gathered from the French that they would have liked to have come into the business, but would not do so unless we were ready to come in also. Now that matters were upon such a friendly footing he did not anticipate any difficulty.

At the earlier interview, before handing to the Emperor my note of the conversation, I had taken it piecemeal, and had begun, after defining the necessity of going step by step with the concurrence of France and Russia, by reading out to him a sentence in which it was stated that the Concession was a German commercial concern belonging to Germany. This pleased the Emperor very much, and he said that, starting with that, the other points seemed to present no difficulty. Finally, I had read out to him, at the earlier interview, the whole of the note before handing it over, having in this fashion explained it first piecemeal.

The Emperor had considered the note with Herr von Schön. I do not think he had shown it to Count Metternich. But at the second interview we went carefully through it.

The result was that the Emperor said that he completely understood the necessity on our part of proceeding at every step with the full knowledge and concurrence of the French and Russian Governments; that in our position this was quite legitimate, and that it was further in accordance with his own wishes.

Count Metternich, at an earlier stage in this second interview, had said that he did not think a conference of the four Powers was desirable. The project belonged to Germany and ought not to be thrown open in such a fashion.

But I had explained that I did not think Sir Edward Grey meant anything more than this; that the business men should meet in Berlin, and should define what each of them wanted. They might not get what they wanted . The Emperor might not be willing to concede things out of his commercial rights. But, on the other hand, the difficulties might be diminished, and even might all disappear.

As a result, after a long discussion, which lasted till 2 in the morning, the Emperor said that he cordially concurred in the note as a basis on which to proceed; that we were " ganz einverstanden," and that what he would like would be to get on as quickly as possible. He was very hopeful, now, that good business would come to all the four

H

Powers concerned, and he would ask Herr von Schön to proceed to London that day (the 15th) to take the initiative by making a proposal from Germany, which he understood Sir Edward Grey desired to have as a first step.

By the end of this interview Count Metternich's critical attitude had become so greatly modified that he observed that there should be no difficulty about a discussion in Berlin à quatre, in the sense now made plain, and that it was not only legitimate, but quite natural that we should wish to proceed in full consultation with France and Russia.

No. 64.

Sir Edward Grey to Count de Salis.

F.O. 371/340.
(No. 335.) Secret.

Sir,

Foreign Office, November 15, 1907.

Herr von Schön came to see me to-day about the Bagdad Railway, in order to follow up the conversations which had taken place with Mr. Haldane at Windsor.([1])

He told me that, a year ago, he had begun discussing the Bagdad Railway question with M. Isvolsky, and had hoped that they were coming to an agreement, when M. Isvolsky had to leave St. Petersburgh for a holiday.

The idea was that Russia should make railways linking up with the Bagdad Railway. But it was exceedingly difficult to get a definite answer from Russia as to what lines she proposed to make in Persia. The fact was that she had not yet made up her mind.

It would be difficult for the German Government to make the Bagdad Railway, which would run close to the Persian frontier, and to forego any right to make an extension into Persia, unless they were assured that some such connection with Persia would be made by some one else.

Herr von Schön expressed great satisfaction at the prospect of now coming to an agreement with us about the Bagdad Railway. He recognised our desire to have a gate at the Persian Gulf end.

I said the question of how our strategical interests could be safeguarded, whether by a share in the general control, or by the control of one section of the line, was a thing to be discussed rather at a meeting of business men than between Ambassadors and Foreign Secretaries.

Herr von Schön said that, as the concession had been given to Germany, it would hardly be legitimate or possible for her to part entirely with a portion of it to any one else. But he recognised that the Note, which Mr. Haldane had made of his conversation with me (copy inclosed),([1]) and which Herr von Schön showed to me, formed a practicable basis for discussion.

I told him I assumed that what we had to do now was to wait till we heard from the German Government, who would of course address the Russian and French Governments also. We should have to tell them what the position was.

Herr von Schön said it might be necessary for Germany to wait while he carried the discussion with Russia a stage further. But he would consult M. Isvolsky to see whether this would be necessary, and whether full discussion between the four Powers might not begin sooner.

[I am, &c.]
E. G[REY].

([1]) [*v. supra*, pp. 95–8, Nos. 62–3.]

[*ED. NOTE.*—Sir Edward Grey's despatch to Count de Salis, No. 355, Secret, of November 26, describes a conversation with Count Metternich which gives some further information as to the position of the Bagdad Railway question at this time. It is printed *infra*, p. 795, *App.* VIII.]

No. 65.

Sir Edward Grey to Sir F. Bertie.

F.O. 371/340.
(No. 654.) Secret.
Sir,   *Foreign Office, November 16, 1907.*
I told M. Cambon to-day that the German Emperor had spoken about the
Bagdad Railway.(¹) He had declared that its object was purely commercial, and that
it was a German Concession which need not concern any one else.

When he had said this, to Mr. Haldane, the latter had replied that, as Minister
for War, he was bound to remark upon the strategical interests which the Bagdad
Railway would have for us if it became the quickest route to India; and that, unless we
had something in the nature of a gate at the southern end, a Railway under exclusively
foreign control might be used to prejudice our position in India.

The Emperor, after consideration, had said that this difficulty could be overcome,
and he had sent a message to me to this effect.

Thereupon, the Emperor had been put in possession of our views, in writing. This
had been done in order that there might be no mistake at Berlin as to exactly what
our views were, and in order that we might be able to let the French and Russian
Governments have them in exactly the same form.

I then gave M. Cambon a copy of the Memorandum,(²) of which a copy was sent
to you in my despatch No. 653A.

He read it with great satisfaction, and then said that Herr von Schön had since
come to see me.

I replied that he had come, in order to give the answer. This was to the effect
that the German Government were very pleased that there was a prospect of coming to
an agreement, and that they considered our Memorandum, which Herr von Schön
brought with him, as a practical basis for discussion.

I had told Herr von Schön that I presumed we must now wait until the German
Government approached France and Russia as well as us.

Herr von Schön had explained that conversations with M. Isvolsky had taken place
some time ago in order to find out how it might be possible to reconcile Russian
interests with the building of the Railway, and that it might be necessary for the
German Government to carry these discussions a stage further before they could
approach all three Powers.(³)

M. Cambon expressed great satisfaction at the progress which had been made, and
remarked that if the Bagdad Railway question could be settled the one great obstacle
in the way of reconciling German interests with English and French interests would
be removed.

I told M. Cambon I was sure, from the way in which the question had been raised,
that the Emperor had raised it without previous consultation with Prince Bülow. And
my impression was that it was the opinion of the Emperor and Herr von Schön only
that we had at present before us.

[I am, &c.]
E. G[REY].

(¹) [*v. supra*, pp. 96–8, No. 63.]
(²) [*v. supra*, pp. 95–6, No. 62. The despatch No. 653A merely enclosed the Memorandum.]
(³) [On November 26, M. Paul Cambon asked Sir Edward Grey for further information as
to these conversations between Herr von Schön and M. Isvolski. The following extract from
Sir Edward Grey's despatch to Sir F. Bertie, No. 676 of the same date, gives the substance
of his reply : " I said I had understood that Herr von Schön had experienced great difficulty in
getting the Russian Government to say definitely what they desired, or what they were prepared
to do; and that he wished to be more clear as to their views before initiating a general discussion.
I gathered that the Russian Gov[ernmen]t were in a delicate position, because there was still
strong feeling in Russia against the Bagdad Railway."]

No. 66.

Sir Edward Grey to Lord Knollys.

Private.(¹)
My dear Knollys,   *November 16, 1907.*

The discussions about the Bagdad Railway are very fragmentary, but I will have what records we have been able to make between us put into shape and sent to the King.(²)

Haldane's conversation with the Emperor gave a most favourable turn to the subject.(³)

The whole visit of the Emperor seems to me to have been a great success, and beneficial from every point of view.

I think, however, it would be desirable that he should not ask Ministers down to Highcliffe afterwards, which might start unfounded rumours. I have no reason to suppose that he thinks of doing so, but I mention it again because it seems so very desirable after his visit to Windsor is concluded that nothing should occur to disturb the excellent effect which has now been produced everywhere.

Yours sincerely,
E. GREY.

(¹) [Grey MSS., Vol. 64.]
(²) [The Editors have been informed that there is no trace of the " records " referred to here in the Windsor Archives.]
(³) [*v. supra,* pp. 96–8, No. 63.]

No. 67.

Sir F. Bertie to Sir Edward Grey.

F.O. 371/263.
(No. 549.) Confidential.   *Paris, D. November 17, 1907.*
Sir,   R. *November 19, 1907.*

Monsieur Pichon asked me yesterday whether I had any information in regard to the visit to Windsor of the German Emperor. I told His Excellency that I heard that it had gone off very well, but that I had no official information on the subject. No great political results were to be expected as there were no important matters at issue between England and Germany for settlement, but if its effect were to improve the feeling between the two countries, France could not be otherwise than glad as it would diminish the risk of war, and I knew there was as little desire in France for a war between England and Germany as there was in England for a war between France and Germany, notwithstanding the assertions of some of the French Nationalist Press. Monsieur Pichon said that the wish of the French Government was that the relations between England and Germany should be good. It was to the interest of France that they should remain so, but there were people who wished them to be much closer. I replied that, notwithstanding the statements that some of the German newspapers might make of the political importance of the visit of the Emperor, His Excellency might feel confident that it would not in any way alter the determination of the Government of His Majesty The King to maintain the existing intimate relations with the French Government. Monsieur Pichon said that he felt sure of it.

I have, &c.
FRANCIS BERTIE.

No. 68.

Sir Edward Grey to Sir A. Nicolson.

F.O. 371/340.
(No. 399.) Secret.
Sir,
                                        Foreign Office, November 19, 1907.
  I told Count Benckendorff yesterday that the German Emperor had spoken on the question of the Bagdad Railway and had said, when pressed as to our strategic interests being guarded, that that could be managed.

  I gave Count Benckendorff a copy of the Memorandum([1]) which had been given to the Emperor in reply, and said that Herr von Schön had informed me that this was a practicable basis for discussion. But Herr von Schön had added that, before his departure from St. Petersburgh, he had had conversations with M. Isvolsky with a view to an agreement with Russia on the Railway question, and it might be necessary to carry the discussion a little further with M. Isvolsky before the German Government could initiate negotiations *à quatre.*

  Count Benckendorff expressed surprise at hearing that the matter had been discussed with M. Isvolsky. He had asked the latter at Karlsbad whether the matter had been raised, and M. Isvolsky told him it had not. Count Benckendorff concluded that his own conversation with M. Isvolsky could have related only to the period after the latter left St. Petersburgh.

  I said this must be so, because I gathered that it was M. Isvolsky's departure from St. Petersburgh that had broken off the discussion.

                                                      [I am, &c.]
                                                      E. G[REY].

([1]) [*v. supra*, pp. 95–6, No. 62.]

[*ED. NOTE.*—The following letter from M. Isvolski to Count Benckendorff is quoted here as it bears directly on the subject of this section :—

Iswolsky, Russian Minister of Foreign Affairs, to Count Benckendorff, Russian Ambassador at London. Confidential Letter, Dec. 6–19, 1907.([1])

  I have read with the liveliest interest your two letters of November 6–19, in which you report on the exchange of views on the Bagdad Railway which recently took place at Windsor between Emperor William and Baron Schön on the one, and the British Government, on the other, hand. I greatly appreciate Sir Edward Grey's attitude and the kind information he sent me through you.

  I beg you to present my best thanks to the Minister and I also take this opportunity of acquainting you in a few words with the standpoint of the Imperial Government on the question of the Bagdad Railway. *The German project has met with no more sympathy in Russia than in England and France.* Without touching on the strategic importance of this enterprise, we must regard with anxiety the influence such a railway would exert in the Turkish neighbouring provinces bordering on the Caucasus, the Black Sea and Persia. Our principal source of concern, however, is the influence on Persia, for we cannot for a moment doubt that the construction of the Bagdad Railway, and its ultimate connection with future railways in Persia, will open this country to German political influence and commercial undertakings.

  If England and France have retained absolute freedom of action in this matter, the position of Russia is not quite the same since the Petersburg Cabinet, at the beginning of the Anglo-Russian negotiations, assured Berlin that it would not enter into any obligations without having come to a previous friendly understanding with Berlin.

  It is quite natural that our attitude towards Germany has led to an exchange of opinions for the exclusive purpose of securing our vital interests in Persia; even England herself recognised these interests as justified in the convention concluded with us. . . . .([2])

([1]) [*Siebert*, p. 478. The notes, spelling, italics, etc., are as in the original. The letter is printed in German in *Siebert-Benckendorff*, Vol. I, pp. 9–11. On December 22, M. Sevastropoulo called to see Sir Edward Grey, and communicated to him the substance of this letter. The conversation is recorded in Sir Edward Grey's despatch to Sir A. Nicolson, No. 438, Secret, of December 31, 1907. F.O. 371/340.]

([2]) [The gap here is in the original.]

No. 69.

Sir Edward Grey to Sir F. Bertie.

Private.(¹)

My dear Bertie, *November* 20, 1907.

Bagdad Railway is the only question of importance and practical politics on which the Emperor touched. He talked at large of questions such as Socialism, etc., just as any one else might do in general conversation.

I have given Cambon a copy of exactly what we replied about Bagdad Railway,(²) and he has reported it to Pichon. It is to be kept secret, for a discussion in the Press at this stage would throw the whole thing into confusion.

I am sure the Emperor mentioned the Bagdad Railway without having consulted Bulow. I doubt whether Bulow will approve of discussion " à quatre," and it may be some time before we hear more.

Schön talked to me at our first conversation of nothing but one or two questions connected with German South West Africa, and evidently had no intention of initiating anything else, though I spoke of Casablanca Claims Commission and Judicial Reforms, and threw in a word about Morocco. I repeated this last very explicitly to Schön three days afterwards, and he received it equally well. . . . .(³)

Yours sincerely,

E. GREY.

I am very satisfied with the German visit. The Emperor was genuinely pleased with his reception, but there was no attempt either on his part or on Schön's to force the pace, or do or say anything inconvenient. In fact, the result has been to mollify Anglo-German relations—at any rate for the time—without in the least weakening our relations with France as far as this side is concerned.

E. G.

(¹) [Grey MSS., Vol. 11.]
(²) [*v. supra*, pp. 95–6, No. 62.]
(³) [The omitted passages refer to details connected with the Algeciras Act and the Norwegian Treaty.]

No. 70.

Mr. L. Buchmann to Sir Edward Grey.

F.O. 371/263.

(No. 114.) *Munich*, D. *November* 20, 1907.

Sir, R. *November* 23, 1907.

I have the honour to transmit herewith extracts in translation from various leaders in the South German press dealing with the recent visit of the Kaiser to England. I may be allowed to add that on the whole the tone of the press in this part of the Empire was most sympathetic and friendly, more especially in the National-Liberal organs, like the Munich " Neueste Nachrichten " and " Allgemeine Zeitung." The Social Democratic " Münchner Post " only recorded the movements of the Kaiser without any comments whatsoever.

Extracts.

(1.) Munich *Bayerischer Kurier*, (Centre Party) No. 314, November 11th 1907.

" . . . .(¹) We would warn our readers not to attach too much importance to the visit and sympathetically as we Germans may view the meeting of the Monarchs yet we must not leave a certain reserved attitude, for we have indeed no reasons to

(¹) [Here and elsewhere in this document these omissions are made in the original.]

rejoice since it was King Edward's turn to pay a State Visit. When Queen Victoria died our Emperor hastened to British shores to show thereby his grief to the whole world. On the other hand, King Edward took a long time to pay his first visit to the German Court—he met the Monarchs of many other countries but he could or would not find his way to Berlin. The King, when travelling to Marienbad, avoided German soil so as to be quite sure not to meet the Kaiser and he still owes his State Visit to Berlin . . . . It is true that political optimists consider our present relations with England as so perfect that we are expected gleefully to shout every moment "The King!" We beg to differ from this point of view; our relations with England have indeed improved; but at whose cost? The British character has not changed and it never will change, for it is as firmly established as the ultimate aim of British policy. However, England has now every reason to show us a friendly face for she has reached her goal and her hunger is satisfied. Let us consider the time of the meeting; it did not take place during that period when Great Britain was still concluding agreements and before the British Government had come to terms with the Powers of the whole world : Japan, France, Spain, Italy, Austria and even Russia. The Emperor is welcome in England after the conclusion of all these "ententes" for there is no game left for him to spoil. On the other hand his visit will prove to the British nation that Great Britain is everybody's friend and that even he who is not her ally prizes her friendship. We would have attached more political importance to the meeting if it had taken place before the conclusion of the agreements; but now the Uncle can show to his nephew what beautiful presents he brought home for his people from his world-wide travels. We may ask ourselves : "What does the Kaiser bring home from his travels?" Tangier! is an answer and a fine one at that . . . . If the German people would learn what enormous sums the policy of King Edward costs us and will continue to cost, their enthusiasm shown on the occasion of the meeting would soon subside; Englishmen may indeed spend something on that visit for it is they who triumph. . . . ."

(2.) Munich *Allgemeine Zeitung*, (National-Liberal) No. 536, November 19th 1907.

" . . . . The Emperor's State Visit to London has yielded positive results neither to us nor to France but the Monarch's speech at the Guildhall will have proved to everybody concerned that nothing can be better for the world's peace than hearty relations between Germany and England. . . . ."

(3.) Stuttgart *Schwäbischer Merkur*, (National-Liberal) No. 627, November 9th 1907.

" . . . . Speaking of the Emperor's stay near the Isle of Wight we could point out many other spots outside England where the Kaiser could recruit his health but if he has chosen Great Britain for that purpose it must be taken as a special compliment to that ͏country. Let us hope that this compliment will be appreciated by those to whom it is paid, else Germans might think that too much amiability has been shown at the wrong place. . . . ."

(4.) *Idem*, No. 530, November 12th 1907.

" . . . . The Emperor's journey will tend to finish at last our mutual misunderstandings and the political meaning of the visit can only further the interests of peace. . . . ."

(5.) *Idem*, No. 537, November 15th 1907.

" . . . . The majority of the German people are agreed with the Emperor's policy and they think—as he does—that good relations between Germany and England form the chief foundation of the world's peace. . . . . The Kaiser is in London the faithful interpreter of German feelings. . . . ."

(6.) *Idem*, No. 542, November 19th 1907.

" . . . . Nobody can possibly think that a great friendship has all of a sudden sprung up between the two nations and it is a question whether the present more friendly sentiments reigning in their relations will continue to exist and in that case whether they will deepen into something more tangible. . . . . "

(7.) *Frankfurter Zeitung*, (Liberal), No. 313, November 11th, 1907.

" . . . . The political crisis between the two countries which reached its most dangerous point during the Algeciras Conference has now been overcome. . . . If we examine the causes of the estrangement betweent the two countries we find that about fifteen years ago we suffered from a certain self-glorification, the effect of Bismarck's successes on the World's political stage and of our great industrial progress. It is no use denying that the dream of Teutonic expansion was actually conceived by public men.   However, we know better now for the failures resulting from our colonial policy have cooled down our aspirations in that direction and even the most inveterate optimist must, when looking at the present grouping of the world's Powers, come to the conclusion that the German nation will have to be on the whole satisfied with that part of the Universe which fate assigned to them. . . . We would not attach any importance to the utterances of the insignificant Socialistic party in England as they can not be considered as being the mouthpiece of the British proletariat but Englishmen must also concede that our press organs employ now quite a different tone from that used during the period of mutual displeasure. . . . The two nations are so closely related to each other that, without interfering with their existence, they can learn from each other, yet such a masterful man and such a good patriot as Prince Bismarck regretted that political circumstances would not allow him of loving the British nation."

I have, &c.
L. BUCHMANN.

MINUTE BY KING EDWARD.

One cannot really expect civility fr[om] the German Press—but it appears to have forgotten King Edward's State Visit to Kiel instead of to Berlin to the Emperor in 1905.

E.R.

No. 71.

Sir Edward Grey to Sir A. Nicolson.

Private.(¹)
My dear Nicolson,   *Foreign Office, November 21, 1907.*
    You will see what passed with Schön about the Bagdad Railway.(²) He gave Haldane the impression that but for Isvolsky's departure from St. Petersburgh in September an agreement with Russia about the Badgad Railway would actually have been signed.   I did not gather from Schön that anything more had passed than conversations with Isvolsky to find out how Russia could be reconciled to the Railway and that the Russian Gov[ernmen]t though no longer opposing in principle could not be induced to say definitely what Russia wanted.
    The Emperor at first saw great difficulties about a discussion *à quatre*, but went completely round when he heard from Schön that discussion with Russia had already taken place. The curious thing is that he had been kept in ignorance of the fact that the subject was being discussed with Isvolsky.

(¹) [Carnock MSS., Vol. II of 1907.]
(²) [*v. supra*, p. 98, No. 64.]

I am sure that the Bagdad Railway was brought up here without any previous consultation with Bülow; it was the Emperor and not Schön who mentioned it first and I am inclined to think that the Emperor did it without premeditation.

What Bülow will think of it remains to be seen. It is possible that Bülow has been trying to buy off Russian opposition to the Bagdad Railway by a favourable agreement about the Baltic. If so a discussion à quatre about the Bagdad railway will not suit his book.

Benckendorff and Poklewsky knew not a word of any discussions having taken place with Isvolsky and though I conveyed this to Benckendorff in its most tentative form, he was puzzled and not at all pleased at the news.

Both Cambon and Benckendorff are very pleased with our reply to the Emperor as they ought to be, for it is clear that the Emperor was ready and perhaps desirous to settle with us à deux. This of course would have been a gross breach of faith on our part towards France and Russia.

Y[ou]rs sincerely,
E. GREY.

No. 72.

Count de Salis to Sir Edward Grey.

F.O. 371/263.
(No. 516.)   Berlin, D. November 22, 1907.
Sir,   R. November 25, 1907.

In my despatches Nos. 498 and 504 of the 12th and 15th instant respectively,([1]) I had the honour to report fully the views expressed in the German Press on the subject of the Emperor's visit to England and the effect which might be expected from it on Anglo-German relations. As a complement to these reports I have the honour to draw your attention to a very friendly article published on the 17th instant in the semi-official *North German Gazette,* of which a very full précis was given in the *Times* of the 18th instant. A copy of the *Times* précis is enclosed for convenience of reference.([1]) The only other article of any importance or interest was one in the *National Zeitung* of the 16th instant. The National Liberal organ considers the reception at the Guild Hall to have been the "pièce de résistance" of the whole visit, as during his long drive to the City the Emperor came into touch with the people, who had turned out in thousands "not so much to see the Emperor as the man." Even in the worst days of anti-German feeling when the Emperor was looked upon in England as the embodiment of all that was hostile, there was still a sub-current of admiration for the manliness of his personality. The London Correspondent of the paper thinks that the visit has been a a decided succes: he says that the English Press have abandoned the reserve they at first maintained and have assumed a very cordial attitude, and the public welcome in the streets was always respectful and often hearty.

I have, &c.
J. DE SALIS.

(1) [Not reproduced.]

No. 73.

Sir F. Bertie to Sir Edward Grey.

F.O. 371/263.
(No. 555.)   Paris, D. November 22, 1907.
Sir,   R. November 25, 1907.

I have the honour to transmit to you herewith an article(¹) from the " Aurore "
of yesterday's date signed by Monsieur Maxime Villaume on the subject of the German
Emperor's visit to England.

Monsieur Villaume comments on the fact that the German " Bundesrath " has
accepted the additional expenditure for the German Navy which is above all directed
against England.   No remarks with reference to the toasts exchanged at Windsor;
" Mais le Bundesrath pendant ce temps-là n'oubliait pas de préparer l'avènement de la
plus grande Allemagne aux dépens bien entendu de la plus petite Angleterre.   Les
affaires sont les affaires; assez causé des idylles d'antan."

I have, &c.
FRANCIS BERTIE.

MINUTE.

(The Germans are a long way behind.   We shall have 7 Dreadnoughts afloat, before they
have one, without our laying down any more.   In 1910 they will have 4 to our 7, but between
now and then there is plenty of time to lay down new ones if they do so.)

E. G.

(¹) [Not reproduced.]

No. 74.

Sir F. Bertie to Sir Edward Grey.

F.O. 371/256.
(No. 604.)   Paris, D. December 21, 1907.
Sir,   R. December 23, 1907.

The " Temps " comments in a leading article on the speech made by you at
Berwick on the 19th instant.   It considers it natural that Anglo-German relations
should have first and foremost been dealt with, and states that France sees no objection
but rather an advantage in an evolution of these relations.   An Anglo-German
" rapprochement " might have been seen with disquietude in France two years ago,
but today it has " une valeur de commodité."

The article agrees that the friendship between England and France has changed
in character since 1904.   Though there exists between the two countries no alliance
properly speaking, the popularity of the *entente* has given it additional force and a
wider scope.   If a European crisis broke out, there is no doubt that the fleets of
England and France would be found side by side. The change which has come over
Anglo-French relations has therefore a practical value and this practical value has
taken a precise shape as is evident from the two simultaneous agreements which
England and France have concluded with Spain, from the not less interesting agreements signed between France and Japan, between Japan and Russia, and between
Russia and England.

The article notes your declaration that none of these agreements are directed
against any other country, which means against Germany, and asks whether it is
necessary to be always striving to re-assure Germany, who perhaps feigns an alarm
not really felt.   If Germany desires to " causer," your speech offers her an opportunity
but while reproaching other countries for their silence, she is in reality the most silent
of them all.   It is, however, right that England, like France in that respect, should
declare that she is ready to discuss any matter though she has need of no one.

The article considers that the references to Persia were well-timed, and notes that
the allusion to the Congo was on the same lines as the recent utterance by the Prime

Minister. It also mentions the fact that you affirmed the necessity of maintaining intact the European concert as regards Macedonia, and resisted, in this respect, the imprudent counsels of a part of the English Press.

The article concludes by remarking that you do not belong to the dangerous school who believe that great political aims can be sought with a mediocre army and navy, that diplomatic success is dependent on military strength and that this is true as regards England but not of her alone.

The "Figaro" of to-day's date also publishes an appreciative article by Monsieur Lautier, in which he compares the lucidity and straightforwardness of your language with that of another foreign statesman. I enclose herein the passage of the article in which this comparison is developed.([1]) The "Figaro" especially welcomes your remarks in regard to the Anglo-French understanding and notes with pleasure the applause which greeted your allusion to the manner in which that understanding had stood the test to which it had been subjected.

The London Correspondent of the "Echo de Paris" says that the chief interest of your speech lies in your silence in regard to the Congo and in your remarks as to the necessity of keeping pace with the naval programme of Germany.

These remarks, he says, are significative of the re-action which has set in since the rejection by the Hague Conference of the pacific proposals put forward by Sir H. Campbell-Bannerman.([2])

I have, &c.
FRANCIS BERTIE.

([1]) [Not reproduced.]
([2]) [This subject will be treated in a later volume.]

[*ED. NOTE.*—A report of Sir Edward Grey's speech at Berwick is given in the *Times* of December 20, 1907. The following extract may be quoted here : " The first subject with which I wish to deal is a safe and pleasant one, and that is to acknowledge the pleasure which I believe the whole country has felt from the visit of the German Emperor. All the public utterances connected with the visit have been most beneficial in tone, and I am sure that the friendly atmosphere of welcome and hospitality on the part of public opinion in this country and the cordial way in which it was reciprocated and acknowledged by the Emperor are bound to have a good effect upon both countries."]

CHAPTER XLIII.
GREAT BRITAIN, FRANCE AND GERMANY, 1908.

I.—GENERAL RELATIONS.

[*ED. NOTE.*—The following minutes are attached to despatch No. 3 from Mr. F. Cartwright, dated Munich, January 8, 1908. The despatch is not printed, as its general tendency is adequately shown by the minutes.

F.O. 371/457.
1308/1308/08/18C.

MINUTES.

A thoughtful review of the situation. Mr. Cartwright does not believe that the recent efforts for a rapprochement between Germany and England denote on the part of the former any cessation of those political designs which must render a violent collision between the two powers inevitable. He thinks that those efforts are made solely for the purpose of gaining time for the necessary preparations.—Mr. Cartwright is a shrewd observer and it would be idle to deny that his view may prove only too true.—I would in this connection refer to a passage in my secret memorandum of Jan[uary] 1, 1907 (p. 33),(1) in which I pointed out that one objection which stood in the way of accepting the view that Germany was deliberately pursuing an anti-English policy, was that pending the necessary development of the German forces, such a policy must compel Germany to make every effort to win and retain England's friendship temporarily. I pointed out that Germany had persistently neglected to make any such effort; the conclusion therefore seemed justified that the design attributed to Germany was not in fact, at least not consciously and deliberately, entertained.

It must be admitted that the very marked change, or at least outward change in Germany's attitude towards us, is well explainable on the hypothesis that she has come to see the mistake she had made; and in fact every indication derived from what is being done and advocated in Germany, does now tend to confirm the impression that the whole energy of her government is directed towards preparing for the coming struggle with England.

E. A. C.
Jan. 14.

A good retrospect. No one is likely to believe in an entente between this Country and Germany in face of the German Naval programme.

W. L.

I am glad he is back and that his reports are coming again. We cannot be comfortable as long as the German Navy is increasing.

E. G.]

(1) [*v. Gooch & Temperley*, Vol. III, p. 414, *App.* A.]

No. 75.

Sir F. Lascelles to Sir Edward Grey.

F.O. 371/457.
1187/1187/08/18.
(No. 11.) Confidential.

Berlin, D. *January 10*, 1908.
R. *January 13*, 1908.

I have the honour to forward, herewith, a despatch, as marked in the margin, which I have received from Colonel Trench Military Attaché to this Embassy, relating to Conversation with the Emperor.

I have, &c.
FRANK C. LASCELLES.

Colonel Trench to Sir F. Lascelles.

Sir,   *British Embassy, Berlin, January 6, 1908.*

I have the honour to report that H[is] M[ajesty] the Emperor, while walking this morning in the Tiergarten with H[er] M[ajesty] the Empress and H[is] R[oyal] H[ighness] Prince Oscar, called me to him and honoured me with five minutes conversation, most of which was personal and rather humorous. His Majesty suddenly said : "What are your allies going to do? Isn't it marvellous the way the centre of interest has shifted to the Pacific? I tell you, you must be very careful! Exactly what I prophesied fourteen years ago is going to happen : there is going to be a life-struggle between the white and black races (H[is] M[ajesty] said "black" not yellow) and woe betide you if you take the wrong side! They'll attack you next! The white race will be turned out of Asia."

The Emperor was looking well and not at all worried, as when I last saw him. His only reference to things in England was a remark about a recent practical joke in high life which bore some resemblance to a burglary.

I have, &c.

F. TRENCH, *Colonel, General Staff.*

MINUTE.

Germany earnestly desires a conflict between Japan and the United States, with a secret reservation that, while both would be exhausted, Japan should win.

E. A. C.
Jan. 13.
W. L.

MINUTE BY KING EDWARD.

On what grounds is above statement made?

E.R.

SEPARATE MINUTE.

Japan, United States and Germany.

The view somewhat shortly expressed in my minute on Sir F. Lascelles' despatch No. 11, is derived, not only from a careful and prolonged study of German opinion as revealed in periodical and other literature, but also, and more particularly, from conversations with a highly-placed and distinguished German naval officer who is in close touch with the leading men at Berlin. Some two years ago I reported privately and confidentially to Lord Lansdowne some of those conversations.[1] I have had others since. My friend has always spoken to me with great frankness on the aims of German policy.

He has explained more than once, what indeed we know well from other sources that America is a country of which Germany is really afraid, because it cannot be tackled by her or exposed either directly or indirectly through other Powers. The attitude of subservience adopted by Germany, as by other States, towards America, is felt to be humiliating, and is often severely criticized by public opinion. Any weakening of America's position as a world-Power would therefore be welcome. (We know of the persistent but hitherto vain efforts made to embroil England and the United States.)

At the same time Germany has come to realize the great mistake she made in offending Japan at the time of the Liaotung cession. She is now determined at all costs to win Japan's good graces and is so confident of success that, as I was frankly told, Germany would altogether supplant England at Tokio in a very short time. The conclusion had been reached that the danger of Japan leading the yellow hosts against the European Powers is a chimæra. On the other hand a conflict between Japan and America—no doubt on the principle that the wish is father to the thought—is considered not only possible but in the long run inevitable. So long as America is not actually strengthened as a result of such a conflict, it would suit Germany. She is not afraid of even victorious Japan.

I had an opportunity, at the Hague Conference, of discussing questions of general policy with the able Japanese delegate, M. Tsudzuki. He confirmed all that I had heard about Germany's changed attitude, and said she was making every possible advance at Tokio. But M. Tsudzuki

[1] [The Editors have recently had access to the Lansdowne private papers, but they have been unable to trace these reports at present.]

did not allow himself to be drawn into any statement of the views of the Japanese government, beyond a decided declaration that Japan meant to go with England as hitherto, and that there was no danger of a war with America.

E. A. C.
Jan. 21.

No. 76.

Sir F. Bertie to Sir Edward Grey.

F.O. 371/484.
3045/2952/08/28A.
(No. 42.)
Sir,

Paris, D. January 26, 1908.
R. January 28, 1908.

The French Press of yesterday and to-day has naturally devoted considerable space to the discussion of the debate on Moroccan Affairs which took place in the Chamber on the 24th instant. It is also natural that Monsieur Delcassé's speech has excited the most interest.([1]) The ex-Minister for Foreign Affairs has received from different organs both the highest praise and the deepest reprobation. . . . . .([2])

I have, &c.
FRANCIS BERTIE.

MINUTES.

M. Delcassé is attacked on all sides. It is however curious that none of his critics seems to be able (or willing) to see exactly wherein the lesson of his fall lay : It is the same lesson that we are said to have failed to learn from the Boer war : namely that policy and strategical preparedness must go hand-in-hand. Failure of such harmony must lead either to military disaster or political retreat. Our own disasters of 1899 were not sufficiently great to bring the truth of the lesson home to us in all its force; that was due to the comparative insignificance of the enemy. With an enemy like Germany we should have been in the same predicament as was the French government when it decided to sacrifice M. Delcassé to placate Berlin. The fact that M. Delcassé now aspires to the control of the French army or navy, seems to show that he now sees the nature of the great error into which he had fallen, of shaping a foreign policy without making sure that there was enough force to carry it through.

E. A. C.
Jan. 28.
C. H.
W. L.

This no doubt is the real criticism.

E. G.

([1]) [On January 24, 1908, M. Delcassé, who had taken no part in the Parliamentary debates since his fall, defended his Moroccan policy against the criticisms of M. Jaurès.]
([2]) [The omitted passages give summaries of various Press articles.]

No. 77.

Sir F. Cartwright to Sir Edward Grey.

F.O. 371/484.
3191/2952/08/28A.
(No. 13.)
Sir,

Munich, D. January 27, 1908.
R. January 29, 1908.

For some time past rumours had been current that Monsieur Delcassé might possibly be sent to St. Petersburg to replace Monsieur Bompard as French Ambassador. The possibility of this has certainly not been viewed with much satisfaction in Germany, but his sudden reappearance at the tribune of the French Chamber may be said to have aroused here little less than a feeling of indignation. This is perhaps not so much due to the fact that so distinguished a politician should seek to reappear again in public life but that Monsieur Delcassé should have come to the front again with all his old energy, his clearness of political foresight and his apparent determination if he returned to power to pursue the policy he always advocated in international affairs. The indignation this has aroused here is not to be wondered at for the

German press had taught its readers to believe that France had been so thoroughly frightened by Germany that nothing would induce her to allow her destinies to be again placed in the hands of so dangerous a statesman. That Germany must be on the watch now cannot be denied: Monsieur Delcassé's speech has changed the position of affairs in the neighbouring country. Ever since the fall of that Minister France has felt herself more or less humiliated, first, for having been drawn to Algeciras against her wish, and, secondly, for being compelled from that moment to look towards Germany before taking any step in Morocco. Now a man appears who still proclaims that France with her ententes needs to be afraid of no one and there is every prospect that by becoming a popular hero he may be lifted to power on a wave of patriotic enthusiasm such as has not been unfrequently witnessed in France. . . . .([1])

I have, &c.
FAIRFAX L. CARTWRIGHT.

([1]) [The rest of this despatch deals with Press comments on M. Delcassé's speech.]

No. 78.

Sir F. Lascelles to Sir Edward Grey.

F.O. 371/458.
3659/3659/08/18.
(No. 40.) Confidential.
Sir,

Berlin, D. *January* 30, 1908.
R. *February* 3, 1908.

At a Court Ball last night, the Emperor deigned to honour me with a conversation of considerable length. During the earlier part of the evening and at supper when I had the honour of a seat at His Majesty's table, the Emperor had been pleased, in a vein of highest good humour, to indulge in the jokes which he frequently makes about the morning visits which he had paid me on two occasions when he found me unprepared to receive him. He had indeed hinted that it was possible that he might again pay me such a visit. After supper His Majesty assumed a more serious demeanour and, taking me aside, said that he felt compelled to speak a word of serious warning to me. The English Press had again begun their attacks upon the German naval programme, by pointing out the great expense to which England would be put by being compelled to build so many more ships in consequence of the increase of the German Naval Forces. This, His Majesty considered, was very unfair. England had the right to build as many ships as she considered necessary, and no one could legitimately complain of her doing so. But why put the blame exclusively upon Germany? Other nations were increasing their naval armaments, some of them, such as France and the United States, to a very considerable extent; and even Brazil was building ships. The English Press, however, took no notice of the increase of the Naval Forces of other powers, which would justify His Majesty's Government in augmenting their programme of naval construction, but singled out Germany as the cause of the increased expenditure. This could not fail to create a feeling of irritation in Germany, which the Emperor might find himself unable to restrain. His Majesty really thought that something should be done to counteract this Anti-German tendency, and he hoped that I would write and say so.

I replied that I would not fail to report to you what His Majesty had deigned to say, but that I did not see what could be done. Personally I had not seen the articles to which His Majesty had alluded, and had been under the impression that the general tone of the Press in England had of late become more friendly to Germany. His Majesty had been able to convince himself during his recent visit to England,([1]) and more especially by the cordial reception which he met with in

([1]) [*v. supra*, pp. 92–8, Nos. 60–3.]

London, on the occasion of his visit to the Guildhall that the influence of the teutonophobe section of the Press was not as great as people in Germany seemed to believe.

This allusion to his visit to England appeared to divert His Majesty's thoughts from his grievance, and he spoke in the warmest possible language of the pleasure which his reception had given him, and of the great kindness shown him by the King and Queen. He had also been much touched by the present which the King had sent him on his birthday and by the very cordial telegrams which His Majesty had addressed to him. He then related at great length his experiences at Highcliffe, and how he had thoroughly enjoyed his life there and been able to make some most interesting acquaintances.

At the close of this conversation, I observed that I rejoiced that the relations between the two countries had greatly improved during the last two years, an improvement which had been greatly enhanced by his recent visit to England, and that therefore the moment was not an unfavourable one for my successor, whoever he might be, to enter upon the duties of the post. The Emperor said that he did not propose to discuss the question of my departure from Berlin. He could read my thoughts and therefore knew what my feelings were. As I gathered this to mean that I myself desired to leave Berlin, I replied that as His Majesty was so fully acquainted with my feelings, I would be indiscreet enough to explain to him, that my mission, having already been prolonged three times, would not be prolonged again, that I was aware that the King had mentioned the subject of my retirement to Count Metternich, and that I was glad to think that the improvement in the relations between the two countries would render the task of my successor more easy than it would have been two years ago. I should certainly have pitied any one who would have been called upon to take my place say in 1905, when I found my position a peculiarly painful one. The Emperor replied that 1905 was indeed a terrible year, and he sincerely hoped that he should never again have to live through such a painful time. There could be no doubt that a very great improvement had taken place since then.

I have noticed on previous occasions, during the reign of Queen Victoria, that the complaints, which the Emperor had to make against England, became more accentuated whenever the Queen made her periodical visits to France, and it has struck me that His Majesty's present grievance may have been in some degree due to the fact that the King and Queen are about to visit the Courts of Copenhagen and Christiania.

I propose to take an early opportunity of giving an account of the conversation with which the Emperor honoured me to Herr von Schoen, but I would suggest that no undue importance should be attached to His Majesty's grievance, which did not appear to me to be based upon anything more definite than a somewhat vague complaint against the tone of certain newspapers, which he chose, on the present occasion, to regard as the Representatives of the English Press.

I have, &c.

FRANK C. LASCELLES.

MINUTES.

The emperor is peculiarly sensitive. The newspapers of which he complains must however have been deliberately submitted to him, because he does not otherwise read foreign papers—which I know on good authority. The responsible people, who submit them, must on their part know quite well that it is not the British government that favours "attacks" on German naval programmes.—As I pointed out in my memorandum on the relations between England and Germany,(2) such an attitude would in the end be impolitic and injurious. Sir E. Grey himself gave the strongest expression quite recently in a public speech to the view that we do not complain in any way of Germany building and arming as much and as quickly as she may think right.

But it is surely asking a good deal that an independent British press should refrain from pointing out that the new German programme must entail a corresponding increase of expenditure

(2) [v. Gooch & Temperley, Vol. III, pp. 397–420, App. A.]

on this country, and from lamenting this obvious but unpleasant fact. It seems a pity that Sir F. Lascelles was apparently unable to make a courteous retort. What if France suddenly decided to make very large additions to her army? Of course the least thing that Germany would do, would be to make corresponding additions to hers. If then, what is not at all improbable, there should appear, even in respectable German papers, articles regretting that by the action of France Germany was being compelled to incur further heavy expenditure, what would the German answer be, I wonder, to a complaint of the French government as to the unfriendliness of the German press?! And how would the argument be received that it was most unfair of German papers to blame France, seeing that not only France, but also Brazil and Austria were increasing their armies?

Could not Sir F. Lascelles be told to say something of this kind to Herr von Schön when he speaks to him, as he proposes to do?

E. A. C.
Feb. 3.

The Emperor can hardly be serious in suggesting that we should restrain our Press, a large section of which will certainly continue to call attention to the German Naval Programme, and the necessity for increased expenditure on our part to maintain our present position. Sir F. Lascelles will find it easier to explain this to Herr v. Schön than to the Emperor, and it is to be hoped that he will do so, though it is as well known in Berlin as here that no restraint is possible even if it were desirable.

W. L.

It would be somewhat absurd if our Naval programme of construction were to be increased on account of Brazil's intention to build a fleet! The Emperor knows as well as we do that the new German navy bill has created a feeling of unrest over here and must naturally be an object of hostile criticism. He knows equally well that the British press is independent.

C. H.

A despatch should be written to Sir F. Lascelles founded on Mr. Crowe's minute.(3) The point might also be made that the Navy League in Germany frequently uses the British Navy as an illustration of the need for increasing the German Navy; in the same way, that section of the Press here which is always afraid that the Gov[ernmen]t especially a Liberal Gov[ernmen]t will let the Navy fall behindhand uses the German Navy to enforce its point. The fact that it pays so much more attention to the German Navy than it does to that of Brazil is due no doubt in part to the nearness of one and the remoteness of the other but may also be taken as a compliment to the quality of the German Navy as compared with that of Brazil.

E. G.

(3) [For this despatch, v. infra, pp. 133–5, No. 84, and encl.]

No. 79.

Sir F. Bertie to Sir Edward Grey.

F.O. 371/454.
3862/3862/08/17.
(No. 54.) Confidential.　　　　　　　　　　　Paris, D. February 3, 1908.
Sir,　　　　　　　　　　　　　　　　　　　　R. February 4, 1908.

Monsieur Delcassé paid me a visit on the 1st instant. He gave me his reason for his speech in the Morocco Debate in the Chamber which was as follows:—

The German Emperor had had a conversation during the Kiel regatta in July with a Frenchman on the relations between Germany and France. His Majesty had said that he had always wished to be on the best terms with France, but M. Delcassé had persistently pursued an Anti-German policy. His Majesty stated that with the view of conciliation he had twice sent word to M. Delcassé that he would like to meet him, but no reply had been made to His Majesty's suggestion which if it had been accepted should have led to a good understanding between Germany and France for there were so many questions that they could settle amicably together.

[17590]　　　　　　　　　　　　　　　　　　　　　　　　　　　　　I

Monsieur Delcassé said that he had never received any intimation of such a desire on the part of the German Emperor and he did not believe that His Majesty had ever sent any message to him, and he therefore determined to take the first favourable opportunity to make a statement of the policy which he had followed during his term of office. Monsieur Jaurès' speech had given him that opportunity and he had taken advantage of it.

Monsieur Delcassé said that he supposed that I knew what had passed between the Emperor and Monsieur Etienne at Kiel.([1]) I replied that I had heard one version which was that His Majesty had suggested an exchange of ideas on various subjects between the two Governments so that they might come to a general understanding which would be of benefit to both countries and that when Monsieur Etienne who had gone to Kiel full of projects for financial and commercial undertakings in combination with Germany had intimated that to render such a general understanding feasible it would be necessary that "La France fût reconstituée" or words to that effect the Emperor had dropped the subject and had soon afterwards terminated the conversation.

M. Delcassé then told me that the Emperor had said more than I had heard and not only to M. Etienne. His Majesty had stated that what he desired was not only agreement about all matters but an understanding between France and Germany against England who was a menace to Europe.

As to the Ministry of M. Clemenceau the faults which he found with it were pandering to the Socialists and consequent unwillingness to maintain proper discipline in the army and navy, and failure to keep sufficiently in touch with The Emperor of Russia, who, say what you may, is Russia; and taking too humble a line towards Germany who does not desire war any more than does France. The French Government would gain nothing; they only tied her hands by such a declaration as that made by the Minister for Foreign Affairs, viz.: "Pas d'immixtion dans les dissensions intestines de l'Empire, pas de protectorat, pas d'action qui nous y conduise, pas d'expédition à l'intérieur. Nous n'irons ni à Fez, ni à Marrakech." M. Denys Cochin had asked M. Clemenceau privately in the Chamber why he allowed M. Pichon to make such a declaration and M. Clemenceau had replied: "It will not prevent us advancing if necessary but the declaration is required in order to keep Germany quiet."

M. Delcassé said that the majority obtained by the Ministry did not indicate confidence in it. It meant that the Chamber was not prepared at present to turn it out.

I asked M. Delcassé his opinion as to the condition of the French army and navy. He stated that from the information which he had and which was quite reliable he was convinced that the French Staff Officers were quite as well educated, intelligent and scientific as those of Germany and as devoted to their profession, the French Artillery was superior to that of Germany. As to the soldiers they were not individually so big or so strong, but they were better marchers and had more "élan" than the Germans. Unfortunately the French Ministry had for political reasons not supported the superior officers in maintaining discipline, and there had been some regrettable incidents in the South during the agitation in the Wine Districts and also elsewhere. If war came everything would depend on the first encounter. If the French troops could obtain a victory he thought that there would be good prospect of success. He believed that the chiefs who would be likely to have commands were capable but the merits of military commanders were an unknown quantity until the hour came for them to show their qualities, viz., actual war. The qualities of the German Chiefs were equally unknown. Germany could mobilize at the outbreak of war more men than France but the problem would be how to feed and supply and utilize a larger number of troops on the German side than could be mobilised, fed and supplied and utilized on the French side.

As to the navy M. Delcassé believed the *matériel* to be good but owing to the weakness of the Ministry on account of the attitude of the Socialists there had been instances of indiscipline in the navy which had not been properly punished. There

([1]) [cp. supra, pp. 58–9, No. 36.]

were sure to be some hotheads amongst such large crews as big ships now carried, but if the Officers were backed up when they took measures to maintain discipline M. Delcassé thinks all would be well.

I have, &c.
FRANCIS BERTIE.

MINUTES.

A most interesting conversation. Two statements made by M. Delcassé call for special attention :

(1) that M. Delcassé never received the two messages which the emperor has repeatedly stated he had sent to him, suggesting a personal meeting;

(2) that the emperor at the famous interview with M. Etienne proposed an understanding against Great Britain.

Sir F. Lascelles has more than once called attention to the habit of the emperor to make statements which have no foundations in fact and which must be heavily discounted; and we know of several instances of this kind. Apparently the alleged intimations to M. Delcassé must be classed with these.

That the emperor gives vent at times to outbursts of a violently anti English kind without taking much precaution as to the discretion of the interlocutary or correspondent addressed we know too well to allow us to treat M. Delcassé's assertion of what passed at the interview with M. Etienne, as unworthy of credit.

E. A. C.
Feb. 4.

M. Clémenceau's answer to M. Denys Cochin rather confirms the impression that the French Gov[ernmen]t have two voices about the Morocco question : one for home use, the other for use in Morocco itself.

W. L.
C. H.
E. G.

No. 80.

Sir F. Lascelles to Sir Edward Grey.

F.O. 371/458.
4552/4552/08/18.
(No. 52.)   *Berlin, D. February 4, 1908.*
Sir,   R. *February 10, 1908.*

I have the honour to forward, herewith, a despatch, as marked in the margin, which I have received from Captain Dumas Naval Attaché to this Embassy, relating to a conversation with Admiral von Tirpitz respecting Anglo-German relations.

I have, &c.
FRANK C. LASCELLES.

Enclosure in No. 80.

Captain Dumas to Sir F. Lascelles.

Confidential.
Your Excellency,   *Berlin, February 3, 1908.*

I have the honour to submit that I called this morning on Admiral von Tirpitz, State Secretary for the Navy, for the purpose of presenting him with a copy of our Royal Navy List from My Lords Commissioners of the Admiralty. In accepting the book His Excellency begged me to return his best thanks and acknowledgments for the courtesy and give expression to his highest respects.

His Excellency went on to say that while deploring the reason (Herr Bebel's speech) he had been very happy last week in being able to express in the Reichstag his profound conviction that there were no possible grounds for any trouble between England and Germany except trade rivalry and that he was sure couldn't be helped by resort to arms.

He deplored Herr Bebel's speech in every way as calculated to re-arouse suspicions on both sides and pointed out how dangerous it was to suggest to a proud people like the Germans that they were not masters in their own house as regards what ships they might or might not build. Such remarks only increased the mad demands put forward by the Navy League and placed a weapon in the hands of the Chauvinists of both countries.

It was most unfortunate that Bebel also should have finished his remarks by suggesting that the day was approaching when England would tell Germany so far and no farther. These things had the worst effect at home even where the man was known and there was no knowing where they stopped abroad.

His Excellency asked me if I thought the feeling in England as regards Germany was better and I answered Yes but at the same time of course their new Navy Bill, through the medium of the newspapers, had frightened many of the less instructed to which he replied that he was really at a loss to know what he could do in the matter and could not believe that in the fleet Bill any thinking man in England could see any harm. After all it was not as if he was constructing anything more in numbers than was laid down to be built in 1900 and to those numbers he had kept and meant to adhere.

I pointed out that it wasn't the numbers but the rapidity of construction of a Dreadnought type of fleet that caused some uneasiness on which the Admiral explained that it was of course incumbent to replace ships as soon as they were out of date and even now it seemed to him that in the future their ships would be close on 25 years old before they could be finally wiped off the list.

Personally he thought, in view of our alliances with France and Japan, that there was from some points of view more possible grounds [sic] for uneasiness in Germany and of course that was worked for all it was worth by the Navy League who had always to be getting up steam but we had no reason of that sort to bring forward and many of our publicists and newspaper writers seemed to him to be mad.

His Excellency went on Take for instance all the nonsense about invasion lately written in England. Out of the 30,000 military Officers in Germany one might expect that one or two sheeps-headed Lieutenants might write such rubbish, yet he was informed that Lord Roberts was gravely bringing it forward in England as possible and probable.

It was incredible to him that a great soldier and a Statesman for whom he had always had the greatest respect could believe in such a thing. So far as he (the State Secretary) knew it was impossible for them to even embark such numbers as say 100,000 men, and none should know better what it meant than the English, and in view of our sea forces, quite impossible that they should be disembarked on the other side. Even Napoleon had found it impossible when only 20 miles off and there were no ten-fold Napoleons in Germany in these or any other days. To carry out invasion two things were absolutely necessary. First to land an amply sufficient number of troops and secondly to maintain the lines of communications.

He had spoken of 100,000 men but that number would be wholly useless in England even if we had no army there to oppose them.

Under circumstances of invasion it was certain that a million semi-trained soldiers would spring up like magic and in that connection he would advise me to think over and study the German halt before Paris in 1870.

Any ideas regarding the keeping open of the lines of communication had only to be thought of to raise a smile. All the fleets of Europe put together against England could not guarantee it. So many articles had been sent him on the subject of late that he had necessarily given it a deal of thought and from his point of view as a Statesman, a Naval Officer and a gentleman he declared plainly that this foolish panic was wholly stupid and impossible to understand.

Finally His Excellency repeated to me almost word for word his speech in the Reichstag of the 29th (already reported) and with renewed friendly messages to our Admiralty said good-bye.

I have, &c.

PHILIP DUMAS,
Captain and Naval Attaché.

MINUTES.

It is rather absurd of Admiral Tirpitz to talk like this. We may have our own idea whether an invasion can be prevented or repelled, but it is too well known that the German military authorities not only regard it as feasible in certain circumstances, but have studied the ways and means and made plans.

I believe it is on record that so great an authority as Moltke regarded the invasion of England as practicable. It is certain that the Great General Staff at Berlin is of the same opinion. It is only 2 or 3 years ago that Baron von Edelsheim then a captain on that Staff published, with the authorization of his chief, a pamphlet dealing in detail with the measures to be taken for the purpose; that the pamphlet was immediately afterwards suppressed; and that Baron von Edelsheim was sent back in disgrace to his regiment, because the Emperor was very angry that the pamphlet having been noticed in the English press, threatened to cause bad feeling and impair the political relations.

It is also a fact which I myself got to know through the indiscretion of one of the officials of the Hamburg-America Line, and which I brought to Lord Lansdowne's notice at the time (some 2 or 3 years ago, I think) that the Emperor with his own hand made a number of blue pencil corrections and alterations in the designs of 2 new liners, then about to be built, because H[is] M[ajesty] maintained that the designs as submitted to him would not permit of these ships taking their allotted part in the transport of 2 divisions to England.

In view of these facts and other considerations of a more general character which need not here be set out, Admiral Tirpitz's bland remarks to Captain Dumas do not, I think, deserve to be taken very seriously. It is of course his business to prevent if possible any suspicions from arising as to possible German plans.

We on our part are not concerned with forming a deliberate opinion as to whether invasion is practicable. That is a matter which only our military and naval authorities can decide. All we can do is to establish whether or not the German authorities consider it practicable. We have strong grounds for believing that they do—or did until recently at any rate.

E. A. C.
Feb. 10.

His views hardly square with his programme.

W. L.

There are many indications that the future invasion of England is being carefully prepared in Germany and, if ever the moment should arise, it will almost certainly be found that no precaution has been neglected to ensure its success.

C. H.

There is no doubt whatever that the Germans have studied and are studying the question, German officers on leave come here and explore our coast and no doubt send in reports which are interesting and welcome to their own authorities. No doubt also the German Staffs work out possible plans. We too continue to work out the best methods of making any such plans miscarry. As long as we have sufficient superiority of Navy the risk will be too great for the Germans to run it in cold blood, but it is a danger to us to be borne in mind in all contingencies.

E. G.

No. 81.

Sir F. Lascelles to Sir Edward Grey.

F.O. 371/458.
6310/6310/08/18.
(No. 71.) Secret.   *Berlin,* D. *February* 12, 1908.
Sir,   R. *February* 24, 1908.

I have the honour to enclose the Annual Report on the German Navy for the year 1907, which has been drawn up by Captain Dumas, Naval Attaché to this Embassy.

Captain Dumas had prepared this Report with the view of my including it in my Annual Report on Germany, but as I propose, in view of the very complicated political situation in Germany to postpone the compilation of that Report until I shall have been enabled to express a more definite opinion than is at present possible.

I have thought it better to forward to you Captain Dumas' very interesting Report without further delay.

I have, &c

FRANK C. LASCELLES.

Enclosure in No. 81.

Captain Dumas to Sir F. Lascelles.

German N.A. Report 9/05.

(Secret.)   *British Embassy,*

Your Excellency,   *Berlin, February* 12, 1908.

I have the honour to submit the following Report on the German Navy for 1907.

In considering the Naval history of the Empire for the year it is, I think, well to recollect that in German eyes they passed through, on account of the Algeciras Conference, a period of terrible humiliation in 1906.

This had arisen, so far as I am able to judge, from the fact that the people as a whole, while fully realising that Germany by means of her army had become one of the greatest land powers of the world, had failed to appreciate the still greater possession of sea and consequent world power and so, prior to the Russo-Japanese war, had only feared Russia.

When therefore, towards the end of that war, she saw the former country shattered and disorganised it may be that a somewhat adventurous policy was embarked upon and especially so with regard to Morocco—always a future colony for Germany in the eyes of the Pan-Germans—but having failed, with incredible foolishness, to first propitiate England and Spain, she was here suddenly foiled and, in the opinion of the people, treated with the utmost contempt by England.

[§ 5.]([1]) The result was an absolute shriek from the Navy League and a consequent immediate desire on all sides for the possession of a great Navy in which alone they now recognized the strong power and might which had thus foiled them and, as has been commonly said, Admiral Tirpitz, had he asked for it in 1906, might have obtained any increase he desired for the fleet. However, on the contrary, studious moderation was observed—too studious in the eyes of the people who were being daily educated by the Navy League—largely because the Admiralty authorities were compelled to hold back owing to the introduction of the Dreadnought type forcing them to delay their building programme by something like a year, and partly because the Admiralty naturally did not desire to be lead [*sic*] by the people and meanwhile for the whole year the Navy League was flooding the country with lectures and pamphlets to the effect that Germany's only possible opening for future greatness, development and proper position as a world power could be attained by the rapid construction of a fleet so strong that even England would hesitate to flout it.

This position having been attained it can well be understood that 1907 opened with considerable disquietude as to the attitude of England in attempting to force Germany to attend the Hague Conference with a view to discussing a scheme of reduction of armaments.([2])

Under these circumstances and in view of their, as they thought, almost foolish moderation of arrangements, it is hardly to be wondered at if, in the proposal of England of all countries, to disarm they discerned the most machiavellian duplicity : first in asking Germany to halt in her progress to world power and secondly, in forcing on her, if she did come to the conference, a rôle as the one determined disturber of the peace of the world.

The feeling as it appears to me now was one of furious exasperation at a second public humiliation to follow that already achieved at Algeciras and the very fact

([1]) [The paragraph numbers inserted in this document in square brackets were written in pencil by Mr. Crowe on a printed version of the report. They correspond to the paragraph numbers used by him in his notes, *v. infra*, pp. 131–2.]

([2]) [This subject will be dealt with in a later volume.]

that there was no general clamour for war shows how profoundly convinced the Admiralty Staff must have been of the certain disaster that recourse to arms must produce.

So impressed were the public with this view that they remained quiet under, as they considered it, humiliation piled on humiliation from England, in which they read a desire to force the country into a ruinous war, and this culminated last April in an almost frenzied outburst of terror caused, as I imagine most such extravagances are, by the innocent facts of a Royal visit in the Mediterranean and the simultaneous issue of a loan at high interest in Berlin, but into which a foolish people read the most sinister meanings.([3])

[§ 10.] In the reaction after such an absurdity the excitement rapidly subsided but the iron had entered their soul and fear of England and her designs has ever since amounted to an absolute obsession. The result was that they considered that their one and only safety lay in the possession of a strong fleet and I am not exaggerating one bit when I say that the new building programme has been received over the country at large with an almost universal sigh of relief, while, were it not for the fact that it might be considered as a menace by England, I believe that a programme of double the proportions would have been most heartily welcomed.

I would also here beg to emphasize that whereas at the end of the Russo-Japanese war there was, to my thinking, almost an outburst of Chauvinism in Germany, to-day the pendulum is at the other end of its swing and there is a great and general distrust of their power to move in any direction.

However that may be all the foregoing seems to me to very clearly determine the attitude which Germany observed, as regards Naval matters, at the Hague Conference and speaking broadly I am of opinion that a sigh of relief was audible all over Germany that England's attitude was not such as to force them into war on account of their determination, at all hazards, to preserve a free hand in the matter of future construction.

[§ 12.] This fear and horror of war is very pronounced in Germany, far more so than in England, and arises first from a possible loss of the breadwinner and secondly from a curious sentimental feeling that going to war means death, whereas in other countries it is more generally connected with glory.

[§ 13.] I mention this because, in so far as it may have any value, public opinion in Germany is always, to my mind, wholly adverse to war and wherever it could exert any influence would certainly make for peace.

[§ 14.] Against that it would be idle not to recognize that the bureaucracy are not so opinionated and would not hesitate to proceed to extremities if any concrete advantages or money was [sic] to be seen in such a policy.

A matter of great Naval interest during the spring was the publication in Paris of some rumours regarding the roping in of Denmark for some sort of an offensive and defensive alliance with Germany.

The effect was electrical in Denmark and disclosed an amazing amount of hate for Germany as still in existence.

This being noted here has, I am sure, made the Germans clearly realise that Denmark, at least in so far as the land contiguous to the Great and Little Belts is concerned, must be overrun and seized by them in case of war with either England or France and *en passant* I would note that Denmark's desires or wishes will probably in the future be treated with severity or even contempt and such efforts as are possible made to get on the best of terms with Sweden who flanks the only other vulnerable approach to Germany in the Baltic.

To that extent it is almost a clearing of the air and simplifies the situation for Denmark who have to choose between Germany who [sic] they hate and fear, and England, of whom, mindful of 1864, they are naturally distrustful. However the dislike shown for Germany is so pronounced that I believe the distrust of England might by judicious support be overcome.

([3]) [cp. *supra*, pp. 28–32, Nos. 15–6.]

As a result of all the above there was an unceasing cry heard throughout the year for an increased rapidity of construction of the German fleet and this resulted in the Amendment to the Fleet Bills of 1900 and 1906, published in November last and certain, I think, to be approved in the Reichstag.

The following tables show its most important provisions.

			1906.		1908.		
			B[attle-ships].	L[ight] C[ruisers].	B[attle-ships].	L[ight] C[ruisers].	Increase.
1908	...	...	2	1	3	1	1
1909	...	...	2	1	3	1	1
1910	...	...	2	1	3	1	1
1911	...	...	1	2	3	1	1
1912	...	...	1	2	1	1	1
1913	...	...	1	1	1	1	...
1914	...	...	1	1	1	1	...
1915	...	...	1	1	1	1	...
1916	...	...	1	1	1	1	...
1917	...	...	2	...	1	1	...
			14	11	18	10	5

It will be thus seen that the whole increase amounts to four extra battleships and a decrease of one armoured cruiser, but the crux of the business as far as we are concerned lies in the fact that those four extra battleships are to be commenced as it were at once and completed, in addition to the previous programme, in 1914: after which date indeed the German armoured ship construction actually falls from that formerly allowed. Of course considering numbers alone our fleet is by so far numerically superior that from that point of view it would not trouble us much but it has to be taken into consideration that with the Lord Nelson and Dreadnought classes, or broadly speaking, the one gun type ship, a new era of shipbuilding construction set in and, to arrive at a due knowledge of our relative strength, tables showing whole numbers and modern ships alone must be considered.

That is to say if we discard ships as they arrive at the age of 20 years in about July of each year the two countries by the present programmes will possess.

	Germany.				England.			
	All Sorts.		Modern.		All Sorts.		Modern.	
—	B[attle-ships].	L[ight] C[ruisers]	B[attle-ships].	L[ight] C[ruisers].	B[attle-ships].	L[ight] C[ruisers].	B[attle-ships].	L[ight] C[ruisers].
1908 ...	32	8	...	...	52	35	3	9
1909 ...	31	8	...	...	55	38	6	12
1910 ...	34	10	4	2	58	...	9	...
1911 ...	33	11	7	3	...	...	...	...
1912 ...	33	12	10	4	...	...	...	...
1913 ...	35	12	13	5	...	...	...	...
1914 ...	37	14	16	6	...	...	...	...
1915 ...	37	15	17	7	...	...	...	...
1916 ...	37	16	18	8	...	...	...	...
1917 ...	37	16	19	9	...	...	...	...
1918 ...	38	17	20	10	...	...	...	...
1919 ...	37	18	21	11	...	...	...	...
1920 ...	38	19	22	12	...	...	...	...

Even this provision has proved as was indeed likely, far from satisfying the desires of the German Chauvinists and the leader of the National Liberals has already put forward a programme suggesting a maintenance of the output of 4 armoured vessels yearly after the present proposed year of 1911.

At 20 years' life such a programme would allow for a fleet of some 43 battleships and 32 armoured cruisers and, judging by the steady increase in desire for a stronger Navy I think it likely that some such programme will shortly be brought forward as the ideal to be arrived at instead of the present one of 38 battleships and 20 armoured cruisers.

A result however of this attempt to lead the Admiralty by the ears has been to put them very much in opposition to the Navy League and other amateur strategists and it is certainly with no good will of the present Secretary of State that an increase in the present numbers will be formulated.

[§ 26.] The greatest reason for this moderation at present is the appalling load of debt that the construction of the fleet is piling up. Great attention has been called to the fact that the Empire's debts have increased from £115,000,000 to no less than £162,000,000 in the past six years but few realise that of this great increase of £47,000,000 no less than a quarter or £12,500,000 has been taken for naval construction and if we add the Kiel Canal, at bottom a strategical work, at least £37,000,000 of the whole debt is Naval in its origin.

[§ 27.] Now by the present Fleet Bill it is proposed to add £37,000,000, to the debt in the next ten years, or if we add the costs of widening and deepening the canal, solely due to the Dreadnought policy, £49,000,000.

[§ 28.] Such sums, especially when read in marks, must stagger even the most extravagant Government and now, immediately following the United States financial crisis and with bad times en evidence everywhere in Germany, so that the bankers are undoubtedly very nervous and cautious it is likely that the spirit will spread throughout the Nation, when could they once realise the source of this debt, some check might possibly supervene against a still greater expansion of the Naval Power.

[§ 29.] I confess however that I do not believe that any such caution will obtain for the fact of Germany's lack of cash is only due to its being all at present absorbed in future productive works. Indeed so far as my enquiries have lead [sic] me I am of opinion that unless some great factor, such as an Imperial preferential tariff or war, supervenes in ten years' time, Germany could comfortably sustain Naval estimates of even £40,000,000.

I have now traced the principal causes of the Fleet Bill of this year and attempted to deduce some lessons therefrom. I cannot but be conscious however of my inability to do so with any completeness and much rests on very slender foundations. Two facts however stand out very clearly :—

1. That the Naval Authorities at present greatly dread the power and aims of England.
2. The whole people are determined to possess a fleet which in quality, if not in quantity, shall leave absolutely nothing to be desired.

[§ 32.] I ought also perhaps to add that a considerable party in Germany are in the greatest hopes that by persistent efforts in the increase of their fleet the people of England will tire of the struggle for the mastery of the sea and finally leave them in possession.

The greatest factor existent in Germany which preserves this feeling and hope is the Navy League.

In the foregoing pages I have already dealt at some length with various doings of this league during the year but as there now seems some possibility of its breaking up as a concrete force for the Empire as a whole I may perhaps note some of the causes.

Under the very capable managership of a General Keim the membership of the League had increased to roughly a million by the end of 1906. Provincial, town and village groups had been formed and there was here a gigantic propaganda which was made use of as far as possible against the Centrum and Socialistic parties by Prince Bülow at the time of the general elections for purely political purposes.

This was possible in the North and West owing to the Centrum having partly sided with the Socialists against the speedy development of the Navy.

Fortunately or unfortunately, owing to the theft of some letters, the fact was disclosed that political rather than patriotic aims were in view in this usage and this was greatly heightened by the Chancellor publicly thanking General Keim for his assistance in the Reichstag.

The result was an outburst of anger in Bavaria and Wurttemburg and all other Catholic centres and, despite a sort of personal effort of the Emperor to smooth matters over at a general meeting held last summer in Cologne, further recriminations against the Catholics as such and Princely personages in the South has now lead to a sort of definite divorce of the Bavarian branch from the remainder while numerous Princes have withdrawn their patronage in sympathy with the Crown Prince of Bavaria.

That this trouble will eventually break up the League I do not believe but it will certainly keep it quiet for some time and possibly do something towards destroying its influence and the pernicious use it has made of England as a bogey in the path of German development and expansion.

[§ 40.] Of late their greatest efforts have been to get at the children and in support of this I may note that two English ladies resident in Germany have told me of their children returning from school and asking if it was true that England really wanted to destroy Germany and could they have some small sum towards the defence of the Empire from that wicked State.

[§ 41.] In another case I spoke to some school children myself who gravely asked why England wished to destroy Germany and told me further that their teacher had begged them always to remember that England was their enemy.

[§ 42.] In themselves of course such stories are ridiculous but they disclose a very serious form of thought which must grow up in the minds of the children and produce a permanent desire for revenge on England.

[§ 43.] When I add to this that England has been constantly held up to hatred by Navy League orators in every village in the Empire and that the grown up members now probably amount to at least 600,000, it can be realised what an overwhelming desire for the downfall of England must now exist in Germany.

[§ 44.] It is true that it is at present masked by fear but I would submit that it cannot be too strongly realised that England is hated throughout Germany and years must elapse before the former friendly feeling, if it ever existed, can again be hoped to obtain and in the meantime friendly meetings, ententes cordiales &c. are only considered by the masses to mask deep and cunning designs to lull their suspicions to sleep. A potent factor in maintaining this atmosphere in a higher circle is the great mass of rubbish which has lately appeared in the English papers and magazines as regards invasion and I would beg here to somewhat elucidate this question.

Even against the Military power of England it would be simply ridiculous to attempt an invasion without at the least a force of 75,000 men.

And in view of the fact of the uncontested superiority of the British Naval forces in home waters any such expedition, unless it can get to sea in absolute secrecy, must be foredoomed to disaster.

Therefore such an invasion must take place in a period of profound peace and, to preserve the secrecy, must either embark and get to sea during a night (say some six hours) or the whole of the telegraphic system must be cut off and all foreigners and sympathisers with England prevented from crossing the borders for many hours.

Further to embark such a body of men in secrecy they must be brought from some distance which presupposes trains, and even if 25,000 men were already collected at the available sea ports it would require some 80 trains, at 600 men to the train, to bring the remainder of the expedition to its point of embarkation.

Therefore a wonderfully organised train service would also be required leading to ports with commodious wharves, far from the borders and served with convenient sidings for the future disposition of the trains on their arrival.

I discount at once the possibility of secretly collecting such numbers in the only city on the German coast which could harbour them—Hamburg—because the town is so full of English shipping, merchants and agents, not to speak of sympathetic foreigners, that it is inconceivable that secrecy under such conditions could be hoped to obtain.

Also, Hamburg lies on a tidal river, some 65 miles from the sea and the passage of a fleet of transports from the docks could but take place slowly and would, in my opinion, be reported before the first ship left the docks thus giving us at least 24 hours to collect an opposing force in the North Sea.

Now the other sea ports on the sea coast of Germany which in some degree fulfil our requirements are Emden, Wilhelmshaven, Bremerhaven, Cuxhaven and Brunsbuttel none of which however I may state offhand could possibly accommodate and dispatch the whole of the expedition and as it must therefore be divided I would therefore take them seriatim.

Emden is close to the Dutch frontier and has numerous semi-Dutch inhabitants besides which there is a resident British Vice-Consul and a foreign staff in the telegraph companies' offices.

It is barely possible that from this port a maximum of ten thousand men might be embarked in secret, if the shipping were already collected, without exciting widespread comment. They would however have to come by train from a considerable distance and I do not think could possibly sail in under twelve hours from the giving of the order which would almost certainly ruin the secrecy.

From Wilhelmshaven, given of course that the necessary shipping could be collected there a very large number could be secretly embarked.

Such troops must however pass en route through Oldenburg and probably Bremen (where there are numerous Englishmen) and it is almost certain that if the numbers were large the secret would leak out.

Probably the maximum number that could get away unseen (ships must pass through the lock gates about high water) would be from ten to fifteen thousand.

At Bremerhaven the facilities are exceedingly good and the shipping in port always ample for a huge expedition. Against that the lock gates must work about high water; troops en route must pass through Bremen and there are always numerous British subjects and ships in port. Consequently I do not think that an expedition of any size could depart unnoticed from this centre.

At Cuxhaven the wharfage is poor but the train service good. Troops however arriving here must have passed on the way through Bremen or Hamburg and again I think that the necessary secrecy in peace time would be out of the question.

There remains Brunsbuttel where both train and embarkation facilities are poor but against that at this port could be embarked just so large a party as could previously have been collected at Neuminster and in Schleswig-Holstein in general without exciting suspicion and this of course would be done while the shipping was collecting in and about the Kiel Canal.

From most of the towns of Schleswig the troops could be brought to the place of embarkation by a line passing no commercial centres, or, so far as I know, where any Englishman resides: but against that, the country swarms with semi-Danes, wholly opposed to Germany, and in view of that fact and the suspicions aroused by the vast collection of shipping about the canal which must be observed by other shipping arriving, I do not think it would be feasible to embark more than 10,000 without the news being spread far and wide over the world.

Summing it up then, I believe that some 30,000 to 40,000 men might possibly embark in secrecy from the various sea ports in separate expeditions but the very fact of that dispersion makes in itself the probability of maintaining the secrecy more and more unlikely.

Given separate expeditions I do not think there would be any great difficulty with the stores. In the first place the ships could load up with a large amount without exciting suspicion and secondly every river and canal in Northern Germany carries vast numbers of huge and strong steel lighters with a capacity up to 800 tons and quite fit to stand being once towed, even at a high speed, across the North Sea.

What it therefore amounts to is that while a raiding expedition is possible an invasion is almost impossible, while, even if either party did arrive, long before they had disembarked their stores and artillery, at least a necessary proceeding, our fleets should have arrived and annihilated them.

Of course from every aspect the affair would be wholly different given a previous period of strained relations but even then I think that organized invasion is impossible.

Present and Future Relations.

Roughly speaking by whatever standard we may judge the present relative strengths of England and Germany the fact emerges that our forces in home waters are at the least twice as strong as those of Germany and this provides the most potent factor for every effort on this side to maintain peace. Even if we carry forward the programmes of the two countries for five years and only allow for the yearly output of four armoured ships from England, the ratio would still amount to better than 2 to 1, which must tend to preserve a healthy feeling of dread of England's power for the whole period while for the approaching two years our ratio of strength is actually increasing.

Again in case of our going to war with Germany it is plain that her ships, if they are to attain any result whatever, must be based on the North Sea where, at the present time, there are but two harbours of refuge for them.

These are Wilhelmshaven and Brunsbuttel, considered as the door of the Canal and Kiel.

But for at least four years Wilhelmshaven, considered in the light of a harbour of refuge, cannot accommodate more than about ten to twelve ships at the utmost whereas, in case of war, they could reasonably expect to have at least 24 battleships in those waters and this is because they can only hope to make any real use of their fleet at the following moments.

1. Directly war is declared when our fleets might not be all in the North Sea and a surprise attack on an isolated squadron or such a valuable asset as the Forth Bridge might cause us severe loss before we had struck a blow.
2. After a series of successful attacks by their torpedo boats on our blockading North Sea fleet.

In the first case their only chance of real success would be to bring out as large a squadron as soon as possible even if the fleet was slow as, having done their work, they must get safely back and as rapidly repair damages.

Therefore before the attack their ships must be already in the North Sea and at least half based on Brunsbuttel which is open to attack by torpedo boats.

In the second case as the ships cannot lie together a junction must first be effected and that fact provides a great danger. But at the same time as the ratio of strength of their fleet to ours is at its least and decreasing, and the works for harbouring the fleet at Wilhelmshaven are incomplete, the works for widening the Kiel canal will also be in hand, and despite every precaution to keep the passage clear there must be a danger of landslips and the blocking of the fairway by the extra draught of a damaged vessel.

[§ 70.] It is also noteworthy that, war or no war, the work must go on, as, until it is completed, the new great ships must make the passage from the Baltic to the North Sea round the Skaw, a very dangerous trip for German ships at such a time. Therefore from these considerations we again see every desire on the part of Germany to postpone any war until both of the works at Wilhelmshaven and on the canal are finished.

[§ 71.] Again so soon as war is declared there must be some movement by Germany infringing the neutrality of Denmark, if only in defence of her own vulnerable position in the Baltic. Any such movement might bring against them the combined power of the Scandinavian States who, while quite ready to bicker among themselves, are by no means ready to see any one of the three sacrificed, and, though their individual power is small, yet in the aggregate it is not to be despised when Germany already has had to concentrate her main forces in the North Sea which would probably leave the 8 Coast defence vessels six small cruisers and some 24 torpedo boats in the Baltic. And yet until the Canal is rebuilt the neutrality of Denmark's territorial waters is certain to be infringed and the benevolence of that country is doubtful enough to give Germany every cause for anxiety.

[§ 72.] Further Russia at the present time possesses about 100 of the most modern destroyers besides other excellent units. With the very uncertain proceedings of that country in case Germany has to fight with either France or England, such a force on a partly undefended flank must cause grave uneasiness and every complaisancy is likely to be shown for the next three or four years to any requirement of Russia.

[§ 73.] Lastly there can be no doubt that the experts of Germany view with the greatest misgivings the present state of their own coast defences and so much is this felt that they are now to be reconstructed at a cost of a million and a half sterling. Taking all these factors together I would submit that from strategic causes alone there is good reason to believe that Germany will keep the peace by every means in her power for the next three or four years though I by no means wish to imply that she has any actual desire for war at any time or that we can afford to relax any efforts to perfect our fleets in the future.

Administration.

except for some very minor alterations in details there is no change to report in the general scheme of administration during the past year.

There have been however numerous changes in the heads of the departments and broadly speaking I gather that the Navy is well satisfied with them especially the relief of Admiral von Ahlefeldt in the dockyard department.

The Inspectorship General of the Navy is at present in abeyance, Admiral of the Fleet von Köster having retired from this practically honorary and wholly impossible position during the year. It is certain however that before long it will again be revived in the person of H[is] R[oyal] H[ighness] Prince Henry at present C[ommander]-in-C[hief] of the High Sea fleet.

No change has occurred at the Admiralty Staff but it is well known that the Chief, Admiral Buchsel, will be relieved in the early spring by Vice Admiral Graf von Baidissin [sic. Baudissin] who is looked upon as more modern.

[§ 78.] In connection with the Admiralty Staff it is worth noting that two senior members are also ex officio members of the Military General Staff and so form a constant go-between for mutual requirements.

Admiral von Müller, head of the Naval Cabinet, has been exceedingly ill during the year, but has now, after a severe operation, recovered. It is feared however that there may be a recurrence when he would have to retire, a serious pity as I am convinced that he is very well disposed towards England. He is considered ruthless and relentless by the Officers and is somewhat of a crank as regards temperance.

Of Admiral von Tirpitz I have seen but little and he is indeed exceedingly unapproachable. When he is met however he is very outspoken—surprisingly so—and I almost fancy he must have schooled himself to this silence and it may be therefore almost a relief for him to talk.

It is a sidelight on his character that his secretary told me that on his return home after an attack on him in the Reichstag he shed tears.

His pursuits are few riding, long solitary walks, music and a sort of philological study of English comprising them all. I have his own word for it that he loves England and English institutions and I truly believe that the perpetual friction between the two countries is a serious trouble to him.

H[is] R[oyal] H[ighness] Prince Henry of Prussia as C[ommander]-in-C[hief] of the High Sea Fleet has kept it very active during the past year and more strenuous work even than usual seems to have occurred in the training at the commencement of the year.

From what little I have heard he seems to have thoroughly justified my remark of last year that under him the rôle undertaken by the fleet would be more of the offensive than the defensive.

This work of reform, as is usual, has not altogether conduced to his popularity but time will of course put that to rights and I do not doubt that in H[is] R[oyal] H[ighness] the command has devolved on the most capable Officer in the Imperial Navy.

Admiral Fischel has retired and his place as second in command has been taken by Vice-Admiral von Holtzendorff of whom personally I know nothing. He is however spoken of very highly by the Officers for his capabilities though not I think popular. The next senior Officer is Rear-Admiral Paschen who is able clever and courteous and most highly thought of throughout the navy.

Admiral Pohl has given up the command of the Cruiser fleet to Rear-Admiral von Heeringen. I only know this Officer from Berlin society, where, to speak plainly, he does not shine, but he is spoken of as clever hardworking and capable and is further I believe a great, almost the only, friend and confidant of Admiral von Tirpitz.

The C[ommander]-in-C[hief] of the East Asian fleet has been taken over during the year by Rear-Admiral von Coerper late Naval Attaché in London. As a tactician and strategist he is spoken of here as the superior of Admiral Breusing but of course a far juster estimate of his capacity could probably be given by our Officers in those waters.

Admiral Ahlefelt took over the command at Wilhelmshaven but has now again been relieved by Admiral Fischel.

The High Sea Fleet.

was employed as usual during the first four months of the year wholly for individual training but towards the end of this period some short cruises were made by ships in company while the cruisers undertook minor scouting operations in and about the Belts.

[§ 91.] It was noticed how frequently the ships made use of the Little Belt about this time and now, having mastered its intricacies, it appears to be preferred for safety of navigation and, in all probability, strategical reasons, to the apparently easier Great Belt. It would therefore seem highly advisable for us I would submit to keep an English Vice-Consul permanently at Fredericia where this use could be noted.

Two series of considerable manœuvres were carried out in May and September of which the fullest available reports, with such lessons as I could deduce, were sent in at the time. The main ones worth mentioning here are.—

1. That Battle tactics as we understand them were carried out for the first time.

2. That England, or anyhow a very superior Naval Power, in each case represented the enemy.

3. That the objective of the enemy in each case was Bremerhaven and Wilhelmshaven rather than the Elbe.

4. That a second and later objective in each case was the Baltic and presumably Kiel.

and their own great lessons learnt sum up into a strong conviction of the inferiority of their coast defences, the necessity for a dry dock on the Lower Elbe and a harbour of refuge for small craft at Heligoland.

Almost equally interesting manœuvres were those carried out during the autumn at Apenrade in Schleswig by landing parties from the fleet repelling a military force sweeping down on the Kiel Canal from Jutland.

There were two inspections of the fleet: one before their Majesties the Czar and the Emperor at Swinemünde in August when actual battle tactics directed by the latter took place.

The second took place before the Emperor off Wilhelmshaven in September after which H[is] I[mperial] M[ajesty] led the fleet to sea for the manœuvres and followed them with the greatest care.

It is worth noting that all the manœuvres of the year have been greatly hampered by bad and foggy weather.

The usual collection of the whole fleet took place at Kiel in June where were two Japanese vessels, invited, it was said, to be impressed by the size of the German fleet. The result was curiously contradictory for the Japanese cruiser proved to be larger than any one of the German battleships and served to point a moral for the Navy League and fleet agitators. During the year the Hannover [sic] and Pommern have been completed and joined the fleet replacing the Brandenburg and Kurfürst Fried[rich] Wilhelm who have joined the reserve; also the Kaiser Barbarossa who has had a refit, entailing considerable lightening, has replaced the Kaiser Friedrich III which is now to undergo a similar refit.

A commencement has been made in replacing the sailing training ships with more modern cruisers.

Some minor changes in the smaller cruisers have taken place. Continual trials with the submarine have been carried out and are now finished.

It has apparently been decided to construct a larger and swifter type and I believe that some 5 or 6 will be laid down in the ensuing year.

The Scharnhorst, a large armoured cruiser, has been completed and joined the fleet, but the Gneisenau, commenced many months earlier and which should have been delivered in July, is not yet completed.

New torpedo boats have joined the flotillas as delivered.

Construction.

Six battleships and three armoured cruisers are now under construction these being.—

Ship.	Laid down.	Probable Date of completion.
Schleswig-Holstein	5.05 ...	July 08.
Schlesien	5.05 ...	July 08.
Ersatz Sachsen...	8.07 ...	January 1910.*
Ersatz Bayern	8.07 ...	November 1909.*
Ersatz Baden	7.07 ...	April 1910.
Ersatz Wurttenburg [sic] ...	7.07 ...	April 1910.
Gneisenau	6.04 ...	March 1908.
E.	3.07 ...	January 1910.
F.	11.07 ...	March 1910.

The completion of these ships at the proper dates depends wholly on the capacity of Messrs. Krupp to provide the guns. Owing to the increase of the shops during the past year these will, in my opinion, be punctually forthcoming.

Considerable steps have been taken during the past year to provide slipways and plant for the construction of the largest ships probable and at present the following establishments possess such facilities.—

Schichau at Danzig	3
Vulkan Yard at Stettin	2
Imperial Yard at Kiel	1
Germania Yard at Kiel	2
Blohm and Voss at Hamburg	3
Vulkan Yard at Hamburg	1
Weser Yard at Bremen	2
Imperial Yard at Wilhelmshaven	1

The Fleet.

Consists at the present day of the following :—

—	Battle-ships.	C[oast] D[efence] ships.	Arm[oure]d Cruis[ers].	Prot-[ecte]d Cruis[ers].	Small Cruis[ers].	T[orpedo] B[oat] Destroyers.	Torp[edo] Boats.	Sub Marines.
Built	22	8	7	5	26	65	47	1
Completing...	2	...	1	...	2	8	...	...
On the stocks	4	...	2	...	3	8	...	(?)
	28	8	10	5	31	81	47	(?)

* These two vessels are of the 1906 programme and their laying down was delayed owing to the introduction of the Dreadnought type and other causes. They can however be quickly completed owing to the time available for collecting materials. Every detail concerning the new ships has been kept a profound secret but roughly speaking their dimensions &c. will be as follows :—

Tonnage	18,000.
Length	475 feet.
Beam	80 feet.
Draught	27·5 feet.
Speed	19 to 20 knots.
Armament	12—28 cm. and other smaller guns.

and they will have reciprocating engines but cruiser F is to have turbine engines and a speed of some 25 knots.

Of this number of 47 torpedo boats some 25 may be considered as hardly modern and certainly not high seaworthy boats. They can of course however be made good use of in the defence of harbours and everywhere in the Baltic.

Of the whole number of 128 Torpedo craft it is probable that about 80 % are always efficient and ready for sea.

During the ensuing year all that are noted here as completing should be turned over to the Imperial Navy.

It is probable that at least one submarine is now on the stocks at the Germania Yard and possibly one at the Imperial Yard at Kiel but not probable that they will be delivered in 1908.

Personnel.

for the year 1908 will consist of the following.—

Admirals	27
Captains	75
Comm[an]ders and Lieut[enant]-Comm[an]ders	581
Lieu[tenant]s and Sub-Lieut[enant]s	952
Mids[hipmen] and Naval cadets	583
Engineer Officers	330
Marine Officers	52
Medical Officers	247
Accountant Officers	203
Seamen W[arrant] O[fficer]s	349
Gunners Seamen Art[ificers]	39
Mining Gunners	35
Eng[ine] Room W[arrant] O[fficer]s	930
Seamen and boys	28,557
Seamen Artillery	2,583
Engine room personnel	10,849
Marines	1,361
Medical corps	506
Ship's steward corps	346
Mining personnel	712

besides which there are of course a large body of technical workmen and officials in the dockyards, at surveying work and in other departments which altogether bring the total for the first time up to 50,000.

During the year it was attempted to increase the number of boys as a first step towards an extended long service system and it is noteworthy that despite free education and numerous other advantages considerable difficulty was experienced in obtaining sufficient entries and the lists had to be kept open for at least a month longer than was intended.

I am told that increasing difficulty is experienced in getting the recruits to volunteer for extra service owing to the higher wages and better standard of living that now obtains on shore.

[§ 114.] This of course is certain to fluctuate with the general state of prosperity of the country but it is very instructive and so great are the consequent number of changes of men that occur in the crews in October that there are many German Naval Officers who frankly state that their ships are not true fighting assets from October to February of each ensuing year and that their ships only attain their real value from May to October.

There are extensive rumours that the authorities are far from satisfied with the Gunnery, Torpedo and Navigating Officers and that specialist corps in these three branches will shortly be introduced.

[17590]

K

A scheme is to be introduced in 1909 to do away partially with the disabilities that attend a clever boy who obtains his pass certificate at school before joining the Navy as a Naval Cadet.

Estimates and Finance.

Owing to the reasons which I have attempted to bring forward in the earlier pages of this report and the fact that at last the people of Germany begin to realise, in the words of their Emperor, that their future lies on the water, the estimates for 1908 clearly indicate that this fact has been grasped by the authorities and show a huge advance in every direction as the following short summary shows.

	£ 1907.	£ 1908.
Recurring expenses	5,913,468	6,546,040
Ship-building and armaments ...	6,235,225	8,366,438
Other non-recurring expenses ...	333,632	429,917
Extraordinary expenses	1,143,600	1,258,569
	13,625,925	16,600,964

These increases are mainly due to the cost of the maintenance of the fleet, both in material and personnel, the huge building programme, allowing for an extra battleship and a fleet of submarines, the commencement of a dock on the lower Elbe at Brunsbuttel (which will in the future become a second Rosyth) and the construction of a harbour of refuge for small craft at Heligoland. Lastly a start is to be made with the expenditure of a huge sum in bringing the coast defences up to date.

Of these increases it is noteworthy that the items of coaling and maintenance of ships in commission show an increase in the past four years of £342,000 and £260,000 respectively.

One of the reasons for the increase in the shipbuilding vote is that battleships and cruisers are in the future to be completed in 33 and 30 months respectively which of course calls for larger yearly contributions than when three years were given but it is noteworthy that for the first time no mention is made of the total cost of any of the new ships, thus following, as they tell me, the lead provided by England.

[§ 121.] Perhaps, looked at all round, the point of greatest interest to note is the immense number of great works which Germany will have in hand for the next five years and which in themselves form a hostage for peace.

In connection with present and future costs a special memo[randum] is added to this year's estimates which I have already fully reported.

According to this the estimates for the next four years—I do not quote further because it is more than likely that a new fleet bill will appear in 1912—are as follows.

1908	£16,600,000 of which £4,500,000 is paid by loan.		
1909 ... · ...	20,250,000 ,,	5,890,000 ,,	,,
1910	22,000,000 ,,	6,350,000 ,,	,,
1911	23,000,000 ,,	6,225,000 ,,	,,

which shows clearly the enormous increase of costs that this determination to possess a strong fleet will bring on the people and the further still more alarming fact that out of these sums no less than £23,000,000 is to be raised by loan during the next four years.

The fact that although these figures have been printed and spread far and wide among the people there is to be heard practically no voice raised in favour of economy should surely bring home to us that there is no probable end in view of this ambition to possess a great fleet, and, as the next increase must begin to touch the margin of superiority which England, in Naval power, has over Germany, it is becoming a matter of enormous interest to check this ambition by every means in our power.

I have, &c.
PHILIP DUMAS,
Captain and Naval Attaché.

MINUTES.

F.O. 6310/6310/08/18.

This is a most interesting report.

What is said at the bottom of page 9 tells a significant tale of how German children are being educated.

On page 19 Captain Dumas says that the Little Belt seems to be preferred to the Great Belt and thinks we should do well to keep a Vice-Consul permanently at Frederic[i]a.

R. H. C.

It appears from para[graph] 2 of the covering desp[atch] that Sir F. Lascelles has still not written the annual report for 1907—it will therefore presumably be a long time before we can expect to see it, and its contents will have encroached far into 1908.

[G. S. S.]

I annex a few Notes on some of the more important points in this interesting despatch.

I think Sir F. Lascelles should be instructed not further to delay the preparation of the annual report for 1907. That report is to deal with the events of last year and there is no reason whatever why it should wait until Sir F. Lascelles finds it possible to form an opinion on, presumably, the present political situation.

If this pretext were once to be admitted, we should never get the annual reports in time.

E. A. C.
March 1.

Ask Sir F. Lascelles not to delay the report and point out that it sh[ou]ld deal with the events of last year only.

Captain Dumas' picture of the peace-loving and panic-stricken German seems rather over-drawn. He does good service in pointing out that the Naval policy is backed by the whole German people and that they can stand the financial strain.

W. L.

NOTES.

§ 10. The panic stated to have been created in Germany by the meeting of King Edward with King Victor Emmanuel at Gaeta in April 1907,[4] is, I think, here somewhat exaggerated. The fear of a British invasion was felt in Germany much more acutely before, for instance in November 1905 when the Emperor partially mobilized his fleet and summoned Count Metternich from London. In the same way it is hardly correct to imply that the conviction of the necessity for a strong German fleet has grown out of the events of 1907. There are few things more certain than that this feeling has reigned supreme in Germany for many years past. In § 5 Captain Dumas himself notes its existence in 1906, after Algeciras. It is of some importance not to allow the fable to become accredited, that the " big-navy " policy of Germany is a reply to alleged British bullying, and recent attempts to " isolate " her. The policy dates at least from the retirement of Chancellor von Caprivi in 1894.

§ 12. I find it difficult to take this paragraph seriously. To say that an Englishman looks at war as a path to glory, and the German as the road to death is really almost absurd. It is quite possible that Germans, who in their last big wars lost on single days of battle as many men as years of campaigning cost the British army, have a more vivid impression of the stern realities of war, than the British public which sits quietly at home enjoying its usual amusements whilst its small professional army is engaged in some distant campaign. But to deduce from this that Germans have an unusual fear of war is to misread the whole of modern history.

§§ 13 and 14. It is dangerously misleading to say that German public opinion would always be against a war. Public opinion in Germany is very largely the outcome of government influence, especially in the domain of foreign affairs. The German (formerly Prussian) government has always been most remarkable for the pains it takes to create a feeling of intense and holy hatred against a country with which it contemplates the possibility of a war. It is undoubtedly in this way that the frantic hatred of England as a monster of personified selfishness and greed and absolute want of conscience, which now animates all Germany, has been nursed and fed.

[4] [*v. supra*, pp. 28–32, Nos. 15–6.]

If ever Germany were to go to war with us, we may be certain that every German will feel convinced that he is fighting the enemy of mankind, and defending the cause of right and justice and carrying out the decrees of the Almighty. (See also §§ 40–43.)

§§ 26–29 call attention to the cost involved in the German naval programme, and the serious financial difficulties which it is creating.

§ 32 gives expression to the German hope that England may, also for financial reasons, be the first to get tired of the struggle of maintaining the superior fleet. This hope rose in proportion as the voices in favour of disarmament grew louder in England, and it is well to remember that the impression made in Germany by the demonstrations of our pacifists who clamour for economies and reductions in naval and military expenditure is not at all that England wants to set an example of peacefulness and eliminate causes of international suspicions, but that England is exhausted and incapable of keeping up the race for supremacy at sea. The greater our efforts in the direction of disarmament, the more persistent will be Germany's endeavour to overtake us.

§§ 40–43 show the action of the German authorities in producing that " public opinion " to which I have above referred (in my observations on §§ 13–14).

At the end of § 44 begin a series of explanations as to the impossibility of a German invasion of England. This subject is abruptly introduced, curiously enough, as one of the elements which *explain* German hatred of England. It is difficult to see the logic of the argument. It looks rather as if this invasion question had been dragged in " by order." And it is rather remarkable that the views now stated with much emphasis are to a large extent flatly contradictory to what Captain Dumas himself said on the same subject in his despatch of Nov[ember] 25, 1906 (No. 40513), which I annex hereto.(5)

§§ 70 and 73 (and 121) call attention to the important fact that for the next 3 or 4 years Germany will be practically unable to begin a war with England owing to the backward state of the necessary preparations. It is implied right through the report that in this respect the situation may be materially altered after 1911.

§ 71 supposes that German policy and warlike operations might be seriously hindered by the opposition of the 3 Scandinavian countries. I am afraid the power of resistance and of offensive action of these countries can hardly be reckoned with as an important factor.

§ 78 notes an interesting arrangement.

§ 91 reports that German sailors devote peculiar attention to the passage of the Little Belt, which is more difficult of navigation than the Great Belt.

§ 114 records an interesting result of the short-service system in the German navy : viz that owing to the large influx of raw recruits in October, the fleet is practically incapacitated between that month of every year and the following February. No doubt this will be carefully noted at our Admiralty.

E. A. C.
March 1.

I have several times talked to Captain Dumas of the possibility of an invasion of these shores and this is the first time that he has expressed the opinion that it is impossible.

C. H.

It is a very interesting report; in dealing with invasion confusion arises unless one makes sure whether it is invasion or raid that is being discussed.

E. G.

(5) [Not reproduced. Marginal comment by Mr. Langley : " He was dealing in that Desp[atch] with the possibility of a *raid*. W. L."]

No. 82.

Lord Tweedmouth to Sir Edward Grey.

Private.(1)

My dear Edward Grey,   *February* 18, 1908.

I send you an astounding communication from the German emperor which has just reached me.(2)

I propose to promptly acknowledge its receipt and thank him for his gracious condescension in writing to me but to say I must take time to fully consider what

(1) [Grey MSS., Vol. 48.]

(2) [The Emperor William's letter to Lord Tweedmouth, the latter's reply, and King Edward's letter to the Emperor are all printed in *G.P.* XXIV, pp. 32–6; *cp.* Sir Sidney Lee : *King Edward VII* (1927), II, pp. 605–10. The Emperor's letter to King Edward is not printed by Sir Sidney Lee, nor is it in *G.P.* XXIV. The Editors have been informed that it is not to be found in the Windsor archives.]

he has written before in detail replying to him and now also send to him a copy of my statement on the naval estimates 1908–9 in strict confidence.

I think it would please him to see it before it is generally published and it will really answer much of his letter. Esher comes in for a bad knock.

Yours ever,
TWEEDMOUTH.

No. 83.

Sir Edward Grey to Lord Tweedmouth.

Private.(¹)
Dear Tweedmouth, *Foreign Office, February* 18, 1908.
I quite agree that you should acknowledge this great(²) letter as you propose and send a copy of the Estimates in confidence.

As to a reply I can supply you with some material but it will have to be adapted in tone to suit the Emperor's letter.(³)

The very fact that we are reducing our shipbuilding programme may produce further articles about the German Navy from those who are nervous in England or who want to attack the Government, but this is quite beyond our control.

You might make this comment now in sending the Estimates.

Yours sincerely,
E. GREY.

(¹) [Grey MSS., Vol. 48.]
(²) [*Sic.* The text of this document is taken from the copy of the original letter, preserved by Sir Edward Grey. The copy is not in his own hand, and it is possible therefore that we should read " queer," or some such word, for " great."]
(³) [*v. supra*, p. 132, No. 82, *note* (²).]

No. 84.

Sir Edward Grey to Sir F. Lascelles.

F.O. 371/458.
3659/3659/08/18.
(No. 49.) Confidential.
Sir, *Foreign Office, February* 19, 1908.
I have received and laid before the King, Your Excellency's despatch No. 40 of the 30th ultimo,(¹) recording an interesting conversation with which you were honoured by the German Emperor.

I note with much satisfaction the expression of His Majesty's gratification at his recent reception in this Country. The complaint, however, which His Majesty made at the same time of the tone of the English press on the subject of the increase in German naval armaments, appears to me somewhat unreasonable, and based on a faulty view of the situation, which an effort should be made to correct, so as to avoid any misunderstanding likely to affect the good relations between the two countries. I therefore desire you to take an opportunity when you see Prince Bülow of communicating to him unofficially and in an entirely friendly manner a copy of the enclosed memorandum, explaining why we cannot admit the Emperor's complaint to be justified.

[I am, &c.
E. GREY.]

(¹) [*v. supra*, pp. 111–2, No. 78.]

Enclosure in No. 84.

Memorandum.([2])

February 19, 1908.

His Majesty's Government have never claimed the right to criticize the action of the German or any other government in determining the extent of their naval or military requirements. They frankly recognise that this is a matter which every independent State must settle for itself. Sir Edward Grey has himself recently given public utterance to this view in unmistakable terms with particular reference to the new German naval programme, and the German Secretary of State for the Navy, when introducing the naval estimates into the Reichstag specially alluded to the dispassionate and friendly tone in which the press and public speakers in England had discussed the German proposals.

It is however alleged that certain English newspapers have made " attacks on the German naval programme," by calling attention to the great expense which this country must necessarily incur if compelled to build so many more ships in consequence of the increase of the German naval forces. No indication has been given as to the particular articles referred to. But as the Emperor has suggested that something should be done to counteract this " anti-German tendency," it seems requisite to explain that His Majesty's Government cannot regard as just cause for irritation in Germany an expression of regret by an independent British newspaper at the growth of expenditure inevitably imposed upon England by the increase of German naval armaments.

The organs of the German navy league frequently use the British navy as an illustration of the need for increasing the German navy, and it is not unnatural that the section of the British press which is always afraid that the Government, especially a Liberal Government, will let the navy fall behindhand, should make similar use of the German navy to enforce its point.

*(If the British press pays more attention to the increase of Germany's naval power than to a similar movement in Brazil—which the Emperor appears to think unfair—this is due no doubt in part to the proximity of the German coasts and the remoteness of Brazil, but might also be taken as a compliment to the superior quality of the German navy.)

The independence and very existence of the British Empire depend on the preservation of its supremacy at sea, and the British Government is bound to organize and keep up such naval forces as are essential for that purpose. It would be futile to pretend that the increase of the German fleet is not one of the factors([3]) which has to be taken into account in any calculation of the strength at which the British Navy must be maintained. To prevent the British Press from freely stating and commenting upon so obvious a fact would be neither equitable nor possible.

*(It might be asked what would be said and done in Germany if France were systematically to increase her army by the formation of large additional bodies of

([2]) [The Memorandum was altered before communication to Prince von Bülow by the omission of paragraphs 4 and 6, as the result of a representation from Sir F. Lascelles (*v. infra*, pp. 135-6, No. 85, and *min.*). The amended draft was then sent to King Edward who minuted it "*An excellent Mem*[*orandum*].—E. R." The Memorandum is printed in *G.P.* XXIV, pp. 36-7.]

*Cancelled in accordance with wish expressed in Sir F. Lascelles' Tel. No. 6 of Feb[ruary] 21. [*v.* immediately succeeding document.]

([3]) [In the first draft the word " principal " occurred before " factors." It was deleted before the memorandum was sent to Sir F. Lascelles as the result of the following minutes :

I should be disposed to omit this word.

E. A. C.

I think it is *the* principal factor and that there is no use in blinking the fact.

W. L.

It is true just now but as this memorandum may reach the Emperor we may omit it; it is not essential to say it.

E. G.]

troops? It is conceivable that proposals for a corresponding increase in the forces of the Empire and for the raising of fresh imperial taxation would be submitted to the Reichstag. If, in such a contingency, voices were raised in the German press giving expression to a sense of discontent with France as the cause of heavy additional burdens imposed on the German taxpayer, would France be considered justified in complaining of the unfriendly attitude of the German press? And, if the Brazilian or even the United States army had simultaneously been enlarged, would much weight be attached to a suggestion that the responsibility of France for the increase in German military expenditure was not greater than that of more remote countries?)

His Majesty's Government regret as much as anyone that the newspaper press should at times be utilized as the vehicle for international recriminations. But even if they had the power to interfere—which it is of course well known they have not—they would not feel called upon to restrain the public but courteous expression of views which reflect the actual situation. This situation, viewed from the standpoint of the British Government is that whilst there is no thought of attributing hostile intentions to Germany or any of Great Britain's neighbours nor of calling in question their right to build what ships they please, the supreme interest of the security of the British Empire requires that the standard and proportion of the British Navy to those of European countries, which has been upheld by successive British Governments must be maintained.

No. 85.

Sir F. Lascelles to Sir Edward Grey.

F.O. 371/458.
6112/3659/08/18.
Tel. (No. 6.)

Berlin, February 21, 1908.
D. 1·44 P.M.
R. 3·0 P.M.

Your despatch No. 49. Confidential.([1])

I fear I must have given a very erroneous impression in my despatch No. 40([2]) of the Emperor's conversation. His Majesty mentioned Brazil in an incidental manner; his principal objections were due to the fact that the considerable increase in the naval armaments of France and the United States were not noticed in the English press and that Germany alone was held responsible for the increased expenditure (group undecypherable? forced) upon England. If therefore Brazil alone is mentioned in the memorandum which you instruct me to communicate to Herr von Schön I shall lay myself open to the retort that I have incorrectly reported His Majesty's language.

I would therefore suggest that the fourth paragraph of the memorandum should be omitted.

I would also suggest that the sixth paragraph of the memorandum should be omitted. The analogy between the increase of the French Army and the German navy is far from being complete and the arguments based upon it could easily be answered.

It appears to me that these two paragraphs greatly weaken the strength of the arguments of an otherwise excellent memorandum.

([1]) [v. immediately preceding document.]
([2]) [v. supra, pp. 111–2, No. 78.]

MINUTES.

I agree.(³)

E. G.

There seems some force in Sir F. Lascelles' suggestion for the omission of the 4th paragraph. His desp[atch] No. 40 did make it clear that the Emperor referred to France and the United States in the same breath as Brazil and with perhaps more emphasis. It would of course be possible to expand and alter the 4th para[graph] to meet the objection but this is perhaps hardly worth while.

On the other hand I do not see the objection to the 6th paragraph, and I do not agree with Sir F. Lascelles that there is not complete analogy between the danger to England of an increase in the German army [navy?] and the danger to Germany of an increase in the French army.

It is one of the habitual offences of German diplomacy to address remonstrances and complaints to foreign Gov[ernmen]ts in regard to matters on which they themselves would never tolerate remonstrances from others, and I think it is well to take an opportunity of bringing this home to them in a specific case like the present.

E. A. C.

There can be no objection to the omission of paragraph 4. The illustration in paragraph 6 appears to me to be very much to the point and it is perhaps rather a pity to cut it out, but the memorandum without it will serve its purpose.

W. L.

(³) [This minute was written by Sir Edward Grey on the decypher itself. The minutes by Mr. Crowe and Mr. Langley appear on the paper cover in the usual place.]

No. 86.

Sir Edward Grey to Sir F. Lascelles.

F.O. 371/458.
6112/3659/08/18.   *Foreign Office, February* 21, 1908.
Tel. (No. 10.)   D. 4·45 P.M.
Your tel[egram] No. 6.(¹)
I agree. You may omit fourth and sixth paragraphs.
You should communicate the memorandum to Prince Bulow and not to Herr von Schön.

(¹) [*v.* immediately preceding document.]

No. 87.

Sir F. Lascelles to Sir Edward Grey.

F.O. 371/458.
7098/7098/08/18.
(No. 76.)   *Berlin,* D. *February* 24, 1908.
Sir,   R. *March* 2, 1908.
The London Correspondent of the Berliner Tageblatt sent a telegram recently to his paper announcing that the Naval Estimates would be brought before the House of Commons on the 20th instant, and that they would not show any essential increase as compared with those of 1907. He further stated that His Majesty's Government would make a fresh attempt to come to an understanding with Germany as to a mutual limitation of naval armaments, and that negotiations in connection therewith would begin shortly.

According to the telegram His Majesty's Government will inform the German Government that, if Germany intends to continue her rivalry in naval construction, England is determined to maintain her maritime superiority by continuing to build new ships. He goes on to say that opinion in London favours the view that, improbable as it may appear, a mutual understanding must sooner or later be arrived at between

England and Germany in which both will agree to limit their naval armaments within certain bounds. In both countries the pressure of taxation for naval purposes has reached such a point that a check on the outlay has become unavoidable.

The correspondent concludes his report by stating that he is informed that, should an Agreement not be arrived at before 1909, England will probably lay down five Dreadnoughts.

The Berliner Tageblatt gives considerable prominence to this message and from the language in which it is couched and the prominence given to it, the idea is conveyed to the public that the correspondent has received official inspiration for his information.

Following upon this communication, the Deutsche Post and other newspapers publish an announcement regarding the attitude of the German Government to the statement made by you that His Majesty's Government were prepared to exchange declarations as to naval construction with other Powers.

According to the press statement, the German Government claim to have already set a good example in this question. The German Naval Law has been discussed entirely in public. The annual naval estimates give an uninterrupted account of the cost of the Navy. Naval proposals not included in the Estimates are freely discussed in the Reichstag and in the Press. More than this could not be attained, since the British Admiralty would be as little inclined as the German, or the Admiralties of any other Power, to disclose secret information regarding construction, armament, signals, and tactics. Should information as to proposed naval construction be exchanged between Governments, international competition in shipbuilding would only be rendered more acute, and thus an opposite end would be arrived at to that which His Majesty's Government by their proposal desire to attain; for naturally each power would endeavour to outbid the others in its proposals. For these reasons the German Government see no cause to make any change in the method which has hitherto been followed by them in presenting their naval programme.

I have, &c.

FRANK C. LASCELLES.

No. 88.

Sir F. Lascelles to Sir Edward Grey.

F.O. 371/458.
7104/7098/08/18.
(No. 82.) Confidential.   *Berlin, D. February 27, 1908.*
Sir,   R. *March 2, 1908.*
At a ball at Prince Eitel Friedrich's Palace on the night of the 22nd instant, the Emperor honoured me by a long conversation of at least an hour's duration. He said that he had received a letter from Lord Tweedmouth in answer to one which His Majesty in his capacity of British Admiral of the Fleet had addressed to His Lordship some days previously. In this letter he had pointed out that in the year 1900 the German naval programme had been drawn up after long and very serious consideration. This programme had been published, and could be bought at any bookseller's shop, and laid down the number of line of battleships which Germany considered necessary. It had not been modified since then, and would certainly be carried out, and in the year 1920 Germany would possess between 30 and 40 line of battleships. Each nation had a perfect right to build as many ships as she required, and no one would be justified in complaining if England thought it necessary to build 100, 150, or even 200 battleships if she considered that her interests required such a number. Germany claimed an equal right for herself. The English Press, however, apparently overlooked the fact that the German programme had been before the public for seven years and sought to prove that the construction of the ships which

was being carried out in accordance with that Programme was a menace to England, which entailed upon her the necessity of incurring enormous expense in building more ships in consequence of Germany's action. His desire for the maintenance of good relations with England, and the interest which he took in all naval matters, had induced him as a British Admiral of the Fleet to address himself to the First Lord of the Admiralty, who had answered in a very friendly spirit and had communicated to him privately the Naval Estimates which were about to be presented to Parliament. His Majesty had also written to the King to inform His Majesty that he had communicated directly with Lord Tweedmouth.(¹)

His Majesty went on to say that he had taken this step entirely on his own responsibility. He had consulted no one, and even the Chancellor himself was not aware that he had written to Lord Tweedmouth until after the letter had been sent. His object had been to avoid what he considered might become a serious danger. I must be aware of the difficulties of the German Naval Authorities in dealing with the Navy League, who were constantly demanding more ships. If public opinion in Germany were to become convinced that England regarded Germany as an enemy, it would be impossible to resist the demand that would then become universal for a far greater Navy than was contemplated in the Programme of 1900, and this result, which he would greatly regret, would be attributable to the British Press. How could any one in England seriously believe that he would ever be foolish enough to attack a Power which was and which would always remain at least five times as strong as he was.

I replied, as I had done on a previous occasion, that personally I was not a bit afraid of him. I had not failed to report to you the language which he had deigned to hold to me at the Court Ball on the 29th ultimo, and I had received your instructions to communicate privately and in a most friendly manner to Prince Bülow a memorandum(²) which you had caused to be drawn up in reply. I might mention to him privately that I had suggested some modifications in the Original Draft of the memorandum, to which you had agreed, and that I should now take an early opportunity of carrying out your instructions.

I had a further short conversation with the Emperor on the evening of the 24th He told me that he had received a letter from the King(³) from which it appeared that he had incurred His Majesty's displeasure in writing directly to Lord Tweedmouth

I have, &c.

FRANK C. LASCELLES.

MINUTES.

The Emperor appears to have now realized the mistake he made in bringing forward his complaint against the English press. H[is] M[ajesty] seems also to have addressed himself direct to Lord Tweedmouth on the subject, which is a most extraordinary thing to do in a constitutional country, and which is a practice that if continued might lead to the most serious consequences. Fortunately The King has evidently intervened with promptitude and with effect

It seems curious that in these circumstances Lord Tweedmouth should have communicated the naval estimates to the Emperor before they were laid before the House of Commons. One naturally wonders what would be said in the House if this fact became known. But we must presume that Lord Tweedmouth's action had the approval of The King.

The substance of the Emperor's remarks bears an apologetic stamp. But the cloven hoof again appears in the attempt to fasten upon the British press the responsibility for the further foreshadowed increase in the German navy.

It was not judicious, to put it mildly, of Sir F. Lascelles to insinuate to the Emperor that he personally had toned down the instructions sent to H[is] E[xcellency] from the Foreign Office. An ambassador ought in his communications to a foreign government absolutely to identify himself with the Secretary of State. As it is, we know that it has been put about at Berlin that the Foreign Office is peculiarly anti-German, and that our ambassador and other important personages are vainly using their influence against this alleged tendency.

(¹) [v. supra, p. 132, No. 82, note (²).]
(²) [v. supra, pp. 134–5, No. 84, encl.]
(³) [Printed in Sir Sidney Lee: King Edward VII (1927), II, p. 606; v. also supra, p. 132 No. 82, note (²).]

The action of Sir F. Lascelles can hardly have any other effect than to corroborate this fable, and it is difficult to see why it should have been taken.

E. A. C.
Mch. 2.

Sir F. Lascelles need not have said this, but it is possible that he thought that a good effect would be produced if he made the Emperor understand that we feel more strongly on the subject than a mere perusal of the memo[randum] would lead him to believe.

W. L.

Sir F. Lascelles' remark is regrettable as implying that he had softened down the communication, which is not the fact, since the two paragraphs omitted merely contained two analogies which were not regarded as complete. He had no right to inform the Emperor of his communications with the F[oreign] O[ffice] and I think this. ought to be pointed out to him privately.

C. H.

I will write to Sir F. Lascelles on this point.
I agreed to the Naval Estimates being sent to the Emperor, but as all that happened was that in answer to his letter he received on Saturday a copy of the actual paper published here on Monday I do not think the fact even if known could have much significance. What would give rise to comment would be the fact of the Emperor having written to Lord Tweedmouth and this should not be divulged.

E. G.

But Lord Tweedmouth must be careful not to divulge it himself.

F.

No. 89.

Sir F. Lascelles to Sir Edward Grey.

F.O. 371/458.
8018/7098/08/18.
(No. 93.) Secret.   Berlin, D. March 2, 1908.
Sir,   R. March 9, 1908.
I have the honour to report that in accordance with the instructions conveyed to me in your despatch No. 49 Confidential 3659 of the 19th ultimo,([1]) I requested Prince Bülow to grant me an interview on February 27th in order that I might have an opportunity of communicating to him the Memorandum which formed the enclosure in your above-mentioned despatch.

I have the honour to enclose copy of the Memorandum([2]) as amended in accordance with the authority conveyed to me by your Telegram No. 10 of the 21st ultimo.([3])

His Serene Highness fixed the hour at 6·30 P.M., but he was unable to receive me as arranged, as he was detained in the Herrenhaus by the debate on the Polish Expropriation Bill, and the interview was fixed for the same hour on the following day (Friday, February 28th). As I had to attend a ball at the Austrian Embassy that evening, it was impossible for me to prepare an official report of my interview with the Chancellor in time for the messenger who left Berlin on the following morning at 11 o'clock.

As usual Prince Bülow talked much but said little. I handed to him the memorandum in reply to the Emperor's remarks about the English Press and the German Navy. He read it through and stated that there was not a word in it of which His Majesty would not thoroughly approve. The line which His Majesty had always taken was that Germany should have the number of ships which she considered necessary for the defence of her coasts and for the protection of her Colonial and Commercial interests, and that it would be ridiculous for her to rival England who would be perfectly justified in building any amount of ships she might

([1]) [v. supra, pp. 133–5, No. 84, and encl.]
([2]) [Not reproduced, as the text is given above, pp. 134–5, No. 84, encl.]
([3]) [v. supra, p. 136, No. 86.]

think necessary to maintain her supremacy at sea, which was a matter of vital importance to her. He enquired whether he might show the memorandum to the Emperor, and I replied that he might certainly do so, and I presumed that such had been your object in instructing me to communicate it to him unofficially and in a friendly manner.

His Serene Highness then informed me that the Emperor had not spoken to him of his correspondence with Lord Tweedmouth. He thought that it must have taken place whilst he was suffering from a slight attack of influenza which had prevented him from seeing the Emperor, and it was probable that His Majesty, after receiving the King's letter disapproving of his having written to Lord Tweedmouth,([4]) may have felt rather reluctant to mention the matter to his Chancellor. Had His Serene Highness known of His Majesty's intentions he would certainly have exerted all his efforts to prevent the letter being sent to Lord Tweedmouth, and he earnestly trusted that the fact that the correspondence had taken place would never become known. He would find himself in a most embarrassing position if he were called upon to explain in the Reichstag a correspondence on political matters between the Emperor and a Minister of a foreign state of which His Majesty's responsible Minister had not been informed. Germany although not a Parliamentary, was a Constitutional State, and it was no easy matter to be the Emperor's Minister.

I have, &c.
FRANK C. LASCELLES.

([4]) [Marginal comment by Sir C. Hardinge : " I wonder how Pr[in]ce Bülow knew this? "]

No. 90.

Sir Edward Grey to Sir F. Lascelles.

Private.([1])

My dear Lascelles,   *Foreign Office, March* 7, 1908.

I am much annoyed that the fact of the Emperor having written to Tweedmouth should have become known. It has been talked about much more than it should have been and at last someone has been found unscrupulous enough to put to public use what he can only have learnt in private conversation.

But the moral is that Emperors must not write about public affairs as if they were private individuals and that correspondence on public affairs should be kept in official channels or to change the metaphor this sudden inpouring of strong Rhine wine has burst the Admiralty bottle, which is not used to it.

I see you told the Emperor that our Memorandum([2]) had been altered a little on your suggestion. I quite agree that the alterations were for the good but the Emperor may think that what was taken out was in some way offensive and if so this would be an unfortunate reflection upon us at this end.

We may be pressed here to clear ourselves of the imputation that we have yielded to German pressure about the Navy. This pressure may take the form of demanding the publication of Tweedmouth's reply. I think we should refuse to publish either the Emperor's letter or Tweedmouth's reply and if we publish anything it should be the Memorandum to which as a matter of fact Tweedmouth referred the Emperor for a reply, though it was drawn up before the Emperor's letter was received.

I did mention to Metternich the other day that German officers are always surveying our coasts; he was already familiar with the statement and stoutly denied that it could be so, saying that such work would only be done by officers on the

([1]) [Grey MSS., Vol. 22.]
([2]) [*v. supra*, pp. 134–5, No. 84, *encl.*]

Staff and why should it be done at all when Ordnance maps were available etc.
To all which the answer is that it might very well be done by Officers who hoped
o get promoted to the Staff by spending their holidays in acquiring information.
But I don't quarrel with this; it is the business of military and naval officers to
prepare for contingencies. What the Emperor and Metternich seem unwilling to
admit is that innocent intentions to-day are no guarantee to us against other
contingencies a few years hence.

[Yours sincerely]
E. GREY.

No. 91.

Sir F. Lascelles to Sir Edward Grey.

Private.([1])
My dear Grey,   *Berlin, March* 14, 1908.
All is well that ends well. It was with this quotation that Schoen greeted me
when I called upon him on Tuesday. He was most complimentary about the manner
in which the Emperor's letter to Tweedmouth had been dealt with in the House of
Lords,([2]) and looked upon the incident, which at one time threatened unpleasant
complications, as finally closed. The German Gov[ernmen]t would have had no
objection to publishing both the Emperor's letter and Tweedmouth's reply, if it had
been necessary to do so, but now happily it would not be necessary to publish anything. The question would no doubt be alluded to in the Reichstag in the debate on the
Chancellor's salary which will take place next week, but then it will probably take the
form of an attack upon the unconstitutional action of the Emperor in writing political
letters without the knowledge of the Chancellor, and the Government will have no
difficulty in dealing with an attack of that kind. I hope therefore that my indiscretion
in telling the Emperor that I had suggested some omissions in the Memorandum in
reply to his complaints of the Press may not have done any harm. I cannot conceive
that what I said should have led him to think that what was taken out was in some
way offensive, but if he should entertain so erroneous an idea I could easily convince
him that this was not the case. . . . .([3])

Yours sincerely,
FRANK C. LASCELLES.

([1]) [Grey MSS., Vol. 22.]
([2]) [v. *Parl. Deb.*, 4th *Ser.*, Vol. 185, pp. 1072–7.]
([3]) [The rest of this letter refers to general matters and the Moroccan question.]

No. 92.

Mr. Cartwright to Sir Edward Grey.

F.O. 371/459.
10815/10815/08/18.
(No. 40.)   *Munich,* D. *March* 28, 1908.
Sir,   R. *March* 30, 1908.
The speeches recently delivered in the Reichstag by Prince Bülow and Herr von
Schön have largely occupied the attention of the German press and I may summarise
the drift of its comments as follows : General approval of Germany's attitude with
regard to the Macedonian question; great reserve as to Prince Bülow's utterances
respecting Germany's good relations with England and general hostility as to the
policy pursued by the Imperial Government towards French action in Morocco.
It may be said that as a general rule Balkan questions interest the average
German very little; he has no personal views on these matters and he forms his

opinions on them from what he reads in his newspaper which in its turn is inspired from Berlin. Therefore one may infer from this that when the German press unanimously approves of the Imperial policy with regard to Macedonia it simply reflects the views of the Berlin Foreign Office and not the spontaneous ones of the German public. So far I have been unable to find a single newspaper in South Germany which has a good word to say in favour of the latest British proposals for reforms in Macedonia; on the other hand, however, much bitter criticism is published on the manner in which the British press has received Prince Bülow's utterances on the subject, though it is conceded in some quarters that the Prince might have been less curt in his declaration that Germany rejected the British proposals as quite unpracticable. That some dread existed here lest Russia should show herself inclined to yield to British pressure with regard to Macedonian reforms, is shown by the satisfaction which is universally expressed at the announcement made by telegrams from Berlin that Monsieur Iswolsky will hold firm to the Murzsteg Agreement and that he will take no action without first consulting Austria.

To keep the South German press well in hand and to give it the desired orientation with regard to Macedonian affairs, a "communiqué" appears in the "Süddeutsche Reichskorrespondenz" this morning to the effect that it is not really to the advantage of British interests that the English press should attack with such vehemence the want of enthusiasm shown by the Chancellor for the scheme proposed by England for Macedonian reforms. A press campaign of this kind will have only one result, namely that at Constantinople the impression will be produced, perhaps unjustifiably, that England's real intentions are to begin a crusade against the Turk for the purpose of driving him bag and baggage out of Europe. The stir which such a press agitation would arouse in the world might compel Germany to assume an attitude of even greater reserve, and nothing would be more regrettable than that the British press should help to spread the erroneous idea abroad that the Balkan question must necessarily lead to antagonism between Germany and England. This idea would be founded on ignorance of the real diplomatic situation at present, for the British proposals have been respectfully received everywhere, and not the least so in Berlin, but in all quarters—even in England—doubts have been expressed as to their being capable of practical application. The "Süddeutsche Reichskorrespondenz" says that one cannot be too careful to avoid approaching the Macedonian question with religious zeal, the question at issue being not so much one of differences of religion as of differences of nationality. Reforms cannot be arbitrarily decreed from above : they must be either peacefully introduced with the consent of the European Concert and the approval of The Porte, or else, by breaking up the Concert, they must be applied by one or two of the Powers without the consent of the Sultan. If this should occur then the proposed introduction of reforms would lead to a breach of the peace.

Professor Schiemann in the "Kreuz Zeitung" declares that the general tone of the debate in the Reichstag showed a distinct desire to maintain good relations between this country and Great Britain but he recognises that there are certain "nuances" in this wish, and in many South German newspapers I have noticed marked expressions of dissatisfaction at the tone of the English press of late, not only as regards Germany's attitude on the Macedonian reform question, but because of a recrudescence of the old grumbling spirit at Germany's naval policy. It is asserted that if Prince Bülow alluded in his speech to the anti-German tone of a portion of the British press, he evidently did so because he believed that those newspapers represented the views of perhaps the more influential part of the British public and also of a section of the British Cabinet. The Chancellor's allusions were therefore in reality made as a warning to His Majesty's Government and it is pointed out here that only last week Prince Bülow in an interview he had with a reporter of the "Novoje Vremyia" made similar complaints against the Russian press which in truth were intended to be taken into consideration by the Russian Government. As further evidence of the misgivings which the attitude of the British press is arousing in Berlin, the letter addressed by the Kaiser to Lord Tweedmouth is pointed at, for more than one newspaper asserts that the letter was written by the Kaiser with no other purport in view but to protect a British Minister from the evil influences which the anti-German section of the English press might possibly exert upon him.([1])

Finally, to turn to the Moroccan question, as I said at the beginning of this despatch, the press here is not satisfied with the Chancellor's declarations on this matter. I have noted for several months past that whenever the Imperial Government have officially stated that they are satisfied with the declarations made by the French Government as to their action in Morocco, the whole German press bitterly attacks France for that very action. Is this done by order from Berlin or does it really reflect the opinion of the writers in these newspapers? It is a question difficult to answer for people here have their own opinions as regards Morocco, but as newspapers in Germany in dealing with foreign questions are so much under the guidance of Berlin it is conceivable that, although in this case they almost unanimously criticise the policy of the Imperial Government, they do so by instruction for a purpose which is not quite clear.

As an example of the criticisms employed by the press in judging of the situation in Morocco, I will draw your attention to the way in which Prince Bülow's recent utterances have been received by the Munich " Neueste Nachrichten," a newspaper which as a rule takes its inspirations from the Prussian Legation here. That newspaper, in commenting on that portion of the Chancellor's speech which relates to Morocco, observes that it does not see why the Imperial Government should not make their views clearly felt in Paris without having the support of the other Powers. It is a mistake to believe that if Germany acted in this independent manner she would thereby complicate matters in Morocco. It thinks that if things have reached the present state of confusion in that country the fault lies to a great extent with Germany who has encouraged France to act as she does by her undecided, wavering and weak attitude of late. The present Moroccan problem would be greatly simplified if Germany could only muster the courage to talk to France in a clear manner. In his speech Prince Bülow described German policy with regard to Morocco as a mixture of resolution combined with reserve. The Munich newspaper declares that if such a policy has not done German interests any positive harm so far, it certainly has not helped to further them very much in Morocco.

The Munich " Neueste Nachrichten " thinks that the moment has come for Germany to have a friendly, loyal but firm exchange of views with the French Government, for if she continues to be silent the politicians in France will take this as a sign that Germany will not impede French action in Morocco. If that should come to pass what was the use of this country going to Algeciras? This is a prospect which cannot be viewed with equanimity, for the solution of the Moroccan problem must not be left to the future to be solved without Germany taking any kind of precaution to protect her real interests.

In reporting the French comments on Prince Bülow's speech, mostly of a laudatory character, the Munich newspapers generally point out that such flattering references by France to German foreign policy cannot sound as entirely satisfactory to German ears.

I have, &c.
FAIRFAX L. CARTWRIGHT.

MINUTES.

Mr. Cartwright notes that the German press freely criticize the Gov[ernmen]t policy in Morocco. It may be that the German Gov[ernmen]t are not unwilling to let feeling in Germany be stirred up against French action in order that later on they may plead the irresistible pressure of public opinion forcing them once more to take up the question.

G. S. S.
E. A. C.
March 30.

([1]) [Marginal comment⸱ by Sir C. Hardinge : " very thoughtful, but suggestive."]

The difference between the official and newspaper view in regard to Morocco is marked. While the official view is comprehensible, the Algeciras Act nothing more or less, there is nothing to show what the Press want. They recommend clear explanations with the French but on what points they do not explain.

W. L.

The Moroccan question still weighs heavily on the political situation, and the tone of the German press shows that it might at any moment again assume an acute form.

C. H.
E. G.

No. 93.

Sir F. Lascelles to Sir Edward Grey.

F.O. 371/459.
12615/12615/08/18.
(No. 169.)   *Berlin,* D. *April* 10, 1908.
Sir,   R. *April* 13, 1908.
I have the honour to forward, herewith, a despatch, as marked in the margin, which I have received from Captain Dumas Naval Attaché to this Embassy, relating to the present Anglo-German Naval Situation.

I have, &c.
FRANK C. LASCELLES.

Enclosure in No. 93.

Captain Dumas to Sir F. Lascelles.

Germany, N.A. Report 20/08.
Confidential.
Your Excellency,   *British Embassy, Berlin, April* 10, 1908.
I have the honour to submit the following translation of an article by Graf Reventlow—one of the best known German Naval writers—in the "Chemnitzer Allgemeine Zeitung" of the 2nd April on the Naval situation as it now exists between Germany and England.

I venture to forward it because I believe that it voices a great wave of distrust of what England may do in consequence of her uneasiness as regards the construction of the German fleet, while the recognition of this uneasiness seems to be coming home to the German people with a feeling akin to amazement and possibly horror.

It is also the only article from a German pen I have ever read which recognizes the danger of having stirred the masses of the British people.

The German Menace.

A dangerous catch word.

Prince Bülow in his political retrospect of the year, usually given to the Reichstag about April or May, has thoroughly dealt with the German-English relations and especially the opinions held in England as to our efforts with regard to our fleet.

A year ago his words—spoken with dignity and firmness—gave general satisfaction throughout the Empire as he repudiated the proposals for disarmament put forward at that time by England and experience has shown that this firmness has matured in the best results.

This year he says somewhat bitterly: "We wish to live in peace and quiet with England and therefore feel it keenly that a portion of the British political writers continue to speak of the German danger although the British fleet is many times superior to ours—and in spite of which it is Germany and ever and again Germany against whom public opinion on the other side of the channel is excited by inconsiderate polemic.'' The Chancellor also remarked that as regards our military defences other people kept quiet and that we do not take it as a threat when England makes every effort to strengthen her fleet and so on—

If however one considers the Chancellor's remarks it must strike one as curious that such sharp and anxious words should be made use of against the ''hate manufacture'' of some of the British publicists if it is true that ''there are many things in the world more important than the scribbling of a portion of the English political press.''

The fact is, unfortunately, that the relations are not so simple as would appear.

But a few days ago when the British Naval estimates were under discussion in Parliament, not only Naval specialists but the most important British Statesmen made long and carefully thought-out speeches and in each of them, without exception, the principal theme and essential point was the German danger.[1]

Mr. Balfour, the leader of the Opposition,—had calculated that in 1911 Germany would possess more modern ships than England :—a calculation based on a false supposition and therefore misleading. Its refutation however on the part of the First Lord of the Admiralty was very feeble and there can be no doubt whatever that Balfour's defective arithmetic resulted in the most effectual excitation against Germany that it is possible to conceive.

In the Upper House the late 1st Lord hurled angry reproaches at his successor not only in the matter of the two-power and the programme of the new ships but he also questioned the readiness for war of the Home fleet and always with reference to Germany.

He said that what the 1st Lord had brought forward sounded very pretty as to the burden on the tax payer of the building programme but this standpoint could in no way be considered as satisfactory for in the first place the efforts made for the superiority of the British fleet had for their object the maintenance of peace and, if the fleet was not kept up to the highest standard, war would soon teach the public what an immense burden must be borne in consequence of this reduced Naval budget. And, apart from this consideration, it was mathematically certain that the comparatively small estimates of this year and the last must result in an increase in future years. It would be more correct, both economically and politically, to spread the costs equally instead of hunting after popularity by present economy. It was not patriotic but simply a party political affair.

According to custom the language made use of in the British Parliament is always carefully chosen and members express themselves with a certain reserve so that even what in itself may be very strong is tempered when given expression to, a custom by the way that our German deputies might well copy with advantage.

But, just because this is not the case with us, we rate those measured utterances much too low as regards their importance and believe that the British press exaggerates and incites when it dilates on the subject matter, the fact being however that the newspapers say no more than the parliamentary debaters whose meaning is preserved while their language is but transformed to a more homely and popular style.

It is therefore above everything indicative of the nature of our relations with England that the Chancellor, in blaming a certain portion of the British press, can

---

[1] [v. Parl. Deb., 4th Ser., Vol. 185, pp. 1138–1234, House of Commons' debate of March 9, 1908. Mr. Balfour's statement is on pp. 1180–82. The debate in the House of Lords took place on March 18, v. ib. Vol. 186; pp. 495–543. Lord Cawdor's speech is on pp. 495–511, Lord Tweedmouth's on pp. 522–40.]

only really mean the British Parliament and just exactly that party which will, apparently, again be very shortly at the helm.

Many German deputies have allowed themselves to be deceived by the highly courteous manner in which the British Parliament handled the case of the German Emperor's letter to Lord Tweedmouth—but the former Minister for Foreign Affairs blamed the 1st Lord in well measured words but none the less sharpness and at the same time deprived the correspondence of any great political influence.

No—it is not only a "portion of the British political press" which steadily refers to the "German danger" but we have now to do with an already very powerful and perceptibly increasing movement among the British People.

The question is urgent whether it is right for the Statesman who is at the head of the German affairs to make such great concessions to international courtesy thus providing an impression so far removed from the actual state of affairs and the actual facts.

Signed   GRAF REVENTLOW.

I have, &c.
PHILIP DUMAS.

MINUTES.

The purport of this article is to show that the British populace and Parliament—though members couch their opinions in temperate language—share the views of the anti-German press.

R. H. C.

Count Reventlow appears to accuse Lord Cawdor in his speech of March 18 in the H[ouse] of Lords of questioning "the readiness of the British fleet for war always with reference to Germany." But the speech in question does not appear to me to contain anything to warrant its being considered as anti-German: it merely criticizes the present policy of putting off increases that will shortly be necessary and utters a grave note or warning as to the dangers we run from unpreparedness and from neglecting to maintain our past efforts. That speech—and the same remarks applies [sic] to all responsible speeches recently made on this subject in either House,—can in no way be considered as deserving to be "blamed" by Prince Bulow, any more than the British Parliament deserve to be "blamed," unless it is to be regarded as a crime against Germany that our statesmen should call attention to the vital necessity for adequate preparations being made to ensure the continuance of peace.

G. S. S.
F. A. C.
14/4.
E. G.

No. 94.

Sir F. Lascelles to Sir Edward Grey.

F.O. 371/459.
15143/12611/08/18.
(No. 202.) Secret. *Berlin,* D. *May* 1, 1908.
Sir, R. *May* 4, 1908.

I have the honour to forward, herewith, a despatch, as marked in the margin, which I have received from Colonel Frederick Trench, Military Attaché to this Embassy, relating to the possibility of a sudden invasion of England by Germany. Colonel Trench's views appear to me to be of a most unduly alarmist nature, which I am unable to endorse.

I have, &c.
F. LASCELLES.

Enclosure in No. 94.

Colonel Trench to Sir F. Lascelles.

SHOULD WARNING PRECEDE HOSTILITIES?

(No. 95.)   Secret.

Sir,   *British Embassy, Berlin, April* 27, 1908.

From the speeches of prominent persons and the actual and proposed organization of the defence forces, both regular and other, as well as the freedom given to foreign officers to acquire local military information in the United Kingdom, there seems good reason to suppose that the belief generally held there is that, should war unfortunately break out between England and Germany, hostilities would be preceded by a period of diplomatic tension and at least three days—or possibly even three months—warning could be counted on.

This view (if it be held) is, I think, quite erroneous, and I respectfully submit my belief that, when Germany comes to the conclusion that her navy is strong enough, or the British fleet sufficiently scattered or otherwise occupied, for there to be a reasonable prospect of success and, for other reasons, the occasion to be a suitable one to contest Englands naval supremacy, the first move will be made without any warning whatever except such as are being given every day by such unmistakable action as the yearly increase by two or three million pounds of the army expenditure, the rapid augmentation of the navy and the strategic enlarging of the Kiel Canal, to say nothing of the hopes and views freely expressed in political and patriotic speeches and publications of all kinds.

I am aware that it is desirable that expression should not be given to so serious an opinion without the production of a certain amount of proof in support, but I submit that the very nature of the case makes this almost impossible to procure.

In the first place, various episodes that played a not unimportant role in the rapid rise of Prussia to wealth and power have so convinced the nation that carefully prepared surprise brings success and that success will always bring pardon for any act no matter how lacking in scruples, that these views have become axiomatic and such matters of common conviction that their expression is superfluous and rare.   In the second, the very nature of surprise makes it a *sine quâ non* that the intention should be kept a secret.   That anything at all is allowed to leak out here can only be put down to a conviction on the part of the Great General Staff that nothing will persuade the English nation to forsake the procedure so often followed in the past of postponing its preparations for war until hostilities have practically commenced.

As far as I can judge, there is a good deal of resentment in this country that Germany's present naval inferiority forces her to accept for the moment hindrances which she encounters in that world expansion which she considers her right and her duty, and this resentment is intimately bound up with a fixed determination to put up with these hindrances no longer than is absolutely necessary, to strain every nerve in every sphere of national and international activity to provide the necessary means and conditions for their removal and to employ these latter in the most profitable way.   Exaggerated punctiliousness is not a Prussian characteristic, when there is nothing to be gained by it, and I can see, as a soldier, nothin[g] in the results of the Hague Conference to prevent " a reasoned declaration of war " being handed in in the Wilhelm Strasse (or in London) *after* the High Sea Fleet with its convoy of transports had passed the Forth Bridge or the Nore Light Ship.

I have already reported the semi official but only half officially acknowledged role, played by the Flotten Verein in the " Imperial " and/or anglophobe education of the people, and, as an example either of the progress the education has made or of the means adopted for carrying it out, beg to attach a copy of a typical publication entitled " The Offensive Invasion of England " which is now on sale.   The pamphlet is, of course, quite valueless either as a strategical study or as an expression of intention, but it is one of the numerous straws which show the direction of the wind.   It is typical of the manner in which the public is being continually reminded that England would, but for certain difficulties at home and abroad, assume the offensive exactly in the same way that Germany hopes herself to be in a position to do before long and it gives an idea of the general knowledge of (but hardly kindly interest in) the British army, navy, and colonies which now exists in Germany.

After some suggestions of the inefficiency of the English staff and of coming difficulties in the colonies and India, the writer describes a surprise attack on some British dockyards, the landing of an expeditionary force and a naval struggle ending more or less in a stalemate and his moral is as follows :—" If the Reichstag, which always places party bargaining before patriotism, had approved of a more rapid construction of the German fleet one would have been better equipped. Unusual measures had to be adopted to equalize the balance." Although the booklet itself has no value whatever some extracts I attach in an appendix have some interest as being an expression of views and hopes which I believe to be those of no small number of persons.

I have, &c.

F. TRENCH, Col[onel],

General Staff and Military Attaché.

(Enclosure to Colonel Trench's No. 95.)

Extracts from " Die Offensiv[-]Invasion gegen England."

" England's animosity to Germany in all parts of the earth and at every possible point of friction had, after all the talk of peace and disarmament, become so bitter that those who controlled German policy could not longer nourish the illusion that even the greatest forbearance could postpone the conflict. On account of the Bagdad railway which it so disliked, England would sooner or later declare war."

(The courses open are discussed.) " Lulled in the proud consciousness of its immeasurable superiority the British fleet would not be prepared for so bold a stroke. Could one not seize a suitable moment to surprise the British military ports and destroy the British mercantile marine by a two-day raid. One knew that British mobilization was too cumbrous to meet the attack at once with readiness for war."

" The offensive in the shape of a sudden attack such as England herself so strongly prefers and such as Admiral Campbell recommended at a public lecture at the very time when the fraternal after-dinner speeches of the German municipal guests were rising to a patient Heaven : this seemed the only way to damage England."

" The authorities having become convinced that England itself when the occasion was ripe would again play on Germany its well known historical joke of the Copenhagen bombardment."

Only regretfully was the decision come to to copy England's fixed doctrine of surprise attack without declaration of war, but there was no choice. How gladly would one live in peace with England if she w[oul]d only be sensible. But England would not learn ! Friendship for her meant Germanys patient contemplation of all British Interference and encroachments and a lamblike neglect to take advantage of any anti-British opportunities that the world offered together with a free hand to England to sap the usefulness of the Bagdad railway."

(The author goes on to describe the steady press campaign against Germany in England) " where the pious belief was held that Germany w[oul]d keep the peace at any price and patiently comply with all Englands exactions." Credit is taken that Germany utilizes the confusion in the colonies only to remonstrate about her interests which were suffering in Egypt and it is suggested that the long suffering patience of Germany has convinced England that she need fear nothing herself and can await the favourable moment to attack Germany.

MINUTES.

Colonel Trench expresses the view that if and when Germany considers her naval power equal to the occasion of defeating the British navy, whether by superior force generally, or by concentrated attack on dispersed units, then Germany is likely to act " by a surprise attack."

Sir F. Lascelles does not apparently share this view, but it is probably quite correct, nevertheless.

E. A. C.
May 4.

It is not clear whether it is the invasion or the surprise attack which Sir F. Lascelles does not agree about.

W. L.
E. G.

No. 95.

Mr. Lister to Sir Edward Grey.

F.O. 371/455.
18593/18165/08/17.
(No. 218.)
Sir,

Paris, D. May 28, 1908.
R. May 30, 1908.

The visit of President Fallières to London(¹) has naturally excited great interest in the Paris papers and long telegrams describing his reception have filled their columns the last few days. Leading articles on the significance of the visit have been printed by most of the papers, and the terms of the speeches exchanged at the Banquet at Buckingham Palace have given rise to much speculation. On the whole it may be said that the idea of strengthening still further the ties that unite France and England has been well received; but a reserve is expressed in one or two papers lest, in view of the present unprepared state of the British land forces, the balance of advantage to be derived from an alliance should incline to the British side.

Two articles published by the "Temps" have been brought to your notice in separate despatches, but articles hardly less remarkable have appeared in other papers. Two, from the pen of M. Lautier, have been printed in the "Figaro." In the first M. Lautier deals retrospectively with Anglo-French relations since 1903. The *entente cordiale*, he states, has been opportune, sincere and efficacious; opportune, because it has supplied to France the international support which she was destined to lose as a result of the disasters to Russia in the Far East; sincere, because it successfully survived the outrageous scepticism and culpable frivolity with which France received the agreements of 1904; efficacious, because, as everyone knows, in the case of conflict at the time of the Algeciras Conference England would have stood side by side with France. Considerations of French policy have become an essential factor in that of England and the road to London passes through Paris. M. Lautier denies that the bargains struck in 1904 were more advantageous to England than to France and he terminates by affirming that the *entente* will be lasting and effective in preserving the equilibrium of the Powers and their freedom from the spirit of conquest if only it will maintain the strength now at its disposal for enforcing the respect of all.

In the second article in the "Figaro" of the 27th instant, M. Lautier notes that the sentiments expressed in the toasts at Buckingham Palace seem to have met with universal approbation in England. Anglo-French friendship has triumphed over obstacles raised rather by ignorance and prejudice than by the compulsion of historical events. It has become more than ever a necessity. The past contains a lesson for the future, and never again will a statesman be found in France so imprudent as to under-estimate the value of England's friendship. How different France's position would be if the intimacy existing between England and France had arisen between England and Germany. But the *entente cordiale* has no longer any dangers to threaten it. "Puisse-t-elle devenir 'permanente' selon le voeu d'Edouard VII, et 'se reserrer' selon le voeu de M. Fallières! C'est de toute évidence notre intérêt; et si tant d'intimité offerte ne rencontrait chez nous que

(¹) [President Fallières, accompanied by M. Pichon, arrived in London on May 25. *v.* Sir Sidney Lee: *King Edward VII* (1927), II, pp. 584–6.]

reserves pusillanimes et un peu blessantes, d'autres seraient ravis de se voir agréés à notre place."

The "Journal des Débats" considers that the present *entente* with England has a more solid and enduring character than those which had been brought about under Louis Philippe and Napoleon III, because the half century which has just elapsed has created immense interests common to the two countries so that their present policy towards each other seems almost to have become an old habit and a part of the thoughts and feelings of the two peoples. The article expresses the usual satisfaction at the pacific objects of the *entente* and states that it is impossible not to endorse the King's wish that it should become permanent. From the material point of view it is of the highest value. Though England has not yet made the effort which a proper anxiety for her own defence requires, yet her command of the sea is a military factor which no Power can afford to ignore.

The "Siècle" points out that the *entente cordiale* is now based not on mere diplomatic hopes and promises but on the mutual confidence of the two Governments and nations. The visits to be exchanged shortly with the Emperor of Russia add importance to M. Fallières' reception and prove the existence of a new triple alliance, which is none the less real for not being committed to paper.

The "Aurore" also points to the importance of the forthcoming visits to Russia of His Majesty and of M. Fallières, and of the Emperor of Russia to France and England. It is now but a step from an Anglo-French 'entente' to a great Anglo-Franco-Russian Triple Alliance whose policy will be purely pacific and at whose existence no one will be able to take umbrage. Perhaps people are moving too fast towards this conclusion, but the change is well within the bounds of possibility and seems very likely to take place.

The "Eclair," the Nationalist Cassandra of the Paris Press, asks whether it is worth while for France to brave on her frontiers the whole weight of German attack in order that British Admirals may satisfy their feverish desire to destroy the German Fleet; if England's strength was such as to guarantee France from all dangers and to enable her to avenge the disasters of 1870, then the journal would abstain from criticisms, but it will not allow itself by silence to encourage illusions as to the risks and obligations which an alliance would entail.

The "Gil Blas" adopts almost exactly the same line in discussing M. Fallières' journey. A European conflagration might result from the explosion of chauvinism which recent events have produced in Germany and England.

The "Petite République" (moderate Socialist) observes that M. Fallières' visit to London undoubtedly marks a new phase in the *entente cordiale*. Now that, thanks to France, an Anglo-Russian *entente* has been brought about no difficulty can possibly arise in the course of the last stage that remains to be traversed. It repudiates the idea that an alliance with England is only permissible on the condition that the latter should strengthen her army to the point of being able to undertake a campaign on the Continent.

I have, &c.
REGINALD LISTER.

No. 96.

Mr. Cartwright to Sir Edward Grey.

F.O. 371/460.
19122/18316/08/18.
(No. 62.)
Sir,

Munich, D. *June* 1, 1908.
R. *June* 3, 1908.

Germany has been passing through a week of discontent and the sound of the festivities on the Thames in connection with President Fallières' visit has considerably ruffled the equanimity of the German press which had just been using the visit of the South German Burgomasters to England as a proof of the ever-increasing friendship between that country and Germany. The views of the German press on this occasion are interesting to watch as they appear to be spontaneous and not inspired from head-quarters; the " Süddeutsche Reichskorrespondenz " so far remains silent with regard to President Fallières' visit to London. It would almost appear as if the Imperial Authorities were hesitating as to what attitude they should assume with regard to this event and as if they were afraid of giving vent to any sentiments which might be seized by the anti-German press in England as a sign of their evil dispositions towards ourselves. Perhaps, however, they are not sorry to allow the German press a free hand on this occasion so that they may be able to point to the discontent which is being aroused here by the action of His Majesty's Government as a warning to them that, however friendly the dispositions of the Imperial Government may be towards England, their hands may be forced by public opinion in a manner which would prove very disagreeable to our country. The visit of President Fallières to London with the one which will shortly be paid by him to Russia and the visit of King Edward to Reval([1]) form for thinking Germans so completely part and parcel of the same diplomatic drama that in criticising the one it will not be long before they take into consideration the total effect likely to be produced by the three, and therefore, although at present it must be acknowledged that the press here on the whole is still very reticent in giving vent to its views, yet we must expect when the State visits to Russia become an actuality to find outbursts of temper and irritation against ourselves in the newspapers of this country. At present a large portion of these try to make light of the presidential visit, and while they profess to smile at the extravagant language indulged in in England, one cannot help detecting behind their smiles a snarl, and Monsieur de Westmann, my Russian colleague here, told me a few days ago that the irritation aroused in official and social circles here at the King's proposed visit to Russia was intense. Monsieur de Westmann is generally considered to be if anything pro-German in his sentiments and people here are therefore more likely to speak openly to him on this subject than they would to me.

I need hardly say that every newspaper article published in France or in England which can be twisted to show any hostility to the idea of converting the Anglo-French *Entente* into an alliance, is at once being laid before the German public by the press of this country, and the incident in the House of Commons, when King Edward's journey to Russia was criticized by the Labour Party,([2]) has been made much use of here as a sign that a large portion of the British public does not approve of it. To calm public anxiety many of the newspapers here are using just now every argument they can think of to prove the inefficiency of the Anglo-French *Entente* as against Germany, and the weakness of England's military forces is held up as evidence that Great Britain cannot be of any real service to France against this country. Therefore all the benefits of the *Entente*, according to these organs of the press, will be on the side of Great Britain and France will discover sooner or later that she will get all the knocks and England all the profits from their union. Consequently England and France cannot long hold together and the day will come when people in the latter country will perceive that their real interests lie in a close friendship with Germany. I might summarise these newspaper arguments in Talleyrand's words, uttered in the early days of King Louis Philip[pe]'s reign, when an understanding with Great Britain was being discussed. The Prince observed that England and France could undoubtedly ride together, the only question was who would play the part of the horse and who that of the rider.

But besides the merely grumbling newspaper articles there have appeared here and there some which deal in a more thoughtful manner with Germany's general political situation in the world at present. In these a feeling of pessimism of a

---

([1]) [For this visit, *v. Gooch & Temperley*, Vol. V, pp. 236–46, Nos. 194–5, and *Ed. note.*]
([2]) [*cp.* Sir Sidney Lee: *King Edward VII* (1927), II, pp. 587–90.]

somewhat pronounced character seems to prevail on this subject. According to the Social Democratic press the chief blame for Germany's unsatisfactory foreign policy is laid to the door of Prince Bülow, and it asserts that Germany is suffering from what it calls "Junkerpolitik"; by this is meant the policy of brag and bluster which has contributed so much to the driving of other nations into alliances against Germany. The originator of this policy was undoubtedly Prince Bismarck with his watchword: "Germans need fear no one but Providence alone," and this phrase has been amplified by the pan-Germans into the maxim: "Wenn nur Deutschland einig bleibt, es einer Welt Gesetze schreibt." If the errors of such a hectoring policy were to a certain extent masked by the vigo[u]r and genius of Prince Bismarck, they become self-evident when such a policy is pursued by men of inferior character and talent. Germany is suffering from the initial mistake made by the Prince when through his bullying policy in Alsace-Lorraine and elsewhere in the world he drove the bourgeoisie of France to seek for safety in an alliance with Russia. Count Caprivi's boast that Germany could face a war on either frontier and Prince Bülow's threat of war against France finally drove that country from a mild *entente* with Great Britain into what has the appearance at present of being a solid alliance. And who remain the friends of Germany? ask the opponents of the present Chancellor. Austria and Italy, it will be said. But they retort that the Sovereign of the first is old and in ill-health and the political views of his successor are still an unknown quantity, while Italy cannot be depended upon, for at the critical moment she will lean towards that side which appears to have most chances of proving victorious.

The pan-Germans clamour for further armaments as a corrective against the coalition of Powers apparently directed against Germany, by which means they hope to increase the moral confidence of the nation in herself. "More soldiers and more ships!" is their present cry; the "Flottenverein" must start a campaign for the rehabilitation of General Keim and for the adoption of his policy, and this at a moment when Germany is face to face with a large deficit—the prospect of a considerable increase of taxation—and a certain shortage of money in commercial circles. Unfortunately, according to the Social Democrats, the creation of the *Bloc* will enable Prince Bülow to pursue his disastrous foreign policy to the bitter end; no restraint is put upon this policy as would be the case in other civilised countries whose Parliaments would long ago have driven from power the man responsible for it. Prince Bülow now holds up to Germany the phantom of an understanding with Great Britain which but few in Germany really believe in, and his organs alternately flatter and attack France. Such a policy will end either in isolation and degradation or in war, and war against the coalitions which Germany will have to face is a risky game to play, and even should it end in a drawn fight it will spell bankruptcy for the Empire.

In other quarters opinions are expressed of a similar kind though not in such pessimistic terms. Everywhere I notice a sullen discontent at the results of Germany's foreign policy. The political sky is continually and rapidly changing and always in a manner unfavourable to this country. A year or two ago it was France who opened out the way to an understanding between Russia and England; now England does her neighbour a good turn by strengthening the alliance between Russia and France which had slightly weakened owing to the insatiable demands of Russia for French money. The visit of the President to England, as a preliminary to the visits of himself and King Edward to Russia, has not only infused new life into the Dual Alliance but has converted it into a Triple Alliance, and the pivot on which this combination now turns is Great Britain. However calmly Germans may look at this political event they cannot help feeling that it bodes them no good; in any case, its accomplishment does not contribute to the prestige of German diplomacy.

If there is one question of foreign policy which excites the German press just now it is that of Morocco. It complains that the Imperial Government have of late shown a timidity and a servility towards France which has been most detrimental to the interests of German trade in Morocco. As a result of President Fallières' visit to London one may expect that in this respect things will go from bad to worse. One of the President's objects in visiting England and later on Russia is to obtain for France some moral support in her present difficulties; these in Morocco are considerable and unfortunately they are driving France more and more into the arms of England. In the first place it is difficult to foresee which of the two Sultans will eventually triumph, and, secondly, France has reached that critical moment when she will have to decide whether she will go on with the Moroccan adventure or withdraw from it. No one here believes that she will follow the latter course; she has gone too far to do so and the only point which remains to be decided is whether she will undertake to settle the Moroccan question for good by a big war, or whether she will pursue the policy of conquest by *étapes*. If the first course is followed, France will deliberately tear up the Algeciras Act, and the Imperial Government will then find themselves in the awkward predicament of either having to ignominiously satisfy themselves with a paper protest, or of going to war. If the latter course is pursued by France and Germany hesitates to enter upon a war with her neighbour, she can with an appearance of more or less dignity shut her eyes to the slow and gradual infringements of the Algeciras Act. What annoys the writers in the German press appears to be that at the present moment threats of war on the part of Germany would no longer intimidate France as they did at the time of Monsieur Delcassé's fall. The rehabilitation of Russia's might and the formation of the new triple understanding are too powerful factors in modern politics to be ignored or trifled with by Germany. Therefore the best thing for her to do, as she cannot prevent it, is perhaps to allow France to thoroughly involve herself in Morocco and so weaken her position in Europe.

In conclusion I may repeat what I have already said, that King Edward's proposed visit to Reval has produced a profound impression on thinking people in this country, and it is feared that if the policy of trying to checkmate Germany by bringing about understandings between European Powers is pursued much further, it must inevitably lead to such exasperation in this country as will produce a situation of the greatest gravity upon the Continent. Nations, like individuals, sometimes get into a state of nervous irritability and they then cease to be responsible for their actions. It should not be forgotten that Germany has received two political shocks in recent times. It was an axiom of German diplomacy that France and England could never really bury their differences and make a solid peace. They succeeded in doing so in 1904, and the visit of President Fallières has put the seal on the *Entente*. Again, Germany counted upon the eternal enmity of Russia against England, an enmity which it was confidently expected would increase as the frontiers of these two Powers drew nearer to each other in Asia. Instead of producing discord this has led to an accord which has all the appearance of being of a lasting character. Some people here are afraid that a third illusion of German diplomacy may before long go overboard and that, should it occur, the consequences might be very grave. So far Germany has counted absolutely on the fidelity of Austria-Hungary; rumours have it, however, that the future Emperor may throw in his lot with the Slav elements in his Empire, and should he do so he will inevitably sooner or later turn towards Russia for support rather than towards Germany.

It is worth noting that on the day the French President left our shores the newspapers here published the information that the Kaiser's health had been so benefited by his stay in England last year that His Majesty contemplates again visiting our country this autumn in a private character, and to calm the present German nervousness it was added that His Majesty will on that occasion no doubt have more than one interview with King Edward.

I have, &c.

FAIRFAX L. CARTWRIGHT.

No. 97.

Sir Edward Grey to Count de Salis.

F.O. 20811/17544/08/38.
(No. 160.)
Sir,
Foreign Office, June 15, 1908.

The German Ambassador, in the course of a visit to-day, asked me whether I had seen Sir Charles Hardinge since his return from Reval.

I said I had just seen him and he had given me a Memorandum(1) of all that had passed, which, however, I had not yet had time to read through. But I told Count Metternich that the things which had been discussed were matters of detail affecting such countries as Persia and arising out of the Anglo-Russian Convention, also points relating to Macedonia. These were all things the nature of which was known to other Governments.

I thought we were practically in agreement about Macedonia, and I hoped that Notes would now be drawn up and sent to the other Powers explaining our joint views.

I observed that some of the Press in Germany seemed to have been displeased because the King was meeting the Czar at Reval. This was very unreasonable, seeing that the German Emperor had already met the Czar several times.

Count Metternich admitted that there was no justification for the dissatisfaction, but there was in some quarters a certain amount of apprehension regarding the King's visit.

I told him there was no reason for any apprehension, and certainly no new Agreement was going to be sprung upon the world as a result of the King's visit to Reval. I thought, however, that the effect of the visit had been very good, for both sides apparently were very pleased with it.

I am, &c.
E. G[REY].

(1) [v. Gooch & Temperley, Vol. V, pp. 237–45, No. 195.]

No. 98.

Count de Salis to Sir Edward Grey.

F.O. 371/460.
22211/22211/08/18.
(No. 284.) Confidential.
Sir,
Berlin, D. June 26, 1908.
R. June 29, 1908.

Mr. Saunders, the Times correspondent who is leaving Berlin in order to take up an appointment in connection with the foreign editorship of the paper, told me this morning that, after making his farewell visits to the Foreign Office, he had been received by the Imperial Chancellor himself and had remained with him in conversation for some two hours.

Prince Bülow, who affected the utmost frankness and begged Mr. Saunders on his part not to hesitate to express his own opinions openly, began the conversation by remarking that Mr. Saunders had been the correspondent of the Times for the last twenty years. During that period the relations between Great Britain and Germany had not improved; on the contrary they appeared to have grown less cordial; what was his opinion as to the causes for this change?

Mr. Saunders replied that, to go back to the beginning, public opinion in England had at the commencement of the period in question been unfavourably influenced by the impression that the Empress Frederick had not been understood or fairly treated in Germany. "I admit," remarked Prince Bülow, "that she did not always have a good time here." Then there was the impression that his friendly policy towards England had been a contributory cause to the fall of Count Caprivi. (Her late Majesty Queen Victoria had, he understood from good authority, held this opinion.) Then a variety of unfortunate incidents had occurred, the Krüger telegram etc. etc. Some of the Prince's own references in the Reichstag to Great Britain had not been taken in good part. (Here the Prince remarked that his remarks about the British army which had excited Mr. Chamberlain's indignation had been quite misunderstood owing to an incorrect summary telegraphed by Reuter's agent.) Coming to more recent times there was the strained situation created by German policy with regard to Morocco, the idea that German interests there were not sufficient to warrant the action taken by the Imperial Government; further the disposition of the press here to give an anti-German interpretation to the understandings arrived at by Great Britain with Spain last year([1]) and Russia this year,([2]) and to the Royal meeting in Italy([3]) though the latter was strictly in accordance with the traditional friendship between Great Britain and that country. There was further the idea that Germany, in the pursuit of her own ends, was disposed to thwart our policy with regard to Macedonian reform.([4]) It could hardly be seriously maintained that the chief cause for misunderstanding was that, as the Prince had suggested, the two peoples did not know each other enough. Better feelings had prevailed at a more distant date when they presumably knew each other even less.

Prince Bülow said that there had never been the least wish on the part of the German Government to use the question of Morocco to test the strength of the Anglo-French *entente*. There was no idea on his part either to use the Macedonian question with any such object, and he quite agreed that anything that could even lend colour to such a view should be most carefully avoided; there might be some difficult negotiation in connection with the matter, but he did not anticipate that grave trouble between the Powers would arise out of it. As regards Morocco, it was only the unreasonable attitude of the French Minister at Tangier which had forced them to take action, solely in defence of their legitimate interests. They had had no ulterior object. Public opinion in Germany absolutely required them to move. As regards the present, he denied that the Emperor had recently used the word "einkreisen"—"surround"—in his speech at Döberitz. He was sick of the word and hoped never to hear it again. At the same time he had to deal with people in Germany who were easily alarmed; there were also such people in England. When the British North Sea fleet had been strengthened at the expense of that of the Mediterranean, a council had been held in the room in which they were sitting, and Admiral Tirpitz had declared that this measure could only mean that an attack against them was meditated. Count Metternich was fortunately present and said that in England there were equally people who were just as persuaded that a German attack was being planned; these fears he felt were equally groundless on either side. It was unfortunate, the Prince added, that at a time when relations were more cordial the two countries had expected, respectively, a little too much of each other. Germany could never have consented, as Mr. Chamberlain had once suggested, to be the sword of Great Britain on the continent. The points on which Germany had expected too much of Great Britain do not seem to have been specified.

I venture to summarize, as far as I can, the substance of this rather discursive conversation since it contains views to which Prince Bülow is apparently anxious to give publicity. It is difficult to avoid remarking that though much detail seems to have been discussed, neither of the parties to the conversation seem to have alluded to what perhaps might be considered to be the real crux of the situation, the vital

([1]) [This subject will be treated in a later volume.]
([2]) [King Edward's meeting with the Emperor Nicholas II at Reval on June 9–10, 1908, is described in *Gooch & Temperley*, Vol. V, pp. 232–46, ch. XXXVII.]
([3]) [*v. supra*, pp. 28–32, Nos. 15–6, and *note*.]
([4]) [*cp. Gooch & Temperley*, Vol. V, pp. 345–6, No. 242.]

necessity of her sea supremacy to Great Britain and the clearly announced intention of the German Government to pursue a forward policy as regards the development of a powerful navy.

I have, &c.

J. DE SALIS.

No. 99.

Sir F. Lascelles to Sir Edward Grey.

F.O. 371/461.
26847/26847/08/18.
(No. 334.) Confidential.
Sir,

Berlin, D. *July* 31, 1908.
R. *August* 4, 1908.

Having returned to Berlin last night, I called by appointment on Herr von Schoen at noon to-day, and had a long conversation with His Excellency.

In speaking of the Macedonian question His Excellency said that he entirely agreed with your suggestion that it would be desirable to suspend any representations to the Porte on the subject of the creation of a mobile force so long as tranquillity prevails in Macedonia.(¹) A new situation had been created in Turkey by the grant of a constitution and His Excellency did not think it would be possible for the Sultan to revoke the constitution as he did in 1876. It would certainly be satisfactory if the reforms, not only in Macedonia, but in Turkey generally could be carried out by the Turks themselves, but there was always a danger in a revolutionary movement of extreme measures being adopted and although the Young Turk party had hitherto shewn great moderation, the reports which had reached him this morning from the German Embassy at Constantinople led him to fear that they might adopt extreme measures against the foreigners employed in Macedonia. There was so far nothing very definite, but there were indications that the Young Turks resented the presence of foreigners in the administration and were beginning to go beyond the bounds of the moderation which they had hitherto observed.

His Excellency expressed his high appreciation of the speech which you had recently delivered in the House of Commons and which had certainly produced a very favourable impression in Germany.(²) I replied that I could tell him very confidentially that your remarks about the relations with Germany were made in reply to the speech of Sir Charles Dilke, and that you had not intended to refer in any way to the so-called isolation of Germany, and had only done so in consequence of what had been said by previous speakers. I added that there was a sincere desire on the part of His Majesty's Government for good relations with Germany and that the only obstacle in the way of a thoroughly good understanding was the vast expenditure on Naval armaments.

I was aware that Count Metternich had been given clearly to understand that it was a vital necessity for Great Britain to maintain her supremacy at sea and that she intended to do so at any cost, and that so long as Germany continued her very large naval armaments it would be necessary for Great Britain to increase hers. Herr von Schoen said that he quite understood this. He would personally be delighted to see a diminution in expenditure on the Navy, and indeed he thought it probable that the Reichstag might raise difficulties about voting the necessary sums, which were constantly increasing. It was however a very delicate question and he was at a loss to find a formula which would justify a reduction. I replied that I did not see the necessity for a formula, but that I thoroughly believed that any diminution of the German shipbuilding programme would do more than anything else to place the relations of the two countries on a perfectly satisfactory footing.

(¹) [v. *Gooch & Temperley*, Vol. V, p. 308, No. 212.]
(²) [v. *Parl. Deb.*, 4th *Ser.*, Vol. 193, pp. 969–70.]

Herr von Schoen said that the German press was causing considerable embarrassment to the German Government, not so much on account of its attitude towards
England as of its violence against France. The French Government gave the most
satisfactory assurances to the German Government as to their action in Morocco, and
these assurances were fully accepted by the German Government, who were convinced
of their sincerity, but the press pointed out that the action of the French in Morocco
was not in accordance with these assurances and accused the German Government of
being hoodwinked. The German Government did their best to influence the press by
the publication of an occasional *communiqué*, but he feared that the anti-French
feeling in Germany was very bitter. He did not however anticipate any complications.
His personal relations with Mr. Cambon were everything that could be desired and he
considered that he was justified in looking forward to a peaceful autumn.

I have, &c.
FRANK C. LASCELLES.

No. 100.

Sir E. Goschen to Sir Edward Grey.

Private.(¹)

Dear Sir Edward Grey, *Marienbad, August 29, 1908.*
I had unfortunately only opportunity for a very short talk with M. Clemenceau;
but as he held to me almost the identic language which he held to the King and
previously to the ''Times'' correspondent, whose notes were forwarded by His
Majesty to Sir Charles Hardinge, the shortness of our conversation was immaterial.(²)
He was, or at all events pretended to be for his own purposes, most nervous about
the situation, and talked in a most pessimistic vein, his theme being '' The smallest
incident may bring about a rupture between Great Britain and Germany; you may
sink the whole German Navy if things go right for you; but how about us? We shall
in any case have to bear the brunt, and shall go to the wall unless you give us military
assistance, which as things now stand, you cannot do. It is a question upon which we
in France are thinking very deeply. Whatever the cause of war might be, Germany
would not hesitate to try and get out of France by land what she might lose to England
by sea. She would at once march upon France through Belgium, for in war time
Generals at the front have no time to think of such small matters as neutrality and
International Engagements, and unless you could send us at least 300,000 men to
create a diversion, she would be able to make such a concentration of her Army Corps
as would place us in a terribly awkward position. It is a great misfortune for us
that at a moment so pregnant with disagreeable possibilities you are tinkering at your
army and have, relatively speaking, neither men, arms nor ammunition.'' I reproached
His Excellency with exaggerated pessimism and he said '' Je suis pessimiste je l'avoue,
c'est à dire, je pense en pessimiste tout en agissant en optimiste.'' He added that he
fervently wished that British Statesmen would do the same. He then observed that
the Franco-Prussian war came about quite unsuspectedly, just because a little simple
question remained unsolved, and that the same thing might easily happen any day
between Gr[ea]t Britain and Germany. I said that as far as I was aware there were
happily no outstanding questions between the two countries which could be made a
pretext for war. As regards the war to which he had alluded, it was quite true that
it had come suddenly without much warning or preliminary discussions—and without
giving the two peoples time for realizing the horrors and disasters it would bring in
its train. The present situation was different. There had been far too much discussion
in the Press of both countries as to the probabilities of an eventual rupture between
England and Germany. This had been unfortunate but it had had its good side, as

(¹) [Grey MSS., Vol. 1.]
(²) [*v.* H. Wickham Steed: *Through Thirty Years* (1924), Vol. I, pp. 284–8.]

it had given time both for Rulers, Statesmen and peoples to reflect upon what was meant, and, in my opinion, it would take more than a slight question unsolved to bring about what everyone had realized would be the greatest possible castastrophe to both the Nations concerned and the world at large. Monsieur Clemenceau admitted that this view furnished some ground for optimism : but he said that as regards there being no dangerous outstanding questions between England and Germany, there was in the first place the question of Naval Armaments and then—" You must not forget that you may quarrel with a woman as much as you like, nag at her and treat her in every way abominably, but she only becomes really dangerous when you show that you have ceased to love her. No! Your Statesmen must realize that a strong effort must be made to cause this country to emerge from its present state of unpreparedness. You may be right and I wrong as to any imminent danger of a quarrel, but in any case for the sake of future peace, Great Britain must be strong on land as well as by sea. Your attitude at Algeciras did much to explode the legend of ' Perfide Albion ' —and the Entente between our two countries is almost universally popular in France : but once let our people realize, as I do, the price which France may probably have to pay for England's friendship, if her military resources are allowed to remain as they are now, and away goes the Entente, away the men who promoted it, and away go the friendly feelings which are so much advantage to both countries.''

Of course the danger to France, if we and Germany were to come to real logger-heads is very patent and real; and Monsieur Clemenceau *says* what a great many people in France only *think* now, but will also say very loudly if things should come to the worst : but in his anxiety that we should be in a position to give to France military assistance if necessary, he omits, or at all events he omitted in his conversation with me, all thought of Russia, who would at least require a large containing force on her frontier, or of the probable lukewarmness of Italy and Austria-Hungary. These two countries would surely be loth to be drawn into a war, in which they would have no direct interest and which could bring them no advantage while exposing them to very real and obvious dangers. . . . .([3])

Yours very sincerely,
W. E. GOSCHEN.

MINUTE BY KING EDWARD.

M. Clemenceau held similar language to me and there is no doubt that he is nervous about Germany, and in his point of view he has reason to be so, because if we have not a soldier to help France were she to be attacked by Germany, she feels she would be unable to hold her own.

E.R.
Sept: 10/08.

([3]) [The rest of this letter quotes a press article.]

No. 101.

Memorandum by Mr. Valentine Chirol.

F.O. 371/461.
37406/28481/08/18.   *Berlin, October* 19, 1908.

I had this morning a two hours' conversation with Baron Holstein, who began by saying that, though we should doubtless differ on many points, he hoped we should at any rate agree to talk frankly and unreservedly.

He surveyed briefly the various stages of Anglo-German differences which, as he had often told me before, originated in the unpleasant impression which the Emperor's conversation with Lord Salisbury at Cowes in the summer of 1895 had left upon His Majesty's mind. Then came the Kruger telegram, which His

Majesty's then advisers had been unable to prevent, though they had mitigated its original asperity. He gave me a fuller account than I had heard before of the circumstances in which it was drafted and despatched. The Emperor had been primed by his military and naval suite before Prince Hohenlohe and Baron Marschall arrived in reply to a summons from His Majesty. He (Baron Holstein) was not present at the council, though he accompanied Baron Marschall. When the latter produced the draft despatch with instructions to send it off immediately, he ventured to express strong objections. "But Marschall, who is an able man, but could never stand up to the Emperor,—he is a South German, and so was Hohenlohe, and only a Prussian can stand up to the Emperor,—told me we must be thankful the telegram was no worse; he and Hohenlohe had done all they could to soften it down, and it was final." Baron Holstein said he had not forgotten the remark I had made to him at the time that this sort of thing could have but one result, namely to pave the way for a reconciliation between England and France. It was a blunder, like the Emperor's visit to Tangier in 1905.([1]) "They are the two big blunders of the reign,—in foreign affairs. But the Emperor, if he lives to be a hundred, will never be a politician. He is an "impressionist," and a "dramatist," and incapable of "reflection." (The conversation was in English, which apart from occasional idiomatic slips Baron Holstein speaks fluently and accurately.)

I remarked that, as far as the Tangier visit was concerned, I had always understood the Emperor had landed reluctantly under pressure from the German Foreign Office, i.e., "from you."

"That is true to this extent. We strongly advocated the visit to Tangier, but as a demonstration of peace, not, as it turned out, as an aggressive demonstration. The Emperor was to have landed in order to demonstrate our right to have a say in Morocco, but he was to have made a very pacific speech of which the tenour had been carefully thought out so as not to wound French susceptibilities. Well, instead of that, the Emperor landed, snubbed the French representative and trotted out the Sultan of Morocco. You know the rest."

Baron Holstein then proceeded to make some rather obscure allusion to "other influences at court,"—presumably the Eulenburg clique,—but he stopped himself. "No, I don't want to enter into these matters which are almost personal." But, he went on, "there are several personal matters which cannot be left out of account, the relations between your King and the Emperor. In former times when King Edward was Prince of Wales, the fault, I believe, was mainly on the Emperor's side. But your King, who is a much cleverer man and has much more experience, has paid him out with a vengeance, and that rankles. I hope things are mending in that direction too, for, believe me, those personal antagonisms are dangerous."

He then told me how the King is believed to have written to President Roosevelt, and also to have told the Tsar, that Germany's Navy was intended as a threat to the United States and to Russia respectively.—I replied that I for one could not believe there was any truth in such stories, and that I had heard on the contrary that the Emperor himself, in conversation with Englishmen, had defended German naval expansion on the ground that Germany had to reckon with the ambition of other Powers, and had notably on one occasion dwelt on the dangers of American spread-eagleism in this connection.—Baron Holstein admitted that that might be so "as the Emperor talks a great deal too much."

He then gave me his own views with regard to the German naval schemes. He had always been opposed to excessive naval expansion, because he knew the English character, and was certain England would never allow Germany to overtake her. It would mean merely a ruinous competition, and possibly the neglect of German military interests which were a matter of life and death. I told him I believed many people in Germany had reckoned upon the advent of a Liberal Government in England which, from considerations of economy and under the influence of its

([1]) [v. Gooch & Temperley, Vol. III, pp. 60–4, Nos. 67–74.]

" pacifist " supporters, was expected to flinch from necessary financial sacrifices. " If so, they never knew anything about Englishmen, and they must anyhow by this time have discovered their mistake." I said I hoped that might be so, and gave him my reasons for believing, with at any rate a very large section of my fellow-countrymen, that the development of the German Navy was directed mainly against us, or at any rate contemplated the possibility or probability of war between the two countries. Baron Holstein did not deny this, nor did he deny the existence of widespread animosity towards England in Germany. He assured me, however, that things were improving, and would further improve under the pinch of increased taxation. He believed it would be impossible for Germany to go beyond the present Navy Bill. I asked whether there was any possibility of allowing it to remain partially unexecuted. He thought that was impossible. He assured me, however, that Prince Bülow's influence would be cast against any further expansion : he would make a Cabinet question of it.

I told him it was difficult for me to place much confidence in Prince Bülow when, within a week of the emphatic assurances he had been good enough to volunteer to me when I was last in Berlin (November 1901), he had started or sanctioned a fresh campaign of unparalleled violence against us under pretext of a speech from Mr. Chamberlain, which had been delivered ten days before my conversation with him (the Chancellor),—a campaign which had culminated in Prince Bülow's provocative speech in the Reichstag about the " rocher de bronze."

Baron Holstein said he had himself regretted that campaign at the time, and had advised the Chancellor to speak in a very different sense : but the Chancellor loved a phrase, and that phrase had unfortunately been suggested to him by his evil genius. He hesitated at first when I asked him who that evil genius might be ; but he ultimately named Herr von Hammann, in the Foreign Office, (who was then head of the Press Bureau), and he went on to tell me that it is Herr von Hammann who prepares the notes for the Chancellor's speeches, and that it was he who suppressed amongst those notes a passage which he (Baron Holstein) had persuaded Prince Bülow to introduce into his great speech on the Moroccan question in the winter of 1905, entirely exonerating England from blame in respect to the non-communication of the Anglo-French Convention to the German Government. " It was not for England, who had conceded rights in Morocco, but for France, who had claimed them, to communicate the new agreement."(²)

Baron Holstein went on, however, to say that he was tarred with the brush of Anglophobia, and probably nothing he could say would destroy that legend. I said that on the contrary I believed he had always sincerely wished to retain England as a friend of Germany—but on terms, i.e. : as a subservient friend, a sort of naval Austria. He took no notice of that remark, but said he had been told (by the Emperor, I think, but of this I am not quite certain) that Sir Frank Lascelles had himself warned His Majesty that so long as he (Holstein) remained at the Foreign Office, the relations between England and Germany could never be cordial. I replied that I could not speak with knowledge, but that I was absolutely convinced Sir Frank never would or could have held such language to the Emperor. We were not in the habit of prying into foreign departments of State and denouncing the real or imaginary sentiments of permanent officials for whom, as far as we were concerned, the Secretary of State himself alone stood responsible.

As time was getting on, I then brought the conversation on to the present crisis.(³) Baron Holstein tried to defend the action of Austria on the usual grounds, i.e. : that Servian intrigues were rendering her position very difficult, and she could not safely have postponed action. I said this seemed to me rather like the fable of the lamb and the wolf. " I assure you, that is not so. When the Archduke Franz Ferdinand

(²) [cp. Gooch & Temperley, Vol. III, p. 217, No. 235, encl., where reference occurs to Prince Bülow's speech of December 6, 1905.]

(³) [For the Bosnian crisis, v. Gooch & Temperley, Vol. V, chs. XL and XLI, pp. 356–815, passim.]

was here some time ago, he explained fully to the Emperor the difficulties of the situation in Bosnia and Herzegovina and told him plainly that it was growing intolerable." I inquired whether he had told His Majesty that Austria contemplated annexation. "Oh, he never said a word about that." "But surely," I replied, "that must have been the conclusion to which his remarks could alone be directed." Baron Holstein simply repeated that the word annexation had never been mentioned, but his manner clearly showed that he had given himself away. "Anyhow, you must not be under any misapprehension. We are not going to desert our ally." I said we should never dream of expecting Germany to do so : but it seemed to me Germany now had a splendid opportunity of acting up to her professions and of making her influence unmistakably felt for a peaceful solution of the present difficulties, merely by advising Austria to defer, as Russia, who was no less powerful and proud a state, had deferred in 1870, to the public opinion of Europe by submitting the annexation of the provinces to the sanction of an European Congress. Baron Holstein replied almost angrily that Germany would neither go into a Conference without Austria, nor advise her to accept the Conference if she were unwilling to do so. "We might have used our good offices in Vienna, had we been consulted : but as usual, we have not been consulted. You and France and Russia have been confabulating for a fortnight and drawing up your terms, and you want us to advise Austria to submit herself to self-appointed judges? That is really too much." I argued the point with him for some time, but to no purpose. He thought that, on the contrary, it was for us to prove our peaceful intentions, by using our influence at Constantinople to secure a direct agreement between Turkey and Austria. "That would be much more practical than all your Conferences,—especially if you allow it to be given out that the object of your Conference is to secure compensations . . . .(⁴) from Austria!"

We then passed on to the situation in Turkey. There, he thought, we might co-operate; for with Germany's great financial and economic interests, and our moral interests in view of our Mahomedan populations in India and in Egypt, we were both equally concerned in the strengthening of Turkey. "You will be much better employed in keeping Bulgaria quiet than in trying to get compensations from Austria." It would also, he added, be much easier, for "you may be sure Prince Ferdinand does not want to go to war. He is not the man to earn any personal glory on a battle-field whereas one of his Generals might!"

Finally, Baron Holstein sought to impress upon me again the danger of irritating Austria, "because, remember, there we come in too. I don't want to say too much about our Emperor, and it is not for me to pose as his champion. He is only too much inclined to blow hot and cold, and his bark is often worse than his bite. He too will never go to war if he can help it; but there are two things he could not help going to war about : if France were to give us any open provocation, or if Austria was threatened. It is not likely to happen, for France knows what she would bring upon herself, and Russia probably also knows that in her present military condition she is not fit even to meet the Austrian Army. Italy might make mischief, for she also has aims that are incompatible with Austria's interests, but she too cannot afford to do anything rash."

In conclusion, I would only add that I was much struck with the tone of complete assurance in which Baron Holstein spoke about German policy. Had he been Foreign Minister, he could not have spoken with more assurance. He was probably conscious of the impression he was making upon me, for as we parted he said : "Of course I no longer speak as a responsible official, but I need not tell you that I still know perfectly well what I am talking about."

VALENTINE CHIROL.

Berlin, 19 October, 1908.

(⁴) [Thus in original.]

No. 102.

Sir F. Lascelles to Sir Edward Grey.

F.O. 371/462.
37100/37100/08/18.
(No. 471.)
Sir,

Berlin, D. October 23, 1908.
R. October 26, 1908.

The German Emperor granted me an audience to-day for the purpose of receiving from me the letter by which the King announced to His Majesty the termination of my mission.

In handing the letter to His Majesty I said that it was with great regret that I was leaving Berlin and I begged to be allowed to express my sincerest thanks for the kindness and consideration which His Majesty had constantly shown me during the 13 years of my official residence at Berlin.

His Majesty deigned to say that he was certainly as sorry to lose me as I was to go, perhaps even more so, and he added that he had made an ineffectual attempt to obtain a prolongation of my mission. I replied by again thanking His Majesty and saying that it was only natural that the older men should make room for younger ones, and that in consequence of the improvement in the relations between the two countries, the moment was a favourable one for the arrival of my successor. On His Majesty's observing that he was not personally acquainted with my successor I took the opportunity of speaking in the most favourable terms of Sir Edward Goschen, as an old personal friend, who, I was convinced, would speedily gain His Majesty's confidence and good-will.

I had subsequently the honour of being received in audience by Her Majesty the Empress who expressed in most gracious terms her regret at the departure from Berlin of my sister Lady Edward Cavendish and myself.

The audiences were followed by a luncheon at which Prince Henry of Prussia and the Princes and Princesses Adolf of Schaumburg Lippe and Frederick Charles of Hesse were present and to which my sister had also the honour of being invited.

After luncheon the Emperor deigned to have some further conversation with me, during which he begged me, on my return to England to do what I could to counteract the idea of his sending spies to England. He believed that he would have far greater reason to complain of the action of certain English Naval Officers in the neighbourhood of the Kiel Canal, of which however he intended to take no notice whatever.

The only political allusion which His Majesty made was that he hoped that the questions which had arisen in the Near East might be settled by direct negotiations between Turkey and Austria-Hungary and Bulgaria. He feared however that further complications might arise, if it was true as stated in a Reuter's telegram that His Majesty's Government had urged the Porte not to negotiate directly with the two Powers.

I replied that I had no knowledge of such action on the part of His Majesty's Government, and the matter then dropped. His Majesty took leave of me in the most gracious manner possible.

I have, &c.
FRANK C. LASCELLES.

No. 103.

Count de Salis to Sir Edward Grey.

F.O. 371/463.
37903/37903/08/18.
(No. 476.)   *Berlin, D. October 27, 1908.*
Sir,   R. *November 2, 1908.*

A report was recently circulated in the German press that the Press Bureau was about to be revised, and that Dr. Hammann, who has been at the head of it was retiring into private life. The latter statement has now been contradicted, but it is understood that certain changes will be made. The chief reform to be introduced is apparently that the Bureau, which has its quarters in the Foreign Office building and is officially part of the "Political Department" will now be divided into two sections, one for home affairs and one for foreign affairs.

The references to this institution in the papers have drawn forth a certain amount of bitter comment upon its political influence and activity from the Liberal Press. Their readers are reminded that Count Caprivi for a time attempted to maintain his position without any Press Bureau, but found it impossible to do so; and it was then that Hammann, the editor of an obscure, anti-Semitic paper, was selected as head of the revised institution. Only in Russia and Austria, it is pointed out, do similar institutions exist; in most *modern* countries each Ministry informs the Press as to the work of its own department, and no special mechanism is required. But the German Press Bureau is a cook's shop, whose duty it is to concoct from the home and foreign news received a dish of political verbiage which will be palatable to the taste of the authorities. Thus in 1905 and 1906, its energies were devoted to preventing the truth about the Morocco fiasco from penetrating into the country; in 1907 during the election time, it was engaged in artificially creating a storm of national enthusiasm; nor is it the fault of Dr. Hammann that recent German semi-official utterances upon foreign affairs have not been as tactful or successful as one might have expected. The Socialist *Vorwärts* developes this theme still further, and explains that Hammann remains in office solely on account of the inestimable services which he has rendered to the present Chancellor, under whose régime his Press Bureau has blossomed into its fullest activity. Germany has received one slap in the face after another during recent years in the sphere of foreign policy and yet Prince Bülow has until quite lately figured in the German Press as an unrivalled master in the art of diplomacy.

I have, &c.
J. DE SALIS.

No. 104.

Sir Edward Grey to Sir E. Goschen.

Private.([1])
Dear Sir Edward Goschen,   *Foreign Office, November 5, 1908.*

I think it is best that you should lose no time in taking up your post at Berlin.

But once you are there, if you think it is necessary or desirable that you should come over for two or three days to see me, I shall be at your disposal at any time.

I think, however, that things are so critical that you ought not to make any arrangements for taking a holiday just yet.

([1]) [Grey MSS., Vol. 22.]

The publication of the interview with the Emperor,([2]) which, according to my information, was entirely his own doing, authorised by himself,—has been a severe blow to him, a great embarrassment to his Government, and a great annoyance to his people. This must be the cause of a great deal of ill-humour in Germany; and when a nation with the strongest Army in the world feels that it has been made a fool of publicly, the fact that it has only itself to blame does not diminish its anger, but only embarrasses it in finding something other than itself on which to vent its ill-humour.

There is already a sign that the Germans are going to make trouble with the French about the Casablanca incident.([3]) They may, and most probably do, intend this only as a means of diverting attention from the results of the interview: but it is playing a dangerous game, and this is not a time when any nation can safely strike sparks.

In the Near East, though the danger of war between Bulgaria and Turkey is not so imminent as it was a short time ago, a strong Slav feeling has arisen in Russia. Although this feeling appears to be well in hand at present, bloodshed between Austria and Servia would certainly raise the feeling to a dangerous height in Russia; and the thought that peace depends upon Servia restraining herself is not comfortable.

I do not think there is going to be war just now: the approach of winter is in itself a sedative. But the situation will be very dangerous next spring unless a settlement has been reached peacefully during the winter; and it is not yet apparent how that settlement can be reached.

So far as the Bulgarian difficulty is concerned, I think that Bulgaria and Turkey will agree in principle that there is to be financial compensation; they will probably disagree as to the amount of the compensation; and they will then, I hope, agree to refer the question of the amount to the Conference, and to abide by the decision of the Conference.

But, in connection with the annexation of Bosnia and Herzegovina, it will be very difficult for Russia to recognise the annexation unless some concessions can be secured for Servia and Montenegro.

Cartwright has suggested to me that a possible compromise might be found by agreeing that a strip of Bosnia and Herzegovina, while remaining under Austrian occupation as at present, should be declared outside the limits of annexation; and that Servia and Montenegro should be guaranteed facilities for railway access to the Adriatic. He thinks that, though d'Aehrenthal could not himself propose this, the Emperor of Austria might at the last moment, for the sake of the peace of Europe, concede this as an act of magnanimity.

It would do no good if we were to suggest anything of the kind to Austria. But it seems to me that if the difficulty between Turkey and Austria, as well as between Turkey and Bulgaria, had been adjusted, thus bringing the prospect of a general settlement so near as to make a great effort worth while, Germany might use her influence with the Emperor of Austria to make some concession of this kind, and so overcome the Servian difficulty.

As yet, it is too soon to make such a proposal: but the appropriate moment might come at any time.

Meanwhile, you will see that I have been urging the Turks to accept the programme proposed for the Conference, on condition that they receive the assurances of the Powers that neither Turkish territory nor Turkish rights will be prejudiced, beyond the annexation of Bosnia and Herzegovina and the recognition of the independence of Bulgaria and Eastern Roumelia.

I am also prepared to encourage direct negotiations between Turkey and Bulgaria, and between Turkey and Austria, as a preliminary to the Conference: but Austria must offer to take over some part of the Turkish Debt, or find some other means to smooth the way for Turkey to recognise the annexation.

([2]) [v. infra, pp. 201–26, Nos. 125–42.]
([3]) [This subject will be dealt with in Gooch & Temperley, Vol. VII.]

I give you these as my own ideas of the situation. Please refer to me freely, on any points; and if you think it necessary, after you get to Berlin, come over to London to see me.

Yours sincerely,
E. GREY.

No. 105.

Sir E. Goschen to Sir Edward Grey.

F.O. 371/463.
39841/39841/08/18.
(No. 496.) Confidential.

Berlin, D. *November* 13, 1908.
R. *November* 16, 1908.

Sir,

I have the honour to report that I was received by Prince Bülow at 7 o'clock this evening, and that I could not have received a kinder nor more cordial welcome. After speaking in the most appreciative and warm manner of Sir Frank Lascelles, he was good enough to express the hope that our relations would be of the same friendly nature. I replied that I cordially reciprocated his wish, that I knew that it was the desire of His Majesty's Government to be on the best possible terms with Germany and that it would be both my duty and my pleasure to contribute to that end by all means in my power. Prince Bülow said that the exceedingly friendly and sympathetic attitude both of His Majesty's Government and the British Press in the lamentable affair of the Daily Telegraph publication([1]) had made a very favourable impression both upon him and the country generally, and that it was a happy augury for my tenure of His Majesty's Embassy here that my arrival had coincided with what he hoped would be a new phase in the relations between the two countries. While on that subject there was one thing to which he would like to call my special attention. This was that the Representatives of every party in the Reichstag, from Conservatives down to Socialists had both in their speeches and in private conversation with him, denied with the greatest warmth the statement attributed to the Emperor that the greater part of his subjects were hostile to Great Britain. This unanimous expression of opinion had been the one and only thing which had been satisfactory in the "Interview" Debate. Great Britain and Germany, he continued, had never fought against each other and he hoped they never would; their interests clashed nowhere, though there was considerable commercial rivalry, and their mutual trade was necessary to both. If there had been any place where the interests of the two countries had perhaps not always run on parallel lines, it had been in Turkey, with whom Germany had been friendly under the old régime and Great Britain had not. Now even that difference was removed and both countries were now at one in desiring to support the new Constitution. The German Ambassador had reported to him that there was no greater error than to believe that British and German interests clashed in Turkey, that there was commercially ample room for both Powers and that by working together they could render immense services both to the rejuvenated Turkey and themselves. He fully shared this view and it was with the greatest pleasure that he had heard of the advance to be made to Turkey by the cooperation of British, German and French financiers. He had, he added, expressed his satisfaction to you on this point through Count Metternich.

He also said that he had been quite delighted with Mr. Asquith's speech at the Guildhall,([2]) which had been in his opinion "quite perfect." It had given the greatest satisfaction throughout Germany.

He also paid a great tribute to Count Metternich's services. He said, after a few humorous remarks with regard to the less brilliant side of his character, that through

([1]) [*v. infra*, pp. 201–26, Nos. 125–42.]
([2]) [*v.* report in the *Times* of November 10, 1908.]

M 3

all the various differences of opinion and passing misunderstandings between the two countries, Count Metternich's despatches had always been moderate and impartial, and that he had always written "like a gentleman." I should agree with him, he knew, if I could go through the Archives of their Foreign Office.

Prince Bülow spoke at some length and in a very depressed tone of the present crisis in Germany. He said that the Emperor meant so well, but the fact was that, as Bismarck had said, there was no longer room for absolutism in Germany. Parliamentary Government was, with their countless parties, impossible, but what people clamoured for and meant to have was Constitutional Government. Germany was intensely monarchical and this crisis, with its unusually hot outcry against the Sovereign, would, he hoped, pass as other similar crises had passed; but nevertheless the present feeling against the personal influence of the Emperor in public affairs was very strong, stronger than it had ever been before, and it caused him considerable anxiety. There must in fact be a change; he spoke feelingly on the subject, because, as I had perhaps noticed, his position as things were now, was anything but comfortable.

In speaking of the Near East he displayed considerable optimism and did not anticipate any serious trouble.([3]) "None of the great Powers want war, so war will not take place," was the line he took. Monsieur Isvolsky had told him that he would do almost anything to avoid war, but had added that it must not be forgotten that the Servians were Slavs and that if Austria-Hungary was too hard upon them, a very dangerous feeling might spring up in Russia which it might be difficult to restrain. For this reason M. Isvolsky had asked him to exercise pressure upon Austria-Hungary with a view to obtaining for Servia some territorial compensation. This request however, for many reasons, he had been compelled to absolutely refuse. Personally, however, he thought Servia would be content with very much less than she asked for, and as for her going to war, the idea was ridiculous. She had no military resources whatever. I told him that Baron d'Aehrenthal had expressed the fear to me, that if by any mischance the Conference should fall through, Servia might, notwithstanding her want of resources, risk some foolish adventure. He replied that it was possible, but not probable. He added that he himself was strongly in favour of a Conference, provided that by previous understandings between the various countries concerned, nothing was left to chance and no surprises were sprung. In the opposite case he considered that a Conference would be more likely to create, than to allay, trouble.

He lamented the unfortunate differences between M. Isvolsky and Baron d'Aehrenthal, but added that the latter had written to him that the negotiations between Vienna and St. Petersburg were proceeding fairly smoothly. The Prince then discussed at some length the incidents in connexion with the announcement of the annexation which had led to the differences between the two statesmen, and stated that personally he had been not at all offended, but rather relieved that the announcement had been made to him later than to M. Isvolsky and M. Tittoni.

He asked me whether I thought that the new régime in Turkey would last.([4]) I told him that nearly all the oriental experts with whom I had talked on the subject, were of the firm opinion that a return to the old system was now practically impossible. He said that Baron Marschall and Mr. Kiderlen-Waechter, both of whom had great experience of the East, were of this opinion, but that M. Zinowiew, the Russian Ambassador at Constantinople took an entirely different view and did not give the new régime more than a few months of existence. He added that the wish was probably father to the thought, as the Russians for many reasons preferred the old system of Turkish Government.

Prince Bülow told me also that M. Isvolsky had sounded him on the question of the Dardanelles,([5]) and that he had strongly dissuaded him from raising the question.

([3]) [For the Bosnian Crisis, *v. Gooch & Temperley*, Vol. V, pp. 356–815, chs. XL and XLI.]
([4]) [*v. Gooch & Temperley*, Vol. V, pp. 247–320, ch. XXXVIII.]
([5]) [*v. Gooch & Temperley*, Vol. V, pp. 881–2, *Subject Index, sub* Straits—Bosphorus and Dardanelles, Question of Egress and Ingress.]

He had said to him, "Turkey can stand, and has stood a great deal: the annexation of Bosnia and Herzegovina makes no real difference to her, though it may touch her *amour propre* somewhat; it is the same with Bulgaria and East Roumelia, and Crete; but touch the Dardanelles or Macedonia and you touch the very marrow of her existence, and that she will not stand without a struggle."

My visit to Prince Bülow lasted for about an hour. He talked with the greatest animation the whole time, but he looked rather harassed and worn as well he may under the present depressing circumstances.

I have, &c.
W. E. GOSCHEN.

MINUTES.

"Words—, words—, words."

E. A. C.
Nov. 16.

It was useful that Pr[in]ce Bülow deprecated raising the question of the Dardanelles.
C. H.
E. G.

No. 106.

Sir Edward Grey to Sir F. Bertie.

Private.([1])

My dear Bertie,   *Foreign Office, November* 24, 1908.

Cambon came to see me to-day about nothing in particular, and I took the opportunity of telling him what a favourable impression the French attitude during the Casablanca affair had made here; I added that I thought it must also have made an impression in Germany.

Cambon told me that the Germans were now saying that they had never asked for apologies from France. This was, of course, untrue, for the French had the German demand in writing.

Cambon considered that the line which France had taken in this affair was the only one which would keep the peace. Had France taken the same line in 1905 and not allowed Delcassé to resign, there would have been an end of the trouble in the same way. He spoke of the spirit of the Army being now very good, and generally spoke as if the French were quite prepared to defend themselves.

He then went on to say that he heard from his Naval Attaché that we should be prepared for an informal discussion as to the form which Naval co-operation should take, if war broke out, just as there had been a discussion about Military co-operation in 1905.([2])

I told him this was the first I had heard of any such idea. I had always assumed that our Admiralty had considered the matter, and might even have spoken informally to the French Naval Attaché; but certainly no proposal had originated with me, the idea had not been mentioned to me before.

Cambon then told me that Haldane, in the course of a conversation with some one connected with the French Embassy, had dropped a remark to the effect that what had been done as regards Military matters in 1905 should be done now with regard to Naval matters. Cambon explained to me that in the event of Military co-operation it was well understood that the chief command should be with the French General; but on the sea the chief command would be ours, and the French would like to know what we should ask of them in case of war.

I said I would speak to McKenna on the subject.

(1) [Grey MSS., Vol. 11.]
(2) [For the Anglo-French conversations of 1905–6, *v. Gooch & Temperley,* Vol. III, ch. XX, pp. 169–203, *passim,* and pp 438–40, *App.* D.]

We had some conversation about the Near East. I expressed the opinion that it was for Austria to find some means of reconciling Turkey, Servia, and Montenegro to what she had done. If Austria could come to some satisfactory arrangement with them, she might feel sure that the Powers would agree to sanction the arrangement at the Conference. Then Austria could waive the point of form, and no longer insist that her action was "indiscutable."

Yours sincerely,
E. GREY.

I also mentioned to Cambon that I thought the King ought to visit Berlin next year. The German Emperor had wished it to be this year, but we had put it off. As, however, the Germans had a fixed idea that all the King's visits were made for the purpose of ringing Germany in, it was desirable that he should make one visit, which could not be so construed and might counteract the impression.

Haldane tells me that Repington or some unauthorized person pressed him on the point of Naval co-operation. He replied that such matters were for the Ambassador and Foreign Secretary, not for him, to open. This is all the foundation for the report that he had instigated it.

E. G.

No. 107.

Sir F. Bertie to Sir Edward Grey.

Private.([1])
My dear Grey,   *British Embassy, Paris, December 4, 1908.*

Clemenceau related to me yesterday evening that at . . . . dinner . . . . on the 23rd of last month he sat next to . . . . who drew him on the subject of Franco-German relations. . . . . nevertheless desired him to speak his mind. He then told . . . . that a Latin race such as the French took always a long time to recover from defeat. France had suffered a crushing defeat in 1870–1. She had embarked on war without any materials for the contest except men, and without thought or plans. Germany had made every preparation for years beforehand; but twice during the war there had been opportunities when, if they had been known to the French, the German successes would have been turned into disasters. One of these occasions was at Versailles when the French could have raised the siege of Paris and cut off the communications of the German army. The French army was very different now to what it was then, and France had recovered from her defeat. She now had confidence in herself and was prepared to defend herself. The French were a peaceful people. They did not want glory. They had had plenty under Napoleon I. They had a horror of war for they had the bitter recollections of 1870–1. They required peace in order as a democracy to carry out great social reforms and they wished to remain on good terms with every one, but Germany must not tread on France's corns (Il ne faut pas qu'on nous marche sur les pieds) for France would take up the challenge, and Germany would have a united people to oppose her. If victories favoured the French arms what would happen in Germany which was a conglomeration of different States not all of the same religion and not all with identic interests, made into an Empire as the result of a successful war abroad by Bismarck, an Empire without a history or traditions and perhaps ready to dissolve again into Separate States? The Emperor William I had warned his grandson to be careful always to do his best to avoid a war with France for the German victories had been due to long and laborious preparations

([1]) [Grey MSS., Vol. 11. This conversation took place with a highly distinguished person of a State neutral in the war of 1914, whose name and that of the host are omitted, as they have no bearing on the matter.]

and it could not be expected that the French would be so unready a second time as they had been in 1870. . . . .

Clemenceau went on to say to me that all Governments desired peace but they were all preparing for war, and the increase in racial animosities and the general feeling of unrest all the world over were very great dangers. He believed the Emperor of Austria to be a very honest straightforward Sovereign, but there did not seem to be any one of his subjects sufficiently intelligent and courageous to point out to him the danger of Aehrenthal's proceedings. In Austria it appeared to be thought that he had made a great and successful coup by the annexation of Bosnia and Herzegovina.

Lord Roberts' speech in the House of Lords respecting the Army([2]) is much discussed in France, and it is thought that the result of it *must* be to make the British public see the necessity of having military forces sufficient not only to resist invasion, but able to spare such an army for operations on the Continent as would be of really important assistance to France if attacked by Germany. It is not believed that we have now or will have such forces unless our system be changed.

Yours sincerely,
FRANCIS BERTIE.

MINUTE.

There is force in what M. Clemenceau said, but of course he said what it was wholesome to have repeated to the German Emperor.

E. G.

MINUTE BY KING EDWARD.

M. Clemenceau's remarks to . . . . were excellent and very much to the point though possibly not very conciliatory.

E.R.

([2]) [*v. Parl. Deb.*, 4*th Ser.*, Vol. 196, pp. 1679–96. The debate took place on November 23.]

No. 108.

Sir E. Goschen to Sir Edward Grey.

F.O. 371/463.
43494/43494/08/18.
(No. 528.) Confidential.
Sir,

Berlin, D. December 10, 1908.
R. December 14, 1908.

I have the honour to report that I had a long conversation with Prince Bülow this evening.([1]) He told me that he had made a speech in the Reichstag in the afternoon on the subject of the limitation of naval armaments. He himself had every reason, from the point of view of there being many better ways of spending money, to be of the opinion that the less outlay on the building of ships the better. For that reason they would never build more ships than were absolutely necessary for defensive purposes. The number of ships required for this purpose was represented by their Naval Programme, which was now a law passed by the Reichstag and the Bundesrat and sanctioned by the Emperor. Therefore like all laws it had to be carried out. I said that we also thought that there were better ways of spending money, but that we had also our programme with which he was acquainted. This

([1]) [For Prince Bülow's brief account of this conversation, *v. G.P.* XXVIII, p. 24.]

was no law, but it was the will of the nation, which would most certainly be carried out. Our programme was of course under certain circumstances open to modification, but that depended on others more than ourselves. Prince Bülow said that he quite understood what I meant, but that I on my part could understand that the German programme as fixed by law would be most difficult if not impossible of modification. He had explained both to the Reichstag and to the Emperor with whom he had had an audience in the morning, that any international agreement with regard to the limitation of naval armaments was fraught with almost insuperable technical difficulties. How was the scale to be fixed on which the proportions of all the different navies were to be calculated? How would it be possible to lay down a fixed rule, when interests, alliances and ententes, not to speak of types of ships and new inventions, were all liable to change? To arrange a fixed scale for all the Sea Powers, one would have to have the power of seeing into the future. No! The more he thought of it the more difficulties such an idea seemed to offer. Things would have to go on as they were, and Germany could only hope that the conviction would be eventually gained that she would certainly not pass in shipbuilding the limits of what was required for her defence. He added that I would read the account of his speech to-morrow and that I would see that he had been careful not to even mention England. "One more thing I must say while on this subject, which is that there is not a man in Germany, beyond those who are qualifying for a madhouse, who dreams that our fleet is being built up for the purpose of invading England, and has the wish that it should be so."

I may mention, in parenthesis, that Colonel Trench attended a lecture last night in which the talk was of nothing else than the best means of carrying out such an invasion.

Prince Bülow further said that it was the idea that people in England, notwithstanding their earnest protestations, believed that the objective of the German Navy was eventually to be Great Britain, that had shocked the Emperor William into the statements published in the Daily Telegraph. He regretted that these statements had been made and published, as they had been generally misunderstood both here and elsewhere, but there was no possible doubt but that they truly represented the Emperor's state of mind. "His Majesty and all his subjects, myself among the first, desire nothing but the best possible relations with England, and people who say otherwise do not know what they are talking about."

I have repeated to you Prince Bülow's words as they were said to me in the pleasant and agreeable manner which is peculiarly his own, but I must admit his account of the friendly sentiments felt towards England by this country do [sic] not quite coincide with what I hear from others of his countrymen who are known to entertain those friendly sentiments.

Turning to other subjects Prince Bülow informed me that he had seen Count Witte the other day who had told him that one of the great dangers of the present situation was that the revolutionary party in Russia actually desired and would do all in their power to push on, a war. Not from love of their Slav brethren, or from any worthy or patriotic motive, but simply in the hope that Russia might be beaten and that a situation might so be brought about which would be favourable to their own designs. Prince Bülow said that that was a point which had not occurred to him, and that he considered Count Witte's remark rather ominous. On the other hand he had reason to believe and he sincerely hoped that the belief was well founded, that the note([2]) which the Austro-Hungarian Government had just sent to St. Petersburg, was of a conciliatory nature and would help to smooth the way to a Conference. "Only," he added, "it is of course not to be expected that the Austro-Hungarian Government will move a hairsbreadth from her contention that the annexation is (? not)([3]) to be made the subject of discussion."

([2]) [This no doubt refers to the Austro-Hungarian *Aide mémoire* of December 8, printed in *Gooch & Temperley*, Vol. V, p. 541. *cp.* also *O-U.A.*, Vol, I, pp. 565–6.]
([3]) [Added by Sir Edward Grey.]

As regards the negotiations between Austria-Hungary and Turkey he said that he was of opinion that the Austro-Hungarian Government should for the moment disregard the boycott in their communications to the Ottoman Government, and find some good basis on which the negotiations could proceed. Then the boycott movement would disappear of itself. I hastened to express my concurrence with that opinion and ventured to say that it would be an excellent thing if he could advise the Austro-Hungarian Government in that sense. He only laughed however and said that he did not know how his advice would be taken. It appears to me however that it is by no means certain that he has not given this advice.

In concluding this long conversation he reiterated his pleasure that under the present change of system in Turkey there was nothing to prevent England and Germany from working harmoniously, side by side in that country, and calling up Herr von Schoen he asked him to take an opportunity some day of showing me Herr von Marschall's despatches on that subject.

I have, &c.
W. E. GOSCHEN.

No. 109.

Sir E. Goschen to Sir C. Hardinge.

F.O. 371/461.
44853/28481/08/18.
Private.

My dear Hardinge,   *Berlin, December* 11, 1908.

Only just a line as I have been working on Bülow's speech up to the last moment —it is so inconsiderate of statesmen to make speeches on the afternoon before the messenger—and also because I hope to get home very shortly after you receive this letter. But I want to tell you at once that Seckendorf came to me again yesterday and talked about the Royal visit to Berlin in a much more enthusiastic tone than on the last occasion. He now thinks it will do a great deal of good and contribute a great deal towards raising the Emperor out of the unpopularity in which recent events have landed him. "And he wants encouragement" said Seckendorf. He expressed the hope that the Emperor's birthday might be the date chosen for the visit as it would imply a great compliment and be regarded as an act of great friendliness. I told him that I didn't know anything about the date but that I imagined that the visit would take place rather later. I wondered whether he was sent to "tâter le terrain."

I dined with Bülow last night and he really out-Bülowed Bülow. He was perfectly splendid. He was in great spirits. I imagine because he had been received by the Emperor in the morning. For ever since the audience after the "Interview" debate the Emperor has left him severely alone. People have commented very much on this and I believe Bülow himself was getting rather nervous. It has been accounted for of course by the Emperor's indisposition but in the meantime other people have been received by His Majesty all along and not Bülow. I asked the latter after the Emperor's health; he told me he was better—much better even, but that recent events had depressed him exceedingly and that his low spirits had evidently retarded his recovery from what had been really a simple cold.

Of course people here (and I know so few) are very careful what they say and it is difficult to ascertain the truth about the Emperor's present state of health but I have heard vague reports which go a little beyond Bülow's expression of "low spirits." Findlay's account is very interesting and I should think contains a good deal of the truth.

You will see in a despatch from me a full account of my conversation with Bülow last night. I wonder while he is talking whether he momentarily believes what he is saying. He is so convincing and speaks with such a glorious air of sincerity that it really looks as if he did. One would think to hear him talk that England possessed nowhere in the world a greater admirer or a sincerer friend, and yet!

On my saying goodbye to him and thanking him for his most excellent dinner, he said " now remember, I am always at your disposal. You have only to telephone and I will see you at any time; it is only by meeting frequently and talking over things together that we can get to that personal and friendly understanding which is so advantageous in the transaction of affairs." I think he would be rather surprised if I took him at his word if what Cambon and Pansa tell me about the difficulty of seeing him is correct. But I think I know why he said all this to me.

Personally I don't think that Germany will be unfaithful to Austria-Hungary in the Near Eastern crisis. There are, it is true, plenty of indications that Aehrenthal's disastrous policy meets with considerable disapproval in Germany—but from that attitude to open infidelity is a long step. Bülow's declarations of unalterable fidelity to Austria-Hungary have been categorical and explicit and have always been received with enthusiastic applause; I think that even he would find it difficult to change now. But he is as supple as they are made and one never knows what he may do. On both occasions when I have seen him he has rather shaken his head over Aehrenthal's action—but he has always said at the same time that he was obliged to support him. What he says to Aehrenthal I don't know but I certainly gathered from the way he spoke last night that he *had* advised him to disregard the boycott and square Turkey by some accceptable financial proposal.

I am so much obliged for your last interesting letter and am hoping that you are enjoying your hard earned shoot.

I am only coming over for a few days—say eight or even ten—but certainly not more.

Yours very sincerely,
W. E. GOSCHEN.

No. 110.

Sir Edward Grey to Count de Salis.

F.O. 371/463.
44600/44600/08/18.
(No. 338.)

Sir, *Foreign Office, December 18, 1908.*

I remarked to Count Metternich to-day that Prince Bülow had stated that no proposals had been made to Germany by us with regard to Naval expenditure.[1]

This might be technically correct, but it must not be forgotten that we had for some time past expressed ourselves ready to compare our Navy Estimates with the German ones, and to discuss them with a view to reduction. This had been expressed in conversations between Count Metternich and me, and also in what Sir Charles Hardinge had said during the King's visit to Kronberg.

Count Metternich remembered this, but remarked that what had been said did not amount to an actual proposal.

I told him that of course we had not made any actual proposal, because we were always met by the statement that German Naval expenditure did not depend upon ours, but was fixed by Law.

Count Metternich said this was so, but the German Naval programme would not be increased. Germany's main consideration was her Army, just as our main consideration was our Navy, and financial circumstances would not allow of an increase in the Naval programme. It might even be that a desire might make itself

[1] [Count Metternich's report is apparently that in *G.P.* XXVIII, pp. 33–5.]

felt, in deference to these considerations, to postpone the laying down of a battle-ship in some year.

I explained to him that our position was that we must build more "Dreadnaughts" [sic] as otherwise in a few years the German Navy would have an actual superiority over ours with regard to vessels of this class. But we should make it clear that what we did depended upon the pace at which the German Naval programme was carried out. For instance, it might very well be the case that early next year we should get Parliament to authorise the building of a certain number of additional "Dreadnaughts," some to be laid down in the early part of the year, some in the summer, and some in the autumn; but, should we find that Germany was not ordering as many ships as had been anticipated, we should at any moment be ready to say to Parliament that, in view of this fact, we proposed not to proceed with some of the ships which had been voted.

I observed to Count Metternich that a reduction of this kind even if made without any agreement between us, and without anything which could be construed, however remotely, as interference with each other's Naval Estimates, would have a good moral effect, not only in Germany and England, but throughout the world. For the whole world was now watching the rivalry between German and English shipbuilding, and if it became apparent that this rivalry was diminishing, this would be taken as real evidence that neither nation cherished hostile intentions against the other.

As Count Metternich once again repeated that Germany built ships solely for the protection of her own interest, I pointed out to him that the other European nations were either not building any "Dreadnaughts" or else building them very slowly, and it was therefore the carrying out of the German programme which necessarily determined the size of our own programme.

[I am, &c.]
E. G[REY].

II.—THE VISIT OF KING EDWARD TO CRONBERG.

[ED. NOTE.—The text of the following memorandum is taken from the Royal Archives at Windsor. The greater part of it is printed in Sir Sidney Lee: *King Edward VII* (1927), II, pp. 616–7; and it is there stated that the memorandum was sent to the King by Sir Edward Grey in view of the forthcoming meeting with the Emperor William at Cronberg. An earlier memorandum of July 31, 1908, quoted by Sir Sidney Lee on p. 615, is not to be found in the Royal Archives. Copies of both memoranda are among the Hardinge MSS. (Vol. IV of 1908), and the text of the earlier one is reproduced from that source, *infra*, p. 779, App. III. It is dated July 31, 1908, instead of July 23, as stated by Sir Sidney Lee.]

No. 111.

Memorandum by Sir Edward Grey.(¹)

Foreign Office, August 6, 1908.

The present and future relations between Germany and England have become in a remarkable degree the subject of attention and pre-occupation not only in the two countries themselves, but in Europe generally.

There is nothing in the relations between the two Governments to cause this anxiety. For the last two years the diplomatic relations between the two Governments have never been difficult. Various subjects such as the North Sea, the Bagdad Railway, Macedonia, several incidents in connection with South Africa etc. have been discussed between them: on some, such as the North Sea, agreement has been easy, and even on those where there has been difference of opinion the discussion has been conducted with frankness and has not led to friction or ill humour. It

(¹) [The copy of this memorandum preserved in the Hardinge MSS. is headed "Mem[orandu]m given to the King and Sir C. Hardinge for their guidance at interview with the German Emperor at Cronberg."]

is therefore not in the dealings of the two Governments with each other that any cause for uneasiness has originated lately.

Nor is it to be found in any deep rooted dislike between the peoples. The stay of the Emperor in England last year was popular here, the reception of such visits as those of Burgomasters and Pastors has been easy and friendly, and the same is believed to be true of corresponding British visits to Germany.

But all this has not availed to quiet apprehension, for the real difficulty is not in the present relations of the two countries, but in a certain anxiety as to their probable relations with each other a few years hence.

A section of opinion in each country speaks and writes as if Germany and England were bound to entertain, increasingly as years go on, unfriendly designs upon each other. In neither country does this opinion appear to be encouraged, on the contrary it is deprecated by the authorities; but it persists, and has come now to found itself upon the rivalry in naval expenditure, the growth of which is now taken by public opinion as the test of what the prospective relations of the two countries are likely to be. Should naval expenditure increase apprehension will be intensified; if the expenditure slackened apprehension would at once diminish.

The British Government would not think of questioning the right of Germany to build as large a Navy as she thinks necessary for her own purposes nor would they complain of it. But they have to face the fact that at the present rate of construction the German Naval programme will in a very few years place the German Navy in a position of superiority to the British as regards the most powerful type of battle ship.

This will necessitate a new British programme of construction to be begun next year. It will be demanded by public opinion; it must avowedly be accounted for solely by reference to the German programme; for the other nations of Europe are either not adding appreciably to their navies or have no navies of importance; and nations outside Europe are too distant or have not armies sufficient to threaten the independence of Great Britain.

Whereas, if the German navy became superior or even attained such a relative proportion to the British as to enable it at an untoward moment to secure command of the sea for a few days, Great Britain would be not only defeated but occupied and conquered; Germany does not run so great a risk as this from any superiority of the British fleet, for the British army is so inferior to the German in size that occupation and conquest are out of the question. Without therefore attributing any sinister motive to the building of the German fleet it is a paramount necessity to increase British naval expenditure to meet the German programme, though we fear that this may be taken as a sign of increasing rivalry and distrust and though we regret anything which is likely to be a barrier to better feeling.

On the other hand a slackening of naval expenditure on both sides would at once be followed by a great rebound in public opinion towards friendly feeling and security. It would be welcomed not in Germany and England alone but everywhere as evidence of pacific intentions, of good understanding and confidence between the two countries. Rightly or wrongly a great part of the world has come of late years to concentrate attention upon the relations between England and Germany, to look in them for the chief indication of whether the peace of the world is likely to be disturbed, and to estimate this by their rivalry in naval expenditure. If this rivalry diminished, still more if the two countries came to any agreement about it, there would be increased confidence throughout the world, a general sense of security such as no other event could produce and the Emperor and King would stand together before the world as the great peacemakers.

It is not desired to force any discussion of this question even in private, if this is deprecated by the Emperor. but the subject is too important not to be mentioned, when the prospect of a visit of the King to Berlin next year is likely to be discussed.

No. 112.

Sir F. Lascelles to Sir Edward Grey.

F.O. 371/461.
28479/26341/08/18.
(No. 347.) Confidential.   Homburg, D. August 12, 1908.
Sir,   R. August 17, 1908.

Prince and Princess Frederick Charles of Hesse were kind enough to invite me to dine and sleep at Schloss Friedrichshof on the night of the 10th Instant in view of the arrival of the King on the following morning.(¹) The Emperor had arrived earlier in the day and, after dinner, honoured me with a conversation of great length.

His Majesty complained bitterly, and with that freedom of language in which he often indulges in his conversations with me, of the suspicion with which he and Germany were regarded in England. If any of his officers went to England and took photographs or made sketches they were at once accused of spying and even the number of German waiters in England created alarm, because they were supposed to be under military control and prepared to join the ranks of the German army as soon as an invasion should take place. All this was, of course, absurd nonsense, and it almost seemed that the English people had gone off their heads, and required something in the shape of a Bogey man upon whom to vent their suspicion. Formerly it was France or Russia, now it was Germany who was to be feared and distrusted. This was all the more disappointing as he had hoped that his visit to England and more especially the speech which he had delivered in the Guildhall would have been taken as a proof of his pacific intentions. That speech had been very carefully prepared in consultation with his Ministers. Every expression in it had been carefully weighed, and he had intended that it should be regarded as a programme of policy which he had definitely adopted. It had produced a very good impression at the time, but now it had been "thrown to the winds" and had been replaced by suspicious animosity.

I replied that I had perfect confidence in His Majesty's pacific intentions, but that I had found it impossible to persuade many of my countrymen with whom I had spoken that the German Fleet did not constitute a menace to England. When I argued that Germany having become a great commercial and colonial Power, naturally desired a Fleet to protect her commercial and colonial interests, I was met by the reply that her Fleet, which had now become a powerful one, was always kept in home waters, "ready to pounce."

The Emperor said that it was simply ridiculous to talk about the Power of the German Fleet in comparison with that of Great Britain. He believed that the British Public and indeed perhaps some departments of His Majesty's Government were deliberately kept in ignorance of the maritime strength of Great Britain. The figures were, however, available and His Majesty sent his aide de camp for a copy of the German publication "Nauticus," which he was good enough to give me. On p. 55 of this work, with which Captain Dumas has supplied the Admiralty, and a further copy of which His Majesty presented to Sir Charles Hardinge, there is a diagram showing the strength in Line of Battle ships of the different nations up to 1909. Germany would then have 24 Line of Battle ships to England's 62. In 1920 when Germany's naval programme would be completed, she would have 38 or perhaps 40 line of battle ships and England would probably about that time have about 75. With regard to my remark that the German ships were always kept in home waters His Majesty said that he could tell me confidentially that the reason was that he had been warned from England that the feeling was so strong against the German Fleet that if the ships were seen cruising

(¹) [King Edward, accompanied by Sir Charles Hardinge, arrived at Cronberg on August 11. cp. Sir Sidney Lee: King Edward VII (1927), Vol. II, pp. 617-20.]

about the Channel and the Atlantic and passing the Straits of Dover public opinion might become dangerously excited and that it was better to keep them out of sight. Now however, that an overwhelming British force had been concentrated in the North Sea, His Majesty thought there could be no objection to his ships cruising in the Atlantic, and he had sent them to the Canaries. He hoped that this would be taken as a proof that he had no fear of being attacked during their absence. It was however really time that something should be done to dissipate the suspicion entertained in England with regard to the completion of the German Navy, which had been sanctioned by law in 1900, and he was thinking of publishing his letter to Lord Tweedmouth[2] in which he fully exposed the German point of view. I replied that, although from what His Majesty had told me on a previous occasion there was nothing in the letter which required secrecy, I always deprecated the publication of a private correspondence.

I had an opportunity of giving Sir Charles Hardinge a brief account of my conversation with the Emperor. He urged me to dissuade His Majesty from publishing his letter to Lord Tweedmouth on the ground that if it were published a demand would be raised for the publication of the reply, which would be most undesirable. I therefore took the opportunity of a further conversation with which His Majesty honoured me, to point out that if his letter were published, it would be impossible to resist the demand for the publication of Lord Tweedmouth's reply, and the outcry that would be raised if it became known that the Naval Estimates had been communicated to His Majesty before being submitted to Parliament would be such as to defeat the object which His Majesty had in view. His Majesty said that under these circumstances it would be better not to publish anything.

I have, &c.
FRANK C. LASCELLES.

MINUTE.

This copy of "Nauticus" will be examined; it may be that some reply to it should be drawn up in the Admiralty.

E. G.

(2) [*v. G.P.* XXIV, pp. 32–5. *cp. supra*, pp. 132–3, Nos. 82–3.]

No. 113.

Sir F. Lascelles to Sir Edward Grey.

F.O. 371/461.
28474/28474/08/18.
(No. 343.) Confidential.
Sir,

Berlin, D. *August* 14, 1908.
R. *August* 17, 1908.

I have the honour to forward, herewith, a despatch, as marked in the margin, which I have received from Colonel Trench, Military Attaché to this Embassy, relating to his conversation with the Emperor at Cronberg.

I have, &c.
(For Sir Frank Lascelles),
J. DE SALIS.

Enclosure in No. 113.

Colonel Trench to Sir F. Lascelles.

(No. 106.) Confidential.
Sir,

Berlin, *August* 12, 1908.

While awaiting the arrival of His Majesty the King at Cronberg yesterday, His Majesty the Emperor did me the honour of speaking to me for a quarter of an hour or so, as well as on three other occasions, including his arrival on Monday and his departure yesterday.

The Emperor, who was wearing German uniform, expressed great pleasure at the long journey made by Count Zeppelin's balloon, and especially at the navigators having been able to find their way about the country at night. He drew my attention to the fact that the destruction of the airship was due to the hostility of the elements and to no structural defect, and told me how their Royal Highnesses the Crown Princess of Greece and Princess Frederic Charles of Hesse had followed the balloon by night, crossed the Rhine on a crowded pont, and finally been able to inspect it *en route* during a temporary stoppage for repairs. The Emperor seemed greatly pleased with the proof of patriotic feeling shown by the German people in spontaneously subscribing enormous sums to replace the lost balloon. He said: "They were so excited about it in Alsace that the Strasburg Cathedral tower nearly tumbled down. I wonder what your friends think of that!" Passing to the way in which the weal of the German people had grown in recent years, he said: "People don't know how great it is owing to it all remaining in the country. Your friends and allies are the greatest money-lenders in the world; they put all their money into stockings, and then when money is wanted they always have it to lend. They are really bankers; they don't put their money into industries. They pay enormous subsidies to shipping lines, but as they don't produce anything their ships travel empty and the money is all thrown away. In Germany, on the contrary, the money is put into business in the country, and not only is it doubly productive, but the mercantile marine is usefully employed, and grows and grows. Look at Tsingtau! Last year there were 900 ships; and that is the growth of only ten years. That's because we have not made it a Colony, and the Chinese flag flies alongside the German one. The Chinese Mandarins see that we want to benefit China as much as ourselves. Look at what we have done in afforestation alone. We have professional foresters there making experiments with all kinds of trees, not only from Europe, but also from Japan. . . . . (1) When Henry was there they were waist-high; now you can hide in them. . . . . Mandarins come from all parts of China to see our nurseries. . . . . The Governor sent from Mukden to borrow a forester. . . . . We lent him one, but we couldn't spare him for all the time they wanted to keep him. . . . . What other nation has tried to cover the plains of Manchuria with trees? And look how we are developing the country round Peking and round Tsingtau. We have no river at Tsingtau, and so there's no bar. We were wise enough in the beginning to make long piers for ships to unload at, and with the railways that are being opened Tsingtau will become the port of Peking, and before long one of the biggest ports of the Far East. Already it's a fashionable watering-place, and your people come there to bathe, and the Japanese come down there to learn about things. We treat it as a 'Musterhaus' (show-room), where we show the Orientals 'this is how we build houses'; this is how we make cranes, ploughs, and so on. And so we get large orders and our commerce benefits. I tell you you're going to have a jolly shindy before long with those allies of yours! What a mistake that was! You're already beginning to feel the effects. The whole East is excited; look at the trouble you're having in Bombay. That never happened before. And then your Colonies won't have them at any price. One of my naval officers reported to me a conversation with the Premier of New Zealand. He said, 'Send us German families, but no yellow men. We won't let them into the country.' You're going to have a lot of difficulties. The Oriental is being excited everywhere. Look at Turkey. Of course we're very glad that Turkey should have a Constitution, but everything is changed now; if any European Power says anything they'll say, 'Please, we are a modern State with a Constitution; and nobody can say anything.' What's the cause of all this? That visit to Reval! At once up went the whole thing! The Turks said, 'England is no longer the friend of Turkey as in the old days of Sir Stratford de Redcliffe, and now she's going to be friends with Russia.' And it's not going to stop there. They'll want a Constitution in

(1) [The omission marks here and elsewhere in this document are in the original.]

Egypt—and in India, too. You bring Baboos to England and educate them at the Universities. That's all very well; they learn a lot of good things, but you don't know all they learn or the use they are going to make of it. One of these days instead of crying out about the German fleet you'll be very glad for it to come and help you."

Referring to South Africa and Simon Copper's misbehaviour, the Emperor said: " Now they'll have to do something. . . . . I had the other day such an interesting report made me by Captain von Hagen. He looked so well with his breast covered with decorations all with swords."*

Speaking of the Imperial manœuvres, His Majesty described the way last year the opposing commanders had to organize their own supply systems, and said that this year they were going a great deal further, and that no special ideas were going to be issued, only general ideas. " The Commanders will have to do their own reconnoitring, and if one of them is badly served by his cavalry—well, he'll get beaten. What's the use of making a lot of suppositions? Let them find out how things really are, and then in war time everything will seem much easier."

His Majesty said he was sorry Captain Dumas had gone, and that his officers had got on well with him and liked him.

The Emperor's manner while talking to me was very gracious, and he condescended to " chaff " me about several little personal matters. He gave me the impression that he wished to convince me of the great wealth and resources of Germany as well as of the high state of training and preparedness of the army. He seemed to take the greatest interest in the popular movements in Egypt and in India, and in the question of yellow labour in the British Colonies. When speaking of the King's visit to Reval and of Turkey he spoke very fast, with less than his usual facility of expression in English—with even the occasional misuse of a word and the interpolation of German expression. This is no doubt a trivial matter, but it is the first time I have noticed it. I may be mistaken, but I gathered the impression that His Majesty was feeling strongly on some of the points on which he touched. The expression of sympathy with the Turkish constitutional movement seemed made, however, rather *en passant* and without conviction.(²)

I have, &c.
F. TRENCH, *Colonel,*
General Staff.

MINUTE BY KING EDWARD.

The Emperor evidently wished to impress on the " gallant Colonel " that there was only one country wh[ich] excelled in civilization and practical benefits for mankind! and that was Germany.

E.R.

* This officer accompanied Major Wilson when the Cape Police relieved Germany of the edoutable Bondelzwart leader, Morenga, and he seems to have received some of the credit and gratitude which Germany owes England and Major Wilson. On my referring to the marked difference between Morenga and the other Hottentot leaders, the Emperor exclaimed : " I should think so; he was the son of an English officer." This is surely an error; Morenga was much blacker than a Hottentot, and his father was believed to be a Herero, *i.e.*, a Bantu. [F. T.]

(²) [The report of a conversation between the German Emperor and Sir Frank Lascelles on this subject on August 10, 1908, is given in *Gooch & Temperley*, Vol. V, pp. 310–1, No. 216.]

No. 114.

Sir F. Cartwright to Sir Edward Grey.

F.O. 371/461.
28599/26341/08/18C.
(No. 89.)   *Munich,* D. *August* 14, 1908.·
Sir,   R. *August* 17, 1908.

The Royal interview at Cronberg is over and a change has occurred in the
tone of the German press with regard to it. For some time past the newspapers
were informing their readers that the Cronberg interview would be an interesting
one as matters of importance would be discussed there and arrangements would be
made for a visit to be paid by King Edward to Berlin. This visit, it was hoped,
would be the first sign of a real desire on the part of Great Britain to come to an
understanding with Germany on serious lines. During the last few days, and
especially since the interview is over, the newspapers continue to assert still more
decidedly that the visit to Berlin will take place very soon, but at the same time
the general tone assumed by the press is one of considerable indifference as to the
importance of such Royal meetings.

On the eve of the King's arrival at Cronberg, the Frankfort Gazette expressed
the belief that the chief result of the Royal meeting would be a certain *détente* in
the nervosity shown on both sides of the Channel, a nervosity which has been
growing visibly in England during the summer and in Germany ever since the
Reval meetings, although in the latter case there was no real justification for it.
The trouble is that on either side mistrust exists which is due in great part to mutual
misunderstandings; the Frankfort organ, alluding to the assertions so frequently
made in the British press that the German newspapers too often seem to give vent
to the ambitious views of "parvenus," says that this reproach is not without some
justificat⸍ ⸗; for whilst Great Britain and other States pursue their policy quietly
and without bluster, Germany is too apt to call attention loudly to herself and this
in an aggressive tone. The result is that by always calling attention to her might,
foreign nations begin to believe that Germany is in great part boasting of possessing
a might which is really weaker than she would like others to perceive it to be.
The "Frankfort Gazette" concludes with these words:—"Even if the meeting,
which takes place to-morrow is merely the outcome of family affection and of a desire
of Uncle and Nephew to see each other, yet the effect will perhaps be a soothing
and calming one in many quarters: people may think that this is not very much,
but yet this much is not to be despised."

It would be wearisome if I were to give you extracts from the newspapers of
every shade which all express their views with regard to this event, but I will try
to summarise for you as briefly as possible the general drift of their comments.

They say that a slight improvement has taken place in Anglo-German relations
of late and that this is in great part due to the improved personal relations between
King Edward and the Kaiser. The danger of the situation has been in part removed
by this personal reconciliation, but the *détente* which has ensued from this, although
not unimportant, should not be over-estimated. In German public opinion King
Edward represents in himself the policy which endeavours by every kind of
diplomatic combination to render unvulnerable and undisputable the supremacy of
Great Britain, especially at sea. This policy leaves Germany out of count, and in
doing so renders the policy itself anti-German, although by Royal and other meetings
and demonstrations this disagreeable fact can in part be glossed over but cannot
be entirely hidden from the public. The assertion that such a policy is peaceful is
deceptive for it means that Germany finds herself at every turn face to face with
an overwhelmingly powerful diplomatic combination which takes little heed of her
interests. In many quarters here it is thought that in England too much praise
is lavished on the King's policy, whereas in Germany it is unfortunate that too

much attention is being called to the apparent success of this policy, whereby an alarming impression is produced in this country for which there is no justification. Whether Great Britain's understandings with France and Russia serve her interests best, may be well doubted, say the Germans, and in their opinion these interests would be better safeguarded by a continuance of that traditional friendship which once for so long existed between Germany and England. The present British policy of endless *ententes* is one which disturbs the tranquillity of the world, for they irritate those who do not take part in them, while they cannot be seriously depended upon by those who do. The newspapers here continually harp upon the influence which, according to them, King Edward unconstitutionally exerts on British foreign policy; His Majesty is accused of using his influence to oppose the views and policy of the great majority of the present Liberal Cabinet who would ask for nothing better than to come to a sincere understanding with Germany; the King stands in the way of this. It is frequently stated that on account of the importance of the Royal influence on British foreign policy it is necessary for Germany to watch with care every indication, such as the visit to Cronberg and the possible visit to Berlin, that there is any change in His Majesty's confidence, however slight, in the wisdom of the policy he has recently pursued. It is also interesting, they say here, to observe whether the King is beginning to show any desire to draw closer to Germany. On this point the Munich "Neueste Nachrichten" says: "The meeting between the Monarchs at Cronberg may be taken as a satisfactory sign. The only question is whether after the meeting British policy will remain the same as before; it must be, however, clearly understood, putting aside all empty compliments and official assurances, that if no change takes place in this respect, and that if influential persons at the British Court, in the Cabinet and at the Admiralty do all in their power to stimulate the hatred of Germany with a view to creating in England a public opinion in favour of an increased naval programme, then all we can say is that German suspicions of England will continue to exist and that it is useless to expect any improvement in the correct but very cool official relations between Great Britain and Germany."

In conclusion I would venture to draw your attention to the fact that all the leading newspapers are beginning to allude to the probability that the Liberal Government in England will next year bring forward a very extensive naval programme for the approval of Parliament. The prospect of this has a very disturbing effect on the equanimity of Germany and is quite eclipsing in the popular mind any satisfactory result which may arise from the Royal meeting at Cronberg. One newspaper after the other declares that if Great Britain should now begin a policy of vast ship-building, then it is no use talking of Germany entertaining friendly relations with her, for until Great Britain sincerely abandons her suspicions of this country and gives up building ships in unnecessary competition with her, there can be no friendship between the two countries. Germany wants a fair share of sea power and England is showing that she will not admit that claim; therefore till she does so, the friction between the two countries will continue to exist till a danger point is perhaps reached. When that comes, in German opinion, the blame must fall upon England.

I have, &c.
FAIRFAX L. CARTWRIGHT.

MINUTE BY KING EDWARD.

The remarks of the German Press are most unfair and misleading. If Germany ceases her extensive ship building—we shall do the same and not otherwise. It is the only chance of a real peaceful solution of the present feeling existing between England and Germany.

E.R.

No. 115.

Sir F. Lascelles to Sir Edward Grey.

F.O. 371/461.
28481/28481/08/18.
(No. 349.)   Very Confidential.   *Homburg*, D. *August* 14, 1908.
Sir,   R. *August* 17, 1908.

After the return of the two Sovereigns to the Castle of Friedrichshof on the evening of the 11th Instant, the Emperor took me aside and spoke at considerable length and with his usual exaggeration of language about the conversation he had had with Sir Charles Hardinge earlier in the day. His Majesty said that Sir Charles seemed to be as suspicious of Germany as any of his countrymen. The words which His Majesty made use of were " He seems to be as mad about Germany as any of you," and he had gone as far as to tell His Majesty that he must stop building ships. Sir Charles really did not seem to know what he was talking about, and when His Majesty showed him the table in " Nauticus," to which he had called my attention last night, he had doubted the accuracy of the figures and said " Oh, that can't be so." He had, however, no figures to quote himself, and His Majesty had presented him with his own copy of " Nauticus," which was perhaps an indiscreet proceeding as he had himself marked and annotated certain passages which struck him as being of especial interest. He hoped, however, that he had not done much harm and that Sir Charles, if he read the book, might acquire a better knowledge of the relative strength of the two navies. Sir Charles had expressed the opinion that it was perhaps a mistake for England to have constructed a " Dreadnought," but it was impossible to prevent the progress of science, and it was only natural that a country who wished to provide herself with a Fleet should seek to obtain the best type of battleship. If therefore the construction of Dreadnoughts by other nations caused embarrassment to England, she had only herself to thank for setting the example.

The Emperor dwelt at considerable length upon the fact that the German Naval Programme had been drawn up in 1900. It had thus been 8 years before the world, and it had not been and would not be increased. Why should Germany and Germany alone, although other Powers were largely increasing their naval armaments, be called upon to diminish her construction of ships? What would be said if he objected to the increase which France was now making in her Field Artillery? For many years past Germany had an enormous superiority over France in the number of Field guns. Now France had decided to bring her field Artillery up to the level of that of Germany. She had a perfect right to do so, and he could imagine the very curt reply which Prince Radolin would receive if he were to suggest to Monsieur Pichon that France should content herself with less. Why then should a demand be addressed to Germany to build fewer ships than she considered necessary?

There was another fact of which Sir Charles Hardinge appeared to be ignorant viz. that by the German Constitution the question of Peace or War was reserved for the decision of the German Emperor. It was not public opinion, it was not Parliament, it was not the Federal Council, but the Emperor himself who had to decide whether Germany should draw the sword, and it was inconceivable to him that any one in their senses could for an instant suppose that he, the grandson of Queen Victoria, whose memory he revered, the nephew of the King for whom he had a sincere affection, should ever dream of attacking England. a country to which he was personally devotedly attached. What possible advantage could he hope to gain even from a successful war against England?

On my observing that I could not believe in the outbreak of a war which would cause incalculable harm to both countries without any appreciable advantage to either, His Majesty said that the only result of such a war would be that the two countries would ruin each other to the benefit of the Americans who would promptly seize on the commerce of both. His Majesty did not believe in the possibility of war, but it was a bitter disappointment to him to find that his pacific utterances at the Guildhall last autumn would have produced so little effect, and that the suspicion of Germany generally entertained in England which he could only attribute to the necessity of the British public for a Bogey man should have been shared by a man in the position of Sir Charles Hardinge.

After dinner on the 11th Instant the Emperor had a further conversation with Sir Charles Hardinge and conferred upon him the 1st Class of the Order of the Red Eagle. I am not aware of what passed on this occasion, but, after the departure of the King from Cronberg the Emperor told me that his second conversation with Sir Charles was far more satisfactory than the first, and that Sir Charles had been good enough to say that he reposed confidence in His Majesty personally.

His Majesty said that he had been highly gratified by a proposal which the King had made to pay a visit to Berlin in the course of the next year and by his asking what time would be most convenient.(¹) This, said His Majesty, would depend entirely upon what the King wanted to do or see in Berlin. If he wished to see something of Berlin society or Court functions, it would be advisable that he should come some time in February. If he should wish to see Berlin at its best, it would be better that he should come in May when the flowering shrubs were in bloom. If he wished to see some military display, it would have to be later in the year, but he would be very welcome at any time.

I have attempted in this Despatch to report to the best of my ability the remarks which the Emperor deigned to make to me and I trust that in considering them, due allowance may be made for His Majesty's habitual exaggeration. The impression left on my mind is that the Emperor was highly gratified by the King's visit and that the relations between the two Sovereigns remained unimpaired. His Majesty no doubt expressed considerable annoyance at the suggestion that he should limit the expenditure on naval armaments, and I would suggest that it would be advisable to refrain from any further allusion to the subject. There is, I believe, a possibility of the Reichstag refusing to vote the necessary sums for carrying out the programme for the coming year, and I am informed that Prince Bülow and Herr von Schoen would be glad to find an excuse for abandoning or at all events postponing the further construction of ships, but any efforts they might make in that direction would be frustrated if it became known that England had suggested a modification of the German Naval Programme. No great Power would consent to interference on the part of a foreign country, and so sensitive a people as the Germans would certainly resent anything which could by any possibility be regarded as a semblance of dictation on the part of England.

I have, &c.
FRANK C. LASCELLES.

MINUTES.

The Emperor's attitude is what was to be expected.

I understand that it may be useful, for British parliamentary purposes, to be able to show that our renewed advances to Germany in the direction of an arrangement for the mutual limitation of armaments have been again rejected. But there can be little doubt that any persistence in bringing forward the subject will produce the worst possible effect on our relations with Germany. We had a foretaste of this when we started the discussion before the Hague conference : we very nearly arrived at a serious breach. It seems therefore regrettable that the Chancellor of the Exchequer should at an interview with a newspaper correspondent have given public and rather crude expression to the proposals for a limitation of armaments.

It seems quite certain that no responsible German statesman—with the possible exception of a second Bismarck—could carry through a policy which would involve a repeal of the German Navy Act providing for the programme of ship-construction. Nor are we left without clear indications of what view Germany would take of such a measure being urged by a foreign gov[ernmen]t. I annex extracts from German inspired papers on the subject, as given by the Times, which are very significant.(²)

It is clear that this question will require most delicate handling and that its public discussion will be full of dangers. It is therefore to be hoped that the Secretary of State will not become embarrassed by communications or utterances on this subject not specially authorized by him

(¹) [The account of King Edward's visit to Berlin is given *infra*, pp. 227–37, Nos. 143–50.]
(²) [Not reproduced.]

There is all the difference in the world between a friendly interchange of views with the Emperor or the responsible German statesmen, and a public appeal to popular sentiment in Germany.

It is not without interest to note the emperor's scorn at the idea of his decision being influenced by public opinion. It has repeatedly been pointed out here how useless it is to advance the alleged peaceful views of the general public in Germany as an argument in proof of the improbability of a conflict. The emperor's remark entirely confirms all that has been said here on the subject, though no doubt this was not H[is] M[ajesty]'s intention.

It will be interesting to scrutinize the marginal remarks in the copy of '' Nauticus '' which the Emperor apparently regrets having allowed to pass into Sir C. Hardinge's hands.

E. A. C.
Aug. 17.

The Emperor's assertion that the decision of peace or war rests with him personally is worth very little : he could not refuse to declare war if his country and Ministers demanded it.

E. G.

No. 116.

Sir C. Hardinge to Sir Edward Grey.

Private.([1])

My dear Grey, *Kimbolton, August* 15, 1908.

. . . .([2]) I will of course prepare you a full report of all that took place at Cronberg and Ischl, but it will take me two or three days to get it into shape. In the meantime I give you this short account.

The King had a very long interview with the Emperor on the morning of our arrival at Cronberg, and talked on every subject except naval armaments. He told me that he mentioned to the Emperor that he had a paper containing the views of his Gov[ernmen]t, but as the latter did not ask to see it or to know its contents he thought it more tactful not to say anything further. On hearing this, I came to the conclusion that it was all the more necessary that I should speak openly to the Emperor, and after speaking both to the Emperor and to Jenisch who was in attendance owing to Schön's illness, I came to the conclusion that it was perhaps a good thing that the King had not touched on a subject which I am sure the Emperor did not like, and after my conversations I advised the King not to raise the subject again.

When the Emperor came and talked to me after luncheon while smoking his cigar I seized an opening he gave me to broach the whole question of the German naval programme and the expenditure of both countries on naval armaments. I developed at considerable length the views contained in your two memoranda.([3]) I pointed out the inevitable consequences of the completion of the German programme on the relations between the two countries and the rivalry in naval construction that must follow. I suggested a possible friendly discussion between the two Gov[ernmen]ts and added that, being far from our wish to dictate or to have the appearance of dictating what German naval construction should be, we only wish to have evident proof that the German naval programme is being modified or deferred, for the Gov[ernmen]t to hold their hand in presenting to the House of Commons a counter programme which no Gov[ernmen]t could under such circumstances avoid doing. The Emperor assumed a most uncompromising attitude, said that the law had been passed and accepted by the country, and that no modification of the programme nor slackening of its completion could be allowed. Nor could any discussion be permitted on a question in which the national honour was involved. He affirmed that our fleet is already far above the two power standard, that next year we shall have 62 first class battleships to 24 German of the same class and that there is no necessity whatever for a programme on our part.

This was the general line he took of which I will give fuller detail in my report and Jenisch, who when I saw him had not had time to compare notes with the

---

([1]) [Grey MSS., Vol. 53.]
([2]) [The omitted paragraph of this letter is of a personal nature.]
([3]) [v. supra, pp. 173–4, No. 111, and infra, p. 779, App. III.]

Emperor, spoke to me in the same sense. I think there is no doubt that the conversation had been foreseen and the reply prepared. It is anyhow good to know where we are.

I had a further long conversation with the Emperor on other matters of less immediate importance which will be dealt with in my report.

My conversations with the Emperor of Austria and Aehrenthal were quite satisfactory and all that could be desired.

Please excuse a hasty scrawl and give me a few days to provide you with fuller information on these interesting subjects.

Y[ou]rs very sincerely,
CHARLES HARDINGE.

No. 117.

Memorandum by Sir Charles Hardinge.

Visit to the German Emperor and Emperor of Austria at Cronberg and Ischl in 1908.

Secret.
(13147*.)(¹)   [*August* 16, 1908.]

The King arrived at Cronberg at 9 A.M. on the morning of the 11th August, and was met at the station by the German Emperor and Prince and Princess Frederick Charles of Hesse.

Owing to Herr von Schön's illness, Herr von Jenisch was in attendance upon the Emperor as representative of the German Ministry for Foreign Affairs.

The meeting between the King and the German Emperor, and the intercourse which took place between their Majesties, were of a most cordial and friendly character, and could only serve to improve and cement the personal friendship between the two Sovereigns. During the course of the morning the King had a long interview with the Emperor, in which every subject of interest to England and Germany was discussed between them, with the exception of naval armaments, and mutual friendly assurances were given on both sides. The King told me that, although he touched on the question of naval expenditure, and mentioned that His Majesty's Government had given him a paper containing their views on the subject, the Emperor neither asked to see the paper nor to know its contents, and the King therefore considered that it would be more tactful on his part not to force upon the Emperor a discussion which he seemed anxious to avoid. After the very clear statements made to me later in the day by the Emperor and Herr von Jenisch, there can be no doubt that the King exercised a wise discretion in not broaching to the Emperor a subject of which the discussion was evidently unpalatable to His Majesty, and which might possibly have spoilt the happy effect of the conversation which had taken place between them.(²)

The King availed himself of the opportunity to propose to the Emperor the appointment of Sir E. Goschen as successor to Sir F. Lascelles, and the Emperor warmly welcomed the proposal, remarking that he had always entertained a feeling of

---

(¹) [This reference is used as the version of the memorandum bound in F.O. 371/461 is a revised one from which certain passages were deleted. This revised version was the one sent to the Embassies at Berlin, Paris and Vienna. The passages omitted in it are here marked with round brackets.]

(²) [*v. The Kaiser's letters to the Tsar* (1920), p. 239. There the Emperor William writes to the Emperor Nicholas on August 18, 1908, " Uncle Bertie was all sunshine at Cronberg and in very good humour. He intends visiting Berlin officially with Aunt Alix next year, date to be fixed. He also talked about Turkey, giving to understand that she was best left alone, to organize herself and to reform Macedonia herself, so that the Powers were able for the time to drop the projected reforms, which seems to relieve him visibly." For the Emperor William's report of his conversations with Sir C. Hardinge, *v. G.P.* XXIV, pp. 122–4.]

great respect for Lord Goschen, the Ambassador's late brother, and that he was just the person whom he himself would have selected. (He was anxious that the British Ambassador in Berlin should occupy the most prominent and an unassailable position in society, and that, as he knew Berlin society to be malicious, he was glad that Sir F. Cartwright's name had been withdrawn, though he had nothing to say against this distinguished diplomatist, whom he had known well and liked in the past, but had not met for several years.)

While smoking his cigar after luncheon, the Emperor did me the honour of calling me up to speak to him. In the course of a conversation on the popularity of military service in Germany, which had become an ingrained principle in the education and development of the national character of the German people, owing to the devastation and misery from which the Germans had suffered during the Thirty Years War, the Seven Years War, and the Napoleonic campaigns, but from which the British Isles had been happily spared, allusion was made to the relations existing between England and Germany, which the Emperor declared to be quite satisfactory, except for the evil results of the campaign of the yellow press in both countries.

I replied that I was sorry to be unable to share the Emperor's opinion, since there could be no concealment of the fact that a genuine apprehension was felt in England as to the reasons and intention underlying the construction of a large German fleet. This preoccupation was being felt, not in England alone, but also in Europe, where happily it remained as the only element of unrest in the international situation. No cause for disagreement existed between England and Germany, and the diplomatic relations between the two countries were perfectly friendly and natural, without the smallest cloud on the political horizon likely to cause anxiety in the future. The knowledge of these facts made it difficult for thoughtful people to reconcile the friendly assurances of the Emperor and German Government with the acceptance by the German Parliament of the extensive naval programme, which could only be realised at considerable sacrifice on the part of the German people. The execution of the German programme would necessarily entail a corresponding increase in our expenditure on naval armaments, since the naval supremacy of Great Britain had now become a cardinal principle of British policy, which no Government of whatever party could afford to ignore. Although nobody could have the right to dictate to any Power a programme of naval construction, it had been fully realised in England that, if the present German programme is completed, the German navy will, in a few years' time, be in a superior position to the British navy as regards the largest type of battle-ship, and British supremacy at sea would thus be endangered. Unless it were possible for some sort of friendly discussion to take place between the two Governments resulting in a modification or a slackening of the present rate of shipbuilding, it would be necessary for the Government next year to submit to Parliament an extensive ship-building programme and to explain how the necessity for it has arisen. There could be no doubt that Parliament would accept whatever burdens the Government might propose, but there could be no doubt that this naval rivalry between the two countries would embitter their relations to each other, and might in a few years' time lead to a very critical situation in the event of a serious, or even a trivial, dispute arising between the two countries.

The Emperor maintained that there was absolutely no cause for apprehension in England as to the German naval programme, and that no sensible person in Germany had ever thought for a moment that the German fleet was intended for an attack upon England. The English fleet had in relation to other fleets already more than a two-Power standard, since in 1909 there would be sixty-two British first-class battle-ships to twenty-four German ships of the same class. The relative proportion of the two fleets in first- and second-class cruisers was also the same. He had only to point out the composition of the fleets of 300 ships of war which had taken part in the North Sea manœuvres to show the absurdity of any comparison now or in the immediate future between the relative strengths of the German and British fleets. He therefore failed to see any reason for nervousness in England, or for any increase in the British fleet on account of the German naval programme. This programme was not a new one; it had been passed by law; and it had become a point of national honour that it should be completed. No discussion with a foreign Government could be tolerated; such a proposal would be contrary to the national dignity, and would give rise to internal troubles if the Government were to accept it. He would rather go to war than submit to such dictation.

I at once pointed out to the Emperor that, in suggesting a possible friendly discussion between the two Governments, there had been no question of dictation and that my words could hardly bear that interpretation, to which His Majesty assented. I said that I was at a loss to understand how His Majesty arrived at the figures of the relative strength of the two navies in battle-ships in 1909, and could only assume that the sixty-two first-class battle-ships of the British fleet comprised every obsolete vessel that could be found floating in British harbours and that had not been sold as scrap iron.

The Emperor at once sent an aide-de-camp for a publication of this year by "Nauticus," giving the above figures, and presented me with a copy for my own edification and conviction.

I told the Emperor that I wished very much that I could accept the figures of "Nauticus" as correct, and that I was quite sure that I could make the same statement as regards His Majesty's Government, who were genuinely anxious to be on the best possible terms with Germany, and who would profoundly regret the necessity of devoting to naval construction funds which could be so much more profitably spent in measures of social reform. Never had there been a more pacific Government than that now in office in England, but they fully realised that no social reforms would be profitable to the country if its security and existence were endangered. It must be remembered that, if there were war between England and Germany and the British fleet received a temporary reverse, the British shores would be open to invasion by the armies of the greatest military Power in the world and the country would be conquered. A large British fleet did not present the same danger to Germany, and, in the absence of large military forces in England, its existence was absolutely essential for the security of the British Isles. The presence at Kiel, within twenty-four hours of the British coasts, of an immense German fleet, which in 1918 would consist of 38 battle-ships, with 20 first-class cruisers and nearly 150 destroyers, would constitute a standing menace and could not be justified by the naval forces at the command of both France and Russia. Nor could it be said that the German fleet was intended for the protection of German commerce, since German trade could not be protected by a fleet lying always at its base.

The Emperor replied with some warmth that the talk of invasion was sheer nonsense, and that such an idea had never been contemplated by any serious person in Germany. Moreover, it was he that directed the foreign policy of Germany, and was it likely that he would ever tolerate such an idea for an instant? He maintained that the figures given by "Nauticus" were correct, and that those given by the Admiralty were intended to deceive public opinion in England. It was in England that the first "Dreadnought" had been built in the greatest secrecy, and on its completion Admiral Fisher and the press had at once announced that she was capable of sinking the whole of the Germany navy. These statements had forced the German Government to begin building ships of a similar type to satisfy public opinion in Germany. Although England had previously increased the size of her battle-ships, Germany had kept to the smaller size of heretofore, until provoked by the action of the British Admiralty to build ships of the largest size. As for the German fleet being kept at Kiel, he kept it there because Count Metternich had reported to him that the Foreign Office and public opinion in England were sensitive, and did not like to see the German fleet passing up and down the Channel. Moreover, Germany had not the numerous bases which England possessed in distant seas, and German ships had in consequence to be kept at home. He had, however, now sent his ships to the Canaries, and, to show his confidence in British policy, he had done so at a moment when the North Sea was full of British war-ships engaged on naval manœuvres. The Emperor repeated that the German naval programme of thirty-eight battle-ships and twenty cruisers must be completed by 1918 at the various stages prescribed by law, and that no further increase would then be made, but that the navy would be maintained at that strength. As for His Majesty's Government, they were, of course, free to build as they pleased.

I replied to the Emperor that the danger of invasion would in that case, unless counter-measures were taken, always be possible in the future, but, I trusted, not probable. Although, from the experience of the last twenty years since His Majesty had been on the throne, His Majesty's Government had the fullest confidence in his peaceful intentions and in those of his Government, it was always possible that a wave of public opinion might, on some pretext which we could not foresee, break down all resistance and precipitate a catastrophe such as war between the two countries. Such an incident would be more likely to happen when a weapon such as the German navy had been forged at great expense and would cost still more to maintain in an efficient state. I admitted that the building of ships of the "Dreadnought" type might in the first instance have been a tactical error, but that that could be no justification for the encouragement of naval rivalry between the two countries. I demurred to the Emperor's statement as to the intention of the Admiralty to deceive public opinion in England by their figures, and added that it was a matter of common notoriety that, if the present shipbuilding programmes are maintained, Germany will, in about three or four year's time, have as many if not more "Dreadnoughts" than England. I expressed my astonishment that Count Metternich should have informed his Government that the Foreign Office were sensitive and disliked the idea of the German fleet passing up and down the Channel. I could say with confidence that such was not the case with the Foreign Office, nor with public opinion as far as I knew. As proof of this I could point out that the passage of the German fleet to the Canaries had provoked no unfriendly comment in England. Reverting to the general question of naval expenditure, I expressed the hope that moderate counsels would still prevail, and that although friendly discussion between the two Governments might as the Emperor insisted, be barred, still I was convinced that His Majesty's Government would require no written formula nor verbal statement from the German Government but only a visible proof that the programme of naval construction had been modified or slackened, in order to make a similar modification or slackening in their own. Without some such proof it would be quite impossible for His Majesty's Government to resist the pressure of public opinion, and a large counter-programme of naval construction would be inevitable.

The conversation here ceased, but two hours later I had an interview with Herr von Jenisch, who had been out with me on a motor drive, and had had no means of communicating with the Emperor in the meantime. I developed the situation to him in much the same terms as those which I had used earlier in the day to the Emperor, only possibly in greater detail. I gave him the most positive assurances of the friendly intentions of His Majesty's Government, and urged upon him with the utmost insistence the necessity of arriving by some means or other at a modification of the present German naval programme or at a postponement of its completion, so as to avoid an insane rivalry in naval construction between the two countries which could only end in their mutual hatred and impoverishment.

Herr von Jenisch gave me precisely the same replies as the Emperor had already given, to the effect that the programme which had been passed by law must be completed; that the date of its completion could not be in any way deferred; and that no changes were possible which could be interpreted in any sense as due to the suggestion of another Power.

I mentioned to Herr von Jenisch that I knew that the King proposed to speak to the Emperor of the possibility of the King and Queen paying an official visit to Berlin next year; but I felt it my duty to warn him that, if the British public had by that time realised the competition in naval construction which was to be initiated between the two countries, such a visit might become very unpopular in England and have consequently to be abandoned.

Herr von Jenisch strongly urged the importance of the visit taking place, since it was ardently desired by all classes in Germany, and there could be no doubt as to the warmth of the welcome which the King and Queen would receive in Berlin. He stated that at the time of the visit of the King and Queen to Reval, although it was well known that their Majesties had not the time at their disposal to pay a visit to Berlin, there had been a feeling of general regret that a visit had not been possible. He was absolutely convinced that a Royal visit to Berlin would create a revulsion of feeling in Germany such as it would be difficult to conceive, and he therefore pressed hard that under no circumstances should the visit be abandoned. He remarked that such a visit would be worth more than one or two battle-ships.

I asked Herr von Jenisch to inform Herr von Schön of the substance of our conversation, and he promised to do so.

From the foregoing account of my interviews with the Emperor and Herr von Jenisch, I think there can be little doubt, from the identity of the views expressed by them, that the conversations had been foreseen and a reply prepared. I do not think it is to be regretted that a clear exposition of the views of the Government on the subject of naval armaments has been placed before the Emperor and the German Government, since their reply offers a complete justification to Parliament and to the world at large for any counter-measures that His Majesty's Government may decide upon taking in the near future. Although it is to be regretted that the German Government have assumed such an uncompromising attitude towards any discussion or modification of their actual programme of naval construction, it is as well to know the worst and to be prepared for it.

What strikes me forcibly in the attitude of the Emperor and of the German Government is their unreasoning fear that any reduction of the German programme may be regarded by their countrymen as due to the dictation of a foreign Power, more especially of England, whose proposals for a reduction of armaments were strongly resisted by the German Government at The Hague Conference last year.[3] If such be the case, it shows that they realise the Chauvinistic spirit of the German public, and that they know they must take it into account. I heard while in Germany that financial difficulties may not improbably hinder or even prevent the realisation of these naval projects, since it is said that Prince Bülow, in order to secure financial equilibrium, proposes to place additional taxes on tobacco and beer. The prosperity of the lower classes has, however, deteriorated of late to such an extent owing to the general financial depression that it is thought probable that on the imposition of the new taxes, they will have to reduce their consumption of beer and tobacco, and that the additional revenue will therefore not be forthcoming. This will make it very difficult for the German Government to build and maintain a large navy at a moment when they are even increasing by two army corps the enormous army which they have already under arms.

The same evening, shortly after dinner, the Emperor, who was in the best of spirits, called me, made me sit down by him, and talked to me for more than an hour in a very pleasant and agreeable manner on every conceivable topic.

In alluding to the recent *coup d'État* at Constantinople[4] the Emperor stated that it had not been organised, as was generally supposed, by the Young Turk party, but by the army, who were afraid that further concessions derogatory to the honour of Turkey would be wrung from the Sultan by the Powers in connection with the Anglo-Russian scheme of reforms for Macedonia. He himself has strongly advised the Sultan to grant a Constitution to the people, and he felt that in its success lay the only hope for a peaceful regeneration of Turkey. General von der Goltz, during

[3] [This subject will be dealt with in a later volume.]
[4] [*v. Gooch & Temperley*, Vol. V, ch. XXXVIII, pp. 247–320.]

his recent visit to Constantinople, had given the Sultan a serious warning that the old system of Palace government could not be indefinitely prolonged, and that he should rid himself of Izzet Pasha and the Palace camarilla, a corrupt and infamous coterie, and he was confident that much good was to be anticipated from their dismissal. He expressed his conviction that there is far greater vitality in Turkey than anybody imagines, and that, with fairly good government, her future will be greater than that of some European Powers.

His Majesty remarked that recent events in Turkey would undoubtedly create difficulties for His Majesty's Government in Egypt and India, but that they should remember that it is a matter of vital importance to Europe to conciliate Mussulman public opinion in Asia, since it was the Mussulman races alone who could oppose an effective barrier between Europe and the yellow races of the Far East. He maintained that his fears of the "Yellow Peril" had not been exaggerated, that the situation would be extremely critical if a Jenghis Khan were suddenly to appear and to lead the yellow hordes of China against the West. The Russians were already beginning to realise the danger, which he considered was a very real one.

Turning to the recent action of the Austrian Government in connexion with the Sanjak Railway,[5] the Emperor said that it had caused his Government much annoyance, since the Austrian Government had acted without consulting them, although it had been generally believed that they had received encouragement from his Government. As a matter of fact, the Russian Government were aware of what had taken place some three weeks before the German Government heard of the project. The German Government were anxious to support and encourage all railway projects in Turkey as a means of developing the country, but they were not disposed to permit the assumption by any European Power of a position of preponderating influence in the Balkan Peninsula. I was able to assure his Majesty that the views of the British Government towards railway development in Macedonia were identical with those of the Russian Government.

(During the course of this conversation the Emperor made several satirical allusions to England's policy and her "new friends," and endeavoured to show what a good friend he had been to England in the past. Thus he repeated the statement previously made (I think) to His Majesty's Ambassador at Berlin that, during the Boer War, he had been approached by the French and Russian Governments to make a coalition against England, but that he had absolutely declined to do so, and had threatened to make war on any Power that dared to make an unprovoked attack on England at that time. I did not think it worth while to mention that this account does not tally at all with that given by M. Delcassé and the Russian Government of this transaction.

So also His Majesty told me that, after our early reverses in the Boer War, he had received a letter from the late Queen Victoria, full of grief at the losses suffered by the British troops, which had touched him deeply. He had at once instructed his General Staff to draw up a plan of campaign, which he had sent to the Queen, and this plan had been followed by Lord Roberts in all its details. "And yet," His Majesty added, "I am said to be the enemy of England!"

The Emperor complained that no British statesmen ever visited Berlin, and that consequently it was impossible for them to understand German sentiment and the German people. He constantly sent his statesmen to England to study various questions, but he could only remember two instances of English statesmen doing the same. The two instances were those of Lord Rosebery many years ago and Mr. Haldane quite recently. To the latter everything at the Ministry of War had been shown and nothing held back. It would be difficult to find an instance where greater confidence had been shown towards a foreign statesman.

Towards the close of the interview an aide-de-camp came to the Emperor and announced that the King was ready to leave for the railway station. As I somewhat hurriedly rose and asked permission to go to fetch my coat and hat, the Emperor stopped me and said in a very emphatic manner:—

"Remember that I fully adhere to and mean every word that I uttered at the Guildhall last year.([6]) The future of the world is in the hands of the Anglo-Teuton race. England, without a powerful army, cannot stand alone in Europe, but must lean on a Continental Power, and that Power should be Germany."

There was no time nor opportunity to continue what might have been an interesting discussion of a somewhat ambitious policy.

On thinking over the Emperor's words and the general trend of his conversation, I cannot resist the conclusion that his last sentences were the climax to which he had been gradually leading, and that he wished to urge once more the greater advantage to England of friendship with Germany over the understandings with France and Russia which have already shown such beneficent and practical results during the past few years.)

The King left Cronberg at 11 P.M. on the 11th instant, and arrived at Ischl on the following morning. . . . .([7])

([6]) [A report of the Emperor William II's speech at the Guildhall was given in the *Times* of November 14, 1907.]

([7]) [The rest of this memorandum describes King Edward's visit to the Emperor of Austria at Ischl, and is printed in *Gooch & Temperley*, Vol. V, pp. 827–30, *App.* IV.]

No. 118.

Sir F. Cartwright to Sir Edward Grey.

F.O. 371/461.
28798/26341/08/18.
(No. 90.)   *Munich, D. August 17, 1908.*
Sir,   R. *August 19, 1908.*
  I have the honour to report that the "Süddeutsche Reichskorrespondenz" publishes a "communiqué" on the results of the Royal meetings at Cronberg and at Ischl, the substance of which is to the following effect.

  The two recent Royal meetings at Cronberg and at Ischl are satisfactory in their character as they show that no attempts were made there to create new groupings of the Powers; on the contrary, the tendency shown at these meetings was against the creation of any new special *ententes*. It must be recognised, however, that Great Britain shows no intention of abandoning her present *ententes*; her understanding with Russia remains firm, but the altered situation of affairs in the Near East has cleared the political horizon in so far as it has removed for the present the probability of an Anglo-Russian joint action in the Macedonian question which might have given rise to serious opposition to it. The Anglo-French *entente* also remains untouched but as far as regards the Near East, France from the beginning always reserved to herself her right of liberty of action. The complicated machinery which was created with a view to bringing pressure to bear upon the Sultan seems for the moment to be held in reserve. The principle of the maintenance of the integrity of the Ottoman Empire which has been advocated by Germany, is for the present accepted by all the Powers and this clears the ground of many minor difficulties. A slight change in the European political situation had already occurred before the meetings at Cronberg and Ischl, but there this fact was rendered more evident. This change may be called a kind of *détente*.

  Side by side with this *détente* there still remains a long and patient up-hill work for the Sovereigns, the Cabinets and the people of Germany and England to accomplish, and this work is to clear up the misunderstandings which exist on both sides with regard to the aims and objects of the fleets which are being constructed. The premature cry of : Halt! would in no way help to solve this difficult question. The idea that the fleets of the two countries have nothing better to do than to knock up against each other will not long prevail; on the contrary, the erroneous belief that a crash is inevitable between England and Germany will be dispelled when it is understood that both fleets have other and pacific duties to perform.

This is the view which Prince Bülow's organ would like South German public opinion to take of the Cronberg meeting. Nevertheless a good deal of confusion is shown in the press with regard to this event, but on the whole the majority of the newspapers of South Germany express satisfaction at its results because they assert that at that meeting Germany did not come off the worst as she did at Reval; the interpretation put here upon the recent Royal meeting is that it shows an inclination on the part of England to turn in a half-hearted manner towards Germany. The Stuttgart " Schwäbischer Merkur " notes that last year King Edward went to Wilhelmshöhe against his wish; " he had found it impossible to reject the Kaiser's invitation as he was crossing through Germany on his way to Marienbad, but he looked upon the invitation as a nuisance and one which was forced upon him against his wish." The same cannot be said of the Cronberg interview, for in this case " the original idea which led to the meeting came from the King and not from the Kaiser. This is what public opinion in Germany finds most pleasant about this event." The Stuttgart newspaper continues by stating that for many years past people have shaken their heads here as to the use of holding out a friendly hand to England. On the present occasion, however, no one can say that Germany has run after Great Britain; even the " North German Gazette " in its welcome to King Edward showed a marked and sensible reserve, very different from what it had done on previous occasions. No doubt can exist that this time England has made advances to Germany. In fact, Cronberg is to be explained by studying the recent speeches of certain British statesmen whose Germanophile tendencies are well known. The change in the tone of official England towards Germany dates from the recent visit paid by the Kaiser to Hamburg, on which occasion His Majesty received such a spontaneous ovation from the population that it must have been evident to English statesmen—who are kept well informed— that the point had been reached where the irritation caused in Germany by the " isolation policy " pursued by King Edward was ready to produce an explosion which might prove dangerous to the peace of Europe. What took place at Cronberg will no doubt in a way help to pacify public opinion here, but as regards the essential points of the political relations between England and Germany no real change will follow this Royal meeting. In conclusion the Stuttgart organ deals with the question of the fleet and it expresses its views in the following words : " Germany seeks to acquire no supremacy either on land or on the sea; but she reserves to herself the right of deciding what armaments she considers necessary for her protection. England, on the other hand, is determined at all costs to maintain her supremacy at sea; if she is in a position to do so, so much the better for her. But it is useless to expect that Germany will help her to achieve this object by artificial means, such as by the creation of international diplomatic understandings. If sincerely cordial relations between the two countries can only be brought about by yielding to Great Britain on this point, then the establishment of good relations between Germany and that country is still far distant."

The naval question is occupying public opinion here more and more and every day it looms up clearer as an irremovable stumbling-block which lies in the way of a friendly understanding between Great Britain and Germany. On this point it may interest you to know what the German public are being told as to what passed at Cronberg between the two Monarchs and between the Kaiser and Sir Charles Hardinge. The Munich " Neueste Nachrichten," in an inspired article says : " It is quite likely that in the explanations given on the German side at Cronberg it has been possible partly to dispel the thick mist of suspicion and misunderstanding which obscures the two views of the naval question. This may have been accomplished so far as King Edward and Sir Charles Hardinge are concerned." The Munich newspaper means that having been enlightened on this point, the King and Sir Charles should in their turn use their efforts to enlighten the British public. The article continues : "Germany must have a fleet commensurate with her requirements and if England should attempt to put a veto upon Germany's efforts in this direction war must ensue. But we are of the opinion that it is worth while to attempt to convince the leading British statesmen that the construction of the German fleet is not intended as a menace to England and that even should the German naval programme be carried out in its entirety in ten years' time, the effective strength of the German navy would still then be only one third of that of Great Britain. May the efforts made in this direction at Cronberg bear good fruit ! "

In conclusion, I may say that the general note which runs through the mass of newspaper articles—inspired from Berlin—which are appearing since the Cronberg meeting, shows a decided hardening on the part of Germany with regard to the naval question. The independent " Frankfort Gazette " which represents the views held in financial circles in that city, gives a warning cry and declares that the present naval programme, when completed, will more than suffice to protect German maritime interests, unless influential circles in this country should be contemplating an aggressive naval policy. It blames the reckless way in which members of the Reichstag have lately voted for the building of ships without troubling themselves very much as to how the money was to be provided for this purpose; hence all the present financial troubles of Germany. The " Frankfort Gazette " lays great stress on the necessity of taking carefully into consideration the financial situation in Germany before the country is allowed to rush into any further wild naval expenditure.

I have, &c.
FAIRFAX L. CARTWRIGHT.

MINUTES.

Public opinion in Germany (led by the government press) remains determined to allow no foreign influence to dictate the size of the German fleet.

The notion that England will soon recognize, with Germany, that navies are not there for war, but have " other, pacific " duties, is peculiar.

E. A. C.
Aug. 19.

The repetition of the refrain that we must not interfere is almost wearisome.

W. L.
E. G.

MINUTE BY KING EDWARD.

I can only reiterate the same remarks I made with reference to Dispatch No. 89.([1])

E.R.

([1]) [*v. supra*, pp. 179–80, No. 114, and *min.*]

No. 119.

Count de Salis to Sir Edward Grey.

F.O. 371/461.
29256/26341/08/18.
(No. 356.)

Berlin, D. August 17, 1908.
R. *August 24, 1908.*

Sir,

The recent meetings at Cronberg and Ischl, and their effect on the European situation, continue to be the main topic of discussion in the press.

The " North German Gazette " in the usual summary of the week's news, which appears every Sunday, devotes several columns to the subject. The semi-official journal records its satisfaction that the British press has adopted an attitude which allows one to hope that, in spite of all efforts to the contrary, a better state of feeling may arise between England and Germany. The Cronberg meeting has proved that there are no questions of magnitude between the two countries. The paper then goes on to quote a communiqué emanating from Berlin which has been published in the " Süd Deutsche Reichscorrespondenz," which frequently serves as the organ of the Chancellor in South Germany. According to this, the recent Royal meetings do not portend a fresh grouping of the Powers, but on the contrary, tend to make the existing grouping more firm (this is evidently an answer to those who seek to prove that England is endeavouring to improve her relations with Austria to the detriment of Germany, and that the German Government have been unable to prevent it). England has in no way modified her situation as regards other Powers. The arrangement between England and Russia remains in the same state as before the two meetings; but the temporary postponement of the Macedonian reform scheme has dissipated the possibility of an Anglo-Russian advance in the East, which has long been threatening on the horizon, and which would have given rise to counter action.

In the same manner the *Entente Cordiale* between France and England remains unchanged.

The complicated machinery put in motion in order to bring pressure on Turkey is for the present thrown out of gear; and the policy of observing the integrity of the Ottoman Empire, initiated by Germany, has become an axiom for all the Great Powers.

The Cronberg interview has relieved the tension. Now the work of monarchs, governments, and people must be to examine carefully and understand the naval policy pursued by each country. The solution of the naval question cannot be reached by simply saying " disarm "; but the idea that the British and German navies have other objects in view besides fighting each other must in the end defeat the nonsensical idea that an armed collision between England and Germany is unavoidable.

The " North German Gazette," while admitting that certain sections of the press take a proper view of the relations between the two countries, expresses regret that papers like the " Morning Post " and the " Standard " should indulge in articles of an anti-German nature. It records the articles of Messrs. Hyndman and Blatchford in the " Clarion " with much satisfaction. This article or so much of it as is of an anti-German nature is quoted at length, and the " North German Gazette " asks its readers whether it is now any longer possible to believe Herr Bebel's Statement that the Social Democrat party in England have no anti-German proclivities.

The " Koelnische Zeitung " also contains a telegram evidently emanating from official sources in Berlin stating that the Emperor in conversation with Sir Charles Hardinge pointed to his speech at the Guildhall as a proof of the pacific intentions of Germany.

An article has appeared in the " Vossische Zeitung" which has caused much excitement here, and a full summary of it appears in the " Daily Telegraph " of the 20th Instant, in which it is stated that the result of the Cronberg meeting is that an agreement will be arrived at between the two countries.

The statement, quoted above from the " Sud Deutsche Reichscorrespondenz," that, in order to arrive at a permanent improvement in the relations between England and Germany, both nations must set to work to study the aims and objects of each other's maritime policy, is criticised in a sensible article in yesterday's " Frankfurter ·Zeitung." No agreement or alliance is wanted says the Radical organ; they would only lead to difficulties. An understanding can be arrived at by means of the facts: one side should know how far the other will go, and when that is done it will be recognised that fear and mistrust of one another are not justified.

Mr. Churchill's speech at Swansea also receives a favourable comment, and the hope is expressed that his utterance will tend to quiet the inflammatory articles in the English press. It is needless to remark that the German press always argues from the standpoint that it is the English press, and the English press alone, which is guilty of utterances calculated to produce bad feeling between the two countries.

I have, &c.

(For Sir Frank Lascelles),

J. DE SALIS.

No. 120.

Sir Edward Grey to Sir F. Bertie.

F.O. 371/461.
29641/26341/08/18.
(No. 402.) Confidential.

Sir,   *Foreign Office, August 26, 1908.*

When calling here on the 22nd instant,(¹) the French Chargé d'Affaires enquired whether any arrangements had yet been made as regards a visit of the King to Berlin next year. I told the Count de Manneville that a visit would probably take place during the course of next year if nothing occurred in the meanwhile to disturb the relations between England and Germany. No date had yet been fixed. The King had not yet been to Berlin since his accession and, as the German press constantly declared that H[is] M[ajesty]'s visits to Reval and other places were hostile to Germany, I hoped a visit to Berlin would put an end to such feeling. It was known that the Emperor was anxious for a visit to take place.

M. de Manneville said he hoped I had observed the calm attitude of the French press in regard to recent events passing between England and Germany. This was due, he said, to the fact that his Gov[ernmen]t had perfect confidence in H[is] M[ajesty's] Gov[ernmen]t.

I told M. de Manneville that so much had been said in the press that I thought it desirable to tell him what the situation was. Last year, as he would remember, when the Emperor came to England, the Bagdad railway and Morocco were both discussed and nothing was said about naval expenditure. At Cronberg neither the Bagdad railway nor Morocco was mentioned and we had endeavoured to impress upon the Emperor and his Government that the relations between England and Germany depended upon the increase or decrease of the rivalry in naval expenditure. If Germany proceeded on her present plan of naval construction we must increase our expenditure and this would next year excite the press in both countries. On the other hand, if a decrease on both sides took place, with or without some arrangement between the two Governments, there would be an improvement in the tone of the press and of public opinion.

M. de Manneville asked whether there was any prospect of an arrangement and I replied that the German Gov[ernmen]t told us that their programme was

---

(¹) [On August 20, M. de Manneville called at the Foreign Office, and held a conversation with Mr. Louis Mallet upon the question of the French tariff; he also asked whether the King and Queen were going to Berlin, to which Mr. Mallet replied that he did not know. Sir E. Grey minuted as follows the record of the above conversation, the substance of his statement being communicated to M. de Manneville by Mr. Louis Mallet on the 21st:

" A visit has been suggested and may very probably take place as the King has never yet been to Berlin, but no date is yet fixed. For the rest if enquiries are made by the French it might be said that no arrangement about anything was come to at Cronberg, though both there and at Ischl an exchange of views showed no difference of opinion as to the attitude to be assumed towards the present development of Turkish affairs. At Cronberg the subject of naval expenditure was mentioned by Sir C. Hardinge, but no arrangement was made."

E. G.]

fixed by law and could not be altered. Our position was that we did not dispute their right to carry out the programme, but we desired them to realise that we should increase our navy and they must not take it amiss if we did so. There things remained for the present.

I told M. de Manneville that the matter had been discussed before the meeting at Cronberg for Mr. Lloyd George, who, as Chancellor of the Exchequer was keenly interested in the question, and myself had had a conversation about it last month with Count Metternich on an occasion when we met at luncheon.

M. de Manneville said he saw Mr. Lloyd George was going to Berlin. I told him that he was already there and that his main object was to study German methods of insurance, &c., from the point of view of our own old age pensions and poor law problems. If, however, he were to be approached with regard to the naval question he would no doubt in private conversation express our views, for this question had now become the one subject of interest to the exclusion of all other political questions between England and Germany.

[I am, &c.

E. GREY.]

No. 121.

Sir F. Lascelles to Sir Edward Grey.

F.O. 371/462.
30939/30584/08/18.
(No. 397.)   *Berlin, D. September 3, 1908.*
Sir,   *R. September 7, 1908.*

Ever since the Cronberg interview the German press has been speculating on the possibility of His Majesty's Government having made proposals to Germany for a reduction of Naval Armaments or for some arrangement regarding future naval construction. In my despatch No. 356 of the 18th ultimo [*sic*],([1]) I had the honour to report a statement in the Vossische Zeitung that the result of the interview between the Emperor and His Majesty the King had been that an arrangement regarding the limitation of armaments had been arrived at. This and similar rumours have given cause for a good deal of uneasiness finding expression in the German press. The Germans are peculiarly sensitive and resent anything which might in any way be construed as dictation from outside or interference on the part of foreign powers in their right to do as they please with their own. The alleged proposals of His Majesty's Government are regarded in the light of interference and even the rumour that such proposals have been made has caused considerable resentment.

The Emperor's speech cleared the air. His Majesty announced clearly and decisively that he had no ground whatever for imagining the peace of Europe to be threatened, that he considered the strength of the armed force of Germany by sea and land to offer a firm guarantee for the maintenance of peace and that Germany would continue to develop her forces as her interests demanded.

His Majesty's speeches do not as a general rule find favour with all his subjects regardless of party, but the Strassburg speech is an exception. With the exception of the Socialist organs the whole press greets His Majesty's words with pleasure and relief—pleasure that the maintenance of peace seems firmly secured, and relief that nothing has been done in the matter of the reduction of armaments which might be considered wounding to Germany's amour propre.

I should but weary you were I to deal at length with the opinions and views of the various organs of the press, especially as they are in the main identical, but all the newspapers except the Socialist organs express the views described above. The Frankfurter Zeitung for example says that the Emperor's words are but another proof

---

([1]) [*v. supra*, pp. 192–4, No. 119.]

of the fact that the peace of Europe is an armed peace and must remain so, and the other newspapers echo these sentiments in but little varying language.

In the chorus of approval with which the speech is greeted, there is but little hostility expressed to England or France. The Magdeburger Zeitung, a National Liberal paper noted for its anti-British sentiments, however, recommends His Majesty's sentences regarding the maintenance of Germany's armaments to the particular attention of England and France.

The Socialist Vorwärts welcomes the statement that the Emperor is convinced that the peace of Europe is not threatened, but goes on to say that the closing words of His Majesty's speech do much to mar the good effect of the previous ones. The latter can only be regarded as an announcement that the policy of increasing the German armaments will be continued and cannot fail to have a bad effect in England.

I have, &c.
FRANK C. LASCELLES.

No. 122.

Sir A. Nicolson to Sir Edward Grey.

F.O. 371/461.
30907/26341/08/18.
Tel. (No. 162.)

St. Petersburgh, September 5, 1908.
D. 2·20 P.M.
R. 3·30 P.M.

Your telegram No. 335.([1])

I told Russian Government that I would be able to give them an account of Cronberg and Ischl interviews but the only document for communication I have received by messenger today is your despatch No. 402([2]) to Sir F. Bertie and this refers solely to Cronberg interview. The Ischl interview would much interest this Government and I do not know if you would wish me to give any information as to that interview taken from Sir C. Hardinge's memo[randum] of Aug[ust] 16?([3])

([1]) [Not reproduced. It announces that an account of the Cronberg and Ischl visits is on its way to Sir A. Nicolson for communication to the Russian Government.]
([2]) [*v. supra,* pp. 194–5, No. 120.]
([3]) [*v. supra,* pp. 184–90, No. 117, and *Gooch & Temperley,* Vol. V, pp. 827–30.]

No. 123.

Sir Edward Grey to Sir A. Nicolson.

F.O. 371/461.
30907/26341/08/18.
Tel. (No. 350.)

Foreign Office, September 5, 1908.

Your Tel[egram] No. 162.([1])

Any account of the Cronberg· interview should be founded on my despatch 402 to Sir F. Bertie.([2]) You may certainly tell Russian Minister confidentially what passed with Baron d'Aehrenthal at Ischl, but it would be better not to repeat what Baron d'Aehrenthal said about German naval armaments.

([1]) [*v.* immediately preceding document.]
([2]) [*v. supra,* pp. 194–5, No. 120.]

No. 124.

Extract from the Times *of October 24, 1924.*

SECRET PAPERS OF TIRPITZ.

Scenes with the Kaiser.

———

THE BUILDING RATIO.

When Grand Admiral von Tirpitz wrote his former volume of "memoirs," Germany was still a monarchy and the German Army and Navy were in existence. Peace had not been signed when they were published. These were among the considerations that influenced him in withholding his secret documents. But after the acceptance of the Dawes Scheme he decided that he could make public his archives without reserve. Under the title of "Political Documents," and edited by Professor Kerns [sic], of the Historical Institute in the University of Bonn, they will shortly be published in book form by the Cotta Publishing Company. In the following article, the first of a short series, we give some indication of their character and contents.

It is something of a surprise to find that in the period of 1905–1906 Admiral Tirpitz was against the scheme for increasing the German fleet, and opposed it with all his power in the interest of maintaining peace with Great Britain. This struggle, long and bitter, was hitherto known only to a few initiated persons. The actual documents relating to it are issued now for the first time.

The documents show that in the first phase of the struggle a state of extreme tension arose between the Kaiser and the Chancellor, Prince von Bülow, on the one side, and Admiral von Tirpitz on the other. The Chancellor had disregarded British overtures for an alliance made at the close of the century, and was chagrined to find in 1904 that Great Britain had allied herself with France. The importance of this step was at once manifest. At the time when the Entente was concluded Lord Rosebery had uttered a warning against it with the prediction that sooner or later it must lead to war. From the end of 1904 onwards opinion gained ground in Germany that the British Admiralty had under consideration the idea of a preventive war. Admiral von Tirpitz asserts that up to the year 1908 Admiral Fisher was advising his Government to "Copenhagen" the German fleet after the manner of Nelson—*i.e.*, to destroy it without any previous declaration of war. From 1912 onwards it was evident that the German fleet would become an important factor in the European balance of power, but in 1904 or 1905 it was undeveloped, and the idea of destroying it in embryo, Admiral von Tirpitz considers, must have been very tempting. His documents certainly show that the responsible administrators of the German Empire stood in some fear of a preventive war of this character. Colour was given to their fears when the Civil Lord of the Admiralty, Mr. Lee, delivered his famous speech, which Admiral von Tirpitz reproduces. He represents Mr. Lee as having said that the British Fleet would in given circumstances know how to deliver the first blow, even before the people on the other side of the North Sea had had time to read the declaration of war in their newspapers. This utterance, he adds, resounded through Germany much as the Kruger telegram had resounded through Great Britain a decade before.

Pulling a Savage Face.

It happened that Admiral von Tirpitz had just invited the British Ambassador, Sir Frank Lascelles. to dinner. Shortly before his guest was due to arrive he received the following autograph letter from the Kaiser :—

Berlin; February 4, 1905.

Dear Maestro,—No doubt you have just read in the newspapers the astonishing speech of the Civil Lord of the Admiralty with its open threat of war against us. I have just had Lascelles

o 3

here, and I have made it clear to him, in a manner not to be mis understood, that this fire-eating corsair must be officially called to order to-morrow by his Government. Otherwise there will be a storm let loose in our Press such as could only be allayed by *the immediate introduction of a colossal new building programme* which would be forced upon us by "public opinion." He was absolutely devastated and distracted, and telegraphed at once. He also intends to talk the matter over with you. Mind you pull *the most savage face* you are capable of when he comes, and mind you make him squirm and get a proper fright.

Yours,
WILHELM, I.R.

The Admiral's reply was formal and terse. It ran:—

To the Kaiser's Majesty,—Your Majesty's gracious letter just received, I will conduct myself towards Lord [*sic*] Lascelles, who is dining with me, in accordance with Your Majesty's directions.

VON TIRPITZ, *Secretary of State.*

In spite of public opinion and the Kaiser's excitement, Admiral von Tirpitz, as he shows, did not share the view that a colossal new building programme should be introduced. The consideration that influenced him most was the fear that the result would be the immediate danger of war. The struggle lasted till February, 1906, between the Admiral and the desires of influential persons. He was attacked by the German Navy League. The Chancellor, who did not believe that war was so probable, was apparently more concerned with retaining the good opinion of the Kaiser and the public. His general attitude in the controversy, as depicted by the documents, is illuminated by the Admiral's remark:—"An oiled eel is a leech compared with Bülow." In the end, however, Admiral von Tirpitz proved victorious, though only after sending in his resignation to the Kaiser. The latter, however, realizing that he could not dispense with the Admiral's talent for organization, gave way. But he did it with a very bad grace. Tirpitz says that the Kaiser in his surprise at receiving the resignation flung out the remark that "he hurled much wilder things at the heads of his other Ministers, and things would come to a pretty pass if they all sent in resignations every time he did so."

Admiral von Tirpitz depicts a lively scene which took place in the Palace in Berlin when the Kaiser realized that he declined to co-operate in accelerating the shipbuilding programme. "So I am not to have the ships?" he exclaimed. "Well, we'll see about that!" Then he turned to the Admiral and said, in an awed voice:—"Supposing some day we *have* no ships!" He went on to depict an imaginary unavoidable war and a lost sea-fight. The Admiral, he declared, would then bear the blame of Germany's having had too few ships. The Chancellor, who was present, remained silent. As his only contribution to the discussion, he remarked to the Admiral as they left the Palace:—"That was the best I could do for you."

A War with England.

Like all the documents of the Wilhelmstrasse which have been made available during the last few years, the numerous memoranda of the German Admiralty and the papers of Admiral von Tirpitz are set forth to bear out the theory that the preservation of peace was the main principle and chief care of the Kaiser and his civil and military advisers. Among them is the Admiral's interesting account of the last great conference held by Prince von Bülow as Chancellor in June, 1909. At this, General von Moltke declared "that, in his view, war with England must be avoided. As Chief of the General Staff, it embarrassed him to think what use was to be made of the Army in the event of a war with England. He would have to request the Kaiser also to bring about a war with France." This ironical observation was made at the end of serious negotiations, extending over almost an entire year, which Prince von Bülow, the Kaiser, Admiral von Tirpitz, and the German Ambassador in London had been carrying on among themselves and with British statesmen. These negotiations were intended to clear up the question whether the building of the German fleet constituted a danger of war, and whether the danger of war between Germany and Great Britain could be avoided by a decrease in the rate of building.

The view is expressed that Admiral Fisher, as First Sea Lord, had made a mistake in going over to the building of Dreadnoughts. The example of Great Britain was followed by all the other navies, and thereby the value of the preponderance of the British pre-Dreadnought fleet, which had been without a rival, was destroyed. In 1908, he says, this was perceived in England.

Nobody, however, cared to acknowledge it, and the responsibility for the consequent increase in the British Fleet was ascribed solely to the German armaments. In reality, however, Germany was building no faster than the rate laid down in the Naval Law of 1900. The Liberal Cabinet of Mr. Asquith and Sir Edward Grey painted the German danger in the blackest colours, in order to goad their unwilling followers to increased sacrifices. It was the year of the Navy Scare, the fleet panic. British newspapers, theatres, cinemas scared the " man in the street " with the bogy of a German invasion. Sir Edward Grey and other leading politicians overwhelmed the German Ambassador with requests that he should urge the reduction of German naval armaments. Count Wolff-Metternich, a weak man, on his part did not cease to bombard the Kaiser and Chancellor with pessimistic reports. King Edward VII., however, chose a more direct route. He took Sir Charles Hardinge, then Under-Secretary in the Foreign Office, with him on his " business journeys."

At the meeting at Ischl, the aged Emperor Francis Joseph was urgently advised to break away from Germany and to save himself by joining the Triple Entente. When the Emperor remained firm, Sir Charles Hardinge remarked at the railway station : " A splendid, exceptional man, this old Kaiser. But I believe he has just missed one of the most favourable opportunities of his long life."

Hectoring Kaiser.

At the idyllic Cronberg in the Taunus (Friedrichshof, the château of the late Empress Frederick is meant), the German Emperor was approached in August, 1908, on the same subject. He sent the following report (written in German, the words italicized being written in English) to Admiral von Tirpitz :—

Hardinge began with the *grave apprehension* which filled all circles in Great Britain with regard to the building of the German Fleet. In a very few years we should have reached the British strength.

Kaiser : That is absolute nonsense. Who has been telling you such rubbish?

Hardinge : It is not rubbish at all, but the authentic material of the British Admiralty.

Kaiser : It is nonsense all the same, even if your Admiralty did tell you so. And it is at the same time a proof how little British statesmen and the British people understand maritime affairs and how little they are informed as to their own strength. You have long ago exceeded the two-Power strength without knowing it.

Hardinge : That is quite impossible. You can have no material more authentic than that given me by the Admiralty.

Kaiser : Your material is false. I am an Admiral of the British Fleet as well. I know it perfectly well, and understand it better than you who are a civilian.

The Kaiser sent for the Naval Handbook and showed him the tables. Hardinge evinced great surprise and said : " This table is quite arbitrary and I do not attach the slightest importance to it." Thereupon he closed the book with a slam and continued : " This competition must be brought to an end; an arrangement must be reached by which the rate of building must be slackened. Otherwise our Government will have to bring in a great new building programme next year, and the country will begin to murmur."

Kaiser : We are not building in competition. Our rate is fixed by law, and the number of the ships it authorizes is known to you. It is you who are building in competition.

Hardinge : *Can't you put a stop to your building? Or build less ships?*

Kaiser : The measure of the maritime armaments of Germany is a defensive one, and it is certainly not directed against any nation, least of all against Great Britain. It is no threat against you, who are all at present suffering one with another from a fear of bogies.

Hardinge : But an arrangement ought to be arrived at to restrict building. *You must stop or build slower.*

Kaiser : *Then we shall fight for it. It is a question of national honour and dignity.*

During this turn to the conversation the Kaiser looked the Englishman full in the eyes. Hardinge got very red, bowed, and asked that his remarks might be regarded as a private blunder. In the evening the conversation was resumed, with the proviso that it should take a conciliatory tone. The Kaiser, who during the afternoon conversation had felt rather like his Grandfather felt towards Benedetti at Ems, sat down beside Hardinge on the sofa and decorated him with a high Prussian order, which awakened memories of Waterloo. King Edward, in view of the strained relations with his nephew, himself refrained from touching upon the subject of the Fleet.

[*ED. NOTE* (*A*).—The material analysed in the article quoted above is contained in the first two chapters of Admiral von Tirpitz : *Politische Dokumente. Der Aufbau der deutschen Weltmacht* (Stuttgart and Berlin, 1924). It is reproduced here because it elicited a reply from Lord Hardinge, which was published in the *Times* on November 10, 1924 :—

To the Editor of the *Times*.
Sir,—In *The Times* of October 24 an account appears, under the heading of " Secret Papers of Tirpitz," of an interview which I had with the German Emperor at Cronberg on August 11, 1908, when I had the honour of being in attendance upon his Majesty King Edward VII.
As it would, in my opinion, be regrettable that the account of this interview given by the German Emperor to Admiral von Tirpitz should be regarded as a complete and authoritative statement I have obtained the permission of the Foreign Office, and through that Department the assent of Viscount Grey of Fallodon, to communicate to you for publication the actual text of the official report of the interview that I addressed to Sir E. Grey on August 16, 1908.
I wish to add that the statement made by Admiral von Tirpitz that " at the meeting at Ischl the aged Emperor Francis Joseph was urgently advised to break away from Germany and to save himself by joining the Triple Entente " is absolutely without any foundation whatever, as is also the remark attributed to me at the railway station at Ischl.
Yours very truly,
HARDINGE OF PENSHURST.
20, Bryanston-square, W. 1, Nov. 4.

This letter was followed by the text of Lord Hardinge's official report of the visits of King Edward to Cronberg. The text published gave only the visit to the German Emperor, and ended with the words " The King left Cronberg at 11 P.M. on the 11th instant, and arrived at Ischl on the following morning." It is identical with that printed *supra*, pp. 184–90, No. 117, except that cross headings were inserted " for the convenience of readers " by the Editor of the *Times*.]

[*ED. NOTE* (*B*).—The following extract from the *Times* of March 13, 1922, describes a speech made by Lord Hardinge at Biarritz, in which he referred to King Edward's visit to Cronberg :—

In June, 1908, when he passed through the Kiel Canal on his way to visit the Tsar, it was realized for the first time that Germany had begun that enlargement of the canal that required five years of time and hundreds of millions of marks to complete. From these and other indications it was easy to deduce that Germany's war preparations would be completed in 1913.
Lord Hardinge then described how, owing to these menacing German preparations, he was instructed, when he accompanied King Edward to Cronberg, to call the Kaiser's attention to the uneasiness caused in England by Germany's attitude and to the naval competition to which it would lead. The Kaiser disavowed any hostile intentions, declaring that it was he who directed Germany's foreign policy, and said that he refused even to think of war with England. Lord Hardinge suggested that even if the Kaiser's personal intentions were pacific, a wave of popular feeling might precipitate a war between the two countries. The Kaiser, however, refused to modify Germany's naval programme.
" It is hardly necessary for me to say that King Edward was profoundly dissatisfied with this refusal, which could only confirm his views upon the real intentions of the Kaiser. The German argument has always been that Germany was pushed into war by what she called the policy of encirclement of King Edward, which had for its object the destruction of Germany. This theory is absolutely devoid of foundation, for King Edward hated war and wished to be at peace with all his neighbours. The title which he loved, and which he so well deserved, was that of Edward the Peacemaker."]

III.—THE "DAILY TELEGRAPH" INTERVIEW.

No. 125.

Count de Salis to Sir Edward Grey.

F.O. 371/463.
37910/37537/08/18.
No. 483.)

Berlin, D. *October* 30, 1908.
R. *November* 2, 1908.

Sir,

The publication in the Daily Telegraph of the 28th instant of the Emperor's interview with an anonymous English personality has created the greatest excitement in all sections of the German Press.(¹) The impression produced on them is on the whole a most unfavourable one. Hardly a paper, even among those which are usually more or less well disposed towards the Emperor's utterances, fails to express regret that His Majesty should have spoken as he is represented to have done, on one or other point in the interview. The National Zeitung for instance, though it closes its leading article in the conviction that "the world-policy of the Emperor is likewise the policy of the German nation," cannot refrain from pointing out that if Germany's policy during the Boer war and since then has been really so Anglophile, it would have been well for the Government to let the German people know this, and so prevent as far as possible the friction which certainly has arisen between the two peoples. Nor will His Majesty's references to the yellow peril be appreciated everywhere. The Cologne Gazette in the midst of an elaborate apology for and explanation of the Emperor's words, expresses similar regret at the references to the Far Eastern question; in other respects the very vehemence of its sympathy with the Emperor's sentiments leaves an impression of lack of conviction underneath.

Few other German papers make any pretence of approving the Emperor's words; the Berliner Tageblatt takes his speech point by point and shows that His Majesty's attitude or action in every case referred to was "mistaken"; the "Deutsche Tageszeitung" takes the opportunity to attack the Emperor vigorously for his habit of interfering in matters of foreign policy, and the Börsen Courier writes in the same strain. "From whatever point they are viewed," observes the latter paper, "His Majesty's remarks are calculated to produce a most unfortunate effect, such as will serve to show afresh the dangerous position in which our foreign policy has been placed for the last quarter of a century, by the impossibility of reckoning with or controlling the personal interference of the Sovereign in diplomatic activity. We do not know whether Prince Bülow has ever taken the opportunity of confronting the Emperor with an 'either—or' on this subject. The present would certainly be a suitable moment for him to do so; and the nation would thank him if he could thus avert similar interference in the future." Meanwhile in official quarters much hesitation and awkwardness prevails. A Berlin correspondent of the Cologne Gazette yesterday reported that the interview, as published in the Daily Telegraph is believed to be a correct reproduction of His Majesty's remarks, but at the Press Bureau of the Foreign Office here, I understand for the moment nothing has been said in answer to the many inquiries made there.

A curious announcement was published last night in the Norddeutsche Allgemeine Zeitung to the effect that "In foreign papers it has been announced that the Imperial Chancellor Prince Bülow has expressed to the Italian Ambassador Monsieur Pansa, his dissatisfaction with Italy's policy. We are authorised to state that this assertion is untrue and unfounded. As far as is known here, no such assertions have been made in the foreign papers; and the vague character of this *démenti* leaves it

(¹) [The incident is fully described in *G.P.* XXIV, ch. 178. For the Emperor's version, v. *My Memoirs: 1878–1918* (1922), pp. 115–7.]

quite uncertain as to the particular sphere of action in which Italy's policy is supposed to have been condemned. The Berliner Tageblatt pointedly remarks that the North German Gazette would give more general satisfaction if instead of denying insignificant press gossip, it would give a decided *démenti* with regard to the Imperial interview.

I understand from Colonel Trench that at the swearing in of recruits to-day at Potsdam the Emperor appeared to be labouring under much excitement and delivered a stirring speech to the soldiers respecting the capacity of Germany to defend herself, should the envy and ill-will of others oblige her to do so.

I have, &c.

J. DE SALIS.

MINUTE BY KING EDWARD.

A very interesting Dispatch.

E.R.

No. 126.

Sir A. Nicolson to Sir Edward Grey.

F.O. 371/463.
38871/37537/08/18.
(No. 484.) Confidential.   St. Petersburgh, D. October 31, 1908.
Sir,   R. November 9, 1908.

M. Iswolsky alluded yesterday to the publication in the "Daily Telegraph" of a conversation between the German Emperor and a British diplomatist; and he said that he had caused a search to be made in the archives of his Ministry for any record of the proposal which it was alleged had emanated from Russia and France for the purpose of calling upon Great Britain to terminate the Boer war. Nothing had been discovered which could justify a statement to the above effect, though I gathered that there had been some desire to express regret at the continued effusion of blood. M. Iswolsky said that he had asked the Emperor whether His Majesty remembered any invitation to Germany to join with France and Russia in urging on Great Britain to conclude the struggle; but the Emperor had replied that he had no recollection of any such step.

I observed that I had always understood that Germany had suggested to Russia that England's difficulties were Russia's opportunities in Central Asia, and that the Russian Government had declined to act upon the suggestion. M. Iswolsky replied that I was perfectly correct, and that the Emperor had mentioned this fact to him at his audience.

The question has been discussed in the Press here, but it is generally regarded as an attempt to sow distrust in England towards France and Russia, and no great importance has as yet been attached to the revelations of the diplomatist.

I have, &c.

A. NICOLSON.

No. 127.

Sir A. Nicolson to Sir Edward Grey.

F.O. 38879/38879/08/38.
(No. 493.)   St. Petersburgh, D. November 2, 1908.
Sir,   R. November 9, 1908.

M. Iswolsky reverted last evening to the conversation which he had had with Prince Bülow as to the solidarity existing between Germany and Austria Hungary, and he told me that he had inquired of Prince Bülow what he meant exactly by the phrase "present grouping of the Powers." Prince Bülow had replied that he naturally alluded to the close understanding existing between France, Great Britain, and Russia; and said that he considered this union was a "very strong combination" which Germany must naturally take into account. M. Iswolsky had explained to him that nothing had taken place between these three Powers. Russia and Great Britain had succeeded in settling certain outstanding difficulties in Central Asia, but that there was no understanding between the two Governments affecting other questions. Prince Bülow had interjected the remark "and what of Reval." M. Iswolsky said that nothing had occurred at Reval of any special significance or which could give the slightest cause of uneasiness to any Power. It was a visit most natural under the circumstances; and there was absolutely no intention either on the side of the Russian or of His Majesty's Government to enter into any arrangements whatever directed against any other Power.

He did not know if he had convinced Prince Bülow, although he had spoken very frankly and clearly. M. Iswolsky added, in referring to the "Daily Telegraph" publication, that he intended to keep under double lock certain documents which would throw a very different light on the communications which had passed between the Russian and German Governments in byegone times.

I have, &c.
A. NICOLSON.

No. 128.

Count de Salis to Sir Edward Grey.

F.O. 371/463.
38492/37537/08/18.
(No. 485.)   *Berlin,* D. *November 3, 1908.*
Sir,   R. *November 5, 1908.*

The statement published in the North German Gazette in explanation of the publication of the Imperial Interview in the Daily Telegraph, as reported in my Telegram No. 61 of the 31st ultimo,([1]) has been received in this country with even sharper criticism.

The few papers which had previously attempted to defend the Emperor's action and had made the best of his latest reported utterances, have ceased to maintain their former attitude and are ready to admit that the whole incident is much to be' regretted. The Cologne Gazette, though it still protests that it can find nothing to blame in the Emperor's words, is compelled to characterise the whole episode as presented in its new light by the official communiqué as a "great blunder." Even the Magdeburgische Zeitung, which was at first one of the warmest apologists of the Imperial Chancellor, now turns round and demands his resignation. "If things are as described," it observes, "one can only ask with horror how Prince Bülow can in the circumstances withdraw his resignation. There is no excuse for his conduct; and he can have no further claim to the confidence of the German nation. His astounding publication has not simplified matters in any way, it has merely accentuated the situation."

The Berliner Tageblatt has some sarcastic remarks respecting the latest development of affairs. The Imperial Interview was "like a mill-stone" upon its head, the "note of apology in the North German Gazette, however, has aroused

---

([1]) [Not reproduced. In Tel. No. 61 Count de Salis stated that a draft of the *Daily Telegraph* article had been shewn to the Emperor and by him sent to Prince Bülow who gave it to the Imperial Foreign Office for examination. As the Foreign Office raised no objection, publication was permitted. Prince Bülow, though he had not seen the document personally, assumed full responsibility and tendered his resignation, but it was refused.]

a pleasant merriment." Saturday evening's announcement found all the official world shaking one another by the hand and congratulating themselves that " he has not read it; no one has read it," and there the matter was thought to end.

The organs of the Centre, while disclaiming any feelings of rancour, urge, as indeed might be expected, that the Chancellor should resign, but the outcry to that effect raised in other sections of the press seems already to be subsiding while it is pointed out in more than one quarter that such a step would not help to re-establish Germany's prestige and would in existing circumstances, in the middle of a crisis in Eastern affairs and on the eve of sweeping domestic reforms as regards finance, be very undesirable. The demands for a change put forward by the Liberal Press give the impression after all of being half-hearted.

The reopening of the Reichstag on the 4th instant is, in consequence of these recent events, looked forward to on all sides with unusual interest; and it will be interesting to see what attitude Prince Bülow will adopt in the face of the storm of attack which is apparently awaiting him. In the meantime it is officially announced that Herr von Schoen was taken ill on Saturday night and has been compelled to give up his work at the Foreign Office for about three weeks. During his absence, the German Minister at Bucharest, Herr von Kiderlen-Waechter will have the direction of the Imperial Foreign Office.

The Cologne Gazette announces that the Committee of the Federal Council for Foreign Affairs has been summoned by the Imperial Chancellor to a meeting at which Prince Bülow intends to make some strictly confidential communications to them on various pending questions of foreign politics, and particularly upon the Eastern question. Prince Bülow does not therefore propose to make any statement at present in the Reichstag on foreign affairs. This news has been received with many expressions of discontent. A further rumour is being circulated this evening that Prince Bülow is to confer to-morrow with the chiefs of the various sections of the *Bloc*, that the terms of the interpellations to be made by them will be settled by agreement, and that after delivering his reply in the Reichstag he will again tender his resignation. It appears that the Austro-Hungarian Ambassador, who has long experience of Berlin thinks that the resignation will take effect and that this view is held by many others. I venture to think that [it] is still doubtful whether there is ground for such an opinion.

I have, &c.

J. DE SALIS.

No. 129.

Memorandum as to the attitude of Germany in regard to intervention during the Boer War.([1])

Private.([2]) *November 6, 1908.*

The precise nature of the action taken respectively by France, Germany and Russia as regards intervention—friendly or otherwise—during the South African war cannot very easily be determined with absolute certainty : there is however no doubt whatever that pourparlers did take place between these countries on various occasions during the period from Oct[ober] 1899 to March 1900.

There is little official information bearing on this question, but the " National Review " of July 1908, and the " Times " of Oct. 29 & 30/08 contain articles which are known to emanate more or less directly from M. Delcassé. Putting these and other accounts together, the following appears correctly to relate the action taken at different times by these 3 Governments.

([1]) [For previous references to this question, *v. Gooch & Temperley*, Vol. III, pp. 411–12, *App.* A; pp. 425–6, *App.* B; p. 431, *Ed. note;* pp. 432–3, *Annex;* and p. 436–7, *App.* C.]
([2]) [Grey MSS., Vol. 53.]

Shortly after the opening of the Boer war, Count Muravieff, Russian Minister for Foreign Affairs, who was in Paris, acting on German initiative sounded M. Delcassé, then French Minister for Foreign Affairs, on the subject of intervention, suggesting that the moment was opportune for making representations to Great Britain in the interests of the restoration of peace. (This is denied by the "Deutsche Revue" of September 1908 which states that if Count Muravieff mentioned the subject at all on this occasion he did so without any prompting from Germany.)

M. Delcassé answered with sympathy and reserve saying that the only representations France was disposed to consider were representations of a friendly character, and that she would in no way associate herself with any further action (see "Times" Oct. 30), whereupon Count Muravieff left Paris for Berlin whence he shortly returned to St. Petersburg without any decision being arrived at between the 3 Governments.

The idea of intervention seems however to have continued to occupy the Emperor's mind—though, according to the "Deutsche Revue," the interchange of letters between the British and German Courts, and the visit of the Emperor to this country were sufficient proof of Germany's attitude to convince the whole world of her absolute refusal to be led into any action hostile to Great Britain—and Sir Cecil Spring Rice reports in his despatch No. 321 of May 16/05 that a "high official of the Russian Foreign Office" (possibly M. Hartwig) told him of a conversation which the German Emperor had held with Count Osten Sacken, the Russian Ambassador at Berlin, in which he had "enlarged on the expediency in the general interests of the world and [e]specially of Russia of addressing joint representations to England with a view to the conclusion of peace. Count Osten Sacken repeated this language to his Government. The Emperor of Russia caused a reply to be drafted([3]) to the effect that the Emperor as inaugurator of the Peace Conference would of course be willing to do all in his power to prevent the further effusion of blood, but that the question as to the precise step to be taken with that object was one on which he was not prepared to offer an opinion. He therefore awaited a further communication from the German Government to which he would give when received its due consideration. An answer was at once received from Count Osten Sacken to the effect that the German Government had no proposal to make in the matter."

(Sir C. Spring Rice suggests that the above communication by Count Osten Sacken was used by the German Government as a documentary proof for a proposal by Russia to intervene.)

Two years later, M. Hartwig in conversation with Sir C. Hardinge (see His Exc[ellenc]y's despatch No. 573 of Sep. 25/05([4])) complained of the "duplicity of the German Government in having declared at the time of the South African war that they were in possession of a document from the Russian Government proposing intervention, while in reality it was a document which he himself had drafted and which Count Osten Sacken had delivered stating that Russia had no interests in South Africa, and that if the German Government were of opinion that intervention was necessary at that stage of the war they themselves should take the first step."

Further confirmation of the belief that Germany desired to place a check on British action is to be found in the fact that a member of the Austrian Embassy at St. Petersburgh showed Sir C. Hardinge a despatch from the Austrian Chargé d'Affaires at Madrid to the Austro-Hungarian Minister for Foreign Affairs stating that the German Ambassador at Madrid had proposed to the Spanish Government that they should join in a coalition against Great Britain consisting of Russia, France and Germany.

([3]) The wording given here "The Emperor . . . . drafted" is a paraphrase of that given in the original despatch, which runs: "By the Emperor's orders an answer was drafted in the Foreign Office which my informant remembered perfectly. It was to the effect that," etc. The despatch is in F.O. Russia 1700.]

([4]) [v. F.O. Russia 1702. Despatch from Sir C. Hardinge No. 573 of September 26, 1905, No explanation seems possible of the statement in the memorandum that the incident recorded in the despatch took place "two years later" than the one referred to by Sir C. Spring-Rice.]

Nothing further seems to have happened till the end of February 1900 when, as M. Mévil says in The Times of Oct. 30, on the successive suggestions of the German Emperor and Prince Bulow, the Russian Government again sounded the French Government as to the possibility of intervention in order to prevent the continuance of bloodshed. M. Delcassé replied as before, with sympathy but with reserve, and dwelt on the necessity of first ascertaining clearly the views and attitude of the German Government in regard to an amicable intervention of the nature contemplated by Count Muravieff.

Count Osten Sacken communicated accordingly with the German Government. The latter appear to have been contemplating a more serious form of intervention for when their reply reached the Russian Government a few days later it was to the effect that intervention would constitute " un acte grave, une œuvre de longue haleine," and that consequently before consenting to join with the other two Powers they required that Germany, France and Russia should reciprocally pledge themselves to maintain the integrity of their territories.

The French Government naturally declined to commit themselves in this way, and the negotiations dropped—for good.

In admitting Germany's demand for a mutual territorial guarantee the " Deutsche Revue " argues that the sole object she had in view was to break off the discussion as to intervention. At the same [? time] it is difficult to blame other Powers for hesitating to accept this explanation.

Foreign Office, Nov[ember] 6, 1908.

No. 130.

Sir Edward Grey to Sir E. Goschen.

F.O. 371/463.
39366/39366/08/18.
(No. 311.)
Sir, *Foreign Office, November 7, 1908.*

Count Metternich having returned to-day after some days' absence, I took the opportunity of saying to him that when I had seen him on the day after the publication of the interview with the Emperor I had not said anything to him about it, because I felt it embarrassing and did not know what to say; also I was not yet aware whether the report would be admitted as authentic.([1])

I hoped, now, that Count Metternich, in reporting what I said to him on the subject, would not report any remarks of mine which he thought likely to cause annoyance.

I had felt, when I read the interview, that it must give offence in France and Russia. I had dreaded that its effect in Germany would be bad,—Count Metternich said this had obviously proved to be the case. I had also feared that our own people would be shocked by hearing, on the authority of the Emperor, that the majority of the German people were very hostile to us.

In fact, one Member of Parliament, who had been received by the Emperor and Prince Bülow at Berlin, had already told me that he had been shocked by this statement as to the hostility of the German people, and had asked me whether it was not the case that the Emperor had been misreported, or his confidence betrayed. In reply, I had of course referred him to the statement which had been made by the German Government themselves as to the publication of the interview.

I was anxious that the effect of the interview should not be to make people think that things had been made more difficult between England and Germany : I wished to remove any impression of this kind.

(1) [For Count Metternich's report, *v.* *G.P.* **XXIV,** pp. 186–7.]

Count Metternich pointed out that a great part of the German Press had already denied that the majority of the Germans were hostile to England.

It was not for him to criticise anything which the Emperor had said. He was sure the intention of the Emperor in the interview had been friendly to England. But, no doubt, the effect of publication had not been what the Emperor hoped.

I told Count Metternich I did not wish the impression to be left that we declined to grasp any hand which was held out to us in good faith : the difficulty was to find some common ground on which we could work together. One barrier between us had, at any rate, been removed lately. The German Government had always supported the Sultan and the old régime in Turkey. Public opinion here, and the Government, had been strongly opposed to them. In the past we had therefore been in opposite camps at Constantinople. But if Germany was now prepared to support the new régime in Turkey, there was no reason why we should continue to work against each other there.

As a matter of fact, I understood that an advance of $1\frac{1}{2}$ millions, which the Turks required, was now to be provided by the Germans, the French, and the English in the following way : one-third by the Deutsche Bank; one-third by the Ottoman Bank, which was mainly French, though it had a branch in London; and the remaining third by British financiers. We were quite willing that this advance should appear as a joint operation of the three countries, acting in common and on the same security. This would show that Germany was working not only with us, but with France too. Any co-operation of this kind must do something to show that the friendship of France and England was not directed against Germany.

Count Metternich knew of this advance to Turkey, and welcomed it. Prince Bülow had said to him at Norderney that now England was supporting the new régime in Turkey it ought to be possible for England and Germany to work on parallel lines.

Count Metternich then referred to the British Press.

He said that the line they took made things difficult. In the Casablanca incident,[2] ·for instance, the British newspapers had at once taken the view that France must be right, and Germany wrong.

I told him that, so far as I was aware, the British Press had not gone much into the merits of the dispute at Casablanca, but had only taken the view that it was not an affair which should lead to a serious quarrel, and that clearly it ought to be referred to arbitration. They understood that Germany had offered arbitration, and that France had accepted it; and they could not see any good reason for reviving the question now.

Count Metternich said it was true that Herr von Schön had mentioned arbitration in conversation, when various other solutions were discussed. M. Jules Cambon had reported this to his Government, who had accepted arbitration. But a despatch from the German Government had crossed this acceptance, pointing out that arbitration had not been formally proposed as covering the whole case.

I told Count Metternich that the French Government had not given me their reports on the merits of the case. They had simply informed me that they were prepared to accept arbitration, and they had explained what had passed with the German Government, and the demand the latter had now made. I had not even seen the report of the French officials on the spot as to the facts of the case; but I gathered that both the law and the facts were in dispute. I knew that the French Government were very desirous of finding some formula which could be accepted, but they could not be expected to make an avowal that they had been in the wrong before the law and the facts had been decided by arbitration.

Count Metternich said that the German Government, he was sure, desired to go as far as they were able in meeting the French half-way.

We then had some further conversation about the Press.

(2) [Reference to this subject will be made in *Gooch & Temperley*, Vol. VII.]

Count Metternich dwelt with emphasis on the mischief done by the hostility of the British Press.

I told him, in reply, that some of the articles from the German Press which were sent to me would be equally exasperating, if I dwelt on them constantly. For instance, only a few weeks ago I saw that there had been a meeting in Berlin presided over by some minor official, who had said in his speech that the object of the Germans must be to build a sufficient number of balloons to capture England.

But I thought it was a great mistake to pay attention to these things. The Press would not lead: it would only follow.

The Press in both France and Russia, a few years ago, was at least as hostile to us as the German Press was now: but the tone of the Press in both these countries had changed, of itself, when the relations between the countries became more favourable.

I feared that the Emperor paid too much attention to cuttings from the British Press, even from publications of no political importance, such as "Vanity Fair."

Count Metternich said that the Austrian press had lately been pointing out how the British Press was envenoming the Casablanca incident.

I answered that of course the Austrian press was hostile to us at present, owing to the line we had taken with regard to Bosnia. But I attached no importance to this hostility: it would pass away in time.

[I am, &c.]
E. G[REY].

MINUTE BY KING EDWARD.
App[rove]d.—E.R.

No. 131.

Sir Edward Grey to Sir E. Goschen.

F.O. 371/463.
39367/39367/08/18.
(No. 312.)
Sir,   *Foreign Office, November 10, 1908.*

Count Metternich came to tell me to-day that he had reported to Prince Bülow what I had told him about the advance which was to be made to Turkey by the co-operation of English, French and German financiers.([1])

Prince Bülow had charged him to express his great satisfaction at this co-operation; and had said that, in view of the excitement which was stirred up by the Press generally, there was all the more reason why the English and German Governments should work for co-operation with calmness and good conscience.

Prince Bülow had to deal to-day with the debate in the Reichstag. He would have to defend the position of the Emperor with regard to the unhappy article in the "Daily Telegraph," and would also have to do his best to overcome the temper and ill-humour which had been caused by it in Germany. But, though Prince Bülow must devote himself to these objects, he was most anxious to speak in such a way as not to create difficulties between England and Germany.

After expressing pleasure on hearing Prince Bülow's views with regard to the joint advance to Turkey, I thanked Count Metternich for what he had told me beforehand about Prince Bülow's speech in the Reichstag: for it gave me an indication of the spirit in which he wished his speech to be read when it reached me. I said I hoped the speech made by the Prime Minister last night in the

([1]) [For Prince Bülow's instructions to Count Metternich and the latter's report, v. *G.P.* XXIV, pp. 187–9.]

Guildhall would in no way make things more difficult for Prince Bülow and the Reichstag. The Prime Minister had talked the matter over beforehand and had felt that it would be embarrassing to make a direct reference to the interview with the Emperor; but I knew that he desired so to speak as to smooth matters, or at least not to make them more difficult for Prince Bülow in the debate in the Reichstag.

Count Metternich expressed himself as entirely satisfied with this aspect of the Prime Minister's speech, and said he hoped a report of it would be telegraphed in time to reach Prince Bülow before he addressed the Reichstag.

[I am, &c.]
E. G[REY].

MINUTE BY KING EDWARD.

App[rove]d.—E.R.

No. 132.

Mr. Findlay to Sir Edward Grey.

F.O. 371/463.
39911/37537/08/18B.
(No. 43.) Confidential.   *Dresden, D. November 10, 1908.*
Sir,   R. *November 16, 1908.*

In my despatch No. 41 Confidential of the 29th ultimo([1]) I had the honour to submit to you an account of the anti-British Press campaign which, in this part of Germany, had been carried on with increasing bitterness during the preceding fortnight in connection with events in the Near East.

This press campaign was interrupted—I cannot say closed—by the publication of the "Kaiser Interview" in the Daily Telegraph, since which time the Eastern crisis has been almost forgotten, and one sensation has followed close on the heels of another.

The authenticity of the Daily Telegraph interview was accepted by the better informed as soon as they saw that it was not immediately contradicted; only the "Stalwarts," like the "Leipziger Neueste Nachrichten" and a few of the minor papers, professed to think that the whole thing was a hateful invention on the part of some perfidious Englishman. This theory, however, did not seem to carry conviction, and though it has been repeatedly put forward, even since the official admission of the general correctness of the account of the Emperor's utterances given by the Daily Telegraph, it may be doubted whether any one seriously believed it.

The public indignation was great, but may be attributed to various causes. The Pan-Germans, and the very large section of the German people who so hotly espoused the cause of the Boers during the South African war, were chiefly furious at the alleged action of the Emperor in drawing up a plan of campaign and placing it at the disposal of the British. Others found fault with the Emperor's assertion that the majority of the German people were not well disposed towards Great Britain, and all felt hurt that His Imperial Majesty should have laid himself and Germany open to a snub.

The effect of the publication of the interview was nothing, however, to that of the explanatory communiqué in the North German Gazette. The news was posted up in the streets in Dresden on Saturday October 31st, and spread like wild-fire

([1]) [Not reproduced.]

in spite of the fact that on the following (Sunday) morning hardly any papers appear. I cannot exaggerate the rage and shame caused by Prince Bülow's announcement. The German, especially the North German, prides himself on his organisation and thoroughness, and though the organisation is ponderous, and the thoroughness often wearisome and pedantic, his pride is justified to a certain extent. The confidence in Kaiser and Chancellor as International statesmen has been rapidly disappearing of late, but the thoroughness of the German official was still an article of faith. Prince Bülow's communiqué, however, showed that the Imperial Interview had passed through his own hands, and had been actually examined and passed by the Ministry for Foreign Affairs. He had not read it, it was true, and, if he had, would have objected to its publication. It was clear, however, that some one must have read it, and that the Chancellor and the Ministry for Foreign Affairs had shown themselves utterly inefficient, or culpably servile. All confidence was swept away, and people went about red in the face with rage and shame.

The next day (Monday) the whole German Press voiced the popular indignation, and the demand for satisfaction of some sort or other was universal. Soon, however, it became evident that though the German people were unanimous that something must be done, and that such things must not occur again, they were by no means unanimous as to the means by which the undesirable recurrence should be prevented. The parties who in their first rage and fury had demanded the immediate retirement of Prince Bülow, constitutional limitations of the Imperial power, and drastic changes in the Ministry for Foreign Affairs, began to reflect that they were part and parcel of the "Block" system of which Prince Bülow was the parent; that if he went they would go too; that it was questionable whether his successor would do better; that there was little hope of mending the erratic régime of the Emperor, and so on, with the result that the speeches of the various leaders in to-day's and yesterday's debates, are a faint echo of what would have been said on November 1st, though a fortnight ago no one would have believed it possible that the sovereign could have been subjected to even the moderate criticism which has been passed on him in the Reichstag.

In spite of this change of attitude on the part of parties and party leaders, I am convinced that a deep and lasting indignation has taken hold on the people, which is combined with a burning desire to vindicate the national honour both at home and abroad, and that the feeling is one which will have to be counted with both by the Emperor, and by all who have dealings with Germany. I was so strongly impressed by the intensity of this feeling that I ventured to telegraph to you that I feared any provocation from abroad would be welcomed.

The following day the Casa-Blanca incident was reported to have assumed a serious aspect, and at one moment it looked as if even that trumpery dispute might lead to war with France. I am assured by persons in a position to know that there has been no such wave of popular excitement since 1870.

Fortunately, however, most of the Liberal papers and the Socialist press took the announcement as a deliberate attempt on the part of Prince Bülow to throw the hounds off his own track by using the Casa-Blanca incident as a red-Herring.

They declared with one voice that Germany was not going to war on such grounds, and I believe that a considerable portion of the more serious military opinion was entirely on the side of France.

The Chauvinist Press and some papers which should have known better endeavoured to convince the people that the attitude of France was provocative. There is no doubt that the mass of the people expected some such attempt to create a diversion, otherwise they might have been misled. As it was the tirades of the yellow press fell flat.

It seems almost incredible that Prince Bülow can have risked playing such a dangerous game as that attributed to him, but many incredible things have happened in the last fortnight.

I am convinced, however, that if the German case had not been so hopelessly weak, and if France had not been so reasonable, there would have been a manifestation of that *furor teutonicus* of which the German papers are so fond of speaking. I am also convinced that the danger is by no means passed.

As soon as it was announced that a meeting of the Committee of the Bundesrat for Foreign Affairs had been summoned by its President, (the Bavarian representative), I endeavoured to ascertain what attitude would be taken up by the Saxon Government. On the 9th I was informed by the Under Secretary for Foreign Affairs that the Saxon Government would do all in their power to support Prince Bülow, and that Count Hohenthal would proceed to Berlin to-day to represent Saxony.

I saw Count Hohenthal immediately after the publication of the interview and he told me he felt as if a bomb had exploded. He did not doubt its authenticity, and had no illusions as to the effect. On the other hand he seemed hopeless of preventing such occurrences, and this hopelessness is a marked feature of the general attitude of the Public.

I believe that it is one ground for the decision of the Saxon Government to support Prince Bülow. The King of Saxony doubtless wishes to support the Emperor, of whom he is believed to be a great admirer. But from what Count Hohenthal said I gathered that he considered the Emperor to be hopelessly erratic, that there was no hope of altering or controlling his impulsive character and action, and that there was equally little hope that any other Chancellor would be more successful in doing so than Prince Bülow had been. In fact the situation was hopeless, and, as a Bavarian friend said to me, using a graphic Bavarian expression : " es wird eben so weiter gewurstelt," *i.e.*, " We shall go muddling on in the same old way."

I have, &c.
M. DE C. FINDLAY.

No. 133.

Mr. Findlay to Sir Edward Grey.

F.O. 371/463.
39912/37537/08/18B.
(No. 44.) Confidential.   *Dresden, D. November* 12, 1908.
Sir,   R. *November* 16, 1908.

In my immediately preceding despatch(¹) I endeavoured to describe the situation created by the publication of the " Kaiser Interview."

I will now venture to submit a few reflections and observations on some of the Emperor's utterances taking them one by one.

1. The middle and lower classes in Germany are said to be ill-disposed or hostile to England. The Emperor and a minority " composed of the best elements " are said to be friendly.

As far as I can judge the Emperor is misinformed. He is certainly misinformed as to Saxony, where the majority of the lower classes are Social Democrats, and as a party, in favour of peace and an understanding with England on the subject of Naval construction. On the other hand Anglophobia is rampant among the officials and the educated classes, especially those who take their tone from the Professors and schoolteachers, whose chauvinism seems to indicate that German education does not always bring enlightenment. There is also, as is perhaps not unnatural, a certain hostility among the officers, though in military circles I have personally always been met in a friendly spirit. I say *personally*, as there is often

---

(¹) [v. immediately preceding document.]

a marked difference in the attitude of a German to individual Britons, and in his attitude towards the British Government and British policy. A certain jealousy, which leads to hostility, is prevalent in Commercial classes and finally the Press is almost entirely hostile. The principal sources of anti-British propaganda are the influential Pan-German Association and the "Flottenverein."

It would therefore appear that unless the feelings of the various sections of the public in the rest of Germany, differ greatly from those prevalent in Saxony, the Emperor is not only misinformed, but the situation is exactly the contrary to what His Majesty believes it to be, *i.e.*, the majority of the lower classes are well disposed towards Great Britain. The majority of the official, educational and journalistic classes, together with a considerable contingent of commercial men and military officers are hostile. It can hardly be doubted that the latter would consider themselves to be the "best elements"; they are certainly the most influential.

2. The Emperor appears to take credit to himself for having averted European intervention in 1899–1900, and he attributes this to his friendly feelings. I do not doubt that His Majesty's feelings have been spasmodically friendly to England. I do doubt, however, that His Majesty's friendly feelings alone would have sufficed to stem the tide of German hostility. Further it cannot be denied that the Krüger Telegram and various other Imperial utterances greatly contributed to create the situation with which His Majesty is now endeavouring to cope. There were also other causes which were quite sufficient to account for German abstention. You will remember that early in 1900 the Emperor Francis Joseph, Germany's most intimate ally, declared himself—(in my own hearing)—"entirely on the side of England." This emphatic and public declaration can hardly have failed to influence German policy.

I have also seen a statement in the papers, which I believe to be authentic, to the effect that Dr. Leyds telegraphed to his Government: "That owing to the <u>Naval Power of Great Britain</u> the European Powers were unable to hold out any hope of intervention."

This last reason would appear to be final and conclusive.

I believe that an American spectator at a British Naval Review once remarked "I guess this makes for peace!" No one at all conversant with the politics of the last twenty years can doubt that he correctly summed up the situation past, present, and future.

I have, &c.
M. DE C. FINDLAY.

No. 134.

Sir E. Goschen to Sir Edward Grey.

F.O. 371/463.
39838/37537/08/18.
(No. 493.)

Berlin, D. November 12, 1908.
R. *November 16, 1908.*

. . . .(¹) Herr Bassermann was followed by Herr Wiemar (Radical), Herr Singer (Socialist) Prince Hatzfeldt (Imperialist) and one or two others.

Then Prince Bülow arose to reply in a speech, translation of which I have the honour to enclose herewith; His Serene Highness, who was looking worn and ill, dropped all his habitual floridness of style and spoke quietly, directly and to the point. It cannot be said however that his speech has given general satisfaction or that it has satisfied public opinion. The Press almost unanimously complain that

---

(¹) [The omitted part of this despatch merely summarises the debate in the Reichstag deploring the *Daily Telegraph* publication.]

it did not answer the interpellations, that it lacked clearness and decision, and especially that it contained no indication whatever as to whether the assurances given that such incidents would not be repeated were given on the authority of the Emperor or not. On the other hand the friends and followers of the Chancellor consider that it was impossible for him to say more than he did and that he emerged creditably from a very trying ordeal.

The day's debate was closed by a speech from Herr von Hertling, of the Centre party which had drawn up no interpellation; and by one from Herr Liebermann von Sonnenberg, who indulged in a violent attack upon both the Emperor and the Chancellor and severely criticised the working of the Imperial Foreign Office.

The debate was continued on the 11th. Herr Gamp of the Reichspartei regretted that the Emperor, to whom the German working man owed so much, should meet with so little sympathy among the masses, but he expressed the opinion that it would be well if His Majesty were brought more into contact with the best men in the nation and if he could be induced to exercise greater restraint in his conversations with foreigners. The next speaker, Herr Schrader, a Radical, criticised the want of harmony in Germany's foreign policy and remarked unfavourably upon the Emperor's absence at this important moment from Berlin. The best speeches of the day were made, however, by Herr Hausmann (Radical) and Herr Heine (Socialist). The former attacked Prince Bülow sharply for his interpretation of the Daily Telegraph publication. The speaker protested that he had not answered the interpellations and hinted that perhaps he had not even read them. The Emperor should have been now in Berlin, and should have authorised his Chancellor to make some statement which would calm the minds of the people. The policy of telegrams and interviews must be put a stop to; the moment had come for introducing a really constitutional form of Government; the Committee of the Federal Council for Foreign Affairs should meet more frequently and obtain better control of affairs.

Herr Heine, whose speech was directed entirely against the person of the Emperor, was followed by Herr von Kiderlen-Waechter, who is temporarily acting as Minister for Foreign Affairs in the absence of Herr von Schoen. It had been hoped that Prince Bülow would have spoken again and considerable annoyance was shewn at his failure to do so. Perhaps it was partly this sense of disappointment coupled with a feeling that Herr von Kiderlen was hardly as yet in a position to make any weighty statement on the question under discussion that caused his words to be received with derision and noise on every side. His remarks were confined to complaints of the short-handedness of the Foreign Office and to the announcement that proposals were under consideration for its reorganisation.

The discussion, an excellent account of which appeared in the Times of the 11th and 12th instants, closed with the rejection of a motion brought forward by two members of the Left for the discussion to-day of the question of presenting an address to the Emperor. The Conservatives and a majority of the House, refused to support this motion, which has accordingly been dropped.

The uneventful character of the proceedings has caused some disappointment in the German Press. Most papers have so far maintained a somewhat reserved attitude with regard to the outcome of the debate; Prince Bülow's speech is on the whole regarded as unsatisfactory; even the Conservative Kreuz-Zeitung can find no assurance in it that such incidents as the Daily Telegraph interview will not occur again. The only guarantee afforded against their recurrence, in the view of the Berliner Neueste Nachrichten, is to be found in the person of the present Chancellor, who would certainly have to resign on the next occasion. Only the National-Zeitung writes as though the incident were now for ever closed. It expresses the hope that the Chancellor may remain in office as long as he considers he can usefully do so, and that the Emperor may learn from this episode to restrain his language, and conform to the policy of his Government. The impression seems to prevail that little has been gained by the discussion, though in the organs of the

Left it is noted with some satisfaction that at least a new and excellent precedent has been started in the fact that the Emperor's words and actions should have become legitimate subjects of debate and criticism.

It is announced in the press that Herr Klehmet, head of the political division of the Foreign Office and one of the ablest men in the office, has been dismissed, in connection with the Daily Telegraph incident; and it is believed that other dismissals will follow. The November number of the "Zukunft" in which Herr Harden characteristically reviews the whole incident, defends Prince Bülow and suggests that the Emperor might abdicate, has been confiscated and removed from general circulation.

It is announced this evening that the Imperial Chancellor, who yesterday summoned the Prussian Ministry to a meeting and to-day presided over a session of the Committee of the Federal Council for Foreign Affairs, will have an audience of the Emperor within the next few days, for the purpose of discussing the situation at present created by the Reichstag debate.

I have, &c.

W. E. GOSCHEN.

Enclosure in No. 134.

Translation of Prince Bülow's Speech.

Gentlemen,

I will not deal in detail here with all the points touched upon by Herr Bassermann. I must have regard to the effect which my words will have abroad, and I will not add anything further to the harm already produced by the publication in the Daily Telegraph.

In reply to the interpellations before me I have the following statement to make :

His Majesty the Emperor did at various times give vent to private utterances to various private English persons, which have been strung together and published in the Daily Telegraph. I must assume that the conversations have not been reproduced correctly in all their details. In one instance I know that it is incorrect. That is the story about the plan of campaign. There was no question of a plan of campaign worked out in every detail so much as of a few purely academic—— (Laughter from the Social Democrats.) Gentlemen, this is a serious debate. The things I am speaking of are of a grave nature and of great political significance. I beg that you will listen quietly to me; I shall speak as shortly as I can. I repeat, then, that there was no question of a plan of campaign worked out in every detail, so much as of a few purely academic ideas—I believe they were actually described as aphorisms—upon the general conduct of the war, which the Emperor inserted into his correspondence with the late Queen Victoria. They were theoretical observations, devoid of practical importance as regarded the course of the operations and the result of the war. General von Moltke, Chief of the General Staff and his predecessor, Count von Schlieffen, have stated that the General Staff did furnish the Emperor with a report upon the Boer War, as they did with regard to every big or little war that broke out anywhere on the earth during the course of the past century. But both have declared that our General Staff never examined or transmitted to England a plan of campaign or any similar work connected with the Boer War, drawn up by the Emperor. I must however further defend our policy against the accusation that it was one of duplicity towards the Boers. We warned the Transvaal Government betimes, as our archives will prove, and told them that in the event of war with England they would have to stand alone, and we urged them directly and through the friendly medium of the Netherlands Government to come to a peaceable understanding, because there could be no doubt as to the issue of a hostile conflict. With regard to the question of intervention the colours are laid on too thickly by the Daily Telegraph article. The circumstances of the case have long been public property. (Hear! Hear!) A short time ago they were the subject of polemics between the "National Review" and the "Deutsche Revue." There can be no question of a revelation. It has been said that the Imperial message to the Queen of England to the effect that Germany had turned deaf ears to a suggestion of mediation and intervention was a breach of the rules of diplomatic usage. Gentlemen, I will not recall the indiscretions in which the diplomatic history of all peoples and all times is rich. (hear! hear! on the right.) The safest policy is perhaps that which need fear no indiscretions. (Hear! Hear! on the left.) To judge whether there have been any violations of confidences, one must have a wider knowledge of the immediate circumstances of the case than appear in the Daily Telegraph article. The declaration might be justified if there had been an effort from any source to distort our refusal to mediate or intervene, or to cast suspicion upon our attitude. Things may have gone before which make reference to the circumstances in a confidential correspondence at least explicable.

Gentlemen, I have already said that many statements in the Daily Telegraph article were too strong. That applies next to the passage where the Emperor is reported to have stated that the majority of Germans are hostile to the British people. Between Germany and Great Britain there have been serious and regrettable misunderstandings. But I know that I am at one with the whole of this august House in the conception that the German people desires to live in peaceful and friendly relations with Great Britain, based on mutual esteem, (applause on all sides) and I can declare that speakers of all parties have spoken in the same sense. (hear! hear!)

The colours are also laid on too thickly in the passage which refers to our interests in the Pacific. It has been expressed in a sense inimical to Japan, and wrongly so. In the Far East we have never had another thought in our mind than this: to win and maintain for Germany a share in the trade of East Asia in the development of the great economic future that lies before it. We have no intention of involving ourselves in a maritime adventure there. German naval construction has no aggressive tendencies in the Pacific Ocean, any more than in Europe. For the rest, the Emperor is in complete agreement with leaders responsible for our foreign policy in recognizing the high political importance the Japanese nation has won for itself by its political activity and its military achievements. German policy has not set itself the task to circumscribe for the Japanese people the enjoyment and development of that which they have won.

Gentlemen, I am of the impression that if the material facts, of course the correct version of them, had been known in detail, the sensation would not have been great; again here their sum total was far greater than all their details put together. Above all, in considering the material side. the psychological side of a tendency must be borne in mind. For two decades the Emperor has endeavoured often in very difficult circumstances, to bring about a friendly understanding with Great Britain. This honourable and sincere effort has had to contend with difficulties that would have disheartened many. The passionate siding of the nation with the Boers, humanly comprehensible—the siding with the weak against the strong—gave rise to unjust and in many cases extravagant attacks on Great Britain. In the same way unjust and malicious attacks were directed on the part of Great Britain against Germany. Our intentions were misunderstood, we are supposed to have made hostile plans against Great Britain of which we have never thought. The Emperor, being firmly convinced and rightly so, that this state of things is a misfortune for both countries and a danger to the civilized world, keeps unswervingly to the aim which he has set before him. Any doubt of the purity of the Emperor's intentions, ideals and sentiments and his deep patriotism is a gross injustice to His Majesty.

Gentlemen, we will draw the line at everything that looks like excessive courting of foreign favour, like uncertainty of pander [sic]. But I understand that the Emperor, just because he was conscious of having zealously and honourably striven after good relations with England felt hurt when he was continually the object of attacks which impugned his best intentions. Have things got to such a pitch that even his interest in the German navy was attributed to secret intentions against the vital interests of Great Britain, which were utterly foreign to him. Then he made an effort to point, in private conversations with English friends, to his attitude in difficult times for Great Britain to show that he was misunderstood and wrongly judged in England.

Gentlemen, the knowledge that the publication of his conversations has not produced the effect which the Emperor intended in England, and has worked deep excitement and painful regret in our country, will—and this is the firm conviction which I have gained during these days of stress—will induce His Majesty in future to observe that reserve even in private conversations, which is equally indispensable in the interest of a uniform policy for the authority of the crown (Cheers on the right). Were that not so, neither I nor any successor of mine could bear the responsibility. (Prolonged cheers on the right and amongst the National Liberals.) For the mistake which was made in dealing with the manuscript I take the entire responsibility, as I have already caused to be stated in the North German Gazette. It is also repugnant to my personal feelings to brand as scapegoats officials, who have done life-long duty, because in a single case they relied too implicitly on the fact that I read and decide almost everything myself. I join with Herr von Heydebrand in regretting that in the machinery of the Foreign Office which has worked faultlessly under me for 11 years, a defect should at last have shown itself. I guarantee that this shall not happen again, and that what is necessary to this end shall be done without injustice and without respect of persons. (Cheers.)

When the article, as to whose sinister effect there could not for a moment have been any doubt, was published I tendered my resignation. The decision was inevitable and was not hard for me. The gravest and hardest decision I have ever taken in my political life was to remain in office, in compliance with the wish of the Emperor. I only resolved to do so because I regarded it as a behest of political duty to continue to serve Emperor and country in this time of stress. (Loud cheers.) How long that will be possible for me remains to be seen. I will only say one thing more. At a moment when the whole situation demands serious attention, when we are called upon to safeguard our external position, and to secure our interests unaggressively but with calm firmness, we must not let foreign countries think us pusillanimous; we must not make a misfortune into a catastrophe. I will refrain from any criticism of the hyperbole which we have had to face of late. The damage done is, as quieter consideration will show, not so great but that with circumspection it cannot be made good. Certainly no one will forget the warning that the recent occurrences have given us all, (cheers on the right) but that is no reason to show a discomfiture that would raise the hope among adversaries that the Empire is crippled within and without.

It is for the elected representatives of the nation to display the presence of mind that the moment demands. I say—not for myself—I say for the country, that in these circumstances support is no favour, it is a duty which this august house cannot avoid. (Loud cheers on the right, hissing amongst the Social Democrats.)

No. 135.

Sir Edward Grey to Sir F. Bertie.

Private.([1])

My dear Bertie,   *Foreign Office, November* 12, 1908.

It may be useful to you to have a line from me to say what a very favourable impression has been produced here by the tone, temper, and attitude of the French Government and of France during the Casablanca crisis last week.

The entire absence of panic, I might say even of excitement, and the way in which conciliation and firmness were combined, so that there could be no mistake about either, was very impressive and satisfactory. If I am not mistaken, it has had a wholesome effect in Germany too.

([1]) [Grey MSS., Vol. 11.]

We wished to ease things as much as we could by smoothing over the difficulty caused by the German Emperor's interview. The Prime Minister had that amongst other things in view in his speech at the Guildhall; and for the same reason I took an opportunity of saying to Metternich that the co-operation of English, French, and German finance in the advance to Turkey was agreeable to us.([2])

The Emperor has made Germany for the time being the laughing stock of the world, and anything we can do with France to keep things quiet I will gladly do, and I think it is wise in the Near Eastern affair to give Germany no pretext for saying that she is being ringed out. It may of course be said that the Emperor's folly is his own affair, and that is true; but he having made his people ridiculous and put them in a bad temper, it is desirable that they should consume their own smoke, which for the present they seem inclined to do.

I am not confident about the future. We can and ought to go the length of giving Germany no excuse for saying that she is being cold-shouldered, isolated, or squeezed; but when she has recovered from the effect of the Emperor's vagaries, she will resume not only her self-respect, but the tendency to resent anything being done without her leave, or any friendship between other countries, in which she is not included. Then there will be trouble. She has reached that dangerous point of strength which makes her itch to dominate.

This is a dull letter, and my last was frivolous : but I haven't time to trouble you much with letters, so you need not be apprehensive.

Yours sincerely,

E. GREY.

([2]) [v. supra, p. 208. No. 131 and note.]

No. 136.

Sir E. Goschen to Sir Edward Grey.

Private.([1])

Dear Sir Edward Grey, Berlin, November 13, 1908.

I must thank you very much for having found time to write me such an interesting letter,([2]) which gave me much valuable information.

From an international point of view things look rather better than when you wrote owing to the satisfactory settlement of the Casablanca Arbitration question; Monsieur Cambon told me that when he saw the agreement in print he was lost in wonder as to how such a simple matter could possibly have taken so long to arrange. I think that the explanation is that Prince Bülow wished to see how the cat jumped as regards the Daily Telegraph publication before finally parting with the useful red herring furnished by the Casablanca incident. It is in any case a good thing that he has parted with it, because the "Interview" crisis has by no means ceased, and the bitterness it has caused is increasing rather than diminishing. Everybody is angry with somebody. The general public are furious because in his speech Prince Bülow did not say enough, and especially because he neither answered the interpellations themselves nor the questions arising out of them. The Conservatives are angry with him because he said too much while not sufficiently defending the Emperor. The latter is *said* to be annoyed for the same reason : while every paper, Metropolitan or Provincial, some in moderate but most in immoderate, language blame the Emperor. To a newcomer like myself, imbued with the idea that H[is] M[ajesty] was more or less outside public criticism, this onslaught upon Him comes as a most striking surprise. Even the word "abdication" has been heard by some of the most violent critics and a number of the Zukunft

([1]) [Grey MSS., Vol. 22.]
([2]) [cp. supra, pp. 163–5, No. 104.]

containing an article by Harden on that subject has been put out of circulation and confiscated. The Chancellor tells me that there have been many previous occasions when the Press has thundered against the Emperor but that he never knew the outcry quite so great as during the present crisis. He seemed to me rather perturbed about it, and he cannot be looking forward to his Audience with the Emperor on Monday (at Kiel I believe) with much pleasure! The Prince received me as you will see from my despatch on the subject,(3) with the greatest cordiality and many expressions of goodwill. As I do not know him at all I am unaware how much value should be attached to the exceedingly friendly language towards England. But I should think he is sincerely grateful for the attitude both of His Majesty's Government and the English Press with regard to the Daily Telegraph publication. As regards my conversation with him, or rather *his* with me, as he did all the talking, he made one statement which appeared to me to be no less than astounding. He was speaking of the fury of Isvolsky against Aehrenthal in the matter of the announcement of the annexation. He said that Isvolsky had raged about it and said that he was a lost man, and dishonoured in the eyes of his countrymen by Aehrenthal's underhand proceedings etc.—but that as a matter of fact Isvolsky knew at Buchlau all there was to be known about the annexation except perhaps the exact date. How, otherwise, had he been able to tell Tittoni that the annexation was imminent : that he had done this was proved because Tittoni had telegraphed to Vienna and asked whether the information given to him by Isvolsky was correct, and Aehrenthal had answered in the affirmative.

All this I have heard before, but what Prince Bülow then said is to me quite new. He said that his own impression was that Isvolsky himself has set the Annexation Ball rolling; that in talking over Balkan matters at Buchlau with Aehrenthal he had asked for the support of Austria-Hungary in the Dardanelles question, and had stated that in return for that support the Russian Gov[ernmen]t would raise no objection should Aehrenthal care to put the project of annexation, which had been given so much prominence in the Austrian Press, into immediate execution! Whence Prince Bülow fished this theory, or whether he really believes it, I haven't the least idea.

The Prince was rather funny about the Plan of Campaign for the Boer War. He said he had taken the trouble to fish it out of the Archives. "But," he added, "please do not ask me my opinion of it or I should have to tell you that it was really a very childish production, consisting partly of extracts from a well-known work on the art of war, and partly of some original thoughts on the same art which would scarcely meet with the approbation of Military experts!"

I have heard that the Emperor has sent a very sharp telegram to the Chancellor criticizing the latter's speech in the Reichsrat [*sic*] with considerable severity.

The Emperor will not return to Berlin for another week : if I had known it would be so long before I could present my letters I think I would have asked you to allow me to come to London for a few days to see you as the position of an Ambassador before presenting his letters is always an embarrassing one. But now I will stop on and will take no leave until things are more settled down.

Thanking you again for your letter.

I remain,
Yours very sincerely,
W. E. GOSCHEN.

MINUTE BY KING EDWARD.

A very interesting letter.

E.R.

(3) [*v. supra*, pp. 165–7. No. 105.]

No. 137.

Sir F. Bertie to Sir Edward Grey.

F.O. 371/463.
40484/37537/08/18.
(No. 468.) Confidential.   *Paris,* D. *November* 19, 1908.
Sir,   R. *November* 20, 1908.

On the occasion of my visit to the Russian Ambassador on the 17th instant in order to carry out some instructions which you had given me the conversation turned on the Constitutional conflict between the German Emperor and the people, the position of Prince Bülow and His Majesty's conversations disclosed with His Majesty's approval in the " Daily Telegraph." Monsieur de Nélidow stated that when he came to Paris as Ambassador at the end of the year 1903 he found from conversations with Monsieur Delcassé that the French version of the circumstances in which an intervention in the War in South Africa was proposed and collapsed was the same as his (Monsieur de Nélidow's) recollection of the Russian participation in the pourparlers which took place on the subject. The German Government suggested to the Russian Government that there should be an intervention by Russia, Germany and France to put a stop to the War and to secure the independence of the South African Republics. The Emperor of Russia though the relations between England and Russia were at that time not of the best was unwilling to take any step that could be regarded as hostile and decided that Russia might join with Germany and France, if the latter were willing, in making friendly representations to His Majesty's Government if there were reason to suppose that they would be acceptable to put a stop to the bloodshed that was taking place in South Africa. It was from a humanitarian feeling and not with a political object hostile to England that the Emperor of Russia consented to enter into discussions on the subject with Germany and France. Advantage was to be taken of some British success which might render His Majesty's Government disposed to listen to mediation, and it was with this intention that at the instance of the German Government the Russian Government sounded the French Government as to whether they would be prepared to join with the Russian and German Governments in making representations to the British Government. Monsieur Delcassé whilst pointing out that France had no particular interests to protect in South Africa asked to be informed what was to be the attitude of the three mediating Powers supposing that England rejected their overtures. The reply from the German Government was that in order to render the mediation or intervention effective it would be necessary that the three Powers should first enter into a guarantee for the maintenance of the *status quo* in Europe. As it was evident to Monsieur Delcassé that Germany's object was not only to put a stop to the War in South Africa by an intervention which would go beyond a mediation but to obtain the support of France to a German interest possibly resulting in a collision with England in which France would probably be the chief sufferer and that a guarantee of the *status quo* would be a confirmation by France of the Treaty by which she had lost Alsace and Lorraine the French Government made no answer to the German reply to their enquiries, and the discussion dropped. The version of the negotiations or discussions given by the German Emperor in his published conversations was of course incorrect said Monsieur Nélidow.

I observed to the Ambassador that those pourparlers were ancient history. We were too practical a people to care now what was discussed then to our detriment and had not succeeded. We quite appreciated the desire of the three Powers, with two of which we were not then on the friendly terms that we were now, to stop the War. It was evident that Germany felt then that Russia and France might act with her and it did not much matter which Power started the negotiations. The important and to us satisfactory result of the discussions was that they had failed in bringing about intervention. We were now on very good terms with Russia and France. We bore no malice on the subject of the negotiations and it was foolish of the

German Emperor to revive the question for the conversations had given offence to Russia and France and they had not persuaded the British public that His Majesty was the person who had saved England from an intervention or that his so-called plan of campaign had insured the ultimate success of the British arms.

I have, &c.

FRANCIS BERTIE.

No. 138.

Sir E. Goschen to Sir Edward Grey.

F.O. 371/463.
40808/37537/08/18.
(No. 503.)   *Berlin,* D. *November* 20, 1908.
Sir,   R. *November* 23, 1908.

A few days before the return of the Emperor from Donaueschingen the following somewhat violent expression of opinion appeared in the " Berliner Tageblatt " :—
" If there is one thing which condemns the present system and points to the absolute necessity of an increase in the Rights of Parliament, it is the present, so-called ' Chancellor Crisis.' What! Here we have a population of over 60 millions, a nation of the highest intelligence, a nation which has come to the front by its own unaided strength, and yet the fate of the Chancellor, whether he is to remain in office or retire, and the choice, in the latter case of his successor, depends on the decision of one solitary individual. This is a state of things intolerable to any self-respecting nation, and the system under which it is possible can only be defended by sycophants and office seekers. The events of the last few days have clearly shown that the German people no longer intends to allow its most vital interests to depend upon the haphazard decisions of one individual, of whose wayward and impulsive moods it has now, but not for the first time, had full opportunity to form a judgment."

I have quoted these words in full, as they appear to me to sum up with the most unmistakable clearness the feeling which is now predominant throughout liberal Germany.

Resolutions embodying similar ideas have been passed by liberal organisations in all parts of the Empire, while even the more Conservative parties have offered but little defence of the present system of Government and have confined themselves in most cases to attempts to shift the responsibility for recent events on to the shoulders of Prince Bülow or his subordinates. Happily an intense monarchical spirit is one of the leading characteristics of the German people, otherwise the present violent outburst of impatience and even anger against the " personal régime " of the Emperor might lead to the belief that a dangerous revolutionary movement was in sight. No one here, however, seems to have regarded the matter in that light, and public opinion as represented by the Press having blown off a sufficient quantity of steam, calmed down as the moment for the momentous meeting between the Emperor and His Chancellor approached, and awaited the result with something approaching to patience.

This meeting which was to have taken place at Kiel, was held at Potsdam on the 17th instant, with the result that the Emperor, after listening to the Imperial Chancellor's report as to the feeling aroused among the people of Germany by the Daily Telegraph publication, and on the attitude which he Prince Bülow had adopted in the Reichstag, expressed His will as follows :—" Without being influenced by what I can only regard as the unjust exaggeration of public criticism, I regard it as My prime Imperial duty to ensure the permanence and continuity of the policy of the Empire by the maintenance of constitutional responsibilities." The final result of the interview was that the Emperor approved the statements of the Imperial Chancellor in the Reichstag, and assured Prince Bülow of His continued confidence.

With this expression of confidence the "Chancellor Crisis" may be said to be temporarily solved, though whether Prince von Bülow will remain very long in office is still to be seen. It is impossible for me with my short experience in this country to form any judgment of my own on the point, but there seems to be a fairly general opinion that the Emperor will not easily forgive either the outspoken criticism of the members of the Reichstag or the somewhat half-hearted way in which it was met by the Imperial Chancellor; and that under these circumstances the latter's position may become so difficult that he will find some pretext for resigning in the near future. What the more radical portion of the Press says about it is that if the Imperial Chancellor had resigned at once he would have left office with the reputation of a great and patriotic statesman, whereas if he retires in a few months' time, as is considered probable, he will be regarded as having been a clever and adroit servant of the Emperor and nothing more.

In the meantime the constitutional crisis, which is of a graver and less easily solved nature, still remains; for it cannot be considered likely that the somewhat vague assurances given by the Emperor will satisfy the people who have during the last fortnight been clamouring for constitutional guarantees and ministerial responsibility. The Emperor says that "He regards it as his first Imperial duty to assure the permanence and continuity of the policy of the Empire by the maintenance of the responsibilities laid down by the Constitution." While the Conservative papers say that by this assurance and by His approval of the statements made by Prince Bülow in the Reichstag, the Emperor has publicly stated his recognition of the fact that henceforth a harmonious agreement between Emperor and nation is a state and national necessity, and that by that statement he has entirely won his way to the hearts of the people; the liberal and radical journals state that His Majesty's assurance means nothing at all, and they point out that it contains no indication as to the nature of the Imperial policy of which the Emperor considers it his duty to assure the permanence and continuity. They maintain moreover that it is difficult to find anything in the Emperor's assurance, at all events in the form in which it was communicated to the Press, to show that His Majesty has any intention of sacrificing what he regards as His constitutional independence of action, or of changing His personal methods of government. The only point which stands out with clearness in the present controversy is Prince Bülow's cleverness in finding a formula which, while committing the Emperor to but little, has nevertheless satisfied a great number of His Majesty's subjects.

The extent, or rather the limit of this satisfaction, is clearly shown by an exceedingly fair and impartial article in the Cologne Gazette of yesterday's date, of which I enclose a précis drawn up by Mr. Mounsey.([1])

One practical result of the discussion caused by the Daily Telegraph publication is, if my information is correct, that it has been decided that the Foreign Affairs Committee of the Bundesrat, whose meetings have hitherto been few and far between, shall in the future meet with far more regularity and frequency.

I have, &c.
W. E. GOSCHEN.

([1]) [Not reproduced.]

No. 139.

Mr. Carnegie to Sir Edward Grey.

F.O. 371/463.
41659/37537/08/18.
(No. 193.)   *Vienna,* D. *November* 24, 1908.
Sir,   R. *November* 30, 1908.

The settlement of the Chancellor Crisis in Germany by the continuance of Prince Bülow in office has caused great satisfaction throughout Austria. The continuity in German foreign policy, promised by the German Emperor and assured by his retention of Prince Bülow, is acclaimed in the Press here as the most necessary factor in the present international situation, and the greatest guarantee that Austria may still depend upon German support. Prince Bülow is a known quantity and it is recognised that it is largely owing to the complete agreement between his views and those of the Austro-Hungarian Government that the latter have been able to carry out their recent policy. So long as the Bismarckian traditions are adhered to—and Prince Bülow is essentially the exponent of these traditions—Austria feels herself secure in the course she is now pursuing, and can face the future, whether a Conference meets or not, with perfect equanimity.

Apart, too, from the specific interests of Austria, a general feeling is prevalent that the dismissal of Prince Bülow or in other words the immediate aggravation of the Crisis by the Emperor, would have been a disaster of incalculable magnitude for Europe at large. At a moment when in the language of the "Neue Freie Presse," "the antagonism between Germany and England keeps reappearing day by day like the uncanny flickering of a will o' the wisp and shedding an eerie light over the grouping of the Powers," and when the friction between Germany and France with regard to the Casablanca incident is barely over, any other solution of the Chancellor Crisis could not but have added to the general unrest and anxiety. Now the "stability of the policy of the Empire" is one factor at least on which the world at large can count.

The Constitutional issues raised by the Crisis are discussed academically without any particular fire or invective.

The now classical assurance that the stability of the policy of the Empire will be safeguarded "without prejudice to the responsibilities imposed by the Constitution" is criticised here as it has been criticised elsewhere. The Emperor's statement does not, it is felt, offer sufficient guarantees for the future Constitutional direction of German foreign policy. His Majesty has yielded for the moment to the pressure of exceedingly severe criticism and it is evident that it will be some time before He is likely to launch forth on another bout of personal policy. But there can be no very great confidence about the future, so long as there are no practical steps taken to insure the constitutional conduct of affairs. Nevertheless it is greatly felt that the Potsdam audience was a historic date for the German Empire, in that for the first time public opinion triumphed over personal policy. Prince Bülow met the Emperor as the spokesman of the German people and the Emperor approved his utterances. The parliamentary education of the German nation has thus made a considerable stride forwards.

I have, &c.
LANCELOT D. CARNEGIE.

No. 140.

Mr. Findlay to Sir Edward Grey.

F.O. 371/463.
41747/37537/08/18B.
(No. 49.) Confidential.

Dresden, D. November 25, 1908.
R. November 30, 1908.

Sir,

In view of the great interest attaching to the recent crisis through which Germany has been passing and to its effect on the future constitutional development of the German Empire, I venture to submit the following observations.

Anyone who has carefully followed the progress of recent events, and the attitude assumed by the various parties in the German Reichstag, can hardly fail to have been struck with the slight hold which constitutional ideas, and constitutional methods have obtained over the German mind.

As far as I am able to judge the "Freisinnige," the Social Democrats and some of the National Liberals alone were impressed with the necessity of obtaining constitutional guarantees that the responsibility of the Chancellor should, in future, be real and not nominal.

The principle that redress of grievances should precede the voting of supplies was mainly advocated by the Freisinnige "Frankfurter Zeitung" and by some of the Socialist papers, and yet with the proposal to add £25,000,000 per annum to taxation actually before them, surely no parliament was ever in a better position to make satisfactory terms.

The Centre is accused, with some show of reason, of having kept out of the fray in order to reserve its strength for an attack on the "Block" by means of its interpellation, the discussion of which is reported to be fixed for Monday or Tuesday next.

The fact is that the various fractions of the Block have entirely different opinions as to what is necessary and desirable. These differences can hardly fail to be clearly emphasised during the impending debates.

The Conservatives and the Pan-German League have declared against any alteration of the constitution. Certain National Liberals and the "Freisinnige" are in favour of reform and of various shades of Ministerial responsibility. It is hardly possible that the "Block" should, under these circumstances, present a firm front towards the Centre on the one side and the Socialists on the other.

As regards the position of the Emperor, and of Prince Bülow I venture to report the substance of a recent conversation with a German friend whose information is almost invariably good. He spoke to me very freely, stating that his information was derived from private sources which he regarded as being reliable. The following is a summary of what he told me:

While the Emperor was at Donau-Eschingen he was perfectly furious with Prince Bülow, and at the same time greatly depressed by the bitter and unanimous criticisms of the Press. This depression was aggravated by the sudden death of his favourite aide-de-camp Count Hülsen Haeseler, by the distress of his family, and by the disaster at Hamm. His Imperial Majesty returned to Berlin utterly dispirited, and with his power of resistance and self-confidence entirely broken down. Prince Bülow was therefore able to carry his point, and to secure the Emperor's assent to what he had stated in the Reichstag. Prince Bülow's position was, therefore, safe for the moment, but could hardly be considered to be so for any length of time. The Emperor's resentment at the failure of Prince Bülow to defend Him against the criticisms of the Press and of the Reichstag was intense, and would become more so as His Imperial Majesty recovered from the depression under which he was labouring for the moment. In a man of the Emperor's sanguine disposition no depression could be lasting.

The Emperor would then feel more and more that he had been exposed to a storm of criticism which had seriously shaken his position owing to the carelessness, or inefficiency of officials for whom Prince Bülow was responsible, even if the Chancellor himself was not to blame; that Prince Bülow, while pretending to defend the Emperor in his official communiqués, and in his speech to the Reichstag, had entirely, and perhaps deliberately, failed to do so. In fact that His Majesty had been deserted by a man who owed everything to Him, whom He had raised to the highest position in the Empire and had treated with every mark of friendship and confidence.

Further if it was true (as had been stated by Count Hohenthal in the Saxon Landtag) that Prince Bülow's masterly speech to the Committee of the Bundesrat on German foreign policy in recent years, had produced the impression on his competent and critical audience that the conduct of German foreign policy was in the best hands, His Highness could only have done so by showing step by step that the failures of German diplomacy were directly traceable to the Emperor's interference, without which his policy would have been successful. Prince Bülow's speech to the assembled representatives must therefore have amounted to a crushing attack on the Emperor. His Imperial Majesty was sure to realise this sooner or later, in fact the Emperor would be sure to rid himself as soon as possible of a Chancellor, intercourse with whom must have become almost intolerable.

My friend had recently been in Berlin where, he said, the Emperor was almost universally regarded as a curious case of atavism, a reincarnation of Frederick William the Fourth, brother of the Emperor William the First. The prestige of the Emperor was gone beyond recall, and all classes of persons with whom he had been in contact, including the military, expressed their feelings of dissatisfaction with equal freedom. It was the general impression that the crisis was by no means over, it was probable that it would break out afresh over the interpellations in the Reichstag next week, and it was impossible to be sure what line the Emperor would then take. No-one could reasonably expect His Imperial Majesty to efface himself for long, it was contrary to His nature to do so, sooner or later there would be similar incidents, and in that case, my friend concluded, there will probably be a general demand for a regency.

I do not pretend to say whether this conclusion is correct. I venture, however, to report these remarks as showing the way in which Germans are talking among themselves.

I have, &c.

M. DE C. FINDLAY.

No. 141.

Sir A. Johnstone to Sir Edward Grey.

F.O. 371/463.
41717/37537/08/18.
(No. 136.) Confidential.

Copenhagen, D. November 26, 1908.
R. November 30, 1908.

Sir,

I met the Austrian Secretary, Count Schönborn, last night at the Russian Legation and in the course of conversation he told me he had just returned from Berlin where he had learnt that the German Emperor was furious with Prince Bülow for not having better defended His Majesty in the Reichstag. Count Schönborn said that he was assured that Prince Bülow had been aware of the communication made to the "Daily Telegraph" and that although the Emperor did not for the moment deem it opportune to quarrel with his Chancellor, yet it was believed in well-informed circles that the Prince's tenure of his office would not be of long duration.

I should not, in most cases, think it worth while to report the utterances of a junior diplomatist about matters not directly affecting his country of residence, especially as Sir Edward Goschen has far better opportunities than I can possibly have of informing you how matters stand between the Emperor and Prince Bülow, but Count Schönborn is the brother-in-law of Prince Fürstenberg, who, as you are aware, is a very intimate friend of the Emperor; and I have little doubt that Count Schönborn has derived his information from his distinguished relative.

I am sending a copy of this despatch by this messenger to Sir Edward Goschen.

I have, &c.
ALAN JOHNSTONE.

No. 142.

Sir Edward Grey to Sir F. Bertie.([1])

Private.([2])

My dear Bertie,   *Foreign Office, December 1, 1908.*

I feel decidedly that things are very well as they are about the German Emperor's interview.

Everyone here is on their guard; nobody believes that France and Russia were more hostile to us than Germany was during the Boer war, and if they did, they would only say that it was a very good thing we were on better terms with France and Russia now, and that what happened in the Boer war was over and done with. All the pro-Germans here have been shaken and shocked by the impulsive indiscretion of the Emperor; they doubt his sanity; and as for the German people, they have been stirred into a greater sense of responsibility, and are taking the Emperor in hand for themselves.

I should like Germany and its Emperor to cease to be talked about; to see them allowed to settle down; and to let the King pay his contemplated visit to Berlin next season, which would have a tranquillizing effect.

I don't believe the German people want war, and if left to themselves, I think they will settle down and the Emperor will never regain his position.

But if they are constantly stirred up and talked about, they will be goaded to great irritation.

The publication of another interview with the Emperor, if it takes place in England or France, will be regarded in Germany as an attempt from outside to damage the Emperor; its accuracy will be denied, which will give the Germans an excuse for saying they disbelieve it; the publication will be resented as a foreign attempt to injure the Emperor, which will create a German reaction in his favour.

Publication in America would not be so bad, but I think even that will probably do more harm than good, and I don't at all like the idea of instigating anything which I am not prepared to own up to. The Americans are beyond my control, and I can do nothing to stop anything coming out there, but as far as my own opinion goes, I should give it, when asked, against any more publication anywhere.

It isn't the attacks upon our King or anything in particular of which I deprecate the publication: if the German Emperor has said rude things, I should be rather glad than otherwise that he should incur the odium of having them known; but on general grounds of policy I should be disposed to let well alone, as the best chance of

([1]) [This letter was in reply to one from Sir F. Bertie of November 30, which is endorsed " Ans[were]d Dec[ember] 1." This letter gave an account of a conversation with M. Clemenceau, in which Sir F. Bertie explained the reasons which led the British government to deprecate the publication of any further interview.]

([2]) [Grey MSS., Vol. 11.]

restoring normal relations with Germany and preventing the Emperor with his megalomania being set up again.

Never since I have been in office has opinion here been so thoroughly wide awake with regard to Germany, and on its guard as it is now. I haven't the faintest tremor of anxiety about that. Never has the Emperor's position been so low in the world.

Why then not let well alone!

Yours sincerely,
E. GREY.

This is written in a great hurry to catch the bag, but the conclusion is clear and I have no doubt about it.

CHAPTER XLIV.
GREAT BRITAIN AND GERMANY, JANUARY TO JULY 1909.

I.—KING EDWARD'S VISIT TO BERLIN.[1]

No. 143.

Sir Edward Grey to Sir F. Bertie.

Private.[2]

My dear Bertie,   *Foreign Office, January 7, 1909.*

The King goes to Berlin in the second week of February. The visit I understand is to be for three days.

If the visit had not taken place, it would have been a cause of offence and made all politics more difficult. For this reason I am glad it is arranged, but otherwise I do not expect much good from it. To please the Emperor does not carry so much weight in Germany as it did.

Feeling here is very strong that a Minister should go with the King. If I went, it would be liable to misconstruction, as I have not been on any other visits; and there is no reason as far as politics are concerned why I should go. I want things to go smoothly between us and Germany. I do not want any special co-operation which would alter the present grouping of the Powers.

It is therefore being arranged that Crewe should go. Dernburg, the German Colonial Minister, has been to South Africa. There are a lot of troublesome boundary and frontier questions with Germany there, which Crewe can discuss, but which are of purely local interest. There is no question of treating any of them in a way which would affect anything outside South Africa; for, apart from other considerations, the South African Colonies themselves will not allow Walfisch Bay to be touched, and that is the only thing there which could conceivably form part of negotiations which would affect Imperial relations.

I think Charles Hardinge will also go with the King, so that if Bagdad Railway comes up it can be referred to him, and he will be instructed to adhere to the position of negotiation à quatre (i.e., : including France and Russia) as a necessary condition. So also with regard to Morocco, or any other matters of foreign policy, which may arise. There will be no new departure. But I do not think the Germans will want to discuss much.

I shall not be in London till the 25th, unless I am forced by untoward circumstances; but you can tell Clemenceau as much as you think necessary or desirable of the circumstances of the visit. None of these special considerations or of the reasons for them should however be disclosed in public in advance.

Your sincerely,

E. GREY.

(1) [The visit, which lasted from February 9–12, is described in Sir Sidney Lee : *King Edward VII* (1927), II, pp. 672–7. *cp.* also *G.P.* XXVIII, ch. 221, especially pp. 85–90. On pp. 85–7 there is an account by the Emperor William dated November 12, 1909, of a conversation with King Edward.]

(2) [Grey MSS., Vol. 12.]

No. 144.

Sir E. Goschen to Sir Edward Grey.

F.O. 1214/1214/09/18.
(No. 12.)   *Berlin, D. January* 8, 1909.
Sir,   R. *January* 11, 1909.

It cannot be said that with the opening of the New Year there is any change for the better in the generally unfriendly tone of the German press towards England. On the contrary, in nearly all the Reviews published in the various papers, of the happenings of 1908, efforts are made to shew that England is mainly responsible for the situation in the Near East. In some of these articles, but not many, there are admissions that Austria might perhaps have managed things a little more tactfully, but even in these cases there is no admission that Austria is responsible for the situation, but only that she gave England the opportunity to raise up trouble and put in movement all the strings of her Machiavellian and baleful policy.

It is difficult to say whether the legend of Great Britain's responsibility was composed in Vienna or Berlin. Personally, I have every reason to believe that it was started by Baron d'Aehrenthal himself; but in any case it is now very current here and is made to do duty in nearly all German Articles on the situation. . . . . ([1])

           I have, &c.
           W. E. GOSCHEN.

([1]) [This despatch proceeds to give summaries of articles in the German Press which do not seem worth reproducing.]

No. 145.

Sir E. Goschen to Sir Edward Grey.

F.O. 1215/1215/09/18.
(No. 13.)   *Berlin, D. January* 9, 1909.
Sir,   R. *January* 11, 1909.

I have the honour to forward, herewith, a despatch, as marked in the margin, which I have received from Colonel Trench, Military Attaché to this Embassy, relating to The Emperor's views as expressed to his Generals.

           I have, &c.
           W. E. GOSCHEN.

Enclosure in No. 145.

Colonel Trench to Sir E. Goschen.

(No. 2.)   Confidential.
Sir,   *Berlin, January* 8, 1909.

I have the honour to draw attention to the views said to have been expressed by His Majesty the Emperor last Saturday on the occasion of his annual reception of the General Officers commanding army corps.

An account of what took place was originally published by the Nationalist Taegliche Rundschau, and although its indiscretion has been blamed by some papers, there has been a general outburst of criticism of the action of the Emperor. What happened appears to have been somewhat as follows (I omit details which have been denied): The Emperor, after dinner, discussed, with maps and in considerable detail, the operations at the manœuvres of the XVth, XVIth XVIIth and Ist Army Corps at which he had been present during the autumn and then read to the Generals either the whole or part of an article which had just appeared in the Deutsche Revue for January, entitled "War in the Present" and which His Majesty said was by General Count Schlieffen, General v[on] Moltke's predecessor as Chief of the Great General Staff. The Emperor appears to have said that there was no need for him to express his opinions regarding the military position of Germany at the commencement of the new year as his views entirely coincided with those expressed in the article. The manner of the Emperor is reported to have strongly impressed his generals and is described as "hoheitsvoll, selbstbewuszt, schlicht und von vornehmster ruhiger Bestimmtheit" (dignified, self-conscious [sic], simple, and determined).

This article, of which I attach a copy in German with a summary of the first portion and a translation of the final political part,(¹) consists of eleven pages of which eight or nine are devoted to an account of the improvements in modern fire arms and their effect on tactic[s.] The last two or three pages of the article are entirely political and describe Germany as standing isolated in the centre of Europe "opposed to a zealous endeavour to unite all the forces round her in a common attack on the centre." With the exception of the Berliner Tageblatt which gives some extracts from the military portion of the article, the press generally ignores the first part of the article and refers only to the political part which many of them quote in extenso.

From the views on tactics which I have had the honour of hearing the Emperor express it seems most likely that it was mainly on account of the military views contained in the first part of the article that he read it to his generals and indeed it is possible that he did not read aloud the last two pages at all. May I, very respectfully, remark however, that I have no reason to suppose that His Majesty disagrees with the political views expressed in them—rather the contrary.

To turn now to the press comments on the episode, the readiness with which the organs of nearly all parties grasp the opportunity of blaming the sovereign is remarkable, and all the more so when one remembers how intimately all but the most independent journals are connected with the Press Bureau in the Foreign Office.

The Frankfurter Zeitung describes the Emperor as "endeavouring to describe the political situation of Germany between the people of Europe by reading aloud from beginning to end an article .... .(²) and declaring his concurrence with the views of the author." The journal goes on to say that "enemies all round" is the pith of this part of the article and it (the F[rankfurter] Z[eitung]) is not surprised to learn that the Emperor substantially shares the views of the author for this is the motto of many a speech he has made." While the journal thinks that the tendency of the military mind is to anticipate situations which will call for the use of the sword, it admits that the description of the military situation is accurate. It compares the expression of Count Schlieffen's views with that of those of Lord Roberts and says that what is uncomfortable is that the Emperor has said that he agrees with them.

The semi-official Koelnische Zeitung makes no better defence than the statement that the Emperor's views were not meant for publication and that for this reason there can be no question of a storm like the one in November.

The Rheinisch-Westfaelische Zeitung declares that it thoroughly agrees with the contents of the article but regrets very deeply that the Emperor should have declared that they were his views. "What are the views of the Emperor? In the most unfortunate interview he declared himself England's best friend who has always done and will always do what he can to maintain friendly relations. In this article he points to England as the 'Implacable enemy,' It is doubtful that King Edward will look upon this as welcoming his visit. What answer will Italy France and Russia give to the Emperor? William II took over the German Empire as the most powerful state in Europe .... now he admits that there is a coalition which forms a standing menace .... that is the captain's statement of the results of the new course."

The conservative Post alone expresses entire approval and says that the German people agree with Count Schlieffen. It adds that while the Emperor considers the

---

(¹) [Not reproduced.]
(²) [The omission marks throughout this document are in the original.]

Q 3

maintenance of peace a sacred duty he will always hold the honour of Germany to be most precious.

I have, &c.

F. TRENCH, *Colonel, Gen[eral] Staff,*
Military Attaché.

[*ED. NOTE.*—In his despatch No. 14 of January 8 (F.O. 1216/1216/09/18), Sir E. Goschen forwarded a copy of the following official communiqué, which had been published in the *Reichsanzeiger* :—

" On January 2, [1909] His Majesty the Emperor and King made a speech, as he does every year, to the Commanding Generals assembled here for the New Year congratulations. What His Majesty said was not intended for publication and ought not to have been the subject of public criticism. In spite of this, news of it has reached the Press. In reply to the attacks which have appeared in the foreign papers we assert that the speech confined itself solely to military questions. Referring to the survey of the tactical experiments made in the last manœuvres, His Majesty mentioned an academic study which appeared recently, in which the form of modern warfare and the influence of modern arms are developed. No reference was made to the political thoughts and views also contained in this military work, in the utterances of His Majesty the Emperor."]

[*ED. NOTE.*—The memorandum which follows gives Sir C. Hardinge's confidential report of his interview with Prince Bülow on February 10, 1909. The earlier part is omitted here as it was printed in *Gooch & Temperley*, Vol. V, pp. 608–9. In this earlier part there were a few omissions, the reason for which was explained in a note at the head of the document. The latter half of the memorandum here printed is given in full.

Memorandum by Sir C. Hardinge.(¹)

F.O. 6767/222/09/18.
Confidential.   *February* 11, 1909.

. . . . On Prince Bülow alluding to the Agreement concluded on the 9th instant between Germany and France relating to Morocco,(²) I took the opportunity of saying that I had before leaving London talked the matter over with Sir E. Grey, and that I had his authority to say that he entirely approved of it, and that he was very pleased to think that this source of friction had, by a wise act of forbearance on the part of the German Government, been now entirely removed. This would undoubtedly have an excellent effect on the relations between England and Germany, since, owing to our engagements with France, any tension between France and Germany relating to Moroccan affairs was liable to create difficulties between England and Germany.

Prince Bülow seemed extremely pleased with what I had said to him, and asked me to express to Sir Edward his very warm appreciation of this friendly message. He fully believed in the excellent effect which the Agreement would produce both in England and France, and, he added, he had for a long time wanted to put an end to the difficulties which had constantly arisen during the last few years, and which, by the exaggeration of the press of both countries, had become a veritable danger to friendly relations and to the peace of the world. He fully realized that France has many reminiscences which it will be difficult for her ever to forget, but all he wanted was that correct relations should exist between the two countries, and he could see no reason why this result should not now be obtained. He begged me to assure Sir E. Grey that the recent Casablanca incident(²) was entirely due to a misunderstanding which had been greatly aggravated by the indiscreet attitude of the press of both countries, but that he could honestly say that he had never contemplated any serious difficulties with France, and much less war, over the fate of three or four miserable deserters, who were worthless and of no account whatever. The question was now to be settled by The Hague Tribunal, and he was able to regard its possible outcome with absolute complacency.

I have since heard that Sir E. Grey's message has created the best possible effect in Government circles.

On my making a reference to the famous " Daily Telegraph " letter,(³) he enlarged at some length on the attitude which he had adopted towards the Emperor in the Reichstag, and his remarks were of an explanatory and even apologetic character. He said that the outburst in

(¹) [For Prince Bülow's report, *v. G.P.* XXVI, II, pp. 551–3, and for the Emperor William II's comments on it, *v. ib.* XXVIII, pp. 85–7. The conversation was also described in Prince Bülow's despatch to Herr von Tschirschky, *ib.* XXVIII, pp. 88–91.]
(²) [This subject will be treated in *Gooch & Temperley*, Vol. VII.]
(³) [*cp. supra*, pp. 201–26, Nos. 125–42 *passim.*]

the German press over the "Daily Telegraph" interview was not to be attributed to any hostility on the part of the German people to the Monarchy in principle, for the Germans are essentially a Monarchical race, nor was it due to the friendly tone adopted by the Emperor towards England, but it was to be attributed to the conviction which had been slowly growing in the mind of the people, that the Government of the Emperor was becoming one of a personal and unconstitutional character. Such incidents as the Tweedmouth letter, certain indiscreet speeches, &c., had forced the conviction upon the people that there was too much personal interference by the Emperor in Governmental and foreign affairs, and that an end must be put to it. Although his own attitude towards the Empera[o]r in the Reichstag had been criticized, the circumstances of the situation were such that he could not have spoken otherwise. The Emperor had been deeply hurt by the attitude of his people, which had come as a great surprise to him, but His Majesty had now entirely recovered his spirits. He expressed his absolute conviction that the sentiments expressed by the Emperor in the interview faithfully represented his feelings towards England and the English people, although, with the Emperor's natural inclination to a certain amount of exaggeration, too much attention should not be paid to the details of some of the statements which the letter contained. The initiative taken by Colonel Stuart-Wortley in submitting the interview to the Emperor for publication was the worst service which a friend of the Emperor could possibly have rendered him.

Prince Bülow expressed the greatest satisfaction at the visit of the King and Queen to Berlin, which had been eagerly awaited, and which he fully believed would contribute to a general *détente*, and to an improvement in the relations of the two countries. The simple and unaffected manner and words of the King and Queen had greatly impressed all classes, and had convinced them of their sincerity.

On Count Metternich's name being mentioned, Prince Bülow praised highly his loyalty and the services he had rendered. I remarked that, although we greatly appreciated his attitude during the Boer war when our relations with Germany were strained, and the fact that he had never created needless difficulties, it was a pity that he had not succeeded in making himself more popular, and that he was always grumbling about something or other. I added that I had heard that, on the other hand, when unfriendly remarks about England are made in Germany in his presence, England can find no more staunch defender than Count Metternich. Prince Bülow said that my remarks were perfectly true and just, and that Count Metternich was loyal to both England and Germany. He had been greatly impressed by him four or five years ago, when the belief spread in Germany that England contemplated an attack on Germany with a view to destroying her fleet. On that occasion he summoned him to Berlin, and introduced him in the room in which we were then sitting into the midst of a crowd of Generals and Admirals who were absolutely convinced that an attack was intended and being prepared. Count Metternich argued at some length, endeavouring to persuade them of the peaceful disposition of His Majesty's Government, but failing to convince them he offered to stake his head, or, what was more, his honour, that no attack was being contemplated. The Generals and Admirals were at last convinced, but what had struck Prince Bülow was that there was no attempt on the part of Count Metternich to hedge, as so many diplomatists would have been inclined to do, but he loyally stated his opinion, and was ready to stand or fall by it.

I took the opportunity of mentioning to Prince Bülow that we greatly appreciate the conciliatory attitude of M. Kriege at the Naval Conference([4]) which had contributed materially to its success. It was all the greater pleasure to bear this testimony to his procedure, since at the opening of the Conference we had had reason to fear that he intended to be obstructive. Prince Bülow replied that he was very pleased to hear this. He admitted that M. Kriege was a type of international jurist, whose motto was "*fiat justitia ruat cælum*," and that he often got on his nerves. He had, however, the highest opinion of his ability, and he looked forward with interest to the impending conflict between M. Kriege and his friend M. Renault over the international intricacies of the Casablanca incident.

During the course of my conversation there was no discussion of the questions of naval armaments or of the Bagdad Railway.

Nothing could have been more friendly or agreeable than Prince Bülow's manner during the course of our conversation, and it may not be out of place to add a few remarks based on information obtained from both German and foreign sources during the few days spent in Berlin.

I took some trouble in trying to discover what Prince Bülow's motive had been in concluding, at the present moment, the Agreement with France relating to Morocco, which was a complete reversal of the policy pursued by Germany during the past four years, and from which it appears that Germany is to reap no material advantage. Various opinions were expressed, based on personal and other motives, but I believe the true explanation to be that Prince Bülow has, since the Casablanca incident, been seriously alarmed at the hostile trend of public opinion in Germany towards England and France for which he has been directly responsible in the past, and which he felt to be gradually growing beyond his control. He has also realized that the encouragement of an anti-English and anti-French public opinion is opposed to the views of the Emperor with whom it is his wish to stand well at present, and it has therefore been in his own interest as well as in the interest of German relations with England and France to check the

([4]) [This subject will be treated in a later volume.]

animosity which he had himself encouraged, and by concluding an Agreement which would have been more appropriate four years ago than now to obtain credit in Germany as a pacifist, and to show the German people that it is quite possible to act in Europe in unison with England and France.

I was told by a member of the German Foreign Office that the explanation of the hostile attitude adopted by Germany towards France in Morocco during the past five years was to be found in the fact that, within a year before the conclusion of the Anglo-French Agreement of 1904, the French Government had approached the German Government with direct proposals for the conclusion of an Agreement relating to Morocco. These proposals had not been rejected, and it was therefore felt to be an insult when an Anglo-French Agreement was concluded in which Germany was entirely ignored. The explanation is plausible, but it is the first time that I have heard it. Recent German policy and its reversal are, in the opinion of some of those with whom I talked in Berlin, largely due to the absence of any fixity in German foreign policy, and to the hopeless confusion created in its direction by the joint activity of the Emperor, the Chancellor, and the Secretary of State for Foreign Affairs, whose views on important questions are constantly divergent.

As regards Prince Bülow's personal position, opinions are divided as to whether he will be able to continue to hold his present office. Much will depend, it is said, on his personal relations with the Emperor and on the success of his financial policy. Outwardly, there is a distinct improvement in his relations with the Emperor, but on the other hand, public opinion in Germany has veered round, and his attack on the Emperor in the Reichstag is severely criticised. I am able, however, to state authoritatively that the Emperor and the Imperial Family entertain the greatest mistrust of Prince Bülow, not only on account of his recent attitude towards the Emperor, but also on account of his close relations with Herr von Holstein, and this fact seems likely to make his fall in the near future probable. It is thought that, in that eventuality, Count Wedel would be his successor, but there is some doubt as to whether the change would be a good one, as he is reported to be headstrong, and likely to quarrel with the Emperor on small provocation.

CHARLES HARDINGE.]

No. 146.

Sir E. Goschen to Sir Edward Grey.

F.O. 5995/222/09/18.
(No. 50.)   Berlin, D. *February* 12, 1909.
Sir,   R. *February* 15, 1909.

I have the honour to report that The King and Queen left Berlin this evening for London.

It is a great pleasure to be able to report that the visit was a splendid success. It passed off brilliantly without the slightest hitch of any sort. The greetings to the King when passing through the streets of Berlin have been wonderfully spontaneous and enthusiastic, the tone of the Press has left nothing to be desired, and as far as I have heard or seen, not one discordant note has been struck which might mar the harmony of the visit.

As the "Kölnische Zeitung" puts it, "The events of the last few days, preceded as they were by Sir E. Grey's friendly tone towards Germany in his speech at Coldstream, the courteous attitude of the authorities in Cape Colony during Herr Dernburg's recent colonial tour, and the unanimous expressions of goodwill towards Great Britain by all parties in the Reichstag on November 10th last, warrant good hopes for the future. The German people ask nothing better than to live in peace and friendship with the People of Great Britain, whose sound good sense, tenacity of purpose, confident strength and eminent achievements in all spheres of life they heartily and honestly admire. . . . .(1) If the visit brings about a gradual and tacit good understanding between the two nations, it will not have been paid in vain. If an 'entente' has not been reached or sought, at all events we can look forward to a progressive 'détente' in the relations between the two countries."

These words in a German paper form very pleasant reading, and all the more that they are devoid of all extravagance such as might have been caused by momentary enthusiasm for a visit which has pleased high and low and which has been such an

(1) [Thus in original.]

unqualified success. The Berlin press teems with articles such as I have just quoted, and it is to my mind satisfactory that, whatever the result of the visit may be in the future, it is its friendly, and not its political side, which is for the present occupying public opinion in Germany.

There is, it is needless to state, but one word throughout Berlin for the great tact and courtesy of the King and the gracious charm of Queen Alexandra, and I have heard not from one, but from many people that they have never seen so much spontaneous and hearty enthusiasm amongst the population of Berlin as on the present occasion.

In the few gracious words which The King was pleased to address to me at the Station, before leaving, His Majesty expressed His great satisfaction at the success of the visit, His appreciation of the Reception He had met with from the Court and the people and His pleasure that everything had passed off so satisfactorily.

The Emperor was pleased to talk to me for a few moments after His Royal Guests had departed. He told me how delighted He had been to receive Their Majesties at Berlin and what a pleasure it was to Him that They had met with such a hearty and enthusiastic reception from His Berlin subjects. He also alluded to the thoroughly satisfactory tone of the Press and added that one of the things which had pleased him most was the account The King had given Him of the proceedings at the Rathhaus. He had also heard an account of them from the First Burgomaster and others present at the reception, and He could tell me that the King's charm of manner and His kindness and affability to all those who had had the honour of being presented to His Majesty had made a deep impression on a class of people not often and not easily impressed.

"One word more"? the Emperor said, "They have telegraphed from London for German paper. Financiers generally know what they are about, and if that is not a sign that the visit has been a signal and brilliant success, I don't know what is!"

I shall have the honour of sending by post an account of the various festivities and receptions, as well as the text of the toasts exchanged between the two sovereigns, which, I may add, have caused widespread satisfaction, and have been very favourably received by the Press.

I have, &c.
W. E. GOSCHEN.

No. 147.

Sir F. Cartwright to Sir Edward Grey.

F.O. 6506/222/09/18.
Tel. (No. 43.) P.([1])   *Vienna, February* 17, 1909.

Baron d'Aehrenthal made a spontaneous reference this afternoon to the good effect which the King's visit to Berlin had produced here. A marked *détente*, which would be felt throughout Europe, would in his opinion be brought about by the visit, combined with the new Moroccan Agreement. He said that the Emperor William had expressed himself as most satisfied with the results of the King's visit in a telegram addressed to the Emperor Francis Joseph. His Excellency said that he had also been informed by Prince Bülow of the good impression which his conversations with Sir Charles Hardinge had created in official circles in Berlin. Baron d'Aehrenthal also expressed great satisfaction at the speech made by the King at the opening of Parliament and at that of the Prime Minister's in the House of Commons. The Press comments in a very complimentary manner on these two speeches.

([1]) [The paraphrase is given as the original decypher cannot be traced.]

No. 148.

Sir Edward Grey to Sir E. Goschen.

F.O. 7379/1780/09/28.
(No. 45.)
Sir, *Foreign Office, February 18, 1909.*

I told Count Metternich that the visit of the King seemed to us to have passed off very well. I heard from every one that the effect had been excellent, and the King himself was evidently very pleased with the visit.

Count Metternich said that this was certainly the feeling in Berlin.

I said the good effect had been increased by the signature of the Agreement with France about Morocco. I had always felt that even when there were no actual difficulties between Germany and France, the anticipation of possible difficulties about Morocco had been an impediment to good relations between Germany and England. I trusted that this apprehension had now been removed.

Count Metternich said that was the intention and desire of the German Government in making the Agreement.

[I am, &c.]
E. G[REY].

No. 149.

Sir E. Goschen to Sir Edward Grey.

F.O. 7942/7942/09/18.
(No. 67.) *Berlin, D. February 24, 1909.*
Sir, *R. March 1, 1909.*

I have the honour to forward, herewith, a despatch, as marked in the margin, which I have received from Colonel Trench, Military Attaché to this Embassy, relating to Opinions of H[is] M[ajesty] the Emperor.

I have, &c.
W. E. GOSCHEN.

Enclosure in No. 149.

The Opinions of H.M. the Emperor.

Very Confidential.
(No. 10/09.)
Sir, *British Embassy, Berlin, February 21, 1909.*

I have the honour to report that, yesterday, at the "Neues Palais," on the occasion of H.M. the Emperor accepting a copy of the British Army List for 1909, His Majesty honoured me by speaking to me for nearly an hour about the recent Visit to Berlin of Their Majesties the King and the Queen, the training and organisation of the British and German armies, and the war between the Yellow and White Races which the Emperor seems persuaded will take place within the next few decades.

His Majesty expressed great satisfaction at the success of the Royal Visit, asked about the King's visits to the Rathaus and to the First Guard Dragoons and said he was greatly pleased, not only that the people of Berlin should have had opportunities of becoming better acquainted with His Majesty, but also that "they should have behaved so well," . . . .([1]) a matter about which he seems to have had some uneasiness. The Emperor expressed especial pleasure at the terms in which the visit to Berlin was referred to in the Speech from the Throne.

The Emperor wanted to know why Lord Charles Beresford was giving up his command before his time, and said he supposed the reasons were personal ones, and what a pity it was that officers did not always think solely of the good of their

([1]) [Thus in original.]

country. He added that he did not at all object to our strengthening the fleet in the North Sea, as he hoped we would come down from the North, on the flank, when all the white men were fighting to defend European civilisation against the Yellow Invasion. This theme seems to have a great interest for His Majesty and he spoke about it for half an hour. He believes that there will be another invasion like that of Genghis Khan, but that this time it will be more formidable on account of the discoveries of modern science, by which the Yellow man is profiting; Russia ought to be strengthening herself against the East instead of "playing with the Bulgarians and Servians"; it is the duty of all European nations to sink their differences and all join together to prevent western civilisation from being overwhelmed by the yellow and brown flood. "We must have the Americans with us and we must also have the Mohamedans." They are monotheists and should be got on our side against the heathen. "That is why I have settled matters with France about Morocco; it would never do for the merchants in Morocco to put the Moors against the white race." "And we must have the Turks too: they're splendid soldiers—I saw that when I was in the East." "I have no reason to approve of the Sultan's government but as he's the ruler of his people I'm friendly with him." After comparing at some length the characters of the Turk and the Arab, His Majesty passed to Egypt where he seemed to think that our rule was tottering. He is reading with great interest and approval a serial by Hall Caine entitled "The White Prophet" which is appearing in the Strand Magazine. The Emperor thinks British rule in India also very shaky—in a small measure owing to the ideas which Baboos bring back from English universities, partly also because the Japanese defeated the (white) Russians in the late war, but mainly "because your dear allies are secretly undermining your rule everywhere there. You will see! Your government there will have to fight for its life before long." "And where is your army!"

His Majesty then criticised the various attempts made to reorganise the British Army, dwelling especially on those points in which he thought sufficient account had not been taken of our peculiarities of character and circumstance. He said the abolition of the militia and volunteers was a great mistake—they were so well suited to our national life; he wondered why we had not formed an army corps of marines, of whom he seemed to have a very high opinion. His Majesty thought we would find it impossible to introduce universal service, certainly by act of parliament, or at short notice. "We've got it; but why? Because we had the French for six years in our country."

The Emperor then compared the training and discipline of the French and German armies (the reserves especially) very unfavourably to the former, and told me how he had organised the mining population in special units and of the excellence of their training and discipline. It was nonsense to say that there was a good deal of social-democratic feeling among them: they would shoot down their own people if ordered to. His Majesty explained with some detail how, in conjunction with the introduction of two years' service, the mobilisation arrangements had been modified, how improvements had been made in the training of the reserves and how the reserve units were now almost as good as those with the colours, &c. (The details were entirely technical and would be out of place here.) Referring to Lord Roberts views, the Emperor strongly deprecated the adoption by a country of systems which, however suitable in other lands, were not adapted to its own peculiarities of life and character, and gave as an instance the unsuitability of our British parliamentary system for Germany (a point on which he expressed himself with a good deal of feeling and emphasis).

His Majesty seemed in excellent health and spoke with his usual animation, and an usual use of expletives, shaking his fist and hammering his left arm. He seemed to want to say all that he said, and on subjects decided on beforehand; the Chief of the Naval Cabinet and the Minister for the Navy were waiting outside all the time. His Majesty seemed to wish to show how sympathetically interested he was in England's difficulties and how closely he had followed her history.

I respectfully beg permission to note being always much struck, whenever the Emperor honours me with the expression of his views on matters outside Europe with his conviction that England's hold on the dependancies [sic] beyond the seas hangs by a thread and that the subject peoples are on the verge of revolt—and several members of his entourage give me just the same impression. Professor Schiemann is, no doubt, responsible for much; but it would be interesting to know whether this conviction is the cause—or the effect—of the journeys to India, Egypt and South Africa of numerous officers—many of them with very small means—, who ask me for letters of introduction to British and native personages. I note, however, that, during the recent operations in German South-west Africa, the view seems to have been accepted that the "Low-german" Boer seems to prefer the Union Jack to "Pangermanism."

I have, &c.

F. TRENCH,

Colonel, General Staff and Military Attaché.

MINUTES.

It is well known that the German Emperor has the Yellow Peril on his brain. He has expressed the same views about our rule in India before. As Colonel Trench remarks, Professor Schiemann, who is one of the most mischievous of German Anglophobes, is responsible for many of the Emperor's views.

G. H. V.

1.3.09.

G. S. S.

1.3.

W. L.

C. H.

MINUTE BY KING EDWARD.

The Emperor's remarks are well worthy of consideration and not to be put on one side as W[ar] O[ffice] would like to do.

E.R.

No. 150.

Sir Edward Grey to Sir E. Goschen.

Private.(¹)

Dear Sir Edward Goschen, *Foreign Office, March 4, 1909.*

You will see from the telegrams the fuss which Prince Bülow has made about the sayings of our Embassy at St. Petersburgh.(²) I am puzzled as to why he has made this storm out of what he must have known was nothing.

I took the opportunity of telling Metternich that as a matter of fact we were exceptionally careful to avoid making mischief.

I had told Cartwright before he went to Vienna to do nothing which would tend to make mischief (if that were possible) between Germany and Austria.

Bülow had spoken to C. Hardinge at Berlin with the strongest disapproval of Aehrenthal's proceedings in the autumn; Hardinge had of course included this in his report to me of what had passed, and I had cut out this passage in circulating it to the Cabinet. I was afraid that if it was known to so many people it might give rise to gossip, which however innocent in intention might do harm by causing the language of Prince Bülow to be repeated.

(¹) [Grey MSS., Vol. 22.]
(²) [v. Gooch & Temperley, Vol. V, p. 643, No. 629.]

The Germans are very difficult people : one never knows with whom one is dealing; sometimes one mind seems to give the impulse,and sometimes another, and they tolerate or encourage mischief makers in their service.

They *seem* not to be pleased at the stiff attitude which Austria has adopted and her failure to respond to Russia's effort of conciliation at Belgrade,([3]) very likely it is true that Schoen is disappointed, but it does not follow that one or more persons more important than Schoen are displeased.

If the Germans would only deal with us as we deal with them there would be no difficulties.

Yours sincerely,
E. GREY.

([3]) [v. Gooch & Temperley, Vol. V, pp. 636–7, No. 619.]

II.—NAVAL PROGRAMMES, JANUARY-JULY 1909.([1])

No. 151.

Sir Edward Grey to Sir E. Goschen.

F.O. 721/721/09/18.
(No. 9.)

Sir,   *Foreign Office, January 4, 1909.*

I told Count Metternich to-day([2]) that we had been considering our Naval Estimates for the forthcoming year : they would have to be very serious.

I reminded him that at the Hague Conference([3]) we had abstained from bringing forward any proposal of an international character, because it was understood that the German Delegates would refuse to take part in the discussion of any concrete proposal. We had, therefore, confined ourselves to bringing forward only such a general resolution as it was understood would be agreed to.

Subsequently, in conversations with Count Metternich, I had dwelt upon the importance of a comparison of the Naval Estimates of the two countries, and the whole subject had been very fully discussed with him in conversation with Mr. Lloyd-George at my house.

We had not made further proposals, because we had been told that the German Naval programme was fixed by law, that it was not dependent upon our Estimates, and that therefore there appeared to be no opening for negotiations.

I had, however, instructed Sir Charles Hardinge before he went to Kronberg to mention the importance of Naval expenditure.([4]) I had done this because I thought that, after the subject had been discussed with Count Metternich, it would never do for a political discussion with the Emperor to take place without any mention being made of the subject. For if the subject was not mentioned, then it might be thought that we no longer considered it as of first rate importance.

I then told Count Metternich that, according to our information, if the German shipbuilding proceeded at its normal rate, Germany would have 13 "Dreadnoughts" completed by February 1912; if materials were collected in advance for the four next "Dreadnoughts", as had been done in the case of four vessels already, Germany

---

([1]) [cp. G.P. XXVIII, ch. 221–2, pp. 85–197, *passim*, and Admiral von Tirpitz : *Politische Dokumente. Der Aufbau der deutschen Weltmacht* (Stuttgart and Berlin, 1924), pp. 111–162.]

([2]) [cp. G.P. XXVIII, pp. 57–8.]

([3]) [This subject will be dealt with in a later volume.]

([4]) [cp. *supra*, pp. 173–4, No. 111, and pp. 199–200, No. 124, and *Ed. note* (B), and *infra*, p. 779, *App.* III.]

would have 17 " Dreadnoughts " completed by February 1912; and if the full German shipbuilding capacity was used without financial restriction, Germany might have 21 " Dreadnoughts " ready by April 1912.

These were formidable figures. Cruisers, rather than " Dreadnoughts " were useful for the protection of commerce; and public opinion here would certainly point to the fact that the " Dreadnoughts " were the most aggressive type of vessel. It might also be noticed that lectures were given in Berlin, publicly, the subject of which was how to invade England. In the absence of any arrangement with Germany, it would be absolutely necessary for us to take as the basis of our programme what it was possible for Germany to do.

Therefore, I wished it to be understood that, if we had to propose a large Naval expenditure, it was not because we had not been ready to discuss the matter or to compare Estimates in advance. While, on our side, we should not complain of Germany's right to build as many vessels as she pleased, she must not take it amiss if we built the number of ships which we thought necessary for our own protection. I could certainly say also that, though in the absence of any arrangement with Germany we were bound to provide for contingencies, yet we should if we found that Germany was not building as fast as we had anticipated, be quite prepared to go more slowly with our building, and not to lay down one or more of the ships for which money had been voted by Parliament.

Count Metternich said, with regard to lectures on Invasion, he believed there had been one given about balloons by a man named Martin, who had been suspended from the Government Service for indulging in politically exciting literature.

As to the German Naval programme, Count Metternich repeated that it was fixed by law. Germany would not exceed it. She was building what was necessary for her own purposes, and the number of vessels she built would not be increased, no matter how many vessels we might build. If, however, we were taking into account what Germany could do, why did we not also take into account what the United States could do? He understood that the Prime Minister's statement about the two-Power standard included every nation.

I told him the Prime Minister's statement meant that we must be prepared to defend ourselves successfully against any other two Powers. In making the calculations for this purpose, the importance attached to vessels at a distance was not the same as that attached to vessels near home. Our object was to maintain such complete command of the sea in our home waters that, even with the small Army we maintained, we should be safe from Invasion. If our object were aggressive, foreign ships at a distance would count for as much or more than those near us; but as our object was defence and not aggression ships at a distance did not count for so much in our calculations as those near home.

Count Metternich evidently thought the figures I had given him were excessive with regard to the number of " Dreadnoughts " which Germany would or could have, and that we need not provide with such care for contingencies which were improbable.

I explained to him that next March we should have to present to Parliament the Estimates which would meet our requirements for a whole year. If, as the year went on, we found that more " Dreadnoughts " had been voted by Parliament than we needed, we could at any time refrain from building one or more of them. But if we found that we had under-calculated the number of ships Germany was going to lay down, or if Germany hastened the date at which her ships would be complete by collecting materials beforehand, then we should have no power to begin building additional " Dreadnoughts " within the financial year unless we summoned Parliament for a Supplementary Estimate. Therefore, if we did not take due precautions, there might come a time when, in spite of all the efforts we might subsequently make, there would be a period of some six months during which Germany's force of " Dreadnoughts " would be superior to ours.

[I am, &c.]

E. G[REY].

MINUTE BY KING EDWARD.

App[roved].—E.R.

No. 152.

Sir Edward Grey to Sir E. Goschen.

F.O. 5222/721/09/18.

(No. 27.)

Sir,   *Foreign Office, February 3, 1909.*

Count Metternich came to see me to-day before his departure for Berlin.

I told him I hoped the King's visit would go off pleasantly. I knew the King was looking forward to it, and he had spoken to me with pleasure about it yesterday.

Lord Crewe, I was sure, would be glad to have a talk with Herr Dernburg, if he wished, about his South African journey. If I remembered rightly, Herr Dernburg had been in London before going to South Africa, but had not been here since.

Count Metternich said there were some questions with regard to the frontier and the police in South Africa. The German Government would like the Cape Government to increase the number of their police.

I told him that I believed the Colonial Authorities were quite anxious to do all they could, but their difficulties were financial. Lord Crewe, however, knew more about these matters than I did.

I went on to say that it was not our desire to raise in Berlin any question which the German Government would rather not discuss. I felt that Naval Expenditure was the most important question, but we should not press it unless the German Government wished to discuss it.

Count Metternich reminded me that I had given him three figures with regard to German shipbuilding. I had told him that in the case of four ships now being built the Germans had collected materials in advance. He had examined this statement, and found it quite true. The materials had been collected in advance for these ships because it was definitely known that they were to be built. In the case of subsequent ships which were not allocated in advance materials would not be collected beforehand, unless the shipbuilding firms cared to do so at their own risk because they found it more convenient to buy at leisure. The building of ships would, therefore, not be quickened in this way. As for my high figure, founded upon the total shipbuilding capacity of the German yards, Count Metternich pointed out that the rate of expenditure was fixed by law and it would be illegal to increase it : though he admitted that the rate might be increased by a vote of the Reichstag, if desired.

I said that we had to take into account the German Naval Programme. We should take power from Parliament to build, from year to year, whatever ships we needed in order to keep pace with the German Programme. If, however, we found that the latter was not being carried out as quickly as we had anticipated, we should not build all the ships for which we had taken power. Should such a step become possible, we should take care that it was announced in such a way as to have the most pacific and soothing influence on our Press and public opinion.

I was afraid our Press was sure to be stimulated—to use an optimistic word—by the increased Naval Expenditure for which we must ask as a result of the German Programme.

Any subsequent slackening in the rate of construction would, however, be looked upon as a very good sign not only here but throughout the world, which was taking a great interest in the competition between German and British shipbuilding.

Count Metternich demurred to the idea that German shipbuilding competed in any sense with British shipbuilding, and said that the talk of invasion in this country was really not friendly attributing as it did hostile designs to Germany. No one in Germany thought of invading England.

I told him that the man in the street in this country naturally asked how man'
" Dreadnoughts " the German Navy would have when the present German Programme
was completed. On being told that the number would be 21, he at once wished to
know how many " Dreadnoughts " we had. He would be told 6, or whatever the
number happened to be. Then he demanded to know what measures were being taken
to ensure that when the 21 German " Dreadnoughts " were ready we should still be in
a safe position. For it seemed to him that, with 21 of the most powerful aggressive
vessels in the world concentrated at Wilhelmshaven and looking straight at our shores
there was a risk of invasion should there be any unfavourable turn in the relations
between this country and Germany. Invasion, for us, meant conquest. It was quite
impossible to avoid such apprehension on the part of people in this country: just as
it would be impossible to avoid a scare in Germany if one of her land-neighbours were
to collect an Army more powerful than the German Army.

[I am, &c.]
E. G[REY].

No. 153.

Sir Edward Grey to Sir E. Goschen.

F.O. 9085/721/09/18.
(No. 57.)
Sir, *Foreign Office, March 5, 1909.*
Count Metternich, in a conversation with me after he had returned from Berlin
recurred on his own initiative to our conversation of February 3rd respecting Nava
Expenditure.
He told me that he found considerable comment was made in conversation here
in political circles and in society upon the quickening of the German programme o.
construction. He wished to explain to me again that, with regard to four of the earlier
vessels of the programme, materials had been collected in advance because, though the
building of the ships had been decided upon, the designs were not finally settled
When, therefore, the contracts were given, the actual laying down of the ships was
deferred till the designs were completed; but the contractors were in a position to
collect and prepare the materials for building. This would not happen with regard to
subsequent vessels.
I said that what he now told me made me feel not quite clear as to whether I
had correctly understood from my previous conversations with him exactly which
vessels he referred to. He would remember that I had at the beginning of January
given him three statements in writing, each of which included certain figures. I had
understood him to say that the first of these statements was correct, but that the other
two would not be realised. He replied that this was the case. As regards the first of
my statements the answer was: Yes. As regards the second and third, the answer
had been: No, it would not be so.
I then observed to Count Metternich that I was not familiar with the details of
Naval construction, and was dependent upon our Admiralty for my information.
I presumed that he was similarly situated with regard to German Naval construction.
The only way to take the matter further would, therefore, be for the German Government to let our Naval Attaché at Berlin see—not of course, the designs of the ships—
but the number of the ships which were actually being built, and the stages in which
they were. We, of course, would give reciprocal advantages to the German Naval
Attaché in London. In this way each Admiralty would be able to know exactly how
it stood with regard to the other.

Count Metternich said that he had not started the conversation with the intention of proposing any arrangement.

I could not, therefore, pursue the subject further.

[I am, &c.]
E. G[REY].

No. 154.

Sir Edward Grey to Sir E. Goschen.

F.O. 9412/721/09/18.
(No. 62:)
Sir,   *Foreign Office, March* 10, 1909.

I told Count Metternich to-day([1]) that the Navy Estimates were coming on next week.

We should have to make a full reference to the German programme, and I was anxious that any reference made should not have a disagreeable character, and should be within the limits of what had passed between us. I therefore gave him a copy of my record of four conversations with him. I regarded these conversations as more or less informal, and therefore not to be published or quoted verbatim; but they were the material out of which our reply would be made to the questions which were sure to be asked as to whether we had proposed any arrangement with Germany, and why it was that no arrangement could be made.

I proposed that we should say definitely that it was the view of the German Government that their Navy was being built solely with regard to their own needs, without any hostile intention towards us : and that they did not intend to increase their programme, however many " Dreadnoughts " we built, but neither would they diminish it. In the view of the German Government, therefore, there was nothing out of which an arrangement could be made.

We should then have to say that, while we accepted the German statements, admitted that our relations with Germany were satisfactory at present, and attributed no hostile intentions to her, it was nevertheless necessary for us to build a Fleet in proportion to the German one, and that German shipbuilding was the factor which determined ours. The German Fleet, though framed solely to defend the interests of Germany, would in a few years time be exceedingly powerful. However good the relations between German[y] and Britain might be at the present moment, we had to build for the contingencies of a few years a-head; and no one could say how the relations between the two countries might be affected if at some future date it was found that the position of naval power had been reversed to our disadvantage.

The German Ambassador confirmed what I had said about the German view, and reminded me that he had gone so far as to state that if we were to build 100 " Dreadnoughts " Germany would still not increase her programme.

I told him I understood it to be equally true that, even if we ceased building " Dreadnoughts " altogether, Germany would not diminish her programme.

He said that this also was true.

He then told me, with regard to a statement I had made to him that Germany would have 13 " Dreadnoughts " by February 1912, that the fact was Germany would not have 13 vessels of this class till the end of 1912.

I said this was a qualification which he had not given me originally, for he had replied to the three statements I had given him by saying that the first was correct and the other two were not.

He told me that he now made this statement to me from the most authoritative source. Germany would not have 13 " Dreadnoughts " till the end of 1912, and would not accelerate her programme.

([1]) [*cp. G.P.* XXVIII, pp. 103–5.]

[17590]

I pointed out to him that it was impossible for us to go before Parliament with a definite statement of this kind unless our Naval Attaché was from time to time admitted to yards, to see the stage in which the various ships were. I did not understand that his statement to me was intended to limit Germany's liberty of action, and it might be that the construction of the vessels might proceed faster than the German Government anticipated. I was informed that the actual date when a ship might be commissioned depended not entirely upon the date at which the ship was laid down, but also upon the number of gun-mountings and turrets which were ready in the hands of the firms who made these things. Our information had been that there were 13 vessels now under construction, or being prepared in some form or another.

Count Metternich said he was assured that this was not so, and if the materials were being collected in advance, for the 4 ships to be laid down in 1909, it must be at the risk of the contractors.

I told him that unless our two Admiralties were able to keep themselves informed, through their Naval Attachés who were allowed to visit the yards, as to the stage in which construction and preparation were, they could never be quite sure when the vessels ordered at any particular time would be completed.

In default of any arrangement between our two countries, it was necessary that we should have some margin on our side.

[I am, &c.]
E. G[REY].

MINUTE BY KING EDWARD.

A most excellent Dispatch.

E.R.

No. 155.

Sir Edward Grey to Sir E. Goschen.

F.O. 10562/721/09/18.
(No. 70.)
Sir,   *Foreign Office, March 17, 1909.*

Count Metternich came to tell me[1] that, though he would not in ordinary circumstances say a word about the Debate on our Navy Estimates, he had read with surprise the statement of the Prime Minister and the First Lord of the Admiralty that Germany would have 13 "Dreadnoughts" in 1911 or early in 1912, after his having told the Prime Minister and me authoritatively that Germany would not have 13 "Dreadnoughts" till the end of 1912.[2]

Count Metternich regretted very much that the statement made in the House of Commons had omitted to take any notice of what he had said. He had not yet heard anything from Berlin, but he evidently expected that his Government would share the surprise and regret which he had himself felt that his statement had been disregarded, and had been passed without notice.

I told him I had recorded his conversation with me, and the statement he had made. I had sent a record to the Prime Minister before the latter had his conversation with Count Metternich, and I had also sent a record to the First Lord of the Admiralty. After sending it, I had not seen the First Lord of the Admiralty till the evening before the Navy Estimates Debate, when he came to me and said he had at first been astounded by Count Metternich's statement, as the Admiralty had positive

(1) [cp. *G.P.* XXVIII, pp. 108–10. The debate had taken place on the previous day, March 16.]

(2) [v. immediately preceding document, and cp. *Parl. Deb.,* 5th Ser., House of Commons, Vol. 2, pp. 934–5 and p. 959.]

information that more ships than were consistent with Count Metternich's statement were already under construction, indeed had actually been seen. On reflection, however, Mr. McKenna said he saw how the misunderstanding had arisen. Count Metternich's statement evidently referred only to what are technically called " Dreadnoughts," and could not include the large armoured cruisers of the " Invincible " type, which for convenience we included in the term " Dreadnoughts," and which I understood were designated in the German programme simply by a letter. This, Mr. McKenna had told me, would reconcile Count Metternich's statement with the information which the Admiralty possessed.

I could but repeat that the only way to prevent such misunderstandings from arising was for the two Admiralties to put all their cards on the table, and to let the Naval Attachés see all the yards in which ships were being built, in order to learn the facts, not of course as to the designs, but as to the actual progress of shipbuilding.

I pointed out to Count Metternich that there was not time for me to have another conversation with him after I had seen Mr. McKenna before the Debate took place. The Navy was a matter of life and death to us in a sense which could never apply to Germany, and we positively must keep on the safe side, and allow for margins of error.

I asked him whether he was in a position to say that his statement to me had included the large cruisers of the " Invincible " type.

He replied that he must make direct enquiry as to that point, and would do so. But he thought that when a direct assurance from the German Government was given in the formal manner this one had been given, it ought to be accepted.

I told him that whatever further information he gave me after he had made his enquiry I would communicate to the Prime Minister and the First Lord of the Admiralty, that we might consider what we should do respecting it. But I impressed upon him that it would be impossible for me to satisfy our Admiralty by conversations between him and myself, just as, if the positions were reversed, it would be impossible for Count Metternich to satisfy his Admiralty. All I could do was to repeat to the Admiralty what he told me. They would naturally be distrustful as to whether I, with no knowledge of naval matters, had fully grasped the meaning of what was said to me; and they would certainly feel when a statement was supplied by the German Admiralty to the German Government, and then passed on from the German Government to the Ambassador, and from the Ambassador to me, and from me to the Admiralty, it must have passed through so many media that there was a great risk of error. We could not satisfy Parliament unless we were in a position to state that the German Government had exchanged information with us, and that our respective Admiralties were convinced that they knew exactly what was the state of the war vessels which were being built in our respective yards.

I am, &c.
E. G[REY].

MINUTE BY KING EDWARD.
App[roved].—E.R.

[ED. NOTE.—The following minute by Sir Edward Grey refers to the five documents immediately preceding, and Sir Edward Grey's despatch No. 338 of December 18, 1908, printed *supra*, pp. 172–3, No. 110.

Minute by Sir Edward Grey.

F.O. 10683/721/09/18.   *Foreign Office, March 18, 1909.*

In view of what has been stated in the German Parliament I circulate to the Cabinet the record of the last six conversations with the German Ambassador upon Naval Expenditure. It will be observed that the fifth of these conversations which modifies previous statements of the Ambassador did not take place till after our Naval Estimates had been settled. It has since been made clear that it is intended to include cruisers as well as battleships. The problem of how it is to be reconciled with other information or statements given to the Admiralty remains to be solved.

E. G.
March 18, 1909.]

No. 156.

Sir Edward Grey to Sir E. Goschen.([1])

F.O. 10996/721/09/18.
(No. 73.)
Sir,

Foreign Office, March 18, 1909.

Count Metternich came to see me to-day,([2]) and I told him that Admiral Tirpitz's reported statement was being construed here to mean that the German Government would have been ready to accept a proposal for the discussion of naval expenditure, and that it was our fault that none had been made. I thought the misunderstanding could be disposed of by the publication of my conversations with Count Metternich.([3])

Count Metternich deprecated the publication of the conversations : they were informal, they had not taken place with a view to publication, and he thought it would be very inconvenient if conversations of this kind with Ambassadors should be liable to publication. Also, in the records I had shown him, there were one or two points which he thought did not give an entirely correct impression of what he had said.

We went through the conversations. None of the points to which he took exception related to the respective dispositions of the two Governments to discuss naval expenditure, but only to what he had said at various times with regard to statements of mine respecting the progress of German ship-building.

He considered the admissions I represented him as having made as to acceleration of certain ships of the German programme were overstated.

I entirely admitted what he had said as to the informal character of the conversations. I had not recorded them with a view to publication, but solely with the object of reporting to my Colleagues. I did not myself see anything in the substance of the records which might not be published; it would, of course, be open to Count Metternich to correct inaccuracies, or to produce his own records.

He held, however, to the opinion that it would be undesirable to publish the conversations, and repeated this before we parted, and I did not press it.

He pointed out to me that the thirteen vessels he had referred to appeared, from Admiral Tirpitz's statement, to have included cruisers.

I agree that this was evidently so.

He asked me what I had meant when I said that this was not something which we could put before Parliament.

I told him that we could of course repeat the declaration in Parliament, just as the declaration about the non-acceleration of the German programme had been repeated. But such an assurance of intention, volunteered by the German Government, an intention which might be changed, or which might be anticipated by the more rapid progress of shipbuilding, coupled with the statement that the German Government were not prepared to enter into any arrangement about naval expenditure, and by a statement that our Naval Attaché was not to be allowed to see the progress

([1]) [The text of this document is taken from the draft which Sir Edward Grey initialled, and which contains corrections in his own hand. There is also in the Foreign Office archives a printed duplicate of the text sent to Sir E. Goschen. It is marked as signed by Mr. W. Langley. Paragraph 4 of the despatch presents some difficulty. The draft contains the words· here· printed but has no capital at the beginning or stop at the end. The printed duplicate has corrected these errors but has omitted the fifth word, " I," Sir Edward Grey's writing being here indistinct.]

([2]) [*cp. G.P.* XXVIII, pp. 113–4. For the statement of Admiral von Tirpitz, *v. infra,* pp. 250–1, No. 160, and *encl.*]

([3]) [*v. supra,* pp. 172–3, No. 110, and pp. 237–43, Nos. 151–5.]

of the building of the ships, such an assurance would not be accepted by Parliament as something which justified us in not building the ships we proposed.

Count Metternich then said that he was authorised to tell me confidently([4]), not for general use, though of course I was free to use the information at my discretion with my Colleagues, that in the case of two of the ships for the financial year 1909–10 tenders would be called for only in the autumn. With regard to the two other ships for this year, the German Government Nad found that the shipbuilders were forming a Trust to put up the prices against the Government, and in order to prevent the formation of this Trust contracts for these two ships were promised in advance to two shipbuilding firms, on the understanding that the Reichstag would be willing to vote the money subsequently.

I said this was exactly what the Admiralty had told me had happened with regard to all four ships. Count Metternich had now told me that it had actually been done but only with regard to two of the ships.

He said this was the case, but added that these two ships would be built at a slow rate, and the contracts for the other two ships of the financial year would be retarded and not given at the beginning of the financial year as had sometimes been done.

I observed that getting information in this way was very confusing. With regard to two of the earliest ships, I had been told that materials had been collected in advance before the laying down, because the designs were not ready. From another source—I thought it had been from him, but he said it was not—I had heard that the building of ships had been accelerated in order to provide against unemployment. Now I had just learnt that, with regard to two of the most recent ships, contracts had been promised in advance in order to prevent the formation of a Trust.

I thought the best plan would be that I should get from the Admiralty a statement of the facts upon which they had based their calculations. If I could get this statement from the Admiralty, and it contained facts which could be proved or disproved by showing our Naval Attaché that they were indisputably true or untrue, we might be able to clear up the matter. This was the best suggestion I could make, and I would ask the Admiralty for the statement.

I then returned to the difficulty in which we had been placed by Admiral Tirpitz's statement, and asked what we were to say in reply to Questions in Parliament next week, if we did not publish the conversations?

Count Metternich suggested that we might say we had left no doubt as to our willingness to discuss a reduction of armaments, though we had not made a formal offer, as we saw no prospect of such an offer being accepted.

I told him that this might do, if the German Government would say it, or authorise us to say it on their behalf.

Count Metternich demurred to the German Government being asked to say anything.

I observed that we were sure to be asked to explain Admiral Tirpitz's statement, and we must have some authoritative explanation. Would it do if I sent him the Prime Minister's statement as to discussion of Naval expenditure, and the German Government authorised us to say that it correctly represented the respective attitudes of the two Governments?

Count Metternich said he did not see any contradiction between Admiral Tirpitz's statement and that of the Prime Minister. No proposal for a reduction of expenditure on armaments had been made, and it was wise that it had not, for the time for such a proposal had not yet come, seeing that we had some ships of the newest type on the water, while Germany had none. He could not authorise me to say this as a statement of the German Government, or at any rate did not think it desirable that it should be put in that way.

I suggested that I should put a direct question to him as to whether I was to understand from Admiral Tirpitz's statement that I had been mistaken in my impres-

([4]) [Sic. confidentially?]

sion of the view of the German Government, as expressed in the Prime Minister's speech, or that, though I had been correct in my impression, the view of the German Government had since changed. If I asked this question, and stated the reply I received, it would dispose of the matter.

Count Metternich strongly deprecated any attempt to extort a formal admission from the German Government that they would not discuss the question of naval expenditure.

In sympathy with this I said that one of the considerations which had determined all our conversations on this subject, so far as I was concerned, was my desire to avoid putting any question to the German Government that would oblige them to reply with a negative. Admiral Tirpitz's statement, however, had made it necessary that we should give some explanation. The only other method of which I could think was that the German Government should publish a statement in their own Press, to the effect that an entirely incorrect inference had been drawn from the Admiral's statement, by supposing that it was meant to invite proposals for a reduction of armaments.

Count Metternich said he was sure no one would be more surprised than the Admiral himself to find that his remarks had been interpreted in this way. He asked me when a question was likely to be put in Parliament.

I said there would certainly be one on Monday. We could put it off by saying that we were in communication with the German Government, but that would of course involve a statement from them later on.

I asked him to think the matter over, and to see what would be the best way to meet the situation.

[I am, &c.]
E. G[REY].

No. 157.

Sir E. Goschen to Sir Edward Grey.

F.O. 10819/721/09/18.
(No. 95.)   *Berlin, D. March* 19, 1909.
Sir,   *R. March* 22, 1909.

The debate on the Navy Estimates in the House of Commons is being followed with the deepest interest here and is the subject of discussion not only in the Press but also in the Budget Committee of the Reichstag, where just at this moment German Naval Affairs are being debated.

The friendly tone towards Germany which has distinguished the speakers on both sides of the House of Commons and the delicacy which characterized the necessary allusions to the German naval policy have met with full recognition in the German Press, but it scoffs with unnecessary vigour at what it is pleased to call the "panic" which has suddenly seized the British nation. It attributes this "panic" to the statement of the First Lord of the Admiralty that Germany can keep pace with England in naval armaments, and that the resources of the German Empire enable her to compete with Great Britain in rapidity of construction. . . . .([1])

I have, &c.
W. E. GOSCHEN.

MINUTES.

In view of the financial straits in which the German Gov[ernmen]t find themselves it would seem as if they might easily have refrained from accelerating their programme.

G. S. S.
22/3.

It is of interest to note how well the German press is kept "in hand." It would be still more interesting to know what that press is being told by the press-bureau in order to keep it

([1]) [The rest of this long despatch gives summaries of various German Press articles.]

quiet. To judge by past experiences, it is not uncharitable to suppose that one thing is said in London, to the British Government, and another thing to the German press, who may be assumed to receive assurances that the German gov[ernmen]t will know in the future, as they have done in the past, to deal with the British gov[ernmen]t in a way that will strengthen the German position.

E. A. C.
Mch. 22.
W. L.

Were the German fleet ready the tone of the press would probably be very different. Soft words are not usual with Germans except when an ulterior object can be attained by them.

C. H.
E. G.

No. 158.

Sir E. Goschen to Sir Edward Grey.

F.O. 11373/721/09/18.
(No. 98.)
Sir,

Berlin, D. *March* 23, 1909.
R. *March* 25, 1909.

I have the honour to report that the Budget Committee of the Reichstag after its sitting of March 19th sent a message to the Chancellor and to the Minister for Foreign Affairs requesting them to appear in the Committee and make a statement with regard to the approaches said in the British Parliament to have been made to Germany for a limitation of Naval Armaments. The Chancellor replied that he would authorize Baron von Schoen to appear at an early date in the Committee and give such information as was possible. He added that he would reserve what he had to say on the subject for a statement in the Reichstag on some suitable opportunity.

According to latest reports Prince Bülow's refusal to make a statement has caused great dissatisfaction in the Budget Committee which, to mark its disapproval, has interrupted the discussion of the Naval Estimates so as to consider to-day (Tuesday) the vote for the Imperial Chancellor's Department.

The discrepancy between the statements made in the English Parliament and Admiral von Tirpitz' assurance in the Budget Committee that no proposal had been made by England to Germany for a restriction of armaments is being much discussed and Press organs of all shades of opinion are pressing for an authoritative ministerial statement on the subject. It is doubtless with the object of stemming this tide of inconvenient curiosity and of preparing public opinion for the official explanation of the apparent conflict on questions of fact between British and German statesmen, that an obviously inspired communication has been published in the " Cologne Gazette " of March 20th. The communiqué, which appears in the form of a telegram from the Berlin correspondent of the paper, after an allusion to the Budget Committee's invitation to the Chancellor to make a statement, remarks that the Imperial Government do not consider it a suitable moment, when the Naval Question is arousing such feverish interest in England, to make declarations which, though having no great consequence in themselves, it would be preferable to defer to a more suitable moment. The " Cologne Gazette " then goes on to say that as a matter of fact confidential proposals had been made by the British Government for a limitation of armaments in reply to which the German Government had pointed out the practical difficulties in the way of an arrangement. In guarded terms the Article proceeds :—
" Probably at that time the competent authorities in Germany drew England's attention to the naval programme laid down by law, at the same time expressing their intention of not exceeding the limits of that programme. Thus interpreted Mr. Asquith's statements do not conflict with what actually occurred." The article concludes by expressing the hope that a feeling of mutual trust may arise between England and Germany which, in its opinion, would obviate the necessity for entering into formal engagements for regulating the relative strength of the two navies.

R 4

Commenting on the statement in the "Kölnische" the "Berliner Tageblatt" observes that every one is quite aware that "Mr. Asquith's statements do not conflict with what actually occurred;" Admiral von Tirpitz's statements on the other hand, it complains, do conflict in a very striking manner with "what actually occurred." After remarking that Admiral von Tirpitz seems very ill-informed with regard to events affecting his Department and that the Minister of Foreign Affairs must have kept him in the dark as to the British proposals the Article concludes by remarking that if the German nation has to wait until the moment which Prince Bülow considers suitable for a public statement, it will indeed have to possess its soul in patience.

The "Kölnische Volkszeitung" remarks that the real reason which prevents Prince Bülow from appearing in the Budget Committee is that he finds it quite impossible to reconcile his own former statements with what has just been announced by Mr. Asquith. It strongly condemns the Government for having tried to maintain silence with regard to the British proposals and considers that such an equivocal policy can only serve to strengthen the suspicions already entertained in England as to the real object of German naval armaments. In parenthesis it should here be mentioned that the "Kölnische Volkszeitung" characterizes the British suspicions as "quite unfounded."

The "Berliner Neueste Nachrichten" is much disturbed at the statement made in the British Parliament that Germany does not mean to accelerate her building programme. "When," it inquires, "was such an assurance given? Is it the result of King Edward's visit to Berlin? After the vain attempts of Sir Charles Hardinge and Mr. Lloyd George to bring about a disarmament, has yet another effort been made to retard German naval construction? And has this effort been successful, at a time too when England is undertaking enormous naval armaments, avowedly directed against Germany? Is the statement of the British Prime Minister really in accordance with facts or is there some misunderstanding? The Imperial Government cannot possibly avoid answering this question."

A survey of independent press comments in Germany on the British naval debate gives the impression that there is a strong feeling of dissatisfaction with the Government for having attempted to keep the country in the dark with regard to the British advances for a limitation of armaments. Another dominant note in the Press is one of complacent self-satisfaction at the close interest with which the development of German naval power is being followed in England. Generally speaking there has up to now been a singular absence of bitterness in the tone of German criticism on the British naval debates, and the possibility and even necessity of some kind of an understanding with England is undoubtedly, as may be seen from the Press utterances, beginning to take root in Germany.

I have, &c.
W. E. GOSCHEN.

MINUTES.

Sir E. Goschen concludes, from a study of the German press that "the possibility and even necessity of some kind of an understanding with England is undoubtedly beginning to take root in Germany."

It would be most unfortunate if this idea should gain ground here and be subsequently found to be erroneous. I would therefore like to sound a note of warning against accepting Sir E. Goschen's statement as any indication that the German government are likely to make an agreement or come to some understanding with England on terms really satisfactory to this country, respecting a limitation of armaments. When the German armaments have reached the size which satisfies Germany, then she may be willing to enter into an agreement for preventing the further growth of British armaments, but there is nothing to show that any amount of discussion in the German press will induce the German gov[ernmen]t to agree to any limitation of their programme. The danger is that they may endeavour to take us in by false and non-binding assurances.

E. A. C.
Mch. 25.

The Press utterances, of which a *résumé* is given in this despatch, do not bear out the conclusion in the last paragraph, which perhaps applies to other articles which Sir E. Goschen has read.

W. L.

The Socialists have always been in favour of an understanding with England but there do not seem to be many traces of a similar feeling elsewhere.

C. H.
E. G.

No. 159.

Sir E. Goschen to Sir Edward Grey.

F.O. 11374/721/09/18.

(No. 99.)

Berlin, D. March 23, 1909.
R. March 25, 1909.

Sir,

I have the honour to report that Baron von Schoen appeared to-day in the Budget Committee of the Reichstag and made, in the name of the Chancellor, a statement on the subject of British advances to Germany for a limitation of naval armaments.

The proceedings were opened by a National Liberal member of the Committee, who said that it was highly desirable that some response should be made by Germany to the British advances, and that an answer should be given to the question of whether Germany could not, while adhering to her Naval Programme, come to some agreement with England.

Baron Schoen in reply, said:—"It is true that the British Government have in a general manner announced their readiness to enter into an Anglo-German understanding with regard to the scope and cost of the Naval Programmes; the British Government have, however, made no formal proposal to the above effect. In the non-binding conversations which took place on this subject between competent German and English persons, no British proposal was ever mooted, which in our opinion could have served as a basis for official negotiations. In communications between friendly Governments it is customary to avoid making formal proposals, if it appears doubtful that they will receive favourable consideration. No doubt for this reason the British Government avoided making a formal proposal to Germany, and we have therefore not had to take up any attitude towards such a proposal. The reasons for our waiting attitude towards the idea of a general limitation of naval armaments were stated by the Chancellor in the Reichstag on December 10 of last year. They obviously also apply to any agreements concluded between separate Powers. Our building Programme, which is fixed by law, is exclusively regulated by our requirements of self-protection; it represents no threat to any other nation, a fact on which we have already repeatedly laid stress."

I have the honour to enclose an extract from this evening's "Norddeutsche Allgemeine Zeitung" giving the text of Baron von Schoen's statement.([1])

I have, &c.
W. E. GOSCHEN.

P.S.—It should be added that at a later stage of the Committee proceedings Baron von Schoen expressed his satisfaction that the entire Committee had given utterance to the hope that Anglo-German relations might, unruffled by agitations with regard to German ship-building continue to become more cordial. Such a result would correspond with the wishes of the entire German nation as well as with those of the German Government.

(For the Ambassador),
R. S. S.

([1]) [Not reproduced.]

No. 160.

Sir E. Goschen to Sir Edward Grey.

F.O. 11375/721/09/18.
(No. 100.)   *Berlin*, D. *March* 23, 1909.
Sir,   R. *March* 25, 1909.

With reference to your telegram No. 106 of yesterday,([1]) asking for a translation of Admiral von Tirpitz's speech in the Budget Committee of the Reichstag, I have the honour to transmit herewith copy and translation of an account of such portion of his statement as relates to the possibility of an understanding between England and Germany for a restriction of naval armaments, and the relative strength of the British and German navies.

The text of this account was supplied to me on my request by Baron von Schoen and is taken from the official minutes of the Committee proceedings.

The greater part of Admiral von Tirpitz's statements in the Committee are of a technical nature. They are being translated by the Naval Attaché and will be forwarded in the course of the next few days.

I have, &c.
W. E. GOSCHEN.

Enclosure in No. 160.

Translation of Admiral von Tirpitz's speech in the Budget Committee of the Reichstag, on March 17, 1909.

I did not till this morning read in the papers what has been said in the English Parliament both by the First Lord of the Admiralty and the Prime Minister Asquith. According to the newspaper reports before me, the latter said " Germany has on several occasions been invited by England to enter with her into an arrangement respecting the carrying out of the naval programme of both countries. Germany has always maintained that she is not building ships with reference to England but in accordance with her own needs. She finally gave the distinct assurance that she would not further accelerate her rate of naval construction."([2]) 1 cannot judge whether the papers have reproduced the speech correctly. With respect to the limitation of naval armaments 1 refer to what the Chancellor said in the plenary sitting of the Reichstag on the 10th of December.

" The Deputy Haussmann touched upon the question of an international limitation of Naval Armaments, as did some of the previous speakers. The question was put in the debate as to why we had assumed a negative attitude with regard to proposals in this sense. I must first of all state that we were not approached with any such proposal. But I will say more. In company with other Powers we have long been of opinion, not only since the discussion of the Finance reforms began, that an international limitation of armaments is in itself a highly desirable thing. Our reserve in the question may be attributed to doubt as to the practicability of putting such proposals into effect."

According to the papers the English Premier said that Germany would not accelerate her ship-construction. We are proceeding strictly in accordance with our programme, it is possible that the construction of one ship may go forward a little quicker but another would on the other hand go more slowly, on an average they will however be ready on the dates provided for in the first instance in accordance with the building programme. And there is no reason why this should undergo any change in the future. Further according to the newspapers, the First Lord of the Admiralty said :—" Should the construction of the German ships be accelerated, as was presumably done in the case of the four ships of the programme of 1909–10, Germany would already have 17 ' Dreadnoughts ' and ' Invincibles ' by April 1912.

([1]) [Not reproduced.]
([2]) [cp. *Parl. Deb.*, *5th Ser.*, House of Commons, Vol. 2, pp. 956–7, and pp. 960–1.]

But even if no acceleration takes place, this figure will be reached in the autumn of 1912.''([3]) With regard to this I declare that in 1912 we will not have 17 " Dreadnoughts " but only 13, and indeed not in the spring but not until the autumn. Where the First Lord derives his information from, I do not know.

Admiral von Tirpitz said :—

In the first place, I should like again to call attention to what the Imperial Chancellor stated in the plenary sitting of the Reichstag : " I state first that we were not approached with any such proposal," and at the end : " In one thing I am certain of the assent of our naval authorities, which is that we should not construct ships beyond the rate determined by our need for protection and legally fixed in accordance therewith."

If an agreement were possible—it cannot however be a one-sided one—it nevertheless appears to me that it would be extraordinarily inopportune, were we in advance to treat the idea of limiting armaments seriously and slacken the fixed rate of construction. That is the most mistaken manner of approaching such an agreement. When it is stated that Germany would have 17 ships in April 1912 should the rate of construction of German ships be increased—which is to be the case with the ships in 1909—this refers to a suppositious act and not to the actual proceeding of Germany. We shall not have 17 ships in 1912 but only 13 in the autumn of 1912. The British estimates however take into account the above-mentioned supposition. As a matter of fact we are not proceeding faster than is prescribed by the law, nor faster than the grants are made; the English assumption on which the new great English demands are based, is not correct.

Admiral von Tirpitz pointed out that the debate in the English Parliament turned on the question whether Germany would have 13 or 17 ships in 1912.

([3]) [cp. ib., p. 936.]

No. 161.

Sir E. Goschen to Sir Edward Grey.

F.O. 11778/721/09/18.
(No. 108.)   Confidential.   Berlin, D. March 26, 1909.
Sir,   R. March 29, 1909.

Herr von Schoen spoke to me the other evening on the subject of the discussion in the House of Commons respecting naval matters. He expressed his great regret at the turn which the discussion had taken but thoroughly recognized that it was impossible for the British Naval Estimates to be laid before Parliament without some mention being made of what was being done by Germany in the way of naval construction. But, even making due allowance for the exigencies of party politics and the heat of debate, he must confess that the Imperial Government had been disagreeably surprised by the fact that notwithstanding the assurances given by Count Metternich in London to the contrary, the Prime Minister and the First Lord of the Admiralty had thought fit to state, the one that Germany *might* have, and the other that Germany *would* have, seventeen Dreadnoughts at the end of 1912.([1]) I said that His Excellency might be sure that there had been no intentional misrepresentations on the part of any one who took part in the debate; but that there was a certain amount of confusion was evident—confusion which might be avoided in the future if our Naval Attaché were allowed to visit the shipbuilding yards from time to time. His Excellency said that the Naval Authorities were for many reasons strongly

([1]) [Marginal comment by Sir C. Hardinge, " Surely the latter statement is incorrect. C. H."]

against such permission; this was perhaps to be regretted; but he must say that it was still more regrettable that the assurances of the German Government should not have been frankly accepted and believed. He did not wish to attach undue importance to this matter but he had not been able to refrain from saying a few words to me on the subject. He would only say one word more, namely that it had puzzled him very much how it had come out that the material for shipbuilding had been collected and stored in some cases before the ships had been commenced. This of course did not in the very least affect the question of the time when the ships would be completed as that was already prearranged, but it had seemed strange to him that it should have become known abroad. The only explanation which occurred to him was that some Argentine Naval Officers at present at Berlin had been allowed to see a good deal and that they had talked. This was rather delicate ground so I expressed no opinion on the subject. It is however true that in their anxiety to secure orders from the Argentine Government, the Imperial Naval Authorities have allowed the above-mentioned officers to see nearly everything that is to be seen in the way of ships now under construction; and Herr von Schoen's surmise is more than probable. His Excellency hoped that his statement in the Reichstag had given you satisfaction. He had done all in his power to avoid anything that might create unpleasantness and to be as conciliatory as possible.

Beyond telegrams from their London correspondents, the Berlin newspapers have as yet made but few comments on the Debate in the House of Commons. They are apparently holding their fire for the moment and awaiting the result of the forthcoming debate on Naval Affairs.

An article, however, has already appeared in the "Kreuz-Zeitung" of which I have the honour to enclose a translation.(²)

I have, &c.
W. E. GOSCHEN.

(²) [Not reproduced.]

No. 162.

Sir E. Goschen to Sir Edward Grey.

F.O. 11781/11781/09/18.
(No. 111.) Very Confidential. *Berlin,* D. *March* 27, 1909.
Sir, R. *March* 29, 1909.
  I have the honour to forward, herewith, a despatch, as marked in the margin, which I have received from Colonel Trench, Military Attaché to this Embassy, relating to Remarks by the Emperor, etc.

I have, &c.
W. E. GOSCHEN.

Enclosure in No. 162.

Colonel Trench to Sir E. Goschen.

(No. 14.) Very Confidential.
Sir, *British Embassy, Berlin, March* 26, 1909.
  I have the honour to report that, at the annual inspection by the Emperor of the First Foot Guards, which took place this morning at Potsdam, His Majesty conversed a good deal with the Austrian Military Attaché, Captain von Bienerth, the brother of the Austrian Premier, and only spoke to one other attaché, while his neglect of his Russian Aide-de-camp, General Tatischeff, was quite marked.

  During the march past, the Emperor called me to him, shook hands and conversed very graciously and kindly for perhaps ten minutes about a present he had given me at Christmas, the museum at Hanover and the troops he was inspecting; then, drawing me away, said: " Tell me, Trench, what's the matter with your people?

All this panic is most unworthy of a great people! And why do they misrepresent us so and tell such stories . . . .(¹) theres no use! . . . . I must say downright lies! Our officials are exceedingly angry about it. I have had to prevent their answering some of the questions they have been asked; if they had, it would have been **very bad** for your government.'' (I understood His Majesty to add here : '' They would have had to go.'') He gave me the impression of being quite as much annoyed with the government as with the opposition, and to take as much exception to the statements made on one side of the House as to those made on the other. He seemed to specially resent that, '' in spite of special information we gave them in March,'' H[is] M[ajesty]'s ministers should have stated that '' we have been accellerating [*sic*] our building. Nothing of the kind has taken place, and they know it! It isn't our way : we have our programme fixed by law years ahead, and we keep to it.'' Here, the movements of the troops having come to a standstill, His Majesty had to be asked for orders, and he did not renew the conversation with me. I could not help receiving the impression that the Emperor's feeling was as much one of disappointment as of annoyance : he seemed to have thought that the information which he referred to as having been given (whatever it was) would have had the effect (or should have had) of convincing the British Government that . . . . say, ... it had no reason whatever to be uneasy about the rapid extension of the German navy.

I have, &c.

F. TRENCH,

Colonel, Gen[eral] Staff and Military Attaché.

Note. I beg permission to observe that I have heard, during the past week, in private circles, a good deal of discussion of the topics of the day without having noticed the slightest exception being taken to the recent events in the House of Commons. The only opinion unfriendly to England that I heard expressed was to the effect that, without England's financial support, Servia would not have been so troublesome.

F. T.

MINUTE.

It is extraordinary how deep the Austrian calumny of England having given financial assistance to Servia has sunk.

C. H.

E. G.

(¹) [The stops here and elsewhere in this document are in the typewritten original. They are not apparently omission marks.]

No. 163.

Sir Edward Grey to Count Metternich.(¹)

Private.(²)

Dear Count Metternich,   *Foreign Office, March* 27, 1909.

I want to be quite sure that what I say in Parliament on Monday does not go beyond what your Government has itself stated in public or intended that I should be free to say.

I propose to say that we have been informed verbally but quite definitely that Germany will not accelerate her naval programme of construction and will not have 13 ships of the '' Dreadnought '' type including cruisers(³) till the end of 1912.

This has been told us not in the form of an undertaking but as a declaration of intention from the most authoritative source. I understand this to mean that 13 ships will or may be ready for Commission as distinct from trials by the end of 1912.

(¹) [This letter is printed in *G.P.* XXVIII, pp. 130–1. Apart from small variations of punctuation, the version given there differs owing to the inclusion of two alterations made by Count Metternich. These are shown in notes (⁴) and (⁵) *infra*.]

(²) [Grey MSS., Vol. 22.]

(³) [This word and the one preceding it are enclosed in brackets in *G.P.* XXVIII, p. 130.]

We have also been told that contracts for two ships of the financial year 1909–10 were promised in advance to certain firms.([4])

I shall probably point out as a necessary inference from all these statements that it is intended that the construction of the two ships last referred to must be intended to proceed at a comparatively slow rate, or at any rate not at an accelerated rate.

You have told me in addition that these two ships will be ready for trial trips at earliest in April 1912 and will not be ready for Commission before October 1912.

You have also told me that, as regards the remaining two ships of the financial year 1909–10, tenders will be called for only in the autumn.([5])

But these two last statements, I understood, were not for general, and therefore of course not for public, use.

There are naturally some points not covered by these statements which our Admiralty must for its own purposes take into account, but my object in writing is not to ask for more information but to make sure that whatever I may say in public is accurate in form and in substance, and does not go beyond what was told me by you for general use.

I return to London on Monday morning.

Yours sincerely,
E. GREY.

([4]) [Addition by Count Metternich : "*provided the money would be granted by the Reichstag.*"]
([5]) [Alteration by Count Metternich to "*late in summer. Orders 2 or 3 months later.*"]

No. 164.

Count Metternich to Sir Edward Grey.

German Embassy,
Private.([1])   9, Carlton House Terrace, S.W.,
Dear Sir Edward,   March 29, 1909.

With reference to your private letter of the 29th [27th] inst[ant], dealing with naval matters and your speech to-day, I wish to say that you may make use of all my information, contained in your letter, in Parliament and that you need not consider anything in your letter as confidential.

Truly yours,
P. METTERNICH.

([1]) [Grey MSS., Vol. 22. The letter referred to is apparently the one printed as the immediately preceding document.]

No. 165.

Sir E. Goschen to Sir Edward Grey.

F.O. 12771/721/09/18.
(No. 117.) Confidential.   Berlin, D. March 30, 1909.
Sir,   R. April 5, 1909.

I have the honour to forward, herewith, a despatch, as marked in the margin, which I have received from Captain Heath, Naval Attaché to this Embassy, relating to a conversation with Admiral von Tirpitz respecting German naval estimates and construction.

I have, &c.
W. E. GOSCHEN.

Enclosure in No. 165.

Captain Heath to Sir E. Goschen.

Confidential.

Sir,   *Berlin, March* 30, 1909.

I have the honour to report that on Sunday the 28th instant I presented Admiral von Tirpitz with a copy of the British naval estimates for the year 1909–10, together with a copy of the First Lord's introductory statement.

The Admiral expressed his thanks for the same, and said that I should receive a copy of the corrected German estimates in exchange.

I congratulated the Admiral on the rapid passage of the German estimates through the Reichstag, and he replied, "I have only to thank your people for that," and added, however, "I wish to talk to you now as one naval officer to another, and not as a politician."

The Admiral at once plunged into the question of certain statements made in the British House of Commons with reference to the German shipbuilding programme. The Admiral became much excited, and said that his word had been doubted, and in fact disbelieved, that notwithstanding his statement that the building of the German ships had not been accelerated, his word had been contradicted by the responsible British Minister. He said that he had been very much tempted to speak his mind in the Reichstag, but that for several reasons he had now handed the whole matter over to "the Wilhelmstrasse." Throughout the whole of the above the Admiral was much excited, and evidently wished to impress on me that he considered that his personal honour had been doubted.

The Admiral then gave the history of the placing of the contracts for two ships of the 1909–10 programme. He had received information that the shipbuilding companies were combining with a view to raising prices, he therefore entered into secret negotiations with two of the firms (one of whom had just completed a similar ship) with the result that he obtained two very cheap contracts on the following lines: The contract was not binding until the estimates had passed the Reichstag. The ships were to be delivered for their preliminary trials three years after the signing of the contract, viz., three years after the passing of the naval estimates, or approximately on the first day of April, 1912. The Admiral added that the preliminary trials would occupy some months, and the ships would be ready to take their places in the line some time in the autumn of that year.

The Admiral was a little scornful about some story which he said had come from England, that he had arranged with certain banks to advance money to the contractors in order to expedite the building of these ships. "Anyone who has the smallest knowledge of our German methods and laws, would know that no Minister would dare to expend the smallest sum without first obtaining the approval of the Reichstag." As regards the remaining two ships of the 1909–10 programme, I was told that the contracts would not be placed before the autumn, and that the ships were to be delivered for preliminary trials three years after the signing of the contract.

The Admiral then went off to the usual remarks as to the German fleet being built entirely and solely for defence purposes, Germany would never attempt to dispute the sea supremacy of England, &c., and then became a little excited again over England's secret method, "England never gives the true cost of her ships in the Budget," "on what possible grounds had the Admiralty decided not to count all England's magnificent earlier battleships," &c.

The Admiral next explained that the alteration in the Navy Law in 1906 did not really produce any acceleration in the building of the fleet, but I did not quite follow nor remember his explanation.

Finally came a complaint that the German navy was talked of as an inveterate enemy, "never for a hundred years had such a use been made of the name of a great friendly Power."

I told the Admiral that anything I might say was simply my own view, and wa
in no way official. I remarked that the first rumours of contracts being awarded i
advance of the programme, appeared in the German press. The Admiral appeared t
doubt this, but I repeated that I had read it with my own eyes, and my statemen
was upheld by the Adjutant, who was present throughout the interview, the Admira
thereupon gave way. I then said that it still seemed possible that if necessity aros
the German programme might be augmented to seventeen ships in 1912, and that thi
number was within the limits of the Fleet Law. This statement rather started th
Admiral off again; he said that to talk of possibilities was nonsense, the possibilitie
of either nation were incalculable, and in any case " I have stated our fixed intention
and my word ought to be trusted."

As regards using the German fleet as our unit of measurement, I said that I coul
not see anything unfriendly in so doing, we had always measured against the nex
strongest, which happened to be the French not so many years ago. However, th
Admiral only replied that in that case we ought to measure against America, and no
Germany.

The Admiral then wished me a friendly good-bye, adding that he was glad o
having had an opportunity of a talk with me.

I came away with the impression that the Admiral is nursing a personal grievance
in that he says his word has been doubted. at the same time I felt that he ha
considerably relieved his feelings in his talk with me.

The Admiral once referred to the Navy League, but only to say that thei
agitation was ill-timed. In my opinion, the German naval programme up to the end
of 1912 is now fully known, although it is as well to bear in mind that certair
well-known writers, such as Colonel Gaedke, are already pointing out that the Flee
Law is not being carried out to its " full capability," and an agitation may arise or
this subject.

I have, &c.

H. L. HEATH,

Captain and Naval Attaché.

No. 166.

Sir E. Goschen to Sir Edward Grey.

F.O. 12646/721/09/18.

(No. 119.)   *Berlin, D. March 30, 1909.*

Sir,   R. *April 3, 1909.*

I mentioned in my despatch No. 115 of to-day's date([1]) that in Prince Bülow's
speech, which was the first of three which he has delivered on the vote on the
Chancellor's salary, no mention had been made of the Naval Questions which are now
occupying public attention in both Great Britain and Germany.

In his second speech, however, which was delivered late on the same evening, he
dwelt for some time on these questions and made the declarations of which I had the
honour to telegraph a summary in my telegram No. 42 of to-day's date.([1])

As you will have seen from this summary the Chancellor stated, in answer to
questions which had been put to him as to whether Great Britain had made proposals
for a mutual arrangement with regard to the limitation of Naval Armaments, that
though unofficial and non-binding conversations had taken place between prominent
British and German statesmen on this subject, no definite proposal had ever been
made from the English side which could form the basis of official negotiations. The
Chancellor's answer is considered by more than one newspaper to be unsatisfactory
and of rather a quibbling nature. They argue that diplomatic negotiations are nearly

([1]) [Not reproduced.]

always preceded by more or less informal conversations, and that in the present case the statement that such conversations had taken place amounted to an admission that proposals for negotiations on the subject of the limitation of armaments had been made. In refusing to make these conversations a basis for negotiations the Imperial Government had practically refused to entertain the official proposal which would otherwise have followed.

Prince Bülow added, while on this subject, that the Imperial Government yielded to no other in their desire for peace, as had been amply proved by their policy during the last 20 years, and that the fact that they hung back in the question of the limitation of armaments must not be attributed to any unfriendly feeling towards another Power but rather to a desire to preserve their undoubted right to maintain their independence of action and to exclude their own internal affairs from all discussion with Foreign Powers. "In any case," he said, "the Imperial Government will continue to regard it as one of their first duties to further to the extent of their ability all tendencies towards friendship between Germany and Great Britain and will strive to bring about such relations between the two countries as will leave no room for feelings of suspicion or mistrust on either side."

These words, and in fact, the greater part of Prince Bülow's speech respecting future Anglo-German relations, correspond almost word for word with some observations made to me by Herr Kiderlen in private conversation a few days ago.

As regards the number of ships building and to be built under the German Naval Law, Prince Bülow reiterated the official statement, that in the autumn of 1912, at the earliest, Germany would have thirteen ships of the new type including the three armoured cruisers. He added that the Imperial Naval Programme had not been inspired by the wish to compete with England; that the Imperial Government had nothing whatever to hide and that they had absolutely no intention of accelerating their naval construction beyond the rate laid down in their Naval Law.(²) All reports to the contrary were false. He added that further details on the subject would be furnished by Admiral von Tirpitz. . . . .(³)

I am, &c.
W. E. GOSCHEN.

(²) [Marginal comment by Mr. Spicer: "This hardly agrees with the preamble to the Navy Bill of 1900, 'Germany must possess a fleet of such strength that a war with her would shake the position of even the mightiest Naval Power.' G. S. S."]

(³) [The rest of this long despatch gives further details of Prince Bülow's speech.]

No. 167.

Sir Edward Grey to Sir E. Goschen.

Private.(¹)

My dear Goschen, *March 31, 1909.*

I took the opportunity of observing to Metternich today that Prince Bülow's speech seemed to have made a favourable impression. It had covered wider ground than our Debate in the House of Commons, during which I had not touched upon Servia, as that would have exceeded the rules of debate,—indeed, I thought I had stretched the rules a little in some of the things I had said.

Metternich said there had not yet been time to see how my speech had been received by the German press.

I told him that with long speeches there was always some risk as to the parts which would reach foreign ears without the context. For instance, in Austria, my statement that the isolation of England brought about by the domination of one great Power on the Continent would lead to a conflict seemed to have been noted without the statement which immediately preceded it, to the effect that the isolation of Germany would just as certainly provoke a conflict. As long as the two statements

(¹) [Grey MSS., Vol. 22.]

were coupled together, I thought they would not convey an unconciliatory meaning; but one statement taken without the other might give an impression of anxiety which was not correct.

I then went on to say that, after he had made it clear to me that he wished the German declarations about naval construction to be repeated in Parliament, I had no choice but to repeat them. I had felt that there was some risk in doing this, because if we made it appear that we were basing our own calculations with regard to the Fleet on declarations of intention which might be changed at any time, it would create an attempt here to discredit these declarations as being too slight a foundation on which to rest our own Estimates. There was, therefore, the risk that the German Government would be disappointed at the comparatively slight importance which public opinion attached, for the moment, to these declarations. But, on the other hand, I had thought it better to take long views. The prophecies of the Opposition with regard to the German rate of construction could be disproved only by the lapse of time; that was the only way in which prophecies ever could be disproved. If, when the year 1911 came, the progress of German shipbuilding was proved by facts to be strictly in accordance with what the German Government had now declared it would be, the fact of their declaration having been made to us and put on record would greatly increase the reassuring effect, and would bear fruit.

Metternich observed, giving his own personal opinion only, that he did not see why it would not be a good thing for us to announce at once that we were going to build the four additional ships referred to in this year's Estimates. By this means, we should end the anxiety and calm the storm which had been raised.

I replied that there was much to be said in favour of taking that course. On the other hand, there were many people here who were anxious to make it clear, by not building in excess of the actual requirements of the moment, that they had no aggressive intentions against Germany.

Yours sincerely,
E. GREY.

No. 168.

Mr. Findlay to Sir Edward Grey.

F.O. 12841/721/09/18.
(No. 17.) Confidential.
Sir,

Dresden, D. *March* 31, 1909.
R. *April* 5, 1909.

Since the second day of King Edward's visit to Berlin([1]) the tone of the Press in this part of Germany has, as regards Great Britain and British policy, been moderate and even courteous, so much so that it would be interesting to know the real reasons of this sudden and extraordinary change. Its suddenness can only have been due to a *mot d'ordre* from head-quarters, wherever they were, and might, therefore, conceivably be attributed to the reassuring effect of His Majesty's visit among those in authority. I have already ventured to report my impression that the King's visit to the Rathaus had a most soothing effect on the middle classes in this part of Germany, and that the results of the Royal visit were entirely beneficial. I trust therefore that I may not be considered to be detracting therefrom if I venture to suggest that the effect of a visit, however successful, which took place over six weeks ago, could hardly be strong enough to restrain a Press so given to vituperation during the great political tension and anxiety of the last fortnight. Nor do I imagine that a *mot d'ordre* could have prevented an outburst on the subject of Naval armaments, unless it were backed by a political reason appealing to all shades of German journalistic opinion. Two months ago the opportunity afforded by the recent

([1]) [*v.* pp. 227–37, Nos. 143–50, *passim.*]

Naval debates in Parliament, and the agitation throughout the British Empire, would have been undoubtedly seized in order to blacken everything British with a deluge of abusive ink.

And yet now these debates are alluded to even in the "Leipziger Neueste Nachrichten" as being courteous in tone and respectful to Germany. That this description is on the whole true is no explanation. Two months ago no lie was too gross, no misrepresentation too malicious, for these very papers. At the same time the Leipzig Pan German papers, which are usually the most warlike, have been publishing criticisms of Baron Aehrenthal's dangerous policy which, as it threatened to result in Germans as a whole being pitted against the orthodox Slavs, should have been very much to their taste. It would appear, therefore, that this section of the Press desired peace for once, unless these articles were also written to command, which is not impossible.

Perhaps this desire for peace supplies the key to the puzzle, and I would suggest that the argument backing the *mot d'ordre* to avoid giving offence to the United Kingdom, which I imagine to have been given, was something to the following effect:

"Austria will probably be involved in a war with Servia and Montenegro, and Germany must stick to her ally through thick and thin. Russia may be forced by public opinion to intervene, and France may take the opportunity to attack Germany; England will then, in support of her partners in the Triple *Entente*, attack and destroy the German fleet. Therefore, in order to avoid the danger as far as possible, no offence must be given to England, at any rate, until peace is assured."

There have been one or two articles to this effect, but only in papers politically so unimportant that they may well have been neglected by the Press Bureau. That these articles were neither criticised nor quoted by the other papers confirms me in the conviction that there has been a *mot d'ordre*, and the argument I have ventured to suggest above is the only one I can think of which would conceivably have been sufficiently cogent to exercise such a strong restraining power.

A few cases of a return to old bad habits of abusing England which have occurred within the last few days (*i.e.*, since peace appeared to be practically assured) also tend to confirm the above theory.

If the suggestion which I have ventured to submit is correct, it is obvious that the fear of British Naval Power must recently have had a considerable effect in restraining German combativeness within certain limits. It is also obvious that as long as the British Fleet is in a position of undoubted and crushing superiority to the German Fleet, Germany will hesitate to bring on a war in which the United Kingdom might take part against her. The more valuable her fleet and commerce, the more will Germany hesitate to do so. I feel sure that you will agree that it is only when Germany realises that it is impossible for her to attain to a position of even temporary and accidental Naval equality with Great Britain that she will be brought to seriously consider the question of a limitation of armaments.

I have, &c.

M. DE C. FINDLAY.

MINUTES.

The explanation is probably correct. The marked change in the tone of the German newspapers during the past few weeks can hardly still be the effect of the Royal visit. Mr. Findlay's last remark is sound.

G. H. V.
5/3/09.

Mr. Findlay is right in suggesting that it is Germany's obvious interest to avoid as far as possible any serious friction with England until the German fleet is considered strong enough to allow Germany to defy us. This has been the burden of some weighty pronouncements in the better German press for some years.

I also agree with Mr. Findlay that Germany is not likely to consider seriously the question of a limitation of armaments until the naval forces have approached to that state of efficiency, strength, and organization which will in the opinion of the German government be sufficient to ensure perfect freedom for them to follow with comparative impunity an anti-British policy.

E. A. C.
Ap. 5.

I read Mr. Findlay's last sentence as meaning that in his opinion Germany will agree to limitation only when she is convinced that she cannot compete with us in building.

W. L.

I think that is the meaning.

C. H.
E. G.

No. 169.

Sir E. Goschen to Sir Edward Grey.

F.O. 12773/721/09/18.
(No. 121.)
Sir,

Berlin, D. April 2, 1909.
R. April 5, 1909.

I have the honour to transmit herewith Précis of a leading article(1) in the "Cologne Gazette," entitled "Straight and Crooked Policy," which discusses some of the issues raised by Prince Bülow in his recent speech in the "Reichstag" on Foreign Affairs.

The views expressed are not particularly new or original but they gain in interest from the fact of the ".Norddeutsche Allgemeine Zeitung" having reproduced them at some length thus conferring on them to some extent the seal of official approval.

The greater portion of the Article is devoted to the discussion of British and German Naval Armaments, a subject which just now is naturally occupying a large share of public attention. Professor Schiemann writing on this question in his weekly survey of foreign policy in the "Kreuz-Zeitung" says:—"It may safely be assumed that with the object of gaining parliamentary sanction to the construction of the 8 Dreadnoughts, the 'German peril' will be painted as black as possible. This 'peril' is an 'idée fixe' which has thoroughly taken hold of English minds, and we must wait till they regain their calm. If the 8 Dreadnoughts help to obtain this result, the English will not have paid too much for their quiet nights. To the whole world which is not the victim of a similar spell there is something supremely ridiculous in the panic of this great nation. But England could free herself from it at a moment's notice if she were willing to enter into an alliance with us, which entailing, as it would, a similar tie with Austria-Hungary, would form the most powerful combination that the world has ever seen. But it is idle to think of that, and therefore we will rest satisfied with our position in the heart of Europe. The result has shown that, with that position too, the peace of Europe can be preserved."

I have, &c.
W. E. GOSCHEN.

MINUTES.

The point of importance is not in the article in the Cologne Gazette, but in Professor Schiemann's article in the "Kreuzzeitung": It is his suggestion that the proper course for England is to make an alliance with Germany. It would be a mistake to treat this suggestion as merely a casual observation. I feel sure that it is meant seriously, and is not put forward without authority. Because we know that this was Bismarck's idea of foreign policy: "make yourself very strong; then show to those Powers which are not willing to submit to you, how disagreeable it is to be opposed by Germany, this will induce such Powers to come to terms and accept German leadership."

Bismarck's policy on these lines invariably failed. His successes were due to crushing victories won in war. But German statesmen still believe in his prescription: witness the attempts to win over France, and, quite lately, Russia.

E. A. C.
Ap. 5.

To France and Russia add G[rea]t Britain.

W. L.

(1) [Not reproduced.]

A combination of England, Germany and Austria would not be durable since it would imply the domination of Germany in Europe, and would inevitably end in war between Germany and England, the latter Power being in a position of complete isolation and without even the sympathy of any of the Powers.

C. H.

Yes: if we sacrifice the other Powers to Germany we shall eventually be attacked.

E. G.
H. H. A.

No. 170.

Sir E. Goschen to Sir Edward Grey.

Private.([1])

Dear Sir Edward Grey,   Berlin, April 9, 1909.

I am very much obliged to you for your letter of the 31st ultimo([2]) recording a conversation with Metternich. It interested me extremely, all the more that the result on the German mind of the building of the four additional ships has been lately much in my thoughts.

After a good deal of consideration I have come to the conclusion that Metternich is right when he says that it would be best were the four extra ships laid down at once. I think that as soon as the Germans are absolutely convinced, and they have nearly reached that point, that we have made up our minds to maintain our superiority at sea and will shrink from no sacrifice in order to do so, they will calm down and, realizing the hopelessness of competition, perhaps be glad at a given moment to ease the strain on their finances by dropping a ship or two.

As you will see from a far too long despatch([3]) I am sending home by this bag, there is already a fairly strong feeling against competition with us, and I feel certain that the idea of the four extra ships has had much to do with it. As long as they are anywhere near us in numbers they will strain every nerve, but they are too practical a nation to persevere much in a task which they see is hopeless. . . . .([4])

Hardinge mentioned in his letter that he was glad Kiderlen had returned to his post and had removed his sphere of action from Berlin. But I fear that it may be regarded as certain that he will be back here before long. He told me himself that Bülow was anxious for his return here, and he hinted in his rather brutal way that there would have to be a change in his position, as he was tired of doing all the work and seeing others get all the credit. I think he intends to get rid of Schoen, who, though pleasant and agreeable to deal with, has not the slightest influence or power and is a mere mouthpiece. Kiderlen is certainly a man to be reckoned with; he ran the whole show here during the crisis and had also much to do with the Morocco agreement. He has made himself indispensable to Bülow, is an intimate friend of Holstein and I do not think he will allow himself to be kept in the background long. He is clever and ambitious, can be brutally frank when it serves his purpose and is not without a certain "finesse" and power of cajolery. He is, I believe, a strong Anglophobe and is altogether a rather dangerous man.

Yours very sincerely,
W. E. GOSCHEN.

([1]) [Grey MSS., Vol. 22.]

([2]) [v. supra, pp. 257–8, No. 167.]

([3]) [This seems to refer to Sir E. Goschen's despatch No. 131 of April 8. It summarises at length three articles which had appeared in the Kreuz Zeitung, the Vossische Zeitung and the Kölnische Volkszeitung.]

([4]) [The omitted paragraphs give further details on the German attitude to naval armaments and British policy in Europe.]

No. 171.

Sir E. Goschen to Sir Edward Grey.

F.O. 14069/721/09/18.
(No. 134.)   Berlin, D. *April* 11, 1909.
Sir,   R. *April* 15, 1909.

The almost ostentatious silence with regard to Italy observed by Prince Bülow in his recent speeches on foreign affairs has naturally given rise to considerable surmise as to the present relations of that country with the other two Powers of Triple Alliance. That Italy was a somewhat shaky partner in that combination during the recent crisis was evident to everyone, and there is a strong feeling here that, had that crisis resulted differently, she would have descended on the "Triple Entente" side of the fence. It is thought, however, that Prince Bülow will soon put things right and that during his visit to Venice he will not have much difficulty in producing arguments to show M. Tittoni good reasons why Italy should display greater appreciation of the advantages of belonging to the Triple Alliance and give greater proofs of consistency and steadfastness in its support. This work will, it is hoped, be begun by Prince Bülow and clinched by the Emperor when He meets the King of Italy on His return journey from Corfu.

In the meantime the Berlin Press is full of extracts from Italian newspapers showing that public opinion in Italy is already clamouring for a 'renewal' of the Triple Alliance and an enlargement of its scope, and it is pointed out that the reason for this change of attitude is the successful display of Austro-German solidarity and strength in the recent crisis. It is also very broadly hinted that the intention of the Austro-Hungarian Government to build four ships of the 'Dreadnought' type has not been without effect in helping Italy to make up her mind as to the direction in which her true interests lie.

It is needless to say that the decision of Austria-Hungary to make such a substantial addition to her naval strength is hailed here with the liveliest satisfaction.([1]) It is admitted that in the case of a naval conflict in the North Sea, the Austro-Hungarian 'Dreadnoughts' would not be of direct service to Germany, but at the same time it is pointed out that indirectly they will be of great assistance, as the presence of a strong Austrian fleet in the Mediterranean must in any case render it more difficult for Great Britain to concentrate her naval forces in the North Sea.

The 'Tageblatt,' writing on this subject, says, "The intention of Austria-Hungary to increase her fleet has naturally added to the apprehensions felt in England with regard to the growth of the Germany navy. It is considered there that to all intents and purposes the German and Austrian fleets are one, and grave doubts are felt as to whether the laying down this year of even 8 ships is sufficient for the maintenance of a two Power standard."

It adds, however, that these apprehensions and doubts are quite groundless both because Great Britain will not have the slightest difficulty in maintaining her naval superiority and because Germany has, for that reason, no intention whatever of contesting that superiority by useless competition.

A short reference is then made to the alarm also created in England by the Zeppelin airships, alarms which the writer of the article is good enough to say is not wholly unnatural in view of the exaggerated estimate of the value of those balloons and their capabilities in time of war put forward by German enthusiasts and propagated by a certain bellicose section of the German Press.

The Article then proceeds to point out that, whether these apprehensions are due to real alarm or only to party manœuvres the fact remains that public opinion in England views Germany's naval policy with profound suspicion and is extremely excited on the subject; that it would be a mistake to treat this feeling with indifference, as it

([1]) [*v. infra*, p. 267, No. 175; and *Gooch & Temperley*, Vol. V, p. 784, No. 836; p. 813, No. 874; p. 824, *App.* III.]

s an incontestable fact that the growing mistrust of Germany felt in Great Britain s one of the most dangerous elements of European Foreign Politics; and that far too much time has already been allowed to elapse without any attention having been paid o the attempts of the Government of Great Britain to come to an arrangement with he Imperial Government on the subject of Naval Armaments.

Like the other Articles to which I had the honour to call your attention in my despatch No. 131 of 8th instant,(²) this Article also maintains that the present moment s favourable for the conclusion of such an arrangement, and gives similar reasons for holding that opinion. Its final sentence is to the following effect. "The Austro-German Alliance has during recent events given effective proof of its superiority on and, while the decision of the Austro-Hungarian Government to increase its Naval strength shews equally plainly that the alliance will soon dispose of a considerable force at sea; we can therefore, without any fear of being accused of weakness and subservience, make overtures for an understanding with England on a footing of perfect equality."

In order that you may see how the question of Naval Armaments is regarded by all sections of public opinion in Germany I have the honour to enclose an article on the subject published in the social democratic organ "Vorwärts" of which Mr. Seymour has furnished an excellent translation.(²)

Since writing the above I see that a Vienna letter announcing that the Japanese Government intend shortly to denounce their treaty with Great Britain, has been reproduced in all the principal Berlin journals. The letter has been published in most cases without comment, but several papers have not lost the opportunity of pointing out that if the report is true the British Government will be obliged to detach a large squadron for service in the far East and so have still further to weaken their Naval Forces in home waters and the North Sea.

I have, &c.
W. E. GOSCHEN.

MINUTES.

Nothing that appears in any German newspaper on foreign, military, or naval questions, can be relied on to have any influence whatever on the decisions of the German gov[ernmen]t, unless it originally emanated from that gov[ernmen]t. For these reasons no importance attaches to what the "Vorwärts" says, and probably none to the effusions of the "Tageblatt."

E. A. C.
Ap. 15.

The last parag[raph] is all wrong. The writer of the "Vienna letter" evidently thinks the Japanese mean to denounce the Alliance Treaty. This is not the case; what the Japanese Gov[ernment] have announced their intention to terminate is the Anglo-Japanese Commercial treaty of 1894.

F. A. C.
16/4.
E. G.

(²) [Not reproduced. For its tenour, v. supra, p. 261, No. 170, note (³).]

No. 172.

Mr. Findlay to Sir Edward Grey.

F.O. 14623/14623/09/18.
(No. 21.) Confidential.
Dresden, D. April 14, 1909.
R. April 19, 1909.
Sir,

I regret to report that the tone of the Saxon Press is again becoming anti-British. During the last fortnight various reports have been circulated which appear to me to be mostly inventions. The obvious tendency of these reports, and still more so of the comments and articles founded upon them, is to spread distrust of Great Britain and to undermine her position with her friends and allies. In several instances Vienna papers such as the ' Wiener Allgemeine Zeitung ' seem again to have been working with the ' Vossische ' and with the Saxon Press, to make mischief.

The following are the principal " canards " to which I allude :

1. That the British and Russian Governments intended shortly to reopen the Macedonian question, and to adopt a different attitude towards Turkey.
2. That Austria was about to lay down a number of " Dreadnoughts," the number of which was variously given as four or six to be laid down at once, eight to be ready in 1917. That consequently, Great Britain would be hard pressed to maintain her Naval position in the Mediterranean, without weakening her fleet in the North Sea, and that in 1917 Austrian supremacy in the Mediterranean would be assured. The report that six Austrian " Dreadnoughts " were to be laid down at once was possibly due to a confusion in the mind of the correspondent, but the satisfaction with which the news was received by the Saxon papers which reproduced it was distinctly significant.
3. That the Triple Alliance would shortly be renewed and strengthened and that Italy has perceived that her best chance of salvation lay in a close understanding with Austria and Germany.
4. That Japan, being thoroughly dissatisfied with the tendency of Great Britain to make friends with her probable enemies, Russia and America, was about to denounce her alliance with Great Britain; that in consequence Great Britain would again have to maintain a formidable fleet of battleships in the Far East; that this news was important for Germany as it would become increasingly difficult for Great Britain to maintain her Naval supremacy in the North Sea, in the Mediterranean, and in the Pacific.

There has also been a considerable amount of not unnatural jubilation at the notable success Count Zeppelin has achieved with his airship; here, at any rate, it is said, Germany has established a marked superiority over her British rival, which it will not be difficult to maintain, and even to increase.

These reports and the comments thereon appear to be intended to keep up the idea that Great Britain is a chronic mischief-maker, that her Naval supremacy is seriously threatened and that consequently her value as a friend or ally is rapidly depreciating.

As far as I can judge there is so far no highly organised anti-British Press campaign such as that which was carried on from October to February last. That may develop later under favourable circumstances. In the meantime it is perhaps worth while to notice the general tendency of these more or less sporadic attacks.

The Press in this part of Germany has not yet adopted any definite attitude towards the revolutionary movement at Constantinople. There have been a few half-hearted suggestions that it was due to British intrigue, but the papers seem to be still in the dark as to what has really taken place.

I have, &c.
M. DE C. FINDLAY.

No. 173.

Sir R. Rodd to Sir Edward Grey.

F.O. 15328/13399/09/18.
(No. 95.)
Sir,

Rome, D. *April* 15, 1909.
R. *April* 24, 1909.

I have the honour to report that the intention of the Austro-Hungarian Government to construct four vessels of the Dreadnought type, which is now stated in the Italian press to have received " officious " confirmation at Vienna, appears, from admissions made to the Military Attaché, to have been known to the Intelligence Departments of the Italian Admiralty as much as three and a-half months ago. To the general public, however, the news has come as an unpleasant surprise which is attracting general and apprehensive attention. It is curious to note that the solidity of the Austro-German *bloc* and the intentions attributed to the Austro-Hungarian Government are almost universally regarded as compromising to the security of Italy, their ally.

Colonel Radcliffe learns from official sources that the problem of the construction will present some difficulty, as at present only Pola and Trieste offer the necessary facilities. It is anticipated that Fiume will also be made available.

I have, &c.
RENNELL RODD.

No. 174.

Sir E. Goschen to Sir Edward Grey.

F.O. 14511/14511/09/18.
(No. 141.)
Sir,

Berlin, D. *April* 16, 1909.
R. *April* 19, 1909.

. . . .(¹) I should not dream of bringing these wild journalistic flights to your notice were it not for the fact that, through all the abuse and deliberate misstatements with which such articles as that which I have quoted are replete, the desire for an understanding with England is always plainly visible. The method employed is tortuous, but the object of the abuse seems to be to convince Great Britain of the error of her ways, to prove to her that her Machiavellian policy is out of date, that, in view of Germany's strength, all her deep-laid plans must fail and that her only salvation lies in an understanding with Germany.

That an arrangement of some sort with England is desired is, I think, absolutely clear; but it is my impression that the only kind of understanding really wished for by Germany is one which would clear the way to her becoming the sole arbiter of the destinies of Europe and relieve her from all anxiety with regard to her only vulnerable side—the sea. The naval supremacy of Great Britain is, in view of Russia's present weakness, the only obstacle to the German domination of Europe, and it is evident that an arrangement which would remove that obstacle would be extremely acceptable to the Imperial Government. The disadvantage to Great Britain of such an understanding is obvious, for though it might obviate temporarily the necessity of abnormal efforts in the direction of naval construction, it would inevitably lead to an upset of the balance of Europe, an endeavour to rectify which might subsequently entail greater and more serious sacrifices upon the country than those which the present naval competition requires.

My impression of the kind of understanding required by Germany is gathered not only from the Press, but also from statements reported to me as having been made by German officers of both services, and more especially from conversations which I have had with M. Kiderlen Waechter.

This gentleman, who may be regarded as Prince Bülow's mouthpiece in questions of policy, has more than once hinted to me the desirability of an understanding between the two countries. His idea of the form which such an understanding should take is either that a political *entente* should be made such as would render increased naval construction on either side a source of satisfaction rather than of suspicion; or a naval convention by which the two Powers should bind themselves for a fixed

---

(¹) [The earlier part of this despatch is omitted because it merely summarises an article which had recently appeared in the *Kreuz Zeitung*.]

period 1) not to make war against each other, 2) to join in no coalition directed against either Power, 3) to observe a benevolent neutrality should either country be engaged in hostilities with any other Power or Powers.

I have, &c.
W. E. GOSCHEN.

MINUTES.

The immediate aim of the present extraordinary Press campaign may be to detach Russia from the " Triple Entente " by showing her that she can expect no help from Great Britain or France, the former of which Powers will only lead her into fresh adventures which will result as disastrously as the last one.

G. S. S.

The German government's desire for an " understanding " with England is of old standing. In the pursuit of the object Germany has steadfastly endeavoured to involve us in one difficulty after another ever since 1884. Formerly the " understanding " was to be of the nature of an expansion of the triple alliance.[2]

The present suggestion is more insidious, but yet so patently absurd that it seems hardly credible that a responsible official like Herr von Kiderlen should have made it, except that the ways of Berlin have of late often been quite absurd.

The end and object of German foreign policy is to frustrate any combination between other Great Powers in which Germany is not the predominant partner. The possibility of a Franco Russian alliance was, as Schuwaloff said, a nightmare to Bismarck. We have witnessed the extraordinarily versatile methods employed by his successors in the effort to prevent the understanding first between England and France and then between England and Russia. Both France and Russia have undergone the traditional German treatment of alternate bullying and cajoling, as well as England. The effect has been disappointing from the German point of view. The present invitation to conclude an agreement represents a renewed effort in the same ultimate direction. Under the terms of such an agreement, Germany would be able—

(a) to increase her fleet to any size desired.

(b) to fall upon France or Russia without fear of English interference.

(c) to impose her hegemony on any of the less powerful States, and in case this provokes resistance, actually to count upon British " benevolent neutrality " in the struggle.

(d) to interfere in any part of the world whilst England would be precluded from offering any serious resistance.

It is true that analogous advantages would simultaneously be secured to this country. But as we have no desire whatever of carrying on a policy of aggression, these paper advantages are in fact null for us. The whole proposal does not merit serious consideration.

E. A. C.
Ap. 19.

It does not, and Germans must see this. Therefore it seems to me more likely that the object of this fresh press campaign against us is to detach Russia from the triple Entente as suggested by Mr. Spicer.

F. A. C.
20/4.

I think there can be no doubt that the re-establishment of the " Drei Kaiserbund " is the main object of German foreign policy, since it is realised that no confidence can be placed on Italy as an ally.

C. H.

We had or were supposed for many years to have an entente with Germany. Count Metternich once complained to me that British Gov[ernmen]ts used " to lean upon Germany " and now did so no longer. During the whole of this period we were kept on bad terms with France and Russia : we were sometimes on the brink of war with one or the other; and Germany took toll of us when it suited her. An entente with Germany such as M. Kiderlen-Wachter sketches would serve to establish German hegemony in Europe and would not last long after it had served that purpose. It is in fact an invitation to help Germany to make a European combination which could be directed against us when it suited her so to use it.

E. G.

(2) [cp. *Gooch & Temperley*, Vol. III, p. 409, *App.* A, where the proposals of 1885 are referred to, and pp. 388–4 which mention *pourparlers* in 1899 and 1901. For those of 1901, *v.* also *Gooch & Temperley*, Vol. II, pp. 60–88.]

No. 175.

Sir E. Goschen to Sir Edward Grey.

F.O. 14935/721/09/18.
(No. 145.)   Berlin, D. April 17, 1909.
Sir,   R. April 21, 1909.

I have the honour to transmit herewith précis of an Article in the "Kreuzzeitung" of April 15th entitled 'Austrian and German Naval Policy'([1]) which seems to me of interest as reflecting what may be assumed to be a fairly general opinion here with regard to the great advantages which would be derived by Germany should the proposed strengthening of the Austrian navy be carried into effect.([2])

Briefly summarized the line of argument followed by the writer is that Germany can well afford to be conciliatory up to a certain point in the question of the limitation of naval armaments, as, should Austria be prepared to give an engagement to annually lay down a certain fixed quota of 'Dreadnoughts,' a rate of construction would be set with which England would find it practically impossible to keep step. Thus Germany would be able to make the concession required by England, while, at the same time, with the help of Austria, gradually getting on terms of equality with the British navy. As regards this statement it will no doubt occur to you that if, as is assumed here, the German and Austrian fleets are to be reckoned as one, the fact of Germany dropping a ship can hardly be regarded as a concession to the requirements of Great Britain.

While the above indicated advantages to Germany are, perhaps, well within the limits of possibility, the writer is unduly sanguine in assuming that Italy, having been forced into increasing her navy by Austria's action, would necessarily be prepared in case of need to place her new 'Dreadnoughts' at the disposal of Germany.

I venture in conclusion to draw your attention to the suggestion contained in the editorial note accompanying the article to the effect that an informal discussion in the Press of projects for disarmament would be of advantage, as, although very likely unproductive, it would serve to calm public opinion in England.

I have, &c.
W. E. GOSCHEN.

([1]) [The précis is not reproduced. The Morning Post published a summary of the article on April 16. A copy of this was circulated in the Foreign Office and the following minutes were written upon it :

This article reveals the real thoughts of those people in Germany who now write and speak in favour of accepting the British " proposals " for a limitation of armaments. British further armaments are to be curtailed in return for Germany's doing likewise. At the same time Austria and Italy are to be encouraged to build Dreadnoughts. It is ingenuously added that this will have the double advantage of dividing the reduced British forces, thereby making any challenge of Germany's power impossible.

This effusion tends to confirm the views which I have expressed respecting the value of German " public opinion " in the matter.

E. A. C.
Ap. 16.

It cuts both ways. It also confirms me in the view that there is an increasing public opinion in Germany against this excessive building. But as this public opinion is not regarded by the German Gov[ernment] it is no use to us at present.

F. A. C.
16/4.

In any case we have to keep at least equal to any two European Powers and if Austria builds Dreadnoughts, we must build more.

E. G.]

([2]) [v. supra, pp. 262–3, No. 171; and Gooch & Temperley, Vol. V, p. 784, No. 836; p. 813, No. 874; and p. 824, App. III.]

No. 176.

Mr. Wyndham to Sir Edward Grey.

F.O. 15331/13399/09/3.
(No. 99.)
Sir,
                                              Rome, D. April 20, 1909.
                                              R. April 24, 1909.

I have the honour to transmit herewith a report drawn up by Colonel Delmé Radcliffe regarding the views held in Italian military and naval circles on the projected increase of the Austrian navy.

Colonel Radcliffe has been much impressed by the anxiety shown in Italian military circles over Austrian intentions and the close accord with Germany.

                                  I have, &c.
                                  PERCY C. WYNDHAM.

Enclosure in No. 176.

Colonel Delmé-Radcliffe to Sir R. Rodd.

(No. 76.)
Sir,
                                              Rome, April 20, 1909.

I have the honour to inform you that I have had some conversations on the subject of the new naval constructions in Austria with several officers of the War Ministry and of the Ministry of Marine in Rome.

There is very great anxiety on the subject in official circles in Italy, and it seems to be accepted as quite certain that the Austrian navy is to be augmented by four ships of the "Dreadnought" type as soon as possible. It is stated that at Muggio, near Trieste, it is possible, or soon will be, to build two of these ships, and at Pola another. It is also stated that there is some activity being displayed at Fiume, though it is not known exactly what constructional facilities there are at this place, in existence or projected. I have also been informed that at Monfalcone, about 10 miles from the Italian frontier, there is a large basin connected with the sea by a canal. It was supposed for some time that this basin and canal were to be used by torpedo craft only, but workshops and arrangements have been made now for the construction simultaneously of four 10,000-ton merchant vessels. It is not known if this plant is being increased or modified to enable ships of greater size to be built, but the canal is being dredged to a depth of 40 feet. Batteries and works on the coast and in the interior have been erected and are in process of erection, surrounding Monfalcone, and covering the mouth of the canal. In particular, there is a heavily armed work at Duino.

The last report received at the Ministry of Marine was to the effect that two of the Austrian vessels were to be, or are being, constructed in Germany, one at Stettin and one at Danzig—but this report is not yet verified. The Italian authorities seem to be convinced that the Austrian and German Governments are working in close accord in this matter, and it is suggested that, even if new Austrian ships are not being constructed in Germany, the designs are being forwarded from Germany to save time in construction, although the ships are officially stated to be designed by the Austrian Naval Constructor Popper.

It is considered that Austria and Germany together would have no difficulty in supplying the armaments and gun mountings as quickly as the ships can be finished, and that the question of expense is one which would be summarily solved in Austria. It is stated that 50,000,000 kroner were saved over the last military account, and that money can always be obtained without waiting for Parliamentary sanction.

In Italian military and naval circles Austria is looked upon as the enemy, in spite of being, by Treaty, an ally, and every step taken by Austria to increase the strength of her army or fleet is watched with the greatest apprehension. It is thought now that it will not be long before Austria organizes another strong base for her fleet in the Adriatic, and that probably Cattaro or Antivari will be utilized.

It appears to be thought that Austria was recently quite ready to fight Italy, Servia, and Russia, all at the same time, and that Germany was prepared to join in and seize the Baltic provinces of Russia. It is supposed that the Austrians are very disappointed at not having taken the opportunity of seizing more. What she has to show now, for the expense and efforts of the last few months, is the possession of Bosnia and Herzegovina, which were practically hers before, and nothing else, except the prestige increased by the display of strength and the proof of the close understanding with Germany. Herr von Radowsky, Vice-President of the Hungarian Chamber, who has recently been in Rome, is reported to have said that Austria has made a great mistake in not going to war, for so favourable an opportunity should not have been lost.

I have, &c.
C. DELMÉ RADCLIFFE,
Military Attaché.

No. 177.

Mr. Wyndham to Sir Edward Grey.

F.O. 16083/15615/09/22.
(No. 107.)   *Rome,* D. *April* 26, 1909.
Sir,   R. *April* 29, 1909.

I have the honour to transmit to you herewith a Report as marked in the margin, which I have received from the Military Attaché to His Majesty's Embassy relative to the intention of the Minister of Marine of asking for a credit of 20 million pounds for naval construction.

I have, &c.
PERCY C. WYNDHAM.

Enclosure in No. 177.

Colonel Delmé-Radcliffe to Sir R. Rodd.

(No. 84.)
Sir,   *Rome, April* 23, 1909.

In continuation of my despatches No. 76 of the 20th April([1]) and No. 83 of the 22nd April,([2]) I have the honour to state that this morning I had a conversation with Captain Conz, of the Ministry of Marine. He confirmed the previous conversation as to the intention of asking for a credit of half a milliard of lire (20,000,000*l*.) for new naval construction in Italy. Captain Conz stated that Admiral Mirabello, the Minister of Marine, regarded the situation as "gravissima," and probably would state that, if the credits for new constructions, for which he would present the demands in May, were not granted, he could no longer be responsible for the Ministry of Marine and would resign.

Captain Conz also repeated that, in the event of its being made clear that the new Austrian "Dreadnoughts" would be ready before the Italian ships of the same class, Italy would certainly have to order at least three "Dreadnoughts" in England or the United States.

He said that it was very unfortunate to be forced to spend large sums for naval construction outside the country, but that it was better to lose a few millions than for the country to lose its liberty.

I have, &c.
C. DELME-RADCLIFFE,
Colonel, Military Attaché.

([1]) [*v.* enclosure in immediately preceding document.]
([2]) [Not reproduced.]

No. 178.

Sir F. Cartwright to Sir Edward Grey.

F.O. 16563/13399/09/3.
(No. 74.)   *Vienna, D. April 29, 1909.*
Sir,   R. *May 3, 1909.*

I have the honour to report that I enquired of Baron von Aehrenthal yesterday whether he could give me any information as to the intentions of the Austro-Hungarian Government with regard to the construction of large vessels of the "Dreadnought" type for the Austro-Hungarian navy. I said to His Excellency that rumours with regard to this matter had attracted a considerable amount of attention in England, and that therefore I should be glad to have some authoritative information respecting the intentions of the Austro-Hungarian Government.

Baron von Aehrenthal replied that it had been decided to lay a proposal for the construction of a certain number of large war-vessels before the Delegations who would probably meet next autumn. He could not at the present moment give me any precise information as to the number of ships which the Government would propose to build, or as to other details of the scheme, as the whole matter was still under the consideration of the naval experts. Anyhow, he did not expect that the Delegations would be asked to approve of the construction of any very great number of these big vessels. On my asking His Excellency whether he anticipated any difficulty in obtaining the necessary funds to carry out this scheme from the two Parliaments, he replied that it was impossible at the present moment to foresee in what frame of mind the Parliaments might be in the autumn with regard to the proposed scheme. He added that no doubt just now public opinion was not very enthusiastic about naval construction; few Austrians ever saw the sea, and the public generally attached more importance to the efficiency of the army than to that of the navy, but the Government could not ignore the fact that they had interests to protect in the Adriatic, and that the Austro-Hungarian navy was falling far behind that of most of the other Great Powers; it was therefore necessary to follow the example of other nations and to build a certain number of "Dreadnoughts."

Baron von Aehrenthal expressed much astonishment that the rumour that Austria-Hungary was about to slightly increase the strength of her navy should have caused so much excitement in England. He assured me that the Austro-Hungarian navy was being strengthened solely for the purpose of defending Austro-Hungarian interests in the Mediterranean. Italy was building bigger vessels, therefore Austria-Hungary had to follow her example. But the new "Dreadnoughts" would not be built with any intention of strengthening the German fleet under any eventualities. In short, he said, what Austria-Hungary was about to do need cause no alarm whatever in England.

I have, &c.
FAIRFAX L. CARTWRIGHT.

MINUTES.

In considering the strength of foreign navies, it is not sufficient to take into account only the present intentions, real or asserted, of the governments owning such navies. In this particular case it may be quite true that no hostility to England is contemplated; but in view of the existence of the triple alliance, it cannot be overlooked that Austria may, whether she likes it or not, find herself engaged in a war against us. The essence of the doctrine of the two-Power standard, is, I take it, that it wisely eschews the almost impossible task of determining whether a particular Power may or may not be opposed to us in war, and seeks safety in the abstract and general principle of superiority over any numerically possible combination of two Powers.

E. A. C.
May 3.

Whatever Baron von Aehrenthal may say there is jubilation in Germany where some papers consider the Austrian move as an answer to the offers of our Colonies.

W. L.
C. H.
E. G.

No. 179.

Sir E. Goschen to Sir Edward Grey.

F.O. 17541/17541/09/18.
(No. 165.)   Very Confidential.   Berlin, D. May 7, 1909.
Sir,   R. May 10, 1909.

In my despatch No. 27 of to-day's date marked Africa([1]) I had the honour to inform you that Herr von Schoen stated to me, in speaking of the Arms Conference, that the German Government was anxious previous to its meeting to come to an understanding with His Majesty's Government on all points which might come up for discussion at that Conference. They were moreover desirous of coming to an understanding not only with regard to the questions which formed the subject of the Arms Conference but upon all Colonial questions. He said that this would have an excellent effect upon public opinion both here and in England and show the Press that the two countries could work well and amicably together. He added that if once we could arrive at an understanding in Colonial Affairs, it would be a great step towards the wider understanding between the two countries which he was most sincerely anxious to promote.

He said that in holding this language to me, he was speaking confidentially and unofficially to an old friend and colleague. He was quite aware that the two countries had not yet reached the point when the question of such an understanding as he desired could be officially brought forward; but he held strongly to the belief that when public opinion was soothed by an understanding in colonial matters, it would only need a little good will on both sides for the other wider and more effectual understanding soon to follow.

I told Herr von Schoen that I cordially reciprocated his sentiments and that I was sure that when the time came for the friendly advances which he foreshadowed, the Imperial Government would meet with nothing but good will from the Government of His Majesty.

I have, &c.
W. E. GOSCHEN.

MINUTES.

I am unaware of there being any " colonial questions " pending between England and Germany which are of any importance.

No doubt Germany desires to acquire Walfis[c]h Bay; but since we do not wish to give it up except for some really valuable concession and as Germany has no concessions to offer, we may reasonably expect that the proposals for a " colonial agreement " will take the usual form of England being asked to make some valuable concessions to Germany in return for the latter's friendship and benevolence coupled with an understanding that England will, generally, follow a German lead in European politics.

We must wait for the actual proposals.

E. A. C.
May 10.

Herr von Schön may perhaps have had Walfis[c]h Bay in his mind but it is more likely that he merely wished to indicate generally his desire to settle amicably the minor Colonial questions which we are discussing with them.

With the exception of the S[outh] A[frican] war claims there will be no difficulty about that. We have been most conciliatory about the German S.W. Africa frontier questions: we are settling M'fumbiro at Berlin: and there is very little prospect of our differing seriously about the Orange River Boundary.

W. L.

([1]) [Not reproduced.]

I think Herr von Schön meant more than the amicable settlement of minor questions which, as Mr. Langley says, will with the exception of the war claims, probably be settled in the near future. I think Herr von Schön has wider ideas upon which it would be useless to speculate. Germany wants a great deal from a Colonial point of view which she might, under certain circumstances get from us. We, on the other hand, want nothing but to be left alone and to be allowed to develop our Colonies in our own way. This will make any agreement on Colonial affairs difficult to devise, but it is for the Germans to make suggestions.

C. H.

The decision with regard to Walfisch Bay would rest in the first place with the Gov[ernmen]t of Federated South Africa. It is not probable that they would entertain any idea of cession and even if they would the view of our Admiralty would remain to be considered. Without a deal about Walfisch Bay I do not suppose Germany would be content.(²)

E. G.

(²) [The Government of South Africa ultimately opposed the cession of Walfisch Bay to Germany, and the project was therefore abandoned. v. reference infra, p. 684, No. 506, Appendix III.]

No. 180.

Sir E. Goschen to Sir Edward Grey.

F.O. 19381/19381/09/18.
(No. 185.)

Berlin, D. May 20, 1909.
R. May 24, 1909.

Sir,

The "Berliner Tageblatt," a paper with a very wide circulation, has for some time past been persistently advocating a better understanding between England and Germany. This morning it devotes a leading article to the subject from the pen of the well-known journalist and writer on questions of Public Law, Herr Friedrich Dernburg. He observes that the danger of the present situation lies not in the warlike sentiments of rulers or statesmen, but in the highly excitable condition of popular feeling in both countries. At such a moment the smallest incident might lead to a general conflagration. Little attention had been paid in Germany to the wild invasion panic in England, and the fairy tales of the forty thousand waiters acting as spies, of the phantom ships stealing up the Humber and of the German aeroplane which nightly hovered over England, were regarded merely as a subject for merriment. But it seemed to be overlooked that the state of public feeling which could lead to the circulation of such legends was in itself a subject for grave apprehensions, as in the case of a popular panic, even a peaceful Government might be driven into taking the most fatal steps. As long as the relations between two countries were satisfactory and devoid of mutual ill-will, an untoward event might occur without great danger of serious consequences; but what, asks Herr Dernburg, would be likely to happen if, by an unfortunate accident or through the fault of some individual in Germany, an incident were to occur analogous to the bombardment of the Hull fishing-vessels by Russian war-ships. The whole of England would at once be in flames; all the pent-up ill-will against Germany would burst out; a war party already existed which would place itself at the head of a popular movement and impose its will on a recalcitrant Government, and before any time had been given for proper reflection, the two countries would find themselves plunged in war. Were the unfortunate incident to occur through the fault of England similar consequences might ensue, as there was no lack of rash persons in Germany who would be only too ready to seize the first opportunity to reply to the everlasting challenges from England. Herr Dernburg then proceeds to point out that the object of all nations really desirous of peace is to safeguard themselves against the consequences which might arise from dangerous and untoward incidents. Many countries had already bound themselves by Treaty to submit, in certain circumstances, to arbitration. No such treaty, however, at present existed between England and Germany—the two countries, by universal consent, in greatest need of such an arrangement, which might be described as an "Insurance Treaty against unforeseen events." England's great grievance against Germany was that a German navy was in course of construction. It should, however, be borne in mind in England that her present naval embarrassments were entirely due to a fault of tactics on her own part as regards naval construction; by introducing the 'Dreadnought' type she had rendered former types obsolete and thus herself destroyed her former absolute predominance. An Agreement for a limitation of armaments would nevertheless be welcomed in Germany—to be negotiated on the basis of the extent of coast-line to be protected in the two countries and of their mutual naval interests. The way to such an Agreement could, however, only be found gradually and on condition of a feeling of mutual good-will being first of all established. In the meanwhile it was most essential that guarantees for present security should be established. It was true that many efforts had been made towards bringing about a popular *rapprochement* between the English and German nations. Repeated visits had been exchanged between English and German members of Parliament; Representatives of Municipal Bodies, journalists and others had exchanged visits, and assurances of friendship had been given and received. Such demonstrations had, however, hitherto not led to any tangible result. People working in the direction of a better understanding between England and Germany would do well to keep before their eyes the practical aim of concluding an obligatory Treaty of Arbitration, which would be a safeguard against any sudden outburst of popular passion and, to repeat a phrase already used, "an Anglo-German Insurance Treaty against untoward events."

I have, &c.
W. E. GOSCHEN.

MINUTES.

It is difficult to take seriously a political writer who calls upon England and Germany to ensure peace by signing an obligatory arbitration treaty, in evident ignorance that such a treaty already exists. (July 12, 1904.)

E. A. C.
May 24.

Except this suggestion of a remedy there is nothing very new in the article, and the suggestion is founded on a misapprehension.

W. L.

No. 181.

Sir E. Goschen to Sir Edward Grey.

F.O. 19382/19382/09/18.
(No. 186.) Confidential.
Sir,

Berlin, D. *May* 21, 1909.
R. *May* 24, 1909.

I have the honour to forward, herewith, a despatch, as marked in the margin, which I have received from Captain Heath Naval Attaché to this Embassy, relating to a conversation with H[is] R[oyal] H[ighness] Prince Henry of Prussia and with Capt[ain] Lans, Chief of the Staff.

I have, &c.
W. E. GOSCHEN.

Enclosure in No. 181.

N[aval] A[ttaché's] Report.

Confidential.
Sir,

British Embassy, Berlin, May 21, 1909.

I have the honour to report that on Thursday the 20th May, I proceeded to Vilhelmshaven, in order to present a copy of the Navy List to H[is] R[oyal] H[ighness] Prince Henry, C[ommander] in C[hief] of the H[igh] S[ea] Fleet.

The arrangement made was for me to be at the "Neuer Einfahrt" by noon, at which hour the "Deut[s]chland" steamed into the lock, on her way into the inner harbour to coal.

[17590]

H[is] R[oyal] H[ighness] was pleased to give me a very gracious welcome on board his flagship, and having expressed his thanks for the Navy List, invited me to remain onboard to luncheon.

The conversation was entirely general, but H[is] R[oyal] H[ighness] remarked that he could not avoid a little chaff about the Air-ship scare as reported in the English Press. He proceeded to explain that he had made several ascents in the different kinds of dirigibles, and had come to the conclusion, that it was not yet time to take them seriously. The air-ship was absolutely unmanageable in a breeze of 6 (Beaufort Scale), and that even in an ordinary way the "lee-way" was tremendous.

H[is] R[oyal] H[ighness] scouted "Aero-planes" as being un-canny, and quite unreliable for Naval purposes.

H[is] R[oyal] H[ighness] referred more than once to the good relations existing "as he thought, and as he hoped would always remain" between the British and German Navies, and toasted me with the health of H[is] M[ajesty] the King and the English Navy.

On taking leave, H[is] R[oyal] H[ighness] again said to me, that he was glad that an opportunity had occurred for my coming on board his ship "For I have purposely and for special reasons, desired to shew my friendship to the British Navy."

I had a subsequent talk with Capt[ain] Lans, the Chief of the Staff who also expressed on behalf of the German Naval Officers, the most friendly feeling for their comrades in the British Navy.

Capt[ain] Lans produced an old "Special Graphic" of Nov[ember] 7th/08, in which was a picture of German subordinate officers, drinking to "the Great Day": viz. that on which the British Fleet was to be wiped from off the seas.

Capt[ain] Lans assured me on his honour, that such a toast was absolutely unknown, and moreover was contrary to the rules of the Service, and he claimed that the publication of "such a lie" in an English newspaper was a gross injustice, he added that these papers were much read by German Naval Officers, and asked whether it would not be possible to put a stop to the publication of such irritable stuff.

Dealing with Naval matters, there was the usual talk of the German Navy being purely defensive &c. "but might be required in case of trouble with America, or with some of the S[outh] American States." I have not had this possibility put before me previously.

I gathered that German Naval Officers recognise that an attack on England, would be shere [sic] madness in the present state of England's superiority at sea. They also seem to recognise that England intends to maintain that superiority.

There was a hint as to the "Naval Law" being the extreme limit of the size of the fleet, but I do not think this was seriously said.

I have, &c.

H. L. HEATH,
Captain and Naval Attaché.

MINUTES.

The usual explanations about the increase of the German Navy are, either, that it is to protect Germany's growing commerce (which signifies the ability to beat any Power interfering with that commerce), or for use in the Far East where side by side with the British Navy it is to face the "Yellow Peril." It is quite new to hear the American continents mentioned as a possible object for the German fleet, and we may at once put aside any idea of the German fleet embarking on ventures against the U[nited] S[tates] while the British fleet remains unbeaten.

As it is the German Press itself explains quite clearly what is the objective of their fleet.

G. S. S.
24/5.

It is not a little curious that the Germans make such a fuss over what they choose to call the English panic respecting aerial invasion, when it is remembered that whatever in the way of alarm may exist on this head in England is entirely due to the rodomontading publications and speeches of the German aerial navigation clubs and patriotic writers. However silly these fantasies may be they were most certainly "made in Germany."

E. A. C.
May 24.

America must have been a happy thought of Captain Lans in default of a better.

W. L.
C. H.
E. G.

No. 182.

Sir Edward Grey to Sir E. Goschen.

Private.([1])

My dear Goschen,   *Foreign Office, June 9, 1909.*

Metternich came to see me to-day, on his return.([2])

He said that he had not been conscious of any change for the worse until he reached this country, but now that he had been here two days he considered that the feeling with regard to Germany was distinctly worse than it had been. It was strange that it should be so, for whenever Englishmen and Germans met : as in the cases of the Burgomasters, Pastors, and other groups which had been meeting lately, they got on particularly well with each other. He told me that he felt very helpless, and did not see what he could do to improve matters.

I replied that I did not think things were worse, except in the way I had foretold : the burden of naval expenditure having an increasing effect in exciting apprehension. Perhaps, if we announced next month that preparations for our four hypothetical ships were to be made this year, some of the apprehension and talk would cease, but till then I did not think there would be any abatement.

Metternich told me, speaking privately, that the German Emperor had been very much hurt by our failure to accept the assurances given by his Government with regard to the number of ships which Germany would have by the end of 1912. In spite of these assurances, public feeling in this country had been worked up.

I said that as soon as the German statements had been made thoroughly clear to us we had put them on record publicly.

But Metternich complained that even subsequently to this the Prime Minister, when speaking at Glasgow in April, had referred to the possibility of 17 German ships in 1912.

I told him that I had not that reference, or the context of it, in mind.

Metternich said that all the restlessness in Europe had arisen since the change of policy on our part in 1904. This had altered the grouping of the Powers.

I replied that Germany might have been conscious of more restlessness, but we had not. On the contrary, before 1904 we had constantly been on the brink of war with either France or Russia. For instance, when I was at the Foreign Office in 1893, we had been thought to be on the brink of war with France about Siam ; soon after that, there had been talk of war with Russia about Port Arthur,([3]) and there had been other instances.

Metternich pointed out that in those years there was, at any rate, no talk of war with Germany : while now there constantly was such talk.

I answered that this talk was not of the same kind as that which there had been in the past in connection with France and Siam, and in connection with Russia and Port Arthur ; in each case an incident, small in itself, leading to a crisis.

Metternich admitted this, but added that he did not think the relations between Germany and England could stand an incident of this kind, in the present state of feeling.

([1]) [Grey MSS., Vol. 22.]

([2]) [For Count Metternich's brief account of this conversation, *v. G.P.* XXVIII, p. 180. Count Metternich had taken part in a discussion of Anglo-German relations held at Berlin on June 3, *cp. ib.*, pp. 178–80, the result of which was embodied in a protocol given on pp. 168–78.]

([3]) [*v. Gooch & Temperley*, Vol. I, pp. 18–30, especially pp. 21–2 No. 32.]

I said that I thought the German Press was responsible for a good deal of this feeling. Take, for instance, the Royal visit.([4]) It was, apparently, regarded as an offence that the King of England should meet the Czar last year. On the other hand, though the German Emperor had met the Czar previously, and was now to meet him again, our Press did not make hostile comments on the subject. But, even now, some of the German Press was writing as if the meeting between the Emperor of Germany and the Czar was intended to show Russia that friendship with England was no use.

Metternich said that some of our Press put forward the view that friendship with Russia and France, especially with Russia, was necessary to keep Germany in check.

I observed that it was a question of preventing the balance of power from being destroyed. If the German Press had its way, and France and Russia were convinced that England was no use and they must abandon her and make friends with the Triple Alliance, the result would be a quintuple alliance which would leave England isolated. Naturally, our Press did not wish this to occur.

Metternich spoke further of Rosebery's reference to expenditure on armaments, endorsed subsequently by me, and by Balfour to-day. He asked why we should necessarily assume that the German Navy was intended for hostile use against us.

I said that we did not put forward any such assumption. The fact was that Germany, according to her programme, was going to have close to our shores a Fleet stronger than any other we had ever had to face before. At the same time, speeches such as the one made by Admiral von Koster lately on behalf of the Navy League showed what pressure was being put upon the German Government to push on the programme. Any attempt here to diminish apprehension as to the increase in naval expenditure would be met by a reference to speeches of this kind, and by definite and pressing enquiry as to whether we knew exactly what was going on in the German dockyards. Besides this, Austria was now about to spend more on ships; Italy was spending more; and it was reported that France intended to spend more. We did not look only at the German expenditure, and we had to take precautions in view of the impossibility of knowing what changes or complications might arise when all these great ships were completed. We were bound to take the question very seriously. I pointed out to Metternich that he had made it a matter of comment to me some time ago that we took into account only Germany, and not the United States. He would have observed from a recent Debate that public opinion here was not at all agreed in omitting the United States from our naval calculations, and all the Government had stated was that, owing to distance, the American expenditure must enter into our calculations on a different basis.

I gathered from some remarks which Metternich made that he himself was depressed by the rapid growth of naval expenditure and would welcome a slackening of it, for he remarked that it was possible that not only the working classes, as Rosebery had said, but the other classes also, who were feeling the pressure of taxation, might join in resisting naval expenditure.

Yours sincerely,
E. GREY.

([4]) [v. Gooch & Temperley, Vol. V, pp. 232–46, ch. XXXVII.]

No. 183.

Sir E. Goschen to Sir Edward Grey.

F.O. 24021/24021/09/18.
(No. 238.) Confidential.   Berlin, D. June 23, 1909.
Sir,   R. June 28, 1909.

Herr von Schoen spoke to me yesterday, at his official reception, on the subject of the meeting between the Emperor and the Czar at Björkö. He said that everything had passed off exceedingly well and that nothing could have been more friendly and more cordial than the meeting between the two Sovereigns. To him it appeared that this meeting and the cordiality of the toasts interchanged had more than usual significance, as it must finally have disposed of the legend that Germany had exercised pressure upon Russia in the last phase of the Bosnian question. For it was clear that, had that been the case, and the German-Russian relations strained in consequence, the Czar would never have sent the Emperor such a pressing invitation not to forget His promised visit, nor have received His Imperial Guest in such a particularly friendly fashion. He was glad to have the opportunity of speaking to me on the subject as judging by the Press the above legend had found a certain amount of credence in England and moreover dark designs against Great Britain had been hinted at as being the reasons for the visit. It was scarcely necessary to assure me that there was nothing more false than this suggestion; the idea that the visit was in any way connected with the detachment of England from Russia or a new grouping of the Powers was sheer nonsense; nothing but the friendliest words had been exchanged about England. The real object of the visit, which had been perfectly successful, had been to dispel the feeling that anything had happened to disturb the good relations which had so long existed between the German and Russian Sovereigns and their respective Governments.

I said that I was not aware that our Press had attributed any hostile designs against England to the visit of the Emperor to the Czar, but that I had seen many articles in the German Press which, to my mind, would have justified people in England in taking that line.[1] Of one thing, however, I was quite sure, namely, that the existence of cordial relations between Germany and Russia could never be anything but welcome to His Majesty's Government, whose leading principle was good and peaceful relations between all countries and a proper balance of Power in Europe.

Continuing, Herr von Schoen said that while of course in conversations between the two Emperors and between him and the Russian statesmen there had been general reviews of the present political situation, no arrangements of any kind or description had been made for the future. Monsieur Isvolsky had of course spoken of Baron d'Aehrenthal in his usual manner, but had said that he desired nothing better than that Russia should be on good terms with Austria-Hungary as with every other Power. Monsieur Isvolsky had added that Russia had need of peace and quiet and time to put her internal affairs in order, and that he fancied that Germany would not object to be free from all external complications for the same purpose; therefore he hoped that the world might be free from surprises for some time to come. Herr von Schoen said that he had expressed his hearty agreement with M. Isvolsky's sentiments.

Herr von Schoen then turned to Anglo-German relations and said that things could not go on as they now were, and that "we must come to an understanding of some sort." He added that of course he did not mean a regular *entente*, but something which would lead to a *rapprochement* and better feeling between the two countries. He added that the difficulty of course was the naval question on which both countries were particularly sensitive. He had since his return from Björkö seen Admiral Tirpitz and asked him whether there was any possibility of an understanding being made in naval matters between the two countries which would remove this sensitiveness; but that the Admiral had replied (very characteristically) that he did not think anything could be done in this direction, all the less that the British Naval Authorities had the bad habit of not believing the official assurances of those in a similar position in Germany. Herr von Schoen then went over a great deal of old ground on the particular subject, finally saying that he wished His Majesty's Government could understand that whatever had been or might be done in the way of preparation or of giving employment, and whatever the Naval League might say, one thing was absolutely certain, namely that not a single ship would be fit for service before its time as fixed by their Naval Programme.

Herr von Schoen said to me in conclusion that he had been speaking to me quite unofficially, as to an old friend and colleague; he had had no instructions to speak to

[1] [Marginal comment by Sir C. Hardinge : "A good reply. C. H."]

me as he had done, but the present state of the relations between the two countries was certainly not as it ought to be, and the matter was a source of the greatest preoccupation both to him and the Chancellor. They wanted to find a remedy, but, to tell the truth, it was a difficult matter to know where to begin.

In reply I said that I was quite certain that His Majesty's Government would welcome anything likely to assure permanent good feeling between England and Germany, and quoted your words to Count Metternich on a former occasion, when you said that His Majesty's Government would be the last to refuse a hand held out to them in good faith. I added that I quite agreed that a ' formula ' was difficult to find; but was a " formula " necessary? Opportunities for a few friendly acts were, in any case, much easier to find than ' formulas ' and such opportunities were seldom wanting. I could name one or two at the present moment. Herr von Schoen said that they were only too anxious to do everything in their power to be agreeable to His Majesty's Government, but that the worst of the whole matter was that the naval question so dominated other questions, that the slightest differences of opinion in small matters were greedily seized upon by the Press of both countries, magnified into serious disagreements, and remembered as such; while any acts of a friendly nature either passed unheeded or were speedily forgotten.

I feel that there is a good deal of truth in at all events the first part of Herr von Schoen's concluding observation.

I have, &c.
W. E. GOSCHEN.

MINUTES.

Herr von Schön exactly hit the nail on the head. The naval question dominates the situation and Germany alone can provide a remedy.

W. L.
C. H.

The only remedy can be exchange of naval information through the respective naval attachés and that the Germans will not adopt. As regards smaller matters between us we will adopt a conciliatory attitude if they will reciprocate.

E. G.

No. 184.

Mr. Bryce to Sir Edward Grey.

F.O. 27359/27359/09/18.
(No. 165.) Confidential.   *North East Harbour, D. July 12,* 1909.
Sir,   R. *July* 20, 1909.

In a conversation which I had with the President on July 8th the subject of the attitude of the German Government was mentioned. The President observed that, though the German Emperor was an erratic personage and had written to Mr. Roosevelt some extraordinary letters, full of alarms and wild suggestions, he did not believe that he had any war-like designs, but was animated more by a sort of megalomania and by a desire to have the glory of possessing a splendid navy. So too he did not believe that the German nation was otherwise than pacific in its intentions. He did not see what would be the end of this incessant increase in armaments, but thought that before long the weight of taxation must arrest their progress.

He had some little while before told me that people had approached him wishing him to take some action in the way of proposing a reduction in the armaments of the Great Powers but that he had not seen his way to such a step.

I gathered that much as he regretted the disquietude these preparations cause, the reports he received from his Representative at Berlin did not make him apprehensive of any disturbance of the peace of the world.

I have, &c.
JAMES BRYCE.

MINUTES.

But still however pacific the German Emperor and German nation may be at present the danger lies in the fact of their possessing a Navy strong enough to enable them to go in for a warlike policy at any moment, when they may feel less pacific. There is the risk that when they have got their big fleet they will be strongly tempted to try to make somebody else pay for it.

G. S. S.
20/7.
W. L.
C. H.

Yes : and it is natural that till they have a big navy they should quiet apprehensions.

E. G.

No. 185.

Sir E. Goschen to Sir Edward Grey.

F.O. 28009/27359/09/18.
(No. 273.)   Confidential.   *Berlin, D. July* 23, 1909.
Sir,   R. *July* 26, 1909.

I had an opportunity of having some conversation with Prince Buelow on the day before he left Berlin for Norde[r]ney.

His Highness, after assuring me that his great desire had always been and still was that Germany and Great Britain should be on the friendliest terms, asked me what impression I had gathered during my recent visit to England, of the feelings of my countrymen towards Germany. I replied that in my conversations with you I had found that you fully reciprocated the desire so often expressed both by His Highness and Baron von Schoen for good relations between the two countries, but that outside official circles I had to admit, if I was to speak quite frankly, that a certain preoccupation existed amongst many of my countrymen with regard to the motives of Germany in developing her Sea Power to the extent she was doing. They seemed, without the least animosity or illwill towards Germany, unable to explain to themselves the efforts made by the latter to supplement her enormous army by a powerful navy, except by attributing to her a desire sooner or later to try conclusions with Great Britain. In this view they were no doubt strengthened by the sort of mental food supplied to them by certain sections of the Press on both sides. Prince Bülow said that he was bound to confess that the German Press was by no means guiltless in the matter and that a great deal of nonsense was written respecting naval matters. He regretted this extremely but, as he had often explained to me, the Imperial Government were powerless in such matters and could exercise no restraint on the Press.([1]) In any case he was sure that I would do him the justice to admit that he had always done his best both in his speeches in the Reichstag and in other ways, to show that there was no real cause for the want of cordiality between the two countries and to make it clear that both he and the Imperial Government as a whole were sincerely desirous to make Anglo-German relations as friendly as possible.([2]) But his task had been rendered difficult by the fanatics on both sides and more especially by the unreasonable suspicions entertained in England with regard to the German Navy, suspicions which were, so to speak, rubbed into the German people by certain sections of the British

([1]) [Marginal comment by Mr. Spicer : " This is scarcely true. The German Gov[ernmen]t have very great power over the Press which depends on the Gov[ernmen]t for its information. G. S. S."]

([2]) [Marginal comment by Mr. Spicer : " Prince Bulow has forgotten the Anglophobe campaign started under his auspices in 1899–1900. G. S. S."]

Press, but which were also, he must admit, justified to a certain extent by the injudicious language held by the members of the German Navy League and reproduced with emphasis in the Press of both countries. But really it needed but a small exercise of common sense to realize how unreasonable these suspicions were. Apart from numerous other considerations, such as the utter impossibility for Germany ever to rival England at sea and the stupendous difficulties of an invasion of England, it would never "pay" Germany to make war on England. In the first place such a war would be highly unpopular with a very large section of the German nation, notably that vast number who had business relations with the United Kingdom and to whom war would spell ruin, and in the second place the war could not possibly be decisive. Germany could not hope to conquer England proper and she had neither the power nor the wish to annex any of the British colonies, having quite enough to do with those she possessed already. On the other hand Great Britain could not hope to defeat sixty millions of Germans : the most she could do would be to destroy the German fleet and her mercantile marine. That might appear to be a temporary success, but Germans, though perhaps slow, were most exceedingly tenacious, and he did not mind saying that such a success might cost England dear, as not a man throughout the Empire would rest until revenge was secured. The idea of war between the two nations was almost unthinkable. If therefore there was no sense in being enemies why could not we be friends? Surely this period of coldness must soon pass. There had been such periods between Great Britain and France and Great Britain and Russia, and now England was on the most friendly terms with both those countries : he hoped the same thing would happen between Great Britain and Germany, all the more that, unlike the cases of France and Russia, where there had been direct causes of friction with England and considerable divergence of interests, there was, as far as he knew, no question whatever between the two countries of sufficient importance to embroil them in a quarrel. In fact he was not sure that the very absence of any acute question, such as might form the subject of negotiation and lead to reconciliation, was not, under present circumstances, almost a disadvantage. It was in fact easier to reconcile people who had a distinct ground for quarrel than people who were simply cold to each other on no tangible grounds. In any case he hoped that this coldness would eventually disappear and he could assure me that his successor, who was animated by the best feelings towards Great Britain, would leave nothing undone to secure that most desirable result.

A day or two after Prince Bülow's departure I saw Herr von Schoen, who also spoke to me respecting the relations between Great Britain and Germany. He spoke on the same lines as Prince Bülow. He said that the suspicion with which a number of people in England regarded the growth of the German fleet was, although there was in point of fact not the slightest reason for it, a matter of no surprise to him. The German 'Flottenverein,' which he termed the "evil spirit of Germany," and the intemperate speeches often made at its meetings, could not but cause distrust, while meetings of Fire-eaters, at which the word 'invasion' was far too freely used, bellicose articles in the Press and long-winded essays from warlike Professors did the rest. At the same time he must say that articles in certain of our magazines and newspapers in which German irresponsible utterances were reproduced with much exaggeration and undue emphasis, were also responsible for a great deal of suspicion and distrust of Germany which was now so common in England. Therefore while he deplored this distrustful attitude on the part of England, he could not regard it as altogether unnatural under the circumstances. That which troubled him was that, while he was convinced that both the rulers, the Governments and the people of the two nations were sincerely desirous of good relations, the situation was such that a very insignificant spark might at any time cause a conflagration.([3]) This situation should not be allowed to continue and both the new Chancellor and he were fully

---

([3]) [Marginal comment by Mr. Spicer : " A very ominous admission, and a proof that much unfriendly feeling towards England *does* exist. G. S. S."]

determined to do all in their power to clear it up. There was absolutely no question between the two countries which could not be easily settled, and he hoped in a very few days to give a proof of the desire of the Imperial Government to meet the wishes of His Majesty's Government in every possible way. He alluded to the question which had arisen with regard to the application of the Egyptian Press Law. He then said that it appeared to him difficult at the present moment, when the respective navies of the two countries were occupying people's minds so much and causing so much controversy, to make any practical step towards a naval understanding, in fact anything in that direction which might be construed into a concession on the part of Germany would raise an outcry throughout the country and place the Imperial Government in an impossible position; but he thought that it was quite possible that as soon as things settled down a little that something might be done in the way of mutual exchange of Programmes or more facilities for the respective Naval Attachés. There were more people than I imagined, both in the Reichstag and out of it, who were antagonistic to the construction of so many vessels of the 'Dreadnought' class and who considered that a smaller type of vessel, built in such numbers as were requisite for coast defence and the protection of their mercantile marine, was better adapted to the needs of Germany. People were already beginning to be appalled by the cost of building 'Dreadnoughts,' a cost which had not been anticipated when the Naval Programme was first laid down; and it was by no means unlikely that when confronted next year with the expense entailed by a rigid adherence to the programme, an agitation would be set on foot for the dropping of one or more of such terribly expensive vessels. If that should take place it would no doubt have a calming effect all round, and then would be the time to make an effort to come to such an arrangement as he had indicated above. He told me this, he said, in order to show the direction in which his mind was working, and he did not at all despair that Great Britain and Germany would one of these days come to a good understanding and exchange a cordial shake of the hand. He then gave me in the strictest confidence an account of the language held by the Emperor at a conversation which took place between His Majesty, Herr von Bethmann Hollweg and himself on the day before His Majesty left for the North. The Emperor had said: "Gentlemen! You must admit that I am a good natured man. I am a grandson of Queen Victoria, I love England, admire the English, and am never happier than when on English soil. I have stated this publicly on many occasions, and have given every assurance that I am a friend of England and wish her nothing but well; and yet I am always held up as a monster of duplicity, and the English people are taught to believe that I harbour warlike designs against them. It is enough to dishearten anyone; but I refuse to be discouraged and shall continue to do my best to bring about friendly relations. In this I count upon your full support."

Yesterday I had the honour of being received by the new Chancellor. His Excellency was extremely friendly and cordial and appeared to be much gratified by friendly messages which he had received from London. He said that I could not expect him, at this early date, to go very deeply into foreign affairs, but he wished to assure me that he was animated by the most friendly feelings towards Great Britain, and that nothing would cause him more gratification than that his tenure of the Chancellorship should be distinguished by the establishment of the good and solid relations which ought to exist between the two countries. "On one thing," he said, "you can thoroughly depend, namely that my policy in foreign affairs will be entirely frank and open."

I have reported these three conversations at some length, because Prince Bülow's valedictory words are not without interest from a psychological point of view; while the language of the new Chancellor and Baron Schoen are interesting as the first utterances under the new order of things. I have always believed that Baron Schoen is personally in favour of friendly relations, and it is quite possible that he will now have a freer hand and that his conciliatory views will carry more weight. If the Chancellor is also as well disposed as he is reported to be there then appears to be some ground for the hope that the new era will result in a quieter, more open and less cantankerous foreign policy. This is all the more likely to be the case as the internal situation requires so much care and watchfulness on the part of the Imperial Government that it will be to their interest to avoid all chance of foreign complications for some time to come.

This consideration may of course have something to do with the very conciliatory and friendly language of the three statesmen.

I have, &c.

W. E. GOSCHEN.

CHAPTER XLV.

HERR VON BETHMANN HOLLWEG'S PROPOSALS, AUGUST–DECEMBER 1909.

[*ED. NOTE.*—The negotiations initiated by Herr von Bethmann Hollweg on August 21, 1909, for which a preliminary overture had been made by Herr Albert Ballin through Sir Ernest Cassel, are fully described from the German side in *G.P.* XXVIII, chs. 223–5. *cp.* Admiral von Tirpitz : *Der Aufbau der deutschen Weltmacht* (1924), ch. 8; E. Jäckh : *Kiderlen-Wächter* (1924), Vol. II, ch. 10; and B. Huldermann : *Albert Ballin* (1922), ch. 8.]

No. 186.

Sir E. Goschen to Sir Edward Grey.

Berlin, *August* 21, 1909.

F.O. 31695/31695/09/18.
Tel. (No. 93.) Secret.

D. 6·27 P.M.
R. 7·30 P.M.

Imperial Chancellor having expressed a wish to see me, I called on him to-day.

He stated that ever since assuming office he had been preoccupied by the question of Anglo-German relations, and he had realised that the naval question was regarded generally as the chief obstacle to real cordiality between the two countries. He had noticed that in the naval debate both the Prime Minister and the First Lord of the Admiralty had stated that England had always been ready to discuss with foreign countries the means for limiting the present enormous naval expenditure, and that door for such discussions was still open.(¹) He wished now to tell me that the Imperial Government were ready to make proposals for a naval arrangement and to bring them forward for discussion at any time which might be suitable to His Majesty's Government.

His Excellency added, however, that the discussion of a naval arrangement could lead to no practical result unless it formed part of a scheme for a good general understanding, and it was based upon a conviction on the part, not only of the two Governments, but of public opinion in both countries, that neither country had any hostile or aggressive designs against the other. I asked his Excellency to what kind of understanding he alluded, as, in view of the present friendships and alliances, it seemed to me personally that the conclusion of any formal *entente* or understanding presented some difficulty. His Excellency replied that the question of outside engagements was, of course, a difficult one, but that he thought that, with good-will and honest intentions on both sides, a satisfactory formula could be found such as would touch no outside susceptibilities.

What, therefore, his Excellency wished to know was whether His Majesty's Government were ready to accept in principle the idea of a revision of Anglo-German relations such as would lead to a good understanding, and to enter at their own time into a friendly exchange of views both respecting the general relations between the two countries and such proposals for a technical naval arrangement as the Imperial Government were now ready to put forward.

His Excellency impressed on me his earnest desire that this conversation, and, in fact, any preliminary negotiations of the kind he had indicated, should be kept strictly secret and neither communicated to other Powers nor the press. He on his side would observe similar secrecy.

(¹) [*cp. Parl. Deb.*, *5th Ser.*, House of Commons, Vol. 8, pp. 878–80 and p. 967.]

No. 187.

Sir E. Goschen to Sir Edward Grey.([1])

F.O. 31696/31695/09/18. Berlin, D. August 21, 1909, 11·45 P.M.
Tel. (No. 94.) Secret. R. August 22, 1909, 8 A.M.

My telegram No. 93.([2])

In speaking of the sort of understanding between the two countries which would render a naval arrangement possible, the Chancellor said that he meant an understanding which would provide on either side necessary sense of security. Germany, for example, could not afford to diminish her rate of shipbuilding unless she was absolutely certain that her moderation would not be used against her. England probably had the same feeling. I said that that was of course the case, and that I presumed no arrangement would be suggested which would have the effect of tying the hands of either country in such a manner as to prevent them from carrying out the lines of action to which they were pledged, either by engagements or by principle, as, for instance, Germany by her alliances, and England by her well-known views with regard to the balance of power in Europe. His Excellency said that to show his idea of what would or would not constitute hostility on the part of England towards Germany he would put following cases : If Russia made an unprovoked attack on Austria, Germany would have to help latter; if England joined Russia he would regard that as indication of hostile feeling; but if Germany made an unprovoked attack on France and England came to the latter's assistance he would consider England's action quite justifiable. Such was the line of thought in which he was contemplating the possibility of an understanding, and it was to considerations such as these that the two Governments would have to turn their minds if His Majesty's Government accepted his proposals in principle. In the latter case he left it entirely to His Majesty's Government to choose the moment they thought most opportune for initiating negotiations.

MINUTES.

It is difficult to imagine any formula for an understanding with Germany which would not fetter our freedom of action and disturb the minds of France and Russia.

Except the increase of her fleet we have no cause of quarrel with Germany and this has been often stated. What then does she want? The Chancellor's illustrations are rather ominous as they point to a desire to limit our right of intervention.

These two telegrams have so far not been printed in the section and have therefore been seen by no one.

W. L.

I already have sent the copies I received this morning to the Prime Minister. The two questions will require much consideration.

We could agree at once to receive proposals for a naval arrangement. They would be in pari materia more or less with our agreements with France and Russia, which are limited to settling differences between us on certain specified points.

The wider proposals indicated by the Chancellor would go beyond anything which we have with France and Russia. It strikes me at first sight that if any general political understanding is to be arranged it should be one not between two Powers alone but between the two great groups of Powers, ourselves France and Russia on one side and the Triple Alliance on the other. Whether any understanding of this sort is possible it is difficult to say, but anything short of it is sure to be regarded as invidious by those who are left out.

E. G.

([1]) [For the Chancellor's report, v. G.P. XXVIII, pp. 221-2.]
([2]) [v. immediately preceding document.]

No. 188.

Sir Edward Grey to Sir E. Goschen.

Foreign Office, August 23, 1909.

Private.([1])
D. 6·10 P.M.

Tel.

Your telegrams 93 and 94.([2])

Prime Minister is away till Wednesday and I go away to-morrow till Monday, but I will consult with him next week about the Chancellor's communication. Meanwhile you might say that the friendly tone of the Chancellor's communication is cordially reciprocated, and that, though I can say nothing further till I have consulted the Prime Minister, the ideas which the Chancellor has put forward will be examined in the most friendly spirit.

([1]) [Grey MSS., Vol. 22.]
([2]) [*v.* the two immediately preceding documents.]

No. 189.

Sir C. Hardinge to Sir Edward Grey.

Private.([1])
Temple House, Waltham Cross,

My dear Grey,
August 25, 1909.

I have been intensely interested over Goschen's two telegrams([2]) and I have been thinking over them the whole time. I was glad to get your letter and to hear your views which I am sure are on the right lines, and I send you a memorandum([3]) which I have written developing the lines on which a reply might be given. " Declarations " are in vogue and I think it is the form most suitable for any agreement to which we and other Powers can subscribe. It would be an advantage to get Germany to subscribe to the policy which I have indicated as the maintenance of the balance of power, since it would be a safeguard for the smaller states. It is however quite evident that an agreement on naval affairs *must* come first. As a matter of fact anything further is really superfluous.

I am so glad that you have polished off Crete for the time being and that you have been able to get away for a few days holiday.

Y[ou]rs very sincerely,
CHARLES HARDINGE.

([1]) [Grey MSS., Vol. 54.]
([2]) [*v. supra*, pp. 283–4, Nos. 186–7.]
([3]) [*v.* immediately succeeding document.]

No. 190.

Memorandum by Sir C. Hardinge.

Private.([1])
August 25, 1909.

The cause of the cool relations between England and Germany is the suspicion aroused by the German Naval Programme with its steady fulfilment and progressive increase during the past nine years. This feeling has been accentuated by certain statements made by German officials and more especially by the German Navy League, which is a recognised and official association. The effect of a technical naval agreement between the two countries would at once remove the feeling of distrust and would re-establish Anglo-German relations on a cordial and satisfactory footing, thus neutralising the cause of recent suspicions. An understanding, therefore, on naval

([1]) [Grey MSS., Vol. 54.]

matters is a primary and essential condition for the improvement of the relations between the two countries, more especially as there are no pending questions of any importance between the two Gov[ernmen]ts such as existed with the French and Russian Gov[ernmen]ts at the time of the conclusion of the Anglo-French and Anglo-Russian agreements. The conclusion of a naval agreement is in reality the only condition that is needed to ensure more friendly feelings between the Gov[ernmen]ts and people of the two countries.

Although it would be difficult to conclude an understanding with Germany which should meet all imaginable eventualities, it might be possible to meet the Chancellor's views by making a declaration of general policy which should satisfy Germany without irrevocably binding the hands of England. Thus it might be stated that the two guiding principles of British foreign policy are :—

1. The preservation of peace ; and
2. The maintenance of the balance of power in Europe.

As regards the first of these two principles Great Britain would declare the firm intention, on her part, of not making an unprovoked attack on any Power or Powers, and of using all her influence to prevent an unprovoked aggression by any one Power or group of Powers on any other Power or Powers.

As to the second of the two principles enunciated above, the traditional policy of Great Britain has been to maintain an even balance of power in Europe, to oppose the domination of Europe by any one single Power or group of Powers, and to prevent the absorption of the weaker European States. For the realisation of this policy Great Britain has made serious sacrifices in the past, and it still remains her policy in the present and (? immediate) future—Great Britain, owing to her insular position, and having no alliance with any Great Power in Europe, stands alone, and is the pacific advocate of a friendly grouping of the European Powers.

I think that a declaration in this form and sense, if made by Germany and ourselves would have a reassuring effect, and the other Powers might be invited to join. I do not see that any special exception could be taken by either France or Russia, but I am not sure that Germany will be satisfied with a declaration of this nature. She may want something much more insidious.

An "unprovoked attack" might be difficult to define, as although the French were apparently the aggressors in 1870, history has taught us that Bismarck, Moltke and Roon were really responsible for the war.

C. H.

Aug[ust] 25, 1909.

No. 191.

Mr. L. Mallet to Sir Edward Grey.

Private.([1])
Dear Sir Edward,   *Foreign Office, August 26, 1909.*

The German proposal is in reality a very clumsy one and betrays the hand of the Master.

If we fell into the trap the *entente* with Russia would at once fall to the ground, a great *revirement* of feeling would take place, and the policy of the last few years would go by the board.

We should then be at the mercy of Germany in the naval negotiations. This is the German calculation. It is so reasonable to say that the Naval agreement must precede a friendly understanding that no one could object.

([1]) [Grey MSS., Vol. 54.]

It seems to me that in any case we must tell the Russians of these overtures; otherwise the German Emperor will tell the Czar that we originated them and will dish it up with some of the indiscretions which will fall from Mr. W. Churchill during the manœuvres.

Yours truly,
LOUIS MALLET.

No. 192.

Sir E. Goschen to Sir C. Hardinge.

Private.([1])

My dear Hardinge, *Berlin, August 28, 1909.*

I thought you would be thrilled by those telegrams.([2]) But I don't mind confessing to you that I penned them with qualms—as tho' no one realises more than I do what a relief it would be to have done with all this mutual suspicion and mistrust —I cannot but feel that the path to a better state of things may be thorny and that it is possible that we may get ourselves a bit disliked by our friends as we march along it. I wouldn't mind so much if we could say openly to France " Our relations with Germany have always been a source of preoccupation to you—we are now going to try to improve them—and at the same time do something to relieve the taxpayers not only of England and Germany but also of all the Great Powers from the enormous burdens entailed by the increasing naval expenditure " : but I do feel that both France and Russia would be furious if with no previous warning an Anglo-German understanding was suddenly sprung on them. A suspicious person might say that this is perhaps what Germany wants : but as far as B[ethmann] Hollweg is personally concerned I believe he is both honest and straight forward. Can we say the same of those above him and around him? That is the question. Stemrich, one of the only, if not the only, men in the Imperial F[oreign] O[ffice] in whom the Chancellor has confided, tells me that B[ethmann] Hollweg is absolutely sincere and can think of nothing else but how to put an end to the present period of mistrust; Stemrich added that the Chancellor had gone further in the way of detachment quâ German views and interests than he himself would have been prepared to go! I think, from considerations such as I have already put before Sir E. Grey—such as the increased cost of battleships, the parlous state of the Imperial Finances, and the need that Germany has of peace for several years at all events—that the Chancellor may have a strong party with him when his efforts become known—but how about the Junkers, the militant professors, and the Army and Navy? But I presume he has counted the cost and struck a balance, or he would not be so keen. At all events he seems to have squared Tirpitz—and persuaded him to agree to naval proposals of some sort or other being put before us. However all the Chancellor wants now is an acceptance of his ideas in principle—as owing to Tirpitz and other Ministers being unavailable, negotiations could not be commenced yet awhile. Under these circumstances as soon as the answer from H[is] M[ajesty's] G[overnment] to the principle of the thing is available, I presume that I shall be able to have a month's leave. I certainly can't have it later. . . . .([3])

Y[our]s ever,
W. E. GOSCHEN.

([1]) [Hardinge MSS., Vol. I of 1909.]
([2]) [*v. supra*, pp. 283–4, Nos. 186–7.]
([3]) [The last part of the letter deals with various subjects unconnected with the Anglo-German negotiations, and a postscript deals with Turkish affairs.]

No. 193.

Notes by Sir Edward Grey.([1])

[*August* **31,** 1909.]

We shall welcome naval proposals at any time the sooner the better.

Effect of a general political declaration on public opinion would be nil unless preceded by or at least accompanied by agreement about naval expenditure.

In case of France and Russia good understanding was subsequent to agreement about particular points of difference and it was not attempted to create it simultaneously.

We have therefore some apprehension lest an exchange of political declarations with Germany alone such as does not exist in case of France or Russia might be liable to a misrepresentation in those countries corresponding to that which was placed in Germany upon our understandings with France and Russia.

We understand and sympathize with Germany's desire for some reassuring declaration and wish to confirm the view of the German Chancellor that the isolation of Germany is not our aim and that our understandings with France and Russia have no such object : but would not this be most completely achieved by a declaration to which France and Russia could be parties. In this way the Triple Alliance and the other three Great Powers of Europe might all be comprehended and a general feeling of confidence created in which all would share.([2])

([1]) [Grey MSS., Vol. 22.]
([2]) [*cp. supra*, p. 284, No. 187, *min.*]

No. 194.

Sir Edward Grey to Sir E. Goschen.

F.O. 31696/31695/09/18.
Tel. (No. 317.) Secret. *Foreign Office, September* 1, 1909.
Your telegrams Nos. 93 and 94.([1])

You can inform Chancellor that as regards naval expenditure we are not only prepared to discuss it at any time, but should cordially welcome proposals; and you should reaffirm the statement that the Chancellor's communication has made a most favourable impression upon H[is] M[ajesty's] Government.

As regards the suggested political understanding, you can say that we must of course have regard to friendships with other Powers, but we shall receive with the greatest sympathy any proposal such as is foreshadowed by the German Chancellor which is not inconsistent with the maintenance of those friendships.

I have told Count Metternich, who asked me, the substance of this reply.([2])

([1]) [*v. supra*, pp. 283–4, Nos. 186–7.]
([2]) [For Count Metternich's report, *v. G.P.* XXVIII, pp. 224–5. The message was conveyed to the Chancellor in a letter from Sir E. Goschen, dated September 2, printed in *G.P.* XXVIII, p. 226.]

No. 195.

Sir Edward Grey to Sir E. Goschen.

Private.([1])
My dear Goschen, *September 1, 1909.*

I have sent you a telegram today([2]) which has the approval of the Prime Minister and the Cabinet. There is nothing in our agreements with France and Russia which is directed against Germany, and therefore nothing to bar a friendly arrangement with Germany. But we have no general political understanding formulated either with Russia or France; and to do with Germany what has not been done with Russia and France would look as if we were intending to change friends. I want a good understanding with Germany, but it must be one which will not imperil those which we have with France and Russia.

I should have thought some formula could be found to which they might also be parties : that would be the best and most reassuring solution, though I see that the French could not be a party to anything which looked like confirming the loss of Alsace and Lorraine.

The bag is leaving and I have no time to do more than to enclose a copy of some rough notes([3]) which I made yesterday to clear my own mind and which show to what my thoughts tend.

Yours sincerely,
E. GREY.

([1]) [Grey MSS., Vol. 22.]
([2]) [*v.* immediately preceding document.]
([3]) [*v. supra*, p. 288, No. 193.]

No. 196.

Sir E. Goschen to Sir Edward Grey.

Berlin, September 3, 1909.
F.O. 33237/31695/09/18. D. 8·1 P.M.
Tel. (No. 96.) R. 9·0 P.M.
(Proposed Anglo-German naval arrangement.)
Your telegram No. 317.([1])

Chancellor thanks you very much for your friendly message. He says that owing to the absence of the Secretary of State & the Minister of Marine he will not be able to go definitely into the matter before the beginning of October.

([1]) [*v. supra*, p. 288, No. 194.]

No. 197.

Sir E. Goschen to Sir Edward Grey.([1])

F.O. 34616/31695/09/18.
Private.
Dear Sir Edward Grey, *Berlin, September 3, 1909.*

The Chancellor was in town yesterday evening for an Imperial dinner. Unfortunately he left the same night before your telegram arrived,([2]) so I was unable to see him. I therefore conveyed your message to him by letter which I asked Herr von Stemrich to forward to him in his daily pouch. Stemrich, to whom I showed my letter was very pleased indeed with its contents. He said that he, personally, had always had good relations with England at heart; both from early associations, (London was the starting-point of his career) and for political reasons; and that he fervently

([1]) [For Herr von Stemrich's report, *v. G.P.* XXVIII, pp. 225–6.]
([2]) [*v. supra*, p. 288, No. 194 and *note* ([2]).]

hoped that the friendly and cordial manner in which you had received the Chancellor's message was a good augury for the future. He then gave me some rather interesting details. He said that the Chancellor had gone into the matter heart and soul, but that no sooner had he taken the first step in the business by sending for me and talking about it, than he began to feel certain qualms. He had asked himself whether he had done right in making a move of so much importance, and one involving so many possible difficulties both from within and without, so soon after he had assumed office. He had also felt doubts as to whether H[is] M[ajesty's] G[overnment] would think it worth while to treat with a Chancellor who had only just got into the saddle, and of whom they might feel doubts as to whether he would be able to stay there for any length of time. This depression had, however, only been momentary, and now he was as keen as possible and full of courage. Stemrich was sure that he would be immensely pleased with your cordial message.

I asked Stemrich from what quarter the Chancellor expected opposition. He replied that that was not an easy question to answer. The Pan-Germans would be furious, that was only to be expected; but the difficult moment would arrive when it was learnt that the initiative had come from the German side. The Chancellor did not look forward to the prospect of making that announcement : but he had his answer ready which would be something to the effect that the British Government had already on several occasions made tentative proposals and had therefore done *their* part; and they had moreover stated openly that notwithstanding that their attempts had met with no response, they would always be glad to listen to any Power who might have some proposal to make for the limitation of the expenditure on Armaments; he would add that England could not be expected to renew proposals which had been more than once rejected, and that if anything was to be done to give effect to the very general opinion that some limit must be put to Naval Expenditure it was Germany's turn this time to make the necessary advances.

Since writing the above I have just received a message from the Chancellor asking me to thank you for your cordial message and saying that as Herr von Schoen is away and Admiral Tirpitz is taking leave after the Naval Manœuvres, he will not be able to submit anything definite to you before the beginning of next month. I therefore propose to avail myself of your permission to go to Austria for a few weeks. I shall however hold myself ready to return at a day's notice at any time and I can always get back in 18 hours.

I am much obliged for the letter which you kindly wrote to me by the Messenger.(³) I have studied its contents and those of the enclosure most carefully, and quite understand the lines on which your thoughts are running. I have assumed that your ideas were not for communication at this early stage but for my enlightenment. I think that your reasons for thinking that a Naval arrangement should precede whatever understanding or political declaration which may be made, can hardly be controverted; but I scarcely think that the Chancellor, up to the present, takes the same view, as he seemed to think that public opinion in Germany would be against a Naval arrangement unless it was preceded by, or at least made at the same time as, some declaration which would clear the air of all mutual suspicion. He admitted at the same time that he had formed no definite ideas as to the exact form his procedure would take.

Yours very sincerely,

W. E. GOSCHEN.

Sept[ember] 4.

P.S. In view of what the Chancellor says I propose to leave Berlin for Austria to-night. I hope it will cause no inconvenience, but I am particularly anxious to go as structural alterations in the Embassy House are going to be made which will turn it completely upside-down. If I do not go the workmen can't begin, and the longer

---

(³) [*v. supra*, p. 289, No. 195.]

I stay the later the House will be ready for us in the Autumn. In fact I expect that even now a Hotel will be my portion when I return at the beginning of October. The Chancellor has promised to give me due warning when he is ready.

W. E. G.

MINUTE BY KING EDWARD.

This subject is one of grave importance—but it is satisfactory that the first move comes fr[om] Germany—through the new Chancellor!

E.R.

No. 198.

Sir A. Nicolson to Sir Edward Grey.

Private.([1])
My dear Grey, *St. Petersburgh, September 22, 1909.*
Iswolsky begs me to express to you his best thanks for the confidence which you have shown in him by letting him know of the German proposal.([2]) You may rely on his discretion. He asked me what was the nature of the general understanding which Berlin has proposed. I told him that it was vague, and in any case the main point was to ascertain how far Germany was prepared to go in moderating the pace of naval construction. Till her proposals on that point were received it was of no use considering further developments. I asked him if he thought that Germany was sincere in suggesting a more moderate tempo in naval armaments. He replied that a year ago v. Schön had mentioned to him the possibility of an arrangement with us as to naval matters, but when he had enquired on what basis such an arrangement could be made Schön had said that he was unable to say precisely how it could be brought about, but that he thought "something might be done." Iswolsky did not seem to think that there was any probability of Germany modifying her present Navy Law. He said that he would welcome any arrangement which would moderate the rivalry between the two countries in respect to naval construction. He was favourably impressed with the new German Chancellor, and I have written a despatch on the interview which Iswolsky had with him.([3]) . . . .([4])

Yours sincerely,
A. NICOLSON.

([1]) [Grey MSS., Vol. 34.]
([2]) [Sir E. Goschen's telegrams Nos. 93 and 94 of August 21 were repeated to Paris and St. Petersburgh. For their texts, *v. supra*, pp. 283–4, Nos. 186–7.]
([3]) [*v. Gooch & Temperley*, Vol. V, pp. 806–7, No. 869.]
([4]) [The rest of this letter refers to Austro-Russian relations in the Balkans, and to Russia's relations with her Polish subjects.]

No. 199.

Sir E. Goschen to Sir Edward Grey.

F.O. 38403/38403/09/18.
(No. 355.) Confidential. *Berlin, D. October 11, 1909.*
Sir, *R. October 18, 1909.*
I have the honour to forward, herewith, a despatch as marked in the margin, which I have received from Captain Heath, Naval Attaché to this Embassy, relating to the Remaining two Battleships of 1909 Programme.

I have, &c.
W. E. GOSCHEN.

Enclosure 1 in No. 199.

Captain Heath to Sir E. Goschen.

Confidential.

Sir, Berlin, October 11, 1909.

I have the honour to report that I lately called at the Reichs-Marine-Amt, and asked informally, if the press statements as to awarding the contracts for the two remaining battleships of the [19]09 programme were correct.

One or two other matters of minor importance were discussed, and my informant (Adm[ira]l von Tirpitz's adjutant) whilst telling me that the above contracts had been awarded, suggested that he had better give me written answers to my questions, so as to save any ambiguity.

After waiting two or three days, a private letter was received from the Adjutant (copy attached).

The purport of the letter is to the effect, that Adm[ira]l von Tirpitz, will not authorise the giving of any more information as to the building of battleships, because he (the Adm[ira]l) is under the impression, that, his official statements have not been officially accepted in England.

Adm[ira]l von Tirpitz intimates, that he has stated officially in the Reichstag, and has supplied data to the British Admiralty indicating the number of German " Dreadnoughts ", which are to be ready for service by autumn 1912, *viz.*, 12.

Notwithstanding these statements it has been officially stated in the British Parliament, " that it must be expected that the number will be 17."

In a subsequent conversation with the Adjutant, it transpired that the attached letter had been written by order of Adm[ira]l von Tirpitz.

It was impressed upon me that the Adm[ira]l is under the impression that he has a real personal grievance. There is good reason to suppose, that if some public acknowledgment were made of Admiral von Tirpitz's official statements, as supplies [*sic*] from time to time, this grievance would be removed.

It is stated that the Admiral's whole life is bound up in the Naval Law, and its rigid and unvariable execution, as regards the number of ships annually to be laid down. (It is admitted that the size of ships must vary according to circumstances.)

In pointing out to the Adjutant that the time allowed for building individual ships was unduly long, he admitted that it was evident that the time could be shortened should circumstances render it necessary, "but in this case no acceleration is contemplated, and if it came to the pinch, I do not know what is the limit of our possibilities."

The whole thing seems to be a mere question of words, and I am given to understand that Adm[ira]l von Tirpitz is still hoping, that his statements as to the number of battleships to be completed by the Autumn of 1912, will be acknowledged as indicating the intentions of the German Gov[ernmen]t, at any rate at the time they were made.

I have, &c.
H. L. HEATH,
Captain and Naval Attaché.

Enclosure 2 in No. 199

Herr von Rheinbaben to Captain Heath.([1])

Translation.

Dear Mr. Heath :— Berlin, October 7, 1909.

I am very sorry, not to be able to procure an answer to your question of the day before yesterday. As you will remember, His Excellency the Secretary of State

---

([1]) [A translation of Herr von Rheinbaben's letter was sent to Sir E. Grey by Sir E. Goschen, as well as a copy of the original. The translation was evidently revised in the Foreign Office, as it bears corrections in Sir E. Crowe's hand.]

explained to you fully in the early part of the year the nature of the allotment of the contracts for our ships, in particular for those of the year 1909, and the nature of our Navy law in general. Further, in answer to your enquiry of July 6th, 1909, the exact dates of the contracts including the dates of delivery were given to you. In that communication it was stated that the period of building provided for the line-of-battleship allotted on April 8th was 36 months. The completion, on which decisive weight is rightly always laid in the debates of the English parliament, and which is clearly alone to the point, falls therefore in the year 1912.

As the other two line-of-battleships of the year 1909 have only now been allotted, the completion of the ships of the year 1909 gives the number of 13 completed Dreadnoughts at the earliest in the autumn of 1912, which is in accordance with the statement of His Excellency the Secretary of State on March 29th, 1909, in the Reichstag.

Having made this precise declaration, the Secretary of State is, as you will yourself remember from your personal conversation with him in the Spring, extremely perplexed at the statement of Mr. McKenna in Parliament. Subsequently to the information given to you, Mr. McKenna expressly confirmed in Parliament on July 26th,[2] his statement of March 1909,[3] according to which England had to expect the number of 13 completed German Dreadnoughts in the Autumn of 1911 and of 17 in the Spring of 1912. He has likewise repeatedly and with emphasis maintained his assertion as to the acceleration of the German building programme, and ignored, in the Navy debates in Parliament on July 26th, the contrary statments of His Excellency the Secretary of State and of the then Imperial Chancellor Prince Bülow.

After careful consideration of the circumstances I regret that I must refrain from approaching the Secretary of State a second time in the matter, since it is to be feared that the misunderstandings which have hitherto arisen from the communication and use made of such declarations will not be removed by the renewal of them.

VON RHEINBABEN.

[2] [v. Parl. Deb., 5th Ser., House of Commons, Vol. 8, p. 965.]
[3] [v. ib., 5th Ser., House of Commons, Vol. 2, pp. 935–6.]

No. 200.

Sir E. Goschen to Sir Edward Grey.

F.O. 38405/31695/09/10.
(No. 356.)   Secret.   *Berlin, D. October 15, 1909.*
Sir,   R. *October* 18, 1909.

At the Imperial Chancellor's invitation I called upon His Excellency yesterday and had some conversation with him on the subject of a naval arrangement and an exchange of pacific assurances between Great Britain and Germany. Herr von Schoen was present during the interview and took notes of what passed between us; His Excellency in fact drew up the *procès verbal* of the conversation of which I have the honour to enclose copy and translation. In his long speech the Chancellor recapitulated what he had said to me on the last occasion adding that he desired that no arrangement or understanding should be made which would interfere in the least with our friendships with other countries or with their own alliances with Austria-Hungary and Italy. As he mentioned the word "understanding" I pointed out to him that as we had no formal understanding with either France or Russia it would scarcely be likely that His Majesty's Government would find themselves in the position to go further with Germany than they had done with those countries; but that if he meant an exchange of pacific assurances would clear away the atmosphere of suspicion which appeared to exist between the two countries, I thought that His Majesty's Government would be quite ready to meet the Imperial Government half way. I said I was not

in full possession of your views on the subject of what assurances could be given—
but that speaking quite personally I thought that His Majesty's Government might
state, for instance, that England would not make an unprovoked attack against any
Power or group of Powers and would use her best endeavours, should occasion arise,
to prevent other Powers doing so and would also give a formal assurance that her
friendships with France and Russia were in no way directed against Germany. I
thought such assurances might be forthcoming, as I knew that it was both the policy
and desire of His Majesty's Government to maintain the *status quo* of the present
European political equilibrium and to promote friendship between the Triple Alliance
and the other Powers. I repeated that these were only personal expressions of opinion
but that I should like to know whether assurances of that or a similar nature would
meet the views of the Imperial Government—should they be offered. (I have thought
it best to give you my account of this portion of our conversation, as Herr von Schoen's
notes, though correct in the main, do not quite give the proper sequence of my
remarks.) His Excellency did not reply to this question, merely remarking that
he was himself fully convinced that the agreements between England and France and
Russia were not directed against Germany but that a formal assurance to that effect
would certainly be of great help in negotiating a naval arrangement.

With regard to the latter I asked His Excellency whether he could give me any
idea as to the naval proposals the Imperial Government were prepared to make.
I presumed that they would not be based on their present naval programme. The
Chancellor reminded me that their programme had become law and could not be
changed except by a vote in the Reichstag. I said that I presumed that I was right in
thinking that the aim and object of the Imperial Government in opening the matters
we were discussing were to bring about a better state of feeling between G[rea]t
Britain and Germany and to limit the naval expenditure which was rapidly becoming
a very heavy burden to the taxpayers of both countries and interfering with other
necessary reforms and schemes for internal development. He replied in the affirmative; I therefore asked him how naval expenditure was to be reduced in either country
if the German programme was to be carried out in its entirety. He replied somewhat
vaguely that, though the programme would have to be carried out, something might
be done in the way of regulating the *tempo* of construction. I asked His Excellency
whether that meant that the time for providing the number of ships now contemplated
for—say the year 1918 would be extended. To this I received no reply from the
Chancellor but Baron Schoen stated that what was meant was that the arrangement
should include a formal assurance that under no circumstances would the speed of
construction be accelerated beyond that laid down in the programme—and this,
he said, would remove the chief ground for the suspicions that seemed to exist in
the minds of the British Admiralty. I said that, still, this did not appear to me
to remove the difficulty which I had indicated, viz., that the rigid execution of
the German programme precluded on both sides, any limitation of expenditure for
many years to come.

The Chancellor said that of course a naval arrangement bristled with difficulties
and that it was therefore, in his opinion, all the more necessary that an exchange of
pacific assurances should, if possible, precede the negotiation of a naval arrangement,
as the rough edge of the difficulties surrounding the latter would be much taken off
by the removal of all suspicion or mistrust from the minds of the negotiators. He
would therefore hope that if His Majesty's Government preferred that the assurances
should not precede the negotiations for the naval arrangement, they might at least be
discussed at the same time.

While on this subject the Chancellor was very strong on the point that in
consenting to make proposals for a naval arrangement Germany was making a great
concession and sacrifice, and that therefore they must have assurances in their hands
such as would justify this sacrifice in the eyes of the Reichstag and the nation.

I gathered from this that the Chancellor thought that such assurances as I had
vaguely intimated were somewhat less than they would be prepared to accept, and I

was confirmed in this impression subsequently by Baron Schoen who said, in private conversation, that they would hope to get something a little more concrete and far-reaching. I asked him what he had in his mind and after some hesitation he said "Well! Something more akin to the wording of the Baltic agreement." Baron Schoen made these remarks to me this morning when he brought me his *procès verbal* of yesterday's conversation for my revision. I took the opportunity of asking him to explain to me what the Chancellor had meant exactly by the "relaxation of the *tempo* of the German programme." He replied that to touch the number of ships provided for by the programme was impossible without a vote in the Reichstag, but that an alteration in the speed with which they were to be built necessitated no such proceeding. That lay in the hands of the Government and they could therefore reduce the number of ships to be constructed in each year. For instance according to the programme four ships were to be laid down each year for a certain number of years. The Government could, without consulting the Reichstag, reduce these to three.([1]) It was true that the whole number to be built according to the programme would not be affected by the proceeding, but the expenses would be spread over a greater length of time and at all events the annual expenditure would be reduced. I said that that might be a temporary advantage but that the gross naval expenditure would finally remain the same; a proposal for reducing this gross expenditure would be more to the point. He replied that that was impossible for the moment, and that therefore he was personally in favour of making at present an arrangement which would only cover two or three years. He explained his view by stating that if at the end of a certain period within that time the arrangement was found to work satisfactorily and, together with mutual pacific assurances, to have tranquillized public opinion on both sides, it would be highly probable that a strong party in the Reichstag would be in favour of reducing the number of ships provided by the programme and that a vote to that effect could be easily secured.

I rather pressed the point with regard to the nature of the arrangement which the Imperial Government proposed to suggest and I put my remarks in such a way as to give him to understand that it was, to my mind at least, doubtful, whether proposals on the basis of the present German programme would be acceptable, and proposals which His Majesty's Government were not likely to be able to accept were better not made at all.

To return to my conversation with the Chancellor, I would mention that there appeared to me to be a disposition on His Excellency's part to throw the initiative of making naval proposals on to His Majesty's Government, or at all events to expect that they would submit their views as to the form a naval arrangement should take simultaneously with the German proposals. I therefore took an opportunity of reminding His Excellency that he had told me in August that, as His Majesty's Government had already informally broached the question of a naval arrangement without result, it was now the turn of the Imperial Government to take the initiative. I had reported this to my Government and it was quite understood by them that they were to expect proposals from the Imperial Government, and these were now being awaited.

My remarks at the close of the conversation with regard to the moment when definite negotiations should be opened were not made, as it would appear from the notes, spontaneously, but because Baron Schoen, in a previous conversation, had expressed to me some doubts as to whether the present moment, when there was such a press of Parliamentary business in London, was propitious for the discussion of such important matters. I told His Excellency that I would, if he wished, ascertain your views on the subject. He begged me, however, to defer doing so until I had seen the Chancellor. The latter did not mention the matter but as Baron Schoen had

([1]) [Marginal comment by Mr. Asquith : " But would they not be obliged (in order to conform to the law) to make up for lost time in the concluding year or years of the statutory period? H. H. A."]

expressed some anxiety on the point I made the observation quoted. The Chancellor said that he would be very glad if I would mention the point to you and ascertain your views.

I have, &c.

W. E. GOSCHEN.

Enclosure in No. 200.

Conversation held on October 14, 1909, between the Imperial Chancellor and the British Ambassador.([2])

Translation.

The Chancellor said :—

In our conversation in August I already had the honour of making the following statements to Your Excellency.

From the repeated utterances of Mr Asquith and of Mr. McKenna we have gained the conviction that England expects from a naval arrangement an improvement in the relations of the two countries. As we also are eagerly aiming at such an improvement, we are gladly willing in reply to this initiative which has been taken by England to offer our hand to conclude a naval arrangement and, if it answers to England's wishes, to make also on our side concrete proposals with this object.

We believe that, if we respond to the English initiative, we are making on our side a concession, as we have always declared, in accordance with the truth, that we only wish to develop our navy to meet our own requirements and not with regard to any other navy. We have repeatedly stated and I repeat again that our navy serves no aggressive purposes but is only destined to protect our trade and, in case of necessity, to defend our coasts.([3]) Whether a naval agreement alone—and this too I have already said to Your Excellency—would be in a position really and lastingly to improve our relations, may appear doubtful. But just because we entertain the earnest and sincere wish, without any *arrière pensée*, to establish the old friendly and confidential relations with England, we are prepared, as far as we possibly can, to meet the English wish for a naval arrangement.

England will further understand that we are in reality, and also bearing in mind public opinion, making a great sacrifice, if in such an agreement we also recognize legally England's actually existing naval supremacy. We can only make such a sacrifice, and in fact we are prepared to make it, on condition that England should declare and show to us that her confidence in us will thereby be restored.

Should that not occur, we should be afraid that a naval arrangement, instead of improving general political relations, would arouse fresh distrust, as ill disposed people would express a doubt as to whether the agreement which had been concluded would actually be kept. Besides we are of opinion that we facilitate the establishment of a naval arrangement if we previously enter into a friendly exchange of opinions of a general character. For in a naval arrangement naval experts would naturally in the first line have the word. And that being so, the fact, as lies in the nature of things, must be reckoned with that the experts will insist with a certain obstinacy on the details of their programme.

As we entertain the serious and sincere wish to arrive at an agreement respecting armaments, we must take precautions that such difficulties as might arise between the experts should exercise no unfavourable influence upon the general mutual relations. We hope that England also shares this view and we would be strengthened in this hope by a friendly discussion of our general political relations to one another. If England thinks that she can declare her agreement in principle to this idea we would be prepared together with her to seek a programme in this direction—a programme which would bring us both nearer to each other and would make us both conscious of

---

([2]) [A copy of the German original of this document was sent by Sir E. Goschen with the translation here printed. *cp. G.P.* XXVIII, pp. 239–43.]

([3]) [Marginal comment : " A swarm of Dreadnoughts is useless for the one purpose, and unnecessary for the other. [H. H. A.]"]

the fact that our navies will not come into conflict with each other. We are ready in this connection to offer to England extensive guarantees based on the principle of reciprocity. We are as ready to meet England's proposals in this connection as on our side to put forward such proposals. Here I would like at once to forestall any possible misunderstanding. We know that there is in certain circles in England a suspicion that we wish to disturb her friendship with other Powers. This is not the case. We do not wish to demand anything of England that is not in consonance with her *ententes*, nothing which could even expose her to the suspicion on the part of her friends that we wish to disturb her relations with them, and *vice versâ*, we also adhere to our treaties. In spite of this however there will be many ways of making the tone of our relations more cordial and of returning to the former mutual confidence.

We beg that the matter may also be considered from these points of view, in order that, in the case of an affirmative reply on the part of England a more detailed discussion respecting a programme of this sort for the regularizing of mutual policies may take place. We believe that the conclusion of a naval arrangement would be most effectively promoted in this manner.

In this connection I finally venture again to express the wish that the utmost secrecy should be observed as regards our negotiations. Nothing could be more calculated to disturb their happy issue than if something connected with them should leak out, because the political parties either in this country or in England would turn the matter into a party question and expose it to the dangers of party passion, and the question can only be settled in a quiet and dispassionate manner. If we should arrive at a positive result it must be reserved for a further mutual understanding as to the manner and extent in which we will each make it known to our friends and the public.

The British Ambassador remarked that England stood in close friendly relations with France and Russia, without any agreement of a general nature having been concluded with them. England could hardly grant Germany more than she had done to the *Entente* Powers, but he had no doubt that a satisfactory formula for mutual pacific assurances could be found. He thought however that Sir Edward Grey was of the opinion that such assurances, unless preceded by, or at least made simultaneously with, a naval arrangement, would have but little effect upon British public opinion.

The Chancellor replied that, as far as the Imperial Government was concerned, the matter stood as follows—that a naval arrangement without an announcement of a general friendly *rapprochement* would remain without favourable effect on German public opinion.

The Secretary of State, Baron Schoen, remarked that the situation between England and Germany was essentially different to the situation between England on the one side and Russia and France on the other. Between the latter three Powers there had existed disturbing (entzweiende) political questions, the settlement of which had paved the way to the *entente*. There were no such questions between Germany and England, and consequently a general declaration of friendship was necessary.

To Sir Edward Goschen's question as to our views respecting the basis of a naval arrangement the Chancellor replied that there could be no question of any departure from the naval Law as a whole, as that would meet with insuperable opposition in the Reichstag; but on the other hand the question of retarding the rate of building new ships might be discussed.

To a remark of Sir Edward Goschen's that the mere fact of retarding the rate of building would not result in any material saving of expense Baron Schoen pointed out that, should Germany bind herself to a certain number of new ships in a given time, such an undertaking would largely contribute towards producing a feeling of calm in England.

Sir Edward Goschen then put a question as to the outlines of a general declaration of friendship. He remarked that he was not in full possession of the views of

Sir Edward Grey on the subject, but that, speaking personally, he thought that His Majesty's Government, whose policy it was to maintain the present *status quo* of the European political equilibrium and who were anxious for the most friendly relations between the Triple Alliance and the other Powers, might be willing to give assurances, for example, that England would not make an unprovoked attack on any Power or group of Powers, and that she would use her influence to prevent other Powers from doing so. His Majesty's Government would also, he was sure, be ready to give an assurance that their friendships with Russia and France were in no way directed against Germany. Sir Edward Goschen asked whether assurances of such a nature would be satisfactory to the Imperial Government.

The Chancellor replied that he was sure there would be no difficulty in finding a formula for the declaration of friendship. It must of course be in such a form as to make it possible for the German Government to uphold in the eyes of the nation the naval arrangement which must be concluded simultaneously and which meant a great concession on the part of Germany.

To the Ambassador's question whether Germany wished to make concrete proposals the Chancellor replied that he would willingly do so if England wished it. He would be equally ready to receive proposals from England.

In Sir Edward's opinion the British Government would wish to receive the German proposals for a naval arrangement as soon as possible.

The Chancellor declared himself ready at any time to open negotiations but pointed out that the question of the naval arrangement must be prefaced by pourparlers by the naval experts which could take place besides, and in connection with, the exchange of views as to a general *rapprochement*.

Sir Edward Goschen said that he was under the impression that it was the opinion of Sir Edward Grey that the sooner such proposals were made the better, but that, in view of the present press of Parliamentary business in England, it would be perhaps well for him to ascertain from Sir Edward Grey whether His Majesty's Government were now ready to receive the German proposals and to open definite negotiations.

The Chancellor replied that in regard to this point he would of course gladly fall in with the decisions of the British Government who had been the first to express a wish for a naval understanding with Germany.

MINUTES.

The German suggestions are still so vague that it is not easy to offer useful criticism. There seems to me to be involved three points deserving of special consideration :

1. An agreement on the lines of the declaration signed in 1908 by Germany, Russia, and Sweden respecting the Baltic,([4]) would probably involve, and may be assumed to be intended by Germany to involve, some sort of solemn recognition of the territorial *status quo*, and the question arises what would be said in France to England putting her hand to such a document. It is hardly to be expected that France herself would in the present circumstances be a party to a formal renunciation of her claim to her lost provinces. It is of course quite true that H[is] M[ajesty's] G[overnment] have no desire to question Germany's title to those provinces, or to encourage or support France in an unprovoked endeavour to wrest them back from Germany. But can we enter into any formal engagement with Germany to this effect without the risk of breaking up the Anglo-French *entente*?

2. It was always to be anticipated that Germany would ask for something " tangible " in return for the mere readiness to enter into a naval agreement. The hints thrown out by Herr von Schoen seem to show that the Bagdad railway, the capitulations in Egypt, " and other matters " are to be subjects of negotiations.([5]) It is a significant relapse into the bad habits of her former diplomacy that Germany should demand fresh concessions in return for being conciliatory in the matter of the capitulations in Egypt. Surely we have already paid for and obtained Germany's assent to the abolition (if necessary) of the capitulations. She wants to sell her goodwill over again, as she has so often done before especially as regards Egyptian affairs. It is further to be noted that the naval agreement is to be only for 2 to 3 years, presumably however the *quid pro quo* which we are to give in the political sphere will have to be something definitive, given outright. These are points to be kept in mind.

3. It seems a question whether the immediate benefits expected from the very modest character of the naval proposals, will not be nullified by the very feature for which it recommends

([4]) [This subject will be dealt with in a later volume.]
([5]) [*v. infra*, p. 301, No. 201.]

itself to the German gov[ernmen]t, namely, the shortness of the period it is to cover. It is apparently thought that the provisional and fragmentary character of the arrangement will have the effect of whetting the appetite of public opinion in both countries for a yet closer understanding. It is of course difficult to prophesy. I understand the idea of H[is] M[ajesty's] G[overnment] to be that if the notion of a necessary naval rivalry can once be got rid of, suspiciousness and sensitiveness will be so diminished that relations will become naturally friendly. But this presupposes a definite settlement of the naval problem. If such a settlement is seen not to be definite at all, is there not a danger that the hotheads in both countries will immediately seize upon this as a further opportunity for criticism and agitation? No doubt a permanent arrangement satisfactory to both parties would knock the bottom out of such agitation. But a mere undertaking to prolong the period of suspense by deferring the building of one ship each year to some convenient after-period (which *may* come round in 2–3 years) and without any guarantee of what is to be done or not done subsequently, seems hardly likely to put an end to nervousness and apprehension as to the future.

Sir E. Goschen seems to have handled a difficult matter exceedingly well, and I have no doubt that Sir Edward Grey would wish H[is] E[xcellency]'s action to be approved.

E. A. C.
Oct. 18.

We have to answer the inquiry whether H[is] M[ajesty's] G[overnment] consider the moment suitable for the proposed discussion, and Sir E. Goschen has suggested a reply on the main question.

It seems useless to speculate about the exchange of pacific assurances until we have a clearer indication of what the German Gov[ernmen]t want, but the Baltic Agreement appears to be a singularly inappropriate model.

W. L.

Sir E. Goschen handled this question cleverly and his suggestions as to the assurances which H[is] M[ajesty's] G[overnment] might be disposed to give were prudent and uncompromising. They evidently did not satisfy Baron Schön who said that assurances of a more far-reaching nature would be required, and referred to the wording of the Baltic agreement as the model upon which they should be based. A glance at the Baltic agreement will show that were England and Germany to make a joint declaration on similar lines, England would find herself bound to recognise and even to preserve the actual *status quo* of Germany's continental and insular possessions and to concert measures with her for the maintenance of the *status quo* in the event of its disturbance. Such a declaration on the part of England would be severely criticised in France as a treacherous action on the part of a friend since it would consecrate the Treaty of Frankfort which the French accepted as it was imposed upon them, but which still remains the last Treaty, either political or commercial that has been concluded between France and Germany. The suggestion of a declaration on the lines of the Baltic agreement must therefore be set aside altogether as unacceptable, although perhaps another formula might be discovered. Great care would have to be taken that umbrage is not given to other Powers, but the statement of the Chancellor that he does not wish to demand anything of England " which could even expose her to suspicion on the part of her friends " provides an opening for the rejection of any formula having that tendency.

The naval programme outlined by the Chancellor is vague but, as far as he has lifted the veil, it may be summed up as containing a recognition by Germany of the supremacy of the British Navy as an accepted axiom, and a less rapid fulfilment of the earlier stages of the German naval programme, which is however to be fully completed by 1918.

It is desired that the recognition of the supremacy of the British navy should be regarded as a great concession, meriting counter-concessions on our side, so far undefined. Such a recognition would be of no value unless the British navy were really supreme, and so long as our navy is supreme it does not matter whether it is so recognised in Germany or not. Consequently the concession is dependent entirely on the intentions of H[is] M[ajesty's] G[overnment] to maintain a supreme navy, and as there is a consensus of opinion on this point in England it thus becomes a paper concession or no concession at all.

According to the Chancellor and Baron Schön, the naval programme having been voted by Parliament must be completed unless modified by Parliament. We are therefore still face to face with a situation in 1918 when Germany will have 38 Dreadnoughts and England will presumably have to have about 60 capital ships, or approximately about 50 more than we now have. This will entail a further expenditure during the next few years of over 100 million sterling, or roughly speaking 10 millions per annum for the next ten years. With the best and most friendly intentions in the world one may ask whether it is really worth while to talk of a naval agreement, except as an empty platitude, so long as it is regarded in Germany as an essential part of German policy that there must be 38 Dreadnoughts by 1918. B[aro]n Schön suggested that if Germany now builds three capital ships per annum instead of four, and if the relations between the two countries improve during the next few years it might be possible for a future Reichstag to modify the programme by reducing it. On the other hand if Germany now lightens the strain upon her finances by building three capital ships instead of four she will be in a better position from a financial point of view to bear this burden than if she keeps to her programme of four ships per annum, and consequently there would be a better prospect of the programme being maintained. There would therefore be less likelihood of a demand being made by a future Reichstag to modify the programme by reducing it, if the naval burden is being more easily borne by the people. The Chancellor held out no prospect of any such modification being possible, in fact he was very categorical as to there being no departure from the naval law as a whole.

On the other hand H[is] M[ajesty's] G[overnment] have always declared themselves in favour of a limitation of armaments and have on more than one occasion stated to the German Gov[ernmen]t their readiness to reduce their programme of naval construction provided that they had clear and indisputable proofs of a similar intention on the part of the German Gov[ernmen]t. Consequently the proposal, if seriously made, that the German Gov[ernmen]t should agree to build only three instead of four capital ships for the next few years and to make no acceleration in their building scheme, is one which it would be difficult for H[is] M[ajesty's] G[overnment] to dismiss as unacceptable without exposing themselves to the charge of insincerity and to the prospect of being held up to the world as the promoters of reckless competition in naval construction, and as the chief obstacle to peaceful stability in Europe.

No indication has been given as to what, if any, limitations are to be placed on British plans of naval construction, but it is presumed that some counter-concessions will be demanded which will require careful investigation.

It is not however merely a question of the number of ships to be constructed within a certain term of years that can inspire mutual confidence between the two countries, but the necessity for both Gov[ernmen]ts to be in a position to know and to realise the ship-building capacity of the other's country, including the possible output of guns, mountings, armour plate, &c. In this way only can the present mistrust be removed and a feeling of confidence be restored. Any suspicion that the savings created by the reduction in the number of ships was being utilised for the preparation of increased building facilities and of a supply of guns, mountings &c., which would enable the German Gov[ernmen]t at a given moment to launch within very short notice a larger number of ships than could be prepared in the same interval in this country would certainly create an aggravated situation in the relations between England and Germany, far worse than that which actually exists at the present time. The ingrained suspicion of the intentions of Germany with a fleet of 38 Dreadnoughts, which from the nature of the ships are suitable neither for the protection of German trade nor for the defence of German coasts as alleged by the Chancellor, will be difficult to remove from the minds of the British public, and it is, in my opinion, very doubtful whether it will be possible to remove this distrust except by a substantial reduction of the present German naval programme.

An answer has to be given to the German Chancellor, and it is for H[is] M[ajesty's] G[overnment] to decide whether it is worth while to open negotiations in view of the Chancellor's categorical statement " that there could be no question of any departure from the naval law as a whole." If H[is] M[ajesty's] G[overnment] decide that it is desirable to meet the German Gov[ernmen]t in the initiative which the latter are now taking, I would suggest a reply on the following lines :—

H[is] M[ajesty's] G[overnment] have read with interest and satisfaction the account of the conversation held on the 14th Oct[ober] between the German Chancellor and H[is] M[ajesty]'s Ambassador, and note with pleasure H[is] E[xcellency]'s desire to re-establish friendly and confidential relations with England.

They will await and will consider in a most friendly spirit the concrete proposals which the German Gov[ernmen]t desire to make to them with a view to arriving at an agreement upon naval construction, which appears to H[is] M[ajesty's] G[overnment] to present the best prospect for securing an improvement in the mutual relations of the two countries.

Although they fully realise that any modification of the German Naval Law would require the sanction of the Imperial Parliament, they are not without hope that this result may in the end be obtained on the re-establishment of more cordial relations between the two countries, and by the removal of the suspicion and mistrust which unhappily exist on both shores of the North Sea. They are of opinion that greater frankness and confidence between the two Gov[ernmen]ts in the treatment of naval matters would largely conduce to the attainment of this object, and they feel confident that the German Gov[ernmen]t will concur in this view. H[is] M[ajesty's] G[overnment] are ready on their side to give to the German Gov[ernmen]t the most friendly and pacific assurances, whilst avoiding at the same time any expressions likely to create suspicion on the part of the friends or allies of both countries.

H[is] M[ajesty's] G[overnment] are prepared to consider any proposals put before them by the German Gov[ernmen]t at any moment which may appear most convenient to them.

C. H.

Oct. 24, 09.

I have spoken in this sense to Count Metternich.([6])

E. G.

([6]) [Probably this was on the 26th, *cp. G.P.* XXVIII, pp. 243–4., *v. infra*, p. 302, *Ed. note.*]

No. 201.

Sir E. Goschen to Sir C. Hardinge.

F.O. 38405/31695/09/18.
Private.

My dear Hardinge, Berlin, October 15, 1909.

You may judge of my feelings when, arriving at the Chancellor's on his invitation to come and have a talk with him, I found, besides the Chancellor, Schoen installed at a table with papers and pens before him. The Chancellor said that he was sure I wouldn't mind his having asked Schoen to take notes of our conversation, as it was better that a record should be kept of what passed between us on such an important matter. "Memories were always deceptive," &c. I of course made no demur but I pointed out to Schoen afterwards that it was not my idea of an informal conversation to have every word that fell from my lips taken down and recorded, and that he must remember that the few remarks I had made consisted chiefly of personal ideas and impressions. Schoen was very airy about it and said that he regarded the conversation as far as I was concerned as quite informal and that they quite recognized that I was merely expressing my personal opinions. As far as what the Chancellor said went Schoen's record was quite correct, as the oration, delivered in German, had unmistakably been prepared. But of course the notes of what I said were pure Schonese, as no one but a shorthand writer could have recorded the exact words. This I found when Schoen brought me his *procès verbal* this morning for revision. I took the liberty of putting in what I really did say and Schoen admitted that my versions were correct: but what is of course missing is the sequence of my remarks as I had to insert them where there was an opening. In indicating what in my opinion were the sort of assurances His Majesty's Government might be inclined to give I purposely did not allude to any idea of France and Russia being brought into an arrangement, as I wished to avoid every appearance of being primed, and that idea would have given me away. I also wished to avoid committing His Majesty's Government in any way at this early stage of the proceedings. But I *did* wish to get some inkling of what sort of assurances they expected, so I indicated what His Majesty's Government might possibly be prepared to give in that way. Schoen evidently wants something more far reaching. He said to me to-day "I won't conceal from you that we Germans have the rooted conviction, founded on sad experience, that wherever we are pushing our legitimate interests we meet with opposition from England." On my saying that I was afraid that there existed people in England who were not devoid of similar feelings with regard to Germany, he said "Yes! I know, and we must have something to put an end to that deplorable state of things. Take the Bagdad Railway for instance; any idea that that enterprise is anti-English or contrary to British interests is quite unfounded, and I know for a fact that our bankers are only too anxious to meet the English half way and come to an agreement with them, while your people only get excited about India and do everything to increase our difficulties. This sort of attitude on their part in the Bagdad and other questions is apt to make our people difficult to deal with, and I can assure you that if an opportunity could be taken by His Majesty's Government during these negotiations to give some assurances which would remove ill feeling and give evidence of a really friendly spirit you would find us much more ready to fall in with your views both as regards the Bagdad Railway, the Capitulations in Egypt, and other matters of importance to England!"

He made one statement to me which I consider of importance, and which I have alluded to in my despatch. He said that his own opinion (which I presume is also that of the Chancellor) was that any naval arrangement which might be come to should only be made to cover two or three years, the idea being that if it worked smoothly and gave satisfaction it would, combined with the pacific assurances, cause the Reichstag to look twice at incurring unnecessary expenditure and incline them to drop ships. This, in my opinion, is worthy of consideration, and it also somewhat tends to remove the haunting anxiety that all they want to do is to tie our hands and then make hay with the rest of Europe. I also consider that it would be a point gained if they gave a formal assurance that no acceleration in their rate of shipbuilding would take place.

As regards the reduction of the *tempo* in their shipbuilding as indicated by the Chancellor, and explained by Schoen to mean that they might spread the construction of their ships over a longer period by laying down at present three ships a year instead of the four provided for by the Programme and subsequently making up the full number by increasing the two provided in later years to three, it is quite true, as I pointed out to Schoen, that, in spite of this, at the end of the Programme all the ships would be there and the gross expenditure for them incurred, while we should have had to build and incur expense in the proportion we thought necessary for safety. Still it must be remembered that they build ships by loan and we out of income so that the spreading process would be more in our favour than in theirs. At least so it appears to me.

As my conversation with the Chancellor and Schoen took place on the evening before messenger day and my morning was chiefly occupied in revising Schoen's notes and making very necessary alterations both my despatch and this letter have had to be written very hurriedly, but I have tried to make things as clear as possible.

By the way you may find a few discrepancies between Schoen's notes and the translation, but I have explained them to Schoen, who quite understood and " passed " them.

He wanted to have them typed on one sheet of paper in separate columns, English and German and signed by me and him; but I refused this as I said it was giving far too much formality to what the Chancellor had himself characterised as a preliminary and informal conversation. He agreed readily, and I think the whole idea of notes being taken of the conversation &c., came from the careful and precise new Chancellor. The whole proceeding was not very pleasant.

You will see from the Chancellor's speech that he expects an answer as to whether His Majesty's Government agree " in principle " to the sort of programme he suggests. Should the answer be in the affirmative I would suggest that it should be stated that His Majesty's Government are awaiting the naval proposals foreshadowed in the Chancellor's communication to me in August last.([1]) For I do not suppose His Majesty's Government would care to go very far before knowing exactly what the German Government have to propose.

Yours very sincerely,

W. E. GOSCHEN.

([1]) [*v. supra*, pp. 283–4, Nos. 186–7.]

[ED. NOTE.—No record has been found in the Foreign Office Archives of any report to Sir E. Goschen of the conversation between Sir Edward Grey and Count Metternich on October 26, described by the latter in *G.P.* XXVIII, pp. 243–4. But see *supra*, p. 300, No. 200, *min.* and *note* ([6]). For Count Metternich's report of the conversation of October 28, *v. G.P.* XXVIII, pp. 250–1, and XXVII, II, pp. 580–2. Sir Edward Grey's despatch was communicated by Sir E. Goschen to the Chancellor on November 4, and is printed in *G.P.* XXVIII, pp. 255–8.]

No. 202.

Sir Edward Grey to Sir E. Goschen.

F.O. 38405/31695/09/18.
(No. 266.) Secret.
Sir,   *Foreign Office, October 28, 1909.*

I asked Count Metternich to come to see me to-day and told him that, though I thought the conversations which had been begun with you in Berlin had better be continued there, I wished to tell him what I proposed to say to you.

I would deal first with the hesitation expressed by Herr von Schoen as to whether the present was a suitable time to continue the discussion and make proposals, seeing that the British Cabinet was already so much occupied. I would say at once that we should very much regret a suspension of the negotiations; business here might occasionally delay our replies, but this would not be so great a drawback as the total suspension of the negotiations.

I approved entirely all that you had already said in conversation. We should have no difficulty in giving general assurances of a peaceable disposition, for we could most truthfully say that we did not desire to direct our understandings with other countries against Germany, and that we had no hostile intentions whatever with regard to her. But it might be difficult to find any formula going beyond this which would not give the impression that we were entering into closer relations with Germany than we had previously entered into with any other Powers. As a matter of fact, we had no such general formula with any other Power, and such engagements as we had made were limited to the terms of the particular agreements which we had concluded.

I understood that it was felt in Germany that some general understanding was necessary, to cause the atmosphere to become more genial, and thus to make a naval arrangement possible. Here, however, there was an opposite feeling: a general understanding would have no beneficial effect whatever on public opinion, and would indeed be an object of criticism, so long as naval expenditure remained undiminished. In order to remove suspicion here, a naval arrangement was essential. Though I had not yet consulted the Admiralty with regard to your last conversation, because it seemed to me that the negotiations had hardly reached the stage at which experts might be consulted, I felt sure that a frank exchange of information between the German and British Admiralties would be the most effective factor in making both countries believe that the naval expenditure of each was intended for general purposes, and had not in view the stealing of a march or the gaining of an advantage at the expense of the other country. The drawing up of satisfactory formulæ would, however, be difficult, and would take time.

Meanwhile, as we were convinced that the German Chancellor really desired to improve relations between the two countries, and we therefore felt that the opening of the discussion had already made the atmosphere more genial, I was anxious that this favourable turn of events should at once lead to some good results, even though they might be indirect. I hoped that one good result would be a greater frankness on points of difficulty between us. . . . . (¹)

Finally, Count Metternich assured me that the object of the German Chancellor was to restore between us and Germany the friendly and confidential relations which used to exist. The German Government had felt of late that, though there might be no actual understanding against Germany, we were somehow or other always found to be acting with France and Russia in opposition to Germany.

I observed that, in the case of Morocco, our action had of course been determined by the terms of the Anglo-French Agreement. In the Balkan crisis last winter Russia and Austria had been violently opposed, and if we had been found acting against Germany at Constantinople this was not because we were opposing German interests.

(¹) [The omitted passage in this despatch refers to the Bagdad Railway and is printed, *infra*, pp. 378–9, No. 277.]

but because Germany had taken up the Austrian side. I reminded Count Metternich that I had told him at the time that we quite understood the action Germany had taken, and that we ourselves should probably have acted similarly in her place; and I pointed out that Germany should also realise that the action we had taken was the action she herself would have taken, had she been in our place.

Count Metternich seemed to think that we were specially responsible for the attitude which Russia had taken up. He was of opinion that France had tried to restrain Russia, and that without our encouragement there would have been no Balkan crisis.

I told him that the language used in London had been exactly the same as that used in Paris, and we had not done anything to make matters worse.

The conversation ended in a résumé of what I had stated at the beginning as to our readiness to receive the German proposals and our desire to prevent by frank explanations the Bagdad Railway, or any other difficulty, from being a cause of soreness.

Count Metternich said that though the German Chancellor was prepared to make suggestions he would also welcome any which we could make.

I said that any suggestions from me at this stage would have to deal with the naval question, and I could not make suggestions of this kind without first consulting the Admiralty.

[I am, &c.]
E. G[REY].(²)

(²) [The text here given is the final draft approved by Sir Edward Grey and initialled by him. This is in accordance with the general rule as to out-going despatches described by the Editors, in *Gooch & Temperley*, Vol. I, p. ix. The text of this despatch, as printed in *G.P.* XXVIII, pp. 255–8, is that of the copy communicated by Sir E. Goschen to Herr von Bethmann Hollweg. It appears from this that the despatch as sent off from the Foreign Office was signed " For the Secretary of State, W. Langley."]

No. 203.

Sir Edward Grey to Sir E. Goschen.

F.O. 38405/31695/09/18.
Tel. (No. 328.) *Foreign Office, October* 29, 1909.
Your despatch No. 356.(¹) I have told German Ambassador of reply which I am sending to you and have said there is no occasion to hang up negotiations on account of business here and that we are ready to receive proposals. Despatch follows.(²)

(¹) [*v. supra*, pp. 293–8, No. 200.]
(²) [*v.* immediately preceding document. The present telegram was probably drafted on October 28, but delayed in despatch.]

No. 204.

Sir E. Goschen to Sir Edward Grey.(¹)

F.O. 40904/31695/09/18.
(No. 371.) Secret. *Berlin, D. November* 4, 1909.
Sir, *R. November* 8, 1909.
On the receipt of your despatch No. 266 of the 28th ultimo marked secret,(²) I at once communicated its contents to the Imperial Chancellor and His Excellency asked me to call upon him this afternoon to hear the observations he had to make upon it.

(¹) [The language used by Sir E. Goschen was approved by Sir Edward Grey in his despatch No. 283 to Count de Salis of November 22, 1909.]
(²) [*v. supra*, pp. 303–4, No. 202.]

Herr von Schoen, as on the previous occasion, was present during our conversation. The Chancellor in the first place begged me to convey to you his best thanks for the exceedingly frank and straightforward statement contained in your despatch—a frankness which he would endeavour to imitate. He was also glad to acknowledge the great friendliness and cordiality with which you had received his first message.

He then in a long speech recapitulated what he had said to me on the last occasion and again laid stress upon the great sacrifice the German Government were making in suggesting a naval arrangement at all. I ventured to remark that before we could judge of the sacrifice we must know what proposals the Imperial Government had to make, because it appeared to me that as things stood, the sacrifice was no greater for one Power than for the other, both Powers being equally anxious to curtail the increasing cost of armaments and to remove from the public mind the impression that aggressive ideas lay at the bottom of that increasing expenditure. His Excellency said that that was the idea, but not the whole idea, and he would come to what he had to propose in a moment.

In the first place, however, he wished to deal with your statement to the effect that public opinion in England would attach small value to political assurances unless they were preceded by a naval arrangement. As regards this he would observe that in Germany the opposite was the case, but that in order to show his goodwill he would suggest as a compromise that a naval arrangement and political assurances should be negotiated and made public simultaneously and side by side.

His Excellency then came to the naval proposals he had to make. They were simply to the effect that during a certain period of years, say, three or four, both countries should bind themselves not to build more than a stated number of "capital" ships; the number of ships to be settled of course by the naval experts of the two Governments. I asked His Excellency whether his proposal would include any arrangement by which fuller information respecting naval construction and building would be exchanged. His Excellency replied that in principle he was not against such an arrangement, but that it was a matter of some difficulty which could only be decided by naval experts. But he could say at once that he deprecated any idea of control—as an arrangement between two such Powers as Germany and England precluded, in his opinion, any idea that control would be necessary.

He then came to the political assurances to be exchanged between the two Powers, with a view to removing suspicion and rendering possible a really good feeling between the two countries. He observed in the first place that the suggestions as to what His Majesty's Government might be able to propose which I had thrown out in our last conversation, which practically amounted to a declaration on the part of His Majesty's Government that their understandings with Russia and France were not directed against Germany, contained nothing that the German Government did not know already; in fact Prince Bülow had more than once made public statements to that effect in the Reichstag. Therefore that assurance—one of an agreeable nature—the intrinsic value of which he would be the last to underestimate, had lost its value as an item in the present negotiations. He would propose that the two Governments should give a mutual assurance, in a form to be afterwards decided, that neither of them entertained any idea of aggression the one against the other, that they would not attack each other, and further that in the case of an attack made on either Power by a third Power or group of Powers, the Power not attacked should stand aside. His Excellency invited an expression of opinion with me with regard to this proposal. I said that it was not for me to pass judgment on a proposal of such a far-reaching nature, but that, speaking for myself personally, I would remind him that I had already pointed out to him that it would be difficult for His Majesty's Government to go further with Germany than they had gone with France and Russia, and that with those countries we had formulated no such definite arrangement. His Excellency replied that as far as that went we had no naval arrangement with those Powers and that the mere fact of a naval arrangement being contemplated between Germany and

neutrality

England created an entirely new situation. I think that he wanted me to understand that as His Majesty's Government had originally suggested a limitation of Naval Armaments and therefore an understanding on that subject, it was His Majesty's Government who had created the new situation of which the political understanding which he now proposed was a natural sequence. For, he explained, it could not be expected from them that, after having consented to reduce their naval plans, they should find themselves opposed subsequently by the Power at whose wish they had done so. This led to another short discussion with regard to their Naval Programme, the scope of which I pointed out would, according to his proposal, be not reduced but only retarded. The Chancellor remarked that to give an assurance that their programme, as formed by Law, would be reduced was impossible, at all events at the present moment; what he proposed was the restriction of their power of rapid construction during a certain number of years, which was certainly a great concession; and it was necessary for them to have some assurance which would be a guarantee that that concession would not be used against them. "Besides," he added, and in this he was supported by Herr von Schoen, "who knows but that circumstances may arise during the years for which the arrangement may be concluded which may render still further reductions possible." I asked whether they meant that if things went well the Reichstag would of its own volition vote for a reduction of the legal programme. They replied that that was possible, but that at all events at the present moment it was out of the question for them to go further than the proposal just indicated. I said that it was difficult for me to give any definite opinion, but that I would not conceal from them my impression that His Majesty's Government might find it difficult to fall in with a suggestion based on the carrying out sooner or later of the entire German programme.

You will see from what I have written that the exchange of political assurances proposed by the Chancellor bears a very striking resemblance to that suggested to me by Herr von Kiderlen-Waechter in the beginning of the year, which I brought to your notice in my despatch No. 141 of April 16 last.(³)

I would mention that in speaking of the Chancellor's political proposal I said that I presumed that in alluding to an attack on either of the Powers by a third Power or group of Powers he meant an unprovoked attack. In reply His Excellency pointed out the difficulty of ever deciding, to the satisfaction of either the attacker or the attacked, which was the provoking party; he would therefore prefer that the word unprovoked should not form part of any formula, and words such as "action aggressive" should rather be used. I would add that in a subsequent conversation which I had with Herr von Schoen, the latter said that it would in fact be well in drawing up a formula that neither the words "war" nor "neutrality" should be used, as they were words of a somewhat exciting character. I said that whatever words were used the Chancellor's proposal could mean nothing else but that in the case of war, the Power not actually concerned should stand neutral. Herr von Schoen replied that all the Chancellor had done as yet was to suggest the line which he thought should be followed; an appropriate formula had yet to be found. It might for instance be stated that in the case of one of the Powers being engaged in an unexpected conflict, the other Power should stand aside unless its vital interests ("Lebensinteresse") were involved.

In bidding me good-bye Herr von Schoen said that he hoped I should bring them on my return a favourable answer to the Chancellor's proposals, which had been made with the honest endeavour of placing the relations of the two countries on a friendly and satisfactory footing. I said that no one could be more anxious than I to see that result attained, but that I could not conceal from him by (? my) personal opinion that while the naval proposals scarcely went far enough, the political proposals went somewhat too far under existing circumstances. In any case he might be certain that both proposals would receive the most careful and unprejudiced consideration at the hands of His Majesty's Government.([4])

I have the honour to transmit herewith copy and translation of the Chancellor's statement and of the notes taken by Baron von Schoen on our conversation.

I have, &c.

W. E. GOSCHEN.

Enclosure in No. 204.([5])

Conversation which took place on November 4, 1909, between Herr von Bethmann Hollweg, Baron von Schoen, and Sir Edward Goschen.

Translation.

The Imperial Chancellor said :

It is with gratitude and satisfaction that I see from the information which Your Excellency, under instructions from the British Government, has just given me, to the effect that Your Government is ready in connection with the negotiations respecting a Naval Arrangement, to enter into a friendly discussion with regard to a general orientation of mutual policies.

Both Governments are convinced that complete and unreserved openness must be the preliminary condition of these discussions. And in view of this fact the following suggests itself :—

From her standpoint, England in the main only interests herself in a Naval Arrangement. Hence it follows that it was England who first suggested the conclusion of a Naval Arrangement, without giving any indication of a desire on her part for a political arrangement. As regards Germany the question is different. We have repeatedly declared that we are only building our fleet to meet our own requirements, for the protection of our trade and to guard against possible attacks on our coasts, without any kind of aggressive designs. It is to our greatest interest that we should again enter into confidential and friendly relations with England. England may judge of the loyalty of this desire on our part by the fact that we are prepared to pay a high price for it, namely the price of limiting by treaty the extent of our Naval Armaments. In the entire course of history no nation has as yet done this as the basis of a friendly understanding.

Two points arise from this situation :—

Firstly in respect to form. England says, and, from her point of view, quite justly :—We can sign no political arrangement until we know what form the Naval Arrangement will take. And, on the other hand Germany says :—We can only conclude the Naval Arrangement when agreement has been arrived at respecting a political arrangement which meets our wants. In other words the negotiations with regard to the political arrangement and the naval arrangement must be carried on simultaneously and concluded simultaneously.

Secondly, in respect to substance. The naval arrangement must offer England so much as to enable her to direct her policy towards us in an amicable way. On the other hand Germany can only fix by treaty the construction of her fleet, which is, moreover, in point of numbers immeasurably weaker than that of England, and which might also conceivably come into conflict with the fleets of other states, when she has the assurance that during the term of the treaty she will not cross swords with England. Without this provision Germany would, in concluding a naval arrangement, renounce her independence as a State. I may presume that England will recognize these premis[s]es.

([4]) [The substance of this statement by Sir E. Goschen was repeated by him in almost identical language in a private letter of November 6. *cp. G.P.* XXVIII, p. 265.]

([5]) [The German original of this record is printed in *G.P.* XXVIII, pp. 259–62.]

As regards the substance of the arrangement in the light in which it now appears to me, I venture to make the following observations :—

The Naval Arrangement should, in our opinion, be founded on the following basis I have repeatedly ventured to point out that we are unable to depart from our Navy Law as such. The general direction of the Naval Arrangement will therefore have to be that for a certain number of years the number of battle-ships will be fixed, which neither of the two countries shall yearly be able to exceed. It would be desirable if England would declare, whether in principle she regards such a measure as a suitable basis for a Naval Arrangement. If the reply is in the affirmative the Naval Experts would at once have to pronounce with regard to the numerical progression of development.

In this connection England has repeatedly put forward a suggestion that both countries might keep themselves informed through their Naval Attachés with regard to their mutual naval construction. I may call attention to the fact that we have already this year given the Naval Attaché very detailed information, which was, however, unfortunately not made use of by Mr. McKenna. If we conclude a Naval Arrangement, in which the number of the battleships to be annually built on both sides is fixed, we already keep each other informed by the arrangement itself, and therefore at first sight further information does not appear necessary to us. Still this question too may be discussed by the Naval experts; for if England urgently desires it, we are in principle also ready to consider this or a similar proposal. But in my opinion we must avoid, in the interests of both countries, giving this part of the Arrangement the faintest appearance of the Naval Attachés having in any way to control the honourable execution of the Agreement. This honesty is to be taken for granted, when England and Germany conclude a treaty.

As regards the Political Arrangement, which is to be made at the same time as the Naval Arrangement, I have already permitted myself to give a general sketch of its contents. It will be the task of further conversations to find a formula doing justice to the interests of both countries. If in respect of this Sir Edward Grey is ready to declare, that no Arrangement has been made with France and Russia, which injure German interests, if England will further also give assurances, for example in the sense that England will make no unprovoked attack on any Power or group of Powers and that she will use her influence to prevent other Powers from doing so, I am far from underestimating the worth of these peaceful assurances. Now England has already repeatedly declared to us that her *ententes* with Russia and France are in no way directed against Germany. Prince Bülow has also repeatedly declared in the Reichstag that assurances to this effect have been given us. From this it appears to me that these offers have not taken into sufficient account the situation which is to be newly created by the Naval Arrangement. In this new situation both sides must in my opinion be offered a certainty of not being involved in hostile complications with one another. That that should not occur through a direct attack of one Power on the other, is postulated as a preliminary condition. It can only be a question of the attitude of England in the case of Germany coming unexpectedly into conflict with a third Power. That Germany is not prosecuting aggressive designs against either Russia, France or any other Power follows from the policy which she has hitherto pursued; for the future I give my personal guarantee that she will not do so. Should, however, Germany be forced into war by provocation on the part of a third Power, she must have the certainty of not finding England on the side of her opponents. I do not need to point out that as regards this point Germany is prepared for reciprocity. Should England be threatened or attacked by a third European or other Power, we would not join her adversaries.

If England considers that she cannot assure more to us that [*sic*] to France and Russia, it must be remembered however that there is the great difference that England wishes to conclude a Naval Arrangement with us—an Arrangement which, as I have already repeatedly allowed myself to state, is only conceivable at all between friends. If England wishes to make France and Russia similar promises of neutrality, we would quite agree to her doing so.

Sir E. Goschen expressed doubt as to whether it would be possible for England to conclude a political arrangement with Germany which would be of wider scope than the *Ententes* with France and Russia. He stated further that a Naval Arrangement which left the German naval programme as a whole untouched would not have the desired effect, for then a limitation of the expenditure on armaments, which was such a heavy state burden, would not be effected.

The Imperial Chancellor answered, if, as was actually the case, England wished to conclude a Naval Arrangement with Germany, that is to say an understanding respecting the limitation of the construction of ships, the wish aimed at the establishment of a quite peculiar relation, it would create a new situation which could not be compared with England's relations with France and Russia. Sincerely friendly relations laid down in a political agreement were the inevitable correlative of a retardation of the building rate. A diminution of the expenditure would at any rate be attained at least for a fixed number of immediately succeeding years by means of a Naval Arrangement. Herein lies a material element of tranquillisation. To tie themselves down now mutually for the entire future with regard to the building of new ships was hardly in consonance with mutual interests, which were decided by other factors besides the relations between the two Powers.

Sir E. Goschen enquired as to the form which the German Government contemplated that the agreement should take.

Baron von Schoen replied that there would be two agreements to be signed simultaneously, one respecting shipbuilding and one respecting political arrangements. The question of eventual publication would be reserved for a later agreement. At the same time an exchange of confidential notes could take place, containing more detailed explanations of the political relations and enumerating some further questions, about which a friendly understanding was contemplated, for instance, the Bagdad Railway and Colonial questions. In reply to a question of Sir Edward Goschen relative to the Bagdad Railway, Baron von Schoen said an understanding respecting the participation of England in the undertaking would meet with no difficulties in this country. France already participated financially. A few years ago we had already negotiated with Russia, by the desire of M. Isvolsky, who had, in view mainly our political disinterestedness in Persia. The course of things since then had proved that we had no other than economic aims in Persia, the ground seemed to us therefore as far as Russia was concerned to be smoothed for an understanding.

MINUTES.

It seems difficult, at first sight to take the German proposals seriously. In order to understand their meaning, the only way is to place oneself at the angle of vision under which the problem appears to the eyes of the German gov[ernmen]t. There is a specious logic in the ideas developed by the Chancellor : Limitation of armament, he says, is possible only as between real friends; for friendship alone precludes the possibility of an armed conflict between two parties. Germany is confiding. She does not doubt England's assurance that there is no intention of an aggressive character. Germany on her part is free from aggressive designs. But in case either country were at war with third parties, the law of friendship requires that the non–engaged friend should remain neutral. If this were thoroughly understood, it would be evident that there was friendship, not otherwise. It is therefore on this condition alone that a limitation of armaments can be agreed upon. It is moreover necessary to eliminate all causes of possible friction between the *new* friends; therefore there must be an amicable arrangement respecting the Bagdad railway and " sundry colonial questions." This is, in the usual guise, our old friend, the demand for English concessions for the sake of sealing Anglo-German friendship.—These conditions being satisfactorily fulfilled, it will be easy to agree not to build more than a fixed number of capital ships within a period of 3 or 4 years. Practical control by inspection of yards, &c., is precluded by the creation of the new friendship which is incompatible with the continuance of suspiciousness. No guarantee is apparently offered as to what is to happen at the end of 3 or 4 years.

The advantages of the proposed compact to this country seem meagre. England will be tied as to the amount of shipbuilding not only as against Germany, but as against the rest of the world. Under the terms of the agreement, Germany would, on the other hand, whilst temporarily abandoning any warlike schemes against England, whether alone or in conjunction with others, be free to deal in whatever way she liked with any other State. She may oppress, constrain, or swallow any small country, she may attack or bully or wipe out big ones. She may leave her allies to build fleets, or she may conclude fresh alliances with the owners of fleets, or buy their ships for a future contingency. She may also oppose British interests, commercial or others, over the whole world; all this without any fear of the interference of the British Government.

The bargain appears a little one-sided. It is very difficult to understand how it can be honestly proposed to us for acceptance.

E. A. C.
Nov. 8.

Like Sir E. Goschen I am unable to see what sacrifice Germany is making in limiting her naval programme and why therefore she should be paid for doing so. But the most objectionable feature in the German proposals is the attempt to tie our hands in the event of a war breaking out between Germany and some other Power.

However worded such a provision must have a disastrous effect on our relations with France and Russia.

W. L.

The German Government have now come into the open and the political proposal put forward by them is practically identical with that which has already been put forward by Baron Kiderlen, and considered by the Foreign Office in the spring of this year.[6] The proposals for a naval arrangement are the same as those which were foreshadowed by the German Chancellor in his previous interview with His Majesty's Ambassador on October 14th.[7] The naval and political proposals may be summarized as follows :—

The German Government are ready to enter into an agreement with His Majesty's Government that during the first few years covered by the German Naval Programme they will build only three instead of four capital ships, the deficiency being completed by the building of three ships instead of two during the latter period of the programme. In the records of the two interviews drawn up by Baron Schön it is categorically stated that there can be no departure from the German Naval Law which provides for the building of thirty-eight Dreadnoughts by 1918.

In return for this so-called concession on the part of the German Government, they will not accept as sufficient the peaceful declarations and assurances which His Majesty's Government have expressed their readiness to make or to renew, but, in view of the situation created by the Naval Agreement, which they profess to regard as a very material concession on their part, they ask as a preliminary condition that England shall not be involved in hostile conflict with Germany, and that, in the event of Germany being forced into war by provocation on the part of a third Power, England shall not be found on the side of Germany's opponents. As regards this point Germany is prepared to offer reciprocity to England.

In a previous Minute on the record of Sir E. Goschen's first interview with the Chancellor I endeavoured to show that the alleged concession offered to His Majesty's Government is in reality no concession at all. The Chancellor now states however that " a diminution of the expenditure would at any rate be attained at least for a fixed number of immediately succeeding years by means of a Naval agreement. Herein lies a material element of tranquillisation."

In this view the Chancellor appears to be entirely mistaken. It would no doubt be advantageous for His Majesty's Government to know that there would be no acceleration of the German naval programme during the next few years, but the root of the distrust in England towards Germany is the suspicion engendered by the creation within a short distance of our shores of a large German battle fleet unsuited to the ends for which it is said to be being built, and doubt as to the intentions of the German Government as to how it is to be employed. A diminution of the expenditure during the first few years can hardly be regarded as a concession of much value, since it would have to be increased during the later years to meet the deficiency and to cover the completion of the German programme in its entirety. The expenditure to be thrown on the shoulders of the British tax-payer would thus remain precisely the same, but, in view of the heavy incidence of taxation in Germany at the present time and the discontent caused thereby, the alleviation from a more even distribution of taxation for naval purposes would react more to Germany's advantage than to our own, and would render more probable the fulfilment of the German naval programme. It is even possible that the German Government may find it desirable to distribute more evenly the German shipbuilding programme whether we come to an agreement with them or not. They have shown that they can do so if they choose.

It must not be forgotten however that His Majesty's Government will also be expected to make a concession to Germany as regards shipbuilding, to which reference is only made indirectly by the Chancellor in the following sentence : " If we conclude a Naval Agreement, in which the number of battleships to be annually built on both sides is fixed . . . ." This implies that our shipbuilding programme will have to be brought into accordance with that of Germany while ignoring those of other Powers such as Austria and Italy, both of which Powers have already prepared programmes for the construction of capital ships in the immediate future. For His Majesty's Government to be restricted in their output of capital ships to meet all and any emergencies might create a very dangerous situtation for British possessions and interests in the Mediterranean at a moment of crisis in the North Sea.

(6) [v. supra, pp. 265–6, No. 174.]
(7) [v. supra, pp. 293–8, No. 200.]

Sir E. Goschen, in his covering despatch, reported an observation made by the Chancellor, in which he was supported by Baron Schön, to the effect that circumstances might arise during the course of the fulfilment of an agreement which might render further reductions possible in the German Naval programme. This is an insidious and dangerous suggestion made in the first instance on October 14th by Baron Schön* and now repeated by the Chancellor, but directly contradicted in the Memoranda given after each conversation. These Memoranda are the only official records of what took place and in each of them any modification of the existing Naval Programme is distinctly precluded. To base hopes on such vague suggestions would be to open the door to disillusion and disappointment. Sir E. Goschen was correct in his impression that "His Majesty's Government might find it difficult to fall in with a suggestion based on the carrying out sooner or later of the entire German programme."

Turning to the German proposals for a political agreement between England and Germany there can be no doubt that they go much farther than would be compatible with the foreign policy of His Majesty's Government. The position of Great Britain on the Continent is happily very different to that of Germany. At the present moment England's only possible foe is Germany, while Germany might under certain circumstances have to reckon with England, France or Russia, or a combination of two or more of these Powers. For Germany therefore to give a pledge to England that, if England be attacked by a third European or other Power, she would not join England's adversaries, no real advantage is to be gained, since any such attack is in the highest degree improbable. Were England to give a similar pledge to Germany, the hands of England would be tied so long as the engagement was in force, and Germany, the only aggressive Power in Europe, would be free to act when and where and how she pleased while England remained a discontented and probably angry spectator. There is no reason to doubt that Herr Bethmann-Hollweg has most pacific intentions and that his guarantee that Germany has no aggressive designs is honest and genuine, but after all he is only human, and one has not forgotten how small a margin there was from war between France and Germany over an incident at Casablanca(8) only a little more than a year ago; yet there is little doubt that Prince Bülow would have been equally ready to give a similar guarantee that he harboured no aggressive designs. Had such an agreement with England as is now proposed been then in force the incident in question might have been decided otherwise than by arbitration. It must be remembered that the one obstacle to German hegemony in Europe has been the strength and independence of the British navy, a fact fully realized in Germany at the time of the Boer war, and for England to tie her own hands and to remain neutral while Germany established her supremacy on the Continent would be a derogation from the honourable rôle which Great Britain has played in Europe for more than three hundred years and which has greatly contributed to the peace of the world.

I venture to quote here an extract from a minute written by me last May upon another question of foreign policy connected with Russia and Germany,(9) in which I referred to the possibility of our coming to terms with Germany, and more especially to the suggestions made to Sir E. Goschen by Baron Kiderlen in practically the same sense as those now put forward by the German Chancellor. I make this quotation in deference to the views of Sir E. Grey who desired that it should be brought up in the event of this question arising.

"It is the apprehension of the danger of German aims to the general peace and independence of Europe that has inspired both the question that has been considered in this memorandum and the reply that has been submitted, but it may be pointed out that there is a yet more serious and more insidious danger to England that must be carefully watched and avoided.

It is quite intelligible that some people, after reading these views, might suggest as an alternative policy that of coming to terms with Germany, and the basis of such an agreement has already been placed quite recently before His Majesty's Ambassador in Berlin by Baron Kiderlen, German Minister at Bucharest, the confidant of Prince Bülow, who has been recently employed at the Foreign Office in Berlin. The basis of the proposed agreement was that either a political entente should be made such as would render increased naval construction on either side a source of satisfaction rather than of suspicion, or that a Convention should be made by which the two Powers should bind themselves for a fixed period :—

"1. Not to make war against each other.
"2. To join in no coalition against either Power and
"3. To observe a benevolent neutrality should either country be engaged in hostilities with any other Power or Powers.

* See Sir E. Goschen, No. 356, Secret. [pp. 293–8, No. 200.]
(8) [This subject will be dealt with in *Gooch & Temperley*, Vol. VII.]
(9) [The extract is taken from a memorandum by Sir Charles Hardinge, printed in *Gooch & Temperley*, Vol. V, pp. 823–6, *App.* III. The Memorandum was undated, and April 1909 was suggested as a possible date by the Editors. A second copy of the Memorandum has now been found in the Hardinge MSS., and this is dated May 4, 1909. The following minutes were entered on this copy :
"I agree with this paper which is very ably stated : it must be brought up if the question arises. E. G."
"This is an able paper, worth thinking over : especially the last two pages. H. H. A."
The part of the Memorandum referred to by Mr. Asquith as the "last two pages" is the extract quoted by Sir C. Hardinge above.]

"Were His Majesty's Government to fall into a trap of this kind, the duration of the agreement would be strenuously employed by Germany to consolidate her supremacy in Europe, while England would remain as a spectator with her hands tied. At the termination of the agreement, Germany would be free to devote her whole strength to reducing the only remaining independent factor in Europe and if, relying upon a profusion of friendly assurances from Germany, which public opinion is always only too ready to believe and to accept as genuine, England had in the meantime neglected to maintain an absolutely predominant naval supremacy, she would richly deserve the fate which would inevitably await her, and compel her for the first time in her history to take her place amongst the satellites of the German constellation. Moreover the mere announcement that England had concluded such an agreement with Germany would result in her immediate isolation, and would entail a loss of prestige and of any confidence for the future in her loyalty and friendship. Although it is unthinkable that any Government should ever be duped by such a transparent proposal as that made by Baron Kiderlen, which would not have been put forward without Prince Bülow's knowledge and approval, it is as well that its dangerous character should be revealed, and that the disastrous consequences which its adoption would entail should be fully realized."

I see no reason to modify these views in any way.

To sum up, no naval agreement can be of any permanent usefulness to restore friendly relations between Germany and England unless it contains some provision for the modification of the present German naval programme. No political agreement between the two Powers would be acceptable on the lines suggested by the German Chancellor which are so far reaching as to be likely to disturb the political equilibrium of Europe.

Now as to the course to be followed in the event of His Majesty's Government concurring in these views, I would suggest that Sir E. Goschen be instructed on his return to Berlin to inform the Chancellor that his proposals are receiving the careful consideration of His Majesty's Government. It would then be desirable to await developments in the internal situation in England, and if there are to be elections in January this fact would afford a sufficient reason for adjourning any decision and for letting the question drop altogether. Any difference of opinion would thus be avoided, and it would not be possible for the German Chancellor to say that we had rejected the right hand of friendship which he had extended.

Should, however, circumstances render it necessary, in the course of the next few months, to reopen this question, it might then be pointed out to the German Government that the ground has been shifted by them from that originally taken up by His Majesty's Government on the subject of a limitation of armaments with a view to the improvement of the mutual relations between the two countries, and that, while His Majesty's Government have always regarded a modification or retardation of the German naval programme as the *crux* of the whole question of improved relations, the German Government consider it from an entirely different standpoint. The German Chancellor is no doubt sincere in his professions of his desire for friendship, but his aim is to secure a political agreement entailing the neutralization of England in schemes where England blocks the way, and, as an inducement or bribe, he makes to England a proposal which is neither one of disarmament nor even of limitation of armaments within the enormous programme already laid down by the German Naval Law. Were England to accept such proposals the advantages would be almost entirely on the side of Germany. It would be impossible to reconcile public opinion in England to an agreement on those bases.

I think Sir E. Goschen's language should be approved.

C. H.

Foreign Office, November 10, 1909.

Approve it: I have spoken both to Sir E. Goschen and Count Metternich and recorded the latter conversation.

E. G.

No. 205.

Sir Edward Grey to Sir E. Goschen.([1])

F.O. 42826/31695/09/18.
(No. 284.) Secret.

Sir,   *Foreign Office, November* 17, 1909.

I told Count Metternich to-day that I had received your report of your last conversation with the German Chancellor and Herr von Schoen.([2]) I had sent it to the Prime Minister, and had had an opportunity of speaking to him about it this morning.

([1]) [For Count Metternich's report, v. *G.P.* XXVIII, pp. 273–5, and XXVII, II, pp. 585–6.]
([2]) [v. *supra*, pp. 304–9, No. 204.]

Since I had last seen Count Metternich, it had become clear that the House of Lords intended to reject the Finance Bill next week. This would very soon be followed by a General Election, and the members of the Cabinet would have several questions to deal with before they separated for the Election. They would have to separate as soon as possible, because all of them, except those who were Peers, would have contested elections. They would certainly not have time to consider the German proposals, and even if they had the time it would not be right for them to settle a question of such importance as this after a Dissolution of Parliament had actually been announced. The question must therefore wait till the General Election was over next January.

From the German point of view, the political side of the question appeared the most important. For us it was rather a matter of naval expenditure : unless whatever was done included a substantial reduction of naval expenditure, people here would regard it as shadow without substance and as worthless. In any case, however, whether the question was to be dealt with by the present Cabinet or by another Cabinet, the matter of naval expenditure would have to be investigated by the Admiralty; and as the experts there had no contested elections to fight I would send on the naval part of the question for their consideration. But this was all I could do for the moment. Count Metternich seemed prepared for this delay and to realize fully that the political situation made it inevitable.

I then reminded Count Metternich that I had told him before that, whatever the difficulty there might be about practical naval proposals and definite political formulæ, I hoped there might be some indirect good results from these negotiations, such for instance as progress with regard to the Bagdad Railway question. I heard that people who were directly interested in the matter had been moving. Herr Gwinner had been talking to Mr. Whittall, who had now come to London ;(3) and the 4% increase of the Turkish Customs Duties seemed to have brought the thing to a head. I was therefore going to give my mind to this question, in the hope of reaching an agreement.

Count Metternich told me again that, in the general negotiations with Germany, the political side of the question must proceed at least *pari passu* with the naval side. The Germans could not possibly reduce their naval expenditure unless it was quite clear that we were not going to be their enemy. It was necessary to find some way of combining these two sides of the question. Count Metternich also pointed out that reduction of naval expenditure meant, from the British point of view, a smaller German Navy.

I replied that this was true. I understood the importance which the Germans attached to the political side of the question. The reason for the precedence which the naval side took in our minds was, of course, that a Navy was vital to us in a sense in which it was not to Germany.

Count Metternich said that he appreciated this.

[I am, &c.]
E. G[REY].

(3) [*v. infra*, pp. 384–5, No. 282 and *min.*]

No. 206.

Sir F. Bertie to Sir Edward Grey.

Private.(1)

My dear Grey, *Paris, November 20, 1909.*

I told Pichon this evening, with reference to our conversation on the 10th instant which I reported to you in my private letter of the next day(2), that you had since informed me that the conversations at Berlin respecting Naval Armaments had

(1) [Grey MSS., Vol. 12.]
(2) [Not reproduced.]

not yet led to any result and that he might continue to rely on the assurance which I had given him that if the negotiations came to anything more than general assurances of goodwill he might rely on your consulting the French Government before committing yourself. You had, I said, told the German Ambassador on the 17th instant that in view of the preparations for a General Election the discussion of Naval Armaments must remain in suspense until after the Elections, for you could not carry on the discussion without consulting the Cabinet and it would not be able to meet to consider the question.

Pichon was very grateful for the information which you had sent to him. He has no faith in German assurances. He is therefore not likely to believe any statements disseminated by the German Government or Press that we are seeking to ingratiate ourselves with Germany to the detriment of our relations with France, but it will be useful to him to be able, if necessary, to refute to the President of the Republic and Briand any misrepresentations which may be made to them or that they may read in the German and the German-paid French newspapers.

Yours sincerely,
FRANCIS BERTIE.

No. 207.

Sir E. Goschen to Sir Edward Grey.

F.O. 43500/31695/09/18.
(No. 388.) Secret and Confidential. *Berlin*, D. *November* 25, 1909.
Sir, R. *November* 29, 1909.

I have the honour to inform you that on my return to Berlin, I called upon Herr von Schoen and gave him the message with which you had entrusted me respecting the German proposals for a naval and political arrangement between the two countries.([1])

His Excellency expressed his regret that I had brought back "bad news," but said that he had been prepared for them by Count Metternich, who had reported a conversation with you([2]) which tallied exactly with the message I had just given him.

Herr von Schoen said that he thoroughly understood that it was impossible for His Majesty's Government to give their attention to such matters at the present moment and that it was evident that the negotiations must lie dormant for some months. He regretted this very much. He was glad however to notice that the feeling in both countries showed already signs of improvement and he could tell me that Mr. Asquith's remarks at the Guildhall upon Anglo-German relations had made a very favourable impression in Germany. He then asked me whether I could tell him anything with regard to the impression made upon His Majesty's Government by the Chancellor's proposals. I replied that in view of the fact that the turn of political events in the United Kingdom had rendered the continuation of negotiations impossible for the moment, you had naturally not gone very deeply into the matter in conversation with me, but that I had heard nothing from you which inclined me to change my opinion, already expressed to the Chancellor, that His Majesty's Government would find it difficult to accept a naval arrangement based upon the eventual fulfilment of the entire German Naval Programme. In fact I had gathered that you held the opinion that the British public would not regard with a favourable eye, or attach any value to, any naval arrangement which did not include a substantial, and more or less immediate, reduction of naval expenditure. To this Herr von Schoen replied that he was afraid that "for the present" it was not possible for the Imperial Government to go further in the way of naval proposals.

I do not gather from this remark that there is any intention on the part of the Imperial Government to come forward at a later date with a more acceptable proposal,

([1]) [cp. *supra*, pp. 310–2, No. 204, *minutes* by Sir C. Hardinge and Sir E. Grey.]
([2]) [v. *supra*, pp. 312–3, No. 205.]

but rather that they cling to the idea that no modification of the Programme is possible without the consent of the Reichstag and that this consent is not likely to be obtained until after the conclusion of at least a political agreement on the lines indicated by the Chancellor.

I told Herr von Schoen that, while pointing out to me the unforeseen difficulties which had arisen respecting the continuance of the discussion of the Imperial Chancellor's proposals, you had expressed the hope that notwithstanding their interruption some good might result from the fact that such negotiations had been initiated, and that you had instanced the Bagdad Railway as a question in which progress might now be made, particularly as you had heard that Herr Gwinner and Mr. Whittall had been having friendly conversations on that subject.(³)

After stating that he entirely shared your views, His Excellency expressed the opinion that it would be best that the two Governments should not move in the matter until the question had been thoroughly thrashed out by the persons directly interested.

I have, &c.
W. E. GOSCHEN.

MINUTE.

This shelves the question for the moment. In fact Herr von Schoen holds out no hope of Germany coming forward with any really serious proposal for a limitation of armaments. Little doubt is allowed to remain that the whole object of Germany is (1) to obtain a political agreement with England under which Germany would be free to deal with third countries without the possibility of England intervening, however inimical to British interests such German dealings might be, and (2) to retain full liberty as to the completion of the German naval programme, subject to the construction of a few capital ships being spread over a slightly longer period than is at present contemplated.

The German proposals reveal no genuine wish to meet the views of H[is] M[ajesty's] G[overnment].

E. A. C.
Nov. 29.
W. L.
E. G.

MINUTE BY KING EDWARD.

The proposed negociations must obviously "lie dormant" but there is no sign of the German Naval programme lying dormant—as the German Gov[ernmen]t seems very active in increasing the numbers of its Fleet!

E.R.

(³) [v. infra, pp. 384–5, No. 282 and min.]

No. 208.

Sir E. Goschen to Sir Edward Grey.

F.O. 167/167/10/18.
(No. 414.) .Very Confidential.   *Berlin,* D. *December 29,* 1909.
Sir.   R. *January 3,* 1910.

An article appeared lately in the "Deutsch-Asiatische Correspondenz" in which the theory was advanced that the Turkish Military Authorities, and especially Schefket Pasha had only consented to the "British Navigation Monopoly in the Euphrates and Tigris" because they were in possession of exact information with regard to the understanding between Great Britain and Germany on the question of Naval Armaments. The Turkish Military Authorities had been in fact originally against this Monopoly as they had foreseen that it would lead to trouble with Great Britain in Mesopotamia, but in view of the Anglo-German understanding they had come to the conclusion that it would be better not to oppose a direct veto to the Concession.

This statement was considered by the better informed Newspapers too wildly improbable to require any comment; the Government however have given it a certain amount of importance by causing the following Communiqué to be published in the "Kölnische Zeitung":

"We cannot see what foundation there is for the assertion of the German-Asiatic Correspondenz with regard to an Anglo-German understanding on the Navy question. The wish to come into better relations with England certainly exists, but up to the present moment (bis zur Stunde) it has led to no agreement with regard to the so called navy question, and it is altogether incorrect to say that Germany intends to recede from the programme of naval construction established by law. False news of the above mentioned kind can in no way alter the Lynch concession, and can at most produce the belief in England that Germany is capable of being induced to effect a change in her building programme."

In informing me yesterday that he had made this communication to the Kölnische Zeitung Herr von Schoen told me that the Chancellor and he were being so much attacked in the Pan-German Press for their "slavish truckling" to Foreign Powers that they had been obliged, in order to be beforehand as regards questions in the Reichstag, to issue a disclaimer of any intention to reduce their Naval Programme.

He added that it was by no means agreeable to him to have been obliged to adopt this course but the attitude of the Pan-German Press had become so hostile that something had to be done. He was sure that I would readily understand this, and that I would admit that nothing had been said in the Communiqué beyond that which was absolutely necessary to reassure public opinion.

These remarks on the part of Herr von Schoen followed some observations he had made to me with regard to Sir E. Cassel's visit to Berlin, and the insistence with which he enlarged upon the manner in which the Chancellor and he were being attacked for their conciliatory attitude towards Foreign Powers, leads me to think that he wished me to understand that even if the British and German Financial Groups came to an agreement with regard to the control and construction of the Bagdad Persian Gulf section of the Bagdad Railway, the moment was very unfavourable for any negotiations on the subject between the two Governments.

I have, &c.
W. E. GOSCHEN.

MINUTE.

The German proposals for a political understanding were accompanied by an intimation that it would, by creating a better spirit between the two countries, bring about in Germany a feeling of willingness to proceed further in the direction of reducing the German naval programme, which was, to begin with, to be somewhat "retarded."

I pointed out at the time that this forecast as to public opinion in Germany was difficult to accept. Events have now shown that in German "influential" circles, that is among the pan-Germans, who are always described to us as mad people of no importance, but to whom the present Chancellor has, like all his predecessors, performed the public kow-tow, no understanding with England is desired except on terms which satisfy all German claims and aims, and which preclude all possible limitation of German naval armaments.

Baron Schoen's communication amounts to the funeral ceremony of the whole negotiation. His notion that we should "readily understand" the harmlessness and obviousness of an official assurance that the one vital element in the negotiation must be definitely abandoned is almost humorous. But what did Sir E. Goschen say? Surely some answer was called for. Presumably H[is] E[xcellency] has, according to his habit, told the rest of the story in a private letter,(¹) with the result that the official record continues incomplete, and may even become misleading to future students.

E. A. C.
Jan. 8.

(¹) [The Editors have not been able to trace a private letter from Sir E. Goschen referring to this subject.]

The *communiqué* is not happily worded but there is this to be said in its favour or in excuse. Although the Germans have held up to us the flattering prospect of a Reichstag voting for a reduction of the legal programme, they have never suggested that this state of things was likely now or in the near future. To let an impression get about that they were in favour of such a reduction would, if this is their policy, effectually defeat their object, and they are not likely to stick at a disingenuous statement if it is required to dispel the impression.

W. L.

Whether it is the secret policy of the Chancellor or not it is quite evident that he will not be allowed by public opinion in Germany to carry it out.

C. H.
E. G.

No. 209.

Sir E. Goschen to Sir Edward Grey.

F.O. 169/167/10/18.
(No. 416.)

Berlin, D. *December* 31, 1909.
R. *January* 3, 1910.

Sir,

The recent visit of Sir Ernest Cassel to Berlin proved to be in some sort an antidote to Mr. Blatchford's articles in the "Daily Mail." The effect of both the articles and the visit has been to make "Relations with England" the chief topic for discussion in the Press. The articles, and, it must be said, some of the political speeches in England founded upon them, raised considerable indignation; whereas Sir Ernest Cassel's visit has been made, on the whole, the subject of friendly remarks, and has been connected with a desire on the part of England, or at least England's financial world, to come to a friendly understanding with Germany, not only on matters such as the Bagdad Railway which was understood to be the primary object of his visit, but also on larger questions such as a general understanding and an agreement on naval armaments.

This view of Sir E. Cassel's visit, while leading to a very unanimous expression of opinion that the German Navy Law must on no account be modified or even form the subject of discussion has been not unfavourably received by a by no means unimportant section of the Berlin Press, and it is really only the Pan-German newspapers which have attacked the Imperial Government for showing a disposition to meet England half way in an endeavour to place the relations between the two countries on a more satisfactory basis.

The "Vossische Zeitung," amongst other papers not always friendly to England, published a few days ago an article on Germany and England of which the gist is that the recent semi-official declaration that the Imperial Government have no intention of altering their Naval Law, should in no way be regarded in England as signifying that Germany has not a sincere desire for establishing friendly relations with England.

In commencing the article the writer refers to the wide-spread report that Sir Ernest Cassel's recent visit to Berlin was in connection with the Bagdad Railway and Naval Armaments.

After quoting the semi-official statement that the German Government have no intention of making any change in the Navy Law, and that there was no connection between the Naval Question and the Bagdad Railway, the article goes on to say that for German readers this declaration was quite unnecessary, and that for the edification of English readers it might be added that it affected in no way the sincere desire on the part of Germany for a friendly understanding with her English cousin.

The writer then discusses the German Navy Law, which holds Germany to a fixed programme known to the whole world. He questions the statement that the construction of "Dreadnoughts" by Germany imperils the British naval supremacy and says that with regard to the type of ships Germany could not let herself be left behind where England led the way. He compares the outlay made by the Great Powers for naval expenditure for the current year and points out that while Germany is only spending £18,000,000, England is spending £35,000,000. And in reiterating the statement that it is absurd to say that the German naval armaments are directed against England, he quotes the words of Herr Paul Koch, a distinguished official in the German Admiralty, which appeared in a recent issue of the "Zeitschrift für Politik," to the effect that the Navy Law made for peace, and that Germany would consult no one but herself should the necessity arise to extend its scope. It is, the article continues, not probable, however, that Germany will extend the scope of her Navy Law within an appreciable time. Her only aim is to complete it for the protection of her trade and coasts, and, once it is complete, to maintain it in a state of efficiency. It is hard to know what Germany should do to allay the feelings of suspicion in England. And nothing has been heard of any kind of plausible proposals for the limitation of naval armaments, a plan which could not be confined to two States only, but which would have to be extended to bring within its scope all the Great Powers, and which demands guarantees for the conscienciousness with which it would be put into effect.

After pointing out the extreme improbability of Sir E. Cassel having been charged with the mission of proposing a plan of this kind, which, under existing circumstances, can only be regarded as Utopian, the writer says in conclusion:—"If the English are in earnest in their desire for a *rapprochement*, the much desired change with regard to armaments and finance would make itself felt, in time, of its own accord, without there being any necessity for a special naval understanding. An agreement entailing alteration of the Navy Law is impossible, in view of the fact that no Great Power can lay herself open to the charge of altering her legislation at the bidding of a foreign State. If England makes plausible proposals it will not be Germany's fault if the negotiations fail. In short a beginning must be made with the naval question, instead of waiting to see whether an understanding on other points does anything to allay the invasion panic, and costly armament fever from which British politics are suffering."

If the article from which I have just quoted goes over a good deal of old ground, it must be at all events admitted that the last sentence constitutes a new departure, as in the innumerable articles which have appeared in the press on the subject of an understanding with Great Britain it has always been pointed out that a naval agreement is impossible between the two nations until a proper atmosphere has been created by an understanding on political questions.

As yet, however, I have seen no trace of the views of the "Vossische Zeitung" on this point being shared by the Imperial Foreign Office.

I have the honour to enclose, herewith, an article from the "Frankfurter Zeitung"([1]) which also deals with Sir E. Cassel's visit and with the reports which have led to the denial on the part of the Imperial Government that a naval agreement has been concluded with England.

I have, &c.
W. E. GOSCHEN.

MINUTES.

It would of course suit Germany very well to complete her naval programme in a more or less neck-to-neck race with England and then to promote an understanding based on the *status quo* of naval armaments. But for this country the attraction of a naval understanding has lain in the hope that a curtailment of the present German programme would make further British expenditure on naval construction on a large scale unnecessary.

It is now abundantly clear that this hope must be definitely abandoned.

E. A. C.
Jan. 3.

([1]) [Not reproduced.]

It is quite evident that no Government in Germany could now propose such a curtailment, and quite probable that the time will never come when they can do so.

W. L.

If the programme is maintained in its entirety an agreement is practically useless and impossible.

C. H.
E. G.

No. 210.

Sir Edward Grey to Sir E. Goschen.

Private.(¹)

My dear Goschen,   *Fallodon, December* 31, 1909.

I have read with much interest your letter of Christmas Eve to Hardinge.

I am not surprised that the German Chancellor is annoyed and disappointed by what seem to him to be anti-German articles and speeches here. They are not really anti-German but alarmist, and in my opinion they arise from two motives. 1. The conviction that if the German fleet was strong enough to challenge ours we should have to choose between war and diplomatic humiliation. This I think is true. I do not mean that it is what Bethmann-Hollweg would intend or desire, but it would be forced upon him. The storm that has arisen in Germany in support of the Mannesmann claims in Morocco shows how easily this might happen.

Such feeling arising about anything in conflict with British interests would force a Chauvinistic policy upon the German Gov[ernmen]t. Hence a genuine anxiety here to stimulate public opinion to keep up the strength of our own forces.

2. The other motive is a desire to create a scare for electioneering purposes : that scare being that the Liberal Gov[ernmen]t is not building enough ships or doing enough for the army. For this purpose it is essential to magnify the aspect of danger.

I do not think it will come to much and if after the election we produce substantial Navy estimates coupled with a statement *on our own information* that Germany is not accelerating her naval programme the fuss will subside. For the present I can only say that Bethmann-Hollweg must discount what is going on now and wait till the election is over to see what substance there is in it. I am not going to be driven out of my course by the Daily Mail and the Peers who are on the stump; but for me or any of us to attempt to moderate their writing and speeches would only lead to the redoubling of their efforts. One result of the Daily Mail efforts is that other newspapers start counter-rumours of advanced negotiations for an entente with Germany and these may cause anxiety in France and Russia.

But I shall continue to ignore the Extremes on both sides unless any of my Colleagues or really responsible men on the other side indulge in loose talk, in which case I may put the position in what seems to me to be its true light.

You put very well my feeling about Bethmann-Hollweg's proposals in their present shape. This must remain in suspense till after the election . . . . .(²)

Yours, &c.
[E. GREY.]

(¹) [Grey MSS., Vol. 22.]
(²) [For the rest of the letter, which deals with the Bagdad Railway, *v. infra*, pp. 418–9, No. 314.]

[*ED. NOTE.*—The following extracts from the Annual Report on Germany for 1909 give a valuable summary of the Anglo-German negotiations. It was sent home by Sir E. Goschen as an enclosure in his despatch No. 184 of June 24, 1910, R. June 27 :—

14. In the meantime, the naval debates in the House of Commons had given rise to considerable feeling and controversy in Germany both in official circles and in the press. There were two

points on which public attention was concentrated. The first related to the approaches alleged in the course of the debates to have been made to Germany for a limitation of naval armaments; the second to the statements of the Prime Minister and First Lord of the Admiralty as to the number of capital ships which Germany would have ready in 1912.

15. The first point was taken up warmly by the Budget Committee of the Reichstag, and a message was sent to the Imperial Chancellor and the Secretary of State for Foreign Affairs requesting them to appear in the committee and give some explanation as to the discrepancy between the statements made in the British Parliament, and the assurances given by Admiral Tirpitz in the Budget Committee that no proposal had been made by England to Germany for a restriction of armaments. In reply to this request, Prince Bülow said that Herr von Schoen would appear in the committee at an early date and give " such information as was possible," but that he would reserve what he had to say on the subject for a statement in the Reichstag on some suitable opportunity. Prince Bülow's reply caused considerable dissatisfaction, and newspapers of all shades of opinion began to press for an authoritative ministerial statement. In order to stem the tide of inconvenient curiosity, an inspired article appeared in the " Cologne Gazette " stating that, in view of the fact that the naval question was arousing such feverish attention in Great Britain, the Imperial Government did not consider the moment suitable to make any statement on the subject. The article, however, added that as a matter of fact Great Britain had made " confidential " proposals for the limitation of armaments, in reply to which the German Government had pointed out the difficulties in the way of arrangement. The article also stated that the Imperial Government had probably called attention to the German naval programme laid down by law, and expressed their intention not to exceed the limits of that programme. " Thus interpreted," the article added, " Mr. Asquith's statements do not conflict with what actually occurred." The article concluded by expressing the hope that a state of feeling would soon arise between Germany and Great Britain which would obviate the necessity of the two countries entering into a formal arrangement for regulating the relative strength of the two navies.

16. This *communiqué* was not well received, and it was pointed out that, while it was clear that Mr. Asquith's statement " did not conflict with what actually occurred," it was equally clear that the same could not be said of the assurances given by Admiral Tirpitz. Either the latter had wilfully misled the committee, which was not likely, or he had been kept in the dark by the Chancellor and the Secretary of State for Foreign Affairs as to events which concerned his department. The Government was therefore strongly condemned for its silence and reproached for carrying out an equivocal policy which could only strengthen the suspicions already entertained in Great Britain with regard to the real object of German naval armaments.

17. A portion of the press also fastened on the sentence in the article alluding to the assurance given that Germany would not exceed the limits of her naval programme, and demanded whether and when such an assurance had been given, an assurance that was singularly ill-timed at a moment when Great Britain was undertaking enormous naval armaments avowedly directed against Germany.

18. A general survey of the independent press at that time shows that there was more dissatisfaction against the Imperial Government for having kept the country in the dark with regard to the British advances than against anything that had been said in the naval debates in the House of Commons; and the language held by several of the leading newspapers seemed to indicate that the possibility, or even the necessity, of some kind of an understanding with Great Britain was an idea which was beginning to take root in the German mind.

19. On the day following the appearance of the above-mentioned *communiqué* Baron Schoen appeared in the Budget Committee, and made, in the name of the Chancellor, a statement on the subject of the British advances to Germany. The statement, which was in reply to a resolution declaring it to be highly desirable that some response should be made by Germany to the British advances and that an answer should be given as to whether Germany could not, while adhering to her programme, come to some agreement with Great Britain, was as follows :—

" It is true that the British Government have in a general manner announced their readiness to enter into an Anglo-German understanding with regard to the scope and cost of the naval programmes; the British Government have, however, made no formal proposal to that effect. In the non-binding conversations which took place on this subject between competent German and English persons no British proposal was ever mooted which, in our opinion, could have served as a basis for official negotiations. In communications between friendly Governments it is customary to avoid making formal proposals if it appears doubtful whether they will receive favourable consideration. For this reason no doubt the British Government avoided making a formal proposal to Germany, and we have therefore not had to take up any attitude towards such a proposal. The reasons for our waiting attitude towards the idea of a general limitation of naval armaments were stated by the Chancellor in the Reichstag last year. They obviously apply equally to any agreements concluded by separate Powers. Our building programme, which is fixed by law, is exclusively regulated by our requirements of self-protection; it represents no threat to any other nation—a fact upon which we have already repeatedly laid stress."

20. Baron Schoen also expressed his satisfaction that the committee had been unanimous in expressing the hope that the agitation respecting German shipbuilding might cease and that Anglo-German relations might become more cordial. Such a result, he said, would correspond to the wishes of the entire German nation as well as to those of the Imperial Government.

21. In defending himself against the charges of ignorance or perversion of facts, Admiral Tirpitz said that, when he had denied that Great Britain had made advances with regard to limitation of armaments, he had been guided by what the Chancellor had stated to the Reichstag last year when asked why the Government had assumed a negative attitude with regard to such proposals. Prince Bülow's reply on that occasion had been to the effect that no proposals had been made, and his Excellency had added that he was sure of the assent of the Imperial naval authorities when he stated that they would not construct ships beyond the rate determined by their need for protection and legally fixed in accordance therewith.

22. In referring to the hope expressed in the committee that some agreement might be concluded between Germany and Great Britain, Admiral Tirpitz said that if an agreement between Germany and Great Britain were possible, it would be extraordinarily foolish were the Imperial Government to begin the negotiations by accepting the idea of limiting armaments in advance and by slackening the rate of their naval construction. That would not be the way to approach anything but a one-sided agreement. As regards the second point, viz., the statements made in the House of Commons relative to the number of capital ships which Germany would possess in 1912, Admiral Tirpitz said—

> "We shall not have seventeen ships in 1912, as stated by Mr. Asquith and Mr. McKenna, but only thirteen in the autumn of 1912. As a matter of fact, we are not proceeding with our shipbuilding faster than is prescribed by the law, nor faster than the grants are made; the British assumption on which the present enormous British demands are based is not correct."

23. The Secretary of State spoke to me on this subject in fairly strong language, but without much conviction. He said that the Imperial Government had been disagreeably surprised by the fact that notwithstanding the assurances given by the German Ambassador in London to the contrary, the Prime Minister and the First Lord of the Admiralty had thought fit to state, the one that Germany might have, and the other that Germany would have, seventeen "Dreadnoughts" at the end of 1912. He talked much in this strain, but admitted that the fact that certain shipbuilding firms, to whom contracts have been given, had collected stores of material and fittings before the date laid down for the commencement of the ships themselves, while it had nothing really to do with the rate of construction, might possibly have led to some confusion on that head. He himself thought that the contracts had been published too soon.

24. The Emperor also spoke strongly to the military attaché. The German press, on the contrary, did not take the matter very seriously, being occupied with abusing its own Government on the subject of the British advances.

25. To return for one moment to the controversy respecting those advances, it should be mentioned that Prince Bülow stated in the Reichstag that, though unofficial and unbinding conversations had taken place between prominent British and German statesmen on this subject, no definite proposal had ever been made from the English side which could have formed the basis of official negotiations. Prince Bülow's reply caused much dissatisfaction. It was pointed out that diplomatic negotiations were nearly always preceded by informal conversations, and that the statement that such conversations had taken place amounted to an admission that proposals for negotiations on the subject of the limitation of armaments had been made. In refusing to make these conversations a basis for negotiations, the Imperial Government had practically refused to entertain the official proposal which otherwise would have followed.

26. After reiterating the official statement that in the autumn of 1912, at the earliest, Germany would have thirteen ships of the new type, including the three armoured cruisers, Prince Bülow stated that the Imperial naval programme had not been inspired by the wish to compete with England; that the Imperial Government had nothing to hide, and that they had absolutely no intention of accelerating their naval construction beyond the rate laid down in their naval law. All reports to the contrary were false. Finally, he said the following words:—

> "In any case, the Imperial Government will continue to regard it as one of their first duties to further to the extent of their ability all tendencies towards friendship between Germany and Great Britain, and will strive to bring about such relations between the two countries as will leave no room for feelings of suspicion or mistrust on either side."

27. This phrase seemed to imply a wish that such relations should be established between the two countries as would render the possession of a powerful navy by Germany an object of desire rather than of suspicion on the part of Great Britain; in other words, that an *entente* should be made between the two countries such as would place the two fleets side by side instead of in opposition to each other in any great European or Asiatic crisis which might arise.

28. As a matter of fact this idea was put tentatively and unofficially before me, doubtless under instructions from Prince Bülow, by Herr von Kiderlen Waechter. At the conclusion of a

long conversation on the subject of the naval controversy, M. Kiderlen Waechter observed that the limitation of armaments by international arrangement was a benevolent dream which it would be impossible to realise in practice; and that, moreover, it would lead to even more suspicion and mistrust than existed under the present circumstances. Speaking quite for himself, he would say that he thought that the question of armaments could be solved in a far better fashion, namely, by bringing matters to a point where an increase of naval strength on either side would be a source of satisfaction rather than of suspicion. He then proceeded to give his ideas as to how that point could be reached. His suggestions may be summarised as follows :—

(1.) That the two countries should bind themselves to engage in no hostile action against each other for a fixed period.
(2.) That neither Power should join a coalition directed against the other.
(3.) That either Power should observe a benevolent neutrality should the other be attacked by another Power or Powers.

29. He contended that a strong navy was as great a necessity for Germany as for Great Britain, as, like the latter, Germany no longer produced sufficient wheat or foodstuffs for her own consumption. If she was attacked by France and Russia, she would have to depend upon her fleets for the safe conveyance of food to her shores. She was exactly in the same position as Great Britain in that respect. I pointed out to him that the cases were rather different, as Germany had her ally, Austria-Hungary, to the south, who could pour foodstuffs into Germany both from Hungary and the wheat-growing countries beyond. To that he replied that one must provide for all eventualities, and that everything changed with time, even alliances. He added that almost everyone in Germany desired a good understanding with Great Britain except sub-lieutenants in the army and navy and the sort of fanatics who saw in Zeppelin's balloon a means for conquering England. He saw no reason why an arrangement such as he had outlined could not be made, since (1) there were no big questions between the two countries; (2) there were no two countries whose commercial classes were in such close touch with each other; (3) as regards colonies, Germany was in too small a way to cause Great Britain any anxiety, especially as the latter possessed all the coaling stations.

30. These suggestions, coming from the confidant of Prince Bülow and an intimate friend of Herr von Holstein, were interesting, but betrayed an unflattering estimate of the perspicacity of His Majesty's Government. The object of the suggestion was palpable, namely, to pave the way for an arrangement which, by tying the hands of Great Britain and neutralising what might possibly be the deciding factor in an European conflagration, viz., the British fleet, would give to Germany a perfectly free hand on the continent. The matter therefore was allowed to drop, which was all the easier, as Herr Kiderlen had maintained throughout the conversation that he was only expressing his private ideas and opinions.

31. In the meantime, beyond rare and isolated articles in the Radical and Independent press, expatiating on the desirability of a good understanding between Great Britain and Germany, nothing occurred to point to any real desire on the part either of the Government or of the great mass of public opinion to make good relations between the two countries an integral part of the Imperial foreign policy. The attitude of the general press was indeed frankly hostile. Every untoward occurrence in the past and in the present, even the military revolt at Constantinople, was laid at England's door, and Russia and France were pitied as the unfortunate tools and victims of her Machiavellian and selfish policy, and were solemnly warned of the danger of continuing to put their trust in such a perfidious country. The arguments on which these warnings were based were that Great Britain desired to use the strength and influence of any Power she could induce to make friends with her, entirely for her own purposes, viz., the isolation of Germany, the ruin of the Triple Alliance, paramount influence at Constantinople, and the gaining over of Italy to her own side. These were put forward as the objects for which Great Britain started the last Balkan crisis, and for which she created a state of anxiety and unrest throughout Europe. In fact, it appeared to be an article of faith among German journalists that the sole object of the policy of His Majesty's Government had been to bring about a general war, and that this object had only been defeated by French reluctance, Russian impotence, and German strength.

32. Subsequently, however, to the conversation recorded above and to Prince Bülow's declarations in the Reichstag, the tone of the press changed and the leading Nationalist and Conservative newspapers dropped their hitherto hostile attitude and strongly advocated an under-standing with Great Britain. As several of these newspapers were known to be in close touch with the Imperial Chancellor and the Ministry of Foreign Affairs, it was fair to assume that their articles reflected the opinions of the directors of German policy, and were intended, by producing a friendly echo in the British press, to prepare the ground for an amicable understanding. One of the arguments employed to accustom public opinion to the idea of an understanding with England was that Germany had given such overwhelming proof of her strength in the solution of the Near Eastern crisis that there now seemed to be no necessity, on the ground of a loss of prestige, for the Imperial Government to turn a deaf ear to the wishes of Great Britain with regard to some arrangement for the limitation of naval armaments. . . . .

44. After Prince Bülow's departure, Baron Schoen spoke to me in the same sense and also abused the Navy League, calling it the "evil spirit" of Germany and saying that he was not surprised that the intemperate speeches made at its meetings caused distrust in England, while meetings of fire-eaters, at which the word "invasion" was far too freely used, bellicose articles in the press and long-winded essays from warlike professors "did the rest." Therefore, while he deplored the distrustful attitude of England, he could not regard it as altogether unnatural under the circumstances. That which troubled him was that, while he was convinced that both the rulers, the Governments, and the people of the two nations were sincerely desirous of good relations, the situation was such that a very insignificant spark might at any time cause a conflagration. This situation should not be allowed to continue, and both the new Chancellor and he were fully determined to do all in their power to clear it up. He then told me that there were more people than I imagined, both in and out of the Reichstag, who were against the construction of so many vessels of the "Dreadnought" class, and who considered that a smaller type of vessel, built in such numbers as were requisite for coast defence and for the protection of the mercantile marine, was better adapted to the needs of Germany. People, he added, were already beginning to be appalled by the cost of building "Dreadnoughts," a cost which had not been anticipated when the naval programme was first laid down; and it was by no means unlikely that when confronted next year with the expense entailed by a rigid adherence to the programme an agitation would be set on foot for the dropping of one or more of such terribly expensive vessels. If that should take place, it would no doubt have a calming effect all round and then would be the time to endeavour to come to an understanding. He told me this, he said, in order to let me know the direction in which his mind was working, and he did not at all despair that one of these days Great Britain and Germany would come to a good understanding and exchange a cordial shake of the hand. He then gave me an account of a conversation between the Emperor, the new Chancellor, and himself, during which His Imperial Majesty had held the following language:—

"Gentlemen, you must admit that I am a good-natured man. I am a grandson of Queen Victoria; I love England, admire the English, and am never so happy as when on English soil. I have stated this publicly on many occasions, and have given every assurance that I am a friend of England and wish her nothing but well; and yet I am always held up as a monster of duplicity, and the English people are taught to believe that I harbour warlike designs against them. It is enough to dishearten anyone; but I refuse to be discouraged, and shall continue to do my best to bring about friendly relations. In this I count upon your full support."

45. From this time on up till the publication of Mr. Blatchford's articles in the "Daily Mail" there was, generally speaking, considerable improvement in the relations between the two countries. Both the Chancellor and Herr von Schoen showed every desire to be conciliatory, and the tone of the press was on the whole friendly. Towards the close of the year most of the newspapers which are supposed to be in close touch with the Imperial Foreign Office published conciliatory though cautious articles on the improvement they were able to discern in the relations between Great Britain and Germany. In these articles the desirability of an understanding was strongly urged, and various reasons were brought forward to prove its possibility. Herr Dernburg's visit to London and Liverpool, to which but little importance was given in the English press, was magnified into an event of high political importance, and alluded to as a possible turning point in the international position. Still greater stress was laid on the fact that the two countries were working hand in hand with regard to matters connected with the Congo, and hints were given that an agreement on this question might be extended to a settlement of all outstanding questions in Africa, to be followed, perhaps, by a general political understanding between the two Powers.

46. To show that the Imperial Government were in sympathy with these articles I may quote a remark made by Herr von Schoen to one of my colleagues. He said that in Germany people were sick of the troubles in which their naval expenditure involved them, and that the one wish of the Imperial Government was to establish such relations with England as would allow the naval difficulty to settle itself in course of time. This remark would seem to indicate not only that the Imperial Government really desired an understanding, but that there was an important section of the public in Germany who would welcome a reduction in the rate of naval construction. . . . .

48. It may therefore be said with every semblance of truth that during the last half of the year 1909 there was a strong desire, both on the part of the Imperial Government and a not inconsiderable portion of the public, to come to an understanding with Great Britain. I feel bound, however, to state that in all the conversations which I had during that period with the leading German statesmen, and in which the subject of Anglo-German relations was touched upon, I never was left with the illusion that the good-will of Germany was to be had for nothing, or that there was to be any departure from the old German principle of *do ut des*.

49. During the last months of the year Sir Ernest Cassel's visit to Berlin aroused general interest, and it proved to be in some sort an antidote to Mr. Blatchford's articles in the "Daily Mail." These articles, and it must be added, some of the political speeches founded upon them,

caused the greatest indignation, whereas Sir Ernest Cassel's visit was made on the whole the subject of friendly remark, all the more that it was considered to indicate a desire on the part of England, or at least England's financial world, to come to an amicable agreement with Germany not only on matters such as the Bagdad Railway, which was generally understood to be the primary object of his visit, but also on larger questions such as a general understanding and an arrangement respecting naval armaments.

50. This view of the object of Sir Ernest Cassel's visit obtained general credence. Except in Pan-German organs the idea of England making friendly overtures was favourably received by the German press, but at the same time it led to a very unanimous expression of opinion that the German naval law must on no account be modified nor even form the subject of discussion.

51. The reports that Sir Ernest Cassel's visit was connected with definite English naval proposals rapidly took hold of the public mind, and in the last days of the year the rumour was current that an agreement on naval armaments, which provided that the completion of the German fleet as laid down by the naval law was not to be carried out, had been actually reached. On the heels of this rumour followed a semi-official *démenti* which stated that no such agreement had been made, that it was quite untrue that Germany contemplated any departure from her naval plans as laid down by law, and that it was extremely to be regretted that these rumours had been spread abroad, as they might give rise to an erroneous belief in England that Germany could be induced to alter her naval law. In commenting on this *démenti*, the editor of the "Frankfurter Zeitung," who was always closely in touch with Prince Bülow and the Imperial Foreign Office, wrote the following words :—

> "Any one who understands the conditions and trend of our policy must realise that the renunciation of our shipbuilding programme is quite out of the question. It is well known that the Emperor, on the occasion of his meeting with King Edward in 1908, rejected the idea, and that soon afterwards, when King Edward endeavoured to induce the Emperor Francis Joseph to act as go-between for the ripening of that idea, he met with the answer, 'Impossible!' It is also known, not only in well-informed circles, but from utterances made by Prince Bülow in the Reichstag, that an agreement respecting the rate of shipbuilding could only date from a period subsequent to the completion of our naval programme, and would consist approximately of an arrangement by which both States would inform each other of what they proposed to do with regard to naval construction in the future, and come to a friendly understanding on the subject. Thus to my certain knowledge Prince Bülow reasoned the matter out to himself. Further, his idea was that an agreement on naval construction was not to be, and could not be, the sole point of an understanding with England, but merely a part of it. The other component parts would be a general assurance of good will, and such arrangements with regard to questions of foreign and colonial policy as might in course of time suggest themselves."

52. This, judging from conversations I have had from time to time with Herr von Bethmann Hollweg and Herr von Schoen, would appear to be the present policy of the Imperial Government, and is evidently a legacy from Prince Bülow.]

CHAPTER XLVI.
THE BAGDAD RAILWAY, 1905-10.

I.—INTERNATIONAL POURPARLERS, 1905-9.

[*ED. NOTE.*—For the previous negotiations in 1903, *v. Gooch & Temperley*, Vol. II, ch. XII, pp. 174–96.(¹) The Konia–Eregli section of the Bagdad Railway was inaugurated on October 25, 1904. In a Memorandum of November 15, 1904, the British General Staff pointed out the disadvantages, political, commercial and strategic, which the control by Germany of a railway line to the Persian Gulf would entail upon Great Britain. The Committee of Imperial Defence at a meeting on April 12, 1905, recorded the conclusion " that it is important that England should have a share in the control of the extension of the Bagdad Railway to the Persian Gulf, with a view to insuring the effective neutralisation of the terminus." For the German side, *v. G.P.* XXV, I, ch. 186, XXVII, II, ch. 216; *cp. Siebert*, ch. 8.]

(¹) [The despatch from Sir N. O'Conor of April 28, 1903, printed in part in Vol. II, pp. 191–3, is reproduced below in full, since some interest attaches to the omitted passages :

Sir N. O'Conor to the Marquess of Lansdowne.

F.O. Turkey 5322.
(No. 217.)   *Constantinople*, D. *April* 28, 1903.
My Lord,   R. *May* 4, 1903.

    I am not yet aware whether the refusal of British capitalists to participate in the Bagdad Railway enterprise is definite and final, or whether the door is left open for the reconsideration of the question after the completion of the first section from Konia to Eregli.

    In any case I think it my duty to lay before Your Lordship such remarks as I have to offer after a careful consideration of the various objections raised in the Press and in Parliament against British participation in this enterprise.

    With regard to the anti-German feeling, which has to a large extent influenced the attitude of the Press and of public opinion in this matter, it is sufficient to point out that the questions involved in the construction of the Bagdad Railway affect our material interests in the regions to be traversed, and that the effect of the solution given to these questions will be felt over a long series of years. It is therefore to be regretted if too much influence is exercised by movements of opinion due to causes which are probably less permanent in their character.

    It is also to be regretted that misapprehensions have been caused by incomplete or incorrect publication of the documents in the case. The Concession for the Bagdad Railway was obtained in the first instance by the Anatolian Railway Company. It is therefore natural that, in the Convention of March 5 1903(²) embodying this concession, that Company appears as the concessionaire of all rights and privileges in question. It does not, however, remain in possession of these rights. Under Article 5 of the statutes of the Société Impériale Ottomane du Chemin de Fer de Bagdad(³) it is provided that the Anatolian Railway Company shall transfer to the new Company " the concession which has been granted to it by the Imperial Ottoman Government with all rights privileges and advantages attached thereto or resulting therefrom, and the new Company becomes owner and proprietor of the said concession and succeeds to all the rights and obligations of the concessionaire " with the exception of those specially relating to the existing line of the Anatolian Railway Co[mpany].

    The important point therefore is to examine the constitution proposed for the new company, for it is on this constitution that the nature of the control over the Konia–Bagdad–Persian-Gulf line depends.

    This constitution is defined in part by Chapter 3 of the statutes and in part by agreements made or proposed to be made between the financial groups in Germany France and England. The Company is governed by a Board of not less than eleven directors, of whom three are named by the Anatolian Railway Co[mpany]. By the agreement between the financial groups this number was to be increased to thirty, eight members being nominated by each of the three above-named groups, two by the Swiss group, one by the Austrian, and three as above by the Anatolian Railway. This distribution was intended to hold good, independently of any transfer of the shares; and, as 75 per cent. of the share capital of the company would be in the first instance in the hands of the three groups, they have the power of securing the acceptance of the nominations by the general meeting of the shareholders, which under the statutes has the right of appointing the directors; and, even if the groups should part with a portion of their holdings, they still would

(²) [Printed in *B.F.S.P.*, Vol. 102, pp. 833–48.]
(³) [*ib.*, pp. 848–55.]

retain control so long as a majority of the capital remained in their hands. If necessary, as an additional security, it would probably have been possible to obtain the acceptance of a condition that no one of the groups should part with any portion of its holding without offering it in the first instance to the other two groups.

It will be observed that the fact that the money for the construction of the line is to be raised by an issue of Government bonds, and that the holders of these bonds will not have any voice in the management of the Company, does not in any way modify the constitution of the company as described above, and does not in any way affect its international character, as is alleged in Mr. Waugh's commercial report of March 16th, a copy of which owing to my absence in England I unfortunately did not see.

The result of the constitution above described would be that any two of the groups could command an absolute majority of the Board and that the Company would be really international in the sense that it would be impossible to direct its policy and working to the benefit of any single country at the expense of the others.

Much stress has been laid on the fact that the guarantee for the construction of the whole line can only be provided by the proceeds of the increase of the customs duties, which would result from the revision of the existing treaties of commerce, and that any increase of the revenue thus produced is already assigned for the benefit of the bondholders under the decree of Moharrem.

This is true—but it is also true that if the bondholders insisted on the satisfaction of their entire claim they would receive nothing at all; for it is not to be anticipated that the Ottoman Government would consent to impose additional taxes on Ottoman consumers without any benefit to its own exchequer. Some years ago before the Bagdad railway question had come into being this fact had been recognised by the Council of the Debt and arrangements were proposed for the partition of the expected increase. It is morally certain that this principle would be accepted by the bondholders whatever the circumstances in which the revision of the treaties were carried out. Not to recognise it would be to act in a manner contrary to their own interests, and indeed might produce the danger resulting from Shylock's insistence on his pound of flesh.

Furthermore, it is evident that the restriction on the Customs duties cannot equitably or practically be maintained in permanence. It is a stipulation resulting from ancient treaties and not involving any reciprocal advantages to the Turks. The Powers deny to the Turks the right to denounce this restriction, but this denial is a limitation of sovereignty to which hardly any other country in the world submits.

It would be contrary to British traditions to refuse to a country a legitimate means of increasing its revenue, and it would be an untenable position to refuse to agree to such increase because the proceeds were to be used for Railway construction, which, whether it pays directly or not, develops the country, increases her other revenues and facilitates the maintenance of order and the defence of the empire against external aggression. The increased customs revenue would be levied to a considerable extent on British trade, but not so as to give a preference against British trade. There may at first be some diminution of the whole volume of trade, but it will be only temporary, and the opening up of the country the creation of new markets, and the increased prosperity of the inhabitants will soon compensate for this loss.

Moreover, it is not to be supposed that England or other foreign Powers will agree to an augmentation of customs dues, whether they are appropriated to the construction of the Bagdad Railway or to other purposes economically less advantageous, unless they obtain in return certain concessions which they consider beneficial to their trade and commerce and a *quid pro quo* for their consent to the increase of the Customs tariff.

It has also been represented that the railway could be worked in a manner detrimental to British commerce by means of direct or indirect advantages, of special rates, through rates rebates, or exemptions accorded to the goods of other countries or to goods arriving by particular routes. This apprehension is not well founded. Such preferences are directly prohibited by articles 24 and 25 of the Cahier des Charges of the Bagdad Railway and by corresponding provisions applicable to the Anatolian Railway. They would also be excluded by a clause of the proposed treaty of commerce; and in any case the execution of these stipulations in the spirit as well as in the letter could undoubtedly be secured by the participation of British capital and of the consequent international character of the Company.

It has been pointed out in the course of the discussions in the Press and elsewhere that so long as the Anatolian Railway from Haidar Pasha to Konia remains in German hands, the international character of the line from Konia onwards will not be a sufficient guarantee for impartial treatment; that the German Company will in fact hold the key of the door by which the through traffic must pass. This is a point of the first importance, deserving careful consideration; but an examination of the whole position will go far at any rate to dispel any anxiety on this account. In the first place the representatives of the Anatolian Railway Company have formally announced their readiness to vest the control of their line in the International Company at some future period; and there are sufficient guarantees for the carrying out of this undertaking in the fact that it would be open to the British Government, in the event of failure to carry it out to refuse the promised facilities for a port in the Persian Gulf, and to withdraw their assurance as to the conveyance of the Indian mails; and also in the fact that, when the Bagdad line has been completed throughout the greater part of its length, it would be so indispensable to the prosperity of the Anatolian line that the latter could not afford to take up a hostile or exclusive attitude. This is the more certain since Haidar Pasha does not afford the only point of access. It is evident that the Bagdad line must have an exit somewhere on the Gulf of Alexandretta, and it is also clear that by combination with the French line from Smyrna to Afioun Kerahissar or the English line from Smyrna to Dineir a competing outlet could be secured at Smyrna.

While insisting upon the extreme importance of the eventual internationalisation of the whole line from sea to sea, I would point out that the drawbacks resulting for British commerce from the existing ownership of the Anatolian line and of the harbour at Haidar Pasha are frequently exaggerated. It has often been stated and gains colour from the remarks in Mr. Vice Consul Waugh's Report that goods arriving by train at Constantinople and ferried to Haidar Pasha without breaking bulk would be specially exempted from quay dues, to which goods arriving by sea are subject. If such a provision existed, it would act unfavourably to German commerce as well as to British, since it is inconceivable that heavy goods coming from Germany should abandon cheap sea-transport for the far more costly land transport. Besides it may be assumed from the statement made in the Times of the 24th instant by Herr Gwinner or some other high official of the Bagdad Railway that no such provision does, as a matter of fact, exist.

If the railway be regarded merely in the light of an industrial speculation it is necessary to bear in mind that without a sufficient kilometric guarantee the construction is more than problematical, and that supported by a kilometric guarantee the shareholders will probably be as well or better protected from loss of their capital than in the average of such undertakings in semi-civilised countries.

No one supposes that the whole railway will pay at once. Whatever may be the final development, many years must pass before the entire line will pay, though certain sections may be remunerative from the start.

Fears have been expressed that at one moment or another either Germany or France or possibly both countries may, for political reasons, come to terms with Russia and find it in their interest to make over their share, or else to buy off her hostility by supporting her claims for Russian access to the shores of the Persian Gulf. These are contingencies, however, which might arise in any case, whether England participates or not in the construction of the Railway. Indeed an arrangement with Russia would be more urgently required and at the same time more easy of accomplishment, if England stands out than if she participates.

As regards the probability of incurring Russian hostility, it must be remembered that French financiers have certainly not engaged themselves in the scheme without the approval of their Government, and I have reason to believe that this approval was given with the knowledge and consent of their ally. Although, therefore, it cannot be expected that Russia will view with indifference any extension of foreign and specially perhaps of British influence in the region of the gulf, it does not seem likely that this enterprise is of a nature to arouse her ill-will towards England in a specially marked degree.

For the reasons given above I can hardly anticipate that it will be the policy of His Majesty's Government to oppose by all such means as are available, the construction of this railway. Such a policy would be, in fact, the exact opposite of that which has been almost invariably pursued by Great Britain, namely the policy of supporting the extension in all parts of the world of the means of communication and commercial intercourse. Our attitude will, I presume, be one of neutrality; and I anticipate that, in that case, the railway will be built, perhaps with some delay and increased difficulty, but still that it will eventually be completed. The German side of the dual partnership will certainly be the stronger, and there will be an increasing tendency for the whole of this great railway and eventually of the other railways in Asiatic Turkey to be drawn into the German orbit.

Nor must it be forgotten that the Railway concession carries with it many valuable privileges and advantages. Apart from the large orders for materials for railway construction etc., it secures extensive mining rights on each side of the line, the right of navigation of the Tigris and Euphrates during the construction of the Railway,[4]—a concession which will probably be unlimitedly extended—, a commercial outlet either at Koweit or elsewhere in the Persian Gulf, an exceptionally favourable position in the future for all enterprise connected with the irrigation of Mesopotamia. etc. Moreover, it can hardly be supposed that no effort will be made to supplant British Navigation in its privileged position in the Persian Gulf, and to take advantage of the opportunity to compete with British shipping in those waters.

It is also to be feared that the preponderance of foreign Powers in the Valley of the Tigris will react upon British influence in Western Persia in the same way as England's exclusion from a public enterprise so intimately connected with the progress and development of the country will affect her prestige and position throughout Asia Minor.

I have, &c.
N. R. O'CONOR.]

(4) [Unsigned marginal comment: " But only for the staff, workmen and materials for the line."]

No. 211.

Memorandum communicated by Board of Trade, June 23, 1905.

F.O. Turkey 5449.

The accompanying Memorandum on the Bagdad Railway,([1]) prepared in this Department by Captain Bigham, summarizes very well the main features—commercial, financial, and political—of the project, and deals with the question of British participation therein.

The available evidence indicates that the Germans are likely to persevere with the scheme and finally to accomplish it, with or without our co-operation, and that they *may* be able to do so even without the raising of Turkish customs duties from 8 to 11 per cent., in order to provide the necessary guarantee—a measure which would require the assent of the Powers. On the other hand, it would probably be difficult to find the necessary funds for the guarantee out of the tithe revenues alone, and the financial difficulty is especially acute at the present time when the Germans are about to enter on the construction of the most costly and difficult part of the railway, involving the piercing of the Taurus Mountains. If the Germans are willing to give us good terms in return for our co-operation, they are much more likely to do so now than they will be after they have overcome the greatest difficulty of construction and the railway has emerged into the plains. We should therefore consider our policy without delay.

The railway, either as a whole or as regards the section from Bagdad to the Persian Gulf (in which we are predominantly interested), is not likely to pay its way without a subsidy for many years to come, though it is impossible to forecast the results that might follow if a large investment of capital took place in irrigation works, which might restore fertility and ultimately attract population to Lower Mesopotamia.

With the kilometric guarantee for construction and working expenses provided in the Concession, the railway is likely to be a safe investment unless the cost of construction should enormously exceed the estimate. It is true that for some years the receipts added to the guarantee for working expenses will probably fall below or only barely reach the expenses of working the line, but there should be a surplus from the guarantee (of about 700*l.* per mile) for interest on the cost of construction which would amply meet any deficit.

Our aim, if any negotiations were undertaken, should be to secure the predominance of British capital and direction in the construction and administration of the section of the line from the Persian Gulf to Bagdad or possibly further, say, to Tekrit or even to Mosul. This would balance the predominantly German character of the existing Anatolian Railway as far as Konia.

Some working arrangement for pooling the general traffic over the whole line would be necessary, giving Great Britain adequate representation on the general directorate. It would be necessary to secure such a modification of the Concession as would permit of the working of the Persian Gulf section of the line as constructed, instead of waiting for the completion of the entire railway which, conceivably, might never take place, as the district between Mosul and Ourfa is exceedingly disturbed, and lawless and unexpected obstacles to railway construction might arise.

An important subsidiary question would be the control of or at least equal rights of participation in the navigation of the Tigris, the steamers on which, with the exception of a limited number of Messrs. Lynch's steamers, are a private adventure of the Sultan.

Until negotiations were opened it would be impossible to say how far the Germans would be ready to meet us with regard to these conditions, but the whole question is too serious to be allowed to drift.

([1]) [Not reproduced.]

The Defence Committee and the Foreign Office have recently been considering it from their points of view.

H.. Ll. S.

June 6, 1905.

No. 212.

The Marquess of Lansdowne to Sir F. Bertie.

F.O. Turkey 5449.
(No. 485.)
Sir, *Foreign Office, July 19, 1905.*

I mentioned to the French Ambassador to-day confidentially that reports had reached me to the effect that another attempt might be made by German financiers to obtain British support for the construction of the Bagdad Railway. It had been suggested that, should British financiers be ready to take the matter up, the Bagdad–Basrah section might be undertaken by Great Britain. The matter was one which we should not like to deal with without previous consultation with the French Government. I asked His Excellency whether I was right in supposing that French financiers were at this moment connected with the project. His Excellency said that the French group had withdrawn in consequence of our withdrawal in 1903, and were at this moment as completely unconnected with it as we were. He had also heard reports that another attempt was to be made to bring us in. The idea of allowing this country to undertake the construction of the Bagdad–Basrah section did not however seem to him a good one. Were such an arrangement to be made, it would be obvious that we had a *visée politique* in the matter. His own idea was that the concern should if possible be dealt with on a strictly international basis.

[I am, &c.
LANSDOWNE.]

No. 213.

Memorandum by Sir T. Sanderson.

F.O. Turkey 5449.
Confidential. *Foreign Office, July 28, 1905.*

Mr. Barry, director of the London Branch of the Imperial Ottoman Bank, called this afternoon and told me that the Paris branch of the Bank had again been approached by an agent of Dr. Gwinner on the subject of the Bagdad Railway. The statement made by Dr. Gwinner's agent appears to have been that the participation of British capital in the Railway had already been decided upon in principle by means of communications with Sir Nicholas O'Conor, that the construction of the Bagdad–Basra section of the line was to be assigned to the British group, that Lord Lansdowne had had a conversation with M. Cambon on the subject and that in view of the present *entente* between the two countries the French Gov[ernmen]t were ready to consent to this and to the participation of French capital, that the joint share of England and France was to be equal to that assigned to Germany and other countries—Austria-Hungary, Italy, &c.,—that Mess[rs]. Speyer and Co. of London were to be charged with the formation of the English group, and that Dr. Gwinner hoped that the Imperial Ottoman Bank at Paris would head the French group.

Mr. Barry's object in calling was to ascertain what foundation there was for all these statements and to suggest that the Ottoman Bank in London was better fitted to head the British group than Messrs. Speyer.

I thanked Mr. Barry and told him that the statement went far beyond anything that was known to me. There had been indications at Constantinople that the

Germans were again desirous of interesting British capital in the Railway, and migl
not be unwilling to leave to the British group the Bagdad–Basra section of the lin
Lord Lansdowne had told Sir N. O'Conor that he should be glad to know how fa
this was the case, and what terms the German group were likely to offer or accep
He had also mentioned the matter in a general way some days ago to M. Cambor
who was entirely without instructions and seemed rather doubtful what view woul
be taken by his Gov[ernmen]t of any special arrangement with regard to th
Bagdad–Basra section. He had not heard Mess[rs]. Speyer's name mentioned i
connection with the matter.

I told Mr. Barry that I mentioned all this to him in confidence and I should b
greatly obliged if he would let me know of any further developments.

T. H. S.

July 28, 1905.

Dr. Gwinner and his friends are apparently well provided with information, which lose
nothing in transmission to them. But the whole story suggests that the German group are ver
anxious for our support.

L.

28/7.

No. 214.

The Marquess of Lansdowne to Sir N. O'Conor.

F.O. Turkey 5449.   *Foreign Office, July* 29, 1905.
Tel. (No. 143.)   D. 10 P.M.
Manager of London Branch of Imperial Ottoman Bank informs us confidentiall
that agent of Deutsche Bank has approached their Paris office on subject of Frenc
and English participation in Bagdad Railway.(¹) The Agent appeared to consider
certain that French and British Gov[ernmen]ts would be favourable and stated tha
France and Great Britain would be offered jointly share equal to that of German
and other countries.

He mentioned Messrs. Speyer of London as the firm who would start th
formation of the English group.

This information goes beyond any facts known to us. We have had n
communications here or at Berlin with Deutsche Bank. I mentioned the subject c
British participation to French Ambassador a few days ago. He had no instruction
but seemed personally unfavourable to assignment of Bagdad–Basra section of th
line to British group.

I should be glad to hear whether you have had any communications wit
German group, and with what result.

(¹) [*cp.* immediately preceding document.]

No. 215.

Sir N. O'Conor to the Marquess of Lansdowne.

Therapia, July 31, 1905.

F.O. Turkey 5449.   D. 5·30 P.M.
Tel. (No. 110.)   R. 8 P.M.
Your telegram No. 143(¹) : Bagdad Railway.
I have reported in my private letter of 12th July purport of my conversatio
with Dr. Zander. Speaking solely for myself, I expressed hope of an eventua
understanding, and dwelt on advantage of some form of private exchange of views t

(¹) [*v.* immediately preceding document.]

ascertain how matters stood. Dr. Zander may have exaggerated or attached undue importance to what I said.

Last Friday I had a few words with M. Hugunenin [*sic*],(²) the present General-Manager of the Anatolian Railway, during which I remarked that I had always been in favour of British participation. I consider it very desirable to keep the door open without, however, in any way pledging us officially.(³)

I have had no further communication with any of the German group.

With regard to French Ambassador's view, would not the French Syrian Railway be considered as a counterpoise to a British Bagdad–Basrah section?

(²) [M. Huguenin succeeded Dr. Zander as General Manager on July 1, and Dr. Zander became Second Director of the Deutsche Bank.]

(³) [This sentence was underlined·by Lord Lansdowne.]

No. 216.

The Marquess of Lansdowne to Sir N. O'Conor.

F.O. Turkey 5449.   *Foreign Office, August 1, 1905.*
Tel. (No. 144.)   D. 3·35 P.M.

Your Tel[egram] No. 110 (of J[ul]y 31).(¹)

It is certainly desirable that door should be kept open, but in present circ[umstance]s we are particularly anxious to avoid making any overtures to the Germans.

In our view internationalization of Railway would be best solution, and if we were invited to join a project in which France, the U[nited] S[tates] and Great Britain were admitted to equal participation with Germany, we should be ready to discuss it.

(¹) [*v.* immediately preceding document.]

No. 217.

Sir G. Clarke to Foreign Office.

F.O. Turkey 5449.   *Committee of Imperial Defence, 2, Whitehall Gardens,*
My dear Sir Thomas,   *August 4, 1905.*

I venture to send you a note on the present position as regards the Baghdad Railway with proposals for an international arrangement.

I do not know whether anything is now possible; but the Germans may perhaps be more amenable than they were, as the difficulties of proceeding further are more fully realized.

           Believe me,
             Yours sincerely,
               G. S. CLARKE.

Enclosure in No. 217.

Memorandum respecting the Bagdad Railway.

The Situation on July 31,·1905, and Suggestions for an Arrangement.

1. As was expected, the Germans appear to be increasingly anxious to secure British co-operation in the Baghdad Railway. If the figures given in the financial statement of the line are correct (*vide* F[oreign] O[ffice] paper, Sect[ion] 1, July 24th, 1905), the cause of this anxiety is evident.

2. The sum available for the construction of the Konieh–Eregli section under the kilometric guarantee was 54.000,000 francs. Of this sum, 48,834,881 francs have apparently been expended on construction, and 771,637 on rolling stock; (total,

49,606,518 francs) so that but a small sum is left available to supplement the guarantee on the more difficult section of the line which must now be undertaken.

The kilometric guarantee of 11,000 francs, when capitalised at 4 per cent., is sufficient to cover the cost of construction at the rate of £17,000 per mile.

3. If it is true that £15,700 per mile has been expended on the construction of the Konieh–Eregli section, it is highly probable that the next two sections, which involve the crossing of the Taurus range, will cost nearly double that sum. Sir N. O'Conor on June 6th reported that the estimated cost of these sections was for a considerable distance at the rate of £25,600 per mile.(1) Thus for many miles there will be an expenditure of about £10,000 per mile not covered by the kilometric guarantee.

4. It is noteworthy that the cost of construction of the line, according to the official statement, has been considerably greater than has been reported from other sources.

Thus Sir N. O'Conor reported in June that only half the sum provided (54,000,000 francs) has been expended on the line (i.e., about £8,700 per mile).

He further stated that about £800,000 has been distributed among the bankers and others who participated in the scheme.

Dr. Zander (Director-General of the Anatolian Railway) is reported to have stated last spring that the cost per kilometre was less than £5,000 (about £8,000 per mile), and that the balance of 54,000,000 francs " went in expenses, including money spent on Turkish officials."

5. These figures are not necessarily inconsistent with the official financial statement, as money distributed among the bankers and others could not be shown in the accounts otherwise than as expenditure on the construction of the line.

6. As railways in India cost about £12,000 per mile, including equipment and rolling stock, it is probable that the above figures (£8,000 or £8,700 per mile) are substantially correct.

7. The point is important, for if the kilometric guarantee suffices only to cover the cost of construction of the section of the line which is the cheapest and easiest not only by reason of its physical conformation, but also on account of the favourable climate and of the ample supply of local labour, then it is clear there will be a large deficit on the more difficult sections; and the deficiency may be so great as to prevent the further extension of the line.

8. If, however, the actual expenditure on the Konieh–Eregli section amounts to only £8,000 per mile, then the guarantee at the capitalised rate of £17,000 per mile would probably suffice if the surplus on the easy sections were used to make good the deficit on the more difficult portions of the line.

9. The directors of the Baghdad Railway Company seem to be in a difficult position. If the cost of construction of the Konieh–Eregli section, as shown in the financial statement, is correct, investors will be chary of advancing money for the more difficult sections which must now be undertaken. If, on the other hand, the actual expenditure on this section is as reported by Sir N. O'Conor, the directors cannot make known the true position without publicly divulging the fact that about £800,000 of the Company's money has been irregularly divided among the bankers and others who participated in the scheme.

10. If the construction of the line is proceeded with, our object must be to secure the control of the Basra–Baghdad section.

11. It seems possible that Germany might be induced to yield that condition if we met her in other directions.

12. M. Cambon, in a recent conversation with Lord Lansdowne,(2) expressed the opinion that the French Government would not favour this proposal; but it is doubtful whether the French Government has given full consideration to the subject.

(1) [Not reproduced.]
(2) [cp. supra, p. 329, No. 212.]

13. At present Germany has complete control over the Anatolian railway; and France has a monopoly of railway construction in Syria as far south as Mezerib.

14. British control of the Basra–Baghdad section might fairly be regarded as a legitimate counterpoise to the French and German railways in Syria and Asia Minor respectively.

15. In view of our present cordial relations with the French Government, it seems probable that, if representations were made, no opposition would be offered to the proposal that we should control this section of the line, more particularly as we should undertake not to establish differential tariffs in our own favour.

16. It is clear from the former negotiations that the German Government is strongly averse from the internationalisation of the Anatolian Railway. We might without serious disadvantage consent to the Anatolian Railway remaining under German control provided that we were given control of the Basra–Baghdad section, and that the 10 per cent. participation and share in the directorate by the Anatolian railway of the Bagdad Railway previously stipulated for were withdrawn.

17. France, Germany, England and the Minor Powers might then combine to participate in the construction, on an international basis, of that part of the Baghdad Railway which lies between Konieh and Baghdad (about 900 miles), together with any branches that might be constructed between these two points, such as those to Alexandretta and Aleppo.

18. The Board of the international section might be composed in the following proportion :—

Great Britain	...	...	...	...	30 p.c.
France ...	...	...	...	...	30 p.c.
Germany	...	...	...	...	30 p.c.
Minor nations	...	...	...	...	10 p.c.

100 p.c.

Or, if there is any possibility of inducing the United States to participate, the proportion might be :—

Great Britain	...	...	...	...	22 p.c.
United States	...	...	...	...	22 p.c.
France ...	...	...	...	...	22 p.c.
Germany	...	...	...	...	22 p.c.
Minor nations	...	...	...	...	12 p.c.

100 p.c.

19. Provision would have to be made to secure to participants proportionate shares in the provision of railway matériel for the international proportion of the line. It would further be desirable that arrangements should be made to pool the receipts of the German, French, English, and International Companies, and that a mutual guarantee should be given by all the Companies that they will not establish discriminating tariffs in favour of or against the trade of individual nations.

20. Such arrangements would concede to the Germans a point which they were clearly unwilling to yield in the former negotiations; and, provided that access to Alexandretta by the international line is assured, the Germans, even if they evaded the Agreement by granting rebates on the Anatolian Railway to German traders, would not be able to injure our trade on any section of the line to Konieh, as goods arriving viâ the Mediterranean would be sent to Konieh as cheaply by Alexandretta as by Haidar Pasha.

21. An arrangement of the nature described above would require the establishment of a Clearing House charged with the duty of apportioning receipts and expenditure on through traffic. The management of the Clearing House would be in the hands of a mixed Committee of the several Boards.

22. If the entire system could be placed under *bonâ fide* international control, British interests would be adequately safeguarded; but the difficulties appear insuperable. It is extremely unlikely that the Germans would consent to internationalise the Anatolian Railway, while the French would probably object strongly to a similar arrangement in regard to the Syrian lines.

23. On the whole, the arrangement above suggested seems the most practical at the present time, and it might be desirable to sound the French Government on the subject.

24. The following is a summary of the proposals :—

(*a.*) Germany to retain control and management of the Anatolian Railway.

(*b.*) France to retain control and management of the Syrian railways.

(*c.*) Great Britain to construct, control, and manage the Baghdad Gulf section.

(*d.*) The intervening section, with branches and connections, to be internationalised.

(*e.*) The international section to be controlled by a Board on which the Great Powers are equally represented.

(*f.*) Materials for the international section to be provided by the Powers in proportion to their financial participation.

(*g.*) The Powers to undertake not to impose differential rates on the sections they severally control.

(*h.*) The receipts on the entire system to be pooled and distributed by a Clearing House managed by a Committee from the several Boards.

G. S. C.

No. 218.

Sir N. O'Conor to the Marquess of Lansdowne.

F.O. Turkey 5449.
(No. 572.)   *Therapia,* D. *August* 20, 1905.
My Lord,   R. *August* 28, 1905.

I have the honour to enclose herewith a Memorandum([1]) prepared by Mr. Mark Sykes, recording some of the phases of the negociations respecting the Bagdad Railway, which may be found convenient for reference at some future date.

My views on the general question were so fully explained in my despatch to your Lordship, No. 217 of the 28th April, 1903,([2]) that I think it unnecessary to review the subject again, or to put forward in detail the reasons that have induced me to favour the participation of England in this important enterprise.

In looking back, however, on the course of negociations, it is well to note that a suggestion made by me, as far back I think as 1899,([3]) to the effect that the construction of the Bagdad–Basra section should be intrusted to British participators, was regarded at the time as impracticable, on the ground that the opposition offered by the Germans to such a scheme would be too strong; however, in the negociations which took place in Paris in 1903 this point was virtually conceded by Mr. Gwinner, as representative of the Deutsche Bank, and I considered the concession on this point augured well for our position in future among the participators.

It has been my view that the railway will eventually be constructed, even without the participation of England, and that a project which has already assumed such definite shape, and is fraught with such immense political and commercial consequences and advantages, will not be allowed to drop easily, whatever may be our

([1]) [Not reproduced.]
([2]) [*v. supra*, pp. 325–7, *Ed. note.*]
([3]) [*cp. Gooch & Temperley*, Vol. II, p. 175, No. 202, para. 1.]

ultimate decision, though no doubt we can impede or advance its development and progress to a considerable and serious extent.

It may not be without interest to state that the Konia–Eregli section was built at a cost of £T. 700,000, and allowing £T. 200,000 for various initial expenses, there remains in the hands of the Deutsche Bank the sum of at least £T. 1,200,000 over from the Bagdad Railway Loan—first series. This surplus is being reserved for the purpose of constructing the next section of the line; which will require a capital of £T. 3,200,000. The Company will therefore be obliged to raise £T. 2,000,000 before commencing active construction.

However the surplus of the revenues assigned to the Fisheries loan and other unhypothecated revenues still at the disposal of the Turkish Government would be ample for guaranteeing this loan.

Taking these facts into consideration, it may be easily conceived that the work may be resumed at no very distant date, and I would lay stress on the fact that every section of the line constructed makes the ultimate completion of the Railway more certain, and that if the Germans overcome the difficulties of the Taurus mountains unaided, they may feel less inclined to share the fruits of their labours with others; for then they will be within reach of the rich tracts of Mesopotamia where the obstacles to construction become less serious and the prospects of success more inviting.

I have, &c.
N. R. O'CONOR.

No. 219.

Memorandum by Sir T. H. Sanderson.

(Confidential.)   *Foreign Office, October 3, 1905.*

Sir E. FitzGerald Law said that while recently at Berlin he had had a conversation with Dr. Gwinner of the Deutsche Bank in regard to the Bagdad Railway, and had been authorized to communicate the following proposals from him.

1. He was ready to give his assistance towards obtaining from the Porte the extension which the Smyrna–Aidin Railway Company desired, if we, on our side, would assist the Anatolian Railway to have the guarantee of the section of the line between Eski Shehr and Konieh put on the same footing as that of the other portions of the line.
2. He was ready also to enter into negotiations with the Smyrna–Aidin Railway Company for amalgamation of the line with the Anatolian Railway on terms acceptable to the British proprietors.
3. If Sir James Mackay and his friends were desirous of building the section of the Bagdad Railway from Bussorah to Koweit he was ready to agree that that section should be in British hands as part of a general arrangement for British participation in the undertaking. It was not in his opinion necessary that Koweit should be the Persian gulf terminus, but he was willing that it should be so, provided some arrangement were made to obviate the inconvenience of a double customs frontier, one for the Sheikh of Koweit and one for the Turkish Government.

Sir E. Law thought that this question offered no serious difficulty.

T. H. S.

Sir E. Law writes that Dr. Gwinner particularly does not wish Sir E. Cassel to be brought into the matter.

No. 220.

Question asked in the House of Commons, April 4, 1906.([1])

Mr. Rees (Montgomery Boroughs): I beg to ask the Secretary of State for Foreign Affairs whether he will make inquiries as to the progress of the Baghdad Railway scheme since the first section was completed in 1904; and whether he will communicate such information as he may obtain.

The Secretary to the Local Government Board (Mr. Runciman, Dewsbury, for Sir Edward Grey): As we are not parties to the scheme, we have no means of knowing anything, except the actual progress of the railway, of which the first section has been completed, and that is all so far. When any more progress is made we shall be kept informed.

([1]) [*Parl. Deb.*, 4th Ser., Vol. 155, p. 499.]

No. 221.

Sir Edward Grey to Sir N. O'Conor.

F.O. 371/148.
(No. 129.)
Sir,   *Foreign Office, April 6, 1906.*

I transmit to you herewith copy of a Parliamentary Question and Answer respecting the progress of the Bagdad Railway Scheme.([1])

In order that I may be in a position to reply to questions of a similar nature in future, I have to request that you will keep me informed of any details which may come to your knowledge as to the further construction of the Railway and as to the progress of the scheme in general.

[I am, &c.
EDWARD GREY.]

([1]) [*v.* immediately preceding document.]

No. 222.

Sir Edward Grey to Sir F. Bertie.

F.O. 371/148.
(No. 205.)
Sir,   *Foreign Office, April 6, 1906.*

I told M. Cambon to-day that I had lately been studying the question of the Bagdad Railway, with a view to seeing what had taken place before I came into Office and what the present situation was.

It seemed to me possible that the Railway would be made in the end anyhow, and if so it would not be desirable for us, or for France, or for Russia to oppose it; but rather that we should all consider on what terms we should be prepared to participate in it. I told M. Cambon that I spoke to him first because we should not like to do anything in the matter without France, and because the difficulty in our way was the opposition of Russia. M. Sazonow had lately spoken to me in strong opposition to the Baghdad Railway, on the ground of commercial competition with the grain-growing provinces of Russia. Very probably, he had political reasons also for his opposition, but he did not state them. I did not wish our Government at this moment to embark on any enterprise in those regions or to take any action which would be regarded as unfriendly to Russia. I assumed that this would be the same difficulty which the French would feel, and it had therefore occurred to me that if the French Government felt the time had come to reopen the question, they might wish to ask the Russian Government whether it would not be better for them to consider on what terms they could join, rather than continue to offer opposition which would not, in the long run, prevent the Railway from being made.

I suggested that the Russians might make a line which would join the Baghdad Railway eventually at such a place as Khanikin, and through it they might share in the joint commercial outlet at Koweit, or wherever else it might be.

M. Cambon told me that the Russians had already an arrangement by which the Sultan had promised them a refusal of any railways to be made in the northern provinces of Asia Minor which bordered on Russian territory, and by which they would have the control of any branch lines from those provinces to the Baghdad Railway. Therefore he was disposed to think that Russia need not continue to offer opposition to the making of the Baghdad Railway.

I said I had no knowledge of what view the Germans would take of the question, and M. Cambon said he had none either. But I told him that I had wished to mention the question to him now, because it might be that negotiations would be re-opened, and before that happened I wished the Russian Government to be prepared to reconsider the question.

[I am, &c.]
E[DWARD] G[REY].

No. 223.

Sir N. O'Conor to Sir Edward Grey.

F.O. 371/148.
(No. 249.) Confidential.   *Constantinople,* D. *April* 12, 1906.
Sir,   R. *April* 23, 1906.

Dr. Zander, the President of the Anatolian and Baghdad Railway Companies arrived here about a week ago and was good enough to call on me to-day.

In the course of our conversation—which it was understood on both sides was entirely private and unofficial—Dr. Zander said that he understood that what Great Britain wanted was the construction and working of the eastern end of the railway from Baghdad south, that he had personally no objection to this arrangement but that he could only speak in his own name and without in any way engaging his own Government of whose views on the subject he was indeed ignorant. If however such an arrangement were to be realized, there was one element in the situation which would require very careful handling, viz:—the necessity of doing nothing to excite the mistrust of the Sultan or lead him to believe that the German Syndicate was ceding to England an important part of the concession which they had obtained for themselves. It was not unknown to me how suspicious His Majesty was of British action and influence in those regions and how essential it consequently became not to arouse his susceptibilities or fears. He (Dr. Zander) believed himself that we could come to an understanding which would give us the full control of the construction and exploitation of the line once we could devise a formula which, while outwardly leaving the Germans ostensibly in the enjoyment of the concession, would give England all the rights, privileges and guarantees which she required.

The Baghdad Railway Company could wait a short time to see if it were possible to come to an understanding with England and France, but they could not stand still indefinitely, and must at no distant date go on with the construction of the line. He was thus naturally anxious to know if I could give him any indication as to the

[17590]   z

views and intentions of the present Government in regard to the general question of participation with the Germans and French.

I said that His Majesty's Government had scarcely been long enough in office to have had time to consider this question, but that no doubt it would come within their purview at no distant date, though I could not say definitely in what way or at what time. I was sure His Majesty's Government would approach the question with the most open mind and with a strong desire to come to terms with Germany if they could possibly do so on terms consistent with the commercial and other interests of the country. The question had not however been touched upon for some months and the last reference I had seen to it was in the shape of a private conversation between Mr. Gwinner and Sir Edward Law.(¹)

Dr. Zander concluded by saying that he hoped both Great Britain and France would join in the undertaking, but that if they did not come to some decision within a reasonable time it would be impossible for Germany to hold open the door indefinitely.

I can take no exception to Dr. Zander's opening remarks respecting the distrust unfortunately entertained by the Sultan of England's intentions in the neighbourhood of Baghdad and the Persian Gulf, nor do I think that he referred to the point to protect the special interests of Germany, but mentioned it simply as a factor that demands consideration.

I have already, and notably in my Despatch No. 217 of the 28th April, 1903,(²) so fully explained my views and opinions of the advantages, under conditions which would have to be carefully studied, of British participation in this great railway enterprise that I need not trouble you with any remarks on the general question which would be mainly a repetition of those which I have already made. I venture to say once more, however, that I believe the railway will probably be constructed with or without the participation of the Anglo-French groups, although obviously in the latter case in circumstances of greater difficulty. I further believe that the sand is running out and if we decide that it is in our interest to join in the construction of the Railway together with the French, without whose participation I should be reluctant to do so, I hardly think we can expect a more propitious moment for opening negotiations. It is improbable that the Germans, if they surmount the difficulties financial and other, attending the construction of the line through the Taurus range and once reach the open plain lying beyond it, will be willing to offer us acceptable terms. These difficulties now loom very large in view of the condition of Ottoman finance and the concentration in the Paris Bourse of Turkish Stock, but a perusal of the careful Memorandum lately prepared by Mr. Mark Sykes (enclosed in my despatch No. 187 of March 20)(³) will show that they may be overcome by judicious financial manipulation and by the personal influence which the German Emperor is sure to bring to bear on the Sultan.

I believe Dr. Zander to be actuated by a sincere desire to see both England and France participate in the scheme as the only means of relieving the Syndicate from a position of immediate difficulty and embarrassment while at the same time it would offer sterling advantages to the Germans from various points of view. He no doubt realizes the political and material advantages of our good-will from Baghdad down to Koweit, and is fully aware of the obstruction which may be felt should the terminal station be within the territory of the Sheikh Moubarak, with whom, he well knows we have special agreements; nor does he lose sight of the material benefit to the Railway should His Majesty's Government decide to send the British Indian Mail by this route. He knows and recognizes the importance of our interests and influence in the region of the Persian Gulf and prefers an amicable compromise to a struggle which might be fruitful of danger to both parties.

(¹) [Apparently that given on p. 335, No. 219.]
(²) [v. supra, pp. 325-7, Ed. note.]
(³) [Not reproduced.]

He also realizes the importance of the good-will of the French Government without whose support he cannot expect to obtain a quotation of any Ottoman Bonds that may be issued in payment of the construction of the railway, and he is well aware that without the co-operation of the Two Powers his labours to obtain security from the Ottoman Government for a kilometric guarantee will be immensely increased.

The advantages to Great Britain of a concession giving her the right of constructing and working the Railway from Baghdad to Koweit are distinct and palpable, but it is not so clear where French interests come in under the arrangement proposed by Dr. Zander. Evidently some compensating advantages must be found for France and the question is not one of easy solution.([4])

In view however of the fact that the extension northwards of the existing French Railway system is rapidly being pushed forward and may even be completed by the end of this summer as far as Aleppo, where a junction with a branch of the Baghdad Railway is eventually to be created, it is possible that the French will be willing to take over the construction of the line from that point to Diarbekir, Mosoul or Tekrit, which last-named place would be a favourable point for us to start from. This however is only an idea which has crossed my mind, but I noticed that it did not appear to meet with disfavour from the French Ambassador to whom I mentioned it casually as a possible arrangement. The idea was new to him, and his remarks cannot therefore be taken as representing the views which either he himself or his Government might hold when the point came to be studied in all its bearings.

Both Monsieur Constans and I were however of opinion that the moment had come when the whole question of co-operation with the Germans must be seriously examined, and in the event of a decision being taken adverse to participation, I venture to think that it behoves us to consider what our policy should be towards the Baghdad Railway as a purely German enterprise.

I have reason to believe that recently Monsieur Auboyneau, one of the Directors of the Imperial Ottoman Bank, gave the German group to understand that if the Algeciras Conference came to a satisfactory issue, the Bank would be ready to confer again about the Baghdad Railway. I learn however from Monsieur Constans that up to the present moment no overtures have been made from Berlin, but I venture to submit that in the event of an exchange of views taking place between the French and German groups, we should be prepared to define our attitude on the general question and to indicate in broad lines the conditions of our co-operation.

There can be no doubt that the Russian Government will regard with disfavour a combination by which Great Britain and France will participate in an enterprise which they have always viewed with suspicion and which, were they in a position to do so, they would oppose with all their former vigour and hostility. So far as I know however the French Government is not disposed to pay much attention to Russian susceptibilities in regard to this matter.

In this review of the situation it ought perhaps to be mentioned that no steps have been taken for the construction of the railway beyond Eregli. The Germans appear to shrink from facing alone the enormous cost of the next section across the Taurus range, and if they are unable to obtain assistance they may find themselves forced to seek another combination involving less expenditure by avoiding the mountains. Such a combination may be found by the construction of a line from Eregli, or more likely from some point West of Eregli, direct to Mersina, whence by utilizing the existing Mersina–Adana railway, in which they have recently obtained a controlling interest, the line can be continued eastwards on the route originally planned.

I have, &c.
N. R. O'CONOR.

([4]) [Marginal comment by Mr Parker: " Perhaps this might be found in control of the Syrian R[ai]lw[a]ys. A P."]

MINUTES.

Dr. Zander's conversation with Sir N. O'Conor affords a suitable opening for taking up the question again. When the French Amb[assado]r returns Sir E. Grey might approach him again and enquire the result of his former conversation on the subject.

E. G[ORST].

I will do this: meanwhile I suppose the record of my previous conversation with M. Cambon was sent to Sir N. O'Conor.([5])

E. G.

This confirms the view how vital time now is. The statement by Dr. Zander that he had no objection to the construction and working of the eastern end of the railway from Bagdad south by Great Britain, is important though only made personally. The last paragraph is not quite clear. I suppose it refers to the old alternative scheme of a route by Alexandretta. But even then the mountains have to be got through at the Cilician gates and if less expensive in one way this route would be longer and more expensive in another.

F.

It would not go through the Cilician gates. Explained to Lord Fitzmaurice.

R. P. M.
Apl. 26.
E. G.

(5) [v. supra, pp. 336-7, No. 222. This despatch was repeated to all Embassies.]

No. 224.

Sir Edward Grey to Sir F. Bertie.

F.O. 371/148.
(No. 287.)
Sir,
Foreign Office, May 29, 1906.

M. Cambon told me to-day that the understanding between the French and German groups of financiers interested in the Bagdad Railway still remained, and, if England, France, and Russia were to come to an agreement as to the terms on which they were willing to participate in the Railway, it would be easy for the French financial group to re-open the question with the Germans on the terms to which these three Powers might have agreed. He thought this would be the most convenient way of re-opening the question.

He said that there would be difficulty in making any arrangement by which the southern section should be entirely controlled by England. The placing of one section under the control of a particular Power might give rise to difficult questions respecting the control of other sections, and would not be altogether in accordance with the general character of an international undertaking. In addition to this, he was sure that the Sultan would never agree to a concession of this section being given to England alone.

I said that statements had appeared in the Press to the effect that we should stipulate for this or that condition as essential to our co-operation, but that these statements had not come from the Foreign Office. As a matter of fact, that to which we attached most importance was that the line should be really international. If this was secured by the co-operation of France, Russia, and Germany, as well as ourselves, I did not think difficulties would be raised by us with regard to the control of a particular section.

M. Cambon said the Russian Government were very much preoccupied with the Duma, but M. Nelidoff had just gone to St. Petersburg, and he was thoroughly conversant with the whole question.

[I am, &c.]
E[DWARD] G[REY].

No. 225.

Sir F. Bertie to Sir Edward Grey.

F.O. 371/148.
(No. 229.) Confidential.   *Paris,* D. *May* 31, 1906.
Sir,   R. *June* 2, 1906.

Monsieur Henry, Commercial Director at the Ministry for Foreign Affairs, came
to see me this afternoon to tell me on behalf of Monsieur Bourgeois, that His
Excellency had thought it right to speak to the German Ambassador on the subject
of the enquiries made of the Russian Government by the German Ambassador at
St. Petersburg in regard to the attitude of Russia in the question of the Bagdad
Railway.

M. Bourgeois had assured Prince Radolin that there was no intention or wish on
the part of the French Government to come to an arrangement either with Russia
or with England irrespective of Germany the holder of the concession from the
Sultan of Turkey. The French Government recognised the special position of the
Concessionnaire. Prince Radolin had not volunteered any expression of opinion on
the question in reply to Monsieur Bourgeois' assurance.

The Minister for Foreign Affairs had also, M. Henry informed me, had some
conversation with the Russian Ambassador on the subject of the Railway, from
which he gathered that the Russian Government had objections—not shared by their
Ambassador—to its construction. M. Bourgeois did not think that these objections
had much force; and from some observations made by M. Henry I conclude that
whereas the Russian Government desire to put difficulties in the way of the
construction of Railways in Turkey in order to keep the country in an undeveloped
condition, the Russian Ambassador is in favour of the projected Bagdad Railway
provided that it be connected with the Russian system.

The eventual object of the Russian Government and the Ambassador is the same
though the means of obtaining the end are different.

I have, &c.
FRANCIS BERTIE.

No. 226.

Sir Edward Grey to Sir F. Bertie.

F.O. 371/148.
(No. 306.)
Sir,   *Foreign Office, June* 8, 1906.

The French Ambassador called on the 1st instant and, under instructions from
his Government, stated that the French M[inister for] F[oreign] A[ffairs] had told
Prince Radolin on the 30th ultimo that he had heard from St. Petersburg of the
démarche made by the German Ambassador respecting the Bagdad Railway, (see
Mr. Spring-Rice's despatch No. 329 of the 24th ultimo).(¹) M. Bourgeois had added
that he wished to assure him that, since the concession was a German one, he had
no intention of taking any step in the matter, but that it was for the Germans to
take the initiative, and that the French Government or bankers would then be ready
to discuss the question with them.

[I am, &c.
EDWARD GREY.]

(¹) [*v. Gooch & Temperley*, Vol. IV, pp. 232–5, No. 218.]

No. 227.

Sir A. Nicolson to Sir Edward Grey.

St. Petersburgh, June 13, 1906.

F.O. 371/148.

Tel. (No. 115.)

D. 8·25 P.M.
R. 10·0 P.M.

Bagdad Railway.

I asked Minister for Foreign Affairs to-day whether he had thought out question of Russian participation. He said he was personally in favour of it, but that he had to gain over Minister of War and Minister of Finance to his views, and then would come question of where to find the financial means. I said banks could manage that without difficulty, but he doubted whether Russian financial houses were at present in a position to do so.

He added that he was strongly of opinion that railway should not be allowed to become a purely German enterprise.

French Ambassador informed me Minister for Foreign Affairs has already sounded a French financier, who is here for a day or two, as to the possibility of making some combination with Russian banks. My French colleague says Chief of General Staff here has no objection to Russian participation, and he appears to consider his support as of more importance than that of the Minister of War.

MINUTES.

The question of Russian participation in this venture is of primary importance and if they decline to take part our future attitude will have to be considered.

C. H.

I do not think they will decline to take part and we must give them time.

E. G.

No. 228.

Sir Edward Grey to Sir F. Lascelles.

F.O. 371/148.

(No. 160.)

Sir,

Foreign Office, June 14, 1906.

The correspondent of the "Times" at Constantinople (Mr. Braham) told me that, on his way through Berlin, he had had an interview with Dr. Zander.

Dr. Zander had told him that the Germans saw their way to construct the next two sections of the Bagdad Railway, but beyond that they were not prepared to go alone. For them to construct a railway to the Persian Gulf which might meet with the opposition of Russia and England would be too great an undertaking. They wished, therefore, for English co-operation, and recognised that, in order to have it, England must control the southern section of the line.

I observed that we did not appear to have so great an interest in seeing the line made as to encourage us to incur the hostility of Russia either, and that if this was the German view it was obvious that the participation of Russia ought to be desired. I further observed that the southern section of the line would, as at present arranged, go through a very unprofitable part of the country.

Mr. Braham said that Dr. Zander was quite aware of this, and admitted that the route to be taken by the line would have to be altered.

[I am, &c.]

E[DWARD] G[REY].

No. 229.

Sir Edward Grey to Sir A. Nicolson.

F.O. 371/148.   Foreign Office, June 15, 1906.
Tel. (No. 103.)   D. 3·10 P.M.

Your telegram No. 115.([1])

Information reaches me that the Germans are anxious to get us to make proposals([2]) about the Bagdad Railway and to commit us to demanding the exclusive control of the Southern end as a condition of our joining. This may create difficulties with Russia and would be opposed by Turkey. I also hear that the Germans are not prepared to carry the line as far as Bagdad themselves. It is therefore unnecessary to press the Russians further at present; though when they mention the subject you should maintain the view that their co-operation in a joint undertaking is desirable; that we are not opposed to the railway but do not wish to participate except on terms which are satisfactory to Russia as well as to us. The participation of France is of course also essential.

([1]) [v. supra, p. 342, No. 227.]
([2]) [The typed copy of this telegram and the paraphrase both read " the Germans are anxious to make proposals." The text given above is that of the draft in Sir Edward Grey's own hand, and the despatch to Sir F. Bertie which follows confirms this reading.]

No. 230.

Sir Edward Grey to Sir F. Bertie.

F.O. 371/148.
(No. 320.)
Sir,   Foreign Office, June 15, 1906.

I told M. Cambon to-day what the "Times" Constantinople Correspondent had told me of his conversation with Dr. Zander about the Bagdad Railway,([1]) i.e.: that the Germans were prepared to make the next two sections of the Bagdad Railway themselves, getting through the Taurus Mountains and reaching Syria, but they were not prepared to make the rest of the line without our co-operation, and they assumed the condition of our co-operation would be the control of the southern end.

I observed to M. Cambon that this assumption that we must have the exclusive control of the southern end had reached me more than once from German sources. But I had not hitherto got so far as to stipulate for or define any special conditions on our behalf. All I had had in my mind was an enterprise under international control. I did not think it was in the British interest specially to promote or encourage the construction of the Bagdad Railway, though I should not like to see a railway made to the Persian Gulf in which we did not participate. I was, therefore, not at all prepared to create friction with Russia by making special conditions in connection with the Bagdad Railway which might alienate Russian co-operation. More than one hint had been given to us that the Germans would like us to make a proposal with regard to the Bagdad Railway. I did not intend to make any proposal. My present opinion was that, if the Germans made any proposal to us, I had better point out to them that, though we were not opposed to the Bagdad Railway, we should want to see it made by international agreement, and the Germans had better consider how Russia might be brought into the enterprise.

([1]) [v. supra, p. 342, No. 228.]

M. Cambon considered the information which had been given me as very interesting, and asked if he might communicate it to his Government.

I said he might do this, provided he made it clear how the information had reached me, and that it was unofficial.

[I am, &c.]
E[DWARD] G[REY].

No. 231.

Sir A. Nicolson to Sir Edward Grey.

St. Petersburgh, June 18, 1906.

F.O. 371/148.
Tel. (No. 118.)

D. 9 P.M.
R. 10·30 P.M.

Bagdad Railway.

French Ambassador informs me that Director of Deutsche Bank has arrived at Paris to discuss matters with Ottoman Bank. He himself has had interview with Minister of Finance here, who is personally opposed to Russian participation, and I do not gather that French Ambassador succeeded in overcoming his scruples. French Ambassador will, I think, continue to press Russian Government to take part in the project, unless I tell him that our information is that Germany does not contemplate carrying line to Bagdad at present, and that I am not to press Government here. At the same time visit of German Bank Director to Paris looks as if Germany were desirous of obtaining French support.

It will take some time to overcome hesitations of Russian Government, and if I held back my French colleague, and ceased from discussing matter with Minister for Foreign Affairs, I am afraid I should cause some confusion. Perhaps in these circumstances you would like me to continue acting with my French colleague.

MINUTE.

There is no reason why Sir A. Nicolson should hold back his French colleague or cease from discussing the question with M. Isvolsky if the latter raises it. All he has to do is to avoid pressing the Russian Gov[ernmen]t to come to a decision to participate and not to hurry the matter.

Explain this to Sir A. Nicolson.

C. H.
E. G.

No. 232.

Sir Edward Grey to Sir A. Nicolson.

F.O. 371/148.
Tel. (No. 112.)

Foreign Office, June 19, 1906.

There is certainly no reason for holding back your French colleague; the French have their own interests to consider and the latest information may increase their desire to have the Bagdad railway project treated as a whole under international auspices instead of carried out piecemeal by Germany independently. I think it desirable that the Russians in their own interest should participate with us and so share in an international commercial outlet on the Persian Gulf; but I do not think it is necessary for us to press them too keenly and as you have already expressed our view to them we might wait for them to return to the subject with us. My present view is that we should not participate unless the Russians come in, but if Germany as it appears really desires our help it is as much her business as ours to overcome the Russian objections.

No. 233.

Sir A. Nicolson to Sir Edward Grey.

F.O. 371/148.
Tel. (No. 165.)

St. Petersburgh, July 25, 1906.
D. 3·20 P.M.
R. 4 P.M.

Bagdad Railway.

My telegram No. 118.(¹)

French Ambassador informs me that director of Deutsche Bank has left Paris for Berlin without having come to any arrangement with Ottoman Bank. He asserts that the line can be concluded without any foreign assistance, and is opposed to British participation as latter would be unfavourably received by the Porte.

MINUTE.

There is an element of bluff in this after an unsuccessful mission to Paris.

C. H.
E. G.

(¹) [v. supra, p. 344, No. 231.]

No. 234.

Sir N. O'Conor to Sir Edward Grey.

F.O. 317/148.
(No. 615.) Confidential.
Sir,

Therapia, D. September 4, 1906.
R. September 10, 1906.

I have received in the Confidential Print a copy of the Annual Report of the Baghdad Railway Company for the year 1905, which was forwarded in Mr. Whitehead's letter to the Foreign Office of July 10.(¹)

In view of the fact that this Railway is supposed to be a purely German undertaking one cannot, I think, help being struck by the number of French Financiers whose names appear in the list of the Board of Directors. Since 1903 another Frenchman, Monsieur Pissard, who was formerly Agent of the Creusot Works at Constantinople and has recently been appointed Director General of the Ottoman Public Debt in the room of Count d'Arnoux, has joined the Board. Monsieur Pissard is very intimate with the French Embassy here and his candidature for the vacant post of Director General of the Debt was very strongly supported by Monsieur Constans.

It will be noticed that not only are all the French Representatives of French interests in the Public Debt Directors of the Baghdad Railway Company but that the French Financiers who are at the head of the Imperial Ottoman Bank at Constantinople and of the Paris Branch of the same institution are also without exception members of the Board.

I venture to think it would be well to ascertain privately from the Imperial Ottoman Bank in London whether the inclusion of these names on the list of Directors may be construed as showing the existence of a private understanding between their syndicates and the Baghdad Railway Company.

Apart however from the question as to what significance should properly be attached to the number of Frenchmen on the Board, I think that Mr. Gwinner's recent visit to Paris, which is reported not to have been attended with any definite result, may result in forcing the Germans to the conclusion that it is only by their own unaided efforts that they will be able to attain the object of their ambitions.

(¹) [Not reproduced.]

If this comes to pass, the declaration made to me in 1903 by Dr. Gwinner (see my despatch No. 831 of December 15 of that year)(^{2}) to the effect that as far as the Anatolian Railway Company were concerned there would be no objection to an arrangement by which the construction of the Persian Gulf end of the Baghdad Railway would be given to a British Syndicate, would presumably no longer hold good, and the possibility of an eventual participation of Great Britain in the enterprise on such a basis, which was reverted to in the course of the private conversation which I had in July of last year with Dr. Zander, and has never in principle been definitely discarded by the German Group, would also disappear.

I venture to think that it is most desirable that we should very carefully consider the consequences of allowing this phase of the negotiations to drop and whether there is any other equally practical and advantageous solution of the question of participation from a British point of view.

I have, &c.

N. R. O'CONOR.

MINUTES.

A large number of the Directors are French and French capital is largely interested in the Co.

A private enquiry might be made to Lord Hillingdon in the sense of Sir N. O'Conor's suggestion.

In view of the recent decision of the Committee of Imp[eria]l Defence,(^{3}) the last paragraphs of this despatch are of great interest.

A. P.
Sept. 10/06.
E. G. L.

I think M. Cambon should be pressed to obtain the views of the Russian Gov[ernmen]t as to their intentions to participate in this enterprise, and the Russian Gov[ernmen]t might be told that, if they are unable to participate at present we must consider the propriety of doing so ourselves, suggesting at the same time that arrangements might be made to give them a share later on.

C. H.
Sept. 10.

M. Cambon might be sounded as to this when he calls. Last time I spoke to him he was in favour of waiting for the Germans to make proposals.

E. G.

Bagdad Railway.
M. Cambon told me to-day that he had heard nothing from his Gov[ernmen]t on this subject since the last time that he spoke to Sir E. Grey. I made the suggestion contained in my minute on this desp[atch] and he said that there would be no difficulty in the French Gov[ernmen]t joining with us in this proposed action and he said that he would write to his Gov[ernmen]t.

C. H.
Sept. 22.

I am glad this has been done.

E. G.

(^{2}) [v. Gooch & Temperley, Vol. II, pp. 195–6, No. 224.]
(^{3}) [Apparently the decision of July 26, 1906, in favour of British participation in the Bagdad Railway, through the placing of the section from Bagdad to the Persian Gulf under a British Manager subject to the general control of an international Board. A copy of this decision is bound in F.O. 371/148 immediately before the paper containing Sir N. O'Conor's despatch.]

No. 235.

Sir A. Nicolson to Sir Edward Grey.

St. Petersburgh, November 3, 1906.

F.O. 371/148.
Tel. (No. 288.)

D. 3·11 P.M.
R. 10·30 P.M.

Bagdad Railway.
M[inister for] F[oreign] A[ffairs] informed me that he gathered generally at Berlin that Germany could provide funds herself to carry line over the Taurus, but he doubted if she could without other assistance prolong it further.

He is in agreement that in regard to last sections at any rate line sh[ou]ld be international and that Russia sh[ou]ld discuss with us as to how we sh[ou]ld come in together.

MINUTES.

Under these circ[umstance]s the sooner the Russians begin to discuss the question the better.

E. G[ORST].

We and the Russians could come in quite easily with the French if the latter are so minded. It would be as well to discuss this with M. Cambon.

C. H.
E. G.

No. 236.

Sir Edward Grey to Sir A. Nicolson.

F.O. 371/148.   *Foreign Office, November 5, 1906.*
Tel. (No. 437.)   D. 1·55 P.M.

Your tel[egram] No. 288.(¹) It will be useful to know what the Russian proposal is for their participation in Bagdad Railway : discussion should not be indefinitely postponed.

(¹) [v. immediately preceding document.]

No. 237.

Sir A. Nicolson to Sir Edward Grey.

St. Petersburgh, November 7, 1906.

F.O. 371/148.   D. 7·53 P.M.
Tel. (No. 290.)   R. 9·45 P.M.

Bagdad Railway : Your telegram No. 437.(¹)

I asked Minister for Foreign Affairs in what manner and in what form he proposed that we should participate. He said that at present he had no definite opinion, and would have to consult his colleagues and obtain consent of Cabinet to participation. He asked whether I had any proposals. I replied that I had no specific ones, but I presumed that, as had been suggested during negotiations in 1902 between British and German financiers,(²) there would be equal division of shares with corresponding representation on Administration.

He inquired if he could have a Memorandum on that subject simply for his own information and guidance, and not as constituting proposals from us. I replied that I would ask you if I could be furnished with a Memorandum. Might I have one?(³)

I asked him how matters stood at Paris in regard to participation. He said that M. Bourgeois had told him that he considered that all four Powers should negotiate in common. France had, he understood, been holding back until Russia had agreed.

I told him that had been our position, but now question should be discussed seriously.

(¹) [v. immediately preceding document.]
(²) [cp. Gooch & Temperley, Vol. II, p. 178, No. 205]
(³) [v. infra, p. 350, No. 241.]

MINUTES.

I understood from M. Cambon some time ago that if it were eventually decided that we and the Russians were, with the French, willing to participate in this scheme their Gov[ernmen]t have means of claiming a share in the undertaking and that this would be a means for bringing us and the Russians in. This may apply merely to the financial and not to the political side of the question and be an entirely inadequate measure. It would be as well however to inform M. Cambon of the Russian adhesion to the proposal of participation and to consult him as to the best means of obtaining German assent to our taking part in it with them.

The next step is to make up our own minds as to what we really want. The proposals contained in Sir G. Clarke's mem[orandu]m of Aug[ust] 1905(4) are hardly possible to realise. Moreover they omit all mention of Russia. They would probably meet with opposition from the French Gov[ernmen]t who, I believe, are in favour of internationalisation. A compromise might be found in a proposal for the construction of sections by different countries with an International Board of Administration for the regulation of traffic, etc. By this means we might get the construction of the Bagdad section, the Russians the Kanikin branch and the French a part of the intermediate section or the linking up of the Railway with the Syrian Railways in which the French Gov[ernmen]t are deeply interested, while the whole would be internationalised and managed by an international board.

In any case the Gov[ernmen]t will have to take a definite decision as to whether we shall participate since it is possible that a Gov[ernmen]t guarantee may become necessary in order to assure that British capital will be found, and we must make up our minds as to what we are to try to obtain. As soon as this is done I would recommend the appointment of a small committee with expert advice to consider the whole question.

C. H.

I must circulate papers to the Cabinet but the Committee(5) may go into the matter first.

E. G.

(4) [v. supra, pp. 331–4, No. 217, encl.]
(5) [An inter-departmental Committee was formed on November 13, 1906, on the initiative of Sir Edward Grey " for the purpose of obtaining all possible information . . . . for submission to the Cabinet."]

No. 238.

Sir Edward Grey to Sir F. Bertie.

F.O. 371/148.
(No. 621.)
Sir,   *Foreign Office, November 8, 1906.*

I told M. Cambon to-day that M. Isvolsky was favourable to Russian participation in the Bagdad Railway, and was consulting with his colleagues, in order to get their consent. He had asked us to give him a memorandum on our views as to participation.

M. Cambon was strongly of opinion that we should wait for overtures from Germany.

I said that it would be desirable that the French Government should let the Russian Government know that that was their opinion. I proposed to say so to the Russian Government, but I thought I must also say something a little more positive to them. I would tell them that the Bagdad Railway did not concern us at its present stage, but if it was to be developed into a through line leading to the Persian Gulf it would raise a political question and should, I thought, be under the international control of the four Powers. Russia would, of course, be one of them, and might secure a direct interest in the line by arranging with the Persian Government to make a line of her own through North-West Persia to join the Bagdad Railway, by which means she would share in the international outlet on the Gulf.

[I am, &c.]
E[DWARD] G[REY].

No. 239.

Sir F. Bertie to Sir Edward Grey.

F.O. 371/148.
(No. 450.)   Confidential.   *Paris,* D. *November 15, 1906.*
Sir,   R. *November 16, 1906.*

Monsieur Pichon told me yesterday that so far as he had learnt the assurances which Monsieur Izvolsky had received at Berlin in regard to the interests which Germany considered that she had in Persia were quite satisfactory to him and were such as to make Monsieur Izvolsky confident that he will be able to come to terms with England without offence to Germany.

Monsieur Pichon understands that the question of Persia was only generally discussed by Monsieur Izvolsky when at Berlin and he does not think that the question of the Bagdad Railway was mentioned.

Monsieur Pichon confirmed to me the rumour which I have already reported to you as having been confirmed to me by Monsieur Clemenceau that the Crédit Lyonnais had been prepared to find money for the German parties who are constructing the Railway, but that the Government of Monsieur Clemenceau on coming into office had prevailed on that Financial Establishment to discontinue the negotiations.

Monsieur Clemenceau told me on the 11th instant that his impression is that the Railway might be completed without financial assistance from Paris and London. Monsieur Pichon does not feel sure that this is so. His Excellency has promised to make enquiries and to let me know the result.

                                                         I have, &c.
                                                         FRANCIS BERTIE.

No. 240.

Sir F. Bertie to Sir Edward Grey.

F.O. 371/148.
(No. 462.)   *Paris,* D. *November 21, 1906.*
Sir,   R. *November 23, 1906.*

I called on the Minister for Foreign Affairs this morning in order to enquire whether he was able to give me the information in regard to the Bagdad Railway which, as I had the honour to report to you in my despatch No. 450, Confidential, of the 15th instant([1]) His Excellency promised to endeavour to procure.

M. Pichon told me that the Minister of Finance who had made enquiries was convinced that the railway could not be completed to the Persian Gulf without the aid of the Paris and London Money Markets.

I asked His Excellency how much further forward from the present completed portion of the Railway at the foot of the Taurus Range of Mountains it could be carried by Germany with German resources only. This Monsieur Pichon was unable to say, but he undertook to make further enquiries, and to endeavour to clear up that point.

                                                         I have, &c.
                                                         FRANCIS BERTIE.

([1]) [*v.* immediately preceding document.]

No. 241.

Memorandum for communication to M. Isvolski.([1])

F.O. 371/148.
Confidential.   *Foreign Office, November 27, 1906.*

H[is] M[ajesty's] G[overnment] have had under consideration the attitude which they should adopt upon the Bagdad Railway question, in the event of the line being prolonged beyond the Taurus Mountains. They are of opinion that no step should yet be taken on their part until Germany reopens the question.([2])

They do not consider that the enterprise in its present stage is of more than commercial importance, but, if it is developed into a through line of communication between Europe and the Persian Gulf, it would raise political questions. In these circumstances it would, H[is] M[ajesty's] G[overnment] Consider, be desirable if an arrangement could be arrived at whereby Great Britain, Russia and France, as well as Germany, might have an opportunity of participating in the undertaking.

It is clear that the possibility of concluding an arrangement of this nature must depend upon the attitude taken up at Berlin in regard to this matter, but it would nevertheless be desirable that the three Governments should arrive at a preliminary understanding as to the lines on which a satisfactory settlement could be made.([3])

([1]) [Communicated by Sir A. Nicolson on December 3, 1906.]
([2]) [This sentence was added to the draft in Sir Edward Grey's own hand.]
([3]) [The original draft ended with a further paragraph : " This settlement might be based on the principle of establishing some form of joint control by the four Powers over the whole railway system, and dividing the construction of the line and its branches into sections to be undertaken by each of the four Powers respectively." This was deleted in consequence of a marginal note by Sir Edward Grey : " Omit this last for the present."]

No. 242.

Sir F. Bertie to Sir Edward Grey.

F.O. 371/148.
(No. 481.) Confidential.   *Paris, D. December 2, 1906.*
Sir,   *R. December 4, 1906.*

With reference to my despatch No. 462 confidential of the 21st ultimo,([1]) I have the honour to report that Monsieur Pichon told me this morning that, as a result of the enquiries which he had made, he had come to the conclusion that the Germans will not with only their own pecuniary resources be able to continue the Bagdad Railway through the Taurus Range of Mountains. They wish to produce the impression that they can do so, but they really depend on being able to obtain further kilometric guarantees through the 3 p.c. additional Turkish Customs Duties, to be levied with the consent of the Powers, and Monsieur Pichon said that he had instructed the French Ambassador at Constantinople to act in concert with His Majesty's Ambassador in dealing with the questions still at issue in regard to the levying of the additional duty.

I told His Excellency that I had been given to understand that the Banque des Pays Bas might be willing to assist the Germans financially. He said that the French Government would certainly oppose any such proceeding until terms in regard to the railway had been come to between the French, Russian, British and German Governments, and that he would make enquiries as to what negotiations might be going on between the Bank in question and the German parties concerned in the Railway.

I have, &c.
FRANCIS BERTIE.

([1]) [*v. supra*, p. 349, No. 240.]

No. 243.

Sir Edward Grey to Sir F. Bertie.

F.O. 371/144.
No. 722.) Secret.
Sir,   Foreign Office, December 29, 1906.

The French Ambassador called at this Office on the 14th instant and gave his own personal views on the measures adopted by the Council of the Ottoman Debt with regard to the hypothecation of certain of the surplus revenues to cover the deficits in the Macedonian budgets. . . . .(¹)

H[is] E[xcellency] subsequently read aloud two telegrams, one from the French Ambassador at Constantinople to the Minister for Foreign Affairs, and the other M. Pichon's reply thereto. In the former M. Constans expressed the opinion that the Bagdad Railway would be built whether the French and English Governments wished it or not. The French Gov[ernmen]t, acting under the advice of their Ambassador in London, were making a great mistake in supporting H[is] M[ajesty's] Gov[ernmen]t in their hostility to the German schemes which were prejudicial chiefly to British interests. Such support must necessarily be regarded by Germany as showing an unfriendly disposition ("malveillance") on the part of France towards herself and would inevitably provoke trouble between the two countries.

M. Pichon's reply to this telegram was couched in very energetic terms. In it he pointed out that French interests and French policy were deeply involved in any Bagdad Railway scheme and that none would be satisfactory unless it combined the participation of France, England, and Russia. All other schemes must therefore be resisted to the utmost. M. Pichon added that since the Anglo-French *entente* England had on several occasions acted "in a most friendly manner" towards France, and that it was the duty and policy of the French Government to meet the views of H[is] [Majesty's] Government as far as possible. On the other hand the German Gov[ernmen]t had recently done everything in their power to be disagreeable to France, and their actions and communications were the reverse of friendly.

[I am, &c.
E. GREY.]

MINUTE.(²)

The contents are very interesting. M. Constans' policy is for France to join Germany in the Bagdad railway and help her to make it to the detriment of England and Russia. He ignores the fact that we are not definitely hostile to the railway and all we ask is that France should not go in without us.

I am clear that the French *Gov[ernmen]t* have done their best for us in this matter of the Debt.

E. G.

(¹) [Here follow long details on the Turkish financial situation.]
(²) [This minute by Sir Edward Grey is attached to a minute by Sir C. Hardinge, which described the interview with M. Cambon and formed the foundation of the above despatch.]

No. 244.

Sir N. O'Conor to Sir Edward Grey.

F.O. 371/346.
(No. 113.) Confidential.   Constantinople, D. February 19, 1907.
Sir,   •   R. February 26, 1907.

I have the honour to transmit herewith copy of a very interesting confidential Memorandum,(¹) accompanied by six tables of figures, with which Mr. Block has kindly provided me, the tendency of which is to show that the present financial situation of this Empire is in such an unsatisfactory condition that the Government

(¹) [Not reproduced.]

would have absolutely no justification in pledging further revenues for new loans or for the construction of railways.

I quite agree with Mr. Block's views as to the financial and administrative disorganisation of Turkey and also that it would be to the advantage of Great Britain as well as of other countries to induce, were it possible to do so, not the Porte, as Mr. Block says,—for this would be a relatively easy matter—but the autocratic and despotic Sovereign of the Empire to adopt a sounder financial policy before embarrassing the exchequer with heavy charges for further kilometric guarantees.

I do not however think that the four Powers would be likely to agree among themselves to interfere in the internal affairs of Turkey in the direct way which would be necessary in order to attain the object in view and still less do I think that Germany would be willing to co-operate with them in a matter of which the primary object was to delay the further construction of the Baghdad Railway respecting which a definite agreement has been concluded between the Ottoman and German Governments.

The situation would, however, be altered if Germany were to agree beforehand with the three other interested Powers to internationalize the Railway, which she is not likely to do at this moment, but even then the task suggested by Mr. Block would be so difficult that probably the Powers would prefer to postpone its consideration until a change of régime here brought it more within the range of practical politics and held out some prospect that their joint endeavours to place the finances of the Empire on a more stable basis would meet with the support and good-will of Turkey herself.

I have, &c.
N. R. O'CONOR.

No. 245.

Sir Edward Grey to Sir F. Bertie.

F.O. 371/340.
(No. 120.)
Sir,   *Foreign Office, March 4, 1907.*

M. Cambon told me to-day that M. Auboyneau had been asked to go to Berlin to consult about the Bagdad Railway.

There he had met M. Zander,([1]) who had proposed to him that the French group should participate in the Bagdad Railway by linking up the Syrian lines with it. The Germans were prepared to make the next section themselves, and the idea was that the Syrian Railway should be extended to meet the extension of the Bagdad Railway, and that the whole should then form one business.

M. Auboyneau had replied that the French group could not participate unless an English group also joined in. M. Zander had said there would be considerable difficulty with public opinion in Germany about accepting the co-operation of an English group. In fact, if an English group was admitted, Germany would find herself in a minority, being in the position of 1 to 2.

M. Auboyneau had suggested that the balance might be redressed by bringing in a fourth group. But M. Zander had replied that this might make matters still worse. Unless Germany was quite sure of the fourth group, she might find herself in the position of 1 to 3.

On M. Auboyneau's return to Paris, M. Zander had followed him there: a fact which appeared to M. Cambon to show that the Germans could not find the necessary

---

([1]) [The spelling was altered to " Zinder " by Sir E. Grey, and so throughout the draft. " Zander " is retained here as it was probably spelled thus in the final despatch.]

money themselves, and were very anxious for French participation. He desired to know my opinion.

I said that Count Metternich had not mentioned the Bagdad Railway to me, but that in talking to others whom he met, and amongst them quite recently the Prime Minister, he had quoted our opposition to the Bagdad Railway as an instance of British hostility to Germany. As soon as Count Metternich returned, I proposed to tell him that I had heard of this, and to say to him that, naturally, we could not look favourably upon the creation of what might be an alternative through route to the East in the control of which we had no share. I would also tell him that, if Germany felt our opposition to the Bagdad Railway to be a political difficulty, it was for her to make proposals with regard to it, as our opposition was not irreconcilable.

I also told M. Cambon that, though the Bagdad Railway formed no part of our negotiations with Russia about Persia, yet it had appeared incidentally in the course of these negotiations, which had lately been making progress, that Russia had ceased to regard the Bagdad Railway as something to be opposed at all costs, and was willing to come to an arrangement with Germany about it. Indeed, she felt that no settlement with regard to Persia would be complete from her point of view unless she had some such arrangement.

M. Cambon said he would report to his Government that, in his opinion, the steps taken by M. Zander clearly showed a desire for co-operation, and that in the meantime the proper attitude was one of expectation and waiting. He would also report what Count Metternich's attitude had been, and what my intention was as to speaking to him.

[I am, &c.]
E. G[REY].

No. 246.

Sir Edward Grey to Sir A. Nicolson.

F.O. 371/369.
(No. 101.)
Sir,   *Foreign Office, March 7, 1907.*

Count Benckendorff came to see me to-day on his return from Russia. . . . .(¹)

We then spoke of the Bagdad Railway.

I explained that Count Metternich had complained to others, though not to me, that our attitude towards the Railway was an obstacle to good relations. I therefore intended to say to him that I thought it was not fair to make a grievance of our opposition to the Bagdad Railway, while Germany refrained from making any proposals to us with regard to it.

Count Benckendorff asked me whether we would initiate any proposal, and I said, No. I meant to confine my statement to the point that, if Germany felt the Bagdad Railway to be a political difficulty, it was for her to make a proposal.

Count Benckendorff said that M. Isvolsky's attitude was that he would prefer that the Railway should not be made. But if it was to be made, the situation must be accepted, and the best terms must be made.

I told him I thought the Railway would be made in the long run. If it became a through route from sea to sea, it was obvious that all the Powers, Russia, France, and ourselves, as well as Germany, would be affected by it, and would be concerned

(¹) [The whole despatch is printed in *Gooch & Temperley*, Vol. IV, pp. 277–9, No. 256.]

in it. If, therefore, Germany made any proposal, I would say that I thought it should include an arrangement with Russia. But I assumed that the German Government were already aware of M. Isvolsky's views. . . . .

[I am, &c.]
E. G[REY].

No. 247.

Sir Edward Grey to Sir F. Lascelles.

F.O. 371/340.
(No. 77.)
Sir,   *Foreign Office, March 8,* 1907.

I reminded Count Metternich to-day([1]) that, in conversation quite recently with the Prime Minister, and I heard with others also, he had expressed himself not altogether satisfied with the relations between Germany and England, and had instanced the Bagdad Railway and our attitude towards it as a cause.

I thought it was not fair to go on quoting the Bagdad Railway, when it was a subject on which we had not received any proposals from Germany.

Count Metternich said he did not suppose Germany would make any proposals. He could not understand why we objected to commercial enterprise on Germany's part in Asia Minor, one of the few places still left open. He had been informed by the late Government that England had no interest in the Bagdad Railway except to see that no fortified port was made on the Persian Gulf. A proposal for co-operation had afterwards been dropped, though Mr. Balfour had been strongly in favour of it. Count Metternich thought the apprehensions expressed in the House of Commons and in the press with regard to the Bagdad Railway were simply due to the suspicion and distrust of Germany.

I observed that, if the Railway became an alternative route to the Far East, going from sea to sea, it could not be a purely commercial enterprise. It must have political consequences which would affect more or less every Power interested in the region.

Count Metternich was unable to see that it could have any political aspect or strategic importance so far as we were concerned.

I maintained the opinion that the change made by so great an enterprise must be a matter of interest to neighbouring Powers.

Count Metternich finally said that he doubted whether this would be a good time for Germany to propose anything. She had now made further progress with the Railway. He did not think any proposal which it would be seemly for her to make with the strong position she now had in the matter would meet the views expressed over here; and she could never consent, after having made so much progress with the enterprise by herself, to be deprived of any part of it.

I said I was not aware that, in any quarter, deprivation had been suggested. Participation was not the same thing as deprivation.

Count Metternich went on to say that he saw our negotiations with Russia were progressing favourably.

I told him it was true they had been more active just lately. But they were concerned with the Indian Frontier, and the scope of them could not be said to affect German interests in any way. I hoped, therefore, he would understand that they were not in any way directed against Germany.

He said that, much more important than the question of the Hague Conference or anything else with regard to relations between England and Germany, was the

([1]) [*cp. G.P.* XXV, I, pp. 244–6.]

Anglo-French *Entente*, and the question of whether it would be developed in a sense adverse to Germany.

I replied that, in this, everything depended on whether the action of Germany was such as to put England and France on the defensive.

[I am, &c.

EDWARD GREY.]

MINUTE.

I told M. Cambon to-day the purport of my conversation with Count Metternich yesterday respecting the Hague Conference and the Bagdad Railway.

E. G.
9 : 3 :'07.

No. 248.

Sir Edward Grey to Sir F. Bertie.

Private.(¹)

My dear Bertie,

April 13, 1907.

. . . .(²) I see an attempt is being made to persuade the French that Germany would do a deal with them about the Bagdad Railway and Morocco.

I expect to be able to give a definite answer about the Bagdad Railway before the end of this month. We do not mean to offer it irreconcilable opposition provided participation can be arranged on terms which would safeguard our interests.

Probably the simplest plan would be that the construction and control of the Bagdad and Persian Gulf end should be our share of the business. But I shall talk to Cambon about it and tell him definitely what our views are when he returns.

Yours sincerely,

E. GREY.

(¹) [Grey MSS., Vol. 11.]
(²) [The opening paragraph of this letter refers to the Franco-Spanish negotiations about Morocco.]

No. 249.

Sir Edward Grey to Sir F. Bertie.

F.O. 371/340.
(No. 256.)

Sir,

Foreign Office, April 25, 1907.

I told M. Cambon to-day that the most essential condition for us of co-operation in the Bagdad Railway was that we should have the construction and working of the southern, or Bagdad, end to the Gulf.

If this could be satisfactorily arranged, we should be willing to participate.

[I am, &c.]

E. G[REY].

No. 250.

Memorandum communicated to M. Paul Cambon and Count Benckendorff.

F.O. 371/340.
Confidential.
(9556.)

Foreign Office, June 4, 1907.

His Majesty's Government have recently had under consideration their future attitude in regard to the Bagdad Railway question, and they consider it desirable in the first instance to communicate their views on the subject to the French and Russian Governments.

[17590]

2 A 2

The interest of Great Britain in a railway which, if completed, would form the most direct mail route to India, is so evident as to require no demonstration; while the attitude of His Majesty's Government towards any radical disturbance of the *status quo* in the Persian Gulf has been clearly enunciated in a declaration made by Lord Lansdowne on the 5th May, 1903.[1]

But apart from the political aspects of the question, the commercial position of Great Britain in the Mesopotamian delta is altogether exceptional. This position has been steadily consolidated since the foundation, upwards of two-and-a-half centuries ago, of the first English factory at Bussorah: in 1766 a British Resident was appointed at Bagdad; at Bussorah there has long been a British Consul, charged with the care of British trade, represented by 96 per cent. of the shipping coming into the port, and by the Euphrates and Tigris Steam Navigation Company, who are the principal carriers of merchandise between Bussorah and Bagdad, and who are subsidised by the Government of India for the carriage of mails. Such is now the nature of these commercial interests that the trade of Bagdad and Bussorah, valued at 2,500,000*l.* in 1903, is predominantly in the hands of British and Indian merchants.

Moreover, the annual pilgrimage of British subjects to the Shiah shrines is continually increasing, the numbers in 1905 exceeding 11,000.

In these circumstances, His Majesty's Government may justly consider, both on political and commercial grounds, that their attitude towards the Bagdad Railway should not be disregarded by the promoters of the undertaking.

They have concluded that this attitude could not be actively favourable, unless British participation in the scheme were assured and rendered permanent on equitable terms; and they are persuaded that such participation can only be arranged if Great Britain secures the construction and control of the railway from a point north of Bagdad to the Persian Gulf. They are prepared to agree, in regard to traffic rates, &c., to equality of treatment for all countries over the entire railway from sea to sea: but they could not be a party to the internationalisation of the line under a system of kilometric guarantees such as the Concession of 1903 has established. Whatever may be the financial arrangements in regard to the rest of the line, His Majesty's Government could not, so far as the British portion were concerned, accept responsibility for a system of which in principle they disapprove. If such conditions, of this nature, as might prove satisfactory could be arranged, His Majesty's Government, in order to ensure their realisation and the completion of this part of the railway, would be willing to consider the question of themselves giving a guarantee to enable the necessary British capital to be raised for that portion of the railway in regard to which their control would cover their responsibility.

His Majesty's Government are further of opinion that the predominant position of British trade would justify the concession to British contractors of such harbour works as might be required at Bagdad, Bussorah, and Koweit.

The further details of British co-operation, such as adequate representation on the international board which would regulate such matters as through traffic and equalisation of rates, would be the subject of subsequent arrangement.

His Majesty's Government fully realise that the initiation and concession of the railway have been due to German enterprise, and are quite willing to consider favourably any practical suggestion for preserving to the Company its German origin which would not impair the international character that the administration of the line should, in their opinion, assume from the moment it becomes a sea-to-sea connection, and consequently an important through route to the East.

[1] [*Parl. Deb.*, 4th *Ser.*, Vol. 121, p. 1348. For this subject, *cp. Gooch & Temperley*, Vol. IV, pp. 465–502, *passim*; an extract from Lord Lansdowne's declaration is given, *ib.*, p. 371, No. 321.]

No. 251.

Sir A. Nicolson to Sir Edward Grey.

F.O. 371/340.
(No. 329.)   St. Petersburgh, D. *June* 18, 1907.
Sir,   R. *June* 24, 1907.

M. Isvolsky mentioned to me yesterday that he had received from Count Benckendorff a copy of a memorandum([1]) setting forth the views of His Majesty's Government in respect to the Bagdad Railway. He intended to study the document carefully and might offer some observations later through the Russian Ambassador in London. He remarked that he doubted if the memorandum would be pleasing to Berlin, and it seemed to him at first sight that Great Britain had taken up an attitude somewhat in advance of that which she had hitherto assumed.

I said that I did not gather that there was any intention of communicating the memorandum to the German Government for the present at any rate, and that my Government had merely communicated their views to the French and Russian Governments for their confidential information. I was speaking without any instructions as I had simply received a copy of the memorandum without any accompanying observations.

M. Isvolsky said that he understood that His Majesty's Government did not intend to address themselves to the German Government until the latter made the first overtures and he then dropped the subject.

I have, &c.
A. NICOLSON.

MINUTE.

My conversation on the subject with Count Benckendorff will by this time have reached Sir A. Nicolson and will tell him what was said in giving it.([2])

E. G.

([1]) [See immediately preceding document.]
([2]) [This conversation is reported in Despatch No. 230 to Sir A. Nicolson of June 6, 1907. Sir Edward Grey informed Count Benckendorff that the memorandum had been drawn up merely to inform the Russian and French Governments of the British attitude to the construction of the Bagdad Railway. At the same time the British Government would be glad to learn the views of the Russian Government. He added that Germany might be glad of an opportunity to join in an agreement with Russia, France and Britain.]

No. 252.

Sir Edward Grey to Sir F. Bertie.

F.O. 371/340.
(No. 432.)
Sir,   *Foreign Office, July* 31, 1907.

I told M. Cambon to-day that I heard there were difficulties both at St. Petersburgh and at Paris about our Bagdad Railway proposal.

I had put it forward as the condition which would be satisfactory to us, in order to prove that we were not irreconcilable in our opposition to the Railway. But if the French Government thought our proposal was impossible, we should be glad to know their objections and to discuss any other suggestion which they had to make. I should like it to be clearly understood that we were not pressing anything at the moment, but that if the Bagdad Railway began to move again the matter would be discussed with us.

M. Cambon said the objections to our proposal were three :—

1. The Sultan would never give such a concession for the Bagdad end;
2. Russia would never agree to the condition we had put forward;
3. It could not be reconciled with the internationalisation of the line.

I said my idea had been that France, Germany, and ourselves should al construct and work different sections, but under an international Board. And Russi would make her own connection, and so come in under the same Board, on the sam sort of terms.

M. Cambon said Russia did not wish the railway connection from the Caucasu to the Persian Gulf, because she thought the result would be to open the way fo British and German trade, to her own disadvantage.

He understood that what I meant was that the proposal we had put forward wa a desire, and not a condition, and he would so inform his Government.

[I am, &c.]
E. G[REY].

[ED. NOTE.—The Bagdad Railway was one of the subjects discussed at Windsor i November 1907, during the visit of the Emperor William II. A memorandum drawn up in th Foreign Office early in November upon the " subjects which the German Emperor may possibl raise " contained a section on the Bagdad Railway (v. supra, pp. 91–2, No. 59). For an account of th discussions which actually occurred, v. supra, pp. 92–4, No. 60; pp. 96–100, Nos. 63–6 pp. 101–2, Nos. 68–9; pp. 104–5, No. 71. A further document giving the substance of conversation between Sir Edward Grey and Count Metternich on November 26 is printed infra p. 795, App. VIII.]

No. 253.

Sir Edward Grey to Sir A. Nicolson.

F.O. 371/538.
6101/5399/08/44.
(No. 44.) Secret.
Sir, *Foreign Office, February* 22, 1908.

Sir C. Hardinge was informed on Saturday by the Councillor of the Russia Embassy that Herr von Schön had been continually pressing M. Isvolsky to com to terms about the Bagdad Railway, and to agree to the construction of a branch lin into Persia viâ Khanikin.

M. Isvolsky had, however, absolutely refused to bind the Russian Governmen to build the branch railway, on the ground that when railway construction was opene in Persia, on the expiry of the Railway Convention, it would probably be to Russia' interest to build some other railway first, and that in any case, before agreeing t the construction of a branch of the Bagdad Railway through Persia, Germany mus recognize the Russian sphere of influence in Persia. When these terms had bee agreed to, the Russian Government would be ready to consider the question o participation in the Bagdad Railway, and would be ready to discuss the term à quatre or separately as the other Powers might decide.

[I am, &c.
E. GREY.]

No. 254.

Sir C. Hardinge to Sir A. Nicolson.

Private.(¹)
My dear Nicolson, *Foreign Office, March* 17, 1908.

. . . .(²) Your conversation with Monsieur Tcharykoff respecting future railwa schemes for Persia is very interesting. We have for some time had the same objec in view and at the present moment there is a sub-Committee of the Committee o Imperial Defence upon which both Sir E. Grey and I are sitting in which this ver question is being studied. There are many other questions in connection with Persi equally under study, on which we have not yet arrived at any definite conclusion.

(¹) [Carnock MSS.]
(²) [The part of this letter here omitted is printed in *Gooch & Temperley*, Vol. **V**, p. 236, No. 193.

I do not think that the idea of a railway from Julfa to Tehran and Kerman to be linked up with our Indian Railway would at all do at the present moment. The Government of India is far too suspicious to regard any such scheme with complacency. A few years more are required to remove prejudices which have existed for more than fifty years. My own idea is that we should suggest to the Russian Government that they should build a railway from Julfa to Tehran and from Tehran to Khoremabad, which should then be linked up with an English railway from Ahwaz which should have its port at Khor Abou Musa on the shore of the Persian Gulf. We have already a concession for a road from Ahwaz to Khoremabad which we have so far not been able to construct owing to the opposition of the tribes. The fact of our having this concession gives us a prior claim to build the railway on the same route. Such a railway would, in my opinion, have an enormous advantage. It would reduce the Baghdad Railway to a purely local railway. The Russian railways already run to Julfa. I have always heard that a permanent way has been constructed from Julfa to Kasvin which is now the actual caravan route. If this is so the construction of a railway along this route would be comparatively cheap. I think the same may be said for the prolongation of the railway, and for that which we ourselves should build in the neutral Zone. This would be the quickest and the best route for both passengers, mails and merchandise to the Persian Gulf and would completely crowd out the Baghdad Railway. A concession giving to us Khor Abou Musa as a port on the Persian Gulf would have the additional advantage of blocking the Baghdad Railway at that port. We have already taken steps to block this scheme at Koweit. This has not yet been considered, but Sir E. Grey and I are strongly in favour of it.

We also want to obtain a concession for a railway from Bunder Abbas to Shiraz with the possibility of prolonging it westwards to Ahwaz or even beyond.

These are our private views, but what I am to tell you from Sir Edward Grey is that you should encourage the discussion of future railway schemes for Persia in principle without going into any details, and you should inform Monsieur Tcharykoff that we are considering some proposals of this kind, and hope to be able in a few weeks to say something definite.

Y[ou]rs ever,
CHARLES HARDINGE.

P.S.—Since dictating the above we have had a further meeting of our Committee, at which we discussed schemes for railways in Persia, and the results of our discussion, which is still inconclusive, were in favour of a line from Mohammerah to Shiraz and thence to Ispahan to link up there with a Russian R[ailwa]y through Julfa and Tehran. The idea of through connection with India was negatived as premature. If these railways are built first the others will undoubtedly follow, but the great thing is to cut out the Bagdad R[ailwa]y in the meantime. Please regard this as private.

C. H.

No. 255.

Mr. G. Barclay to Sir Edward Grey.

F.O. 371/538.
11413/5399/08/44.
Tel. (No. 83.)

Pera, April 3, 1908.
D. 9·10 P.M.
R. 11 P.M.

I hear on private but reliable authority that the German Ambassador is pressing the Sultan for prolongation of the Bagdad Railway for three further sections, the security for the construction loan being the surplus ceded revenues, but that the Grand Vizier and Minister of Public Works have reported strongly against the scheme, in view of Turkey's present financial straits.

No. 256.

Sir Edward Grey to Mr. G. Barclay.

F.O. 371/538.
11413/5399/08/44.
Tel. (No. 66.)   *Foreign Office, April 4, 1908.*

Your tel[egram] No. 83.(¹)

It appears that this would prevent any chance of getting the Macedonian deficit paid off. Unless this deficit is paid off we should be entitled to withdraw our consent to the 3% Customs increase; it might be well to give a timely hint to the Sultan and Grand Vizier that though we do not wish to embarrass the Porte by taking such a step at this moment it would be necessary to consider it, if surplus revenues were charged for other purposes, while Macedonian deficit remained unpaid.

(¹) [*v.* immediately preceding document.]

No. 257.

Mr. G. Barclay to Sir Edward Grey.

F.O. 371/538.
12665/5399/08/44.
(No. 171.) Confidential.   *Pera,* D. *April 7, 1908.*
Sir,   R. *April 13, 1908.*

Referring to my Telegram No. 83 of the 3rd instant,(¹) in which I reported that I was informed on private but reliable authority that the German Ambassador was pressing for the prolongation of the Bagdad Railway, I now have the honour to forward herewith a copy of a Memorandum(²) which has since been furnished me by my informant. As you are aware the surplus of the ceded revenues which is looked to as security for the necessary construction loan was at the end of last year already pledged well into 1910. Since then Sir Nicholas O'Conor has reported a further charge upon it of £T. 200,000 as security for a loan made to the Government by the Anatolian Railway Company, and quite recently this charge has been increased by a further £T. 100,000. I do not know how it is proposed to clear off these charges so as to free the surplus for the purpose now in view.

A notice in the Turkish press which appeared two or three days ago to the effect that the Anatolian Railway Company (*sic*) had applied to the Minister of Public Works for the extension of the Bagdad Railway to Aleppo afforded me a favourable opportunity for delivering the hint indicated in your Telegram No. 66 of the 4th instant.(³) I conveyed the message yesterday to the Grand Vizier, who in his reply confirmed my information that he was opposed to the prolongation of the railway. As regards the Macedonian deficit His Highness said that if the proceeds of the 3% surtax came up to expectations the deficit would gradually be cleared off in the natural course. This is no doubt true if the next two or three years show

(¹) [*v. supra,* pp. 359–60, No. 255.]
(²) [Not reproduced.]
(³) [*v.* immediately preceding document.]

avourable Customs receipts, but the outlook for the current year is not promising
as the depression following the recent commercial crisis is likely to react for some
ime on the import trade.

The hint given the Grand Vizier will of course reach the Sultan, and it should
strengthen His Highness' hands in resisting the German demands.

I have, &c.

G. BARCLAY.

No. 258.

Annual Report for France for the Year 1907.

F.O. 371/456.

21042/21042/08/17.

Paris, D. April 15, 1908.

Sir,

R. *April* 18, 1908.

I have the honour to submit to you my Report for the year 1907. . . . .

Bagdad Railway.

87. The position with regard to the Bagdad Railway appears to be that the
Germans cannot find the money requisite for the completion or even any large
extension of the present line without the assistance of the Paris market, and that the
French Government will not open that market to them except on conditions which,
down to the present, the Germans refuse to accept. There have not been any
negotiations between the French and German Governments or definite ones between
the British and German Governments. The policy of the British and French Governments has been to await advances from the German Government. The financiers
have, meanwhile, been discussing the question, and it is supposed that French
capital has been passing to Germany for the railway though ostensibly intended for
other purposes.

88. On the 11th and 15th March, the French Ambassador left at the Foreign
Office proposals communicated to M. Auboyneau, of the Paris Branch of the Ottoman
Bank, by M. Zander, of the Deutsche Bank, and Dr. Gwinner, for the internationalization of the Bagdad Railway. M. Auboyneau had told these gentlemen that
the scheme would not be acceptable to the British and French Governments as it gave
preponderance to German influence. To their declaration that the German Company
would never abdicate the position which it had acquired by its own energy and on
its own initiative, M. Auboyneau had replied that further concessions were necessary
specially as regarded placing the French and English groups in a position of equality
with the German group in the Council of Administration.

89. On the 5th June you communicated to the French Ambassador a
Memorandum([1]) embodying the views of His Majesty's Government, which were that
their attitude towards the railway scheme could not be actively favourable unless
Great Britain secured the construction and control of the railway from a point north
of Bagdad to the Persian Gulf. His Majesty's Government would agree to the
equality of traffic treatment for all countries over the railway from sea to sea, but
not to the internationalization of the line under the kilometric guarantee system
of the 1903 Concession. If in other respects satisfactory terms were arranged, His
Majesty's Government might be willing to guarantee the necessary British capital
for the Persian Gulf portion of the railway to be under their control. They, moreover, considered that any harbour works required at Bagdad, Bussorah, and Koweit
should be entrusted to British contractors. Further details as to British co-operation
and representation on the Board regulating through traffic and rates to be the subject

([1]) [Dated, Foreign Office, June 4, *v. supra*, pp. 355-6, No. 250.]

of arrangement. They would also be ready to consider suggestions for preserving for the Company its German origin, whilst not impairing the international character of a sea to sea line. The Memorandum was also communicated to the Russian Ambassador. M. Cambon informed you on the 31st July([2]) that the objections to your proposals were that the Sultan would never give such a concession for the Bagdad end; that Russia would never agree to the condition which you had put forward, and that it could not be reconciled with the internationalization of the line. To your observation that your idea had been that France, Germany, and Great Britain should each construct and work different sections under one international Board, and that Russia should make her own connection with her lines on the same sort of terms, M. Cambon replied that Russia did not desire railway connection between the Caucasus and the Persian Gulf, for she thought that it would open the way for British and German trade to her own disadvantage.

90. As you thought that the question of the Bagdad Railway might be raised during the visit of the German Emperor to England in November, you instructed me on the 11th September to inform the French Government that His Majesty's Government would be glad to have their observations on your Memorandum communicated to M. Cambon on the 5th June. These observations which though frequently applied for were not forthcoming till the 26th October were to the effect that the proposals of His Majesty's Government would render impossible any Agreement between the Powers and any combination between financial groups in the absence of which the execution of the enterprise would appear to be incapable of realization for many years to come. In the opinion of the French Government the means best suited for bringing into harmony all the rights and interests involved would be to endeavour to find a formula of internationalization. Such an attempt had been made in 1902 and might be renewed as soon as the Governments concerned were favourably disposed for the discussion of the question. M. Pichon's note concluded as follows :—

"Le Gouvernement Français, qui reconnaît volontiers l'importance des intérêts que possède l'Empire Britannique dans cette partie de l'Empire Ottoman, ainsi que dans le Golfe Persique, et qui se propose de faire valoir ceux qu'il possède lui-même sur toute la ligne considérée soit dans son ensemble, soit dans certaines de ses parties, particulièrement dans celle où aboutit la ligne Française du Chemin de Fer de Syrie, se montrera toujours très disposé à s'entendre à ce sujet avec le Gouvernement Britannique et à rechercher avec lui une formule susceptible d'amener l'accord entre les Gouvernements intéressés à la réalisation de cette entreprise."

In my despatch No. 518, Secret, of the 29th October, 1907,([3]) I gave my reasons for thinking that M. Pichon's note might not be the considered judgment of the French Government, and I recommended that they should be informed that, in view of the paramount interests of England and her Indian Empire involved in the establishment of a sea-to-sea railway terminating on the shore of the Persian Gulf, His Majesty's Government feel it quite impossible for them to concur in the views expressed in the Memorandum communicated to me by M. Pichon, which they trust are not the definitive opinions of the French Government in regard to the weighty arguments advanced by His Majesty's Government in support of the position which they claim to occupy in respect to the railway. . . . .([4])

([2]) [v. supra, pp. 357–8, No. 252.]
([3]) [Not reproduced. The reasons suggested were that the note had been compiled in haste and that probably M. Pichon had not had time to consider it himself.]
([4]) [Paragraphs 91–2 merely summarize the German Emperor's visit to England which is more fully described elsewhere, v. supra, pp. 91–107, Nos. 59–74.]

No. 259.

Mr. G. Barclay to Sir Edward Grey.

.O. 371/538.
7281/5399/08/44.
el. (No. 110.)

Pera, May 19, 1908.
D. 7·50 P.M.
R. 8 P.M.

In view of revival of rumours respecting the extension of the Bagdad Railway, have taken the opportunity to remind the Grand Vizier of the communication which I made to him on 6th April, as instructed in your telegram No. 66.(¹)

His Highness' opposition has evidently been overruled, as I found his tone ntirely changed since my despatches No. 171(²) and 187.(³) He was very reticent, ut, while assuring me that the Macedonian indebtedness would be paid off, left me in ittle doubt that the surplus of ceded revenues was about to be, if it had not already een, pledged for the extension of the line.

MINUTES.

This is a most cynical proceeding on the part of the German Gov[ernmen]t and deserves howing up in Parliament, quite as much as the Austrian Railway scheme.(⁴)

There is a large debt of over £300,000 to be cleared off on the Macedonian Budget, the owers are now considering a scheme of reforms which will undoubtedly lead to greater civil xpenditure whatever may be said to the contrary; the outlook for the present year of Customs eceipts is "not favourable" according to Mr. Barclay, and the Germans choose this moment or hypothecating about the only possible remaining security on which the Porte can raise money.

As soon as a Note is agreed upon, the question of the Macedonian deficit must be raised nd we should then make it clear that, unless the deficit is paid off we shall withdraw our consent o the 3% and that we shall take the same course if any difficulties are made by the Porte bout the passing of the Budget—we might telegraph this to Mr. Barclay.

The news quite justifies our proposal, about which Mr. Barclay is doubtful, that the civil equirements shall be the first call on the Budget, as it will be more difficult in future for the 'orte to find money to make up deficits.

In regard to the Bagdad Railway, the situation has been modified by the decision of the ersian Committee to approach Russia with a view to the construction of an Anglo-Russian Line hrough Persia.

Sir C. Hardinge will doubtless discuss the whole question with M. Isvolsky and lay stress n the advisability of our early decision.

L. M.

The report has now been confirmed by a later tel[egram] from Mr. Barclay.(⁵)

I think Mr. Barclay might be instr[ucte]d to mention to the Grand Vizier the report which e has heard and to ask if it is true. If the reply is in the affirmative he should express the urprise of H[is] M[ajesty's] G[overnment] that the Porte should devote its resources to such bjects while a heavy deficit on the Macedonian. budget remains unpaid. He should at the ame time state that unless equilibrium is re-established in the Macedonian budget within the ear future it will be impossible for H[is] M[ajesty's] G[overnment] to allow British trade to ontinue to pay the additional 3% import duties so long as the conditions accepted by the Porte re not observed.

It would also be well if Sir E. Grey would speak to M. Cambon of the proposal to continue he Bagdad R[ailwa]y for a further extension. If the French Gov[ernmen]t maintain their olicy of the past it is not unlikely that the Turks will be unable to raise the requisite loan to pay he kilometric guarantee.

There is absolutely no doubt that the only means of bringing the Germans to reason is y agreeing at once with the Russian Gov[ernmen]t to press for a concession for a line in 'ersia from Julfa to Tehran and Mohammerah. When the Germans realise that we mean business hey will quickly change their attitude.

C. H.

(¹) [v. *supra*, p. 360, No. 256.]
(²) [v. *supra*, pp. 360–1, No. 257.]
(³) [Not reproduced. It enclosed a table shewing the rate at which the floating charges n the surplus of the ceded revenues were to be cleared off, and stated that the Grand Vizier as opposed to the hypothecation of the surplus of the ceded revenues for the Bagdad Railway.]
(⁴) [v. *Gooch & Temperley*, Vol. V, ch. XXXIX, pp. 321–55, *passim*.]
(⁵) [v. immediately succeeding document.]

We must be careful to base anything we say on the actual conditions stipulated for in the 3%. Mr. Barclay should draw the Grand Vizier's attention to these and point out that we are getting anxious about some of them and that if the Turkish Gov[ernmen]t has difficulty in fulfilling them and at the same time is depriving itself of the means of doing so by pledging its resources for other purposes we shall have to withdraw our consent.

E. G.

On the general question of the Bagdad railway the last paragraph of Sir C. Hardinge's minute gives the solution.

[E. G.]

No. 260.

Mr. G. Barclay to Sir Edward Grey.

F.O. 371/538.
17340/5399/08/44.
Tel. (No. 111.)

Pera, May 20, 1908.
D. 11 A.M.
R. 11 A.M.

(Bagdad Railway.)   My immediately preceding telegram.([1])

I learn from a private but reliable source that at Sunday's Council of Ministers a Mazbata was sent to the Palace in favour of continuing the Bagdad Railway as far as Halif junction for Mardin 840 kilometres.   Security is the surplus of the ceded revenues.

([1]) [v. immediately preceding document.]

No. 261.

Mr. G. Barclay to Sir Edward Grey.

F.O. 371/538.
17816/5399/08/44.
(No. 271.)
Sir,

Pera, D. May 20, 1908.
R. May 25, 1908.

With reference to my two Telegrams Nos. 110 and 111 of yesterday([1]) respecting the Bagdad Railway, I have the honour to report that the Grand Vizier's assurances yesterday as to the payment of the arrears in the three Vilayets were of the most positive kind, His Highness declaring that the debt would be paid *argent comptant.*

It may be that this confident assurance is based on expectations of accommodation from Paris now that the Heraklea question is settled, but it seems more probable that it points to a financial arrangement with Germany which would no doubt, besides supplying the money required to pay off the arrears in Macedonia, enable the Turkish Government to clear off the temporary charges on the surplus of the ceded revenues which, as you are aware, would not in the ordinary course be paid off before 1911

The favourable turn in the German negotiations is doubtless due to the pressure of the German Emperor when he received Turkhan Pasha's Mission sent by the Sultan to greet His Majesty on the occasion of his visit to Corfu.   I cannot otherwise account for the Grand Vizier's apparent change of attitude noticed in my telegram No. 110 of yesterday.

I have, &c.
G. BARCLAY.

MINUTE.

If the Germans pay off the Macedonian deficit we need not complain.

L. M.

([1]) [v. supra, pp. 363–4, Nos. 259–60.]

No. 262.

Sir Edward Grey to Mr. G. Barclay.

F.O. 371/538.
17281/5399/08/44.
Tel. (No. 80.)

Foreign Office, May 21, 1908.
D. 6·30 P.M.

Y[ou]r tel[egram]s Nos. 110 and 111.([1]) (Bagdad Railway.)

The Porte have an undoubted right to dispose of their financial resources in such manner as they think best, except in so far as they are bound by International engagements, but the hypothecation of the surplus of the ceded revenues for the extension of the Bagdad Railway Line seems to H[is] M[ajesty's] G[overnment] to be a proceeding hard to justify in the light of the financial situation.

Although this source of revenue was not specially pledged to cover possible deficits in the Macedonian Budget, H[is] M[ajesty's] G[overnment] cannot but view with apprehension the assumption of further liabilities by the Porte at the present moment.

You should take an opportunity of reminding the Grand Vizier of the Porte's engagements under Article XII([2]) of the arrangement with the Ottoman Bank : to [*sic*] the delay in fulfilment of their pledge to spend £100,000 on the improvement of the Custom House and to the large outstanding deficit on the Macedonian Budget and you should remind him that H[is] M[ajesty's] G[overnment] only consented to the increase of the duties on condition of the Porte's continuing to fulfil the engagements which they have undertaken.

([1]) [*v. supra*, pp. 363–4, Nos. 259–60.]
([2]) [Marginal minute added to the draft by Mr. Mallet : " *i.e.*, to make up deficits."]

No. 263.

Sir Edward Grey to Sir F. Bertie.

F.O. 371/538.
17281/5399/08/44.
(No. 220A.) Secret.
Sir,

Foreign Office, May 21, 1908.

I told M. Cambon to-day that a report had reached Mr. Barclay([1]) at Constantinople that the Germans had made an arrangement with the Turks to secure the surplus of the ceded Revenues, as soon as they were free in 1910, for an extension of the Bagdad Railway. This would lead to further developments, and I told M. Cambon that I was anxious to act with the French.

M. Cambon suggested that the report might not be true.

I told him that Mr. Barclay had spoken to the Grand Vizier about it when he first heard it, and had pointed out that if Turkey pledged her revenues in such a way as to prevent her from fulfilling the conditions of the 3% increase we might have to raise the question of withdrawing our consent to the increase. The Grand Vizier had, at first, been satisfactory in his reply ; but when approached more recently he had given the impression that an arrangement with Germany was either concluded or on the point of being sanctioned.

I also told M. Cambon that, now the Heraclea question was settled, I hoped the French Ambassador would be instructed to support the Quays Company, who had been waiting for some time for an Iradé to settle a matter in which they were interested. Mr. Barclay informed us that there was a hostile disposition towards

([1]) [*v. supra*, p. 364, No. 260.]

the Company on the part of the Turks, and that it would be necessary for us and France sooner or later to make it clear to the Turks that they must not obstruct the affairs of the Company.

M. Cambon said he would ask his Government to send instructions in this sense.

[I am, &c.]

E. G[REY].

No. 264.

Mr. G. Barclay to Sir Edward Grey.

F.O. 371/538.
17850/5399/08/44.
Tel. (No. 114.)

Pera, May 23, 1908.
D. 4·30 P.M.
R. 7 P.M.

My Tel[egram] No. 111 (of May 20).([1])

Iradé sanctioning the extension of Bagdad Railway to Halif was issued last night. For the construction and working kilometric guarantees, surplus of ceded revenues, supplemented by surplus of tithes assigned for the Anatolian Railway, are to be hypothecated from 1913.

It is not quite clear why the hypothecation is only to date from 1913 as the temporary charges on the surplus of ceded revenues should be cleared off by 1911.

([1]) [*v. supra*, p. 364, No. 260.]

No. 265.

Memorandum communicated to M. Pichon, May 27, 1908.

F.O. 371/538.
17606/5399/08/44.

D'Après les renseignements parvenus au Gouvernement de Sa Majesté Britannique, S[a] M[ajesté] le Sultan aurait autorisé par iradé impérial le prolongement du Chemin de fer de Bagdad jusqu'à Halif, situé à 840 kilomètres au delà de Bourgourlou, et l'affectation à ce but du surplus des revenus cédés et de l'excédant des revenus appropriés au Chemin de Fer d'Anatolie.([1])

Il s'agirait donc dès à présent pour la Compagnie de Bagdad de réaliser, au moyen d'un emprunt, la somme requise.

Sir E. Grey, s'inspirant de l'accord intervenu entre les Gouvernements de France de Russie et de la Grande Bretagne de ne pas soutenir cette entreprise sans entente préalable, prie instamment M. Pichon de vouloir bien faire les démarches nécessaires pour que cet emprunt ne soit pas coté à la Bourse de Paris.

En attirant l'attention bienveillante de M. Pichon sur cette affaire, Sir E. Grey croit utile de signaler tout spécialement à S[on] E[xcellence] les observations faites à ce sujet par M. Henry à Sir F. Bertie au mois de Décembre 1906, ainsi que l'attitude du Gouvernement de Sa Majesté lors de la visite de l'Empereur d'Allemagne en Novembre passé.

([1]) [The Convention authorizing this extension was signed on June 2, 1908. It is printed in *B.F.S.P.*, Vol. 102, pp. 884–6.]

No. 266.

Memorandum respecting the Bagdad Railway.

.O. 371/538.
3503/5399/08/44.   *Foreign Office, July 3, 1908.*

On the occasion of the German Emperor's visit to Windsor last November the
subject of the Bagdad Railway came under discussion

Mr. Haldane, who discussed the subject with His Majesty at two separate
audiences, handed to His Majesty a memorandum of a private conversation with
Sir E. Grey([1]) intimating that H[is] M[ajesty's] G[overnment] could not discuss the
question with Germany alone, but only together with France and Russia, whose
interests were also involved.

The Emperor at first expressed doubt as to whether discussion *à quatre* was
practicable; but, after learning from his Foreign Secretary that certain *pourparlers*
with Russia had already taken place, he modified this view and, in the second
interview with Mr. Haldane which was in the early morning of November 15th, he
stated that he did not anticipate any difficulty. At this interview Herr von Schoen
and Count Metternich were both present.

As a result, after a long discussion, the Emperor said that he cordially concurred
in the memorandum which had been handed to him as a basis on which to proceed;
that the understanding was complete; and that he would like to get on as quickly
as possible; he was very hopeful that good business would come to all the four Powers
concerned; and he would ask Herr von Schoen to proceed at once to London to
take the initiative by making a proposal from Germany.

By the end of this interview Count Metternich's attitude, which had at first
been critical, had become so greatly modified that he observed that there should be
no difficulty about a discussion *à quatre*, and it was both legitimate and natural that
H[is] M[ajesty's] G[overnment] should wish to proceed in full consultation with
France and Russia.([2])

On November 15th Herr von Schoen called at the Foreign Office and saw
Sir E. Grey.([3]) He expressed great satisfaction at the prospect of now coming to an
agreement with H[is] M[ajesty's] G[overnment] about the Bagdad Railway, and
recognised their desire to have a gate at the Persian Gulf end. He recognised that
the memorandum communicated by Mr. Haldane formed a practicable basis for
discussion.

Sir E. Grey assumed that H[is] M[ajesty's] G[overnment] should wait till
they heard from the German Government. Herr von Schoen said he must consult
M. Isvolsky to see whether full discussion between the four Powers might not be
begun without further carrying discussion with Russia a stage further.

On June 25th Count Metternich called at the Foreign Office([4]) and, in the course
of conversation with Sir C. Hardinge, stated that his Government had renounced
the idea of summoning a Conference *à quatre* at Berlin. The Ambassador himself
had strongly opposed such an arrangement, and he had not at all approved of what
had taken place at Windsor, on the ground that such a Conference as that proposed
was foredoomed to failure and would only serve to accentuate the difference between
Germany and the three other Powers. It was therefore no longer proposed to have
such a Conference, but Germany would always be ready to discuss with H[is]
M[ajesty's] G[overnment] the question of a terminus on the Persian Gulf.

Foreign Office, July 3rd, 1908.

([1]) [*v. supra*, pp. 95–6, No. 62.]
([2]) [For this interview, *cp. supra*, pp. 96–8, No. 63.]
([3]) [*v. supra*, p. 98, No. 64.]
([4]) [*v. infra*, p. 368, *Ed. note*, and No. 267.]

[*ED. NOTE.*—The following despatch was based upon a minute drawn up by Sir C
Hardinge on June 25, 1908, after his conversation of that date with Count Metternich
Sir Edward Grey added the following note at the end of Sir C. Hardinge's minute:

This would mean a quarrel with Russia: and if we bargain alone we shall not ge
good terms.(¹) The Germans have now arranged for some further sections of the railway t
be built; these will take some years and for the present I can see nothing for it, but to ge
as many levers into our hand as possible with which to bring pressure to bear later on
The renewal of the 3% increase of Customs will be one lever a few years hence.

E. G.]

(¹) [Marginal comment by Mr. Asquith: "I agree. H. H. A."]

No. 267.

Sir Edward Grey to Count de Salis.(¹)

F.O. 371/538.
22501/5399/08/44.
(No. 176.) Secret.
Sir,
Foreign Office, July 13, 1908.

The German Ambassador called at the Foreign Office on the 25th ultimo and
in the course of a conversation with Sir C. Hardinge on Anglo-German relations
he quoted the Bagdad Railway as one of the questions open for settlement in which
a friendly attitude might be shown by H[is] M[ajesty's] G[overnment].

Sir C. Hardinge replied that after the friendly discussions which had taken place
last autumn both at Windsor and in London,(²) H[is] M[ajesty's] G[overnment]
were waiting for the initiative of the German Gov[ernmen]t, since it had then been
decided by Herr von Schoen, apparently with the Emperor's approval, that, after
certain discussions with the Russian Gov[ernmen]t had been concluded,
"*Conférence à quatre*" should be summoned at Berlin, when a scheme of co-opera
tion should be discussed; for this step H[is] M[ajesty's] G[overnment] were still
anxiously waiting.

Count Metternich said that his Gov[ernmen]t had renounced the idea of
summoning such a Conference, and, in reply to a further enquiry, he said that he
himself had strongly opposed any such arrangement, that he had not at all approved
what had taken place at Windsor, and that he had given as his reason that such a
Conference was foredoomed to failure and would only serve to accentuate the
difference between Germany and the three other Powers, since Germany would alway
be in a minority of one to three. It was, therefore, no longer proposed to have such
a Conference but Germany would always be ready to discuss with H[is] M[ajesty's]
G[overnment] the question of a terminus on the Persian Gulf.

[I am, &c.
E. GREY.]

MINUTES.(³)

Please see annexed Memorandum,(⁴) which I have had prepared.

I think that H[is] M[ajesty's] G[overnment] should realize what has happened, in cas
we are accused of an uncompromising stiffness about the Bagdad Railway. Sir F. Lascelle
is one of those who cannot understand our attitude he thinks that the Germans are quit
right not to approach us and that it is for us to go to them.

I told him of what had passed in November of which he professed utter ignorance but it di
not seem to modify his opinion.(⁵)

(¹) [For Count Metternich's detailed report of this conversation, *v. G.P.* XXIV, pp. 81–7
and especially pp. 83–4.]
(²) [*v. supra,* pp. 91–107, Nos. 59–74, and *infra,* p. 795, App. VIII.]
(³) [These minutes were attached originally to the minute by Sir C. Hardinge which formed
the basis for the despatch.]
(⁴) [*v. supra,* p. 367, No. 266.]
(⁵) [Marginal comment by Sir C. Hardinge: "He was staying at Windsor at the time!"]

There are probably members of the Cabinet who hold the same view and I would suggest that this Memo[randum] should be sent round because it is a first rate instance of the difficulty of negotiating with a Power whose representatives have no idea of the meaning of good faith and who are openly influenced by Bismar[c]kian principles in this respect.

I would also suggest that it should be embodied in a despatch to C[oun]t de Salis and that he should be instructed to read it to Herr v[on] Schoen with a[n] expression of regret on the part of H[is] M[ajesty's] G[overnment] that the German Gov[ernmen]t should not [sic] have withdrawn from their undertaking. It will look very well in some future bluebook.

Copies should be sent to Paris and St. Petersburg and left with M. Pichon and M. Isvolsky.

L. M.

Count Metternich's communication was not made in a form which invites us to raise the matter at Berlin and I am afraid that our doing so would give Germany an opportunity of saying that Russia is opposed to the Railway and that we must choose between Russia and Germany and decide whether we will accept a German offer without waiting for Russia. Germany would then be in a position to say that we had again refused a friendly offer from her. What Count Metternich has said is that Germany refuses to negotiate with us and Russia; what I fear Herr von Schoen will say is that as Russia cannot make up her mind he must make us an offer alone; the offer will probably not be one, which we could on its merits accept, and even if it were Germany would make a grievance of our making our consent to it dependent upon Russia. For the moment Germany sees her way to the next Sections of the line and we cannot yet bring effective pressure to bear on her. I should therefore be disinclined to say anything at Berlin([6]) which would invite negotiations at this moment.

The Prime Minister,
Lord Morley,
Lord Crewe,
Mr. Haldane,

should see this latest developement. The Cabinet have not yet had the previous papers I think and I will decide as to circulating the whole after the four Ministers have seen this.

E. G.

([6]) [Marginal comment by Mr Asquith : " I agree. H. H. A."]

No. 268.

Count de Salis to Sir Edward Grey.

F.O. 371/538.
25928/5399/08/44A.
(No. 326.)   *Berlin*, D. *July 24, 1908.*
Sir,   R. *July 27, 1908.*

In course of conversation this evening Herr von Schoen remarked that there was an outstanding matter between the United Kingdom and Germany in connection with which, unlike the Macedonian reforms to which we had just alluded, the material interests of both countries were deeply involved. He alluded to the Bagdad Railway. He considered that the relations between the two Courts were at present good, as well as between the two Governments. There was however a certain tension of public opinion, and there was danger that this feeling would not subside as long as questions like this remained unsettled. He had not been able to agree to the proposal that there should be a discussion " *à quatre.*" This would expose Germany to the certainty of being in a hopeless minority. In view of the importance of their interests this was impossible. He wished to say, however, that he quite understood our anxiety at the idea of a railway being brought down by another Power to the Persian Gulf which was the " *avant-port des Indes,*" and was prepared to take due account of it. For his own part he was convinced that the matter was one which could be arranged.

I answered that His Majesty's Government had made great efforts of late years in the pursuit of the policy of removing causes of friction with other Powers. But I could not of course express an opinion offhand as to how far you might find it possible to discuss the matter in such a way. Besides before proposing the Conference "*à quatre*" you had presumably exchanged views with other Powers towards whom due loyalty would have to be observed.

Herr von Schoen again rejoined that he was convinced that the matter was one that could be arranged. It was desirable that a cause of possible misunderstanding should be removed.

I have, &c.
J. DE SALIS.

MINUTE.

This communication was probably due to C[oun]t Metternich having reported his conversation with me.(¹)

C[oun]t de Salis' reply was quite suitable.

C. H.
E. G.

(¹) [*v. supra*, p. 368, No. 267, and reference there to *G.P.* XXIV, pp. 81–7, especially pp. 83–4.]

No. 269.

Sir Edward Grey to Sir F. Bertie.

F.O. 5946/5946/09/18.

(No. 80.)

Sir,
Foreign Office, February 10, 1909.

M. Cambon handed me to-day the text of the Franco-German Declaration about Morocco, with a covering Note.(¹)

M. Cambon then said that the reception of the King appeared to be good in Berlin, and the speeches were excellent. He thought Germany would now propose something to us, but he did not know what. Possibly it might be about the Bagdad Railway.

I told him we should be quite willing to discuss the Bagdad Railway, on the terms I had previously indicated. I had been approached recently by one or two British financiers, who had been in communication with German financiers. They had asked me whether the British Government were prepared to favour negotiation with Germany about the Railway. I had always replied that we were prepared to do so on proper terms, provided there were negotiations *à quatre* between France, Germany, Russia, and ourselves. The difficulty lay in the Russian Government. had not, however, had any proposal about anything from Berlin.

M. Cambon said that Naval Expenditure would be a great difficulty. Did I think the Germans would agree to compare Estimates, as I had suggested some time ago, with a view to reduction?

I told him I was afraid the Germans would not do this. We should have to decide what expenditure was necessary to enable us to maintain a sufficient superiority as the German programme of construction advanced, and I thought the Germans ought not to resent this.

[I am, &c.]
E. G[REY].

(¹) [The texts of the Declaration and Note will be printed in *Gooch & Temperley*, Vol. VII.]

No. 270.

Sir G. Lowther to Sir Edward Grey.

F.O. 20290/2074/09/44.
(No. 375.)   Constantinople, D. May 25, 1909.
Sir,   R. June 1, 1909.

I have the honour to transmit herewith copy of a despatch and its enclosures(¹), which I have received from His Majesty's Resident and Consul-General at Bagdad in which he advocates as being in the interests of both Turkey and Great Britain the acquisition of a concession for a railway connecting Mesopotamia with the Mediterranean at Alexandretta by way of the Euphrates valley and Aleppo.

The Importance of the results which the realization of such a scheme would have for our commerce and for our political influence in this country are, I am aware, thoroughly appreciated by His Majesty's Government, and I need not therefore dilate upon them. As to the commercial prospect of the proposed line, I am in no position to express a decided opinion as it appears to me that until Sir W. Willcocks's scheme for the irrigation of Mesopotamia(²) has been advanced far enough to afford approximate data as to the economic development to be anticipated in these regions, the matter must remain largely speculative, and I therefore propose only to offer a few observations on some of the points raised in Col[onel] Ramsay's despatch together with some remarks of a general character.

Col[onel] Ramsay dwells with some insistence on the necessity, for the success of the scheme under discussion, of preventing the German Bagdad railway Company from acquiring the concession for the line between Aleppo and Alexandretta, for, he argues, the German Company, if they obtained it, would be enabled, by applying over this section the maximum tariff permitted by their "cahier des charges," to maintain through rates for goods carried by the Euphrates Valley Railway to Alexandretta at a figure higher than for similar goods carried by the all German line, and thus secure the latter against effective competition. I am not convinced that this apprehension is well grounded. The German Company possesses its preference for the line connecting Aleppo with the sea only on condition that the prior similar rights of the Damascus–Hamah–Biredjik are [sic] Railway are respected (see Young's Corps de Droit Ottoman, Vol. 4, pages 166–7 and 228). Now supposing the French Company is willing to cede its right, it seems to me certain that whatever other conditions they may attach to the agreement, they would certainly stipulate for favourable treatment in tariff matters for themselves, and in such case it is hard to conceive that the Turkish Government would not insist on equally favourable treatment for any railway starting from Aleppo for which they might grant a concession. Thus, though no doubt serious, I doubt whether the competition of the Bagdad Railway would be as formidable as Col[onel] Ramsay anticipates, especially when the advantage which the Euphrates valley line would possess in its shorter route is taken into account. However this may be, there can be no question but that it would be desirable that the concession for this important line should be in the hands of more friendly parties than the Bagdad Railway is likely to prove. Perhaps, if there were a reasonable prospect that the French Railway Co. and the French financial houses interested in it were disposed to follow a policy more in harmony with that of their Government, some arrangement with the Damascus–Hamah–Biredjik Company might offer a satisfactory solution of the difficulty. I hear however that the saying "l'argent n'a pas de patrie" is of too true application in Paris to allow of hopes in this direction.

Col[onel] Ramsay also suggests that, thanks to the double guarantee, for construction loan and for working expenses, which the Bagdad Railway enjoys under its concession, that Company could without loss to itself lower rates to a point which a less favoured rival Company could not afford. This in practice would

(¹) [Not reproduced.]
(²) [Sir W. Willcocks's scheme is more fully explained, infra, pp. 381–4, No. 281.]

probably prove to be the case but this advantage again is considerably neutralized by the shorter route along the Euphrates valley. It appears to me also that there is a limit beyond which the German Company could not cut rates, and that limit would be reached when the kilometre receipts of the line were so reduced as to fall below francs 4,500, the amount of the working expenses guarantee, and the Turkish Treasury became liable to make good the difference.

In any case it seems indubitable that the Germans will make a strong effort to obtain a concession of the Alexandretta–Aleppo line. It did not need the debate on the Bagdad Railway concession to show the Germans what the country at large think of the bargain they succeeded in making with the late Sultan, for the Germans had already hastened to assure the Minister of Public Works of their readiness to discuss that instrument and, if need be, to modify it, but, so far as I am aware no definite proposal for a basis of discussion has been put forward on either side. The Germans however, will hardly consent to make a concession wihtout [sic] some quid pro quo, and an alteration of the tracé of the railway so as to bring Alexandretta and Aleppo on to the main line, which they can colourably represent as being a modification as much in favour of Turkey as of the Company, will assuredly be one of their requirements. On the other hand they are still less likely to abandon the whole of the advantages in the nature of guarantees they now possess, and as Turkey with the resources at present available to her, is quite unable to provide even for a reduced expenditure under that head, it seems probable that negotiations between the Company and the Government will be deferred until the latter has obtained the consent of the Powers to an alteration of the existing Customs Régime.

In conclusion, I would hazard the opinion that whatever may be the prospect of a Euphrates Valley Railway, such as advocated by Colonel Ramsay as a purely commercial enterprise, the unsettled political condition of this country is likely to deter capitalists from engaging in so important an enterprise without some assured guarantee, at least for the interest on the capital invested. To expect Turkey to furnish this would, I fear, be vain, but it seems to me that in view of the magnitude of the interests involved it would be worth while carefully to examine whether the prospects of such a railway are not sufficiently good to warrant His Majesty's Government in doing so. If the result of such examination is favourable the annuity should be required for only a few years and provision might be made for the repayment by securing to the Treasury a participation in the eventual profits of the line.

I have, &c.

GERARD LOWTHER.

MINUTES.

After reading this despatch and Sir W. Wil[l]cock[s]'s memorandum to the Porte in which he strongly advocates the construction of the Euphrates Valley Railroad, I am not sure that our draft to Sir G. Lowther is on the right lines.[3]

We say that " if Great Britain were enabled to participate in the construction and control of the Bagdad Railway . . . . , H[is] M[ajesty's] G[overnment] would be willing to accept the proposed increase of the Turkish Customs—if, on the other hand agreement . . . . . should be impossible, then the only condition on which H[is] M[ajesty's] G[overnment] would be able to agree to the Turkish proposal would be the granting of a concession for a railway from the Persian Gulf to Basra and Bagdad along the Valley of the Tigris with the option to prolong it along the Valley of the Euphrates to Tripoli or some other port on the Mediterranean."

If, therefore, this menace brings the Germans to terms with us about the southern end of the Railway, we shall not get the Euphrates Valley Railway, which the Turks will certainly wish to build now that Wil[l]cocks has urged them to do so.

I should like to invert the order of the draft and demand as a price of our consent to the increase of the Customs the Euphrates Valley line, with a prolongation from Bagdad down the

(3) [The draft referred to here was apparently drawn up in the first instance immediately upon the receipt of the communication from Jevad Bay on May 27. (v. infra, immediately succeeding document.) The draft was then sent to the Board of Trade for criticism on May 29, but the arrival of Sir G. Lowther's despatch and enclosures caused a change in procedure, as these minutes show. The new procedure is indicated infra, pp. 373–4, Ed. note, and the despatch as finally sent is printed infra, pp. 374–5, No. 272.]

Tigris, the latter portion to be abandoned if the Germans will grant our terms for participation in the construction etc., of the southern portion of the Bagdad Line.

I think that in this way we stand a better chance of getting something.

L. M.

This is a most important despatch, and it is curious that Col[onel] Ramsay at Bagdad should be advocating simultaneously and without any indication from us precisely the same railway for which it is suggested that a concession should be obtained in exchange for an increase of the Turkish Customs dues. The proposed despatch to Sir G. Lowther should now be reconsidered in connection with Colonel Ramsay's views, and I would suggest that the small sub-committee which previously sat upon the Bagdad R[ailwa]y question(⁴) should be re-assembled as quickly as possible and should reconsider the d[ra]ft desp[atch] to Sir G. Lowther in the light of the additional valuable information which has now reached us. In view of the importance of the Euphrates valley R[ailwa]y being in our hands, if ever built, I think that the policy sketched out in our desp[atch] to Sir G. Lowther will require some modification.

C. H.

This should be done.

E. G.

(⁴) [cp. supra, p. 348, No. 237, note (⁵).]

No. 271.

Jevad Bey to Sir Edward Grey.(¹)

F.O. 20101/659/09/44. Ambassade Impériale de Turquie, Londres,
Monsieur le Ministre,   27 Mai, 1909.

Le Gouvernement Anglais connaît l'état précaire des finances Ottomanes, état qui est un des funestes héritages de l'ancien régime. Le nouveau Gouvernement prend des mesures presque draconiennes pour diminuer les dépenses afin d'équilibrer le budget. Mais il n'y arrive pas; il lui faut de nouvelles ressources tant pour les dépenses ordinaires que pour les travaux publics. Le Gouvernement de Sa Majesté Britannique sait mieux que nul autre qu'une bonne administration s'obtient avec de bonnes finances. En fait de nouvelles ressources, le Gouvernement Ottoman ne peut en avoir d'autres en ce moment qu'avec l'augmentation des droits d'entrée à quinze pour cent (15%) ad valorem. Rifaat-Pacha en avait déjà causé avec Votre Excellence et le Gouvernement Britannique avait donné son assentiment sous une condition que la Sublime Porte avait acceptée.

D'ordre de mon Gouvernement, j'ai l'honneur de porter aujourd'hui à la connaissance de Votre Excellence que la Turquie compte sur l'amitié de l'Angleterre pour voir réaliser au plus vite son désir si légitime.

Le Gouvernement Impérial a déjà le consentement de l'Autriche-Hongrie et de l'Allemagne et il ne doute pas que le concours bienveillant du Foreign Office, toujours prêt à aider le nouveau régime, ne lui fera pas défaut en cette occu[r]rence.

Je serais reconnaissant à Votre Excellence de vouloir bien me mettre prochainement à même de transmettre à mon Gouvernement la bonne nouvelle qui est attendue à Constantinople avec tant de confiance.

J'ai, &c.
DJÉVAD.

(¹) [A copy of this communication was sent to Sir G. Lowther on September 3.]

[ED. NOTE.—In accordance with Sir C. Hardinge's suggestion in his minute to Sir G. Lowther's despatch (v. supra, p. 373, No. 270, min.), a departmental committee was appointed ' To reconsider the answer to be given to the Turkish Government to their request for an increase of the customs dues from 11 per cent. to 15 per cent. in the light of further information received from His Majesty's Consul-General at Bagdad in connection with a proposed concession for a railway from the Mediterranean to Bagdad and Bussorah.'' The committee reported on July 24. Their report confirmed the suggestions made by Mr. Mallet in his minute upon Sir G. Lowther's despatch and included recommendations for an application to the Turkish Government on the lines indicated in Sir Edward Grey's despatch to Sir G. Lowther, No. 245 of August 18 (*infra*, pp. 374–5, No. 272). This despatch was the first formal reply to Sir G. Lowther's despatch, but an exchange of private letters had taken place in the meantime. Sir E. Grey's letter of July 14 is of considerable interest. Its text is as follows:

Sir Edward Grey to Sir G. Lowther.

F.O. 28402/2074/09/44.
Private.
My dear Lowther,   *July* 14, 1909.

I have been reading your letter to Hardinge of July 6th, urging that the Bagdad Railway and the increase of the Customs Dues should not be connected. You even say that by treating the two questions separately we could put forward, and possibly obtain, larger demands than by connecting them. I should be very glad if you would explain this a little more.

I am much more anxious to secure our interests against being damaged by the construction of the Bagdad Railway than to secure special advantages for ourselves, and I do not quite see how we are to guard against the construction of the Bagdad Railway without our participation unless we take advantage of such opportunities as the increase of the Customs Dues may give us for making conditions. In what other way are we to secure any conditions?

Now, I wish you to realise the position as it appears from this end.

The Germans have the Bagdad Railway Concession; we cannot object to that as it stands; we cannot alter it, or make holes in it. But what we do object to is that the Turks should go on pledging new revenue for kilometric guarantees to enable the Railway to be made. When we are asked to give the Turks more money, I think the least we can expect is that they should promise to use this money in ways which are not wasteful for themselves and damaging to us.

Of course, it may be said that the increase of the Turkish Customs Dues to which we are asked to agree is not regarded as supplementing the revenues upon which the Germans have a lien for kilometric guarantees; but that does not really meet our point; because, as a matter of fact, we are asked to place more revenue at the disposal of the Turks, and this revenue is levied to a very large extent upon British trade. Will the Turks give an undertaking that, as long as the increase of the Customs Dues remains, they will not pledge revenue for kilometric guarantees without consulting us? If they give an undertaking of this kind I shall be exposed to the charge here that I am helping the Turks to find money which may be used to damage British interests. Even the old Jewish law forbade that a kid should be seethed in its mother's milk; and it would be an analogous proceeding to that which shocked the Jews if the Turks were to derive increased revenue from British trade with our consent, and with that revenue enable a new through-route to the East to be made and kept exclusively in the hands of our rivals.

I am most anxious to find some way of agreeing to the increase of the Customs Dues. In any case, there will be opposition to it here on commercial grounds; but I am prepared to meet that. Unless, however, I can get some understanding about kilometric guarantees for the Bagdad Railway, I shall be in a position which I cannot defend, and the effect will be very unfavourable to the good feeling which at present exists here with regard to Turkey.

E. GREY.]

No. 272.

Sir Edward Grey to Sir G. Lowther.

F.O. 27901/2074/09/44.
(No. 245.) Secret.
Sir,   *Foreign Office, August* 18, 1909.

Y[our] E[xcellency] is aware that the question of railway communication between Bagdad and the Persian Gulf has been recently under consideration by an Inter-Departmental Committee, in conjunction with the question of the proposed increase in the Turkish Customs duty on imports. A copy of the report of the Committee, whose recommendations I have approved, is enclosed herewith.([1])

I have to request you to apply to the Turkish Gov[ernmen]t for a concession for a railway between Bagdad and the Persian Gulf, viâ Bussorah and the Tigris valley, the concession to be without any financial guarantee from the Turkish Gov[ernmen]t, and the concessionnaires to have the first option of prolonging the railway along the valley of the Euphrates to the Mediterranean, should the development of irrigation and trade render such a course desirable.

([1]) [Not reproduced.]

It might be worth considering by Y[our] E[xcellency] whether, in the first instance, it would not be as well that the Turkish Gov[ernmen]t should be sounded by Sir A. Block, or by some other person unconnected with H[is] M[ajesty's] Embassy in whom you have confidence, so that the ground may be prepared before H[is] M[ajesty's] G[overnment] are formally committed to the proposal. I leave, however, the whole question of procedure to Y[our] E[xcellency's] discretion.

The question of the consent of H[is] M[ajesty's] G[overnment] to the proposed increase of the Customs duty on imports will be treated in a separate despatch.(²)

I am, &c.

E. G[REY].

(²) [No trace can be found of a despatch answering to this description until that of September 23, which is printed *infra*, pp. 791-2, *App.* VI. On September 3, however, a copy of Jevad Bey's communication of May 27 was sent to Sir G. Lowther, and on September 14 a copy of the *aide-mémoire* printed immediately below.]

No. 273.

Aide-mémoire communicated by Tewfik Pasha, September 14, 1909.

F.O. 34716/659/09/44.

Par sa note du 27 Mai dernier, No. 4587/48,(¹) Djevad Bey avait eu l'honneur d'exposer à Son Excellence Sir Edward Grey la nécessité où se trouve le Gouvernement Impérial d'augmenter de 4% ses droits de douane sur les marchandises importées dans l'Empire. Cette augmentation subordonnée à l'assentiment des Grandes Puissances, s'impose, en ce moment, pour des raisons impérieuses. Au nombre de celles-ci présente, en premier lieu, le déficit budgétaire qui atteint 4 millions de Livres Turques. Pour le combler et subvenir, en même temps à d'autres besoins immédiats, le Gouvernement Impérial vient de procéder à la licitation d'un emprunt de 7 millions de Livres Turques. Il dispose actuellement des ressources nécessaires à l'intérêt et à l'amortissement de cette somme. Mais il ne lui restera plus de recettes disponibles pour de futurs emprunts. D'ailleurs, en affectant les recettes normales du Trésor à des opérations exceptionnelles, on crée, à la longue, une situation financière onéreuse, qui a pour conséquence de paralyser le développement du pays. Ne pouvant donc combler constamment ses déficits au moyen d'emprunts, le Gouvernement Ottoman a besoin d'augmenter ses ressources régulières.

D'autre part, il est résolu à poursuivre l'œuvre de réorganisation entreprise.

La justice, la gendarmerie et les Travaux Publics le préoccupent au premier chef. Il tient, en même temps, à perfectionner le service des douanes. L'engagement de Mr. Crawford, dû à la courtoisie si appréciée du Gouvernement de Sa Majesté Britannique et qui a produit de si bons résultats, dans un laps de temps relativement restreint, en est une preuve. La Sublime Porte ne considère point Mr. Crawford comme un simple Conseiller spécialiste : il dispose d'une latitude illimitée pour diriger, à son gré, les services ; il est, de fait, le chef des douanes de l'Empire et vient d'être chargé d'inspecter toutes les douanes en province, afin que celles-ci soient dotées des améliorations réalisées dans la capitale En fin, le Gouvernement Impérial demandera le renouvellement de l'engagement de Mr. Crawford pour une période minima de trois ans. Mais tout le bon vouloir, tous les efforts du Gouvernement ne sauraient produire leurs fruits s'il continuait à avoir un budget à découvert. Voilà pourquoi il tient à majorer de 4% les droits de douane.

On serait, de prime abord, tenté peut-être de croire que la majoration projetée pourra diminuer le chiffre des importations. C'est là une hypothèse sans base réelle. En effet, lors de l'augmentation de 3%, on avait constaté une baisse dans les importations. En l'année 1322 (1906) la valeur des marchandises importées se

(¹) [*v. supra*, p. 373, No. 271.]

montait à 3,639,294,700 piastres. En 1324 (1908), après l'application du nouveau tarif le chiffre baissa à 3,508,123,362 piastres. Mais, outre que cette baisse, ne se maintint que durant une courte période, on constata qu'elle était due non à l'augmentation douanière, mais à un habile procédé des commerçants importateurs, lesquels ayant eu connaissance de la majoration, avant qu'elle ne fût appliquée, avaient fait venir de l'étranger une très grande quantité de marchandises, afin de les vendre plus tard en profitant de la plus-value provoquée par l'élévation à 11% des droits de douane.

Il est ainsi établi que l'augmentation douanière ne pourra faire baisser le chiffre des importations et que, si le fait se produisait comme il a déjà eu lieu, ce serait pour une durée insignifiante. D'ailleurs, les recettes douanières de 1908 accusent une augmentation de 17%, ce qui eu égard aux événements qui ont agité le pays, constitue là preuve mathématique de ce qui précède, en même temps que celle de l'amélioration des services douaniers de l'Empire.

Les recettes produites par la majoration de 4% tout en contribuant à équilibrer le budget, auront pour résultat de permettre, dans la suite l'émission d'un grand emprunt que le Gouvernement Impérial se propose de faire en faveur du développement de l'agriculture, des Travaux Publics et surtout du perfectionnement du service judiciaire.

Dans cet ordre d'idées, parmi les réformes arrêtées, une partie, telle que la création de tribunaux de paix est déjà en voie d'application. Cependant toutes ces améliorations appelées à relever le pays, entraînent des dépenses que les ressources actuelles du Gouvernement sont loin de couvrir.

Le Gouvernement de Sa Majesté Britannique dont l'appui est si précieux à la Sublime Porte, voudra bien lui donner une nouvelle preuve de son amitié en acquiesçant à l'augmentation de 4% qui, ainsi qu'il a été dit dans la note susmentionnée de cette Ambassade, est agréée par l'Autriche et l'Allemagne.

Il est bien entendu que les sommes provenant de cette majoration ne seront point affectées à des entreprises dans lesquelles le Gouvernement Impérial se trouve déjà engagé et nommément au chemin de fer de Bagdad.

Enfin, l'augmentation en question permettra au Gouvernement Impérial de réaliser au bout de quelques années son projet d'abolir les droits de transit et d'exportation, mesure qui avantagera considérablement le commerce étranger.

Londres, le 14 Septembre 1909.

No. 274.

Sir G. Lowther to Sir Edward Grey.

F.O. 35011/2074/09/44.
(No. 746.) Secret. *Therapia, D. September* 14, 1909.
Sir, R. *September* 20, 1909.

In obedience to the instructions contained in your despatch No. 245 Secret of August 18,(1) and your telegram No. 665 of the 9th instant,(2) I yesterday asked the Grand Vizier whether the Turkish Government would be disposed to grant in principle a concession to a British syndicate for a railway between Bagdad and the Persian Gulf viâ Basrah and the Tigris valley, the concession to be without any financial guarantee from the Turkish Government, and the Concessionnaires to have the option of prolonging the railway along the valley of the Euphrates to the Mediterranean in the event of the development of irrigation and trade rendering such a railway desirable. I added that should such a concession be granted, a

(1) [*v. supra*, pp. 374–5, No. 272.]
(2) [Not reproduced. It directed Sir G. Lowther to apply without delay for the **Tigris** Valley concession.]

substantial syndicate would be forthcoming without delay to discuss details with the Ottoman Government.

His Highness took notes of the proposal and replied that personally he would favour such a scheme, but he would have to consult all his colleagues individually and confidentially before laying the matter before the Cabinet. He hoped however to give me a reply in a week's time. His Highness added however that he could not conceal from me that the granting of such a concession would be deeply resented by Germany who would probably seize every opportunity of injuring this country both internally and externally as a punishment for the granting of the concession to Great Britain, and Turkey would then have to rely more than ever on England to help her out of such difficulties.

There was no disguising the fact that this country was not yet in a strong or independent position. He likened its state to that of a severe wound which had been festering for years, and which was cicatrizing successfully, but the slightest rupture of the skin might retard its healing for a long period. He hoped we would understand that they must not run any risks of the wound being reopened. I observed that the proposed concession was not in contravention to the Bagdad Railway convention, and Germany would have no more right to resent such a concession being granted than she would have to resent the acceptance of the Glasgow and other railway schemes which have recently been put forward, which opened up a different part of the country from that which it was contemplated the Bagdad Railway would open up.

I have, &c.

GERARD LOWTHER.

[ED. NOTE.—On September 23, Sir Edward Grey handed to Tewfik Pasha a memorandum in answer to the Turkish aide-mémoire of September 14. It is printed infra, pp. 791-2, App. VI.]

No. 275.

Sir G. Lowther to Sir Edward Grey.

Therapia, September 27, 1909.

F.O. 36009/2074/09/44.
Tel. (No. 335.)

D. 9 P.M.
R. 9·45 P.M.

My telegram No. 321.(¹)

Grand Vizier, while prepared in principle to granting of a concession to British syndicate for a railway from Bagdad to Bussorah, suggests that it would be advisable to postpone the actual demand for the concession until after question of 4 per cent. has been settled, fearing that Germans, with the knowledge of such a concession having been asked for, may impose as a condition of acceptance the refusal to us of the concession.

Speaking generally on question of 4 per cent. and intimation received that Italian Government would ask for settlement of all outstanding claims, his Highness said that if all the Governments were going to impose conditions he would rather drop the matter of 4 per cent. altogether.

(¹) [This telegram briefly reported the conversation more fully given in the immediately preceding document.]

No. 276.

Sir G. Lowther to Sir Edward Grey.

F.O. 38360/2074/09/44.

(No. 839.)   *Therapia,* D. *October 11, 1909.*

Sir,   R. *October 18, 1909.*

I asked the Grand Vizier to-day whether General Mahmoud Chefket Pasha had, while in Germany, had any official communication with the authorities on the subject of the future of the Bagdad Railway. His Highness said that the Emperor had strongly recommended the Railway to the General's attention but that he was unaware of his conversation having taken any definite shape. The Grand Vizier had however spoken with the General on the matter and they were both of the opinion that some modification must be made in the present Convention. When the line was completed the Turkish Government would be called upon to pay in kilometric guarantees a yearly sum of £T. 1,250,000. Granting that the Railway earned £450,000 this would leave this Government saddled with a liability of £800,000, which was more than its finances could stand. His Highness said that he himself was in favour of a narrow gauge line but he believed that the military authorities were opposed to it though the matter had not been examined with them but he believed that a narrow gauge would mean a saving to the Ottoman Government of £400,000 a year in kilometric guarantees. He himself, he said, was in favour of an arrangement being come to between the German Company and the English regarding the construction of the remaining sections of the line and he had instructed General Mahmoud Chefket Pasha to broach the subject with the German Ambassador.

I have, &c.

GERARD LOWTHER.

No. 277.

Sir Edward Grey to Sir E. Goschen.([1])

F.O. 38405/31695/09/18.

(No. 266.) Secret.

Sir,   *Foreign Office, October 28, 1909.*

. . . .([2]) Herr von Schoen had mentioned our opposition to the Bagdad Railway as one of the things which caused irritation. I would, therefore, take this opportunity of explaining why it was impossible for us to agree to the 4% increase of the Turkish Customs Duties without a promise that the additional revenue would not be used for the Bagdad Railway. About one-third of the increase of the Duties would fall on British commerce, and this in itself would be much disliked. But, if the money thus secured at the expense of British trade was to be used to make a new through-route to the East and to establish means of communication which would supersede all others in carrying trade from the Persian Gulf into Mesopotamia, and all this under the exclusive control of one foreign Power, then the position of a British Government which had agreed to this would become untenable. It was, therefore, impossible for us to agree to the increase of the Turkish Customs Duties unless we had proper safeguards against the use of the additional revenue for the purpose of displacing British trade in Mesopotamia. We felt that we must either have a part in the Bagdad Railway itself, or else we must have a concession which would enable us to establish other means of communication by which we could trade with Mesopotamia on equal terms.

([1]) [*cp. G.P.* XXVII, II, pp. 580–2.]

([2]) [The omitted passages at the beginning and end of this despatch are printed, *supra,* pp. 303–4, No. 202.]

With regard to the participation of France and Russia in the Bagdad Railway, I knew that Count Metternich had objected to a discussion à *quatre* because such a discussion would put Germany in a minority. But I explained to him that this had not been our object in proposing the discussion. French financiers had already an interest in the project before I came into Office, and it was certainly not I who had brought them in. As regards Russia, the position was this. We had on previous occasions been instrumental, or been supposed to be instrumental, in defeating the Russian plans for securing outlets on the sea, first in the case of the Mediterranean, and then in the case of the Far East; this had caused much illwill in Russia towards us. Now we had succeeded in overcoming this illwill and I was very anxious not to revive it as regards the one remaining outlet which Russia was thought to desire, the Persian Gulf, by participating in the Bagdad Railway, when Russia was opposed to it and excluded from it. I had told the Russian Government more than once that I thought they ought not to oppose, in principle, the construction of the Bagdad Railway, but ought instead to make up their minds as to the terms on which they could join in the project. I did not think it would be impossible for the German Government to overcome this difficulty of Russian opposition; indeed I knew that before the visit of the German Emperor to this country Herr von Schoen had spoken to the Russian Government on the subject.([3])

I told Count Metternich that my object in giving these explanations to the German Government was to prove to them that our action was not dictated by illwill to Germany, but by the necessities of the case, and that the attitude we were obliged to take up with regard to the increase of the Turkish Customs Duties was not an attitude taken up behind the back of the German Government in a way to cause irritation and introduce friction into what we hoped would be a friendly discussion.

Count Metternich replied that there would be no objection to British financial co-operation in the Bagdad Railway, but Germany must have the control : in the sense of having a majority on whatever Railway Board controlled the line. He asked me whether we should be satisfied with some measure of control on the southern section of the Railway.

I told him it was the southern part that interested us principally.

He asked how much we meant by the southern section, because he thought that the part of the line that went through Mesopotamia would probably prove to be the most valuable part of the whole line.

I replied that this was a question for experts at a later stage in the discussion.

Count Metternich observed that the Bagdad Railway did not, as it was at present intended, touch Russian territory, or prevent Russia from making a separate outlet for herself to the Persian Gulf.

I said that this was no doubt the case, but in my opinion the Russian needs would best be met not by the making of a separate route to the Gulf, but by establishing, under Russian control, connections with the Bagdad Railway. This would give Russia an interest in the outlet created by the Bagdad Railway.

Count Metternich asked whether, if participation was arranged for us, we should be willing that the additional revenue secured by the 4% increase should be used to make the Bagdad Railway.

I answered that if we came to an agreement about participation we should, of course, not wish to hinder the progress of the Railway; but we had promised the new régime in Turkey that we would not apply for any kilometric guarantees in connection with concessions in which we were interested, and therefore we could not press the Turkish Government to allocate any more of their funds to kilometric guarantees. I should have to consider how far this question was involved in the further progress of the Bagdad Railway. . . .

[I am, etc.]
E. G[REY].

([3]) [*v. supra*, p. 98, No. 64, p. 99, No. 65, and *note* ([3]).]

II.—THE GWINNER-CASSEL NEGOTIATIONS, 1909-10.

No. 278.

Mr. Marling to Sir Edward Grey.

Constantinople, October 31, 1909.

F.O. 39959/2074/09/44.
Tel. (No. 346.)

D. 1·35 P.M.
R. 3·30 P.M.

Bagdad Railway.

Grand Vizier informed me voluntarily yesterday that he understands that the Germans are willing to agree to British participation on basis of equality of representation on board, and said he would give me definite assurance in a few days. He would give no indication of other conditions.

No. 279.

Mr. Marling to Sir Edward Grey.

Constantinople, November 5, 1909.

F.O. 40694/2074/09/44.
Tel. (No. 351.)

D. 2 P.M.
R. 4·45 P.M.

My telegram no. 346.([1])

Dr. Gwinner has informed Babington Smith([2]) that he would welcome British co-operation on the basis of British control and construction of the Bagdad–Gulf section, provided the Turks agree; Dr. Gwinner denies that the Germans are ready to abandon their lien on the 4 per cent. and he has suggested the foregoing to the Grand Vizier as a possible solution of the Customs question.

Gwinner's proposal did not contemplate giving us participation in other parts of the railway but Smith is disposed to think that this, if desired, would not be impossible.

Gwinner leaves tomorrow evening. I have heard no more from the Grand Vizier.

([1]) [*v.* immediately preceding document.]
([2]) [For a fuller account of Dr. Gwinner's proposals, *v. infra*, pp. 384–5, No. 282, and pp. 793–4, *App.* VII.]

No. 280.

Mr. Marling to Sir Edward Grey.

F.O. 41726/2074/09/44.
(No. 889.)
Sir,

Constantinople, D. November 5, 1909.
R. November 15, 1909.

The Bagdad Railway Company announces that the Turkish Government have now accepted the Company's plans for the continuation of the line from Bulgurlu over the Taurus to Aleppo and thence across the Euphrates to El Helif, a distance of 840 kilometres, and that work on this section will be started on at once.

As in the case of the first section a construction company is to be formed for this section, with a capital of £400,000, having its headquarters in Switzerland. There will be a Board, composed of 12 members, of whom 5 are to be Germans, 4 French, 1 Austrian and 2 Swiss. Dr. Gwynner [*sic*] will be President, and M. F. Kautz, Director-General adjoint of the Anatolian Railway, one of the German members; the French are M. Gaston Auboyneau, administrator, and M. C. de Cargat director of the Imperial Ottoman Bank, Comte d'Arnoux and M. Benac of the Banque de Paris et des Pays-Bas.

The executive committee of three will have Regierungsrat Riese as President, and Messieurs Huguenin and Helfferig [sic] as members. The Work of construction is in the hands of Messieurs Winkler and Mavrogordato for the part from Bulgurlu across the Taurus to Adana, while Meissner Pasha, builder of the Hedjaz Railway, has been entrusted with that portion over the Amanus mountains. Work is to be begun simultaneously from four points, at Bulgurlu, and at Adana towards the Taurus, and from Adana towards the Amanus, as well as at Aleppo. It is anticipated that the climate of the Adana plain will allow work to go on all through the winter, so as to make up for lost time and give employment to the many unemployed and sufferers from the Adana massacres.

The Bagdad Company's announcement would seem to imply that the Government have agreed to the *tracé* of the whole section as presented to them, but I believe this is not actually the case and that no decision has been reached regarding the stretch from Adana onwards; the Ministry of War favouring the original *tracé*, which would go northward from this point, whereas strong local pressure is being brought to bear to have the line curve round the bay to touch Alexandretta. The Germans have however prevailed on the Government to allow them to commence work on the parts agreed on, pending their final decision on this point.

A syndicate formed by the Imperial Ottoman Bank of Paris, the Vienna Bank-Verein and the Swiss Credit Anstalt and headed by the Deutsche Bank will take over the loans Series II and III, amounting to £9,080,000 with the proceeds of which the Railway Company will gradually pay for the construction of the new section.

The announcement of the continuation of work on the Bagdad Railway line coincides with the opening of the new Railway Terminus at Haidar Pasha, which took place with great ceremony on the fourth instant, as a delicate compliment to the Sultan on the occasion of his birthday, in the presence of representatives of the Sultan, all the Turkish Ministers, the German Ambassador and all the prominent members of the Anatolian Railway Company. After a short speech by M. Gwynner Director of the Deutsche Bank, and a long oration by M. Kautz, the Minister of Public Works, Haladjian Effendi said a few words in the name of the Turkish Government, thanking the Anatolian Company for their enterprise and activity and announcing that the Government had changed their attitude with regard to questions of progress and development since the days of the old régime. They welcomed the influx of foreign capital into the country, but in granting new concessions and sanctioning new enterprises·it was their aim now, not to benefit certain individuals but to augment the wealth and power and encourage the development of the Ottoman Empire.

He added that, as a first step to the encouragement of free circulation, the Government were preparing a Bill for the abolition of passports within the Empire, and that revenues derived from this source were struck out from this year's Budget.

I have, &c.

CHARLES M. MARLING.

No. 281.

Minutes by Sir C. Hardinge and Sir Edward Grey.

F.O. 41576/2074/09/44.

Sir Edward Grey, *Foreign Office, November 6, 1909.*

Sir William Willcocks called upon me yesterday, having arrived from Constantinople on the previous evening.

I asked him to explain to me as far as he was able his views and plans in connexion with the irrigation schemes in Mesopotamia.

He told me that the Turkish Government had decided for the present not to employ any contractors to carry out the survey and preparatory measures for the big irrigation scheme. The idea had been that Messrs. Pearson should be employed for six months in executing the most urgent part of the repairs to the existing *barrage* and canals, but the Turkish Government had come to the conclusion that it would be better that they should do it themselves, and that later on the big scheme of irrigation should be submitted to tender. He (Willcocks) had asked the Turkish Government for a certain fixed sum, with which he considered he would be able to complete these preliminary works, and every farthing for which he had asked had been granted to him. He had now come over to England to engage competent engineers, and to make contracts for various materials which would be necessary before he commenced operations. He hoped to be able to get Messrs. Pearson to lend him one of their principal engineers for the space of one year. After he had concluded these arrangements, he proposed to return to Constantinople at once, and to go thence to Mesopotamia.

I annex a map, in which I have roughly indicated what he proposes to do as regards irrigation.([1])

You will observe that there is between Baghdad and the Euphrates what is marked as the Saklawiyeh Canal. The people in Baghdad are always afraid that, when the Euphrates is in flood, the banks of this Canal may give way, in which case Baghdad would be flooded. In the middle of this Canal there is a lake which does not appear on the map, but which I have marked as drawn by Willcocks. He proposes to build a *barrage* where the Canal joins the Euphrates. This *barrage* will stop much of the silting which, he says, is very considerable, so that clear water will come into the lake. From the lake he proposes to make a canal two hundred kilometres long in a straight line on the right bank of the Tigris. From this canal, others at right angles to it will be made, covering the country intervening between the Tigris and the Euphrates. All this country will, he declares, become an enormous wheat granary or cotton-growing country, and the exports from thence should, in a few years' time, be of very considerable value.

Were a railway to be constructed from Baghdad to the Gulf, the only line for it to follow would be one between the Tigris and the canal of two hundred kilometres, which he proposes to construct. It would then have to take a South Easterly direction, and cross the Euphrates close to Azanieh, and go thence to the Gulf. Such a railway is, however, in his opinion, absolutely useless for the export of the grain or cotton that would be grown near Baghdad.

Instead of such a railway, he strongly urged the construction of one following this line:—It should pass straight from Baghdad to Hit on the Euphrates, where the rocks on each side of the River would form a suitable foundation for the building of a bridge. From Hit the line should, instead of following the course of the River, which has deep ravines on each side of it, continue along the high ground at some distance from the River to a town called Abou Kemal, which has a considerable stationary population. From Abou Kemal the line should go straight to Tadmor, and from thence follow the carriage road to Damascus, where connexion would be made with the Syrian Railway. Willcocks explained that anyone who now went to the Euphrates would find both banks of the River more thickly populated than could be imagined, and crowded with enormous flocks of sheep, and with cattle, horses, goats and buffaloes, all waiting for the first rain, when the grass springs up like magic and grows all over the desert. Then slowly and on foot the natives drive these enormous herds to the coast for sale, losing many on the road by robbery and death. To reach the coast takes these people several months while, if a railway were to be constructed, all these cattle could reach the coast within the space of two days. The result of this would be that the breeding of cattle would be enormously increased, and the Syrian desert would

([1]) [Not reproduced.]

become as valuable a breeding-ground for cattle as the grass lands of Argentina and Texas. He argued also that such a railway is essential for the export of the cotton or grain which is to be produced on the irrigated lands. Were these products to be dependent for export on the Bagdad–Persian Gulf Railway, the cost would be so great as to make it hardly worth while to cultivate the crops. After arriving at the Persian Gulf, the crops would be taken to Bombay, and probably re-exported to Europe, passing through the Canal, with its heavy dues. There would thus be very great delay, before the crops reached Europe, and a much longer sea journey than if there were an exit at Tripoli or Haifa.

Sir William further expressed his conviction that this railway would become the chief route for pilgrims on their way to Mecca from Transcaspia, Afghanistan and Northern Persia. They would pass through Kermanshah and, reaching Baghdad, would take the new railway to Damascus, from whence there is a direct route by rail to Mecca and Medina.

Were this railway to be built, he felt quite convinced that the Baghdad Railway would never go further than the four sections which are now being built, since the line from Mosul to Baghdad, instead of following the populated country on the left bank of the Tigris, was to follow the right bank through an absolute desert.

He further added that, were such a railway to be built, it would form an excellent channel for the importation of British goods, especially of British cottons, which would be able to compete successfully at Baghdad with Indian cottons, and for which there was a great demand. He realized that this might be disadvantageous to Indian trade on account of the competition which it would meet with from British manufactures; but he could see no reason why British trade should not also have its opportunity.

He strongly urged the absolute necessity of Great Britain taking a leading part in the construction of this railway. He understood that the French were ready to go in for it, but that they recognized that British interests were predominant at Baghdad, and they would do nothing without British participation. He was strongly opposed to the construction of a big railway, such as the Germans were building in Asia Minor. He preferred that it should be a light railway, such as is being built in Nigeria at a cost of about Three thousand pounds per mile. The length of the line would be five hundred and fifty miles, and he calculated that, in leaving a fair margin, it might be built for Two and a half million sterling. He expressed his absolute conviction that, within a very short time, it would be a paying railway and, were a guarantee given for the first few years, he felt certain of its future success.

Sir William intends, I understand, to lecture before the Royal Geographical Society on his irrigation schemes in Mesopotamia, and we may thus be able to obtain from his lecture fuller information than he has given me. I asked him, in view of the importance of the question which he has raised, to go to the Board of Trade and put his views on the Baghdad–Damascus Railway before them, in order to discuss the commercial questions which the construction of such a line will bring into being. He agreed, and I have arranged for him to see Mr. Stanley of the Board of Trade to-day.

C. H.

Foreign Office, November 6th, 1909.

This is very important and has a bearing on Lynch concession as well as on Bagdad R[ailwa]y. I do not quite gather whether Sir W. Willcocks thinks a railway from Bagdad to the Gulf will be useless or not, if the Bagdad–Abou Kemal–Damascus railway is made.

We cannot contend that navigation concessions on the Euphrates or Tigris should stand in the way of irrigation. The object of means of communication is to develop country not to block the development.

It seems to me that if the Turks would give us a concession for the Bagdad–Abou Kemal–Damascus R[ailwa]y with a right to prolong it to the Gulf, we might let the Bagdad R[ailwa]y alone. The Turks would have a free hand in irrigation and the steamer concessions below Bagdad would become relatively unimportant. The Germans would probably claim that we must come

to terms with them about any railway from Bagdad to the Gulf, but this might be arranged
We ought as soon as possible to have a complete scheme to put before the Turks. The information
points to something of this kind :
1. The Turks to go ahead with Sir W. Willcocks as to irrigation.
2. We to have the Bagdad to Damascus R[ailwa]y concession.
3. An arrangement with Turks and Germans as to Bagdad to Gulf R[ailwa]y. The Turk
will probably insist upon dropping the Lynch Concession if all this is to be done, and if so
I do not see how we can help that.
The sooner the Bagdad R[ailwa]y Committee(²) can put this into shape the better.

E. G.

(²) [For this Committee, *v. supra*, pp. 373–4, *Ed. note.*]

No. 282.

Mr. Marling to Sir Edward Grey.

F.O. 41730/2074/09/44.
(No. 893.)   *Constantinople,* D. *November 9, 1909.*
Sir,   R. *November 15, 1909.*
With reference to my telegram No. 351 of the 5th instant(¹) informing you
briefly of the proposals outlined by Dr. Gwinner to Sir H. Babington Smith for
British participation in the Bagdad Railway, I have the honour to transmit herewith
a copy of the memorandum(²) which the latter is sending to Sir Ernest Cassel of the
conversation which took place between them.
Mr. Edwin Whittall, the Administrator of the National Bank called on me
subsequently and informed me that he had at Dr. Gwinner's request arranged the
interview between these two gentlemen, and added that, after a long discussion of
the situation in which Dr. Gwinner had developed his views as to our participation
in considerable detail, Dr. Gwinner had finally requested him to go at once to London
to try to induce Sir Ernest Cassel to come to some arrangement with the German
Company. It is natural that Dr. Gwinner should prefer to approach the National
Bank through Mr. Whittall rather than through its official representatives, as
Mr. Whittall has not only very large dealings with the German Railway Co[mpany]
but has also for some time past been a strong advocate of British participation in
the Railway; and when he asked me whether in my opinion he should go to London
as requested, I urged him to do so provided that Sir H. Babington Smith concurred
Mr. Whittal[l] started for London this morning travelling viâ Bucharest.
It will at any rate be of advantage that His Majesty's Government should obtain
possession of Dr. Gwinner's views, and no one is better qualified to convey them
than Mr. Whittal[l] who is a personal friend of Dr. Gwinner and who, moreover, is
acting in the matter as a private person.
You will have noted that Dr. Gwinner's proposal to give us control of the Bagdad
–Gulf sections is not on all fours with the communication made to me by the Grand
Vizier (as reported in my telegram No. 839 of the 11th October)(³) and again repeated
by His Highness to me with somewhat more assurance on the 5th instant, that the
Germans were prepared to accept our participation on the basis of equal representation
on the Board. In spite of this discrepancy I have no reason to suppose that
Dr. Gwinner did not, as mentioned in Sir H. Babington Smith's memorandum, urge
on the Grand Vizier that the Ottoman Government should agree to our acquiring
control of the Gulf sections of the line; and I think the explanation probably is that
the Grand Vizier, while really anxious to bring the Germans and ourselves together

(¹) [*v. supra*, p. 380, No. 279.]
(²) [*Printed infra*, pp. 793–4, *App.* VII.]
(³) [*v. supra*, p. 378, No. 276.]

shrank from making officially a proposal which might be represented as calculated to advance British political interests at a moment like the present when a certain stir has been made in the press about our supposed designs of aggrandizement at the expense of Turkey in those regions.

I have, &c.
CHARLES M. MARLING.

MINUTES.

Mr. Whittall came to see me this afternoon and gave me a full account of *his* interview with Dr. Gwinner which preceded Sir H. Babington Smith's interview. There is one important discrepancy in the account of the two interviews. According to Mr. Whittall Dr. Gwinner agreed to British control over the Bagdad–Gulf section and with that end in view British interests in that section and in the provision of material etc. should be 50%, the remaining 50% being divided amongst the German, French, Belgians etc. This would give, according to his views, British control over this section. Mr. Whittall told me that he made a point of inquiring about material and that Dr. Gwinner had said that the British Company would supply half, and that the remaining half would be supplied by any of the other participants at the lowest tender.

From Mr. Whittall's version it seems to me clear that Tewfik Pasha's statement to me the other day should have been that the Bagdad R[ailwa]y Co. were ready to allow British participation in the Bagdad–Gulf section on equal terms with the Co[mpany]. This is not what we want.

We must have nothing less than what Sir H. Babington Smith has stated that Dr. Gwinner is ready to concede. We must always remember that this is Dr. Gwinner's first offer and that we can get more if we want it. I do not consider that we should have the control over the section if we only had 50% of the voting power. We must have a good deal more.

Dr. Gwinner further told Mr. Whittall that in the event of an agreement being arrived at his Company would be ready to agree to recognise England's predominant interests in Mesopotamia south of Bagdad. This, I think, would be a valuable admission.

C. H.

Our position is a very strong one and we must now take care to get all that we want.
[C. H.]

Everything points to its being our objective to induce the Turks and Germans to eliminate from the Bagdad R[ailwa]y concession all interest in any line south of Bagdad and to promise us a concession to make a railway from Bagdad to the Gulf. The quid pro quo for this would be an unconditional consent on our part to the 4% increase of Customs dues. We must also consider how our interest should be secured in a line west from Bagdad to the Mediterranean such as Sir W. Willcocks proposes.

E. G.

No. 283.

Sir Edward Grey to Mr. Marling.

F.O. 41367/2074/09/44.
(No. 350.) Secret.

Sir,
Foreign Office, November 12, 1909.

The Turkish Amb[assado]r called at the Foreign Office on the 8th inst[ant] and was received by Sir Charles Hardinge. H[is] E[xcellency] stated that he had been instructed by Rifaat Pasha to inform me unofficially that he had been in communication with the Bagdad Railway Company and that he had, not without difficulty, succeeded in persuading them to agree to British participation in the railway on equal terms. This statement Tewfik Pasha repeated more than once.

He was further instructed to ask that a British Representative should be appointed to discuss with a representative of the Germany Company the agreement to be arrived at in conjunction with the Ministry of Public Works at Constantinople.

Sir Charles Hardinge informed Tewfik Pasha that the news he gave was some-what of a surprise since the question had been seriously under discussion six or seven years ago and, but for German pretensions an agreement might then have been reached. We had constantly heard since that these pretensions had not been abated and we had been patiently waiting for a moment such as this to arrive. He would understand that there was no Company in existence to undertake participation with the German Company, and that it would not be possible to select anybody to enter upon negotiations without further delay.

Sir C. Hardinge requested the Amb[assado]r to convey my thanks to the Min[ister] for F[oreign] A[ffairs], and to say that the matter will be taken into consideration at once.

[I am, &c.
E. GREY.]

No. 284.

Sir A. Nicolson to Sir Edward Grey.

St. Petersburgh, November 15, 1909.

F.O. 41981/2074/09/44A.
Tel. (No. 490.)
Bagdad Railway.

D. 8·29 P.M.
R. 9·30 P.M.

M. Isvolsky read to me some secret information which had reached him. Hilmi Pasha had been made acquainted with possibility of an English company asking for concession of a railway from Koweit to Bagdad without requiring any guarantees. Hilmi Pasha did not himself like proposal, but thought it might be found pleasing by Assembly. He had therefore spoken to German Ambassador at Constantinople, and had proposed that for the last section of the railway an Anglo-Franco-German combination should be made.

German Ambassador said he would recommend this combination on condition that no difficulties were made to German company coming to a final arrangement as to the Bu[l]gurlou–Hilif section. Minister for Foreign Affairs asked if I knew anything of above. I reminded him of the possibility of our asking for a railway, and that he had made no objection, but that I had heard nothing of the proposed combination "à trois." I told him that he could remain perfectly assured that we would not enter into conversation as to Bagdad Railway except "à quatre," and that I would answer for my Government that they would not do so.

No. 285.

Sir A. Nicolson to Sir Edward Grey.

F.O. 42638/2074/09/44A.
(No. 610.) Confidential.
Sir,

St. Petersburgh, D. November 16, 1909.
R. November 22, 1909.

Monsieur Iswolsky told me yesterday that he had some secret information to give me. He had learnt that Mr. Winston Churchill, when recently in Germany, had informed Mahmet Chefket Pasha that an English Company would shortly apply to the Ottoman Government for the concession of a railway from Koweit to Bagdad without requiring any guarantees, and that similar information had been communicated to Tewfik Pasha in London. I observed to Monsieur Iswolsky that this was in all probability the scheme as to which I had given him private information some little time ago, and to which he had made no objection.

His Excellency said that he quite understood that, but he wished to communicate to me the subsequent developments which he thought might be of interest. Hilmi Pasha had naturally received intelligence of the project, and had not viewed it favourably, though he admitted that it would probably be pleasing to the Turkish Parliament in view of the fact that no guarantees were required. He had, in order to block an exclusively British project, suggested to the German Ambassador whether the German Railway Company would not be disposed to form a combination for the last section of the railway with French and English concessionnaires. Baron Marschall said that he had no objection to such a combination, provided that no further difficulties were raised in regard to the Bulgurlou–Hilif section. He would be prepared in such circumstances to recommend the combination which Hilmi Pasha suggested.

I told Monsieur Iswolsky that I had heard nothing whatever as to the proposed combination, but he could be assured that my Government would not enter into any discussions as to the Bagdad Railway unless Russia was a party to them. He knew well that my Government had consistently declined a conversation à *deux*, and had maintained that it should be à *quatre*; and I felt confident that they would not move from that position. His Excellency said that he had no doubts on that head, but he had chiefly desired to draw my attention to the attitude of Hilmi Pasha.

I have, &c.
A. NICOLSON.

No. 286.

Sir Edward Grey to Mr. Marling.

F.O. 41726/2074/09/44.
(No. 355.)
Sir,   *Foreign Office, November 16, 1909.*

I have rec[eive]d your despatch No. 889 of Nov[ember] 5(¹) reporting that the plans for prolonging the Bagdad Railway eastward from Bulgurlu to Adana, Aleppo and El Helif have received, in principle at any rate, the approval of the Turkish Gov[ernmen]t.

It would appear from information received in this Dep[artmen]t from Sir A. Block which is probably in your possession, that the revenues assigned by the Porte as guarantees for the interest on the railway loans, not including any of the proceeds of the prospective 4% increase of the Customs duties, will suffice for the construction of Series II of the Bagdad Railway, but not for the construction of Series III. I have to request you to communicate to me your views as to how the Bagdad Railway Company propose to finance the construction of Series III of the Railway.

I am, &c.
E. GREY.

(¹) [*v. supra*, pp. 380–1, No. 280.]

No. 287.

Sir Edward Grey to Sir A. Nicolson.

F.O. 41981/2074/09/44A.   *Foreign Office, November 18, 1909.*
Tel. (No. 1334.)   D. 2·45 P.M.
Your tel[egram] No. 490.(¹)

The Russian Gov[ernmen]t are aware that H[is] M[ajesty's] Ambassador at Const[antino]ple applied some weeks ago for a concession for a railway from Bagdad to the Gulf by the valley of the Tigris with the option of prolonging it along the valley of the Euphrates from Bagdad to the Mediterranean.(²)

(¹) [*v. supra*, p. 386, No. 284.]
(²) [*v. supra*, pp. 376–7, No. 274.]

[17590]   2 c 2

The Russian Gov[ernmen]t may also be aware that one of the conditions imposed by H[is] M[ajesty's] G[overnment] for the acceptance of the 4% surtax is that none of its proceeds is to be applied to the payment of kilometric guarantees and that the Porte is to obtain a written assurance from the German Gov[ernmen]t in this sense.([3])

The Bagdad R[ailwa]y Co: realise that the required kilometric guarantees will not be forthcoming unless the Powers agree to the additional surtax on imports and unless its proceeds are devoted to them at least in part. Consequently the German Gov[ernmen]t are not likely to give the required assurance.

Two days ago I received a memorandum from Babington Smith at Const[antino]ple([4]) giving an account of an interview he had with Gwinner in which the latter expressed his readiness now to agree that the section of the Bagdad Railway from Bagdad to the Gulf should be under British control and should be constructed by British Agency and with British material, other interests taking only a subordinate share and the British group having nothing to do with the line north of Bagdad.

I have told German Amb[assado]r that we must oppose increase of Turkish Customs dues failing an agreement about Bagdad R[ailwa]y, and that one difficulty in participating in that scheme is that Russian as well as French co-operation must be invited. We are now given to understand that the Germans might waive in our favour all rights to construct their railway south of Bagdad leaving it to us to make an arrangement with Turkey for a line from Bagdad to the Gulf. This is what H[is] M[ajesty's] G[overnment] have always demanded and what it is imperative for British interests in Mesopotamia to obtain. If this were conceded we would probably agree unconditionally, as other Powers including Russia seem inclined to do, to increase of Turkish Customs dues and make no conditions as to participation in Bagdad Railway. We should be much more interested in a railway going due west from Bagdad by a different route altogether than in the German line north of Bagdad. Question of increase of Turkish Customs dues has made decision urgent; for we cannot maintain opposition to increase of duties alone, and if conceded this will place the Germans in a position to complete the Bagdad Railway.

You are authorised to give this information to M. Isvolsky and to endeavour to ascertain his views.

([3]) [cp. infra, pp. 791–2, App. VI.]
([4]) [This is the memorandum sent to Sir Edward Grey by Mr. Marling in his despatch No. 893 of November 9 (supra, pp. 384–5, No. 282). It is printed infra, pp. 793–4, App. VII.]

No. 288.

Sir A. Nicolson to Sir Edward Grey.

F.O. 42457/2074/09/44.
(No. 494.)
(Telegraphic.) P.([1])　　　　　　　　　　St. Petersburgh, November 19, 1909.

Please refer to your telegram dated yesterday, No. 1334 :([2]) Bagdad Railway negotiations at Constantinople.

In accordance with your instructions I saw M. Isvolsky this afternoon, and communicated to his Excellency a paraphrase of your telegram under reference.

([1]) [The original decypher of this telegram cannot be traced. The paraphrase given above is taken from the *Confidential Print.*]
([2]) [v. immediately preceding document.]

He said he would defer giving me his views until he had studied the question in detail, but the following are some points on which he commented :—

It appeared to his Excellency that (so far as he could see) Germany was to take all the line as far south as Bagdad, and England the continuation of the line from that place to the Persian Gulf. In fact the railway was to be divided between these two Powers; and in that case all idea of a conversation à quatre had been abandoned, and Russian interests were not to be taken into account. All rights over the Bagdad–Persian Gulf section had, it seemed to him, been waived by Germany in order to obtain the consent of Great Britain to the surtax on Turkish customs without any conditions, and in return England had given Germany a free hand as regards the whole line north of Bagdad. It was, he said, inaccurate to suppose that no conditions would be made by Russia before she assented to the surtax. When in 1907, or earlier, discussions had begun as to the railway between Russia and Germany, with special reference to how future railways in Persia might be affected by it, he had let the matter drop on learning that in view of His Majesty's Government all four Powers should take part in the discussion. M. Isvolsky's memory is, I think, at fault in this, for the reason why discussions were then dropped was, so far as I can remember, that Germany would not abandon her claim to extend the railway to the east, and no agreement could be reached on this point. M. Isvolsky observed that the Governments of Berlin and London would seem to be desirous of settling the question " on the backs of all other parties," and the communication made by me showed that His Majesty's Government had embarked on an entirely new and unexpected course.

Please regard the following as confidential :—

It was clear to me that M. Isvolsky was considerably displeased by my communication. Although I impressed on him the language held by you to Count Metternich, his Excellency apparently did not attach much importance to it.

No. 289.

Minutes by Sir C. Hardinge and Sir Edward Grey.

F.O. 43161/2074/09/44.
Sir E. Grey,   *Foreign Office, November* 19, 1909.

Sir E. Cassel called last night and talked of the Bagdad and Hit railways.

He regards the Bagdad–Gulf railway as the most important of the two, and believes that for grain transport the Persian Gulf route will always be cheaper than the route across the desert viâ Hit. He said that it is also absolutely necessary that we should obtain the Khanikin branch which must start from Bagdad and not from Sadijé. I remarked that the Germans would not be likely to give this up. He replied that he thought they would give it up, and that we must have it on account of the Persian trade coming from the Gulf.

As regards the Hit railway it would no doubt compete with the Bagdad railway and might in the end be a paying concern. Sir W. Willcocks had told him that you had suggested the possibility of the Gov[ernmen]t taking shares in the railway, and that Sir W. W[illcocks] had talked a good deal of a Gov[ernmen]t guarantee, but that he was opposed to both ideas and wished that the two railways should be constructed and run on purely commercial lines. He thought that the French would not co-operate in the Hit line, as they have 30% interest in the Bagdad R[ailwa]y. The line would have to be a metre gauge, as nothing less would do for heavy transport. He thought that Sir W. Willcocks had greatly underestimated the cost of construction. He intends therefore to send an engineer to report. He wishes to know as soon as possible the views of H[is] M[ajesty's] Gov[ernmen]t and will himself as head of the National Bank negotiate with Dr. Gwinner whom he knows very well.

He remarked that there must be a conflict between the Germans and the Turks since the Germans want the 4% for kilometric guarantees while the Turks want i for a large loan as guarantee. That, I remarked, is no concern of ours, if we can get all we want.

C. H.

Nov[ember] 19, 1909.

I never suggested that the Gov[ernmen]t should take shares in the Hit railway it was Sir W. Willcocks who made some suggestion of the kind to me when I pointed out the difficulties of a Gov[ernmen]t guarantee: I made no comment on the suggestion, which does not differ much from a Gov[ernmen]t guarantee. If Parliament would agree to one it would probably agree to the other.

The Khanikin branch may complicate matters with the Russians. We cannot go further with that till we hear the result of our communication of this week to St. Petersburgh.

E. G.

No. 290.

Sir A. Nicolson to Sir Edward Grey.

Private.(¹)

My dear Grey,   *St. Petersburgh, November 19, 1909.*

I have an opportunity of sending you this letter by a private hand tomorrow. I communicated to Iswolsky this afternoon the latest developments in regard to the Bagdad Railway question, and I could clearly see that he was much annoyed and was under the impression that we were disposed to come to an arrangement with Germany over the head of Russia. I quite understand that as a question of Imperial interest it would be an immense gain to obtain from Germany a waiver of her rights over the Bagdad–Gulf section and her consent that this section should become a practically exclusively British concern. This no doubt would be more than we had expected, and from a British point of view would be a valuable prize. But I think that I should explain to you that my impression is that Iswolsky considers that in order to acquire a concession on terms more favourable than were anticipated we have waved on one side Russian interests, consulting solely our own, and have abandoned our standpoint to discuss Bagdad Railway matters with Russia and the two others—in short that the conversation *à quatre* has gone by the board. I could see that he had some difficulty in suppressing his annoyance, and when I said "Frankly you must admit that you would prefer seeing us have charge of the southern section than that it should be in German hands," he replied "That may or may not be; but I thought we should all come into the railway or at any rate have a voice in the matter, but you seem to be settling affairs with Germany on the backs of us and France." He said that the interests of Russia, strategical, political and economical in the Bagdad Railway were important and he had always thought that we would enter into no discussions without consultation with her and France. To put it crudely he seemed to me to think that the bait offered to us was so tempting that we were willing to leave all our former declarations on one side and come to terms with Germany for what was practically a division of the railway between us both. These were in short his first impressions, and later doubtless he will give me his reasoned views. It is unfortunate that the question should have cropped up just now. There are already

(¹) [Grey MSS., Vol. 34.]

ome misgivings as to the constant reports as to a rapprochement between us and
Germany, and though Iswolsky himself would not and does not regard a rapprochement with disfavour—indeed he would perhaps welcome it—he would not like and
would resent it being accomplished to the neglect of the interests of Russia and to
e extended to matters in which she was directly and seriously concerned. More-
ver I am afraid—I am writing quite frankly—that he feels on first impressions of
he communication I made today to him that we have not fully acted up to our
ssurances, and that we are inclined to jump at a tempting offer made by Germany,
ndifferent as to how it may be regarded by Russia. There may arise in his mind
certain distrust of us, and what would be still more regrettable mistrust in the mind
f the Emperor. This distrust I myself have little doubt Germany would be glad
o see implanted, as by that means she could the more surely detach Russia from
s, or in any case break down that complete confidence which has hitherto existed
etween us. I shall be curious to see in what frame of mind I shall find Iswolsky
when I next see him, and when he has had time to reflect over the whole question.
The first impressions were decidedly not favourable, and his attitude towards me at
he end of our interview was frigid. To these various phases of his disposition I
m accustomed and they do not disturb me; but I should much regret if I found
fter he has had time to look into the question that he considers that we have not
reated Russia well and fairly. France I think is already well provided for in the
Bagdad Railway and would not complain; moreover the question has not that direct
nd immediate interest to her as it has to Russia. I don't know whether it will
urn out to our advantage if Russia is left alone to discuss with Germany questions
s to the railway north of Bagdad, especially if Russia feels that she is entirely free
nd unfettered from any obligations to us and can come to any terms she may
consider desirable in her own interests. Valuable as the offer of Germany undoubtedly
s to us, I am a little afraid that it may prove to be the first rift in the lute on which
we and Russia have been playing so harmoniously together.

Y[ou]rs sincerely,
A. NICOLSON.

No. 291.

Sir F. Bertie to Sir Edward Grey.

F.O. 42694/2074/09/44A.
No. 455.) Secret.   Paris, D. November 20, 1909.
Sir,   R. November 22, 1909.
    1 received on the night of the 18th instant the Telegram([1]) which you had
despatched that day to His Majesty's Ambassador at St. Petersburg relative to the
application to the Porte by His Majesty's Government for the concession for a railway
rom Bagdad to the Persian Gulf by the Valley of the Tigris with the option of
prolonging it along the Euphrates Valley from Bagdad to the Mediterranean; the
condition attached to the consent of His Majesty's Government to the 4% increase
n the Turkish Customs Duties as regards kilometric guarantees to Railways; the
apparent readiness of Mr. Gwinner to agree that the section of the Bagdad Railway
rom Bagdad to the Gulf should be under British Control and should be constructed
by British Agency and with British material; the communication which you made
on the subject of the Bagdad Railway and the increase of Customs Duties to the
German Ambassador; the conditions subject to which His Majesty's Government
would be prepared to forego any participation in the Bagdad Railway North of Bagdad
and give their consent to the increase in the Customs Duties.

([1]) [v. supra, pp. 387–8, No. 287.]

In view of the fact that you authorized Sir Arthur Nicolson to give to the Russian Minister for Foreign Affairs the information contained in your Telegram and that if you had not already made a like communication to the French Ambassador in London, the information would reach the French Government from Petersburg thought that it would be advisable to inform Monsieur Pichon of the communication which you had directed His Majesty's Ambassador at Petersburg to make to Monsieur Isvolski. When therefore I called on His Excellency yesterday evening, I reminded him of the observations which he had made to me on the 7th ultimo (see my Despatch No. 402 of October 8th(²)) on the question of connecting the consent of His Majesty's Government to an increase in the Customs Duties with a stipulation that an assurance should be given by the German Government in regard to the Bagdad Railway, and I asked him whether he had made or received any further communication on the subject. His Excellency said that he had drafted a formula which whilst having the effect of precluding any part of the proceeds of the additional Customs Duties being employed for the purpose of the Bagdad Railway would he thought safeguard the interests of all the Powers in other matters. As he told me that he had not quite recently received any communication from the French Ambassador in London on the subject of the Bagdad Railway I read to His Excellency your Telegram of the 18th instant to Sir Arthur Nicolson and he expressed satisfaction at there being a prospect of a settlement of the question. He further said that he did not think that the Ottoman Bank and their German Partners in the Combination for raising money for the Railway would be able to obtain all the requisite funds without recourse to the Paris Market and the French Government did not intend to allow a quotation of the loan on the Bourse except on conditions which hitherto the German Company had not been willing to accept.

I have, &c.
FRANCIS BERTIE.

(²) [Not reproduced.]

No. 292.

Sir Edward Grey to Sir A. Nicolson.

F.O. 42457/2074/09/44.
(No. 1340.)
(Telegraphic.) P.(¹)   *Foreign Office, November 23, 1909.*
British participation in the Bagdad Railway.
Please refer to your telegram No. 494 of the 19th instant.(²)
You should make the position of affairs clear to M. Isvolsky as follows: The 4 per cent. increase of customs is designed by Germany to supply her with funds. A free hand she has already by virtue of the concession itself, and not owing to anything we are doing. What we have to do now is to protect ourselves in the matter of the customs by making our consent to the increase conditional on some stipulation about the railway. Russia is at liberty to make a similar stipulation, although the other Powers do not appear to be desirous of doing so; in fact, we are marking time in the matter until we learn the views of the Russian Government. I informed M. Isvolsky of the state of affairs as soon as the question was first raised, and up to now I have made no communication to the German Government other than the two statements that, first, an obstacle to an Anglo-German agreement about the railway—an obstacle which I would do my best to overcome—lay in the obligation

(¹) [The original decypher of this telegram cannot be traced. The paraphrase given above is taken from the *Confidential Print.*]
(²) [*v. supra*, pp. 388–9, No. 288.]

we were under to come to an understanding with Russia, and, secondly, that our consent to the customs increase must be conditional. We have not yet entered into official negotiations with the German Government, so that it should be noticed that we have no authority for our ideas of the terms likely to prove acceptable to the Germans except that of the information volunteered to us by Dr. Gwinner, and conveyed to us indirectly through unofficial channels.

We have always demanded—and we still refuse to waive our claim—the construction of the section south of Bagdad and its control when built. More than ever is this important now, since we are in some danger of losing the river transport for our Indian trade in Mesopotamia, which we have controlled for half a century, owing to irrigation schemes now being initiated by the Turkish Government in Mesopotamia of a kind probably calculated to render the rivers non-navigable, in which case no means of transport would be available until the completion of the railway. These being our requirements, it is essential that we should learn on what conditions Russia would be willing to participate in the line north of Bagdad. Whether England and Russia so participate or not, the line will assuredly be built. His Majesty's Government must therefore take steps to meet the situation, and they desire to know the views of the Russian Government before going further with the offer made to them.

With reference to your private letter,([3]) we have kept M. Isvolsky informed, we have made no bargain, we put Russian Government in possession of Gwinner's views within two days of hearing them ourselves through private channels. I am therefore at a loss to see the justification for M. Isvolsky's annoyance.

([3]) [v. supra, pp. 390–1, No. 290.]

No. 293.

Sir Edward Grey to Sir F. Bertie.

F.O. 43281/2074/09/44.
(No. 470.)

Sir,   Foreign Office, November 23, 1909.

I told M. Cambon to-day that a little time ago Herr von Schoen had observed, informally and in the course of general conversation with Sir Edward Goschen, that irritation was caused in Germany by the fact that we appeared so often to be obstructing the Germans in commercial enterprises.([1]) Herr von Schoen had mentioned coaling-stations and the Bagdad Railway.

A few days after this, I had taken an opportunity of telling Count Metternich frankly exactly what we were doing about the Bagdad Railway.([2]) I explained to him the condition which we had made with regard to the increase of the Turkish Customs Duties. It was impossible for any British Government not to make this condition, owing to the fact that the construction of the Bagdad Railway and the carrying out of the irrigation works now projected to the south of Bagdad would displace existing means of communication in which we were largely interested, and would introduce changes into the whole trade of Mesopotamia, in which we were also largely interested. I pointed out to Count Metternich that it was out of no illwill to Germany, but out of the necessities of the case, that we had stipulated that the revenue derived from the increased Customs Dues should not be used for the construction of the Bagdad Railway. I then pointed out to Count Metternich that we had always felt that France and Russia were interested in the question of this Railway too. French participation presented no difficulty. But Russian participation

([1]) [cp. supra, p. 301, No. 201.]
([2]) [Probably this refers to Sir Edward Grey's conversation of October 28, for which v. supra, pp. 378–9, No. 277. But see also G.P. XXVII, II, pp. 585–6.]

had not yet been arranged, and we had no wish to quarrel with Russia about thi
question. It was therefore for Germany to arrange how the difficulty with Russi
could be overcome. For my own part, I was prepared to give my attention to th
question of the Railway, in order to find a solution.

I told M. Cambon that this was all that had passed with the German Govern
ment. I had, however, heard from a private source that Herr Gwinner had beer
talking to Sir William Whittall(³) and others at Constantinople, and had beer
saying that Germany must have the new revenue from the increased Duties fo
the Bagdad Railway, and that to secure this she might be prepared to eliminate
from the Railway Concession the section of the line between Bagdad and the Persiar
Gulf, and hand this section over to Great Britain. If that was done, it was clear tha
British interests would be safeguarded, and there would be no further need fo
objection on this point to the increase of the Customs Duties.

I explained to M. Cambon that, within two days of hearing Herr Gwinner'
views, I let M. Iswolsky know what the new situation was; and I then com[muni
cate]d to M. Cambon the substance of the telegrams which I had sent to Sir Arthu
Nicolson on the subject. M. Iswolsky was now very much disturbed, and h
considered that we were departing from the agreement to discuss the Railway questior
à quatre.

I thought that M. Pichon ought to know what had happened, and I had kep
Sir Francis Bertie informed. We could not go on for ever opposing the increas
of the Turkish Customs Duties if our own interests were safeguarded, and I had beer
obliged to put the situation before M. Iswolsky in order that he might decide wha
line to take.

M. Cambon said that as far as France was concerned there was of course n
difficulty. He was much interested in the advance which Herr Gwinner had made
and he looked upon it as auspicious. He then told me that he heard Sir Willian
Willcocks was negotiating with an important English and French group concernin
the Hit Railway, which he regarded with favour.

I replied that Sir William Willcocks had explained his project to me.(⁴) I feare
that it would cost more than he expected. But in any case we were much mor
interested in it than in the Bagdad Railway to the north of Bagdad, and we wer
favourable to it. I then showed M. Cambon on the map how the irrigation work
would render impossible the river traffic in which we were interested. It was there
fore essential that we should get a concession for a railway from Bagdad to th
Persian Gulf to take the place of this river communication.

[I am, &c.]

E. G[REY].

(³) [This is the first reference that has been found in the British archives to a conversatior
between Dr. Gwinner and Sir William Whittall. Reference is made to such a conversation ir
G.P. XXVII, II², pp. 585–6, but this is contained in a report from Count Metternich of hi
interview with Sir Edward Grey of November 17, of which Sir Edward Grey's own accoun
describes the conversation as having taken place between Dr. Gwinner and Mr. Edwin Whittall
Sir William Whittall's son (*v. supra*, p. 313, No. 205). A fuller account of Mr. Edwin Whittall'
conversation with Dr. Gwinner is given *supra*, pp. 384–5, No. 282.]

(⁴) [*v. supra*, pp. 381–4, No. 281.]

No. 294.

Sir A. Nicolson to Sir Edward Grey.

St. Petersburgh, November 24, 1909.

F.O. 43086/2074/09/44A.

Tel. (No. 495.)

D. 10 P.M.

R. 10·30 P.M.

Bagdad Railway. Your telegram No. 1040.(¹)

I have seen M. Isvolsky, and found him in cheerful and rational mood.
communicated to the Minister for Foreign Affairs substance of your telegram above

(¹) [This is probably a mistake for 1340, for which *v. supra*, pp. 392–3, No. 292.]

mentioned. He said that he had been looking into the question since our last conversation, and he read me the telegram which he addressed to Russian Ambassador in London in September 1907,(²) after the overture made to us at Windsor. He explained that since then he had abstained from all discussion with the German Government, and had awaited patiently the commencement of conversation à quatre. Now it appeared that the Germans had informally suggested that we should undertake southern section, and abstain from any interest in railway north of Bagdad. If we accepted that proposal, and he said that we would be quite within our rights in doing so, it was clear it would be an arrangement à deux, and Russia, in those circumstances, would be at liberty to endeavour to make an arrangement herself with Germany as to the railway north of Bagdad. But then the conversation à quatre would be abandoned. He thought that his reply to our communication would be in that sense. I asked him to keep it back until I had communicated again with you.

I told him that I wished him to remove from his mind any doubts as to our having accepted any proposals or even entered into negotiations in regard to any. We had received certain information, which we had immediately communicated to him, and asked for his views, and I had also communicated to him what had been said to German Ambassador. What we wanted to know were the views of the Russian Government, and conditions on which they would wish to participate in the railway. He said that he quite understood this, and had no desire whatever to make any reproach or to express any doubts. He quite understood our attitude as to the southern section, but it seemed that Germany would not give us a free hand there unless we agreed to abstain from taking any further interest in railway north of Bagdad. Were we disposed to enter into more formal and official negotiations on that basis if the German Government approached us in that sense?

My personal impression is that now that he has thought over the matter he would not be vexed if we did come to terms with the German Government and leave him to try and settle matters with the latter on behalf of Russian interests. But I should like to have one more talk with him before giving you a more decided opinion than an impression. I do not think that he has any clear views as to the conditions on which Russian Government would participate in the railway. Perhaps you would kindly send me a telegram somewhat to the effect that the matter is so urgent that you will shortly be obliged to discuss matters on the basis of Mr. Gwinner's proposals, and that it is of importance that if the Russian Government wish us to continue to insist on maintaining the standpoint of a conversation à quatre, they should lose no time in giving us full information as to their conditions. I think that with this in my hand I could obtain some more definite proposal from him.

As to the surtax of 4 per cent., he said that Russian Government had not yet replied to the Ottoman Government and that they considered that Turkish memorandum of 14th September(³) distinctly stated that surcharge would not be devoted to guarantees for Bagdad Railway (see penult[imate] paragraph of Tewfik Pasha's memorandum). If the above interpretation was incorrect it was very possible that Russian Government might make the same reservation as His Majesty's Government on that point.

(²) [sic. The date is probably a mistake for " December 1907," cp. M. Isvolski's letter to Count Benckendorff, of December 6/19, quoted supra, p. 101, Ed. note.]
(³) [v. supra, pp. 375–6, No. 273.]

No. 295.

Mr. Marling to Sir Edward Grey.

F.O. 43494/2074/09/44.
(No. 933.) Secret.   *Constantinople*, D. *November* 24, 1909.
Sir,   R. *November* 29, 1909.

 I have the honour to acknowledge the receipt of the dispatch No. 355 secret of Nov[ember] 16(¹) in which, after informing me that from information derived from Sir Adam Block it would appear that the revenues assigned by the Porte as guarantors for the interest on the construction loans of the Bagdad Railway (excluding the proceeds of the prospective 4% increase of the Customs duties) will suffice for the cost of building of the second and third sections of the line, but not for the fourth and fifth sections, You are so good as to ask my views as to how the Railway Company propose to finance the construction of the latter two sections. I am not aware of the substance of the communications you have received from Sir Adam Block nor, so far as I can ascertain, has he recently expressed any such view to the Embassy. Sir A. Block who called on me this morning cannot recall the communication to which you allude. The only expression of that gentleman's views that I can find in the Embassy is contained in some notes appended to a memorandum of a conversation he had with M. Huguenin, the director of the Anatolian Railway Company, on August 4 last in which he says; " I consider that normally the Public Debt Revenues will shortly(²) increase and will eventually suffice for sections 4 and 5."

 Sir A. Block sent a copy of this memorandum to Sir C. Hardinge about the same time that he communicated it to Sir G. Lowther.

 To return to the question of how the Company now intend to find the security of the 4th and 5th sections of the Railway, Sir A. Block informs me that there are three sources of revenue handled by the Debt which might be drawn on, viz. : 1. Surplus of the tithes collected by the Debt for Railway guarantees, amounting to something between 60,000 Turkish pounds and 100,000 per annum. 2. The interest on the reserve fund of the Debt when that fund reaches £T. 2,000,000. This may very well occur within 12 months and the interest available may be put at £T. 80,000 and 3. The advance of £T. 250,000 which the Debt undertook to make to the Government for the needs of Macedonia. It is clear that with the anticipated increase of the Debt's surplus, the Sublime Porte will eventually dispose of more than sufficient revenues to find the £T. 244,000 required for the third series.

 From Sir A. Block I have also learnt that there has been an exchange of views between the Minister of Finance and Mr. Kau[t]z the director of the Bagdad Railway as to the revenues, other than the 4% which could be assigned to the service of series 2, (sections 2 and 3) and with the following result : Djavid Bey proposed the surplus revenues of the Debt, about £T. 200,000, the sheep tax of the vilayets of Adana and Aleppo set free for 40 years by the recent transaction concerning the Russian loan indemnity and estimated at £T. 40,000 and lastly the surplus of the tithes collected by the Debt, which may be placed at between £T. 60,000 and £T. 100,000 per annum. Mr. Kautz admitted the adequacy of these revenues but stipulated that they should be paid to the Railway by the Debt. The Minister of Finance demurred, however, and said that the moneys would be paid into the Government by the Debt, and the Minister of Finance would make the requisite payments to the Railway Company; to this Mr. Kautz objected and said that if the Government insisted he must ask for a *quid pro quo*, viz., an undertaking by the Government to conclude the financial arrangements for the prolongation of the line from Halif to Mosul. He said he would telegraph to Berlin to ask for authority to treat on these lines.

(¹) [*v. supra*, p. 387, No. 286.]
(²) [Unsigned marginal comment : " a misquotation ' shortly ' should be ' slowly.' "]

This move on the part of the Germans is a clever one, and it implies that they do not intend to renounce their claim on the 4% without obtaining a valuable concession in exchange. They can moreover argue to the Turkish Government that to see the line carried to Mosul is in the interests of the Treasury, for the Aleppo El-Halif section ending as it would *en l'air* would not pay, and the kilometric guarantee will be a drain on the Government whereas if the line is prolonged to Mosul the through traffic thence would greatly increase the receipts and diminish the amount required as kilometric guarantee accordingly.

Mr. Kautz, with whom Mr. Fitzmaurice had some conversation yesterday afternoon speaks with great confidence of the strength of the German position. He says that by making it a condition that the 4% should not be utilized for Railway guarantees, His Majesty's Government had declared war on the Bagdad Railway which it was in the Turkish interest to have built, but that if the germans did not obtain satisfactory financial arrangements to carry out their engagements with the Turks, they themselves would withhold their assent to the increase of the Customs duties and the Turks would logically conclude that their refusal was owing to the attitude of Great Britain in the Railway question. This attitude of Mr. Kautz is no doubt a bargaining one and he gave it to be understood that he would prefer some business-like *entente* with the British as regards the completion of the line.

I have, &c.
CHARLES M. MARLING.

No. 296.

Sir C. Hardinge to Sir A. Nicolson.

Private.(¹)

My dear Nicolson,   *Foreign Office, November* 24, 1909.

. . . .(²) I cannot help thinking, from your telegram and private letters, that Isvolsky is very unreasonable about our attitude towards the Bagdad Railway. Nothing could have been more loyal than the way in which we have acted towards him. Without waiting to discuss the advantages of the proposals made privately to us, we at once informed him of their substance. Nothing has been done behind his back, and no agreement has been come to. I can quite understand that Isvolsky would like to profit by our opposition to the Baghdad Railway, so that it should never be built; but he has yet to realize that, in the long run, the railway will be built, and that the best thing that he can do is to find a means of coming into it with us and the French. The latter are quite pleased at the proposals put forward by Dr. Gwinner, and I feel sure that they will indirectly use their influence to induce the Russians to state the conditions upon which they would be willing to participate, and as to which we are so far absolutely in the dark. I believe that we could, if we wanted, also come to terms with Germany as to the construction of the Baghdad–Kanakin branch; but we do not intend to raise this question, in deference to the susceptibilities of Russia. In the Baghdad–Gulf section we are on strong ground, as it has always been the sphere of British influence, and we intend to keep it so. There is absolutely no ground for Isvolsky's ill-humour or for suspicion that we have come to an arrangement with Germany " at the backs of Russia and France," as he expresses it. . . . .(³)

[Yours ever,
CHARLES HARDINGE.]

(¹) [Carnock MSS.]
(²) [The opening paragraphs of this letter refer to the Balkan situation.]
(³) [The passages which close this letter are of a general character, and are unimportant.]

No. 297.

Sir Edward Grey to Sir A. Nicolson.

F.O. 43086/2074/09/44A.   *Foreign Office, November 26,* 1909.
Tel. (No. 1343.)   D. 5·15 P.M.
    Your telegram No. 495.([1])
    We have, as you are already aware, given no reply so far to Gwinner's proposals,([2]) but have confined our action to informing the French and Russian Governments of their substance.([3]) The proposal made to us is the minimum of what would satisfy British public opinion and safeguard British interests, and to obtain this we should be willing to waive our interests in the railway to the north of Bagdad, although some pressure has been put upon us by the British group to endeavour to obtain the concession of a branch from Bagdad to Khanikin. We realise, however, that Russian sphere of interests might be involved in a line terminating at a point on the limit of the Russian sphere of interest in Persia, and although we should be glad to obtain a concession for such a line, or to participate with Russia in its control and construction, we have refrained from giving any support to such a proposal, and shall not do so without the concurrence of the Russian Government. Although the German Government are aware that proposals have been made to us by the Bagdad Railway Company, we propose to allow the negotiations to be carried on by the English group on a purely commercial basis.
    The matter is one of some urgency, as a decision about the increase of Turkish customs dues cannot be indefinitely postponed, and we are as yet in complete ignorance of the views of the Russian Government as to participation. Two years ago Russian negotiations with Germany fell through owing to the refusal of the latter to recognise Russian interests in the Russian sphere of influence in Persia. To this condition we should naturally have no objection, but we could hardly remain indifferent if, in return for this recognition, any concessions were made by Russia to Germany in the neutral zone. Such a possibility would seem to be precluded by article 3 of the Persian Convention of 1907.([4]) We should certainly raise no objection to the opening of negotiations between Germany and Russia as to participation in the railway to the north of Bagdad, but we trust that the Russian Government would keep us informed of their progress.
    We shall expect to receive in due course a reply from the Russian Government to the communications which you have made to them.
    (Repeated to Paris, No. 737.)

        ([1]) [*v. supra*, pp. 394–5, No. 294.]
        ([2]) [*v. supra*, pp. 384–5, No. 282, and *min.*, and *infra*, pp. 793–4, *App.* VII.]
        ([3]) [*v. supra*, pp. 392–4, Nos. 292–3.]
        ([4]) [*v. Gooch & Temperley*, Vol. IV, p. 618, *App.* I.]

No. 298.

Sir A. Nicolson to Sir Edward Grey.

                                          St. Petersburgh, November 27, 1909.
F.O. 43445/2074/09/44A.   D. 8 P.M.
Tel. (No. 497.)   R. 8 P.M.
    Bagdad Railway.
    Your telegram No. 1343.([1])
    I communicated to Minister for Foreign Affairs substance of above telegram to-day. As to the line from Bagdad to Khanikin, he remarked that German

        ([1]) [*v.* immediately preceding document.]

company had already a concession for a line to Khanikin from a point to the north of Bagdad. He said that if we were to enter into negotiations with Germany on the basis of proposals of Herr Gwinner Russia would of course have to commence discussions on behalf of her own interests with Germany, but that she would enter into them with her hands much weakened if Germany had already come to an arrangement with us. He would have of course to be in a position to have something in hand wherewith to bargain with Germany. I said that bargain should not in any case be in the neutral zone of Persia, as this would hardly be in accordance with our convention. (Personally I have my doubts on the point.) He replied that he did not say that he would look for a bargain in that direction, but that he must be prepared to offer something. He would, in the event of our falling in with new proposals, find Germany very (? stiff) in negotiating with him. I asked him, after some further conversation, what reply I should send you, but I regret to say I could extract nothing from him beyond that he must examine question very carefully, and would let me have a reply later. I explained to him that if we all sat still and did nothing Germany would perhaps withdraw all offers and construct line herself without co-operation of either of us. He said that he had not had an answer to the question which he put to me at our last interview. I asked him to what he alluded. He said were we or were we not going to accept Herr Gwinner's proposals and abandon our interests to the north of Bagdad, *i.e.*, give up the conversation *à quatre* and enter into one *à deux*? I replied that we had decided nothing as yet, and were awaiting his views, but that it was probable we should have to do so if further delay occurred. He asked whether we thought that his interpretation of the paragraph in the Turkish note as to the surtax was correct, namely, that Turkey promised not to devote proceeds to any enterprises already commenced, and that thereby she could not give them to Bagdad Railway. I said I had not had a reply on that point.

I cannot pin M. Isvolsky down, and perhaps you would wish me to tell him positively that you would inform British group that they had better proceed without delay with negotiations with Herr Gwinner. I am a little uneasy still, as I mentioned in my private letter, as to leaving him to discuss alone with Germany, but perhaps we had better run that risk and secure southern section.

MINUTES.

It seems to me that any misunderstanding with M. Isvolsky is one of words rather than of fact.

H[is] M[ajesty's] G[overnment] are quite uncommitted to Germany in regard to the Railway, they have not even decided that negotiations should be conducted *à deux*, and all they desire is that, since there seems a prospect of the Bagdad Railway question being reopened shortly, M. Isvolsky should formulate the views of the Russian Gov[ernmen]t as soon as possible and communicate them to H[is] M[ajesty's] G[overnment] who would then be in a position to determine their own attitude before any negotiations with M. Gwinner take place.

I think it is very undesirable to leave M. Isvolsky to discuss with Germany alone, as it might lead to discussions as to concessions in the neutral zone in Persia, such as an extension of the Bagdad Railway into Persian territory, which would be clearly opposed to Indian interests. I think therefore that we should inform him that Herr Gwinner's proposals (which as a matter of fact are widely divergent in the form reported by Sir H. Babington Smith and in that reported by Mr. Whittall)(2) are in a purely tentative stage, but that it is urgent that we should know, as soon as possible, the attitude of Russia towards the whole question, what participation, as to finance, control, or construction, she would desire, and that we will give his wishes most attentive consideration.

It is of course difficult, after our attitude in 1907, to abandon the position that discussion must be conducted *à quatre*. It is certainly not the case that we propose to abandon our interests north of Bagdad, since even if we built the S. Section of the Bagdad Railway, we should not *ipso facto* be debarred from making a line from Bagdad to the Mediterranean, if the alignment were not that of the proposed Bagdad Railway from Aleppo to Bagdad.

The point about the Turkish note (end of last paragraph but one of Sir A. Nicolson's telegram 497) seems to me immaterial, for if Turkey gets the increased customs other revenues will be set free and could be devoted to the Bagdad Railway kilometric guarantees.

(2) [*v. supra*, pp. 384–5, No. 282, and *min.*, and *infra*, pp. 793–4, App. VII.]

I think the proposal in the last sentence would be a very injudicious line of action to adopt, and it might have very serious consequences.

A. P.
November 29th, 1909.

It would be interesting to know what Herr von Gwinner really proposes : so far we have two different sets.

H. N.
C. H.

No. 299.

Sir A. Nicolson to Sir Edward Grey.

F.O. 44303/2074/09/44A.
(No. 628.) *St. Petersburgh*, D. *November* 28, 1909.
Sir, R. *December* 6, 1909.

I would beg leave to summarise certain conversations which I have had with Monsieur Iswolsky in regard to the Bagdad Railway. Monsieur Iswolsky is now perfectly well aware that matters have not hitherto proceeded further than the reception by the British group of certain proposals made by Monsieur Gwinner to the effect that the former should have the construction and control of the section south of Bagdad, and that, if this proposal were accepted, the British interests in the railway north of Bagdad would be waived. He further understands that His Majesty's Government lost no time in informing him of these proposals, and that hitherto they have not entered into any negotiations with the German Government on the subject. It has also been brought to his knowledge that the objections of His Majesty's Government to their consent to the increase of Turkish customs duties cannot be indefinitely maintained, and that the control and construction of the southern section of the railway are the minimum which would satisfy British public opinion and British interests : that, if necessary, Germany would of herself construct the whole railway without outside co-operation : and that His Majesty's Government are anxiously awaiting information as to the views of the Russian Government in regard to participation in the railway. The above are the chief points which have been brought to the knowledge of Monsieur Iswolsky. His present attitude may be summarised as follows. He considers that the proposals of Monsieur Gwinner constitute an entirely new departure : he does not question the right of the British group or of His Majesty's Government to accept them, and he expects that eventually they will do so : he fully appreciates the loyalty of His Majesty's Government in so promptly informing him of the proposals, and of abstaining from accepting immediately proposals which are so eminently satisfactory to British interests. He regards an arrangement between England and Germany on the basis of the proposals of Monsieur Gwinner as dispelling any expectation that the Bagdad Railway will be discussed between Germany, England, France and Russia. It will necessarily amount to an arrangement between Germany and England, by which the latter will secure for herself the southern section, and in return abandon all interest in the line to the north of Bagdad. In these circumstances he considers that Russia will be left alone to discuss matters with Germany so far as Russian interests are concerned. These interests he regards, from the political, strategical and economical points of view, as of great importance : and he is of opinion that Russia will enter into negotiations with Germany with her hands much weakened. Had he been able to have the continuation of British co-operation in these negotiations he would be more hopeful of their success. France he considers is already in a sense a partner in the Bagdad Railway, and moreover her interests in the project are small in comparison with those of Russia. He has at present, so far as I have been able to ascertain, no definite views as to the basis on which he would endeavour to obtain a Russian participation in the railway. I do not think that he so much desires an actual participation in the railway: he rather wishes to assure himself that Germany will not endeavour to push railway enterprise in those portions of Persia in which Russia possesses direct and immediate interests. In what manner he may secure such assurances he is not at present very clear, but he is well aware that in order to do so he will probably be obliged to offer Germany a *quid pro quo*. Of what character such a *quid pro quo* will be he does not know, nor is he decided as to the quarter in which he could find it. I do not think that he would consider himself precluded from seeking it in the neutral zone of Persia, but he will keep His Majesty's Government informed of the progress of his negotiations with Germany whenever they may be commenced. Personally I doubt if Monsieur Iswolsky would be inclined to admit Germany into the neutral zone of Persia; but I hardly think in case of such an endeavour we could appeal to the Anglo-Russian Convention, though we might have other grounds for raising objections. By Article 2 of the Convention each party agreed not to support concessions to third parties in the zones of the other, but as regards the neutral zone there was, I submit, no restriction on third parties seeking concessions and no obligation on either party to abstain from supporting third parties in that respect. It was simply provided in Article 3 that Russia would not oppose British concessions nor England Russian concessions in that zone.([1]) So far as I can recollect it was understood that there should be no mention of the liberty of action of third parties in the neutral zone, so as to obviate opening the door to observations on their part, and to keep the convention strictly within the limits of an understanding regarding British and Russian interests. It was for this reason that in my *written* paraphrase of your telegram No. 1343 of November 26([2]) I omitted any reference to Article 3, though in conversation I alluded to the point without dwelling upon it, as I did not feel sure of my ground.

As regards the question of a line from Bagdad to Khanikin, Monsieur Iswolsky remarked that the Germans had already a concession for a line from a point to the north of Bagdad to Khanikin, and he seemed to think that this would render superfluous a second branch from Bagdad to that place. With respect to the increase of Turkish customs duties, Monsieur Iswolsky stated very positively that the Russian Government had as yet given no reply to the Turkish request, and he read the last paragraph of the Turkish note as debarring the Ottoman Government from devoting any portion of the proceeds of the surtaxe to kilometric guarantees of any enterprise already commenced: and within that category he placed the Bagdad Railway. He would like to have the views of His Majesty's Government on that point.

As matters at present stand, I should say that Monsieur Iswolsky fully anticipates that His Majesty's Government will negotiate with the German Government, or allow the two groups to do so, on the basis of the proposals of Monsieur Gwinner: and that therefore Russia will be left to come to the best terms she can with Germany. As to what offers he may be disposed to make in order to tranquillise his mind as to possible eventual German enterprise to the east of the Bagdad Railway I cannot say. My own impression is that if he feels he has a perfectly free hand, he may be disposed to offer a good deal: and on that point I confess I am not entirely at ease.

I have, &c.
A. NICOLSON.

([1]) [Marginal comment by Sir C. Hardinge: " This is quite true but if Russia supported a German concession which we wished to obtain she would be opposing us. C. H."]
([2]) [*v. supra*, p. 398, No. 297.]

No. 300.

Sir A. Nicolson to Sir Edward Grey.

F.O 43850/2074/09/44.
Tel. (No. 499.)

St. Petersburgh, November 30, 1909.
D. 3·58 P.M.
R. 5·5 P.M.

Bagdad Railway.

French Ambassador had a conversation with M. Isvolsky yesterday on the above subject. He found the Minister for Foreign Affairs much preoccupied and perplexed as to the basis of (? on) which he might have to approach the German Government in order to safeguard Russian interests in the event of His Majesty's Government accepting the proposal of Herr Gwinner. French Ambassador said that M. Isvolsky intended to speak to me as to Persian railways and as to the concession to provide for linking up a connection with Indian Railways. French Ambassador expressed the hope that we would be conciliatory on this point. If Minister for Foreign Affairs approaches me on the subject should I remind him that the Russian Government have already agreed in principle to a Julfa–Mohammerah line and that we are still waiting for a reply to our memorandum of October of last year?(¹) Or if we obtain construction and control over the southern section of the Bagdad Railway would His Majesty's Government still claim Mohammerah line? As to connection with Indian railways should I maintain former *non-possumus* attitude or would you be inclined to allow such a concession to be applied for in order to exclude other competitors and so earmark it, leaving construction to an indefinite future? I remarked to French Ambassador that I understood that his Government had no objection to Herr Gwinner's proposals. He replied that possibly not, but that his Government might ask for a compensation.

(¹) [Not reproduced. The memorandum was dated October 14, 1908. It concerned railway concessions in Persia, and the question of a Persian loan. *cp. infra*, p. 452, No. 343, *min.* by Mr. Alwyn Parker, and *note* (³).]

No. 301.

Sir Edward Grey to Sir A. Nicolson.

F.O. 43445/2074/09/44A.
Tel. (No. 1346.)

Foreign Office, November 30, 1909.
D. 12·40 P.M.

Your telegram No. 497.(¹)

You should explain to M. Iswolsky that no negotiations are taking place with Germany but that Herr Gwinner has opened communications with English financiers and we have been informed of what has passed.

We are not yet clear exactly what proposal will be the outcome of these communications. Till it is submitted to us with the approval of the German Gov[ernmen]t we cannot be sure that it will be acceptable : if acceptable we shall not accept it, till we have discussed the question with the French and Russian Gov[ernmen]ts in order that whatever agreement is reached may be *à quatre*. Meanwhile we have informed the French and Russian Gov[ernmen]ts of what is passing(²) in order that they may be prepared to come to a decision, when the need for one arrives, and we hope M. Iswolsky will be equally frank with us as to his views.

(¹) [*v. supra*, pp. 398–9, No. 298.]
(²) [*v. supra*, pp. 391–3, Nos. 291–2; pp. 393–4, No. 293 for France, and pp. 394–5, No. 294 for Russia.]

No. 302.

Sir A. Nicolson to Sir Edward Grey.

St. Petersburgh, December 1, 1909.

F.O. 43959/2074/09/44A.

D. 7·57 P.M.

Tel. (No. 500.)

R. 8·45 P.M.

Bagdad Railway.

Your telegram No. 1346.(¹)

M. Isvolsky appeared pleased with the communication which I made to him to-day, and said he hoped to let me have shortly a reply to various communications which he had received, but it would hardly comprise all the points which the Russian Government would have to consider. These would require time to examine. He again asked me if I had received a reply as to the views of His Majesty's Government in regard to his interpretation of penultimate paragraph of Turkish note respecting the surtax.(²)

He then spoke on Persian railways, but, as this is not an immediately urgent matter, I will send his observations by to-morrow's messenger.

(¹) [v. immediately preceding document.]
(²) [v. supra, p. 395, No. 294.]

No. 303.

Sir F. Bertie to Sir Edward Grey.

F.O. 44041/2074/09/44A.

(No. 470.) Secret.

Paris, D. December 1, 1909.

Sir,

R. December 3, 1909.

To-day was M. Pichon's weekly receiving day and I had a conversation with His Excellency on the subject of the Bagdad Railway. I found that the French Ambassador in London had fully reported to M. Pichon what you had said on the subject to the Ambassador on the 23rd ultimo as recorded in your despatch to me No. 470, Secret, of that day(¹) which I had the honour to receive last night.

I read to M. Pichon in French the portion of Sir Arthur Nicolson's telegram No. 495 of the 24th ultimo(²) beginning " I communicated to the Minister for Foreign Affairs your telegraphic instructions. He said that he had been looking into the question " and ending " But then the ' conversation à quatre ' would be abandoned." I also read to His Excellency the first part of Sir Arthur Nicolson's telegram No. 497 of the 27th ultimo(³) beginning "I communicated to the Minister for Foreign Affairs," omitting the words "hardly" and " (personally I have my doubts on the point)," and ending "in negotiating with him." I further read to M. Pichon the whole of your telegram No. 1346 of yesterday(⁴) to His Majesty's Ambassador at St. Petersburg, with the purport of which His Excellency expressed himself as very satisfied.

M. Pichon said that he quite appreciated the necessity for England, in view of her commercial interests, her political interests in the Persian Gulf and her interest in a railway on the high road to India, to have a control over the portion of the Bagdad Railway from Bagdad to the Persian Gulf. It would be necessary to make sure that no part of the increase in the Turkish revenues consequent on the proposed surtax of 4% in the customs duties should be assignable to the German Company

(¹) [v. supra, pp. 393–4, No. 293.]
(²) [v. supra, pp. 394–5, No. 294.]
(³) [v. supra, pp. 398–9, No. 298.]
(⁴) [v. supra, p. 402, No. 301.]

2 D 2

as kilometric guarantee([5]) except on conditions acceptable to France, England and Russia. His Majesty's Government had made their consent to the surtax conditional and if England obtained the control of the Bagdad–Persian Gulf section of the Railway it would be necessary that France should have some *quid pro quo* for her consent. The French Parliament would naturally expect it. He had given directions for a study of the matter, but he had avoided bringing it before the Cabinet for the present for fear that something might leak out and hamper the negotiations between the English financial group and the German Company through Mr. Gwinner.

M. Pichon having told me, in reply to my enquiry as to the Minister with whom it would be necessary for him to arrange the terms to be submitted to the Cabinet, that it was the Minister of Finance, I asked him whether he did not think that it would be advisable to consider at once with M. Cochery confidentially what France should require, so that if and when the negotiations with the German Company came to a conclusion acceptable to the German Government and His Majesty's Government there might not be further delay owing to the French Government not being prepared to state the terms on which they would be ready to join in an agreement between the four Powers interested in the matter. M. Pichon authorised me to inform you that he would do so. He told me that his personal opinion was that the stipulation to be made by the French Government should be a connection (*raccordement*) of the French Railways in Syria with the Bagdad Railway. He would be averse to any land concessions for it would have the appearance of spheres of influence and would meet with strong opposition from the Young Turk Party.

With regard to M. Isvolsky's observations to Sir Arthur Nicolson, M. Pichon said that the Russian Minister for Foreign Affairs was two years ago strongly opposed to the Bagdad Railway scheme and his feeling against it had probably not diminished. As I would remember, M. Isvolsky's fear was that to connect Persia with the Bagdad Railway system would have the effect of diverting Persian trade, now passing through Russia, westward and southward to the Persian Gulf, and M. Pichon feared that it would be rather difficult to persuade him to come to an agreement with the French and British Governments on the subject of the Railway.

I suggested to M. Pichon that if the French Government showed to M. Isvolsky that whether he liked it or not the Railway would eventually be constructed by the German Company without the participation of Russia, France and England if those three Powers did not come to terms now with the German Company and Government M. Isvolsky might feel inclined to come into an *arrangement à quatre* instead of attempting to enter into a separate agreement with Germany. M. Pichon said that he hoped that it might be possible to persuade M. Isvolsky to arrange terms with the French and British Governments so that the three Governments might be united in their negotiations with the German Government, but he thought that it would be difficult.

I have, &c.
FRANCIS BERTIE.

MINUTES.

Interesting.
M. Pichon is apparently contemplating demanding compensation in the shape of a railway on the lines suggested by Sir W. Willcocks.

R. C. L.
3/12.
R. P. M.

We shall not obtain the Mediterranean Line for ourselves but we must endeavour to make it Anglo-French.

L. M.
E. G.

The above minutes are based on a misunderstanding. What the French want is not a connection between the Syrian railways and the Bagdad Railway at Bagdad but a junction by means of a short railway from Aleppo due north to meet the Bagdad Railway somewhat to the east of Alexandretta.

C. H.

([5]) [*cp. supra*, p. 388, No. 287, and *infra*, pp. 791–2, *App.* VI.]

I understood this from the despatch and had overlooked the point in the minutes or rather had taken it to be that we should have to come to terms with the French about any railway from Bagdad to the Mediterranean. This of course is so, because they have the Mediterranean side already. But for the present Sir W. Willcocks' scheme is outside the Bagdad R[ailwa]y negotiations.

E. G.

No. 304.

Mr. Marling to Sir Edward Grey.

F.O. 45122/2074/09/44.
(No. 946.) Secret.
Sir,
Constantinople, D. *December 5, 1909.*
R. *December 13, 1909.*

In their report of July 24 last the Mesopotamian Railway Committee state that they "understand that His Majesty's Government would be willing to guarantee a reasonable rate of interest on the capital invested by any British syndicate which might be formed" for the purpose of acquiring a concession for a railway in those regions; and so far as I am aware financial support in some such form is still under the serious consideration of His Majesty's Government. I would however venture to point out that the fact, if it became public, that His Majesty's Government intend to take a direct financial interest in any railway scheme in Mesopotamia would make the acquisition of a concession for that purpose very problematic. As you are aware the designs of England for territorial aggrandisement in the regions about the Turkish [Persian?] Gulf was, under the old régime, a favourite card to play with those who desired to thwart any British interests there, and this notion has been sedulously fostered of late so that a widespread, if vague distrust of our policy now exists in certain circles. How easily it can be aroused is shown by the excitement which ensued on the publication of the alleged text of your recent communication to Tewfik Pasha on the Lynch affair, and I make no manner of doubt that the Turkish Parliament with its unreasonably susceptible patriotism would look on the fact that His Majesty's Government were granting a guarantee to a British Railway syndicate as so positive a proof of our alleged designs that it would never sanction a concession even if a Ministry could be found strong enough to decide in favour of granting it.

I would therefore venture to urge that, if possible, the utmost secrecy should be used in regard to the proposed guarantee, or that it should be granted in some form that need not necessarily become public.

I have, &c.
CHARLES M. MARLING.

No. 305.

Sir C. Hardinge to Sir A. Nicolson.

Private.([1])
My dear Nicolson,
Foreign Office, December 8, 1909.

It is satisfactory that Isvolsky's ill-humour in connexion with the Baghdad Railway has disappeared. I can quite imagine that our first communication was somewhat of a shock to him, as he must for some time have been relying upon our opposition in order to block indefinitely the construction of the Railway. It is extraordinary that he should have no alternative scheme as to what Russia would want. I am not yet at all certain whether the present negotiations will come to anything; they are being, or will shortly be, conducted by Cassel with Gwinner in Berlin. Cassel knows our views, and we have yet to see whether it will be possible

([1]) [Carnock MSS.]

to obtain from Gwinner all that we demand. The difficulty which I anticipate is in connexion with kilometric guarantees, as Gwinner will probably want guarantees for the Baghdad–Gulf section to be utilized for the remaining part of the line, while we wish that section to be built without any guarantee whatsoever.

We are doing what we can to press the India Office to consent to the earmarking of railways in Persia, and more particularly to a trans-Persian line to be eventually connected with the Indian system. I do not see any harm in such a scheme, since it does not entail the construction of the railway by us in the near future, while we know that the Russians have no money available for such enterprises. We may expect, however, to meet with considerable opposition from the Government of India. That such a railway will some day be built is quite inevitable, and it should, I think, be of immense advantage to us in India, both for mails and passengers. I have no fear as to any military danger. . . . .([2])

Yours ever,
CHARLES HARDINGE.

([2]) [The closing paragraphs are of a general character.]

No. 306.

Mr. Bax-Ironside to Sir Edward Grey.

F.O. 45620/2074/09/44A.
(No. 58.)
Sir,

Berne, D. December 13, 1909.
R. December 16, 1909.

With reference to Sir Conyngham Greene's despatch No. 56 Confidential of November 21st, 1908,([1]) on the subject of the Baghdad Railway, I have the honour to report that, as announced by the "Times" correspondent in Berlin, a new Company has been constituted at Glarus in Switzerland, termed the "Société pour la Construction de Chemins de Fer en Turquie" with a capital of 10,000,000 francs (£400,000) for the purpose of further railway construction in Asiatic Turkey.

The immediate object is to extend the Baghdad Railway for a distance of 840 kilomètres from Bulgurlu.

The real reason for constituting the new Company in Switzerland appears to be that the enterprise thus commenced will be judged to have an International character, and the founders hope by this means to attract more capital from France, Switzerland, and even Italy, than would be the case were the company to have been formed in Berlin.

As a matter of fact, it is understood here that the undertaking will practically be in the hands of the Deutsche Bank.

Messrs. Escher and Frey, of Zurich, are the only men of Swiss nationality represented on the board.

I have, &c.
H. O. BAX-IRONSIDE.

([1]) [Not reproduced. It gave details as to the composition of the company and announced that French influence had apparently succeeded in eliminating Swiss participation in the enterprize.]

No. 307.

Mr. Marling to Sir Edward Grey.

F.O. 46060/2074/09/44A.

(No. 966.)   *Constantinople,* D. *December* 13, 1909.

Sir,   R. *December* 20, 1909.

The German Ambassador, on whom I had occasion to call last Saturday, asked whether I knew that Mr. Whittall had been to London and Berlin in connection with the Bagdad Railway, and if so if I had heard what had passed. I said that Mr. Whittall had undertaken his journey on the suggestion of Dr. Gwinner, who had also invited Sir H. Babington Smith to discuss with him the question of British participation in that undertaking, that I did not know what had passed, but that I understood that Mr. Whittall had been commissioned by Sir E. Cassel to arrange for a meeting with Dr. Gwinner, a meeting which was to take place in one or two days, but that he had not been authorised to make any definite statement on behalf of Sir Ernest.(¹) The meeting was to have taken place in Paris, but owing to injuries received in a motor-car accident Dr. Gwinner had been unable to travel. Sir H. Babington Smith I added had just left Constantinople to take part in the conference. His Excellency said that he hoped that some result would be reached; he had never been able to understand on what grounds the " Times " had led the campaign against British co-operation, which had resulted in a breakdown of the negotiations in 1903 which he knew to have had the support of the Foreign Office :(²) he understood that one principal requirement now was the control of the Bagdad end of the line; as for Sir W. Willcocks's scheme of a Bagdad–Homs–Damascus railway,(³) that was financially impossible, as the line was to pass over 400 kilometres of desert, where it could earn nothing, besides which, Sir William's estimate of its cost, £2,500,000, was much too low. I said that I did not know what His Majesty's Government's views were, but I thought it probable that they would communicate them to Sir E. Cassel but otherwise leave him a free hand to deal with the financial aspects of the matter. Baron von Marschall again repeated his earnest wish that some arrangement satisfactory to the Powers could be reached, so as to put an end to the friction between them here.

I should perhaps remark that since the re-establishment of the Constitution the German Embassy has made several efforts to regain its prominence in the councils of those who really control the Government, and as those efforts have so far been ineffectual, their Government has reason to wish to come to terms with us, and thus take the line of least resistance and secure the co-operation instead of the rivalry of British prestige and influence in this country. It may also have occurred to Baron von Marschall that should the Germans fail to come to terms with us in the matter of the remaining sections of the Bagdad railway, and should Great Britain throw the whole of her weight into the Bagdad Mediterranean line advocated by Sir W. Willcocks coupled with the navigation of the two rivers, the prospects of the German line ever being completed on its present conditions and *tracé* becomes [*sic*] very problematical. The Ottoman Parliament found it impossible to upset the convention for the sections of that Railway up to Halif, but, as may be gleaned from the tone of the discussion over the Mesopotamian Navigation project, it would almost certainly withhold its consent to any convention for the further sections on the old conditions.

I have, &c.

CHARLES M. MARLING.

(¹) [The record of these meetings is printed *infra*, pp. 410–1, No. 309, *encl.*]
(²) [*cp. Gooch & Temperley*, Vol. II, pp. 195–6, No. 224, and *min.*]
(³) [*v. supra*, pp. 381–4, No. 281.]

No. 308.

Sir E. Goschen to Sir C. Hardinge.

F.O. 46381/2074/09/44A.   Berlin, D. *December* 15, 1909.
My dear Hardinge,   R. *December* 21, 1909.

At the close of a conversation on general matters which I had with Herr von Schoen at his last official reception, he referred to Sir E. Cassel's visit to Berlin and to the discussions concerning the Bagdad Railway between that gentleman and Herr Gwinner.([1])

He said that he would speak to me quite frankly and loyally upon this subject. It was quite possible that Sir E. Cassel and Herr Gwinner might come to a satisfactory agreement, as far as the commercial interests involved in the question were concerned, but, he would have me to understand, it did not follow that the Imperial Government would see their way to confirming such an agreement—at all events at once. He did not wish me to think that the Government had any objection to British participation, because that was by no means the case. But public opinion in Germany would be up in arms and make things very unpleasant for the Imperial Government unless the latter could show that there was some return for what they would certainly regard as a concession. The so-called Lynch monopoly would add fuel to the flame and there would certainly be an universal cry that German interests were being sacrificed with nothing to show on the credit side of the account.

Herr von Schoen then again repeated that the Imperial Government had no wish to raise any objection to British participation in the Bagdad Railway and gave me to understand that, as owing to events in England, there was no hurry about the matter, there would be plenty of time to discover some means by which German public opinion could be satisfied that the advantage was not wholly on the side of England. Perhaps even such means might be found on the resumption of the discussion with regard to the future relations between Great Britain and Germany. I told Herr von Schoen that he need not regard events in England as any obstacle to coming to an understanding about the Bagdad Railway, for, as I had already had the honour to inform him, Sir E. Grey was perfectly ready to discuss the matter with the Imperial Government as soon as the parties directly interested in the matter as a commercial understanding had exchanged their views on the subject; I had understood that this was the point of view of the Imperial Government also. In any case until the two Governments were aware of the result of the discussions he had alluded to between Herr Gwinner and Sir Ernest Cassel, it was obviously impossible for me to agree or disagree with him as to the effect any agreement they might come to might have on German public opinion. I could only express the personal view that as the discussion with regard to British participation had apparently been initiated by Herr Gwinner and were in his capable hands, it seemed fairly certain that the interests he represented were not likely to suffer much in any arrangement that he might suggest or accept, at all events not in a degree which was likely to shock German public opinion.

From the remark which Herr von Schoen casually dropped with regard to what might happen when the discussions concerning Anglo-German future relations were resumed, it may, I think, be fairly surmised that it is in the mind of the Imperial Government that the construction and control of the Bagdad Persian Gulf section of the Bagdad Railway may be utilized as a lever to push His Majesty's Government further in the direction of a political understanding than they have yet shown any disposition to go.

This alleged inability or reluctance on the part of the Imperial Government to face the Reichstag or Public Opinion unless they can show that they have got the best of a bargain has become chronic and it has to be taken into serious account in all negotiations with which they are concerned.

([1]) [*v.* immediately succeeding document.]

I have had some talk with Sir E. Cassel upon the subject of his conversations with Herr Gwinner and he read to me a Memorandum recording the latter's proposals. As you will have seen him before you get this, it is not necessary for me to say anything about it, all the more that he read it too quickly for me to seize all the details. But of course I could not help remarking that kilometric guarantees play a certain rôle in Gwinner's proposals. I reminded Sir Ernest Cassel that His Majesty's Government particularly wished to avoid kilometric guarantees, but he said that that must be a matter for the Governments to discuss afterwards. The chief thing was to get the control and construction. He hated the principles of kilometric guarantees as much as anyone, but he would sooner have the concession with them than no concession at all.

Yours very sincerely,
W. E. GOSCHEN.

MINUTE.

Draft a despatch on these lines([2]) for me to consider : a further point might be added viz; that the *quid pro quo* which we give is our consent to the increase of 4% in the Customs dues : a burden upon trade of which about ⅓ is British and upon which the Bagdad Railway has a lien. It might also be pointed out that the railway concession which we shall get is not an advantage additional to the Lynch concession, but may possibly impair and will at any rate cover the same ground as that concession. It might also be pointed out that even when the new Lynch concession and the railway are both accomplished facts we should only have a controlling interest in means of communication in which we have for a long time had a vested interest through Lynch; and that all we shall have accomplished will have been essential to prevent that long established interest from being crushed out by new developments.

E. G.
C. H.

([2]) [This refers to a long minute by Mr. Louis Mallet of which the following extract may be given :

. . . . Sir E. Goschen might be told to inform Herr v[on] Schoen in a friendly way, that you are somewhat surprized at his attitude, as he will remember no doubt that it was Herr Gwinner who made the first overtures and not H[is] M[ajesty's] G[overnment], that although H[is] M[ajesty's] G[overnment] would be glad to arrive at an understanding with the German Gov[ernment] in regard to the Bagdad Railway, as an understanding on so important a matter would re-act favourably on the general relations of the two countries, the improvement of which H[is] M[ajesty's] G[overnment] have much at heart, they consider that any advantage which might accrue to them, if an agreement were arrived at, would be more than equally shared by the German Gov[ernmen]t and the suggestion that H[is] M[ajesty's] G[overnment] should pay for advantages shared by both parties, cannot, of course, be entertained. . . . .

L. M.]

No. 309.

Sir E. Cassel to Sir C. Hardinge.

F.O. 46237/2074/09/44.

My dear Hardinge,   21, *Old Broad Street, London, December 20, 1909.*

I send you herewith copy of a Memorandum of my conversations with Mr. Arthur von Gwinner. This Memorandum was partially drafted by Mr. von Gwinner, and the whole has been approved by him.

Yours very sincerely,
E. CASSEL.

Enclosure in No. 309.

Berlin, December 15, 1909.

Memorandum of Conversations between M. Arthur von Gwinner and Sir Ernest Cassel, December 13, 14, and 15, 1909.([1])

Mr. von Gwinner formulated his ideas on behalf of the Bagdad Company as follows :

With the consent of the Ottoman Government a separate Company, English or Ottoman, to be formed to take over that part of the concession of the Bagdad Company which relates to the line from Bagdad to the Persian Gulf.

The capital of the new Company to be £300,000 nominal (£150,000 paid up), or a less amount as may appear sufficient for working the line.

A construction company to be formed, in Switzerland or elsewhere, upon lines similar to those of the construction companies formed by the Bagdad Company.

In both these companies an interest of 50% is claimed, which is to be distributed as follows :

> 30% for the Bagdad Company,
> 10% for the Anatolian Railway, and
> 10% for the Turkish Government.

Mr. von Gwinner says that he has discussed the question of the distribution of the participations with Hussein Hilmi in the presence of Djavid Bey; Hussein Hilmi wished the English participation not to exceed 50%. So far as the Bagdad Company was concerned, they would have no objection to the English interests having a controlling proportion.

Mr. von Gwinner stated that the origin of this idea was Hussein Hilmi's remark asking him to come to an understanding with the English. Owing to the refusal on the part of the British Government to sanction the 4% additional Customs unless an undertaking were given that the proceeds should not be pledged to the Bagdad Railway, there might now be a moderate deficiency in the provision of the security for the 3rd series of Bagdad Bonds which are to be issued for the purpose of completing the line up to Helif. This security is based upon the excess at the Public Debt to which the Government is entitled, and which would be increased immediately if an augmentation of the Customs Tariff were agreed to. It is not expected that this issue will have to be made for several years yet, when the other income will cover all requirements, but both the Turkish Government and the Bagdad Company recognize that it would be an advantage to all parties if a definite arrangement relating thereto could be come to without much delay, and the Germans distinctly object to a change of the existing contract and bonds. Accordingly, the Grand Vizier in the presence of the Minister of Finance suggested to Mr. von Gwinner to see whether arrangements could not be made by the Bagdad Company with English interests. The discussion of the terms was confined to the respective participations.

Mr. von Gwinner explained that he had verbally informed the Turkish Government that the Bagdad Company would not insist upon the application of the 4% additional Customs beyond the Bagdad loans Series 2 and 3. Their contract entitled them to this, but as they were anxious to meet the wishes of the Turkish Government and desirous not unduly to burden Turkish finance, it would in such case be left to the Government to fix themselves a future date on which they would provide the security for the construction from Helif to the Persian Gulf.

Mr. von Gwinner states that no arrangement for handing over the Bagdad end of the line to the control of other interests would be satisfactory to the Bagdad Company nor to the Turkish Government unless it ensured the whole construction

([1]) [*v. G.P.* XXVII, II, pp. 605–7.]

from Helif to the Gulf; this for the reason that whereas a line terminating some-where in Upper Mesopotamia would be a burden on the Turkish Treasury, a through line would soon pay itself and immediately increase the revenue of Turkey by a larger amount than the subvention loans would require. Mr. von Gwinner sees no other way now of carrying this out, except by assigning part of the additional Customs dues to the guaranty of the Bagdad subvention loans from Helif to the Persian Gulf. These loans would require about half a million £ Sterling per annum, the distance being some 1,100 kilometers, whereof about 560 kilometers are between Bagdad and Basra (outside of about 106 kilometers from Zobeir Junction to Kazima on the Gulf of Koweit; this section may be built later). It appears from the Bagdad concession that the Turkish Government is to pay about Frs. 269,000 in 4% Bonds per kilometer, being, at 80%, about £8,500 cash per kilometer. Now Mr. von Gwinner explained this amount is an average, there are kilometers that cost six times the average, and further the Bagdad Railway requires to set aside a sum not inferior to £2,000 on the 1,100 kilometers unfinished towards a reserve required for the working of the entire line, towards gradually increasing the rolling stock and generally to fulfil the burdensome clauses of the concession. Accordingly his proposal is that, of the subvention loan for the section from Bagdad to Basra, a sum of £2,000 per kilometer should be left to the Bagdad Railway Company, the remaining £6,500 per kilometer being amply sufficient to construct the line from Bagdad to the Gulf to provide its rolling stock and leave a sufficient reserve in the new Company's treasury for fulfilling on this section the working of the line and conditions of the general concession. This concession for the line between Bagdad and the Persian Gulf would have to be transferred with the consent of the Turkish Government to the new company to be formed. The share which the old Bagdad Railway Company claims as its consideration, viz., the 30% interest in the new Railway and Construction Companies, would remain in the old Company's treasury.

MINUTES.

Sir E. Cassel called to-day and communicated the enclosed mem[orandu]m.

On reading it through I remarked that the British control would with the proposed arrangement be insecure but Sir E. Cassel said he was confident that we could obtain more than 50% from the Bagdad R[ailwa]y by negotiation.

I pointed out that the scheme reeks with kilometric guarantees to which we are so strongly opposed. To this Sir E. Cassel remarked that he is quite as much opposed himself to these guarantees, but that he considered the important point to be kept in view is the acquisition of the Bagdad–Gulf section and that some arrangement about these guarantees might possibly be arrived at later.

He said that he found Gwinner with his mind absolutely made up and that the views contained in the mem[orandu]m represent absolutely the lines on which he will agree to participation. The only concession which he seems to think obtainable being the reduction of the 30% claimed by the Bagdad Co.

I suppose we should send this to the Board of Trade for their views.

The question of kilometric guarantees seems a difficult one. Yet it would be a pity to lose a most important political concession on that account, if the Turks raise no objection. I wonder if we could not find some other way of re-imbursing them?

C. H.

Sir E. Cassel goes to Egypt on the 23rd.

[C. H.]

This will take some time. The Board of Trade must express their view and we shall then have to talk it over with France and Russia.

E. G.

No. 310.

Sir Edward Grey to Sir A. Nicolson.

F.O. 46357/2074/09/44.

(No. 325.)

Sir,   *Foreign Office, December 21, 1909.*

In the course of conversation with Sir Charles Hardinge on the 18th inst[ant] the Russian Ambassador said that M. Izvolski realised that H[is] M[ajesty's] G[overnment] have acted quite loyally with regard to the Bagdad Railway.

M. Izvolski's policy in connection with this line had always been a negative one and at present he was at a loss what to do. He was anxious to prevent the north of Asia Minor from becoming a German sphere of influence and he wanted to have something to show the Russian public as a gain on his part in the event of H[is] M[ajesty's] G[overnment] coming to an agreement with the German Gov[ernmen]t with regard to the section of the line from Bagdad to the Persian Gulf.

Sir C. Hardinge pointed out to Count Benckendorff that the obvious policy of the Russian Gov[ernmen]t was to acquire the right of construction and control of the Khanikin branch of the Bagdad Railway and that if M. Izvolski obtained a concession for the construction of a line in the north of Asia Minor by way of Sivas and Diarbekir, regarding which discussions were already in progress he should have no difficulty in satisfying the Russian public.

Sir C. Hardinge added that I was in favour of earmarking those railways which the two Gov[ernmen]ts might desire to construct in Persia but that I was not yet in possession of the views of the India Office.

[I am, &c.

E. GREY.]

No. 311.

Sir A. Nicolson to Sir Edward Grey.

F.O. 153/100/10/44A.

(No. 677.) Secret.   *St. Petersburgh,* D. *December 27,* 1909.

Sir,   R. *January 3,* 1910.

I have the honour to transmit herewith copy of an *Aide-Mémoire* which M. Iswolsky handed to me yesterday, and which is a reply to various communications which, by your direction, I have from time to time made to him in regard to the discussions between the British and German financial groups respecting the Bagdad Railway. M. Iswolsky explained to me that this memorandum must not be considered as an exhaustive statement of the views of the Russian Government, but merely as preliminary observations. The memorandum carries the question but little further forward and leaves the views of the Russian Government still in the region of conjecture. It seems to me that the Cabinet of St. Petersburg has been in full possession for some weeks past of the nature of the proposals made by the German group, and that their enquiries as to the memorandum of 1907(¹) have in reality little bearing on the new development which has recently taken place. I had hoped that M. Iswolsky would have been able to have given some general indication as to the conditions on which the Russian Government would wish to participate in the railway, and it would have been of especial interest to have known on what bases he proposes to negotiate with the German Government. I will endeavour later to ascertain whether he is willing or able to give some further enlightenment on this point.

(¹) [That of June 4, 1907, *v. supra*, pp. 355–6, No. 250.]

M. Iswolsky read to me a letter and a telegram which he had received from Count Benckendorff reporting what he had gathered of the results of the mission of Sir E. Cassel and also giving the substance of a conversation with M. Paul Cambon who had related to him what Hilmy Pasha had said to M. Bompard at Constantinople. M. Iswolsky enquired of me whether I had received any information on the latter subject. I replied that M. Louis had been good enough to acquaint me with the statement of Hilmy Pasha. M. Iswolsky said that the question seemed to be confused, as if the Turkish Government were really to oppose any bisection of the line the proposed arrangement between the German and British groups might have to be considerably modified.

I beg leave to enclose copies of the *Pro-memoriâ* and of the communications from me to which reference is made in the Russian *aide-mémoire*.

I have, &c
A. NICOLSON.

Enclosure 1 in No. 311.

Aide-mémoire by M. Isvolski.

(Confidentiel.)

Le Ministère Impérial des Affaires Etrangères n'a pas manqué d'examiner l'aide mémoire du 6/19 novembre dernier(²) ainsi que les quatre communications subséquentes de Son Excellence Sir A. Nicolson en date des 9/22, 11/24, 14/27 novembre et du 18/1 décembre(³) relativement à la question du chemin de fer de Bagdad.

Le Ministère Impérial croit devoir tout d'abord relever un malentendu évident concernant la question de la surtaxe douanière en Turquie. Si le Cabinet Impérial n'a pas posé jusqu'ici comme condition de son assentiment à cette surtaxe que celle-ci ne serve pas à défrayer la garantie kilométrique du chemin de fer de Bagdad, c'est uniquement parce qu'il considérait que la Porte a donné elle même une assurance explicite dans ce sens dans le dernier alinéa de sa Note du 5/18 septembre dernier.(⁴) S'il se trouve que cette assurance n'a pas de force obligatoire pour la Turquie, le Gouvernement Impérial ne manquera pas de formuler à ce sujet des réserves analogues à celles qui ont été faites par le Gouvernement Britannique.

Le Ministère Impérial des Affaires Etrangères a appris avec une grande satisfaction que les récents pourparlers anglo-allemands au sujet du chemin de fer n'ont eu lieu jusqu'ici qu'entre les deux groupes financiers et que le Gouvernement Britannique n'acceptera aucune proposition avant que cette question n'ait été discutée avec les Gouvernements de Russie et de France, en vue d'arriver à un arrangement à quatre.

Vu l'extrême complexité des intérêts russes en cause, le Gouvernement Impérial ne pourra formuler d'une manière détaillée les conditions auxquelles il pourra se joindre à un arrangement à quatre qu'après avoir soumis cette question à une étude approfondie; il lui est d'autant plus difficile de se prononcer immédiatement, que les communications de Sir A. Nicolson ne définissent pas clairement les bases de l'arrangement projeté; le Cabinet de Londres renonce-t-il dès à présent aux idées énoncées dans le mémoire du 6 (*sic*) juin 1907 remis par Sir E. Grey au Comte Benckendorff(⁵) et qui diffèrent essentiellement de celles dont s'inspirent les propositions allemandes? Ainsi par exemple, le mémoire du 6 (*sic*) juin prévoyait la création d'une direction internationale tandis que les propositions de M. Gwinner tendent à un sectionnement absolu de la ligne. Le même mémoire étendait la sphère des intérêts anglais jusqu'à un point " au nord de Bagdad,'' tandis qu'actuellement il est question d'abandonner à l'Angleterre le tronçon de la ligne à partir de Bagdad. Il importerait au Gouvernement Impérial d'être fixé sur le point de vue du Cabinet de Londres avant d'émettre de son côté une opinion déterminée.

(²) [*v. infra, encl.* 2, and *cp.* Sir E. Grey's telegram *supra*, pp. 387–8, No. 287.]
(³) [*v. infra, encls.* 3–6, and *cp.* Sir E. Grey's telegrams *supra*, pp. 392–3, No. 292, p. 398, No. 297, and p. 402, No. 301.]
(⁴) [*cp. supra*, p. 376, No. 273. The memorandum is dated September 14, 1907.]
(⁵) [This refers to the memorandum dated June 4, 1907, *v. supra*, pp. 355–6, No. 250.]

Enfin la réalisation du chemin de fer de Bagdad pouvant gravement menacer les intérêts russes en Perse, le Gouvernement Impérial devra tâcher de s'entendre directement avec l'Allemagne sur ce côté de la question; il constate avec plaisir que le Gouvernement Britannique est favorable à une pareille entente; de son côté le Gouvernement Impérial ne manquera pas d'observer strictement à cette occasion les arrangements précédents qu'il a conclus au sujet de la Perse avec l'Angleterre et de tenir le Cabinet de Londres au courant de ses négociations éventuelles avec l'Allemagne.

St. *Pétersbourg,*
   le 12/25 *décembre,* 1909.

Enclosure 2 in No. 311.

Pro-memoriâ by Sir A. Nicolson.

It will be within the knowledge of the Imperial Government that some weeks ago an application was made by Sir G. Lowther to the Sublime Porte for a railway concession for a line to connect the Persian Gulf with Bagdad *viâ* the valley of the River Tigris; and it was at the same time asked that the option should be granted to connect the Mediterranean Sea with Bagdad by a prolongation of the above-mentioned line along the Euphrates valley.[6]

It may also be known to the Imperial Government that the 4% surtax on the Turkish Customs duties received the assent of His Majesty's Government on certain conditions, among which was one to the effect that no kilometric guarantees should be defrayed out of the proceeds of the surtax, and that an assurance in writing to this effect should be obtained from the German Government by the Sublime Porte.[7] It is however unlikely that this assurance will be given; for the Bagdad Railway Company are aware that unless the additional surtax on imports is assented to by the Powers and unless some, at least, of the proceeds therefrom are applied to pay kilometric guarantees, these guarantees cannot be defrayed.

A few days since Monsieur Gwinner informed Sir H. Babington Smith that he is now ready to consent to the following conditions :—

1. Control over the Bagdad–Persian Gulf section of the Railway is to be British :
2. The construction of this section is to be carried out with British material and by British agency :
3. Non-British interests are to participate in this section only in a subordinate capacity : and
4. The Railway north of Bagdad is to be in no way connected with the British group.

Sir E. Grey had informed Count Metternich that unless an agreement was reached respecting the Bagdad Railway, His Majesty's Government would be unable to consent to the Turkish Customs duties being increased; and he had also observed that the necessity of inviting the co-operation of Russia as well as France constituted one of the difficulties in the way of His Majesty's Government participating in the Railway. He now learns however that all rights to continue their railway south of Bagdad may possibly be waived by the German Government in favour of Great Britain, who would be left free, as regards the Bagdad–Persian Gulf Railway, to come to an arrangement with the Sublime Porte. It is essential for British interests in Mesopotamia to obtain this, which is the very point on which His Majesty's Government have invariably insisted. Other Powers, including Russia, are apparently disposed to agree unconditionally to the Turkish Custom duties being increased; and His Majesty's Government would probably do likewise if the above-mentioned point were conceded by the German Government.

[6] [*v. supra*, pp. 376–7, No. 274.]
[7] [*cp. supra*, p. 388, No. 287, and *infra*, pp. 791–2, *App.* VI.]

The German line north of Bagdad is a matter of very much less interest to His Majesty's Government than a line following an entirely different route from Bagdad due westwards.

A decision in the matter is urgently needed, as the question of increasing the Turkish Customs duties is involved. Opposition to such an increase cannot be maintained by His Majesty's Government alone; and once this point is conceded there will be no obstacle to the completion of the Bagdad Railway by Germany.

St. Petersburg, November 6/19, 1909.

Enclosure 3 in No. 311.

Sir A. Nicolson to M. Isvolski.

Mon cher Ministre, *St. Péter[s]bourg, le 9/22 novembre, 1909.*
. . . .(⁸) Je serai toujours à votre disposition pour causer de nouveau sur la question du chemin de fer de Bagdad quand vous avez étudié la dernière phase de la question.

J'espère que j'ai bien expliqué que les propositions faites par M. Gwinner à Sir H. Babington Smith ne sont parvenues à Sir E. Grey que deux jours avant mon *Pro Memoria* et que nous n'avons pas perdu du temps en vous en faisant part.

Votre, &c.
A. NICOLSON.

Enclosure 4 in No. 311.

Sir A. Nicolson to M. Isvolski.(⁹)

Confidential.
Mon cher Ministre, *St. Petersburgh, November 11/24, 1909.*
After our conversation of Friday last in regard to the Bagdad Railway I communicated to my Government the substance of some observations which you were good enough to make as being merely your first impressions and not your final views. I have now received some further explanations from Sir E. Grey which I doubt not will entirely clear up any doubts. In the first place I would wish to state that no bargain has been concluded, and no negotiations have as yet taken place with the German Government.

My Government are not giving Germany a free hand, as in fact she already had it by the concession. Germany hopes to obtain the necessary funds by an increase of the Turkish Customs duties, and all the Powers, with the exception of England, were apparently ready to concede this increase without any stipulation about the Bagdad Railway. My Government were obliged to consider what stipulation they should make to protect themselves in giving their consent to the increase of Customs duties. Russia can of course equally do the same and my Government are waiting for your views before going further. Nothing more has been said to the German Ambassador than what I communicated in my *Pro Memoriâ* of the 6/19 November. As I informed you in a private letter two or three days ago, as soon as the proposals of M. Gwinner reached my Government they were immediately communicated to you. Moreover the impressions as to the terms on which Germany might agree with my Government were based on the information spontaneously given by M. Gwinner, and not on any negotiations with the German Government for none has taken place. My Government are most anxious to know the decision to which the Imperial Government may arrive as to the conditions upon which they would be willing to participate in the railway north of Bagdad. My Government have always demanded the control

(⁸) [The omitted part alludes to the question of trade routes in the south of Persia.]
(⁹) [This enclosure and the one following are reproduced from the typed copies sent to the Foreign Office by Sir A. Nicolson. They have, as shown here, an English text, in spite of the use of French for the address.]

and the construction of the line south of Bagdad and they could not be satisfied with less. There can be little doubt that the line will be built eventually whether England and Russia participate in it or not; and therefore my Government must consider with great attention the present situation and the offer which M. Gwinner has mooted; but before going further with the matter Sir E. Grey is anxious to know the views of the Russian Government. There is one matter which renders the question of the southern section of extreme urgency. The Turkish Government are now commencing irrigation works south of Bagdad, and there is a probability of the river's being unnavigable from want of water. The river transport of British Indian trade which has been in British hands for over 50 years would thus become lost with nothing to take its place until the railway is built.

You will see then that my Government as soon as they received information as to what M. Gwinner proposed lost no time in informing you; and that they have entered into no negotiations and made no bargain with Germany. My Government are anxious to have your views as soon as possible as to Russian participation in the railway north of Bagdad, and as to the conditions you may wish to lay down in regard to increase of Customs duties.

yours, &c.
A. NICOLSON.

Enclosure 5 in No. 311.

Sir A. Nicolson to M. Isvolski.

Mon cher Ministre,   *St. Petersburgh, November* 14/27, 1909.

In order to complete the information which I have already given you, I should like to tell you that all that His Majesty's Government have done at present is to inform you and Paris of the substance of Monsieur Gwinner's proposals and have hitherto given no reply to these proposals. These proposals are the minimum of what would satisfy British public opinion and British interests, and in order to obtain the southern section my Government would be willing to waive their interests in the railway north of Bagdad. The British group wish that a concession should be obtained of a branch line from Bagdad to Khanikin, and although my Government would be glad to obtain such a concession or to participate with the Russian Government in its control and construction they have refrained from giving any support to such a proposal and would not do so without the concurrence of the Russian Government. My Government realise that Russian interests might be involved in a line terminating at a point on the limit of the Russian sphere of interest in Persia. The German Government are aware that Monsieur Gwinner has made certain proposals, but my Government propose to allow negotiations to be carried on by the English group on a purely commercial basis. My Government are most anxious to have the views of the Russian Government (of which they are at present in complete ignorance) as to participation in the Bagdad Railway, as a decision as to the increase of Turkish Customs duties cannot be indefinitely postponed. My Government would naturally have no objection to the recognition by Germany of Russian interests in the Russian sphere of influence in Persia; but they could hardly remain indifferent if, in return for this, Russia were to make any concession to Germany in the neutral zone. My Government would certainly raise no objection to the opening of negotiations between Russia and Germany as to participation in the railway north of Bagdad, but they hope that the Russian Government would keep them informed of the progress of such negotiations.

Yours, &c.
A. NICOLSON.

Enclosure 6 in No. 311.

Sir A. Nicolson to M. Isvolski.

Mon cher Ministre, *St. Petersburgh, November* 18/*December* 1, 1909.

Referring to previous communications in regard to the Bagdad Railway I beg leave to inform you that no negotiations are taking place with Germany, but that M. Gwinner had opened communications with the British group of financiers. It is not clear as yet what proposal will be the outcome of these communications, and until it is submitted to the British Government, with the approval of the German Government, it is not sure that it will be acceptable. If it be acceptable, His Majesty's Government will not accept it until the question has been discussed with the Russian and French Governments so that whatever agreement may be reached may be *A quatre*. My Government feel sure that you will explain your views fully to them, and that as the Russian and French Governments have been kept fully informed of what is passing they will be prepared to come to a decision when the need for one arrives.

Yours, &c.
A. NICOLSON.

No. 312.

Sir Edward Grey to Sir F. Bertie.

F.O. 46697/2074/09/44A. *Foreign Office, December* 30, 1909.
Tel. (No. 743.) D. 8·30 P.M.

I told French chargé d'affaires to-day that I had seen with satisfaction what M. Pichon had said about Bagdad Railway.(¹) As far as we are concerned, position is as follows: Gwinner's overtures led to negotiations with Cassel, which may result, but have not yet resulted definitely, in an offer to British financiers of assured control of construction and working of railway from Bagdad to Gulf.

When financiers agree, His Majesty's Government will have to consider whether arrangement proposed would justify them in agreeing to increase of Turkish customs dues without condition. I should then let French and Russian Governments know what the agreement between financiers was and what was our opinion of it before taking any step. It would then be for French and Russian Governments to let us know what conditions as regards Bagdad Railway would ensure their consent to increase of Turkish customs dues, so that we may all act together.

Questions of internationalisation and of any concession of parts of railway north of Bagdad have not come at all into negotiations between British and German financiers, and we should await views of French and Russian Governments as to how these points should be dealt with before raising them. Essential point for us is to ensure that railway from Bagdad to Gulf does not pass into foreign hands, though British financiers have expressed to me desire to secure interest in Khanikin branch also.

Assuming that terms agreed between Cassel and Gwinner are found satisfactory by His Majesty's Government on this point, it would still remain to be ascertained whether German and Turkish Governments would agree about them. No negotiations have as yet taken place between us and German Government about Gwinner's proposals, and we assume only that German Government know of them. You should communicate substance of this telegram to M. Pichon.

(Repeat to Sir A. Nicolson and instruct him to make same communication to M. Iswolski adding that we hope he will keep us similarly informed. E. G.)(²)

(¹) [*v. supra*, pp. 403–4, No. 303.]
(²) [The sentence in brackets was added by Sir E. Grey to his own first draft of the telegram.]

No. 313.

Sir Edward Grey to Sir A. Nicolson.

F.O. 47012/2074/09/44A.
(No. 335.)
Sir, *Foreign Office, December 31, 1909.*

The Russian Ambassador called at this Office on the 21st inst[ant] and enquired of Sir C. Hardinge as to what had happened in connection with Sir E. Cassel's visit to Berlin, and as to what would now take place.

Sir C. Hardinge stated, as he had stated the day before to M. Cambon, that M. Gwinner had indeed expressed his readiness to make what could only be regarded as solid concessions on the part of the Bagdad R[ailwa]y Co[mpany], but that no agreement had been come to between M. Gwinner and Sir E. Cassel as there were points which would require serious consideration and possibly further negotiation.

Count Benckendorff enquired what procedure would be followed in the event of Sir E. Cassel coming to terms with M. Gwinner, and Sir C. Hardinge replied that he supposed the German Gov[ernmen]t would then inform H[is] M[ajesty's] G[overnment] that the Bagdad R[ailwa]y Co[mpany] were ready to allow participation by a British Company on certain terms, and would ask whether H[is] M[ajesty's] G[overnment] would approve. The reply would then probably be that before answering France and Russia must be consulted, or that much as H[is] M[ajesty's] G[overnment] approve the terms, they would like to learn how France and Russia were to be satisfied. It was made clear to Count Benckendorff that once the financiers had come to terms, H[is] M[ajesty's] G[overnment] would not in any case bind themselves to accept those terms without consulting the French and Russian Gov[ernment]s, and discussing the terms which they also might make with Germany.

Count Benckendorff appeared satisfied with this statement. He had seemed to fear that, because Sir E. Cassel's mission to Berlin was approved, whatever agreement was arrived at with M. Gwinner would be binding on H[is] M[ajesty's] G[overnment]. Sir C. Hardinge also remarked that, although an agreement might be arrived at between Great Britain and Germany, that agreement would also have to be accepted by Turkey, and he anticipated that there might be considerable objections on her part to the proposed solution. Count Benckendorff agreed.

[I am, &c.
E. GREY.]

No. 314.

Sir Edward Grey to Sir E. Goschen.

Private.([1])
My dear Goschen, *Fallodon, December 31, 1909.*

. . . .([2]) Here is a sketch of the proper course for the Bagdad R[ailwa]y negotiations to take:

1. An agreement between Cassel and Gwinner.
2. Consideration by H[is] M[ajesty's] Gov[ernmen]t of that agreement, to see if it secures our interest sufficiently to justify us in agreeing to increase of Turkish Customs dues without a condition.

If 2 is answered by us affirmatively, we must then:

3. Discuss with France and Russia to ascertain what they will require to enable them to agree to the increase of Turkish Customs dues.

([1]) [Grey MSS., Vol. 22.]
([2]) [For the first part of this letter, *v. supra*, p. 319, No. 210.]

4. The German Gov[ernmen]t will then have to say whether it is prepared to agree to all this.

5. The Turkish Gov[ernmen]t must have its say. If 4 and 5 are settled affirmatively then

6. The increase of Turkish Customs dues will be agreed to.

All this must take time. I want an agreement with Germany about the Bagdad R[ailwa]y in order to heal that sore, but when we have ascertained that an agreement to safeguard our interests is possible we must wait till France and Russia are in line. For we promised to keep in touch with them and the consent of one of us to the increase of Turkish Customs is no good without the others.

Yours etc.,
[E. GREY.]

No. 315.

Sir A. Nicolson to Sir Edward Grey.

F.O. 1745/100/10/44A.
(No. 3.) Secret. St. Petersburgh, D. January 3, 1910.
Sir, R. January 17, 1910.

I had the honour to receive your telegram No. 743 to Sir F. Bertie of the 30th ultimo([1]) regarding the present situation of the discussions in respect to the Bagdad Railway, and the attitude present and future of His Majesty's Government in the matter. I communicated the substance of this telegram to Monsieur Iswolsky, who desired me to convey his best thanks for the information which had been given him. He observed that matters seemed to be pretty well where they were : and I agreed that they had not moved appreciably of late. As you will have received since the despatch of your above mentioned telegram the *aide-mémoire* of Monsieur Iswolsky([2]) in which he engages to keep His Majesty's Government informed of the course of any negotiations which he may have with the German Government, I stated in my written summary of your telegram that His Majesty's Government were " glad to hear " that they would be kept acquainted with his discussions with Berlin, instead of expressing the hope that this would be the case.

I have, &c.
A. NICOLSON.

([1]) [v. supra, p. 417, No. 312.]
([2]) [v. supra, pp. 413–4, No. 311, encl. 1.]

No. 316.

Sir C. Hardinge to Sir A. Nicolson.

Private.([1])
My dear Nicolson :— Foreign Office, January 5, 1910.

I have returned to-day from my Christmas holiday, and write these lines to catch the bag this evening.

I am very sceptical as to the result of the negotiations in connexion with the Baghdad Railway. There appears now to be an uproar in Germany created by the Pan-Germans, who are attacking Schön, and the latter seems to wish that nothing should be done for the time being, and that the negotiations should not be pursued further.

([1]) [Carnock MSS., Vol. I of 1910.]

Although it is quite possible that Gwinner and Cassel may come to terms, I do not believe that the Turkish Government will accept the view that we should have the control and construction of the Baghdad section. What they would like would be the internationalization of the line, in which case we should have a certain percentage of interest, but no control. Then again there is the difficulty about the kilometric guarantee; Cassel would like to have the guarantee, and Gwinner wants a portion of it. Our only chance of getting the terms we want lies in being able to tell the Turks that we renounce the guarantee for that section of the line. The latter would resent a British guarantee as a breach of their sovereign rights, and I do not think that it will be easy to find a Company to build the line, unless a guarantee of some sort is offered. It appears to me that we are moving in a vicious circle.

We have received an unsatisfactory note from the India Office in reply to ours on the subject of Persian railways. The military authorities are strongly opposed to the trans-Persian line linking up the Russian and Indian systems. They maintain that this would afford facilities for a concentration of Russian troops fed from Russia at Kerman, and would constitute a serious menace to the safety of the Indian Empire. We are going to answer this letter and to propose that each country should demand a preferential right for construction of railways in the North and the South. This is, I think, the only way out of it and, if we obtain a preferential right to construct in the South, while the Russians enjoy the same right in the North, it is inevitable that, in the course of a few years, the Northern and Southern railways will be linked up. . . . .(²)

Wishing you a happy New Year,

Y[ou]rs ever,
CHARLES HARDINGE.

(²) [The last two paragraphs refer to the return of the Russian Court to Tsarkoe Selo and to the detention at Shiraz of the Russian Consul-General of Bushire.]

No. 317.

Sir Edward Grey to Sir E. Goschen.

F.O. 46381/2074/09/44A.
(No. 7.)
Sir,   *Foreign Office, January 10, 1910.*

I have received your telegram of the 14th and your despatch of the 15th ultimo,(¹) reporting a conversation you have had with the German Minister for Foreign Affairs respecting the Bagdad Railway. You should inform His Excellency that I am obliged to him for his very frank explanation of the attitude of the German Government towards the participation of His Majesty's Government in the construction and control of the Gulf section of the line, although it is somewhat disappointing to learn that even if an agreement were arrived at between the financiers, which was acceptable to His Majesty's Government, the German Government might find it difficult, at any rate at the present time, to confirm it owing to the opposition which is to be anticipated from German public opinion.

You should remind Herr von Schoen that, so far as His Majesty's Government are aware, it was Herr Gwinner who first approached Sir E. Cassel on the subject of British participation and that the initiative in no way proceeded from the British group, still less from His Majesty's Government, who have made no move in the matter since the discussions which took place at Windsor in November 1907.(²) When

(¹) [*cp. supra*, pp. 408–9, No. 308.]
(²) [*v. supra*, pp. 92–102, Nos. 60–9.]

His Majesty's Government were first informed that Herr Gwinner had made overtures to the British group they assumed that the German Government were not unaware of the proposals which had presumably been put forward, after due consideration of the advantages and disadvantages of British participation.

The German Government are aware of the attitude of His Majesty's Government towards the present discussion. Should an agreement be arrived at by the Germans which is in all respects satisfactory to His Majesty's Government, they would be perfectly willing to sanction participation after due discussion with the Governments of France and Russia, and they would welcome the conclusion of an agreement on a question which has been long outstanding and which has, they fear, occasioned some soreness of feeling between the two countries.

But the suggestion that the German Government regard British participation in the light of a concession and that some *quid pro quo* will be required from the British Government in return, in order to make the arrangement acceptable to the German people, is one which His Majesty's Government cannot entertain.

His Majesty's Government consider that any advantages which may accrue to them from participation in the railway will be more than equally shared by Germany, especially when it is remembered that the consent of His Majesty's Government to the increase of the Turkish customs duties by 4 per cent. would follow upon the conclusion of an agreement, thus imposing for the advantage of the Bagdad Railway, which has a lien upon the customs revenue, an additional burden upon the foreign trade of Turkey, of which such a large proportion is British.

Public opinion in this country would, it may safely be said, welcome an agreement with Germany on equitable lines but any attempt on either side to obtain special advantages or to overload the agreement with extraneous questions might over-reach the mark and, far from improving the feeling between the two countries, react injuriously upon the harmonious relations now existing between the two Governments.

As Herr von Schoen has mentioned the Lynch concession, it may be as well to explain to His Excellency that this question seems to be the subject of some misunderstanding in Germany. British vessels were accorded the right to navigate the Euphrates and Tigris by Firmans of 1834 and 1841 and a Co[mpany] was formed by Messrs. Lynch in 1862 for the purpose of navigating these rivers. Ever since that time this firm have maintained their steamers on the rivers. The present negotiation merely relates to the amalgamation of Lynch's concession with the Turkish Hamidie Company and the transformation of what has been an entirely British concession for so long a period into a Turkish company in which Lynch has a share.

No new rights have been acquired: on the contrary Mr. Lynch is surrendering rights which he has enjoyed many years and is amalgamating his interests with those of a Turkish Company.

It is also to be observed that the contemplated participation of British interests in the Bagdad R[ailwa]y is not an advantage additional to the Lynch Concessions, but may possibly impair that concession and at any rate will be in the same region. Even if the new Lynch concession were granted and a participation of British interests in the Bagdad R[ailwa]y admitted, Great Britain would only have a controlling interest in means of communication in which this country has for a long time had a vested interest through the Lynch steamers. Nothing more will have been accomplished than what will have been essential to prevent that long established interest from being crushed out by new developments.

[I am, &c.]
E. G[REY].

No. 318.

Memorandum by Sir Edward Grey.(¹)

F.O. 1355/100/10/44.   *Foreign Office, January 10,* 1910.

I cannot help feeling that we should be careful not to be dragged into the vortex of kilometric guarantees, as established by the Convention of 1903,(²) and that it is necessary to put our foot down at once to prevent ourselves being placed in a hopelessly false position in relation to our declared policy of the last few years. Were we to accept any scheme of co-operation in the Bagdad Railway which included participation by this country in the kilometric guarantees under the Convention of 1903, it would be almost impossible to defend our action in Parliament against the attacks which would undoubtedly be made on it both there and in the press. There have already been indications in this sense in the press.

To put the matter very briefly, there are, under the Convention of 1903, two forms of kilometric guarantee : (1) a 99 years' annuity to be capitalized and devoted to the construction of the line and the provision of rolling-stock and (2) A guarantee for the working expenses.

The construction annuity is fixed at such a figure as to far exceed the cost of building the line and the supply of rolling stock, and to leave large sums for allocation, thus encouraging extravagance and fraudulent finance, as exemplified in the first section.

The guarantee for the working expenses is not conducive to the encouragement and development of traffic since, owing to the terms in which the concession is drawn up, the most favourable situation for the Company, from a financial point of view, would be that there should be the smallest possible amount of traffic or, better still, none at all.

This brief outline is sufficient to show that the extension of the system of kilometric guarantees is very injurious to the interests of Turkey, since it involves mulcting the Turkish tax-payer of sums largely in excess of the actual requirements, while it tends to restrict the development of traffic on the line. These are very serious objections, which have already been recognized as sufficient to justify His Majesty's Government in refusing to participate in the Baghdad Railway scheme on the basis of kilometric guarantees for construction and working expenses.

It is desirable to find a solution of the situation created by Sir E. Cassel's negotiation with Gwinner, which at present involves the system of kilometric guarantees with all its faults and objections.

There are three alternatives to kilometric guarantees :

> (*a.*) No guarantee at all.
> (*b.*) A British guarantee.
> (*c.*) A Turkish guarantee.

Now as regards the question of constructing the line without any guarantee at all, it is not possible to express an opinion as to whether such a course is possible or not; but I would draw attention to the case of the British Smyrna–Aidin Railway which, ever since it was constructed in 1856, has been worked without a kilometric guarantee. Naturally all the shareholders of this line are British and, although an incomparably poorer country than the Mesopotamian Delta is served by it, it has paid a regular and continuous dividend of 6%. If British investors were sufficiently enterprising to find capital for the construction of the Smyrna–Aidin Railway, it

(¹) [This memorandum was drafted by Sir C. Hardinge. It is endorsed " comm[unicate]d privately to Mr. Winston Churchill."]

(²) [The Convention of March 5, 1903, is printed in *B.F.S.P.*, Vol. 102, pp. 833–48. Article XXXV deals with the kilometric guarantees.]

should not be impossible to find British capital for the construction of the Baghdad section, with all its prospects of irrigation of the adjoining districts.

The second alternative is that of a British guarantee of three per cent. on the capital spent on the Gulf section of the line, any earnings above this three per cent. being shared equally between the guarantors and the shareholders. This was recommended by Sir James Mackay at the Baghdad Railway Committee of 1907, and subsequently submitted to the Cabinet. Assuming the distance from Baghdad to the Gulf to be 450 miles, and the cost of construction with rolling stock £8,000 sterling a mile, the cost would be £3,600,000, and the annual guarantee £108,000, the latter to be shared by the Imperial and Indian Exchequers. It has been stated as an objection to this proposal that the Turks would regard it as a dereliction of their sovereign rights. It would, however, if that were so, be a dereliction for which they would receive good money value, since they would be relieved of some of the onerous conditions of the Convention of 1903. I think it not unlikely that they would in the end accept a proposal on these lines if it were put before them, as it undoubtedly could be, in an attractive form.

The other alternative which might be suggested to the Turkish Government is that they should themselves give a guarantee. In their case it would have to be one of five per cent. on the capital actually expended on the Baghdad–Gulf section, and in return Article 35 of the Convention of 1903 might, in so far as it relates to this portion of the line, be modified so as to relieve Turkey of both the construction annuity and working expenses guarantee. The gain to the Turkish Exchequer would be considerable for the following reasons :—

The construction annuity works out at £700 sterling per annum per mile, and is a fixed charge for 99 years. From Baghdad to Koweit the distance is about 450 miles, therefore the annual charge to Turkey for 99 years would on this account amount to £700 multiplied by 450, that is to say £315,000 a year.

The working expenses guarantee is not a fixed charge, but it might, at its maximum amount, reach £290 per annum per mile which, for 450 miles, works out at £130,500 a year.

The liability of Turkey in respect of the 450 miles from Baghdad to Koweit would thus, under the 1903 Convention, be a minimum annual amount of £315,000, and might reach £445,500 each year.

On the other hand the five per cent. guarantee on the capital of £3,600,000 (which, assuming £8,000 per mile, would be the actual cost of constructing and financing rolling stock for 450 miles) would be only £180,000 sterling, the maximum annual liability of Turkey and, which is an important point, this liability would not, like the other, continue for 99 years, but it would cease as soon as the railway realized a net profit of five per cent., while Turkey would share equally in any profits over and above this five per cent. It would be almost incredible that she should refuse a modification in this sense.

There yet remains the point of the £2,000 per kilometre which Gwinner demands should be paid to the Baghdad Railway Company from the construction guarantee for the Bagdad Gulf section. We need not trouble about this, as it should form a subject of agreement directly between Gwinner and the Turkish Government, and need not be in any way connected with our own negotiations with the latter.

The Foreign Office Memorandum of June 4th, 1907,([3]) of which copies were given to the French and Russian Governments, represents the attitude which we should now uphold as regards our participation in the Baghdad Railway. There are one or two points in it which might be modified, but, as a whole, our policy should remain unchanged.

I have noticed in Sir E. Cassel's Memorandum([4]) that no mention is made of the ports which are to be constructed at Baghdad, Basra, and Koweit. It may be presumed

([3]) [v. supra, pp. 355–6, No. 250.]

([4]) [Apparently the memorandum of December 15, 1909, v. supra, pp. 410–1, No. 309, encl.]

that, if the Gulf section is to be under our construction and control, the building of the ports on that section would be naturally included. It is very desirable that there should be no doubt upon this point, and the fact must not be overlooked that we are paying £4,000 a year to the Sheikh of Koweit, precisely in order to control the terminus of the line. It might therefore be as well to stipulate that the terminus should actually be there and under our control.

Sir E. Cassel's proposals contemplate a certain proportion of the share capital being in British hands; but no attempt is made to show how this proportion should be permanently so secured. The following is a suggestion which has been made to me, and which, I think, is worth considering:

The bonds for the Bagdad Gulf section may be issued to the investing public at say par. We could stipulate that the Bank of England should have the right to buy up any bonds allotted to British shareholders at any time at, say 105 or 108 per cent., or any price that might be considered fair. This would leave us free from any active intervention in the concession unless, for some political reason, such intervention should at any time prove expedient. The Japanese and other Governments constantly reserve the right of redeeming their bonds at a fixed price.

A copy of the Memorandum of June 4th, 1907, to which I have referred, is enclosed.

E. G.

January 10, 1910.

No. 319.

Sir F. Bertie to Sir Edward Grey.

F.O. 1493/100/10/44A.
(No. 13.) Secret.
Sir,

Paris, D. *January* 11, 1910.
R. *January* 14, 1910.

M. Pichon thanked me to-day for the information which, as I had the honour to report to you in my despatch No. 5 secret of the 1st instant,([1]) was given to M. Conty for communication to His Excellency respecting the attitude of His Majesty's Government in regard to the Bagdad Railway negotiations between Sir Ernest Cassel and Mr. Gwinner.([2])

M. Pichon observed to me that the French Government had all along been in favour of the internationalization of the Railway. Before he left Paris ten days ago for a holiday he had informed the Ottoman Bank that he considered that when Mr. Gwinner came to Paris to negotiate with French Financiers the Bank Representatives should listen to Mr. Gwinner's proposals and report them to the French Government, but should not commit themselves in any way. If, M. Pichon said to me, the French Financiers accepted terms not approved by the French Government, the loan would not be allowed a quotation on the Paris market.

The information which M. Pichon had in regard to the negotiations between Sir Ernest Cassel and the Deutsche Bank was that the conditions offered by Mr. Gwinner, viz., a 50% British participation in the Bagdad to the Persian Gulf section of the Railway, were not at all acceptable to His Majesty's Government.

I have, &c.
FRANCIS BERTIE.

([1]) [Not reproduced.]
([2]) [*cp. supra*, pp. 418–9, No. 314.]

No. 320.

Sir C. Hardinge to Sir A. Nicolson.

Private.(¹)

My dear Nicolson :—   Foreign Office, January 18, 1910.

. . . .(²) I wonder if Isvolsky has yet made up his mind as to what he intends to ask for in connexion with the Baghdad Railway. The French Government have decided to press for the internationalization of the line, but, as they realize that this scheme is opposed to our wishes, they propose to claim the right to connect the Syrian Railways with the line to Baghdad, the restitution of certain rights previously held by them in connexion with branch lines which have now been conceded to the German company, and the concession for a line to the Mediterranean from Baghdad viâ Homs. Such are the French demands, and it would be rather interesting to know whether Monsieur Isvolsky has yet made up his mind as to what the Russians want. As a matter of fact, I think that the negotiations will all come to nothing, as I cannot conceïve that the Turks, in their present frame of mind, would agree to any scheme which contained a proposal to create spheres of influence for foreign Powers. . . . .(³)

Yours ever
CHARLES HARDINGE.

(¹) [Carnock MSS., Vol. I of 1910.]
(²) [The first part of this letter refers to Persian railways.]
(³) [The last two paragraphs merely give personal details about the Russian Court.]

No. 321.

Sir Edward Grey to Sir F. Bertie.

F.O. 2075/100/10/44.

No. 38.)

Sir,   Foreign Office, January 22, 1910.

The French Ambassador called at the Foreign Office on the 13th inst[ant] and informed Sir C. Hardinge that he had two days before had a long conversation with M. Pichon who had explained to him the views of the French Gov[ernmen]t on the question of participation in the Bagdad Railway and had authorised him to communicate to me what had been said.

M. Pichon foresaw that there would be very great difficulty in obtaining from the Turkish Gov[ernmen]t and Parl[iamen]t their assent to the British proposal for the control and construction of the Gulf section, since the Turkish Gov[ernmen]t would oppose any scheme which had the appearance of creating a sphere of influence, and would be very suspicious of British aims in Mesopotamia. He said he was in favour of internationalization of the whole line on equitable terms, a scheme which would not be likely to meet with any opposition on the part of the Turkish Gov[ernmen]t. He realized, however, that such a scheme presents no attraction to H[is] M[ajesty's] G[overnment]. In the event therefore of H[is] Majesty's G[overnment] adhering to their present demands he had decided what the demands of the French Gov[ernmen]t would be. They are as follows :—

1. Facilities for the junction of the Syrian R[ailwa]ys with the Bagdad R[ailwa]y.
2. Restitution to the French Syrian Co[mpany] of certain rights in branch lines abandoned by them to the Bagdad R[ailwa]y Co[mpany].
3. A concession for a railway from Bagdad to Homs and the Mediterranean.

The demand for the latter concession would be absolutely essential.

M. Cambon said that an Anglo-French group of a sound character is alread being formed with a view to financing the irrigation projects in Mesopotamia, an that Sir E. Cassel is in the group. The French Gov[ernmen]t would propose tha the Bagdad-Homs line should also be financed by British and French capital. It wa estimated in Paris that the line could be built for £3,000,000.

On Jan[uary] 20th Sir C. Hardinge took an opportunity of explaining to th French Amb[assado]r that H[is] M[ajesty's] G[overnment] have no intention o pressing upon Turkey any proposal which is disagreeable to her, and that our firs step, when matters are sufficiently advanced to enable progress to be made, will b to ascertain the views of the Turkish Gov[ernmen]t before pressing anything. I was pointed out to His Excellency that it is the Turkish desire to increase th Customs Duties by 4%, and not any action on the part of H[is] M[ajesty's G[overnment] which has set the whole matter in motion.

[I am, &c.
E. GREY.]

[ED. NOTE.—The despatch printed above was based on a memorandum by Sir C. Harding describing his interview with M. Cambon. At the end of this memorandum Sir E. Gre wrote a minute the substance of which was communicated to M. Cambon by Sir C. Harding on January 20. This minute is the basis of the final paragraph of the above despatch.]

No. 322.

Sir H. Babington Smith to Sir C. Hardinge.

F.O. 5227/100/10/44.   *Constantinople,* D. *February* 8, 1910.
Dear Hardinge,   R. *February* 14, 1910.

1 have waited to write to you about the Bagdad Railway and other matters unt I had time to take stock of the situation here.

There is considerable sensitiveness here regarding any proposal for internationa ising the Bagdad Railway, not by participation throughout, but by what the Turl are inclined to regard as a division into "spheres of influence." This sensitivenes has become very acute in connection with the Lynch affair, the opponents of th scheme having made great play with the argument of British designs on Mesopotami It will subside; but it could easily be stirred up again; and the exaggerate chauvinism of the new régime is a fact which we must take into account.

I discussed the matter confidentially with Djavid Bey immediately after m return. He said that, having regard to the feeling which had been excited, it wa not the moment to bring forward any proposal for British participation in th Bagdad–Gulf section; and while he did not absolutely exclude the possibility of Britis participation in this section only, he expressed a decided preference for a schem under which the participation should be extended to the whole line.

I had also some conversation with Nazim Pacha, who is about to go to Bagda as Vali. He expressed much the same opinion.

It is clear, therefore, that even if the other aspects of the matter presented n difficulties, the time has not arrived for pressing it on here. It is necessary to wa for a suitable opportunity.

In the meanwhile our engineer, Mr. Money, has left for Konia, Aleppo an Bagdad whence he will go to Basra and Koweit. When he has traversed th proposed route of the line we shall have at our disposal a more accurate estima of the probable cost of construction. Such an estimate is a necessary prelimina for any arrangement.

In my last conversation with you before I left London you told me that Sir Edward Grey was not inclined to support a scheme which would involve our taking over the kilometric guarantees provided in the existing convention of the Bagdad Railway.

We are all agreed that the arrangement of the convention is a bad one; but it exists, and the question is whether it is practicable to carry through a negociation involving a complete modification of the system of guarantees.

The position of the Germans is strong. They have a convention which the Turks cannot repudiate, and under which they will be compelled sooner or later to find the revenues for the guarantee of the whole of the line. It is true that no definite period is fixed, and that the Turks are adepts in the art of delay, but the Germans can afford to wait. Revenues have been assigned to provide for the next four sections, and the construction of these sections will take perhaps six years. Before the end of six years the Germans are certain to have opportunities of bringing pressure to bear, or of offering inducements. They have also behind them the fact that the military party here are anxious to see a broad-gauge, high-speed line carried through to Bagdad and the Gulf. The Germans, therefore, have no great reason to be dissatisfied with the prospect for the future, and will certainly not give up their present strong position, except for a suitable inducement.

You know the position under the existing contract. It is very favourable to the Bagdad Company as regards the amount provided for construction. The cash product of the Bonds provided to meet the construction cost is about £8,500 per kilometre. This is a large sum, but not so excessive as has often been represented, because : (1). the type of line required under the concession is a very solid and expensive one; (2). in certain sections there is heavy and costly engineering work; (3). the company has to pay interest on capital during construction.

On the other hand, the arrangement as regards the guarantee for the working of the line and the division of the traffic receipts between the Government and the Company is unfavourable to the Company. The Government guarantees an annual receipt of Fcs. 4,500 per kilometre; but if the traffic receipts exceed this sum, the whole of the surplus up to Fcs. 10,000 per kilometre goes to the Government, and the Company receives nothing more until that sum is exceeded. Any receipts above that amount are divided in the proportion of 40% to the Company and 60% to the Government. This means that the Company has precisely the same sum to meet the working expenses, whatever the traffic receipts may be, so long as the receipts do not exceed 10,000 Frcs. per kilometre; and that out of the receipts above that sum, the Company receives only 40%, a proportion insufficient to meet the additional cost of the additional traffic. The Germans admit the perversity of the arrangement; and say that, in order to meet the future charge arising from it, they propose to put aside as a reserve a sum of £2,000 per kilometre from the margin on the construction of the easy sections.

What, then, are the objects of the Germans in proposing British co-operation? They probably foresee that if British capital does not participate, British opposition will grow stronger and stronger as the line approaches the Persian Gulf. Such opposition would probably not prevent the ultimate completion of the line, but it would delay it. In the second place, they wish to secure for their guarantee the proposed addition to the customs duties, and consequently they are anxious that there should not be any condition which would exclude this. Thirdly, they would not be sorry to obtain the assistance of Paris and London in issuing the Bonds; fourthly, looking further into the future, they perhaps think that British co-operation would facilitate the use of the line for Indian mails and passengers.

With these advantages in view, they agree to cede to British capital a preponderating interest in the Persian Gulf section, provided that arrangements are made for them to retain the £2,000 a kilometre on which they count. On the other hand, they are unwilling to contemplate any modification in the terms of the concession, even if the modification were such as to leave their prospective profits

untouched, since they are of opinion that any negociation of the kind would be very
difficult to carry through in the present state of affairs, and might endanger the
concession in general. Cassel brought away from his conversations at Berlin the
strong impression that they would not listen to a proposal involving a general
modification of the convention, and that the only practical course was to accept
substantially the terms they offered.

The objection which Sir Edward Grey sees to this proposal is that it would
involve accepting the kilometric guarantees, and that this would expose the Government to the charge of inconsistency, and to damaging criticisms in the Press and
in Parliament.

As regards the *system* of the guarantees under the Bagdad convention, the
criticisms which have been made apply specially to the *working* guarantee. This
might with great advantage be modified; and it is worth considering whether we
might not dispense with the working guarantee altogether, if the division of the
traffic receipts were arranged on a rational basis. I do not at present put this
forward as more than a suggestion for consideration. Mr. Money's investigations will
give us the materials for judging whether it is practicable.

As regards the *construction* guarantee, the *system* is not open to the same
criticisms. It merely amounts to a guarantee of interest and sinking fund on the
estimated cost of construction, given in the form of bonds. The criticism is that
the amount allowed for construction is exaggerated. This may be true, if the easy
sections are considered separately and if the £8,500 remains intact; but if the
£2,000 per kilometre is deducted from the £8,500, the remainder, (£6,500), will
probably not leave an excessive margin. Here again Mr. Money's reports will give
us a more accurate basis; but taking into consideration the gauge and the substantial
nature of the line, the provision of rolling stock, the cost of terminal arrangements
at Bagdad, Basra, and Koweit, and of one or more bridges over the Euphrates, and
finally, the payment of interest during construction, the cost cannot be low.
Dr. von Gwinner has given the actual construction cost of the Konia–Eregli section
(a very easy one, with no big bridges) as £5,000 per kilometre, without interest
during construction.

In any case it cannot be expected that British capital will take the matter
up without a reasonable prospect of profit and, if it is a condition of obtaining control
of the Bagdad–Gulf section, that £2,000 per kilometre should be assigned to the
Germans, there is not much room for reduction in the amount of the guarantee.
It has been suggested that the British Government might give a guarantee; but
the Turks would have the strongest objection to this, and would far rather pay the
guarantee themselves. If, therefore, the Government regard it as an object of great
importance to obtain control of the Gulf section, it may be inevitable to take the only
course open for arriving at this end, even though it should lead to some criticism.
If we could start with a clean slate the case might be different; but we have to start
from things as they are, with the Germans in the position of *beati possidentes.*

The position is further complicated now by the question of irrigation in
Mesopotamia and the Bagdad–Damascus Railway which has been proposed by
Sir William Wil[l]cocks.

Wil[l]cocks's irrigation schemes require large sums of money. The Ottoman
Government will not be able to find these sums out of their ordinary budget. If
the schemes are successful, there will be a large return to the Government, in tithes
and other taxes and perhaps from the sale of irrigated lands. It was evident that
there was an opportunity here for foreign capital to assist the Government in carrying
out remunerative works, and that it was desirable that British capital should take
a leading part in it.

You are aware that when Cassel was in Paris before Christmas he had some
conversation on the subject with Bardac, who is in close alliance with the Ottoman
Bank. A general understanding resulted, that there should be co-operation between
the English and French group as regards Mesopotamian irrigation. There was no

detailed agreement, and no discussion of any actual scheme. Cassel's view was that it was necessary to obtain further information, and to have the opinions of other experts on Wil[l]cocks's projects before they could form the basis of a financial arrangement. With this object we have retained the services of Webb and Garstin, and Webb will go to Mesopotamia this Spring. Our idea of the procedure to be followed was that when this information was obtained, the time would have arrived for discussing a concrete scheme with the French group and with the Government.

The French group have, however, gone ahead. They have been carrying on negociations here through Mr. Ornstein. When I left Constantinople in December their proposals appeared very vague and indefinite; but in the last few days Mr. Ornstein has laid before the Government three draft conventions, indicating the terms on which they are prepared to find money for the irrigation schemes and the Bagdad–Homs Railway. I have given copies of these documents to the Ambassador. The general idea of the proposals is that the money for the irrigation schemes and the railway is to be provided by means of Government Bonds, which the financial group undertakes to issue. The tithes, etc., of the irrigated lands are to provide the interest on these bonds; and the capital is to be repaid out of the proceeds of the sale of Government lands. It is probably intended that the Government should guarantee interest on the Bonds and any deficit on the working of the railway; but the drafts carefully refrain from specifying what is to happen if the revenues from the irrigated lands do not suffice for these purposes. Any profit from the railway, and the surplus receipts from the sales of land are to be divided between the Government and those who provide the money. The financial interests are to have a voice in the control of the undertaking generally.

It may appear strange that the Ottoman Bank should put forward a railway scheme which must obviously be hostile to the Bagdad Railway, in which they have a substantial share. But the French participation has never been recognised by the French Government, and the Bagdad–Homs line would be in the interest of the French railways in Syria. What view the French Government take I do not know; but presumably the Ottoman Bank have not put forward the scheme without the approval of their Government.

In any case, the linking of the railway scheme with the irrigation proposals is somewhat embarrassing as far as we are concerned, having regard to the provisional understanding between Cassel and Gwinner.

It is also necessary for us to consider whether we should come to any more definite arrangements with the French group now or whether we should endeavour to induce them to hold back the negociations until the further information which we regard as necessary has been obtained.

I must apologise for the length of this letter; but I thought it might be convenient to you if I gave a full statement of the position as it strikes me.

Yours sincerely,
H. BABINGTON SMITH.

No. 323.

Sir C. Hardinge to Sir H. Babington Smith.

F.O. 5227/100/10/44.
Private.
Dear Babington-Smith,   *Foreign Office, March* 12, 1910.

I am very much obliged to you for your interesting letter of the 8th Feb[ruary],(¹) containing an able statement of the arguments in favour of accepting Gwinner's offer to Cassel.

(¹) [v. immediately preceding document.]

I quite agree that the present moment is not an opportune one for pressing our views at Constantinople about the Bagdad Railway, owing to the chauvinism which has been created by interested parties around the Lynch Concession. It is difficult, however, to believe that when the proper moment comes, any insuperable objection can be raised by the Turks against British interests acquiring 60 per cent. of the total capital of the Gulf sections of the railway. Were there any apprehensions on the part of Turkey, a clear statement of our intentions should suffice to dispel them, and to show that no challenge to Turkey's sovereign rights would be involved. All that we want is to maintain and foster, under the protection of the Turkish Government, the trade interests which this country has been developing for over two centuries. The method by which we propose to attain this object is that British investors should hold a certain percentage in a *Turkish* Railway Company's share capital, and that they should be adequately represented on the Board of that Railway Company, whose total share capital will revert to the Ottoman Government on the expiration of the Concession. Much will depend upon the attractiveness of the form in which the matter is presented to the Turks.

I do not believe that the position of the Germans is quite as strong as you seem to think. The 1903 Concession is bound to call forth increasing discontent as the line progresses and the payment of the annuities for each successive section is exacted from the Turkish taxpayer. My belief is that the Germans are anxious for our co-operation because they realize the strength of *our* position. They fear that we may get a competing line down the Tigris. Also they probably know of our privileged position at Koweit, and that the terminus can hardly be made elsewhere, and they do not want opposition to their interests in Mesopotamia on account of the political uncertainty which is at present affecting enterprise in Turkey. They realize, moreover, that so long as we are hostile to the project their bonds will not obtain quotation on the Paris market.

It is not impossible that, if His Majesty's Government decline to approve of British participation in the Bagdad Railway unless there is a modification of the Concession, the Germans may give way and agree to suggest a modification to the Porte. Were the Germans to unite with us in such a course it is probable that the opposition of the Turks would disappear, especially if the prospect of the 4 per cent. customs increase were held out to them. The Germans might then stipulate that the whole benefit of such a modification should not be enjoyed by Turkey alone, but should be shared by them, and they could then arrange matters as they liked best.

Our objections to the kilometric guarantees remain, and to accept them would expose us to very damaging criticism from the public. It is true that the working guarantee has been criticized, because it militates against the railway being sufficiently worked to make it pay. It should be noted, however, that in the sections as far east as Mosul the gross traffic receipts may well be under 4,500 fr. a kilometre, as the population is sparse and the traffic would be relatively small, so that the Germans will probably derive their profits on those sections, not from traffic receipts, but from the Government working guarantee. On the other hand, the gross receipts on the Bagdad–Gulf sections would probably exceed the 4,500 fr. per kilometre, and there the Government would not have to pay any guarantee to the Company. Why therefore should the Bagdad–Gulf sections be mulcted 2,000l. per kilometre in order to meet the working expenses of the western sections of the line, which must almost certainly be lower than those of the Gulf sections?

As for the construction annuity, we look upon it as altogether in excess of what the actual cost is likely to be. The Committee which examined the question here in 1907 stated that, owing to the size of the kilometric guarantees, a profit of 5,000,000l. was expected to be realized by the promoters on the construction alone of the Bagdad Railway. Such a Concession would be utterly inconsistent with the interests of Turkey.

I enclose a short statement showing how the Committee arrived at this estimate of profit,([2]) and from it you will see that, while recognizing the substantial nature

([2]) [Not reproduced.]

of the permanent way, they estimated the cost of construction, including rolling-stock, at 4,375*l.* per kilometre on the first section, as against Dr. Gwinner's figure of 5,000*l.*, which you quote. We draw our own conclusions as to the disposal of the difference.

Now as to the Gulf sections. You say, "The cash product of the bonds provided to meet the construction cost is about 8,500*l.* per kilometre." If 2,000*l.* per kilometre is surrendered to Dr. Gwinner in respect of the western portion of the line there will remain 6,500*l.*, and this sum, you urge, will not leave an excessive margin, taking into consideration the gauge and the substantial nature of the line, the provision of rolling-stock, the cost of terminal arrangements at Bagdad, Bussorah, and Koweit, and of one or more bridges over the Euphrates, and, finally, the payment of interest during construction.

I do not think it correct to include in the cost of constructing the Bagdad–Gulf sections of the railway the expense of "terminal arrangements" other than stations. It is expressly stipulated in Article 23 of the Concession of 1903 that "le concessionnaire aura la faculté de construire, *à ses frais*, des ports à Bagdad," &c.; and it is provided that there shall be special port dues, which would of course be regulated on such a scale as to cover not only the current expenditure of the port authorities, but also the interest and sinking fund on the original outlay in construction.

With regard to bridges, so far as I can see, over the Euphrates there need only be one.

As to payment of interest during construction, this item need not be very considerable on the Gulf sections, where the engineering obstacles are few. If, as in any case would be necessary, Article 29 were modified, it might be possible to undertake work on all the Gulf sections simultaneously, thus lessening the period of construction during which interest would have to be paid.

You do not think that 6,500*l.* per kilometre would leave an excessive margin after construction; it is impossible to estimate cost with precision in the absence of detailed surveys, but such information as we have does not point to so high a figure. The Committee of 1907, after an examination of all available data, put the cost of the Konia–Eregli section at 4,375*l.* per kilometre, *including rolling-stock;* and they fully recognized that the first section was relatively easy and that the line is substantially built. As a fair estimate of the cost on the Bagdad–Gulf sections Sir James Mackay, who has some Indian experience, suggested 8,000*l.* a mile (5,000*l.* a kilometre); *i.e.*, 625*l.* per kilometre in excess of what the first section is believed to have cost.

So much for the cost of construction. I now take the liability of the Ottoman Government under the Concession of 1903, in so far as concerns the sections from Bagdad to Koweit—a distance of approximately 450 miles, or say 716 kilom.

The construction annuity yields, to take your figure, 8,500*l.* per kilometre; and as the loans, after allowing for discounting and bankers' charges, produce only slightly over 80 per cent. of their nominal amount, interest must be reckoned at 5 per cent.

The capital sum on which interest would be payable would be 8,500*l.* × 716, or 6,086,000*l.*; and interest at 5 per cent. would be 304,300*l.*, and this amount of interest would be subject to reduction only by the operation of the sinking fund, which is spread over the whole period till the expiration of the Concession.

The working expenses guarantee is not a fixed charge, but it might at its maximum amount reach 4,500 fr. per annum per kilometre, which works out at 128,880*l.* a year.

The liability of the Turkish tax-payer in respect of the Bagdad–Gulf sections would thus be interest to the amount of 304,300*l.*, reducible only by the gradual operation of the sinking fund, and, with the working guarantee, it might reach 433,180*l.*

An alternative plan would be the adoption of what, for the sake of convenience, I may term the "Indian" system. This could be introduced on the most

advantageous basis if His Majesty's Government were to offer a guarantee of 3 pe
cent. on the actual cost of construction, which we put up at, say, 3,600,000*l*
including rolling-stock. It has been suggested that the Turks would regard thi
proposal as a dereliction of their sovereign rights.

The other alternative which might be suggested to the Turkish Government i
that they should themselves give a guarantee. In their case it would probably hav
to be one of 5 per cent., and the guarantee would have to begin from the momen
the money was required for construction. A 5 per cent. guarantee would onl
amount to 180,000*l*. a-year, plus, say, 20,000*l*. in respect of bankers' profits an
discounting, if such were necessary in connection with the financial operations; and
an important point, this liability would not continue for ninety-nine years, but i
would cease as soon as the railway realized a net profit of 5 per cent. (a state o
affairs which ought soon to come about in the fertile districts of Mesopotamia); whil
Turkey, under the "Indian" system, would share equally with the Railwa
Company in any profit over and above 5 per cent.

Now to contrast the two systems :—

Under the Concession of 1903 the Turkish Government might have to pay, a
stated above, the maximum amount of 433,180*l*. Should, however, Dr. Gwinne
insist on having 2,000*l*. of the construction guarantee (viz., 2,000*l*. × 716 makes
capital sum of 1,432,000*l*., which, at 5 per cent., represents an annual charge o
71,600*l*.) on the Bagdad–Gulf sections, and make arrangements on that basis wit
the Turkish Government, while the "Indian" system was adopted by the Britisl
capitalists, the cost to the Turkish Government would be 71,600*l*. for the guarante
and 200,000*l*. a-year as the "Indian" maximum, making a total of about 270,000*l*

The "Indian" system has the great advantage that the guarantee reall
corresponds to the actual cost of construction; it is a far cleaner plan than the other
it would benefit the Turkish tax-payer; and it would foster and develop Britisl
trade, getting us out of what you call the "perversity" of the working guarantee
which renders the railway incapable of being worked as a commercial success. If
on the other hand, we accept Dr. Gwinner's proposal, the Germans will be reapin
the lion's share of the profits under the 1903 Concession, while we shall merel
incur the odium of it, as neither the Turkish tax-payer nor the British public wil
be able to discriminate the innocent from the guilty of the two parties to th
transaction.

We are not opposed to kilometric guarantees as a system; they exist, as you
know, in Egypt; what we object to is the scale of the guarantees allotted under th
Concession of 1903, imposing as they do, in our opinion, burdens altogether in exces
of what is fair upon the Turkish tax-payer.

As regards the Bagdad–Homs Railway and the irrigation schemes ir
Mesopotamia, the French Government are very anxious that British capital shoulc
participate in the railway upon which they have bestowed their blessing, and the
themselves are equally desirous of participating in the irrigation schemes. If the
railway is to be built, we think it very desirable that British finance should participate
in the scheme, so as to have a voice in the construction and control of a line which
may in the future be of considerable advantage to British trade. The question o
the extent of the participation of a British group and other details can be decidec
later. I understand, however that the French Government have no knowledge whatever of the Ornstein group and that the Ottoman Bank is not represented in it.
Moreover the French Gov[ernmen]t will take good care that no group gets the
concession except through them. I may add that they have already announced
their claim to a concession for this railway as a condition of the 4% surtax.

In view of my earlier statement that we agree with you that, owing to the
prejudices aroused by the Lynch Concession, it may be advisable to postpone
temporarily any further pressure to obtain for British capital the construction and
control of the Persian Gulf section of the Bagdad Railway. it appears to us that for

the present it would be well for British finance to concentrate on encouraging sound irrigation and railway projects, which will cover the ground in Mesopotamia, and so minimize the importance of the southern end of the Bagdad Railway.

C. H.

MINUTES.(³).

I have drawn up a reply to Sir H. Babington Smith dealing with the question of the Bagdad R[ailwa]y, and if its terms are generally approved I would suggest that this letter and my reply should be submitted to the B[oar]d of Trade before my reply is despatched.

C. H.

Proceed as proposed. I entirely agree with the draft reply. It seems to me that for the present it would be well for British finance to concentrate on encouraging sound irrigation and railway projects, which will cover the ground in Mesopotamia and so minimize the importance of the Southern end of the Bagdad R[ailwa]y concession.

E. G.

(³) [These minutes are attached to the draft of the above letter. They follow a long minute by Mr. L. Mallet which has not been thought worth reproducing.]

No. 324.

Sir Edward Grey to Sir G. Lowther.

F.O. 10397/100/10/44.   *Foreign Office, March 30*, 1910.
Tel. (No. 59.)   D. 1 P.M.

My immediately preceding tel[egram].(¹)

The information which you have given me shows that the Turkish Gov[ernmen]t have practically bound themselves afresh to the very course of action from which we have endeavoured to protect them, and which Hilmi Pasha declared to you that the Porte would never allow to be carried out on the lines of the present Convention. In my desp[atch] No. 245(²) of last year you were instructed to ask for a concession for the Tigris valley railway and on the 23rd Sept[ember] last I told the Turkish Ambassador that the attitude of the Porte towards this and other matters in Mesopotamia would influence the eventual decision of H[is] M[ajesty's] G[overnment] on the question of the 4 p.c. increase.(³) Unless we receive the concession for which you have applied which is necessary to put us on equal terms with the Bagdad railway in the Persian Gulf region or unless the Turkish Gov[ernmen]t secure for us participation in the Bagdad R[ailwa]y scheme on terms satisfactory to ourselves, while accepting the condition imposed for the liberty of Egypt to raise loans in future, there can be no question of our adhesion to the proposed Customs increase.

(¹) [Not reproduced.]
(²) [pp. 374–5, No. 272.]
(³) [*v. infra*, pp. 791–2, *App.* VI.]

CHAPTER XLVII.

ANGLO-GERMAN NEGOTIATIONS, 1910.

No. 325.

Sir E. Goschen to Sir Edward Grey.

F.O. 886/167/10/18.
(No. 1.) Confidential. Berlin, D. *January* 1, 1910.
Sir, R. *January* 10, 1910.

I have the honour to report that, in accordance with custom, the Ambassadors accredited to this Court proceeded to the Palace this morning for the purpose of offering their good wishes to the Emperor and Empress on the first day of the New Year.

The Emperor, who was looking exceedingly well, said a few words to each Ambassador. To me, after cordial inquiries after the health of the King and Queen His Imperial Majesty observed that he could not find much trace in England at the present moment of the "Peace and Good Will" which was supposed to be usual at this time of the Year. He then said somewhat impetuously: "They are all mad in England, and people seem to think that I am standing here with my battle axe behind my back ready to fall upon them at any moment."

I murmured something to the effect that too much importance should not be attached to all that was said during the heat and turmoil of an impending General Election, but His Majesty said that he knew that very well and had tried to make allowance for it, but that some of the speeches made had gone much too far and that he felt them all the more as they came from a class of men from whom he had not expected such utterances. His Majesty added that his Chancellor was 'very angry about this 'Hetzerei,' as, having gone out of his way in his Reichstag speeches to emphasize the improvement in Anglo-German relations and to show by quotations from the utterances of leading politicians in England how suspicion had given way to more friendly feelings, he was now being subjected to attacks from his political opponents for having misled public opinion.

Though it may be gathered from the language held by the Emperor on this occasion, that He is somewhat irritated by what he considers to be a revival of Anti-German feeling in England, the tone in which he spoke was, nevertheless, quite good humoured except when he alluded to Mr. Blatchford's articles in the "Daily Mail," which, he said, very seriously, were, in his opinion, very mischievous and singularly ill-timed. On saying good-bye His Majesty said that he supposed he must have patience, and expressed the sincere hope that after the Elections this wave of Anti-German feeling would subside and no more be heard of it.

The Chancellor, who was in attendance upon the Emperor spoke a few friendly words to me afterwards and in wishing me a happy New Year said that notwithstanding what was now being said in England, he had every hope that before the close of 1910 the united efforts of the two Governments to bring about good relations between Germany and England would show some tangible result.

I have, &c.
W. E. GOSCHEN.

No. 326.

Mr. Bax-Ironside to Sir Edward Grey.

F.O. 680/680/10/43.
No. 3.)　Confidential.　　　　　　　　　　Berne, D. *January* 1, 1910.
Sir,　　　　　　　　　　　　　　　　　　　R. *January* 7, 1910.

I have the honour to report that I had a conversation recently with a high German Official, who is in the close confidence of the Kaiser, and with whom I am well acquainted.

He informed me that he had recently been to Paris and had seen a good deal of the official world—amongst others Monsieur Briand, with whom he had held several conversations.

The real object of my informant's visits to Paris is to supply His Imperial Majesty with reports of the general state of public feeling, both in the French capital and throughout France, towards the personality of the Emperor in particular, and towards Germany in general. These visits are paid periodically both to France and to Great Britain.

My informant was, he stated, now able for the first time to report favourably to the Emperor. The policy of the latter had for some years past been one of the utmost conciliation. It was hoped that by unvarying kindness, scrupulous attention in avoiding French susceptibilities, and careful representation at all National Fêtes, accidents, or disasters, the atmosphere of distrust and dislike—not to use a stronger term—which had lasted since the war would eventually be dissipated, and be succeeded by one of, at least, friendly tolerance. This was, in his opinion, now the case.

French Statesmen and politicians had become quite friendly with Prince Radolin, whose tact and fitness for his position was welcomed by his Imperial master. The German Military Attaché, who presented wreaths from the German Emperor and Nation on the sad occasion of the death of the four aeronauts by the destruction of the French air-ship "La République" was received with cries of "Bravo!—C'est bien fait!" and even some cries of "Vive l'Empereur!" A few years ago such an action was always received in cold and deadly silence. They now hoped and believed in Berlin that their policy would meet with eventual success. The late war was always placed on the shoulders of Prince Bismarck, if it had to be mentioned at all. The French Nation were volatile and easily led, and even such violent patriots as Monsieur Déroulède had to stimulate national hatred by spicy and exciting speeches.

As regards Great Britain, my informant, who is returning to Berlin in a few days to take up his official duties, said, "The English are temporarily mad, and nothing can be done for the present in that direction."

He added that the German Naval Programme would go steadily forward, and it was for Great Britain to continue to endeavour to hold her supremacy, should she see fit to do so.

I have, &c.
H. O. BAX-IRONSIDE.

No. 327.

Sir E. Goschen to Sir Edward Grey.

Private.(¹)
Dear Sir Edward Grey,　　　　　　　　　　　Berlin, *January* 8, 1910.

I have written all my items of news to Hardinge as I did not want to bother you while you are so busy about other things : but I must write you one line to

(¹) [Grey MSS., Vol. 23.]

thank you for your wonderfully clear and concise statement with regard [to] matters at issue between us and Germany.(²)

This statement is invaluable to me and will be of the greatest assistance when the Chancellor talks to me.

He is still very sore and complains bitterly still of the position in which the anti-German tone of the Election speeches has placed him. I have endeavoured to soothe him down to the best of my ability, but both he and the Emperor are evidently very angry. Of course we are receiving a good doing in the Press, but they are beginning to say that after all Election speeches don't count for much, and to hope for better times when the Elections are over. The struggle is watched with *intense* interest, in fact they are almost as keen as if they were on the spot. Their keenness is not to be wondered at, in view of their business relations with the United Kingdom. . . . .(³)

Yours very sincerely,
W. E. GOSCHEN.

(²) [Apparently this refers to the letter given in two parts, *supra*, p. 319, No. 210, and pp. 418–9, No. 314.]

(³) [The closing remarks refer to the internal situation in Germany.]

No. 328.

Sir E. Goschen to Sir C. Hardinge.

F.O. 4953/167/10/18.
Private.
My dear Hardinge,

Berlin, D. January 28, 1910.
R. *February* 11, 1910.

I have a fearful cold which I caught coming back from Weimar and have increased a little day by day, but particularly yesterday in the draughty Royal Chapel and the still draughtier Opera House. I only mention this in order to excuse what will be a short and illwritten letter; also it may account for a somewhat depressed feeling as to the way things are going. The Chancellor is all right and very friendly and cordial, and so is Schoen; Stemrich is also welldisposed; but I feel that amongst the Heads of Bureaux in the Foreign Office there is antagonism towards us. I am going to have a talk with Schoen about it one of these days, and I shall tell him that I thoroughly appreciate his friendliness and cordiality, but that it is no good our trying to smooth matters to make things pleasant if the Tchinovniks under him are to be allowed to administer pinpricks and always place the smallest little difficulty in the most disagreeable light. Leaving aside big things, the difficulty of getting answers, the curt refusals and the grudging consents, I will mention two little things as an example of what I mean. When Shackleton expressed the hope that he might be received by the Emperor the answer brought to me by one of the leading officials in the F[oreign] O[ffice] was that the request could not be supported because Shackleton had used anti-German language in his speeches. I proved to him that he was wrong, that Shackleton had never used the language attributed to him, but my explanation was received with a very Prussian sneer and it was only after Shackleton had buttered them up in his lecture that the same official telephoned that under the circumstances the Emperor would say a few words to him after a lecture which was to take place at Dernburg's. The whole thing was not nicely done.

The same official yesterday, speaking to de Salis on the subject of Boyle's appointment, said, "We have given him his exequatur, but I may tell you that we granted it with a great deal of hesitation owing to his anti-German action in Egypt." De Salis was as usual quite equal to the occasion. He said that he had been with Boyle in Egypt and had never noticed anything of the kind, though of course the arrival of Baron Oppenheim in Egypt and his subsequent activities had been after his (de Salis') time. On de Salis saying that as the exequatur had been

granted and the matter settled he would not mention the matter, the official said
that on the contrary he would be much obliged if de Salis would bring it to my
notice! It is not so much what they do as the nasty way they do it which is
so annoying.

The French are very much up for the moment, and the Emperor is showing
Cambon much attention. He went, accompanied by the Empress and the Crown
Prince and Princess to a Fete at the French Embassy the other night (a very pretty
and successful one), this being the first Embassy party He has attended since I
have been here. He is making a great fuss over the French Art Exhibition here
and has conferred a high decoration on a French artist; in fact He is doing all in
his power to be civil to the French and Russians. To me H[is] M[ajesty] is quite
friendly in a way, but never loses an opportunity of rubbing it into me how much
put out He is by recent utterances in England. Last night He attacked me again.
He began by saying that He had received a beautiful present from the King together
with a charming letter which had given Him great pleasure; but He very soon
began about the speeches and again said that what He couldn't stand was that
the abuse of Germany came from the upper classes. I told H[is] M[ajesty] that
I had not noticed abuse so much as endeavours to stimulate people to imitate
German activity and go-aheadness, and to make people realize that Germany was
so strong by land and by sea that England must bestir herself if she was not to be
left behind. This could scarcely be regarded as abuse of Germany, rather the
contrary. He said, "No! No! you are quite wrong about that; the speeches were
not on those lines at all; besides *I* am not the strong man; you must look elsewhere
for him!" This cryptic remark, which he made with great emphasis, tapping me
on the breast to enforce it, left me in a maze from which I have not yet emerged
—unless he means that the King's navy is so much stronger than His that we
needn't make a fuss about the German's attempts to compete? One would wish to
have a chance of finishing an answer or developing an argument sometimes—but
that I never have—a volcanic remark or two—a momentary cyclone of words—
and before one has time for anything but the *beginning* of an answer H[is] M[ajesty]
is talking to someone else. I am happy to say that my opinion as to the sincerity
and straightness of Bethmann-Hollweg is confirmed from all sides. Only yesterday
Prince Halzfeldt [*sic*: Hatzfeldt] said to me, "Buelow, though probably very pleasant
with you, was always a bitter enemy of England. You couldn't trust him an inch—
and none of us did. You will find the present man the exact contrary; he is fond of
England, and he is as honest and singleminded a man as is to be found in Germany."
I have lots more to say on this subject, but have no time and must say it in my next.

Schoen tells me that the answer about de Pass has come from the Colonial
Office and that I will get it in a day or two. "You won't like the answer," he
said, "but it can't be helped and you must console yourself with the thought that
the members of the firm are Germans." When I get this note I will see whether
there is anything I can do, but I don't think that I shall be able to do much, as
if I go to Schoen he will say that he knows nothing about the case (which is true)
and if I go elsewhere I shall only get disagreeable answers.

Yours sincerely,
W. E. GOSCHEN.

No. 329.

Sir E. Goschen to Sir Edward Grey.

F.O. 4251/4251/10/18.

(No. 26.) Berlin, D. *February* 3, 1910.

Sir, R. *February* 7, 1910.

I was unfortunately prevented by indisposition from attending the Court Ball
which took place yesterday evening. Count de Salis informs me that during the

Ball, which was a very brilliant function and to which some 1,500 guests had the honour of being invited, the Emperor was pleased to converse with him for some time. His Majesty again alluded to the pleasure which he had derived from the charming letter he had received from the King on the occasion of his birthday, and added that his pleasure had been enhanced by the fact that for the first time in 21 years the King had alluded to political matters. His Majesty's allusions had been moreover of the most friendly and reassuring nature. The Emperor used almost identical language in conversing with Colonel Trench—so it is evident that he was really very much gratified and pleased by the friendliness of the King's letter. He added however to Count de Salis, speaking in a very good humoured manner, that He had been striving for many years to make the relations between His country and England more cordial and satisfactory and that He would continue to do so, but that He must admit that He was getting rather tired of being set up as a target and shot at.

The Emperor was much amused, I am told, by Count de Salis' rejoinder that, as an Irish landlord, he had every sympathy with His Majesty.

I have, &c.

W. E. GOSCHEN.

No. 330.

Mr. Vaughan to Sir Edward Grey.

F.O. 4294/4294/10/15.
(No. 18.) Confidential. *Copenhagen, D. February* 3, 1910.
Sir, *R. February* 7, 1910.

I have the honour to report that a Foreign Diplomatist told me in private conversation some days ago that he had recently been discussing the merits of the German navy with a German naval officer, and my informant appeared greatly impressed with what he had heard. As an instance of the high pitch of excellence to which the Imperial navy had attained, the officer cited their large guns, which he maintained were superior to the British. In speaking of these he explained that Germany possessed one distinct advantage over Great Britain in that when the life of a gun had expired, the inner tube could be immediately replaced, as there was a duplicate ready in every case. I cannot judge whether such a statement as the above has any value, but I was recently told by an expert that it took nearly four times as long to bore and reline a gun built on the English wire-bound system as one cast on the Krupp system. The German officer further maintained that with regard to men, Germany also possessed a decided superiority over Great Britain.

I have thought it worth while to report the foregoing, as, apart from the question of their accuracy, the statements are interesting, as showing the opinions probably held by German naval officers, and expressed to third parties who cannot fail to be impressed by them.

Another diplomatist, who has been accredited to Russia, told me yesterday that he gathered that the general opinion was that war between Great Britain and Germany must come sooner or later, although he knew that both King Edward and the German Emperor would do all in their power to avert it.

I told him that nothing was more ardently desired by Great Britain than the maintenance of peace and that there appeared to be no reasons whatever to occasion a quarrel.

I regret to say that the possibility of an eventual Anglo-German war appears to be very generally believed in by foreigners in Denmark, and I have no hesitation in stating that nine-tenths of the educated classes in this country believe such a war to be not only probable but inevitable. That this view is also shared in Danish Government circles would appear from your despatch No. 43 of September 3 last to Sir Alan Johnstone and his despatch to you No. 114 of September 11, 1909.([1])

I have, &c.
J. C. T. VAUGHAN.

([1]) [Not reproduced as the tenour is indicated.]

No. 331.

Sir F. Bertie to Sir Edward Grey.

Private.([1])

My dear Grey,   *Paris, February* 10, 1910.

I met Pichon at luncheon yesterday. He told me à propos of the proposal to be made to the Chamber to spend in the course of the next ten years £56,000,000 on ship-building that when the matter was discussed in the Cabinet Council presided over by the President of the Republic it was strongly opposed by the Minister of Finance (M. Cochery) but Briand had been splendid for he had said that he would not remain at the head of a Government which did not observe its moral obligations. Besides the necessity for France to have a Navy able to defend her she had moral obligations towards England. There had been pourparlers with the British Authorities as to the respective parts to be played by the Navies of the two countries in the event of a war in which they became allies. A duty had been assigned to the French Navy and it must be rendered fully able to carry it out, and the shipbuilding programme was considered by those competent to judge to be necessary. He could not accept the position of its being said with any show of accuracy that France could not fulfil her moral obligations and was of no reliable aid at sea to England. M. Fallières and the Cabinet generally sat on the Minister of Finance and Briand had his way . . . .([2])

Yours sincerely,
FRANCIS BERTIE.

([1]) [Grey MSS., Vol. 13.]
([2]) [The closing sentences describe changes in the French Cabinet.]

No. 332.

Sir Edward Grey to Sir F. Bertie.

Private.([1])

My dear Bertie,   *February* 12, 1910.

Your letter([2]) as to what passed in the French Cabinet about ship-building is very interesting.

The disposition towards us shown by M. Briand is very gratifying but the form it has taken may raise some embarrassing questions later on. I would rather that the French spent all they could afford to spend on their Army and not on the Navy.

However there is nothing for us to say about it : they must do as they think best : and meanwhile I will reserve the subject till you next come here, when we will talk about it.

Yours sincerely,
E. GREY.

([1]) [Grey MSS., Vol. 13.]
([2]) [v. immediately preceding document.]

No. 333.

Sir F. Bertie to Sir Edward Grey.

Private.(¹)

My dear Grey,   *Paris, February 17, 1910.*

We may prefer, as you say in your letter of the 12th instant,(²) that the French should spend all they can afford on their Army, and not on their Navy. They cannot be expected to see things in that light. The Commission of Inquiry has brought before the Public some of the great defects of the French Navy and the French Parliament and the Country are prepared to make sacrifices for it. The Ministry are consequently obliged to propose an extensive programme of Shipbuilding. At present as France is dependent on England for her defence at sea we are in the position of being able in the last resort to dictate to the French Government as regards a war with Germany. They desire, and small blame to them, to free themselves from such entire dependence on us not only in that respect, but in general policy. What the French navy, even with the increased ship power, may be worth at sea is another matter.

Yours sincerely,

FRANCIS BERTIE.

(¹) [Grey MSS., Vol. 13.]
(²) [*v.* immediately preceding document.]

No. 334.

Sir Edward Grey to Sir F. Bertie.

Private.(¹)

My dear Bertie,   *February 19, 1910.*

What I said in my previous letter is true but so is what you have said in yours of February 17 about French Naval Expenditure.(²) French opinion will demand the expenditure and the Government cannot help themselves. They also desire to free themselves from entire dependence on us as *you* truly say : but what *Briand* said to his colleagues as reported in your letter of the 10th(³) was that France must spend money on her Navy in order to fulfil her moral obligations towards England.

Having done this she will of course say that what she has spent on her Navy for the sake of her obligations towards us adds force to our obligations towards her.

It was what Briand said and this reflection upon it that drew from me my previous letter. What really strengthens the moral obligations between us is that France should keep up an Army and we a Navy at the highest possible pitch of strength.

Yours sincerely,

E. GREY.

(¹) [Grey MSS., Vol. 13.]
(²) [*v.* immediately preceding document.]
(³) [*v. supra*, p. 439, No. 331.]

No. 335.

Sir E. Goschen to Sir Edward Grey.

F.O. 8718/167/10/18.
(No. 62.) Confidential.   *Berlin, D. March 7, 1910.*
Sir,   R. *March 14, 1910.*
   I have the honour to forward, herewith, a despatch, as marked in the margin, which I havé received from Captain Heath, Naval Attaché to this Embassy, relating to a conversation with H[is] M[ajesty] the Emperor.

                                              I have, &c.
                                              W. E. GOSCHEN.

Enclosure in No. 335.

Captain Heath to Sir E. Goschen.

Confidential.
Sir,   *Berlin, March 7, 1910.*
   I have the honour to report that His Majesty the Emperor was graciously pleased to hold a few minutes' conversation with me on the occasion of the annual dinner to the Ambassadors, given at the Berlin Schloss on the 4th March.
   His Majesty expressed his great satisfaction that the "naval scare" in England appeared to be passing away. His Majesty remarked that he believed that nothing approaching the recent scare had taken place in England since the years immediately following the Crimean war.
   His Majesty complained that no allowance appeared to have been made for his own close blood relationship with His Majesty the King, nor to the fact that he had ruled Germany for twenty-two years, and had never shown any desire but for the maintenance of peace and good relations between Great Britain and Germany.
   His Majesty expressed great surprise that the "scare" seemed to extend from the "dukes to the lowest in the land." As for certain remarks made in connection with the possible conversion of Belfast into a German naval base, His Majesty remarked that he could find no words in which to express his wonder.
   His Majesty referred to the strange "stories" told by the leaders of both the principal parties in the House of Commons as to the number of German 1st class ships to be completed by early 1912.
   His Majesty added, "If only they would read and understand the conditions of the Naval Law, they would have been saved all these false statements."
   It is perhaps the best illustration of His Majesty's good spirits that he wound up his remarks somewhat as follows :—

   "I really get so puzzled as to the state of mind of some of my friends in England that I was constrained to finish up one of my letters with the lines of the old song—
          "'Oh, Julia, oh, Julia,
          Why are you so peculiar?'"

                                              I have, &c.
                                              H. L. HEATH,
                                              Captain and Naval Attaché.

MINUTE.

   The feelings of the German Emperor may at any time be swept aside by a wave of Chauvinism arising from some more or less trifling incident. In such cases one cannot count on blood relationship.
                                              C. H.
                                              E. G.

No. 336.

Sir Edward Grey to Sir E. Goschen.(¹)

F.O. 10740/167/10/18.
(No. 71.) Secret.

Sir,   *Foreign Office, March* 22, 1910.

Count Metternich remarked to me to-day that I had said nothing about the negotiations with Germany since the general election. I replied that the Cabinet had been so much occupied since the election and the political future was so uncertain that I had not attempted as yet to bring the question before them. Count Metternich seemed to be prepared for this reply and to understand the difficulty of the situation.

I observed that there had been no indication when the negotiations were suspended that the German naval programme could be modified. Count Metternich asked whether I meant the German Naval Law, and I replied that I meant the naval programme as fixed by law. His Excellency said that it had always been made quite clear on the German side that this could not be altered. I observed that this was the key of the situation, for I was sure that public opinion here would expect a diminution of our naval expenditure to be a consequence of any agreement, and our present naval expenditure was based on the German naval law as it was now.

[I am, &c.
E. GREY.]

(¹) [For Count Metternich's report, *v. G.P.* XXVIII, pp. 308–10.]

No. 337.

Sir Edward Grey to Sir E. Goschen.(¹)

F.O. 11445/8445/10/34.
(No. 80.)

Sir,   *Foreign Office, March* 31, 1910.

I observed to the German Chargé d'Affaires to-day that, though I was not speaking officially or with the object of bringing forward anything for discussion, I had been reflecting upon what Count Metternich had said to me as to the non-renewal of the discussions started by Herr von Bethmann-Hollweg last autumn with regard to a general arrangement between England and Germany.(²)

A reduction in naval expenditure was in our view essential to any arrangement of this kind, and Count Metternich had reaffirmed the impossibility of altering the German Naval Law. An arrangement of this kind was, therefore, not possible at present; but it seemed to me that the key to smooth relations in many respects between the two countries might be found in a settlement of the Bagdad Railway question. This had been suggested to me by the representations which Germany had recently made here and in St. Petersburgh respecting Persia. The German Government did not wish to have a discussion of the Bagdad railway *à quatre;* but we on the other hand though we might discuss the question separately, could not have a settlement except *à quatre; i.e.,* we could not have a settlement with Germany ourselves unless France and Russia also had a settlement with Germany. With regard to France, there was no difficulty. With regard to Russia and ourselves, perhaps a settlement might now be made which would include the Persian question.

(¹) [For Herr von Kühlmann's report, *v. G.P.* XXVIII, pp. 313–4, and *ib.* XXVII, II, pp. 634–6. On April 1, Sir A. Nicolson was instructed by telegram to inform M. Isvolski of this conversation.]

(²) [*v.* immediately preceding document.]

The German Chargé d'Affaires received this very sympathetically. He said that he had felt for some time that a frank discussion of Persian affairs, though in a non-committal way, would be desirable to prevent the growth of a bad sentiment. Germany did not wish to be made to feel that a monopoly was being established against her in Persia in favour of England, Russia, and eventually France.

I told him that we were bound to watch very carefully our strategic and political interests. This would not be so necessary if Persia were a strong country, able to hold matters in her own hands; but, as she was so weak we were obliged to guard against her giving away concessions which would injure us strategically or politically. On the other hand, however, we had no desire to exclude foreign commerce by establishing a commercial monopoly. There was a certain analogy between the situation in Persia and the situation in Morocco. The analogy was not exact, because in the case of Persia there was no Convention of the nature of the Algeciras Act. But, still, as Germany had been able to come to a working arrangement commercially with France about Morocco, I did not see why she should not get on in a similar way with Russia and ourselves about Persia.

The German Chargé d'Affaires remarked that he had known something of Morocco when he was there, and in his opinion there need have been no trouble had it not been for the bad sentiment which was aroused some time ago. He saw no reason why an arrangement should not be come to with regard to Persia, and why the arrangement should not be satisfactory to our position in the Persian Gulf. He understood that we had considered our position in the Gulf to be prejudiced by the Bagdad Railway project.

I said that a great deal of Indian and other British trade went to the Gulf, for generations we had done all the work there, and the Lynch Concession had control over one of the means of communication into Mesopotamia. Control over means of communication had much to do with the flow of trade, and if the Railway were made down to the Gulf and irrigation took place in Mesopotamia the means of communication now in our hands would be entirely superseded. It was in this sense that our position in the Gulf was at stake. So far as the northern sections of the Railway were concerned, Germany was not displacing anything of ours; but if Germany had control over the southern section she would be displacing our vested interests.

The Chargé d'Affaires told me that it was believed to be our view that, even if Germany did give us control over the southern section, this would not be a concession for which we owed anything to Germany.

I pointed out that the investment of British capital in the completion of the line would be a *quid pro quo*, and so would be our consent to the 4% increase of the Turkish Customs Dues,[3] which would help the Turks to find the money for the other sections of the Railway.

The Chargé d'Affaires dwelt upon the difficulty which his Government experienced owing to the pan-German feeling. This feeling made it hard for them to appear to make concessions without getting substantial considerations in return. At the same time, he did not think this was a reason for not preparing the way for a settlement.

I said my reflections had been much influenced by the impression made upon me of a good disposition and a genuine desire to smooth matters on the part of Herr von Bethmann-Hollweg, and I would add of Herr von Schön also.

[I am, &c.]
E. G[REY].

[3] [*cp. infra*, pp. 791–2, *App.* VI.]

No. 338.

Sir A. Nicolson to Sir Edward Grey.

F.O. 12142/8445/10/34A.
(No. 169.)   *St. Petersburgh,* D. *April* 2, 1910.
Sir,   R. *April* 11, 1910.

I had a conversation this afternoon with Monsieur Iswolsky in regard to possible German action in Persia, and I gave him in a Pro memoria the substance of your observations to the German Chargé d'Affaires, as communicated to me in your telegram No. 156 of the 1st instant.(¹) I explained that the conversation with Monsieur de Kühlmann had been quite informal and unofficial, but that you thought it might interest him to know what had passed. Monsieur Iswolsky expressed his best thanks and remarked that your observations were most interesting. He would, he added, naturally keep me fully informed of the course of any discussions which might take place between him and the German Government in regard to the Bagdad Railway, but he doubted if they would lead to any results. I thought it as well to give Monsieur Iswolsky a summary in writing of your remarks as they will be a useful guide to him in any conversation he may have with the German Ambassador.

I told Monsieur Iswolsky that I was glad we had come to an agreement as to the text of the communication to be made to the Persian Government, and that the necessary instructions had now been sent to Sir George Barclay and Monsieur Poklewski.(²) It would be well that the Persian Government should receive a warning as soon as possible. His Excellency remarked that as long as Great Britain and Russia held firmly together they were on very strong ground. He had not heard positively that there was any immediate intention on the part of German financiers to make an advance, and they would find obstacles in their way very serious if they seriously contemplated such a step. As to railway concessions, he was beginning to regard that question with a certain quietude. Even supposing that the Persian Government, in spite of our warnings, granted a concession, it would be impossible for the Germans to put it into execution, in any case until the Bagdad Railway was constructed. The Russian Government would decline to allow any material to go in transit through Russian territory. I remarked that material could be imported from the south by sea. The cost of transport would perhaps be very great for northern lines, but for lines in the south the same difficulties would not exist.

Monsieur Iswolsky remarked that in his view the action of Germany was prompted by various motives. The Government perhaps wished to show the German public that they were ready to encourage and promote German enterprizes in a new field; and they also might think that they could put pressure on Russia to be conciliatory in matters connected with the Bagdad Railway. There was, further, the desire to ·impress on Russia that her understanding with England did not preserve her from admonitions from Berlin, and there was possibly a hope that some divergence of views might be developed between England and Russia. "Enfin," he said, "il y a un peu de tout" in this last move of Germany.

I observed that the press had now got wind of what was passing and he said that some Russian journals had already taken up the matter.

I asked if Count Pourtalès had again referred to the subject, and he replied in the negative. He expects to receive a written communication before long, and I think he is quite prepared for it not being couched in very agreeable terms.

I have, &c.
A. NICOLSON.

(¹) [Not reproduced. Its substance is given in greater fulness in the immediately preceding document.]
(²) [For the substance of this communication, *v. infra*, p. 452, No. 343, *note* (²).]

No. 339.

Sir G. Lowther to Sir Edward Grey.

F.O. 12167/100/10/44.
(No. 197.)   Constantinople, D. April 2, 1910.
Sir,   R. April 11, 1910.

I arranged to see Rifaat Pasha at his house to-day and told him that I wished to make clear the position of His Majesty's Government as regards their consent to the 4 % increase of the Customs dues, if it was still the intention of the Ottoman Government to impose that increase, as information had reached us that negotiations were proceeding between the Ottoman Government and the Bagdad Railway Company which, if completed, would, five years hence, give to the Bagdad Railway Company the excess of the tithes for the kilometric guarantees, amounting to about £T 500,000, for the construction of the final portion from El Halif to Bagdad.

Rifaat Pasha made no attempt to deny the existence of the negotiations but said they had not terminated. He could not see how we could object to the giving of tithes as a guarantee, it was the giving of the 4 % increase about which we had made the reserve. I reminded His Excellency that in the original communication made to your department on September 14 of last year, requesting agreement to the 4 % increase, the following phrase had occurred "Il est bien entendu que les sommes provenant de cette majoration ne seront point affectées à des entreprises dans lesquelles le Gouvernement Impérial se trouve déjà engagé et notamment le chemin de fer de Bagdad."(¹) This obviously had been introduced in order to get over the objections that our goods would be handicapped with the extra 4 % in order to benefit the Bagdad Railway in fact that the money would go out of the pockets of British merchants into those of German contractors, a position difficult to justify before our Parliament, and it was obvious that the receipts other than the 4 % should be available and be reserved for works of general utility and advancement and should not be used for furnishing exaggerated guarantees against which we have always inveighed and against which we have endeavoured to protect them.

Rifaat Pasha said he was the more surprised at the view of His Majesty's Government thus expressed by me because he had recently instructed Tewfik Pasha to ask at the Foreign Office whether there would be any objection on the part of His Majesty's Government to the ordinary revenues being given as guarantees for the prolongation of the line from Halif [sic. Helif] to Bagdad and he had understood from Sir Charles Hardinge that there would be none, and that it was only the 4% about which we were concerned.(²)

Rifaat Pasha then went on to say that our attitude could only be interpreted by the hypothesis that we wished to obstruct the completion of the line and to leave it as it were "in mid-air" at Halif. The Turkish Government were committed in principle to Germany as regards the completion of the line to Bagdad and they could not risk a disagreement with that Power on the matter. He did not, however, state, which is the fact, that the military authorities are pressing very hard for the conclusion of the line to Bagdad. I observed that they were committed when funds were available for the guarantees, and these were not available unless the 4 % or their equivalent were released. The only way in which they could become available was by some satisfaction being given to British commerce either by some participation in the Bagdad Railway scheme or by the granting of a concession to us for a Bagdad–Basrah Railway. This latter, I reminded His Excellency, had in principle been approved of by the ex-Grand Vizier Hilmi Pasha after consultation

(¹) [v. supra, pp. 375–6, No. 273. The passage here quoted ends in the original text " nommément au chemin de fer de Bagdad."]
(²) [Unsigned marginal comment: " This is not the case see 11372." The reference is to Tel. No. 51 from Sir G. Lowther of April 2, which gives a shorter account of the above interview. Sir Charles Hardinge wrote a minute on this telegram saying that he had spoken " in exactly the contrary sense " to Tewfik Pasha.]

with some of his colleagues.(³) To this His Excellency observed that he had not been one of them and this was the first he had heard of the suggestion. I then briefly recounted to him my conversations with Hilmi Pasha, the conclusion of which was that Shevket Pasha who had recently returned from Berlin should speak to Baron Marschall with a view to bringing about some participation of Great Britain in the continuation of the line. I reminded him of the conversations that had taken place between Sir Ernest Cassel and Dr. Gwinner in Berlin, negotiations not broken off, but only suspended. His Excellency seemed to suggest that it would be time enough to consider this proposal when the Halif Bagdad section was completed, and if necessary Turkey could build the Bagdad–Basrah line herself. This, however, is obviously out of the question. In the first alternative we should have no lever left with which to negotiate with the Germans, and in the second it is clear that they could, once in possession of the line to Bagdad, make their own terms with regard to the Turkish Bagdad–Basrah line.

I also took occasion to remind His Excellency that Hilmi Pasha, when Grand Vizier, had frequently declared to me that he would never agree to the continuation of the line on the old conditions, to which His Excellency merely observed that Hilmi Pasha was in the habit of giving promises very lightly. But the fact must not be lost sight of that the military element is still supreme and perhaps makes its influence more felt than it did last autumn.

In the course of the conversation Rifaat Pasha, while still suggesting that a British participation with the Germans in the Halif–Bagdad portion would not get over our objections as to the existence of exaggerated kilometric guarantees asked whether, in the event of such a solution being found, we would grant the 4 % but pending the clearing up of the misunderstanding referred to I thought it wiser not to enter on a field which might be fruitful of lengthy discussion especially as I am not aware as to how far His Majesty's Government would support a British participation that necessarily involves kilometric guarantees.

Finally Rifaat Pasha said that he would refer to Tewfik Pasha's telegram recording his conversation with Sir Charles Hardinge which he had not at hand, and that he would confer with the Grand Vizier, but in a somewhat desperate tone he added that the only way he could see out of the matter would be to abandon the request for the 4 % increase of the Customs dues.

It may not be out of place to observe that the entering into arrangements for the completion of the line from El Halif to Bagdad impliedly on the old onerous conditions with the new one, and that too in connection with the 4 % is clearly at variance with what was generally believed to be the intention of their Government last year, namely not to proceed with the construction of the line beyond Helif or even Aleppo unless some considerable modification more favourable to the Ottoman Treasury were brought about.

I have, &c.
GERARD LOWTHER.

(³) [cp. supra, p. 377. Nos. 274–5.]

No. 340.

Sir Edward Grey to Sir G. Lowther.

F.O. 11372/100/10/44.   *Foreign Office, April* 4, 1910.
Tel. (No. 61.)   D. 6 P.M.

Bagdad Railway. Your telegram No. 51 (of April 2).(¹)

Y[our] E[xcellency] should explain to M[inister for] F[oreign] A[ffairs] that our present attitude is not open to the interpretation indicated: all we maintain is that we cannot agree to the customs increase if that increase is to be used,

(¹) [Not reproduced. *v. supra*, p. 445, No. 339, *note* (²).]

whether directly or by liberating other revenues, to facilitate the prolongation of a railway which must, as at present controlled, have a prejudicial effect on our established trade interests in Mesopotamia. Our attitude will only be changed subject to the fulfilment of one of two alternative conditions : either we must be admitted on acceptable terms to participation in the Gulf sections of the Bagdad Railway, or we must be granted a substantial interest in a " protective " concession for a line down the Tigris.

We are in favour of railway construction in Mesopotamia, but not on terms calculated to handicap British interests.

You should emphasise the fact that you did apply to Hilmi Pasha for a concession, and that your application was agreed to in principle (see your tel[egram] No. 335 of Sept[ember] 27)(²): to avoid all ambiguity it might be well to make this communication in writing.

As to the last paragraph of your telegram, it is difficult to express any opinion without knowing the details of what M[inister for] F[oreign] A[ffairs] has in contemplation and what safeguards he would propose for securing our commercial position.

(²) [v. supra, p. 377, No. 275.]

No. 341.

Sir G. Lowther to Sir Edward Grey.

F.O. 11887/100/10/44.
(No. 198.) Confidential.   *Constantinople,* D. *April* 4, 1910.
Sir,   R. *April* 8, 1910.

I have the honour to transmit to you herewith an account, courteously communicated to me by Sir H. Babington Smith, of a conversation that gentleman recently had with the German Ambassador on the subject of the Bagdad Railway.

You will notice that the tone of Baron von Marschall's remarks seems to indicate that in his opinion the construction of the line on to Bagdad is assured, so that he is disposed to contemplate with comparative indifference the construction of a line from Bagdad to Homs and Tripoli, whether or not the proposed irrigation schemes are carried into effect, as he does not fear for the German line the competition of this latter railway.

He seems, in fact, to consider the German position to be so strong as to be able to defy competition, though he is evidently apprehensive of being too uncompromising in regard to the Bagdad–Basra section where he recognises that British interests are predominating.

I have, &c.
GERARD LOWTHER.

Enclosure in No. 341.

Memorandum of Conversation between Sir H. Babington Smith and Baron Marschall von Bieberstein on March 24, 1910.

After various other matters had been discussed, I referred to the question of the Bagdad Railway.

Baron Marschall said that he was now, and always had been, in favour of an agreement with England as regards the Bagdad–Gulf section, since English interests were necessarily predominant in that region, owing to the extent of her commerce, her position in the Persian Gulf, and the nearness of her Eastern possessions. He had seen Gwinner's memorandum of his conversation with Sir Ernest Cassel,(¹) and Cassel's letter to Gwinner. He quoted the phrase " nothing short of absolute

(¹) [v. supra, pp. 410–1, No. 309, encl., and G.P. XXVII, II, pp. 605–7.]

control'' from the latter; and said that he thought that condition would create great difficulty. He suggested that "participation" was a better word than "control," and that a participation of 50 % would, in fact, give real control, without offending in the same way the susceptibilities of the Turks as regards spheres of influence. The assent of the Turks was necessary, since, under the Bagdad Convention, the concessionnaires must obtain the assent of the Turks for handing over any part of the concession to another party. I reminded him that it would also be necessary to obtain their assent to the removal of the bar on the use of the Bagdad–Gulf section before the rest of the line was open to traffic. He thought that if the participation were limited to 50 %, the assent of the Turks might be obtained; though he did not know whether Hakki Pasha's views were as favourable to such an arrangement as Hilmi's had been. I said that the matter was in suspense at present for various reasons. It was not a good moment for pursuing the matter at Constantinople; also we were awaiting the result of Money's investigations. I did not refer to the objections of the British Government to any scheme involving the acceptance of the kilometric guarantees in their present form. Baron Marschall agreed that it was not a good moment here, since, he said, there were too many irons in the fire—the new Mahsousseh, the Lynch Affair, Willcocks and Mesopotamian irrigation,([2]) and the Bagdad–Homs railway, as well as the question of the Bagdad–Persian Gulf section.

As regards irrigation and the Bagdad–Homs railway, Ornstein had explained to him the nature of his schemes, and had endeavoured to convince him that the Bagdad–Homs line would not compete with the German Bagdad line. Baron Marschall did not accept this though he did not lay strong stress on the competitive character. He held that heavy traffic, such as grain, from Bagdad and country to the south of Bagdad would find its natural exit in the Persian Gulf, and he did not expect that a Bagdad–Homs–Tripoli line would secure that traffic. He therefore, if I understood him rightly, considered that the Bagdad–Tripoli line would compete, if it competed at all, not so much with the Bagdad–Mossoul–Alexandretta line as with the route to Basra, but even on this route he thought that water carriage would defeat the railway.

He referred in this connection to Art[icle] 12 of the Bagdad Convention,([3]) which reserves to the Bagdad Company the exclusive right to "embranchements reliant le chemin de fer faisant l'objet de la présente convention à la mer en un point situé entre Mersine et Tripolis de Syrie." I suggested that this article did not cover a line reaching the sea at Tripolis itself, since Tripolis was not "un point situé entre Mersine et Tripolis de Syrie"; but Baron Marschall said that in his opinion the definition included the two points specified as the limits.

(We had not the exact words before us at the time but on looking at them again, I venture to think that the Ambassador's view is quite untenable. Even if the words themselves admitted of any doubt, the meaning is clearly indicated by the fact that, when the Convention was signed, a railway was actually in existence from Adana, a point on the line, to Mersina; and it was therefore obviously impossible to reserve to the Bagdad Company the exclusive right of making a branch from their railway to Mersina.)

Baron Marschall said that Ornstein had claimed to represent "Bardac's group, including the Ottoman Bank, Cassel and the Rothschilds." I said he represented Bardac's group, and that though I believed the Ottoman Bank had not taken formal engagements, or committed themselves to the detail of Ornstein's schemes, they were fully aware of what had been done, and there was undoubtedly an understanding that they would take part in the scheme. As regards our position I thought it well to be frank, and said that there was a general understanding that we would act with the French group as regards irrigation in Mesopotamia, but we were not responsible for the details of Ornstein's proposals, and, indeed, thought

([2]) [cp. pp. 381–4, No. 281.]
([3]) [v. B.F.S.P., Vol. 102, pp. 837–8.]

that Willcocks's projects and estimates required checking by cooler judgments before they could be taken as a basis of a large scheme. The understanding with the French group referred primarily to Willcocks's irrigation schemes. The railway had been joined with these schemes by the French group, in response, as we are told, to an invitation expressed by the Turks. We were inclined to share Baron Marschall's doubt whether a railway to the Mediterranean could get much of the export traffic from Bagdad; but, if the railway scheme ever came to anything, it could only be in close connection with the irrigation schemes, and we should, of course, regard the understanding for common action with the French as applying to it. Marschall agreed that the railway project was necessarily closely united with the irrigation. He added that notwithstanding the claim that might be based on article 12 of the Bagdad convention, he did not think that Germany would oppose the Bagdad–Homs railway.

Ornstein, who was, he said, " un peu naïf," had suggested that the Germans should participate in the Bagdad–Homs scheme and give up *their* Bagdad scheme. He evidently did not treat this suggestion seriously.

As regards the attitude of the Turks to the Bagdad–Homs railway, he thought it probable that they were attracted by the assertion that no kilometric guarantee was claimed; and they would be less favourable to it when they discovered that the arrangement suggested amounted in fact to a guarantee both for construction and working.

The general impression I derived from the conversation was that he was strongly in favour of an arrangement for the Bagdad–Gulf section and much less hostile than I anticipated to the Bagdad–Homs project.

H. BABINGTON SMITH.

No. 342.

Sir E. Goschen to Sir Edward Grey.

F.O. 12136/100/10/44A.
(No. 99.) Very Confidential. *Berlin*, D. *April* 8, 1910.
Sir, R. *April* 11, 1910.

During a visit I paid to Herr Stemrich yesterday he alluded to the conversation which had taken place between you and the German Chargé d'Affaires on the Bagdad Railway([1]) and your suggestion that perhaps some arrangement might be made which would include the Persian question. He said that I knew very well that no one desired more than he did to see good relations established between Germany and England, but that the attacks recently levelled against the Imperial Foreign Office rendered it excessively difficult for the Imperial Government to come to any arrangements which would entail concessions, on their part, particularly if there was no substantial consideration in return to be placed on the German side of the account. The Bagdad Railway loomed very largely in the public mind at present as a purely German undertaking; speaking for himself, and he had no authority to speak for the Government, he considered that any concession made with regard to the Railway would be severely criticized by Public Opinion and would be held up as yet another example of weakness in the Imperial Foreign Policy. I said that surely he recognized that in the case that an arrangement was come to giving us control over the Southern Section of the Line there would be something to show on the German side of the account, as, as you had pointed out to Mr. Kühlmann, such an arrangement would facilitate the completion of the whole line and place us in a position to give our consent to the 4 % increase of the Turkish Customs Dues.

(1) [Apparently the conversation described in pp. 442–3, No. 337.]

Herr Stemrich replied that this might be so but that he was quite certain in his mind that Public Opinion would not view the matter in that light or see any *quid pro quo* for what would be regarded as a concession. I replied that if the Imperial Government recognized that the *quid pro quo* existed and was sufficient, it would not perhaps be difficult to educate Public Opinion and bring it to a proper knowledge of how the matter really stood. He replied that on the contrary it would be extremely difficult; it was not only the Pan-Germans who were ill-disposed towards the Imperial Government for its management of Foreign Affairs, but unfortunately there was a general feeling amongst the influential industrial classes that German interests abroad were not meeting with sufficient support. I asked Herr Stemrich whether I was to gather from his remarks that he considered the present moment inopportune for any conversations with regard to the Bagdad Railway and kindred matters. He said that he would not go so far as that, as it was of course quite possible by mutual consideration of each other's interests for the two Governments to come to some understanding; but he had wished to show me that for the reasons he had given the Imperial Government had to move very carefully and avoid anything that might have the appearance of concessions to Foreign Powers without due compensation in return. He begged me at the same time to regard his observations as confidential and as merely the expression of his own personal opinions. I would hear the views of the Imperial Government from the Chancellor who he knew would shortly wish to have a conversation with me on these subjects.

As an example of the interest which the public is now taking in the Railway Question, Herr Stemrich sent me this morning the enclosed article by Professor Wirth,[2] a well known publicist, whose writings, Herr Stemrich says, are eagerly read by a very wide circle.

I have, &c.
W. E. GOSCHEN.

MINUTES.

This puts on official record that the German Gov[ernmen]t are unable or unwilling to grant us any participation whatever in the Southern end of this Bagdad Line, *even in return for an arrangement in regard to Persia.*

We have decided on the policy which we are therefore forced to pursue *i.e.* to obtain a railway concession for ourselves from Turkey and if complaints are made on the side of Germany we shall have an overwhelming answer.

Personally I am of opinion that we must now completely abandon the idea of coming to terms with Germany over the Bagdad Line, although their overtures will probably be renewed when they hear that we are in earnest about the Tigris Line.

When we have obtained our concession, we shall be able to bargain on equal terms.

L. M.

As Sir E. Goschen has put it in a private letter to me " The Chancellor has come to a certain extent into the open. His idea seems to be to use the southern end of the Bagdad Railway, and our vital interests in the Persian Gulf, as levers to force us into the sort of understanding he wants, an understanding which, as it would leave Germany practically mistress of the European continent, would no doubt be acceptable to the Reichstag and public opinion and crown its engineers with laurels."[3]

We must go on with the Tigris valley R[ailwa]y.

C. H.

Yes : and if we find the Germans opposing the Tigris valley railway we can retort that they are claiming monopoly in Mesopotamia.

E. G.

[2] [Not reproduced.]
[3] [This extract is taken from a private letter from Sir E. Goschen to Sir C. Hardinge, April 14, 1910. *v. infra*, p. 463, No. 348.]

No. 343.

Sir E. Goschen to Sir Edward Grey.

F.O. 12218/100/10/44A.
Tel. (No. 25.)

Berlin, April 10, 1910.
D. 1·8 P.M.
R. 8 P.M.

Chancellor sent for me this evening.

Referring to your conversation with German Chargé d'Affaires([1]) he said that he regretted not to have been able to fall in with your views respecting Bagdad railway. Public opinion would not allow him to give preponderance of influence on most valuable section of railway without very substantial compensation. What H[is] M[ajesty's] Gov[ernmen]t seemed to regard as such was no compensation at all. It was something for Turks but nothing for Germany.

After listening to my enumeration of advantages to Germany of British participation he said that they amounted to nothing. I asked him whether he had in his mind any compensation which he and public opinion would deem sufficient. His reply was to the effect that the only way he could make such a great concession palatable to public opinion was to make it form part of a general political understanding such as he had indicated last year. Any other way was impossible. After pointing out once more the difficulties in the way of a political understanding on his lines, I said that surely fact that suggestion of British participation had come from German side would have a tranquillising effect on German public opinion. He said that, on the contrary, in the first place the Deutsche Bank was not Germany and secondly much had changed since Cassel's visit to render German public opinion sensitive with regard to concessions. No one was more anxious than he to have good relations with England but he could assure me that nothing was more certain than that if he gave away this valuable concession for what public opinion would regard as nothing the relations between the two countries would become far worse than ever.

Alluding to your remarks about Persia, he said that, in his opinion, that was another question which should form part of the general political understanding. His views were that British and Russian Gov[ernmen]ts should renew assurances as to open door. That Germany should engage not to apply for railway, telegraph or such like concessions in the British sphere, while in return G[rea]t Britain should give Germany a fair share of supply of material etc. in any British enterprises under such concessions. Germany would also ask for equal participation with other third Powers in loans and situations under Persian Gov[ernmen]t. I also understood he [sic] to say that as regards Russia Germany would require that line between Teheran and Khanikin should be constructed and that on completion of that line and the German Bagdad–Khanikin line carriages and trucks from German line should be allowed to run through to Teheran without prohibitory customs dues or other disadvantages. As long as this was not promised, and the matter was almost as important to British commerce as to German, any assurance of the open door was illusory.

MINUTES.

This telegram deals with very important questions, but it does not appear to require an immediate reply.

As regards the Bagdad Railway, as a matter of fact it is not so much a question of what German public opinion would allow, it is rather a matter for the German Gov[ernmen]t to consider whether German interests would best be protected by allowing us to co-operate in the Bagdad Railway (Gulf sections) or by running the risk ot our getting an alternative concession for a line down the Tigris valley. It is probable that if we succeed in getting a concession down the Tigris, the German Gov[ernmen]t will alter their present conception of British participation in the Bagdad Railway. I have minuted a letter from a firm in the City, and proposed that a detailed and reasoned despatch, in a form suitable if it should ever be required for publication, should be drawn up to Sir G. Lowther, in order to explain fully our attitude in regard to the Customs increase in Turkey and the question of railway construction in Mesopotamia, and so

([1]) [Apparently that in pp. 442–3, No. 337.]

[17590]

2 G 2

I do not cover the same ground again in this minute, except to say that it does seem very desirable that we should concentrate upon a concession for the Tigris Valley Line.

As regards Persia, it seems hardly advisable that we should enter into any written understanding with Germany as she might, to judge from her past conduct in other regions, utilise such an understanding for justifying a policy of gradual commercial absorption. It would seem rather that we should inform the Persian Gov[ernmen]t in explicit terms that we should regard it as an unfriendly act if concessions for railway construction in Persia were given to third Powers (other than Russia and ourselves) since such concessions would possibly have a very harmful influence, from political and strategical aspects, upon vital British interests.(²) As long ago as October 1908 we wrote a long memorandum to the Russian Gov[ernmen]t(³) indicating the concessions for railways in Persia for which we should apply, and there has been much correspondence of a desultory character since, but it does now seem desirable that we should definitely approach the Persian Gov[ernmen]t on the subject. As to Germany having equal rights with third powers as regards loans and official posts, it does not seem quite clear whether this alludes to Powers other than G[rea]t Britain and Russia, or whether it includes those two Powers. One thing must be borne in mind about the Germans having running powers over what would presumably be a Russian line from Khanikin to Tehran, and that is that such running powers would be very unwelcome to Russia, since it would involve the line from Tehran to Khanikin being built on the German gauge (4 foot 8 inches) whereas the Russian gauge is 5 foot. This would render it necessary for the Russians to " break bulk " at Tehran.(⁴)

The Germans in discussing these questions, more especially the Bagdad Railway, overlook the important fact that we have been building up our commercial position in Mesopotamia for over two centuries, and that it is only natural that we should seek to protect those interests when they are threatened.

Mr. Crowe to see in first instance.

A. P.
April 11th, 1910.

I do not think that we should surrender to this ultimatum without a most serious endeavour to obtain from Turkey the Tigris concession. If that policy fails together with the Bagdad-Homs scheme and we find ourselves at the end of our resources so far as Turkey is concerned, then there will be time to consider whether participation in the Bagdad line is so valuable to us, as to induce us to modify our views as to a general understanding. With regard to which, the German Gov[ernmen]t have frequently been told that it is impossible without a preliminary naval agreement.

It is to be noted that concessions in Persia is [*sic*] only a part of the general understanding. We do not know what other concessions will be asked for in other parts of the world. And this is the modest payment we are to make for the privilege of finding money to complete a Railway which will not benefit us.

It is indeed very doubtful whether it will benefit anyone except the Turks strategically. There is a great deal of bluff in the Chancellor's communication.

Our participation in the Bagdad Railway would undoubtedly be of advantage to Germany, apart from such incidental benefits as the carriage of the Indian Mails. Our opposition, is at any rate disagreeable to them and our possession of the Terminus at Koweit a good card in our hands. The Chancellor perhaps does not yet know of our last intimation about the 4%.(⁵) It may have the effect of nipping in the bud the recent negotiations with Germany respecting the prolongation to Bagdad.

My point is that Germany is asking a very great deal and conferring very little. We must not be driven into a corner over this business. Our way out is through the Tigris Valley, and if we can possibly secure this concession, then the whole attitude of the Germans must change.

Possibly even now they would grant us some sort of participation in the Railway in exchange for an agreement about Persia only. As to this we should have to examine very closely whether— *if we can't get the Tigris Valley railway*—it would be worth our while to enter upon such a bargain— Russia would have to be consulted—. Another point must be remembered German consent would be useless as the Deutsche Bank have told Cassell [*sic*. Cassel] unless Turkey was squared—so that

---

(²) [Marginal comment by Mr. Parker : " Since writing this I have seen the note of April 7 to the Persian Gov[ernmen]t. A. P."

The note of April 7, to which Mr. Parker refers, was presented to the Persian Government jointly by the British and Russian representatives at Tehran. It was to the effect that the two Powers had no objection to loans being concluded by Persia with any other Powers provided certain conditions were fulfilled. The conditions included the requirement that no concessions should be given to other foreign Powers " qui puissent porter atteinte à leurs intérêts politiques ou stratégiques en Perse." (F.O. 15837/8172/10/34) *cp. infra*, p. 490, No. 375, *note* (¹).]

(³) [Memorandum of October 14, 1908 (F.O. 371/503). It indicated as " the Concessions which most closely concern " Great Britain, " besides the southern section of a line which may be built from Julfa to Mohammerah ", " the lines Bunder Abbas to Kerman, and Bunder Abbas, viâ Shiraz, to Ahwaz, with the option to construct a port at Khor Musa." *cp. supra*, p. 402, No. 300.]

(⁴) [Marginal comment by Mr. Mallet : " This would be a matter for negotiation. L. M."]

(⁵) [*cp. infra*, pp. 791-2, *App.* VI.]

after we had made our concessions in Persia, Marschall would only have to put up Turkey to refuse us a preponderant share and bleed us twice over. They would certainly do this, unless we stipulated that the Persian concessions were to become valid only on Turkey having given her consent. The Persian terms will require careful examination. It looks as if they might serve as a basis for an agreement but we must remember the Yangtse Valley agreement and act with great caution.([6])

We may await a despatch from Berlin, before making up our minds.

L. M.

Whilst I do not feel competent to express an opinion on the details of the particular arrangements suggested by the German government, I venture to offer a few remarks from the point of view of their probable effect on Anglo-German relations.

There is one aspect of the proposals to which it is well, preliminarily, to give some attention : They are the outcome of a secret negotiation which was started on a very different basis, and it is difficult to resist the suspicion that the German government deliberately opened up the false prospect of an agreement respecting the limitation of armaments, in order to entangle H[is] M[ajesty's] G[overnment] once more in the meshes of an Anglo-German agreement of the well-known type, under which it is the part of Great Britain to pay compensation to Germany.

It was recognized at the outset to be little short of a mystery how it was possible for the German Admiralty to be represented as ready to enter into an agreement for the limitation of armaments. Is it possible to doubt, now, that this was a blind? It is unnecessary to assume that Herr von Bethmann-Hollweg was consciously misleading H[is] M[ajesty's] G[overnment]. He may himself have been misled and " used " by others.

The present move closely resembles in character and method of proceeding, former German proposals for understandings with England, of which we have had such long and uniformly unhappy experiences; and it is a fair inference from those experiences that if we now enter into a fresh understanding, it should be done with our eyes open to the fact that we shall not have advanced one step in the direction of better general relations with Germany. On the contrary we must make up our minds that if we see advantages in the German proposals on their own merits, we shall have to buy them at the price not only of the compensation we are openly asked for, but of finding Germany, now entrenched in a fresh position, gained at our expense, as hostile as before.

These considerations ought to be carefully weighed if an exact calculation is to be made of the balance of advantages and disadvantages that may be involved in the German proposals. We are called upon to buy off German hostility in certain restricted fields in Turkey and Persia. The bargain even if honourably kept,—which with Shantung, the " Yang-tsze " agreement,([6]) and the evacuation of Shanghai in our memory is a large assumption—will involve no more than just so much German opposition in that particular field given up. This must form the basis of any sound judgment of the general advantages of coming to terms.

Unless the advantages are found to be very substantial, we should probably fare better without any agreement. I understand we have certain vital political and strategical interests in Persia; we also have rights as towards the Persian gov[ernmen]t in the shape of pledged revenues, &c. We are presumably prepared, whatever happens, to defend those interests and enforce those rights. Apart from these and from our obligations to Russia, we have no desire, I believe, to stand in Germany's way. The Persian door is open. Let her walk in. There is no occasion for us, to tie our hands further by special engagements towards Germany nor do we ask for any German assurances. But this is a subject on which I am not sufficiently informed to have a decided opinion.

E. A. C.
Ap. 11.

I agree generally with all the above minutes, but I wish to point out the change which has taken place in the attitude of Germany towards a naval agreement coupled with a political Convention and our participation in the Bagdad Railway, since the month of November last.([7]) At that time Germany was ready to offer us her recognition of British naval supremacy while maintaining her own naval programme, in return for a Treaty or Convention, on the lines proposed by B[aro]n Kiderlen to Sir E. Goschen,([8]) by which the hands of Great Britain were to be tied for a period of years during which she would be pledged neither to attack Germany nor to join a coalition or alliance against her. At the same time the German Gov[ernmen]t were fairly well disposed to a deal between Sir E. Cassel and Dr. Gwinner for our participation in the Bagdad R[ailwa]y, although her statesmen always said that, when an agreement had been made by the financiers, it would then be the moment for the two Gov[ernmen]ts to intervene. The Germans now realise that, so long as they persist in the maintenance of their naval programme

---

([6]) [The " Yangtse Agreement " is treated in *Gooch & Temperley*, Vol. II, ch. IX, pp. 1–31; and *ib.*, Vol. III, p. 413, *App.* A, pp. 426–8, *App.* B. For the negotiations relating to evacuation of Shanghai, *v. ib.*, Vol. II, ch. XII, pp. 138–53.]

([7]) [*cp. supra*, pp. 304–12, No. 204; pp. 312–3, No. 205; and pp. 314–5, No. 207.]

([8]) [*cp. supra*, pp. 265–6, No. 174.]

we are not so foolish as to tie our hands in Europe for the sake of a theoretical recognition of our naval supremacy, and they evidently believe that we might yet be induced to accept the Kiderlen proposals for a mess of pottage in the shape of participation in the Bagdad R[ailwa]y.

"A general political understanding such as he (the Chancellor) had indicated last year " is out of the question, and really never was feasible. So also is any understanding about Persia unless coupled with the Bagdad R[ailwa]y question.

The change of attitude in Berlin towards the latter question is probably due to the fact that the German Gov[ernmen]t see a prospect ahead of funds being available for kilometric guarantees independently of the 4% Customs dues to which the assent of the Powers has not yet been given. The fact that such funds are being set aside by the Turkish Gov[ernmen]t is probably due to pressure from the Military party who lay stress on the strategic importance of the Bagdad R[ailwa]y.

The course I would recommend is that we should steadily press for a railway concession in the Tigris valley, withholding our assent to the Customs increase until we receive it and support any Company that is approved by France in obtaining a concession for the Bagdad–Homs R[ailwa]y. As regards Persia, we should tell the German Gov[ernmen]t, if they refer to this matter again, that we have always maintained the open door in Persia for commercial purposes and that to make any special agreement with them on the subject of commercial concessions in Persia would entail similar agreements with all the other Powers. We should add at the same time that it is our intention to strenuously resist any encroachment by the Persians [sic] or any other foreign Power on our political and strategic interests in Persia.

In the meantime, no action is necessary until and unless the question is reopened by the German Gov[ernmen]t.

C. H.

I agree generally as to the course we should take and the view of the German ideas. The despatch respecting them can be considered when it arrives.

E. G.

No. 344.

Sir E. Goschen to Sir Edward Grey.

F.O. 13071/100/10/44A.
(No. 102.)   Very Confidential.   *Berlin, D. April* 11, 1910.
Sir,   R. *April* 18, 1910.
    I have the honour to report that at the Imperial Chancellor's request I called upon His Excellency yesterday evening. He said that he wished to speak to me on the subject of the Bagdad Railway question and that he also desired to say a few words with regard to Persia and Germany's position in that country.

His Excellency began the conversation by stating that he was grateful for the frank and open manner in which you had stated your views on these subjects to the German Chargé d'Affaires.([1]) He would be equally frank with me and if his views did not agree altogether with those of His Majesty's Government, he would ask me to bear in mind that it was none the less the sincere desire of both Herr von Schoen and himself to establish good relations between Germany and Great Britain. This desire had been the mainspring of his policy ever since he had become Imperial Chancellor, not only from personal inclinations but because he had realized the all-importance of the question of Anglo-German relations. It was not a question which concerned the two nations alone, it was not even only a European question, it was a question which concerned the whole world. The main point was to create an atmosphere of good feeling between the two peoples and this could only be done by a process of give and take, by mutual concessions, and by making an arrangement which would not only be acceptable to the two Governments but satisfactory to the two nations behind them.

([1]) [Apparently the conversation of March 31, *v. supra*, pp. 442–3, No. 337.]

He had rather gathered that His Majesty's Government were of opinion that he Naval proposals which he had made last year[2] were not such as would recommend hemselves to the British Public. He feared he must say that the idea that Germany should hand over the Southern section of the Bagdad Railway to Great Britain would be equally unacceptable to the people of Germany. The Bagdad Railway had become an Imperial idea in Germany; it was regarded as a great national undertaking; and as I had probably noticed from the newspapers, the people regarded any proceedings connected with it with a very watchful and suspicious eye. This was, in his opinion, unfortunate, but he felt bound to add that this regrettable feeling was chiefly due to the opposition shown by Great Britain to the undertaking from its very commencement—an attitude which was subsequently adopted by Russia and France. How would it be then if it was suddenly announced that the Imperial Government had handed over the most valuable section of the whole line to the very Power who had all along been the most bitter opponent of the scheme and placed every obstacle in the way of its fulfilment? The Imperial Government would first be asked what return they had secured for such an enormous concession. The reply would have to be " None whatever;" and the anger of the nation would have no bounds. Their anger moreover would not only be directed against the Imperial Government but also against Great Britain. Under such circumstances the relations between the two countries, instead of being improved would be far worse than before. I pointed out to His Excellency that this might possibly be so if the people were told that they got no return for the concession. The Imperial Government would, however, be able to show that they had secured very important advantages in return for their consent to British participation. They would be able to point out, amongst other advantages, that the consent of His Majesty's Government to the 4 % increase of the Turkish customs dues—in itself a great concession in view of the great preponderance of British Trade interests in Turkey—would place the Ottoman Government in a position to find the money for the other sections of the Railway, and thus facilitate their construction, and that the investment of British Capital in a portion of the line would indubitably give life to the whole undertaking and enable the whole Railway to be completed in a far shorter period than would be otherwise possible. His Excellency replied that all this amounted practically to nothing and would be regarded as nothing by German public opinion. The withdrawal of our opposition to the 4 % increase of Turkish customs dues would be a concession to Turkey—not to Germany; while the shortening of the period required for the completion of the line was a matter of convenience certainly, but not of vital necessity. The line would be completed in any case, and whether a few years earlier or later was a matter of comparatively little moment. If he was to lay such considerations before Parliament and the Public as an adequate return for such a great concession, he would be laughed out of office. His Excellency then went at some length into the reasons why the Imperial Government had to be specially careful at this moment with regard to concessions to Foreign Powers; and reminded me of all the attacks which had been made upon him, directly and indirectly, on account of the alleged want of back-bone in his foreign policy. I ventured to observe to His Excellency that the opinion of the public upon any given question depended very much on the way it was put before them. He said there was some truth in that remark, but that it did not apply in the present case, when the mind of the people was made up and public feeling was so strong. I replied that surely if the people knew, or were brought to know, that the suggestion of British participation had come from the German side and from people whose interests were bound up in the undertaking, they would realize that the advantages of the transaction were not likely to be wholly on the side of Great Britain. The Chancellor answered that Mr. Gwinner was not the Imperial Government nor the Deutsche Bank the German Empire. I said that Herr von Schoen had often spoken to me of the

[2] [These proposals are described, *supra*, pp. 283–324, ch. XLV, *passim*.]

conversations between Mr. Gwinner and Sir E. Cassel and had never expressed disapproval of them([3]); he had certainly said that the matter would ultimately have to be discussed between the two Government[s], but surely if the Imperial Government, who were cognizant of what was passing, had held such strong views on the subject as those which he had just laid before me, it would have simplified the situation if they had let the two groups know that nothing could come of their negotiations. His Excellency replied that since Sir E. Cassel's visit the situation had changed. They had had the Mannesmann question([4]) and the violent attacks on the Imperial Government to which it had given rise. He then spoke more to the point and said: "After all you must remember that the concession is ours; that we have it in our pocket; and the very fact that British interests in the Persian Gulf make His Majesty's Government desirous of controlling the Southern Section of the line is a clear proof that what they require is worth a substantial return." I subsequently asked His Excellency whether he had in his mind any return which he and the German public would consider adequate. He replied that after much consideration and anxious thought he had come to the conclusion that the only way in which an agreement respecting the Bagdad Railway in the form His Majesty's Government desired could be made palatable to the German people would be that it should form part of a general political understanding between Great Britain and Germany. I asked His Excellency to what sort of a political understanding he alluded. Did he mean a regular *entente* between the two Powers? He replied that he meant the kind of understanding which he had proposed last year. I reminded His Excellency that in our former conversations I had placed before him some of the difficulties in the way of such an understanding. He replied that he could not think they were in any way insurmountable; in any case he did not, to his great regret, see any other way of meeting the wishes of His Majesty's Government with regard to the Bagdad Railway. Nothing less than what he proposed would satisfy public opinion or place him beyond the reproach of yielding or truckling to Great Britain.

As His Excellency seemed to wish for an expression of opinion from me as to the merits of his proposal, I said that beyond pointing out to him as I had done that there were great difficulties connected with its acceptance, it was hardly for me to pronounce upon it and I could only promise to put it as fairly and accurately as I could before His Majesty's Government.

The Chancellor then proceeded to discuss the Persian question, to which you had referred in your conversation with the German Chargé d'Affaires. He said that this question, which in his opinion offered no great difficulty, should also form part of the political understanding he had suggested. German interests in Persia were purely commercial and Germany had no desire to acquire political influence.([5]) His views were that an arrangement might be made somewhat on the following lines: Germany should engage not to apply for Railway, telegraph or road concessions in what was termed the British sphere of influence. That in return His Majesty's Government should give an assurance that German capital and German industry should not be excluded from a fair share of the contracts and supply of material necessary for the working of such concessions of the above nature as His Majesty's Government might obtain from the Persian Government. Germany would also wish that His Majesty's Government should renew their assurances with regard to the Open Door in Persia, by which he meant amongst other things, that Germany should have equal participation with other Third Power in loans and such official positions under the Persian Government as might be open to foreigners.

The Chancellor proceeded to explain that the arrangement he had just proposed

---

([3]) [cp. *supra*, pp. 408–9, No. 308.]
([4]) [Reference to this subject will be made in *Gooch & Temperley*, Vol. VII.]
([5]) [Marginal comment by Mr. Mallet: "This is simply misleading as a commercial stake in the country brings with it political influence. It is merely a phrase which means nothing. L. M."

was on similar lines to the proposals which the Imperial Government had made to the Russian Government in 1906(⁶)—proposals to which M. Isvolsky had up till now not replied. These proposals were still open and in return for the concessions which Germany was ready to make—and they must be regarded as concessions as Germany really had an entirely free hand in Persia,—the Imperial Government would require that the Railway projected by Russia between Teheran and Khanekin should be constructed and that on its completion an assurance should be given that the Russian Government would not throw obstacles in the way of international traffic between Bagdad and Teheran by special tariff and customs measures. His Excellency explained that an assurance of this kind was of as much importance to Great Britain as to Germany. Ever since the year 1883 the transport through Trans-Caucasia of foreign merchandize for North Persia had been prohibited by Russia, thus leaving the old caravan road to Teheran through Trebizond, E[r]zeroum, Tabris the only route available to foreign trade. The heavy transport rates on the caravan road were an effectual bar to any competition with the Transcaucasian routes; if therefore Russia now completed the North Persian Railway system by the addition of a line from Julfa to Teheran, and at the same time did not construct the line from Teheran to Khanekin, she would practically assure to herself a trade monopoly in North Persia. Under such circumstances an assurance of the Open Door would be illusory.

His Excellency added that he had now reason to believe that Mr. Isvolsky contemplated sending his long-delayed answer to the German proposals, and he hoped very much that it would be of a satisfactory nature, all the more that an understanding with Russia would obviously smoothe the way to an arrangement with Great Britain on the lines he had indicated. This was the close of our conversation.

As I saw the Chancellor spoke from copious type-written notes, I told His Excellency that, in view of the length and importance of the conversation, it would perhaps be safer and ensure the accurate repetition of his views if he would let me have a memorandum of what he had said. His Excellency kindly said that he would do so and would if possible send me a memorandum the following day. As, however, it did not arrive, and I had to go to Mecklenburg Strelitz on the day after, I thought it best to wait no longer and to telegraph to you the chief points of the conversation as I remembered them.(⁶ᵃ) On my return from Neu-Strelitz Herr von Stumm brought me round the memorandum, and as I found that the Chancellor had somewhat amplified the part dealing with Russia, it seemed to me advisable to send you an additional telegram giving more or less His Excellency's exact words.

I have now the honour to transmit, herewith, copy and translation of the Chancellor's memorandum, which, except for the amplifications as regards Russia, agrees in substance with my first telegram.

The memorandum naturally differs from the conversation as regards the form and order in which the various statements and arguments were developed. The substance is however the same, with perhaps one exception. According to my recollection the Chancellor, in his conversation with me laid more stress on the necessity for Russia to build the Teheran–Khanekin Railway than would appear from the Memorandum. But I would venture to observe that the pointed allusion made by the Chancellor to the consequences which would ensue if the Russian Government determined to build a line from Julfa to Teheran and to leave the Teheran–Khanekin line unbuilt, would seem to show that my recollection was correct and that the construction of the latter line was put forward by His Excellency as one of the requirements of the Imperial Government.

I have, &c.
W. E. GOSCHEN.

(⁶) [cp. supra, p. 98, No. 64, p. 99, No. 65, and note (³).]
(⁶ᵃ) [v. immediately preceding document.]

Enclosure in No. 344.

(Translation.) *Memorandum by the German Chancellor.*([7])

I received with interest Sir Edward Grey's suggestions which were conveyed to me by the Imperial Chargé d'Affaires, and I welcome them as a proof of confidence which I sincerely reciprocate. I am gladly prepared to fall in with Sir E. Grey's suggestions and to explain fully and confidentially my standpoint in respect to the Bagdad Railway and the Persian Question.

I see from the reports of the Chargé d'Affaires that Sir E. Grey regards the unreserved consent of England to the proposed increase in the Turkish Customs as sufficient compensation for the cession to England of the preponderating influence in the Gulf section of the Bagdad Railway. I cannot agree with this view.

The Bagdad Railway Company has been definitely granted the concession by the Porte to build the railway from Konia to a point on the Persian Gulf which is still to be fixed. The section from Bagdad to the Gulf constitutes one of the most important parts of the whole line and one which has the richest future in store for it. In view of these facts any agreement yielding to England preponderating influence in this section would be regarded by public opinion in Germany as a weak concession to England on the part of the Imperial Government. Sir E. Grey is not unaware how far I have to reckon with German public opinion. This was recently made additionally clear by the proceedings arising out of the Mannesmann's mining claims in Morocco. Public opinion in Germany is following the Bagdad Railway question with quite exceptional interest. I am only stating the facts when I say that the Press has—much against the wish of the Imperial Government and the financial circles concerned—stamped this question almost as one of first class national importance, chiefly on account of the opposition which the British Government raised with regard to the project—an opposition which was also taken up by Russia and France. In these circumstances even Germans of quiet and moderate views would not understand a special agreement about the railway, by which the Imperial Government, without sufficient equivalent in return, renounced in England's favour rights granted by the Porte in the exercise of her sovereignty. Under no circumstances can England's unreserved consent to the 4 % increase of Turkish Customs be regarded as a sufficient equivalent. This step would in reality be more a measure taken by England to meet the wishes of Turkey, in that it would facilitate the Porte's task in fulfilling her obligations with regard to the Bagdad Railway Company. Besides even the maintenance of the reserve would only have the effect of delaying the construction of the line. It would by no means completely frustrate it, because the Porte would by degrees be in the position to fulfil its obligations in respect to the Bagdad Railway Company in another way. As therefore England's unreserved consent to the increase of the Customs cannot be considered as an equivalent, it remains to be seen whether, in return for the renunciation of German preponderance in the Gulf Section other concessions can be found which could be regarded as a *quid pro quo* on the part of England.

I have considered this question thoroughly and am convinced that no *quid pro quo* can be found which would justify from the German standpoint a separate agreement respecting the Bagdad Railway. I should, by the conclusion of a separate agreement, lay myself open to the just reproach of weakness and exaggerated *complaisance* in respect to England. As Sir E. Grey is aware I cherish sincere wishes for the lasting establishment of confidential and friendly relations between Germany and England. But by this reproach I would, without doubt, thwart the realization of these wishes, and give German public opinion genuine ground for animosity not only towards myself, but also towards England. Under these circumstances I see, to my regret, no other possibility of an understanding about the Bagdad Railway than the conclusion of a general political agreement (Gesamtabkommen) between Germany and England, of which this question should

([7]) [For the German original, *v. G.P.* XXVII, pp. 636–8, and *ib.*, pp. 772–4.]

form a part. I am convinced that a general agreement of this kind is the only thing that can save me from the charge that in the Bagdad Railway question 1 have openly sounded the retreat before England.

An understanding with regard to Persia ought, on the other hand, scarcely to offer especial difficulties. Germany is prosecuting commercial aims in Persia. Her interests are served, if England and Russia respect—in accordance with the assurances given in their Agreement of August 31, 1907,([8])—the independence and integrity of Persia, and keep the door there open for the commerce of all nations.

As early as 1906 M. Isvolsky submitted to the Imperial Government the proposal for an understanding with regard to Persia.([9]) In reply to this the Imperial Government declared itself ready to renounce, in favour of Russia and within a part of Northern Persia to be subsequently more accurately defined, obtaining concessions for Railways, Roads and Telegraphs. In return for this Germany's essential demands are for the complete recognition of her equal rights in all other economic questions, the linking up of the railway lines planned by Russia in Northern Persia with the future Bagdad–Khanekin line and for the assurance, that Russia will not prejudice the international traffic on this line by customs and tariff measures. This demand is equally in the interest of Germany and in that of England. At the present time Russia places a serious obstacle in the way of the penetration of foreign trade into Northern Persia by the interdiction which has existed since 1883 against the passage in transit of foreign goods through Trans-Caucasia. The foreign import trade to North Persia therefore passes at present by the caravan route of Trebizond–E[r]zeroum–Tabriz–Tehran. On account of the high transport dues this caravan route can even now no longer compete as a trade route to North Persia with the way of importation by Trans Caucasia. If Russia should now develope [sic] the railway system of Northern Persia by a line from Julfa to Tehran and should on the other hand not establish the Tehran–Khanekin connection, she practically succeeds in securing to herself a monopoly of the trade of Northern Persia.

M. Isvolsky recently held out hopes to me of a reply to the German proposals. I hope that it will contribute to the settlement in a satisfactory manner of the questions which have now arisen in regard to Persia between the Cabinets. An understanding with Russia would materially smooth the way to a corresponding agreement with England. For an agreement of this kind similar concessions in Southern Persia might well come into consideration as those quoted above. An assurance on the part of England might perhaps be taken into consideration as a *quid pro quo* to the effect in the exploitation of the concessions in question a percentage of participation should be kept open for German industry. An authentic interpretation of the open door in Persia would also be of value to me to the effect that in Loan Questions and in questions affecting the reorganization of the Persian Financial Administration Germany should be placed on a par with all other third Great Powers.

From the German point of view an Agreement of this nature with regard to Persia could also best be included in a general political Agreement with England.

MINUTES.

This is a full report of what has already been summarized in Sir E. Goschen's two telegrams,([10]) and there is little to add to the departmental minutes written on those tel[egram]s.

([8]) [*v. Gooch & Temperley*, Vol. IV, pp. 502–4, No. 456, *encl.*, and pp. 618–9, *App.* I.]

([9]) [*cp. G.P.* XXV, I, pp. 231–4. The negotiations which followed are described, *ib.*, ch. 185.]

([10]) [For Tel. No. 25 from Sir E. Goschen, *v. supra*, pp. 451–4, No. 343. Tel. No. 26 gives an account of the German proposals to Russia as described in the above despatch, and bears minutes relating to these negotiations. As a result a telegram was sent to Sir A. Nicolson (No. 174, Secret of April 13) directing him to ask at St. Petersburgh " to be informed of any communication which Germany may have made to Russia."]

The bargain proposed to us is :

1. No naval agreement.
2. A general political "understanding," by which Great Britain would engage to stand aside and not interfere if Germany makes war on any third countries.
3. Special agreements, on the terms now set out, respecting (*a*) the Bagdad Railway and (*b*) Persia.

It is difficult to understand how Great Britain could entertain such a scheme. If very tempting offers were made to her in Mesopotamia and Persia, one might understand the German view of making really valuable and important concessions to us for the sake of acquiring an absolutely free hand for Germany in dealing with France, Russia, or other Powers. If H[is] M[ajesty's] G[overnment] were minded to abandon France to Germany, they would probably at least demand an enormous price. But to ask us for such abandonment of France, and make, in addition, onerous conditions about the Bagdad Railway and Persia, is a plan to characterize which it is really difficult to find the appropriate adjectives.

E. A. C.
Ap. 18.

No action at Berlin appears to be called for at present : we should concentrate our efforts on the one hand on the Tigris Valley Concession and on the other on impressing upon the Persian Gov[ernmen]t that for political and strategic reasons we shall regard it as an unfriendly act if railway concessions either in the British or the neutral sphere are granted to third Powers without our previous consent.

A. P.
April 18th, 1910.

Mr. Crowe puts the case in a very clear way.

The proposal is a stupid one from the German point of view, for the slightest reflection would have shown the Chancellor that it is one which no Government in this country could possibly accept.

The despatch bears out our suspicion that Germany only renounces concessions in the British sphere retaining freedom of action in the Neutral sphere. The Memorandum, it is true, speaks of Southern Persia, but this must mean that Persia is divided into Northern, Central and Southern Persia. In any case we need not consider this at present.

A despatch must eventually be written in reply to this; pointing out that it was not Great Britain who made overtures to Germany to participate in the Railway, but Germany who from the beginning, has made overtures to us. They recognized in those days that our participation was necessary for political as well as for economical and financial reasons.

The terms they offered were not sufficiently good but H[is] M[ajesty's] G[overnmen]t did not complain on that score—they waited until the German Gov[ernmen]t made further overtures. The assent of the Emperor to a discussion *à quatre* seemed at one moment to offer a prospect of a solution of this question but this assent was withdrawn subsequently and no further mention was made, on our side, of participation until Herr Gwinner approached Sir H. B. Smith, with the cognizance of the German Gov[ernmen]t.

The German Gov[ernmen]t now apparently have withdrawn their patronage to these negotiations and now demand, as a price of our participation, for the first time concessions which, in so far as they relate to a General Entente they are aware that H[is] M[ajesty's] G[overnment] are unable to give, and there the chapter closes.

But we had better let the German Gov[ernmen]t remain under the delusion that we are considering these proposals until we are sure of our Tigris concession or at any rate for some time longer.

We have secured Koweit and we should now, as Mr. Parker said the other day turn our attention to securing Khor Musa.

Sir E. Goschen should be told semi-officially of the line of action it is proposed to take.

L. M.

The proposals of the Chancellor are clearly inadmissible. I think it would be better for the moment to give no reply at all. In a private letter to Sir E. Goschen yesterday I foreshadowed this attitude on our part.([11]) There is nothing to be done about the Bagdad R[ailwa]y, but we must press for the Tigris valley concession and exert pressure upon Persia to prevent concessions being given to Germany that might prove injurious to our political and strategic interests in that country.

C. H.

([11]) [*cp. infra*, p. 468, No. 351.]

We must wait for the present at any rate, and as to the future—

1. We cannot enter into a political understanding with Germany, which would separate us from Russia and France, and leave us isolated while the rest of Europe would be obliged to look to Germany.

2. No understanding with Germany would be appreciated here unless it meant an arrest of the increase of naval expenditure.

3. We do not want to deprive Germany of the Bagdad Concession, which as the Chancellor says is in her pocket already. All we want is that Germany should not have the only door for trade into Mesopotamia. This can be secured by Turkey giving us another door and we cannot therefore pay a high price for entrance into the Bagdad Railway.

E. G.

No. 345.

Sir Edward Grey to Sir A. Nicolson.([1])

F.O. 12430/100/10/44A.

Tel. (No. 175.)

Foreign Office, April 13, 1910.
D. 5·50 P.M.

With reference to my preceding telegrams, the following observations occur to me :—

No mention seems to be made of any concession respecting the Bagdad Railway.

It is presumed that Germany is to construct and manage the Bagdad–Khanikin line, and will insist on the German gauge from Khanikin to Tehran.

We do not wish to throw obstacles in the way of an arrangement between Russia and Germany, but we think that the matter should be handled with great caution and firmness, and that no special status should be given to Germany in Persia which is not shared by other Powers, and there should be no agreement about rates which would place our trade at a disadvantage.

Germany's requirements in regard to the British sphere are another matter.

So far as appears from telegraphic account of the interview with the Chancellor, the German Gov[ernmen]t do not offer us any serious *quid pro quo*.

A settlement of the Bagdad Railway question is absolutely barred without a general political understanding, in regard to which you are aware of my views.

The German Gov[ernmen]t are prepared to renounce railway and other concessions in the British sphere, in return for a share in any concession we may obtain there.

The only railway project which has been seriously considered within our sphere is a line from Bunder Abbas to the interior, and, under the German proposal, the Germans would be free to obtain concessions say from Bushire to the frontier of the Russian sphere, or along the Gulf in continuation of the Bagdad line. No corresponding share is offered in such concessions, and we should be jeopardising our position in the Persian Gulf, if we allowed such concessions to go to Germany.

By entering into such an agreement we should, moreover, be giving to Germany a special position in Persia, and we could not reconcile such action with maintenance of our present relations with other Powers.

For these reasons we are not attracted by the German offer.

We should be glad of a frank exchange of views with Russia.

([1]) [This telegram was endorsed " Repeat Berlin, adding at end : ' Nothing should be said at present to German Gov[ernment.' "]

No. 346.

Sir Edward Grey to Sir F. Bertie.

Private.(¹)

My dear Bertie,   *April* 13, 1910.

I told Cambon on his return to-day that the negotiations with Germany, which had been mentioned last autumn,(²) had not been taken up again. There was no prospect apparently of an arrangement as to naval expenditure and the position of the Government here at present was not such that we could deal with negotiations of that kind just now.

I told Cambon what had passed with Germany about Persia, &c., but that I will record separately.

Yours sincerely,
E. GREY.

(¹) [Grey MSS., Vol. 13.]
(²) [*v.* references given, *supra*, p. 402, No. 301, *note* (²).]

No. 347.

Sir A. Nicolson to Sir Edward Grey.

St. Petersburgh, April 14, 1910.

F.O. 12751/100/10/44A.   D. 8·25 P.M.
Tel. (No. 124.)   R. 10 P.M.

Germany and Persia.

Sir E. Goschen's telegrams Nos. 25 and 26.(¹)

I communicated to Acting Minister for Foreign Affairs substance of above telegrams, and gave him a summary of your observations as received in your telegram No. 174.(²)

He was most grateful for communication. In reply to an enquiry, he said that nothing fresh had been received from Berlin, but that German Ambassador had verbally expressed willingness to reopen conversations which had been interrupted in 1907. Ambassador had stated that Germany would ask for no concessions in Russian sphere if Russia undertook to link up any railways which she might construct in North Persia with the Bagdad line, and had also suggested that Russia should make no opposition to a German or two being taken into the employment of the Persian Government.

I told Acting Minister for Foreign Affairs that it was essential that the Russian and British Governments should maintain the closest solidarity, and that I hoped that Russian Government would take no steps without consulting with His Majesty's Government. I think, though I did not tell him so, that this is very necessary, as the Russian Government might be led into arrangements which might be inconvenient to us. Acting Minister for Foreign Affairs replied that he perfectly agreed with me, and that closest understanding and fullest exchange of views were most desirable. I said that I proposed to speak to the Emperor to-morrow in the same sense. He replied that he hoped that I would do so.

I mentioned withdrawal of troops from Kazvin, and expressed hope that this would be accomplished without delay. He said that the Russian Government had

(¹) [*v. supra*, p. 451, No. 343, and p. 459, No. 344, *note* (¹⁰).]
(²) [Tel. No. 174 is not reproduced, but its substance is indicated *supra*, p. 459, No. 344, *note* (¹⁰). It is probable that Sir A. Nicolson means here to refer to Tel. No. 175, *v. supra*, p. 461, No. 345.]

put two conditions on the withdrawal: (1) settlement of the question of attack on the Russian consul-general on his way to Bushire, and (2) arrangements for the retention of Russian officers in Cossack brigade. He himself rather regretted that these conditions had been imposed, and if he found that they had not been already communicated to the Persian Government he would not raise them. I said that it would be well to abandon them and get troops away.

(Sent to Tehran.)

No. 348.

Sir E. Goschen to Sir C. Hardinge.

F.O. 15622/167/10/18.(¹)
Private.

My dear Hardinge,   Berlin, April 14, 1910.

It was a nuisance that the Chancellor asked me to call upon him on Saturday as it made a whole week before the messenger. That necessitated long telegrams, which are unsatisfactory things at best, as they must always lack details and atmosphere.

Well! the Chancellor has come to a certain extent into the open. His idea seems to be to use the southern section of the Bagdad Railway and our vital interests in the Persian Gulf, as levers to force us into the sort of understanding he wants, an understanding which, as it would leave Germany practically mistress of the European Continent, would no doubt be acceptable to the Reichstag and public opinion and crown its engineers with laurels. The Chancellor is of course working the attacks against him and Schoen, and the Mannesmann business, for all they are worth, and they have no doubt something to do with his present attitude. He *has* suffered from these attacks considerably and now he sees his way to getting some profit out of them. I think, however, with all due respect to the Chancellor, that the plan of using the southern section of the railway as a lever, or perhaps a bait, for a political understanding dates from further back than the attacks on the Foreign Office and that we should have heard of it last year if our negotiations had continued. I am confirmed in this idea by a remark dropped to me by Stemrich who said that they had regarded the Cassel–Gwinner conversations with a benevolent eye because at the time they took place things pointed in the direction of a satisfactory political understanding.

If the Chancellor sticks to his present attitude as regards the Bagdad Railway —and he seemed very decided on the subject—the only thing to be done, I suppose, is to devote all our energies to getting an opposition line of our own. If he means what he says, namely that nothing will satisfy him but a political understanding as a return for our control of the southern section, and if he insists on an understanding on *his* lines and the carrying out of the entire German Naval Programme, it is difficult to see any other way of safeguarding our interests in the Persian Gulf.

Talking of the carrying out of their naval programme I must tell you what Stumm said when he brought me round the Chancellor's memorandum. He asked me what I thought of the Chancellor's proposals. I told him that the Chancellor had told me that in all transactions he liked to get his money's worth—for instance, he had added, if he arranged with a shoemaker to pay him 30 marks for a pair of boots, he expected to get boots worth that sum and not a pair which he would be ashamed to wear before his friends. I considered that in the present case, to continue H[is] E[xcellency]'s simile, the Chancellor wanted the honest tradesman to supply him with the most expensive pair of patent leather boots in the shop at the price of an ordinary pair, asking the shoemaker to give him a heavy discount

---

(¹) [The original of this letter is in the Hardinge MSS., Vol. II of 1910. The text here given is taken from a typed copy filed in the Foreign Office archives.]

and some backsheesh into the bargain. That was *my* idea of the Chancellor's proposal but that was only quite a personal opinion. Stumm said that he knew I thought there were difficulties in the way of a political *entente* between the two countries. So there were, he admitted that, but he could not think they were unsurmountable. "Where there's a will there's a way." I said that leaving out difficulties of an international character there was always this difficulty :—Our people would not, both for financial and other reasons, think anything of an understanding which did not carry with it a reduction of armaments, and as long as Germany insisted on the rigid carrying out of her naval programme there could be no reduction. Our taxpayers would readily pay their money for the ships necessary to ensure supremacy at sea, there was no doubt about that, but to make them take to their bosoms the people who had made the process so expensive would be a difficult matter for any Government. He said, "Yes! but there are ways and ways of carrying out our programme." I said I knew that, but that I had not yet heard of a way which would alter the fact that at the end of the programme period we should have had to build fifty or sixty capital ships in order to maintain what we considered to be our proper and necessary naval standard. The conversation then drifted on to other subjects.

While I am on the subject of naval matters I must tell you that on Heath's calling at the Ministry of Marine the other day to ask some very trifling question, he was told that their orders were to give him no information whatever on any subject! One of Tirpitz's grievances is apparently that Mr. McKenna had stated that dates given in the *Norddeutsche Allgemeine Zeitung* could not be regarded as official and Heath was told that he ought to know by this time that everything that appeared in that paper *was* official. On referring to his notes of a previous conversation Heath finds that he was told, on mentioning that he had gathered certain information from the paper in question, "Oh! we can't be responsible for everything that appears in the papers!"

To return to the Persian question Pansa tells me that he asked Stemrich what de Ruete was doing in Persia, and that Stemrich had replied that he didn't know and didn't want to know, as he wished to be in the position to tell people who might make inquiries that he knew nothing of the matter and that the Government had nothing to do with the private affairs of the Deutsche Bank. This does not tally with the information I received from a financier in touch with that institution, to the effect that it was the Government that had asked the Deutsche Bank to send out a man to Persia. The information was quite gratuitous and arose out of a conversation about de Ruete who had once been in my informant's employ and of whom he had but a mediocre opinion.

I saw Stemrich for a few minutes to-day. He wanted to make out that as far as Persia was concerned they were offering us splendid terms, on the ground that as they were not parties to the Anglo-Russian Convention they had a perfectly free hand. Their abstention from any endeavour to acquire political influence was in itself a concession, but they recognized our special position and intended loyally to adhere to their self-denying attitude. But it was very trying for them to be told whenever they applied for the smallest commercial concession that it could not be granted because it affected British or Russian political interests. This was always the answer he got from Spring-Rice and Hartwig when he was in Persia and on making the smallest request. All they required in return for their loyalty was the Open Door and a fair field for German capitalists and exporters. It was not as if Persia wanted to shut them out; on the contrary she was very anxious indeed to get German money—all the more anxious because she knew that Germany had no political aspirations.

One more thing. I notice that in his telegram to Nicolson([2]) Sir E. Grey says that it is to be presumed that Germany will insist on German gauge from Hannekin [*sic*]

([2]) [*v. supra*, p. 461, No. 345.]

to Tehran. This *is* to be presumed from what the Chancellor said to me—but in his memo[randum] I notice that he only speaks of the junction of the two lines. That looks as if he at all events hopes that it will be arranged that the gauge should be the same. The Chancellor was just a trifle vague about the line, for instance he always talked of the German projected line as starting from Bagdad, whereas Samara would be the starting point. I asked Stemrich today about the gauge but he too rather slurred over the point and said that all they cared about was that German goods should get through without prohibitive customs dues.

It is all very complicated and I am dying to know what the next move will be. I am awfully sorry to have inflicted such a long letter upon you, but I hope you will find some interest in it.

Hoping that you enjoyed your little leave, I remain

Yours very sincerely,
W. E. GOSCHEN.

No. 349.

Sir A. Nicolson to Sir Edward Grey.

St. Petersburgh, April 15, 1910.

F.O. 12895/8445/10/44A.
Tel. (No. 125.)

D. 8·21 P.M.
R. 10·15 P.M.

I explained at my audience this morning of the Emperor the proposals of the German Government as indicated in the conversation between the German Chancellor and Sir E. Goschen.([1]) His Majesty observed that request of Germans to participate in concessions in British sphere was a remarkable suggestion. He said that one of the objects of German Government was to separate Russia from England, as they had already endeavoured to do on more than one occasion. His Majesty was emphatic in stating that two Governments must present a firm and united front, and keep each other fully and frankly informed. This would be the best means of inducing the German Government to modify their present attitude with which I could see His Majesty was by no means pleased. The Emperor will receive this afternoon the memoranda which I left yesterday with Acting Minister for Foreign Affairs,([2]) and their perusal, in addition to my statements, will, I feel sure, strengthen His Majesty in his intention to work cordially and unitedly with us.

His Majesty observed that M. Isvolsky had pointed out to him that the present action of the German Government was on all fours with that which they had pursued in regard to Moroccan question, and the only result on that occasion had been to draw France and England closer together. I remarked that I hoped that a similar result would now be the outcome, to which His Majesty replied that undoubtedly it would. His Majesty said that he heard that German Ambassador here was now speaking in more conciliatory terms, and I observed that it was more important to listen to what was said at Berlin than to what a representative here might let drop in conversation.

Emperor quite appreciates seriousness of recent German action.

He expressed high satisfaction with the replies which you recently gave in the House of Commons to questions on Persian affairs.([3])

Emperor also spoke of affairs in the Far and Near East. His Majesty was quite convinced there was no danger of any aggressive designs on the part of Japan, and that, on the contrary, she was desirous of developing the arrangement made in 1907. His Majesty was grateful for attitude of His Majesty's Government in regard to Manchurian railways.

([1]) [*cp. supra*, p. 451, No. 343.]
([2]) [*cp. supra*, p. 462, No. 347.]
([3]) [*cp. Parl. Deb.*, 5th Ser., House of Commons. Vol. 16, pp. 571–4.]

[17590]

2 H

As to the Near East, His Majesty said that King Ferdinand's visit to Constantinople had had an excellent effect, and that King had informed Russian Ambassador at Constantinople that he had completely changed his views as to Turkish aims and policy, and had admitted his former appreciations had been erroneous. His Majesty said he trusted that His Majesty's Government recognised that visits of the two Balkan Sovereigns to St. Petersburgh could but be productive of good to the general peace. I had no difficulty in reassuring His Majesty on that point.

The audience was entirely satisfactory and came at an opportune moment.

I should add that His Majesty is very desirous that the through line to India should not be entirely abandoned.

MINUTES.

As to the last sentence, it will take time to remove Indian suspicions but I certainly think that the question should not be entirely abandoned.

L. M.

It can hardly make progress however with Russian troops in Persia and Persia in such a precarious state.

E. G.

No. 350.

Sir Edward Grey to Sir G. Lowther.

F.O. 13013/100/10/44.
(No. 96.)   Secret.
Sir,   *Foreign Office, April 18, 1910.*

The Turkish Ambassador called upon me on the 13th instant, at my request, to discuss the financial negotiations now proceeding between the Porte and the German Gov[ernmen]t for facilitating the extension of the Bagdad Railway from El Halif to Bagdad.

I informed Tewfik Pasha that H[is] M[ajesty's] G[overnment] had heard of these negotiations with much surprise and concern, in view of the fact that they had previously been assured that the line would on no account be extended without the introduction of considerable modifications in the Bagdad Railway Convention of 1903,[1] as also in view of the further fact that they could not, as the Turkish Gov[ernmen]t were aware, regard with equanimity the progress to the Persian Gulf of a railway which, as at present controlled and without any British participation, would seriously modify, and was indeed intended to modify, the economic position of this country in regard to the trade of Mesopotamia; would affect the political situation in the Persian Gulf to the detriment of British interests; and would assuredly have an important influence in regard to the Indian Empire.

I impressed upon Tewfik Pasha that H[is] M[ajesty's] G[overnment] were not actuated by any hostility to the railway, as such; and, under proper safeguards, would view the progress of railway construction in those regions with favour.

As, however, the present Administration in Turkey were acting in this matter in complete disregard of the views and wishes of H[is] M[ajesty's] G[overnment], and since,—(in spite of all that H[is] M[ajesty's] G[overnment] had done to assist the new régime, and of the friendly and even enthusiastic support, both moral and material, which had been extended by this country to Turkey, more especially during the crisis of 1908/1909[2]),—the application of H[is] M[ajesty's] G[overnment]

[1] [Printed in *B.F.S.P.*, Vol. 102, pp. 833–48.]
[2] [For the Young Turkish Revolution, *v. Gooch & Temperley*, Vol. V, pp. 247–320, ch. XXXVIII, *passim.*]

for a "protective" concession for a railway along the Tigris Valley from Bagdad had latterly been ignored, it showed very feeble appreciation of our friendship on the part of the Sublime Porte.

Needless to say in these circumstances, and until the attitude of the Turkish Gov[ernmen]t changed with regard to the Tigris Valley concession, H[is] M[ajesty's] G[overnment] could have nothing to say to the increase of customs duties.

I remarked that the Turkish M[inister for] F[oreign] A[ffairs], in a recent interview with Y[our] E[xcellency], had denied any knowledge of our application for the concession in question(³),—a circumstance which, in view of the reports which Y[our] E[xcellency] furnished to me last September,(⁴) seemed to me most extraordinary.

The Turkish Ambassador cordially agreed with me, and stated that he had repeatedly pressed the subject upon the attention of the Turkish M[inister for] F[oreign] A[ffairs]. H[is] E[xcellency] added that he himself was of opinion that an arrangement whereby G[rea]t Britain would obtain this concession would be an equitable and easy solution of the difficulty.

I assured Tewfik Pasha that we should be perfectly willing that the proposed railway along the Tigris Valley should be nominally Turkish provided British interests were adequately represented, that H[is] M[ajesty's] G[overnment] had no political designs whatever on Mesopotamia, that they merely wished to preserve the economic position which had been steadily built up in those regions by the enterprise of British subjects during upwards of two centuries, and prevent it from being displaced by another foreign Power, and that they would be fully prepared to give to Turkey the most binding assurances of political disinterestedness in this respect.

I concluded by begging H[is] E[xcellency] urgently to support the specific proposals which you will be instructed to put forward in a separate despatch.(⁵)

When carrying out the instructions referred to, I have to request Your Excellency to read this despatch both to the Grand Vizier and to the M[inister for] F[oreign] A[ffairs].

[I am, &c.]
E. G[REY]

(³) [v. supra, p. 446, No. 339.]
(⁴) [v. supra, pp. 376–7, Nos. 274–5.]
(⁵) [v. infra, pp. 468–72, No. 352.]

No. 351.

Sir C. Hardinge to Sir E. Goschen.

Private.(¹)

My dear Goschen :—   *Foreign Office, April* 19, 1910.

I only returned yesterday afternoon, and have been overwhelmed with work since my arrival, so I must ask you to excuse a rather short letter.

The Chancellor's interview was very useful,(²) as he has come out into the open and has cleared the air. I think your replies to him were admirable. There is evidently now no question of our participation in the Baghdad Railway, according to the views of the German Government at this moment. We shall therefore now concentrate all our attention upon obtaining a concession for a railway in the Tigris Valley, and also upon supporting the demand for a French concession for a railway from Baghdad to the Mediterranean. There can be no possible question of any political arrangement with Germany by which we might obtain a modified control of the Gulf section, and sacrifice for this mess of pottage our position in Europe and our interest in Persia and the Persian Gulf. I am surprised that Stumm should

(¹) [Hardinge MSS., Vol. III of 1910. An extract of a copy of this letter is preserved in the Foreign Office, F.O. 15622/107/10/18.]
(²) [v. supra, pp. 451–61, Nos. 343–4, and pp. 463–5, No. 348.]

have thought that anything would come out of the Chancellor's naval proposals: he ought to have known us better. As regards Persia, if we and the Russians present a solid front and co-operate very closely in that country, I think we shall in the end defeat the Germans, as we are the two Powers on the spot, who are in a position to exert pressure. The Russians seem ready to play up, and neither they nor we are likely to throw up the sponge without a serious struggle. I will even go so far as to say that I should be ready to advise the exercise of the severest form of coercion upon the Persians, if there were any question of their yielding privileges to Germany which could in any way injure our political and strategic interests.

We think that our best policy now is to say no more to the Germans, and we do not intend to send you any instructions as regards a reply to the Chancellor.

I will bring to the notice of the Admiralty the difficulties of your Naval Attaché. It is evidently a case in which retaliation is necessary.

[CHARLES HARDINGE.]

No. 352.

Sir Edward Grey to Sir G. Lowther.

F.O. 11933/100/10/44.
(No. 107.) Secret.

Sir, *Foreign Office, April 20*, 1910.

In your Excellency's despatch No. 197 of the 2nd instant(1) you reported that the Ottoman Minister for Foreign Affairs, while denying that negotiations on the subject had as yet reached a binding or final conclusion, had admitted that active discussions were in progress between the Sublime Porte and the parties concerned, with a view to facilitating the ultimate prolongation of the Bagdad Railway from El Halif to Bagdad by means of the allocation of the surplus revenues of the tithes which would be available for kilometric guarantees in 1915.

This information, as your Excellency is aware, has been received by His Majesty's Government with surprise and concern : in the first place it appears to indicate a fundamental change in the attitude assumed by the Ottoman Government only a few months ago in regard to the Bagdad Railway concession of 1903,—a concession which could hardly meet with the approval, let alone the encouragement and support, of an enlightened administration under the new régime, unless and until it had undergone drastic revision and substantial modifications : in the second place it tends to confirm an impression that the Ottoman Government, by disregarding the well-known views and wishes of His Majesty's Government, no longer recognise that community of interest which, in the critical period following upon the revolution of July 1908, induced His Majesty's Government on their part to extend to Turkey, with no small measure of success, their whole-hearted and consistent support : while finally, it foreshadows the progress of an enterprise which, as at present controlled and unless rendered innocuous by the execution of protective and countervailing measures, is calculated to involve increasing injury to long-established British commerce in Mesopotamia, as well as to affect political issues of the greatest magnitude in the Middle East, and more especially in the Persian Gulf, where, owing to the proximity of the Indian Empire, the commercial interests of Great Britain have long been recognised as predominant to those of all other European States.

It will be convenient that I should deal with these important subjects under distinct and separate headings.

Firstly, as regards the Bagdad Railway Convention of 1903, your Excellency was categorically informed by Hilmi Pasha, in his capacity as Grand Vizier, that the Bagdad Railway would not be continued unless the terms of the concession negotiated under the corrupt and obscurantist rule of the ex-Sultan Abdul Hamid

(1) [v. supra, pp. 445–6, No. 339.]

were first materially altered.([2]) His Majesty's Government had cordially shared the estimate formed by Hilmi Pasha of the concession : and the failure both in 1903 and subsequently to enlist British participation in the undertaking is largely due to the recognition in this country of the onerous nature of the concession,—imposing upon Turkey burdens altogether out of proportion to the advantages it is likely to confer,—while certain *pourparlers* which took place in Berlin in the closing months of last year have not led to any concrete result owing to some extent to the disinclination of the present holders of the concession to consider certain financial modifications advantageous to the Turkish Exchequer, which His Majesty's Government desired to see introduced into the scheme of the concession as regards its application to the Persian Gulf section.

I do not intend in the present despatch to enter upon a detailed exposure of the objections to which the terms of the convention of 1903([3]) might reasonably be subjected, the more so since those objections are sufficiently patent from a perusal of the document in question : but I shall touch upon certain salient points which appear particularly disadvantageous to the interests of the Turkish Government and taxpayer.

Under article 35 two guarantees are instituted, the one a working-expenses guarantee, the other for purposes of construction : the first is arranged upon such a scale that it directly militates against the progressive development of traffic, and therefore against the commercial success of the line; the other is calculated upon a basis so extravagant that, even if the main line alone be taken into consideration, there should remain at the disposal of the promoters funds exceeding by several millions of pounds the actual cost of construction, while, if the branch lines were included in the estimate, the surplus would be still higher. It is on these grounds that His Majesty's Government are unable to approve of the financial burdens underlying the Bagdad Railway concession : they consider that there would be manifest advantages in substituting a form of guarantee approximating to that adopted by the Government of India, whereby a *minimum* rate of interest is assured upon the capital actually employed in constructing and working a railway, and any surplus profits over and above that guaranteed *minimum* are equally divided between the Government and the railway company : this system is productive of economy in construction and efficiency in working, factors which are indispensable in order to secure commercial success and satisfactory results.

Secondly, as regards the attitude of the Sublime Porte towards British interests, His Majesty's Government are far from suggesting that the Ottoman Government are at liberty to disregard their contractual obligations under the Bagdad Railway Convention simply and solely because those obligations, though concluded with evident disregard of her real interests, are burdensome to Turkey; what they do take exception to is the fact that the Ottoman Government, while showing no inclination to treat on their merits the applications for concessions and trade facilities, however modest in character, from British subjects, have apparently contemplated certain financial arrangements tending to facilitate and to hasten the progress of the Bagdad Railway towards the Persian Gulf : and inasmuch as those arrangements cannot become operative until the year 1915, the solicitude of the Ottoman Government to bind themselves *without further delay* and to smooth the way for a monopoly of the economic exploitation of the country cannot but cause serious misgiving and some perplexity to those who have at heart the financial regeneration of the Ottoman Empire. His Majesty's Government, by manifestations of practical sympathy, have given tangible proof of their desire to contribute towards that regeneration which is the foundation of all administrative reform; yet it appears that the Ottoman Government, at a time when they are desirous, on the one hand, of raising the customs duties on foreign imports from 11 per cent. to 15 per cent., are ready on the other hand to go out of their way to promote the prosecution of an enterprise

([2]) [*cp. supra*, p. 378, No. 276.]
([3]) [Printed in *B.F.S.P.*, Vol. 102. pp. 833–48.]

admittedly burdensome to the Turkish Exchequer, without so much as attempting by negotiation with the concessionnaires to bring about an alleviation of the burdens which that enterprise will involve.

In the face of these considerations, His Majesty's Government are reluctantly constrained to believe that the Ottoman Government, oblivious of the services rendered by Great Britain during the Near Eastern crisis of 1908–1909, are deliberately promoting at all costs the progress of the Bagdad Railway on its present basis and thereby undermining the commercial position of this country in Mesopotamia which has been firmly established in those regions for the last 200 years: they can only conclude that the Ottoman Government have allowed themselves to be influenced by prejudiced and unworthy suspicions in regard to British designs in that region. The policy of Great Britain in Mesopotamia is directed towards the maintenance of the *status quo*, His Majesty's Government emphatically disclaim any designs of territorial aggrandisement in those regions, and they are prepared to furnish the Ottoman Government with the most binding assurances to this effect.

I now pass to the final points to which I have alluded: British commercial interests in Mesopotamia, and the disturbance of the *status quo* which the Bagdad Railway is calculated to effect.

The commercial position of Great Britain in the Mesopotamian delta is altogether exceptional: that position has been steadily consolidated since the foundation, upwards of two and a-half centuries ago, of the first English factory at Bussorah; in 1766 a British Resident was appointed at Bagdad; at Bussorah there has long been a British consul, charged with the care of British trade, represented up to a recent date by 96 per cent. of the shipping coming into the port; in short, such is now the nature of these commercial interests that the trade of Bagdad and Bussorah, valued at 2,500,000*l*. in 1903, is predominantly in the hands of British and Indian merchants: moreover, it may be mentioned incidentally that the annual pilgrimage of British-Indian subjects to the Shiah shrines of Kerbela and Nejef is continually increasing, the numbers in 1905 exceeding 11,000,—a circumstance which serves to emphasise the interest which this region must possess for British Indian traders and commerce.[4]

The position attained by this country upon the waters and on the shores of the Persian Gulf has been won not without the expenditure of many millions of money and the sacrifice of many valuable lives: in the early years of the nineteenth century the slave trade was rampant in the Gulf, and the vessels of the Indian Marine were engaged in a long and arduous struggle with the Arab pirates who infested its southern coasts: this conflict, which was conducted entirely by British agency and means, without any help from the Ottoman Government, resulted in the establishment of treaty relations with the Arab chiefs, under which they bound themselves to observe perpetual peace and to refer all disputes to the British Resident at Bushire. The *pax Britannica* which has ever since, with rare exceptions, been maintained, is the issue of these arrangements and is the exclusive work of this country. It is owing to British enterprise, to the expenditure of British lives and money, that the Persian Gulf, not excluding the approaches to the Turkish ports of Bagdad and Bussorah, is at this moment open to the navigation of the world: indeed to these causes alone it may be said that the seaborne trade of Mesopotamia owes its very existence. The situation of Great Britain in the Persian Gulf has been well described as unique: for although she has not sought territorial acquisitions in those regions, she has for generations borne burdens there which no other nation has ever undertaken anywhere, except in the capacity of sovereign; she has had duty thrust upon her without dominion; she has kept the peace amongst people who are not her subjects; has patrolled, during upwards of two centuries, waters over which she has enjoyed no formal lordship; has kept, in

[4] [*cp. supra*, p. 356, No. 250.]

strange ports, an open door through which the traders of every nation might have as free access to distant markets as her own.

I have dwelt at some length upon the position of Great Britain in Mesopotamia and the Persian Gulf because it is desirable that the Ottoman Government should be able to appreciate fully the disturbance of long-established interests which the Bagdad Railway, the most direct route between this country and the Indian Empire, is likely to entail. This will appear the more accurate when it is recalled that under the terms of the concession, the promoters of that enterprise not only are entitled to establish ports at the important trade centres of Bagdad and Bussorah, but under various articles a number of minor but valuable rights are conferred upon them: exemption from customs dues for all materials, machinery, rolling-stock, iron, wood, coal imported from abroad during the period of construction, and exemption from taxation of the company's entire property and revenue during the whole term of the concession; mining and quarrying and forest rights within a zone of 20 kilom. on either side of the railway; the right to establish warehouses, elevators and shops; to manufacture bricks and tiles, and to make free use of any natural water power in the vicinity of the line—all tending to confer a monopoly of the economic development of the country.

It has been incumbent on His Majesty's Government to consider most carefully in what manner they can legitimately, and with due regard to the economic and general welfare of the important Ottoman provinces concerned, prevent the establishment of such a monopoly expanding throughout the whole region of Mesopotamia; forestall the destruction of British commercial interests which it would perforce accomplish; maintain an open door for the trade of all nations; and protect the larger interests in India and the Persian Gulf which the completion of the Bagdad Railway, as at present controlled, is destined to influence.

They have come to the conclusion that the only course now open to them which could at the same time promote the objects in view would be the construction of a "protective" railway. I have therefore to request your Excellency to renew the application which you have already made to the Ottoman Government for a railway concession along the valley of the River Tigris[5]: the precise course of the line would be a matter for subsequent arrangement; what His Majesty's Government at present desire is that the Sublime Porte should accede to their application forthwith in principle; and for this object it does not appear necessary to go further than to say that the line would approximately follow the valley of the Tigris from Bagdad to Kut-el-Amara, and that from that point it would proceed in a south-easterly direction to Bussorah, and from that point to Koweit. The cost of the railway would naturally depend upon the gauge and the results of the surveys, but His Majesty's Government would not call upon the Ottoman Government for any guarantee whatsoever, and they would be prepared to recommend a group of financiers of high standing who would provide for the construction and working of the line under a *Turkish* company.

Such a railway, when constructed, could not be looked upon as involving any prejudice to the Bagdad Railway Company, since in the first place it would serve a region which is distant in places over 160 kilom. from that company's proposed alignment, while in the second place its object,—an entirely legitimate one,—is to protect long-established British interests which the Bagdad Railway is calculated to displace: British trade is indeed interested in the district in question in an especial degree, since the annual volume of our trade passing into Persia alone viâ Bussorah and the Tigris valley is estimated at 750,000*l.*

I have accordingly to request your Excellency to read this despatch, in translation, both to the Minister for Foreign Affairs and to the Grand Vizier, and to communicate a copy to them. I desire your Excellency at the same time to press them to give an early and favourable reply to the application of His Majesty's

[5] [*cp. supra*, pp. 374–5, No. 272, pp. 376–7, No. 274, and p. 433, No. 324.]

Government, with facilities for a preliminary survey at an early date, and I have to emphasise to your Excellency, for the information of the Ottoman Government, that His Majesty's Government will in no circumstances agree to the desired increase of the customs duties until the Ottoman Government show a disposition to meet their wishes with regard to this concession, and that the future attitude of this country towards the Ottoman Empire will be largely affected by the reception with which your Excellency's application may meet.

I am, &c.
(For the Secretary of State),
CHARLES HARDINGE.

No. 353.

Sir E. Goschen to Sir C. Hardinge.

F.O. 15623/167/10/18.
Private.

My dear Hardinge, *Berlin, April 23,* 1910.

Many thanks for your interesting little letter by last Messenger,([1]) which, though unavoidably short, was just what I wanted.

I have nothing to tell you this time, as things are quiet for the time being. The Chancellor is sure to ask me what H[is] M[ajesty's] G[overnment] think of his conversation with me! But, unless he sends for me, I don't expect I shall see him before Roosevelt's arrival; at all events I hope not. By the way it seems to be the Emperor's intention to meet Roosevelt at the station on his arrival. I can hardly believe it, but Stemrich says so. I know that H[is] M[ajesty] wished to do so, but I had heard that his entourage were so much against it that he had given it up. If H[is] M[ajesty] really does this it will be going rather far. I haven't reported it to the King as I thought the idea had been given up. I still cannot believe it.

Cambon saw the Chancellor the day before yesterday and found him uncommunicative and rather depressed, chiefly about the Mannesmann case. He was very plucky in the Reichstag, spoke quite frankly and knocked the bottom out of the Mannesmann's case: now he is worrying about them, is frightened at the support they get from all sides and says he will eventually have to do something to propitiate them, if only for the sake of his own position in the country! This is quite in the picture I have always drawn of him, doing what he thinks right and then worrying as to whether he *is* right. Cambon tried to draw him about Persia but could get nothing out of him, except that he was rather astonished that Isvolsky had not gone to see him on his way through Berlin, while he had gone to see Pichon on his way through Paris! By the way the Russian Chargé d'Affaires tells me that he thinks Isvolsky will soon resign and be succeeded by Sassonow. Is this true? Cambon was very keen to know what the Chancellor had said to me the other day. I told him that he had raised some difficulties about the southern section of the Bagdad Railway, but I did not tell him what he had asked for in exchange, or indeed that he had asked anything. Cambon said that if he made too many difficulties about the Railway France and England would have to set to work to get concessions of their own and to build alternative lines; but he seems to think that the Germans have got almost as firm a hold upon the Young Turks as they had upon Abdul Hamid, and that we should have great difficulty in getting what we wanted. Supposing we don't get a concession for the Tigris line and the Germans refuse to give us the southern section and build it themselves, what happens then? What sort of opposition should we make to their building a terminus to their railway on the Persian Gulf? I should like to know this very much some day. But *perhaps* when they hear that we intend to build an alternative line they will be more

([1]) [*v. supra*, pp. 467–8, No. 351.]

amenable. But the Chancellor is no doubt right when he says that the Bagdad Railway has taken a very firm hold on the imagination of the German Public, so that there will be sure to be some effervescence. Better however now than later! and the Bagdad Railway question has got to be settled one way or the other.

I am glad to see that Russia is inclined to be firm about Persia; it seems to me that we shall both want all the firmness we have got, and I don't look forward to an agreeable time. Nizamy *lives* at the Wilhelm Strasse and one of his secretaries told one of mine that they were being worked night and day.

Please excuse a dull letter and believe me to be

Yours very sincerely,
W. E. GOSCHEN.

It is snowing hard!

No. 354.

Sir A. Nicolson to Sir Edward Grey.

F.O. 14510/100/10/44A.
Tel. (No. 134.)

St. Petersburgh, April 27, 1910.
D. 8·40 P.M.
R. 9 P.M.

Bagdad Railway.

Acting M[inister for] F[oreign] A[ffairs] tells me that Russian Ambassador at Constantinople telegraphs that discussions as to southern section of railway have recommenced and that it was possible that some arrangement would be arrived at in regard to British participation. He asked me to ascertain whether anything new was passing on the subject.

No. 355.

Sir Edward Grey to Sir A. Nicolson.

F.O. 14510/100/10.
Tel. (No. 196.)

Foreign Office, April 28, 1910.
D. 2·30 P.M.

We are unaware of any negotiations for participation in the S[outhern] end of the Bagdad Line.

German Gov[ernmen]t have informed us categorically that they will not admit our participation without a general agreement on European questions.

You may tell the Russian G[overnmen]t for their confidential information that, in these circumstances, we shall apply for a separate concession from Bagdad to the Gulf *viâ* the Tigris.

No. 356.

Sir A. Nicolson to Sir Edward Grey.

F.O. 15876/100/10/44A.
(No. 211.)
Sir,

St. Petersburgh, D. April 28, 1910.
R. May 9, 1910.

Monsieur Sazonoff informed me yesterday that he had heard from the Russian Ambassador at Constantinople that discussions had been resumed as to British participation in the Southern section of the Bagdad railway and that there were some prospects that the discussions might lead to an arrangement. He asked if I had heard anything on the subject. I replied in the negative and said that I would make enquiries.

Monsieur Sazonoff added that the Emperor had lately been speaking to him on the subject of the Bagdad railway and had enquired whether England had any " legal right " to claim a share in the construction and control of the Southern section. I told His Excellency that of course no "legal right" existed; but it was clear that a line debouching on the Persian Gulf where British interests were of the highest importance was a matter of the greatest concern to us. We considered, therefore, that in respect to the Southern section we should endeavour to obtain at least a preponderating interest. We were consequently desirous of inducing the German Government to recognize and accord to us what we considered to be essential to the safeguarding of our interests. He was aware of the methods by which we were, so to speak, exercising pressure towards that object, and he was acquainted with the proposals, not perhaps entirely harmonious, which had been severally made by the German Government and the Deutsche Bank.

I have, &c.
A. NICOLSON.

No. 357.

Sir Edward Grey to Tewfik Pasha.

F.O. 11933/100/10/44. *Foreign Office, April 30, 1910.*

From a careful perusal of the terms of the Bagdad Railway Convention of 1903 (of which a copy is enclosed for facility of reference)([1]) it will be observed that there is no clause which confers on the holders of the concession a monopoly of railway construction in Mesopotamia : indeed according to article 42 it is laid down that the land to be expropriated shall be strictly confined to the area which is necessary for the railway. Moreover it cannot equitably be contended, apart altogether from the terms of the convention of 1903, that, because a concession for a railway has been granted to certain promoters along one specified alignment, the Ottoman Gov[ernmen]t are *ipso facto* debarred from granting a further concession to other parties, when that concession is for a railway destined to serve another district : such a contention, if advanced, would be utterly preposterous; and inasmuch as it is stipulated in article 34 that all disputes respecting the execution and interpretation of the convention of 1903 shall be settled in the Ottoman Courts, the ultimate decision as to what the Ottoman Government may and may not do with regard to granting further concessions would rest with those Courts and with no foreign Power.

The German Gov[ernmen]t have definitely informed H[is] M[ajesty's] G[overnment] that British participation in the Bagdad Railway will not be admitted on terms which H[is] M[ajesty's] G[overnment] could possibly approve : in these circumstances, H[is] M[ajesty's] G[overnment] renew the application, to which the ex-Grand Vizier acceded in principle in September last, for an entirely separate concession as indicated in the enclosed despatch to H[is] M[ajesty's] Ambassador at Constantinople.([2]) The reception with which this renewed application may meet, will, as stated in the despatch, affect the future relations of this country towards the Ottoman Empire.

([1]) [Not reproduced. For the text, *v. B.F.S.P.*, Vol. 102, pp. 833–48.]
([2]) [*v. supra*, pp. 468–72, No. 352.]

No. 358.

Sir Edward Grey to Sir F. Bertie.

F.O. 14472/183/10/44.
(No. 225.)
Sir,   *Foreign Office, April 30, 1910.*

When discussing with the French Ambassador on the 21st instant the question of the Bagdad–Homs Railway, Sir C. Hardinge remarked to him that France and England were more interested almost than any other Powers in the well being and financial stability of Turkey. His Majesty's Government had not pressed the Turkish Government to give orders for ships to British Shipbuilders, although naturally they did nothing to hinder the transaction, but they felt that all this naval expenditure together with the large sums being spent upon the army could hardly be justified by the present financial condition of Turkey, and that to continue the present reckless scale of expenditure would in the end bring Turkey to a state of bankruptcy and place the country in a worse position than under the old régime. He told Monsieur Cambon that he had been reliably informed that by next autumn the Turks would be in need of a loan of between nine and ten million sterling, and that although they might have an excess in customs receipts during the course of the summer which they would probably pledge, they would if they continued in this course ruin the future of their country by mortgaging in advance their available revenues and finally be without a penny. He alluded to the proposal to allocate the excess of the tithes to kilometric guarantees five years' hence.

He added that I was of opinion that the British and French Ambassadors in Constantinople should co-operate not only in affairs relating to Mesopotamia but in impressing upon the Turks the absolute necessity of maintaining their financial stability and of developing the country on progressive lines, and that they should warn the Turkish Government that in the event of their continuing this reckless course of expenditure they would find it hard to find money in Paris or London to meet their requirements.

Monsieur Cambon entirely agreed with all that Sir C. Hardinge said, and remarked that he would put my views before the French Minister for Foreign Affairs.

[I am, &c.
E. GREY.]

No. 359.

Sir G. Lowther to Sir Edward Grey.

F.O. 15938/100/10/44.
(No. 276.) Secret.   *Constantinople, D. May 3, 1910.*
Sir,   R. *May 9, 1910.*

I to-day read to the Minister for Foreign Affairs and to the Grand Vizier your despatches Nos. 96 and 107, of the 18th and 20th ultimo,([1]) setting forth the point of view of His Majesty's Government with regard to the negotiations which are in progress between the Ottoman Government and the Bagdad Railway Company for the prolongation of the line from El Halif to Bagdad, and I renewed the application which I had already made last year for a railway concession along the valley of the Tigris on the lines indicated in your despatch No. 107 Secret, of the 20th ultimo, of which I left His Excellency a translation.

Rifaat Pasha said that this proposal required careful study, which he and his colleagues would give it. Meanwhile he would merely observe that it was not the Ottoman Government that had urged the continuation of the line from El Halif to

---

([1]) [*v. supra*, pp. 466–7, No. 350, and pp. 468–72, No. 352.]

Bagdad: it was the attitude assumed by Great Britain in connection with the increase of the 4 % Customs dues and the demand made from the Bagdad Company to abandon their claim to this that had led the Company to negotiate with a view to obtaining guarantees for the conclusion of the Halif–Bagdad section. The Ottoman Government, His Excellency observed, were now placed in such a difficult position with regard to the 4 % that it appeared as if it would be necessary to abandon it if the Powers maintained their present attitude. Monsieur Bompard had, before leaving for Paris a few days ago, repeated that the French Government asked for no conditions, but that if other Powers insisted on such France would ask for a concession for the Homs–Bagdad line.

Italy had intimated that further conditions might be asked for beyond the settlement of the claims. Even the American Government had stated that their consent would depend on the Chester concession being granted and the order for the battleships being given to an American firm of shipbuilders. The Minister for Foreign Affairs and the Grand Vizier had been obliged to reply somewhat sharply to these latter suggestions of my American colleague.

His Excellency said he hoped that His Majesty's Government would not for a moment believe that the Ottoman Government were oblivious of the services rendered by Great Britain during the crisis of 1908–9. Their object in negotiating with the Bagdad Railway was merely to satisfy our demands regarding the 4 %. Nor did the Ottoman Government entertain any suspicion regarding British designs on Mesopotamia. They were most anxious to find a way out of the difficulty without offending Germany to whom they were morally bound for the completion of the line when funds were available. As regards the section Bagdad–Persian Gulf it seemed to His Excellency possible to exclude it from the domain of the Bagdad Railway Company and perhaps the best solution would be for the Turkish Government to construct that section of the line themselves. He would not, however, offer any definite observation on the proposals of His Majesty's Government until he had consulted his colleagues.

The Grand Vizier, whom I saw later, spoke in much the same sense, but said it was incomprehensible to him that his predecessor should have given anything in the nature of assurances regarding a modification of the Bagdad convention, for they found themselves confronted by the terms of the convention and by the legal obligation to continue the line to Bagdad.

It was also absolutely necessary in their own interests and to justify the sacrifices they were now making for the working guarantee that the line should have its terminus at a big centre instead of stopping in mid air as it were at El Halif. What however he was determined to endeavour to obtain from the Germans concurrently with any arrangement for the continuation of the line to Bagdad was an abandonment of their claim to build the section Bagdad–Persian Gulf. It would no doubt be very difficult to succeed in this as it obviously entailed a considerable sacrifice for the Germany Company, but he felt that he would be able to obtain it. His idea was that that section should be built by the Ottoman Government, if necessary with foreign capital. Beyond that he had not considered the question in detail. The specific proposal now put forward by His Majesty's Government would have the careful attention of the Ottoman Government and a reply would be sent in the same form in which it had been received.

I reminded His Highness that you, Sir, had all along been placed in a somewhat difficult position in having to justify to the British mercantile interests the imposition of an additional duty of four per cent. which would contribute to the success of a line ultimately destined to injuriously affect our commercial position in portions of the country traversed by it—an argument which was all the stronger as Great Britain was a Free Trade country which practically left all Turkish imports untaxed.

His Highness specially begged that his intentions as regards inducing the German Government to abandon the Bagdad–Gulf section, as well as the British proposal now made, should be kept strictly confidential, as any suspicion of a bargain being made would militate against the success of their negotiations for obtaining the 4 % increase.

I have, &c.
GERARD LOWTHER.

No. 360.

Sir Edward Grey to Sir E. Goschen.([1])

F.O. 16610/100/10/44.
(No. 121.)   Secret.

Sir,   *Foreign Office, May 5, 1910.*

To-day the German Chargé d'Affaires, after mentioning a point of detail about Persia which I have recorded separately, enquired what was my view as to proceeding to discuss an agreement with Germany as to Persia in the light of what Herr von Bethmann-Hollweg had said.

I replied that I had not seen much material for an agreement in what Herr von Bethmann-Hollweg had said about Persia, and with regard to the Bagdad Railway his attitude had been discouraging.([2])   I had sent his proposals to the Prime Minister: but I had not seen the latter for about three weeks now, I knew he had been very fully occupied before Parliament rose last week, and I did not expect to see him until a fortnight hence.   Therefore, although I intended to write my own personal reflections to you, I did not think I could discuss the matter further in conversation at present.

The German Chargé d'Affaires had evidently anticipated that we would be disappointed by what had been said about the Bagdad Railway and the Navy, and he explained to me that as these questions might take a long time to settle it would be well to make progress first with the Persian matter.   Herr von Bethmann-Hollweg was quite willing to recognise the special position which we had in Persia, and our sphere of influence there; but he could not make this recognition, and thereby give up the full commercial rights which Germany had in Persia by Treaty, unless he was able to prove to German public opinion that he had obtained some *quid pro quo.*   The Persian question might become urgent soon because, though the negotiations for a loan had fallen through for the moment, the Persian Government were much in need of money, and we and Russia might secure all the railways in return for a loan.   The Chargé d'Affaires mentioned the promise which we already held with regard to railways in the south, and he said that if Germany waited she might find herself entirely excluded, whereas if she took advantage of the present situation she might perhaps get some concessions.   His idea was that, in return for a German recognition of our special position and sphere in Persia, we might agree to give the Germans orders for about 25 % of the materials for such railways as we built in that country.

I told the Chargé d'Affaires that the idea of a separate agreement about Persia seemed to be receiving more emphasis from him now than it had when Herr von Bethmann-Hollweg had spoken to you, and I asked whether the Chancellor's view had changed in this direction since last he saw you.

The Chargé d'Affaires gave me to understand that there had been a change, for the reason he had already mentioned: that the Persian question might become urgent soon, while the other matters might take months to settle.

I said that I supposed a similar arrangement with Russia was contemplated.

([1]) [*cp. G.P.* XXVII, II, pp. 638–9.   A summary of this despatch was sent to Sir A. Nicolson in Tel. No. 221 of May 11, 1910, which was repeated to Berlin and Paris.]

([2]) [*v. supra,* pp. 451–9, Nos. 343–4.]

The Chargé d'Affaires replied that this was the case. It was proposed to have a similar agreement with Russia, and to sign it simultaneously. His Government feared, however, that Russia might build railways in the north of Persia to promote her own trade, but would be unwilling to link these lines with the Bagdad Railway; and they wished to guard against this.

I then said that in writing to you I would bear in mind what he had told me as to the Chancellor's most recent view with regard to a Persian agreement. One difficulty, however, which occurred at once with regard to it was that, if we were to give Germany a participation of 25 %, why should other countries not ask us for a similar participation, and what were we to say to them?

The Chargé d'Affaires urged that Germany was in a special position, owing to her rights in the Bagdad Railway; and he asked me what other countries I thought likely to put forward a claim for participation.

I answered that France would certainly wish to participate, and Austria also, for she had taken exactly the same attitude with regard to Persia as Germany had taken. Other countries would probably follow suit.

He suggested that this difficulty might be met if we and Germany took 55 % in every case, and left the remaining 45 % to be disputed for by the other countries.

I concluded by saying that all I could promise for the moment was to bear in mind the special desire for an agreement as to Persia when I was writing my views to you.

I am, &c.
E. GREY.

No. 361.

Sir Edward Grey to Sir E. Goschen.

F.O. 26089/167/10/18.
Private.

My dear Goschen, *Foreign Office, May 5, 1910.*

I have not seen the Prime Minister for three weeks, but even if I had seen him I am sure he has been far too busy, during the last weeks of the part of the Session just closed, to be able to go into Bethmann-Hollweg's proposals. So what I send you now are my own personal reflections; but you may use them as such at your discretion if you are pressed in further conversations with the Chancellor or Schoen.

I entirely understand the Chancellor's difficulty in giving us the southern end of the Bagdad Railway without getting in return something which Germany will look upon as a *quid pro quo*. I have the same difficulty here in giving what he asks: for British public opinion is not less exacting than German.

Crawford, of the Turkish Customs Service, tells me that 65 % of the trade with Mesopotamia is British. On this trade, in the first instance, will fall the burden of the 4 % increase, until it is passed on to the Turkish consumer. There will be a great outcry when the increase is made, and I shall have all I can do to get public opinion here to recognise that participation in the Bagdad Railway is an adequate *quid pro quo* for a new burden upon British trade, only a part of which is interested in Mesopotamia. This is my first difficulty. It would be insuperable if I had to make another set of concessions as well.

In the next place, with regard to any understanding with Germany: the attention of public opinion here is concentrated on the mutual arrest or decrease of naval expenditure as *the* test of whether an understanding is worth anything. In the first overtures of Bethmann-Hollweg last year I felt that the naval question was not sufficiently prominent. Since then it has receded into the background, and the perspective of his last proposals is therefore even less advantageous. This is an important point.

In the third place, there is this difficulty with regard to any general political understanding : we cannot sacrifice the friendship of Russia or of France. There is no intention of using either for aggressive purposes against Germany. When Germany settled her difficulty with France about Morocco, not only was I free from jealousy, but I had a sense of absolute relief. I had hated the prospect of friendship with France involving friction with Germany, and I rejoiced when this prospect disappeared. My attitude is the same with regard to Germany's difficulty with Russia about Persia. Also, I am quite sure that neither France nor Russia wishes to quarrel with Germany; indeed, I know that they wish to avoid a quarrel. So on this ground I am quite easy. But I cannot enter into any agreement with Germany which would prevent me from giving to France or Russia, should Germany take up towards either of them an aggressive attitude such as she took up towards France about Morocco, the same sort of support as I gave to France at the time of the Algeciras Conference and afterwards until she settled her difficulty with Germany. Any agreement which prevented the giving of such support would obviously forfeit the friendship of France and Russia, and this is what makes me apprehensive of trouble in finding a political formula.

Since I formed the intention of writing this to you, Kühlmann has pressed the Persian question upon me. I have recorded that separately, and later on I will give you my reflections upon what he has said. He has made it clear that Bethmann-Hollweg wishes to shift the whole discussion on to the Persian question for the present. Meanwhile I think that it may be worth while for you to have my own views at first hand on the general question, though I believe that Hardinge has already told you what I wrote briefly on a previous paper.(¹)

Yours sincerely,
E. GREY.

(¹) [This evidently refers to the minute written by Sir Edward Grey upon Sir E. Goschen's despatch No. 102 of April 11, *v. supra*, p. 461, No. 344, *min.* The substance of these minutes was sent to Sir E. Goschen in a private letter from Sir C. Hardinge of April 26, 1910. This letter is in the Hardinge MSS., Vol. III of 1910.]

No. 362.

Sir Edward Grey to Sir E. Goschen.

F.O. 16757/100/10/44.
(No. 122.) Secret.
Sir, *Foreign Office, May 10, 1910.*

Count Metternich, in the course of conversation to-day,(¹) told me that during his absence from London he had seen the German Chancellor, who had spoken to him about Persia.

The substance of what Herr von Bethmann-Hollweg had said was that the German Government would continue to be willing to respect the strategical and political interests of England and Russia in Persia. Also, in the economic sphere the German Government would recognise the English and Russian claim to a sort of favoured optional right with regard to railways, roads, and telegraphs in their respective spheres of interest. The German Government had no thought of interfering with the political interests of the two countries; but England and Russia ought to recognise that the economic concessions which Germany was prepared to make included the waiving of her right to most-favoured-nation treatment, which she has under her commercial treaty with Persia. In order to come to a friendly agreement with England and Russia, Germany was willing to give up her claim to most-favoured-nation treatment to the extent suggested. There had long been a sincere desire to come to a friendly agreement, and the German Government had therefore refrained from influencing the Persian Government, although at times the latter Government had probably wished that German influence should be exerted.

(¹) [*cp. G.P.* XXVII, II, pp. 789–90.]

Germany had manifested her desire for an understanding as long ago as in 1906, when she had made certain proposals to Russia. M. Iswolsky had now made a communication from which it appeared that an answer to these proposals would be sent soon. The German Chancellor had also expressed his desire for an agreement in his conversation with you on April 10th last.([2]) Of course, there might be difficulties in the way of such an agreement. Germany might, for instance, have to mention at Tehran that her right to most-favoured-nation treatment had been impaired as a result of the diplomatic action of England and Russia. Germany would, however, do this very reluctantly, if only because of the effect upon German public opinion; and this difficulty would not arise if England and Russia would come to an understanding with Germany before obtaining the condition which they desired from Persia as to the granting of concessions. Count Metternich added that an agreement of this kind would very likely facilitate matters with regard to the Bagdad Railway.

I told him that I could not continue the discussion just at present. I explained to him, however, that what I had said to Herr von Kühlmann in his absence([3]) did not raise any difficulties of principle, though I had not gone into any details; and therefore, although I was not at present prepared to continue the discussion, I had no wish to close it.

Count Metternich asked me whether I was drawing up any reply to the communication which the Chancellor had made to you.

I replied that I had already written to you to give you my private impressions before the recent events here had suspended business. You might, perhaps, make use of these in conversation with Herr von Bethmann-Hollweg, but as you would now be coming to London for the Funeral, and would see me then, I thought you would probably wait until you had talked over the matter with me before you said anything further.

I am, &c.
E. GREY.

([2]) [v. supra, pp. 451–61, Nos. 343–4.]
([3]) [cp. supra, pp. 477–8, No. 360.]

No. 363.

Sir Edward Grey to Sir A. Nicolson.

F.O. 16649/100/10/44.   *Foreign Office, May 11, 1910.*
Tel. (No. 222.)   D. 1 P.M.

German chargé d'affaires called on the 6th May and read to Sir C. Hardinge a telegram from Herr von Schoen to following effect:—

German Government had learnt that British and Russian Governments had asked Persian Government for an assurance that no concessions of a political or strategical character, such as railways, roads, telegraphs, mines, etc., should be given to foreign companies without their consent and that Russian Minister had stated that all concessions in Persia must be of a political character. Herr Kühlmann was instructed to state that such a declaration on the part of Persia would render illusory the principle of open door and the prospect of any negotiations such as Chancellor had outlined for an agreement upon Persian affairs; and that his Government considered that German firms had had opportunities for obtaining concessions in Persia, but that German Government, out of deference to British and Russian interests in Persia, had given no encouragement to such projects.

Sir C. Hardinge replied that long before the Chancellor had made any proposals about Persia we had asked the Persian Government for assurances that they would not give concessions of a political and strategic nature, such as railways, roads, and telegraphs, without first consulting British and Russian Governments, and that we were pressing them to give these assurances. Sir C. Hardinge added that we were not demanding any monopoly in Persia, but merely that in such matters our political and strategic interests, which, as a limitrophe Power, were undeniable, should not be ignored; all we asked for in such cases was an option.([1]) Sir C. Hardinge further stated that he failed to see that this attitude clashed with the proposals made by German chargé d'affaires on 5th May.([2])

Herr Kühlmann intimated that he thought that a limitation of concessions to those for railways, roads, and telegraphs would greatly alter the situation, but asked whether it would not be possible to delay the demand for these assurances from the Persian Government until an agreement had been reached with Germany.

Sir C. Hardinge replied that the matter had gone too far; that pressure upon the Persian Government need not hinder negotiations on the lines suggested by the Chancellor: that the principal objection to those negotiations seemed to be that they contained no mention of a possible settlement of the Bagdad Railway question; and that whereas that railway had been urged as a reason for Germany's interest in the affairs of Persia, our position in Persia would present a reciprocal argument.

Herr von Kühlmann stated that Germany could not, without being placed at a disadvantage in negotiating with England, give assurances about the Bagdad Railway.

Sir C. Hardinge urged that owing to the special position of Great Britain and Russia in Persia, Germany must necessarily be in a less advantageous position than either of these two countries.

Your Excellency may inform M. Isvolsky.

([1]) [cp. supra, p. 452, No. 343, min., and notes ([2]) and ([3]), and infra, p. 490, No. 375, note ([1]).]
([2]) [v. supra, pp. 477–8, No. 360.]

No. 364.

Sir F. Cartwright to Sir Edward Grey.

Vienna, May 13, 1910.
D. 12·10 P.M.
R. 1·10 P.M.

F.O. 17017/100/10/44A.
Tel. (No. 24.)
Persia.

The editor of the Austrian Foreign Office newspaper has come to me to warn me as to the serious view held at the Austro-Hungarian Foreign Office with regard to Persian question. He tells me that German Ambassador in London has had an unsatisfactory interview with you and a still more unsatisfactory one with Sir C. Hardinge. This information has no doubt been supplied to Count von Aehrent[h]al by Germany. Evidently Germany is trying to secure Austro-Hungarian support and is creating considerable alarm here by perhaps magnifying the crisis. German Ambassador here is saying that if Great Britain and Russia are not more conciliatory the Persian question will cause a crisis more dangerous than that brought about by Morocco and by Bosnian an[n]exation. A few days ago Count von Aehrent[h]al told me that he knew that he knew but little about Persian affairs and that he took but small interest in them. Now I learn that a memorandum on these matters is being prepared by the Austrian Foreign Office for Count von Aehrent[h]al's information. As far as I can ascertain Count von Aehrent[h]al is reluctant to be dragged into the dispute over Persia but he will be driven to give his support to Germany if a serious crisis arises. French Ambassador came to me last night somewhat alarmed at Germany's action here. He is however under the impression after a conversation with Austrian M[inister for] F[oreign] A[ffairs] that the latter would be glad if he could see his way to use his influence at Berlin to moderate Germany's attitude.

I am to see Count von Aehrent[h]al tomorrow morning before my departure to London and I should be glad to have your views on these matters before I see him.

No. 365.

Sir Edward Grey to Sir F. Cartwright.

F.O. 17017/100/10/44A.
Tel. (No. 23.)

Foreign Office, May 13, 1910.
D. 6 P.M.

On March 31st, I suggested to the German Ch[argé] d'Affaires(¹) that although a general arrangement with Germany, which did not include a reduction in Naval expenditure was out of the question, possibly an arrangement might be come to with Russia and ourselves to include the Persian and the Bagdad R[ai]l[wa]y questions. With regard to France, there would be no difficulty.

I explained that, as regards Persia, we were bound to watch very carefully our strategic and political interests and obliged to guard against a weak Gov[ernmen]t giving political and strategic concessions to others. We had, on the other hand, no desire to create a commercial monopoly. In reply to this friendly commun[icatio]n, I received very shortly afterwards, an intimation both verbal and in writing that, without a general understanding, the German G[overnmen]t, were not prepared to negotiate at all, respecting the Bagdad R[ai]l[wa]y—but that, if a general and political entente were arranged, then our participation in the Bagdad Gulf section of the Railway might be admitted, if, in addition, we would agree to give to Germany, a share in any concession we might obtain in Persia.

In return for this, Germany w[ou]ld recognize our special interests in the British sphere—(not in the neutral sphere).

I have not yet returned any formal reply to this proposal, which I was not able to discuss with the Prime Minister before his departure abroad. In the meantime, however, the German Ch[argé] d'Affaires intimated on the 5th May,(²) that it would be well to make progress at once with the Persian agreement—see my Tel[egram] to Sir A. Nicolson No. 221.(³) On the following day the German Ch[argé] d'Affaires saw Sir C. Hardinge (see my Tel[egram] No. 222 to Sir A. Nicolson.(⁴) On the 10th inst[ant], I saw the German Amb[assador](⁵) who said that the German G[overnmen]t would recognize the British and Russian claims to " a sort of favoured optional right with regard to Railways roads and Telegraphs in their respective spheres of interest " a far less advantageous proposal, as you will observe, than that of the Chargé d'Affaires, if we and Russia would come to an agreement with her, before obtaining from Persia the conditions which we are now asking—namely that Persia shall not give political or strategical concessions to other Powers.

(¹) [*v. supra*, pp. 442–3, No. 337.]
(²) [*v. supra*, pp. 477–8, No. 360.]
(³) [Not reproduced. For its contents, *v. supra*, p. 477, No. 360, *note* (¹).]
(⁴) [*v. supra*, pp. 480–1, No. 363.]
(⁵) [*v. supra*, pp. 479–80, No. 362.]

He hinted that an agreement of this kind might facilitate an agreement about the Bagdad Railway—but no undertaking was given that the agreement would include a settlement of that question.

I replied that I w[ou]ld not continue the discussion at present but had no wish to close it.

No. 366.

Sir Edward Grey to Sir G. Lowther.

F.O. 15938/100/10/44.   *Foreign Office, May 13, 1910.*
Tel. (No. 103.) Secret.   D. 6 P.M.

Your despatch No. 276.([1])

German interpretation of second paragraph of additional convention of 20th February, 1908,([2]) that debt surpluses have been assigned to Bagdad line in general and not merely to prolongation to El Halif, for which alone second and third series of loan provides, is quite untenable, since paragraph clearly refers to preceding paragraph respecting decision to continue line to El Halif only.

There was therefore every reason for the Turkish Government at any rate to delay their assent to the company's proposal, and, in view of the well-known wishes of His Majesty's Government on the subject, it might have been expected that they would have done so.

You should point this out to Turkish Minister for Foreign Affairs, and also impress on his Excellency consideration that there does not appear to be slightest ground for hope that German Government will voluntarily abandon right to construct line from Bagdad to Gulf without compensation, and that it is immaterial whether they do so or not, for, as we have already shown, there is nothing to prevent Turkey from constructing other lines to Gulf and from giving concessions for such lines.

He has quite misunderstood our proposals if he is under the impression that we are urging him to approach the German Government.

([1]) [*v. supra*, pp. 475–7, No. 359.]
([2]) [Printed in *B.F.S.P.*, Vol. 102, pp. 884–6. The date of the additional convention is June 2, 1908.]

No. 367.

Sir C. Hardinge to Sir Edward Grey.

Private.([1])
My dear Grey,   *Foreign Office, May 13, 1910.*

. . . . .([2]) According to a tel[egram] from Cartwright([3]) the Germans are working up the Austrians to support them in the Persian question. It is curious how pressing the Germans are, it looks as though they want to make trouble at once. My own idea is that we should tell them that we are quite ready to negotiate the Persian question with or concurrently with the Bagdad R[ailwa]y question, and that we should hold out for this. I think from the hint let drop by C[oun]t Metternich to

([1]) [Grey MSS., Vol. 54.]
([2]) [The opening paragraph refers to the arrival of the new Italian Ambassador, the Marquis Imperiali.]
([3]) [*v. supra*, pp. 481–2, No. 364.]

you that we would get it, if we press for it, without any condition about a political agreement which the Germans must see by this time is unrealisable.

I have never seen Metternich so agitated as today. I cannot make out the meaning of it.

Y[ou]rs very sincerely,
CHARLES HARDINGE.

No. 368.

Sir G. Lowther to Sir Edward Grey.

Constantinople, May 16, 1910.

F.O. 17313/100/10/44.
Tel. (No. 90.)

D. 7·10 P.M.
R. 8·30 P.M.

Your telegram No. 103([1]) (Bagdad Railway).

I again to-day repeated to Grand Vizier argument contained in first paragraph of your telegram.

His Highness argues that original convention and additional convention of 1908 read together imply an obligation to find guarantees for continuation of line to Gulf, but prefers not to discuss question here, or to reply to your despatch No. 96, Secret,([2]) until he learns result of Rifaat Pasha's conversations with you on the subject.

He, however, added that he trusted that Germans would be reasonable about waiving their rights over the Gulf section, but if they insisted on their rights to continue to the Gulf the Ottoman Government could bring pressure to bear by stating their inability to find the guarantees.

MINUTES.

Sir G. Lowther apparently only mentioned the first point in our telegram. At least he makes no mention of the argument that Turkey has a right to give others concessions to the Gulf; but as the Grand Vizier does not wish to discuss the questions and Rifaat will soon be in London, it is hardly worth while explaining further.

L. M.

The Grand Vizier appears to be living in a fool's paradise if he imagines that the Germans will surrender a part of their concessions without compensation.

C. H.
E. G.

([1]) [*v. supra*, p. 483, No. 366.]
([2]) [*v. supra*, pp. 466–7, No. 350.]

No. 369.

Sir Edward Grey to Count de Salis.

F.O. 17808/8445/10/34.
(No. 133.) Secret.
Sir,

Foreign Office, May 21, 1910.

I have to inform you that the German Ambassador called on the 13th instant,([1]) and made a statement to Sir C. Hardinge on much the same lines as that which he made to me on the 10th inst[ant], respecting concessions in Persia (see my desp[atch] No. 122 Secret of that day to Sir E. Goschen).([2]) He added that,

([1]) [*cp. G.P.* XXVII, II, pp. 791–2.]
([2]) [*v. supra*, pp. 479–80, No. 362.]

according to information which the German Government had received, the **Persian** Government had partly acceded to the demands of the British and Russian Governments, and the German Gov[ernmen]t feared that, in the event of pressure being applied by the two Governments, Germany would find herself face to face with a *fait accompli* and would be compelled to resort to a protest against a breach of most-favoured-nation treatment by the Persians. He said that I had appeared favourably disposed to the idea of negotiations, and he pressed Sir C. Hardinge for a reply as to whether His Majesty's Government intended to negotiate an agreement with Germany, or to exert pressure on the Persian Government to obtain a declaration in the sense which they desired.

Sir C. Hardinge told His Excellency that the information which he had received from Tehran was, as far as he knew, inexact. His Excellency had seen me a few days before, and I had then told him that I would speak to Sir E. Goschen when he came here for the funeral. In the meantime nothing further had been said to the Persians, the last communication being dated five or six weeks ago, and H[is] M[ajesty's] Gov[ernmen]t were not pressing the Persian Gov[ernmen]t at this moment.

[I am, &c.
E. GREY.]

No. 370.

Translation of Extract from Letter from Dr. Gwinner to Sir E. Cassel.
(Communicated by Sir H. Babington Smith, May 26.)

F.O. 18846/100/10/44.
(Translation.)
(After personal expressions.) *Berlin, May 21, 1910.*

Concerning our Bagdad negotiations, you have not been quite accurately informed, and the expressions of the German Government have not been quite rightly understood.

It is obvious that the German Government will not consider English concurrence in the 4 % increase of the Turkish Customs as an equivalent for my resigning to you the control of the section from Bagdad to the Persian Gulf. You know that we can build the Bagdad railway without the increase of the Customs duties. It is Turkey who has the principal interest in the Customs increase, not Germany. Moreover, you demanded 60% of the capital for the last section, while Hilmi and Djavid had told me expressly, as I repeated to you, that we must not go beyond 50 %, Hilmi meanwhile has fallen and Djavid, at least for the moment, has got into a fright. The concurrence of the Young Turk Government would also not be obtainable at the present time, for the arrangement discussed between us, as Hilmi would have had it. But that is not Germany's fault.

With united forces we should be able gradually to bring the Turks round to our view; if we oppose each other, neither will get much more than he already has; but *we* are, in this case, not only the compliant and friendly party, but also the *beati possidentes*. The German Government has obviously no interest in seeing merely the proclamation of an English victory. In the sense in which we discussed it, a friendly co-operation ought of course to be announced simultaneously, and consequently, there should be a reciprocal granting of minor participations in the irrigation business and similar matters. It is obvious that Germany cannot concur in an English monopoly of the navigation of the Euphrates and Tigris. If, however, without a monopoly, you wish to set up half a dozen English Navigation Companies, for the development of Mesopotamia, I shall be delighted. Finally, it can hardly be expected that one should come to an understanding in an affair, while one finds oneself exposed to the danger of being opposed and maligned on that very point and everywhere else.

For the rest, I take note that you formally resume your liberty. Practically this makes very little difference in the facts. That the National Bank of Turkey is jointly interested in, and co-operate with the endeavours of Mr. Ornstein and his associates was stated by Sir H. Babington Smith himself to Baron von Marschall.

Accordingly I say with Shakespeare,

> " Fight valiantly,
> But eat and drink as friends."

In this spirit I greet you,
As yours always obediently,

No. 371.

Count de Salis to Sir Edward Grey.

F.O. 19042/8445/10/34A.
(No. 151.)   *Berlin,* D. *May* 24, 1910.
Sir,   R. *May* 30, 1910.

Baron von Schoen told me this evening that he was sending instructions to Count Metternich not to approach you further, for the present, on the subject of Persia. The German Government felt that it was not the moment to do so, while in view of the recent explanations given to them on the subject the question had lost much of its acute character. There had been a misunderstanding about it. He had, as I was no doubt aware, seen Monsieur Iswolsky, and had spoken to him about the manner in which, as they considered, German rights were being menaced. Monsieur Iswolsky had retorted by accusing them of coming into Persia with offers of loans and demands for concessions, to the detriment of the position and interests which Russia had acquired in that country. He had of course rejoined that this was not the case. Though they were not bound by any agreement or obligation to do so, they had expressly refrained from countenancing any proceedings of the kind. He would give his word of honour to that effect. The misunderstanding had thus been cleared up.

Moreover the German Government had now learnt that the two Powers were proposing to the Powers an "exchange of views" with the Persians before the grant of concessions which might injure British or Russian political interests. This was quite different from the original idea that the "permission" of the two Powers was to be required before any concessions were examined. The German Government had been very sensitive on this point but the first-mentioned formula seemed to be in accordance more or less with a private suggestion he had made for the two Powers to act discreetly (agir discrètement) but not to make a parade of anything (de ne rien afficher). Meanwhile no actual difficulty in practice had arisen but, as I must know, their Press was extremely susceptible and ready to raise an outcry that German interests were in danger. I remarked on this that it was to be noted that some organs, by no means backward in the defence of German rights, had sounded a distinct note of moderation.([1]) Baron von Schoen replied that this was the case; they had been accused in some quarters of trying to make a second Morocco affair out of the business. This was the last thing in the world they wished to do.

Baron von Schoen spoke at some length, more than once repeating himself, especially in insisting that there had been a misunderstanding (malentendu). But I think that the foregoing is an accurate summary of the purport of his remarks.

([1]) [Marginal comment by Sir E. Crowe : " Notably the official Pan-German organ the Alldeutsche Blätter.' E. A. C."]

he impression left on me from the very first was that of a carefully prepared, if
ot very convincing explanation of a change of front with regard to the recent
ttitude of the German Government relating to Persia. As regards the causes which
ıay have contributed to dictate this action, I can only venture so far to
ıggest one or two ideas. Monsieur Jules Cambon in the course of conversation
eemed to be struck with the idea that the Emperor's visit to London and his
eception there by The King and by the public had rendered His Majesty more
esirous of avoiding causes of friction. Perhaps the lukewarm attitude of Austria
ıight furnish a more plausible explanation—a view which receives some confirmation
om the information respecting Count Aehrenthal's ideas which you were good
ıough to communicate to me on the 21st instant. A further article by Count
.eventlow in the "Tageszeitung" urges that it must be borne in mind that should
ιussia be hard pressed as regards her legitimate aspirations in Northern Persia,
ıe must in self-defence end by declaring some sort of protectorate. Germany
ould not prevent her from doing so, though she would of course find that the
ıange would be by no means to her advantage. A story reached me privately
ıat this consideration has been urged upon the German Government by Count
.ehrenthal himself who was not however the author of the suggestion which was
ıpposed to form part of what a Pan-German newspaper recently called "English
ıtrigues viâ Vienna." In any case there have been, as I have ventured to report
efore, marked traces of a disinclination on the part of the non-inspired press to
ee matters develop into a "second Morocco affair." On the other hand it is
vident that anything like a promise from the British Government to guarantee
articipation in the supply of railway material would be hailed by more than one
ectión of the German press as an important diplomatic triumph and would increase
ıe prestige of the Chancellor in quarters where such a result would at the present
ıoment be welcome to him. The National Liberal party which represent to a
reat extent the manufacturers who would directly benefit by any such arrangement,
re just at the present moment in a fairly strong position in Prussia. The fate of
ıe electoral reform' law introduced by the Government is in their hands, for unless
certain number of them can be induced to support the very Conservative form
ñich has been given to this measure, it must inevitably be lost and the struggle
n the subject must be recommenced afresh next session in the less favourable
onditions which would arise from the discredit of failure. It may be further
emarked that the Centre party, at present not on the most cordial terms with
Ierr von Bethmann-Hollweg, who is in some need of their goodwill, derives some
f its influence in Westphalia from the iron industry. After the recent trouble with
ıe Mannesmanns and their supporters, the Imperial Foreign Office may be expected
ɔ be doubly anxious to avoid an accusation of indifference to German commercial
ıterests. In all the circumstances therefore it would seem possible that, although
ıey have interrupted discussions with His Majesty's Government for the moment,
ıe German Government may be quite ready to return to the subject later if the
ıoment is found to be favourable and especially if the progress of separate
.egotiations with Russia should encourage them to do so.

I have, &c.
J. DE SALIS.

No. 372.

Count de Salis to Sir Edward Grey.

'.O. 18921/18921/10/18.

No. 152.)   Berlin, D. *May* 26, 1910.
                                             R. *May* 28, 1910.
ıir,

I have the honour to report that the "Norddeutsche Allgemeine Zeitung" of
ɔ-day's date contains the following communiqué respecting a conversation held in

London between His Majesty the German Emperor and the French Minister fc Foreign Affairs.

"The foreign press is occupying itself with a report of the 'Matin according to which the Emperor in a conversation with M. Pichon in Londo is alleged to have spoken of the foundation of an European Confederation. is correct that His Majesty expressed to the French Minister his confidenc in the maintenance of the peace of Europe and his firm intention of doing a in his power to contribute thereto. The idea of forming an Europea confederation of States was not a subject of the conversation and is far fror His Majesty's thoughts."

Reference is also made to the conversation between the German Emperor an M. Pichon in an apparently inspired communication from the Berlin corresponder of the "Kölnische Zeitung." The writer observes that the friendly language hel by M. Pichon in talking of his meeting with the Emperor had not remaine unnoticed at Berlin. Referring then to certain rumours from Paris regarding th alleged conclusion of a Secret Agreement between France and Germany th "Kölnische" denies the existence of any such arrangement between the tw Governments. It says that latterly negotiations have only been in progress wit regard to the Morocco Mining Laws and Morocco Loans. The Loan question ha now been settled and there were grounds for hoping that a satisfactory compromis would soon be arrived at about the Mining Laws. In addition to these two question negotiations had been conducted in Paris between private French and German group with the object of securing concerted action on the Cameroon frontier on the par of French and German parties interested.

The writer says that, while the successful conclusion of these negotiations woul naturally be hailed with much satisfaction, such an issue could scarcely be described unless an unusually large magnifying glass were used, as a highly important politica Agreement.

"It is enough for us," he concludes, "that Franco-German relations have ever without a secret Agreement, taken an eminently satisfactory form. This fact ha an importance greater than that of all commentaries more or less to the point."

I have, &c.

J. DE SALIS.

No. 373.

Sir E. Goschen to Sir Edward Grey.

F.O. 19040/168/10/18.
(No. 149A.) Confidential. *Berlin, D. May 28, 1910.*
Sir, R. *May 30, 1910.*

I have the honour to forward, herewith, a despatch, as marked in the margin which I have received from Captain H. L. Heath, Naval Attaché to this Embassy relating to a conversation with His Majesty, the Emperor, at Potsdam, on feelin towards Germany in England and arrangements for the Kiel Regatta.

I have, &c.

W. E. GOSCHEN.

Enclosure in No. 373.

Sir,

I have the honour to report that in accordance with instructions I proceede to Potsdam on the 16th instant and presented a copy of the Navy List t His Majesty the Emperor.

His Majesty remarked on the loss sustained "not only by England but by th whole world" by the death of His Majesty King Edward VII.

The Emperor then dealt with Naval questions. His Majesty gave it as his opinion that the so-called panic in England was dying down. His Majesty referred again to "certain speeches and newspaper articles" published in the English press and magazines which had caused much irritation to the German people "to say nothing of my own personal feelings." His Majesty then somewhat altered his tone and said "Now I hear that several English Naval Officers are thinking of visiting Kiel during the regatta week. I wish you to represent to the proper authorities that if any English Naval Officer wishes to visit any of the ships of my Fleet the following are the steps to be taken:—

1. The name and rank of all such officers must be notified by the British Naval Attaché to the Commander-in-Chief of the Kiel Station.

2. The Commander-in-Chief at Kiel will submit the names for my approval.

3. British Naval Officers whose names are approved will be notified the time at which their visit is to be made. The visitors must wear the uniform of their rank."

I have, etc.,
H. L. HEATH,
Captain and Naval Attaché.

No. 374.

Sir E. Goschen to Sir C. Hardinge.

F.O. 21715/167/10/18.
Private.
My dear Hardinge,   *Berlin, May 28, 1910.*

I have an idea that you are returning to the F[oreign] O[ffice] on Monday so I am going to write you one line as I have seen no-one except Pansa since I came back on Thursday evening. Pansa told me he had just seen Stemrich, who had appeared rather upset about Persian matters, because, said Stemrich, Isvolsky had stated that the communication to the Persian Gov[ernmen]t(¹) would be put in such a form as to require no answer, whereas Quadt had reported that the Russian Minister at Tehran had informed or was going to inform the Persian Gov[ernmen]t that an answer would be required. This of course did not suit the German book. Pansa begged me to regard this information as confidential.

I had a very nice audience with the King. H[is] M[ajesty] told me that the Emperor had been exceedingly nice, most thoughtful and tactful in every way. He added that he should do all he could to keep the "family" relations on the good level on which they had now started. As the Emperor spoke to me in equally high terms of the King it is to be hoped that things will continue to work smoothly between the two monarchs and cousins. The King also told me that he had not talked any politics with the Emperor.

I saw Metternich the day I left and found him fairly reasonable. But I had to talk to him like a father when he told me that he had heard privately that Mr. McKenna's rejection of the assurances given by the Imperial Gov[ernmen]t with regard to naval cons[t]ruction was due to erroneous information supplied by Captain Heath. I told him that both Prince Henry and other high German naval officers had spoken to me in the highest terms of Heath and had praised the tactful and conscientious manner in which he performed his duties. I added that Heath was extremely careful in his reports and at all events tried to check any information he received by consulting the German Admiralty. If he had ever sent erroneous information which I very much doubted it was the fault of the Admiralty officials who often refused to give him any information whatever either positive or negative.

(¹) [*v. infra*, p. 490, No. 375, *note* (¹).]

If he, Metternich, could use his influence to get Tirpitz to consent to information being given to the Naval Attaché it would be a great point gained as there would be any amount of reciprocity on our side and the atmosphere of suspicion would be gradually removed.

B[ethmann]-Hollweg has had a nasty shock over the Prussian electoral reforms.

Yours ever,

W. E. GOSCHEN.

No. 375.

Sir Edward Grey to Sir E. Goschen.

F.O.19706/100/10/44.
(No. 148.)   Secret.

Sir,

Foreign Office, May 31, 1910.

Count Metternich came to inform me to-day that he was going to Berlin for some days, and after some general conversation he asked me whether I had anything to say to him before he went upon the subjects which had recently been under discussion between ourselves and Germany.

I replied that I had nothing new to tell him about Persia. Within the last ten days we had made at Tehran the communication which, as I had previously told him, contained the least that we could say.(¹) I repeated the substance of it, and added that as we had not asked for a reply pledging the Persian Government to give us any monopoly the communication was not open to the objection which the German Government had apprehended.

Count Metternich said that his Government had received the same information from M. Iswolsky; but, in order to prevent any misunderstanding arising from the reports which they received from the German Minister at Tehran, who got what information he could, Count Metternich would like to be quite sure of the dates. He understood that about a month ago we had made a written communication asking for a reply, and he seemed in doubt as to whether I was now referring to a written or a verbal communication.

I informed him that the first communication was a written one on April 7th. The Persian Government had replied satisfactorily to that on the two financial points, but had asked for an explanation of what exactly we meant with regard to concessions. We had now, within the last ten days, given this explanation in a written communication which required no reply.

Count Metternich then said that he understood I had told you my views on the subjects of your conversations with the German Chancellor, and he asked whether I had written to you.

I answered that I had not given you any written communication to make, but I had told you in a letter what my views were. As Count Metternich was anxious to know them, I said that I had told you how impossible it would be for me to make an arrangement about Persian railways unless an arrangement with regard to the Bagdad Railway were included.

Count Metternich argued that the *quid pro quo* for a share in Persian railways would be the renunciation by Germany of her right to apply for railway concessions

---

(¹) [This is the note of May 20. It was in answer to the Persian reply (dated May 7) to the previous joint note of April 7 (*v. supra*, p. 452, No. 343, *note* (²)). The Persian Government had asked for an explanation of the words '' concessions qui puissent porter atteinte à leurs intérêts politiques ou stratégiques en Perse.'' The joint note of May 20, proposed that an exchange of views should take place between Persia and the two Powers, before any concessions were granted to other foreign Powers with respect to communications, telegraphs or ports. The Persian reply of May 7 and the Anglo-Russian joint note of May 20 are in F.O. 20032/8172/10/34.]

in the part of Persia in which we were interested. He could not see why the Bagdad Railway should be brought into the discussion, or why we should expect participation in it without giving some *quid pro quo*.

I observed that financial assistance and the 4 % increase of the Turkish Customs Dues would be a *quid pro quo*. I also reminded Count Metternich that on the occasion of the German Emperor's visit it had not seemed unreasonable to the Germans, in the conversations which then took place, that we should have participation in the southern end of the Bagdad Railway, "a gate" as the Emperor had called it,(²) without any talk of a *quid pro quo* other than financial assistance. Even the 4 % increase of the Turkish Customs, which was directly or indirectly to provide money for the Bagdad Railway, was not mooted then.

Count Metternich said that he would like me to know what the attitude of the late Conservative Government had been with regard to the Bagdad Railway, as they were certainly not less Imperialist than the present Government. Lord Lansdowne had expressed himself favourable, in the interests of general commercial development, to the making of the Bagdad Railway by Germany. All he had stipulated was that an arrangement should be made with Great Britain when a port was actually selected on the Persian Gulf, as it would prejudice our interests if a fortified harbour were constructed there. No mention had been made of British control of the line from Bagdad to the Gulf: a most valuable part of the Railway. Since the Emperor's visit two years ago, more political feeling had been aroused about the Railway, and this had made things more difficult.

I told Count Metternich that, early this year, Herr Gwinner and Sir Ernest Cassel had been in negotiation, and I had thought that the financiers would probably be able to come to some arrangement; but progress had been blocked by political considerations.

Count Metternich did not dispute this, but rejoined that it was over here that the question had been made a political one.

I observed that what I meant was that the negotiations between the financiers had been blocked by political considerations in Germany.

Count Metternich explained that he meant that the political feeling in Germany had been aroused by the political considerations which had been urged here.

I am, etc.
E. GREY.

(²) [This phrase was used by the Emperor and by Herr von Schoen during the visit to Windsor of 1907, *v. supra*, p. 96, No. 63, and p. 98, No. 64.]

No. 376.

Sir Edward Grey to Sir H. Babington Smith.

F.O. 18846/100/10/44.
Confidential.

Dear Sir Henry Babington Smith :—   *Foreign Office, May 31, 1910.*

In order to avoid all ambiguity I think it may be as well that I should put on paper my views with regard to British participation in the Bagdad R[ai]l[wa]y, in the light of Dr. Gwinner's letter of May 21st to Sir E. Cassel.(¹)

I see no objection to your negotiating with Herr Gwinner on the basis of that letter: but I think that the British share should be 55 %, and that we should construct the harbour at Koweit and have a large share in its subsequent control.

We should decidedly prefer that the "Indian" system should be substituted for the existing arrangement of kilometric guarantees; we believe that the Turkish Gov[ernmen]t could hardly object to such a modification, but if they definitely express a preference for the 1903 arrangement we should, though reluctantly, agree

(¹) [*v. supra*, pp. 485–6, No. 370.]

to it. You are however fully aware of the drawback of the existing arrangement for the "working expenses" guarantee, viz., that it militates against the development of traffic, and for this reason it should if possible be modified.

It would be well for you to make sure that any proposals put forward by Herr Gwinner have the approval of the German Gov[ernmen]t; and you must clearly understand that we can approve no agreement definitely without consultation with the French and Russian Gov[ernmen]ts.

[I am, &c.]
E. G[REY].

No. 377.

Sir Edward Grey to Sir G. Lowther.

F.O. 18636/100/10/44.
(No. 155.)
Sir,   *Foreign Office, June 6, 1910.*

On the 19th May the Ottoman M[inister for] F[oreign] A[ffairs] called upon me and had a long conversation with Sir C. Hardinge and myself in regard to the Bagdad Railway.

Rifaat Pasha introduced the subject by referring to the instructions contained in my despatch No. 107 of April 20th([1]); and I explained to H[is] E[xcellency] that it would be impossible for H[is] M[ajesty's] Government] to agree to the proposed increase of the Turkish customs duties from 11 % to 15 %, and that I should even be reproached if I were to consent to the prolongation of the existing 3 % increase after 1914, if Turkish revenues were to be pledged for the construction of the Bagdad Railway, the increases in the customs duties being thus used, either directly or indirectly, to create a monopoly which would destroy that part of British trade which had so long been established in Mesopotamia.

H[is] E[xcellency] pointed out the difficulty which Turkey would have in granting a concession for any railway which would become a rival of part of the Bagdad Railway, and so make heavier the burden of kilometric guarantees to which Turkey was pledged in connection with that railway; the greater the competition which the Bagdad Railway had to meet, the greater the burden would be.

Finally, Rifaat Pasha suggested that Turkey might induce Germany to give up the Bagdad–Gulf sections of the concession, and let Turkey make that part of the line herself, and he enquired whether such a solution would satisfy H[is] M[ajesty's] G[overnment].

I replied that it would be a necessary condition that if Turkey in making the railway employed foreign capital or material a proportion of say 60 % should be British; also, if a foreign contractor were employed, he should be British.([2]) Sir C. Hardinge and I expressed doubts as to whether Germany would be willing to agree to an arrangement of this sort, but Rifaat Pasha seemed hopeful and was anxious to try.

([1]) [*v. supra*, pp. 468–72, No. 352.]

([2]) [The following notes were written against this sentence in the margin, though apparently their substance was not included in the final despatch:

I hope we should also insist on a British Manager if foreign officials were employed, and also on non-differential rates. A. P.

The first ought to be as a condition of providing the capital and the second we must also stipulate for: it cannot be refused. We shall consult the Board of Trade on the subject of rates generally if the question becomes a practical one. There ought I should think to be some arrangement as to rates with the main Bagdad R[ailwa]y. E. G.]

We explained to H[is] E[xcellency] that we had thought it very unfortunate that Turkish revenues should have been pledged for four sections of the Bagdad R[ai]l[wa]y just before the end of the old régime; but we had not made this a fatal objection to an increase of the customs, because the new régime could not be held responsible for it; now, however, when the new régime was endeavouring to find revenues and to pledge them for four additional sections the situation with regard to the 4 % increase of the customs duties would become intolerable unless some arrangement satisfactory to H[is] M[ajesty's] G[overnment] and British interests could be made.

I have to instruct Y[our] E[xcellency] to press the Ottoman M[inister for] F[oreign] A[ffairs] for a written reply to my despatch of April 20th, setting forth his reasons for being unable to grant a concession for a railway along the Tigris Valley, and what his counter-suggestion is, as stated in conversation with me already.

I may add, for Y[our] E[xcellency]'s information, that Rifaat Pasha had an interview with Mr. Mallet on May 23rd, when H[is] E[xcellency] said that the Ottoman Gov.[ernmen]t were not prepared to "froisser" the Germans by giving a concession to a British company—an argument which is not very convincing—and that if such a concession were granted the German Gov[ernmen]t on their part would certainly refuse their consent to the proposed 4 % customs increase. Furthermore, H[is] E[xcellency] contended that if they gave a concession to a British Company in return for British assent to the 4% increase, they would likewise have to give a concession in return for French consent, but that the Ottoman Gov[ernmen]t did not intend to give a concession for the Homs–Bagdad R[ai]l[way], which the French Gov[ernmen]t desired, since such a line would compete with the Bagdad R[ai]l[way], and the burden of the financial guarantee which was an obligation upon the Ottoman Gov[ernmen]t in respect of the latter undertaking would be of longer duration in consequence of such competition.

[I am, &c.]
E. G[REY].

No. 378.

Sir G. Lowther to Sir Edward Grey.

F.O. 22859/100/10/44.

No. 392.)   *Therapia,* D. *June* 20, 1910.
                                            R. *June* 27, 1910.
Sir,

In obedience to the instructions contained in your despatch secret of the 7th Instant No. 155([1]) in regard to the Bagdad Railway, I to-day told Rifaat Pasha that you were expecting a reply to your despatch of the 20th of April([2]) translation of which I had read to him and left with him on the 3rd of May last.

I added that I had understood from the conversation I then had with him and the Grand Vizier that he would have some more satisfactory reply to give you than that given to me on that occasion, as he had undertaken to discuss the matter with the Grand Vizier and lay certain proposals before you. His Excellency however merely repeated what he had said to you as recorded in your despatch No. 155 secret of the 6th Instant and added that as Baron Marschall had left on leave of absence he had had no opportunity of speaking to him and he did not know whether the Chargé d'Affaires would be authorised to discuss the matter with him. In the contrary case he would instruct the Turkish Ambassador in Berlin to induce the

([1]) [*v.* immediately preceding document.]
([2]) [*v. supra,* pp. 468–72, No. 352.]

German Government to give up the Bagdad–Gulf section of th; Concession an
let Turkey make part of the line herself, and in spite of the doubts expressed by yo
as to the success of the negotiations, he was still sanguine.

Rifaat Pasha eventually promised to reply in the same manner in which ou
communication had been made—namely in a despatch to be addressed to Tewfi
Pasha—copy of which would be left with you.

I may add that Rifaat Pasha made no allusion to the fact that they were nc
prepared to *froisser* the Germans by giving a concession to a British Company, bu
he did say that they would be confronted with great difficulties if they began
bargaining process over the 4 % Customs increase, as once it was known that
concession was to be made to us, the French would demand another and other Power
would follow suit.

I have, &c.
GERARD LOWTHER.

No. 379.

Sir E. Goschen to Sir Edward Grey.

F.O. 24880/24880/10/18.
(No. 194.) Confidential.
Sir,

Berlin, D. *July 3, 1910.*
R. *July 11, 1910.*

I have the honour to report that the Imperial Chancellor left Berlin yesterda
for his summer holiday. At his request I called upon him before his departur
and had a short conversation with him on general topics. His Excellency sai
that, with the exception of the ever recurring Cretan Question, there appeared t
be a general lull in European Politics. Monsieur Isvolsky, who when passin
through Berlin had given it to be understood that he would shortly send an answe
to the German Persian Railway Proposals of four years ago, had made no sign, nc
had His Majesty's Government, he added with a smile, shown any particula
anxiety to continue the conversation with Germany on Persian affairs. This wa
all His Excellency said respecting Foreign Politics . . . .([1])

The Chancellor then spoke of Herr von Kiderlen Waechter and expressed th
hope that I would have the same pleasant relations with him as I had had wit.
Herr von Schoen. I said that I should miss the latter very much as we wer
friends and colleagues of many years' standing. I had always found him ver
friendly and well disposed towards my country and I hoped that Herr von Kiderle
entertained the same sentiments. The Chancellor replied that Herr von Kiderle
had somehow or other got the reputation of being somewhat brusque an
overbearing in his manner. He did not think that this reputation was deserve
and he was sure that I would find him very pleasant to deal with. " As for hi
sentiments" His Excellency added, "it is I who direct the Foreign Affairs of th
Empire, and as long as I hold my present office those under my orders will hav
to adapt their sentiments to mine."

The Chancellor said this very stiffly and his words were almost identical wit
those which he had used to my French Colleague a few days before. Personally
think that the language held by the Press in writing upon Herr von Kiderle
Waechter's appointment has rather got upon His Excellency's nerves. There i
scarcely a newspaper which does not allude to the probability of a more active polic
as soon as the conduct of affairs comes into Herr von Kiderlen's capable an
energetic hands, and though some of them speak of the Emperor's controllin;
influence, the Chancellor seems to be entirely left out of their calculations.

([1]) [The part omitted deals with German internal affairs and is unimportant.]

The Berliner Tageblatt at the conclusion of an article respecting the appointment writes as follows :—

" How far Herr von Kiderlen Waechter will succeed in making his mark is very doubtful. More than ever the deciding word in Imperial affairs rests with the Emperor. The Debates of November 1908 have remained a mere episode. Personal Régime still holds the field and is to-day more in evidence than ever."

The Chancellor himself called my attention, somewhat pointedly, to the "excellence of Herr von Kiderlen's Press."

I have, &c.
W. E. GOSCHEN.

No. 380.

Sir F. Cartwright to Sir Edward Grey.

F.O. 25932/167/10/18.
(No. 113.)   Vienna, D. *July* 16, 1910.
Sir,   R. *July* 18, 1910.

I have the honour to report that the speech made by Mr. Asquith on July 14th[1] in connection with the Naval Estimates has aroused great interest here, and forms the subject of leading articles in all this morning's newspapers.

The tone of these articles is on the whole friendly, and a very general appreciation is shown of that portion of the speech in which the Prime Minister refers to the zenith of naval expenditure as being in sight : while his intimation that His Majesty's Government have not given up hopes of ultimately arriving at some arrangement with Germany has been received with particular interest. The friendly tone of Mr. Asquith's speech towards Germany is hailed with great satisfaction as indicating the amelioration in the relations between the two countries which has recently taken place.

The semi-official "Fremden-Blatt" declares that Mr. Asquith's "masterly speech" will not be misunderstood, even though he appears to adopt the Triple Alliance in lieu of the Two Power standard. The necessity for England of a considerable reserve of power is fully admitted, as is the right of every State to be strong enough to have no reasons for fear. Mr. Asquith's statement that Germany also must be permitted to take the measures which she considers necessary for this end is, says the "Fremden-Blatt," the most valuable part of the Prime Minister's speech. His declaration that national security must precede the introduction of social reforms deserves special emphasis in Austria-Hungary . . . .[2]

I have, &c.
FAIRFAX L. CARTWRIGHT.

[1] [*v. Parl. Deb..* 5th *Ser.*, House of Commons, Vol. 19, pp. 636–45.]
[2] [The concluding paragraphs of this despatch summarise various articles in the Press.]

No. 381.

Sir Edward Grey to Sir E. Goschen.

F.O. 25383/8445/10/34.
(No. 181.)   Confidential.
Sir,   *Foreign Office, July 18, 1910.*

Herr von Stumm, lately Councillor of the German Embassy in London and now an official of the Ministry of F[oreign] A[ffairs] at Berlin, paid recently a short visit to this country.

In the course of his stay in London he arranged to call on Mr. Parker, of this Office, at his private house and spoke to him of the relations between Great Britain and Germany.

Herr von Stumm criticised with considerable warmth the attitude of H[is] M[ajesty's] G[overnment] towards the German Gov[ernmen]t and, amongst many other expressions of dissatisfaction, complained of their delay in replying to the recent memorandum of the German Chancellor(¹) suggesting a method of settling the questions at issue between the two countries.

In the light of a reperusal of my recent despatches on this subject, more especially of my desp[atch] to Y[our] E[xcellency] No. 148 of May 31(²) and after reading your desp[atch] No. 194 conf[idential] of July 3rd(³) containing an account of your recent interview with Herr von Bethmann-Hollweg, I feel that too much importance need not be attached to Herr von Stumm's complaint.

Only six weeks have elapsed since my interview with the German Ambassador here, recorded in my desp[atch] No. 148 of May 31, and in the circumstances there appears to me to be no pressing need for a reply, while the policy of not moving further till the Russian Gov[ernmen]t have given their long-promised answer respecting a Russo-German understanding with regard to Persian affairs offers certain advantages.

As Y[our] E[xcellency] is aware, H[is] M[ajesty's] G[overnment] are at this moment in communication with the Russian Gov[ernmen]t for the settlement of the question whether the negotiations between the two Powers and Germany should be conducted jointly or only simultaneously.

[I am, &c.
E. GREY.]

(¹) [*v. supra*, pp. 458–9, No. 344, *encl.*]
(²) [*v. supra*, pp. 490–1, No. 375.]
(³) [*v. supra*, pp. 494–5, No. 379.]

No. 382.

Sir Edward Grey to Sir E. Goschen.(¹)

F.O. 26336/167/10/18.
(No. 185.)
Sir,   *Foreign Office, July 18, 1910.*

Count Metternich informed me to-day that the German Chancellor had expressed his appreciation of the friendly language used by the Prime Minister in his speech last week on the Navy Estimates, and his pleasure at seeing the good effect which this had produced in Germany. The Chancellor was, however, rather anxious as to whether some expressions used by the Prime Minister might not have put public opinion on the track of the negotiations which had taken place last year. What the Prime Minister had said might be taken to mean that we had made proposals to the German Government about naval armaments, to which they had

(¹) [For Count Metternich's report, *v. G.P.* XXVIII, pp. 341–2.]

pposed a *non possumus*. Such an impression would be commented upon by Radical newspapers in Germany; indeed, it was already being commented upon. t did not correspond with the actual facts of the case, and the Chancellor might e obliged to take some exception to it. He would regret this, especially as he ordially appreciated the friendly language which the Prime Minister had used.

I said that I was sure that what the Prime Minister had had in view was he desire of the German Government that no impression should be given which night lead German public opinion to suppose that they had at any time contemplated ampering with, or modifying, their Naval Law. It had been impressed upon us hat this was a thing which should be avoided, in the interest of the German Gov[ernmen]t, and I had no doubt that the Prime Minister's language was inspired by his desire to avoid doing anything which could possibly cause difficulties for the German Government with that section of their own public opinion which was attached to the Naval Law.

Count Metternich, while appreciating this, observed that in the course of the negotiations last year it had been made clear that some alleviation might be produced by reducing the rate of naval construction without altering the Naval Law.

I said that I had recently been looking through the collection of papers on the subject, and as a matter of fact I had sent them to the Prime Minister, though not till after the Naval Debate was over. The impression made upon me by re-reading the papers was that we had been given to understand that German opinion this year was stiffer than ever against any alteration of the Naval Law, and that the question of Persia had been placed in the forefront.

Count Metternich while admitting this about Persia doubted whether anything had been said by the German Government to show that they were less disposed to come to a naval arrangement. He thought I must have derived the impression from reports which I had received from Berlin.

I told him that, in any case, I had been referring to the papers again, because I thought it desirable that the whole situation should be reviewed by the Government before we were all separated for the summer Recess of Parliament, and I would examine the papers once more.

[I am, &c.]
E. G[REY]

No. 383.

Sir H. Babington Smith to Sir Edward Grey.

F.O. 26703/100/10/44.　　　　　　　　　　　*Constantinople,* D. *July* 19, 1910.
Dear Sir Edward Grey,　　　　　　　　　　　　　R. *July* 23, 1910.

I must apologise for my delay in thanking you for your letter of the 31st May.(¹) I received it on my return to Constantinople; but since then I have been laid up with an attack of fever, and have not been able to resume work until a few days ago.

Sir Ernest Cassel replied to Dr. Gwinner on June 3rd in the sense suggested in the course of our conversation at the Foreign Office. I understand that Sir Charles Hardinge saw the letter before it was sent, and approved of its terms. Since then I have not heard anything further from Dr. Gwinner, nor, so far as I am aware, has Sir Ernest Cassel.

As regards the extent of the British share to be claimed in any future negociations, I may mention that when the question was raised before, Dr. Gwinner explicitly stated that there would be no objection on the part of the Bagdad Company to a preponderant British share but he anticipated objection on the part of the

(¹) [*v. supra*, pp. 491–2, No. 376.]

Turks. In their present frame of mind I think it is likely that their objections would be difficult to overcome; and I venture to suggest that, if this should prove to be the case, the point after all is not an essential one. A 50 % interest in one hand would, I believe, as a matter of fact, give absolute control, as against 50 % divided among several interests. It would, of course, be essential that the 50 % should remain intact; but I do not think there would be difficulty in devising arrangements to secure this.

As regards Ports, Article 23 of the original concession gives the concessionnaires the right of constructing and managing ports at Bagdad, Basra and the terminus of the Koweit section. Whatever arrangements are agreed upon as regards the line south of Bagdad would no doubt apply also to the ports of Basra and Koweit. The point is not mentioned in Dr. Gwinner's memorandum of December 15th,(²) and we will bear it in mind in any future negociations.

With reference to the last paragraph of your letter, may not an inconvenient situation arise if the conditions on which the French and Russian Governments will agree to an arrangement are not ascertained till after the arrangement has been negociated? If their conditions were ascertained beforehand, they could be kept in view in the course of the negociations.

Believe me,
Yours very truly,
H. BABINGTON SMITH.

MINUTE.

I doubt if the public would be satisfied with a 50% participation.

C. H.
E. G.

(²) [v. supra, pp. 410–1, No. 309, encl.]

No. 384.

Sir Edward Grey to Sir G. Lowther.

F.O. 27274/100/10/44.
(No. 215.) Secret.

Sir, *Foreign Office, July 26, 1910.*

The Turkish Ambassador and Djavid Bey had some conversation with Sir Charles Hardinge and me to-day, in the course of which we explained how impossible it was for us to grant the 4 % increase of Customs Dues without some arrangement about the Bagdad Railway.

In any case, British commerce would object to the increase of the Duties, but I should be prepared to defend the increase if I could prove that the additional revenue would be for the good of the Turkish Government, and would not be applied to purposes which would injure us. If, however, the additional · revenue was devoted, directly or indirectly, to the Bagdad Railway, it would not help the Turkish Government in securing good administration, and it would assist in the creation of a German monopoly of means of transport which would exclude our trade from Mesopotamia. Trade there always had a tendency to fall into the hands which controlled the means of communication. Some of these means had for a long time been in British hands, and almost for centuries we had had considerable trade interests in Mesopotamia. If these interests were now to be undermined and eventually replaced by a foreign monopoly, created as a result of our having agreed to the increase of the Turkish Customs Duties, it was too much to expect that we should agree to the increase.

Djavid Bey protested that the 3 % increase of Dues, agreed to two years ago, had not injured trade. He argued that therefore the 4 % increase would not do so either. He went on to say, however, that no decision had yet been taken as to the allocation of revenues for the Bagdad Railway beyond El Halif; the Germans would be asked to renounce their right to claim the proceeds of the 4 % increase during the next five or six years, and to give up part of the Concession beyond Bagdad; this part of the Railway could then be made by the Turks themselves.

It was arranged that Djavid Bey should further discuss the details of the Railway with Mr. Parker.

Djavid Bey also explained to us the desire of the Turkish Government to establish a petroleum monopoly and to impose a "patent tax" on foreigners trading in Turkey.

We promised to examine these questions.

I am, &c.
E. G[REY].

No. 385.

Sir Edward Grey to Mr. Carnegie.

F.O. 27647/167/10/18.
(No. 358.)

Sir,   *Foreign Office, July 27, 1910.*

In conversation with me to-day, M. Cambon referred to the speech made by the Prime Minister on the Naval Estimates the other day.([1]) M. Cambon wished to know whether I could tell him exactly what was meant by the allusion which had been made during the Debate to German engagements respecting naval construction.

I said that there were no engagements on the part of the German Government in the sense of a binding undertaking. The allusion had been to the declaration of intention on the part of that Government, and the statement of what was required by their naval programme, which had been given to me by Count Metternich at the beginning of 1909.([2]) It had been explained at the time that these were the intentions of the German Government, but that they were not a binding undertaking, and that the German Government were under no obligation not to change their minds. I had read out this communication to the House of Commons in March 1909.([3]) There had been no other German engagements, and it was to this that the Prime Minister referred in his speech the other day.

[I am, &c.]
E. G[REY].

([1]) [*v. Parl. Deb.*, *5th Ser.*, House of Commons, Vol. 19, pp. 636–45.]
([2]) [Apparently this refers to Sir Edward Grey's conversation with Count Metternich of March 10, 1909, *v. supra*, pp. 241–2, No. 154.]
([3]) [*v. Parl. Deb.*, *5th Ser.*, House of Commons, Vol. 3, pp. 61–2.]

No. 386.

Sir E. Goschen to Sir Edward Grey.

F.O. 27754/167/10/18.
(No. 210.)   *Berlin, D. July 29, 1910.*
                                                        R. *August 2*, 1910.

Sir,

The comparison of the British and German Naval Armaments is still occupying public attention in Germany to the exclusion of nearly every other topic except the reported desire of Turkey to join the Triple Alliance and the meeting between Count Aehrenthal and Herr von Kiderlen Waechter at Marienbad. Some interest is also being attached to the struggle between the party in favour of a naval understanding with Great Britain and the Pan-German party over the body, so to speak, of Admiral Tirpitz.

Heated discussions between the respective Presses of Germany and the United Kingdom never fail to arise whenever naval matters come up for discussion in Parliament. The present occasion has been no exception to this rule, the only difference being that the subject of naval armaments has become, or is rapidly becoming, a German party question, and that now the German newspapers are not concentrating their broadside upon Great Britain but are also firing on each other. This is to a certain extent a gain, but I venture to think that it would be a still greater gain if both countries were allowed to build the ships they require without violent polemics in the Press every time a keel is laid down or the Naval estimates of either country come up for discussion. There is now evidently a growing desire in German liberal circles for a diminution of Naval expenditure. But what with violent articles in the pan-German Press and scarcely less violent recriminations in a certain portion of the British Press, this desire runs a very poor chance of bearing any fruit. A certain amount of energy of language may at one time have been opportune; on the German side to make public opinion feel the necessity of a large fleet and prepare for the sacrifices necessary to attain this object; on the British side to arouse in the public mind a sense of the danger which threatened British Naval supremacy. But now violent articles would seem to be out of place as the naval situation is quite clear. Everyone now knows that Germany has a well defined Fleet Law which she intends to carry out in its entirety, and that Great Britain, in the face of this intention, is firmly resolved to take the measures necessary to ensure her naval supremacy. No amount of violent writing can change this situation for the better, while on the contrary it can do a great deal of harm by embittering public opinion on both sides, and thus rendering any moderating influence quite powerless.

The German Press is at present teeming with articles on British and German Naval Armaments, but I do not propose to trouble you with them as they merely say what has been said a hundred times before. There is however a slight difference to be noted. It has been the habit, hitherto, both in official circles and in the Press to ridicule the idea that British naval supremacy is in any way threatened by German competition. The "Berliner Neueste Nachrichten" takes a different and more defiant line. It gives it to be understood that the nervousness of Great Britain is not without justification, as, though the Nassau class is armed with eleven inch guns the subsequent German Dreadnoughts carry guns equal in calibre and superior in their arrangement to those of the latest British ships. The article also alludes to the probability that Messrs. Krupp will shortly be in a position to manufacture guns superior in calibre to the proposed British 13·5 gun and with twice the resisting power of the latter weapon. The 'Berliner Neueste Nachrichten' states further that it is the knowledge of these facts which has made the Government and people of Great Britain so anxious to come to a naval understanding with Germany.

The 'Berliner Tageblatt' which, as you are aware, is at present a strong advocate of a naval arrangement, recently stated in its morning issue that Admiral Tirpitz was certainly about to send in his resignation partly because he required a rest and more particularly as a protest against the strong movement in favour of a reduction of expenditure and a naval understanding. It added, however, that after all it was not so much Admiral Tirpitz as the Emperor himself who stood in the way of a naval arrangement with Great Britain.

In its evening issue of the same day the 'Tageblatt' was obliged to publish a semi-official statement to the effect that there was not a word of truth in the rumour of Admiral Tirpitz's retirement.

In commenting on this statement the 'Tageblatt' expressed some doubt as to its accuracy, but added that, if it was by any chance true and the position of Admiral Tirpitz was secure, the only conclusion to be drawn was that the Chancellor, whose anxiety to obtain the reduction of the naval expenditure was well known, might himself find it rather difficult to remain in office.

The argument on which the 'Berliner Tageblatt' bases this conclusion is that while the services rendered to German naval power by Admiral Tirpitz are indisputable, nevertheless it is under his administration that the relations between England and Germany have become seriously strained and that the expenditure on the fleet has piled up the debt of the Empire to such an extent that, if the extravagant outlay continues, the financial ruin of the Empire is only a question of time. Further that both these results of the Admiral's administration are so much at variance with the Chancellor's pacific and careful views that with the prospect of the same administration of the naval department being continued he may well feel inclined to withdraw from further responsibility.

It is quite possible that the pacific and careful views attributed to the Chancellor by the ' Tageblatt' do actually exist, but he is pledged to the execution of the Fleet Law in its entirety and as long as its limits are not exceeded there can be no question of any disagreement between him and Admiral Tirpitz on that account. What the ' Berliner Tageblatt' is evidently hinting at is that the continuance of Admiral Tirpitz in office means that the scope of the law will be still further enlarged. That is, however, pure conjecture, and the same may be said of the statement in the same paper that the 38th battle-ship (to complete the number laid down in the Law) will be provided for in the naval estimates of 1911.

I have, &c.
W. E. GOSCHEN.

No. 387.

Sir Edward Grey to Sir E. Goschen.

F.O. 28050/167/10/18.
(No. 203.) Secret.
Sir, *Foreign Office, July* 29, 1910.

The German Chancellor having expressed some apprehension lest words used by the Prime Minister, during the Debate on the Navy Estimates this month, should have given rise to misapprehension respecting the attitude of the German Government towards an agreement between Germany and us about naval expenditure,(¹) H[is] M[ajesty's] Government have thought it well to put on record in a Memorandum their view of the situation.

You should take an opportunity, when it is convenient to Herr von Bethmann-Hollweg, of expressing to him in conversation the views of H[is] M[ajesty's] Government, and of leaving with him a copy of this Memorandum.

[I am, &c.]
E. G[REY].

Enclosure in No. 387.

Memorandum.(²)

The German Chancellor has, through Count Metternich, expressed the apprehension that the speech of the Prime Minister on the Navy Estimates may be construed as meaning that the German Government has opposed a *non possumus* to every suggestion of agreement respecting naval expenditure. It is therefore well that His Majesty's Government should explain their point of view, not only or chiefly to summarize the past, but also to examine what may be possible in future. Up to the present two ways of reducing or arresting naval expenditure have been considered or suggested from one side or the other.

1. An alteration of the existing German Navy Law. This the German Chancellor has declared to be at present impossible, a statement which was reaffirmed by the communication made to and published by the "Kölnische Zeitung" on the 28th December, and again by Count Metternich in conversation on the 22nd March of this year.(³)

(¹) [*cp. supra,* p. 495, No. 380, and *note* (¹), pp. 496–7, No. 382.]
(²) [The memorandum is printed with some interesting comments by the Emperor William II in *G.P.* XXVIII, pp. 351–4.]
(³) [*v. supra,* p. 442, No. 336.]

2. A modification of the tempo of the rate of shipbuilding in Germany. To what extent this would be possible without an alteration of the Naval Law is not apparent. In any case the gross naval expenditure would finally be the same, but His Majesty's Government recognise the immediate value that would attach to an agreement of this kind and would readily discuss it.

We have been given to understand that no naval agreement could take place unless it were preceded or accompanied by a political understanding. There would be difficulty in accepting any formula which would give the impression of an understanding different in kind from that which exists between His Majesty's Government and any other European Power, and might therefore affect adversely the relations between His Majesty's Government and certain other Powers, unless these Powers could also be made parties to it. His Majesty's Government have, however, always been ready to give assurances that there is nothing in any agreement between themselves and any other Power which is directed against Germany, and that they themselves have no hostile intentions respecting her.

There is a third suggestion, which has not yet been considered. An Agreement might be made, based on an understanding that the German Naval Programme should not be increased, accompanied by an exchange of information from time to time between the two Admiralties, which, without revealing those details that are never disclosed, would satisfy each that they were kept informed of the actual progress of shipbuilding in the yards of the other country. Such an arrangement would of course be on the footing of reciprocity.

It is true that the effect of such an agreement upon the naval expenditure of either country would be less substantial and definite than in the case of the first, and possibly of the second, of the above suggestions. But it would remove the apprehension of indefinite future increase; and it would have a moral effect considerable and very favourable. Such an agreement, especially the exchange of information between the two Admiralties, would dissipate in the public mind the suspicion (which increased expenditure has hitherto inevitably aroused, in spite of all that the two Governments can say), that either Government has hostile intentions, or desires to steal a march upon the other. To put an end, in the public mind, to suspicion with regard to present, and to limit anxiety as to the amount of future, naval expenditure would have an effect on the political atmosphere in each country of which the extent and consequences might be greater and more favourable than can be foretold. It might easily be followed by a state of good feeling, which would make the arrangement of minor matters easy, and might even lead eventually to a diminution of naval expenditure, for which public opinion is thought not yet to be prepared.

In submitting these suggestions, it is not desired to press the Chancellor to enter upon a discussion which he may consider inconvenient. During the first five months of this year circumstances were not favourable, owing to the political situation at home, for reviewing the possibility of an agreement; there were also debates in prospect on Navy Estimates, which might have had, as they did last year, an unfavourable effect on public opinion. Those debates are now concluded, and have had, so far as His Majesty's Government can judge, a favourable, rather than an adverse, influence; the time has not yet come for deciding the naval expenditure of next year; and it seemed well to summarize the situation and to review the prospects in the hope that nothing, which may seem to the German Chancellor to be possible, should be overlooked, discarded, or discouraged, owing to any doubt on his part of the good-will of His Majesty's Government.

July 26, 1910.

No. 388.

Memorandum communicated to Jevad Bey,(1) *July* 29, 1910.

F.O. 27275/100/10/44.

His Majesty's Government have given their careful attention to the important considerations laid before them by his Excellency the Minister of Finance on the subject of the proposed increase in the Turkish customs duties from 11 to 15 per cent. *ad valorem.*

They fully appreciate the motives which have determined the Imperial Ottoman Government to approach the Powers with a view to securing assent to this proposal, but unfortunately, as the Ottoman Government are aware, the question is complicated owing to its relation to the Bagdad Railway,—an enterprise which, under the existing concession, has not been conceived in the best interests of the Ottoman Empire, while it offers, as at present controlled, an undoubted menace to the legitimate position of British trade in Mesopotamia, which now rests upon the uninterrupted efforts of well-nigh three hundred years.

His Majesty's Government are satisfied that any increase in the Turkish customs duties under present conditions must, if not directly then indirectly by the mere fact of setting free other revenues, hasten the completion of the Bagdad Railway, with its consequent effects prejudicial to the interests of this country.

In view of this conclusion, His Majesty's Ambassador at Constantinople was recently instructed to represent to the Ottoman Government that British assent to the increased customs duties must be chiefly dependent upon the satisfactory solution of the Bagdad Railway question, and, as a means of attaining this object, it was suggested either that British participation should be secured on acceptable terms in the portion of the Bagdad Railway between Bagdad and the Persian Gulf, or that the Ottoman Government should grant, along the valley of the River Tigris, a " protective " concession for a second railway, which was to be under the *ægis* of a Turkish company.(2)

The latter suggestion did not commend itself to the Ottoman Government; while, as regards the former, no concrete scheme has as yet been brought before His Majesty's Government.

In the course, however, of tentative discussions which have taken place within the past few days, the Ottoman Minister of Finance has put forward two alternative proposals as affording the basis of a possible agreement : the first is an arrangement for internationalisation, the second is for the construction of the line by the Turkish Government; both proposals are confined to the portion of the railway between Bagdad and the Persian Gulf.

With regard to internationalisation, His Majesty's Government are aware of what has been discussed by Herr Gwinner with Sir Ernest Cassel. In their opinion, a solution might be found on these lines, but to be satisfactory to all parties it

(1) [Ottoman Minister of Finance.]
(2) [*v. supra,* pp. 374–5, No. 272; pp. 376–7, No. 274; p. 433, No. 324; pp. 471–2, No. 352.]

should not be financially onerous to the Turkish Government nor prejudicial to the future working and development of traffic on the railway.

As His Majesty's Government understand that the purport of the negotiations between Sir E. Cassel and Herr Gwinner is known to Djavid Bey, they think it right to communicate to him confidentially a copy of the letter to Sir H. Babington-Smith, in which they have already expressed their own view.[1]

As for the construction of the line by the Turkish Government, His Majesty's Government would, under certain safeguards, regard such a solution as satisfactory; but certain questions would arise the settlement of which might present some difficulty. For instance :—

Would the Ottoman Government *permanently* control the railway when completed; would they guarantee that British merchandise should not be subjected to adverse manipulation of rates; would they be able to secure equality of treatment for goods of British origin or destination on the sections of the railway west of Bagdad; would they give to British railway contractors a share (proportionate to the volume of British trade in those regions, say 60 per cent.) in the provision of railway material and rolling-stock; if, as would probably be the case, foreign engineers and foremen are employed, and if a foreign staff is required to work the railway when completed, would application be made to this country for suitable candidates, and would this country be given equality of treatment with others in regard to the posts to be filled?

Then His Majesty's Government, realising the immense importance of the railway as constituting the future highway for fast traffic between this country and the Indian Empire, feel confident that the Ottoman Government will appreciate the necessity of selecting as the terminus of the railway a point best adapted to economy of time. His Majesty's Government are advised that there is a consensus of opinion amongst those interested in shipping that the most suitable place for a port would be the harbour of Koweit : there ocean-going steamers of large tonnage could enter at all states of the tide and at all seasons of the year and, within a few minutes of leaving the open sea, could come alongside a quay where passengers and merchandise might, without loss of time, be transferred to the railway adjoining.

On the other hand, the town of Bussorah is obviously not suited for the maritime terminus of a great trans-continental railway : situated as it is several kilomètres from the mouth of a river which presents exceptional difficulties of navigation, especially at times of drought, if it became the terminus it would entail, even in the most favourable conditions of tide and weather, a delay of from ten to twelve hours in reaching the open sea : moreover, the tendency of modern steamers is to increase in tonnage, and ultimately the larger vessels would not be able to approach Bussorah, with the consequence that transhipment to smaller vessels would be necessary.

His Majesty's Government are further of opinion that, in view of the great predominance of British trade interests in the Persian Gulf, it would only be just that British contractors should build the harbour at Koweit; if His Majesty's Government agreed to the customs increase while merely insisting that Turkey herself, and not Great Britain, should control the line of railway between Bagdad and the Persian Gulf, the least they could expect would be that Turkey should allow Great Britain to construct, and to have a share in the control of the port at Koweit : indeed, short of some arrangement of this nature, it would be quite impossible to satisfy British public opinion and to defend the assent of His Majesty's Government to the increase of customs.

His Majesty's Government, in making this proposal to the Ottoman Government, have an earnest desire to co-operate with them in an amicable settlement of a question which, if it remains in suspense, may give rise to much inconvenience in future.

[1] [*v. supra*, pp. 491–2, No. 376.]

There is one further point to which His Majesty's Government wish to draw attention :—their desire that the Ottoman Government should consent to the removal of existing restrictions on the borrowing powers of Egypt: they feel confident that the Ottoman Government will not fail to recognise how reasonable is this request, and to take it into their favourable consideration.

From certain observations which his Excellency the Minister of Finance has made, His Majesty's Government are led to conclude that the Imperial Ottoman Government would deprecate the assent of the Powers being made subject to conditions to be embodied in a formal convention : His Majesty's Government fully realise the importance of this consideration and, with a view to meeting the wishes of the Ottoman Government on the subject, they would suggest that the Ottoman Minister for Foreign Affairs should address to them a note, which if desirable could be regarded as confidential, conveying assurances with regard to the points enumerated in this communication : in such an event, and on learning that the other Powers had notified their assent to the Ottoman Government, His Majesty's Government would be prepared to agree to an increase of the customs for an initial period of three years, terminating in April 1914 when the seven years during which the former increase was to continue will come to an end.

If, at the expiration of the period in question, the arrangements which have been outlined were being executed in a satisfactory manner, His Majesty's Government, who are keenly interested in the economic prosperity of the Ottoman Empire, would make no difficulty in assenting to the continuance of the increased duties (up to 15 per cent.) for a further period, subject to the agreement of the other Powers.

Foreign Office, July 29, 1910.

No. 389.

Sir G. Lowther to Sir Edward Grey.

F.O. 28558/100/10/44.
(No. 533.)   *Therapia,* D. *August 2, 1910.*
Sir,   R. *August 8, 1910.*

With reference to my despatch No. 392 of the 20th of June last([1]) I have the honour to report that Rifaat Pasha yesterday told me that he had been in verbal communication with the German Chargé d'Affaires as to the proposal for the abandonment by Germany of the construction of the Bagdad Gulf section of the line and as to an undertaking on the part of Turkey to construct the line herself and that latter after having submitted the suggestion to his Government had informed Rifaat that it was considered that this might form a basis for negotiation.

His Excellency said that this being so he hoped that Great Britain would no longer place any obstacles in the way of giving her consent to the increase of the 4 % Customs' duties.

I asked Rifaat Pasha whether he had received this German consent in writing and added that I presumed that if this were so he was now in a position to reply to your despatch to me (secret) of the 20th of April([2]) copy of which I had left with him on the 3rd of May last. His Excellency replied that he was not yet in possession of any written document from the German Government but that such was obviously necessary. He was considering however the form in which the agreement should be recorded, the communication to His Majesty's Government &c. Until something is committed to paper it seems premature to offer any opinion as

([1]) [v. *supra,* pp. 493–4, No. 378.]
([2]) [v. *supra,* pp. 468–72, No. 352.]

to whether the pourparlers with the German Chargé d'Affaires are likely to offer an acceptable solution. Moreover as I understood that you were likely to have some conversation with Djavid Bey, the Turkish Finance Minister, during his stay in London I told Rifaat Pasha that I preferred for the moment to refrain from offering any opinion.

I have, &c.
GERARD LOWTHER.

No. 390.

Sir E. Goschen to Sir Edward Grey.

F.O. 28577/167/10/18.
(No. 215.) Confidential.   *Berlin, D. August* 6, 1910.
Sir,   R. *August* 8, 1910.
    I have the honour to forward, herewith, a despatch, as marked in the margin, which I have received from Captain Heath, Naval Attaché to this Embassy, relating to a general summary of naval matters in Germany on vacating his post as Naval Attaché.

I have, &c.
W. E. GOSCHEN.

Enclosure 1 in No. 390.

Captain Heath to Sir E. Goschen.

Confidential.
Sir,   *Berlin, August* 6, 1910.
    I have the honour to submit a general report on German Naval Affairs.
I have, &c.
H. L. HEATH,
Captain and Naval Attaché.

Enclosure 2 in No. 390.

Report by Captain Heath.

Confidential.
    As the time of my service as Naval Attaché to the British Embassy at Berlin has reached its conclusion, I venture to submit a few remarks, summing up the impressions I have gained during my two years' service.
    I wish first to put on record the unfailing kindness with which I have been received by His Majesty the Kaiser, on the different occasions on which it has been my honour to be before His Majesty. Although the conversation has generally been more in a matter [*sic*] of chaff, generally at the expense of the so-called panic-mongers in England, His Majesty has on occasions.spoken seriously on Naval matters, shewing his intense knowledge and grasp of detail. It is noticed that His Majesty has no desire that the internal economy either of ships or of the service generally should be known to other nations. I am quite unable to see any weakening of His Majesty's often-expressed opinion that Germany's future lies on the water, and the consequent necessity for the construction and maintenance of a powerful fleet.
    It need hardly be added that so far as can be seen the whole Navy, without exception, are absolutely devoted to His Majesty, not only as being their Emperor, but also particularly in a personal sense.
    His Royal Highness Prince Henry of Prussia was in command of the Home Service Fleet when I assumed the duties of Naval Attaché. Here again on the few occasions on which it has been my privilege to meet His Royal Highness, his manner

has been most kind and cordial. I believe the Naval opinion on His Royal Highness's capabilities is that he is a better seaman than administrator. It was due to his initiative that the annual "Blue Water" cruise of the Home Service Fleet was undertaken. Being more practical than theoretical, it is understood that during his command the officers and men took part in many interesting exercises, as compared with the more stolid instruction which is most in favour with the German mind. His Royal Highness is no believer in Air-ships for Naval purposes but is all in favour of continued experiments, with a view to overcoming defects.

Admiral von Tirpitz is, in my opinion, one of the foremost men in Germany. Coming from a Bürgerlicher family, he has won his way to his present high position solely by merit. He appears to have the whole Navy absolutely under his thumb, for although theoretically the various Admirals who command stations, fleets, &c., are responsible to the Kaiser alone, it seems that if they differ from Tirpitz, it generally ends in their losing their appointments.

The Admiral's whole thought is devoted to the carrying out of the Navy Law, with the amendments and additions thereto. No power on earth would induce him to in any way modify the Law.

In the interviews that I have had with him from time to time, he struck me as being a man of wide knowledge, but of an excitable disposition, and might almost be said to be seeking for an excuse to consider himself insulted, or his word doubted by English Ministers. He is devoted to secrecy, and will have nothing to do with the "cards on the table" policy. There have been from time to time rumours of both his retirement and promotion, if either of these takes place it seems that the German Navy will lose a good administrator and stout champion. There is no doubt that he has the complete confidence of the whole Navy.

Of other German Naval Officers, my experience is that they are extremely formal, and reticent on Naval matters. It is known without doubt that they have orders not to be intimate with Naval Attachés.

A German officer stated privately that the exclusion of the Naval Attachés from the ships' entertainments during the Kieler Woche is intentional.

Turning to the Navy as a whole : one might live in Germany for ever without learning much of the internal economy or efficiency. On no occasion have I been able to induce German Officers to talk of their drills and exercises, or of life on board. I have seen the ordinary harbour drills carried out by individual ships at Kiel, but never a " General drill day."

The German Officer, especially when married, has a strong hankering for shore billets, his heart is not really on the sea. They infinitely prefer sitting at a desk, pondering over official papers, to the more active sea life, and it appears that few if any of them have any dread of growing stout.

At the same time those that cannot get shore billets make the best of it and do all that in them lies to make the service efficient. There is no reason to suppose that either " personnel " or " matériel " are anything but first class. The Torpedo service is probably having an effect on both officers and men, and this effect will be shewn in the battle squadron in a few years' time. One can generally detect a Torpedo Boat Officer, his whole manner and bearing being so different to those who are serving in the line of battle ships.

The men as a rule look smart and well set-up, but their clothes are ugly and ill-fitting, this more especially applies to the working rigs. I have absolutely seen only one drunken Blue-jacket, but the returns of punishments and suicides work out rather high.

Gun Practice.

From the few photographs obtainable it appears that German targets are built in much the same proportions as our own, and considering the very variable results obtained from different ships in our own service, it is to be assumed that German gunnery results are somewhat similar, the performances of any one or two ships cannot be taken as exemplifying the whole. It is reported that battle practice is carried out at moving targets, at ranges up to 10,000 metres, and that the system of 25 % of short shots has been adopted, as the best control, and found to produce the greatest number of hits. All reports concur that the Germans do not " calibrate " as is done in the English service.

Experimental towing targets have been seen in which netting only is used, a broad vertical line in the centre, and a three foot broad horizontal line at the base of the target, (the two making an inverted " T "), is marked by having the netting three parts thick.

Photographs were obtained last year shewing that Fleet firing is carried out, but under what conditions is unknown.

In my opinion most exercises are copied from our own and in many ways the British Navy is still taken as the model.

Coaling has become a fleet exercise, the time occupied in this work has been much reduced, which has, however, been the case [? cause] of some accidents and loss of life.

Preparation for War.

Last year a number of reserve ships were mobilized for manœuvres and remained with the Home Service Fleet for about four weeks. The time occupied in mobilizing those vessels was, for men in the reserve, three days' notice. Officers and men serving in the depôts had no notice of mobilization, which went off however quite satisfactorily, the ships getting away in about a week from the order to mobilize being given.

All the usual war exercises were carried out : the squadrons were divided into convenient units for carrying out, or frustrating, combinations. Battle exercises (P Z) were carried out on a large scale : the effective concentration of fire on certain of the enemy units, and " change of object " being much practised.

Torpedo attack by night, and defence against the same were frequently practised. Submarines worked in conjunction with the Fleet for the first time.

The transfer of wounded to a hospital ship at sea was practised. It was stated in the press that " Fleet auxiliaries " were chartered, but no details could be obtained.

As is usual a number of military officers were detailed to embark, in order to get instruction in Naval work, but one of them told me that going on board our own Dreadnought as a visitor, he had been permitted to see more than he had in any German man-of-war, where the soldier pupil is not even permitted to see the interior of a turret.

Ship-building.

In actual output of ships, in capabilities of output, and in the class of ships constructed, the growth of German sea power has been most remarkable.

In the Autumn of 1908, it was apparent that there would be no difficulty in the carrying out of the construction required by the new Law. In addition to four " Nassau " class, one " Von der Tann," one " Blucher," all in various stages of construction and completion, it was made known that the material for the battle ships and cruiser of the 1908 Programme was well in hand in the shops. A further revelation, was the admission by the German authorities, that provisional contracts for two large ships of the 1909 programme, had been signed in Autumn 1908.

The German Naval Authorities did their best to shew that this meant no acceleration of the building programme, but there is no getting over the fact, that work on at least one of these ships, was commenced in the Schichau Yard before the estimate had received the approval of the Reichstag.

A good deal of excitement was raised both in England and Germany when these facts became known. The feeling in Germany, can best be shewn by the fact, that he Reichstag voted their approval of the Naval Estimates for 1909 without lebate.

The principal improvements in Ship-building facilities are as follows:

1. Complete new dockyard by "Vulkan" at Hamburg, with two large slips.
2. Considerable enlargement of the yard and appliances at Blohm and Voss.
3. Completion of electrical gantries over Howaldt's slips.
4. Completion of a new large slip by Schichau at Danzig.

All the above firms, also the Imperial Yards at Kiel and Wilhelm[s]haven, have installed machinery for the manufacture of turbines.

The only private yard which does not manufacture its own turbines is the "Weser" at Bremen.

At the Imperial Yard, Danzig, slips have been completed, on which at least five submarines can ⸴ built simultaneously.

In the estimates for 1910, eleven battleships and four large cruisers are shewn in various stages of construction. The "Vulkan" Company of Stettin, completed a Home Service Torpedo Boat of some 620 tons, in ostensibly eight months from the date of the order. This is a good example of rapidity of construction, and shews the capabilities of German firms.

The German Naval Authorities state officially, that their ships are built, viz. are ready for steam trials in from 36 to 42 months, from the first of April of the year in which they are authorised. An endeavour was made to shew that this meant, that no ship would be completed in less than 36 months. This fable was dispelled last year when it was officially stated (letter of 12th July 1909) that neither the plans, nor the contracts for the battleships "E Heimdall," and "E Hildebrand" had been completed before the Autumn of 1909, and yet these ships must be completed in 36 to 42 months from the 1st of April of that year.

The remarks on pages 69 and 70 of "Nauticus" for 1910, do not quite agree with the above official letter.

Again, in the above quoted letter, it is stated that the cruiser "G" is to be delivered in 33 months, presumably from the 1st of April 1908, although the contract was only completed in September of that year.

There is no reason to doubt the capability of rapid building, nor of the ability to build vessels of any size or power. Tonnage, armament, and engine power, increase every year, and it looks as if the German authorities had determined that, ship for ship, their's should be in no way inferior to those of other nations.

Krupp is reported to be well ahead with his contracts, but as permission to visit this establishment was refused, no definite statement can be made. As regards armour, that for the "Oldenburg" was seen lying in Schichau's yard some months before the ship was launched.

Rumours of the probable adoption of a fourteen inch gun, have appeared from time to time. It is pretty well known that Krupp has experimented with guns of this calibre. It has also been reported, that last year at the meeting of the Kaiser with the Czar, the former gave it as his opinion that guns of larger calibre than the 12 inch, must shortly be introduced.

As regards small craft, the construction seems equally good, great speeds have been obtained by some vessels, but the introduction of turbines has brought preliminary troubles. Oil fuel is being introduced, it is said that all ships will be fitted with a proportion of boilers, burning oil only.

No information has been obtained as to the general efficiency of engines and boilers.

Education.

As the Fleet grows, the training establishments grow with it. A new submarine boat division has been formed, and many officers and men are now under instruction, and the German Navy is well abreast of the times in this respect, with this one exception, that no money has been voted for air-navigation. One Naval Officer has been sent to Zeppelin for a course of instruction.

As regards shore work and communications, it is sufficient to call attention to the broadening and deepening of the Kiel Canal now in progress.

The deepening of the Ems–Yade Canal.

The completion of a large and fully equipped, fortified harbour at Wilhelmshaven.

The completion of a Torpedo Boat Harbour at Helgoland.

The projected docks and works at Brunsbuttel.

The (according to the press) projected Torpedo Boat Station at or near Emden, in connection with the Ems–Yade Canal.

The High Power Wireless stations are believed to be equal with any elsewhere, communication is reported to have been established between Nauen and a Woerman Line steamer off the Cameroon Coast.

It is understood that endeavours have been made to obtain sanction for a Wireless Telegraphy station (worked by Germans) to be established at Teneriffe.

New cables have lately been laid from Emden to the Azores to be continued to South America, with perhaps a branch to South Africa.

In one respect only is there a leak, it is believed that so far, no coaling station or concession for such, exists between the German coast and the nearest South African possession.

On the 1st of April 1910, one half of the Home Service Fleet was permanently transferred to the North Sea. As each new battleship and armoured cruiser takes the water, she is designated officially, as "belonging to Wilhelmshaven."

Thus the German Naval Front, together with the principal fighting force, is being moved from the interior defensive position in the Baltic, to the open waters of the North Sea.

No. 391.

Sir E. Goschen to Sir Edward Grey.

Private.([1])

Dear Sir Edward Grey,   Berlin, August 6, 1910.

I found your letter on my return from a two days' visit to friends in Silesia. The Chancellor is away at his country house but he comes in now and then and I will try to get hold of him. I wish now that I had not made it quite so clear that a naval understanding on the basis of the fulfilment of their Fleet Law in its entirety would not satisfy British Public Opinion. However nothing definite or official on this point has been said from here.

I have never quite understood what the Chancellor really meant by a modification of the tempo of their rate of shipbuilding. His allusions to it have always been extremely vague and there never seemed much disposition to make it clear. After next year the rate of building according to the Programme is one battleship and one large Cruiser—it is not clear to me how they can reduce that rate and still carry out the Law in the specified time. It may also have been in their mind to reduce the tempo by paying for the ships in say, five or six money instalments instead of four. That would certainly reduce the 'tempo,' but it would also mean an alteration of the Fleet Law, as by this method they could not possibly have even *laid down* by 1918 all the ships required by the Law. I doubt very much whether the Chancellor knows himself what he means by a 'reduction of the tempo' but I will try and extract an explanation from him when I see him. The third

([1]) [Grey MSS., Vol. 23.]

suggestion in the Memorandum(²) would seem to be the most feasible, but up to the present Admiral von Tirpitz has been very much against any exchange of information between the two Admiralties. As regards an understanding that the German Naval Programme should not be increased, there is, as you are aware, a growing movement in Liberal circles against any acceleration of the rate of Shipbuilding and any increase of the Programme. On the other hand, there is a disposition on the part of the Navy League and the Pan-Germans to agitate for an increase and perhaps the latter combination is the strongest.

An understanding satisfactory to both countries seems for the moment to be rather hopeless, but I have not seen the Chancellor since Mr. Asquith's speech, and, as he has of late seemed rather anxious to cultivate the good opinion of the National Liberal Party, he may now be in a better frame of mind.

Thanking you very much for your letter, I remain,

Yours very sincerely,
W. E. GOSCHEN.

(²) [v. supra, pp. 501–2, No. 387, encl.]

No. 392.

Sir Edward Grey to Sir E. Goschen.

Private.(¹)

My dear Goschen,   *Fallodon, August* 11, 1910.

It was my view too that nothing which did not modify the fleet law in Germany would seem worth much to public opinion here, but the Cabinet thought it would be better than nothing and in that view I concur especially if it be combined with exchange of information to which I have always attached importance. I am afraid Tirpitz will fight hard against anything. He uses all that we say or do as a pretext for standing off from us.

[Yours sincerely,
E. GREY.]

(¹) [Grey MSS., Vol. 23.]

No. 393.

Sir E. Goschen to Sir Edward Grey.

F.O. 29834/167/10/18.   *Berlin, D. August* 15, 1910.

Tel. (No. 42.)   *R. August* 16, 1910.

Secret. Your despatch No. 203.(¹)

I saw Chancellor yesterday and after some conversation handed him your memorandum. He wishes me to thank you for it and to say that he will give it careful consideration and let you know his views as soon as possible. He will be in Berlin this week when he will have a further conversation with me. Till then he wished me to regard any remarks which he might make as quite private and unofficial.

(¹) [v. supra, pp. 501–2, No. 387, and encl. The enclosure is the memorandum to which reference is made here.]

As a matter of fact he went into no detail but with regard to third suggestion in the memorandum I could see that he was puzzled as to no mention having been made as to what H[is] M[ajesty's] Gov[ernmen]t would do on their side if the German Gov[ernmen]t promised not to increase their naval programme. He is sure, I think, to raise the question and I should be glad to know what you would wish me to reply.

His Excellency did not mention Persia

No. 394.

Sir Edward Grey to Sir E. Goschen.

F.O. 29834/167/10/18.   *Foreign Office, August 18, 1910.*
Tel. (No. 86.)   D. 1·10 P.M.
    Your secret telegram No. 42.([1]) We should of course restrict our shipbuilding programme to what was necessary to preserve safe proportion to existing German programme, as long as that continued to be as it is at present the chief factor in determining our shipbuilding. I cannot give a more specific answer without consulting Prime Minister and it would probably need consultation with Admiralty experts. This would be more appropriate at a later stage after principle of agreement and reciprocity had been accepted.

([1]) [*v.* immediately preceding document.]

No. 395.

Sir E. Goschen to Sir Edward Grey.

Private.([1])
My dear Grey,   *Berlin, August 19, 1910.*
    Many thanks for your letters—on one of which you will see that I am acting.
    The Chancellor after reading Your Memorandum([2]) the other day said that he would like to study it a little before expressing any definite views with regard to its contents. He therefore begged that anything he might say in the course of conversation might be regarded as talk between friends and not reported officially. On coming to the third suggestion in Your Memorandum he said "Yes, but there is no mention of what G[rea]t Britain proposes to do in return for a promise on our part that we will not increase our Naval Programme." I replied that, as we had for many years been trying to obtain a general decrease in the enormous expenditure on Armaments, I presume that we should seize the opportunity of knowing exactly what Germany proposed to build, to reduce our Naval construction as far as we safely could having due regard to our position as a Power to whom strength at sea meant everything. He naturally said that that was rather vague and asked how he was to know how far our reduction would go. "If you had a Programme" he said "that point could be made clear: but you have none." I replied that if we had no programme we had at all events a Naval principle—namely the Two Power Standard: and that to that principle as far as I knew both H[is] M[ajesty's] Government and public opinion adhered. The Chancellor said that we always talked about the two Power Standard but that it seemed to him that we only built against Germany. Why didn't we build for instance against the

([1]) [Grey MSS., Vol. 23.]
([2]) [*v. supra,* pp. 501–2, No. 387, *encl.*]

United States. I answered that that was just the point. We did not, and could not, only build against Germany, but had to keep our eyes open to what other Powers were doing: therefore beyond saying that we would do our best to uphold our principle of the Two Power Standard, it was difficult for us to lay down a fixed programme at any given moment. Of course the more exactly we knew what other Powers were doing in the way of Naval Construction the nearer we should get to having a fixed Programme. "Yes" he said, "that is all very well but you want us to fix our Programme now. How do I know what we shall want in 1918?" I said that Germany was in quite a different position. Their Army was, and from their geographical position must be, their first line of defence and they had to regulate its strength according to the strength of their neighbours. On the other hand they could easily calculate what they required in the way of a Navy for the protection of their commerce and coasts; and in fact they had done so when they had brought in their Navy Law. He had spoken of the United States. Well it was natural that for the moment we should be more preoccupied by a large fleet which was growing up at our very doors than by one which was a week off. To this he only made the rather grim remark that Japan was still further off from Russia but that that had not prevented war between the two countries.

I asked him what he thought of the idea that the two Admiralties should reciprocally supply each other with information with regard to their respective Naval Construction. He reminded me in reply that in former conversations he had always been rather against that idea as tending to increase, rather than decrease, suspicion and recrimination. He added, however, that that was a question on which Naval Experts (meaning of course Admiral Tirpitz) would have the most to say. Those are the principle [sic] points of our conversation. No! there was one other point upon which I touched. I asked him whether he could explain to me what exactly was meant by "a reduction in the tempo" which he had formerly suggested as a means for arriving at a Naval understanding. He answered, as vaguely as ever, that it meant that for a series of years they would reduce the number of ships to be laid down. I asked him whether that would not affect the Naval Law, as if they reduced the small number of ships to be laid down annually after 1911 they could not possibly have the number required by the Law at the end of the period which it covered, unless, of course, they crammed a large number into the last few years, and then I did not quite see, beyond a short respite, what advantage was to be gained. He said that the "reduction of the tempo" would not affect the Law but only the Naval Programme. But he did not make it at all clear to me, and, honestly I don't think it is very clear to his own mind, as when I pressed him a little more he said that it was a question with which Naval Experts were more competent to deal. But it is a most important point and I wish I could find someone who could really explain it. . . . .(³)

Believe me,
Yours very sincerely,
W. E. GOSCHEN.

(³) [This letter closes with a reference to the Bagdad Railway, and to the Press in Germany and France.]

No. 396.

Sir E. Goschen to Sir Edward Grey.([1])

Private.([2])

My dear Grey,   *Berlin, August 25*, 1910.

Before going off on leave to-night to Austria I want to write you a line to thank you for letting me go and to finish up the few things I have to say before my departure. I saw Kiderlen on Tuesday and found him a little sceptical, rather reserved and quite friendly. He only told me what I telegraphed to you namely that the Chancellor was very gratified at your cordial message and your evident wish to reopen discussions in a frank and friendly manner, but that he couldn't answer at once as the important matters of which Your Memorandum treated required due consideration. He, Kiderlen, also wanted to know what Great Britain proposed to do should Germany promise not to add to her Programme, and I answered him in the sense of your telegram on that subject.([3]) But he rather shook his head over it and changed the conversation. Our new Naval Attaché, who seems very wide awake saw Tirpitz to-day and appears to have talked to him on the subject of the suggestion that the two Admiralties should give each other reciprocal information. Watson seemed to think that Tirpitz was not unfavourable, which would be a change; but it appears that Tirpitz has a great admiration for Sir Arthur Wilson and maybe that he is anxious to stand well with him. In any case Tirpitz, though he began rather stiffly, was finally very friendly with Watson and kept him for over half an hour. Watson is sending a full report home. The Emperor seems also to be in a better frame of mind. My French colleague tells me that His Majesty had talked a good deal on the subject of Anglo-German Relations with the French Minister at Christiania and had said that He was v[ery] glad to say that they had much improved of late; that the English were gradually getting over their belief that the German Fleet was being built for the purpose of attacking G[reat] Britain and were taking a calmer view of things and that generally he was very much encouraged! He also said that His sisters who had been in England had told him that during Their stay They had heard nothing but the friendliest sentiments expressed with regard to Germany. As regards Russia His Majesty had not been quite so cordial in his language. He had inveighed bitterly against her alliance with Japan and had said (I do not know on what authority) that England did not approve of the alliance any more than He did! He had added that He thought that the English were not so keen about their yellow allies as they used to be. I give you these remarks of the Emperor as they were told to me, but I can't help thinking that the French Minister *must* have embroidered a little. . . . ([4])

Yours very sincerely,

W. E. GOSCHEN.

([1]) [For Herr von Kiderlen-Waechter's brief report, *v. G.P.* XXVIII, pp. 354–5.]
([2]) [Grey MSS., Vol. 23.]
([3]) [*v. supra*, p. 512, No. 394.]
([4]) [The omitted paragraphs refer to Servia and the Balkan situation, and to Turco-German relations.]

No. 397.

Count de Salis to Sir Edward Grey.

F.O. 31333/167/10/18.

(No 235.)   *Berlin*, D. *August* 27, 1910.

Sir,   R. *August* 29, 1910.

I have the honour to forward, herewith, a despatch, as marked in the margin which I have received from Captain Watson, Naval Attaché to this Embassy relating to a conversation with Admiral von Tirpitz.([1])

I have, &c.

J. DE SALIS.

([1]) [An account of this conversation is given in Admiral von Tirpitz : *Politische Dokumente Der Aufbau der deutschen Weltmacht.* (Stuttgart and Berlin, 1924), pp. 179–81.]

Enclosure 1 in No. 397.

Captain Watson to Sir E. Goschen.

No. 31.)

Sir, *Berlin, August 25, 1910.*

I have the honour to report an interview I had yesterday with his Excellency Admiral von Tirpitz.

With reference to the notes I handed to his Excellency, those contained in No. 2 I was authorised by the First Lord of the Admiralty to put before Admiral von Tirpitz.

Those in No. 3 the Director of Naval Intelligence suggested that I could put them [*sic*] forward as views of British Admiralty to Admiral von Tirpitz should opportunity arise.

I have, &c.

HUGH D. R. WATSON,

Captain and Naval Attaché.

Enclosure 2 in No. 397.

Précis of Conversation held with his Excellency Admiral von Tirpitz by Captain Watson, R.N.

His Excellency was only making a brief stay in Berlin on his way from his home to Dantzig to attend the combined naval and military parade there before His Majesty the Kaiser.

As the Emperor had expressed his intention of receiving me on the 1st September, I suggested to Reichs-Marine-Amt the desirability of reporting myself to Admiral von Tirpitz prior to that.

This his Excellency was good enough to accede to, in spite of his brief stay in Berlin; as will be seen subsequently, the interview lasted some time.

His Excellency thanked me when I reported myself as relieving Captain Heath. After some personal conversation, his Excellency spoke of the younger age at which our officers become captains (39 years), as compared with their 42 years, and wondered how we managed it. Also dwelt on the desirability of having young captains. I thanked his Excellency for receiving me when so busy on only passing through Berlin.

I then handed his Excellency a statement of points which the First Lord of the Admiralty had said I could bring before Admiral von Tirpitz should I find convenient opportunity. (A copy of the statement is herewith attached.)

His Excellency read it attentively, and then said he would require time to think over it, as it raised so many important points. He then went on to say he had given Captain Heath some statements as to shipbuilding programme, which had appeared in House of Commons in totally different form.

I said I had read the correspondence, and was certain that we regretted exceedingly a misunderstanding should have arisen. At use of this word Admiral Tirpitz observed somewhat forcibly: "There could be no misunderstanding; my statement to Captain Heath was perfectly clear." I suggested to his Excellency that the statement he so much resented indicated a possibility, and not a certainty, of Germany having seventeen "Dreadnoughts" ready in 1912. His Excellency observed that if it came to possibilities Germany could build as big a fleet as England—it was purely a question of money; but no money could be taken for any new ships before the 1st April without Parliament's consent.

I pointed out, as one who had read the correspondence as a new-comer, and therefore had a somewhat impersonal point of view, the necessity of an agreement on the terms to be used for indicating commencement and completion was obvious, and that some of the recent unfortunate misunderstandings had arisen from lack of such agreement. That the proposals contained in the written statement I had just given his Excellency would avoid such misunderstanding, and that the proposals were only practicable if the same terms were adopted by each nation.

Admiral Tirpitz then said the proposals would require thinking over, and that we should have a meeting at a later date on the question.

Admiral Tirpitz expressed his pleasure that so high-minded and able an officer as Admiral of the Fleet Sir A. K. Wilson is now at the head of the British naval officers.

I informed Admiral Tirpitz that Mr. McKenna had authorised me to speak to him on the proposal as to visits to shipbuilding yards, and the Director of Naval Intelligence (Rear-Admiral Bethell) in regard to rest of proposals.

That Sir A. K. Wilson had not spoken to me on the subject, but that I felt sure, with his knowledge and appreciation of Admiral Wilson, his Excellency would endorse my opinion that Admiral Wilson would entirely support any proposals leading towards declaration of intentions and honesty of purpose, so far as it did not interfere with efficiency of our navy.

I assured Admiral Tirpitz that any information given me should be given by me to our Admiralty in exactly same form as received.

The Admiral then enquired to whom my information would go.

I replied to Mr. McKenna and the Admiralty generally.

His Excellency showed pleasure when I assured him that any information he gave me should be placed by me before Admiral Wilson personally as well as before the First Lord.

Admiral Tirpitz bade me present his compliments to Admiral Wilson.

I submitted that, having read the correspondence, I was convinced Captain Heath had reported everything exactly as Admiral Tirpitz had told him. The Admiral was evidently not pleased at the subject, and observed again that Captain Heath could have made no mistake as to what he had said; though he, Admiral Tirpitz, did not know the intricacies of the English language, still what he had said to Captain Heath was absolutely clear and represented what Germany is actually doing not what they possibly might do. I again urged that Captain Heath reported exactly as informed, and requested his Excellency to believe it of a brother naval officer.

In regard to general matters the Admiral dealt on the attitude of England towards Germany for past twelve years. Germany had observed with regret that the political party in England had latterly used Germany as an excuse to put naval estimates through.

He went on to say that it was not natural a military nation of Germany's size should stand such treatment as England had directed at them.

I observed that, whatever the attitude of the newspapers might be, I asked his Excellency to believe that our navy looked on the German navy as respected comrades; and that any steps, such as the proposals handed to him, or others which would have the effect of making mutual good-fellowship between the two navies more real, were very desirable in the interests of both nations.

Further, that our navy regretted very much that misunderstanding should exist.

His Excellency observed Germany does not want England's colonies, she does not want to take Canada or Australia, &c., but she does want an open market; and, in view of nations arising other than European, it behoves us to make common cause.

His Excellency then rose and said that as he had a lot to do, he must go, that he would think over what I had said and given him.

Notes on Interview.

Generally speaking, his Excellency was most pleasant; the interview may be summed up as follows:—

1. Pleasant reception of new naval attaché; conversation on ordinary daily topics.

2. Consideration of the proposals, not unaccompanied by doubt or suspicion, and some irritation at remembrances of 1909 controversy being revived.

3. Subsequent to this, a readiness to discuss proposals in a general aspect and to discuss previous occurrences without rancour.

4. Evident pleasure at the appointment of Admiral of the Fleet Sir A. K. Wilson as First Sea Lord.

On leaving his Excellency I spoke to Korvetten-Kapitän Seebohm (chief of Central-Abteilung), who was present at interview, and agreed that a further conversation should take place later as mentioned by Admiral Tirpitz.

His Excellency is now going to Dantzig, and will return to Berlin about the 1st September, but only for a brief stay, as he then goes to his home again for two weeks, returning to Berlin finally about third week in September.

Submission.

I would submit that further points in regard to the proposals handed to Admiral von Tirpitz may be given me for my instruction as to limits to be observed.

Also submitted that prior to any further discussion, should Admiral Tirpitz fix a date, I may be permitted to have the advantage of a personal interview at Admiralty with :—

> First Lord.
> First Sea Lord.
> Director of Naval Intelligence.

Submit for consideration that German naval attaché in London may be invited to confer at Admiralty on the points raised.

HUGH D. R. WATSON,
Captain and Naval Attaché.

Berlin August 24, 1910.

Enclosure 3 in No. 397.

Statement handed to his Excellency Admiral von Tirpitz by Captain Watson, R.N., August 24, 1910.

Any information that his Excellency Admiral von Tirpitz gives Captain Watson shall be transmitted exactly as given, and Captain Watson guarantees it shall be laid before First Lord of British Admiralty exactly as given.

2. Visits to shipbuilding yards. Mr. McKenna, First Lord of Admiralty, authorised Captain Watson to inform his Excellency Admiral von Tirpitz that the German naval attaché is welcome, on making application, to visit British ship-building yards, counting battle-ships, cruisers, destroyers, and submarines or other vessels for navy on the stocks : provided a reciprocal treatment is accorded to British naval attaché in Germany. Visits to be six-monthly.

3. The British Admiralty would be prepared to furnish to German Admiralty, in exchange for similar information :—

(*a.*) The numbers and nature of ships and vessels it is proposed to build annually.

(*b.*) Dates of laying down ships and vessels.

(*c.*) Dates of intended delivery for trials under German or British naval flag.

(Also as a matter for consideration : Nature of armament. The British Admiralty would probably be prepared to exchange information on this point also.)

4. Submit that the visits to all shipbuilding yards and the exchange of information would—

Promote good feeling between the navies of the two countries, and would assist towards a good understanding between the two countries generally. Would also lessen expense to both countries by reason of fuller knowledge of each other's intentions.

HUGH D. R. WATSON,
Captain and Naval Attaché.

No. 398.

Sir E. Goschen to Sir Edward Grey.

F.O. 36518/167/10/18.
(No. 276.) Confidential.
Sir,

Berlin, D. October 7, 1910.
R. October 10, 1910.

I have the honour to forward, herewith, a despatch as marked in the margin, which I have received from Captain Watson, Naval Attaché to this Embassy, relating to the proposals for the improvement of the relations between the English and German Navies.

I have, &c.
W. E. GOSCHEN.

Enclosure in No. 398.

Captain Watson to Sir E. Goschen.

(No. 41.) Confidential.
Sir, Berlin, October 7, 1910.

I have the honour to report that Korvettan [*sic*] Kapitan Wide[n]mann, German Naval Attaché in London, called on me this morning at his own request.

2. Kapitan Wide[n]mann informed me that he saw Admiral von Tirpitz yesterday on the subject of the proposals put forward to His Excellency on August 24th last (my letter No. 31 August 25th 1910).([1]) That His Excellency had expressed himself in favour of a better understanding on Naval matters, and generally in favour of the proposals indicated above.

3. Kapitan Wide[n]mann expressed a desire to call on the First Lord of Admiralty, the First Sea Lord, Controller, and Director of Naval Intelligence on his return to England shortly. I suggested that if he did he should see the First Lord first. I observed that it would no doubt help to a good understanding if he could convey to the First Lord of the Admiralty and the principal Naval Officers an expression of Admiral Tirpitz's concurrence with the principle underlying the proposals, and with the proposals themselves.

4. I observed however that the question of these proposals is in the hands of the British Ambassador, and that proceedings must be conducted through Foreign Office. Further that the settlement of the details of these proposals must come later.

5. In regard to the proposals I observed that they represented a desire for better understanding on Naval matters, but that the wording of them was my own, and that they would no doubt require amendment.

6. I would however submit most respectfully for your consideration Your Excellency, that it would not be desirable to depart from these proposals as they stand at present; until a definite expression of opinion on them, or counter proposals, are obtained from Admiral von Tirpitz. Should negotiations lead to further consideration of them by Naval Officers, amendments can then be made.

([1]) [*v.* immediately preceding document.]

7. In event of future discussion I would respectfully submit for consideration that it should be conducted by two Flag Officers, representing the respective Admiralties. This would help to strengthen relations between the two Admiralties, and I would submit that the points for consideration are of sufficient importance to warrant this.

8. In conclusion, I would submit to Your Excellency that under the proposals, the British Naval Attaché will be of infinitely more use to his Government by being able to give them a better general idea of German Navy, by virtue of seeing much more of them than has been possible latterly. In support of this view I beg to submit my very cordial and frank reception at Kiel recently. I would bring to your notice that under other conditions my predecessor has at times either been refused permission to visit Shipbuilding Yards and Gun Factories, or else has been granted permission with the impossible reservation that he could see no Naval work.

I have, &c.
HUGH WATSON,
Naval Attaché.

MINUTES.

It was inevitable that Captain Watson's injudicious proceedings should lead us into a difficult position.

It is not desirable that negotiations of this kind should be conducted by the German Naval Attaché here with the First Lord. Either the communications he has to make relate to purely technical matters, in which case he can talk to the D[irector of] N[aval] I[ntelligence] or some officer in the Admiralty conversant with the subject, or the question touches on political considerations, in which case they should be discussed by Count Metternich with Sir Edward Grey.

If we once allow the German naval or military attaché to conduct negotiations direct with our authorities, we shall, unless the subject and scope of the discussion is strictly defined and limited, find ourselves in serious trouble.

Qu[ery]: So write to the Admiralty and send copy to Sir E. Goschen, for the information and guidance of Captain Watson.(2)

E. A. C.
Oct. 12.

It would perhaps be advisable to put on record our view that no discussion as to details should take place at the Admiralty until the questions of principle have been settled here. I rather think that that is what Captain Watson himself has intended to convey to Captain Wide[n]man[n], but the first overtures made by him at Berlin have put matters into the wrong channel.

W. L.

The discussions as to a naval understanding are still in progress between the two Gov[ernmen]ts through the Chancellor and H[is] M[ajesty's] Amba[ssado]r. It is clear that until these discussions have advanced considerably further confusion and misunderstandings will occur if the naval auth[ori]ties at the present stage interchange views as to details.

The best course would be to ask the Admiralty (if we have not already done so) to give us conf[idential]ly a clear and concise statement of what they would wish us to formulate to the German Gov[ernmen]t through our Ambas[sado]r when the proper time arrives for so doing. We might express to the Adm[iral]ty the hope that they will inform the German naval attaché, should he approach them, that they understand that discussions as to a naval understanding are still in the hands of the F[oreign] O[ffice] and the German Gov[ernmen]t and that it would be premature to confer with him until they hear from us that the question is sufficiently matured to enable them to do so with advantage.

Also inform Sir E. Goschen of above and ask him to impress once more on Capt[ain] Watson that he should be very cautious as to what he says and suggests to the naval officers with whom he comes into contact.

A. N.

This will do—if it is known that Bethmann Hollweg doesn't object to the Naval Attaché knowing. Send by private letter to Mr. McKenna.

E. G.

(2) [A letter in these terms was sent to the Admiralty on October 24, and a copy forwarded to Sir E. Goschen with Sir Edward Grey's despatch No. 279 secret of the same date.]

No. 399.

Sir E. Goschen to Sir Edward Grey.

Berlin, *October* 12, 1910.

F.O. 37093/167/10/18.
Tel. (No. 62.) Secret.

D. 8·30 P.M.
R. 10·0 P.M.

The Chancellor handed to me to-day his answer to the mem[orandum] contained in your despatch No. 203 Secret of July 29.(¹) The answer is to the effect that the Imperial Gov[ernmen]t have no objection to the proposal that information in regard to shipbuilding should be furnished reciprocally by the two Admiralties and that greater facilities should be given to the Naval Attaché; but that, if this proposal presupposes an obligation on the part of Imperial Gov[ernmen]t to give up their right to expand their existing fleet law, they must before considering suggestion know what counter-concession H[is] M[ajesty's] Gov[ernmen]t are prepared to offer in return for this obligation. The mem[orandum] then recalls the fact that Imperial Gov[ernmen]t have already admitted in principle their readiness to arrange for a modification of their rate of shipbuilding within the limits of their fleet law, adding that such a modification had not yet been discussed by experts of the two countries owing to interruption in negotiations which took place by wish of H[is] M[ajesty's] Gov[ernmen]t.

The mem[orandum] then repeats the conviction of the Imperial Gov[ernmen]t that as any naval arrangement must necessarily affect the defensive power of the nations concerned, assured good relations should form a prior indispensable condition. On this ground Imperial Gov[ernmen]t consider a political understanding highly necessary, and hope that H[is] M[ajesty's] Gov[ernmen]t will not reject idea of a simultaneous exchange of views corresponding to interests of both countries. Memo[randum] adds that as H[is] M[ajesty's] Gov[ernmen]t have repeatedly declared that their understandings with other Powers are in no way directed against Germany, Imperial Gov[ernmen]t feel convinced that it will be possible to find a formula which will take into account Germany's wishes without prejudice to Great Britain's other International agreements.

A report of the long conversation which ensued will be forwarded by messenger.

MINUTES.

The Germans criticize the vagueness of our proposals. Sir E. Goschen has called attention to the nebulosity of the German suggestions. It seems desirable to contribute to a clearing of the situation by formulating on our part, if possible in the shape of draft clauses of an agreement, exactly what we wish to stipulate for.

The German offer to reduce the rate of shipbuilding amounted to nothing more than dropping " perhaps " one capital ship, not out of the total programme, but out of the programme of one year, the programme being ultimately completed by building the deferred ship (or ships) in subsequent years. I do not see how this offers the basis of an agreement, seeing that the period within which the German programme is laid down by law, is very shortly terminating. Any agreement of a practical nature would have to deal with the new programme which a new German law may lay down.

The allusions to the contents of the proposed political agreement are as vague as the rest of the suggestions. But we know from the former correspondence that what Germany wants is both precise and unacceptable.

E. A. C.
Oct. 13.

The mem[orandum](¹) to which the Chancellor has given his answer is at page 43 of the annexed print.

(¹) [*v. supra*, pp. 501–2, No. 387, *encl.*]

I agree with Mr. Crowe that it would be most useful, if possible, to have a draft of what would satisfy us from the naval point of view.

W. L.
A. N.

We must wait till the text of the German answer and the record of the conversation come, before dealing with it.

E. G.

No. 400.

Sir E. Goschen to Sir Edward Grey.[1]

F.O. 37598/167/10/18.
(No. 280.)   Secret.   Berlin, D. October 12, 1910.
Sir,   R. October 17, 1910.

I have the honour to report that the Imperial Chancellor asked me to call upon him yesterday for the purpose of discussing with him his reply to the Memorandum which, in accordance with the instructions contained in your despatch No. 203 of July the 29th last[2] I had handed to him on the 14th August.

After handing to me his statement, copy and translation of which I have the honour to enclose herewith, His Excellency opened the conversation by expressing his gratification at the good-will shown by His Majesty's Government in reopening the discussions which, for reasons which he quite understood, had been temporarily interrupted. He then reminded me that in the course of those previous discussions negotiations between the two Admiralties had been foreshadowed by his repeated allusions to the possibility of a modification of the tempo of the rate of German naval shipbuilding within of course the provisions of the existing naval law. In the face of these allusions he had never been able to understand Mr. Asquith's statement in Parliament to the effect that the Imperial Government had declared their inability to fall in with the views of His Majesty's Government on the subject of a Naval Agreement. This statement had not only gone very near disclosing the fact, for which he had repeatedly implored the greatest secrecy, that negotiations had been taking place between the two Governments, but had also given a wrong impression of the attitude of the Imperial Government. He did not wish however to dwell on that point, which Count Metternich had been instructed to discuss with you at the time. What he wished to do on the present occasion was to explain to me the general point of view of the Imperial Government with regard to the naval question. In drawing up their naval programme they had been exclusively guided by their desire to possess sufficient naval strength for the adequate protection of their coasts and their commerce. They felt, as far as they were concerned, no necessity for making a reciprocal agreement with any other Power on the subject of their respective naval forces. Nevertheless they were prepared to fall in with the views of His Majesty's Government and to discuss such suggestions with regard to naval matters as had just been put before them, in the hope that by this means the relations of friendship and confidence which had formerly existed between the two countries might eventually be restored.

His Excellency then proceeded to discuss the suggestions, contained in the fifth paragraph of your memorandum, relating to the interchange between the two Admiralties of information on the subject of their mutual progress of shipbuilding. He said that the Imperial Government were quite willing to accept the proposal for such an exchange of information and to agree to the wider facilities for Naval Attachés which the arrangement entailed. He added however that if, as appeared from your memorandum, the arrangement was to include and, in fact, to be based upon, a hard and fast undertaking on the part of the Imperial Government that they would not depart from the provisions of their existing Fleet Law, it would be necessary

[1] [A memorandum by Mr. Crowe upon the subject of this despatch is printed infra, pp. 533–6, No. 404.]
[2] [v. supra, pp. 501–2, No. 387, and encl.]

for him to know what equivalent engagement would be taken by His Majesty's Government. "We have always stated," he said, "that we have no intention of going beyond our Fleet Law; but it is another thing to give a solemn engagement not to do so. You cannot expect me to promise to take the edge off my knife while you remain at liberty to keep yours sharp!" He added that he had all the less hesitation in requiring information on this point as he had understood from your memorandum that reciprocity was one of the conditions of your proposals. I said that for the moment it was not possible for me to give him a specific answer on this point, but that I thought I was right in saying that the general idea underlying your suggestions was that His Majesty's Government would on their side restrict their shipbuilding programme to what was necessary to preserve a safe proportion to the existing German programme as long as the latter continued to be, as it necessarily was at present, the chief factor in determining British naval construction. I added that at the time you had drawn up your memorandum you had not had any discussion with the Admiralty on the particular point he had raised, and that I was under the impression that you had thought that the necessary consultations with naval experts would come more appropriately at a later stage after the principle of the agreement and reciprocity had been accepted.

The Chancellor then dropped this point and came to the question as to whether the exchange of information which you had suggested would have the effect desired. He said that he must return to his old contention, namely, that unless such an arrangement as you had proposed came as a natural sequence to a political understanding harmonizing with the interests of both countries, it would have but little effect and would not be unlikely to render the atmosphere of suspicion and mistrust which at present hung over the two countries denser than it was before. I observed that I could not agree with him that it would have that effect. It would, I was sure, not be the case on our side of the Channel. There was no denying the fact that as far as the British public were concerned the primary cause of what feeling of mistrust they might feel against Germany was the enormous expansion of German Naval Power during the last few years. There existed amongst them a widespread notion that this expansion was directed in some way or another against England, and that their supremacy at sea, a vital question for all Englishmen, was threatened. The knowledge that Germany had shown herself disposed to come to a friendly arrangement with regard to naval construction, such as might eventually lead to a diminution of expenditure on naval armaments would, I was sure, tend to allay their feelings of mistrust and would be a first and very important step in the direction of the good and friendly relations between the two countries which their Governments were both so desirous of seeing established. The Chancellor said: "Do you really think so?" I replied that it was my firm opinion. His Excellency answered that he looked upon the matter in a different light. If the arrangement you had suggested was preceded by a satisfactory general understanding then he had no doubt that it would prove acceptable to his countrymen and in fact it would be his business to make it so. If, however, the arrangement stood by itself, with no political understanding to account for it, he felt sure that the German public would say that German naval interests were being sacrificed to those of Great Britain, and that German official assurances carried so little weight with British statesmen that special arrangements had had to be made to allow them to be checked by the British Admiralty. I said that I thought that the German Public were too sensible to regard a reciprocal arrangement in that light; but he maintained that it was only too likely that that was the point of view which would be generally held. Any naval agreement between two countries must necessarily restrain their liberty of action as regards expenditure for national defence and consequently affect their naval strength. It followed therefore that such an agreement was only possible between countries whose relations stood on a firm and friendly basis. It was on this ground that the Imperial Government held the firm conviction that it was absolutely necessary that a political understanding should precede or at all events be made concurrently with a naval agreement. Continuing, the Chancellor said that one thing was quite certain, namely that at one time Anglo-German relations were good and that now they left much to be desired. Ever since he had taken office *as Imperial Chancellor he had had the re-establishment of the former good relations constantly in his mind. He was also certain that you, Sir, and His Majesty's Government generally were equally anxious to secure that result. What was the impediment? Of course, as far as the British Public was concerned, the construction of the Fleet which Germany considered necessary for the protection of her coasts and commerce had something to do with the present unsatisfactory state of things; but there were other and stronger causes which were more than sufficient to produce whatever irritation might be felt in Germany against England. His Majesty's Government had stated in the Memorandum under discussion and also on former occasions, that their understandings with other Powers were in no way directed against Germany. The Imperial Government fully appreciated the value of this declaration and they would never dream of doing or asking anything which might disturb those understandings; but at the same time they could not shut their eyes to the fact that British Foreign Policy in its general tendency followed a course opposed to that of Germany, often even in cases when British and German interests were more or less identical and called for co-operation. He could give me volumes of instances in which German interests were systematically opposed by the British Government. He would only mention a few of them: Algeciras, Persia, the Bagdad Railway, and quite recently the Turkish Loan. At Algeciras we had supported France in her aspirations for a monopoly of political influence, notwithstanding the fact that Germany had gone there to maintain the old British principle of the Open Door. As regards Persia, during last spring the Imperial Government, whose interests in that country were purely commercial, had made the most self-denying and considerate proposals to His Majesty's Government. What had been the result? They had received no reply. On the contrary His Majesty's Government had stood side by side with Russia and by exercising pressure on the weak Persian Government had endeavoured to reduce German commercial relations with that country to the narrowest possible limit. The Imperial Government had asked that German subjects might have a fair participation in posts under the Persian Government. There, again, American subjects had been accepted while the applications of German subjects had been steadily refused. The Bagdad Railway question, the Chancellor continued, was another case in point. The Imperial Government had endeavoured to come to an arrangement with regard to the southern section of the Railway; their proposals had not only been rejected by His Majesty's Government but the latter had also tried to put obstacles in the way of the German projects by refusing to support the raising of the Turkish Customs dues on the ground that part of the sums realized by that increase would find its way to the concessionnaires of the Bagdad Railway. Nevertheless this attitude of hostility to the German Bagdad Railway had not prevented His Majesty's Government from supporting the French scheme for a Bagdad Railway projected by M. Tardieu.

Finally in the question of the Turkish Loan His Majesty's Government had set themselves in opposition to Germany, and had, as it appeared to the Imperial Government, supported the recent efforts of France to replace the " Dette Publique " by the Ottoman Bank notwithstanding the fact that such an arrangement must be as distasteful to Great Britain as it was to Germany.

In completing the list of grievances the Chancellor made the somewhat extraordinary statement that it had been brought to the knowledge of the Imperial Government that British Representatives abroad now took the line of treating their German colleagues with the greatest reserve while ostentatiously affecting the greatest intimacy with their colleagues of " other nations " !

After making a few obvious remarks on the question of Algeciras, I endeavoured to explain to the Chancellor the attitude of His Majesty's Government as regards

Persia and the reason why no formal answer had been returned to their proposals. I pointed out to him that you regarded the question of Persian Railways etc. and the Bagdad Railway as interdependent. It was your conviction that Public Opinion in the United Kingdom would take a very unfavourable view of a promise to give to Germany participation in Railways through Southern Persia, while Germany maintained the monopoly of railways in Mesopotamia. His Excellency said "What monopoly? We have no monopoly." I replied that as a matter of fact the Bagdad Railway was a monopoly as under the system of kilometric guarantees attached to the concession, it was out of the question that the Ottoman Government could afford to sanction any other line which would in the least compete with it. His Excellency said: "Well, in that sense it may perhaps be called a monopoly, but only in that sense." He added that it seemed to him that formerly we had been more moderate in our demands for participation. A former British Government had only demanded a small portion of the Southern Section. Now we seemed to want the whole of that section. I then reminded him of all I had said to him during former conversations respecting our enormous interests in Mesopotamia and the Persian Gulf, and expressed my regret at the tendency of the Imperial Government to regard the legitimate efforts of His Majesty's Government to defend British political and commercial interests as deliberate and premeditated opposition to Germany. He said that he was afraid that this tendency to which I had alluded was not without justification. "But still" he added, "we must try and alter this state of things and place our relations on a better footing. It is in the hope that we may succeed in this that I have talked to you frankly and openly and not held back anything which appears to us as a cause for irritation. I must say one more thing. You said that the primary cause for mistrust against Germany in the British mind is the expansion of our navy. I maintain that if the British people had not been *taught* by their Governments to regard Germany as an enemy, the expansion of the German Fleet would have caused them as little anxiety as the expansion of the Navy of the United States."

Finally the Chancellor said that in order to prevent outside influences from affecting the result of our negotiations, he must impress upon me once more the necessity for absolute secrecy. In this connection he felt bound to tell me that Sir E. Cassel, on the occasion of his last visit to Berlin, had spoken of our negotiations to his friends and had stated that the discussions of last year had fallen through because Germany had demanded as a condition for an understanding that Great Britain should renounce her *ententes* with France and Russia. It was unnecessary for him to point out to me the gravity of such an indiscretion, for there was nothing more likely to bring to nought such delicate negotiations as those upon which we were engaged than the dissemination of false reports by irresponsible persons.

Throughout the conversation the Chancellor spoke from voluminous notes, of which I have had the advantage of seeing a summary.

I have, &c.
W. E. GOSCHEN.

Enclosure in No. 400.

Memorandum.([3])

(Translation.)([4])

The Imperial Government have been gratified to learn from the Memorandum of His Britannic Majesty's Government that they are willing to resume the

([3]) [For the German original of this Memorandum, *v. G.P.* XXVIII, pp. 367–8; *v.* also *ib.,* pp. 368–73. The British reply of March 8, 1911, is printed *infra*, pp. 598–600, No. 444, *encl.*]

([4]) [The translation of this document was forwarded by Sir E. Goschen with a copy of the original. The translation bears many corrections in the hand of Mr. Crowe, and it is his corrected text which is here reproduced.]

discussions which they had been led to interrupt for a considerable period, owing to political situation in the United Kingdom.

The Imperial Government, desirous of meeting the wishes of His Britannic Majesty's Government, have once more carefully examined the question, whether it would be possible to give effect to the suggestion of His Britannic Majesty's Government for a limitation of naval expenditure upon the basis of a mutual understanding.

The Imperial Government have in the first instance examined the proposal for a mutual exchange of information as to the state of progress at any given moment of the vessels of both parties under construction recourse being had to the Naval Attachés in this connection. The Imperial Government have no objections to raise to this proposal. But if the proposal is based on the assumption that the Imperial Government will engage to renounce any extension of the existing German Fleet Law, then the Imperial Government must certainly reply that they cannot take this suggestion into consideration, until it is made clear what equivalent His Britannic Majesty's Government would be willing to offer in return for such a formal undertaking, since such an Agreement, as His Britannic Majesty's Government have themselves pointed out, can only be founded upon the principle of reciprocity.

The Imperial Government would wish however once more to recall that they have recognised the possibility of considering the question of a retardation of the rate of naval construction within the limits laid down by the Fleet Law, and have intimated their readiness, in principle, to do so. Owing to the fact that negotiations have been interrupted at the wish of His Majesty's Government, the Naval Authorities of the two countries have not yet discussed the manner in which such a retardation could be effected.

The Imperial Government wish once more to express their conviction that assured mutual good relations are an indispensable preliminary condition for any naval agreement, seeing that such an agreement affects the armed strength of both countries parties to it. To this end the Imperial Government certainly consider a political agreement to be necessary. Since according to the declaration of His Britannic Majesty's Government no agreement concluded by them with any other Power contains anything that is directed against Germany, the Imperial Gov[ernmen]t believe it to be possible to find a formula, which will meet German wishes in this respect, without prejudice to the Agreements of His Britannic Majesty's Government with other Powers. The Imperial Government therefore hope that His Britannic Majesty's Government will not fail to recognize the necessity of a simultaneous political exchange of views (" Aussprache ") which shall take account of the interests of both parties.

MINUTES.

I have in the attached memorandum([5]) called attention to the points of chief importance which arise on this despatch. The Eastern Department add a separate minute dealing with the particular questions raised by the German Chancellor in regard to eastern affairs.

Herr von Bethmann-Hollweg has put before Sir E. Goschen a written memorandum, and at the same time made a lengthy verbal communication. The memorandum treats mainly of the naval question, and I think we shall do well to answer it by putting clearly before the German Government, also in writing, what should in our opinion be the contents of a naval agreement. For this purpose I have suggested that we should now invite the Admiralty to draw up, in the form of draft clauses of an agreement, the precise stipulations by which they consider effect can be given satisfactorily to the plan of a mutual reduction of armaments. The preparation of such a document will require the most careful consideration from the naval, the political, and the juridical point of view. More especially the relative naval strength of this country in comparison with that of third States, whether allied to Germany, or reliably neutral, must be taken into account, if the policy of the two-power standard is to be adhered to.

The German memorandum winds up with a reiteration of the German claim that a political agreement must accompany the naval one. If and when we are in a position to lay before the

([5]) [v. infra, pp. 533–6, No. 404.]

German government precise proposals for a naval agreement, we shall be in a good position to ask that the German gov[ernmen]t should on their part put down in black and white what exactly they propose should be put into a political agreement.

Meanwhile it is not desirable to leave unanswered the grave accusations and complaints brought forward by the German Chancellor. The best course would be to send to Sir E. Goschen a full statement of Sir E. Grey's views on the several questions involved, and instruct H[is] E[xcellency] to take an opportunity of presenting them to the Chancellor, in a verbal communication in the first instance, explaining that H[is] M[ajesty's] G[overnment] do not wish or propose to enter into controversy with the German gov[ernmen]t in this connection, but that they cannot allow the Chancellor to remain under the impression that H[is] M[ajesty's] G[overnment] accept his criticisms as well founded or his version of facts and events as an accurate presentation. We ought to make a clear and temperate statement of the attitude of H[is] M[ajesty's] G[overnment] in respect to Algeciras, Persia, the Bagdad Railway, and the Turkish loan.

It appears to me essential that we should take formal and very decided objection to being told that H[is] M[ajesty's] G[overnment] have deliberately incited the British people to enmity against Germany. Sir E. Goschen might well be directed to put some warmth into his protest on this point and to say that H[is] M[ajesty's] G[overnment] have welcomed a friendly discussion with the German government, which they earnestly hope may ripen into a satisfactory agreement; but a continuance of this friendly discussion will become impossible if unwarranted statements of this kind, which are derogatory to the honour of the British government, are put forward. Sir E. Goschen should express the confident expectation that the offensive remark will be withdrawn.

In regard to the attitude of British Representatives towards their German colleagues, Sir E. Goschen might well refer to the O'Beirne incident and add that only the desire of H[is] M[ajesty's] G[overnment] not to envenom the discussion prevents them from commenting on the attitude of Germany's representatives, which however they assume to reflect the views and wishes of the German government.

The question of secrecy of the negotiations will require some delicate handling. We might perhaps safely give the explanation of Mr. Asquith's statement which I have suggested in my memorandum. But as regards Sir Ernest Cassel I confess it appears to me that the less we say, the better.

E. A. C.
Oct. 20.

MINUTES BY THE EASTERN DEPARTMENT.

The questions which concern the Eastern department in this despatch and are specifically alluded to are three :—

(i.) Persia. (ii.) The Bagdad Railway. (iii.) The Turkish loan.

The questions of Persia and the Bagdad Railway must, in so far as Germany is concerned, be considered together, except as regards one point,—the Chancellor's grievance that Americans are considered eligible for posts under the Persian Government, while the applications of German subjects for such posts have been steadily refused.

In the first place, the Medjliss decided in favour of Americans (see Sir G. Barclay's telegram No. 355 of September 7th),(⁶) and, in the second place, the view of Great Britain and Russia has been that the engagement of Americans is unlikely to give rise to political difficulties, as they are not subjects of a *Great European* Power (see Sir G. Barclay Tel : No. 392 of September 30th).(⁶)

I think that this might be pointed out to Herr von Bethmann-Hollweg.

It is only accurate to say that we have given no *written* reply to the proposals of the German Government made last spring. On May 31st Sir E. Grey told the German Ambassador his views,(⁷) pointing out how impossible it would be for H[is] M[ajesty's] G[overnment] to make an arrangement with Germany in regard to railway construction in Persia unless it included a satisfactory settlement as to British participation in the Bagdad Railway as a *quid pro quo*. The remarks of Count Metternich, who it is true was not speaking under instructions from his Gov[ernmen]t, were so unfavourable to this view of the question that it can hardly be said that H[is] M[ajesty's] G[overnment] received much encouragement to press forward negotiations.

It is wholly misleading to say that by exercising pressure on the weak Persian Gov[ernmen]t, Great Britain and Russia have endeavoured to reduce German *commercial* relations with Persia to the narrowest possible limits.

On May 31st Sir E. Grey informed Count Metternich of the action actually taken at Tehran by Great Britain and Russia, viz., of the joint notes of April 7th and May 20th, 1910,—notes which asked that, before granting any concessions for means of communication, telegraphs or ports to foreigners, the Persian Gov[ernmen]t should enter into an exchange of views with G[rea]t.

(⁶) [Not reproduced.]
(⁷) [*v. supra*, pp. 490–1, No. 375.]

Britain and Russia, in order that the political and strategic interests of the two Powers might be duly safeguarded.([8])

The fact is that such concessions in Persia cannot in many cases be considered purely commercial, especially if they involve an extension of such an enterprise as the Bagdad Railway into Persia.

As regards the Bagdad Railway, the German Gov[ernmen]t seem unable to appreciate the fact that our attitude is one of defence and not of aggression.

It would be tedious to argue this point in the present minute, but I would submit that it might be expedient to draw up a detailed though conciliatory statement or despatch for Sir E. Goschen's use, in case, as appears not improbable, the Chancellor should revert to the subject. Such a statement would review our attitude in regard to the Bagdad Railway concession ab ovo, and incidentally explain our reservations as to the proposed increase of the Turkish customs duties. I think it is very desirable that we should not allow a strong case, such as we undoubtedly have in regard to this question, to suffer through not being cogently represented if criticism is renewed at Berlin.

Before leaving this subject I venture to express the view that sooner or later the Bagdad Railway is likely to be completed, even if we withhold our assent to the customs increase. If this is a correct view, then, at an opportune moment, we must reach some agreement as to British participation unless we are prepared to be left out in the cold. The position appears to be this : the Germans are ready to accept our capital for the Bagdad Railway but not, in corresponding measure, our control. In order to obtain control we must, it would seem, give some quid pro quo, such as a share to Germany in the provision of material for any railways we may ultimately build in Persia. The time does not seem to have come yet for such a bargain : but eventually, if an arrangement as to British participation in the Bagdad Railway is to be reached at all, it would seem to be more feasible on these than on any other lines.

In view of the approaching meeting at Potsdam the question of railway construction in Persia may be forced upon us by the trend of the negotiations which we know are to take place between Russia and Germany.

(iii.) *British opposition to Germany in regard to the Turkish loan.*

H[is] M[ajesty's] G[overnment], in this question, expressed to the French Gov[ernmen]t their concurrence in the view that it would be only prudent to make an advance to Turkey conditional upon some satisfactory form of control, and also upon adequate guarantees that the loan should not be swallowed up in unproductive expenditure. Such a reservation appears eminently desirable, not only in the interests of all Turkish bondholders of whatever nationality, but above all in the interests of Turkey herself. H[is] M[ajesty's] G[overnment] have never wittingly supported efforts to replace the Public Debt Administration by the Ottoman Bank.

I think this might be brought to the notice of Herr von Bethmann-Hollweg, who at the same time might be informed that H[is] M[ajesty's] G[overnment] are at a loss to appreciate how their attitude in this question has been one of opposition to Germany, since no indication had been vouchsafed to them as to the views of the German Go[vernmen]t regarding the loan, while they still have no certain knowledge as to what those views may be, and now learn for the first time that they exist at all.

From the remarks of the Chancellor on this subject it might be concluded that the contentions of Turkey, as to the conditions upon which she should be allowed to borrow foreign money, are in fact the contentions of *Germany*.

There is also the statement of Herr von Bethmann-Hollweg that " British foreign policy in its general tendency followed a course opposed to that of Germany, and *that* even in cases when British and German interests were more or less identical and called for co-operation." Although this statement does not primarily concern the Eastern Department, instances have occurred in recent years in the Near East where the opposition to co-operation has emanated from Germany, who has created not a few difficulties for Great Britain, as indeed also for the other Powers, particularly on account of the German attitude towards the obligations incurred by Europe under the Treaty of Berlin.

I need only instance two cases, though it would not be difficult to add to the number.

Under the Treaty of Berlin, the Powers assumed a moral responsibility to see to it that reforms were introduced in certain provinces of the Ottoman Empire.

The attitude of Germany, in detaching herself from the other Powers, was the principal reason why the Macedonian reforms (1904/5/6/7)([9]) did not meet with greater success.

Again as regards Crete, the action of the German Emperor in " laying down his flute " as H[is] M[ajesty] called it, and thus deserting the concert of the Powers, has very greatly increased the difficulty of the Protecting Powers in dealing with this problem. If Germany had cordially co-operated Turkey would have been more reasonable, especially of late; and the same may be

([8]) [*v. supra*, p. 452, No. 343, *note* ([2]), and p. 490, No. 375, and *note* ([1]).]
([9]) [This subject is treated in *Gooch & Temperley*, Vol. V.]

said in regard to the Turkish attitude towards Greece. I am not sure that it would not be expedient to take advantage of the Chancellor's remark to rub this in and to try and induce Germany to act with the other Powers in the cause of peace.

A. P.

Oct. 20th, 1910.

I entirely agree with Mr. Parker's minute.

R. P. M.

Oct. 20/10.

The minutes of Mr. Crowe and of Mr. Parker are so much to the point that I have nothing to add.

The whole question requires a careful study, and I forward the despatch and minutes as they stand preliminary to a fuller examination of them.

A. N.

No. 401.

Sir E. Goschen to Sir Edward Grey.

Private.(¹)

My dear Grey, *Berlin, October 14, 1910.*

I am sending you by this Messenger a despatch giving an account of the long conversation I had the day before yesterday with Bethmann-Hollweg.(²) I must tell you that his *tone* throughout the conversation was perfectly friendly—much more so, in fact, than you will gather from my despatch. The catalogue of grievances he read out from the voluminous notes which he had before him, and which had been, if I am not mistaken, supplied to him by Kiderlen. He read them as quickly as possible and slurred over many of the severer criticisms of our policy; he seemed in fact to be very glad when he had got that portion of his remarks over. He said however that he would wish me to peruse these notes before I wrote my report to you as they would assist me in reporting accurately what he had said—and what he had not said. Under these circumstances, after reading a summary of his notes I had to put in my despatch what he was supposed to have said—rather than what he actually said. Thinking that probably the notes which he wished me to read would not arrive in time I first wrote an account of the conversation as I remembered it and I confess it read much milder. In any case his tone was friendly in the extreme—much friendlier than the language which was put into his mouth. I did not care, and I hope you will approve, about entering into a wrangle about our respective policies. I have gone into it all before with him, and, except for a few remarks about Algeciras and Bagdad I confined myself to an expression of regret that the German Gov[ernmen]t persisted in regarding legitimate defence on important British Interests as deliberate and carefully thought out aggression against Germany. You will see that as regards the interdependence, in our view, of the Bagdad and Persian Railways question I used the private letter you were good enough to send me on that subject.

There is one thing which is not clear to me. The Chancellor began by saying that he accepted your proposals as regards the interchange of information between the two Admiralties and then proceeded to say: (1) that if they were based upon an undertaking to be given by Germany that she would not add to her existing Programme, he must, before coming to any decision, know what equivalent H[is] M[ajesty's] G[overnment] proposed to offer; (2) that he regarded a preceding or concomitant Political Understanding as a *sine quâ non* for a Naval agreement. I asked him two or three times whether he meant that he accepted the 'Interchange' proposals in any case or whether he meant that he would only accept them as part of a general Understanding. But I could not get an answer and [he] always flew off

(¹) [Grey MSS., Vol. 23.]

(²) [*v. supra*, pp. 521–8, No. 400. The interview took place on October 11.]

at a tangent and continued to harp on the necessity of a general Understanding and of a clearance of the atmosphere. Finally, when I pressed him, he said I would see what he meant from his notes which he would ask Kiderlen to show me. But the notes contained no elucidation of this point. I hope there is no confusion in his mind between your proposals and those made by the Naval Attaché. Curiously enough I don't think that he wanted me to see Kiderlen before I wrote to you—as on my saying that I would call on Kiderlen and ask him to show me the Notes —he said "Oh no! don't do that, send a Secretary and Kiderlen will dictate a summary to him." The notes say: "We have adopted the suggestion of an Interchange of naval information" and then proceed with a series of "buts." I cannot see that either the German counter Memorandum or the conversation help us forward very much. The German Government seem very querulous about Bagdad and Persia and their frame of mind does not seem to be much improved by the Turkish Loan business. It was only when speaking of that subject that the Chancellor's tone was at all unpleasant. He was also somewhat bitter when he spoke of Cassels indiscreet remarks about our negotiations. I told him I could hardly believe what he had told me and that there must have been some misunderstanding. But he assured me that it was quite true.

I think that the Chancellor is all right, that he really [is] desirous of establishing better relations between the two countries but I think that Kiderlen is doing, and will continue to do, all he can to prevent him from being too conciliatory. Kiderlen's friends are always coming to me and telling me how anxious he is to be friendly with me and to work harmoniously with me for the good of the two countries: but I feel that if he wants an arrangement with us at all he wants to make the path leading up to it as thorny as possible, and to make us feel that after all our iniquities it is very kind of Germany to be willing to be friends with us. It is thus that I account for the long catalogue of our misdoings which he served up to us through the Chancellor's mouth. . . . .(3)

Yours very sincerely,
W. E. GOSCHEN.

(3) [The closing remarks are on personal matters.]

No. 402.

Sir E. Goschen to Sir A. Nicolson.

Private.(1)

My dear Nicolson,   *Berlin, October* 14, 1910.

. . . . (2) I had a tremendous talk with the Chancellor on Wednesday, which I have faithfully reported in, I am sorry to say, a very long despatch. He was personally excessively friendly, as he always is, with me, (especially since I went out to his farm and admired his cattle and pigs) but he had somewhat unfriendly words put in his mouth by Kiderlen. At the end he said that he hoped, by his frank exposition of their numerous grievances against us, to clear the atmosphere! I longed to tell him that it was a dubious way of attempting to secure good relations to rake up everything they had against us from Algeciras to the Turkish Loan and to put all our proceedings in the most disagreeable and prejudiced light. As I have told Sir E. Grey I did not think it worth while to go in for recriminations. They

(1) [Carnock MSS., Vol. II of 1910.]
(2) [The omitted passages of this letter refer to the proposed visit of Emperor Nicholas II to Berlin and to the Russian Embassy.]

could only have taken the form of ' Tu quoque ' and I could only have told him that if it was irritating to Germans to find Englishmen always in possession it was equally irritating for Englishmen, wherever they had vested and important interests, to have Germans poking their noses in and demanding shares in concerns and interests which had been built up by years of British hard work and enterprise. Of course I allowed myself to make a few remarks, but they were not worth reporting as I have made and reported them so often. I have supplemented my despatch by a private letter to Sir Edward Grey(³) which he will no doubt show you. . . . .(⁴)

Yours ever,
W. E. GOSCHEN.

P.S.—I forgot to mention in my despatch one remark of the Chancellor's. He said at the close of our conversation '' I can see no reason for the suspicion that we are trying to come to an understanding with England in order to disturb her relations with other Powers. Nothing can be further from our intentions. On the contrary we are of the opinion that a frank exchange of views and a subsequent understanding with His Majesty's Government will have the result that the relations between Gt. Britain and her friends will suffer no change and that at the same time German Relations with those Powers will gain in cordiality.'' (I presume that this utterance was prompted by the allusion he had just made to Cassel's alleged indiscretion).

This, if you think worth while, postscript to my despatch.(⁵)

W. E. G.

(³) [*v.* immediately preceding document.]
(⁴) [The closing paragraphs refer to Balkan affairs.]
(⁵) [It was added by the Foreign Office as a postscript to Sir E. Goschen's despatch No. 280 of October 12, *supra*, pp. 521–4, No. 400.]

No. 403.

Sir E. Goschen to Sir Edward Grey.(¹)

F.O. 38552/167/10/18.
(No. 288.) Secret.   *Berlin, D. October* 16, 1910.
Sir,   R. *October* 24, 1910.

I have the honour to report that I had the honour to-day of presenting to the Emperor the letters by which The King has been pleased to appoint me his Ambassador Extraordinary and Minister Plenipotentiary at this court.

Immediately I had presented my letters The Emperor began to speak to me in a very animated manner regarding my recent conversation with the Imperial Chancellor and the general question of a political understanding with Germany. '' The present state of things,'' His Majesty said, '' must not continue and the time is come when an understanding *must* be made. I have waited patiently, and I told my Ministers last spring to mark time, as I wished to give His Majesty King George time to make up His mind as to what course with regard to us He wished and intended to pursue. Now, to my satisfaction, the interrupted conversations have been reopened by His Majesty's Government(²) and the question must be gone through with.'' I said that I was sure both the King, my August Sovereign, and His Government were equally anxious that the relations between the two countries should be as friendly as possible; upon which His Majesty said that in that case it was to be hoped that this anxiety would bear fruit in the discontinuance of the

(¹) [An account of this interview by the Emperor William II is given in Admiral von Tirpitz : *Politische Dokumente. Der Aufbau der deutschen Weltmacht* (Stuttgart and Berlin, 1924), pp. 182–4. The date of the interview is there given as October 17.]
(²) [It will be observed, *v.* p. 521, No. 400, that the initiative came from Germany, as was admitted by Herr von Bethmann Hollweg.]

systematic opposition to all German schemes which he regretted to find existing in so many quarters of the globe. I rather demurred to this and said that I hoped His Majesty would not regard defence of our interests always as deliberate opposition to Germany. "But I," he rejoined, "am here also to defend the commercial interests of my country. I am a commercial man; you are commercial men too; but with you politics and commerce go hand in hand—too much so."

His Majesty then proceeded to discuss the naval question. He said that he had no particular objection to the idea of the two Admiralties exchanging information; he did not believe that it would be of the slightest use, as even without an arrangement to that effect the two Admiralties generally knew pretty well what was going on in each other's Dockyards. If however His Majesty's Government thought that it would do good, He had nothing to say against the proposal. "But to one thing," he added, "I will never consent, and that is to bind myself not to add to my existing programme. I do not *wish* to add to it, but it is asking too much to request me to make an engagement not to do so. I have two neighbours, each with a number of corps d'armée close to my frontiers, who are only waiting for an opportunity to jump at my throat. I cannot afford to weaken my Power on land or to place any restriction upon my right to bring up my naval strength to the standard which I consider necessary." He reminded me that I had once told Him that the man in the street in England wanted to know why He was building such a large Fleet when He had already such an enormous and efficient army. "I will tell you why," He said, "because I want to make myself safe. Safe against France and Russia and safe against England should she at a given moment feel called upon to come to the assistance of her friends. I have another reason which is this. I am all for the white man against the black, whether they be Chinese, Japanese, niggers or Slavs; and I foresee the time when the overweening ambition of the black and yellow races, grown out of bounds since the victory of Japan over Russia, will show us the necessity of white men standing shoulder to shoulder; and then you will come crawling on your knees to me, not to beg me to diminish my naval strength, but to increase it to the utmost of my power." I ventured to state that my imagination could not travel quite so fast, but He maintained that that time would assuredly come. He said that we talked a great deal of the necessity of keeping up our supremacy at sea. He had nothing against that, if we could do it; and if we continued to build four or five capital ships a-year it would not upset his equanimity in the least; but if we began to build dozens every year it would give Him cause for reflection and He would have to take measures accordingly. His Majesty added that it was the impression in England and elsewhere that Germany had no money. That was a mistake; they had plenty; more perhaps than in Paris. The proof that they had money was that they had been perfectly ready to advance money to Hungary and to Turkey. In the case of the latter we had deliberately opposed Germany and supported France manifestly against our own interests.

The mention of the Turkish loan brought His Majesty to the general question of British opposition to all German financial and commercial schemes. He told me that He had spoken to the Chancellor before the latter had seen me and had told His Excellency what He wished him to say. He had even written some of the points down in English so that there might be no mistake. I told His Majesty that as a matter of fact the Chancellor had communicated to me the list of our iniquities in German but that I could assure His Majesty that there had been no want of clearness in his language. His Majesty laughed and said that he was glad of it, as we were really behaving too badly, and He was anxious that we should know how our proceedings were regarded in Germany. He added that it was not as if Germany ever did anything to oppose or annoy us. Only lately the British Government had annexed, or taken under their protection, an enormous tract of land in Siam. It had not been a very "pretty transaction," but Germany had not said a word. If the position had been reversed what a storm would have been

2 м 2

raised in England. His Majesty then talked about Persia and said that we had not even returned any answer to the generous proposals Germany had made. I endeavoured to lay before His Majesty the point of view of His Majesty's Government on this question in the same language I had held to the Chancellor as reported in my Secret Despatch No. 280 of the 12th instant(³) and I spoke to him in general terms of the work we had done in the Persian Gulf and the trade interests we had there, but His Majesty however did not seem much inclined to pay any heed to our point of view as to the interdependency of the Persian and Bagdad Railway questions or indeed to our views on any question.

Finally His Majesty alluded to our understandings with France and Russia and said that we ought to have come to Germany first, as the country to which we were bound by ties of blood, old comradeship and intellectual sympathy. I said that between France and Russia and ourselves there had been definite and long existing sources of irritation and friction with regard to which it had been absolutely necessary both in our own and general interests to come to a settlement. Between Great Britain and Germany there had been, happily, nothing of the sort. It seemed to me therefore perfectly natural that His Majesty's Government should have decided to settle their differences with the two Powers rather than to approach a Government with whom none such existed, at all events of a definite and pressing nature. His Majesty replied that that was all very well but that he must remind me that the French and Russian alliance had been directed entirely against Germany; England, without saying a word to Him had joined that alliance, that is to say had made understandings with the members of that Alliance. That had naturally caused irritation in Germany. "We, as champions of the principle of the open door" (His Majesty said this without a smile) "are the people to whom you ought to have come instead of to the two peoples who of all others are the advocates of political and economic monopolies." Before I had time to get my breath, His Majesty added that Great Britain was also, in her best moments, a champion of the open door and the two champions ought to stand together. In any case an understanding between the two countries had become absolutely necessary and he sincerely trusted that it might soon be made in some form or other, but preferably with the open door as its main and leading principle.

At that moment the Empress came in to say that it was long after luncheon time. His Majesty then only added that He had spoken as a Friend to Great Britain, frankly and openly as a good friend should. He had wanted me to understand the reasons for such irritation as existed in Germany and he hoped he had made them perfectly clear. I replied that His Majesty could not have spoken with greater clearness but that——. His Majesty laughed and said, "We have not time for any 'buts,' as we must not keep the Empress waiting any longer."

I have, &c.
W. E. GOSCHEN.

P.S.—Since writing the above despatch I have taken an opportunity of calling the attention of the Secretary of State for Foreign Affairs to the discrepancy between the Emperor's remarks with regard to the non-increase of the existing German Naval Programme and those made on the same subject by the Chancellor during our recent conversation. I explained that His Majesty had stated that He must refuse to give any pledge that he would not add to the Programme, while the Chancellor had merely said that he could come to no decision on the subject before he knew what equivalent His Majesty's Government was prepared to give in return. Herr von Kiderlen replied that the Emperor, who had, as I had probably observed, become very animated, had expressed himself badly and gone beyond what He had really meant. What His Majesty had intended to say, and this was clear from the Notes which He had furnished to the Chancellor, and upon which the latter's

(³) [v. supra, pp. 521–4, No. 400.]

remarks to me had been chiefly founded, was that he could not bind himself not to add to the existing Naval Programme without a previous understanding such as would prove to him our friendly intentions. I said that I only knew what the Emperor had actually said and that in such an important matter it would be well that there should be no confusion. Herr von Kiderlen entirely agreed with me and said that he would speak to the Chancellor on the subject and ask him to clear the matter up on the occasion of his next audience with the Emperor which would take place very shortly.

W. E. G.

MINUTES.

The Emperor's re-entry on the scene is marked by all H[is] M[ajesty's] usual impulsiveness and disregard for facts and his total want of consideration for the interests of other nations. It must be exceedingly difficult for an ambassador to listen to these imperial fulminations with respect and the outward forms of civility.

As for the actual observations of the Emperor, they hardly call for any fresh comment since they evidently served as the basis of his Chancellor's recent remarks to Sir E. Goschen, to which answers have already been suggested.

The only point of importance is the Emperor's emphatic statement as to his never consenting to any agreement for a limitation of armaments. I have more than once stated my conviction that the German gov[ernmen]t have merely held out the bait of their possibly consenting to such agreement, for the purpose of getting their political agreement. We have already been told both that Admiral von Tirpitz would never consent to a naval limitation agreement which he regarded as impossible of achievement, and that he is favourably disposed towards it and ready to conclude one on conditions. We now hear that the Chancellor is ready to consider the question of such an agreement, and that the Emperor, who had just instructed the Chancellor at length, declares that he will never never agree to such a thing.

They are none of them to be believed on their word

E. A. C.
Oct. 24.

It is admitted that the Chancellor was only the mouthpiece of the Emperor.

W. L.

Approve Sir E. Goschen's language.

A. N.
E. G.

[ED. NOTE.—The following memorandum by Mr. Crowe was written in connection with Sir E. Goschen's despatch No. 280 of October 12 (v. supra, pp. 521–8, No. 400).]

No. 404.

Memorandum by Mr. Crowe.

Herr von Bethmann Hollweg's Memorandum of October 11, 1910.

F.O. 37598/167/10/18/   *October* 20, 1910.

1. I propose to deal briefly with the principal points in the German Chancellor's communication(1) which deserve consideration :

(a.) *What equivalent does Great Britain propose to offer for an engagement on Germany's part not to exceed the limits of the German Naval Law?*

2. The question is a legitimate one and requires an answer. Sir E. Goschen, being unable to answer it, fell back upon a suggestion which amounts to this : Let the two governments agree in principle that there shall be limitation of armaments; then the details of how this principle is to be applied may be left for subsequent discussion between the naval experts of the two countries. It is not likely that the German government will or can accept such an arrangement, because it is obvious

(1) [v. supra, pp. 524–5, No. 400, encl.]

that this is one of those cases where the whole essence and principle of an agreement consists in the detailed particulars and that without the particulars there is really nothing to agree upon.

3. The German government have repeatedly declared that they see great difficulty in indicating any method by which the desired object can in practice be obtained. Their only contribution towards a solution of this difficulty has been the suggestion that the completion of one or perhaps two ships included in the existing naval programme might be slightly deferred. It can hardly be supposed that the German Chancellor seriously counts on this suggestion being accepted by Great Britain as a working basis for an agreement, more especially if so meagre an offer is to be coupled with a demand for important concessions in the political field.

4. In these circumstances I venture to repeat what I submitted in my minute on Sir E. Goschen's telegram No. 62 (37093)(²) that the moment seems to have come when the Admiralty should be asked to formulate in the shape of articles of a draft agreement, not necessarily for communication at this stage to the German government, but for the clearer guidance of the Secretary of State in conducting the negotiations, exactly what we desire to stipulate for and what we are prepared to undertake.

(b.) *Probable effect on the relations between the two countries of an arrangement for the mutual, systematic, and periodical exchange, through their Naval Attachés, of exact information, verified by them, respecting the rate and actual progress of shipbuilding for the two navies respectively.*

5. The German Chancellor believes that the effect of such an arrangement, unless accompanied by a general political agreement, would tend to aggravate rather than to relieve the existing tension. Sir E. Goschen, on the other hand, has argued in reply that the contrary would be the case at least in England. This is largely a question of opinion and speculation. Probably both the Chancellor and the ambassador are right, each in respect to his own country. But the matter practically loses its importance owing to the fact that the Chancellor seems determined in any case to make the conclusion of a far-reaching political agreement a *conditio sine quâ non* of any, even the most modest, naval understanding.

(c.) *General relations between England and Germany.*

6. The Chancellor throws no fresh light on what the proposed political agreement is to contain. But we know enough about his intentions from previous communications to render it necessary for us to be very cautious in approaching this matter. By way of illustrating the need for such an agreement, the Chancellor refers to the relations between the two countries, which, he says, were formerly good, as now leaving much to be desired. This is not the place for explaining how it has come about that our relations are not good. It is however well to remember that it is necessary to go back a good number of years in order to reach a period when those relations were genuinely satisfactory, certainly as far back as the Krüger telegram, since when the mutual animosities have been steadily growing. Even that telegram would be unexplainable except as the outcome of a feeling of pent-up irritation, which in fact we know it was. Germany may be inclined to hark back with some gratification to the long period during which by constant pressure and threats she induced Great Britain to do her will time after time. We have less reason to wish for a return of those days of "good relations."

7. The Chancellor is therefore right in suggesting that it is not merely or even principally the question of naval armaments which is the cause of the existing estrangement. The building of the German fleet is but one of the symptoms of the

(²) [*v. supra*, p. 520, No. 399.]

disease. It is the political ambitions of the German government and nation which are the source of the mischief.

8. When the Chancellor on his part assigns what he considers the cause, his statements show that he is either very imperfectly informed—which would easily be explained on the hypothesis that he is dependent for his "facts" on Herr von Kiderlen and some of the notoriously shoddy officials of the German Foreign Office —or that he disposes of a good fund of cynicism. He complains of the deliberately anti-German policy of Great Britain. Besides accusing H[is] M[ajesty's] G[overnment] in express words of *teaching* the British people to regard as an enemy, which none but a Prussian official could do without being conscious that this is a gross impertinence, he particularly mentions four or five instances of English hostility, out of the "volumes" which he says he could quote.

9. He begins by a reference to the Algeciras conference, and it is difficult to take him seriously. Sir E. Goschen does not report what he rejoined. But our answer is as simple as it is conclusive : What H[is] M[ajesty's] G[overnment] did on the occasion of the Algeciras conference was to afford France that diplomatic support which they were bound to give under the solemn engagement of the Anglo-French Declaration of 1904, an instrument of which Prince Bülow publicly declared at the time of its conclusion that he regarded it as in no way objectionable from the German point of view.

10. The Eastern Department are dealing in a separate minute with the other instances of alleged English ill-will adduced by the Chancellor.

(d.) *Attitude of British Representatives abroad towards their German colleagues.*

11. It is one of the least estimable traditions of the German Foreign Office to direct personal attacks against British officials who are obnoxious to them because believed to stand in the way of the realization of particular German plans or ambitions. Few of our most deserving diplomatists have escaped their censure, and it is quite in accordance with this policy that the Chancellor should bring a general indictment against all our Representatives.

12. It is not desirable that H[is] M[ajesty's] G[overnment] should follow in the German footsteps. They will no doubt continue to act on the assumption that the proceedings of the German Representatives abroad is such as their government prescribes or approves. But it is useful for us to remember what the record of those proceedings has been. Although we do not address complaints to the German gov[ernmen]t directed against the personality of their agents, we do not overlook, or fail to appreciate the tendency of their action. If we find Baron Marschall at Constantinople, Herr von Quadt at Tehran, Count Tattenbach at Lisbon, M. Rosen at Tangier, Count Bernstorff at Cairo and at Washington, the German Minister at Peking do things, not here and there, but systematically, which are incompatible with professions of friendship for Great Britain but quite intelligible from the point of view that hostility against her should be created and fostered at every possible point, we are entitled to draw and we do draw our conclusions as to the *bona fides* of the demand that British diplomatists shall go out of their way to show- in their intercourse with foreign embassies or legations which are active centres of persistent anti-British intrigues, the same degree of cordiality as with those of Powers which act in loyal co-operation with us on the basis of a clear political understanding.

13. Moreover it is well to remember that the views of German diplomatists as to the principles governing private intercourse with their colleagues differ somewhat from that which is in England considered honourable; and in view of such incidents as the O'Beirne affair at St. Petersburg, or the proceedings some years ago of a German naval Attaché in a London club of which he had been made an honorary member, prove how necessary it is that a certain amount of that reserve

of which the Chancellor complains should be observed in any dealings with German diplomatists.

(e.) *Secrecy of the Negotiations.*

14. Germany has her own reasons for accentuating the necessity of absolute secrecy. The Chancellor complains that the secret was nearly betrayed by Mr. Asquith's statement in Parliament that the German government had declared their inability to fall in with the views of H[is] M[ajesty's] G[overnment] on the subject of a naval agreement. This is captious criticism. The views of H[is] M[ajesty's] G[overnment], which are known to all the world, are that it would be desirable to arrive at an understanding with Germany for the purpose of limiting the actual output of shipbuilding by agreement between the two countries. H[is] M[ajesty's] G[overnment] have never concealed the fact that what they desire is a curtailment of the German naval programme. The German gov[ernmen]t in December last published an official communiqué to the effect that "there had been up to then no agreement with regard to the so-called navy question" and that "it was altogether incorrect to say that Germany intended to recede from the programme of naval construction established by law. False news of this kind can at most produce the belief in England that Germany is capable of being induced to effect a change in her building programme."

15. In the face of this declaration it is surely childish of the Chancellor to find fault with the statement of the Prime Minister.

16. More serious is the allegation that the secret of the negotiations has been divulged to Sir E. Cassel. If he really used the words attributed to him, it does look as if he had some inkling of the German demand for a political agreement which, as has been pointed out here, would in fact amount to an abandonment of our *Entente* with France and Russia. I had an opportunity yesterday of speaking on the subject to Lord Hardinge. He assured me that so far as he was aware, nothing was at any time said to Sir E. Cassel at this Office about the negotiations.

17. Whether somebody has been indiscreet in Paris, or whether Sir E. Cassel himself put two and two together from what he learnt at Berlin, I have no means of verifying.

E. A. C.
Oct. 20.

No. 405.

Sir E. Goschen to Sir A. Nicolson.

Private.([1])
My dear Nico, *Berlin, October 22, 1910.*

A few quite private lines about my other letter.([2]) I wonder what the German game is, and why they are so fearfully keen about a political understanding. I suppose it is something in this way : We know that the phrase "Balance of Power" stinks in their nostrils. In fact they have told me so. They want the Hegemony of Europe and to neutralize the only thing which has prevented them from getting it, viz., England's naval strength. They want an understanding which would have that effect. Kiderlen proposed it long ago—and this has been the tendency of all my conversations with the Chancellor: Should we fall in with their

([1]) [Grey MSS., Vol. 23.]

([2]) [This letter, of October 21, opens with some general remarks on Russo-German relations and the Bagdad railway, and continues in the same sense as despatch No. 288 of October 16, printed *supra*, pp. 530–3, No. 403.]

views of a general understanding it appears to me that the balance of advantage must be against us. It would stand thus—I mean the balance sheet:

Gain.	Loss.
England.—Diminution of Naval Expenditure. S. Section of Bagdad R[ailwa]y.	Good will of Russia and France.
Germany.—Diminution of Naval Expenditure. Free hand on the Continent. Facilitation of completion of B[agda]d Railway by raising of Turkish Customs 4 %. Participation in B[ritis]h Enterprises under Persian Concessions. Wedge between G[rea]t B[ritai]n and France and Russia and our possible isolation.	S. Section of B[agda]d Railway.

This is how I can't help looking at it—and the balance would be so heavy on the German side that I cannot see how it would remove "that atmosphere of mistrust and suspicion which has so long hung over the two countries."

It remains to be considered how far the latest "idea" of taking Russia and France into the Naval Agreement would improve our position.[3] I can't see how it would change it at all, as 'Diminution of Naval Expenditure' would still be nearly our only gain, and the political understanding with Germany would still make France and Russia look askance at us. So that the new 'idea' can only be a gain to us if France and Russia are included in the Political Understanding also, on the lines suggested by Sir E. Grey. Even then the balance would be slightly against us —but that *would* clear the general atmosphere and so be a gain all round. Don't you think that when the 'idea' is put forward officially or definitely and we find that it is only to apply to a naval arrangement we might suggest as an amendment that it should apply to the political understanding too? It is *so* important that our friendships with Russia and France should not be endangered. . . . .[4]

Yours ever,

W. E. GOSCHEN.

[3] [Sir E. Goschen referred to this subject in a private telegram to Sir Edward Grey of October 21. Herr von Kiderlen-Waechter had informed him, " very confidentially," in the course of explaining the Emperor William's conversation of October 16 (*v. supra*, pp. 530–3, No. 403), that " an idea was germinating that France and Russia might also be invited to join in a naval arrangement." Grey MSS., Vol. 23.]

[4] [The closing sentences touch on the subject of the Bagdad Railway, and refer to personal matters.]

No. 406.

Sir Edward Grey to Sir E. Goschen.

Private.[1]

Tel.

Foreign Office, October 25, 1910.

D. 1·25 P.M.

I cannot admit justice of Chancellor's criticisms of our general policy, but I will reply to those separately in a way, which will not impede discussion of other points.

[1] [Grey MSS., Vol. 23.]

I have sent his Memorandum to the Prime Minister who will not be in London for some days. We must of course have time to consider it, but you may say at once that I accept it as showing the Chancellor's desire to continue the discussion in the same spirit as we resumed it in our last communication.

No. 407.

Sir Edward Grey to Sir E. Goschen.

Private.([1])

My dear Goschen, *October* 26, 1910.

A despatch shall be drafted in the Office on the subject of the German Chancellor's strictures upon our attitude towards Germany.([2]) Meanwhile, I will give you some reflections which his words suggest to me.

Metternich some time ago complained to me that we used to lean upon Germany, or towards Germany, and now did so no longer. It is quite true that this is the case, but the Germans have themselves to blame for it.

In 1892, Lord Rosebery began his term of Office by informing the Ambassadors of the Triple Alliance that he meant to continue the policy of Lord Salisbury: a policy which included an attitude so benevolent towards the Triple Alliance that the French Press some times wrote about the "Quadruple Alliance." The German Government, and I suppose the other two also, expressed great satisfaction.

What was the result as far as our relations with Germany were concerned? The Germans worried us about Witu: they showed no consideration for our interests anywhere in Africa, though we asked for it at least once when they were themselves negotiating a boundary arrangement with the French in the region of Nigeria; and the general impression left on my mind was that we were expected to give way whenever British interests conflicted with German interests, and that we got no diplomatic support from Germany anywhere and continual friction. It is true that the Germans did support us in Egypt, but I remember once at any rate a threat to withdraw that support if we did not clear the way for German railway concessions in Turkey. In the meantime, we were always on bad terms with France or Russia, and the German Emperor openly expressed his satisfaction in conversation when it seemed that we were on the brink of war with France about Siam.

I am telling you all this from my own recollection of my time in the Foreign Office as Under-Secretary from 1892–95. I have not attempted to verify from papers the instances which I have given, but I remember most clearly that the position was anything but comfortable, and that we appeared destined to be for ever on bad terms with France and Russia, with Germany as a "tertius gaudens."

After 1895, when I left Office, I followed Foreign Affairs only to the extent which was necessary to enable me from time to time to take the part which was expected from me in the House of Commons. Naturally, I welcomed the settlement of our differences with France and with Russia: had they not been settled, they must sooner or later have led to war with one country or the other. My impression is that Lord Salisbury and Lord Lansdowne always desired friendship with Germany, but that they were worried into a more distant attitude by finding that ostensible friendship with Germany meant no return from Germany, and constant trouble with Russia and with France.

This does not mean that we do not still wish to be friends with Germany. I desire friendship: but it must not be on terms which would involve the old disadvantages.

([1]) [Grey MSS., Vol. 23.]
([2]) [*cp. supra*, pp. 523–4, No. 400. For the despatch to Sir E. Goschen on this subject, *v. infra*, pp. 546–54, No. 414.]

The German Chancellor complains of our recent attitude. At the Algeciras Conference we were bound to France by an engagement which was public to all the world. It was Germany who forced that Conference. Our attitude was as obligatory in honour upon us as that of Germany was upon her when she supported Austria recently in the Bosnia-Herzegovina case. Indeed, our attitude may have been even more obligatory, for I do not know how far the letter of the Triple Alliance covers the support which Germany gave to Austria. But whether it covers it or not, I have never resented what Germany did. I told Metternich once that I understood her attitude, and that in her circumstances we would have done the same. Germany therefore ought to be able to understand our attitude at Algeciras. As to Persia. How can I defend before British public opinion a concession to Germany about Persian railways which would give her participation in every railway we may get in Persia, while leaving her a railway monopoly in Mesopotamia? For the Bagdad Railway is a monopoly : the Turks, having to pay kilometric guarantees, cannot allow the construction of any other line which would compete with it. As to the Bagdad Railway itself. The Germans ask too much when they request that we should agree to a large additional burden upon Turkish trade, the greater part of which burden would fall upon British trade with Turkey, and the proceeds from which would be applied to the creation of a railway monopoly in Mesopotamia, to displace such interests as we have there already. I could not defend such a thing for a moment in Parliament. In suggesting that we might give Germany a large participation in all orders for materials, etc., for railways in the southern half of Persia, and agree to an increase of the Turkish Customs Dues unconditionally, in return for the controlling interest in the southern end of the Bagdad Railway, (which after all is only an end, and not a half), I have gone as far as any British Minister could possibly go, if he was to have any chance of carrying the Cabinet and Parliament with him.

As to a Turkish Loan : even if I had the desire, I have not the power to prevent Germany from lending to Turkey. But I do not wish to see British money lent to Turkey to help her on the road to bankruptcy, without control and without conditions.

I do not want to provoke controversy by saying all this to the Chancellor. You can use bits of it in conversation if the occasion seems to require it and you think it desirable.

Yours sincerely,
E. GREY.

No. 408.

Sir E. Goschen to Sir A. Nicolson.

Private.([1])
My dear Nicolson,   *Berlin, October* 28, 1910.

I am much obliged to you for your letter and for the nice words it contained. Of course I thoroughly enjoy the work, the most interesting I have ever had in my long career : but I wish I had more light and that I could be more hopeful of the result of all these conversations. I so thoroughly agree with you as to the danger of worse relations should our negotiations ' run into the sand.' But there is no help for it. The lines upon which negotiations might have had a practical and satisfactory result were those originally suggested by Sir Edward Grey, namely that in return for a satisfactory Naval Agreement we should give Germany an assurance of our peaceful intentions together with a declaration that our Ententes

([1]) [Carnock MSS., Vol. II of 1910.]

were not directed against Germany in any way and that we would use our influence to obtain similar declarations from France and Russia. Unfortunately the Germans said that that was very pretty as far as it went but that it was not sufficient for them. Then the negotiations drifted into the inclusion of the Bagdad and Persian questions and there at once the outlook became very dubious and as a matter of fact beyond getting a fairly clear idea of what Germany has at the back of her head we have not got an inch more forward. The *probability* is that in the end our relations will not be much more cordial than they were before the negotiations began, but it is also just possible that the conversations, strictures and explanations may have cleared the air a bit, shown at least a certain amount of goodwill on both sides and have the result that we may become as friendly as such rivals can be, and that without any definite understanding or naval agreement between us. That is the most I feel we can hope for. But to attain even that to my mind it is absolutely necessary for us to make them respect us as a Naval Power whose supremacy they cannot dispute. If we depart from that principle they will not think us worth conciliating and our relations will get worse than ever. I think they are feeling now that we are determined not to be caught up or to let our Naval strength down and hence their burning desire for a political understanding which will neutralize our strength in another way. I don't think anything of Kiderlen's last idea if it is only confined to a Naval Agreement. In the first place I thoroughly agree with you that France and Russia will not consider it at all advantageous and if they did agree to it it would ease Germany's mind on the Naval question and enable her to devote her whole mind to maintaining her enormous supremacy on land. In any case the ' idea ' is unthinkable unless Italy and Austria are also included. It will, however, as Sir Edward Grey says, be a splendid test of Germany's real aspirations when we see how a proposal should such have to be made to extend the idea to a general political agreement to which France and Russia and even the other two Triplice Powers should be parties, is received by the Imperial Government. In this sense Kiderlen's hinted idea, whatever its scope may be, will be of the greatest service. . . . .(²)

Yours very sincerely,
W. E. GOSCHEN.

(²) [The omitted passages refer to German action in Turkey and Persia, and to the relations between M. Isvolski and Count von Aehrenthal.]

No. 409.

Sir E. Goschen to Sir Edward Grey.

F.O. 40878/168/10/18.
(No. 310.)   *Berlin,* D. *November* 4, 1910.
Sir,   R. *November* 7, 1910.

The article which appeared in the "Daily Telegraph" of the 27th instant [October] under the sensational headings "German Ships Delayed," "Dramatic Surprise," not only conveys erroneous impressions to the British Public, but has again brought the intricacies of British and German naval construction into the arena of press polemics, a result which on all grounds is to be much deprecated.

From the despatch addressed to me upon the subject by Captain Watson, which I have the honour to enclose herewith,(¹) you will see that according to his information, and according to the statement made by the German Admiralty to the Daily Mail correspondent, there is no idea of any delay in shipbuilding, or relaxation of the rate of construction laid down by the Naval Law, either because of the manufacture of guns of larger calibre or for any other reason. Nothing in fact

(¹) [Not reproduced.]

has occurred, beyond the inappreciable delay caused in some cases by the recent strike, to prevent the battleships under construction from being ready at the time specified for their delivery.

The Press is also unanimous in denying the allegations of the Daily Telegraph and state that they constitute a piece of bluff which will altogether fail in its object.

It is perhaps as well that the German Admiralty and the German Press have taken so much pains to deny the statements of the "Daily Telegraph" as it might perhaps have been more to their advantage to let them pass uncontradicted and allow them to sink into the minds of that section of British public opinion which is ready to seize any excuse for demanding the reduction of our naval expenditure.

I think that from this point of view the Berlin correspondent of the "Daily Mail" has rendered great service by obtaining an authoritative contradiction of the Daily Telegraph's statements direct from the German Admiralty.

I have, &c.
W. E. GOSCHEN.

No. 410.

Sir E. Goschen to Sir Edward Grey.

F.O. 41336/167/10/18.
(No. 320.)   *Berlin,* D. *November 9,* 1910.
Sir,   R. *November 14,* 1910.

The report on Anglo-German relations furnished to the Daily Chronicle by its Berlin correspondent and which appeared in last Monday's issue of that paper was reproduced in most of the leading newspapers here with comments, for the most part, of a not very agreeable nature. The vicious "Hamburger Nachrichten" gave a short résumé of the Article under the headline "An English manœuvre for the limitation of Naval Armaments." After calling attention to the fact that the "Daily Chronicle" endorses the "view of its correspondent that a political understanding must precede a limitation of Naval Armaments," the "Hamburger Nachrichten" adds :—"As pointed out in our headline, everyone must see in these somewhat pompous and bombastic utterances of the London paper a new attempt to drive Germany into an agreement for the limitation of armaments. To be sure it is very questionable whether such an attempt, which can only result in failure, is seriously meant, but still the manœuvre is there clear to the eye and its obvious intent is to show 'England's good-will' and to put Germany morally in the wrong in the case of a large augmentation of the British fleet being again submitted to Parliament."

The 'Vossische Zeitung' draws attention to the fact that the Correspondent was told in Berlin that a political understanding was an absolutely necessary prelude to an agreement for the limitation of armaments, and lays much stress on the fact that it was from his conversations with German officials that he gathered that there existed in German official circles a widespread complaint of Great Britain's arrogance and ambition and of her determination to check the commercial expansion and world energies of Germany by joining any ally to oppose Germany's interests in places even where British interests are not concerned. In commenting upon the Leading Article in the Daily Chronicle on the report of its correspondent, the "Vossische Zeitung" fastens on the sentence in which it is asked "whether British and German statesmen have not sufficient courage and wisdom to attempt to achieve such an understanding covering the whole international field?" To this question it replies : "First and foremost let it be said that the notorious antipathy felt by the British Foreign Minister, Sir Edward Grey, against Germany, would be in itself a well nigh insurmountable obstacle to the conclusion of an Anglo-German understanding. Therefore there is but little hope that any attempt in this direction will be crowned with success.''

It will not have escaped your notice that the language of the officials with whom the Daily Chronicle's special correspondent seems to have conversed is almost exactly similar to that held to me by the Emperor, the Imperial Chancellor and both Herr von Schoen and Herr von Kiderlen.

On seeing the latter to-day at his diplomatic reception I called His Excellency's attention to this extraordinary coincidence. He admitted that it seemed rather extraordinary but said that as he had only seen short extracts from the Report, as published in the Berlin Press, he could not express any opinion. As he said that he would like to read the whole report I sent him a copy of the Daily Chronicle. He returned it to me to-day with a short note saying that the report was certainly rather curious, and asking at the same time whether I was sure that it really came from Berlin.

To return to my conversation with Herr von Kiderlen I would mention that before leaving I called his attention to the statement in the '' Vossische Zeitung '' with regard to your antipathy to Germany, and expressed my astonishment and regret that such a mendacious and misleading statement should have appeared in a leading German paper. I pointed out to him that the attacks on our general policy, of which the Berlin Press was at present so full, gave me but little concern; but that such a widely read journal as the '' Vossische Zeitung '' should attribute that policy to a personal feeling on the part of a statesman who, as he knew, had repeatedly shown unmistakable good-will towards Germany and was doing all in his power to improve the relations between the two countries, was, as I was sure he would agree, a most mischievous and uncalled for proceeding. Herr von Kiderlen replied that he was entirely of my mind and expressed his regret that such an insinuation, which he agreed with me was entirely unjustified, should have been served up to the German public.

Dr. Schiemann in his weekly article in the '' Kreuz '' has also a few words to say on the '' Daily Chronicle '' report. But he takes a different view from the papers from which I have quoted, and gives it unstinted praise. He says :—'' The writer of this report when in Berlin had occasion to converse with some of our own Diplomats, with Ambassadors of Foreign Powers, and a number of eminent financiers, politicians and officials. These conversations enabled him to form a judgment upon the actual state of Anglo-German relations and the means of improving them, which I do not hesitate to qualify as the best and soundest which has been published by an Englishman ever since the beginning of the great anti-German agitation. Nothing in fact could be more thoughtfully or more impartially written than this excellent report.''

After a short summary of the contents of the report Dr. Schiemann concludes his article with the following words on his own account : '' I must add one point to those enumerated in the Report. An Anglo-German understanding would at one stroke alter for the better the relations of Great Britain with her colonies. Canada would certainly not allow herself to be involved in a war between Great Britain and Germany, while Australia already feels that the massing of the British Fleet in the North Sea may leave her unprotected. Such considerations and other misgivings which England must feel with regard to her future will promptly disappear once the great source of preoccupation is removed.''

I have, &c.
W. E. GOSCHEN.

No. 411.

Mr. O'Beirne to Sir Edward Grey.

F.O. 42209/167/10/18.
(No. 454.)   Secret.   Confidential.   *St. Petersburgh, D. November* 15, 1910.
Sir,   R. *November* 21, 1910.

I have the honour to report that the Acting Minister for Foreign Affairs gave me the following account of a statement made to him at Potsdam by the German Emperor,(¹) which may throw some light on the future intentions of Germany with regard to naval armaments.

The Emperor said that it had always been the policy of England to crush any naval Power which threatened her supremacy at sea. She had crushed the Dutch, and she had destroyed the Danish fleet, and she would now like to do the same to Germany, but Germany had no intention of being subjected to such treatment. Germany, His Majesty went on, proposed to carry out her present naval programme. When that was accomplished, further developments would depend on the action of England. If England was content to acquiesce in the proportion in her favour that would then exist between the two fleets, and allowed matters to rest there, well and good. But if England attempted to alter that proportion to the disadvantage of Germany, the latter would stop at no expenditure in order to continue the struggle.

I have, &c.
HUGH O'BEIRNE.

(¹) [The subject of this interview will be treated in a later volume.]

No. 412.

Sir Edward Grey to Sir E. Goschen.(¹)

F.O. 42552/167/10/18.
(No. 308.)   Secret.
Sir,   *Foreign Office, November* 19, 1910.

Count Metternich told me to-day that questions were sure to be put in the Reichstag which the Chancellor would have some difficulty in answering. These questions would be a consequence of a statement which our Prime Minister had made in the summer, to the effect that Germany could not come to a Naval Agreement without altering her Naval Law, which she was unable to do. As a matter of fact, a year ago the Chancellor had intimated that it might be possible to slacken the German rate of construction, without altering the Naval Law, and that an Agreement might be based on this slackening. The Chancellor had therefore instructed Count Metternich to give me the accompanying statement, which Count Metternich asked me to have translated, showing what the Chancellor proposed to say.

I said that I would put a translation before the Prime Minister, so that anything which he might have to say should correspond with the German Chancellor's statement.

Count Metternich added that the Chancellor would like to have the statement back by the end of next week, with any comments which we might have to make.

He showed me a rough translation which he had made of the statement.

Having read it, I said that *primâ facie* it seemed to me that the same idea was contained in it as was in the Prime Minister's Guildhall speech : namely, that the desire for peace amongst nations ought to make the political atmosphere more genial, and that that would react favourably upon expenditure on armaments; but the Prime Minister had not mentioned Germany, and had made his words of general application.

[I am, &c.]
E. G[REY].

(¹) [For Count Metternich's report, *v. G.P.* XXVIII, pp. 376–7.]

Enclosure in No. 412.

Statement communicated by Count Metternich.(²)

(Translation.)

In regard to our relations with England and alleged negotiations with her respecting a conventional limitation of naval armaments I must in the first place point out that it is notorious that the British Government have repeatedly given expression to the view that an agreement fixing the naval strength of individual Powers would tend to have a materially tranquillizing effect on international relations. This is a view which, as is well known, England expressed as far back as the time of the Hague Conference. Since then England has repeatedly revived this idea without, however, making proposals which we could definitely accept or definitely reject.

We too share England's desire to avoid rivalry in respect to armaments but during the informal and friendly conversations which have taken place from time to time we have always laid stress on the consideration that a frank and loyal discussion, followed by an understanding respecting the economic and political interests on either side, would offer the safest means of dissipating all mistrust as to the relative strength of the two countries on sea and on land. The continuance of an open and unreserved exchange of views respecting all questions connected with these matters is in itself a guarantee of the amiable spirit animating both parties and may be expected gradually but surely to put an end to the suspiciousness which unfortunately has in many ways affected, not the two Governments, but public opinion.

(²) [For the German original, *v.* *G.P.* XXVIII, pp. 375–6.]

No. 413.

Sir Edward Grey to Sir E. Goschen.(¹)

F.O. 42654/167/10/18.

(No. 311.) Secret.

Sir,   *Foreign Office, November* 19, 1910.

Count Metternich came to see me to-day and, after some preliminary remarks about the approaching General Election, he asked me whether the Naval question would play some part in it.

I replied that apparently Tariff Reform was not as good a card now as it had been a year ago, and the most might be. made of other things, including the Naval question : though I thought that there was less material for this question than there had been at the last Election.

Count Metternich then gave me the enclosed statement from the German Government as to what the position would be with regard to German "Dreadnoughts" in commission up to April 1913.

I asked whether this statement was based on the German Naval Law, and whether it had been made public in Germany.

Count Metternich said that it was based on their Law; it had been communicated by the German Admiralty to the Imperial Chancellor and the Foreign Office, and it was now placed in my hands.

He observed that, before the last General Election and during it, very erroneous statements had been made as to what the position would be with regard to German "Dreadnoughts" at various dates. These dates were now falling due, and the exaggerated statements had not been realised.

I said that I was glad to have the information he had given me; but there was a difficulty in making public use of it. We could not meet the attacks of the

(¹) [For Count Metternich's report, *v.* *G.P.* XXVIII, pp. 376–7.]

Opposition by quoting German figures which were not part of any Agreement, and from which the German Government were at liberty to depart whenever they liked. For instance: if a year hence the German Government thought it desirable to "speed up" the rate of shipbuilding, they could, I assumed, have more than 17 "Dreadnoughts" by April 1913.

Count Metternich said that this could not be done without asking the Reichstag for more money.

I asked him whether it would not be possible to save money on one Vote and apply it to "Dreadnought" construction if desired. He admitted that he did not know whether this could be done, and I said that I also was not aware whether our own Admiralty could do anything of this sort.

Further, I pointed out that, with regard to construction, the German Government must always have in hand some margin of time, for the delay caused by strikes in Germany would not prevent their "Dreadnoughts" from being ready at the time originally contemplated, and I observed that if there was controversy here about the Navy the only effective way of meeting attacks made upon the Gov[ernmen]t was to show that we were prepared for any reasonably possible contingencies of shipbuilding abroad.

[I am, &c.]
E. G[REY].

Enclosure in No. 413.

GERMANY'S "CAPITAL SHIPS."

By April 1911 the following are to be delivered from the shipyards:

Ships of the Line.	*Large Cruisers.*
None.	None.

Ships ready: 5.

By April 1912 the following are to be delivered from the shipyards:

Ships of the Line.	*Large Cruisers.*
6. Helgoland June 1911.	10. Moltke June 1911.
7. Thüringen June 1911.	11. "H" Spring 1912.
8. Ostfriesland Aug[ust] 1911.	
9. Oldenburg Spring 1912.	

Ships ready: 11.

By the Spring of 1913 the following are to be delivered from the yards:

Ships of the Line.	*Large Cruisers*
12. Ersatz Heimdall Summer 1912.	17. "J" Spring 1913.
13. ,, Hildebrand Autumn 1912.	
14. ,, Hagen Spring 1913.	
15. ,, Ægir ,, 1913.	
16. ,, Odin ,, 1913.	

Ships ready: 17.

No. 414.

Sir Edward Grey to Sir E. Goschen.

F.O. 37598/167/10/18.
(No. 312.) Secret.
Sir,   *Foreign Office, November* 23, 1910.

The matters which form the subject of your Excellency's despatch No. 280, Secret, of the 12th ultimo([1]) are receiving, on the part of the Cabinet, the careful attention which their importance demands. I am consequently not as yet in a position to express the views of His Majesty's Government on the two main points of the memorandum handed to your Excellency by the German Chancellor on the 11th October, namely : the precise conditions to be stipulated for in an understanding between Great Britain and Germany respecting a limitation of naval armaments, and the exact form which it might be possible to give to a general political agreement such as the German Government consider a necessary concomitant to any naval understanding. I hope, however, in due course to indicate more definitely the lines which the contemplated arrangement should, in the opinion of His Majesty's Government, follow, and meanwhile I would say that the willingness to exchange information respecting the progress of shipbuilding has produced a very favourable impression here.

2. The object of my present despatch is to offer some comment on the observations of a more general character which the Chancellor made to you in conversation, with regard to particular incidents in the past and present political relations between our two countries. I do so not with any intention of entering into controversy with Herr von Bethmann-Hollweg, nor with any desire to suggest that the subject is one requiring discussion in connection with the proposed understanding for the limitation of armaments, to which, indeed, I think such a discussion would be irrelevant, and with which I do not wish to see it connected. But the light in which the Chancellor has placed the action of the British Government in respect to those incidents, and the inferences which he apparently considers himself justified in drawing therefrom as to the general attitude of this country towards Germany are in such direct conflict with facts and events recorded in the archives of this department that I should be only fostering a dangerous misunderstanding if I allowed to pass unchallenged an account of the decisions and motives of His Majesty's Government, which is clearly based on an entire misapprehension of what has occurred.

3. I am sincerely anxious to see that misapprehension dispelled, and to induce, if possible, on the part of Herr von Bethmann-Hollweg a less biased view and a more accurate understanding of the position as it presents itself to the British Government. I leave it to your Excellency's discretion to make, in your further conversations with the Chancellor, such use of the observations and explanations I am about to offer as may appear to you best calculated to attain this object, without provoking further polemics or recriminations as to past history, which I deprecate as unlikely to serve any useful purpose, and as tending rather to aggravate than to smooth the existing difficulties of the situation.

4. Before taking up the several statements made by the Chancellor which I think it incumbent on me to correct, I feel constrained to refer to his remark, made, I gather, with particular emphasis, that " if the British people had not been *taught* by their governments to regard Germany as an enemy, the expansion of the German fleet would have caused them as little anxiety as the expansion of the navy of the United States." I deeply regret that the Chancellor should have allowed himself to make, in speaking officially to the accredited representative of Great Britain, an insinuation of this kind, reflecting dishonourably on the conduct

([1]) [*v. supra*, pp. 521–8, No. 400.]

of His Majesty's Government. I trust he will on reflection see that he used words for which he had no justification. Only shortly before, he had spoken of his determination to work for better relations between the two countries, and had, in that connection, expressed his conviction that His Majesty's Government, and I personally, were equally anxious to secure that result. I should be happy to believe that these words more truly represented the Chancellor's considered views. I have no desire on my part to point to the manifestations of open hostility and ill-feeling to this country which have, from the beginning, accompanied and invigorated the German national propaganda for a fleet strong enough to deal with that of the biggest naval Power, an agitation which, having regard to the moment of its inception, the circumstances of its growth, and the machinery by which it has been directed, alone offers a sufficient explanation of the popular feeling of anxiety with which the expansion of the German navy has been watched in this country. I also refrain from enumerating the acts of unmistakable unfriendliness and provocation by which the German Government have, often without any concealment of their intention, endeavoured from time to time to create political difficulties of His Majesty's Government. For I want to see the obstacles in the way of a better understanding removed, not multiplied. But if this end is to be attained by loyal co-operation, it is essential that the Imperial Chancellor should not put forward a charge, as grave as it is unfounded, which, if meant to be taken seriously, must, as he will no doubt himself recognise, render it impossible to continue our discussions on the lines we both desire. I trust he will see the propriety of withdrawing it.

5. Herr von Bethmann-Hollweg, whilst accepting the assurance that the existing understandings between Great Britain with certain other Powers are in no way directed against Germany, complains nevertheless "that British foreign policy in its general tendency follows a course opposed to that of Germany." His Majesty's Government have had much unhappy experience of the ready inclination of the German Government to regard as "opposition" to German plans or desires the legitimate defence of important British interests which it is the bounden duty of British Governments to safeguard, or the fulfilment of treaty obligations to which this country is solemnly pledged. I enclose, for your use, a memorandum illustrating this very position with special reference to each of the several concrete instances with the Chancellor has adduced as evidence of the truth of his contention. An impartial examination of the facts and explanations therein stated should convince him that the aspersions which he has so readily cast upon His Majesty's Government are not merited. This memorandum is not intended for communication to the German Government as a formal document prepared in this Office. I should prefer that its contents should form the subject of a verbal communication. But I see no objection to your Excellency leaving with the Imperial Chancellor, in strict confidence, informal notes of what you say verbally, and of your practically reproducing for this purpose the text of the memorandum. You should, however, emphasize that the object of the communication is explanatory and not controversial.

6. His Majesty's Government have at no time contemplated, far less pursued, an anti-German policy. On the contrary, on the many occasions when grave embarrassment to British interests have threatened to result, or have actually resulted, from the course of action adopted by Germany, His Majesty's Government have invariably endeavoured to minimise the danger of serious friction, as far as was in their power, by going to the very verge of possible concession and conciliation. The Chancellor has been pleased to contrast the present situation, which he characterises as unsatisfactory, with the happy days when Anglo-German relations were "good." I am in doubt as to the precise period to which he wished to refer. But the impression which an attentive survey of our foreign relations during the last twenty-five years has left on my mind is that the German complaint of English unfriendliness has been practically chronic. At recurrent intervals of rarely more than a few years the German Government have put forward demands involving the

abandonment of some well-established British rights or interests as the price for a "continuance" of their friendship, frankly declaring, and not infrequently illustrating in practice, how disagreeable Germany could be to this country if her desires were not acceded to. I need not recite the series of agreements and understandings by which Great Britain again and again made the concessions demanded, receiving in return the assurance that German friendship was now secured. But obviously this is a process which cannot be repeated *ad infinitum*, and I should lose all hope of Anglo-German relations ever being bettered, if Herr von Bethmann-Hollweg were seriously to expect that, in order to replace them on what he considers to have been their old amicable footing, His Majesty's Government should abandon the protection of British interests whenever their maintenance is looked upon by the German Government as an obstacle in the way of some enterprise or ambition of their own. I have, however, a greater faith in the justice of his political aims, and I would gladly believe that a frank explanation as to the necessary course of British policy and the reality of the interests which it is the object of that policy to protect, will lead him to a clearer and more sympathetic appreciation of the attitude of His Majesty's Government in the particular matters to which he has called attention.

7. There is one allegation which, coming from the Imperial Chancellor, has caused me even greater surprise than the general reproach of an anti-German attitude. I allude to his statement that Great Britain has maintained such an attitude "even in cases where British and German interests were more or less identical, and called for co-operation." Assuming for the moment that there are cases where the real interests of the two nations are genuinely conflicting—an admission which I am by no means prepared to make—I may remind your Excellency that I have more than once during the last few years urged upon the German Government, through the Imperial Ambassador at this court, the advantage of paving the way for a better feeling between the two countries by our co-operating in just such cases as the Chancellor has referred to, when neither our own direct interests nor considerations arising out of obligations imposed by our respective alliances and understandings with third Powers stood in the way of our acting together. I was given to understand at the time that the German Government approved this suggestion, and agreed to put it into practice when opportunity occurred. When, however, occasions presented themselves for following the course indicated, with the prospect, as it appeared to me, of undoubtedly beneficial results, I was met with polite but distinct refusals from Berlin. I refer more particularly to the question of reforms in Macedonia prior to the Turkish revolution, and to co-operation in the Cretan problem. I have never complained of the attitude of the German Government in these matters. I do not complain now. But if Herr von Bethmann-Hollweg regrets the loss of such opportunities, it does not seem just that he should lay the blame on His Majesty's Government.

8. There remains the last item in the list of the Chancellor's grievances : the complaint that "British Representatives now take the line of treating their German colleagues with the greatest reserve, while ostentatiously affecting the greatest intimacy with their colleagues of other nations." It can scarcely be profitable to discuss such a vague and general charge. The specific complaint which occurs to me in this connection is that of the accusations made last year against the members of His Majesty's Embassy at St. Petersburgh. I was somewhat disappointed that no regret was expressed for this charge when it proved to be unfounded.

I am, &c.

E. GREY.

Enclosure in No. 414.

Memorandum.

(Confidential.)

Speaking on the 11th October to His Majesty's Ambassador at Berlin, the Imperial Chancellor mentioned four instances in which German interests had been systematically opposed by His Majesty's Government, viz. :—

1. The Turkish loan;
2. The Bagdad Railway;
3. Persia; and
4. The Algeciras Conference.

It will be convenient to reproduce, in italics, the substance of the criticisms made by Herr von Bethmann-Hollweg; and to subjoin, in ordinary type, the observations to which those criticisms severally give rise.

1. THE TURKISH LOAN.

"*In the question of the Turkish loan His Majesty's Government had set themselves in opposition to Germany, and had, as it appeared to the Imperial Government, supported the recent efforts of France to replace the Dette Publique by the Ottoman Bank, notwithstanding the fact that such an arrangement must be as distasteful to Great Britain as to Germany.*"

His Majesty's Government, in the month of September, expressed to the French Government their concurrence in the view that it would be only prudent to make an advance to Turkey conditional upon some satisfactory form of control, and also upon adequate guarantees that the loan should not be wholly swallowed up in unproductive expenditure. Such reservations appeared to His Majesty's Government eminently desirable not only in the interests of Turkish credit and of all Turkish bondholders of whatever nationality, but also with a view to avoiding, if possible, undue encouragement at a critical moment to those influences in Turkey which might make for disturbance of peace.

On the other hand, His Majesty's Government have never wittingly supported efforts to replace the Public Debt Administration by the Ottoman Bank.

In these circumstances, His Majesty's Government are at a loss to appreciate how their attitude in this question has been one of opposition to Germany. At the date (11th October) of the Imperial Chancellor's remarks no indication had been vouchsafed to His Majesty's Government as to the views of the German Government regarding the Turkish loan question, and it was on receipt of Sir E. Goschen's despatch recording those remarks that they learnt for the first time that such views existed at all, though they still have no certain knowledge as to what they may be, unless indeed it is to be inferred that the contentions of Turkey in regard to borrowing operations in Paris and London are in fact the contentions of the German Government. Upon such an assumption alone does the criticism of Herr von Bethmann-Hollweg appear to be intelligible.

2. THE BAGDAD RAILWAY.

"*The Bagdad Railway question, the Chancellor said, was another case in point. The Imperial Government had endeavoured to come to an arrangement with regard to the southern section of the railway: their proposals had not only been rejected by His Majesty's Government, but the latter had also tried to put obstacles in the way of the German projects by refusing to support the raising of the Turkish customs dues on the ground that part of the sums realised by that increase would find its way to the concessionnaires of the Bagdad Railway. Nevertheless, this attitude of hostility to the German Bagdad Railway had not prevented His Majesty's Government from supporting the French scheme for a Bagdad Railway, projected by M. Tardieu.''*

The last sentence appears to focus the German representation of the attitude of His Majesty's Government: it is indispensable that the misconception which underlies such censure should be corrected.

The attitude of His Majesty's Government is not of opposition to railway construction as such or of distinction between enterprises of German and French origin: it is, moreover, in so far as concerns the Bagdad Railway Convention of 1903, not aggressive but defensive.

So far as His Majesty's Government are aware, the project referred to as that of M. Tardieu did not assume any very definite form: but be this as it may, they have never denied that railway development is essential to the prosperity of the Turkish Empire, and they were accordingly prepared to welcome, provided the terms were acceptable, British participation in any railway—whether projected by M. Tardieu or another—which might be constructed between the Mediterranean and the Persian Gulf; they were confirmed in this tendency because—such participation not having been satisfactorily arranged under the concession of 1903—it could not appear advantageous to British interests that all railway communication in Mesopotamia should be a monopoly under the virtual control of one nationality.

So much for the policy of His Majesty's Government in regard to railway construction in general: if their attitude, based upon the entirely legitimate object of defending British interests, is not actively favourable to the concession of 1903, the justification of that attitude must be sought in the peculiar conditions of the concession and the circumstances in which it is proposed to exploit it. To this aspect of the question further reference will presently be made; in the first place, however, it is convenient to indicate, in some detail, what are the interests which His Majesty's Government have to defend in the regions in question.

The commercial position of Great Britain in the Mesopotamian delta is altogether exceptional: that position has been steadily consolidated since the foundation, upwards of two and a-half centuries ago, of the first English factory at Bussorah; in 1766 a British Resident was appointed at Bagdad; at Bussorah there has long been a British consul, charged with the care of British trade, represented up to a recent date by 96 per cent. of the steam tonnage entered at the port; in short, such is now the nature of these commercial interests that the trade of Bagdad and Bussorah, valued at 2,500,000*l.* in 1903, is predominantly in the hands of British and Indian merchants: moreover, it may be mentioned incidentally that the annual pilgrimage of British-Indian subjects to the Shiah shrines of Kerbela and Nejef is continually increasing, the numbers in 1905 exceeding 11,000—a circumstance which serves to emphasise the interest which this region must possess for British Indian traders and commerce.

The position attained by this country upon the waters and on the shores of the Persian Gulf has been won not without the expenditure of many millions of money and the sacrifice of many valuable lives: in the early years of the nineteenth century the slave trade was rampant in the Gulf, and the vessels of the Indian Marine were engaged in a long and arduous struggle with the Arab pirates who infested its southern coasts: this conflict, which was conducted entirely by British agency and means, resulted in the establishment of treaty relations with the Arab chiefs, under which they bound themselves to observe perpetual peace and to refer all disputes to the British Resident at Bushire. The *pax Britannica* which has ever since, with rare exceptions, been maintained, is the issue of these arrangements and is the exclusive work of this country. It is owing to British enterprise, to the expenditure of British lives and money, that the Persian Gulf, not excluding the approaches to the Turkish ports of Bagdad and Bussorah, is at this moment open to the navigation of the world: indeed, to these causes alone it may be said hat the seaborne trade of Mesopotamia owes its very existence. The situation of Great Britain in the Persian Gulf has been well described as unique : for although she has not sought territorial acquisitions in those regions, she has for generations borne burdens there which no other nation has ever undertaken anywhere, except in the capacity of sovereign; she has had duty thrust upon her without dominion; she has kept the peace amongst people who are not her subjects; has patrolled, during upwards of two centuries, waters over which she has enjoyed no formal lordship; has kept, in strange ports, an open door through which the traders of every nation might have as free access to distant markets as her own.

Such are the interests, such is the historical position, which His Majesty's Government are called upon to uphold : it may indeed be confidently asserted that no European Power is concerned in these regions, by reason of long-established interest and influence, to the same extent as this country : and when, moreover, it is borne in mind that the most direct route to the East has always in the past been controlled by the Rulers of India—that the Portuguese acquired Algoa and Delagoa Bays as ports of call to and from Goa, that the Dutch East India Company established a fort at Table Bay in 1652 for a similar purpose, that the Cape was subsequently, in 1814, ceded to the British Crown, and that the port of Aden was occupied by the British as an outpost of India—when all this is taken into consideration, it cannot give rise to surprise if His Majesty's Government—though they emphatically disclaim any desire to disturb the territorial *status quo*—regard with some measure of concern the advent of a great trans-continental railway under the *ægis* of a foreign Power, accompanied by a rigorous exclusion of British control and its consequent effect upon the Oriental mind.

The Bagdad Railway Convention of 1903, apart altogether from the financial clauses, is no commonplace concession—it confers rights of wide and exceptional nature : thus the promoters of the enterprise not only are entitled to establish ports at the important trade centres of Bagdad and Bussorah, but under various articles a number of minor but valuable rights are conferred upon them : exemption from customs dues for all materials, machinery, rolling-stock, iron, wood, coal imported from abroad during the period of construction, and exemption from taxation of the company's entire property and revenue during the whole term of the concession; mining and quarrying and forest rights within a zone of 20 kilom. on either side of the railway; the right to establish warehouses, elevators and shops; to manufacture bricks and tiles, and to make free use of any natural water power in the vicinity of the line—all tending to confer a monopoly of the economic development of the country.

Having regard to certain clauses of the " cahier des charges," His Majesty's Government do not contend that it is proposed to establish differential rates against British trade; but they do apprehend that, in practice if not in theory, the advent of this railway, with its great terminal ports, the whole under German control, must react adversely upon British trade interests in Mesopotamia, while German commerce, supported by the great local organisation of the railway and its powerful officials, will almost inevitably compete with weighted dice.

But the Bagdad Railway concession, as has been urged in Germany as well as in England, is a political enterprise; it is not exclusively commercial; it will have an undoubted and important political influence upon the primitive minds of the Arab population, not to mention the natives of British India; and finally it is based upon such remarkable financial guarantees, that it is in the interest of the Turkish Exchequer, as the Turkish Government themselves contend, that no other railway concessions should be granted in the adjoining regions : it must in fact be a monopoly.

His Majesty's Government have no wish to enter here upon a detailed discussion as to those financial guarantees : they would confine themselves to the general comment that whereas the construction annuity appears to be more than sufficient even if due regard be had to the cost of crossing the Taurus and to the substantial character of the permanent way, on the other hand the working expenses guarantee is apparently arranged upon such a scale that it actually militates against the progressive development of traffic.

Neither of these results is perceptibly advantageous to the Turkish taxpayer.

In view of all these considerations, His Majesty's Government frankly admit that they have not been able, for the reason indicated by the Imperial Chancellor, to accede to an additional duty being imposed upon British commerce: they believe that they would not be justified in assenting to this measure if, in effect, it were to hasten the completion of the Bagdad Railway under existing conditions, conditions which involve the total exclusion of British control in the enterprise.

Thus the attitude of His Majesty's Government is, as has already been contended, defensive and not aggressive. It may be that the construction of the railway can be completed without any British participation; but it is not for His Majesty's Government actively to co-operate to this end at the expense of British commerce.

It remains to consider the Imperial Chancellor's grieva_ y that the German Government have attempted to reach an arrangement with regard to the southern section of the railway, but that their proposals have been rejected by His Majesty's Government.

On three occasions proposals have been adumbrated from the German side.

(1.) In 1903 the proposals, it will be recalled, had reference to the whole railway: these proposals, if accepted, would have secured the assistance of British capital while involving the exclusion of British control in any effective degree.

(2.) In the autumn of 1907, as a result of prolonged discussions at Windsor,([2]) it was virtually agreed, as appears from the records made at the time, that negotiations on the subject of the Bagdad Railway should take place à quatre between Great Britain, Germany, Russia, and France; and it was recognised as both legitimate and natural that His Majesty's Government should wish to proceed in full consultation with France and Russia.

In pursuance of this understanding, Herr von Schoen called at the Foreign Office on the 15th November and saw Sir E. Grey:([3]) his Excellency expressed great satisfaction at the prospect of now coming to an agreement with His Majesty's Government on the subject, and recognised their desire to have a "gate" at the Persian Gulf end: he further admitted that a memorandum([4]) communicated at Windsor formed a practicable basis for discussion. Sir E. Grey assumed that His Majesty's Government should wait till they heard further from the German Government; and Herr von Schoen replied that he must in the first instance consult the Russian Minister for Foreign Affairs, in order to ascertain whether full discussion might not be begun between the four Powers without first carrying discussion with Russia a stage further.

On the 25th June, 1908, seven months later, the German Ambassador called at the Foreign Office and stated that his Government had renounced the idea of summoning a conférence à quatre at Berlin: his Excellency further professed that he himself had always strongly opposed such an arrangement, upon the ground that such discussion was foredoomed to failure and would only serve to accentuate the difference between Germany and the three other Powers.

(3.) Finally, in the autumn of 1909, Herr von Gwinner intimated to Sir H. Babington-Smith at Constantinople that he was desirous to have British co-operation in the Bagdad Railway; and, in consequence, certain discussions relating to British participation in the southern section of the line, and in regard to British control of the terminal port, took place between Sir E. Cassel and Herr von Gwinner

([2]) [v. supra, pp. 96–107, Nos. 63–74.]
([3]) [v. supra, p. 98, No. 64.]
([4]) [v. supra, pp. 95–6, No. 62.]

at Berlin.([5]) These discussions, as the German Government are aware, were only interrupted in consequence of the attitude of the Imperial Government themselves, who intimated that political factors were involved.

Such then are the causes which have rendered all negotiation for British participation in the Bagdad Railway ineffective : the concession has been obtained by Germany, and from her must come definite proposals for British participation if it is decided that it should be admitted.

3. Persia.

"*As regards Persia, during the last spring the Imperial Government, whose interests in that country were purely commercial, had made the most self-denying and considerate proposals to His Majesty's Government. What had been the result? They had received no reply. On the contrary, His Majesty's Government had stood side by side with Russia, and by exercising pressure on the weak Persian Government had endeavoured to reduce German commercial relations with that country to the narrowest possible limit. The Imperial Government had asked that German subjects might have a fair participation in posts under the Persian Government. There, again, American subjects had been accepted, while the applications of German subjects had been steadily refused.*"

It is only accurate to say that His Majesty's Government have given no *written* reply to the proposals of the German Government made last spring. On the 31st May Sir E. Grey told the German Ambassador his views verbally,([6]) pointing out how impossible it would be for His Majesty's Government to make an arrangement with Germany in regard to railway construction in Persia, unless it included a satisfactory settlement as to British participation in the Bagdad Railway. The remarks of Count Metternich, who, it is true, did not profess to be speaking under instructions from his Government, were so unfavourable to this view of the question that it can hardly be said that His Majesty's Government received much encouragement to press forward negotiations.

His Majesty's Government cannot subscribe to the view that, by exercising pressure on the weak Persian Government, Great Britain and Russia have endeavoured to reduce German *commercial* relations with Persia to the narrowest possible limits. On the 31st May Sir E. Grey informed the German Ambassador of the action actually taken at Tehran by Great Britain and Russia, viz., of the joint notes of the 7th April and 20th May, 1910([7])—notes which expressed the wish that, before granting any concessions for means of communication, telegraphs or ports to foreigners, the Persian Government should enter into an exchange of views with Great Britain and Russia in order that the political and strategic interests of the two Powers might be duly safeguarded.

The fact is that Russia and Great Britain are, from geographical considerations, vitally interested in the political and strategical aspects of such concessions in Persia; moreover, it is now twenty years since the Persian Government gave to Her Majesty's Government an assurance that if any railway concession were given to Russia in the north of Persia, a concession for a line in the south should simultaneously be given to a British company.

His Majesty's Government can only repeat that they have no wish whatever to exclude German or any other commerce from Persia; they adhere to the principle of the open door in regard to that country.

Finally, there is the complaint that Americans are considered eligible for posts under the Persian Government, while the applications of German subjects for such posts have been steadily refused.

([5]) [*v. supra*, pp. 410–1, No. 309, *encl.*]
([6]) [*v. supra*, pp. 490–1, No. 375.]
([7]) [*v. supra*, p. 452, No. 343, *note* ([2]) and p. 490, No. 375, and *note* ([1]).]

The Persian Medjliss, in September last, decided in favour of Americans; and the view of the British and Russian Governments has been that the engagement of Americans is unlikely to give rise to political considerations, inasmuch as they are not subjects of a *Great European* Power.

4. ALGECIRAS CONFERENCE.

"*At Algeciras, Great Britain had supported France in her aspirations for a monopoly of political influence, notwithstanding the fact that Germany had gone there to maintain the old British principle of the open door.*"

If the German delegates at the Algeciras Conference found themselves in opposition to their British colleague, this was the inevitable result of the German Government at the time pursuing a policy in regard to Morocco, which His Majesty's Government were precluded from supporting by the express stipulations of the Anglo-French Declaration of the 8th April, 1904. Under that Declaration, as the Marquess of Lansdowne had occasion to remind the German Ambassador here, Great Britain, whilst making no attempt to dispose of the rights of other Powers, did make certain important concessions in respect of the rights and opportunities to which she was herself entitled.

It was provided in article 2 that—

"His Britannic Majesty's Government for their part recognise that it appertains to France more particularly, as a Power whose dominions are conterminous for a great distance with those of Morocco, to preserve order in that country and to provide assistance for the purpose of all administrative, economic, financial, and military reforms which it may require."

And article 9 further stipulated that—

"The two Governments agree to afford to one another their diplomatic support in order to obtain the execution of the clauses of the present Declaration."

The German Government could therefore be under no illusion as to the binding nature of the obligation which lay on this country, to support France in her Moroccan policy so long as that policy was in conformity with the principles embodied in the Declaration. That Great Britain, in setting her hand to that instrument, in no way disregarded or ignored German interests in Morocco, was frankly and explicitly acknowledged by Prince Bülow when he made his speech in the Reichstag on the 13th November, 1904.[8] His Majesty's Government cannot therefore with justice be reproached for unfriendliness to Germany merely because they acted loyally up to their solemn engagements under the Declaration.

In the autumn of 1908, when Great Britain contended that international treaties ought not to be altered arbitrarily without the consent of the Powers parties to them, the German Government gave no support to this contention, but on the contrary lent their active support to Austria, though there was no public instrument obliging them to do so.[9] I might therefore have complained then of the action of the German Government with more reason than they now complain of our action at Algeciras. But I did not make any complaint, as I understood the delicacy of their situation.

[8] [cp. *Gooch & Temperley*, Vol. III, pp. 348–9, *Ed. note*, and p. 431, *App.* B, *encl.* 2, where Prince Bülow's speech of April 12, 1904, is cited. That this is the speech intended is clear from a minute by Mr. Crowe, *infra*, p. 569, No. 424, *note* (2).]

[9] [cp. *Gooch & Temperley*, Vol. V, p. 397, No. 316, p. 440, No. 376.]

No. 415.

Sir Edward Grey to Sir E. Goschen.

F.O. 43410/167/10/18.
(No. 321.)
Sir,
Foreign Office, November 25, 1910.

In the absence of Count Metternich, Herr von Kühlmann came to see me to-day,(¹) and I informed him that I had shown to the Prime Minister the form of words which the Imperial Chancellor intended to use in the Reichstag(²) à propos of what Mr. Asquith himself had said.

We had naturally been exceedingly busy preparing for the General Election which was now to take place, but I had taken an opportunity of seeing the Prime Minister and I wished the Chancellor to know that Mr. Asquith thanked him for the communication which he had made in this friendly way, and did not think that the use of the words proposed would be embarrassing.

[I am, &c.]
E. G[REY].

(¹) [cp. G.P. XXVIII, p. 378.]
(²) [v. supra, pp. 543–4, No. 412.]

No. 416.

Sir E. Goschen to Sir Edward Grey.

F.O. 43965/167/10/18.
(No. 337.) Secret.
Sir,
Berlin, D. November 30, 1910.
R. December 5, 1910.

With reference to your despatch No. 311 Secret (42654) of the 19th instant,(¹) in which you inform me of a conversation you had had with the German Ambassador respecting the part which the naval question was likely to play in the approaching General Election, I have the honour to transmit, herewith, for your consideration, a despatch by Captain Watson, Naval Attaché to His Majesty's Embassy, containing his observations on the statement left with you by Count Metternich, which I submitted to him for any remarks he might have to make.

I have, &c.
W. E. GOSCHEN.

Enclosure 1 in No. 416.

Captain Watson to Sir E. Goschen.

(No. 46.) Germany. Confidential.
Sir,
Berlin, November 29, 1910.

In regard to statement as to German rate of naval construction, I have the honour to submit the attached remarks for your consideration.

I have, &c.
HUGH WATSON, Naval Attaché.

Enclosure 2 in No. 416.

Remarks on German Statement.

In regard to powers of Admiralty in respect of money in Germany, though it might be impossible to lay down new battle-ships before Reichstag had voted the money, it would probably be within the powers of Government, in time of crisis, at its discretion, to obtain necessary money, &c. (without reference to Reichstag)

(¹) [v. supra, pp. 544–5, No. 413, and encl.]

to speed up the construction of ships already in process of construction or voted by Reichstag. In support of this I would adduce the following points :—

(a.) Contracts for two ships of 1909 Estimates were given to private firms in autumn of 1908 before assent of Reichstag was obtained. (Admiral von Tirpitz in Reichstag, the 29th March, 1909.) Strong evidence existed at the time to show that these two ships were commenced some three months before the estimate year 1909 began (the 1st April).

(Admiral von Tirpitz on same date, the 29th March, 1909, stated that time of German ship-building is thirty-six months; Imperial yards, forty months.)

This does not include trials, and is from the 1st April in year in which money is first voted for a ship to date of commissioning for trials. The date in case of these two ships should have been the 1st April, 1909; in view of early contract and commencement their thirty-six months (both built in private yards) should be dated from about January 1909 and not the 1st April, 1909.

(b.) It is reported now that the firms to which contracts were given were assured financially by allocation of Savings Banks funds.

(c.) That further evidence of the powers of Government and Admiralty, independently of Reichstag, exists in the recent sale of battle-ships to Turkey. The sum accruing from it must be regarded as a fund available in addition to Naval Estimates.

2. *By April* 1911.—Statement appears correct. I would point out, however, that the total time allowed for building (three years from first vote of money being made) allows considerable margin for delays; further, that actual dates of following ships completing, as given by German Admiralty, are so near to April 1911 as to make it possible to hasten them on to completion by that date if required. In view of remarks made before, possibly this might be done, Reichstag's assent being obtained after :—

"Helgoland"   ...   . ⎫
"Thuringen"   ...   . ⎬ June 1911.
"Moltke"   ...   . ⎭

("Ostfriesland" may be reckoned as only slightly behind the others.)

By April 1912.—In regard to the ships mentioned :—

"Helgoland."   "Thuringen."   "Ostfriesland."   "Moltke."

(By their German official dates they will be ready considerably before April 1912.)

"Oldenburg."   Cruiser "H."

(In view of Admiral von Tirpitz's statements as to the contracts of these ships being placed earlier, and the strong evidence that existed at the time of these ships being commenced either late in 1908 or early in 1909; it would seem that the probable and possible date for completion should be antedated by three months from that given in the German statement. The latest information of present state of progress of "Oldenburg" rather confirms this.)

By the spring of 1913.—In respect of these ships :—

"Ersatz Heimdall."   "Ersatz Hildebrand."

(The contracts for these ships were not placed until late in 1909, and taking Admiral von Tirpitz's statement of thirty-six to forty months for building, dates given for completion would appear in accordance with statements previously made.

They do not, however, confirm [*sic*] to allowing three years from the 1st April of year in which money is first voted.)

" Ersatz Hagen."   " Ersatz Ægir."   " Ersatz Odin."   Cruiser " J."

(The dates in these cases appear to stand investigation.)

3. In general, I would point out that whereas in 1909 there appears to have been both acceleration or anticipation of programme and delay, in 1910 the contracts for *all* the ships voted were placed somewhat earlier than usual, at the beginning of the 1910 financial year.

HUGH WATSON,
Captain and Naval Attaché.

MINUTES.

This interesting despatch illustrates one of the cardinal difficulties of the proposed understanding. What if one side to the arrangement does not play scrupulously fair? It is probably out of the question that we should argue about these points with the German Admiralty. I am sure that if we did, the result would be fatal to any arrangement being agreed to at all. But if the German statements cannot be trusted accurately to reflect the real position in a matter of this kind, which is not, for Germany, of vital importance, would it be safe, would it be even right, to place implicit reliance on assurances as to Germany's general policy, and its real aim?

E. A. C.
Dec. 5.

There are statements in Captain Watson's despatch which show that there is some elasticity in the German programme and that at a pinch ships might be advanced.

W. L.
A. N.
E. G.

No. 417.

Sir E. Goschen to Sir Edward Grey.([1])

F.O. 43968/167/10/18.
(No. 340.)   Secret.   *Berlin,* D. *December* 2, 1910.
Sir.   R. *December* 5, 1910.

I have the honour to report that I called upon the Imperial Chancellor yesterday and laid before him, in conversation, some of the observations suggested to you by the perusal of his last memorandum,([2]) as detailed in your despatch No. 312 Secret of the 23rd ultimo.([3]) I prefaced my remarks by telling His Excellency that any observations I might have to make in the course of our conversation were not in the least to be regarded as dictated by a spirit of recrimination or controversy, but rather as a clearing of the air. His Excellency in his last conversation had spoken with the greatest frankness with this object; I now, by your direction, proposed to do the same. When both Governments were thoroughly acquainted with the various views and standpoints of the other, there would be no need for further discussion of matters irrelevant to the real object of our conversations, namely the establishment of better relations between the two countries and any arrangements tending to that end. His Excellency said that that had been his idea in putting forward the points in our policy which he had considered open to criticism and that he quite agreed with me that a frank interchange of opinions, the franker the better, was a very desirable preliminary for the important work which we had before us. He would therefore be very glad to hear your views.

([1]) [An *aide-mémoire* embodying this conversation, with a covering note by Sir E. Goschen, was communicated by Sir E. Goschen to Herr von Bethmann Hollweg on December 2, *v. G.P.* XXVIII, pp. 379–82.]

([2]) [*v. supra*, pp. 524–5, No. 400, *encl.*]

([3]) [*v. supra*, pp. 546–54, No. 414, and *encl.*]

After telling His Excellency that his memorandum was under the consideration of the Cabinet and was receiving the attention which its importance deserved, I informed him that for that reason you were unable for the moment to furnish him with the views of His Majesty's Government on the main points with which it dealt, namely the conditions for a naval agreement and the precise form which could be given to a general understanding such as he desired, but that in due course you hoped to be able to do so. His Excellency was much gratified when I told him that his willingness to exchange information with regard to the progress of shipbuilding had made a very favourable impression upon yourself and His Majesty's Government.

I then told His Excellency that my chief object in calling upon him was to lay before him the point of view of His Majesty's Government upon the particular incidents in our past and present political relations to which he had drawn especial attention. I observed however that before dealing with his observations with regard to those incidents, I should like to say a few words respecting certain remarks which had fallen from him during our last conversation. I said that to one of those remarks especially you had taken very grave exception. This was his observation that if the British people had not learnt from their Government to regard Germany as an enemy, the expansion of the German Fleet would have caused them as little anxiety as the expansion of the Navy of the United States of America. His Excellency, who appeared very much perturbed, expressed some doubts as to having used those words, but I assured him that there could be no doubt of the matter, as the words were taken verbatim from the notes of the conversation with which he had been good enough to supply me. After a few moments' thought he gave me to understand that the speeches of prominent statesmen, like Mr. McKenna and others, had justified him in drawing the above conclusion. I said that as far as my recollection went of the speeches which had been made by members of the Government, they had been confined to the perfectly justifiable endeavour to show that the vigorous expansion of German Naval Power was a serious matter for England and that in order to ensure that supremacy at sea which was of vital interest to her, His Majesty's Government had to take into account not only the existing German Navy Programme, but also other circumstances, including not only the increase in the rate of shipbuilding in Germany, which German skill and enterprise had undoubtedly rendered possible should occasion require such increase, but also the naval plans of other Powers. His Excellency said that he wished he could regard the speeches which he had in his mind with equal benevolence, but that he was really unable to do. His Excellency then asked me whether you had made any further remarks on the subject—on which I told him that you had expressed deep regret that His Excellency should have made to me, as an accredited Representative of Great Britain, an insinuation which reflected dishonourably on the conduct of His Majesty's Government, and that you trusted that he would see that he had used words for which he had no justification. I also reminded him of the appreciative language he had held in the same conversation with regard to the earnest wish of His Majesty's Government to establish better relations, and said that you would be glad to think that this language more truly represented his considered views. I touched very lightly, but I hope clearly, on what might be considered the real reasons for the popular feeling in England with regard to the expansion of the German Navy, and hinted that I might say more but that you had expressly told me that you did not wish to enter into recriminations of any nature, as you wished to remove, and not multiply, obstacles in the way of a better understanding. But I pointed out that if that end was to be attained by loyal co-operation it was essential that such charges, as grave as they were unfounded, should not be brought against His Majesty's Government.

His Excellency said that at all events the Press had certainly led the people to regard Germany as an enemy and that His Majesty's Government had never taken the slightest step to put a stop to that mischievous campaign. I told His

Excellency that to muzzle the Press in England was a matter of impossibility and that in any case the words he had used to me were of a very different character. His Excellency said that he must think over the matter and that he would be very much obliged if, as he had done on the last occasion, I would let him have notes of my foregoing remarks and any others I might have to make to him. I said that I would do so, but that I must beg him to treat them as strictly confidential. I then came to His Excellency's complaint that British Policy in its general tendency followed a course opposed to that of Germany. I told him that you viewed with regret the general inclination of the Imperial Government to regard as opposition to German plans and desires the legitimate defence by His Majesty's Government of important British interests, or the fulfilment of treaty obligations to which Great Britain is solemnly pledged. His Excellency said that he had never denied the right of His Majesty's Government to defend British interests—he would never deny them a right which he claimed to the full for himself in the case of German interests. What he had said, he added, was that His Majesty's Government maintained an antagonistic attitude to Germany even in cases where no British interests were involved, and where co-operation was indicated. I said that I was coming to that directly; that of which I was then speaking was an impression forced upon the minds of His Majesty's Government by the numerous complaints against their attitude which had been continually made by the Imperial Government and which had been formulated by him in his last memorandum. Continuing, I said that the remarks I had been authorized to offer upon those complaints, and to which I would come immediately, were to be regarded as explanatory and not controversial, and that you hoped that they would dispel from his mind any idea that His Majesty's Government was in the habit of pursuing, or even contemplating an anti-German policy, and that they would lead His Excellency to a clearer and more sympathetic appreciation of the attitude of His Majesty's Government in the particular matters to which he had called attention.

Referring to his contention which he had just mentioned, namely that His Majesty's Government opposed Germany even in cases which called for co-operation, I communicated to His Excellency the views expressed in paragraph eight [seven] in the despatch under reference, and recalled to his mind the efforts you had made during the last few years to secure German co-operation in cases when nothing stood in the way of the two Governments acting together and in which, in your opinion, such co-operation would have had beneficial results; and reminded him of the way in which your proposals had been met. He at once asked me to what cases reference was made. I said that the cases you particularly referred to in this connection were the question of reforms in Macedonia prior to the Turkish revolution and to co-operation in the Cretan problem : there were other cases but these were uppermost in your mind. Beyond saying that the Macedonian Reforms question, at all events, was before his time as Chancellor, he made no remark on this subject. I especially pointed out to His Excellency that you had never complained of these matters, nor did you do so now, but that as His Excellency appeared to regret the loss of opportunities for co-operation you had wished to show that the blame for such loss should not be thrown upon His Majesty's Government.

Before passing to the Chancellor's four chief grievances I referred as briefly as possible to the vague complaint he had formulated with regard to the attitude of British diplomatists towards their German colleagues. I said that the matter appeared scarcely worthy of serious discussion, but that, as both His Excellency and Herr von Kiderlen appeared to be convinced of its truth, I would say a few words about it. I then scouted the idea as being utterly at variance with the habits and traditions of His Majesty's diplomatic service and told him what you had said on the subject : His Excellency made no reply.

I then began a conversation with him on the subject of his specific complaints. In the course of our conversation he had mentioned Persia, so I took that subject first and endeavoured to explain to His Excellency the point of view of His Majesty's

Government as explained in your memorandum. I was turning to the other subjects when His Excellency, observing that I was speaking from notes, asked me whether I did not think it would simplify matters, particularly as our conversation had already lasted a considerable time if I left my notes with him and returned another day to develop them and hear his views. As the notes had been carefully prepared and were practically a reproduction of your memorandum, I did not see any objection to the course proposed. So I left my notes with His Excellency on the condition that he would regard them as notes for a confidential conversation and not as a formal document. He said he would certainly regard my wishes in this respect.

Except for being obviously troubled by the allusion to his remarks upon the reasons for the anxiety of the British public respecting German naval expansion, His Excellency remained imperturbable throughout our conversation. At its close he expressed the opinion that the frankness shown by the two Governments was in itself a gain on former relations, and in all respects advantageous and he shared my view, although I cannot tell how far he will act upon it, that now that the two Governments have unloaded their minds as regards the past and present the way was now much clearer for the establishment of better relations.

I have, &c.

W. E. GOSCHEN.

MINUTE.

Sir E. Goschen has done it very well.

E. G.

No. 418.

Admiralty to Foreign Office.

F.O. 44161/167/10/18.
Secret and Confidential.

Sir, *Admiralty, December 3, 1910.*

I have laid before My Lords Commissioners of the Admiralty your letter of the 24th October([1]) on the subject of the exchange of certain information between the British and German Naval Authorities and enquiring whether the Admiralty would prepare, for the confidential information of His Majesty's Ambassador at Berlin, a statement showing clearly and concisely what he should formulate to the German Government when the proper time may arrive for opening negotiations.

In reply I am commanded by their Lordships to acquaint you that the information as to the German Shipbuilding programme which their Lordships would like to have should comprise the following data :—

(a.) Dimensions of vessels to be laid down :
(b.) Protection, armament, speed and Horse Power.
(c.) When to be laid down, and when completed.

Respecting these data, it must be borne in mind that important details as regards our own ships generally become known publicly either through the Navy Estimates or from the Press, especially when the vessels are launched, whereas similar information as regards German Ships is not published until the vessels are completed or approaching completion.

As supplementary to the proposed arrangement, My Lords would therefore suggest for Sir E. Grey's consideration that the Naval Attachés of the respective Governments should be permitted to visit periodically Government and private Shipbuilding Yards, every facility being given them to see the progress of ships under construction.

([1]) [Not reproduced. Its substance is indicated, *supra*, p. 519, No. 398, *min.*, and *note* ([2]).]

I am to add that My Lords have noted the views of the Secretary of State in regard to the manner in which the German Naval Attaché should be received, should he call with the object of discussing any matter of high naval policy.

I am, &c.

W. GRAHAM GREENE.

MINUTES.

It is a question for consideration whether the discussion respecting the particular point of mutual exchange of information should be pursued now, and independently of the larger question of an understanding respecting naval armaments in general, or whether it should continue to be treated as an integral part of the larger scheme. Much depends on the value attached to the smaller question by the Admiralty and by H[is] M[ajesty's] G[overnment] : If they are very anxious to secure the information respecting German naval construction in any case, even if the larger negotiations should not at present lead to anything practical, then it might be well to instruct Sir E. Goschen at once to take the first suitable occasion for sounding the German Chancellor as to his willingness to proceed on the lines indicated by the Admiralty.

On the other hand, it may perhaps be assumed—seeing how great was the irritation caused in Germany by the secrecy kept here concerning our Dreadnoughts—that Germany is herself anxious to obtain the information to be hereafter supplied as a matter of course respecting British construction. If this were so, it might be more prudent not to dissociate the proposals for reciprocal exchange of information from the larger scheme, but use it, as far as possible, as a pawn in the game of negotiating the latter.

E. A. C.
Dec. 5.
W. L.

I should think that the minor question—(interchange of inform[atio]n) and the larger one (limitation of armaments) must be kept distinct. We might instruct Sir E. Goschen as Mr. Crowe suggests.

A. N.

It is doubtful whether the German Chancellor will discuss this separately. It must wait till I have been able to see Mr. McKenna.

E. G.
9.12.10.

No. 419.

Sir E. Goschen to Sir Edward Grey.

Berlin, December 5, 1910.

F.O. 44186/167/10/18.   D. 8·55 P.M.

Tel. (No. 74.) (? Secret.)   R. 10·45 P.M.

Your despatch No. 312, Secret.([1])

Your observations on the Chancellor's statement respecting His Majesty's Government and the British public have caused great trouble at the Imperial Foreign Office.

The note dictated by Secretary of State to Embassy Secretary,([2]) on which my despatch No. 283, Secret,([3]) was founded, contains the following passage :—

"Si le peuple anglais n'avait pas appris par ses Gouvernements([4]) de regarder l'Allemagne comme un ennemi,([5]) il ne serait pas ému de l'aggrandis[s]ement de la flotte allemande. Les grands progrès de la flotte des États-Unis le laisse[nt] calme."

([1]) [*v. supra*, pp. 546–8, No. 414.]

([2]) [*v. infra*, pp. 564–6, No. 420, *encl.*]

([3]) [Despatch No. 283 from Sir E. Goschen merely enclosed a report from Captain Watson describing an interview with Admiral von Müller. It is not reproduced as the information it contains has already been indicated in previous reports. Sir E. Goschen's reference in the above telegram to No. 283, Secret, is clearly an error for No. 280, Secret, for which *v. supra*, pp. 521–8, No. 400.]

([4]) [*Sic.* The version sent by Sir E. Goschen as enclosure in his despatch No. 345, Secret, of December 9, has here "gouvernants." *v. infra*, p. 565, No. 420, *encl.*]

([5]) [In the later version this read "considérer l'Allemagne comme l'ennemi." *v. infra*, p. 565, No. 420, *encl.*]

The Chancellor, speaking from the notes subsequently dictated, certainly said the same thing to me with great emphasis and a little more strongly.

Secretary of State denies that he ever dictated the above French passage which appears in the dictated notes, and has shown me the memorandum from which Chancellor spoke and from which he dictated. It certainly contains nothing like the dictated passage, and merely says, " The unconcern with which the British public regards the expansion of the United States navy is a proof that the possession of a large fleet by a friendly Power need not necessarily cause anxiety." This, I am assured, is what the Chancellor was to say, and what the Secretary of State dictated.

It is clear that the latter is not the case, as the discrepancy is far too great.

MINUTES.

The incident is instructive. It shows (1) how right we were in expressing our resentment at the impertinence of the Chancellor's statement, and (2) the sorry shifts to which even the highest German officials stoop.

They will no doubt be rather more careful in future. I have the impression that if we insisted, we should succeed in getting an apology. But I doubt whether it would be wise to press the matter further. It is customary in Germany to issue a " revised version " of any public utterance that is subsequently found to have caused just offence. Such versions are nearly always " prepared " of the Emperor's speeches, for instance. It was also done when Admiral von Tirpitz had in the Committee of the Reichstag referred to the " false statements contained in the British navy estimates." The object lesson for us to remember is that there is little regard for truth in responsible quarters at Berlin.(6)

E. A. C.
Dec. 6.

We have had the satisfaction of causing them " great trouble " for their rudeness and shall, I venture to think, getting [sic] nothing more out of the German Gov[ernmen]t even if it were wise to attempt it. The suggested tel[egram](7) makes a good termination to the discussion on this incident.

W. L.
A. N.
E. G.

(6) [Here follows on the file the text of Sir E. Grey's telegram No. 126, Secret of December 12, 1910, v. infra, pp. 566–7, No. 421.]

(7) [v. infra, pp. 566–7, No. 421.]

No. 420.

Sir E. Goschen to Sir Edward Grey.

F.O. 44824/167/10/18.
(No. 345.) Secret.
Sir,

Berlin, D. December 9, 1910.
R. December 12, 1910.

In my despatch N . 340 Secret of the 2nd instant(1) I had the honour to report to you the substance of the conversation with the Imperial Chancellor in which I conveyed to him your answer to the complaints of the Imperial Government against the policy of His Majesty's Government. You will remember that on hearing your remarks respecting the charge he had brought against His Majesty's Government of having taught the British public to regard Germany as an enemy, His Excellency had expressed some doubt as to having used that phrase, but that on my insisting and saying that he had not only done so, but that the phrase was to be found in the notes of the conversation which had been supplied to me, he instanced certain speeches which might have had that effect.

Two days afterwards, Herr von Stumm came to this Embassy and said that I had been mistaken in saying that the phrase in question had been found in the notes dictated to Mr. Seymour by Herr von Kiderlen, as in the original notes from

(1) [v. supra, pp. 557–60, No. 417.]

which the latter had dictated there was no such phrase to be found. He would therefore be much obliged if I would lend him the dictated copy of the notes for the purpose of comparison. To this I agreed and on the following day he brought back my dictated copy and also the original notes from which the dictation had been made. He showed me these notes, and, in effect, there was a very wide difference between the language used in the two copies. The following is a translation of the phrase found in the notes stated to be those on which the Chancellor based his conversation :—

" That the existence of a big fleet in the hands of a friendly Power is not in itself a source of anxiety is proved by the indifference with which the British people regard the expansion of the United States Navy."

The phrase in the notes dictated by Herr von Kiderlen, in French runs thus :—

" Si le peuple anglais n'avait pas appris par ses gouvernants de considérer l'Allemagne comme l'ennemi, il ne se serait pas ému de l'agrandissement de la flotte allemande. Les grands progrès de la flotte des États Unis le laissent calme."

Herr von Stumm told me that Herr von Kiderlen stoutly denied ever having dictated these words. I asked how in that case they came to be written down. He said that he could not explain it; he was only sorry that he had not been in the office at the time, as the dictated notes taken down by Mr. Seymour had been read over by a Foreign Office official who was not at all acquainted with what was intended to have been said. Had he been there, he would have seen the mistake at once and corrected it, as he knew that the impression which was intended to have been conveyed was not that His Majesty's Government had deliberately set to work to rouse the British public against Germany, but that the speeches which had been made by members of the Government and highly placed people in England had had that unfortunate result. I said that I neither saw that language in the original nor in the dictated notes nor had I heard it from the Chancellor when he formulated his indictment. Herr von Stumm said he could not explain the discrepancy in the two sets of notes and added that perhaps I had misunderstood the Chancellor. I said that my recollection of what the Chancellor had said had been fully corroborated by the dictated notes, and that as a matter of fact His Excellency's language had made such a vivid impression that I had written it down immediately I had returned to the Embassy. On Mr. Seymour bringing me the dictated notes I had first of all asked him to find the passage in question and read it to me, as I wished to see whether I had reported it correctly. I found that it tallied except that to me the Chancellor had said that the Government had ' taught ' the British public, while the notes said that the British public had ' learnt ' from the Government. I had reported what the Chancellor had said. I asked Herr von Stumm whether he did not think the phrase in the dictated notes was a very strong one and one likely to cause offence to His Majesty's Government. He said " Certainly! ", but that it had neither been said nor meant. As to how it got there he could offer no explanation whatever.

On Tuesday afternoon I saw Herr von Kiderlen. He at once came to the point, and said that he had seen our version of the notes and that he denied ever having dictated the disputed phrase. He could not have done so, he said, because it was not to be found in the original from which he had dictated. It was therefore evident that Mr. Seymour had misunderstood him. He added, as a great secret, that he himself had prepared the original notes for the Chancellor, and that the latter had more or less read them out to me. I said that as regards the particular phrase we were discussing it was rather " less," as the Chancellor's language coincided with that in the dictated notes. He said that he could offer no explanation except that I had misunderstood the Chancellor and that he himself had been misunderstood by Mr. Seymour. I said that even granting that I had misunderstood the Chancellor, it was inconceivable that Mr. Seymour in writing quickly from dictation should have had the time, not to speak of the imagination, to compose a sentence which beyond the reference to the United States Fleet bore absolutely no resemblance to the phrase which he claimed to have dictated. His Excellency murmured something to the effect that perhaps Mr. Seymour in typing the notes had "retouched" the phrase which he (Herr von Kiderlen) had dictated in order to make it look better! I said that from a literary point of view one version was as good as the other; but that I was sure that he was not speaking seriously as his statement that Mr. Seymour had altered the phrase was tantamount to a charge that the latter had, for the purpose of rounding a sentence, not hesitated to make mischief between the two Governments.

Herr von Kiderlen said that he certainly brought no such charge—all he meant was that in translating from the German into the French he might have put the phrase clumsily, and that Mr. Seymour might have unwittingly changed its meaning when endeavouring to improve it. I again pointed out the utter unlikelihood of such a thing having happened. Herr von Kiderlen, who throughout the conversation had not shown the slightest irritation, then said that as neither of us could explain what had happened it was not much use our discussing the matter further. He added that no harm would have been done, as he would furnish me with a copy of the Notes from which the Chancellor had spoken as well as with an explanatory memorandum. You would see from these documents what the Chancellor had really meant to say.

I said that however difficult it was to explain what had occurred I was sure that you would hear with pleasure that His Excellency had no intention of bringing a charge of such gravity against His Majesty's Government.

I may mention that as Herr von Kiderlen had informed me that he was the author of the indictment against British Policy I took the opportunity of placing before him your views with regard to Anglo-German relations in the past, as stated in paragraph 6 of your despatch No. 312 secret of the 23rd ultimo.([2])

I have, &c.
W. E. GOSCHEN.

P.S.—The documents promised to me by the Imperial Foreign Office (see my telegram No. 75 secret of the 6th instant)([3]) have not yet been received.

Enclosure in No. 420.

Notes of conversation dictated by Herr von Kiderlen-Waechter to Mr. Seymour at the Imperial Foreign Office, October 14, 1910.

Le Gouvernement Impérial a appris avec satisfaction par le mémoire anglais que le Gouvernement Britannique était prêt à reprendre les pourparlers interrompus en printemps pour des raisons de politique intérieure. Au cours de ces pourparlers on avait aussi prévu des négociations entre les deux Départements de la Marine sur la restriction ou le ralentissement des armements navals. Le Gouvernement allemand n'a pas bien compris comment Mr. Asquith a pu dire au Parlement que le Gouvernement allemand avait déclaré ne pas pouvoir tenir compte des désirs du Gouvernement britannique au sujet d'un "Naval Agreement." Ce n'était que le désir britannique qui a interrompu les négociations entamées—du reste le Comte Metternich a déjà été chargé de vérifier ce point. Je ne reviens pas à ce point mais je voudrais de nouveau expliquer à Votre Excellence notre manière de voir dans

([2]) [*v. supra*, pp. 547–8, No. 414.]
([3]) [Not reproduced. It repeated the statement made in Sir E. Goschen's telegram No. 74 of December 5 (*v. supra*, pp. 561–2, No. 419) that Herr von Kiderlen-Waechter denied having dictated the words quoted in that telegram. The documents promised are those printed *infra*, pp. 570–4 No. 424, *encls.*]

la question des flottes. Nous n'avons été guidés dans notre construction navale que par le désir d'être assez forts pour pouvoir protéger nos côtes et notre commerce. Pour nous mêmes nous ne sentons pas un besoin de nous arranger avec une autre Puissance sur l'étendue de la force navale réciproque—nous sommes prêts à entrer dans les vues du Gouvernement britannique et à nous entretenir avec lui sur les questions qu'il nous a posées dans l'espoir de revenir ainsi aux anciennes relations d'amitié et de confiance. Dans cet examen nous avons adopté les propositions d'échange des renseignements à l'aide des Attachés navals, et le Gouvernement britannique nous propose en outre de nous lier formellement aux armements prévus dans notre dernière loi. Nous avons toujours dit que nous n'avons pas l'intention de dépasser la loi. Si on nous demande cependant de nous y engager formellement nous devons demander au Gouvernement britannique quels seraient ses engagements. Le principe de la réciprocité est cependant aussi reconnu dans le mémoire anglais. Dès le commencement des premières négociations nous avons exprimé notre opinion, qu'un "naval agreement" ne pouvait que suivre une détente et entente politique. N'importe quel "naval agreement" restreindrait la liberté d'action des Puissances dans les dépenses pour leur défense nationale, et touche par ça à leur force maritime. Un "naval agreement" n'est donc possible qu'entre pays dont les relations ont une base solide. Pour arriver à de pareilles relations entre nous et l'Angleterre nous croyons une entente politique absolument nécessaire. Le Gouvernement Britannique dans son mémoire déclare à différentes reprises que ses ententes avec d'autres pays ne contiennent rien qui soit dirigé contre l'Allemagne. Nous savons apprécier toute la valeur de cette déclaration, aussi nous ne songerions jamais à mettre entrave à ces ententes entre l'Angleterre et de tiers pays. Nous ne saurions cependant nous cacher le fait que la politique anglaise dans sa tendance générale poursuit une route opposée à la politique allemande et qu'en s'appuyant sur d'autres Puissances elle suit souvent des tendances contraires aux intérêts anglais même là, où les intérêts des deux pays dictent une coopération. Il en est ainsi en Perse et en Maroc, où l'Allemagne ne défendait que le principe de l' "open door." Dans les deux pays où nous n'avons que des intérêts commerciaux nous trouvions l'Angleterre du côté des Russes et des Français qui aspiraient à un monopole politique. Nous avons promis [le] printemps dernier au Gouvernement anglais les plus grandes avances possibles. L'Angleterre n'y a pas répondu. Elle a préféré essayer de nous restreindre dans nos relations commerciales en Perse par une pression exercée sur le faible Gouvernement persan. Quand il s'agissait d'employer en Perse des sujets de la Triplice on leur a fait des difficultés de concert avec les Russes. Pour des sujets américains il n'en était pas ainsi. Je rappelle l'attitude dans la question de Bagdad. Notre effort de nous entendre sur le dernier tronçon n'a pas été accepté mais en revanche le Gouvernement Britannique a tâché d'entraver nos projets en refusant aux Turcs les moyens nécessaires. On a dit aux Turcs nettement qu'on ne leur concédait pas l'augmentation de $4\frac{1}{2}$% des droits d'entrée pour cette seule raison qu'une partie de cette augmentation reviendrait au chemin de fer de Bagdad. La lutte ouverte contre la route de Bagdad allemande n'a pas empêché le Gouvernement Britannique de favoriser une route de Bagdad française projetée par Monsieur Trarieux [sic].[4] Les derniers efforts français de remplacer la dette publique par la Banque Ottomane ont été vivement soutenus par le Gouvernement Britannique quoique ce dernier soit aussi intéressé à la dette publique que nous. Partout nous voyons auprès des Représentants anglais à la place de l'ancienne intimité une certaine réserve envers leurs collègues allemands. On affiche partout l'intimité avec les représentants des autres Puissances. Cette politique est dans une certaine limite la raison pour laquelle le peuple anglais s'est ému des armements allemands. Si le peuple anglais n'avait pas appris par ses gouvernants de considérer l'Allemagne comme l'ennemi, il ne se serait pas ému de l'agrandissement de la flotte allemande. Les grands progrès de la flotte des États-Unis le

[4] [? Tardieu. *cp. infra*, p. 573, No. 424, *encl.*, and *G.P.* XXVIII, p. 371.]

laissent calme. Le Gouvernement ne sait pas si l'échange de renseignements aura l'effet espéré. Les renseignements donnés jusqu'à présent par le Gouvernement allemand n'ont pas empêché des membres du Gouvernement britannique de donner en publique des renseignements contradictoires à ceux fournis par le Gouvernement allemand. Il serait à craindre que les renseignements donnés par le Gouvernement allemand en raison de l'échange de nouvelles proposé rencontreraient la même méfiance. L'organisation d'un contrôle de renseignements par les attachés navals des deux parties, comme l'a proposée le Premier Lord de l'Amirauté, devrait être considérée par l'opinion publique, vu l'état actuel des rapports entre les deux pays, comme une preuve (Dokumentierung) de cette méfiance. Un arrangement de la sorte ne saurait être compris et accepté par l'opinion publique allemande que dans le cas où il corresponderait à un rapprochement politique qui aurait pris des formes positives et c'est seulement dans ce cas aussi, que cet accord pourrait créer en Angleterre l'apaisement désirable. Dès le premier jour en prenant la direction de la politique extérieure de l'Empire j'ai considéré comme ma tâche la plus importante de faire disparaître l'atmosphère de méfiance existant entre nos deux pays. Je suis convaincu que le Gouvernement anglais ne reconnaît pas moins la nécessité d'un échange de vues politique qui aurait pour but de jeter les fondements de relations assurées d'amitié et de confiance. Pour écarter les influences étrangères des pourparlers qui pourraient nuire à leur résultat je sousligne encore une fois qu'il me paraît de la plus haute importance de les tenir absolument secrets vis-à-vis de qui que ce soit. Sir Ernest Cassel lors de son dernier séjour à Berlin a parlé à ses amis de nos pourparlers de l'année dernière et leur a dit qu'ils avaient échoué parce que du côté allemand on avait posé la condition que l'Angleterre renonce à ses ententes avec la Russie et la France. Ce fait suffit pour prouver la nécessité de la discrétion la plus absolue en cas de pourparlers de ce genre, car il est clair que le succès des pourparlers serait définitivement compromis si des nouvelles tendancieuses et fausses se répandaient à leur sujet. Comme le Gouvernement anglais nous a déclaré à plusieurs reprises, que ses arrangements avec d'autres Puissances n'ont aucune tendance hostile à l'Allemagne je ne vois pas de raison pour le soupçon que nous essayons de nous arranger avec l'Angleterre dans le but de troubler ses relations avec d'autres Puissances. Nous sommes loin de poursuivre un but de ce genre—au contraire nous sommes d'avis qu'un échange de vues sincère et une entente avec le Gouvernement britannique aura pour suite que les rapports de l'Angleterre avec ses amis resteront les mêmes et qu'en temps nos rapports avec ces mêmes Puissances en gagneront.

No. 421.

Sir Edward Grey to Sir E. Goschen.

F.O. 44824/167/10/18.
Tel. (No. 126.) Secret.   *Foreign Office, December* 12, 1910.
     Your despatch No. 345.([1])
     I warmly approve your proceedings. The explanation offered is obviously irreconcilable with the facts, but as I am anxious not to embitter the discussion, I am prepared in the circumstances to consider the German denial as disposing of the incident and to let the matter drop. You may so inform the Chancellor, avoiding however anything that could justify his declaring afterwards that I was satisfied with his explanation.

([1]) [*v.* immediately preceding document.]

As for the reference to the fleet of the United States the Chancellor ought to realize that for us whose policy is defensive and not aggressive the growth of a fleet at the other side of the world is a much less vital matter than the growth of a fleet close to our capital.

No. 422.

Sir E. Goschen to Sir Edward Grey.

F.O. 45129/45128/10/18.
(No. 349.)   Berlin, D. December 12, 1910.
Sir,   R. December 14, 1910.
.... ([1]) Speaking on Anglo-German relations the Chancellor admitted that His Majesty's Government had repeatedly supported the point of view that a treaty limitation of the naval armaments of the various Powers would materially contribute towards the improvement of international relations. England had however never made proposals which could have given Germany occasion either for a definite acceptance or refusal. The Chancellor continued in the following words: "We also meet England in the desire to avoid rivalry in regard to armaments, but in the non-binding pourparlers which have from time to time taken place and which have been conducted on both sides in a friendly spirit we have always advanced the opinion that a frank and sincere exchange of views, followed by an understanding with regard to the economic and political interests of the two countries, offers the surest means to allay all mistrust on the subject of their relation of power to each other on sea and land. The continuance of a frank and unconstrained exchange of views on all questions connected with these matters is in itself a guarantee of the friendly intentions entertained on both sides and should gradually but surely lead to the dissipation of the mistrust which has unfortunately manifested itself in many cases—not in the case of the Governments—but in public opinion." .... ([1])

I have, etc.
W. E. GOSCHEN.

([1]) [This despatch gives an account of the speeches in the Reichstag of Herr Bassermann and Herr von Bethmann Hollweg on German foreign policy, on December 10, 1910. The omitted passages contain references to the Triple Alliance, Russo-German relations, German policy in Turkey and Morocco, and the interview of the Emperor Nicholas and the Emperor William at Potsdam.]

No. 423.

Sir Edward Grey to Sir E. Goschen.([1])

F.O. 45899/167/10/18.
(No. 332.) Secret.
Sir,   Foreign Office, December 16, 1910.
Count Metternich told me to-day that he had informed his Government, after giving me the figures as to German naval construction, that I had said it would be more effective for us to dwell upon our own state of preparation than to make use of these figures publicly. His Government supposed that we did not doubt that the figures had been given in good faith, and hoped that, if we were unable to

([1]) [For Count Metternich's report, v. G.P. XXVIII, pp. 385–9.]

make public use of them, our Cabinet Ministers would not put forward different figures as to German shipbuilding.

I said that I had not intended to convey that we should not make public use of the figures. All I had meant to say was that, if we quoted the figures, and were then pressed as to whether there might not be in future some acceleration in German shipbuilding, our only effective reply would be to say that there was a margin in our state of readiness sufficient to meet any acceleration which might take place.

Count Metternich then said that, as a matter of fact, he had noticed that I had used the figures.

I replied that I had made use of them several times, and with all the greater satisfaction because they were included in a table which I had obtained from the Admiralty before I made any speeches. As far as I had observed, the elections had passed over without anything being said about the German Navy to which any exception could be taken.

Count Metternich cordially agreed with this, and expressed his satisfaction. He remarked that Mr. Balfour had made one or two statements, but they had been in general terms, without any reference to Germany to which exception could be taken.

⌐I am, &c.
E. GREY.⌐

No. 424.

Sir E. Goschen to Sir Edward Grey.

F.O. 45714/167/10/18.
(No. 356.) Secret.   *Berlin,* D. *December* 16, 1910.
Sir,   R. *December* 19, 1910.

I have the honour to report that, in response to an invitation from the Imperial Chancellor I called upon His Excellency to-day.

His Excellency opened the conversation by stating that, having observed from the remarks which during our last conversation,([1]) I had made upon his October utterances that he had been misunderstood upon several points, he thought it best to furnish me with a copy of the Notes on which those utterances had been founded, and which it had been his intention in conversation with me to reproduce as far as possible textually. The points on which he had been misunderstood were the phrase respecting His Majesty's Government and British public opinion to which you had taken exception, and the expression "political monopoly" in the conversation respecting Morocco and Algeciras.

The first of these misunderstandings was of course the most serious and his Excellency assured me that he had never used the sentence which I had reported. He could not have done so, he said, because it did not represent his opinion. He appealed to me as one who had seen him a good deal since he assumed office, and knew how desirous he was that Germany and England should be friends, as to whether it was likely that he should deliberately have used words which could not fail to give offence to His Majesty's Government. I repeated to him all the arguments which I had used to Herr von Kiderlen, and said again that the sentence had made such an impression on me that I had written it down on returning to the Embassy. His Excellency again assured me that I *must* have misunderstood him as he was quite certain that he had not made use of the phrase. I then read to him the sentence taken down from Herr von Kiderlen's dictation, on which he said that the latter denied having dictated any such thing. I said that to discuss the matter

([1]) [This would seem to refer to Sir E. Goschen's conversation with Herr von Bethmann Hollweg on December 2, *v. supra*, pp. 557–60, No. 417. But if this is so, it was not the "last conversation" as one of December 12 on other subjects is quoted *supra*, p. 567, No. 422. No record can be found of a conversation on the "October utterances" after December 2.]

further would only be to argue in a vicious circle. I added that I had in the meantime furnished you with a full report on the subject and that you had authorised me to say that, although the matter was by no means clear, you proposed, in your wish to avoid all acrimony in the discussions, to regard His Excellency's denial of having used the phrase attributed to him, as disposing of the affair and to drop the subject.

His Excellency then came to the second point on which he had been misunderstood. He said that the Imperial Government had not complained of the "*political*" support given by His Majesty's Government to that of France at Algeciras. The word he had used was "commercial" and not "political." Germany had not gone to the Algeciras Conference with any political aims. In his conversation with me he had only wished to emphasise the fact that the endeavours of the German Negotiators to uphold the principle of the open door in opposition to the efforts of France to establish a commercial monopoly in Morocco had met with no support from the British side. He added that in the text of the Anglo-French Declaration of April 8, 1904 there was nothing, as far as he could see, which should have prevented His Majesty's Government from adopting an attitude corresponding to the interests of Great Britain and Germany which in this particular question were identic. He also stated that as a matter of fact Prince Buelow made no speech in the Reichstag on the 13th of November 1904.[2]

I said that as regards the phrase "political monopoly" being found in the dictated notes instead of "commercial monopoly" I was quite ready to admit the possibility of a mistake. I had in this case relied upon the dictated Notes alone and had reported what I found there. In dictation an error with regard to a single word might easily be made. It was different when a whole sentence was concerned.

The Chancellor then turned to your remarks with regard to the Bagdad Railway and Persia, which I had conveyed to His Excellency at our last conversation; and asking me to regard it as a summary of a conversation and not as an official document, read to me the memorandum of which I have the honour to enclose copy and translation herewith.

In a short conversation which ensued, His Excellency said that his point of view with regard to the Bagdad Railway and Persia was that he had the railway concession in his pocket and that he had a most favoured nation treaty with Persia. It was indifferent to him whether the two questions were treated separately or together: but it was asking too much to expect him to make concessions in both questions without receiving anything in return which would be in the least likely to satisfy German public opinion.

His Excellency then said to me "Well, I hope we have now cleared up all misunderstandings."

I said that I too hoped that the fact that the two Governments knew each other's minds on so many important questions would tend to facilitate discussion, but that as regards the particular misunderstanding to which he had alluded at the beginning of our conversation, I could not conceal from him that neither you, Sir, nor I were able to make clear to our minds how it had occurred.

As however you had said that in order to avoid anything which might embitter future discussions between the two Governments you were prepared to let the matter drop, I would not refer to the matter again. I said this in order to show, as you wished, that the explanations which had been offered had not carried conviction to your mind.

On the Chancellor again returning to the subject I said that although there was no mention of it in the notes which he had just supplied to me I was sure that he would remember that he had at all events used the expression that the British people regarded Germany as an enemy. He said that if he had used that expression and

[2] [Marginal comment by Mr. Crowe: "It was a misprint. The speech was made on April 12."]

it was quite possible that he had done so, he had meant that owing to many reasons such as articles in the Press on both sides, election speeches and other circumstances, British public opinion had come, not been taught, to regard the growth of the German Fleet as entailing hostility against Great Britain; in this sense they regarded Germany as a probable or at all events a possible enemy. To get rid of this suspicious feeling on the part of England he had been anxious all along to come to a political understanding with Great Britain such as would remove all feeling of anxiety or suspicion with regard to the growth of the German Fleet. "For," he added, "a great country like ours with so many oversea interests must have a fleet." I said that I quite understood that but that it was its size and its rapidity of expansion and its possibilities in the way of still further development that disturbed the British mind and raised thoughts of a lost naval supremacy. His Excellency said that none of these things would cause anxiety if Germany and England were really friends and had a general political understanding. I said that there I could not quite agree with him, as, personally, I could conceive of no political understanding, however far-reaching, which would make the British public indifferent to the growth of a fleet nearly if not quite equal to their own at their very doors. He said that there was no chance of the German Fleet ever being equal to ours. I replied that I hoped not. I had only taken an hypothetical case in support of my view that a political understanding would in itself not necessarily remove all anxiety with regard to the growth of the German Fleet. On the other hand the removal of anxiety on this head would no doubt facilitate if not a general political understanding such as His Excellency had in his mind, at all events the establishment of such cordial relations as ought to exist between the two countries, which had no irreconcilable differences between them. As His Excellency then alluded to our indifference as to the growth of the navy of the United States I pointed out to him, in accordance with your instructions, that as British policy was defensive and not aggressive, therefore the growth of a fleet at the other side of the world was a much less vital matter than the expansion of a huge navy close to our capital.

His Excellency replied that because German policy also was defensive it was necessary for Germany to have a fleet which, besides looking after her overseas interests, could have some chance of defending itself and the coasts under its protection in the, he hoped, very improbable event of hostilities breaking out between England and Germany.

The Chancellor's tone was most friendly throughout and he again expressed the hope that now that the two Governments had unburdened their minds some further advance might soon be made in the direction of a good understanding between the two countries.([3])

I have, &c.
W. E. GOSCHEN.

Enclosure 1 in No. 424.

Memorandum.([4])

(Translation.)

Your Excellency's answers to the statements made by me in October justify me in the conclusion that I am misunderstood on several points. I hand you herewith a memorandum([5]) on which my remarks made at that time were based, the sense of which it had been my intention to convey.

([3]) [Sir E. Goschen's language was "entirely" approved by Sir Edward Grey in his despatch No. 344 of December 30, 1910.]
([4]) [For the German version, *v. G.P.* XXVIII, pp. 382–4.]
([5]) [Translation amended by Mr. Crowe to "the Notes."]

The memorandum shows([6]) that it was far from my intention to level against the English Government the reproach of having taught the English people to see in Germany an enemy.

A further misunderstanding seems to have crept in about Morocco. It was not to the support which the English Government gave to the French Government in respect of their political aims in Morocco that the Imperial Government took exception. We had no political aims even at the Algeciras Conference. I merely wished to point out that the advocacy by the German negotiators in Algeciras of the maintenance of the principle of the Open Door in Morocco, as opposed to the French efforts to secure an *economic* monopolization of the country, found no support from England. It is not apparent that the wording of the Anglo-French declaration of April 8, 1904, would have stood in the way of such a trend of English policy in this matter which equally affected German and English interests. It may further be remarked that Prince Bülow made no speech in the Reichstag on November 13, 1904.

As far as the Bagdad Railway is concerned, the Imperial Government have always been alive to the great political importance which the English Government attach to the section from Bagdad to the Persian Gulf. With this fact in mind and in the attempt to meet the wishes of the English Government, I again informed Your Excellency in April of this year of the readiness of the Imperial Government in principle to consider the idea of England's participation in the section in question. In doing so I merely pointed out the fact that, in view of the political importance which the whole question has gained on account of the construction put upon it by the English Government and of their attitude towards it, I could not regard an economic concession and especially the renunciation by the English Government of their opposition to the 4 % customs increase as a *quid pro quo* which could be defended to German public opinion.

With regard to Persia Sir Edward Grey remarks that he declared to Count Metternich on May 31 of this year([7]) that it was impossible for the English Government to come to an agreement as to railway construction in Persia without a simultaneous settlement of English participation in the Bagdad Railway. Count Metternich's remarks were, according to Sir Edward Grey, so unfavourable to this point of view that they had given the English Government little encouragement to press for a pursuance of the negotiations.

Count Metternich reported simply the following as to this conversation :—

> "We discussed the whole Persian question and the question of the Bagdad Railway, without the discussion producing any new views except that the English Government appear to have met with a refusal from the Turkish Government with regard to their attempts to acquire a rival([8]) line to the Persian Gulf. The Minister was of opinion that we were claiming a railway monopoly in Asia Minor. If England was doing the same in South Persia that would equalize matters. When I contested that we had a railway monopoly Sir Edward Grey replied that the prohibition to build any other railways in the district traversed by ours hung together with the kilometric guarantee on the Bagdad Railway. I remarked that the Bagdad Railway was based on acquired rights and treaties, whereas the question of English concessions in Persia was not."

Count Metternich in the above conversation accurately recorded the point of view of the Imperial Government, according to which it is a question, both in the Bagdad Railway question and the Persia question, of a renunciation by Germany of

---

([6]) [Translation amended by Mr. Crowe to " The notes show."]
([7]) [*v. supra*, pp. 490–1, No. 375.]
([8]) [Translation amended by Mr. Crowe to " competing."]

well founded treaty rights and of a consequent meeting of(9) England's wishes. From this it should be clear that it was a matter of indifference to the Imperial Government whether both questions were treated separately or together.

Finally, as regards my remarks concerning the attitude of English diplomats abroad, I was far from wishing to make any reproaches. I merely thought that I ought not to conceal from the English Government the conclusions come to as the result of observation on the part of many German diplomats.

Enclosure 2 in No. 424.

Memorandum.(10)

(Translation.)

The Imperial Government have observed with satisfaction from the Memorandum of the British Government, that the latter are prepared to resume the negotiations with regard to the question of the diminution of expenditure in Naval Armaments, which the internal political situation in England caused them to break off for some considerable time. In the course of the earlier negotiations we had stated that we were able and also prepared in principle to undertake a moderation of the rate of naval construction within the limits of the Navy Law. In consequence of the interruption of the negotiations which ensued in accordance with the wishes of England it never came to an exchange of views between the Naval Authorities of the two countries with regard to the manner in which such a moderation in the rate of construction could be effected. In these circumstances, it naturally caused surprise here that Mr. Asquith should have stated in Parliament that the German Government had declared that they were unable without an act of Parliament in any way to meet the wishes of the British Government with regard to a Naval Agreement. The interruption of the negotiations which had been commenced took place *exclusively* in conformity with the wish of England. Count Metternich has already made this clear. I may therefore refrain from going into this point again. I gladly however take this opportunity once more to define our attitude in the Naval Question. 1 should like in the first place once again to affirm that the development of the German fleet is carried out solely in accordance with the standard of what is requisite in expert opinion for an effective protection of the German coasts and German commercial interests. In itself therefore we do not feel a Naval Agreement to be a necessity, and if we met the wishes of the British Government in regard to the conclusion of such an Agreement, we based our action in doing so on the expectation that the question of armaments would smoothe the way to the re-establishment of the former relations of amity and confidence between the two countries. This wish also caused us, on the ground of the Memorandum of the British Government, once more to subject to a careful examination the question of an Understanding with regard to naval expenditure, and, in doing so, we directed our attention in first line to the most recent proposal of the British Government, which aims at the introduction of a periodical exchange of information on both sides with the help of the Naval Attachés with regard to the state for the time being of naval construction in the two countries. We are quite ready to accept this proposal. But if it is further proposed that we are to *pledge ourselves* to renounce an extension of the existing Navy Law, we could not take this proposal into consideration, until after the British Government had stated what *quid pro quo* (Gegenleistung) they were prepared to undertake on their side in return for such a *formal* engagement. It has also been recognized in the Memorandum that an Agreement of this nature could solely be based upon the principle of reciprocity.

We have never disguised the fact that we regard a Political Understanding between the two countries as a necessary correlative of a Naval Agreement. On

(9) [Translation amended by Mr. Crowe to " concession to."]

(10) [Translation amended by Mr. Crowe to " *Notes.*" For the German version, *v. G.P.* XXVIII, pp. 368–73.]

whatever foundation a Naval Agreement is concluded it will always limit the two Contracting Powers in respect of expenditure to be made for purposes of national defence and it therefore affects their position as an armed Power. It follows from this that an agreement of this kind is only possible between countries, whose relations are based upon an absolutely assured foundation. We certainly consider a political understanding requisite for the establishment of such relations between Germany and England. The British Government repeat in their Memorandum the assurance that their agreements with other countries ˙contain nothing directed against Germany. We are far from underestimating the importance of this declaration. Also nothing is further from our minds than the wish to prejudice, even in the smallest degree, the relations, which bind England to other countries. We cannot however close our eyes to the fact that the general tendency of British policy is to work in an opposite direction to German policy, and that it works against our policy in supporting other Powers even in questions, in which the identity of their (German and English) interests indicates a common line of action. In this connection I should in the first place like to call to mind the attitude of the British Government towards our efforts to maintain the " open door " in Morocco and in Persia. As in Algeciras British policy gave its unrestricted support to France in her efforts to acquire the economic monopoly of Morocco, so is it now trying, in collaboration with Russia, to place obstacles in the way of all German economic activity in Persia also. Its efforts in this line found emphatic expression in the attitude adopted last spring by the British Government towards my announced intention to meet their wishes up to the furthest possible point in the Persian question. The British Government avoided making use of this conciliatory attitude and preferred to make an attempt, in collaboration with Russia, to bring about a limitation of Germany's economic interests in Persia by influencing the Persian Government which was in a critical situation; which limitations I had declared to the British Government ŏur readiness in principle to take upon ourselves voluntarily and by means of conventional friendly agreements with England. According to information received here from a reliable source, the resistance offered by the British Government to the appointment of subjects of the Triple Alliance Powers to posts in the Persian service, as opposed to subjects of other Powers, such for instance as the United States, betrayed a similar tendency.

The attitude of the British Government in the question of the Bagdad Railway is also evidence of their disinclination to settle any questions which may arise in a spirit of friendly agreement with Germany. In spite of our readiness in principle to come to an understanding with England with regard to the carrying out of the last section of the railway from Bagdad to the Persian Gulf, the British Government is attempting to attain their end by trying to rob the Ottoman Government of the possibility of fulfilling the guarantees taken over by them with regard to the railway, instead of by negotiating with us. On the other hand the opposition against the German Bagdad Railway project does not prevent the British Government from lending their sympathy to projects for railway communications between the Mediterranean and the Persian Gulf, which are in the hands of the subjects of other Powers (Monsieur Tardieu's project). England was just as ready to further French efforts to displace the Dette Publique, in the maintenance of which England was no less interested than Germany, and in its stead to assure a commanding position in Constantinople to the Ottoman Bank, which is under French influence.

Moreover the disinclination of the English Government to any political co-operation or even to an attitude of sympathy with German policy is clearly indicated in the numerous smaller questions. This is borne out by the attitude of the English representatives abroad. In the place of a former confidential cooperation with their German colleagues, a certain reserve has crept in, together with the attempt to emphasize the greater intimacy of English policy with other Powers. It is inevitable that this trend of English policy must cause an ever increasing estrangement between the two countries. It contains the germ of the danger of conflicts between the two countries in the future; even now its consequences are perceptible. Weighty interests, equally important to Germany and to England, must suffer from the antagonism of English policy to Germany. But above all this policy is, in the opinion of the Imperial Government, primarily responsible for the uneasiness which has seized upon wide circles of the English people with regard to Germany's naval policy. That a powerful fleet in the hands of a friendly power need not be a cause for anxiety for England is shown by the equanimity with which England regards the growth of the fleet of the United States.

The Imperial Government doubts whether the periodical exchange of information proposed by the English Government, as to the state of the shipbuilding operations on both sides, without the simultaneous explanation of English policy elsewhere, would have the effects hoped for by the English Government. These doubts are probably especially justified in view of the fact that the definite official declaration made by the Imperial Government in the past as to the carrying out of the German Navy Law has not prevented even members of the English Government from making public statements in contradiction to these declarations.

It is to be feared that the statements of the Imperial Government made on the strength of the proposed exchange of information would encounter the same mistrust. The introduction of a control of these statements by the Naval Attachés of both countries as proposed by the First Lord of the Admiralty would, however, in the present condition of the relations of the two countries, be sure to appear to the public mind to be an actual record of that mistrust. Such an agreement would only be understood and accepted by public opinion in *Germany* and cause the desired feeling of reassurance in *England* if it were to be accompanied or preceded by a political rapprochement in a tangible form between the two countries.

I have, from the first day when I took over the conduct of the foreign policy of the Empire, regarded it as my most cherished task to dispel the atmosphere of mistrust existing between the two countries. I continue therefore to trust that the British Government will not shut its eyes to the necessity of a political exchange of views the object of which would be to lay the foundation of assured relations of friendship and confidence between Germany and England.

Once more I wish to lay stress on the fact that I consider that it is a matter of urgent necessity that the negotiations should be kept strictly secret from everybody in order to keep away from them all outside influences, which might prejudice their result. What serious consequences a failure to preserve secrecy can have, is shown by the fact that Sir Ernest Cassel, when last in Berlin, spoke to acquaintances about our negotiations of last year and made the statement that the negotiations had been wrecked owing to the demand put forward by Germany that England should abandon her *ententes* with Russia and France. It is obvious that if such partial and malicious misrepresentations should become public, the fate of the negotiations would be definitely sealed.

Since the English Government has again and again explained to us that her agreements with other Powers are in no way directed against Germany, it is impossible to understand how the English Government can come to suspect that we were seeking an understanding with her, in order to disturb her relations with other Powers. Such aims are far removed from our minds.

A frank exchange of views and an understanding with the English Government will on the contrary, in our opinion have the result that England's relations to her friends will remain undisturbed, and at the same time our relations to these Powers will be improved.

MINUTES.

The conversation here recorded does not lead us any further. Our statements were furnished by way of explanation. So far as they are now answered, the answers are vague and not much to the point.

Sir E. Goschen acquitted himself well in dealing with the objectionable statement originally made by the Chancellor respecting the action of H[is] M[ajesty's] G[overnment] in fomenting anti-German feeling. It is characteristic of official German methods that they do not even follow a consistent line in their denials. We were first given the French text of the notes of the original conversation, as dictated by Herr von Kiderlen. In those notes the offensive passage had been remodelled and changed out of all resemblance to the spoken words. (I have underlined the passage in the revised version on p. 3 of the annexed print.) Now we have the Chancellor's own notes from which he professes to have spoken. Of these notes, M. von Kiderlen's version was a French translation. But—*mirabile dictu*—in the original from which the translation must have been made, there is neither the passage as verbally delivered by the Chancellor, nor the revised version given by Herr von Kiderlen; there is a simple blank, and the revised version must apparently now be also regarded as a myth! The Chancellor would have been wiser to obey the 11th commandment: " If you tell a lie, stick to it."

The arguments, if they may be honoured by that name, advanced in the German counter-memorandum, hardly require further comment.

I regret that owing to a misprint the date of Prince Bülow's speech respecting the Anglo-French agreement of 1904 was wrongly given as the 13th Nov[ember], instead of the 12th of April 1904. Sir E. Goschen should be asked to correct the error. That Germany when entering the Algeciras conference, had no political aims, is so manifest a perversion of facts that it is not worth while to dwell upon it, beyond recalling the conversations with Sir A. Nicolson at the time in which the German Representatives so clumsily tried to persuade him that the proper policy of Great Britain was to join with Germany for the purpose of crushing France.

As regards the Bagdad railway and Persia, the German gov[ernmen]t take up the position that their railway concession is a formal contract sanctioned by treaty, whilst the British claim to a control over Persian railway schemes is not. It is of interest to note that the German ambassador's report refers to the British scheme of a Tigris railway and to its failure as something which he learnt for the first time from Sir E. Grey in his conversation on May 31 last.

On the subject of the complaints against the attitude of our diplomats, the Chancellor, in the way with which we are familiar, takes refuge in generalities, so soon as we point to the necessity of being specific.

E. A. C.
Dec. 19.

The question as to the proper version of what was said and dictated could now be dropped—no advantage would be gained in pursuing it. I suppose the Cabinet will be consulted as to what our next step will be.

A. N.

The record of my conversation with Count Metternich last week has explained the present position([11]) : the general question will come before the cabinet next month.

Meanwhile Count Metternich has told me that the German Gov[ernmen]t accept our proposal for exchange of information absolutely,([12]) *i.e.*, apart from the general question. There was a letter from the Admiralty some time ago on that point and we should proceed with it. My idea was that this point left to itself might be proceeded with by the two Admiralties through the naval Attachés, but I should like to know the view of Sir E. Goschen on this before proposing to the Admiralty that we should suggest this to the German Gov[ernmen]t.

E. G.
21.12.10.

([11]) [This refers apparently to Sir Edward Grey's interview with Count Metternich of December 16, which was recorded in two despatches to Sir E. Goschen one of which is printed *supra*, pp. 567–8, No. 423, and the other *infra*, pp. 575–6, No. 425.]
([12]) [*v.* immediately succeeding document.]

No. 425.

Sir Edward Grey to Sir E. Goschen.

F.O. 45900/167/10/18.
(No. 333.) Secret.
Sir,
Foreign Office, December 16, 1910.

Count Metternich reminded me to-day that I had asked him whether the adhesion of the German Government to the idea of the exchange of information between the German and British Admiralties was dependent, as any general arrangement respecting naval armaments was, upon a political formula. He was now able to tell me that the German Chancellor's adhesion to the proposal for the exchange of information was absolute, and not dependent upon any political formula.

I said that I was very glad to hear this, and it would enable us to proceed on this point.

I then told Count Metternich that the whole question of a political formula and the German naval programme had been brought to the notice of the Cabinet before we separated for the General Election this month, in order that, if we remained in Office, the question might be considered when we reassembled. We were now confirmed in Office, the Cabinet would meet after the Christmas holidays, and we should then in due course consider the question.

Meanwhile, the question in my own mind was the difficulty of finding a political formula which would improve our relations with Germany without being open to misconstruction in France or Russia. I wished to find some way of bettering our relations with Germany without impairing those with either France or Russia. It was to the overcoming of this difficulty that I was addressing my mind. No doubt the German Government would understand how natural this difficulty was.

Count Metternich did not dissent from this.

I added that I hoped the German Government might also be considering how the difficulty could be overcome. I should like to see something which would make it clear that the Triple Alliance and what was called the " Triple *Entente*," though they were regarded by some as different camps, were not really opposite camps.

Count Metternich said that this was just the awkward part of the situation. These groups were looked upon as maintaining the balance of power, and therefore they were each considered to exist in order to be a check on the other.

I agreed that this was the way in which these arrangements came into existence : first the Triple Alliance had been formed, then the Alliance between France and Russia, and so forth. But, during the last five years, since Germany settled her difficulty with France as to Morocco, I had been increasingly conscious that there were not antagonistic aims between the different European Powers.

Count Metternich said that this would only be true if France entertained no idea of a war of *revanche* to recover the lost provinces, she had not renounced this, but did not embark upon it because she knew that Germany was too strong.

I said France could hardly be expected formally to renounce the lost provinces, but as a matter of fact I was not conscious that an attack upon Germany to recover them played any part in her relations with other Powers : I did not know the terms of the Franco-Russian alliance, but I did not suppose it embraced this point.[1]

Count Metternich said it certainly did not.

[I am, &c.]

E. G[REY.]

(1) [On August 3, 1914, Sir Edward Grey repeated this in the House of Commons. " We are not parties to the Franco-Russian Alliance. We do not even know the terms of that Alliance." *Parl. Deb.*, *5th Ser.*, House of Commons, Vol. 65, p. 1815, *cp. Gooch & Temperley*, Vol. IV p. 256.]

CHAPTER XLVIII.

NAVAL NEGOTIATIONS,
JANUARY 1911—FEBRUARY 1912.

No. 426.

Sir R. Rodd to Sir Edward Grey.

F.O. 2007/2007/11/22.
(No. 3.) Very Confidential. Rome, D. *January* 12, 1911.
Sir, R. *January* 18, 1911.

I have the honour to report that I had this morning a long conversation with Signor Luzzatti, the Prime Minister. Although I do not think it probable that he will be able to retain control of the Chamber very long after it reassembles on the 24th instant, and his prospect of remaining in power is therefore very doubtful, his views are always interesting, and he will continue to exercise a certain weight, as he has done for many years past, in Italian political life. I will therefore endeavour to set before you the substance of what he said to me, clearly stating that he was not speaking officially and was only talking to me as a personal friend and a friend of Italy, in a manner in which he maintained he would not do to any one of my colleagues.

Signor Luzzatti began by asking me my impressions of the situation at home and repeated the fears I have heard several times expressed in this country that preoccupation with internal politics would prevent my countrymen from giving sufficient attention to what he described as the menacing position in Europe. I observed that in my opinion this assumption was apt to be too readily made abroad, and that on such questions as national defence and the maintenance of our just rights and liberties the country would always be found united. Do they realize, he then asked, in England the strength of the influence which Germany and Austria have now acquired in the Turkish Empire, an influence which was having a sinister effect on the interests of Italy. Italy had always supported the integrity of the Ottoman Empire. His own administration like that of his predecessor in office had been most categorical in their declarations on the subject and had given every encouragement to the new régime, but the existing conditions in Turkey were in reality those of a military autocracy disguised under constitutional forms, and the admiration of the military element for Germany had resulted in an imitation of her arbitrary methods of procedure.

He then went on to talk of clerical influences which at the present time were a more potent factor than was realized in shaping the policy of nations, citing in this connection the power of the Irish Catholics to turn the balance in Great Britain the great strength of the centre in Germany and of the Catholic party generally in Austria-Hungary. While deploring the recent indiscretions of the Syndic of Rome which had unnecessarily stirred up so much violent resentment, he sustained the argument that clerical influence was generally an element of discord and danger.

There were, he went on to say, at the present time two and only two aggressive Powers in Europe, one of which was a standing menace to ourselves as the other was to Italy. The liberal States must stand together against the two aggressive empires and look out for their defences. The two most liberal countries in Europe were Great Britain and Italy. "Where else," he said, "but there and here, if confirmation of my contention is necessary, would it be possible for me, being what I am, to occupy the position which I hold?" He referred of course to his Jewish origin. Their friendship was the only disinterested friendship in modern history, and was really inspired by sentiment and affection. Our interests moreover seconded our inclinations. Being both of us threatened with a similar danger it was imperative that we should uphold the bond.

I observed that Italy was in some ways at least in a more fortunate position than we were as regards the menace to which he had referred, for so long as she remained in the Triple Alliance, this menace was surely discounted. Signor Luzzatti smiled grimly and said : "Alliance or no alliance, do you really seriously think that if Austria made a further step forward in the Balkans, to which we should be bound to object, that she would hesitate to attack us?" But what, I suggested, if she were to offer you compensation? He replied that it was not Austria's way to offer compensation to Italy. The Austrian naval programme and the manner in which propaganda was being made for it very seriously disquieted him. There was nothing left for Italy to do but to anticipate it and always to maintain the lead. No reliance could be placed on the efficiency of the French fleet, and the balance of power in the Mediterranean was at stake. It was deplorable with all the crying needs for internal development and social reform that continued increase of naval and military expenditure should be forced on Italy, and she would struggle to maintain the equilibrium of the Budget which the Italian nation had supported with admirable patience. But on this point there could be no compromise, and when the Italians had nothing left but their shirts to wear, they would if need be sacrifice them also for the national defence. He then made a somewhat striking pronouncement. The Italian ships were good and he had reason to know that their marksmanship was very good, the material of the Navy was better than that of the Army and it was an instrument not to be despised. We feel, he said, that we can count on your fleet, as you can always count on our's. The only thing to do is to keep them up to the highest standard.

I have in former conversations had opportunities to realize how very high Signor Luzzatti's anti-Austrian sentiments can run, and he is typical of a large number of men of his class and age who remember the white coats in Venetia. But I must confess that I was not prepared for quite such a frank profession of faith as he made this morning. He showed considerable feeling and much uneasiness, and he spoke throughout as though Italy were the ally of Great Britain and France, and not of Austria and Germany. The interest of his statement lies I think in the indication which it affords of the real explanation for the increase of Italian armaments, an increase which I have often heard set down as an additional asset of the Triple Alliance.

The ideas which the Prime Minister thus expressed are, I think, very generally held in Italy, and it is probable that so long as our naval strength is sufficiently maintained in the Mediterranean to give the Italians a feeling of reliance and support, their material resources would never be used against us. Such maintenance of our strength however at a point sufficient to turn the scale would seem to be a necessary condition of our permanently exercising the stronger attraction, inasmuch as the weakness of the Italian frontier on the north-east and the great military strength of Austria might conceivably scare her into a coalition to which she would very reluctantly adhere. As things at present are it is probably still open to us to retain a support the transference of which to an opposing camp would count as two in the division of the Powers.

I have, &c.
RENNELL RODD.

MINUTES.

This is an important declaration on the part of the outgoing Italian prime minister. The substance is that Italy is arming against Austria and that she relies, for the maintenance of her position on Great Britain and more especially on British naval forces in the Mediterranean. He gives us to understand that a weakening of our naval position in the Mediterranean must inevitably lead to Italy's collapse. This is a consideration which must have an important bearing upon the distribution of our naval forces and the maintenance of our fortified places in the

Mediterranean. The despatch should therefore be communicated to the Committee of Imperial Defence.

E. A. C.
Jan. 18.

Signor Luzzat[t]i did not explain how our naval preponderance was to be made effective against the great military strength of Austria mentioned in the last few lines of this despatch.

W. L.

I should doubt if Ms. di San Giuliano would speak in regard to the Triple Alliance in the same tone as M. Luzzat[t]i. The military strength of Austria and Germany will compel Italy to remain within the alliance. We were given to understand by the King of Italy that Austrian Dreadnoughts and destroyers were being built for service in waters far distant from the Mediterranean.

A. N.
E. G.

No. 427.

Sir Edward Grey to Sir E. Goschen.

Private.([1])

My dear Goschen, *Foreign Office, January* 24, 1911.

Some time ago Metternich somewhat pointedly informed me that an arrangement for exchange of information between the Admiralties might be *independent* of any political formula, and that the German acceptance of this part of our proposals was to be construed in that sense.([2])

We must therefore go forward with it, and I am sending you an official instruction.([3])

The Germans may jib at the idea of a signed document. I am content that the document should be an exchange of notes in the most simple form possible : but there should be some document, which can be made public. I desire this because it would have some effect in dissipating an impression in the public mind here, in Germany, and in third countries that either nation is preparing for a sudden spring upon the other.

I do not mean that we should not agree to exchange of information without a signed document, if the Germans insist upon it, but the moral effect would be much less, and if, as they say, the German Navy is being built only to enable Germany to defend her commerce, etc., and not with aggressive designs upon our fleet, I can see no objection to emphasizing the exchange of information.

Yours sincerely,
E. GREY.

([1]) [Grey MSS., Vol. 23.]
([2]) [*v. supra*, p. 575, No. 425.]
([3]) [*v.* immediately succeeding document.]

No. 428.

Sir Edward Grey to Sir E. Goschen.

F.O. 45714/167/10/18.

(No. 25.) Secret.

Sir, *Foreign Office, January* 27, 1911.

From my despatch No. 333 Secret of the 16th ultimo([1]) Your Excellency will have learnt that the German Government are now prepared to adhere, independently of any general political agreement being previously reached, to the proposal that certain information in regard to naval matters should be periodically exchanged between the British and German naval authorities.

I consider that the time has accordingly arrived when negotiations may be initiated with the German Government as to the details of the arrangement in

([1]) [*v. supra*, pp. 575–6, No. 425.]

contemplation; and I should be glad to learn Your Excellency's views as to the manner in which the decision arrived at should be recorded, whether in the shape of an exchange of notes between the two Governments, or in that of a more formal agreement:—the object of His Majesty's Government being that any understanding should be based upon some precise(²) document exchanged between the two Governments.

As to the details of the proposed arrangement, I enclose, for Your Excellency's guidance, a letter, dated December 3rd,(³) from the Admiralty setting forth the views of the Lords Commissioners as to the points which are of importance.

It would, however, be desirable that the scope of the agreement should be sufficiently elastic to permit the inclusion of other items which, with the development of ship construction, or owing to changes in naval warfare, might hereafter acquire importance and special significance. This object would probably be best attained by stipulating for reciprocity as a general principle.

You will no doubt consider that the actual terms of the agreement should, in whatever form, be settled in direct communication between Your Excellency and the German Government: but there will of course be no objection to your availing yourself of the expert services of the naval attaché, in so far as you may deem expedient, in dealing with the technical details of the negotiations.

[I am, &c.

E. GREY.]

(²) [In the first draft of this despatch the words " and binding " appeared after " precise." These were omitted by Sir Edward Grey as the result of discussion with the Admiralty. The last but one paragraph of the despatch was added as the result of a suggestion made by the Admiralty at the same time.]

(³) [v. supra, pp. 560–1, No. 418.]

No. 429.

Sir Edward Grey to Sir F. Bertie.

F.O. 4453/4451/11/18.

(No. 54.) Secret.

Sir, *Foreign Office, February* 3, 1911.

I reminded M. Cambon to-day that, some time ago, he and M. Pichon had been informed very confidentially and secretly that certain negotiations had been entered upon between us and Germany.

These negotiations had been interrupted by the General Election of January 1910. After that Election, the Government here had been too insecure at home to resume the negotiations until the autumn, and then there had been another interruption, owing to the General Election of December 1910. Now, however, we were in a position to renew the discussion with Germany.

Originally, the negotiations were concerned with naval expenditure. As long as they were concerned with that alone, and nothing political came into them, there was no reason why I should say anything about them. But what had occurred with Russia at Potsdam(¹) made it clear that, in all conversations of this kind, the Germans desired that some political assurance should be given. They had evidently obtained some thing of this sort from M. Sazonow, that had enabled Herr von Bethmann-Hollweg to make a speech giving the impression that there had been a political *rapprochement* between Russia and Germany. The question of whether we should say any thing of the same sort to the Germans might, therefore, at any moment come up for consideration.

I felt that, after Potsdam, if first Russia and then we did something which gave the impression of a political *rapprochement* with Germany, France would appear to have been isolated. I wished to avoid this, and I should like to say to the

(¹) [Reference to this subject will be made in a later volume.]

Germans, if the situation arose, that the real guarantee of peace would be that Germany should exchange with us something which she could also exchange with Russia and France.

Of course, when Germany had proposed the North Sea Agreement to us, it had been simple enough for us to say that France ought to be a party to it. But France might feel much more difficulty with regard to joining in a larger arrangement, owing to the question of Alsace-Lorraine. Therefore I wished M. Cambon to turn over the matter in his mind. The situation might never arise, and perhaps I might never have to refer to it again. But if it should arise, this was the direction I should like to give to the negotiations.

M. Cambon said that he would write to M. Pichon on the subject. It was quite true that what had passed at Potsdam had given rise to apprehension in France. No doubt this was the reason for the sensitiveness which had been shown by the French Press with regard to a report from Constantinople that we were on the eve of concluding an arrangement as to the Bagdad Railway.

I told M. Cambon that the idea in my mind was that, since France had come to an understanding with Germany about Morocco,([2]) and since the settlement of the Bosnian question had been recognised by all of us, there was nothing to bring the two groups of European Powers into conflict; and it could therefore fairly be said at any time that, though there were two separate groups of Powers, these groups were not necessarily hostile.

I impressed upon M. Cambon that all I said was most confidential and unofficial.

[I am, &c.]
E. G[REY].

([2]) [The Morocco question will be treated in *Gooch & Temperley*, Vol. VII.]

No. 430.

Sir E. Goschen to Sir Edward Grey.

F.O. 4294/1244/11/18.
(No. 25.) Confidential.   Berlin, D. *February* 3, 1911.
Sir,   R. *February* 6, 1911.

I have the honour to acknowledge the receipt of your despatch No. 10 of the 13th ultimo([1]) asking me, on behalf of the Lords Commissioners of the Admiralty whether I can corroborate Captain Watson's statement that there is reason to believe that the scope of the rumoured amendment to the German Fleet Law with the object of increasing the number of ships to be commenced in 1912 and subsequent years, is dependent on the British programme of naval construction for 1911–12.

I would venture to state that it is a difficult matter to corroborate impressions. Captain Watson sees a great many naval officers, reads German naval papers, and keeps his eyes and ears open for naval information of every kind, and after due consideration has formed the above impression. I have a very high opinion of his intelligence in naval matters, therefore I considered and still consider his remarks on this subject worthy of attention.

But it is impossible for me to say that I "corroborate" his impressions, as this would be tantamount to saying that I know for a fact that the Germans are waiting to decide as to any increase of their Programme until they know the British programme of construction. I do not and cannot know this for a fact. I can only

([1]) [Not reproduced.]

say that I share Captain Watson's impressions in regard to the general naval situation as stated in paragraph 5 of his report No. 44 of November 10th, 1910, and for the following reasons. I consider that there is but small doubt that up till now Germany has always taken advantage of any slackening in British naval construction to increase her own activity in shipbuilding and that *vice versâ* her activity in this direction has slackened off in years when the British naval estimates increased. This, I think, can be gathered from a glance at the naval estimates and shipbuilding programmes of recent years. In fact there is every indication that the increase of British shipbuilding in the years 1909 and 1910 checked the extreme activity which prevailed in German dockyards in the preceding years.

As regards the possibility of further naval expansion it must be borne in mind that a "strong Navy" Party (*i.e.*, the Navy League and Messrs. Krupp and their supporters) has for some time past been urging the Government to build more armoured cruisers and has filled the Press with articles pointing out the necessity for such a step. Whether such an expansion of the Navy Law would meet with the general approval of a public already inclined to murmur at naval expenditure is doubtful, especially in view of the reiterated assurances of the Government that they have no intention of going beyond the Programme laid down in the Law. But it must be remembered that amendments of the Navy Law have already been made in the past, and that, moreover, it would not be difficult if the "strong navy" Party carried their point, for the Government to show that their proposals did not go beyond the replacement of old protected cruisers by modern armoured cruisers, and therefore only entailed a readjustment and not an expansion of the Navy Law. The idea of such a readjustment would certainly meet with less criticism both in Germany and abroad than an addition to the number of ships laid down in the Programme. A modern armoured cruiser does, I believe, not differ greatly from a battle ship, but to the public it has a less formidable sound than a "Dreadnought."

From this point of view I consider that there is nothing to preclude the possibility of the Government yielding to the demands of the "Strong Navy" Party, should they think fit to do so.

The question then remains as to whether considerations of expense would stand in the way of the Navy League's carrying this point.

In this connection it must be remembered that the expenditure on naval construction reaches its highest point this year 1911, and that in the years to follow, according to present arrangements, there will be a large decrease in the naval vote. There is therefore no reason for believing that there would be any insuperable financial difficulties in the way of acceding to the requirements of the Navy League should the naval expansion for which they are pressing be found desirable.

Another point to which I would call attention is the decrease of employment in the German dockyards which must necessarily synchronize with the decrease, beginning next year, of shipbuilding and naval armaments. The fact that a large number of men will be thrown out of employment will no doubt be made full use of by the "Strong Navy" Party and will no doubt greatly strengthen their hands in their efforts to influence the Government in the direction of naval expansion.

To sum up, I consider that the history of naval construction in recent years shows that the activity in German dockyards has a tendency to increase or decrease in the inverse ratio to that of Great Britain and that there is every reason to suppose that the same course of procedure may be expected in the future. Also that if, proceeding on this system, the German Government should wish to take advantage of a reduced British shipbuilding programme to meet the wishes of the "Strong Navy" Party, there are no reasons, financial or otherwise, except perhaps an adverse public opinion, to prevent them from doing so.

In view of these considerations I consider that there is strong reason for the belief that the British shipbuilding programme of 1911–12 will not be without influence on German naval construction in 1912.

I must candidly admit that these are mere impressions, but in the absence of facts I would venture to observe that they are perhaps worthy of being borne in mind when the British naval estimates come to be framed.

As my views on the naval situation have been called for I have but little hesitation in stating my opinion that a British shipbuilding programme showing a steady rate of increase in 1911–12, and a determination to continue on that basis annually in subsequent years would go far towards leading people in Germany to the feeling that if Great Britain goes on steadily increasing her naval strength, further competition in shipbuilding would be useless and would lead to expenditure which would either starve the army or entail an intolerable burden on the nation.

I have, &c.
W. E. GOSCHEN.

No. 431.

Sir E. Goschen to Sir A. Nicolson.

Private.([1])

My dear Nicolson,   *Berlin, February 4, 1911.*

. . . . ([2]) I hope to see the Chancellor in a day or two and to begin work with him on the exchange of Naval Information question. I know that he agrees with me in thinking that we should go as far as possible together before calling in Naval Experts. When an agreement has been reached I should *personally* be in favour of an exchange of notes for recording purposes. I should think that, bearing in mind possible susceptibilities of Third Parties, that this would be a safer method than recording the agreement in a more formal document. I shall no doubt soon hear the Chancellor's views on this subject. He has however such a poor opinion of the utility of the proposed agreement that he *may* not relish the idea of a signed document.. But even if he holds that opinion I do not think that he will refuse to have the agreement recorded, as he is a reasonable man on the whole—and will see that an unrecorded agreement would be rather futile.

Yours very sincerely,
W. E. GOSCHEN.

([1]) [Carnock MSS., Vol. I of 1911.]

([2]) [The omitted parts of this letter refer to the Bagdad Railway scheme and Anglo-French relations.]

No. 432.

Sir E. Goschen to Sir Edward Grey.

F.O. 4788/4788/11/18.

(No. 28.)   *Berlin, D. February 6, 1911.*

Sir,   R. *February 9, 1911.*

I have the honour to transmit herewith a translation of a leading article in the " Kölnische Zeitung,"([1]) which is quoted in the rest of the Press as being officially inspired. The article is an answer to the attacks on the Foreign Policy of Germany which have recently appeared in the foreign press. It draws a sharp contrast between the calm and correct attitude of Germany in the question of the Flushing fortifications and the excitement displayed on this question in England and France ; and is at pains to show that the Bagdad Railway, which is continually dragged into discussion as if it were an international affair, is a question which primarily concerns Turkey and " at most in a second degree " the German Companies who have obtained the concession for its construction. In any case, the article adds,

([1]) [Not reproduced.]

it is an undertaking in which foreign financial participation would be welcomed and by no means opposed.

The article also alludes with pride to the self-restraint exhibited by Germany with regard to the "Anglo-French negotiations concerning military measures."

I may mention that the Imperial Chancellor, in the course of a conversation with me on other matters, made a semi-jocular allusion to these negotiations, saying that, if it was not indiscreet, he would like to ask me about them. I told His Excellency that I could not tell him anything as I had never heard of any such negotiations. . . . .(²)

I have, &c.
W. E. GOSCHEN.

(²) [The rest of this despatch summarises a press report on Russo-German negotiations.]

No. 433.

Sir E. Goschen to Sir Edward Grey.

Berlin, February 7, 1911.

F.O. 4636/4451/11/18.
Tel. (No. 4.)

D. 1·50 P.M.
R. 3·25 P.M.

Secret. Your despatch No. 25.(¹)

I laid before the Chancellor to-day views of H[is] M[ajesty's] G[overnment] respecting the scope to be given to an agreement for the exchange of naval information between the two Gov[ernmen]ts. His Excellency, while as before a little sceptical as to the value of such an agreement, said that he was perfectly ready to go on with it and that personally he saw nothing to object to in the suggestions I had put forward as to the class of information which would be desirable. He must however consult the Minister of Marine before going into details.

His Excellency told me that he would not have the slightest objection to any agreement arrived at being recorded either by an exchange of notes or a more formal document. Of the two he perhaps preferred the former.

He said that at a future meeting we might discuss a formula for whatever recording document might be decided upon and agreed that it should be as short and simple as possible.

(¹) [v. supra, pp. 579–80, No. 428.]

No. 434.

Sir E. Goschen to Sir Edward Grey.

Berlin, February 7, 1911.

F.O. 4679/4451/11/18.
Tel. (No. 5.) Secret.

D. 8·20 P.M.
R. 9·45 P.M.

My telegram No. 4, Secret, of to-day.(¹)

In speaking to Chancellor, I made no mention of any engagement on the part of Germany not to increase her programme as laid down by the fleet law. This I presume to be beyond scope of present contemplated agreement. I only ask because it formed part of our last suggestions for naval agreement, and was put forward at the same time as the exchange of naval information proposals.

(Group omitted : ? See) your memorandum of 26th July last.(²)

(¹) [v. immediately preceding document.]
(²) [v. supra, pp. 501–2, No. 387, encl.]

MINUTES.

I think it was Sir Edward Grey's opinion (see minutes on 44161/10([3]) and 45900/10([4])) that the agreement for the exchange of naval information should be proceeded with independently of the question of a more general agreement which would deal with (a) a limitation of armaments, and (b) a political understanding.

E. A. C.
Feb. 8.

There can be no doubt that this is the meaning of the minutes on the papers mentioned by Mr. Crowe, and of the conversation recorded in 45900.

W. L.

There is no doubt whatever that the present discussions are strictly and solely limited to the minor question of an exchange of naval information. The other two larger questions are under the consideration of the Cabinet Committee.([5])
Telegraph as proposed to Sir E. Goschen.([6])

A. N.
M.

([3]) [v. supra, p. 561, No. 418, min.]
([4]) [v. supra, pp. 575–6, No. 425. There are no minutes written on this document.]
([5]) [v. infra, p. 590, No. 440.]
([6]) [v. immediately succeeding document.]

No. 435.

Sir Edward Grey to Sir E. Goschen.

F.O. 4679/4451/11/18.
Tel. (No. 10.) *Foreign Office, February 8, 1911.*
Your tel[egram] No. 5.([1]) You were quite right. Agreement for exchange of naval information should be treated quite independently of general understanding respecting limitation of armaments and political formula.

([1]) [v. immediately preceding document.]

No. 436.

Sir E. Goschen to Sir Edward Grey.

F.O. 5168/4451/11/18.
(No. 32.) Secret. *Berlin, D. February 8, 1911.*
Sir, R. *February 13, 1911.*
I have the honour to report that, in accordance with the instructions contained in your despatch marked Secret No. 25 of the 27th ultimo,([1]) I called yesterday on the Imperial Chancellor and, after reminding him that in our former conversations he had expressed the willingness of the Imperial Government to make some arrangement for the exchange of naval information between the two Governments, stated that I was ready, if it was agreeable to His Excellency, to go further into the matter.

The Chancellor said that he was quite willing to meet the wishes of His Majesty's Government in this matter although, as he had often told me before, he had still some doubts as to the practical value of the arrangement proposed.

I pointed out to His Excellency that, as I understood the matter, the value of an exchange of naval information, such as His Majesty's Government had in their minds, lay in the fact that if both Governments were officially aware of what was

([1]) [v. supra, pp. 579–80, No. 428.]

going on in each other's Dockyards and were in possession of accurate data respecting the number of ships laid down and to be laid down and respecting the dimensions, speed and armaments etc. of such vessels, they would be in a position to dissipate the misapprehensions and suspicions with regard to naval construction which had of recent years been so often the cause of needless public excitement. The removal of such misapprehensions could not, I thought, fail to be a great gain. It would show a spirit of friendliness and go far to dispel from the public mind in both countries any suspicions which might exist of unfriendly designs on one side or the other. It would, moreover, have a tendency, at all events, to clear the political atmosphere and thus prepare the way for amicable arrangements of such minor matters as might in the future come up for discussion between the two Governments. I also pointed out to His Excellency that a fuller knowledge of each other's intentions with regard to ship-building, would remove from the minds of both Governments any apprehensions of future indefinite increase, and thus tend towards the reduction of naval expenditure—a result desired by everyone, both Governments and Public.

The Chancellor said that I knew his mind well enough to feel assured that no one more than he would welcome the beneficial results which I had depicted, but he felt strongly that the arrangement contemplated could only bring about those beneficial results in a clear atmosphere, and when the relations between the two countries were good. In a bad atmosphere, and he could not say that it was at present good, the arrangement would not, he thought, be particularly beneficial, and might even be the reverse.

I said that I was sorry to hear from him that he considered the present atmosphere bad, as I had been under the impression that the relations between the two countries, if not especially intimate, were at all events quite friendly and cordial. A strong evidence of this was that we were at that moment discussing in such a friendly manner an amicable arrangement respecting naval matters. His Excellency said that that was certainly an advance, but that I must admit that our Press had recently been very unpleasant on the subject of the Russo-German negotiations. I said that there had perhaps been a certain amount of criticism on the part of irresponsible persons, but I was sure that he had observed that no member of His Majesty's Government had spoken in anything but the friendliest spirit with regard to those negotiations. His Excellency acquiesced and added that he could have wished that M. Pichon had adopted the same friendly tone, and not informed the world that England and France were engaged in conversations on military measures. This statement had made a deplorable impression on German public opinion, as I had no doubt seen in the papers, for there was no reasonable doubt as to for whose benefit these measures were being discussed. I said that M. Pichon only put a hypothetical case, on which His Excellency replied with a smile that the deductions from his hypothetical case were easy to divine. He added that he did not wish to be indiscreet, but he would like very much to know more about these conversations. I told him that I had never heard a word respecting any such conversations.

Returning to the matter in hand, he said that I must not think from anything that he had said that he was in the slightest degree indisposed to accept the arrangement we proposed, and he would be glad if I could tell him or let him know generally the sort of naval information which His Majesty's Government would wish to exchange. I told him that His Majesty's Government thought that the two Admiralties might communicate to each other periodically the following data[2]:

1. The dimensions of vessels to be laid down;
2. Protection, armament, speed and horse-power of such vessels;
3. The dates of the laying down of such vessels and of their completion.

[2] [An *aide-mémoire* containing the substance of Sir E. Goschen's statement on this point was presented to the Chancellor on February 8. It is printed in *G.P.* XXVIII, pp. 390–1.]

I added that it was also thought that the arrangement should include permission for the Naval Officers attached to the Embassies in London and Berlin to visit periodically Government and private ship-building yards with every facility for seeing the progress of ships under construction.

His Excellency said that he personally saw nothing whatever to object to in these proposals, but that of course he must consult with the Naval Authorities before going into details and giving me a definite answer. He added that he presumed that it would be necessary to record any arrangement which might be decided upon in some sort of document, either a formal agreement or an exchange of notes. Personally he would prefer the latter course, and his opinion was that it should be drawn up in the shortest and simplest form possible. On my saying that I thought either form would be agreeable to His Majesty's Government the Chancellor said that when he had seen Admiral Tirpitz he would ask me to pay him another visit, when we could discuss details and perhaps endeavour to find a suitable form for placing any arrangement we might come to on record.

I have, &c.
W. E. GOSCHEN.

No. 437.

Sir E. Goschen to Sir A. Nicolson.

Private.([1])

My dear Nicolson,
Berlin, February 10, 1911.

. . . . ([2]) You may remember that in speaking to me towards the end of last year on the subject of Naval Construction the Emperor said that there was a general idea abroad that Germany had no money, and that as a matter of fact she had plenty, more perhaps than France or England had at their disposal. His Majesty reiterated this statement to one of my colleagues the other day and said that as a matter of fact the money put by now every year in Germany exceeded French economies by several millions. Personally I should think this an over-statement, but at all events the Emperor fully believes it. His Majesty also alluded to the alleged decrease in the German birth rate. He said that it was true that there was a slight decrease but nothing like that in the French birth rate. He added that this decrease in the French birth rate which had been going on for years had an important effect on the French army, and would have more effect in the future. The French, in order to keep up their numbers, had, and would have still more as time went on, to accept for service a large proportion of the physically unfit. Germany with her superiority as regards birth rate had a great advantage in this respect, as she had, and would have, larger numbers to draw her soldiers from, and could therefore afford to reject those whose physical deficiencies rendered them unfit for military service. As a result the German army was, and as far as he could see, would always be, a far more efficient fighting machine than that of France. . . . .([3])

Yours very sincerely,
W. E. GOSCHEN.

([1]) [Carnock MSS., Vol. I of 1911.]

([2]) [The opening paragraphs of this letter make passing reference to Persian and Turkish railway schemes and Russo-German negotiations.]

([3]) [The omitted passages refer to other subjects. They include mention of the negotiations for a general political understanding, but do not add any new information.]

No. 438.

Sir E. Goschen to Sir Edward Grey.

F.O. 6105/6104/11/18.
(No. 42.)   *Berlin, D. February* 15, 1911.
Sir,   R. *February* 20, 1911.

I have the honour to forward, herewith, a despatch, as marked in the margin,
which I have received from Captain Watson, Naval Attaché to this Embassy, relating
to German Navy Estimates.

I have, &c.
W. E. GOSCHEN.

Enclosure in No. 438.

Captain Watson to Sir E. Goschen.

(No. 4.)   Confidential.
Sir,   *Berlin, February* 17 [*sic*], 1911.

I have the honour to report that the German navy estimates, having passed
the Budget Committee, have been under discussion in the Reichstag this week.

Considerable criticism has been directed by the Social Democrats at the saving
effected by cutting down the stokers' allowances, and they have coupled that with a
recent case of ill-treatment of a stoker in order to stir up opposition to the navy
estimates, and also a feeling of unrest in the fleet. The empty state of the Reichstag
and other indications point to very little interest being taken in their efforts; and it
is unlikely that their efforts to reduce the naval expenditure will have any effect in
that direction now or in the near future.

That Germany is wedded to a strong naval policy finds expression in several
leading papers, but perhaps the most important pronouncement is in the
"Norddeutsche Allgemeine Zeitung" of the 18th December, 1910, in a leading article
which reads as follows :—

"First of all it is satisfactory that in discussing our foreign policy both
Government and Reichstag were in perfect accord. There seems to be a
thorough understanding on all sides that it is useful to our prestige among foreign
nations if this domain is not the subject of party discussion. The confidence
reposed by the Reichstag in the management of our foreign affairs forms a
valuable asset in our foreign policy. The same applies to the steady treatment
of our land and sea defences. Without wasting many words the 'Bourgeois'
parties are in harmony with the Government in the preservation of national
interests."

2. In regard to the articles appearing of late in other journals, they form a
valuable aid in preparing the way for a further naval increase; the arguments for
which were put forward strongly by Admiral Koester at Navy League last autumn,
as reported in my letter No. 43 of the 4th November, 1910.(¹) They have also
received the support of Graf Reventlow and other influential writers.

3. In my letter No. 44 of the 10th November, 1910,(¹) I reported that various
items of information had come to my knowledge which indicated that the activity
of naval preparation in Germany, prior to England laying down more ships in 1909
and 1910, was incessant. I have now seen a good deal more of naval affairs in
Germany, and have every reason to corroborate what I then had heard.

The execution of the navy law still continues, and I submit there is an
extremely influential party in Germany who are desirous of seeing a further
strengthening of their naval policy.

(¹) [Not reproduced.]

Those desirous of a curtailment of naval expenditure are at present in Reichstag small in number, but they will receive more adherents, which would be reflected in the German general election, if the relative naval estimates of England and Germany hold out no hope to the latter country to compete with England without further naval expenditure.

4. It is widely believed here that 1912 estimates will see the commencement of the replacement of the five cruisers of the "Hansa" class by modern armoured cruisers. It is needless to point out the great accession in capital strength to the fleet by such replacement. It would appear doubtful if it could be considered as an expansion of the navy law, rather a step for which no new law is necessary.

I submit that it is probable that German naval estimates for 1912 and succeeding years will provide for the construction of three armoured ships per year, instead of two as at present proposed by navy law. I would point out that such provision of armoured cruisers is a logical development of Germany's naval strength. It would also keep up the employment and work at the ship-building and armament yards, and avoid the difficulties consequent on the curtailment of amount of building work at present likely to take place. Also this replacement is urged by the Navy League; the league has considerable power in Germany towards educating public opinion and influencing the Government, however unconscious the Government may be of being so influenced.

In regard to naval expansion, press articles in favour of more submarines also appear, and now the initial steps have been taken a rapid development of this arm may be expected. It is unnecessary to point to the increase in numbers of High Sea German destroyers of great power, it is an accomplished fact, and is still proceeding annually.

I have, &c.
HUGH WATSON, *Naval Attaché.*

No. 439.

Sir Edward Grey to Sir E. Goschen.

F.O. 5930/4451/11/18.
(No. 45.) Secret.
Sir,
Foreign Office, February 16, 1911.

In the course of conversation to-day,[1] Count Metternich reminded me that, before the Christmas holidays, I had held out the expectation that after the Cabinet had reassembled a reply would be sent to the German Chancellor's Memorandum.[2] He asked whether I could give him any further information.

I said that we had already sent a reply about the exchange of naval information.[3] I had sent that without waiting for the Cabinet to meet, as Count Metternich had informed me that this was decidedly a matter which could be discussed independently of the general political discussion.[4] You had already had a conversation with the German Chancellor about it.

Count Metternich said that he had lately heard that a communication had been received on that point.

As to the larger question, I told him, informally and privately, that the week before last I had drafted something which I thought might be given to the German Chancellor in the form of a Memorandum of conversation, as the German Chancellor had given his communication to you. My absence last week, and that of the

[1] [*cp. G.P.* XXVIII, pp. 393–4.]
[2] [*v. supra,* pp. 524–5, No. 400, *encl.* The British reply was sent finally on March 8, and is printed *infra,* pp. 598–600, No. 444, *encl.*]
[3] [*v. supra,* pp. 579–80, No. 428, and pp. 585–7, No. 436.]
[4] [*v. supra,* p. 575, No. 425.]

Chancellor of the Exchequer, had delayed matters a little. But the draft would be considered by the Cabinet now, and I hoped to be able to send the communication soon. I also hoped that it would advance matters a little further.

I saw nothing in what the German Government had stated on definite points, such as the Bagdad Railway or railways in Persia, that should prevent an agreement between us. In Persia, we had special political interests, not because we desired to push our own political influence, but because we did not wish to see the *status quo* disturbed in a way which might alter the political situation to our disadvantage. But this *status quo* did not, in our view, comprise exclusive commercial arrangements; and if, as I understood, the object of the German Government in Persian affairs was purely commercial and not political, I did not see why our respective commercial interests should not be susceptible of agreement.

Count Metternich entirely assented to the statement that German interests in Persia were commercial and not political.

He then asked me whether I had much news from Turkey; he mentioned the troubles in the Yemen, and finally asked whether anything was passing with Turkey about the Persian Gulf.

I said that Rifaat Pasha had informed us confidentially that he hoped to make proposals to us about the Bagdad Railway. We had expressed our willingness to receive and consider whatever proposals he made. But these conversations did not amount to much yet, and no doubt Rifaat Pasha had kept the German Ambassador in Constantinople informed of them. Our reply to the German Chancellor would probably touch upon the question of the Bagdad Railway, and it was a little difficult to know whether we were to negotiate with Germany or with Turkey.

[I am, &c.]
E. G[REY].

No. 440.

Sir A. Nicolson to Lord Hardinge of Penshurst.

Private.([1])

My dear Hardinge, *Foreign Office, March 2, 1911.*

. . . . ([2]) As regards the larger questions which we have to discuss with the German Government, that is to say the political arrangement and the reduction or limitation of naval armaments, the matter is at present in the hands of what is called the Cabinet Committee. This Committee has been quite recently constituted, and is composed of Grey, the Prime Minister, Lloyd George, Morley, Crewe and Runciman. I have seen one or two revised drafts of the instructions which are eventually to be sent to Goschen on the subject. I do not gather that the views of the Committee are entirely harmonious, and there seems a tendency to- fall in with the view of the German Government that a political arrangement is the more important question of the two. I am keeping a very close eye upon the drafting of the instructions, and am continually impressing upon Grey that it is essential that we should not move too far from our original position, which was that in any case reduction of armaments was a vital point, even if it did not precede the question of any political agreement. Then in regard to such an agreement, it was essential that it should in no-wise impair our understandings with Russia and France, and that it should, if possible, be made sufficiently elastic to permit those two Powers to participate in it, should they desire to do so. I do not know in what shape the instructions will eventually emerge from the Committee or what treatment they are

([1]) [Carnock MSS., Vol. I of 1911.]
([2]) [The opening paragraph refers to the exchange of naval information between the British and German Governments.]

likely to meet with when they are submitted to the whole Cabinet. Personally
I do not see how it is possible that we should ever arrive at a satisfactory agreement,
either with regard to reduction of armaments or as to a political formula, and I intend
to press very hard that in any case Goschen shall not be authorized to deal with
the larger questions until we have come to an agreement in respect to the minor
one of exchange of naval information, with which he is now dealing. I may tell
you quite privately—and it is a satisfactory piece of news—that the Government
intend to lay down five more Dreadnoughts this year, and I hope that, if we continue
to show a determination not to be caught up in naval construction, we may give
the Germans some reason to become more amenable as to reduction of armaments.
At the same time the Emperor has on more than one occasion intimated that we
are quite wrong if we consider that the question of finance can at all hamper
Germany in developing her navy. Grey is perfectly sound on the whole matter,
but I am afraid there are in the Cabinet several members who desire to come to
what they term a " friendly understanding " with Germany at almost any cost, and
there are no doubt sections of the Radical party who are still more emphatic on
this point. . . . .(³)

[A. NICOLSON.]

(³) [The last part of this letter gives details about the general European situation.]

No. 441.

Sir E. Goschen to Sir Edward Grey.

F.O. 8051/4451/11/18.
(No. 52.) Berlin, D. March 3, 1911.
Sir, R. March 6, 1911.
    I have the honour to transmit, herewith, translation of an article which
appeared in the " Deutsche Tageszeitung " of March 1st comparing Mr. McKenna's
replies in the House of Commons on March 16th, 1909,(¹) to questions respecting
German naval armaments with his statements made on February 8th last(²) on the
same subject.

I have, &c.
W. E. GOSCHEN.

Enclosure in No. 441.

Extract from the " Deutsche Tageszeitung " of March 1, 1911.

MR. McKENNA IN 1909 AND MR. McKENNA IN 1911.

(Translation.)
    Nearly two years ago on March 16th 1909 the memorable debate took place in
the English Parliament in which the Prime Minister and the First Lord of the
Admiralty declared that the German programme of naval construction was secretly
and silently undergoing material acceleration and that in consequence of this from
the year 1912 on the number of German Dreadnoughts would only be very little
behind that of England. These statements were at once contradicted by the
German Minister of Marine in the Reichstag on March 17th 1909, and the
disclaimer was repeated on March 29th by the Chancellor in general terms and by
the Minister of Marine with all details : in short everything was done to give in
the most authoritative manner full publicity to the real truth of the case.

(¹) [cp. Parl. Deb., 5th Ser., House of Commons, Vol. 2, pp. 933–6.]
(²) [cp. Parl. Deb., 5th Ser., House of Commons, Vol. 21, pp. 266–8.]

Nevertheless up to February 1911 no notice of this was taken by the British Government, but in 1909 and 1910 they repeatedly and publicly emphasized and used for purposes of agitation what they knew to be untruths. The panic which was thereby produced assumed the most grotesque forms. The object of the Liberal Government in kindling and keeping alive this panic was to assure their position which was at that time threatened. Contrary to what they had originally intended they found themselves obliged to draw up a programme of construction which was much larger than what had first been contemplated, that is to say, unless they wished to see themselves thrust out of office by the far more comprehensive naval proposals of the Opposition. The sudden change in their naval attitude was based on the assertion that they had been completely surprised by the German intention to accelerate and that now, as a matter of course, they were obliged to regard England's position as a very serious one. By this trick the Government overcame the Opposition in their own party too, especially that of the extreme Left, which, without a credible proclamation of national danger, would not have sanctioned larger demands for the navy. The result of this was, as we are aware, the passing of a programme for eight large ships.

Those declarations of the First Lord of the Admiralty of March 16, 1909 contained, in the doubt which they cast on the assurances already given in German official quarters, considerably more than what is termed unfriendliness and the lack of justification for these doubts, which were only means for agitation, was increased by subsequent German declarations. It appears also that diplomatic negotiations on this subject took place in 1910; further the Minister of Marine quite recently once more expressed in the Reichstag his surprise that the English Admiralty had not yet put right their false assertions of 1909. The result then is that on February 8th of this year Mr. McKenna replied to the questions of Mr. Robert Harcourt. It is true that it should first be observed that these replies are given in the habitual form of English Ministerial statements, which consist in an arrangement of clauses almost unintelligible to the lay mind. This form sometimes makes it difficult even for English people to grasp the far-reaching import of the short speech. Consequently, there cannot be the slightest doubt that the general public in England has not in the least noticed that these replies constituted a retraction on the part of the First Lord of the Admiralty. We do not hope to influence the English public opinion, but it would be a good thing if people in Germany would realize with what conscious levity the English Liberal Government consciously adopted in 1909 false statements simply in order to keep the Opposition out of power. The other necessary consequence, namely a feeling of the deepest mistrust and enmity on the part of the English people towards Germany was faced with a light heart, and representatives of the English Government have nevertheless often had the courage to speak with regret of the "irresponsible agitations" on both sides of the Channel!

We give here Mr. McKenna's answers of the year 1909 and then his recent ones in order that the difference may be clearly shown.

The first question in both cases was to the following effect :—

" At what time during the autumn of 1910 the 4 German Dreadnoughts of the 1908–1909 Programme would be ready, as they would bring the total number of Dreadnoughts to 9 ships as early as the autumn of 1910 " (corresponding to a period of construction of only about two years).

(To-day, in the spring of 1911, we only have 5 and not 9 of the large new ships ready. E.R.([3]))

On March 16, 1909 Mr. McKenna answered :—" The Admiralty expects the ships of the building programme of 1908–09 to be finished not in February 1911 but as early as the autumn of 1910."

Mr. McKenna on the 8th April 1911 (sic) said : " The ships are not yet ready."

([3]) [The initials are those of Count Ernst Reventlow, the writer of the article.]

The second question put to Mr. McKenna was: "When in 1911 will the four German Dreadnoughts of the building programme (Budget) 1909/10, bringing the total number of German Dreadnoughts up to 13, be ready?"

Mr. McKenna's answer in 1909 was: "In August 1911 Germany will dispose of 13 ships," and in 1911, "Not one single one of the four ships will be ready this year."

The third question put to Mr. McKenna was: "When in 1912 will the four German Dreadnoughts of the 1910/11 Budget be ready?" Mr. McKenna's answer in 1909 was: "If their construction is hurried on they will be ready in April 1912, otherwise, in the autumn of 1912," and in 1911 he said "In the spring of 1913."

The fourth question was: "Must one really assume that in the course of the year Germany will have 21 Dreadnoughts ready?" Mr. McKenna answered in 1909: "Germany will in 1913 dispose of a total number of 21 Dreadnoughts," and in 1911 he said: "These ships will not be ready till 1914."

The fifth question was : "Were there in March 1909 13 German Dreadnoughts in course of construction?" Mr. McKenna's answer in 1909 was: "I have received information (!) that the building material and the artillery of the ships of the 1909 Budget have been commenced." In 1911 he said: "If under the term 'course of construction' the hulls of the ships are to be understood, my answer is No!"

The First Lord of the Admiralty could, and strictly speaking should, have given exactly the same answers on the 16th of March 1909 as he actually gave on the 8th of February 1911. The reasons which prevented him from doing so in 1909 are not calculated to increase the value of the declarations of friendship which he and the Government in general have so liberally handed out to Germany in the last few years.

MINUTES.

As the article in the German newspaper was probably inspired by Admiral von Tirpitz, it might perhaps be useful if we had the official commentary of our Admiralty on the allegations made. Such criticism would be of advantage if, as is not unlikely, Count Metternich again refers to the subject.

Qu[ery]. Ask Admiralty to furnish Sir E. Grey with a statement dealing with these German allegations which he could if necessary use if the subject is mentioned by the German Ambassador.

E. A. C.
Mch. 8.
W. L.
A. N.

The German newspaper omits all reference to the amount to be spent on the new ships, which I understand is larger than we anticipated, and which may account for their not being ready so soon, but may also mean that when ready they will be of increased power. This would justify precautions on our part.

E. G.

No. 442.

Sir E. Goschen to Sir Edward Grey.

F.O. 8053/4451/11/18.
(No. 54.) Secret.

Berlin, D. *March 4*, 1911.
R. *March 6*, 1911.

Sir,

I have the honour to forward, herewith, a despatch, as marked in the margin, which I have received from Colonel Russell, Military Attaché to this Embassy, relating to his conversation with the German Emperor.

I have, &c.
W. E. GOSCHEN.

2 Q

Enclosure in No. 442.

Lieutenant-Colonel Russell to Sir E. Goschen.

(No. 4.)   Secret.

Sir,   *Berlin, March* 3, 1911.

I have the honour to bring to your notice the tenour of a long conversation I had to-day with His Majesty the Emperor.

The occasion was the annual inspection in riding by His Majesty of the subaltern officers of the I[mperial] Guard Dragoons, which was followed by a luncheon at the officers' mess.   By invitation of the Officer commanding the Regiment and by permission of His Majesty, I was present at the inspection and remained to luncheon afterwards.

Immediately after luncheon the Emperor called me up to him and conversed with me for nearly an hour.   We were standing out of earshot of the remainder of those present.

After some remarks of a general nature, His Majesty passed to politics and in very vehement terms urged his passionate desire for a good understanding with England.   The general drift of the Emperor's observations were [*sic*] to the following effect:—An exchange of naval information is no use whatever; what we want is a proper political understanding.   "The matter is quite easy" His Majesty repeated several times.   "We all want it here in Germany."

"Every one knows that the alliance between Russia and France is merely to fight Germany and now you have gone and joined them.   You had the choice of joining with us or with Russia and France and you chose the latter.   England and Germany together would ensure the peace of the world.   We do not want to fight you.   If we did fight you, who would reap the benefit?   Undoubtedly the nations which had not taken part in the war."

"France will not try to regain Alsace and Lorraine; if they did attempt such a thing, they would get a worse beating than they ever dreamt of."

His Majesty then urged the decadence of the French nation in general and the French army in particular.   He said that he had read reports of the health of the French army, which were deplorable.   Infectious diseases were rife amongst the French soldiers.   The number of cases of typhoid fever, mumps, etc., was appalling.   These diseases did not exist in the German army.   He had agents and watchers (*sic*) who told him all about these things.   One of his officers had told him that on the French manœuvres the ditches were full of men who were too weak to continue marching.   The sanitary conditions in French barracks was [*sic*] terrible.   It was reported to him that in quite a new barracks in France there was not a single w.c.!

Why, therefore, did we join with a dead nation like that.   The Emperor said he was quite certain that the German ships of war were better than the British.   If we joined with Germany it would thus be a great thing for us.   Every German bayonet too would be on our side.   To this I ventured to ejaculate "and Your Majesty has a great many bayonets" to which the Emperor replied "Yes and very good ones too."

His Majesty urged that our panics in England were very undignified.   There could be no panics in Germany, because every streetboy knew quite well that the French could not suddenly arrive in Berlin.

"All my life," the Emperor continued, "I have worked for a good understanding with England, but you do not help me.   Look at Repington's letters to the Times, saying that you ought to practise the same tactics as the French, so that you can fight side by side against the Germans.   Excuse my saying so, but the few divisions you could put into the field could make no appreciable difference."

"And then this question about Flushing; it is ridiculous.   As if I wanted Flushing!   Have I not enough to look after at home without bothering myself about Flushing.   The hundredth anniversary of Waterloo is coming round very soon.   We fought side by side a hundred years ago. I want our two nations to stand together again in front of the Belgian monument at Waterloo.

"One of these days you will implore German help against the yellow races. You made a terrible mistake allying yourselves with Japan. Your prestige all over the world has suffered in consequence and you have given life to a new Power in the Far East.

"I have always been loyal and friendly to you. I wanted a coaling station. I asked you, if I took one, where would it be least inconvenient to you. Lord Salisbury said later on he would see me damned first.

"We have now a wonderful situation which will never occur again. The German Emperor grandson to Queen Victoria. The English people ought to be proud of it. They ought to come round me and ask what they can do for me." His Majesty appeared very hurt on the other hand that the British Regiment, of which he was Chief, should have been sent abroad to India.

His Majesty then referred in very reverential terms to Her Majesty Queen Victoria.

Returning to the earlier part of the Emperor's conversation, I might add the following observations :—Referring to a war between England and Germany, His Majesty said: "What do I gain by a war with England? Do I want Australia? With its labour politicians? No thank you. Do I want India? What could I do with India. I can assure you that the Japanese are stirring up trouble for you there."

I have only given the most salient points of a long conversation, perhaps not quite in the right sequence, but the whole drift of the Emperor's remarks gave evidence, in my opinion, of a passionate desire on His Majesty's part of a political understanding with England.

I have, &c.
ALICK RUSSELL, Lt.-Colonel,
Military Attaché.

MINUTES.

A very characteristic outburst. Many words, but little substance. There is however one remark of the Emperor's which merits close attention :

H[is] M[ajesty] clearly objects to the understanding respecting the reciprocal exchange of naval information, which we had been led to believe was practically settled in principle. What H[is] M[ajesty] (and therefore the German gov[ernmen]t) wants, therefore, is a political agreement by which England abandons her Franco-Russian understanding, and joins Germany, apparently in a definite crusade against France and Japan! Such agreement not to be accompanied by any naval understanding at all, not even as regards the exchange of naval information!

It is to be feared that this is the real explanation of why the *pourparlers* with Admiral von Tirpi[t]z are making no progress.

H[is] M[ajesty's] G[overnment] however have this particular game in their hands. The German gov[ernmen]t want from us something they are evidently very keen about. In return, as their attitude as regards a naval agreement, and also as regards the Bagdad Railway, shows, they propose to give nothing. The course for H[is] M[ajesty's] G[overnment] seems clearly indicated.

Encl[osure] to W[ar] O[ffice] in orig[inal]. (Secret.)

E. A. C.
Mch. 6.

It is quite clear that the Germans want a political understanding and has been clear for a long time. It is not so certain that the Emperor's words can be construed to indicate a dislike of the exchange of naval information, but that will appear when we get the official answer.

W. L.

It seems to me that Germany is striving to isolate France and is desirous that we should come to a political understanding irrespective of any naval agreement at all. Were we to fall in with this plan we should be unfaithful to our friend, upset the balance of power, and abandon the position which we originally took up that no political understanding could be acceptable to the public of this country unless accompanied by a naval agreement. The difficulties attendant on the simple question of exchange of naval information do not augur well for the acceptance of the wider agreement as to Limitation of armaments. I would submit that H[is] M[ajesty's] G[overnment] should not enter upon discussions as to the wider agreement until the minor question of exchange of naval information is settled. Were we to act otherwise I am afraid that we might become entangled in some political understanding to which France and Russia would not be admitted while we should lose the main object of our discussions viz., a naval agreement.

A. N.

The Emperor forgets recent history. In 1892 Lord Rosebery began by assuring the representatives of the triple Alliance that he would continue Lord Salisbury's policy of cordial relations with them. Great satisfaction was expressed I think by the German Gov[ernmen]t, for there had been some idea that the Liberal Gov[ernmen]t of that day might draw towards France.

But the result was not the halcyon days which the German Emperor says would ensue from this policy. We had constant diplomatic trouble with Germany from that day till the French agreement was made in 1904 and we had in addition constant diplomatic trouble with France and Russia.

E. G.

No. 443.

Sir F. Bertie to Sir Edward Grey.

F.O. 8320/6834/11/17.
(No. 104.)
Sir,

Paris, D. *March* 5, 1911.
R. *March* 7, 1911.

On the 3rd instant I received the visits of M. Delcassé, the Minister of Marine, and M. Cruppi, the Minister for Foreign Affairs, and yesterday those of M. Perrier, the Minister of Justice, who was accompanied by his Under-Secretary M. Malvy; M. Berteaux, the Minister for War, who came with M. Pams, the Minister for Agriculture; M. Massé, the Minister for Commerce; M. Boncour, the Minister for Labour and M. Monis the President of the Council. All those Ministers expressed their satisfaction at the friendly understanding existing between their country and England.

To M. Delcassé I expressed my personal regret that I should not be renewing with him as Minister for Foreign Affairs the agreeable relations which I had with him when he was in office in 1905. I quite realized, I observed, that it would have been difficult in present circumstances for him to undertake that office, but his presence in the Cabinet would be a guarantee if any were required that there would be no departure from the cordial and intimate relations of confidence which, begun by him, had been ever since the policy of the French and British Governments and I had no doubt that M. Cruppi who had only a short and indirect experience of foreign affairs would find in him a valuable counsellor.

M. Delcassé said that he would have preferred to remain out of office but he found himself by the vote of the Chamber and the appeal of M. Monis, bound to answer to the call of duty. He knew that for the time being he could not hold the post of Minister for Foreign Affairs and he feared that in addition to his onerous labours as Minister of Marine he would be constantly appealed to in regard to Foreign Affairs. As I probably knew he had made the Navy his special study, he had been reporter of the Parliamentary Commission and he was thoroughly acquainted with the state of the navy, its organisation and its needs. He intended to build sufficient Dreadnoughts and other ships to enable France to be more than a match for Austria and Italy combined in the Mediterranean and able to hold that sea. By the year 1920 there would be twenty French Dreadnoughts.

With regard to the foreign relations of France, as M. Cruppi would tell me, the Ministry intended to continue the policy which he had initiated and which had been followed by successive French Governments and his presence in the Cabinet was the best proof possible of its desire to have the most intimate relations with His Majesty's Government. It was for the benefit of both countries.

I had some further general conversation with M. Delcassé on the subject of the Potsdam interviews, Persian Affairs, and the Bagdad Railway and Turkey. When I make my return visit to him I propose to suggest that he should examine the dossier in his Department concerning the Aerial Conference and confer with the Minister for Foreign Affairs on the subject. I also propose to speak to the same effect to M. Berteaux, the Minister for War.

With M. Cruppi, whom I had known when he was Minister of Commerce in M. Clemenceau's Cabinet, I had only a short conversation. He reminded me that his sentiments were not protectionist and how desirous he had shown himself when last in office to meet as far as he could the representations of His Majesty's Embassy in commercial questions. He had always been an advocate of a good understanding between France and England and he was happy to know from a long interview with M. Pichon how cordial and intimate the relations of the two countries were and he requested me to assure you that he would devote his best energies to continuing the policy of his predecessor at the Ministry for Foreign Affairs as regarded His Majesty's Government with whom he would desire to have the closest relations in all matters in which the interests of France and England are concerned. I had the honour of so reporting to you by my telegram No. 16 of the 3rd instant([1]) and I informed His Excellency yesterday of the reply which you directed me to make to his message.

M. Berteaux said that he was glad to find on his return to office that the excellent relations which existed between the French and British Governments when he was Minister for War in M. Rouvier's Cabinet continued. Nobody could be a more convinced advocate of the *Entente* than he had been and was and I might be sure that any Cabinet of which he was a member would cultivate the best relations with England.

M. Monis referred in a cursory way to the Potsdam interviews which the German Chancellor had made the most of as a German success in the Reichstag and the Press, to the newspaper campaign in Germany and France on the subject of the "Légion Etrangère" which he much regretted, to the apparent instability of the present Turkish Ministry, to the ignorance in which the Emperor of Russia seemed to be kept of what was being done by his Ministers, to the advantage for the peace of the world which the Agreement between Russia and England had been and to the necessity for those two Powers and France to be watchful but very circumspect in regard to Germany. He intended to be very correct towards that country so as to avoid affording to the German Government any pretext for complaint. He had been glad to avail himself of M. Delcassé's services for the Navy. He had incurred the risk of offending the German Government by including M. Delcassé in his Cabinet, but it was a risk which he considered it his duty to incur in the naval interest of France and he had on the whole no reason to complain of the way in which his selection of M. Delcassé had been treated by the German Press. It was necessary for France to have a strong fleet and it would be one of the points on which his Cabinet would insist in the Declarations which would be made in the Chambers. On my observing that M. Delcassé's experience of foreign affairs would no doubt be very useful to his colleagues M. Monis whilst concurring stated that the foreign policy of the Ministry would be that of himself and the whole Cabinet. M. Delcassé would have his say and his opinions would carry great weight but he would have his own work to attend to and it would be quite sufficient to occupy all his energy. As regarded England and France M. Monis stated and requested me to assure you in his name that he and his Ministry were unanimous in desiring to continue the intimate relations with His Majesty's Government which had been of so much benefit to both countries. He considered the *entente* between them and the treatment of matters in consultation with each other and with Russia to be a great guarantee of peace. He could not suppose that the German Emperor or his Government desired war. The danger was that the internal political condition of Germany was bad. There was great discontent at the growing expenditure. The Government in order to justify that expenditure and to divert the attention of the

([1]) [Not reproduced.]

people from their home grievances might agitate foreign questions, and the Government might be pushed by the Press, the military party and public opinion to take up an uncompromising attitude in some matter not of itself important.

I have, &c.

FRANCIS BERTIE.

No. 444.

Sir Edward Grey to Sir E. Goschen.

F.O. 9045/4451/11/18.
(No. 60.) Secret.
Sir,

Foreign Office, March 8, 1911.([1])

I told the German Ambassador to-day([2]) that the Cabinet had now agreed to the Memorandum in continuation of what I would call, as Herr von Bethmann-Hollweg had called them in his speech in the Reichstag, our "non-binding pourparlers."([3]) I would now send it to you, and instruct you to have a conversation with Herr von Bethmann-Hollweg, and leave the Memorandum with him. I thought that the German Government would find that the Memorandum showed a friendly spirit.

I then said that I was rather disappointed that we had not yet received an answer to our last communication about the exchange of naval information.([4])

Count Metternich said that this was a technical matter which the German Government no doubt had to discuss with their experts.

Two copies of the memorandum referred to are sent herewith, and I request Your Excellency to communicate its purport to the Chancellor, leaving a copy with H[is] E[xcellency] should he so desire.

I am, &c.

E. GREY.

Enclosure in No. 444.

Memorandum.

Foreign Office, March 8, 1911.

His Majesty's Government have considered the reply of the German Chancellor communicated to Sir Edward Goschen.([5])

They note with much satisfaction that the Imperial Government have no objection to a mutual exchange of information through naval attachés. They are ready to proceed with this proposal without making it dependent on any other conditions, such as the Imperial Government deprecate, and have therefore already sent instructions to Sir E. Goschen on the subject. His Majesty's Government are convinced that the mere fact of such an exchange of information being agreed to by the two Governments will have considerable effect in convincing public opinion in both countries and elsewhere that the two Governments do not cherish any hostile designs against each other.

Apart, however, from any effect that an agreement so limited may have upon naval expenditure, His Majesty's Government wish to discuss the larger question in the spirit of the German Chancellor's latest communication, and to reciprocate

---

([1]) [The actual date of despatch was clearly some days after this, as a private letter from Sir A. Nicolson of March 14 was sent by the same messenger. *v. infra*, p. 603, No. 449.]

([2]) [*cp. G.P.* XXVIII, p. 395. The interview is there described as having taken place on March 7. The attached Memorandum, presented to the Chancellor on March 24, is printed in *G.P.* XXVIII, pp. 403–5.]

([3]) [This refers to Herr von Bethmann Hollweg's speech in the Reichstag of December 10, from which an extract is given *supra*, p. 567, No. 422.]

([4]) [*v. supra*, pp. 585–7, No. 436.]

([5]) [*v. supra*, pp. 524–5, No. 400, *encl.*]

his earnest desire to remove causes of misunderstanding and to promote feelings of cordial friendship between the two countries.

The view of His Majesty's Government originally was that a reduction or slackening of naval expenditure in both countries would in itself produce such an effect as to make the political atmosphere more genial. The Imperial Government, on the other hand, hold the view that assured mutual good relations are an indispensable preliminary condition for any naval agreement. To this end the Imperial Government consider a political agreement to be necessary and believe it to be possible to find a formula which will meet German wishes in this respect, without prejudice to the agreements of His Majesty's Government with other Powers.

There is certainly nothing in the engagements of His Majesty's Government with other Powers to prevent frankness, good feeling, and assured friendly relations on the part of His Majesty's Government in their dealings with the Imperial Government. It has never at any time been their purpose or their policy to establish or encourage understandings with any foreign Power or group of Powers, which were aimed directly or indirectly against Germany; no such understandings exist, and they are ready to give their sympathetic attention to any formula which the Imperial Government may suggest.

They would like to indicate in advance—but solely with the desire to attain the end in view—certain considerations that they cannot leave out ot sight.

The arrangements which His Majesty's Government have entered into with other Powers have not hitherto been based upon a general political formula. They have had their origin in certain specific questions which are defined in the agreements, and on which, happily, a satisfactory understanding had been reached. An arrangement, therefore, as foreshadowed by the Imperial Chancellor, embodying a general political formula, might be considered as something more comprehensive, far-reaching, and intimate than any arrangement that His Majesty's Government have with any other Power, short of actual alliance. In particular, such a construction of any new agreement made by His Majesty's Government might tend to impair their relations with France and Russia. The almost continuous friction and constantly recurring discord, which had lasted for years between these two Powers and the United Kingdom, have during the last seven years been transformed into relations of friendship and confidence which His Majesty's Government are naturally anxious to preserve. They have, in the last few years, seen with satisfaction the settlement of certain differences, and a consequent improvement of relations, between each of these Powers and the German Government. To-day His Majesty's Government believe that the special interests, which have led to the present grouping of Powers, do not involve anything in the nature of opposition and still less of hostile purpose among them. But they feel that in any general formula care must be taken to avoid on the one hand undue vagueness and on the other the risk of possible misunderstanding. With this object His Majesty's Government think that an endeavour to come to an agreement upon certain specific questions should form part of the negotiations.

The Bagdad Railway has from time to time been mentioned on one side or the other as one of these questions. The interest which His Majesty's Government feel with regard to it was fully explained on the occasion of the German Emperor's visit to Windsor in 1907.([6]) The difficulties which His Majesty's Government must experience in agreeing to the Turkish request for an increase of customs dues without some arrangement to safeguard commercial and strategical interests in connection with the railway have also been explained.

His Majesty's Government recognise that the Government of Turkey must be consulted, and that its sanction will be required for any arrangement respecting the Bagdad Railway, and they do not desire in any way to ignore the rights of Turkey or of the German concessionnaires.

([6]) [v. supra, pp. 92–8, Nos. 60–4.]

A further subject for agreement, which has been suggested by the German Chancellor himself, is that of railways in Persia, which is closely connected with that of the Bagdad Railway. His Majesty's Government have never seen, in what has been said respecting either of them by the German Government or on its behalf, anything which in principle rendered an agreement impossible.

The German Chancellor will perceive that, in sending this reply, His Majesty's Government are accepting his view that some wider agreement is essential to any arrangement about naval expenditure.

In assenting to negotiation on this basis, His Majesty's Government assume that the discussion of naval expenditure will not be postponed, but will proceed so that an agreement on that point shall be simultaneous with the conclusion of any political understanding.

No. 445.

Sir E. Goschen to Sir Edward Grey.

F.O. 9094/4451/11/18.
(No. 64.) Secret. Berlin, D. March 11, 1911.
Sir, R. March 13, 1911.

I have the honour to report that this evening the Chancellor expressed to me his regret that he had been unable to furnish me with a reply on the subject of the proposals of His Majesty's Government for the exchange of naval information between the two Governments. He said that in the first place Admiral Tirpitz had been busy with his estimates and that then he had been away at Wilhelmshaven on business connected with his department, and that finally he had accompanied the Emperor on a visit to Heligoland and other places from which His Majesty had only just returned. His Excellency assured me that he would now take the earliest possible opportunity of discussing the matter with Admiral Tirpitz and that he would let me have an answer at an early date.

I have, &c.
(For the Ambassador),
RICHARD SEYMOUR.

No. 446.

Sir E. Goschen to Sir Edward Grey.

F.O. 10035/4451/11/18.
(No. 69.) Berlin, D. March 12, 1911.
Sir, R. March 20, 1911.

I had the honour to be present yesterday evening at the dinner which the Emperor gives annually to the Ambassadors accredited to the Court of Berlin.

After dinner His Majesty was pleased to converse with me at some length. After alluding to the pleasure with which He, the Empress and Princess Victoria Louisa were looking forward to their visit to England and to the cordial letters of invitation which they had received from the King, His Majesty told me that He had read your speech with much interest and that both He and His Government had been much pleased with your clear and straightforward statement respecting the Bagdad Railway. His Majesty then was pleased to give me His own views respecting this question. He said that that railway, with or without foreign participation, would most certainly be completed; they had the concession and they had the money to carry it through; there was no doubt about that, and if He were in the position of His Majesty's Government, He would look at the best side of things, recognise that the Railway would serve the commercial interests of all nations and that it would be the shortest route to India, and make up his mind to start a line of steamers connecting the terminus of the Railway with the nearest available Indian port. "That," His Majesty said, "is your best plan. Why throw difficulties in the way?"

His Majesty then turned to general politics and went over a great deal of old ground. He reproached England with having joined Russia and France instead of Germany, saying that every child in Germany had known that the Franco-Russian alliance had been directed against Germany, and that the German nation as a whole still felt very sore that England had attached herself to that combination. I said that I could see no reason for soreness. We had had uncomfortable questions with both those countries, which for our own and for the general interests it had been prudent and wise to set at rest, and then, as His Majesty knew, and as the German Press had often pointed out, the balance of power in Europe was a fetish worshipped by the British nation and a principle which in the past it had made great sacrifices to uphold and for which it had always fought. His Majesty said with a smile that the present grouping did not, as events had shown, represent a real Balance of Power. I said that that was a question which I should not like to enter into, that the present grouping was at all events numerically equal and so appeared a satisfactory arrangement to British public opinion. Moreover if we, as His Majesty seemed to hint, were on the weakest side, that would not be a reason, given British ideas and traditions, for leaving it. His Majesty laughed and said : " No! you ought to be with us. What is perpetually in my mind is this : The Greeks and Romans each had their time; the Spaniards had theirs and the French also. The Latin races have in fact had their fair share of power and influence in the world. It is now for the Anglo-Saxons and Teutons to come to the front; not to be striving against each other and quarrelling over petty questions, but to join hand in hand and lead the world. People in England, though, I am pleased to see, now taking a more sensible view of things, have long been pleased to regard me as a sort of monster only waiting for an opportunity to fall upon them. You and I know that this is nonsense. Why should I? Your people say, because I am striving for the hegemony of Europe. There was never a more nonsensical idea. I can tell you I have quite enough to do with managing my own country and my own Reichstag. Besides such ambitions are entirely against the tradition of my House. No Hohenzollern has ever suffered from megalomania;—two of my ancestors, for instance, refused the Crown of Poland, and I certainly am not going to be the first of my House to suffer from that disease. The Russians have come to us and now you must come. We *must* have a political understanding, and then a naval arrangement tending to limit naval expenditure, to follow." As His Majesty paused for a moment, I ventured to remark that our view was that a naval arrangement should come first. After giving his reasons why his view was the sounder, reasons with which you are now familiar, His Majesty said that if we did not come to some sort of an understanding, things would drift on as they were now, with constant bickerings on subjects of no real importance and an atmosphere electrified up to the danger point, when the slightest spark might cause an explosion, "and," His Majesty added, "we don't want a Waterloo with Germans and English fighting against each other instead of side by side, and with the Slavs and yellow men as *tertia gaudentia*."

The Emperor then said a few words with regard to our estimates and, on my remarking that I hoped His Majesty had observed how moderate they were, said laughingly that he had not been particularly struck by their moderation. His Majesty also made a few remarks with regard to the Two Power Standard, which He said was impossible for us to maintain. " Not impossible, Sir," I said, " but necessarily its maintenance involves a certain amount of patriotic sacrifice, which I think the country is quite prepared to make." He said, " No! You have talked too much about it, that was your mistake. You should have built as many ships as you required without giving reasons. But clamouring about the Two Power Standard in and out of season put other Powers on the *qui vive* and now, if you don't like me to say the word impossible, it will at all events be extremely difficult for you to maintain that standard."

You will see that most of this is old ground and that the language of His Majesty was very similar to that He has held to me before. It is for instance not new that he should put the " Slavs and the Yellow Men " together in one class,([1]) but it is new that he should almost in the same breath use the phrase that " Russia had come to Germany."

I have, &c.
W. E. GOSCHEN.

MINUTE.

The Emperor went so far as to speak of an agreement for the limitation of armaments, to follow the proposed political agreement. The burden of H[is] M[ajesty's] previous utterance was that a naval agreement he would never, never, never, ...([2]) etc.

The train of thought on which the emperor dwelt when saying " Russia *had* to come to us . . . .([2]) " and " now you *must* come " bears a very close resemblance to what Sir E. Goschen alluded to under the designation—German desire for hegemony.

Qu[ery]. Approve his language.

E. A. C.
Mch. 20.
W. L.

([1]) [*cp. supra*, p. 531, No. 403.]
([2]) [Thus in original.]

No. 447.

Sir Edward Grey to Sir F. Bertie.

F.O. 9827/4451/11/18.
(No. 89.)   Secret.

Sir, *Foreign Office, March* 14, 1911.

I told M. Cambon to-day, very confidentially, that we were resuming the " non-binding pourparlers" with the German Government, and that there were four points in our last communication to them.([1])

The first point was the question as to a political formula. On this, we had made no proposal, but had pointed out that we had no political formula with France or Russia, and that there might therefore be difficulty in finding one not open to the construction that we were drawing away from France and Russia : which we were determined not to do. For this reason, I hoped that any *rapprochement* which took place between the Germans and ourselves would be one in which France and Russia might also share in some way simultaneously.

The second point was the Bagdad Railway, which we had said was a desirable subject for an agreement. We had not made any proposal with regard to it, but had pointed out that of course the sovereign rights of Turkey could not be ignored, and her sanction would presumably be required for any agreement.

The third point was Persian railways. With regard to these, we had stated that there was nothing in what Germany had said to prevent an agreement between us. My own idea was that, so long as we obtained the concessions for railways in southern Persia, and thus prevented the control of the lines from falling into foreign hands which would prejudice our political and strategical interests, the commercial advantages of participation in the railways might be shared with France, Germany, and Russia : so that there would be no commercial exclusion.

The fourth point was the question as to a naval arrangement : which could be discussed only within the limits explained in the speech which I made last night in the House of Commons.([2])

[I am, &c.]
E. G[REY].

([1]) [*v. supra*, pp. 598–600, No. 444, *encl.*]
([2]) [*v. Parl. Deb.*, 5th *Ser.*, House of Commons, Vol. 22, pp. 1977–92.]

No. 448.

Sir Edward Grey to Sir G. Buchanan.

F.O. 9828/4451/11/18.
(No. 77.)   Secret.
Sir,   *Foreign Office, March* 14, 1911.

I spoke to Count Benckendorff to-day, in similar terms to those I had just used to M. Cambon,(¹) with regard to our negotiations with Germany : with the addition that, as regards a political formula, something had passed already between Russia and Germany, though only verbally at Berlin, and there could of course be no objection, so far as Russia was concerned, to our doing something of the same sort as Russia was doing.

We wished to be on more friendly terms with Germany, but in such a way that Russia and France might be included in any *rapprochement.*

I asked Count Benckendorff what was to be done with the information I had given him, as it was very confidential, and not for the general information of the Russian Foreign Office, and M. Sazonow was at present very ill.

Count Benckendorff said that he would not telegraph it, but would send it to M. Neratoff, through whom it would reach the Emperor.

[I am, &c.]
E. G[REY].

(¹) [*v.* immediately preceding document.]

No. 449.

Sir A. Nicolson to Sir E. Goschen.

Private.(¹)
My dear Goschen :—   *Foreign Office, March* 14, 1911.

Many thanks for your letter.

The Germans are certainly taking their time in replying to our proposals in regard to the exchange of naval information, but I daresay they may have been waiting to see what our naval estimates for the coming year were likely to be. It is curious that I have noticed no reports in our papers as to the views of the German press on the subject, but they may be waiting to get a full report of the discussions of the naval estimates which commence on Thursday. You will see that we are sending you by this messenger a memorandum to be communicated to the Chancellor.(²) It seems to me that we have gone as far as we possibly can towards meeting his wishes, and I think the tone of our memorandum is as friendly as it can well be made. To my mind, the whole gist of the memorandum is contained in the last paragraph, and I daresay that it will be over this paragraph that the Chancellor may jib. In my opinion it is essential that we should not be induced to proceed to any political agreement until we have come to some understanding as to what is now termed the mutual reduction of naval expenditure. Sir Edward intends to inform both Cambon and Benckendorff very confidentially that we are reopening discussions with the German Government on the subject. We shall, of course, only tell them so in general terms, and we shall not give them a copy of the memorandum, or enter into any details. I believe that you will hear also from Sir Edward to the effect that you may inform the Chancellor that we have mentioned

(¹) [Carnock MSS., Vol. I of 1911.]
(²) [*v. supra,* pp. 598–600, No. 444, *encl.*]

the matter to France and Russia.([3])   I do not see how the Chancellor can possibly take exception to this course, as in fact it has become public property that both Governments are desirous of arriving at some understanding on these questions. . . . .([4])

[A. NICOLSON.]

([3]) [*v. supra*, pp. 602–3, Nos. 447–8.]
([4]) [The closing paragraphs of this long letter touch on British relations with Russia and Germany in general terms.]

No. 450.

Sir A. Nicolson to Sir G. Buchanan.

Private.([1])
My dear Buchanan,   *Foreign Office, March 14, 1911.*
. . . . ([2]) After considerable delay—and this I tell you for your own private and confidential information alone—we are about to reopen discussions with Germany in regard to the two questions which are respectively termed the political agreement and the mutual reduction of armaments.   I do not for one moment myself believe that these discussions will ever come to any result, but it was impossible for us to leave the Chancellor's overtures unanswered.   Sir Edward intends to inform both Benckendorff and Cambon to-day in general terms of what we propose to say to the German Government.   We have no desire to keep them in the dark, and we intend to let the German Chancellor know that we have informed our friends of the fact that certain discussions have been commenced.   It will be best, however, that you should say nothing at all in regard to the matter, and no doubt whoever is in charge of the Foreign Office will let you know what Benckendorff reports. . . . .([3])

([1]) [Carnock MSS., Vol. I of 1911.]
([2]) [The opening paragraphs of this letter refer to Anglo-Russian relations and have no bearing upon those between England and Germany]
([3]) [This letter closes with detailed reference to the Bagdad Railway schemes.]

No. 451.

Sir E. Goschen to Sir Edward Grey.

F.O. 10036/10036/11/18.
(No. 70.)   *Berlin, D. March 16, 1911.*
Sir,   R. *March 20, 1911.*
     The speech which you made in the House of Commons on Monday last, the 12th [13th] instant,([1]) has aroused the greatest interest in Germany and with the exception of violent Pan-German newspapers like the "Hamburger Nachrichten," who affect to doubt the sincerity of your utterances, the Press recognises to the full both the importance and the conciliatory tendency of your statements as far as Germany is concerned.
     The manner in which your speech is regarded in official quarters is to be found in a *communiqué* published in the "Norddeutsche Allgemeine Zeitung," and its tone is one of such hearty and unreserved appreciation that the Liberal "Tageblatt" is drawn to the conclusion that there must have been a preliminary arrangement with the Imperial Government as to the language which you should hold! The communiqué runs as follows :—

     "The House of Commons was on Monday last the scene of a most important political declaration on the part of the British Minister of Foreign

([1]) [*cp. Parl. Deb.*, 5th *Ser.*, House of Commons, Vol. 22, pp. 1977–92.]

Affairs. We are able to welcome with the most sincere satisfaction his state-ments both with regard to the international situation in general and Anglo-German relations in particular. The same thing holds good of the declarations devoted to the question of armaments—declarations which do justice in so high a degree to the German point of view also, that they yield a cheerful prospect for the further development of Anglo-German relations. According to the reports of his speech the Minister repeated and emphasized the declaration of the Imperial Chancellor in the Reichstag, that mistrust has not manifested itself in the case of the two Governments, although in many cases it has manifested itself in the public opinion of the two countries. If agreements can contribute anything in the sense that the Minister hinted to the removal of this mistrust as far as public opinion in England is concerned, there will be readiness on the German side to give a hand. From this to the ideal of a world peace based upon arbitration is certainly, as Sir Edward Grey himself said, a long step. However sympathetic one's attitude may be towards the idea of arbitration agreements, one will not be justified in regarding them as a secret specific against misunderstandings and disagreements. Only quite recently a special instance showed that this is not the case, and that differences may arise concerning the application of arbitration just as well as about other things. An agreement between the Governments that are at variance will in such a case, precisely as in all other cases, depend upon the more or the less conciliatory spirit in which the negotiations are conducted. And it is precisely the conciliatory spirit with which the whole speech of the English statesman is permeated that will awake sympathies for the speech throughout the world."

In commenting upon this communiqué, in addition to the observation quoted above, the "Berliner Tageblatt" states that the sceptical tone of its remarks respecting arbitration may be safely disregarded at a moment when the possibility of a genuine and straightforward Arbitration Treaty with the United States was engaging the fascinated attention of all parties in the English Parliament. The German Government would also no doubt sooner or later adopt more progressive views on such matters. This was proved by their present favourable attitude towards a naval understanding with Great Britain. "The very pith of the communiqué," the 'Tageblatt' says, "is to be found in this change of attitude. The idea which year after year and day after day German Liberals have in vain advocated and pressed upon the Government, has at last been acknowledged as possible of realization. At last there seems to be a prospect of some tangible agreement which will have the effect of stemming the rising tide of naval armaments. One cannot help asking whether it was really necessary that the flood should have risen so high and whether, if we had only wished it, it could not long ago have been restrained within due limits to the benefit of both nations. The Imperial Govern-ment will now have the satisfaction of feeling that in this new attitude they will have the great majority of the nation behind them. In Parliament also they will, we wish and hope, receive hearty support from the policy they have just indicated. It is a thousand pities, indeed, that up to now, even on the Liberal side, these ideas have not been more actively put forward in Parliament, and that more pressure has not been brought to bear on the Government to adopt the only sensible and profitable course. If that had been done we should by this time be probably well advanced on the path which to our great satisfaction and pleasure the Government now propose to follow."

The same newspaper, in a leading article on the speeches made by you and the First Lord of the Admiralty,[2] takes as its text the declaration of the latter that the high-water mark of British Naval expenditure had been reached. The article renders useful service in calling special attention to the reservation which both

[2] [cp. Parl. Deb., 5th Ser., House of Commons, Vol. 22, pp. 1915–21.]

Mr. McKenna and yourself attached to that declaration, namely that its application to the future must necessarily depend upon whether the Naval Programmes of other Powers, and especially Germany, followed their normal and avowed course. "This reservation, the ' Tageblatt' says, brings the declaration out of the realms of hopes and wishes into the area of practical politics. . . . . "(³)

I have, &c.
W. E. GOSCHEN.

(³) [The omitted paragraphs of this despatch contain further comments of the *Tageblatt* in the same strain, and summaries of other friendly Press comments.]

No. 452.

Sir F. Cartwright to Sir Edward Grey.

F.O. 10027/10027/11/3.
(No. 44.)   *Vienna, D. March 16, 1911.*
Sir,   R. *March 20, 1911.*
    I have the honour to inform you that the speech made by you, Sir, in the House of Commons on March 13(¹) in regard to the European political situation has met with a very favourable reception in the Austrian Press.
    The "Fremden-Blatt" welcomes your declaration that England is anxious to resume her former friendly relations with Austria-Hungary, and goes on to remark that your statement that England never wished her dealings with a third Power to make friendly relations with Germany impossible is a most conclusive denial of the so-called "hemming-in" policy. The "Fremden-Blatt" is of opinion that the Bagdad Railway question is the only serious ground for difference between England and Germany, and notes with satisfaction the probability of an amicable settlement of this matter. "Yesterday's speech," it says, "does away with the Anglo-German conflict. It goes even further: it proves that the supposed antagonism between the Triple *Entente* and the Triple Alliance belongs to the misunderstandings of the past."
    The comments of the "Neue Freie Presse" on your statements are conceived in much the same spirit. This paper heartily welcomes your message of peace and the improvement in Anglo-German relations which that message implies. It greets with particular satisfaction your friendly references to Austria-Hungary. The desire to return to the traditional good relations between the latter and England is, it declares, general: while your attempts to find a means of mutually reducing expenditure on armaments will, says the "Neue Freie Presse," find ready support in this country.
    In a second article the same paper interprets your speech as removing the "sting" from the *Entente* policy. France will, it says, now be left alone if Monsieur Delcassé attempts to carry out an aggressive policy. The "Neue Freie Presse" hopes to see the Bagdad Railway question shortly settled between Germany and England.
    The portion of your speech, Sir, which has attracted most attention in the Austrian Press is, however, that relating to the question of armaments. Your reference to the burden of naval and military expenditure as a "bleeding to death in time of peace" has in particular created a great impression here, and is quoted by the entire Press. "No other Foreign Minister in Europe," says the "Zeit," "has ever admitted in so downright a manner that the rivalry in armaments leads to financial ruin." The Socialist "Arbeiter-Zeitung" remarks that if your words had been used by an anti-militarist they would have been denounced as the exaggerations of a demagogue: coming from such a source, it welcomes your admission with extreme satisfaction, and proceeds to point a moral for Austria by asking how this country, poor as it is, can possibly support a burden which even

(¹) [*v. Parl. Deb.*, 5th Ser., House of Commons, Vol. 22, pp. 1977–92.]

England finds too heavy. Both of these papers willingly recognize the high importance and value of your statements regarding the reduction of armaments, though they are unable to refrain from accusing you of inconsistency in defending a Budget which you admit to be an intolerable burden.

The "Zeit" as usual qualifies its approval by a considerable amount of sarcasm. It speaks of England's "renunciation of alliances which she cannot find," and of the adoption of a specific policy by Great Britain as making a virtue out of a necessity. The world would, it says, be still more grateful for your utterances if it could forget that it was England who started and still keeps up the competition in 'Dreadnoughts.' This paper is doubtful of the feasibility of your proposal to exchange information on the subject of ship-building. Germany is, it says, already sufficiently well informed in regard to England's armaments : it is only the latter country which is notoriously ill supplied with information. It also points out that England, as the *beatus possidens*, is naturally anxious for a limitation of armaments which would leave her in her position of supremacy—a position which according to the "Zeit" she has no historical right to claim. The "Zeit," after begging England to set the example by reducing her own armaments, concludes its article by an eulogy of your speech, which it says is "worthy of being taken to heart by the War and Finance Ministers of all the Great Powers."

The "Neues Wiener Tagblatt" describes your speech as "a world programme of peace." "It is," it declares, "well known that Sir Edward Grey is free from every tendency to indulge in political fantasies or Utopias, that his plans proceed from mature consideration of the facts, that his whole official career has shown not the smallest deviation from the path which he has marked out for himself." All the more importance is therefore to be attributed, in the opinion of the "Tagblatt," to your statements, which are a final proof of the desire for peace now existing among all the Powers. Your courteous references to Germany and her fleet are, it says, in particular welcome, and will put an end to the misunderstandings which have so long existed between the two countries. As for Austria-Hungary, your friendly statements are welcomed by this paper as a sign of the renewal of the traditional good relations between this country and England, which you emphasized in your speech to the International Press Association in 1909.

The remaining newspapers discuss your speech with much the same cordiality : the unanimity of the Viennese Press in welcoming your statements is indeed complete, while the interest aroused by your reference to President Taft's arbitration proposals is also very general.([2])

To-day's "Fremden-Blatt" devotes a leading article to the question of the record height of the English Navy Estimates. It severely censures His Majesty's Government for the conclusion, now shown to be false, that Germany intended to accelerate her ship-building. It says that Germany's declarations on that head ought never to have been doubted. Your words in regard to the burden of naval and military expenditure are, it considers, a proof that opinion in England is undergoing a change, and that it has now become possible for the Government to make an energetic stand against the misleading of the public. It draws the conclusion that England is now beginning to realize that in these days of world-commerce the supremacy of the sea by one State has become impossible. It looks upon the resolution adopted by the British Chambers of Commerce against the ratification of the Declaration of London([3]) as a proof of the increasing prevalence of this point of view.

I have, &c.
FAIRFAX L. CARTWRIGHT.

([2]) [v. Parl. Deb., 5th Ser., House of Commons, Vol. 22, pp. 1988–90.]
([3]) [This subject will be treated in a later volume.]

No. 453.

Sir E. Goschen to Sir Edward Grey.

F.O. 9985/4451/11/18.
Tel. (No. 8.) R.

Berlin, March 18, 1911.
D. 10·40 P.M. [sic].
R. 10·30 P.M.

Exchange of naval information.

Secretary of State informs me that answer of German Government is ready, but that, as it has to be submitted to the Emperor, the Chancellor will only be able to communicate it to me after his return from Kiel, where he will be with His Majesty until 24th March.

Secretary of State said that the answer accepted our proposals and made a few additional suggestions.

No. 454.

Sir E. Goschen to Sir Edward Grey.

F.O. 12050/4451/11/18.
Private and Secret.
My dear Grey,

Berlin, March 24, 1911.

The Chancellor having returned from Kiel asked me to call upon him this evening when he gave me his answer to the Exchange of Information proposals. But he asked me not to communicate it to you officially before I had seen Herr von Kiderlen who would explain to me more fully this point of view.

The answer, which he gave me in the form of a memorandum,(¹) is, as far as it goes at present, that the Imperial Government accept the suggestions of the Admiralty as to the data on which information is to be exchanged. But it expresses the opinion that reciprocity in this matter can only be fully observed if the information is exchanged *simultaneously*.

This, the Chancellor explained, means that it will not do for one side to furnish information and for the other to use that information as a basis for increasing its programme of shipbuilding. For instance, the Chancellor said: "We might tell you that we were going to lay down two ships; it will not do for you then to say 'Aha! they are going to lay down two, so we must lay down four or five.' We must both make up our minds what we are going to build, give each other that information and stick to it."

On this principle the Imperial Government proposes in the Memorandum that the information arranged for should be exchanged between the 1st of October and the 16th [sic] of November every year.

The Memorandum further states that as regards the periodical visits of the respective Naval Attachés to shipyards for the purpose of inspecting ships under construction the Imperial Government would suggest that the details should form the subject of a direct agreement between the Naval Attachés and the naval authorities of the two countries.

It seems to me that the Imperial Government have reason on their side in asking that the information should be exchanged simultaneously; but how will it be if, after we have given information as to the number of ships we intend to build, circumstances should arise or be foreseen which, apart from considerations connected with the German fleet, might render it absolutely necessary for us to increase our programme? Such a case might give rise to unpleasantness, as it might be inopportune to have to explain our reasons. It might even happen, though

(¹) [v. infra, p. 610, No. 455, and reference there to G.P. XXVIII, p. 402.]

1 scarcely like to put the suggestion on paper even privately, that, after the Germans saw for instance that we intended to have a small programme they might persuade their allies to increase theirs, and they would in the meantime say to us "What other people build is no concern of ours; you have told us the number of ships you are going to build and you must stick to that number." To an inexpert mind like mine the arrangement they propose seems to have a too binding effect. Again as regards the date fixed, won't it be rather awkward for us to say in October what we propose to do in March or April? After saying that Kiderlen would go further into the matter with me the Chancellor asked me whether I could give him your views respecting the wider questions which had formed the subject of our last conversation. I then handed him your memorandum(²) saying that I was sure he would find that it evinced a sincere desire on the part of His Majesty's Government to remove all causes of misunderstanding and to promote cordiality between the two countries.

After I had given His Excellency a short account of the substance of the Memorandum the Chancellor read it through very carefully and then made a few remarks stating that I was to regard them as his own personal views and not in any sense as criticisms on the contents of the memorandum which he would have to study very carefully before giving me his official views.

He said that your idea of a political understanding seemed to be a settlement of the Bagdad Railway and Persian Railway questions and that, in return for that, you wanted an agreement for the mutual reduction of naval expenses. Such an agreement was, he thought, a good deal to ask for such a limited political understanding. Warming to his subject he reminded me that he had always said that the atmosphere must be thoroughly cleared and a good understanding secured before any reduction of naval armaments could be made. Arbitration and reduction of armaments were excellent things in their way, but they were only possible between two countries whose relations were so stable that there was no possibility of their ever being pitted against each other. The idea was, as a matter of fact, Utopian, as where did two such countries exist? "I certainly cannot see myself making any arbitration treaty or promising to reduce armaments unless absolutely certain of the lasting sentiments of the country who might approach me on the subject. Besides, talking of reduction of armaments, supposing you and we made an agreement for the mutual reduction of expenditure on naval armaments what about the United States, Japan, Russia, France and even Austria and Italy! No! The more one thinks of these things the more difficult they appear."

As he shook his head over the last paragraph of the memorandum I reminded him that in former conversations he had rather seemed to agree that if a political understanding was arrived at it should be made simultaneously with a naval agreement. You had been in favour of the latter and he in favour of the former taking precedence; that they should be made simultaneously seemed a fair compromise. He said that he would go into that matter with me as soon as they had studied the memorandum. As yet he has said nothing about proposing a formula.

I should mention that I gave him your message with regard to the communication made to the French and Russian Ambassadors.

Before I left he again reiterated that he had only given me his private opinions, but I feel bound to tell you of them as it may be useful to you to know his frame of mind.

Amongst other things he told me that I must not gather from the perusal of the daily Press that anything was settled about the Gulf section of the Railway. The papers made out that any future negotiations about that section would have to be carried out with Turkey. This was by no means the case. Nothing definite had been arranged, only the Bagdad Railway Company had given it to be understood

(²) [v. supra, pp. 598-600, No. 444, encl.]

that perhaps, under certain circumstances, they might be induced to give up their right to build the line on the Southern Section and allow the Turks to form a fresh Company for its construction.

On the whole I cannot see that the Chancellor takes a very optimistic view of the future of our negotiations; but his official views may differ from his private ones.

I shall try to see Kiderlen tomorrow afternoon and get through with the Exchange of Information business at all events.

I got your private telegram this evening. I had already communicated the Memorandum. The Chancellor could not see me before owing to his absence at Kiel. When I wrote and told him that I had a memorandum for him he himself expressed the wish that we should clear off the Naval Exchange business first.

Yours very sincerely,
W. E. GOSCHEN.

No. 455.

Sir E. Goschen to Sir Edward Grey.

F.O. 11015/4451/11/18.
Tel. (No. 9.) Secret.

Berlin, March 25, 1911.
D. 8 P.M.
R. 9·50 P.M.

Exchange of naval information.

The Imperial Government has furnished me with a memorandum, of which following is a translation(¹) :—

"The Imperial Government adhere to view of British Government in accordance with which contemplated exchange of information in regard to naval armaments on both sides would have to extend to—

" 1. The dimensions of the ships to be laid down.
" 2. The protection, armament, speed, and horse-power of the ships.
" 3. The dates of their laying down and completion.

" The Imperial Government are of opinion that reciprocity of exchange will only be completely guaranteed if communications to be made on both sides are delivered at the same time. They propose that this simultaneous exchange should be made every year in period between 1st October and 15th November.

" As far as periodical inspection by naval attachés of both sides of the ships under construction is concerned, details might be reserved for direct arrangement between naval attachés and the naval authorities of both countries."

The Secretary of State explained that this somewhat ambiguous paragraph meant that whenever naval attachés desired to visit a dockyard they should apply direct to naval authorities.

On my observing that that was the present practice, his Excellency said that difference was that at present permission was often withheld, whereas under this agreement it would be granted.

I asked his Excellency what would happen if permission was refused. He replied that he supposed that in that case the matter would have to be referred to the two Governments. He added, however, that (group undecypherable) was an unlikely supposition, as principle of our proposals had been agreed to.

As regards date for exchange of information, he said that date suggested in memorandum was approximately time when naval budget was communicated to Minister of Finance, but that date was comparatively immaterial so long as exchange was simultaneous.

(¹) [For the German original, *v. G.P.* XXVIII, p. 402.]

MINUTES.

The proposed terms do not contain the general statement of the principle of reciprocity which, at the request of the Admiralty (see the 4th paragraph of our instruction of Jan[uary] 27, No. 45714(²)) Sir E. Goschen was asked to get included.

I think we should press for the inclusion in the agreement of a specific reference to the facilities for periodical visits of the naval attachés; and this would perhaps afford the opportunity of bringing in the principle of reciprocity in general. It would be highly undesirable to leave the question of the naval attachés visits " to be settled by themselves." What we desire is an arrangement that shall inspire confidence. As at present suggested the terms of the arrangement are unfortunately calculated on the contrary to give rise to a suspicion that fair and straight dealing will be evaded.

Qu[ery.] Copy to Admiralty, with observation in above sense, saying that it is proposed to instruct Sir E. Goschen accordingly.

E. A. C.
Mch. 27.

When Sir E. Goschen sends the memo[randum] he will perhaps give us his views as to the manner in which the decision arrived at is to be recorded. He has not replied on that point.

W. L.

We should wait till we receive the memo[randum] with the observations of Sir E. Goschen.

A. N.
E. G.

(²) [v. supra, pp. 579–80, No. 428.]

No. 456.

Sir A. Nicolson to Sir E. Goschen.

Private.(¹)

My dear Goschen, Foreign Office, March 28, 1911.

. . . . (²) Your observations in respect to exchange of naval information are exceedingly sound and valuable and will be communicated to our Naval Authorities. On the whole it seems to me that the Germans have met us very fairly well on this point. I do not quite follow the reasoning of the Chancellor that if we mutually consent to reduce or limit naval expenditure we should make a concession to Germany. He seems to regard reduction or limitation as a great sacrifice on the part of Germany for which they will be entitled to receive some valuable quid pro quo. We might equally claim the same. For my part I do not regard the matter in any light as a bargain but as a simple desire on the part of both Governments to lighten the burdens which are at present imposed on both peoples. I daresay he may have at the back of his mind an idea that if the problem is put crudely it really amounts to a recognition by Germany of the permanent naval superiority of this country and therefore Germany should receive something in exchange for such an admission. I do not agree with him, but I daresay in his reply he will let us know more clearly what his views really are. I hope that we shall maintain firmly our present attitude of insisting that the conclusion of the naval arrangement should be simultaneous with that of the political understanding. If we allow the latter to be definitely settled before we have come to terms with respect to the former we shall find ourselves in a very awkward position. I am quite sure that the naval arrangement would in those circumstances be indefinitely postponed. . . . .(³)

[Yours sincerely
A. NICOLSON.]

(¹) [Carnock MSS., Vol. I of 1911.]

(²) [The opening sentences of this letter refer to the Bagdad Railway, and the proposed Anglo-German political understanding.]

(³) [The letter closes with a discussion of the general political situation.]

No. 457.

Sir E. Goschen to Sir Edward Grey.

F.O. 12050/4451/11/18.
(No. 83.)   Secret.   *Berlin,* D. *March* 30, 1911.
Sir,   R. *April* 3, 1911.

I have the honour to inform you that on Friday last, the 24th instant, the Chancellor handed me the enclosed Memorandum which contains the answers of the Imperial Government to the proposals made by His Majesty's Government on the subject of an exchange of naval information.([1])   In handing me this Memorandum His Excellency begged me not to forward it to you until I had seen the Secretary of State for Foreign Affairs who would explain to me the point of view which had guided the Imperial Government in drawing up their answer.

I accordingly called upon Herr von Kiderlen Waechter on the following day.

Herr von Kiderlen said that I would see from the Memorandum that the Imperial Government accepted the proposal that the two Governments should on the principal of reciprocity communicate to each other periodically information comprising the following data :—

1. Dimension of vessels to be laid down.
2. Protection, armament, speed and horse-power of such vessels.
3. The date of (*a*) the laying down of such vessels (*b*) their completion.

Herr von Kiderlen then stated that it was the opinion of the Imperial Government that, in order to ensure strict reciprocity, the exchange of such information should be so arranged that neither Power could use the information obtained for the purpose of amending their own ship-building programme.   For instance if Germany announced that she was going to build say three ships in a certain year and Great Britain had made up her mind to build five, the latter should not on the strength of the German information bring up her programme for that year to six or seven or *vice versâ.*   In order to avoid any proceeding of that nature they had proposed that the exchange of information should be made simultaneously and had suggested, as a convenient time for the simultaneous communication of the information arranged for, the period between the 1st of October and the 16th [*sic*] of November.   This he said was the time when the Minister of Marine submitted his shipbuilding estimates to the Imperial Ministry of Finance.   I said that I was somewhat uncertain as to our exact procedure with regard to our year's programme but that I was under the impression that our naval estimates were only brought forward in March.   If this was the case it might be difficult for His Majesty's Admiralty to say in October what they were going to do in March.   Herr von Kiderlen replied that the date of the exchange of information was a minor question which could be settled later : the main point was that the exchange should be made simultaneously.

From Herr von Kiderlen's remarks and from those made to me privately by the Chancellor, it would appear that the Imperial Government consider that the information exchanged would include a statement as to the number of ships to be laid down in each year by the two Governments and that this statement should be of a binding nature.

This would seem to be going rather beyond the *data* suggested by the Admiralty, which, as I understand them, relate only to the dimensions, armament, speed and other details of the class of ships to be laid down without mentioning their number.   The number would of course be incidentally known but I can see nothing in the Admiralty Memorandum providing for the exchange of a formal statement of the number of vessels to be respectively laid down, while the idea that

([1]) [*v. supra*, pp. 585–7, No. 436.]

any such statement exchanged should be incapable of modification or amplification seems to go further than what is contemplated in these minor negotiations. The arrangement would no doubt cut both ways, but I feel sure that you will agree that all things considered the balance of the advantage would rest with Germany.

I asked Herr von Kiderlen what, under such an arrangement, would happen if either country suddenly found, for reasons quite unconnected with the information given by the other, that their programme was insufficient.

His Excellency said that I must remember that the information exchanged would only relate to a single year and that it was highly unlikely that either Power would be under the necessity of reconsidering their programme in such a short space of time. I agreed that it might be highly unlikely but events moved rapidly now-a-days and such an eventuality was not outside the bounds of possibility. It would be decidedly awkward if one Power by its engagements to another Power was debarred from making such arrangements as it might suddenly consider necessary for its own interests *vis-à-vis* of what was going on in the rest of the world. Herr von Kiderlen said that he presumed that in a case such as I had outlined the matter would form the subject of a friendly discussion between the two Governments.

I told His Excellency that the remarks I had made to him were purely my own personal ideas and that I would lose no time in forwarding the Chancellor's Memorandum to His Majesty's Government communicating to them at the same time the explanations he had been good enough to give me.

Since writing the above I have received from Captain Watson the inclosed despatch in which he has furnished me with his views respecting the Chancellor's Memorandum. These views appear in the main to agree with the personal impressions which I have ventured to lay before you in this despatch.

I have, &c.
W. E. GOSCHEN.

Enclosure 1 in No. 457.

Aide-mémoire communicated to Sir E. Goschen by the German Foreign Office.([2])

Enclosure 2 in No. 457.

Captain Watson to Sir E. Goschen.

Confidential.
Sir, Berlin, March 30, 1911

In regard to the general tenor of the reply of the German Government as to exchanging naval information and the date suggested for such exchange, I have the honour to submit the following remarks for your consideration. My remarks are based on the experience I have gained as naval attaché in Germany.

1. I submit it would appear that the German idea of an exchange of information is considerably wider in scope than the exchange of details of the ships.

2. My experience as naval attaché of the naval situation in Germany obliges me to submit my firm belief that a naval agreement, based on the lines of an exchange of programmes which should be binding on each nation, would be extremely convenient at the present time to those responsible for the naval requirements of Germany.

It is, I respectfully submit, all to the advantage of England not to enter at all into such a binding agreement, but still more not to do so until the German Fleet Law has shown by its provisions for 1912 whether it is going to be adhered to or not.

At the present time (March 1911) the moderate character of the English naval

(2) [For the text of this *aide-mémoire*, v. *G.P.* XXVIII, p. 402. A translated version is given, *supra*, p. 610, No. 155.]

estimates, and perhaps the political situation in Germany, have to some extent cut the ground from under the feet of the Large Navy party in Germany.

It is, I submit, desirable to wait before entering into an agreement of so binding a nature and see what Germany's naval intentions and naval difficulties really are; they will probably show themselves at the end of 1911.

In support of my submission in regard to the German proposals, I would observe that the number of ships to be laid down are already exchanged by means of the naval estimates of the two countries.

3. I would submit that any exchange of information at the present time should be limited to exchange of information of details of ships and dates of laying down, to be made subsequent to each nation's programmes having been made public, and that a further guarantee of good faith should be the exchange of visits of the naval attachés to the ship-building and armament yards.

I respectfully submit that what is required for a better understanding on the naval question is an alteration of the present practice of keeping secret the details and dimensions of the German ships. Information on this, which is available in England on the date of launch, is not in Germany until even later, or, rather, until the details have gradually leaked out. In addition to the incentive to distrust thereby supplied, expense to both countries in "going one better in the dark" is incurred in bringing out something better than it is probable the other has. Also the precautions taken in Germany to prevent ships being seen prior to and after their launch are obstacles in the way of frank avowal of intentions.

As the question of exchange of information as to the number of ships to be laid down is unnecessary, an early date for the exchange of information is not required, and information on the details of the ships to be laid down and dates for so doing can, I submit, be as conveniently exchanged after both countries have issued their naval estimates, *i.e.*, at latter end of March or the early part of April.

4. In regard to exchange of visits by naval attachés, I submit that the principal point to ensure is that they shall, on the occasion of these visits, see all naval vessels in process of building, and not, as in the past, be informed by private ship-building yards in Germany that it is impossible to show vessels building for, or work in hand for, the Imperial German navy.

It would, I submit, be desirable that the principle that visits are to be six-monthly or at some defined period should be recognised in terms of any agreement on this point, otherwise difficulties may arise. Within such recognition the actual dates to be settled by the naval attachés with the Admiralty concerned.

I have, &c.

HUGH WATSON,
Naval Attaché.

MINUTES.

The German government now proposes an arrangement which, under the guise of exchange of information, really involves an engagement to effect a limitation of armaments. It is very desirable to keep these things apart.

As regards the exchange of information, see my minute on Sir E. Goschen's telegram No. 9 (11015).(3) Captain Watson confirms my suggestion that something more definite and precise respecting the periodical visits of inspection by naval attachés should be embodied in the agreement.

Sir E. Goschen's remarks about the date on which information is to be annually exchanged, concern rather the question of the limitation of armaments. They touch upon one of the most fundamental difficulties which, as I have repeatedly pointed out, stand in the way of H[is] M[ajesty's] G[overnment] making an agreement respecting limitation of armaments with one Power only, whilst third Powers, some of them allied, and others perhaps in secret understanding with Germany (Turkey, Brazil, Sweden?) remained free to build what they liked and as rapidly as they liked. This is a practical consideration raising issues so important that it is essential not to mix them up with the question of the exchange of naval information concerning rate of construction, &c. As Captain Watson judiciously remarks, the numbers of

(3) [v. supra, pp. 610–11, No. 455.]

ships to be built are, under existing arrangements, given in the naval estimates of each country. What the special arrangement we desire to conclude is intended to secure, is that the information given in the estimates shall not be falsified by the actual proceedings in ·the dockyards.

If the limitation of armaments is to have any practical value for this country, it must be based on a far more comprehensive foundation than the present German proposal, and any negotiation concerning it would be sure to be protracted, and in view of the German Chancellor's recent speech, of doubtful success.

It seems curious at first sight that the Chancellor at the very moment when he declares any limitation to be absolutely impossible, because contrary to first principles, should put forward a proposal which does, in however modest a form, take the shape of a limitation to be agreed upon from year to year. We must assume that this particular form has advantages for the German government. It is not difficult to see why this is so. The German government has in reality no apprehension that H[is] M[ajesty's] G[overnment] may suddenly start a new building scheme of maximum dimensions. They rely on our being reasonable. They do not therefore fear that, having made up their minds how many ships they are going to lay down, their plans will be seriously upset by the British programme. But are we in the same position? Supposing we reckoned with an existing German navy law and, on the basis of a reasonable forecast of German action thereunder, proposed to lay down 4 ships; and supposing that at the moment we so inform the German gov[ernmen]t, they announce a modification of their navy law, such as has twice been made, or that they reduce the official age of their ships, before they are to be regarded as obsolete, from 20 years to 15 or 10; we should under this proposed agreement be precluded from building more than 4 ships whilst Germany would be entirely free to lay down 8 or 10. It will not do to leave such a contingency out of account, when you are asked to tie your hands by a formal agreement. I do not say that the present Chancellor contemplates some such action as I indicate as possible, but he may not be in office, and the German gov[ernmen]t is giving no pledge not to do what is clearly open to them. There is, further, the other possibility, to which Sir E. Goschen has called attention, that whilst England would at a given date (as early before the commencement of the English financial year, as possible) be tied down to a fixed number of new ships, Austria, Italy, and other Powers whom Great Britain has to take into account, could shortly afterwards lay down an unexpectedly large number of extra ships? Moreover Germany, under her system of a fixed navy law, does at present tie herself in a certain way for years in advance (notably as regards providing the money) whereas the British programme is undetermined until the estimates are, each year, made up. Germany would gain by knowing something definite and rigid beforehand, beyond which Great Britain could not go for, say, 15 months. Such an arrangement as the 4 " contingent Dreadnoughts " of 1909–10 would be made impossible for us.

Qu[ery]. Invite the observations of the Admiralty in the first instance, pointing out that it would seem desirable not to mix up in the same document the comparatively simple question of the exchange of naval information, and the suggested limitation of numbers by annual undertakings.

E. A. C.
Ap. 3, 1911.

Captain Watson's advice to confine this agreement to an exchange of naval information seems sound. To tie our hands for a year in ignorance of Germany's programme or those of her allies might give them an advantage which would not be easily recovered.

W. L.

The two questions of (1) exchange of information and (2) limitation of armaments should most certainly be kept distinct. We can await the views of the Admiralty as suggested by Sir E. Crowe.

A. N.

Refer to Admiralty in first instance pointing out the German proposal seems to have a wider scope than ours.([4])

It is unnecessary to say more than this as the matter will have to be discussed with the Prime Minister.

Personally, I do not see how we can in the autumn name any figure for number of ships to be laid down without making it conditional upon at any rate the German and Austrian programme ·being what we anticipate.

E. G.

([4]) [*v. infra*, p. 617, No. 459.]

No. 458.

Sir E. Goschen to Sir Edward Grey.

F.O. 12051/12051/11/18.
(No. 84.)   *Berlin, D. March* 31, 1911.
Sir,   R. *April* 3, 1911.

The speech which the Chancellor delivered in the Reichstag yesterday, and of which I have the honour to enclose a translation,(¹) is characterized by the greater part of the Conservative, and even the moderate Liberal, Press as the finest exposure of the disarmament and arbitration illusions that has ever been made in any parliament. On the other hand the Liberal and Radical papers look upon the speech as a "declaration of war" against the disarmament idea, and express the greatest disappointment that His Excellency should have thrown so much cold water on resolutions which expressed the feelings of a large portion, if not the majority, of the German people.

These resolutions which were moved by the Social Democratic and People's Parties, were firstly a request to the Imperial Chancellor to express his readiness to enter into negotiations with other Great Powers as soon as proposals should have been made by one Power for the simultaneous and proportional limitation of expenditure on armaments; secondly a demand for the conclusion of arbitration treaties with other Powers. . . . .(²)

The 'Tageblatt' opens a long leading article on the Chancellor's speech with the following words :—

"'If, so far as public opinion in England is concerned, understandings can contribute to the removal of this feeling of suspicion, as Sir Edward Grey has intimated, then on the side of Germany there will be every inclination to put her hand to the work.' These words were to be found only a fortnight ago in the 'Norddeutsche Allgemeine Zeitung.' Therefore it was possible to say, 'At last!' The English Minister for Foreign Affairs has now spoken in the most conciliatory form possible of an understanding with Germany and of a future mutual reduction of expenditure on naval armaments.(³) The German Empire was, according to the semi-official newspaper, ready to put its hand to the work. The outlook seemed fair and full of promise. But since the Chancellor's speech of yesterday this promising outlook has, like a beautiful Fata Morgana, melted into thin air. 'Reduction of expenditure on armaments?' asked the Chancellor, answering his own question with the words, 'We have found no practicable formula,' adding, 'The question is incapable of solution, as long as men remain men and States States.' 'Arbitration treaties?' asks the Chancellor; and again he answers the question himself, 'I consider international Arbitration Treaties imposed by a world's congress to be as impossible as the idea of international disarmament.' From these utterances it would appear that armament, ever increasing armament, is the beginning and the end of the wisdom of our leading statesman."

The 'Tageblatt,' in this outburst, seems, as is clear from the rest of the article, which I have no time to quote, to regard the Chancellor's utterances as a refusal on his part to accept the hand held out by Great Britain. Personally I do not think it should be regarded as anything of the sort. It does not evince, it is true, a very hopeful state of mind either as regards Arbitration treaties or the limitation of armaments, but there is nothing that I can see in what he said to show that he is

(¹) [Not reproduced. A full account of the speech was published in the *Times* of March 31, 1911.]
(²) [The omitted paragraphs contain a detailed description of the debate in the Reichstag.]
(³) [*v. supra*, pp. 604–7, Nos. 451–2 and reference there to *Parl. Deb., 5th Ser.,* House of Commons, Vol. 22, pp. 1977–92.]

any way disinclined, as the 'Tageblatt' maintains he is, to come to an understanding with Great Britain. His speech was, in my view, a philosophical dissertation rather than an exposition of policy. But I do rather agree with the "Tageblatt's" opinion that the speech was somewhat of a diplomatic blunder and that it was a mistake on his part to answer your speech as he has done, even though the ideas he expressed were merely his own reflections on the general question of the possibility of arrangements for international disarmament and the utility of international arbitration treaties.

You will notice that there is scarcely anything in his speech which he has not repeatedly said to me in the course of our conversations.

I have, &c.
W. E. GOSCHEN.

No. 459.

Foreign Office to Admiralty.

F.O. 12050/4451/11/18.
Secret.
Sir,   *Foreign Office, April 6, 1911.*
With reference to the F[oreign] O[ffice] letter No. 5168 of Feb[ruary] 16th last([1]) and previous correspondence I am directed by Sec[retar]y Sir E. Grey to transmit to you, to be laid before the Lords Commissioners of the Admiralty, the accompanying copy of a despatch, dated March 30th, from H[is] M[ajesty's] Ambassador at Berlin,([2]) forwarding a memorandum([3]) from the German Government in reply to the proposals of H[is] M[ajesty's] G[overnment] respecting a periodical exchange of naval information.

The despatch from Sir E. Goschen also contains a memorandum by the Naval Attaché at Berlin. It will be observed that the German proposal has a wider scope than that contemplated by H[is] M[ajesty's] G[overnment].

Sir E. Grey would be glad to be furnished with the observations of the Lords Commissioners on the German Gov[ernmen]t's memorandum.

[I am, &c.
W. LANGLEY.]

([1]) Not reproduced.]
([2]) [*v. supra*, pp. 612–3, No. 457.]
([3]) [*v. supra*, p. 610, No. 455, and reference there to *G.P.* XXVIII, p. 402.]

No. 460.

Sir F. Bertie to Sir Edward Grey.

F.O. 13392/13392/11/17.
(No. 163.) Confidential.   *Paris, D. April 9, 1911.*
Sir,   R. *April 11, 1911.*
I have the honour to transmit to you herewith, a despatch which I have received from Colonel Fairholme, the Military Attaché to this Embassy, reporting a conversation with General Foch, Commandant of the Staff College, on international politics.

I have, &c.
FRANCIS BERTIE.

Enclosure in No. 460.

Colonel Fairholme to Sir F. Bertie.

(No. 4.)   Confidential
Sir,
                                                                Paris, April 8, 1911.
I have the honour to submit to your Excellency the following statement of
some views expressed by a prominent French general, in the course of a conversation
which I had with him yesterday.

The officer in question is General Foch, Commandant of the Staff College, and
he is in the closest touch with the French General Staff, and with its chief,
General Laffon de Ladebat, so that his views may, I think, be taken as representative of the best-informed military opinion in this country.

The general expressed himself as profoundly impressed by the astuteness,
activity, and continuity of German policy all over the world, and he lamented the
fact that he was unable to detect those qualities, at least in the same measure, in
the foreign policies of France, England, and Russia.

The last-named Power, he said, is being fooled by Germany, and induced,
unmindful of recent Manchurian experiences, to weaken herself by embarking on
fresh adventures, in Persia, which will infallibly result in ultimate discontent at
home, and in consequent revolutionary outbreaks which will tend to immobilise the
Russian armies.   This he considers to be the inward meaning of the recent
Potsdam meeting.

He alluded to the outwitting of M. Isvolsky by Count Aehrenthal, and it may
interest your Excellency to learn that he spoke of the new Russian Ambassador as
notoriously under German influences here in Paris.

General Foch dwelt on the flattering manner in which the German Emperor
lavishes personal attentions and favours on all Russian missions and officers who
visit Germany, a policy which is not without its effect on the Russian army, and
against which republican France is unfortunately not in a position to compete.

Similarly, he continued, by fostering Moslem hostility against England, in
Turkey and Egypt, Germany is preparing difficulties for the former Power, which
will hamper her action on the continent of Europe when the day for action comes.

Germany is daily extending her influence over the minor European States,
Belgium, Switzerland, Holland, &c., as well as in the near and Far East, in all of
which regions there is a corresponding decline of British prestige.

"Germany," the general went on to say, "will never declare war against us,
she will go on her way, gradually encroaching in all directions, always armed to the
teeth and ready to fight if her pretensions should be challenged, until one day, at
a moment when Russia and England have their hands full elsewhere, she will bring
about a situation in which the *entente* Powers will find themselves confronted with
the choice of making war on her or of suffering injury to vital interests.   They will
then have to decide between war at an unfavourable moment and effacement in
the future."

It is thus that General Foch considers that war with Germany will come, and
his forecast is that big events may be expected " à partir de 1912."

To remedy this state of affairs the general is of opinion that it behoves France
and England to pursue a more active policy towards the minor European States, with
a view to encouraging them to resist German influence and to oppose German
incursion in case of war.

If Belgium, for instance, could be induced to contemplate a resolute defence of
her frontier, with her 120,000 men, on the line of the Meuse, instead of a useless
concentration back in Antwerp, the German advance would find itself seriously
hampered.   Similarly with Switzerland and Holland.

None of these States have any special love for Germany, but they fear her
and naturally want to be on the winning side.   They have constant evidences of

German power and self-assertion, which are not counterbalanced by corresponding activity on the part of English and French diplomacy.

The general further considers that the French and British Governments ought to settle beforehand exactly what they are prepared to concede, and what to resist, in the many political questions of the moment, so that they may not be perpetually faced by fresh minor encroachments of German policy all over the world, which become *faits accomplis* before a joint decision has been arrived at to resist them.

But, above all, General Foch is firmly convinced of the urgent necessity for an understanding between His Majesty's Government and that of the republic regarding the form which joint action should take in the event of war between France and Germany.

It will by no means suffice that a decision to co-operate should be arrived at after war has been declared, or even on the eve of a rupture.

The most acceptable and the only really effective form which British help could take would be the dispatch of the strongest possible expeditionary force, in time to take part, side by side with the French armies, in the decisive battle or battles between the main forces of France and Germany, where it would help materially to neutralise the considerable numerical superiority of the German army, and where its early arrival and subsequent presence would enormously enhance the confidence, and hence the fighting value, of the French troops, who are always particularly susceptible to moral influences.

The collision may be expected to take place any time after the thirteenth day of the French and German mobilisation, when the main opposing forces will probably meet on a front of some 190 miles, extending from Namur on the north to about Epinal on the south.

In order that the British expeditionary force should be in its place by that date, it would have to be mobilised simultaneously with the French army, and it would have to be transported to the continent, and railed to the front without a moment's delay.

It must be evident to anybody in the least familiar with the complicated mechanism of modern war, aptly described by General Foch as "de l'horlogerie," that an operation on such a scale could only be undertaken, with the slightest hope of success, if the whole plan had been worked out beforehand on both sides of the channel in its minu[t]est details, down to the sequence and composition of the hundreds of troop-trains, as well as the exact hours and minutes of their respective departures from the selected ports of debarkation and of their arrival at their ultimate destinations.

The preparation of such a scheme offers no special difficulties to the British and French general staffs, and it is obviously their function and duty to study and work out beforehand the military problems connected with any course of action which their respective Governments may be expected to adopt under any reasonably probable circumstances.

But General Foch points out that, however fully such a scheme might be prepared beforehand by the two general staffs, the French Government, when the time came, could not possibly afford to earmark railway lines and rolling-stock for such a purpose at a moment when all its resources must be so urgently required, unless indeed it had received a previous assurance that it could count with certainty on the arrival of the British contingent.

Hence the absolute necessity for a clear previous understanding between the two Governments. Upon its existence may depend the result of the war and, consequently, the fate of Europe.

A British contingent dispatched at a later moment than as above might pr bably just as well stay away.

General Foch observed that no doubt there might be insuperable difficulties in the way of getting a majority in the British Parliament to vote for such an agreement at the present moment, but he pointed out that the Anglo-Japanese Alliance had been arranged without the previous consent of Parliament having been obtained.

I have, &c.

W. E. FAIRHOLME,
Military Attaché.

MINUTES.

General Foch's remarks are worthy of the most serious attention. He sums up the situation in the paragraph marked on page 2, and his forecast agrees with that of many shrewd observers. The General however does not tell us how we are to stimulate Belgium, Denmark, Holland, etc., against Germany. What possible chance have these little States against an army whose *peace* strength is about to be raised to 5 millions.

The question of a definite military Convention with France is one fraught with such immense consequences that it can hardly be considered in a departmental minute.

War Office in original.

G. E. V.
11/4/11.

I think that General Foch's description of German policy is accurate, and that the danger he depicts is both real and urgent. Germany's immediate efforts are at present concentrated on—

1. Ostentatiously seeking British friendship;
2. Doing everything to create friction between Great Britain and other States, by action in Russia, in France, in Turkey and elsewhere; with a view to the levy of political blackmail;
3. Being absolutely prepared for a war when it comes;
4. Encouraging the pacifist movement in England—so diametrically opposed to all German principles of policy—in order to prevent Great Britain from taking any serious measures for combining with France and Russia to resist the German attack.

It looks as if Germany were meeting with success in all these endeavours.

E. A. C.
Ap. 11.

Colonel Foch's diagnosis is probably correct but nothing that we may say will persuade the small Powers to show a bold front to Germany if they think, and they probably do think, that on land at least she has the big battalions and that a day of reckoning will come for them in which their independence will be jeopardized.

W. L.

This is too wide a question to discuss by minutes. Should it not go to the Cabinet Committee?

A. N.

Prime Minister
Lord Morley
Lord Haldane
       in first instance.

E. G.

Sir E. Grey thinks this circulation sufficient.

W. T.

No. 461.

Sir A. Nicolson to Lord Hardinge of Penshurst.

Private.([1])

My dear Hardinge,   *Foreign Office, April* 19, 1911.

. . . . ([2]) Now as regards European affairs. We are still awaiting the reply to our last memorandum which was communicated to Berlin two or three weeks ago.([3]) As I anticipated the Germans do not much like our making an agreement in regard to limitation of armaments a necessary condition to any political understanding and

([1]) [Carnock MSS., Vol. II of 1911.]
([2]) [The opening passages of this letter refer to personal matters and to the Bagdad Railway.]
([3]) [*v. supra*, pp. 598–600. No. 444, *encl.*]

I think that they see that we shall limit the latter to an agreement to certain specified questions such as the Bagdad Railway and Persia and not come to any engagements of a wider and more general scope. We could, of course, put into any formula general expressions of goodwill and friendship but I sincerely hope that we shall keep clear of any understanding which would tie our hands in any way or which would in the slightest degree affect our understanding with France and Russia. I hope that our Government now fully realise that the aim of Germany in these negotiations is to smash up as far as she is able to do, the Triple *Entente* and that her chief object is to isolate France as much as possible. I am not completely at ease in my own mind that she may not succeed in this respect to a limited extent as it is known that at the present moment there is a wave in many circles here towards a friendly understanding with Germany. The Anglo-German Friendship Society, of which Lascelles, I believe, is Chairman, has induced the Lord Mayor to convene a meeting at the Guildhall on May the 1st in favour of an understanding and I daresay that the visit here of the German Emperor next month will encourage all those who consider that the true way to salvation for us lies in our marching hand in hand with Germany. I think that this is unfortunate as it is impossible to convince the adherents to this policy that Germany does not admit a friendship on equal terms and that we should find ourselves before long compelled to act in accordance with German wishes in every question which might arise. On the other hand it is, of course, impossible for us to take up an attitude adverse to the friendly understanding as we should be immediately accused of placing obstacles in the way of what these good people consider to be one of the strongest guarantees for peace. I look forward to a troublesome time during the next few months but so far as my voice is heard it will always be in favour of a firm maintenance of our understanding with France and Russia. It is most unlucky that at this moment the French Government is not in a strong position and that the position of Stolypine is shaken while Sazonow will not be able in the best of circumstances to return to work for some time to come. Again, a projected visit of members of both Houses of Parliament to Russia does not seem to be feasible owing to the internal situation here and this, of course, will be a source of much disappointment in St. Petersburg. The field therefore is pretty well open to Germany and the stars in their courses are, for the moment, in her favour. . . .(⁴)

[Yours sincerely,
A. NICOLSON.]

(⁴) [The omitted passages refer to the internal affairs of Turkey, the Moroccan situation, and Austro-German relations.]

No. 462.

Sir E. Goschen to Sir Edward Grey.

Berlin, May 9, 1911.

F.O. 17617/4451/11/18.
D. 7·21 P.M.
Tel. (No. 26.) Secret.
R. 9·40 P.M.

The Chancellor has just handed to me his answer to your last memorandum.(¹) The position he takes up is this : The time has gone by when his original proposal for reducing tempo of construction within naval law could be put into effect. He has now nothing to propose, but will give his best consideration to any proposal for mutual reduction of expenses from His Majesty's Government. He sees basis for political understanding in your last memorandum, but as His Majesty's Government

(¹) [*v. supra*, pp. 598–600. No. 444. *encl.*]

hold view that naval agreement must at all events be simultaneous with political understanding, he must await British proposals for former before suggesting formula for latter.

Last paragraph runs thus:—

(R.) "The Imperial Government maintains its opinion that a general understanding would exclude all idea of an attack by one party on the other, and would guarantee friendly discussions of any questions which might arise between the two Powers, would be the best means of allaying suspicion with regard to each other's armaments; such an understanding should not clash with agreements of either Power with other Powers, and should enable His Majesty's Government to fulfil their wish to invite the accession of the Powers with whom they have special agreements."

MINUTES.

The German government now at last confess what we suspected from the outset to be the case : they have definitely withdrawn from their promise to submit proposals for a reduction of armaments, on the ground that they consider any such scheme impossible. In view of the repeated public utterances of high German officials, including successive Chancellors; and of the Emperor himself, it is clear that they never did believe that they could put forward such proposals. Their statement to the contrary was used, as was pointed out here at the time, for the purpose of leading H[is] M[ajesty's] G[overnment] on to the conclusion of a general Anglo-German agreement, such as they knew Great Britain was unwilling even to discuss. They have gone some considerable way in gaining their point. They have induced H[is] M[ajesty's] G[overnment] in the first instance to abandon their original attitude which was that no discussion of a reduction of armaments was of any use if the existing German naval programme was to be carried out in its integrity. The Chancellor on the contrary explained that any negotiation would have to start from the basis of the actual completion of that programme. We abandoned our position, and continued the discussion.

Germany insisted that before a naval understanding could be thought of, there must be a general Anglo-German agreement of a political nature, which would preclude the possibility of war between the two countries in any circumstances. The essential feature of such an agreement was that not only would the two countries refrain from ever attacking the other, but they would undertake each to remain neutral in any war in which the other was engaged. The object of this clearly is to allow Germany to deal with other Powers, such as France and Russia, without any fear of British intervention.

H[is] M[ajesty's] G[overnment] at first declined to enter into any general political agreement at all. After a time, they declared their willingness to discuss it if and when a naval agreement had been come to. Germany declined to accept this, and we again went a step back, and declared our readiness to consider an arrangement by which both agreements were to be concluded simultaneously.

Since then, Germany has manœuvred to throw the naval agreement overboard altogether. The speeches delivered by the official spokesmen of the German government ought never to have left us in doubt that Germany never intended to agree to any reduction of armaments. But her disingenuous professions have achieved what was intended : Great Britain has been induced to discuss the terms of a political agreement.

With the view of assuring the success of this negotiation, the German government, being always farsighted in these matters, have for a considerable time carefully laid their plans for leading H[is] M[ajesty's] G[overnment] further on in the same road. The means employed have been those placed at their disposal by the organization of their press bureau, the direct and indirect influence they exercise over the British press, and personal connection, through the Berlin Foreign Office, and through the German ambassador in London, with the leaders of the so-called "pacifist" propaganda in this country. By these means the German gov[ernmen]t have encouraged, if not created, over here an agitation—to which nothing in practice corresponds in Germany—in favour of an Anglo-German understanding as such, of the exact purport of which its promoters and supporters have not the shadowiest notion.

Finally, in order to put still further pressure on H[is] M[ajesty's] G[overnment], they have so played their cards that, if the negotiations come to nothing, they will be able to say,—and they will say it loudly and have it re-echoed throughout Europe—that it is all the fault of H[is] M[ajesty's] G[overnment]. For, as has always been anticipated, they have now turned round and thrown upon us the burden of producing definite proposals for a reduction of armaments. Great Britain having so insistently urged such reduction, will be placed in an unfavourable light if she fails to bring forward practical proposals. Whether such proposals can be framed at all I know not. Neither the Admiralty nor anyone else in authority has ever produced any. Unless we can and do produce them, we shall be in the dilemma of either having to bear the unfavourable comment to which our failure would no doubt expose us, or to make the further, and this time radical, concession of abandoning the one and only thing for which we declared we could ever accept some general political agreement with Germany, that is an agreement for the reduction of armaments.

The latter we shall now no doubt be urged to do both by the Berlin-inspired public opinion in this country, and by the direct pressure of the German gov[ernmen]t, beginning with the German emperor during his forthcoming visit.

We are fast drifting back into the position which was summarized in the memorandum of Jan[uary] 1st, 1907.(²) Now again, as on former occasions, the German gov[ernmen]t after a period of much unfriendliness on their part, come to woo us with assurances that if we will only do what they wish, it will lead to peace, the end of all friction, and the definite establishment of Anglo-German friendship. This time, if we fall into the same trap, the consequences will be still more serious than before. We shall have to reckon not only with renewed German unfriendliness, and further German demands, pressed by the added weight of a strengthened Germany, but we run the imminent risk of practically breaking up the *entente* with France and Russia.

Detailed criticism of the German answer must be deferred until we have the text.

E. A. C.
May 10.

The " tempo of construction " proposal has turned out as shadowy as was expected.

Whatever unfavourable comment our failure to conclude an Agreement may expose us to, an agreement which leaves the naval question unsettled would, I believe, command still less support.

W. L.

Sir Eyre Crowe's minute is an admirable summary of what has passed and merits the most careful consideration. I entirely agree with his views and am also of his opinion that the object of the German Gov[ernmen]t is to lay on one side the naval agreement and lead us into " a general understanding." We have hitherto resisted, and rightly resisted, going further with Germany as regards an understanding than we have done with France and Russia. I trust that we shall firmly maintain this attitude. Unless we intend to reverse our foreign policy of preserving the equilibrium in Europe, we cannot tie our hands in the manner which Germany proposed to us on a former occasion and to which doubtless she would revert were she to find us pliant. The Chancellor will not suggest his formula till he is in possession of our proposals for a mutual reduction of armaments. I presume that when we originally entered into the negotiations we had in our minds some proposals for mutual reduction, and that the competent authorities were then ready, and would be ready now, to draw up a project. It would be well if they were to do so, and we should then present it to the Chancellor and request him to supply us with his formula. We should also inform him that when we received his formula we should take advantage of his willingness that we should consult our friends as to whether they would be ready to accede to it. We should make it perfectly clear 1 that a naval agreement must be simultaneous and 2 that we could not subscribe to any *general* formula without the concurrence of the Powers with whom we had special agreements. The question is one which should be dealt with most carefully and cautiously especially at this moment.

A. N.

It would be well to have the papers put together, which give the history of the question and will bring out the points of Sir E. Crowe's minute. I remember one occasion on which Count Metternich reproached us because the Prime Minister had stated in Parliament that there could be no question of Germany altering her naval law and had thereby ignored the offer to reduce the " tempo." I am sure I recorded this conversation and it should be included in the collection of papers.(³)

The last decision of the Gov[ernmen]t was that an agreement under which Germany undertook not to increase her naval programme might be worth consideration. From the point of view of naval expenditure the German reply is most unsatisfactory. On the other hand the last paragraph apparently makes it easier for us to avoid being entangled in separate political negotiations with Germany to which other Powers are not parties.

We must wait for the full text, which I will circulate to the Cabinet when received.

E. G.

(²) [Printed in *Gooch & Temperley*, Vol. III, pp. 397–420, *App.* A.]

(³) [*cp. supra*, pp. 496–7, No. 382. The collection of papers to which Sir Edward Grey refers was a volume of *Confidential Print* in which documents relating to the Anglo-German negotiations were collected.]

No. 463.

Sir C. Spring-Rice to Sir Edward Grey.

F.O. 18074/730/11/18.
(No. 175.) Confidential.   *Stockholm, D. May 9*, 1911.
Sir,   R. *May 13*, 1911.

I have the honour to state that Count Taube spoke to me today with regard to his speech on the question of disarmament, which formed the subject of Lord Kilmarnock's despatch No. 48 of March 23.([1]) His Excellency said that the Swedish Government was placed in an embarrassing position in consequence of the effect produced by your speech in the House of Commons on the question of peace and arbitration.([2]) So great was the effect of this speech here that it looked as if it would be impossible for the Government to induce the House to vote the sums necessary for the support of the army. He had been obliged to speak with great frankness as to. what he considered the facts of the case and the necessity for the small powers of taking adequate measures of defence. He was happy to find himself in agreement with the German Chancellor but he was also extremely fortunate in having to make his speech before that made in the Reichstag by Herr von Bethmann Hollweg. For if his speech had been made subsequent to the German pronouncement everyone would have said that it had been made under German influence and not independently. The fact was that he had consulted noone except the Prime Minister. Recently in the course of a long and interesting visit which he had paid the Chancellor, he, Count Taube, had talked over the European situation. The Chancellor had told him of the negotiations which were going on with England on the subject of the limitation of armaments and had stated that he perfectly appreciated the English point of view that the existence of Great Britain depended on her retaining the command of her own waters. But, he had added, how can any German Chancellor come to the German people with an agreement by which Germany accepted formally for all time a position of inferiority at sea? It was quite out of the question. I gathered that neither of these two statesmen in their conference attributed much practical importance to the pending negotiations. Count Taube went on to say that the military situation of Sweden was good if she took adequate measures of defence and that her means allowed her to take adequate measures. But the Swedish people were not like the English who perfectly well understood that their safety depended on a sufficient navy. It seemed impossible to convince a large section of the population that military sacrifices were incumbent on them if Sweden was to retain that position of complete independence which every Swede desired. He had no fault to find with what you had said, but he found it very hard to make people understand that you had been as decided in your advocacy of adequate measures of defence as you were eloquent in the cause of peace.

To morrow takes place the debate on the Government proposals for the construction of a battleship on which the present Cabinet has staked its existence. There is a good deal of excitement on the subject and as the elections take place in the Autumn the votes of the members will be closely scrutinized. The general feeling seems to be that the Government will be defeated in the lower House but will carry their proposals on the joint vote.

I have, &c.
CECIL SPRING RICE.

([1]) [Not reproduced.]
([2]) [*v. Parl. Deb., 5th Ser.*, House of Commons, Vol. 22, pp. 1977-92.]

No. 464.

Sir E. Goschen to Sir Edward Grey.

F.O. 18222/4451/11/18.
(No. 135.)   Secret.   *Berlin*, D. *May* 10, 1911.
Sir,   R. *May* 13, 1911.
   I have the honour to report that, by the Imperial Chancellor's invitation, I
called upon His Excellency yesterday for the purpose of receiving the answer of
the Imperial Government to the Memorandum respecting Anglo-German negotiations
which in accordance with your instructions I handed to His Excellency on the
24th March last.(¹)
   The answer is contained in the *Aide-Mémoire* of which I have the honour to
enclose a copy and translation.
   Before handing me the *Aide-Mémoire* the Chancellor gave me a brief account
of its substance and of the views held by the Imperial Government of the present
phase of the negotiations.
   His Excellency said that the year before last, in fact immediately after he had
assumed office, he had expressed the willingness of the Imperial Government to
reduce the *tempo* of their Naval construction as far as it was possible within the
limits of their Fleet Law.   This suggestion had been made with the idea that,
although it could not affect the number of ships to be ultimately built under that
Law, it would, by reducing naval expenditure during, say, a couple of years, allay
suspicion, create a better atmosphere, and give to the world in general the reassuring
idea that the relations between Germany and Great Britain were so friendly that
there was no necessity for either Power to display any special activity in their
respective shipbuilding yards.   His Majesty's Government, however, for various
reasons, had never shown any particular desire for the development of this proposal
and the subject had been allowed to drop.   Now, in view of the fact that next year
the rate of German Naval construction would reach its lowest limit, it was of course
impossible that this offer could be renewed.   Moreover, anxious though they were
to meet the wishes of His Majesty's Government that some agreement should be
made for the mutual reduction of expenditure on naval armaments, the Imperial
Government had in this connection nothing further to propose; they must therefore
leave it to His Majesty's Government to put forward proposals such as might form
the basis of negotiations for the object desired by Great Britain.   He need hardly
say that any proposal put forward by His Majesty's Government would receive the
earnest and sympathetic attention of the Imperial Government.
   His Excellency went on to say that as far as a political understanding was
concerned he saw in your Memorandum a basis for negotiation, but that as it was
the view of His Majesty's Government that public opinion in England would attach
but little value to a political understanding unless it were preceded by, or at least
made simultaneously with, a naval agreement, it was obviously unnecessary for the
Imperial Government to suggest a formula for the former until a negotiable basis
had been found for the latter.
   His Excellency spoke at some length on the great difficulties which surrounded
the question of a naval agreement and maintained his former standpoint that an
adequate political understanding such as would render a naval agreement unnecessary
was the best policy for both countries.   "I know," he said, "that it is the best
policy for Germany, and I think it is the best for England also."
   In conclusion, he called my special attention to the last sentence of his
Aide-Mémoire, saying that I would find that the idea of a political understanding

(¹) [*v. supra*, p. 609, No. 454.   The memorandum is printed *supra*, pp. 598–600, No. 444, *encl.*]

which it adumbrated was in harmony with the views originally put forward by you, namely, that it should be one in which France and Russia could be invited to join.

I have, &c.
W. E. GOSCHEN.

Enclosure in No. 464.

Aide-Mémoire *handed to Sir E. Goschen by the Imperial Chancellor,* May 9, 1911.([2])

(Translation.)([3])

In the course of the negotiations with the British Government respecting the conclusion of a Naval Agreement, the Imperial Government have repeatedly referred to the possibility of allowing, within the limits of the German Navy Law, a retardation of the rate of naval construction to take place. In fact, the Imperial Government would, during the two financial years which have elapsed since the commencement of the negotiations that have now been in progress for almost 2 years, have been in a position to effect a material diminution in the number of ships to be begun, without calling in question the complete execution of the general programme for the expansion of the German fleet as laid down in the Navy Law. The interruptions, which at the desire of the British Government delayed the negotiations, have rendered it impossible to give effect to this idea during the past financial year. In view of the little progress made in the negotiations owing to this delay, it was equally impossible to contemplate a diminution in naval construction for the current year when settling the estimates for the Imperial Budget.

Now as regards the financial years following the current one, the Navy Law provides for a minimum number of new ships, to fall short of which would appear impossible for several reasons. In the first place the necessity of making up in later financial years the arrears of delayed construction, so as to comply with the provisions of the Navy Law, would result in irregularities in the demands upon the Imperial finances, which would be incompatible with the principles of sound finance. Moreover, such a course stands self-condemned by reason of the consideration due to the German shipbuilding industry, which would thus be incapacitated from rationally and profitably working its establishments, organized as these are, on the basis of having to deal with a definite quantity of government orders.

Whilst therefore the Imperial Government must, to their regret, forego their original intention, of coming forward, on their part, with proposals for retarding the complete execution of the Navy Law, they will nevertheless be most happy to continue the exchange of views on the subject of how it may be possible, to meet the wishes of the British Government as to the conclusion of a naval agreement going even beyond the proposed exchange of information. The Imperial Government will in any case readily enter into an examination of any proposals that may be made by the British Government, the adoption of which would render possible the realisation of the idea repeatedly expressed by Sir E. Grey, and a mutual reduction of expenditure on armaments. They look forward with interest to receiving from the British gov[ernmen]t any proposals of this nature, not involving a departure from the requirements of the Navy Law.

As regards the question of a political understanding, the Imperial Government continue to adhere to their view that a suitable agreement of that kind is a necessary corollary of any naval agreement. They even believe that such an agreement might possibly render a purely naval agreement superfluous, but they are willing, on this point also, to have regard for the views of the British Government. The Imperial Government do not therefore hesitate to declare at once that they think they see a suitable basis for such an agreement in the explanations contained in the last Memorandum presented by the British Government.

([2]) [For the German original, *v. G.P.* XXVIII, pp. 409–11.]
([3]) [The translation as given here is taken from a copy of the Berlin Embassy version corrected by Sir Eyre Crowe.]

They adhere to their view however that a general understanding which would exclude all possibility of an attack by one party on the other, and guarantee the friendly discussions of any questions that might arise between the two Powers would be the best means of allaying all suspiciousness concerning each other's armaments. Such an understanding would hardly clash with agreements of either Power with third parties and should meet the wish of the British Government to invite the accession of the Powers with whom they have entered into special agreements.

MINUTES.

The general purport of the German reply has already been reviewed and criticized in the minutes on Sir E. Goschen's telegram([4]) which gave a provisional summary of the present despatch.

There are however a few new points deserving attention :

It is of interest to note the general character of the reasons given as justifying, or rather compelling, the German government now to withdraw their previous offer concerning a slight temporary retardation of the rate of naval construction within the limits of their Navy Law. It is impossible not to see that these reasons would have been equally conclusive against the proposal when first made. It follows that if they are to be regarded as valid, either the original proposal was not seriously meant, or, although made in good faith, it was in fact impracticable from the outset.

Of the two reasons put forward, the first, based on the sacrosanctity of sound finance sounds perhaps a little hollow, if regard be had to the ease with which the German government appear at times to juggle with the figures of their naval expenditure and the extraordinarily elastic terms of the financial provisions of their Navy Law.

The second reason is at once more solid and also more ominous. It means, if true, that the ring of ship-building, gunmaking, and allied industries is so powerful as to compel the government to show " due consideration " to its interests by continuing in the path of large orders for armaments. It incidentally explains one side of the popularity of swollen armaments in a country where industrial organization has reached so high a state of efficiency as in Germany.

As regards the desired political agreement, I venture to put on paper some further reflections :

The German gov[ernmen]t continue, without committing themselves to tangible proposals, to lay stress upon the necessity of obtaining binding guarantees that Germany will not, whatever happens, be attacked. It is obvious that they would welcome such guarantees all the more eagerly if they were not restricted to Great Britain, but were to include France and Russia. To encourage the participation of these two Powers in such an arrangement, is not a concession to Great Britain : it is an extension of the demand.

An arrangement which enthusiasts without much political experience would perhaps consider themselves justified in describing as one for the abolition of war between the three Great Powers, might at first sight appear as a triumph of international justice and human progress. I believe such a conclusion would be fallacious. It is not the object or desire of any State to go to war. The object is to attain certain political ends, which may, in given circumstances, be attainable with or without a resort to force. If without the use of force, so much the better for the State desiring the particular end. Every Power must obviously prefer to secure the objects of its policy without the inordinate sacrifice of lives and treasure, and the widely ramifying other calamities entailed by a war. If this be achieved, there will no doubt be the satisfaction that war was avoided. But what if the object aimed at, and attained without war, be in itself one dangerous to the peace of the world, the independence of free communities, the rights and liberties of civilized peoples? In that case, the absence of war, being the result of a prohibition of warlike measures for the defence of right and justice, acts not as a progress of civilization, but as an encouragement to conquest and oppression. The abolition of war would have been bought at too high a price. An absolutely necessary condition precedent to any undertaking not to use force by way of attack, must be a sufficient reduction of force on the other side to prevent its use for unjust ends. This is probably not obtainable under the political conditions prevailing at this moment.

It is the openly avowed policy of Germany to make herself so strong that in all matters in which she considers German interests to be involved, she will have her own way. The ambition is not deserving of any moral censure. It inspires the policy of every Great Power worthy of the name, to a certain degree. But the uniform experience of history shows that if this ambition is absolutely realized, the unquestioned supremacy of one State reacts disastrously on all the others. It is for this reason that Great Britain has, for centuries, stood for the balance of power.

(4) [v. supra, pp. 622-3, No. 462, min.]

2 s 2

Now an agreement on the lines which we know Germany desires, will undoubtedly enable her to alter the balance of power very materially in her favour. It is true that, theoretically, the other contracting powers would be in the same position. Of these other Powers (England, France, Russia) it is doubtful whether any at present are ardently bent on a policy of ascendency. Great Britain is certainly not. And neither France nor Russia, if they were, have the forces which are at Germany's disposal for such a purpose. Therefore the arrangement would in practice be purely one sided, in favour of Germany alone.

Germany has the means, quite apart from the employment of force, of putting considerable pressure on other States. By the application of tariffs, shipping subsidies, financial combinations, navigation dues, emigration and frontier regulations, &c.,' she does already at this moment exercise such pressure on countries like Holland, Belgium, Switzerland, Denmark, Sweden, and Norway that she often compels from them an attention to German demands which is certainly not always given willingly. Even in the case of countries in the position of Spain, Portugal, or Italy, the fear of German displeasure is well known to have a powerful influence in obtaining concessions to German claims and ambitions which those countries would in their own better interest desire to resist. The apprehensions of those and other countries would no doubt be considerably allayed if, by some miraculous means, they were absolutely guaranteed against the use of force by Germany. But Germany at least has never hesitated frankly and loudly to proclaim that, for her, the appeal to force is the *ultima ratio* of upholding what she holds to be her rights and obtaining due consideration of her interest and for her position as a Great Power.

This being the situation, it would be but natural, and there can be no unfairness in supposing, that Germany, if for a period definitely freed from any fear of attack by her three most formidable rivals, would use the opportunity to consolidate and strengthen her position in other countries, extending her political influence, creating fresh interests and rights, and above all acquiring positions of strategical value and importance in case of any future wars with the three other contracting States. She would certainly strain every nerve to obtain, whether by purchase or cession, or in return for an exchange of colonial possessions, or by any other means, those foreign ports, islands, and bases which are known to have been for years the aim of her keenest national ambitions : Spanish islands, Portuguese islands, Dutch islands, Greek or Turkish islands, Moorish ports, any possible footing in fact in regions flanking the ocean trade routes and the lines of communication with the colonial possessions of other Powers. To this end, and to others, Germany under an agreement such as she appears to desire, could, without fear of interference, use all the means at her disposal to establish her influence in the councils of other governments, so as to win their acquiescence in, or disarm their hostility to, the necessary bargains or transactions.

It is quite conceivable that in this way, and without violating any explicit treaty right of Great Britain for the vindication of which reliance could be placed on the process of arbitration, Germany might, simultaneously with a further rapid expansion of her navy, acquire coaling stations and naval bases abroad which could have no other object than to strengthen her hands in a naval conflict, and in the possession of which she could perhaps hope with a reasonable prospect of success to challenge British supremacy at sea, when necessary.

However legitimate all this may be from a German point of view, it cannot be the object of British policy to encourage it or assist in bringing it about. For if and when Germany shall thus have fortified her position, what chance will there be for Great Britain, for France, for Russia, or in fact for anything short of a general combination of all the world, to resist German dictation? Of what avail will it then be that the friends of peace may boast that war has been avoided? All that Germany could ever hope to obtain through a war, she would have gained without war.

We may readily credit the *bona fides* of the German claim that in no case would she ever use her power except to make right prevail, and that no one has to fear any injustice at her hands. But is it possible to believe that what Germany considers right and her due, will always appear such in non-German eyes?

Until the day has arrived when all international differences are settled by judicial or arbitral process, only the determination to defend and uphold its own standard of right and wrong, by force if necessary, will guarantee a State against the loss of that essential part of its sovereignty which consists in the power, on supreme occasions, to realize its own conception of national rights and liberties. There is a large element of safety for a State in the absence of any rival political force or combination outside it strong enough to extinguish this power of self-determination. So long as the power to order the national life in accordance with the nation's own conceptions of rights and duties is likely to be threatened by the political hegemony of one State or group of States, only the maintenance of the balance of power—and, as a possible alternative, some sort of all-embracing federal organization for regulating international relations—stand between the independence of nations and their subjection, direct or indirect, to the predominance of a militarily powerful and ambitious State.

The balance of power, as the term implies, consists of a balance of force, actual or latent. Anything that prevents the employment of force in the defence of national interests against a particular Power or set of Powers, whatever their aims or actions, abolishes the balance of power. The two things are not compatible with one another.

Great Britain would definitely upset the balance the day she signed away the right to use force against any particular State in the position held by Germany at present. To do this without substituting any other effectual method of ensuring the maintenance of British rights, interests, and independence, cannot be a proper policy for a British government.

E. A. C.
May 14.

I agree and hope that we shall never allow our hands to be tied.

W. L.

Before the desp[atch] and encl[osure] are circulated to the Cabinet, I believe the Dep[artmen]t will submit a memo[randum](⁵) and original doc[umen]ts regarding the history of the negotiations.

A. N.

Yes; the memo[randum] should be quite dispassionate bringing out the facts only.
Meanwhile circulate to the Cabinet Committee in the first instance with the short covering note that I enclose.

E. G.

I send the German reply that the Cabinet Committee may see it without delay.
I am having a memo[randum] prepared on the history of the negotiations, which seems desirable in order to understand the point now reached.
When this is ready I propose to circulate the whole paper to the Cabinet.

E. G.

(⁵) [v. infra, pp. 631–6, No. 468, encl.]

No. 465.

Admiralty to Foreign Office.

F.O. 18876/4451/11/18.
Confidential.
Sir,
Admiralty, May 16, 1911.

I have laid before my Lords Commissioners of the Admiralty your letter of the 5th April, No. 12050,(¹) and in reply I am commanded by their Lordships to request you to represent to Secretary Sir Edward Grey their satisfaction that the Imperial Government adhere to the view of the British Government in regard to the subject-matter of the proposed exchange of naval information.

The Imperial Government express the opinion that the reciprocity of exchange will only be completely guaranteed if the communications to be made on both sides are delivered at the same time, and they propose that this simultaneous exchange should be made every year in the period between the 1st October and the 15th November. It is believed that these dates are suggested as being those within which the German naval estimates for the year are printed and published. The naval estimates of the British Government, however, are usually not printed and published before 15th March in each year; and while accepting in principle the proposal for simultaneous exchange, my Lords suggest that the exchange should more properly be made in the period between the 15th November and 15th March.

It would be impossible, however, for the information at this date to cover more than the bare number of ships of each type included in the programme for the ensuing year. Questions of tonnage, speed, and armament are subject to modification up to the moment of laying down, and the exchange of information on these matters would necessarily have to be made in each case when the keel is first laid.

It appears from the covering letter, dated 30th March 1911,(²) of H[is] M[ajesty's] Ambassador at Berlin that Herr von Kiderlen considered that the information exchanged, so far as it related to the number of ships to be laid down in each year

(¹) [v. supra, p. 617, No. 459. The letter was dated April 6, 1911.]
(²) [v. supra, pp. 612–3, No. 457.]

by the two Governments, should be of a binding character. It should be observed that the suggestion as here made extends an arrangement for the exchange of information into an arrangement for the limitation of armaments, even though the limitation be for one year only. Whatever opinion may be formed on political grounds as to the desirability of such a limitation, my Lords do not think that it ought to form part of an agreement for the exchange of information. They agree that when information has once been communicated, there should be no variation of the programme thus made known without previous and further information being given to the other party, but would suggest, for Sir Edward Grey's consideration, that H[is] [Majesty's] Ambassador at Berlin should be instructed not to pledge H[is] M[ajesty's] Government to anything beyond the proposals contained in this letter.

With regard to the question of Attachés visiting dockyards and private yards, any arrangement involving strict reciprocity might well be agreed to.

I am, &c.

W. GRAHAM GREENE.

No. 466.

Sir Edward Grey to Sir E. Goschen.

F.O. 18222/4451/11/18.
(No. 116.) Secret.

Sir,   *Foreign Office, May 18, 1911.*

Count Metternich told me to-day(¹) that, while he was away on leave, he had learnt the views of the Imperial Chancellor on certain points. On my saying that we had now received the Chancellor's Memorandum(²) in reply to ours about a naval and political agreement, Count Metternich somewhat amplified in conversation the Chancellor's Memorandum, explaining in the same way as the Chancellor why the *Tempo* of naval construction, as fixed by the Naval Law in Germany, could not be reduced now, though it might have been reduced two years ago.

He then went on to say that the Chancellor felt that a political arrangement, removing any apprehension in England of aggressive intentions on the part of Germany, would be more effective than anything else. The Chancellor would prefer to have an undertaking from us not to join in a war against Germany, rather than an extended Treaty of Arbitration. The only thing which could cause war between England and Germany would be our joining with France and Russia when the two latter were engaged in war with Germany. The Chancellor thought that apprehension might be removed by some undertaking to which our arrangements with France and Russia would be no obstacle.

I asked whether it was meant by this that Russia and France should be made parties to it, and Count Metternich assented.

I observed that what he had told me agreed with the Chancellor's Memorandum, but made it a little more explicit. That Memorandum had already been sent to the Prime Minister, and it would be considered by the Government.

[I am, &c.]
E. G[REY].

(¹) [*cp. G.P.* XXVIII, p. 418.]
(²) [*v. supra,* pp. 626–7, No. 464, *encl.*]

No. 467.

Sir Edward Grey to Sir F. Bertie.

F.O. 20050/20050/11/18.
(No. 178.)
Sir, Foreign Office, *May* 23, 1911.

In telling M. Cambon to-day that there had been no conversation with the German Emperor on questions of foreign politics,([1]) I informed him of the substance of my conversation on the 18th instant with Count Metternich on the subjects of Morocco and the Bagdad Railway.([2])

I am, &c.
E. GREY.

([1]) [The Emperor's visit to London for the unveiling of the memorial to Queen Victoria lasted from May 15 to May 20. *cp. G.P.* XXVIII, pp. 415–7, and XXIX, pp. 120–1.]

([2]) [Sir Edward Grey's conversation with Count Metternich on the 18th was described to Sir E. Goschen in two despatches of that date. One is printed above (*v.* immediately preceding document); the one relating to Morocco will be printed in *Gooch & Temperley*, Vol. VII.]

No. 468.

Minute by Sir Edward Grey.

F.O. 19557/4451/11/18. Foreign Office, *May* 24, 1911.

I circulate to the Cabinet Committee a Memorandum summarising the history of the negotiations with Germany. It may be useful in considering the point at which we have now arrived.

E. G.

Enclosure in No. 468.

Memorandum respecting Agreement with Germany.([1])

1. In consequence of the last communication from the Imperial Chancellor,([2]) the negotiations with Germany have reached a point at which it may be useful to summarise the several stages through which they have passed.

I.

2. The first intimation of Germany's desire for an arrangement with Great Britain was given by Herr von Kiderlen-Wächter, then Acting Minister for Foreign Affairs, to His Majesty's Ambassador at Berlin, and by him reported in April 1909. The plan then put forward was that of either— Sir E. Goschen, No. 141, April 16, 1909.([³])

  (*a.*) A close political understanding under which an increase in the navy of either Power would be an advantage to both; or
  (*b.*) A convention by which each would engage, for a fixed period—

   (i.) Not to make war against the other;
   (ii.) To join in no coalition directed against the other;
   (iii.) To remain neutral in a war in which the other was engaged with a third Power.

([1]) [The draft of this memorandum was sent to Sir Edward Grey by Sir A. Nicolson with a minute attached in which he attributes its authorship to Sir Eyre Crowe.]

([2]) [*v. supra*, pp. 626–7, No. 464, *encl.*]

([3]) [*v. supra*, pp. 265–6, No. 174.]

3. These suggestions did not recommend themselves to His Majesty's Government. They appeared incompatible with the maintenance of the *ententes* with France and Russia. As, however, they were not put forward officially, nothing was said in reply.

II.

Sir E. Goschen, No. 93, Aug. 21, 1909.([4])

4. In the following August the German Chancellor informed His Majesty's Ambassador that, in response to the declarations repeatedly made by His Majesty's Government in favour of an agreement for the limitation of naval expenditure, he would shortly make proposals for a naval arrangement with Great Britain: at the same time he observed that it would be useless to discuss a naval arrangement unless it formed part of a scheme for a general political understanding, of a nature to preclude the possibility of war between the two countries.

To Sir E. Goschen, No. 317, September 1, 1909 ([5])

5. This seemed to foreshadow a revival in a more formal manner of Herr von Kiderlen's proposals. But with the prospect of Germany seriously approaching the question of a limitation of naval expenditure, it was decided to encourage negotiations on the lines indicated, whilst making reservations as to the difficulties inherent in a political agreement. His Majesty's Government accordingly replied that they would cordially welcome the naval proposals and that they would receive with sympathy any proposals for a political understanding, provided these were not inconsistent with the maintenance of existing friendships. It was at the same time intimated that a naval agreement must precede whatever political understanding was arrived at.

Sir E. Goschen, No. 356, Oct. 15, 1909.([6])

III.

Sir E. Goschen, No. 356, October 15, 1909.

6. A more precise indication of the nature of the naval arrangement contemplated was received in October 1909, when the German Chancellor informed His Majesty's Ambassador that whilst there could be no question of curtailing the programme of construction embodied in the German Navy Law, a retardation of the rate of building might form the subject of discussion. The exact nature of the proposal has never been fully explained, but it was understood that the number of new ships might, in the then current year and that immediately following, be restricted to three instead of the four provided in the programme, the full number being subsequently made up by raising from two to three the keels to be laid down in the later years covered by the programme.

Sir E. Goschen, No. 356, October 15, 1909.

7. This suggestion was accompanied by the declaration that the concession which Germany was ready to make in putting forward naval proposals at all, could only be justified to German public opinion by the announcement that a general *rapprochement* with England had been effected.

To Sir E. Goschen, No. 266, Oct. 28, 1909.([7])

8. A naval agreement which did not carry with it a definite reduction of the total German programme was at this time considered by His Majesty's Government to be of little practical value, and the German Ambassador was accordingly informed that a general political agreement without a diminution of naval expenditure would have no beneficial effect on British public opinion and would indeed be an object of criticism so long as naval expenditure remained undiminished. In order to remove suspicion in England, it was essential to have an agreement which involved a substantial and more or less immediate reduction of naval expenditure.

9. On neither of the points declared by His Majesty's Government to be essential, did the German Government at either this or any later stage modify their attitude, beyond expressing their readiness to let the political and the naval agreements be negotiated simultaneously instead of proceeding with the former before the second was concluded.

([4]) [*v. supra*, p. 283, No. 186.]
([5]) [*v. supra*, p. 288, No. 194.]
([6]) [*v. supra*, pp. 293–300, No. 200.]
([7]) [*v. supra*, pp. 303–4, No. 202.]

IV.

10. In giving more concrete shape to their scheme in November 1909, the German Government proposed that both countries should bind themselves for three or four years not to build more than a stated number of capital ships, but insisted that although the execution of their programme might in this way be retarded, its eventual completion must remain assured. They might, perhaps, though not very willingly, consider an arrangement for the periodical exchange of more detailed information, through the Naval Attachés of the two countries, concerning the ships to be laid down, but no system of mutually checking or controlling such information by inspection could be allowed. Priority was again demanded for a political agreement, of which the scope was now defined as providing that neither Power was to attack the other, and that in case of war of either with third parties the Power not involved should remain neutral. *Sir E. Goschen, No. 371, November 4, 1909.(⁸)* *Sir E. Goschen, No. 371, November 4, 1909.*

11. Consideration of these proposals by His Majesty's Government was unavoidably delayed in consequence of the parliamentary crisis and the resulting general elections in England. But the German Ambassador was once more told, in anticipation of a detailed examination of the scheme suggested, that an arrangement not including a substantial reduction of naval expenditure would be regarded in England as worthless. *To Sir E. Goschen, No. 371, November 17, 1909.(⁹)*

V.

12. In the interval of suspended negotiations the German Government published, and brought to the notice of His Majesty's Ambassador, a declaration to the effect that Germany would never recede from the naval programme as established by law. This was followed up by a further statement in an "inspired" article that an agreement respecting naval construction could only start from the completion of the naval programme. *Sir E. Goschen, No. 414, December 29, 1909.(¹⁰)* *Sir E. Goschen, No. 416, December 31, 1909.(¹¹)*

13. In March 1910 the discussion was resumed. The German Ambassador was informed at the Foreign Office that, as a reduction in naval expenditure was in the opinion of His Majesty's Government essential to any general arrangement, and as the impossibility of altering the German navy law had been reaffirmed, no such an arrangement was possible. It was suggested, however, that some agreement might be arrived at for settling the question of the Bagdad Railway and that of railway concessions in Persia. *To Sir E. Goschen, No. 80, Mar. 31, 1910.(¹²)*

14. The reply of the German Government was to declare that any settlement of these questions must form part of a general political agreement on the lines proposed by them. The naval agreement was on this occasion only mentioned to be dismissed, since—as the German Chancellor said—his naval proposals had not recommended themselves to His Majesty's Government. *Sir E. Goschen, No. 25, Telegraphic, Apr. 10, 1910.(¹³)* *Sir E. Goschen, No. 102, Apr. 11, 1910.(¹⁴)*

15. The decision arrived at on this communication was recorded in the following terms :—

" (i.) We cannot enter into a political understanding with Germany which would separate us from Russia and France and leave us isolated, while the rest of Europe would be obliged to look to Germany.

" (ii.) No understanding with Germany would be appreciated in England unless it meant an arrest of the increase of naval expenditure."

VI.

16. A few months later (July 1910) the German Chancellor expressed apprehension lest words used by Mr. Asquith during the debate on the navy *To Sir E. Goschen, No. 185, July 18, 1910.(¹⁵)*

(⁸) [*v. supra*, pp. 304–9, No. 204.]
(⁹) [*v. supra*, pp. 312–3, No. 205.]
(¹⁰) [*v. supra*, pp. 315–6, No. 208.]
(¹¹) [*v. supra*, pp. 317–8, No. 209.]
(¹²) [*v. supra*, pp. 442–3, No. 337.]
(¹³) [*v. supra*, p. 451, No. 343.]

(¹⁴) [*v. supra*, pp. 454–7, No. 344. The decision quoted in the next paragraph was entered as a minute on this document, *v. supra*, pp. 460–1, No. 344, *min.*]
(¹⁵) [*v. supra*, pp. 496–7, No. 382.]

estimates should mislead public opinion by giving rise to the idea that the German Government had opposed a *non possumus* to proposals put forward by His Majesty's Government for a reduction of armaments, whereas, as a matter of fact, it had been made clear that, in the opinion of the German Government, some alleviation might be effected by temporarily retarding the rate of construction.

To Sir E, Goschen, No. 203, July 29, 1910.(¹⁶)

17. This message was made by His Majesty's Government the occasion for a formal reconsideration of the whole situation, and their views were recorded in a memorandum which was communicated to the Chancellor in August 1910. The memorandum intimated that His Majesty's Government were now prepared to approach more closely to the German position by agreeing—

(*a.*) To abandon their previous contention that any agreement must be based on a reduction of the German naval programme;

(*b.*) To discuss the suggestion for a retardation of the rate of construction without any alteration in the German navy law;

(*c.*) To negotiate an agreement on the basis that the present German programme should not be increased, accompanied by an exchange of information which would ensure that each country was kept informed of the actual progress of shipbuilding in the other.

18. As regards a political understanding, His Majesty's Government maintained their attitude, and formulated their point of view as follows:—

"We have been given to understand that no naval agreement could take place unless it were preceded or accompanied by a political understanding. There would be difficulty in accepting any formula which would give the impression of an understanding different in kind from that which exists between His Majesty's Government and any other European Power, and might therefore affect adversely the relations between His Majesty's Government and certain other Powers, unless these Powers could also be made parties to it. His Majesty's Government have, however, always been ready to give assurances that there is nothing in any agreement between themselves and any other Power which is directed against Germany, and that they themselves have no hostile intentions respecting her."

Sir E. Goschen, Aug. 19, 1910.(¹⁷)

19. When communicating these fresh overtures to the Chancellor, His Majesty's Ambassador took the opportunity of asking for some more precise indication of what was really meant by the retardation of the rate (" *tempo* ") of construction. The answer given was vague; and when further pressed, the Chancellor said the question was one best left to be dealt with by the naval experts. The impression produced on Sir E. Goschen was that the Chancellor himself was not clear in his own mind as to what his proposal amounted to in practice.

Sir E. Goschen, No. 280, Oct. 12, 1910.(¹⁸)

20. The formal reply of the German Government was received in October 1910. It recalled that they had from the outset expressed their willingness to discuss a retardation of the rate of shipbuilding, without, however, throwing any fresh light on the exact nature of the arrangement contemplated.

21. With reference to the British proposal that negotiations should be resumed on the basis that the German naval programme was to be completed, but not further enlarged, the German Government asked what equivalent engagement would be taken by His Majesty's Government.

22. The suggested agreement respecting a periodical exchange of naval information was, in deference to the desire of His Majesty's Government, accepted in principle, although the Chancellor expressed himself very sceptically as to its practical value.

(¹⁶) [*v. supra*, pp. 501–2, No. 387, and *encl.*]

(¹⁷) [This reference is apparently to Sir E. Goschen's private letter printed *supra*, pp. 512–3, No. 395.]

(¹⁸) [*v. supra*, pp. 521–5, No. 400, and *encl.*]

VII.

23. The consideration of the German answer had to be deferred owing to the intervention of fresh general elections in England, but a preliminary reply was sent merely to explain the British point of view in regard to the special political questions which the Chancellor had touched upon. To Sir E. Goschen, No. 312 November 23 1910.([19])

24. In the meantime the German Emperor, at an audience granted to Sir E. Goschen, stated with marked emphasis that he had no intention of allowing, and would on no conditions ever consent to, any agreement binding Germany not to enlarge her naval programme. Herr von Kiderlen, the German Secretary of State for Foreign Affairs, to whom Sir E. Goschen pointed out the discrepancy between the attitude on this question taken up by the Emperor and by the Chancellor respectively, endeavoured to explain away His Imperial Majesty's words by suggesting they had been misunderstood. A promise was given to have the matter definitely cleared up, but nothing has since been heard on the subject, and the Emperor's declaration has not been disavowed. Sir E. Goschen, No. 288, Oct. 16, 1910.([20])

VIII.

25. Negotiations were resumed, after the elections, in January 1911.

26. The German Government having consented to proceed with the proposed agreement for an exchange of naval information independently of any political understanding being previously arrived at, Sir E. Goschen communicated to them the views which the British Admiralty had formulated as to the points to be covered by such an agreement. These did not include any mention of the desired engagement on Germany's part not to increase the naval programme, as His Majesty's Government desired that the exchange of information should be treated separately and apart from any general agreement respecting reduction of naval expenditure and any political understanding possibly to be connected therewith. To Sir E. Goschen, No. 333, December 16, 1910,([21]) and No. 25, Jan. 27, 1911.([22])
Sir E. Goschen No. 5, Telegraphic, Feb. 7, 1911.([23]
Goschen, No. 10, Telegraphic, Feb. 8, 1911.([24]

27. As regards the political understanding, His Majesty's Government advanced a step further by submitting to the German Government the following considerations as possibly affording a basis of discussion for the purpose of settling the terms of an arrangement :— To Sir E. Goschen, No. 60, Mar. 8, 1911.([25]

" The arrangements which His Majesty's Government have entered into with other Powers have not hitherto been based upon a general political formula. They have had their origin in certain specific questions which are defined in the agreements, and on which, happily, a satisfactory understanding had been reached. An arrangement, therefore, as foreshadowed by the Imperial Chancellor, embodying a general political formula, might be considered as something more comprehensive, far-reaching, and intimate than any arrangement that His Majesty's Government have with any other Power, short of actual alliance. In particular, such a construction of any new agreement made by His Majesty's Government might tend to impair their relations with France and Russia. The almost continuous friction and constantly recurring discord, which had lasted for years between these two Powers and the United Kingdom, have during the last seven years been transformed into relations of friendship and confidence which His Majesty's Government are naturally anxious to preserve. They have, in the last few years, seen with satisfaction the settlement of certain differences, and a consequent improvement of relations, between each of these Powers and the German Government. To-day His Majesty's Government believe

([19]) [v. supra, pp. 546–54, No. 414, and encl.]
([20]) [v. supra, pp. 530–3, No. 403.]
([21]) [v. supra, pp. 575–6, No. 425.]
([22]) [v. supra, pp. 579–80, No. 428.]

([23]) [v. supra, p. 584, No. 434.]
([24]) [v. supra, p. 585, No. 435.]
([25]) [v. supra, pp. 598–600, No. 444, and encl.]

that the special interests, which have led to the present grouping of Powers, do not involve anything in the nature of opposition and still less of hostile purpose among them. But they feel that in any general formula care must be taken to avoid on the one hand undue vagueness and on the other the risk of possible misunderstanding. With this object His Majesty's Government think that an endeavour to come to an agreement upon certain specific questions should form part of the negotiations.''

28. Among the specific questions so indicated, the Bagdad Railway and railways in Persia were mentioned.

29. In thus explicitly assenting to the German view, hitherto combated, that some wider agreement was essential to any arrangement about naval expenditure, His Majesty's Government declared they assumed that the discussion of naval expenditure would not be postponed, but would proceed so that an agreement on that point should be simultaneous with the conclusion of any political understanding.

IX.

Sir E. Goschen, No. 83, Mar. 30, 1911. (²⁶)   30. After a brief delay, the German Government presented a memorandum embodying specific proposals for settling the terms of the agreement respecting the exchange of naval information. The views of the British Admiralty were in the main adopted, but a stipulation was added that the information should be exchanged at a particular date once a year, and should include a statement of the number of ships to be laid down in each year by the respective Governments, from which there must be no departure during that year.

Admiralty, May [16], 1911. (²⁷)   31. His Majesty's Government, after examining these proposals, have adhered to the view that this element of restriction of numbers ought to form part not of the agreement respecting the exchange of information, but of a wider arrangement for a reduction of naval expenditure. Exception has also been taken to the particular date proposed for the exchange. These criticisms are about to be communicated to the German Government through His Majesty's Ambassador at Berlin.

Sir E. Goschen, No. 135, May 10, 1911 (²⁸)   32. The German answer on the subject of the general naval and political understanding is conveyed in the despatch from Sir E. Goschen now under consideration.

Foreign Office, May 20, 1911.

(²⁶) [*v. supra*, pp. 612–4, No. 457.]
(²⁷) [*v. supra*, pp. 629–30, No. 465.]
(²⁸) [*v. supra*, pp. 625–7, No. 464, and *encl.*]

No. 469.

Sir Edward Grey to Sir E. Goschen.

F.O. 21107/4451/11/18.
(No. 121.) Secret.
Sir,   *Foreign Office, June 1, 1911.*
Y[our] E[xcellency] should take an early opportunity of seeing the Chancellor and giving to him the enclosed memorandum in reply to that given by him on the 24th March.(¹)
You should explain to the Chancellor that we are most anxious now to arrive at a practical agreement in this matter, and that the memorandum, though

(¹) [*v. supra*, p. 610, No. 455. The Memorandum, communicated by Sir E. Goschen on June 9, is printed in *G.P.* XXVIII, pp. 419–20.]

restricted to a statement of the points in discussion, has been drawn up with an earnest desire to conclude it and to adjust our own arrangements to meet the German suggestions.

[I am, &c.
E. GREY.]

Enclosure in No. 469.

Memorandum.

His Majesty's Government have learnt with satisfaction that the Imperial Government adhere to the proposal for a periodical exchange of naval information.

The Imperial Government express the opinion that the reciprocity of exchange will only be completely guaranteed if the communications to be made on both sides are delivered at the same time, and they propose that this simultaneous exchange should be made annually in the period between the 1st October and the 15th November. It is believed that these dates are suggested as being those within which the German naval estimates for the year are printed and published: the naval estimates of the British Government, on the other hand, are usually not printed and published before the 15th March in each year; and while accepting in principle the proposal for simultaneous exchange, His Majesty's Government would suggest that the exchange would more properly be made in the period between the 15th November and the 15th March.

It would be impossible, however, for the information at this date to cover more than the bare number of ships of each type included in the programme for the ensuing year: questions of tonnage, speed, and armament being subject to modification up to the moment of laying down, the exchange of information on these matters would necessarily have to be made in each case when the keel is first laid.

His Majesty's Government further understand, from the remarks made by the Secretary of State for Foreign Affairs to His Majesty's Ambassador, that the Imperial Government consider that the information exchanged, so far as it relates to the number of ships to be laid down in each year by the two Governments, should be of a binding nature. This proviso would seem more relevant to an arrangement for mutual limitation or reduction of naval expenditure, such as has hitherto been dealt with as part of the larger negotiations, distinct from the mere exchange of information: but His Majesty's Government agree that when information has once been communicated, there should be no variation of the programme thus made known without previous and further information being given to the other party.

With regard to the periodical visits of naval attachés to dockyards and private yards, His Majesty's Government are in principle prepared to agree to any suitable arrangement involving strict reciprocity, and they attach great importance to this, apart and distinct from any other arrangements, as a means of setting at rest in future any apprehensions that may arise in the public mind as to the respective progress of the shipbuilding programme in either country.

Foreign Office, June 1, 1911.

No. 470.

Sir E. Goschen to Sir Edward Grey.

F.O. 21735/21735/11/18.
(No. 153.) Confidential.   *Berlin*, D. *June* 2, 1911.
Sir,   R. *June* 6, 1911.
    I have the honour to forward, herewith, a despatch, as marked in the margin,
which I have received from Captain Watson, Naval Attaché to this Embassy, relating
to the Eleventh General Meeting of the German Navy League.
                                     I have, &c.
                                     W. E. GOSCHEN.

Enclosure in No. 470.

Captain Watson to Sir E. Goschen.

(No. 20.) Confidential.
Sir,   *Berlin, May* 30, 1911.
    I have the honour to forward report of eleventh general meeting of the German
Navy League,([1]) which took place on the 28th May last.
    I have before submitted to you that the Navy League, as heading the Large
Navy party in Germany, are in favour of a naval policy which will earlier replace
the cruisers of "Hertha" class by battle-ship cruisers.
    I submit now to your notice the resolution, unanimously arrived at by the Navy
League without debate, from which there can be no doubt as to the nature of pressure
that will be brought to bear on the Government to build three armoured ships per
annum from 1912 on. The chief points of Admiral Köster's speech are shown on
pp. 200 and 201, and the resolution as passed on p. 201.
    2. I believe there is not the slightest doubt that three armoured ships per annum
will be built, but consider it possible that this may not take place before the estimates
for 1913 are prepared. The estimates for 1912 are published before the general
election takes place, and the Government may wish to adhere to the present Navy
Law until after the elections for political reasons, and also to allay the suspicions of
England for a little longer.
    The earlier replacement proposed constitutes an alteration of the Navy Law, in
respect of the age limits originally ordered. I submit my conviction that, if this or
similar alterations take place, the only way to bring the German Large Navy party
and German people to their sense of proportion is by an answering addition to British
naval strength.
    3. I submit that the party in favour of naval increase, of which I have before
reported in my letters from October last, is becoming more active as the preparation
of the next naval estimates approaches. Further, that it is probable the Government
will yield amiably to it, if not this year, then the next.
    4. It is to be hoped that representatives of Reichs-Marine-Amt were at the
meeting of the Navy League, but as they send representatives to all interesting
meetings this is of no particular importance in the case of this special resolution,
though it shows naval authorities' close interest with league generally. The positions
which His Royal Highness Prince Henry of Prussia and Gross-Admiral Köster occupy
in regard to the league, lead one to infer that the association of it with the naval
authorities of the present day is considerably closer than is acknowledged by the
German authorities, and makes the league more of a Government instrument and
more far-reaching in its influence than the British Navy League.
                   I have, &c.
                     HUGH WATSON, *Naval Attaché.*

([1]) [Not reproduced.]

No. 471.

Sir C. Spring-Rice to Sir Edward Grey.

F.O. 22449/4451/11/18.
(No. 94.) Confidential.   Stockholm, D. *June* 5, 1911.
Sir,   R. *June* 10, 1911.

I venture to think that it may be of interest to report a conversation which I have recently had with an American gentleman who has been lecturing in Berlin in pursuance of the arrangement for the interchange of professors between American and German Universities.

He tells me that his stay in Berlin and his intercourse with his colleagues at the university have upset all his preconceived notions of German professorial life and thought. Speaking of Berlin, where he lectured (and carefully excluding other parts of Germany with which he was less acquainted) he could say that the university professor looked to the Government for all hopes of advancement, titles and decorations and was guided in all his out spoken opinions by the spirit which ruled in the Prussian bureaucracy of which he formed an inferior and subordinate part. With regard to foreign policy and the expansion of *Deutschtum* the spirit which prevailed in the Prussian bureaucracy and which was fully shared by the professors was one of pure and unqualified aggression in which questions of right played no part whatever. It was no longer the Bismarckian doctrine that force was stronger than justice, but a new doctrine that force *was* justice. With regard to the subject nationalities, embraced in the German Empire, Poles, Frenchmen and Danes, it was openly maintained that their language and their national traditions must be relentlessly destroyed. As to the lesser nationalities, neighbours to Germany, the official view appeared to be that their independence could be allowed, so long as it was not used in a manner inconsistent with German interests, but that, inasmuch as Germany's power and organisation were superior to theirs, it would be a wiser and better course for all parties concerned if the administration of these lesser countries and their possessions passed to stronger and more competent hands.

With regard to England and America there appeared to prevail a deep-rooted antagonism, not of race so much as point of view, appearing frequently in every sort of accusation, innuendo and misconstruction, as if the Anglo-American idea of Government as much as the English and American Commonwealths, were the obstacles which prevented Germany coming to her rights.

My informant added that the longer he stayed in Germany and the closer was his intercourse with the professorial class, the stronger grew his conviction that the idea which ruled the great bureaucracy of Germany was that the world must be ruled, that Germany can and shall rule it; and that all opposition must be "ridden down." In his view these opinions, which he characterized as a return to mere barbarism, are not those of the great majority of the German nation, nor (he is convinced) of the Emperor himself. But they are the opinions of that class which has been in the past, and which is still, dominant in politics : and what from his point of view is the most important aspect of this question, the bureaucracy has gained complete ascendency over that body of professors whose enlightenment and independence has been so long the glory of Germany.

My informant has recently been on a lecturing tour in several countries in Europe and he tells me that he is a good deal struck by the ignorance which appears often to prevail in the most enlightened circles, as to the movement of opinion in dominant quarters in central Europe. He added that what struck him more painfully was the fact that where ignorance did not prevail, he had often found in its stead a sort of dull acquiescence.

I trust that, for obvious reasons, this despatch may be treated as confidential.

       I have, &c.
         CECIL SPRING RICE.

No. 472.

Count de Salis to Sir Edward Grey.

F.O. 26212/4451/11/18.

(No. 187.)   *Berlin, D. July 1, 1911.*

Sir,   *R. July 5, 1911.*

I have the honour to transmit to you herewith copy and translation of a Memorandum handed to me by Herr von Kiderlen-Waechter, in reply to the Memorandum transmitted in your secret Despatch No. 121 of June 1st 1911.([1])

I have, &c.

J. DE SALIS.

Enclosure in No. 472.

Aide-Mémoire communicated to Count de Salis by Herr von Kiderlen-Waechter(.[2])

(Translation.)   *[June 27, 1911.]*

1. The Imperial Government agree to the proposal of the British Government according to which

a. the exchange of information would be postponed to the period between the 15th of November and the 15th of March,

b. the bare number of ships of the programme for the following year would be communicated at this date with the proviso that as soon as the information has been communicated there should be no variation of the programme thus made known without previous and further information being given to the other party,

c. the exchange of technical information, as detailed in Nos. 1 to 3 of the *Aide-Mémoire* from the Imperial Government of the 24th of March, 1911([3]) would *as a matter of principle not be made till the time of the laying of the keel.

2. The Imperial Government note that the British Government agree in principle to the German proposal that the communications should be delivered simultaneously. As the exchange of information is to be made at the time of laying the keels, but as the keels in both countries will not be laid at the same time, and, moreover, as several keels will be laid in each year, the Imperial Government consider that further discussion as regards this date is desirable, and are of opinion that the decision as to this point would best be left to the respective naval authorities.

In order to maintain the principle of complete reciprocity, the Imperial Government are of opinion that it should be agreed that after the technical information respecting a ship has been communicated no alterations in the details thus communicated should be made until after the other State has been informed of them.

The Imperial Government entirely agree with the statements of the British Government respecting the visits of Naval Attachés to dockyards and suggest that the details of these visits should be agreed upon by the respective naval authorities.

MINUTES.

This should in the first instance go to the Admiralty for their observations and any suggestions they may have to make.

My own opinion is that this is not the moment for continuing these discussions, and that we should not be in a hurry to answer.

Under the head of paragraph 2, the German memorandum proposes that the settling of certain details should be "left to the respective naval authorities." I take this to mean that the

([1]) [*v. supra,* p. 637, No. 469, *encl.*]

([2]) [The German original, communicated to Count de Salis on June 27, is printed in *G.P.* XXVIII, pp. 423–4.]

([3]) [*v. supra,* p. 610, No. 455.]

* The German word is "grundsätzlich." The word used in the corresponding passage in the English memorandum of June 1st is "necessarily."

proposal is to conclude an arrangement which provides, among other things, that the details in question shall be left to be so settled thereafter. If this is what the German gov[ernmen]t means, I am of opinion that the proposal ought not to be accepted. We have had repeated and unhappy experience of the practice of concluding agreements and leaving some essential part to be arranged subsequently. It is to my mind an absolutely unsound method, and almost invariably leads to Great Britain being jockeyed out of what she thought had been settled—I need only recall what occurred in regard to the stipulations about Zanzibar and about the Newfoundland fisheries in the Anglo-French agreements of 1904.

The only prudent and safe course is to have everything settled and agreed to before anything is signed.

Qu[ery.] Point this out briefly in writing to the Admiralty, and send copy of the correspondence to Berlin.

E. A. C.
July 5.

The agreement should be complete with all details embodied in it. Any other arrangement would give opportunities for wrangles and accusations of bad faith.

W. L.

I quite agree with the above minutes. We could comm[unica]te with the Admiralty—but can well defer continuing this negotiation until other more important matters have been settled.

A. N.

Send to Admiralty as proposed.

E. G.

No. 473.

Foreign Office to Admiralty.

F.O. 26212/4451/11/18.
(Secret.)

Sir, *Foreign Office, July* 10, 1911.

With reference to the F[oreign] O[ffice] letter (12050) of Ap[ril] 6th last,([1]) I am directed by Sec[retar]y Sir E. Grey to transmit to you, to be laid before the Lords Commissioners of the Admiralty, a memorandum([2]) which has been received from the German Gov[ernmen]t in reply to the last communication from H[is] M[ajesty's] G[overnment]([3]) on the subject of the exchange of naval information.

It will be observed that under the head of paragraph 2) the German Gov[ernmen]t propose that the settlement of certain details should be left to the respective naval authorities. If this means that the details in question shall be left to be so settled after the arrangement between the two Gov[ernmen]ts has been concluded in outline, Sir E. Grey is of opinion that it would be imprudent to accede to the proposal. He considers that the proper course would be to have all details settled before any agreement is concluded or signed.

Sir E. Grey would be glad to be furnished with the views of the Lords Commissioners on the German memorandum, but in view of recent political events it may be convenient to postpone replying to it for the present.

I am, &c.
W. LANGLEY.

([1]) [*v. supra*, p. 617, No. 459.]
([2]) [*v.* immediately preceding document, *encl.*]
([3]) [*v. supra*, p. 637, No. 469, *encl.*]

No. 474.

Admiralty to Foreign Office.

F.O. 33264/4451/11/18.
(Confidential.)
Sir,   *Admiralty, August* 21, 1911.

With reference to your letter of the 13th ultimo, No. 26212/11,(¹) on the subject of the exchange of Naval information with the German Government, I am commanded by my Lords Commissioners of the Admiralty to acquaint you, for the information of the Secretary of State for Foreign Affairs, that they agree (*a*) that the bare number of ships of the programme for the following year be communicated annually with the proviso that as soon as this information has been communicated, there should be no variation of the programme thus made known without previous and further information being given to the other party, (*b*) that the above communication be made at a convenient date in the period between the 15th November and the 15th March.

2. As regards the date for the exchange of technical information, namely the dimensions of the ships to be laid down, the protection, armament, speed and horse power of the ships, and the dates of their laying down and completion, my Lords agree that there might be some difficulty in arranging for strict reciprocity owing to the indefiniteness of the date of laying the keel and this difficulty would not be removed by leaving the matter to the respective Naval Authorities. To meet this difficulty my Lords would suggest that provision should be made for this technical information to be communicated when the number of ships to be laid down in the *next* programme is given, *e.g.* at the time when the two Governments communicate the number of ships to be laid down in the 1912–13 programme, the technical details of those belonging to the 1911–12 programme would be given.

I am, &c.
C. I. THOMAS.

(¹) [*v.* immediately preceding document. The letter is dated July 10.]

No. 475.

Sir F. Bertie to Sir Edward Grey.

F.O. 34109/34109/11/17.
(No. 377.)   Secret.   *Paris, D. August* 25, 1911.
Sir,   R. *August* 29, 1911.

I have the honour to transmit to you herewith a despatch as marked in the margin which I have received from Colonel Fairholme, Military Attaché to this Embassy reporting a conversation with General Joffre, Chief of the French General Staff, respecting strategical problems which would arise in a war between Germany and France and other matters.

I have, &c.
FRANCIS BERTIE.

Enclosure in No. 475.

Colonel Fairholme to Sir F. Bertie.

(No. 12.)   Confidential.
Sir,   *Paris, August* 24, 1911.

I have the honour to report to Your Excellency that I was to-day received by General Joffre, the newly appointed Chief of the French General Staff, who, under the recent reorganisation of the High Command, occupies the position of supreme head of the main French Armies in Peace and War.

General Joffre, who took part in the defence of Paris as a Sub-Lieutenant in the Siege Artillery, and was transferred to the Engineers after the war, has seen service in several Colonial Expeditions, including Tonkin, in all of which he rendered eminent services. He commanded the IInd Army Corps (Amiens) up to last year, when he was appointed a member of the Supreme Council of War.

I was favourably impressed by the personality of the new Chief, who is a big, square-built man, quiet in manner, but with an unmistakable air of confidence and resolution. He is 59 years of age.

I found the General extremely well-disposed towards England, and anxious to maintain the cordial and intimate relations which have existed of late between the two Armies. He expressed his intention of affording all possible facilities for the interchange of information, and of visits by French and British officers, with a view to mutual improvement and understanding.

When the first reserve had worn off, he became more communicative than most French Generals in responsible positions, and it may interest Your Excellency to know what he said about the present political and military situation.

General Joffre considers that, though relations with Germany are undoubtedly very strained, ("très tendues"), the principal danger of the protracted negotiations lies in the possibility of incidents occurring which might inflame public opinion on either side.

The French Military Attaché in Berlin, who was formerly Chief Staff Officer to General Joffre, had, in letters to his late commander, for some time past predicted the present difficulties with regard to Morocco, but, in his opinion, Germany does not want war at the present moment. He thinks it probable that an unsatisfactory agreement, wanting in finality, will be patched up. He writes, however, that the German General Staff is very busy just now with war preparations.

On the French side, General Joffre said that he and his Staff have been, and are still, hard at work settling the details of their plans of campaign, which, he stated, will be ready in every particular in a few days' time.

The General then went on to discuss the stragetical problem.

The one unknown factor is whether the Germans mean to come through Belgium or not. "I wish I knew that," he observed, "and I wish I knew that they intend doing so; it would be better for us. It would greatly hamper our dispositions if we did not know their intentions in this respect by about the fourth day of mobilisation, as it would be difficult to get back any considerable force in time for employment in the main theatre of operations which had been originally sent to oppose an advance through Belgium. Recent German preparations, construction of railways and detraining platforms, &c., point to an intention to move considerable bodies of troops in these regions."

The new Chief attaches the very greatest importance to the co-operation of a British expeditionary force, which concentrating somewhere between Douai and Cambrai, and falling on the right flank of the German advance, might produce great, and even decisive, results. But it would have to be sent early in the day; its intervention, for instance, on the 18th day of the French mobilisation, might not prove a bit too soon. As regards the provision by the French authorities of the requisite railway transport to convey the British Contingent to the points of concentration which might ultimately be fixed on, he anticipates no difficulty, even should all the six British Infantry Divisions be dispatched.

He stated that arrangements have recently been made by which the carrying powers of the French railways in War have been considerably increased.

"In any case," he said, "Germany must pour a large force into Alsace and Lorraine, as if they allowed us to gain a footing there the populations of both provinces would rise. *This we know for certain.* And then every possible difficulty would be created for their transport, &c."

I gathered that, if the Germans should advance in force viâ Belgium, the French plan would be to hold them in check on that flank, and to attack vigorously on Alsace and Lorraine.

General Joffre remarked that if the Germans did not attack in force through Belgium, the front of contact between the two armies would become very restricted for such large forces.

I ventured to suggest that such a contingency might not prove disadvantageous to France in view of the notorious superiority of the German forces in numbers.

"That superiority," General Joffre replied, " does not trouble me very much. It would only amount to two or three Army Corps. Against the German Reserve Corps we have our Reserve Divisions, and we can count on the active intervention of the Russian army, which would be on the move certainly before the 30th day of our mobilisation. But we should very much like to know what Austria would do."

On my mentioning Italy, the General said very positively, "Italy will make no move. Her interests lie on our side, not on that of Germany and Austria."

Speaking of the abandonment of the French Army Manœuvres, which has now been definitely decided on, General Joffre said that this is due to the prevalence of foot-and-mouth disease in the North of France; from his manner, and from the details he gave me, I am satisfied that this, and not the possibility of war, is the true reason for the change of plans.

He informed me that the manœuvres of the VIIth Army Corps, (Besançon), which, like the VIth, is a frontier corps of three Infantry Divisions, will be transformed into Army Manœuvres, but on a smaller scale than those originally contemplated, and that the Foreign Officers will be invited to witness these instead of those which have now been cancelled.

I have, &c.
W. E. FAIRHOLME *Colonel*
Military Attaché.

No. 476.

Sir E. Goschen to Sir Edward Grey.

F.O. 38377/4451/11/18.
(No. 295.) Confidential.   *Berlin,* D. *September* 28, 1911.
Sir,   R. *October* 2, 1911.

I have the honour to transmit to you herewith a despatch which I have received from Captain Watson, Naval Attaché to His Majesty's Embassy, in regard to a report that it is proposed that German Naval Estimates should in future be published in March each year instead of in November.

Captain Watson points out the significance of this change, and I would invite your attention to his observations.

I have, &c.
W. E. GOSCHEN.

Enclosure in No. 476.

Captain Watson to Sir E. Goschen.

(No. 25.) Confidential.
Sir,   *Berlin, September* 27, 1911.

In my immediately preceding letters([1]) and my letter No. 26 of this date,([2]) I have had the honour to call your attention to the efforts of the Navy League and others in influential positions to secure a more rapid replacement of cruisers.

I would bring to your notice that I have just heard confidentially, on the best authority, that it is under consideration, and will probably be brought into force, that

---

([1]) [cp. *supra*, p. 638, No. 470, encl.]
([2]) [Not reproduced.]

the next German naval estimates and those in succeeding years should be published in March, and not in November as heretofore.

It is within recent memory that in the negotiations between England and Germany as to interchange of information the latter country desired to obtain a date for such exchange as would suit their usual date of publication, *i.e.*, November. This would incidentally do away with the advantage England at present derives from issuing her naval estimates at a later date than Germany, viz., March.

As His Majesty the Emperor remarked to me on the 5th June last, in a chaffing manner, " Ah, yes; you want to fix a date which will enable you to first find out what we do and then lay down something to beat us."

His Majesty was, in my opinion, only voicing the ideas of his Minister.

It will be further remembered that Germany subsequently acquiesced in the English date for the exchange of information, namely, the date of or about the production of the English estimates. The reason for acquiescence appears more clear now. It is unnecessary for me to point out the disadvantage the production of the English naval estimates will be under if the German proposal I report is brought into force, and my information goes to show it probably will be.

I respectfully submit that the evidence of German naval politics and activity of past few years leads one to the opinion that the authorities concerned in this country, from His Majesty downwards, have been steadily building up the German fleet, with admirable consistency and political strategy, to rival the English fleet, if not alone, at least with the aid of naval allies in the Mediterranean.

I submit the proposal now reported is principally designed to further the advantage she has gained, in the hope that the English Government will not vote large naval estimates when the advantage of comparison with the formerly earlier-produced German estimates is no longer available.

The shipbuilding resources of Germany have become so efficient, and are known to be capable of such rapid further development, that their possibility of output renders it possible for that country to overtake a narrow margin possessed by a naval rival.

Bearing on this point, I would submit to your notice that I have recently been informed, on what appears to be a good source, that an amalgamation of Erhardt's gun, armour, and ammunition firm with Krupps is planned, and is likely to be carried out very shortly. The advantage of a second source of supply for guns to the German navy is obvious, in view of its largely increasing size and the frequent changes made in present time in matériel.

Under the proposed alteration of date for production of German estimates, it would appear that the possession of a very considerable margin, or double Germany's possible annual number of ships to be laid down, with a further increase if Germany's estimates reveal that the increase asked for by Navy League, and influentially supported, is to be made, is necessary to avert the possibility of her rapidly gaining on us in one year, and following up her advantage in the next from her own ship-building resources, or from those of her allies.

2. Though trenching on matters which concern higher authority, I would bring to your Excellency's notice that after the completion of the present navy law, the German rule of replacement of ships makes it necessary for her to build three armoured ships per annum merely to replace. This number is exclusive of any increase of numbers that may arise out of the Navy League's present proposals, as reported on in my letters No. 21 of the 3rd June last, and No. 26 of this date.([3])

I submit that after the completion of the navy law, England will have a formidable task to meet the German replacement building with an added margin of superiority; and that if she is called on to further meet a German increase, or increase on the part of Germany's allies, it will be a very formidable financial task.

Prior to 1917, it is possible for England to make her superiority one that leaves no doubt to the German people that we intend to retain the superiority we have

([3]) [Not reproduced.]

possessed in the past. Doubt in the German mind on this point has assisted her authorities to press forward with her fleet development.

The increase of the German navy, the steady replacement of not only each German ship, but also small armoured ships by large, the growth in strength of the navies of her allies are factors which present themselves to one's mind.

The close relations between Germany's and Austria's navies are shown by the visits this year of the German Emperor to the Austrian squadron, and of the Archduke Ferdinand of Austria and the Austrian Minister of Marine to the German fleet at Kiel; by a German naval attaché being appointed for Vienna alone, and an Austrian naval attaché to Berlin; and by other evidences of close naval confidences.

Of the German naval relations to Turkey during past year, and of her naval connections with Sweden, Norway, and Denmark, I am reporting in a later letter.

3. I submit the proposed change of date for production of German naval estimates arises out of the recent negotiations for interchange of information. The German naval authorities, having failed to secure an advantage by getting England's consent to her date, now propose to alter their own date for publication of estimates to the English date.

I have been gradually led to the opinion by previous incidents that, though no doubt the German naval officers would like a better understanding with British naval officers, the German admiralty authorities have only used the negotiations to gain an advantage.

I would bring to your notice that no one who has closely studied the actions of the German naval authorities of past few years can help being struck by the clever way they have manipulated events and German public opinion to their advantage, and submit that the clever series of pretexts and methods of allaying English doubt and awakening the German people are clearly visible if a retrospect is made of German naval politics during past few years.

Their discouraging attitude towards an agreement for lessening of armaments is a matter of history of recent growth. Negotiations with Germany on a question of naval strength appear to be of little use unless the English strength is so great as to stop Germany increasing.

I submit the people of Germany are being led along the road of naval rivalry with England, not yet realising where and to what cost it is leading them, by the influential though small party of Admiral von Tirpitz, the navy, the armament interests, and the Navy League, acting under the support of His Majesty the Emperor.

Their sense of proportion and cost will only be restored by the magnitude of English naval estimates for several years running.

It is unnecessary for me to further allude to the support a stronger German naval policy will derive from the Moroccan affairs. The German people are, or have been, inflamed against England. I heard a few days ago that they are so inflamed against us that the "Man in the street is talking of taking that little island in three or four years' time."

I have, &c.
HUGH WATSON,
Captain and Naval Attaché.

MINUTES.

The change in the date of publication of estimates is of great importance and will have to be carefully borne in mind if and when the suspended negotiations are resumed. The anti-English feeling in Germany is at present so violent that there seems little prospect of their successful resumption for some time.

Captain Watson's subsequent remarks, when one has grappled with his peculiarities of style and original punctuation, emphasize again what has so often been brought out in F[oreign] O[ffice] minutes.

G. H. V.
2/10/11.

In view of the present situation and of the emphatic warning given by Captain Watson as to German intentions and motives in putting their hand to the proposed agreement, it is for earnest consideration whether we should proceed at all with its signature.

The whole object, so far as H[is] M[ajesty's] G[overnment] were concerned, was to promote an arrangement by which the element of suspicion should be removed from the naval dealings of the two Powers with each other. It would be useless to pretend now that this object can be attained in this manner. The German naval authorities will, as Captain Watson observes, use and manipulate the agreement so as to serve some peculiar advantage to themselves and they will endeavour to entangle us in something that will prove to us embarrassing.

It has already been decided to defer any further action in this matter for the present, and it will be well to remain inactive indefinitely.

E. A. C.
Oct. 2.

We can only wait for better times before going on, I should say.

F. A. C.
3/10.
A. N.
E. G.

No. 477.

Sir E. Goschen to Sir Edward Grey.

F.O. 43699/38119/11/18.
(No. 357.)

Berlin, D. November 3, 1911.
R. November 6, 1911.

. . . .([1]) In the course of conversation the Chancellor alluded somewhat bitterly to the fact that our previous negotiations, in which he had shown so much good will and anxiety for good relations with England had been twice interrupted by His Majesty's Government and that he was still waiting for an answer with regard to the exchange of naval information. I did not think it advisable to go deeply into this subject and only said that if there had been interruptions in our negotiations they had been owing to unavoidable circumstances which had been fully explained at the time. . . . .([1])

[I have, &c.
W. E. GOSCHEN.]

([1]) [The rest of this long despatch will be printed in *Gooch & Temperley*, Vol. VII.]

No. 478.

Admiralty to Foreign Office.

F.O. 49986/4451/11/18.
Secret.
Sir,

Admiralty, December 12, 1911.

Adverting to your letter, No. 26212, of the 13th July,([1]) and Admiralty reply of the 18th August, relative to a suggested exchange of naval information between this country and Germany, I am commanded by my Lords Commissioners of the Admiralty to state that they have recently reviewed this question with an earnest desire to arrive at a useful and practical result, which should be convenient to the two Governments and beneficial to the relations between the two countries.

2. My Lords do not see any difficulties of an insuperable character in the exchange of technical information, whether as regards substance or time. The wider publicity given to details of new construction in England renders the information probably less valuable to Germany than to this country, and my Lords would not allow any question of mere procedure to stand in the way of an agreement, the

([1]) [*v. supra*, p. 641, No. 473. The letter was dated July 10, 1911.]

object of which is to remove uncertainty and to disarm suspicion. It should, however, be recognised that the difficulties of arranging for an interchange of technical details increase markedly as the details become more minute. More room for differences as to the bases necessary for fair comparisons arise at every step. There is a danger that this in itself might become the vantage ground of suspicions and disputes, while all the time the value of the information for the main purpose in hand would steadily diminish. They recognise moreover that what may be called the professional secrets of construction, which are the signs of the progress of naval science in either country, are in a peculiar sense the private property of the respective Governments, and that it would be discouraging to the designers and architects of either nation were an arrangement come to by which each new contrivance should be immediately imparted to the naval authorities of a foreign Power. In strongly supporting the policy of a fair and reasonable exchange of naval information, my Lords have never had in mind an attempt to pry into or a willingness to disclose the special features upon which naval experts rely for the superiority of this or that point in the construction of any vessel. They are quite content to assume that every ship in each class will represent the last word of the naval science of the constructing Power upon the subject. What they wish to know, and what they are perfectly willing to disclose, is not so much the technical quality and specifications of the different vessels, as the scale of warlike preparation upon which the Admiralties of the two countries have embarked; and it is with the sole object of freeing this vital matter from the atmosphere of doubt and anxiety with which it has been from time to time surrounded, that my Lords put forward the following observations.

3.   They do not seek to know the intentions of the German Government so far as the future is concerned, or to lead that Government into any arrangement which would fetter reciprocally the free discretion of either Power to alter, vary, diminish or extend their naval programme. They are concerned with the exact situation in fact at given and agreed periods in each year. They wish to know how many vessels of each class or type are being constructed at such given times in all the yards, public and private of the German Empire, whether for the German Government or foreign sale. They are prepared similarly to satisfy the German Government beyond doubt or question as to the general position of all warship construction within the United Kingdom. What they desire is, indeed, an exchange of simple and easily verifiable facts. It will be sufficient if at any dates convenient to the two Governments when communicating the programme for the ensuing year, the number of ships of each class upon whose construction or preliminary preparation for construction money is actually being spent, could be made known to each other by the two Governments, if the dates of their laying-down, launching, and completion, could be exchanged, and if the first two conditions could be tested by the periodical and reciprocal visits of the naval attachés, who should be permitted at the agreed periods to inspect the building slips in all the yards capable of constructing war vessels.

4.   So far as further information upon the character of the vessels in each class is concerned, my Lords do not think that there would be any difficulty in arriving at an understanding. The main data of the ships building or to be built, such as are published in the annual Dickinson Return, i.e., displacement, horse-power, and the number of guns constituting the primary armament, could readily be exchanged. To this might be added with great advantage a simple statement of the amount of money which, according to the contract price, was to be expended on the hulls, armament, and the engines, respectively. The last, without trenching at all upon the peculiarities of construction, would probably be found in practice to provide a much truer measure of the scale of naval preparations than any other which could be adopted. My Lords agree with the German Government that any contemplated variation in facts which have once been communicated should be notified before it is made. It is therefore all the more desirable to confine that information to broad and main features of construction and armament, and thus avoid the need of repeated communications on minor details.

5.   With a view to freeing the naval preparations of both countries from all sinister suspicions which may be fostered by newspaper activities, and so undermine the feeling of mutual confidence which they earnestly desire to see prevail, my Lords are also very anxious that the above proposals for the interchange of information shall include all cases of the arming of merchant or passenger vessels.   They would be prepared to use their influence with the shipping companies of the United Kingdom, in order to secure opportunities of inspection at agreed periods by the German Naval Attaché of all such vessels over and above a speed which might be fixed at 14 knots; and they would ask that similar facilities should be accorded to the British Naval Attaché or other officer who may be agreed on as convenient between the two Governments.

6.   My Lords feel most strongly that an agreement upon these lines is, so far as they are concerned, practicable and most valuable to all; that it would be entirely equal and reciprocal between both countries; that it would not prejudice the natural enterprise of the naval architects of either country; that it would not bind the freedom of action of either country; and that it would afford no foothold for disputes or suggestions as to discrepancies in the bases adopted for the various data; and they are prepared promptly and frankly to facilitate the carrying out of any such agreement, not merely in the jealously regarded letter but in fullest confidence and sincerity.

I am, &c.

W. GRAHAM GREENE.

MINUTES.

These are, I think, excellent observations both in substance and in spirit.   I feel however less sure as to whether they would or would not be particularly well received at the moment.   Possibly the German gov[ernmen]t might consider that we are trying to force them to disclose at once their new naval construction scheme, supposing such a scheme to be in contemplation.   I have some doubt also as to the proposal in § 5 of the present letter being welcome to the German gov[ernmen]t, although I fully agree as to its value.

I would suggest sending copy of the letter to Sir E. Goschen and asking him in the first instance whether he considers the present moment a favourable one for re-opening this discussion, and if so, instructing him to make a communication to the German gov[ernmen]t embodying the substance of the Admiralty letter.

E. A. C.
Dec. 13.

Are we also now to send to Sir E. Goschen the previous letter from the Admiralty(²) of which § 2 deals with the date at which the technical information is to be communicated?

W. L.

Sir E. Goschen sh[oul]d have full information—and he could be consulted as to whether the moment is favourable for approaching the German Gov[ernmen]t.

A. N.

Send to Sir E. Goschen as proposed making sure that the Admiralty still desire the previous letter to hold good.

(There is a new First Lord and a new Board since the previous letter was written to us.)

E. G.

(²) [v. supra, p. 642, No. 474.]

No. 479.

Foreign Office to Admiralty.

F.O. 49986/4451/11/18.

Sir,   *Foreign Office, December* 18, 1911.

I am directed by Sec[retar]y Sir E. Grey to acknowledge the receipt of your letter M. 0941/11 of the 12th instant(¹) with regard to the suggested exchange of naval information between this country and Germany.

(¹) [v. immediately preceding document.]

Sir E. Grey proposes to send a copy of your letter to H[is] M[ajesty's] Amb[assado]r at Berlin asking him in the first instance whether he considers the present moment favourable for reopening the discussion on this subject with the German Gov[ernmen]t and if so, instructing him to make a communication to that Gov[ernmen]t embodying the substance of the proposals and observations of the Lords Comm[issione]rs. Before doing so, Sir E. Grey would be glad to learn whether your present letter supersedes that of August 21, M. 0941,([2]) Confidential, or whether copies of both these letters should be communicated to Sir E. Goschen, and the substance of both embodied by him in a note to be communicated to the German Gov[ernmen]t at a suitable opportunity.

[I am, &c.
W. LANGLEY.]

([2]) [v. supra, p. 642, No. 474.]

No. 480.

Sir Edward Grey to Sir E. Goschen.

F.O. 51342/51342/11/18.
(No. 304.)
Sir,   *Foreign Office, December 20, 1911.*
Count Metternich came to see me to-day.([1])
He said that he had no instructions to propose anything to me. Indeed, he had turned over in his own mind whether it would not have been better to wait till January or February before saying anything; but he had come to the conclusion that he ought not to wait so long.

It would be very desirable if the tension in Germany could in some way be relaxed. Much, no doubt, must be left to the soothing influence of time; but in talking to people here, whether they were Conservatives or others, he found a disposition favourable to any steps which would produce more cordial relations with Germany.

He reminded me of what I had said during the negotiations as to Morocco, about not standing in the way of Germany and of the phrase which the Prime Minister had used in Parliament as to a "place in the sun" for Germany. Even if no territorial questions arose, perhaps where German and British interests were concerned some occasion might be found for the two countries to work together, instead of in opposition, without prejudicing the friendships or *ententes* of either.

I said that I doubted whether any progress could be made until the German elections were over. At present the favourable effect of anything that might be done was very liable to be upset by some untoward incident such as Captain Faber's speech: a most trivial thing, founded on gossip, but one that had had a most prodigious effect in Germany. However, if what Count Metternich aimed at was some means of showing that, though we had been in opposite camps in regard to the question of Morocco, the motive on our part was not a desire to thwart German interests everywhere, I should be very glad to prove that that was true. I asked what he had in his mind, but he had no suggestion to make.

I mentioned that the Bagdad Railway was the case which occurred to me.

We then went over some old ground as to the Railway, after which Count Metternich said that to ask Germany to give up a part of her concession to England could hardly be taken as a marked evidence of goodwill on our part.

([1]) [For Count Metternich's report and annotations by the Emperor William, v. G.P. XXXI, pp. 81–6.]

I explained our difficulties in connection with the Railway, and the concession which we should be willing to make as to Turkish Customs Dues.

Eventually, when I dwelt upon the importance of rates, he suggested that an equal share to us in controlling rates from Bagdad to the Gulf, coupled with an agreement about the terminus, might be a possible arrangement, if Germany was left with the controlling voice in the construction and management of the line apart from the question of rates.

I said that it had never occurred to me that the control of rates could be separated from the management of the line. It was a point which I should have to consider. I suggested that possibly an agreement about the Bagdad Railway, if it appeared to be too one-sided in a sense adverse to Germany, might be combined with some agreement in matters of a kindred kind elsewhere. In other words that if British participation came into a German enterprise in the case of the Bagdad railway, German enterprise might be assured of participation in British in some other part of the world.

Count Metternich proposed that we should look at the map of Africa. We did so, and he drew special attention to the Portuguese Colonies, saying that Portugal was in a very bad financial position, and that the disposal of her Colonies might become a question of practical politics. He commented upon the "enclave" reserved for us in Portuguese West Africa under the secret agreement.(²)

I said that it was not apparent to me what the exact value of that "enclave" was to us; and I could not say without enquiring, why it had been arranged originally.

He then talked about the Belgian Congo.

I pointed out that, if there were territorial changes, there might be some rectifications of the frontier on the side of East Africa that we should require, and there was the Katanga district coming right down into Rhodesia. But, apart from these small things, we had no territorial ambitions; and if the Congo should be for sale it would be no object of ours, as some people supposed, to prevent German territory from extending across Africa from East to West as it would do if Germany purchased part of the Congo between Angola and German East Africa and eventually acquired Angola; though no doubt we would ask for wayleave for a railway from North to South.

We agreed, however, that Belgium did not show any disposition to part with the Congo.

Finally, I said that I would discuss the matter with the Prime Minister and Mr. Harcourt. We should need the Christmas holidays to consider it. We had every goodwill to show that we did not desire to thwart German interests. The difficulty was to find any concrete expression of our friendliness, especially as a good many opportunities had already been disposed of by the Secret Agreement as to the Portuguese Colonies, and by the arrangement for the transfer of Heligoland to Germany.

[I am, &c.]
E. G[REY].

MINUTE.

I wish to direct the special attention of the Cabinet to this conversation with Count Metternich. It will have to be considered after the Christmas holidays and there [are] some things that may be possible but that I do not like to mention to Count Metternich till they have been put before the Cabinet.

E. G.

(²) [v. Gooch & Temperley, Vol. I, pp. 71–2, No. 90, encl.]

No. 481.

Admiralty to Foreign Office.

F.O. 51194/4451/11/18.
Secret.
Sir, *Admiralty, December 21, 1911.*

In reply to your letter of the 18th instant, No. 49986,(¹) I am commanded by my Lords Commissioners of the Admiralty to state that Admiralty Letter of the 12th instant M. 0941(²) was intended to be a full and final statement of the views of the Board as to the suggested exchange of naval information, and they therefore see no advantage in communicating Admiralty Letter of the 21st August(³) to H[is] M[ajesty's] Ambassador at Berlin.

I am, &c.
W. GRAHAM GREENE.

MINUTE.

Sir E. Goschen being now on leave (but not in England) it would appear desirable to defer sending the proposed instruction to Berlin until he returns to his post. No time will really be lost because the combination of Christmas and preparations for the elections will practically preclude early attention being given to this matter just at this moment.

E. A. C.
Dec. 22.
W. L.
A. N.
E. G.

(¹) [v. supra, pp. 649–50, No. 479.]
(²) [v. supra, pp. 647–9, No. 478.]
(³) [v. supra, p. 642, No. 474.]

No. 482.

Sir Edward Grey to Sir E. Goschen.

F.O. 51194/4451/11/18.
(No. 2.) Secret.
Sir, *Foreign Office, January 2, 1912.*

With reference to my despatch No. 185 Secret of the 3rd August last,(¹) I transmit to Y[our] E[xcellency] herewith copy of a letter from the Lords Commissioners of the Admiralty,(²) containing a full statement of their views on the subject of the proposed exchange of naval information between this country and Germany.

While H[is] M[ajesty's] Gov[ernmen]t are most willing to resume the conversations which have been temporarily suspended, it is a matter for serious consideration whether the present moment is a favourable one for them to place before the German Gov[ernmen]t the proposals now made.

Before therefore requesting Y[our] E[xcellency] to make a communication to the German Gov[ernmen]t embodying the substance of the accompanying letter from the Lords Commissioners, I shall be glad to be favoured with an expression of your views as to the advisability of reopening the discussion at this time.

[I am, &c.
E. GREY.]

(¹) [Not reproduced.]
(²) [v. supra, pp. 647–9, No. 478.]

No. 483.

Sir E. Goschen to Sir Edward Grey.

F.O. 1151/1151/12/18.
(No. 4.)
Sir,

Berlin, D. *January* 3, 1912.
R. *January* 9, 1912.

The articles with which a certain portion of the German Press have opened the New Year are not pleasant reading. The 'Hamburger Nachrichten,' in reviewing the events of the past year, observes that, while the settlement of the Morocco Question by the Chancellor and Herr von Kiderlen may be regarded as a success in that it has removed a source of friction with France, the tension between Germany and England still remains a source of anxiety and is carried on into the New Year with undiminished force. This tension, the article says, is the blackest storm cloud on the international horizon, and will continue in the future to be a point of danger as long as Germany remains the sole target for English policy. . . . .([1])

The "Lokal Anzeiger," after calling attention to the undiminished irritation felt by German public opinion at the "strange and inexplicable hostility" of England against Germany which the events of the past year brought to light, makes a strong bid for Russian, and to a certain extent French, friendship. . . . .

These remarks lead up to a dissertation upon the advantage to Germany of close relations with Russia, the only country, the article states, whose interests *vis à vis* of England are identic with those of Germany. . . . .

The article then points out that alliances and *ententes* founded, not on community of interests, but on the hatred of a third Power, cannot last, that Germany and Russia have common aims and no fundamental points of difference, and that it would be to the interests of both Germany, Austria-Hungary and Russia if a return could be made to the policy which formed for nearly a century the ground work of European development.

"The present moment" the article says, in conclusion, "and the present political constellations in Europe may perhaps be unpropitious for such a change, but the re-establishment of the 'Drei-Kaiser-Bund,' which would not necessarily exclude Italy, or be necessarily directed against France, should in the future be the constant aim of our statesmen. It is our firm hope that the Potsdam Agreement has cleared the path in this direction."

Of course there is nothing new in this attempt to stir up antagonism between Russia and ourselves and to revive the idea of the "Drei-Kaiser-Bund," still I do not remember that it has ever been made in quite so barefaced a manner and in such plain and even hostile language. This must be my excuse for quoting the article at such length. . . . .

I have, &c.
W. E. GOSCHEN.

([1]) [The omitted parts of this despatch contain summaries of and quotations from German Press reports.]

No. 484.

Sir E. Goschen to Sir Edward Grey.

Private.([1])
My dear Grey,

Berlin, *January* 7, 1912.

I should like to reflect a little on the question of reopening the 'Exchange of naval information' negotiations before answering your despatch on the subject officially.([2]) No time will be lost, as obviously nothing can be done before the Reichstag Elections.

([1]) [Grey MSS., Vol. 23.]
([2]) [*v. supra*, p. 652, No. 482.]

There seem to be two points to bear in mind in considering this question. The first is whether, in view of the present irritation felt against us by a large section of public opinion and the violent manner in which we are being abused by its Press, it would be advisable at this moment to make proposals which presuppose a certain amount of friendliness between the two nations or whether it would not be better to wait a little time in order to give this irritation time to evaporate.

The second is whether, considering the time that has elapsed since the German Government accepted our proposals in principle, we should not take the earliest opportunity after the Elections to renew the negotiations; in which case we should have a perfectly natural reason to give for the delay which has occurred, namely that we had chosen the first moment when the German Government, having got rid of the Moroccan Question and of the Elections, could give the question their full attention. If on the other hand we delay our answer much longer we should have less excuse for the delay which has occurred, and we might be suspected of motives for springing our answer on them at some particular moment and for some particular reason—for instance a possible increase in the German Naval Programme or an increase in the Socialist vote.

As, for the reason I have indicated, the renewal of the negotiations as soon as the elections are off the German mind, would be a perfectly natural and easily explained proceeding on our part, I am inclined to think that that is the course we should follow. It seems to me to outweigh the consideration that our friendly proposals, if made while public opinion is excited against us, might be regarded as the result of hostile language on the part of a section of the German Press.

There remains to be considered the possibility of the Imperial Government saying that the time has gone by when our proposals would have been acceptable to them. I think that it is unlikely that the German Government will adopt this course. Both the Chancellor and Kiderlen have on several occasions made it a grievance that our answer has been so long delayed, but neither of them have ever given any indication or hint that they were inclined to let the matter drop in consequence. But even should our desire to reopen the negotiations meet with a refusal I think we should be on strong ground. We could easily show why our answer has been delayed and let public opinion here become aware of our reasons, and if the party of the left return, as anticipated, to the Reichstag as the strongest single party in that house, they would make it hot for the Government as soon as they knew that proposals from Great Britain, intended to remove the distrust and suspicion which have had so much to do with the increased expenditure in armaments, have once more met with a rebuff from the Directors of German foreign policy.

These are my views, but before writing them officially I should like to think them over a little longer and also to consult Captain Watson as to the present feeling in naval circles with regard to this question. He is, however, at present in Holland and I am not sure when he returns. Should you agree with my present views and wish to act quickly, I would send you a despatch by next messenger without waiting to consult with him.

Yours very sincerely,
W. E. GOSCHEN.

P.S.—Captain Watson has just returned. I shall tell him of course that I only want his opinion and that he is to make no inquiries.

No. 485.

Sir E. Goschen to Sir Edward Grey.

F.O. 1909/1909/12/18.
(No. 14.)   Secret.
Sir,

Berlin, D. *January 12, 1912.*
R. *January 15, 1912.*

I have the honour to acknowledge the receipt of your despatch marked Secret No. 2 of the 2nd instant,([1]) in which you desire me to furnish you with an expression of my views as to whether the present moment is favourable for placing before the German Government the proposals for the "Exchange of Naval Information" contained in the letter addressed to you by the Lords Commissioners of the Admiralty on the 12th December last.([2])

In reply I would venture to state that, while seeing some advantage in communicating these proposals to the German Government at the earliest moment possible, I see nothing in the present situation which renders their postponement necessary or desirable. Both the Chancellor and the Secretary of State for Foreign Affairs have made it somewhat of a grievance that, although they have signified their willingness to fall in with the views of His Majesty's Government on this question and notified their acceptance in principle of the views of the Lords Commissioners of the Admiralty as to the form the Agreement should take, no further steps in the matter have been taken by His Majesty's Government nor any answer returned to their last Memorandum on this subject. This delay is of course very easily to be explained particularly if, as I would venture to suggest, His Majesty's Government should decide to present their new proposals to the German Government as soon as the Reichstag elections are over and therefore at a moment when the German Government may be presumed to be free to give their full attention to the matter.

That public opinion in Germany is still in a high state of irritation against Great Britain is an unfortunate fact which cannot be gainsaid, and at first sight it might appear inopportune to lay before the Government proposals which presuppose a certain amount of cordial feelings between the two nations. I venture however to express the opinion that in this matter, in which in any case the first negotiations will probably be of a secret nature, the state of public opinion in Germany should not be allowed to interfere with the communication of proposals which have been long looked for by the Imperial Government and which moreover may perhaps, at all events from our point of view, be regarded as an answer to the frequently expressed desire that "acts and not words only" should be forthcoming from His Majesty's Government.

I would accordingly suggest that the proposals should be placed before the German Government as soon as possible after the elections are completed, and before any proposals for the increase of the German Shipbuilding Programme, if such, as is confidently expected, are to be made, can be submitted to the new Reichstag. For I consider that no time for reopening the negotiations on this subject would seem to be more natural and suitable than the moment when the German Government will, for the first time since their last communication on this subject, be free from serious preoccupations, such as the Morocco-Congo negotiations and the Reichstag elections.

The question remains as to whether there is any likelihood that the Imperial Government will refuse to entertain these proposals with the excuse that the time has passed when they would have been acceptable.

I do not consider this at all likely. But in any case His Majesty's Government could give strong reasons for the delay which has taken place, reasons which could not fail to carry weight with the more reasonable portion of the German public. In

([1]) [v. *supra*, p. 652, No. 482.]
([2]) [v *supra*, pp. 647-9, No. 478.]

fact I feel sure that the knowledge, which would sooner or later reach the public, that naval proposals from His Majesty's Government of a friendly nature had again met with a rebuff would cause great dissatisfaction at all events in liberal and radical circles and would not tend to smooth the path of the Government in the new Reichstag where, according to all accounts, the party most opposed to expenditure on armaments, will be considerably reinforced.

I have consulted Captain Watson, Naval Attaché to this Embassy, with regard to the probable attitude of German naval officers towards the present proposals. He has stated his views in the enclosed Memorandum, to which I beg to call your attention. The Memorandum covers a good deal of ground but the gist of it is that, notwithstanding the irritation caused in Germany by recent events, Senior Naval Officers, at all events, would, in his opinion, welcome anything that might lead to a better understanding between the two Navies, and that a more favourable opportunity than the present for presenting the present proposals is, as far as naval opinion is concerned, not likely to occur.

The elections to the Reichstag are taking place to-day; in a fortnight the second Ballots will take place and the new Reichstag is expected to meet on or about the 9th of February.

I have, &c.
W. E. GOSCHEN.

Enclosure in No. 485.

Proposals for exchange of Naval information between England and Germany.

Remarks by Captain H. D. R. Watson, Royal Navy, on the probable reception of them by German Naval Officers.

Confidential.   *January 9, 1912.*

1. Evidence that has come to me during the past 17 months goes to show that during the years in which the British Naval Estimates were reduced and prior to the introduction of the additional 4 British Armoured Ships being laid down (making 8 in one year), the activity in German ·Naval circles, Ports, and Yards was extremely great. During this period the German Naval Officers appear to have had an idea that they might be able to build sufficiently near to the British Naval strength as to be able by means of Allies and assiduous work on their own part to successfully compete with the British Fleet weakened, as they thought, by lack of financial support and divided in action by Strategical considerations, whereas the German Naval Officers have had only one object in view, the British Fleet. Further, people were not wanting, inside the German Navy as well as outside of it, who decried the state of efficiency of the British Fleet and lauded that of the German. I have myself come across echoes of this in Germany, Holland, and Denmark.

Whether the German Senior Naval Officers, who knew the British Navy by virtue of previous experience, really believed this is a matter of some doubt. I am under the impression that the average Senior Officer did not, and was really full of admiration for his "big Naval British brother" and his larger opportunities for acquiring Fleet experience, and that he further was in some doubt as to the likelihood of an ultimate German Naval success in a war, even given equal numbers. However the Newspapers, etc., helped to lull his fears, and to promote the hopes of the younger generation; and the day was carried by the Admiralty Officers, whose ambitions and those of others for a greater German Fleet led them on, and who were helped by the younger generation of the Navy who, not knowing the British Fleet like their Seniors, were fully conscious of their own hard and really good work and, having no standard of comparison to go by, believed the disparaging reports of the British Fleet, and also doubted the desire or ability of England to continue bearing the Naval financial burden. They were encouraged in this doubt by proposals for limitations of Armaments emanating from England. These same proposals were regarded by the German Admiralty Authorities with some suspicion because the German Fleet Law was decided on and was on its way to the zenith of its Ship-building programme, which was to be reached in 1911. Without going further one may say that the proposals, made at the time they were, provoked suspicion at the German Admiralty, and wonder in that they, having laid down a regular programme to meet their own requirements, should be thought likely to reduce it for apparently England's benefit.

This situation continued until the addition of the 4 British Armoured Ships before referred to, and the subsequent years' programmes of 5 or 6 Armoured Ships per annum in England. Up to the last it was thought in German Naval circles that the 8 Armoured Ships, voted in one year, would not be laid down; and when they actually were, evidence in Germany goes to prove that the before prevailing general Naval activity was greatly diminished.

Since that the general Naval opinion has been gradually accustoming itself to the thought that England will always build to have a strong proportional strength over Germany. The opinion of the older and more moderate Senior Officers began to have more weight as compared with that of the special Admiralty Officers and the young generation. Further the personal resentment of the Minister of Marine against the First Lord of the British Admiralty and against the then Naval Attaché in Berlin, on which I have before reported, at certain statements in the English House of Commons which Admiral von Tirpitz alleged impugned his personal honesty and truth, began to diminish with the process of time.

2. When suggestions for the interchange of Naval information were handed to Admiral von Tirpitz by me on August 24th, 1910,[1] matters in the Naval world were therefore in this condition :—

(a.) That the Minister of Marine was still nursing a personal grievance, and he was also being urged on by the Navy League and the Armament and Ship-building Firms to further increase the Navy when the zenith of the ship-building of present Navy Law was reached. Also having built up the Navy Law it was impossible for him not to have a feeling of pride in his achievement; while he would have been hardly human if regret did not enter his mind at a thought of the possible reduction of the ship-building programme during his concluding years of office. Also it is fair to say that looking at the German Fleet it does appear to be deficient in Armoured or Battle Cruisers.

(b.) The Admiralty were naturally of his views.

(c.) The large mass of the German Navy were beginning to think a better understanding with the British Navy was desirable. I have strong evidence of this desire on the part of the Senior Officers who were free of the Admiralty influences.

I am bound to say I believe the Ship-building policy of England, by its magnitude in recent years, has had its effect in this respect and has helped the friends of England in the German Navy.

3. On the proposals for the exchange of information being made in 1910, the first opinion of the Minister of Marine, still labouring under a sense of personal resentment, was I considered and still think, adverse to them particularly as the suspicion the previous proposals for limitation of armaments had aroused was again awakened in his mind; and he feared having his hands tied during the lean years of German Naval Ship-building soon to come under the present Navy Law. Naturally his idea permeated his immediate entourage at the Admiralty.

I have reported in September 1910 on the events subsequent to speaking to the Minister of Marine about the above proposals, and on how well proposals making for a better knowledge of each other and for an improved feeling between the British

[1] [v. supra, pp. 514–8, No. 397, and encls.]

and German Navies, were received by the Senior Flag Officers not immediately under the Admiralty.

In the light of my subsequent experience, I now beg to report that I consider the opinion I then formed that the majority of the Senior Officers of the German Navy would welcome a better understanding between the two Navies, was entirely correct; and I believe would have grown steadily but for the events of Morocco, etc.

Even allowing for the Moroccan affairs, and the bitterness of the Newspapers, I would report that the attitude of the more Senior Naval Officers was uninfluenced thereby; and that they still desire sincerely a better understanding, and would welcome steps leading thereto.

Naturally the Naval Officer is in favour of a larger Navy as it means more appointments, and the senior Officers are beginning to suffer from unemployment. But in spite of recent political events and the heat engendered thereby, the senior Naval Officers as a whole were somewhat lukewarm over the Morocco affairs, they shared the opinions held by many moderate Germans that the Government action in this matter was injudicious in the beginning and weak in its continuing steps. More travelled than other Germans, and conscious of the inferiority of Numbers of the German Fleet, they were not optimistic as to the chances of German success in an encounter with the British Fleet. Of the younger Officers it is unnecessary to speak, except to say that they and perhaps some of the Senior Officers, being Teutons, were excited against England later by the German Newspapers' publications in the Naval ports of reports of the British Fleet being off Borkum at a critical stage of the proceedings.

4. The attitude of the Admiralty towards the proposals for exchange of information from being first one of antipathy changed to one of encouragement for a few months last winter, tempered by a desire to establish the proposals on a basis which might be favourable to Germany's interests.

Then Moroccan affairs supervened, and I am bound to say that the attitude of the Admiralty had been such during the previous months as to decidedly convey the impression to me that the proposals had not been to the liking of the Admiralty, that they had given the German Naval Authorities some food for thought as to how they could benefit their own Country over them (particularly in the matter of postponing production of their Naval Estimates to the same date as the British); and further that when the Morocco affairs rendered it necessary to delay matters with the onus of reply to the proposals on the British side, to put it mildly they were glad and hoped to benefit by the experience.

5. Whether the renewal of the proposals for exchange of information at present time would be agreeable it is difficult to say for certain in view of so recent a state of high feeling in Germany. The Moroccan affairs have undoubtedly, whether conducted with a purpose or not, given a better chance of a Naval increase being carried out. But it is patent to all moderate naval men that the process of getting a little more and a little more for the Navy is becoming played out. The Army demands are clashing with the Naval, and other political factors are making it more and more unlikely that even if the Reichstag votes the Naval increases put forward by the Navy League, the limit of expansion is nearing its end, and the Liberals at any rate are realising that one German ship more means two British. The cry of the Ship-building Yards to have the next 6 years bridged over, coupled with the Moroccan agitation, may result in one more Armoured Ship per annum, (though that is a political question). But I believe the opinion, already existing in the Nation, is extending to the Navy that a limit to Naval expansion is nearing, that further efforts in this direction will jeopardize relations with England, and that it is in their interests to have a rest from the ceaseless activity and jealousies, the former of which bears more hardly on the permanent Personnel of the German Navy than on the British. Further the Senior German Naval Officers look back to the old friendly relations they have had with their British Colleagues and would like their renewal. Another factor in favour of a favourable reception of the proposals for

exchange of information by the German Admiralty is that time and other factors have diminished the personal resentment of the Minister of Marine, before referred to. Also if one may judge by one's personal relations with him and the senior Naval Officers recently, I should say the time is as ripe as it is likely to be.

6. Allowing therefore for the temporary irritation caused to some of the Naval Officers by Moroccan affairs, I believe that it is probable the renewal of the proposals for exchange of information would probably be now favourably received by the German Admiralty; but I desire to emphasize that I am strongly of opinion that this favourable reception is made possible only by the increased and maintained relative strength of the British Fleet to the German, and by reason of the possibility of failure of the German Estimates to continue providing in the future for a large Navy as well as a large Army. My remarks in regard to the former reason apply to the future as well as the past.

7. I submit these remarks with all deference, observing that as they are only impressions I cannot guarantee their accuracy in all respects. But as my study of the German Navy has been a close one, extending over 3 years, first at the War College; then visiting German, Dutch, Danish, and Swedish Naval centres; at the Intelligence Department of the Admiralty; and subsequently as Naval Attaché in Berlin, I feel the more confident that my remarks contained herein are correct in the main. Owing largely to my speaking to the Minister of Marine and other Naval Officers in 1910 about the proposal for exchange of information, and other reasons, I have been personally very intimately received by German Naval Officers.

HUGH WATSON.

Captain and Naval Attaché.

No. 486.

Sir E. Goschen to Sir A. Nicolson.

F.O. 5986/5569/12/18.
Private.

My dear Nicolson,   *Berlin, January 12, 1912.*

I have heard a rumour that you are back in London so I write you a few lines on the chance. There is for the moment nothing new to report. I wish I could give a better report of Anglo-German relations, but as my few England-loving German friends tell me that they have never known the feeling of irritation against England so strong and so widely spread as it is at present, I am afraid that that is the case.

Well! there is nothing to be done for the moment as far as I can see: but I can't help thinking that the bad feeling is just a little artificial and that we shan't hear quite so much of it after the Elections are over. I think that Lord Lonsdale, meaning doubtless excessively well "manque une bonne occasion de se taire"! but the Pan-German Press has been really too silly about it, and it really takes some ingenuity to represent the interview as an insult to the Emperor. I was afraid at one moment that we were going to have another 'Daily Telegraph' incident over again, but thank goodness the matter seems to have fizzled out. The poor little effort of the Standard to put the Crown Prince right with his English Friends also gave rise to unfriendly comment here. In fact both these well meant attempts have been represented here as part of a deep and insidious policy on the part of H[is] M[ajesty's] G[overnment]! it would be interesting to look into the minds of the German journalists who write this sort of nonsense.

The Emperor talked no international politics with me on New Year's day, but he talked a good deal with Cambon—condoled with him on being abused in France for his conduct of the negotiations and said 'never mind! in a year's time they will erect a statue in your honour.' He then said a thing which Cambon has not reported to his Government, and which he told me under the seal of secrecy, with a reservation in favour of you; the Emperor said "Your Press is very bad and very hostile to Germany, but I don't blame France for it as I happen to know that all those anti-German Articles are paid for by my friends on the other side of the Channel."

My information is still that there is an intention to submit to the New Reichstag, as soon as possible after it meets, proposals for an increase of the shipbuilding Programme for 1912. But there is apparently a controversy going on as to whether it is not the Army that should be attended to rather than the Navy, and it seems rather uncertain as to which will carry the day; possibly both may come in for an increase.

I am rather tired of sending home anti-English Articles in the Press, particularly as I think I have done enough in that line to show the state of public opinion at the present moment. For that reason I have not made any analysis of Professor Schiemann's last weekly Article in the Kreuz. But looking over it tonight I see that there are one or two points which might interest the Foreign Office, so I will just mention them to you now. In speaking of the strong probability of an increase in the Naval Programme for this year he says that the experiences of last summer, when England, unasked and unbound by any Treaty, placed her fleet and an expeditionary force unreservedly at the disposal of France for a war that would have had no justification whatever, had caused the whole of Germany, with the exception perhaps of the socialists, to unite in the desire that precautionary measures should at once be taken by the Imperial Government. "Sir E. Grey" he continues, "has only allowed Parliament a very superficial glance at the cards he holds in his hand. We know that he is our deadly enemy, and it is not us, but he, who will be responsible, if the costly and, to both sides, exhausting, competition in the building of super-Dreadnoughts has to be resorted to again." Later he adds that there is no reason to doubt that the friendly hand which is held out to Germany by those who sympathise with the sentiments expressed in a recent Article in the "Nation" (from which he quotes largely) will be heartily grasped, and he points out that he has always maintained that an understanding honourable to both sides would be the interest of both Germany and Great Britain. Moreover the Kaiser had never concealed his desire for such an understanding and had only recently stated that if 1912 saw the attainment of that result it should be a year marked with a white stone —but . . . . here the Professor gives a long list of English statesmen both in and outside the Cabinet, beginning with the Secretary of State for War and ending with Mr. Hobhouse, who have an understanding with Germany profoundly at heart— but he expresses some doubt as to whether their influence is strong enough to effect any change in the attitude and tendencies of the Foreign Office!!

The 'Kreutz Zeitung' is I think you told me an old 'friend' of yours!

The Elections are over by this time. I have heard nothing about them yet; but the opinion has lately been very generally expressed that the Socialist gains will not be as great as they were expected to be. The Chancellor used to tell me that he feared that about 120 Socialists would be returned, but the latest estimate was between 80 or 90. Tomorrow we shall know more about it, but there are of course the supplementary Ballots to be taken yet. I am very glad to hear that you are feeling quite rested, I hope it is true.

Yours very sincerely,
W. E. GOSCHEN.

MINUTE.

The Emperor's statement that anti-German articles in France are paid for from England is untrue and very mischievous.

E. G.

No. 487.

Sir Edward Grey to Sir E. Goschen.

F.O. 1909/1909/12/18.
(No. 11.)   Secret.

Sir :—   *Foreign Office, January 17, 1912.*

In your despatch No. 14 Secret of the 12th instant,([1]) Your Excellency informed me that you considered that it was desirable that the proposals of His Majesty's Government with regard to an exchange of naval information should be in the hands of the German Government immediately after the close of the present Reichstag elections.

I inferred from Your Excellency's despatch that you further considered that it might be advisable for His Majesty's Government in communicating these proposals to explain the reasons why they have not replied at an earlier date to the last memorandum from the German Government on the subject. The reasons for such delay appear to me to be so patent as hardly to require any explanation—certainly no excuses—on the part of His Majesty's Government; unless such explanations are invited by anything said or suggested by the Chancellor.

I should be glad if Your Excellency will choose a suitable moment for making known to the German Government the proposals of His Majesty's Government with regard to the exchange of naval information, and I leave to Your Excellency's discretion the form in which the communication should be made.

I am, &c.
[E. GREY.]

([1]) [*v. supra*, pp. 655-6, No. 485.]

No. 488.

Sir E. Goschen to Sir Edward Grey.

F.O. 2894/1909/12/18.
(No. 29.)   Secret.   *Berlin, D. January 19, 1912.*

Sir,   *R. January 22, 1912.*

I have the honour to acknowledge the receipt of your despatch marked Secret No. 11 of the 17th instant.([1])

I propose to take the earliest possible opportunity after the conclusion of the Elections to lay before the Imperial Government the proposals of His Majesty's Government with regard to an exchange of naval information.

I would venture to state with reference to my despatch No. 14 Secret of the 12th instant([2]) that it was by no means my idea that any explanations or excuses should be given or made in communicating the proposals to the Imperial Government. What I intended to convey was that if, as seemed possible from recent remarks by the Chancellor and Herr von Kiderlen, any observations were to be made respecting the delay which has occurred, His Majesty's Government had very strong reasons wherewith to explain that delay.

I have, &c.
W. E. GOSCHEN.

([1]) [*v.* immediately preceding document.]
([2]) [*v. supra*, pp. 655-6, No. 485.]

No. 489.

Sir E. Goschen to Sir Edward Grey.

F.O. 4980/1909/12/18.
(No. 47.) Secret.   *Berlin,* D. *January* 28, 1912.
Sir,   R. *February* 5, 1912.

With reference to your despatch No. 11 Secret (1909/12) of the 17th instant,([1])
I have the honour to report that I saw Herr von Kiderlen-Waechter to-day and
handed to him a Memorandum, copy of which is enclosed herein, containing the
proposals of His Majesty's Government with regard to an exchange of naval
information.

His Excellency, who has only just returned from Italy, stated that he was
leaving Berlin again immediately. He promised however to examine the matter
closely and he hoped to have an opportunity of speaking to me again on the subject
next week.

I have, &c,
W. E. GOSCHEN.
Enclosure in No. 489.

Memorandum communicated to Herr von Kiderlen-Waechter.([2])

His Majesty's Government have had under their consideration the *Aide-Mémoire*
of the Imperial Foreign Office dated June 27th, 1911,([3]) in regard to the suggested
exchange of naval information between Great Britain and Germany. They have
reviewed the question with an earnest desire to arrive at a useful and practical result
which should be convenient to the two Governments, and beneficial to the relations
between the two countries and they do not see any difficulties of an insuperable
nature in the exchange of technical information whether as regards substance or
time.

His Majesty's Government would not allow any question of mere procedure to
stand in the way of an agreement the object of which is to remove uncertainty and
to disarm suspicion; at the same time, however, it should, they consider, be
recognized that the difficulties of arranging for an interchange of technical details
increase markedly as the details become more minute. More room for differences
as to the bases necessary for fair comparisons arise at every step. There is a danger
that this in itself might become the vantage-ground of suspicions and disputes, while
at the same time the value of the information for the main purpose in hand would
steadily diminish. They recognize, moreover, that what may be called the professional secrets of construction, which are the signs of the progress of naval science
in either country, are in a peculiar sense the private property of the respective
Governments, and that it would be discouraging to designers and architects of either
nation were an arrangement come to by which each new contrivance should be
immediately imparted to the naval authorities of a foreign Power. His Majesty's
Government whilst anxious to arrange for a fair and reasonable exchange of naval
information, have never had any desire to ascertain or disclose the special features
upon which naval experts rely for the superiority of this or that point in the construction of any vessel. They are content to assume that every ship in each class will
represent the last word of the naval science of the constructing Power on the subject.
The information which they would wish to obtain, and which they are perfectly willing
to furnish, concerns not so much the technical quality and specifications of the various
vessels, as the scale of warlike preparation upon which the Admiralties of the two
countries have embarked; and it is with the sole object of freeing this vital matter
from the atmosphere of doubt and anxiety with which it has been from time to time
surrounded that the following observations are put forward.

([1]) [*v. supra*, p. 661, No. 487.]
([2]) [Printed in *G.P.* XXXI, pp. 50–3.]
([3]) [*v. supra*, p. 640, No. 472, *encl.*]

His Majesty's Government do not seek to know the intentions of the German Government so far as the future is concerned, or to lead that Government into any arrangement which would fetter reciprocally the free discretion of either Power to alter, vary, diminish or extend their naval programme. They are concerned with the exact situation, in fact at given and agreed periods in each year. They would desire to know how many vessels of each class or type are being constructed at such given times in all the yards, public or private, of the German Empire, whether for the German Government or for foreign sale. They are prepared similarly to satisfy the German Government beyond doubt or question as to the general position of all war-ship construction within the United Kingdom. What is desired, indeed, is an exchange of simple and easily verifiable facts. It would, it is considered, be sufficient if at any dates convenient to the two Governments, when communicating the programme for the ensuing year, the number of ships of each class upon whose construction or preliminary preparation for construction money is actually being spent, could be made known to each other by the two Governments, if the dates of the laying down, launching and completion of the ships could be exchanged, if the first two conditions could be tested by the periodical and reciprocal visits of the Naval Attachés, who should be permitted at the agreed periods to inspect the building slips in all the yards capable of constructing war-vessels.

So far as further information upon the character of the vessels in each class is concerned it is not considered that there should be any difficulty in arriving at an understanding. The main data of the ships building, or to be built, such as are published in the annual " Dickinson Return," *i.e.*, displacement, horse power and the number of guns constituting the primary armament, could it is thought readily be exchanged. To this might be added with great advantage a simple statement of the amount of money which, according to the contract price, was to be expended on the hulls, the armament and the engines, respectively. The last, without trenching upon the peculiarities of construction, would probably be found in practice to provide a much truer measure of the scale of naval preparations than any other which could be adopted. His Majesty's Government agree with the German Government that any contemplated variation in facts which have once been communicated should be notified before it is made. It is therefore considered all the more desirable to confine that information to broad and main features of construction and armament, and thus avoid the need of repeated communications on minor details.

With a view to freeing the naval preparations of both countries from all sinister suspicions which may be fostered by newspaper activities, and so undermine the feeling of mutual confidence which it is earnestly desired to see prevail, His Majesty's Government are also anxious that the above proposals for the interchange of information shall include all cases of the arming of merchant or passenger vessels. They would be prepared to use their influence with the shipping companies of the United Kingdom, in order to secure opportunities of inspection at agreed periods by the German Naval Attaché of all such vessels over and above a speed which might be fixed at 14 knots; and they would ask that similar facilities should be accorded to the British Naval Attaché or other officer who may be agreed on as convenient between the two Governments.

It is most strongly felt that an agreement upon these lines is, so far as His Majesty's Government are concerned, practicable and most valuable to all; that it would be entirely equal and reciprocal between both countries; that it would not prejudice the natural enterprise of the naval architects of either country; that it would not bind the freedom of action of either country; and that it would afford no foothold for disputes or suggestions as to discrepancies in the bases adopted for the various data; and His Majesty's Government are prepared promptly and frankly to facilitate the carrying out of any such agreement, not merely in the jealously regarded letter, but in fullest confidence and sincerity.

No. 490.

Sir Edward Grey to Sir F. Bertie.

F.O. 5331/1909/12/18.
(No. 48.)

Sir,   *Foreign Office, February 3, 1912.*

I told M. Cambon to-day(¹) that Sir Arthur Nicolson had reported to me his question whether anything was proceeding between Germany and ourselves as to the Portuguese Colonies.

I said that nothing was proceeding. Count Metternich, some time ago, and not, as I understood, under instructions from his Government, had spoken to me of the possibility that Portugal might sell her African Colonies of Angola and Mozambique. He had not mentioned any other Portuguese Colonies. In Berlin neither the Imperial Chancellor nor Herr von Kiderlen had said a word about any Portuguese Colonies at all. M. Cambon would, however, remember that some time ago I had informed him that we had begun negotiations, or rather conversations, with Germany from the starting-point of naval expenditure. These conversations had been interrupted by our Elections. We had resumed them after the last Election, and the Germans had sent us a reply as to naval information. We had held back our answer to this, owing to the electricity in the air during the discussion of the question of Morocco; but now we had sent our answer, and the conversations would be resumed.

M. Cambon said that he heard the impression in Germany was that, if Germany made an increase in her naval expenditure, we should at once precipitate a war with her; at the same time, an increase of German naval expenditure was inevitable. Of course, he did not believe that we should act in this way.

I said that it was believed throughout Germany that we had intended, either with or without France, to attack Germany last September, by surprise, without any warlike step having been taken by Germany. This was, of course, absolutely untrue; but the state of feeling created in Germany was such that things must get either worse or better. We felt, therefore, that it was necessary to talk with the German Government. We would do all we could to remove the absurd suspicion that we had intended to make an unprovoked attack.

M. Cambon said he assumed that, if conversations were to be renewed, it meant that it was not absolutely certain that Germany would embark on an increase of naval expenditure.

I replied that this was one of the things which we had to find out in the course of discussion. At present, everything was very vague, and I could not tell how the conversations might develop; but, whatever developments occurred, we should take care that they were not such as to impair the relations between France and ourselves.

I impressed upon M. Cambon that it was essential to regard what I had said to him as very confidential.

[I am, &c.]
E. G[REY].

(¹) [M. Paul Cambon's account of this interview is given in *D.D.F.*, 3rd *Ser.*, Vol. **I**, pp. 603–4.]

No. 491.

Sir Edward Grey to Lord Granville.

F.O. 4980/1909/12/18.
(No. 30.) Secret.

My Lord,   *Foreign Office, February 6, 1912.*

I have received Sir E. Goschen's despatch No. 47 Secret of the 28th ultimo([1])
and I approve the terms of the memorandum handed by H[is] E[xcellency] to
Herr von Kiderlen-Waechter, containing the proposals of H[is] M[ajesty's]
G[overnment] with regard to an exchange of naval information.

[I am, &c.
E. GREY.]

([1]) [*v. supra*, pp. 662–3, No. 489, and *encl.*]

CHAPTER XLIX.

THE HALDANE MISSION, 1912.

[ED. NOTE.—For references from the British side to the Haldane Mission and the subsequent negotiations, v. Lord Haldane : *Before the War* (1920), pp. 55–72, *Autobiography* (1929), pp. 238–245; W. S. Churchill : *The World Crisis, 1911–1914*, (1923), pp. 94–108; Lord Grey : *Twenty-Five Years* (1925), Vol. I, pp. 249–253; H. H. Asquith : *The Genesis of the War* (1924), pp. 97–102. For the German side, v. *G.P.* XXXI, ch. 243; Bethmann Hollweg : *Reflections on the World War* (1920), pp. 47–61; Admiral von Tirpitz : *Politische Dokumente. Der Aufbau der deutschen Weltmacht* (Stuttgart and Berlin, 1924), pp. 279–338; Kaiser Wilhelm II : *My Memoirs* (1922), pp. 142–158; B. Huldermann : *Albert Ballin* (English translation), (1922), pp. 167–184.]

No. 492.

Mr. Winston Churchill to Sir E. Cassel.

Private.(¹)

My dear Cassel, *Admiralty, January 7, 1912.*

It will not be wise for me at this juncture to have any parley with y[ou]r august friend. If the King were to visit Germany, and I went with him—both hypothetical conditions—I sh[oul]d be honoured by being permitted to discuss the great matters wh[ich] hang in the balance. But the occasion w[oul]d have to arise naturally, and I sh[oul]d have to be empowered by Grey and the P[rime] M[inister].

Even then, all that c[oul]d be said on our part w[oul]d be that till Germany dropped the naval challenge her policy w[oul]d be continually viewed here with deepening suspicion and apprehension; but that any slackening on her part w[oul]d produce an immediate *détente*, with much goodwill from all England. Failing that I see little in prospect but politeness and preparation.

I deeply deplore the situation, for as you know I have never had any but friendly feelings towards that great nation and her illustrious sovereign, and I regard the antagonism wh[ich] has developed as insensate. Anything in my power to terminate it I w[oul]d gladly do. But the only way I see open is one which I fear Germany will be reluctant to take.

Will you then as you think best disengage me with the greatest respect from the suggestion, using, so far as your judgment inclines you, what is written here. Always my dear Cassel,

Your very sincere friend,
WINSTON S. CHURCHILL.

(¹) [Grey MSS., Vol. 48. A copy of this letter was sent to Sir Edward Grey by Mr. Churchill on February 13.]

No. 493.

Mr. Winston Churchill to Sir Edward Grey.

Private.(¹)

Secret and Personal.

My dear Grey, *Admiralty, January 20, 1912.*

Cassel has received a letter in reply to the answer he conveyed from me (wh[ich] I showed you and the Prime Minister) to this effect :—

" Herr Ballin's friend is pleased and interested : Churchill w[oul]d have a very good reception in Berlin whether he came in the King's suite or alone :

(¹) [Grey MSS., Vol. 48.]

the difficulties are quite understood : if they c[oul]d be surmounted he might have some⋅ very useful conversation with Admiral Tirpitz :'' lastly, '' It is necessary that there should now be increases both in the Army and in the Navy.''

Will you send this to the Prime Minister when he returns.

Yours very sincerely,

WINSTON S. CHURCHILL.

No. 494.

Sir Edward Grey to Sir E. Goschen

Foreign Office, February 2, 1912.

Tel. Private.(¹)   D. 6·30 P.M.

Some communications have taken place with Emperor and German Chancellor through Ballin and Sir Ernest Cassel, a channel that was selected in first place by the Emperor. I wish to inform you of what has passed and of what we intend to do and to consult you as to future developments. I shall be glad if you will come to London at once so that I can talk things over with you fully on Monday.(²)

(¹) [Grey MSS., Vol. 23.]

(²) [No record has been found in the Foreign Office archives of the conversation which took place between Sir Edward Grey and Sir E. Goschen during this visit. M. Paul Cambon reported, after his interview with Sir Edward Grey on February 7, that Sir E. Goschen was in London for twenty-four hours only, and that '' On lui a fait verbalement connaître le véritable but de la visite de Lord Haldane sur laquelle on entend garder un secret absolu.'' *v. D.D.F.,* *3rd Ser.,* Vol. I. p. 630.]

No. 495.

Sir Edward Grey to Sir G. Buchanan.

F.O. 5632/5569/12/18.   *Foreign Office, February 7, 1912.*

Tel. (No. 96.) Secret.   D. 7·15 P.M.

You should inform the Minister for Foreign Affairs very confidentially that conversations about naval expenditure that began some time ago, as Russian Government were informed at the time,(¹) but were suspended first by General Election here in 1910, and then by Morocco crisis,(²) are being resumed.

Lord Haldane has gone to Berlin on a private and unofficial visit, having some enquiries to make about university education; he presides over a commission here on that subject. But he will have a frank interchange of views with German Chancellor informally, and explore the ground to find out whether there is a favour- able prospect for negotiations to put the relations of the two countries on a less unfavourable footing.

(¹) [*v. supra*, p. 291, No. 198, and *note* (²).]

(²) [This subject will be treated in *Gooch & Temperley*, Vol. VII.]

Till Lord Haldane reports I cannot say what the prospect is, but in any case there will be no developments to impair our present good relations with Russia. France has made her agreement with Germany about Morocco, and Russian Minister for Foreign Affairs settled some questions at Potsdam last year. It is very desirable that we should also settle some of our questions, if possible, or present relations with Germany may get worse.

No. 496.

Sir Edward Grey to Sir E. Goschen.

F.O. 5631/5569/12/18.   *Foreign Office, February 7,* 1912.
Tel. (No. 8.) R.   D. 7·45 P.M.

I have told German Ambassador([1]) that when press enquire as to visit of Secretary of State for War to Berlin they will be told that, as president of a commission here on university education, he is with his brother, Professor Haldane, making some enquiries, especially about scientific education in Germany, but that, as he is well known to many leading people in Germany, he will no doubt have general conversations on the political situation and relations between the two countries. German Ambassador said he would inform his Government, and hoped they would answer enquiries in the same way.

([1]) [*cp. G.P.* XXXI, pp. 107–8.]

No. 497.

Sir Edward Grey to Sir E. Goschen.

Private.([1])
My dear Goschen,   *London, February 7,* 1912.

I told Metternich today that I had seen a letter from Mr. Allen Baker, M.P., giving an account of an interview which he had had with Herr von Bethmann-Hollweg. Mr. Allen Baker had gathered that the Chancellor intended to send instructions to Count Metternich, in continuation of the conversation which we had had before Christmas. But, as I had heard nothing further from Metternich, I assumed that he had not yet received instructions.

Metternich said that he had himself suggested to the Chancellor that the conversation should not be resumed until after the holidays.

I then told him that, since we last met, a communication had reached one of my Colleagues from the German Emperor through an unofficial channel; and we had replied to the communication through the same channel; but things could not be taken beyond a certain point in an unofficial channel. The Emperor had been good enough to express a wish that I should go to Berlin to negotiate; he had indeed sent an invitation though the unofficial channel. I did not wish it to be supposed that I did not appreciate the Emperor's wish and the kind words in which, as reported to me, it had been expressed; but I had felt that a visit on my part to Berlin would be unfortunate unless there was some definite result to be announced at the close of the visit. It was, however, convenient to Haldane to make some enquiries in Germany about scientific education. He was the Chairman of a University Committee for that purpose here, and he was going to Berlin with his Brother, Professor Haldane. At the same time he would be ready to enter upon a frank exchange of views with Herr von Bethmann-Hollweg, to explore the ground

([1]) [Grey MSS., Vol. 23.]

thoroughly, and to see whether ground could be found on which more formal negotiations could proceed to a satisfactory conclusion. In informal discussions of this sort, the exchange of views could be more frank and full than in actual negotiations. I had discussed with Haldane the whole question of our relations with Germany, and I knew that he was prepared to speak frankly and without reserve about the past, present, and future situations.

I had also asked you to come to London, in order that I might inform you of everything that had passed hitherto.

Count Metternich told me that he had been kept fully informed by his Government of what had passed in the unofficial channel. He understood that certain bases had been proposed.

I said that every thing which had passed in the non-official channel must be regarded as non-committal; but no doubt we had stipulated on our side that naval expenditure must be open to discussion, and had said that we would welcome suggestions as to how we could show that our policy was not opposed to German expansion and German interests. Every thing had, however, been very vague, and nothing definite had been stated as to German naval expenditure.

Metternich remarked that the unofficial channel had suggested, amongst other things, that possibly I might visit Berlin in company with Lord Haldane and Mr. Winston Churchill.

I replied that the suggestion of this combined visit was new to me; when more than one person was engaged in an unofficial channel, various suggestions were apt to be made.

Metternich said that we must now wait to see what report Haldane brought back from Berlin.

To this I agreed.

Yours etc.,
E. GREY.

No. 498.

Sir Edward Grey to Sir F. Bertie.

F.O. 5569/5569/12/18.
(No. 59.) Secret.

Sir,   *Foreign Office, February 7, 1912.*

I told M. Cambon to-day very confidentially for his information and that of M. Poincaré, that Lord Haldane was now on his way to Berlin.([1]) It was convenient to him to make some enquiries about scientific education in Germany, and he was going to do so with his Brother. But, while he was in Berlin, he would also have a frank interchange of views with Herr von Bethmann-Hollweg, and would explore the ground, in order to find out what Germany intended and what she wanted, and whether there was a favourable prospect for negotiations which would put the relations of the two countries on a better footing. I observed that France had made her Agreement with Germany as to Morocco; Russia had made hers as to the Bagdad Railway; but so far since I had been in Office we had not made any Agreement with Germany as to any of the difficulties between us.

M. Cambon said that he supposed the important point was naval expenditure. If an agreement on this point could be come to between England and Germany, it would be a very good thing; but he feared that it would be very difficult.

I remarked that the question was certainly a difficult one. We would have to find out what Germany wanted before we could say whether anything could be done.

[I am, &c.]
E. G[REY].

(1) [M. Paul Cambon's report on this subject is given in *D.D.F.*, *3rd Ser.*, Vol. I, pp. 630–3.]

No. 499.

Sir Edward Grey to Sir F. Bertie.

Private.(¹)
My dear Bertie,   *London, February 7, 1912.*
    The record of my conversation with Cambon will show you what I have said to him about our conversations with Germany.(²)
    Last month a communication reached one of my Colleagues from the German Emperor through Ballin and Cassel. It was brought to me, and some further communications passed through the same channel. The Emperor expressed a strong wish that I should go to Berlin, and he sent me an invitation. I thought that this would never do; but I also thought that the communications should not go any further through unofficial channels.
    It happens to be convenient for Haldane to go to Berlin about the business of a University Committee for Scientific Education, over which he presides here. He is to see Bethmann-Hollweg, and have a very frank exchange of views about naval expenditure and other things, in order to discover whether the Germans will do any thing in connection with that expenditure, and what they want in return.
    I have discussed the whole ground thoroughly with him and with Goschen. The question is not very easy. The Germans are very vague about what is possible as regards naval expenditure; and, though we are quite prepared to satisfy them that we have no intention of attacking them or supporting an aggressive policy against them, we must keep our hands free to continue the relations which we already have with France.
    I spoke to Cambon for his information and that of Poincaré, so that it is not necessary for you to make a communication; but I think that you ought to know how things stand, in case that Poincaré should say anything to you.
                                      Yours sincerely,
                                    EDWARD GREY.

(¹) [Grey MSS., Vol. 14.]
(²) [*v.* immediately preceding document.]

No. 500.

Sir E. Goschen to Sir Edward Grey.

                                        Berlin, February 9, 1912.
F.O. 5855/5569/12/18.   D. 4·15 P.M.
Tel. (No. 9.) Secret.   R. 6·45 P.M.
    Lord Haldane had yesterday friendly conversation with Chancellor at the embassy. He spoke in language arranged. Chancellor expressed satisfaction at explanation of military preparations last summer. As regards an understanding, Chancellor asked Lord Haldane's opinion as to the formula he had proposed in memorandum sent to England.(¹) After some discussion his Excellency admitted that unprovoked attacks on allies of either Power would be fatal to his formula. Lord Haldane then asked, speaking for himself only, whether mutual undertakings against aggressive unprovoked attacks and against all combinations, military and naval plans having for their basis aggression or unprovoked attack would meet his views. His Excellency was inclined to agree, but said he must consider question. The new

(¹) [*cp. infra*, pp. 682–4, No. 506, Appendices I–IV.]

German Navy Law was then discussed. Chancellor said that third squadron was absolutely necessary, so Lord Haldane pointed out measures Admiralty would have to take in consequence. He added that new construction programme was a more serious matter, and would affect value of agreement in British public opinion. Two keels for one to every one German addition would have to be laid down. Chancellor asked whether that would really be Admiralty programme. Lord Haldane said that there was no doubt of it and that some modification of German new programme would materially assist agreement. Chancellor said he would consider matter, but that some new ships would be necessary in view of third squadron. The new plan would have fundamentally to be adhered to; could Lord Haldane suggest any way out of the difficulty? Latter suggested spreading plan over a number of years. Chancellor said he would reflect on suggestion, but seemed to anticipate difficulty with German Admiralty.

The possibilities which might arise out of an agreement on above points were then discussed, and Chancellor seemed both surprised and pleased at disposition of His Majesty's Government to talk over territorial questions in Africa in friendly spirit. Lord Haldane said that of course he could not commit his colleagues in these matters, but that he was sure that if an agreement was come to on two great topics his Excellency would find His Majesty's Government in excellent mood for discussion. His Excellency said he would be in equally good mood.

Lord Haldane touched lightly on Bagdad Railway question, and Chancellor gave it to be understood that in the event of agreement he thought that he might meet our wishes.

Lord Haldane lunches with Emperor to-day.

No. 501.

Sir G. Buchanan to Sir Edward Grey.

St. Petersburgh, February 9, 1912.

F.O. 5856/5569/12/18.
Tel. (No. 49.) Secret.

D. 8·10 P.M.
R. 8 P.M. [*sic*]

Your telegram No. 96.([1])

Minister for Foreign Affairs desired me to convey to you his sincere thanks for your friendly communication, and to say that he would welcome an improvement in Anglo-German relations as making for European peace. His Excellency added that he personally rather regretted that His Majesty's Government should have taken initiative, as he believed that, had they waited a little, Germany would herself have made advances to them, and this, he thought, would have been preferable.

I observed that, if Germany now rejected olive branch which His Majesty's Government were holding out, fact of their having taken this initiative would greatly strengthen hands of His Majesty's Government should they have, in consequence of Germany's attitude, to present increased naval estimates. His Excellency admitted that there might be something in this.

([1]) [*v. supra,* pp. 667–8, No. 495.]

No. 502.

Sir E. Goschen to Sir A. Nicolson.

Private.(¹)
My dear Nicolson,   *Berlin, February 9, 1912.*(²)

I found, when I arrived here, that the Chancellor had said that he would receive Lord Haldane at 11 this morning. I didn't think that quite a good plan, so I arranged that I should go and see His Excellency at 11 and that he should come and lunch with me here to meet Lord Haldane. In conversation with the Chancellor the latter said that he had just received a despatch from Metternich and that there was evidently some misunderstanding. The idea seemed to prevail in London that Ballin had acted under instructions from the Emperor. This was far from being the case, as neither the Emperor nor he himself had anything to do with Ballin's first step! In fact he had been most surprised that Cassel had been chosen by his Majesty's Government as our intermediary in an important matter which concerned the two Governments and when there was a German Ambassador in London. I said that I had certainly understood that Ballin had acted with some authority, but the Chancellor denied it absolutely. In any case, he added, now that the matter is in the hands of the two Governments Messrs. Cassel and Ballin can now drop out. In this I agreed. Coming back here I at once telephoned to Lord Haldane asking him if possible to come in a few minutes before lunch as I had something that I wished him to know before he saw the Chancellor. I then told Lord Haldane what the Chancellor had said, and which, by the way, Stumm had said to Granville last night, viz. "Why on earth did His Majesty's Government employ Cassel?"

I was rather of the opinion that this matter should be put straight, but Lord Haldane said that he considered the matter should be passed over as lightly as possible, all the more that he suspected that the Chancellor's words to me were dictated purely by a wish to save Metternich's face.

After his conversation with the Chancellor I asked Lord Haldane whether he had mentioned the point. In reply he told me that he had begun by saying "In consequence of the Emperor's message through Ballin" &c.

You will see from Lord Haldane's memorandum(³) that the Chancellor was very pleased with the conversation. The Chancellor also told me that it had caused him the greatest satisfaction, and that he hoped it was the beginning of a real step forward in the direction of good relations.

Knowing Admiral Tirpitz' position I agreed with the Chancellor's remark that, as regards the slackening of the tempo of construction under the new plan, he might encounter some opposition from the German Admiralty. But Lord Haldane tells me that he was informed last night by Herr Ballin that Admiral Tirpitz was not likely to raise difficulties. Ballin had come straight from the Emperor, so Lord Haldane thought he would be likely to know.

I spoke to my French colleague yesterday (he came to see me at once) in the sense of Sir Edward Grey's communication to M. Paul Cambon.(⁴) He said that personally speaking he would be glad, providing there was no weakening of the 'entente cordiale,' to see the resumption of our conversations lead to a satisfactory result, as it would mean the elimination of a danger which must always be a source of anxiety to France; but he was afraid that when French public opinion came to hear of our talking to Germany there would be a certain amount of outcry. To tell you the truth Cambon himself seemed to be a little nervous about the effect which a 'rapprochement' with Germany would leave on the 'entente cordiale,' and his looks rather belied his words.

(¹) [Carnock MSS., Vol. I of 1912.]

(²) [It appears from the contents of this letter that, with the exception of the last paragraph, it was actually written on the 8th.]

(³) [v. infra, pp. 676–84, No. 506, and note (¹).]

(⁴) [v. supra, p. 669, No. 498.]

Lord Haldane is anxious that his memoranda should be sent to the King as he had promised His Majesty to keep Him well informed.

Since writing the above, Lord Haldane has informed me of the substance of his conversation with the Emperor and Admiral Tirpitz. As I pointed out to Sir Edward Grey and you in London, the difficulty to be foreseen in the whole business was—Tirpitz. The Admiral during his long term of administration has had the joy of seeing England's naval superiority over Germany substantially reduced. But the events of last summer showed that the German fleet was still not ready for serious business. Therefore, at the cost of a severe struggle with the Chancellor and the military authorities, he succeeded in getting his proposals for a still further increase of construction accepted. No doubt he threatened to resign if he did not get his way, and he is practically irreplaceable. He cannot be expected, after winning his battle, to be ready to give up all the fruits of it; and it is my firm opinion that if Lord Haldane had talked to him till Doomsday he could not have persuaded him to diminish the number of ships for which he has applied and which there is but little doubt the Reichstag will sanction. Even to spread their construction over a number of years, as Lord Haldane suggested, will be, if the suggestion is finally accepted, gall and wormwood to him, and I feel certain that nothing more favourable to our views can be obtained. Whether the firm intention of His Majesty's Government, about which Lord Haldane left no possible doubt in the mind of those with whom he conversed, to lay down two keels to one would ultimately bring the German Government to a more yielding frame of mind is another matter. There is a large section of public opinion in Germany with whom that forcible argument would have more effect than any other. But, as matters stand at present, with the public in full possession of the new Government proposals, there is perhaps a still larger section who would raise a storm against any reduction of the proposals and who will certainly make it very hot for the Government if they learn that even a reduction of the ' tempo ' of the new construction is contemplated. Under these circumstances I think that it was impossible for Lord Haldane to obtain from the Imperial Government any further concession as regards the new law than that of which they have foreshadowed their willingness to make.

Yours very sincerely,
W. E. GOSCHEN.

No. 503.

Sir Edward Grey to Sir G. Buchanan.

F.O. 5856/5569/12/18.
Tel. (No. 110.)   *Foreign Office, February 10, 1912.*
    (Your telegram No. 49.([1]))

You may inform M[inister for] F[oreign] A[ffairs] very confidentially that first communication of those [advances?], which eventually led to Lord Haldane's visit, came to us from Berlin, and was an invitation to a British Minister to visit Berlin.([2])

([1]) [v. supra, p. 671, No. 501.]
([2]) [cp. supra, pp. 666–7, Nos. 492–4.]

No. 504.

Sir E. Goschen to Sir A. Nicolson.

Personal and Private.([1])

My dear Nicolson, *Berlin, February 10, 1912.*

You will see from my other letter([2]) and from Haldane's memoranda([3]) how the conversations have gone.

The Chancellor's remarks to me about Ballin and Cassel were queer and there must be some—well call it misunderstanding—somewhere. Haldane says that the Chancellor was only trying to save Metternich's face, and that it was hardly necessary for him to allude to it. But then how about *my* face if the Germans are allowed to give the impression that H[is] M[ajesty's] G[overnment] opened the conversations through Cassel and not through H[is] M[ajesty]'s Ambassador at Berlin. That however doesn't matter—at all events it affects no one except myself. But from a public point of view I thought that it was a matter which should be put straight at once, as I don't at all like the idea that the world should think that, perturbed by the new German fleet proposals or frightened by the bellicose attitude of German Public opinion, we came to the Emperor through an underground channel with proposals for an understanding. I told this to Haldane but he would not listen. I also told him that the Chancellor was of the opinion, without any prompting from me, that now that matters were in the hands of the two Governments, Cassel and Ballin should be given to understand that they must drop out. Haldane said that that was not his idea, as the presence of those gentlemen in Berlin was most useful to him. He therefore would try and persuade them to stop. He dined with them that evening at the "Adlon" restaurant and implored them not to leave Berlin—but Ballin, who had come straight to the dinner from a long interview with the Emperor said that the latter had intimated to him that his task was now over and that he could go and he was therefore off.

I have now Haldane's second Memo[randum] before me giving his conversation with the Emperor and Tirpitz and reporting what it was possible to obtain from the German Government. And what does it amount to? That if what has been suggested is carried out the Germans get what, under Grey's instructions, I have been opposing for two years, namely a political understanding without a naval agreement. For I cannot regard a relaxation in the 'tempo' of a brand new and additional Naval Programme as a naval arrangement. We more or less rejected a relaxation of the 'tempo' of the original naval law as a rather worthless concession, and now it is proposed that we should accept a relaxation of the 'tempo' of a new Law, which will add a number of ships to the German Navy and bring up its 'personnel' up to about 80,000 men as a quid pro quo for the realization of Germany's dearest wish viz. a political understanding, an agreement which however carefully drawn up as regards the 'aggressive' point (B[ethmann] Hollweg is going to suggest a formula this afternoon) is only too likely to hamper us in the future. I pointed out most of this to Haldane—and to tell you the truth he was rather depressed at not getting more—but he said that after all a political understanding was the main thing. So said the Emperor and so said the Chancellor, and so they have said for two years! That it was possible for Haldane to get more I do not believe, but I am not surprised that both the Emperor and the Chancellor are "in a good mood"! Besides the understanding we appear to be willing to give them Zanzibar &c. and facilitate at a given moment their acquisition of certain Portuguese possessions, besides a share under our Concessions in S. Persia. On the other hand what do we get? No Naval arrangement such as might relieve our tax payers—only a relaxation in the 'tempo' of construction outside the old Naval Law and fair promises about Timor and the Bagdad Railway. I told Haldane that in my opinion they were getting, more or less,

([1]) [Carnock MSS., Vol. I of 1912.]
([2]) [*v. supra*, pp. 672–3, No. 502.]
([3]) [*v. infra*, pp. 676–84, No. 506.]

their hearts' desire at a cheaper price than we had fixed before. And I think this is a pity as recent events have shown that our position, unhampered by a political understanding, is a strong one, and our price should therefore have been raised not lowered. That is however only a personal opinion. Thank goodness Haldane has been firm enough on the two keels to one question. That is a practical argument which may yet have some influence on their Construction Programme. Tirpitz is evidently very exercised by Haldane's assurances that the two keels to one are inevitable.

Cambon is pale but calm,' but whatever he says I can see that he is not comfortable, and I *hear* (through Russell from his Russian colleague) that the Russian Embassy is rather in dismay: but then they don't in the least know what Haldane has been doing. Hullo! they want to close the bag.

Yours ever,
W. E. GOSCHEN.

P.S.—Watson has sent a fearfully long—unnecessarily so—report upon Naval matters. I should like you to skim through it—as though his pen is prolix—he *does* know his job—and he has exceptional facilities for knowing what is going on owing to his large acquaintance—and I think popularity—among German naval officers—senior and junior.

W. E. G.

No. 505.

*Copy of telegram from M. Jules Cambon to M. Poincaré communicated by
Lord Haldane.*

Private.([1])

Lord Haldane, que j'ai vu hier soir à l'Ambassade d'Angleterre, souhaiterait que la tension existant actuellement entre l'opinion anglaise et l'opinion allemande, put prendre fin. Il était naturel qu'au moment de la formation de la triplice, les puissances qui n'en faisaient pas partie, gravitassent les unes vers les autres pour contrebalancer l'Allemagne et l'Autriche unies. Par suite, le maintien des relations existant entre l'Angleterre, la France et la Russie doit être la condition de tout essai de conversation entre les cabinets de Londres et de Berlin.

L'impression laissée par le Chancelier à Lord Haldane est que cette manière de voir est la sienne. Sans renoncer à leurs unions particulières, les grandes puissances pourraient chercher à d'accorder entre elles, dans leur commun désir de maintenir la paix.

J'ai fait remarquer à Lord Haldane que dans ces conditions, son voyage avait en vue l'établissement d'une détente et non d'une entente entre l'Angleterre à l'Allemagne. Lord Haldane trouva la distinction correcte, mais il espère qu'une détente conduirait à quelque chose de préférable, qui serait cependant en harmonie avec le maintien absolu de l'entente entre l'Angleterre, la France et la Russie.

Je repondis que dans ces conditions la détente ne comporterait pas dans le présent d'arrangement sur des points précis, notamment sur les questions qui occupent la presse, la limitation des armements maritimes, les accords territorials en Afrique, le chemin de fer de Bagdad.

Lord Haldane ne parla que de la question navale et comme je disais qu'il serait difficile au Gouvernement Allemand d'arrêter le developpement de la marine de guerre, il me repondit que l'Angleterre ne permettrait jamais que sa supériorité navale fût mise en question.

([1]) [Grey MSS., Vol. 63. The interview between Lord Haldane and M. Jules Cambon took place on February 9, 1912. The date of the communication of a copy of the above telegram by Lord Haldane to Sir Edward Grey is uncertain, as the following minute attached to it is dated only " February 1912."

" This is a copy, given to me by Lord Haldane, of the telegram sent by M. Jules Cambon to M. Poincaré after M. Jules Cambon had seen Lord Haldane at Berlin. E. G."]

Je m'en felicitai en remarquant que toute diminution de la puissance navale de l'Angleterre devrait entrainer par contre une augmentation de sa force militaire.

En terminant, Lord Haldane me répéta qu'il était venu simplement ici *tâter le terrain*.

No. 506.

Diary of Lord Haldane's Visit to Berlin.

I.

F.O. 6063/5569/12/18A. *February* 10, 1912.(¹)

Thursday, February 8, 1912.

I arrived at Berlin at 7·30 this morning, and was met at the Friedrichstrasse station by Sir Edward Goschen's motor and the embassy porter. I proceeded with my brother and servant to the Hôtel Bristol, which is close to the embassy. I saw Sir Edward Goschen before 10 o'clock. He informed me that he had arranged with the Chancellor that the latter should lunch at the embassy, and that after luncheon I should have a private talk with him *à deux*. Before luncheon I saw Sir Edward, who had in the meantime seen the Chancellor. The Chancellor had asked the question whether I was to talk to him officially, the difficulty being that he, the Chancellor, could not divest himself of his official position, and it would be awkward to talk with me in a purely private capacity. I said I should tell the Chancellor that I had come here officially with the approval of the King and the Cabinet, but merely to talk over the ground, and not to commit either himself or my own Government to any propositions.

At the interview with the Chancellor, which took place at 2 o'clock, and lasted for more than an hour and a half, I began by giving him the message of good wishes for the conversations and for the future of Anglo-German relations with which the King had entrusted me at the audience I had before leaving. He was pleased with this message, and intimated that he would write through the German Ambassador to thank the King. I then said that perhaps it would be convenient if I defined the capacity in which I was in Berlin, and there to talk to him; and I defined it as above intimated. I proceeded to ask whether he wished to make any observations or desired that I should begin. He wished me to begin, and I went on at once to speak to him as arranged in a conversation I had had with Sir Edward Grey before leaving London.

I told him that I felt there had been a great deal of drifting away between Germany and England, and that it was important to ask what was the cause. To ascertain this, events of recent history had to be taken into account. [Germany had built up, and was building up, magnificent armaments, and with the aid of the Triple Alliance she had become the centre of a tremendous group.] The natural consequence was that other Powers had tended to approximate. I was not questioning for a moment Germany's policy, but this was the natural and inevitable consequence in the interests of security. We used to have much the same situation with France when she was very powerful on the sea that we had with Germany now. While the fact to which I had referred created a difficulty, the difficulty was not insuperable; for two groups of Powers might be on very friendly relations if there was only an increasing sense of mutual understanding and confidence. The present seemed to me to be a favourable moment for a new departure. The Morocco question was

---

(¹) [This date is given as that on which Sir E. Goschen sent to Sir Edward Grey the text of the first two parts of the Diary. A note on the despatch says that Part III and the Appendices were " added later by Lord Haldane " (*cp.* also *infra*, p. 709, No. 532, where Lord Haldane states that Parts I and II were written on the 8th and 9th " within an hour " of the conversations recorded, and Part III on the morning of February 10). Sir E. Goschen's despatch arrived on February 12. It seems clear that Part III and the Appendices were still lacking when Sir Eyre Crowe wrote the minute printed *infra*, pp. 684–5.]

now out of the way, and we had no agreements with France or Russia except those that were in writing and published to the world.

The Chancellor interrupted me, and asked me whether this was really so. I replied that I could give him the assurance that it was so without reserve, and that in the situation which now existed I saw no reason why it should not be possible for us to enter into a new and cordial friendship carrying the two old ones into it perhaps to the profit of Russia and France as well as Germany herself. He replied that he had no reason to differ from this view.

In connection with my remarks as to the events of last summer, he interposed that we had military preparations. I replied that no preparations had been made which were other than those required to bring the capacity of the British army in point of mobilisation to something approaching the standard which Germany had long ago reached and which was with her a matter of routine. For this purpose we had studied our deficiencies and modes of operation. This, however, was a purely departmental matter concerning the War Office, and the Minister who did it was the one who was now talking to him and who was not wanting in friendly feeling towards Germany. We could not be caught unprepared, and in Germany they would say that my preparations ought to be matters of routine. They certainly were not evidence of hostility or of any design of attack.

The Chancellor seemed much pleased with this explanation, and said there had been much talk of our fleet and our army, and the steps we had taken, but that he understood the position I had indicated. I said, in reply, that it was a pleasure to me to hear this, and that I hoped I should carry him with me still further in my belief that if Germany had really, which I did not at all suppose, intended to crush France and destroy her capacity to defend herself, we in England would have had such a direct interest in the result that we could not have sat by and seen this done.

He said he did not dissent from this view, nor did he wish to hamper our freedom in such a case. But he wished to propose a formula; the balance of power was a phrase he did not like, though he admitted that the historical considerations I had referred to made it natural that some grouping should take place, and that England should lean towards the weaker side. He had, however, proposed, in his communication to us, a formula of neutrality which might go a long way to help.

I said I cordially agreed with the good intention of his formula, the wording of which was that neither was to enter into any combinations against the other. If this meant combinations for attack or aggression, I was entirely of his mind. But I must put on spectacles in looking at his words, and first of all I would put on German spectacles. How would Germany find herself if, when bound by such a formula, we were so wicked as to attack her ally Austria or to try to grab Denmark, which was of deep strategical interest to her? She would certainly have to combine against us and attack us. Again, suppose Germany joined in an attack on Japan or Portugal or Belgium—he then interposed, "Or Holland"—but I said I really hadn't all our treaties sufficiently in my head to be as sure about Holland as I was about the others. Or if, I added, Germany were to pounce upon France and proceed to dismember her, what would happen? He answered that these cases were not at all likely, but he admitted that they were fatal to his formula. I asked him whether he would be satisfied with mutual undertakings against aggressive or unprovoked attacks and against all combinations, military and naval agreements, and plans directed to the purpose of aggression or unprovoked attack. He said it was very difficult to define what was meant by aggression or unprovoked attack. I replied that you could not define the number of grains which it took to make a heap, but one knew a heap when one saw one. I did not know what my colleagues would think of such a formula as I had suggested, but it struck me, as at present advised, as not only consistent with all our engagements with other Powers, but as of much more value if it was introductory to substantive clauses about other things. He said that he was inclined to take the same view, but he would like to consider the question. He saw how difficult it was for both countries to make an unrestrictive neutrality agreement which would be consistent with their treaty and moral obligations, but he thought there was something to be said for what I had suggested. The spirit, he said, was everything; and, if there was the real spirit, such words as these might express all that was necessary.

We then passed on to the question of the German fleet, as to which he asked me whether I would like to make any observations. I said I must. He and I had been talking with the most absolute candour and friendliness to each other, and I felt he would regard me as wanting in character were I not very frank with him about the new Navy Law. What was the use of entering into a solemn agreement for concord and against attack if Germany at the same moment was going to increase her battle fleet as a precaution against us, and we had consequently to increase our battle fleet as a precaution against her? This was vital from our point of view, because we were an island Power dependent for our food supplies on the power of protecting our commerce, and for this we needed the two-power standard and a substantial preponderance in battle fleets. He said that it was absolutely essential to Germany to have a third squadron in full readiness for war. At present, owing to her system of recruiting, for three months in the year she had virtually, owing to the necessity for training recruits, no fleet ready at all. I said I did not contest this; she was quite entitled to have it if she thought it necessary, but the result would be that we should not be able to rely on the two battle squadrons and reserve squadrons which had sufficed hitherto, but that we should be compelled to have five or even six squadrons ready in home waters, perhaps bringing ships from the Mediterranean to strengthen them. He asked me was that necessary if we had a friendly agreement? I said it would be a less convincing proof of friendliness if Germany prepared her third squadron, and we should have no option. Still, I said, this was not so serious as the proposal to add a third ship every second year to the German construction programme. This would put us in great difficulties so far as securing the good opinion of the public in England about the value of an agreement. We should certainly have to proceed at once to lay down two keels to each one of the new German additions, and that would cost money and cause feeling. It was true that each country could bear the additional cost without difficulty. They were rich and so were we. If it was for the purpose of the navy our people would not complain, in my opinion, of the addition of another shilling to the income tax, but it would be a great pity. He asked was that really likely to be our programme, the laying down of two additional keels for each German one. I said I had no doubt that that would be the result, and the Government would be turned out if they failed to accomplish it; and therefore some modification seemed to be of the utmost importance, if the agreement was to be a real success.

After a pause he said he would consider this and "die Sache überlegen." The conversation up to this point had been largely in German, I taking to English whenever there was a delicate topic, and the Chancellor occasionally speaking English, but nearly always German. In order to avoid misunderstanding we sometimes repeated sentences in the other language. I was impressed by his evident desire to meet us whenever he could, and I derived considerable hope from the manner and emphasis with which he said that he would reconsider the question of the ships. But I must add that he went on to say that the question of the new squadron was vital and that some new ships would be necessary in it. Could I suggest any way out, for they must keep to the plan of a new law? I observed that it was not for me to venture to make any suggestion to his Excellency, but that a spreading out in time of the new programme might make a difference. He said, "Perhaps, eight or nine years"; I added, "Or twelve, if he could not do better." He again said that he would take this matter into serious consideration and consult his experts. "My admirals," he said, "are very difficult." "That was an experience," I observed, "which we sometimes found in England also." He then said to me, "Suppose we were to come to an agreement on the two topics already discussed, what would follow?" I replied that such an agreement would open up a vista of other topics. We were free traders and believed that the more trade Germany developed the more we should develop. He said "Yes! we each give each other the open door." I said I wished we could work in the world together a great deal more. He said, "In Africa, for instance." I said, "In Africa particularly."

We then went over various possibilities in Africa, on which I had been instructed pretty fully by Harcourt and by Grey. He seemed much pleased and I thought a little surprised at our openness to talk over territorial questions in Africa. He never mentioned Walfisch Bay, but when I said that the Island of Timor, to which I thought Germany had a right under the secret agreement, might land us in difficulties with Australia, he added, at once, that he would gladly meet us on that. I said that I could not commit my colleagues on this subject or on anything else further than this, that if we agreed on the two great topics, he would find us in an excellent mood for discussion. He said he would be in an excellent mood for discussion also.

On this I observed that there were one or two little things of which we should then wish to speak, and I mentioned the Bagdad Railway. He smiled and said that he thought he could meet our wishes about that. We discussed it a little, satisfactorily, and then I hinted that there might be commercial enterprises in our sphere of interest in Persia which would possibly be open to discussion as regards German participation, though this must for the present necessarily remain vague.

This brought a very long conversation to a conclusion. He asked me whether, if we could agree on the two first matters, I would like to return to London and take the sense of my colleagues before we talked about the other questions. I replied in the negative. I thought I knew enough of their ideas to be able to do all that we could do at this stage, which was to talk over the ground fairly fully. My instructions were not to bind or commit them, but I knew their intentions so intimately that, with this reservation, I had felt myself in a position to say as much as I had said. I had done my best to express myself to him with the most perfect frankness, keeping nothing back of what was passing in my mind. He said that he had appreciated that throughout our talk, and had liked the conversation all the better on that account; it had been very helpful to him. For two and a half years he had been striving to bring about an agreement between Germany and England. This had been the aim of his policy. He recognised that we desired to preserve to the fullest degree our existing relations with France and Russia; and Germany also had analogous obligations which we would not desire to interfere with. I had said that I could commit nobody in what I had said, and he on his part wished likewise to say that he could commit nobody. He would take counsel over our talk and communicate with me shortly again.

I have reason to think that he went immediately to see the Emperor. There is no saying what difficulties may not crop up. It is evident to me that, as regards others than the Emperor, the Chancellor has not an easy task before him, but I was impressed with what appeared to me to be his absolute sincerity and good-will, and I have confidence that so far as he is concerned he wishes to do his very best. I shall doubtless know much more for better or for worse shortly.

II.

Friday, February 9, 1912.

I lunched at 1 o'clock with the Emperor at the Schloss. Besides the Empress and Princess Victoria Louise there were present the Chancellor and Admiral Tirpitz and one or two others. After luncheon the Emperor withdrew with me to his study along with Admiral Tirpitz. I found the relations excellent and the atmosphere genial. The Emperor tried, as I did myself, to bring his mind to the standpoint of the other country. After expressing the opinion that an agreement, if it could be come to, would improve things enormously for all of us and indeed for the whole world, and speaking of my conversation with the Chancellor the evening before in terms which showed that he was minutely informed of what had passed, the Emperor invited me to proceed to naval matters. He sat on one side of the table at the head of which I sat, and on the other side Admiral Tirpitz.

I began by saying that I was not a technical expert in naval things and that of course the navy was not my department, but that I understood it would be agreeable to the Emperor to explore the ground with me in this as in previous matters. I might from my want of knowledge use language that was inapt or inaccurate, as indeed might the Emperor himself. But neither of us would be bound, and I might be able to carry back ideas *ad referendum*. A long discussion then ensued, part of it in German, part of it in English, and part in a mixture of both. [Admiral Tirpitz, and indeed the Emperor himself, said that the original programme was to have a new Fleet Law with a new ship every year of the six; that they had cut it down to three ships in six years beginning in 1912, and it was very difficult to get out of this. Admiral Tirpitz said that he had to take care of the Emperor's position before the German public, and that the three new ships were, moreover, essential for the third squadron, which they desired to introduce for the purpose of having a fleet available all the year round.] They could not get the men without the ships. A fundamental law gave them the complement of men only when and if the ships were laid down, and it was therefore necessary to lay down the ships, or at least to get them voted, in order to produce their squadron. I remarked that I did not doubt what Admiral Tirpitz told me, but I pointed out that if we were to enter into an agreement for settling differences and introducing a new spirit into our relations, that agreement would be bones without flesh if Germany began new ship-building immediately. Indeed, the world would laugh at the agreement, and our people would think that we had been befooled. I did not myself take that view, because I thought the mere fact of an agreement was valuable; but the Emperor would see that public opinion would attach very little importance to his action unless the agreement largely modified his ship-building programme.

We then discussed this programme at great length. Admiral Tirpitz struggled for it. [I insisted that fundamental modification was essential. The tone was thoroughly friendly, but I felt that I had come to the most difficult part of my task of getting materials fit to bring back for the consideration of my colleagues. The utmost I was able to get to was this: the Emperor was so disturbed at the idea that the world would not believe in the reality of the agreement unless the ship-building programme was modified that he asked me what I would suggest. I said that it was a too technical matter for me to discuss here, but that if he could not drop the new law—which I saw he felt he could not—he might at least drop out a ship.] This idea was never abandoned, but Admiral Tirpitz combated it so hard that I said, "Well, can we not spread the *tempo*?" After much talking we got to this, that, as I insisted that they must not inaugurate the agreement by building an additional ship at once, they should put off building the first ship till 1913, and then should not lay down another till three years after (1916), and lay down the third till 1919.] Admiral Tirpitz wanted us to give some undertaking about our own ship-building. He thought the two-Power standard a hard one for Germany, and, indeed, Germany could not make any admission about it. I said it was not a matter for admission. Germany must be free and we must be free, and we should probably lay down two keels to their one. In this case the initiative was not with us but with them. The idea occurred to all of us on this observation that we should try to avoid defining a standard proportion in the agreement, and that, indeed, we should say nothing at all about ship-building in the agreement, but that if the political agreement was concluded the Emperor should at once announce to the German public that this entirely new fact modified his desire for the Fleet Law as originally conceived, and that it should be delayed and spread out to the extent we had discussed. For the rest, each of us would remain masters in our own houses as far as naval matters were concerned. The Emperor thought the agreement would affect profoundly the tendency in ship-building, and he certainly should not desire to go beyond the three ships. The fact of the agreement was the key to everything. The Chancellor, he said, would propose to me this afternoon a formula which he had drafted. I said that I would see the Chancellor and discuss any further territorial questions with him, and would then return as speedily as I could and report the good disposition which I had found to my colleagues, and leave the difficulties of not being able to stop ship-building more completely, and, indeed, all other matters, to their judgment. I could only assure the Emperor that I had been much struck with the friendly disposition in Berlin, and that he would find a not less friendly disposition in London.

III.

Friday, February 9, 1912 (Later).

After my interview with the Emperor I dined with the Chancellor—Herr von Kiderlen-Waechter was there, but I had no private conversation with him. Indeed, such conversation was unnecessary, for I had thought it prudent to call on him earlier in the evening at his house in the Foreign Office. I had had a quite friendly but not very long talk with him and had touched on politics, but only in general terms, for I had and have the strong impression that the Chancellor did not want him to have a part in the conversation. However, we made friends. At the dinner at the Chancellor's, Baron Stumm, Professor Harnach [sic: Harnack], Herr Zimmermann, of the Foreign Office, and others were present. After dinner the Chancellor took me into a room with him alone. I saw that he was disturbed by a remark I made as to the difficulty I was sure my colleagues would feel about the smallness of the slackening in German ship-building in the proposals Tirpitz had made to me that afternoon at the Emperor's. I had remarked to the Emperor that I would rather make no observation on them, beyond that I must take them *ad referendum* to the British Cabinet. The Chancellor said that if we could not meet them in their necessity for a new Fleet Law, the idea of agreement must go to pieces (" scheitern ") and that things would grow worse. He had done and was doing his best—what the result of failure would be was matter of destiny (" Schicksal "). I observed that we were now speaking as man to man, that I was as anxious for an agreement as he was, and my colleagues were anxious too. But how would our agreement look if it were followed by more ship-building? And that this was to be so arose from, I did not for a moment say the fault, but the initiative of Germany. He looked depressed.

I then left, for I had to meet M. J. Cambon at 10 o'clock at the British Embassy. With him I had a talk alone. I found him a little nervous, so, without telling him anything, I said emphatically that we were not going to be disloyal to France or Russia, that the Chancellor agreed that it would be dishonourable in us if we even talked of departing from the existing agreements, and that we believed a better state of public opinion between England and Germany would benefit France. With that he said he agreed. He suggested that my conversation had no other end than to create a *détente*, as distinguished from an *entente*. I said this was so as regards my conversation. I had not come there to draw up an agreement, or to do more than *tâter le terrain*. But that I hoped more than a *détente* would follow later on—if my very limited mission succeeded. He said he wanted to telegraph the gist of our talk in cypher to M. Poincaré. I said I had no objection, especially if, as he kindly said he would, he would let me see his telegram before it went. This he willingly agreed to, and I saw it the next day and modified it, so that it went in the words of the copy which I have brought with me.(²) As the conversation was in French, this was a useful precaution. Sir E. Goschen also saw him, and I am pretty sure, from a remark of the Chancellor's next day, that he knew that M. Cambon had seen me.

(²) [*v. supra*, pp. 675–6, No. 505.]

On the Saturday I lunched with Baron von Stumm, of the Foreign Office, who was formerly at the German Embassy in London as Secretary. After luncheon he took me aside and said he had something to tell me. It was that the Chancellor was unhappy over what he had gathered from his talk with me last night was my impression that my colleagues would consider Tirpitz's concession too small to be accepted by English public opinion. The Chancellor, said Baron Stumm, was not going to let this agreement—which was the dream of his life—founder because of Tirpitz, and it would help him, Stumm thought, if I took a very strong line to the effect that there must be further naval concessions. I took the hint, and when I went, as I had previously arranged with the Chancellor to do, to his house at 5 o'clock, I began by saying that continued reflection had made me even more unhappy than I was after leaving the Emperor's Palace on the previous day. English public opinion would not improbably be unmanageable and, I thought, with reason. He said he saw my point. He would do his best. But the forces he had to contend with were almost insuperable. Public opinion in Germany expected a new law and the third squadron, and he must have these. I said we could not contest Germany's right to do in these matters and indeed in other matters as she pleased. But why not postpone the ship-building for longer and adapt the law accordingly? It was a serious situation. No doubt Germany wanted the third squadron for her recruits, and it was mainly a question of organisation. But it would make her stronger at sea. If an agreement were come to, and it was a success, it would matter much less whether Germany built a few ships more or less. For instance, we did not look closely at how France built. But keep the two-power standard we must, and our people would resent the increasing burden Germany proposed to put on us. It might be fatal to the much-desired "Verständigung." The Chancellor said he would try. He asked me to consult the experts in London and make a suggestion. I had said, he remarked, that everything was good only on balance, and Germany must for a greater end give up a minor advantage. The new squadron and the new Fleet Law she must have, but it was a question for the experts, on which he did not pronounce, whether a retardation of greater magnitude than Tirpitz proposed might not be possible. I promised to let him know privately the state of feeling here about the Tirpitz proposals on my return.

We then sat down at a table with pencils and paper and went on a voyage of discovery about other matters which are indicated in the notes which I have brought back (printed as appendices). I can only say that the attitude of the Chancellor was that of a high-minded sincere gentleman, and left me nothing whatever to desire. When we parted he held me by the hand and said that whether success or failure crowned the effort which was the greatest object of his life now, he should never forget that I had met him with an openness and sympathy for his difficulties which made the recollection of these days for him a delightful one. I reciprocated his sentiments not less warmly, and said I should now be able to leave next Sunday and lay my impressions before my colleagues.

APPENDIX I.

Sketch of a Conceivable Formula.

The high contracting Powers assure each other mutually of their desire for peace and friendship.

2. They will not, either of them, make any unprovoked attack upon the other or join in any combination or design against the other for purposes of aggression, or become party to any plan or naval or military combination alone or in conjunction with any other Power directed to such an end.

3. If either of the high contracting parties becomes entangled in a war in which it cannot be said to be the aggressor, the other will at least observe towards the

Power so entangled a benevolent neutrality, and use its utmost endeavour for the localisation of the conflict.

4. The duty of neutrality which arises from the preceding article has no application in so far as it may not be reconcilable with existing agreements which the high contracting parties have already made. The making of new agreements which render it impossible for either of the high contracting parties to observe neutrality towards the others [*sic*: other] beyond what is provided by the preceding limitation is excluded in conformity with the provision contained in article 2.

5. The high contracting parties declare that they will do all in their power to prevent differences and misunderstanding between either of them and other Powers.

Appendix II.

Further Proposals given me in Writing by the Chancellor.

England to make no objection to the completion of the Bagdad Railway (*e.g.*, England will not object to the raising of the Turkish customs dues).

2. Thereupon Germany, so far as concerns the Bagdad–Bussorah section, will meet the English wish to have an exceptional position.

3. In the event of England making railways in her zone in Persia she will be willing that Germany should have a participation.

4. Thereupon Germany will agree with England that she will fully recognise the political interests of England in the Persian Gulf and in South Persia. For instance, that England should obtain from Turkey an extensive concession for the Bussorah–Koweit section. Germany gives up claim to that section and will diplomatically assist England to obtain it.

5. Further, Germany will assist England to obtain from Turkey a concession for a harbour in Koweit—a concession similar to that which a German company has at Haidar Pasha.

6. The two contracting parties undertake for the future to exchange views about all questions which may arise, and to endeavour to bring about a solution suitable to the reciprocal interests of both parties.

7. Each of the two Powers will make use of its own good and friendly relations to third Powers in order to influence the relations of the other Powers to such third Powers in a friendly sense.

8. Agreement, say, for ten years, with automatic prolongation.

Appendix III.

Memorandum.

After discussing formulæ, we passed to territorial questions. Each of us had a map. The sum and substance of the discussion amounted to this :—

Germany would like to have Zanzibar and Pemba. In exchange, she would give us what the Chancellor defined as " eine sonderbare Stelle " (a special position) in the Bagdad–Bussorah section of the Bagdad Railway.

I replied : " Nicht nur eine sonderbare Stelle, aber eine kontrollirende Stelle."

He answered : " Ich werde Ihren Wünschen entgegen kommen." He did not wish that this should be done by bringing other Powers into the controlling share. He said that he would arrange that we should have what we desired in a form which he would work out with us.

The other proposals in connection with the Bagdad Railway and Southern Persia appear in the memorandum which he handed to me.

He was anxious to have the piece of Angola reserved for Britain by the secret agreement.

I said that we would like to have the Island of Timor.

He agreed to this at once.

I told him that if Germany ever obtained a belt across the Lower Congo—as to which she would have to make a friendly bargain with France as well as with Belgium—we would ask her to let us have the Katanga triangle.

He agreed; but said that he would like very much to have Seal and Penguin Islands, off Angua Pequeña.

I observed that I feared these islands might prove to belong to the South African Union, in which case it would be difficult to exchange them; but I would look into this point.

He replied that he would make no difficulties for us if we could not help him, and I would notice that he had not even mentioned Walfisch Bay, because he knew how difficult our position was with the South African Union.([2a])

We went over the map of Africa, but I cannot recall that any further question was raised.

He was thoroughly desirous of meeting our wishes, and said to me: "I am not here to make a bargain with you. We must look at this thing on both sides from a high point of view, and if you have any difficulties, tell me, and I will see whether I can get round them for you."

APPENDIX IV.

First Suggestions of Chancellor—abandoned in further Conversation about Formulæ.

The high contracting Powers assure each other mutually of their desire for peace and friendship.

2. They will not either of them make any combination, or join in any combination, which is directed against the other. They declare expressly that they are not bound by any such combination.

3. If either of the high contracting parties becomes entangled in a war with one or more other Powers, the other of the high contracting parties will at least observe towards the Power so entangled a benevolent neutrality, and use its utmost endeavour for the localisation of the conflict.

4. The duty of neutrality which arises from the preceding article has no application, in so far as it may not be reconcilable with existing agreements which the high contracting parties have already made. The making of new agreements which make it impossible for either of the contracting parties to observe neutrality towards the other beyond what is provided by the preceding limitations, is excluded in conformity with the provisions contained in article 2.

5. The high contracting parties declare that they will, in the case of either of them having differences with third Powers, mutually give their diplomatic support for the purposes of settling their differences.

MINUTE.([3])

I am not in a position usefully to comment on this paper as a whole; the policy indicated is of course a reversal of the attitude hitherto taken up by H[is] M[ajesty's] G[overnment] as regards the German naval law. There is one point of special interest:

The German gov[ernmen]t declared, with some emphasis that whatever England did in the way of ship-building, nothing would in any circumstances be added to the German programme as fixed by law.

([2a]) [*v. supra*, p. 272, No. 179, *note* ([2]).]

([3]) [At the head of Sir Eyre Crowe's minute a note by Sir Edward Grey was written as follows: "Lord Haldane is having his papers that are to be circulated to the Cabinet printed: these papers are not complete." *cp. supra*, p. 676, *note* ([1]).]

I have not myself ever attached any value to these assurances, but there is some interest in calling attention to the way in which they are now completely ignored.

H[is] M[ajesty's] G[overnment] took up the line that unless there were a real *reduction* in the German programme, an agreement had no value. The German government ultimately offered to slacken the rate of building by spreading the execution of the programme over a slightly longer period of years. Later on H[is] M[ajesty's] G[overnment] accepted this as a possible solution, provided it preceded any political agreement. Whereupon the German gov[ernmen]t withdrew their proposal altogether and proposed to proceed with a political agreement alone, without any naval arrangement.

So far as I can gather from the present memoranda, the suggestion now is to conclude a political agreement on a basis of (1) a general formula and (2) special bargains on the principle of give and take. [Any naval understanding is to be excluded from the agreement. The German gov[ernmen]t is merely to give an assurance (not to this country, but to their own parliament) that there will be less rapid completion of a big new programme than would have been necessary in the absence of the political agreement with England. Such a form of " understanding " has of course no binding effect. If a political incident intervened, or if merely the German gov[ernmen]t were to renew the press campaign against this country which they allowed to flourish during the last 6 months, they would be fully justified in saying that, in view of the state of public feeling, they could not, with the best intention, avoid going beyond their assurances.

Therefore an assurance, having no conventional force, is useless for the only purpose for which we should require it. An alternative would be to put the understanding respecting naval construction into a secret treaty, to be signed simultaneously with the political agreement. I do not, however, suppose, after all that has recently been said about secret engagements, that H[is] M[ajesty's] G[overnment] would willingly consent to such an arrangement.

In these circumstances there seems to remain nothing for practical consideration except the political agreement. I gather from the German Chancellor's remark that he realizes the difficulty of finding any " formula " with a positive content that could reasonably be expected to suit all parties. So soon as anything very precise and binding is said, the formula becomes inapplicable. It must remain vague, and a vague formula really means nothing beyond an assurance that neither party harbours any hostile designs. That is no more than what every State is bound to profess to its neighbours. It is nothing justifying any counterconcession on either side.

There remains the special bargain on the basis of ' Do ut Des.' There is of course no difficulty in seeing quite a number of concessions, territorial and other, that Germany would welcome from us. The difficulty is in finding the counterconcession that is to represent our share of the bargain. This has always been the difficulty in our previous understandings with Germany. It was generally solved by England making the concessions, and Germany replying by an assurance of general friendship. The result was invariably found to be disappointing, and the reason is not really obscure. Germany made the experience [experiment] and saw it repeatedly confirmed that the policy of first getting up great public excitement against England and then offering more friendly relations in return for some tangible token of British good will, in the shape of a definite concession, invariably led to her getting a good deal, if not all of what she wanted.

It could hardly be doubtful that if, after having with conspicuous success carried on a policy on different lines for 8 years, H[is] M[ajesty's] G[overnment] were now to revert to the system of political concessions without adequate return, Germany would feel rewarded for the trouble she has taken to make herself as disagreeable as possible to England, and encouraged to pursue the same course in future. It would be a distinct invitation to her to act as she did last summer.

The essential point of any possible agreement seems therefore to lie in the discovery of something that Germany should give us in return for anything we may be asked to give.] I am not well enough informed as to what has passed to make any definite suggestions on this point. But some ideas present themselves as possible : We might perhaps stipulate for a larger share of Mozambique, so as to give Rhodesia (and possibly, in future, the Katanga) a direct access to the east coast, as well as to the west coast (which we already enjoy under the 1898 agreement[4]); also Timor should fall to us; Germany should not only accept everything we desire in respect to the Bagdad railway, but should definitely recognize our exclusive political influence in the Persian gulf, and refrain from any activity in either the British or the neutral sphere in Persia itself. These are not really serious concessions for us to ask. Others may suggest themselves. The essential thing is that if we are to have no naval agreement, and a political agreement is nevertheless decided upon, then there should be an overwhelming advantage for us in any merely political agreement. For public opinion in this country will be seriously disappointed at the failure to get a naval agreement and will naturally look askance at any political bargain not including such an agreement. If, in addition, the new pact is not favourable to this country on its merits, the feeling against Germany will inevitably become more bitter than it already is, which clearly ought, at any reasonable cost, to be avoided.

E. A. C.
Feb. 12.
F. D. A.
A. N.
E. G.

(4) [*v. Gooch & Temperley*, Vol. I, pp. 71–3, Nos. 90–1, *encls.*]

No. 507.

Notes by Sir A. Nicolson on the " Sketch of a conceivable Formula." Appendix I
to Lord Haldane's Diary.

Private.([1])

1. Could certainly stand.

2. Could be improved by omitting the words after "aggression"—if we engage to abstain from entering into *any naval or military combination* involving a possible offensive line of action, we should be debarred from any arrangements which are "defensive" in policy but "offensive" in the strategical sense.

3. We have, I believe, always consistently maintained that there is no such thing as a "*benevolent* neutrality" as it involves a contradiction in terms. If a country is neutral it is neutral and nothing else—*benevolence* towards one party is distinctly a violation of that neutrality. Who can say, further, who is in reality the aggressor? A country, and history furnishes many examples, may be forced by the political action of her adversary to assume the rôle of an apparent aggressor. To use "best endeavours" for localising a war might very conceivably involve belligerent operations. I should omit the whole of No. 3.

No. 4 has no meaning without No. 3, and is open to the objection that it permits the Triple Alliance to act as it may think fit, but definitely precludes us from entering into any engagements of the same nature. Our hands would be definitely tied for the future. I would therefore omit No. 4.

No. 5 could remain. The formula would then consist of No. 1, part of No. 2 and No. 5. It is true it would be then a brief document—but it is even then going further than anything we have signed hitherto, our Japanese Alliance of course excepted.

([1]) [Carnock MSS., Vol. I of 1912.]

No. 508.

Sir F. Bertie to Sir Edward Grey.

F.O. 6855/5569/12/18.
Private.

My dear Grey:—   *Paris, February* 11, 1912.

Baron von Stumm paid me a visit yesterday. He explained that his stay here, beyond the intention expressed to me when I last saw him, was due to incompleted business. He also said that Germany was not at the present time an agreeable country for him to be in for he found himself, when there lately, in disagreement with almost all his friends on the subject of England. He had no patience with such men as Kiderlen Waechter. He was an intelligent but common vulgar fellow with bad manners and worse methods. Evidently he has deserted that gentleman for present purposes. The Emperor has taken a dislike to him, but cannot get rid of him. Bethmann Hollweg is still Stumm's right man in the right place, but unfortunately he has a horror of foreign politics which he has not studied and does not fully understand. Stumm found him anxious to be on good terms with England and so was the Emperor who constantly referred to the English blood in his veins. Advantage ought to be taken of these favourable dispositions. After beating about the bush a little more he referred to Lord Haldane's visit or rather mission to Berlin, for nobody affects to believe in the University business on which he is said to have gone to Germany. Did I, Stumm asked, think that an arrangement could be come to. I said that I thought that it would be very difficult in view of the German Naval budget and we had nothing to give away to satisfy German ambitions we had no spare Heligolands which the British public would be prepared to present to Germany as gifts and we could not give away the goods of others.

Stumm had when in Germany deprecated the proposed increase in the German Naval budget as it must inevitably be met by a proportional increase in the British Programme. He thought it senseless. The answer had, he saw, already been made by Mr. Churchill and very naturally and though he objected to the German fleet being considered a luxury he admitted that supremacy at sea must be [a] necessity for England. The chief argument successfully used in Germany for an increase in the fleet was that all the world over Germany was opposed by England, in China, Turkey, Africa, including Morocco where there had never been any intention on the part of Germany to establish herself territorially; and even in Persia. It ought to be possible to come to an understanding. It would be so easy for England to facilitate matters for Germany by concessions of some sort not necessarily by giving up British territories as gifts.

I replied that Germany had arrived late on the scene and expected without the expenditure of life and money as had been the case with England for years and years, to step into the front rank of colonial powers. In the case of Persia we had for a century past preserved peace at sea in the Persian Gulf and it was due to our money and efforts that Germany and other countries were enabled to carry on trade there. Germany could not expect like the late arrived labourer in the biblical vineyard to occupy the same position in Persia as the Russian neighbour and England. In Persia except in regard to merely trade questions Germany must be regarded by Russia and England as somewhat of a poacher.

On my remarking that it was not an indication of very peaceful intentions that Germany should be adding to her army as well as to her navy Stumm said that the German Government did not know how otherwise to dispose of the surplus of young men resulting from the annual increase in the population. I suggested that if the German Government were at a loss as to how to dispose of them the recent acquisition of the French Congo might be a field on which to exercise their energies. Emigration to that country might be encouraged. Stumm smiled a faint smile and said that even if the two Governments did not become friends we two would remain so. He finally made some observations, intended to be flattering to myself, in regard to my reputation with Bethmann Hollweg, Kiderlen Waechter and Co. with which I need not trouble you. They were not, I may verily believe, repeated to me textually by Stumm.

Yours sincerely,
FRANCIS BERTIE.

No. 509.

Sir F. Bertie to Sir A. Nicolson.

Personal.(¹)

My dear Nicolson,
Paris, February 11, 1912.

Many thanks for your letter of the 8th.(²)

I think that the Haldane Mission, which it was absurd and of no use to surround with mystery, is a foolish move, intended I suppose to satisfy the Grey-must-go radicals. It certainly creates suspicion here, not with Poincaré and perhaps not with those of the Ministry who are in his confidence, but with many political people. We ought to bear in mind that in any territorial arrangements or exchanges which we may make with the Germans we may injure the interests of our friends if not our own. The French consulted us in the course of their negotiations with the Germans whether we would have objection to certain cessions of territory including

(¹) [Carnock MSS., Vol. I of 1912.]
(²) [Not reproduced.]

islands. We ought to act similarly in regard to the French if there be questions of cessions of British territories to Germany.

[It is evident that the German Government whatever they may pretend to us will not abate their intention to compete with us at sea. The more dignified course for us would be not to waste words, but to go on in increasing ratio to construct against the German building programmes.] Any undertaking given to us by the German Government would not be observed in the spirit as would any engagements entered into by us. We have many examples of this. . . . .(³)

Szécsen in conversation with me a few days ago whilst deprecating German naval competition with us said with regard to the increase proposed in the German Army that it was justified by the position shown during the Morocco crisis in September. On my showing ignorance as to his meaning he reminded me that the British Gov[ernmen]t had prepared 150,000 men for service on the Continent and it was to meet such an addition to the French Army that it was necessary for the German Government to make additions to the German Army.

Yours ever,

FRANCIS BERTIE.

(³) [The omitted part of this letter refers to personal details.]

No. 510.

Sir Edward Grey to Sir E. Goschen.

F.O. 6420/5569/12/18.
(No. 40.) Secret.
Sir, *Foreign Office, February 12, 1912.*

Count Metternich asked to see me to-day,(¹) and when he came he enquired whether I had yet seen Lord Haldane.

I replied that I had just seen him, and had heard his account of the conversations which he had had in Berlin. The conversations had, of course, disclosed the difficulties of coming to an arrangement on particular points. But I was immensely impressed by what Lord Haldane had told me of the desire which the Chancellor had shewn to lift the discussion on to a high plane, and of the spirit in which he had approached the whole question. He evidently wished a great effort to be made to rise to the occasion and to do something that would make peace more secure, not only between Germany and England, but in the whole of Europe.

I felt most strongly that we, on our side, must endeavour to rise to the occasion in the same spirit. Some thing, I thought, had been gained already. Before Lord Haldane went to Berlin, I had agreed with him that, if he found it possible, it would be desirable that he should be quite frank about the object of our military and naval preparations last Summer. He had been frank about these preparations, and I thought that he must in this way have dispelled the suspicion that we had meditated an unprovoked attack upon Germany, even if she herself took no warlike step. This frankness might not of itself have made the atmosphere more genial, but I felt that it must have made it more clear. This by itself would be something gained.

Count Metternich said that the King had sent a friendly message to the German Chancellor. Count Metternich had been instructed to convey a message in reply, and he would do so through Lord Stamfordham. It would be to the effect that the Chancellor felt that something had been gained already. Count Metternich added that he agreed that something had been gained, and he hoped that more might follow.

[I am, &c.]

E. G[REY].

(¹) [For Count Metternich's report and annotations by the Emperor William, *v. G.P.* XXXI, pp. 121–2.]

No. 511.

Sir Edward Grey to Sir E. Goschen.

Private.([1])
My dear Goschen,   London, February 12, 1912.

Metternich referred, in conversation with me to-day, to what I had said as to the first communications through the Ballin–Cassel channel having come from Germany. The German Government thought that the first communications had come from us, with the knowledge of the Prime Minister, Lord Haldane, myself, and he thought some one else.

I said that the communications themselves had not been made with the actual knowledge of the Prime Minister, because he was in Sicily at the time. But, just before he went to Sicily, an invitation, or at least a desire or suggestion,—I could not be quite sure of the wording,—had been conveyed from the Emperor through Ballin and Cassel to Winston Churchill for a visit to Berlin.([2]) I myself, through indirect channels, had had intimations that the Emperor would like me to go to Berlin. We felt that an official visit would be premature, but at the same time we did not wish to give the impression of leaving any stone unturned, or rejecting any channel by which it was suggested that conversations could be facilitated.

Therefore, after Churchill had received a message from the Emperor through Ballin and Cassel, we had made use of the same channel for our reply; and we had wished to avoid the appearance of not responding to the desire that a Minister should go to Berlin, though we thought that if one did go he must do so unofficially.

Yours sincerely,
E. GREY.

([1]) [Grey MSS., Vol. 23.]
([2]) [cp. supra, p. 666, No. 492.]

No. 512.

Sir R. Rodd to Sir Edward Grey.

Private.([1])
My dear Sir Edward,   Rome, February 12, 1912.

After Lord Haldane's visit to Berlin, it may seem rather unnecessary that I should write to you from Italy about the relations between Germany and Great Britain. But if the matter I have to report confirms what comes to you from other sources it may not be altogether useless to put it on record. My German colleague came to see me this afternoon, on a question connected with the protestant cemetery here, and talked to me about many other matters. He is one of my oldest diplomatic friends and has always been very frank with me. Referring to Lord Haldane's visit he said he hoped very greatly that good would come of it, and that he knew there was a ready disposition in Berlin to lead relations into a better channel. I said I knew there was a very sincere desire to do so with us; the difficulty seemed to be where to begin, in restoring confidence and dissipating mutual suspicion. He said it was clear to him that it was the limitation of armaments which should furnish the common ground for departure, and he was quite sure the Chancellor appreciated this and was favourably disposed to entertain consideration of the question. But in Germany they wished the question to be approached in connection with, or rather simultaneously with one or two political questions. First of these he believed to be a settlement of the Bagdad railway issue. Perhaps the Governments had never approached each other in a frank and friendly spirit on this matter. As far as Germany was concerned, the Bagdad railway was in the first place a question of

([1]) [Grey MSS., Vol. 25.]

prestige, and secondly one involving important commercial interests. He could honestly assure me as an old friend that Germany was not moved therein by any ambitions or covetings which could cause us misgiving. Nothing in any respect aggressive or detrimental to our interests had been contemplated, but her prestige was seriously involved, and therefore opposition was resented. He then went on to talk of last summer, and said that the situation produced in Germany had been desperately dangerous. He had not realised how serious it was until he went on leave and he found that it was especially in Bavaria and Southern Germany that public opinion was most fiercely aroused. The culminating point had been the Chancellor of the Exchequer's Guildhall speech,(²) which had produced an effect quite out of proportion to the actual words employed, due to the particular psychological moment at which it was made. Until then he had always believed that the anti-English feeling reported to exist in Germany was exaggerated, but the experiences he had had at that time convinced him that it was then intense and formidable. He hoped and believed it would pass and felt sure there were openings, as there was an earnest desire on the part of the controlling elements, for a rapprochment. During the twelve years that I have known Herr von Jagow I have always found him a consistent advocate of a good understanding with us, and so far as one can feel sure of anyone in this world, I feel sure he is sincere in this respect. He has always before tended rather to make light of our dissensions regarding them more as matters to occupy the pen of journalists than as proving any real national animosity, but this time I found him sadly convinced that the matter was very serious, and one for which a remedy must be sought before it was too late.

Very sincerely yours,
RENNELL RODD.

MINUTE.

The German Ambassador's comment on Mr. Lloyd George's speech is in itself a justification of it. It came at a moment when it had real influence in restraining Germany.

E. G.

(²) [Extracts from this speech and comments upon it will be printed in *Gooch & Temperley*, Vol. VII. It is the one made by Mr. Lloyd George on July 21, 1911, during the Agadir crisis.]

No. 513.

Sir Edward Grey to Sir F. Bertie.

F.O. 6556/5569/12/18.
(No. 79.)
Sir,   *Foreign Office, February* 13, 1912.

I told M. Cambon to-day, very confidentially, that Herr von Bethmann-Hollweg had enquired as to the possibility of our ceding Zanzibar and Pemba to Germany.

We did not see any *primâ facie* objection to a transaction that would involve the cession of these places, as they lay off the coast of a German Colony, and Germany already had in Dar-es-Sal[a]am a better harbour than she could get in Zanzibar or Pemba, but it would, of course, be essential to get in return sufficient to satisfy British public opinion with regard to the cession of territory.

For several reasons, I thought it right to mention to M. Cambon, very confidentially, the possibility even of such a cession, though I had not mentioned it to Count Benckendorff. One reason was that France had territory, such as Madagascar, in that region, whereas Russia had none. Another reason was that, during the negotiations between France and Germany last year, France had always told us of any cession of territory that she proposed to make to Germany, in order that we might satisfy ourselves that British interests would not be prejudiced. M. Cambon would remember that, when the question was raised of the cession by France to Germany of some territory adjoining the Bar-el-Ghazal, I had said that, though such a change was not of the sort which we desired, we would not plead British interests as a barrier to a satisfactory arrangement between France and Germany. I thought that France, in a converse case, might take the same view as to Zanzibar and Pemba. I found, however, that there were certain Treaties between France and Zanzibar, and between France and ourselves as to Zanzibar; and of course the special rights which France might have under these Treaties would be examined and considered. These were the reasons for which I had mentioned the matter to the French Government at this stage.

I impressed upon M. Cambon that it was most essential that this should be kept quite secret: it might come to nothing and in that case it should not be known that it had ever been discussed.

[I am, &c.]
E. G[REY].

No. 514.

Sir Edward Grey to Sir F. Bertie.

F.O. 6559/5569/12/18.
(No. 80.)

Sir,   *Foreign Office, February* 13, 1912.

I gave M. Cambon to-day the following résumé of what had passed in connection with Lord Haldane's visit to Berlin.

I said that the idea that a British Minister should visit Berlin had not originated with us: the intimation that the visit of a British Minister would be welcome and would facilitate discussion had reached us first from Berlin. When we had shown our readiness to discuss matters and to send a British Minister, the first suggestion from Berlin had been that I should go. We thought that matters were not sufficiently advanced for a step as formal as this; and therefore Lord Haldane, who must sooner or later have made a private visit to Berlin, had gone there.

Lord Haldane had had discussions with the Emperor, with Herr von Bethmann-Hollweg, with Baron Stumm once—acting under instructions from the Chancellor—, and with Admiral von Tirpitz. The main discussions had been direct with Herr von Bethmann-Hollweg. There had been but one perfunctory conversation of civility of a general character with Herr von Kiderlen-Waechter, who had taken practically no part in the discussions.

Nothing had been concluded, but the ground had been explored, and there were three questions before us :—

(1.) The question of naval expenditure.

As regards this, we had made it quite clear that we could suffer no diminution of the ratio of superiority that we considered necessary with regard to German shipbuilding. I did not think that there was a prospect of either the Germans or ourselves binding ourselves to definite limitation of expenditure; but Germany might in practice regulate the pace of her shipbuilding faster or slower, and our expenditure would vary accordingly.

(2.) We had discussed the Bagdad Railway.—The part of the Railway to the north of Bagdad had not entered into the discussion, our point of view being that we required a controlling influence over the section from Bagdad to the Gulf, and also that our position with regard to Koweit and the Gulf generally should not be disputed. I considered that we were free to secure these things by negotiations with Germany, if we could. But, just as, when M. Sazonow had concluded his arrangement with Germany last year,([1]) I had said to him that the understanding between us was that he would not agree to an increase of Turkish Customs Duties until we had secured a satisfactory arrangement about the Bagdad Railway: so now, of

([1]) [Reference to this subject will be made in a later volume.]

[17590]   2 Y 2

course, if we did secure a satisfactory arrangement with Germany, we could not give our consent to the increase of the Turkish Customs until France also had secured a satisfactory arrangement with Germany. This had for some time been the understanding between France, Russia, and ourselves : that we should negotiate separately, but should not give our consent until we were all satisfied. Russia, of course, was already satisfied.

(3.) The impression was widely held in Germany that we had intended an attack upon her last Summer.—This idea was absolutely untrue. We were ready to assure the German Government that there was not in our understanding with France, or with Russia, or in any agreement which we might have with any Power whatever, any preparation to be aggressive towards Germany, or to make an unprovoked attack upon her. There was nothing of this sort, and we did not intend that there should be anything. On the other hand, Lord Haldane, in talking to Herr von Bethmann-Hollweg, had made no secret of the fact that we made military and naval preparations last year that would have enabled us, if we had thought it right, to go to the assistance of France if Germany had made an aggressive or unprovoked attack upon her : and Lord Haldane had explained that we could not tie our hands with regard to such an event. The difficulty was to find a formula that would express our attitude.

M. Cambon thanked me for what I had told him, and remarked that the discussion of military and naval expenditure would probably take a long time before an agreement could be arrived at.

I said that there might not be any formal agreement. Any understanding that might be come to would probably be rather with regard to the exchange of information, and what each Government did in practice, without any binding agreement.

M. Cambon did not comment further upon what I had told him, except to say that what I had said on the third point would, he was sure, be satisfactory to his Government.

I said that the spirit of Herr von Bethmann-Hollweg was most friendly and, I was convinced, quite sincere. We had now to continue our survey of the ground; but already the frank exchange of views that had taken place, even if it had not of itself made the atmosphere more genial, had, I thought, made it more clear by dispelling some of the suspicion between the German Government and ourselves.

M. Cambon said the Germans were increasing the strength of their army; having come to the conclusion there was last year approximately in practice an equality with the French army. He feared that predominance in Europe was what Germany desired.

[I am, etc.]
E. G[REY].

No. 515.

Sir Edward Grey to Sir G. Buchanan.

F.O. 6557/5569/12/18.

(No. 51.)

Sir, *Foreign Office, February* 13, 1912.

I spoke to Count Benckendorff to-day substantially to the same effect as I spoke to M. Cambon, about Lord Haldane's visit to Berlin.(1) I did not, however, say anything to Count Benckendorff about Zanzibar and Pemba.

[I am, &c.]
E. G[REY].

(1) [v. immediately preceding document. A copy was sent to St. Petersburgh as No. 55 of February 13.]

No. 516.

Minute by Sir A. Nicolson.

Private.([1])
Sir Edward Grey,   *Foreign Office, February 13, 1912.*

If it be seriously contemplated to hand over Zanzibar and Pemba to Germany, we should certainly, before coming to any decision, enquire of France if she has any objection. The French Gov[ernmen]t, during their negotiations with Germany, always enquired of us whether we should object to any proposed cession of territory. It should not be forgotten that Zanzibar is near Madagascar. I trust no great stress will be given to the point as to whether a locality is of immediate use to us strategically or otherwise. Utility is not everything, and if we were ready to part with all possessions which were not strictly useful, the Empire would shrink considerably.

A. N.

([1]) [Carnock MSS., Vol. I of 1912.]

No. 517.

Sir Edward Grey to Sir C. MacDonald.

F.O. 6848/5569/12/18.   *Foreign Office, February 15, 1912.*
Tel. (No. 9.) K.   D. 11 P.M.

I have told Japanese chargé d'affaires that Lord Haldane did not at Berlin discuss anything nearer to the Far East than the Persian Gulf, that nothing had been settled then, but that frank discussion had taken place quite informally about Bagdad Railway, questions connected with South Africa, naval expenditure, and the possibility of a formula assuring each party against unprovoked attack or aggression by the other. There could be no question of our reducing our proportion of naval superiority to the German, and if any formula was drawn up it would not in any way be inconsistent with the Japanese alliance, and I should inform the Japanese Government of its terms.

You should inform Japanese Minister for Foreign Affairs confidentially.

No. 518.

Minute by Sir A. Nicolson.

Private.([1])
Sir Edward Grey,   *Foreign Office, February 15, 1912.*

M. Cambon came today to express M. Poincaré's thanks for the communication which you had made in regard to Lord Haldane's mission.([2]) The French Gov[ernmen]t made no comments, probably awaiting further developments. I told M. Cambon that, for the moment in any case, the question of territorial cessions or exchanges had receded into the background.

I said that the letter from the French Mil[itar]y Attaché in Berlin was very interesting([3])—but I was surprised that no mention had been made of Russia. He said that the Chief of the French General Staff visited St. Petersburg about 6 months ago—and went into the whole question with the Russian General Staff. The Russians are changing their organization and mobilization schemes, and are, therefore, in a transition state. They said they would not be ready for taking a *serious* part in

([1]) [Carnock MSS., Vol. I of 1912.]
([2]) [*v. supra*, pp. 690–2, Nos. 513–4.]
([3]) [This refers to a letter from the French Military Attaché in Berlin to the French Military Attaché in London, an extract from which is in the Carnock MSS., Vol. I of 1912. The letter is endorsed as having been received in the Foreign Office on February 9, 1912, but it probably relates to an earlier period, as its substance is much the same as that of another letter by Lieutenant-Colonel Pellé, printed in *D.D.F.*, 3rd *Ser.*, Vol. I, pp. 343–7, under date December 16, 1911.]

a campaign for two years from then, or about 16 to 18 months from now. The Germans are, of course, aware of this, and are also aware that our 6 divisions would have brought the contending parties practically to an equality. Consequently the Germans were hastening their military increase and preparations to be able to obtain the necessary numerical superiority before Russia was ready.

M. Cambon added that his Gov[ernmen]t, and the press under their control, were not uneasy as to the pourparlers between us and Berlin, but he would not conceal from me that among the French public there were uneasiness and doubts. If Germany could tie our hands and retain her own free, she would very soon be in a position to face a contest with France with equanimity—which was not the case last Autumn—and would not be the case 18 months hence.

The Spanish Amba[ssado]r, who had [been] speaking today with M. v[on] Kühlmann, said that the latter had expressed great doubts as to whether an agreement could possibly be reached as to reduction of naval expenditure.

M. Cambon expressed privately his opinion, in a friendly way, that he thought the Prime Minister had yesterday(⁴) held out hopes of an arrang[emen]t with Germany in terms a little more positive than he (M. Cambon) thought the circum[stan]ces justified.

A. N.
E. G.

MINUTE.

A comparison of what I said and what the German Ch[ancello]r said yesterday in the Reichstag does not bear out this opinion of M. Cambon.

H. H. A.
16 Feb.

(⁴) [cp. Parl. Deb., 5th Ser., House of Commons, Vol. 34, pp. 31–3.]

No. 519.

Sir G. Buchanan to Sir A. Nicolson.

St. Petersburgh, February 17, 1912.

Tel.
Private.(¹)

D. 4·30.
R. 5 P.M.

King's letter received. Before asking for audience I should like to be in a position to make a confidential communication to His Majesty with regard to the results of Lord Haldane's visit. Language used to Mr. O'Beirne by one of the Grand Dukes shows that there is a certain soreness in court circles on the subject and as Regent of Brunswick is here on a visit I am afraid that Germans may mis(?)represent what we are doing to Emperor.

I should also like to know what I may say to him as to our policy in South Persia, as on new year's day he suggested that we should restore order there. I am not quite clear as to what is contemplated with regard to despatch of troops in connection with proposed negotiations with tribes for maintenance of order.

(¹) [Carnock MSS., Vol. I of 1912.]

No. 520.

Sir A. Nicolson to Sir G. Buchanan.

Tel.
Private.(¹)

Foreign Office, February 18, 1912.
D. 10·45 P.M.

Your private telegram of yesterday. Full information has been given to Russian Ambas[sado]r here as to what passed at Berlin and has been recorded in a despatch

(¹) [Carnock MSS., Vol. I of 1912.]

to you. But you could say that Lord Haldane's visit to Berlin was much less formal than that of Russian M[inister for] F[oreign] A[ffairs] last year and that there can be nothing but advantage from relaxation of tension between England and Germany which is now greater than that between France and Germany or than it has ever been between Russia and Germany.([2]) You should assure the Emperor that nothing will be arranged which would in any way weaken or impair existing relations between us and Russia and add that H[is] M[ajesty's] G[overnmen]t are considering the reply to be sent to the German overtures and that the main object is to remove unfounded suspicions and misapprehension and enable the two Gov[ernmen]ts to talk frankly and freely with each other on any question which may arise between them.

As to South Persia we are considering with India Office and Gov[ernmen]t of India as to what steps can best be taken for re-establishment of order. You could express to H[is] M[ajesty] the satisfaction which H[is] M[ajesty's] G[overnmen]t feel in the cordial co-operation they are receiving from the Russian Gov[ernmen]t for alleviating the situation in Persia generally and affording all practicable support moral and material to the Persian Gov[ernmen]t. The removal of the ex-Shah and other disquieting elements is very necessary and we were glad that on this essential point the Russian Gov[ernmen]t are in complete accord with us. You could also express to H[is] M[ajesty] how highly we have appreciated the gracious reception accorded by him and also the welcome preferred by his Ministers, public bodies and the Russian people generally to the British visitors and say that the latter have returned here with the most grateful recollections of the generous and kindly hospitality extended to them during their visit to Russia.

([2]) [This sentence was written on the draft by Sir Edward Grey, the rest of the draft being in Sir A. Nicolson's hand.]

No. 521.

Sir Edward Grey to Sir C. MacDonald.

F.O. 7806/5569/12/18.
(No. 33.)

Sir,   *Foreign Office, February 19, 1912.*

The Japanese Chargé d'Affaires conveyed to me to-day the sincere thanks of his Government for the information which I had given as to Lord Haldane's visit to Berlin.([1])

I said that we were still considering the situation, and we had had no further communication with the German Government. If there were any developments which affected the common interests of Japan and ourselves, I would, of course, keep him informed.

[I am, &c.]
E. G[REY].

([1]) [*v. supra*, p. 693, No. 517.]

No. 522.

Sir G. Buchanan to Sir A. Nicolson.

Private.([1])

My dear Nicolson,   *St. Petersburgh, February 22, 1912.*

. . . .([2]) The Russians, I am glad to say, seem now quite to realise that Haldane's visit to Berlin is a matter to which they cannot possibly take exception. At first, however, it came upon them as a disagreeable surprise, more especially as it followed so closely on the British visit here.   The Grand Duke Alexander, who has of late become quite an Anglophil, spoke to O'Beirne on the subject and plainly showed that he considered it a poor return for the hospitality and cordial reception accorded to our countrymen.   Though no importance need be attached to his utterances, they are curious as showing how touchy people are in certain quarters here about such matters.   As another instance of their sensitiveness on such points I may mention that the Grand Duchess Xenia—the Emperor's sister—asked me the other day whether the King was coming to St. Petersburg this year, as she had seen in the papers that He was to go to Berlin and Vienna.   I replied that I knew nothing whatever about His Majesty's movements: but I fear that should the reports published in the papers prove correct, there will be considerable heartburnings if his visit is not extended to St. Petersburg. . . . .

Ever yours,

GEORGE W. BUCHANAN.

([1]) [Carnock MSS., Vol. II of 1912.]

([2]) [The omitted parts of this letter refer to Persian affairs, Austro-Russian relations, and the Balkan situation.]

No. 523.

Memorandum by Sir Edward Grey.([1])

F.O. 8612A/5569/12/18.   *February 22, 1912.*

At ten o'clock this morning, (22 February, 1912) the German Ambassador called at Sir Edward Grey's private house, in Queen Anne's Gate, and met Sir Edward and Lord Haldane.

The conversation with the Ambassador took place on the lines discussed at the meeting of the Cabinet earlier in the . week, and the genuine desire of H[is] M[ajesty's] Gov[ernmen]t for cordial relations was emphasized.   The difficulty was pointed out to the Ambassador of making any Agreement which was coincident with a substantial increase in the German Fleet.   It was explained that the proposed new Fleet Law went a great way farther than was necessary for merely providing such a squadron as would relieve the active squadrons of the High Sea Fleet of Germany from the duty of training recruits.

The Ambassador said that he was not sufficiently expert to be able to discuss the details of the proposed Fleet Law, or the extent to which it went beyond what had been indicated.

Reference was made to the increased number of torpedo craft and of " personnel," beyond what a new Fleet Law limited to the purpose above defined would necessitate.

The Ambassador said that he would like to have more precise information on this point; and he was promised such information in a definite form.

Sir Edward Grey remarked that, at all events, something had been gained; the speeches in this country and in Berlin evidenced a substantial increase in the frankness of our relations, and that in any case this might be maintained.

([1]) [Count Metternich's report of the conversation noted in this document is printed in *G.P.* XXXI, pp. 128–30.]

The Ambassador expressed pleasure at this; cordially reciprocated it and said that he regarded this statement as very important. What he was anxious to attain was a state of things in which the two nations should not join in hostile combinations against each other, and in which the British nation should not be in any way in an attitude hostile *per se* to Germany. He referred to a possible formula.

Sir Edward Grey and Lord Haldane touched on the difficulty that the suggestion made by the German Chancellor went too far. They were aware that a formula limited to aggressive action left room for divergencies of interpretation, but the spirit which even a formula so limited would introduce would be a very valuable one.

The Ambassador did not dissent from this view.

Further questions, of a territorial character, were touched on only very lightly. It was pointed out that the Treaty rights of other nations might give rise to some complications: as, for instance, the Dutch title to Timor.

The conversation occupied nearly an hour.

E. G.

No. 524.

Sir Edward Grey to Sir E. Goschen.

F.O. 8613/5569/12/18.
(No. 48.) Secret.

Sir, *Foreign Office, February* 24, 1912.

I gave the enclosed Memorandum to Count Metternich to-day.([1])

In doing so, I explained that, after our last conversation, Lord Haldane had seen Mr. Churchill, and had told him of the point on which a Memorandum was required. As a result, the Memorandum which I was handing to Count Metternich had been drawn up in the Admiralty. It must be regarded purely as supplementary to our conversation, and anything in it that was other than technical must be construed in the light of our conversation, and must not be regarded as modifying or displacing anything that had been said on the general aspect of the questions which we had discussed.

Count Metternich said that he had gathered an impression, though neither Lord Haldane nor I had said anything direct on the subject, that we were rather receding from the proposals respecting Zanzibar and Pemba that Lord Haldane had made with our knowledge in Berlin.

I replied that it was true that the Government felt that the cession of Zanzibar and Pemba would require some corresponding territorial concession; and that there would be difficulty in reconciling public opinion here to a cession of territory in exchange only for prospective rights in the Bagdad Railway, which would be rights conceded mainly by Turkey, and rights in the Persian Gulf, which would not be an acquisition of territory by us, but rather a maintenance of the *status quo.* The Government also felt that, if a large increase of naval expenditure was to take place and could not be avoided, it would be better that any bargain should follow rather than precede it. But I did not wish him to suppose that we had put on one side the question of territorial arrangements. Time was required for the consideration of their full bearing. We had spoken of a cession of Zanzibar and Pemba and a strip across Angola. These were considerable assets, and would require compensation in *pari materiâ.*

Count Metternich observed that Timor had been suggested as a concession on the German side.

([1]) [*cp. G.P.* XXXI, pp. 132–4. The text of the memorandum there given has a few slight differences of punctuation, etc.]

I remarked that, as the Dutch Government had a Treaty with Portugal giving them a right of pre-emption to Portuguese Timor, there was some difficulty as to the title to the island. The Cabinet considered that they had better deal first with the question of naval expenditure and the question of a formula : but we did not wish to rule out of discussion the question of territorial arrangements on. their merits.

[I am, &c.]

E. G[REY].

Enclosure in No. 524.

Memorandum communicated to Count Metternich.

The increases under the new Navy Law comprise 3 capital ships, 15,000 men, and 13,000,000 of money, of which the men are to be spread over 9 and the ships and money over 6 years. These great augmentations are to be devoted to developing the already high efficiency of the German Navy and its immediate readiness for offensive or defensive operations at all seasons of the year. The Admiralty compute, from the materials so courteously supplied them, that nearly 4/5ths of the whole German Navy will by these means be kept in permanent full commission. These increases go far beyond the standard of Naval strength prescribed by the 1900 Fleet Law and its subsequent amendments. They are more than is necessary either to provide for the increased complements of modern ships or for the institution of such a Training Squadron as would be adapted to relieving the 1st and 2nd squadron of the High Sea Fleet from their present burden of training recruits during the winter months, which, it appears, the formation of a 3rd Active Squadron is to effect. The Admiralty hesitate very much to dogmatise upon matters which require a more intimate knowledge than they possess of the manning system of the German Navy, but, so far as they can tell, it would not be impossible to provide for the commission-ing of the 3rd Squadron out of the large annual increases in personnel at present being made : and the numbers required to meet the increased complements of modern ships would not appear to exceed 4,000 men, according to Appendix 3 of the Novelle.

2. All increases of whatever kind in the strength of the German Navy will of course require corresponding measures of due proportion here. If the new Law were carried out in its present form, the Admiralty would find it necessary to add at least 4,000 men to the Fleet each year for the next 6 or 7 years, to maintain in full permanent commission four Battle Squadrons of 8 ships each and to keep two other Battle Squadrons ready at very short notice without a mobilisation, as well as two further Battle Squadrons (making eight in all) dependent upon the calling out of the reserves. They would also deem it necessary to raise their Flotillas to the number of 9 in the next 5 years, and to lay down two keels to one for every capital ship added to the German Navy above the existing law. These measures would, so far as can be foreseen, involve an additional expenditure of £18,500,000 spread over the next 6 years, together with a certain further concentration of the Fleet in Home Waters. It is difficult to understand how the public opinion of both countries could be brought to regard these serious measures and countermeasures as appropriate to the coincident re-establishment of cordial relations.

3. If the British Government, in asking Parliament to sanction some modified increases much less than the above, were able to make it clear that the new German Navy Law did not go beyond the limits of the old Law and the memoranda accompanying the Naval Estimates of 1906 and 1908, except in so far as was necessary to provide for the increased complements of modern ships or the necessities of a new Training Squadron to relieve the existing High Sea Fleet of training duties, it is possible that the difficulties might be surmounted.

In illustration of the extent to which the new Law seems to go beyond the limits above defined, the construction of 3 additional Battleships to be begun within the next 6 or even 9 years, the provision of full crews for all the Torpedo Boat

Destroyers and Submarines, the proposals for additional Submarines on a very large scale, and the addition to personnel of 11,000 men more than are needed for the increased complements above referred to, may, with great respect, be mentioned.

No. 525.

Sir F. Bertie to Sir Edward Grey.

F.O. 8481/391/12/436.
(No. 103.)   Secret.   Paris, D. February 24, 1912.
Sir,   R. February 27, 1912.

M. Poincaré in conversation with me yesterday referred to the mission of Lord Haldane to Berlin. He expressed his high sense of your loyalty in making the French Ambassador acquainted with the desire of the German Government to acquire Zanzibar and Pemba. His Excellency asked me whether they had made any proposals in regard to the Portuguese possessions in Africa. There was he said some anxiety on the subject amongst some members of the Senate and Chamber. I replied that, as he was aware, a Secret Treaty had been entered into by Germany and England in 1898 regarding those Possessions[1] but no proposals had recently been made concerning them by the German Government.

I have, &c.
FRANCIS BERTIE.

[1] [v. Gooch & Temperley, Vol. I, pp. 71–2, No. 90, encl.]

No. 526.

M. Jules Cambon to M. Poincaré.[1]

Conversation avec Monsieur de Bethmann-Hollweg.

F.O. 9572/5569/12/18.   18 février, 1912.

J'ai eu ce matin un long entretien avec le Chancelier de l'empire. Après m'avoir dit un mot de la situation intérieure et du Reichstag, Monsieur de Bethmann-Hollweg a abordé la question des rapports de l'Allemagne avec les autres puissances, et s'est plaint de la nervosité qui se manifeste partout. C'est ainsi qu'il en est venu à me parler de l'état des esprits en France, "qui, m'a-t-il dit, est pour lui une cause de préoccupation constante." Il a été frappé du ton qu'a pris la discussion au Sénat au sujet des accords du 4 novembre dernier. Il fait la part des entraine-ments de la discussion, mais il n'en trouve pas moins que le langage de certains orateurs n'était pas celui d'hommes qui ont connu les responsabilités du gouverne-ment et qui peuvent être appelés à les connaître encore. Je répondis que cela était naturel en raison du sacrifice auquel notre Parlement était appelé à consentir. Il me dit qu'il ne partageait pas ma manière de voir et qu'il n'y avait pas à parler de sacrifice, quand en réalité la France acquérait un grand empire qu'elle convoitait depuis de longues années. Je ne voulus pas le laisser sur ce mot et je repris : "Au fond du débat de sénat, il n'y avait pas seulement le côté matériel, la question territoriale, mais bien autre chose : il y avait surtout le sentiment français blessé par l'envoi de la "Panther" à Agadir. Je vous l'ai déja dit ajouté-je : vous avez fait ce jour-là une grande faute; vous en avez commis une plus grande en ne retirant pas votre bateau aussitôt après la reprise des négociations." "Je suis de votre avis,* me répondit le Chancelier, mais auriez-vous négocié si nous n'avions pas

[1] [This document is endorsed " Given to me confidentially by M. Paul Cambon, Feb[ruary] 27, 1912." It is typed on Foreign Office paper, and it seems probable that it was dictated by M. Paul Cambon in the Foreign Office.]

*In a private letter to his brother, M. Jules Cambon goes further, and explains that the Chancellor said that he himself was opposed to the despatch of the Panther and only yielded at the last moment, to the re-iterated insistence of M. de Kiderlen.

A. N.

manifesté nos intentions? Assurément, lui dis-je, mais c'est vous et vous seul qui d'une négociation destinée à écarter un malentendu entre nos deux pays, avez fait une source d'amertume.''

Enfin nous exprimâmes tous deux l'espoir que peu à peu l'apaisement se ferait dans les esprits et que, l'opinion publique reprenant son sang-froid dans les deux pays, les gouvernements pourraient faire triompher la raison dans le règlement des différentes questions qui vont occuper l'Europe. Cet ordre d'idées nous conduisit naturellement aux conversations que Lord Haldane est venu entamer à Berlin. Il me paraissait nécessaire de ne manifester aucune préoccupation à ce sujet, et je me félicitai purement et simplement de ces conversations, dont le résultat ne peut que faciliter l'apaisement des esprits. Je pris la liberté de demander au Chancelier s'il pourrait me donner quelque indication sur la direction de ces conversations: ''Mon dieu, me répondit-il, vous m'aviez parlé le 11 juin dernier de ce qu'avait fait votre frère autrefois à Londres lorsqu'il avait mis sur la table pour les comparer tous les griefs que la France et l'Angleterre avaient l'une contre l'autre: nous voudrions faire la même chose.'' ''Oui, lui dis-je, mais il y a la question des armements: est-ce que vous voulez les limiter?'' ''Assurément non, reprit le Chancelier; la limitation des armements est une chimère entre deux pays, qui peuvent avoir à défendre l'un vis à vis de l'autre leur honneur ou leur indépendance. Est-ce qu'il nous serait possible de vous demander de limiter vos armements? Et vous, pourriez-vous nous demander de limiter les nôtres?'' ''Il est vrai, remarquai-je, mais deux Gouvernements raisonnables, sans limiter leurs armements, peuvent s'entendre pour apporter de la mesure dans le développement de leurs propres forces.'' ''Ceci, me répondit le Chancelier, c'est autre chose; je dois même vous avouer que la question posée ainsi se posera un jour, et peut être bientôt, non pas seulement pour l'Angleterre et l'Allemagne, mais pour toute l'Europe. Nous approchons du moment où la limite des forces des Etats va être atteinte, et où ni leur population ni leurs finances ne pourront plus suffire aux sacrifices qu'on exige d'elles. Vous aurez, vous autres Francais, une grande part de responsabilité: vous inventez toujours, et voici maintenant qu'il faut vous suivre pour la création de la quatrième arme, comme il a fallu suivre l'Angleterre quand elle a lancé son premier Dreadnought.

Je crois savoir en effet que le Gouvernement allemand étudie en ce moment l'organisation d'un service plus complet d'aéroplanes et de dirigeables; mais je me contentai de dire que cette remarque rendait hommage au génie d'invention francais.

Nous en vînmes à parler de l'Afrique comme je l'indique dans ma dépêche 66.

Enfin Monsieur de Bethman-Hollweg me dit qu'il s'entretiendrait avec Monsieur de Kiderlen au sujet des travaux de la commission de délimitation qui doivent commencer après l'échange des ratifications des accords du 4 Novembre. Je lui dis que je serais heureux de faire connaître à mon Gouvernement les vues qu'il pourrait avoir à ce sujet, et je convins avec lui que je le reverrais dans quelque temps.

No. 527.

Lord Granville to Sir Edward Grey.

F.O. 9163/1151/12/18.
(No. 101.) Confidential.   *Berlin,* D. *February* 29, 1912.
Sir,   R. *March* 2, 1912.

With reference to my despatch No. 99 of yesterday's date,([1]) I have the honour to transmit, herewith, three copies each of two pamphlets which have been published here within the last day or two, entitled respectively '' Englands Weltherrschaft und die deutsche Luxusflotte '' and '' Die Kriegsbereitschaft der englischen Flotte im

([1]) [Not reproduced.]

Jahre 1911.''(²) Both these pamphlets are being widely advertized and copies have been sent to all the Berlin correspondents of foreign newspapers.

An American gentleman with English connections, who has long resided in Berlin and whom I believe to be very well informed, had long conversations yesterday with Captain Watson and with me on the subject of the present state of German opinion with regard to naval questions.

He has been so kind, on his own initiative, as to record the substance of what he said to us in the form of a Memorandum, which appears to me of such interest that I venture to enclose a copy.(³) Everything in the Memorandum is either confirmed by Captain Watson's and my own information or seems to fit in so well with known facts as to be regarded as almost certainly correct. One point to which I would draw your attention is my informant's statement that Admiral von Müller, the Chief of the Naval Cabinet, is one of the strongest advocates of an increase of the navy, and is the man who at this moment has the greatest personal influence over the Emperor : I am not in a position to confirm or dispute this.

My object, however, in writing this despatch and in troubling you with these pamphlets, which, taken individually are not perhaps of very great importance, is to bring to the notice of His Majesty's Government the undoubted fact that a desperate effort is being made at the present time to whip up public opinion in Germany in favour of a strong and active policy of naval increase. There is not the least question that the Navy League and Admiral von Tirpitz, and probably

(²) [Not reproduced.]

(³) [It has not been thought necessary to reproduce the whole of this memorandum, which comments on Articles which had recently appeared in the German press. The following extract refers to the pamphlet entitled *Englands Weltherrschaft und die deutsche Luxusflotte* which was signed " Lookout."

Herr Stein (whom I assume to be the author) spends most of his time in the lobbies of the Reichstag. I have the impression he is a professional lobbyist—that is to say, he seems to devote himself to the *Bearbeitung* of Reichstag deputies " for national purposes." I have no doubt every Deputy has been supplied with a copy of " Lookout's " pamphlet.

Stein told me categorically that Tirpitz is keen on the 3 : 2 idea; that Tirpitz is exactly in favour of such a policy as Von Gottberg outlines in the " Daheim " article herein quoted. Stein went on to say that the German official crowd is divided into two pretty sharply-defined camps on the subject of a naval understanding with Britain. He says the two camps may be so subdivided :—

In favour of some form of understanding.	Against any understanding limiting naval construction.
The Kaiser.	Admiral von Müller.
The Imperial Chancellor.	Admiral von Tirpitz.
Herr Wermuth.	Herr von Kiderlen-Waechter.

Many people have told me in recent times that Admiral von Müller, contrary to general knowledge or belief, is strongly Anglophobe, and a " Big-Navy " man of incorrigible sentiments. He is said, moreover, to be in the highest possible favour with the Emperor and to have more influence over him at present than any other man in Germany. I was told by a certain well-known Berlin society woman that " Von Müller is a man I ought to know; he is the power behind the throne; it is he who prevents Anglo-German friendship; he has the Kaiser in his pocket."

I do not pretend, of course, to be able to vouch for the accuracy of these statements. I reiterate them for what they may be worth.

To sum up : Mr. Churchill's Glasgow speech(⁴) has caused the utmost chagrin in German " Big Navy " circles. Von Tirpitz is said to admit privately that the speech illuminates so clearly the hopelessness of German ambitions to outstrip Britain at sea that he fears his proposed Supplementary Naval bill may be in imminent jeopardy. He is afraid that Reichstag deputies, who are on the fence, so to speak, with regard to further expansion of the Fleet, may now have been swung definitely into line against expansion, as Mr. Churchill has made it plain that the competition must go on, and at an accelerated pace, if Germany keeps increasing the pace. If these fears are genuinely cherished by Tirpitz, the sudden launching by the 3 : 2 idea is explainable: he means to make the doubters see that the case is not hopeless for Germany, if the past rate of construction is kept up, and a little more so. " *Lookout's* " *figures—the table of percentages which appear at the close of his book—are meant to prove that Germany has successfully and steadily brought down the margin of British naval superiority since 1898, and can continue to do so if only she will.*]

(⁴) [*v.* report in the *Times* of February 10, 1912. The speech was delivered on February 9 at a luncheon given by the Clyde Navigation Trustees.]

Admiral von Müller, work hand in hand, that their great object is to reduce the ratio of difference between the British and German fleets, and that recent events such as the growth of the Left in the Reichstag, Lord Haldane's visit and the statements made by Mr. Asquith, yourself and the Imperial Chancellor, not to mention the attitude towards increased naval expenditure which seems almost certainly to have been adopted by the Chancellor and by the Secretary of State of the Treasury, have given the strong navy party great cause for alarm and have thus brought about this violent propaganda.

I have also the honour to enclose a further despatch on the subject by Captain Watson.(⁵)

I also enclose a copy, the only one we have been able to obtain, of the "Leipziger Illustrierte Zeitung" of December 21, 1911, an article which was referred to in Sir E. Goschen's despatch No. 9 of the 10th ultimo.(⁵)

I have, &c.
GRANVILLE.

MINUTES.

The thing that matters is that we should clearly see the facts as they are.

These despatches show beyond possibility of controversy the determination of the German Admiralty, by every means in their power to continue the race in which they claim to have already materially diminished the distance between German and British naval power, and which they still hope they may yet, ultimately, win.

It is suggested that the purely naval influence, which is frankly opposed to any slackening in the race, is counteracted by the opposition of the Emperor, the Chancellor, and the Finance Minister. I should attach more importance to this suggestion if some evidence were adduced for it. So far as I know, the only pieces of evidence brought forward have been certain remarks recently made by the Emperor and the Chancellor, and reinforced by a minor official in the German Foreign Office, to the effect that they would favour an agreement for the limitation of further increases in German shipbuilding, if only the German Admiralty could be persuaded that this was compatible with the requirements of German naval defence. It was difficult in a negotiation to be polite and say less, and indeed it would have been extraordinary, and displayed a want of diplomatic capacity which we have no right to attribute to the Emperor and his distinguished advisers, if, at a moment when they openly showed their anxiety to draw this country into Germany's political orbit, and to gain valuable concessions by the way, their conversations had not been so conducted as to create the impression that there was a genuine disposition to meet our desires so far as possible on the subject of naval armaments.

Of the Chancellor, it should be remembered that, however well-meaning he may personally be considered, he has shown himself altogether powerless to prevent a provokingly anti-English policy designed to inflame the passions of his country. Nor ought it to be forgotten that, at the critical moment, he did not refrain from publicly fanning those passions and from actually exploiting them in the interest of the very policy of further naval expansion, by agreements difficult to reconcile with the fact that he was in possession of information which he could have used effectively for the purpose of dispelling the popular illusions.

As for the Emperor, surely we know too much of his naval ambition, we have too much positive proof of the versatility of mind which enables him at the same time tenaciously to pursue a given course and to profess opinions and sentiments irreconcilable with his actions, we have suffered too often from the inaccuracy and insincerity of his statements, to justify us in taking the imperial assurances literally, and building upon them with any confidence as to their reliability.

It cannot be too clearly borne in mind that it would be absolutely impossible for Admiral von Tirpitz to carry on the propaganda once more illustrated in the present despatch, if the Emperor did not desire it. In such matter the Emperor is his absolute master. The German navy is governed almost entirely by four men, who work together in the closest and heartiest co-operation : The emperor himself; Admiral von Tirpitz; Admiral von Müller; and Admiral von Holtzendorff. This is a fact well known to anyone in touch with German naval circles; I have had more than one occasion to hear it affirmed by Admirals von Müller and von Holtzendorff themselves. Only last autumn, the latter told me most solemnly never to believe anyone who asserted that the emperor favoured, or would ever consent to, a limit of any kind being placed on Germany's liberty to increase her navy to any dimensions she desired. It will be remembered that the Emperor himself said as much to Sir E. Goschen as lately as Oct. 16, 1910,(⁶) when the question of a limitation of armaments was being discussed at Berlin on the invitation of the German Chancellor. When we had entered into that discussion, we were at once met by demands for a political agreement; the naval proposals, after a good deal of fencing, resolved themselves

(⁵) [Not reproduced.]
(⁶) [v. supra, p. 531, No. 403.]

into a nebulous suggestion for putting off the building of one or two ships for one or two years; and when H[is] M[ajesty's] G[overnment], in their genuine desire to conclude something however modest, expressed a willingness to treat even on that basis, the Chancellor himself promptly withdrew his proposal, such as it was, and declared, as indeed he had unequivocably done before in one of his biggest parliamentary speeches, that he considered the whole plan of limitation, in any sense, entirely impractical.(7)

These incidents are worth remembering when we are asked to pin our faith on assurances as to the real views and intentions of the German government which are utterly belied by their past actions and by the policy nakedly advocated and followed by them in Germany itself at this very moment.

Herr Adolf Stein, the author of the pamphlets, whose activity is described in the present despatch, is the well-known agent of the press-bureau, and their regular go-between in their relations with the German papers in regard to subjects of foreign policy. He is on the staff of the Frankfurter Zeitung, and during the whole of the Morocco campaign against England, was used by Herr von Kiderlen almost as his amanuensis. Sir F. Oppenheimer, who has personal and inside knowledge of the organization and working of the Frankfurter Zeitung, was able to ascertain that the leaders on Morocco and England were practically dictated "ipsissimis verbis" by the German Secretary of State. It is impossible to believe that Herr A. Stein wrote the pamphlet without the knowledge and encouragement of the government.

No one who understands the machinery of government at Berlin, is therefore likely to have any doubt that the policy propagated in the manner reported in the present despatch is the policy of the German government, and not that of an Admiralty clique fighting in opposition to the Emperor and the Chancellor. In fact such an hypothesis is almost unthinkable.

That policy has a well defined object : namely to go on steadily increasing the military and naval strength of the German Empire until it is sufficient to overawe any and every foreign opposition. Hand-in-hand with this strengthening of the armed forces, goes the effort to prevent or break up any combination between other Powers than those allied to Germany. It is obvious what would be the consequences for other nations of the success of such a policy. They would all have to take their orders from Berlin, and those orders are not likely to be very congenial to them, however little it might be thought, by those who attribute the friendliest motives to the German government, that Germany wished to domineer over others.

If this is the policy we have to face—and, so far as I am aware, no-one competent to judge has ever expressed a contrary opinion—there is no help for us but to keep up our own strength and to consolidate our international friendships. I do not see how this German policy could be deflected by concessions on our part, territorial or otherwise. These might cause a lull, they could never conquer the storm. Good relations with Germany are to be had by any Power with which she is afraid to go to war, and by no other.

E. A. C.
Mch. 3.

The minute by Sir Eyre Crowe and the accompanying papers are well worth consideration. L[or]d Granville's desp[atch] with its enclosures might be printed for Admiralty and the Cabinet.

A. N.
F. D. A.
E. G.

(7) [cp. supra, pp. 616–7, No. 458.]

No. 528.

Lord Acton to Sir E. Crowe.

F.O. 10797/5569/12/18.
Private.

My dear Crowe, *Buckingham Palace, March 2, 1912.*

I had some conversation yesterday with Kühlmann which may interest you. He says that although he is next for promotion he has asked to remain on as he hopes to see some result before he leaves. But he is rather despondent. He is certainly in favour of a naval agreement but thinks that it should be preceded by a colonial arrangement and he is against concurrent or inverted negotiations. The recent disclosures by Reuter about the 1898 agreement are traced to Eckardstein. This agreement ought to be the basis of the future arrangement. He thinks that a Declaration ought to be published, defining the British and German spheres of interest in the Portuguese colonies. The conditions of 1898 are no longer quite the same. If a substantial colonial agreement were reached, the Emperor would be-able to appease the Navy League and to retard naval expansion. The Chancellor is strongly in favour of an understanding; he has much influence with the Emperor, but his influence would be greater if he received incentive and support from the London Embassy. Metternich is apathetic and a fatalist and will do nothing to help. Kühlmann does not think that an Anglo-German agreement would weaken the entente, although it would render the chance of the re-insurance maturing more remote. He warmly repudiates the suggestion of Anglophobes, that we check German expansion and that we make promises that are hollow.

Kühlmann believes that if Metternich were to go, Jenisch would probably be proposed as his successor; and that Bernstorff will replace Kiderlen. Bernstorff is the best man they have. He says that Mr. Bryce would be 'persona gratissima' at Berlin.

Yours sincerely,
ACTON.

No. 529.

Memorandum communicated by Count Metternich, March 6, 1912.([1])

F.O. 10205/5569/12/18.
(Translation.)

The British Government had let it be known here that they were prepared to enter into negotiations with the German Government.

The German Government have, it is true, equally declared themselves to be ready to negotiate, but pointed out at once that the preliminary naval estimates for the current year, 1912, must be regarded as included in the present fleet programme, since all preparations had already been concluded.

The British Government caused a reply to be returned that a German supplementary naval law would render necessary an immediate and considerable increase in the present English naval estimates, these being based upon the supposition that the German fleet programme would not undergo any alteration. In these circumstances the negotiations would be difficult, if not impossible. If however the German naval expenditure on the fleet, whether by a change in the rate (*tempo*) of construction or in some other manner, could be so altered as to render unnecessary a material increase of expenditure for the purpose of meeting the German programme, the British Government would be prepared to continue the negotiations, for they would conclude that there was a possibility of discussing the question of expenditure on naval armaments and that there was a prospect of arriving at an agreement.

The German Government has returned the following answer :—

"We are prepared to continue the conversation in a friendly spirit. As regards the Navy Bill, which will lead to a discussion of the respective naval programmes, it seems possible that we could go some way to meet English wishes if we receive at the same time adequate guarantees that English policy will be directed in a sense friendly to us. The agreement would have to make it clear that either Power engages not to take part in any plans, combinations or warlike complications which are directed against the other. Such an agreement would render possible at the same time an understanding relative to mutual expenditure on armaments.

"Assuming, as we do, that England shares this view, we should be gratified if, as proposed by Great Britain, a British Minister were to come for the purpose, in the first instance, of a private and confidential exchange of views."

([1]) [For the German original *v. G.P.* XXXI, pp. 150–3.]

Thereupon, Lord Haldane arrived in Berlin and, although without full powers to conclude a binding arrangement, but still under authority from the whole British Cabinet, declared that the British Government were prepared :—

1. to conclude a general political agreement with the German Government which should preclude an aggressive policy directed by England or Germany against each other;
2. to support such plans for the acquisition of the Portuguese colony of Angola, as well as of parts of the Congo State, as it may eventually be the policy of Germany to entertain;
3. to cede Zanzibar and Pemba to Germany.

Lord Haldane on his part demanded :—

a. a retardation of the rate of construction as regards the three battleships provided for in the German Navy Bill;
b. the renunciation of the German claims to Timor arising under the treaty with the British Government of 1898;
c. due consideration of the wishes of the British Government respecting the Bagdad Railway.

The Imperial Government have accepted Lord Haldane's offers. For the purpose of the political agreement, both sides, while not committing themselves, drew up formulas, without any irreconcilable divergence of views appearing. As regards the demands of the British Government, the Imperial Government have met their wish for a retardation of the rate of construction by offering to defer until the years 1913, 1916 and 1919 respectively, the building of the three new battleships. Due consideration for the wishes expressed by England with respect to Timor and the Bagdad Railway was promised. Lord Haldane, in the course of his conversations with the Imperial Chancellor, has expressly recognised that the introduction of a bill providing for a third active squadron was, for the German Government, a necessity. Against the increase in personnel Lord Haldane had no objection to make. He declared repeatedly that England was primarily interested in the rate of construction of the battleships on account of her own considerable expenditure.

It is difficult to reconcile with these declarations, and it amounts to a shifting of the basis on which the negotiations have so far been conducted, that the British Government should now criticise the increases of personnel provided for in the Navy Bill and the additional vote demanded for submarines. The Imperial Government further feel constrained to regard as a departure from the point of view which appears to have inspired Lord Haldane's mission to Berlin the fact that Sir E. Grey, in his conversation with Count Metternich on Feb[ruary] 24th,[2] should have made reservations with regard to the cession of Zanzibar and Pemba, which had been offered unconditionally by the Secretary of State for War; that he should have termed it a cession of territory, although it is only a question of a protectorate and that he should have endeavoured to minimise the value of the concessions asked for by England from the German Government and agreed to by the latter with reference to the Bagdad Railway and Timor. Above all, however, the simultaneous arrival at an understanding respecting the proposed neutrality agreement has always formed, in the eyes of the Imperial Government, the indispensable preliminary to any agreement respecting the rate of construction under the Navy Bill.

If, nevertheless, the Imperial Government are prepared to abide by the bargain proposed to Lord Haldane and are ready to restrict their demand for the construction of the new battleships under the Navy Bill to the years 1913 and 1916, that is, a third of a ship for each year, and altogether to refrain from indicating at present any year for the construction of the third ship, they are inspired with the hope

[2] [v. supra, pp. 697–8, No. 524.]

that the British Government will come forward with a proposal as regards the political understanding agreed to in principle and that they will thereby offer the possibility of a continuance of the negotiations.

MINUTE.

This memorandum is being printed as an enclosure in the despatch to Sir E. Goschen recording the conversation with Count Metternich on March 6,[3] and will be circulated to the cabinet as soon as the printer delivers the copies. It will no doubt require detailed consideration at the hands of the Admiralty.

Meanwhile there are in it certain points which have a more general bearing on the negotiation and which deserve special notice, as they are in marked contradiction with Lord Haldane's account of what passed at Berlin :

Notwithstanding Mr. Asquith's public declaration, care is taken again to assert that the initiative in sending Lord Haldane to Berlin came from the British government.

The German memorandum makes out that although Lord Haldane was not furnished with Full Powers to sign an agreement, he made, on the authority of the British Cabinet, certain distinct offers, such as the cession of Zanzibar and Pemba *unconditionally*, and that in return he presented *demands*. These demands were formally *accepted* by the German government, who are now at a loss to understand how the agreement so arrived at can be repudiated on the ground that the German navy law includes an increase of personnel, an increase which Lord Haldane, they say, admitted to be necessary, and against which he made no objections whatever.

I venture to think that the spirit shown in their distorting Lord Haldane's proceedings and the attitude of H[is] M[ajesty's] G[overnment] is ominous. It is of course possible that Lord Haldane did not make his meaning so clear to the German Chancellor as in his own written record of his visit. But a reference to the several passages which I have marked on the attached copy of that record, make this difficult to believe. I am afraid this will prove another instance of the well-known practice of the German Foreign Office to make profitable use of the ambiguities which so easily glide into confidential and unguarded conversations, in order to tie the other party down to statements and promises and engagements never made. We need only remember the incidents of the " Yangtse " agreement, the occupation of Kiao-Chow, the alleged promise of Great Britain not to seek a connection between the Sudan and South Africa through the Belgian Congo; the alleged assent of the Powers to the Waldersee appointment in China; the recent assertion that the Emperor obtained, when in London, the formal approval of the King and H[is] M[ajesty's] G[overnment] to the German occupation of Agadir etc.

I cannot believe that Lord Haldane at Berlin agreed to Great Britain " supporting such plans (? designs) as German policy may hereafter entertain for the acquisition of Angola and the Belgian Congo."

This would compel us to put pressure on Portugal and Belgium to part with their colonies, and would so far as Portugal is concerned be contrary to our express treaty stipulations to defend those colonies, besides involving a degree of obliquity in dealing with an allied and friendly country which would run counter to all ideas of national honour.

According to the present memorandum, the German government consider us bound to swallow their naval programme with its large extension, without any remark or criticism; to conclude a political agreement according to the well-known " formula "; and, besides " unconditionally " ceding Zanzibar and Pemba, to join in pressing for the cession of Angola (in its entirety apparently, as no mention is made of the British-reserved portion of it for which we so strongly held out in 1898) and also of the whole of the Belgian Congo minus the Katanga.

As a result, we shall have to meet the increased naval expenditure demanded by the German naval expansion; lose Zanzibar, for which we gave away Heligoland and our rights in Madagascar; stand before Europe as the despoiler of our ally, and of Belgium; admit Germany to a position in Persia from which she will be able to renew there the part she has recently played in Morocco; and get in return : the reversion of Timor to Holland, instead of to us; an empty promise respecting the Bagdad railway which is meaningless if not mischievous, and will embroil us with Turkey; and—lastly—Germany's friendship !

This is a very much worse bargain than any of the numerous ones by which we have been persuaded to buy this same German " friendship " so many times already.

I am afraid all our experience goes to prove that this is the way not to get better, but to get a perpetuation of worse, relations.

E. A. C.
Mch. 8.
F. D. A.
E. G.

[3] [*v.* immediately succeeding document.]

No. 530.

Sir Edward Grey to Sir E. Goschen.

F.O. 10066/5569/12/18.
(No. 50.)

Sir,

Foreign Office, March 6, 1912.

The German Ambassador read to Lord Haldane and to me to-day([1]) the enclosed Memorandum.([2])

He then informed me that the German Chancellor could not conceal from himself that the turn taken in the negotiations had come as an unpleasant surprise to the German Government, after the satisfactory declarations which had been made by me to Count Metternich respecting Lord Haldane's visit([3]) and after the Prime Minister's statement.([4]) They had hoped, from these statements, that a basis of mutual confidence had been established that would render possible an agreement satisfactory to both parties. The German Government felt that there would be to some extent a relapse into want of confidence if doubt were cast upon the German official declarations concerning the aims of the latest amendments of the German Naval Law, and if suspicion were expressed that further new formations, beyond the present Novelle, were contemplated. This suspicion could rest on no foundation. The Novelle provided, as clearly appeared by its wording, for nothing more than an increase of fully commissioned ships, by three ships of the line, three large cruisers, and three small cruisers. The formation of torpedo-boats was not changed since 1906, when the Reichstag had voted full active complements for all torpedo-boats except those kept as reserve for "matériel." The increase of "personnel" that would not be absorbed by the increase of ships kept in full commission and by the crews of submarines would be needed to fill existing gaps. As another instance of want of confidence might be taken the British objection to the increase in the number of German submarines. It was difficult to see how this could influence the British Naval Budget. Lastly, the German Government confidently expected that we would come forward with a proposal about a neutrality agreement. No success in the negotiations was possible unless political and naval questions were treated *pari passu.* The German Government could not be expected to discuss naval questions as an isolated issue, if they did not see any prospect of coming to a satisfactory political agreement. The German increase in shipbuilding was only one new battleship in three years : this was very moderate. The Novelle must now be laid before the Reichstag. An attempt to cut down " personnel " needed for existing units, and to drop altogether the three battleships needed for the completion of the third squadron, —the building of which battleships was to be spread over a long period—would be a thing that public opinion in Germany would not accept, especially as the German Government could not point to any corresponding concession from England.

I said that parts of this communication were very technical, and we should have to refer them to the Admiralty. One observation of a general character, however, occurred to me : as I had already said in speaking to Count Metternich, even if the negotiations did not result in a definite public agreement between the two Governments, I hoped that nevertheless the better atmosphere created by Lord Haldane's visit to Berlin, and the relations of frankness then established, would continue. In other words, I hoped that Count Metternich and I should go on talking together as freely as Herr von Bethmann-Hollweg and Lord Haldane had talked. I observed to Count Metternich that the communication which he had just made to

([1]) [*cp. G.P.* XXXI, pp. 158–9.]
([2]) [*v.* immediately preceding document.]
([3]) [*cp. supra*, p. 688, No. 510, and pp. 696–7, No. 523.]
([4]) [For the statement of February 14, *v. Parl. Deb.*, *5th Ser.*, House of Commons, **Vol. 34**, pp. 31–3.]

me gave me the impression that the German Government felt that, unless some definite agreement was reached, nothing at all would have been gained.

Count Metternich said that he had emphasised, in communicating with his Government, what I had said as to the gain which had been made in the increased frankness of our relations, and he would not fail to emphasise it again. But our latest Memorandum(5) had given his Government the impression that there was want of confidence.

On this I observed that the Memorandum was a technical document, and that in giving it to Count Metternich I had expressly stated that no sentence in it which appeared to have a political meaning must be regarded as displacing or superseding what Lord Haldane and I had said during these negotiations. The object of the Memorandum was to point out that the German Novelle would entail upon us an increased expenditure of £18,000,000 in five years, beyond what we had anticipated; and, of course, if this were to be the firstfruits of a definite public agreement between the two Governments, public opinion would be much disappointed.

Count Metternich observed, with regard to the three new battleships, that the first of them was not to be laid down until 1913, the second not until 1916, while no date was fixed for the laying down of the third.

At the end of the conversation I told Count Metternich that I had settled with Mr. Harcourt, who had been looking into territorial questions, that we should meet Count Metternich here to discuss them on the map.

[I am, &c.]
E. G[REY].

(5) [v. supra, pp. 698–9, No. 524, encl.]

No. 531.

Sir Edward Grey to Sir E. Goschen.

F.O. 10678/5569/12/18.
(No. 53.)
Sir,

Foreign Office, March 9, 1912.

Having arranged with Mr. Harcourt that we should both see Count Metternich to-day,(1) I prefaced the interview by saying that it would be informal and non-committal, but that a survey of possible territorial arrangements would no doubt be useful. Further than that we could not go without consulting the Cabinet. I was submitting to them the last Memorandum from the German Government,(2) and as soon as possible I would let Count Metternich have our views.

I explained to Count Metternich that I was much disappointed that he persisted in regarding the discussion in Berlin as having taken the form of a complete offer from us with regard to territorial exchanges. I said that we were most desirous of arranging with Germany about our position in the Persian Gulf, the Bagdad Railway, and so forth. But, as regards the Bagdad Railway, Germany had already sold to Turkey the concession from Bagdad to the Persian Gulf and had been compensated by a concession to Alexandretta. Turkey regarded herself as free to dispose of this concession, subject only to the condition that Germany was to have as large a share in it as any other foreign country. The only thing which Germany had to give in connection with the railway from Bagdad to the Gulf was the waiving of this condition. Moreover, the waiving of this condition would not give us any territory, or even give us the concession for the railway. We should have to purchase our share in the concession from Turkey by an increase of the Customs Dues: an increase which, incidentally, would go to develop the main part of the Bagdad Railway concession, which was German, and in which we had no share.

(1) [cp. G.P. XXXI, pp. 255–60.]
(2) [v. supra, pp. 704–6, No. 529.]

Count Metternich referred to the promise of German diplomatic support for us in Constantinople

I said that that would be very welcome, though it should be remembered that an inconvenient effect might be produced in the Mohammedan world if Germany and England joined in putting pressure upon Turkey to give a concession. I thought that an agreement with Germany about the region of the Persian Gulf and the railways there would be very desirable, and I did not wish to belittle its importance; but, in setting it off as a *quid pro quo* against a cession of territory, the considerations which I had urged must naturally be borne in mind.

The interview was a long one and the record of the main part of it has been made by Mr. Harcourt and is being sent to you separately.([3])

[I am, &c.]
E. G[REY].

([3]) [A memorandum was drawn up by Mr. Harcourt describing this interview. It relates to the question of the Portuguese colonies and will be printed in a later volume.]

No. 532.

Observations by Lord Haldane on the Memorandum communicated by Count Metternich on March 6, 1912.

F.O. 10786/5569/12/18A. *March* 11, 1912.

The memorandum now communicated([1]) contains some statements on which I desire to comment briefly. The notes which my colleagues have of my conversations in Berlin([2]) were made, in the case of the first and second conversations, within an hour of their taking place. The note of the third was written by me in the train on the following morning. They represent, as I believe, accurately the substance, and, as far as was possible in a condensed statement, the language of the discussions. Although my confidence in the good feeling of the Imperial Chancellor was great, I thought it prudent to be precise about my position. I informed him at the outset that, while in Berlin with the full approval of the King and the Cabinet, and while intimately acquainted with their feelings and intentions as regards the topics in question, I had no authority to make any agreement or to bind them. · I had come merely to explore the situation (*pour tâter le terrain*), and it was this very fact that enabled me to discuss possibilities without restraint. A reference to the conclusion of my first conversation with the Chancellor, as recorded in my notes, will show that I made it quite clear that I was communicating no offer, and was committing nobody. It also appears from the note that the Chancellor made it equally clear that he committed nobody. Both with him and in speaking with the Emperor and Admiral Tirpitz I was careful to employ the phrase that the discussions could only be "*ad referendum*," and that I was only there to see whether there were materials on the two sides for a possible agreement. I emphasised the necessity for us of considering particular questions not in isolation, but as part of a general bargain of which our people would approve, and I said that the naval prospect would profoundly affect the problem of what was practicable. It was only subject to these several times repeated reservations that I conducted my conversations. The concluding passages of the notes of the conversation at the Schloss, and of the second conversation with the Chancellor, showed this clearly.

There is no justification for several of the statements in the memorandum communicated on the 6th March. It is not plain what is meant by saying that although I stated that I was without "full powers to conclude a binding agreement," I said I was "under authority from the whole British Cabinet" to do the things

([1]) [*v. supra*, pp. 704–6, No. 529.]
([2]) [*v. supra*, pp. 676–84, No. 506.]

set out. Moreover, I never used such a phrase as that the British Government were prepared "to support such plans for the acquisition of the Portuguese Colony of Angola, as well as of parts of the Congo Free State, as it may eventually be the policy of Germany to entertain." On the contrary, I have the most definite recollection of saying that we were on good terms with Portugal and Belgium and could put no pressure on them to sell; and that, as regards the Congo, France had certain rights of pre-emption. I made no offer to cede Zanzibar and Pemba: I merely stated that these were places which might very well come into a general bargain. It is ridiculous to suggest, as is done, that I "offered them unconditionally." Timor was a very small point, and I mentioned (although the German document omits them) the Mozambique and Katanga questions, as to which the Chancellor replied in the same generally favourable spirit as had characterised my own suggestions as to Angola, Zanzibar, and Pemba.

As to naval matters, I was given the new Fleet Bill only at the end of my conversation at the Schloss. The Emperor said it was very technical, but that Captain Dumas could explain it clearly. I took care not to look at it, but put it into my pocket and said I would take it home for consideration by the naval experts. I was told nothing and knew nothing of the increases in personnel or submarines. Indeed, I was cognisant of nothing but what appeared to be the quite reasonable desire for a new training squadron, and of the three new battle-ships as to which I told the Chancellor that they might give rise to trouble. A reference to the notes will show this clearly.

I have read with care the German text of the memorandum of 6th March. I do not think that it is written by the Chancellor. He has a distinctive style, of which the quotation in it from his previous memorandum is a good example. The document suggests quite a different pen, and perhaps more pens than one. I suspect that differences of opinion have emerged between the Chancellor and his colleagues, and that the naval party have got the matter partly out of his hands, and have assisted the officials of the Berlin Foreign Office to prepare this document with a view to making out a case for themselves. The concluding paragraph is significant. It seems to contain a new offer to indefinitely postpone the third battle-ship if a formula can be agreed on; and the earlier part of the document, in stating that no irreconcilable divergence of views has appeared about the formula, seems to hint that the limited principle suggested by Sir E. Grey would be accepted.

H. OF C.

March 11, 1912.

No. 533.

Memorandum by Lord Haldane of a conversation with Count Metternich.

Very Secret.(¹)   *Tuesday, March 12, 1912.*
This evening I received a note from Count Metternich expressing a wish to see me immediately, as he had "something of importance and urgency to tell me." I saw him at the German Embassy at 10·45. He informed me that he had a communication from the Chancellor in reply to his report that serious exception was taken here to the magnitude of the changes contemplated by the New Fleet Law, and especially to the large increase of perso[n]nel. What he had learned he wished in the first place to tell me quite privately and informally. He gathered from Berlin that if the British Government would offer a suitable political formula the proposed Fleet Law as it stood would be withdrawn. Some Fleet Law there must be, but one of less magnitude would be introduced. I asked him whether

he could tell me the extent of the reduction. He replied that he gathered that it would be considerable, but that he was not in a position to define it. I gathered that he thought it extended to person[n]el. I asked whether he wished this communication to be treated as merely between him and me. He said no, he was officially instructed, but he had wanted to see me in the first place to say that time pressed, as a statement would have to be made almost at once in the Reichstag about the Fleet Law, and the Chancellor wished to be provided with the offer of a formula from us as a reason for not proceeding with the original proposals. I asked whether the formula need go beyond the disclaimer of aggressive intentions and combinations. He indicated that he thought it need not. He added that he was instructed to say that if, having offered the formula, we were dissatisfied with the naval reductions when they came out we were to be regarded as quite free to withdraw it, in other words it was to be conditional on our being satisfied in this respect.

I said I would see Sir Edward Grey at once.

H. of C.

No. 534.

Sir A. Nicolson to Sir E. Goschen.

Private.([1])

My dear Goschen :— *Foreign Office, March 13, 1912.*

I am much obliged to you for the two letters which I received by last Messenger.([2]) The story you relate as to the Emperor's indiscretion, I agree with you that it was a studied indiscretion, is very interesting and significant. I shall treat your letter in regard to it as one which can be shown to the King and Haldane, as I think it is desirable that the latter especially should be cognisant of the remarks which have been made in respect to his alleged statements. Needless to say they are quite unfounded, as he never intimated, even in the most indirect manner, any unfriendliness towards France. On the contrary, as you know, he made it as clear as he possibly could that any understanding or arrangement to which we might come with Germany must in no wise impair the friendly relations which at present existed between us and France and Russia. All the documents which record the conversations which have taken place during the last two or three days are being sent you by to-night's messenger and will give you a full account of the latest German proposals and moves, and, I may add, of their misrepresentations which, to my mind, surpass anything that can well be imagined. I need not further comment upon them, as you will be able to draw your own conclusions in respect to them.

I am going to draw up a rough draft of our reply([3]) to the German memorandum,([4]) which, of course, will have to be submitted to the Cabinet, and which I am prepared should be continually modified, if necessary, by them. I am, on the whole, glad that the Germans have shown their hands in the way which they have done. I will not touch further on this question as I should only take up your time unnecessarily, and you will be kept fully informed as to any further developments which may take place.

In regard to other European questions, I do not think that anything of much interest has taken place during the last week, and I am glad to say that no very startling events occurred as I was away on holiday, and have returned very much refreshed by it.

([1]) [Carnock MSS., Vol. II of 1912.]

([2]) [Not reproduced. The story referred to in the next sentence relates to a statement said to have been made by the Emperor in a private conversation at dinner. The Emperor was reported to have said that he had " no confidence " in England " and that no reliance could ever be placed on her. ' For instance,' he continued, ' I don't mind telling you that when Lord Haldane was here his references to France were not at all friendly.' "]

([3]) [v. infra, pp. 713–4, No. 537, encl.]

([4]) [v. pp. 704–6, No. 529. cp. pp. 709–10, No. 532.]

You will see that we and the French have agreed to follow the procedure suggested by Sazonoff in respect to making enquiries at Rome in the first place. I still am of opinion that the French proposal was the more reasonable of the two, and that we should have made simultaneous enquiries both at Constantinople and Rome. We are perfectly well aware what the Italian reply will be, and I do not quite see how the five Powers can carry it in their hands to Constantinople, as whatever may be said, the Turks will undoubtedly consider that in the mere fact of the Powers being the channel for such a communication a certain amount of indirect pressure is being brought to bear upon them to accept it. At the same time I have certain doubts as to whether we shall be able to secure unanimity among the Powers for acting in this manner, and I expect that the whole effort to mediate will consequently be once more shelved to a future date.

The very latest communication which was made last night by Metternich,[5] and a copy of which will be forwarded to you to-day, is a somewhat extraordinary step to have taken. I am waiting to see Haldane and have a talk with him on the subject, as Grey, unfortunately, is entirely absorbed in these Coal Conferences and has no time to attend to foreign affairs except intermittently, so I shall do my utmost to find a formula we may submit which will be of as non-committal a character as possible, and also one which will not bind our hands in regard to any eventualities which may possibly arise in the future.

Churchill intends to make a very full and clear statement on Monday next in introducing his naval budget. I should advise you to read it carefully. I think from the summary which he gave me verbally yesterday it will be made very clear that we intend to maintain preponderance in naval construction at all costs, and I trust that this will show the Germans that it is useless for them continuing this naval competition.

I have just seen Haldane and I had a long talk with him, and I think that the formula which has been drawn up is a perfectly innocent and clear statement, and one to which neither France nor Russia can take the slightest objection. I cannot send you a copy of it as it is to be submitted to the Cabinet, and it is just possible that they may modify it in some respects, but I sincerely trust they will not.

[A. NICOLSON.]

(5) [v. immediately preceding document.]

No. 535.

Sir Edward Grey to Sir A. Nicolson.

Private.(1)
My dear Nicolson,   3, *Queen Anne's Gate, S.W., March* 13, 1912.

This German move is very extraordinary. Please read Haldane's pencil memo[randum](2) and consider my pencil draft of a formula(3) which I will discuss with you today when I can get time : I must submit a formula to the Cabinet tomorrow (Thursday). I have told Haldane to come to see you this morning. I shall be at the coal conference.

Yours sincerely,
E. GREY.

You can show it all to Mallet also.

(1) [Carnock MSS., Vol. II of 1912.]
(2) [v. *supra*, pp. 710–1, No. 533.]
(3) [v. *infra*, pp. 713–4, No. 537, *encl.* No pencil copy of this has however been found. There is a second draft in Grey MSS., Vol. 23, but this also is written in ink.]

No. 536.

Sir Edward Grey to Sir E. Goschen.

F.O. 11234/5569/12/18.
(No. 58.) Secret.
Sir,   *Foreign Office, March 14, 1912.*

Count Metternich said to me to-day that the Admiralty Memorandum(¹) in reply to the German communication(²) was greatly exaggerated. He could give me explanations : but, as he was not a naval expert, and I was not a naval expert, our Admiralty would never be satisfied with explanations given through him and through me.

We discussed the possibility of our sending a naval expert to Berlin, who would have no Mission and would not touch upon the political side of the question, but who might go into the Novelle with a German expert, and make notes to bring home with him : notes which he could show to the German expert when the investigation was concluded, so that it should be quite clear what the British expert view of the Novelle was, and how it had been arrived at.

Finally, I said that I would consult the Admiralty on this point, and if I found that it recommended itself to Mr. Churchill I would communicate with Count Metternich again.

[I am, &c.]
E. G[REY].

(¹) [*v. supra*, pp. 698–9, No. 524, *encl.*]
(²) [This may refer to the verbal communication of February 22, *v. supra*, pp. 696–7, No. 523.]

No. 537.

Sir Edward Grey to Sir E. Goschen.

F.O. 11235/5569/12/18.
(No. 59.) Secret.
Sir,   *Foreign Office, March 14, 1912.*

Count Metternich, in conversation to-day,(¹) reminded me that the German Chancellor had already invited the proposal of a formula from us, and had emphasised the point that a formula and naval expenditure were inter-dependent questions.

Count Metternich went on to say that, if we came forward with a formula, matters would proceed with regard to negotiations respecting the German naval programme. He had no authority to say that the Novelle would be changed, but he said that any proposal of a formula made by us would be without prejudice and not binding unless we were satisfied that our wishes were met on the naval question.

On this understanding, I gave Count Metternich a copy of a draft formula which had been approved by the Cabinet.

I am, &c.
E. GREY.

Enclosure in No. 537.

Copy of Draft Formula given by Sir Edward Grey to Count Metternich.

March 14, 1912.

England will make no unprovoked attack upon Germany and pursue no aggressive policy towards her.

(¹) [*cp. G.P.* XXXI, p. 178. The text there is identical with the above version, but in the word " understanding " the final " n " is omitted.]

Aggression upon Germany is not the subject and forms no part of any Treaty understanding or combination to which England is now a party nor will she become a party to anything that has such an object.

No. 538.

Count Metternich to Sir Edward Grey.

Kaiserlich Deutsche Botschaft,

Private.(¹) 9, *Carlton House Terrace, S.W.,*

Dear Sir Edward, *London, March* 14, 1912.

I am afraid that the political formula you left with me to-day will not be found sufficient at home, as no mention is made of neutrality. Neutrality formed the most important part of the draft Haldane made in Berlin with the Chancellor. I should like to suggest some additions to your formula at your earliest convenience.

Yours sincerely,

P. METTERNICH.

(¹) [Grey MSS., Vol. 23.]

No. 539.

Sir Edward Grey to Sir E. Goschen.

F.O. 11541/5569/12/18.

(No. 60.) Secret.

Sir, *Foreign Office, March* 15, 1912.

Count Metternich asked to see me to-day.

He told me that he had submitted the formula(¹) which I had given him to the German Chancellor. He had not heard from the latter, and did not expect to hear from him; but he was sure that the formula would not be sufficient by itself. Time pressed: for important decisions must be taken in Berlin in the next few days. He then urged me very strongly that it was necessary that an addition should be made to our formula, and he suggested two alternatives: "England will therefore observe at least a benevolent neutrality should war be forced upon Germany," or "England will therefore as a matter of course remain neutral if a war is forced upon Germany." This would not be binding unless our wishes were met with regard to the naval programme. The Novelle could not be withdrawn, but it might be cut down. It was necessary, if our proposed formula was to affect the political situation in Berlin, that it should be accompanied by a sketch of the reductions in the Novelle that would satisfy us. A postponement of ships would be comparatively easy; a reduction of men would be more difficult. He pressed for our views, and was anxious to have them to-morrow, both as regards the formula and as regards the Novelle. Monday (the 18th) might be too late.

I said that I would ask Mr. Churchill whether he could come at once to see me, and I would consult the Prime Minister; but I could not deal with the question of the formula without consulting my Colleagues, and it seemed to me almost impossible to deal with it by to-morrow. Count Metternich had pointed out that our intention to remain neutral, if a war was forced upon Germany, might be inferred from the formula which we had proposed. This I said was true: but I thought that our formula, as it stood, exactly expressed the situation, and need not be added to. I told him quite frankly how the growing strength of Germany had given rise to an anxiety in this country that a day might come when a German Government might

(¹) [*v. supra*, pp. 713–4, No. 537, *encl.*]

desire to crush France. If such a contingency arose, though our hands were quite free, as they were now, we might not be able to sit still: for we should feel that, if we did sit still, and allowed France to be crushed, we should have to fight alone later on. All the military conversations or preparations of which he might have heard had meant simply that, improbable as such a contingency might be, we had considered what we should do if it arose and we decided to take action. On the other hand, I had given France clearly to understand that, if France was aggressive towards Germany or attacked Germany, no support would be forthcoming from us, or would be approved by British public opinion. Our formula, as it stood, exactly expressed this situation. I was afraid that the words which he suggested would give an impression going beyond the literal sense of the words, and might be taken to mean that under no circumstances, if there was war on the Continent, could anything be expected from us. I told him frankly my difficulties, and I had hoped that the formula which we had suggested would be sufficient.

Count Metternich urged me very strongly to consult the Prime Minister and some of my Colleagues to-morrow morning, if a meeting of the whole Cabinet was not possible. He told me that he had emphasised my opinion that, even if the Novelle were proceeded with, the frank relations established by Lord Haldane's visit to Berlin should be preserved; but he was afraid that, if the Novelle were proceeded with, the negotiations would come to an end. He gave me to understand that this would be due to a change of "personnel" in Berlin. Count Metternich gave me the following copy of the formula which the German Chancellor had sketched to Lord Haldane as being what he would like.

[I am, &c.]
E. G[REY].

Enclosure in No. 539.

Formula sketched by German Chancellor.([2])

1. The high contracting powers assure each other mutually of their desire of peace and friendship.

2. They will not either of them make or prepare to make any (unprovoked) attack upon the other or join in any combination or design against the other for purposes of aggression or become party to any plan or naval or military enterprise alone or in combination with any other power directed to such an end. And declare [themselves] not to be bound at present by any such engagement.

3. If either of the high contracting parties becomes entangled in a war with one or more powers in which it can not be said to be the aggressor, the other of the high contracting parties will at least observe towards the power so entangled a benevolent neutrality and use its utmost endeavour for the localisation of the conflict. If either of the high contracting parties is forced to go to war by obvious provocation from a third party they bind themselves to enter into an exchange of views concerning their attitude in such a conflict.

4. The duty of neutrality which arises [out] of the preceding article has no application in so far as it may not be conciliable [sic]([3]) with existing agreements which the high contracting powers have already made.

5. The making of new agreements which render it impossible for either of the contracting powers to observe neutrality towards the other beyond what is provided by the preceding limitation, is excluded in conformity with the provision in article 2.

6. The high contracting parties declare that they will do all in their power to prevent differences and misunderstandings arising between either of them and other powers.

([2]) [cp. pp. 682–3, No. 506, Appendix I.]
([3]) [On the typed copy in the file " reconcilable " has been written over " conciliable " in pencil.]

No. 540.

Sir Edward Grey to Sir F. Bertie.

F.O. 11711/5569/12/18.
(No. 135.)
Sir,
                                                     Foreign Office, March 15, 1912.

I saw M. Cambon to-day, and told him that our discussion with the German Government as to naval expenditure had continued. Count Metternich had told me yesterday that some assurance of policy on our part was essential to any naval arrangement.(¹) I had replied that I was quite willing to give such an assurance, and I had suggested a form of words. I gave M. Cambon a copy of these, very confidentially for his information and that of M. Poincaré. This form of words, of which I enclose a copy, was not to be exchanged as a formula unless the naval arrangements were satisfactory, and in any case it did not impair any other agreements which we had.

M. Cambon read the words, and seemed satisfied with them. He took away the copy of them which I had given him.

[I am, &c.]
E. G[REY].

(¹) [*v. supra,* pp. 713–4, No. 537, and *encl.*]

No. 541.

Sir E. Goschen to Sir A. Nicolson.

Private and Secret.(¹)
My dear Nicolson,
                                                     Berlin, March 15, 1912.

The first German memorandum of the 6th of March(²) is a wonderful tissue of misrepresentations; but what fairly beats me is the *volte-face* in the second.(³) "He gathered from Berlin that if the British Government would offer a suitable formula, the proposed Fleet Law as it stood would be withdrawn," and then "He added that he was instructed to say that if, having offered the formula, we were dissatisfied with the naval reductions when they came out we were to be regarded as quite free to withdraw it."

Unless the German Government have something up their sleeve of which we know nothing these sentences would seem to indicate that the Chancellor has finally got the better of Admiral Tirpitz and Kiderlen. I add Kiderlen because the first memorandum has quite the Kiderlen touch. It was, I presume, an attempt to nail down Lord Haldane as Sazonow was nailed; a try-on to which the Chancellor may have given a grudging consent, while resolved to try a milder process should the bluff fail, as it apparently has. The Chancellor and Tirpitz have been having a long struggle in the matter of the new Naval Law and represent two distinct forces :— The Chancellor who said to me only the other day that if he could only arrange a satisfactory understanding with England he wouldn't care tuppence what was said about the rest of his work as Chancellor, and who may therefore be supposed to be willing to make considerable sacrifices to obtain his object; and Tirpitz who has made it the business of his administrative life to reduce the superiority of England at sea, and may therefore be supposed to be very *unwilling* to sacrifice what he doubtless considered would bring him a step nearer his object. Has the Chancellor won the day? On the surface it would appear so, but I think we must see a little

(¹) [Carnock MSS., Vol. II of 1912.]
(²) [*v. supra,* pp. 704–6, No. 529.]
(³) [*v. supra,* pp. 710–1, No. 533.]

further into the matter before arriving at that conclusion. Tirpitz has the strongest will of the two, I should think, and he has probably Krupp and the whole ' armour plated' crew and the Pan Germans behind him. I can't therefore quite see him in my mind's eye coming before the Reichstag and saying that owing to certain assurances which England has given he was not going to ask them to pass the naval ' Vorlage' which he had had in his mind (and which he might add he had trumpeted in the Press as being absolutely necessary for Germany's needs) and was only going to ask them to pass a very modified version of his proposals.

I should think he would sooner resign, and *that* the Emperor would hate, as Tirpitz is practically, at the present moment, irreplaceable. Of course he may see from Churchill's attitude, as set forth in the Admiralty memorandum,(⁴) that it is useless to go on trying to reduce our supremacy at sea; and that is a possible explanation, but it would be a tremendous climb down and his followers would raise a tremendous outcry. Again the increased vote of the Socialists may have something to do with the matter, though they cannot do much without the National Liberals who have hitherto been as hot as anyone for increased armaments, and who would scarcely be tempted by the formula we have proposed to give up their ideas in that respect—connected as they are with those who get their living from the manufacture of warlike material!

I must confess that the sudden difference of tone between the two memoranda is beyond my comprehension for the moment.

I received to-night the formula which His Majesty's Government have proposed.(⁵) I don't see that it can arouse the susceptibilities of our friends. I am wondering what they will think of the formula here.

Yours very sincerely,
W. E. GOSCHEN.

(⁴) [*v. supra*, pp. 698–9, No. 524, *encl.*]
(⁵) [*v. supra*, pp. 713–4, No. 537, *encl.*]

No. 542.

Sir Edward Grey to Sir C. MacDonald.

F.O. 11711/5569/12/18.
(No. 45.) Secret.
Sir, *Foreign Office, March 15, 1912.*

I saw the Japanese Chargé d'Affaires to-day, and spoke to him in the same way as to M. Cambon, as to our discussion with the German Government as to naval expenditure. I gave him a copy of the form of words which I had suggested.(¹)

I enclose a copy of my desp[atch] to Sir F. Bertie,(²) recording my conversation with M. Cambon.

[I am, &c.]
E. G[REY].

(¹) [*v. supra*, pp. 713–4, No. 537, *encl.*]
(²) [*v. supra*, p. 716, No. 540.]

No. 543.

Sir Edward Grey to Sir G. Buchanan.

F.O. 11711/5569/12/18.
(No. 88.) Secret.
Sir. *Foreign Office, March 15, 1912.*

I saw Count Benckendorff to-day, and spoke to him in the same way as to M. Cambon, as to our discussion with the German Government as to naval expenditure. I gave him a copy of the form of words which I had suggested.

I enclose a copy of my despatch to Sir F. Bertie,([1]) recording my conversation with M. Cambon.

⌈I am, &c.⌉
E. G⌈REY⌉.

([1]) [v. supra, p. 716, No. 540.]

No. 544.

Sir Edward Grey to Sir E. Goschen.

F.O. 11712/5569/12/18.
(No. 62.) Secret.
Sir,   *Foreign Office, March 16, 1912.*

I told Count Metternich to-day([1]) that we had considered his suggestions as to the formula.([2]) There could be no objection to a preface, which would make the beginning less abrupt; and we might say : '' The two Powers being mutually desirous of securing peace and friendship between them, England declares that she . . . .'' I then explained to Count Metternich my apprehension that, if we used the word '' neutrality,'' it would convey an impression that more was meant than was said; and I suggested that the substance of what we wished would be obtained and most accurately expressed by saying, instead of the words '' will make no unprovoked attack,'' '' will neither make nor join in any unprovoked attack.''

Count Metternich said he feared that unless the word '' neutrality '' was used it would be impossible to secure reduction in the Novelle.

Bearing in mind what he had said to me yesterday, I told him that we had been given the impression that some change of '' personnel '' in Berlin was possibly impending. I could not see how words used in our formula could have any effect upon the position of the German Chancellor personally, as there was no dispute between him and Admiral von Tirpitz about the Novelle, to which the Chancellor had been a consenting party before Lord Haldane went to Berlin; which he proposed to cut down only if he obtained from us what he considered to be satisfactory; and which, it was therefore to be assumed, he was free to go on with if what we said did not satisfy him. It would not be useful for us to exchange a formula if a naval increase was impending, because the naval increase would destroy the good effect produced by the formula. But, if public opinion had been excited by the naval increase, we might afterwards consider the territorial questions, and exchange some formula which would have a calming effect.

I went on to tell Count Metternich that, as far as Herr von Bethmann-Hollweg personally was concerned, I wished to say that he had inspired the greatest confidence in Lord Haldane, who knew him personally, and in myself. We believed genuinely that he wished to pursue a straightforward policy of peace; and, as long as he remained German Chancellor, he might rely upon our co-operating with him to preserve the peace of Europe, each of us not only abstaining from aggression upon the other, but each also using what influence we had with others to prevent war. If this was likely to be of use in personal questions now pending in Berlin, Count Metternich might certainly report it.

I observed that a formula could not be personal. For instance, if we were to exchange with Germany now a formula which made relations between us and any other country more distant, we could have no security that Herr von Bethmann-Hollweg might not be overthrown a month or two hence : when we should be in the

([1]) [For Count Metternich's report and annotations by the Emperor v. G.P. XXXI, pp. 181–3.]
([2]) [v. supra, pp. 714–5, No. 539, encl.]

position of having gained nothing as regards the policy of Germany, and we should have lost something elsewhere.

Our conversation was most friendly, and Count Metternich did not show any of the anxiety which there was in his manner yesterday.

In the course of conversation, he referred to the feeling which had been aroused in Germany by the impression that we might attack her.

I said that we were helpless with regard to an impression of this sort, unless the German Press Bureau could take some action to prevent things like Captain Faber's speech from being used in the way they had been used. As long as the question of Morocco was not settled, I understood that it gave occasion for those people who desired to circulate unfavourable reports as to our policy and intentions with regard to Germany; but I hoped that these occasions would disappear when the question of Morocco was settled.

I went on to tell Count Metternich, that since the beginning of this year, when the question of mediation between Turkey and Italy had been discussed, I had stipulated that all five Powers, including Germany, should be in agreement before any action was taken. I had stipulated for this in Vienna and in St. Petersburg, when approached on the subject. Similarly, with regard to the questions which might arise in connection with the Balkans, I had said to the Representatives of other Powers: "Do not let us fall into two groups over these Balkan questions. Let us keep in touch with one another." It was true that I should be glad to see Russia and Austria come to an agreement which would prevent their getting into a war with each other about the Balkans: a war which would be very inconvenient to their allies and friends. But such an agreement would not make separate groups, for it would bring together two Powers which belonged to different groups. In time this line of policy, if it was given a fair chance, would have a good influence.

Count Metternich asked for the words of alteration in the formula and I wrote them out and gave them to him.

[I am, &c.]

E. G[REY].

No. 545.

Sir Edward Grey to Sir E. Goschen.

F.O. 12081/5569/12/18.
(No. 66.) Secret.
Sir, *Foreign Office, March 19, 1912.*

Count Metternich informed me to-day([1]) of the following communication from the German Chancellor:

> The Chancellor said that our promise not to make or join in an unprovoked attack upon Germany was so elastic as to be valueless: it even left room for the idea that, hitherto, such an attack had been a thing with which Germany had to reckon. The German measures for expenditure on armaments were already known, and the German Government were asked to abandon them for our proposed formula, without getting the necessary guarantee against an attack. In the opinion of the German Naval Authorities, the German measures of armament were necessary to maintain an efficient defence against the combined fleets of the Triple *Entente*. In the English calculations, account had been taken of the possibility of a future change in German policy. But, if an agreement were come to, German policy would be bound, no less than English policy, for a considerable period. Though we, on the one hand, might apprehend that, in consequence of a future change in German policy, we might

([1]) [*cp. G.P.* XXXI, pp. 191–2.]

lose the friendship of France : Germany, on the other hand, had to consider that a future change in English policy might leave Germany, who had renounced the Novelle by her agreement with us, in maritime inferiority to the Powers of the Triple *Entente*. Quite apart from this, the person of the German Emperor was a guarantee that German policy would be conducted on friendly lines, and in the peaceful path which had never been abandoned during the time of the Emperor's government. What we offered now could, therefore, not be a basis for serious negotiations. Count Metternich was instructed to make it quite clear that the German Chancellor could recommend the Emperor to give up the essential parts of the Novelle, and justify this action to the public opinion of Germany, only if we could conclude an agreement guaranteeing neutrality of a far-reaching character, and leaving no doubt as to any interpretation.

Count Metternich then went on to say, speaking personally on his own account, that he was afraid that, when the ground on which Lord Haldane took his stand in Berlin was abandoned, what we proposed could not be useful. Lord Haldane had spoken of neutrality, and of large ships only; but, when he had brought the Novelle to us, we had found that there were things in it much larger than Lord Haldane had known in Berlin. When Count Metternich had asked us to specify what reductions in the Novelle would be satisfactory to us, Mr. Churchill had said that we should prefer no increases in the German Navy Law, and that we could not say that we liked any part of any increase.

Count Metternich added that he was afraid that what Mr. Churchill had said in the House of Commons yesterday,(²) as to our having now a One-Power Standard instead of our previous Two-Power Standard, would not have a soothing effect.

I said that Mr. Churchill's speech represented only actual facts, which had often been put forward in discussion between the German Government and ourselves; and I thought that his reference to the One-Power Standard should rather be taken as a compliment to the great strength which the German Navy had attained, as compared with that of other Powers.

I told Count Metternich that I was surprised that the German Chancellor estimated our draft formula at so low a value. I could not help thinking that the exchange of it would have a favourable effect. No doubt it was true that we had never meditated an unprovoked attack on Germany : but German public opinion thought otherwise. What the Chancellor now asked amounted to an agreement of absolute neutrality, which was more than conditional neutrality.

Count Metternich said that the Chancellor had not used the word " absolute," but in effect his wish amounted to that.

I said that I would refer the communication to the Prime Minister and my Colleagues, but I was still in some doubt as to the exact extent of its meaning. I understood the Chancellor to mean that, failing a guarantee of absolute neutrality, the Novelle must proceed.

Count Metternich confirmed this.

I went on to say that I understood clearly this, and the German point of view with regard to it; but, if the Chancellor meant to infer that, failing a guarantee of absolute neutrality, the relations between the two Powers could not be cordial or satisfactory, I thought that such an idea would be unreasonable. In effect, the Chancellor was asking us for an agreement which went much further than anything which we had with any other country except the Japanese alliance and our ancient Treaties with Portugal : it went further than anything we had with France or Russia.

Count Metternich said that we had not had with France or Russia the acute differences which we had had with Germany.

I replied that, at the end of last century and the beginning of this, we had been more than once on the brink of a war with France or with Russia; yet our relations with these two countries had improved, without any agreement so far-reaching as

(²) [*v. Parl. Deb.*, *5th Ser.*, House of Commons, Vol. 35. pp. 1549–74, especially pp. 1555–6.]

the Chancellor now suggested that we should have with Germany. If the Novelle must proceed, I thought that it should be possible, after public opinion had been stirred by it, to negotiate something which would have a calming influence. In any case, I was ready to continue to discuss from a friendly point of view all the questions which arose between the two Governments; and I saw no reason why this readiness should not be reciprocated by the German Government. In the interests of good relations between us, I would much rather have the Novelle proceeded with, and the Morocco question out of the way, than have no Novelle and the Morocco question still between us.

I added that, as far as we were concerned, we were prepared to continue the territorial discussions surveyed with Mr. Harcourt the other day, if the German Government desired to do so.

Count Metternich said that the Chancellor had not made any reference to these.

Finally, I repeated that I would report the Chancellor's communication to the Prime Minister and my Colleagues.

[I am, &c.]
E. G[REY].

No. 546.

Sir Edward Grey to Sir C. MacDonald.

F.O. 12203/5569/12/18.
(No. 47.) Secret.
Sir,
Foreign Office, March 20, 1912.

The Japanese Chargé d'Affaires informed me to-day that his Government felt some apprehension lest the wording of the draft formula(1) which we had proposed to Germany might interfere with our power to assist Japan under Article II(2) of the Anglo-Japanese Alliance. If Japan were to be involved in a war with Germany, and we had bound ourselves not to attack Germany unless provocation had been offered by her to us, we might be unable to go to the assistance of Japan in accordance with the provisions of the Alliance, inasmuch as Germany might have attacked Japan without giving us provocation. The Chargé d'Affaires showed me the accompanying translation of a telegram from his Government, in explanation of what he had said.

I replied that it had never occurred to me that it might be possible to put such a construction upon the formula which we had proposed to Germany. An attack by Germany upon our Ally would certainly be regarded as provocation to us.

The Chargé d'Affaires then said that this had been his view too, and that when he had read the draft of the formula it had not seemed to him to be open to objection.

I told him that Germany was not content with our draft formula. She had asked for a declaration of neutrality on our part in the event of her being at war with another Power. I had said that if another Power, France for instance, made an unprovoked attack upon Germany, we would not join in it; and I had offered to insert in our formula the words "not join in any unprovoked attack."(3) But we had not been able to promise neutrality in the form which Germany asked, and Germany had decided that the formula which we offered was not sufficient to justify her in reducing naval expenditure. For the moment, therefore, the question of a formula had dropped. It might be revived, and if so I would bear in mind the point which the Japanese Government had raised, for it was not our intention to say anything which would interfere with the Alliance.

[I am, &c.]
E. G[REY].

(1) [*v. supra*, pp. 713–4, No. 537, *encl.*]
(2) [*v. Gooch & Temperley*, Vol. IV, p. 166.]
(3) [*v. supra*, p. 718, No. 544. The phrase there reads "nor join in any unprovoked attack."]

Enclosure in No. 546.

Translation of Telegram received by Japanese Chargé d'Affaires from his Government.

In reference to your telegram of the 15th instant on the subject of the Anglo-German relations, the Imperial Government note with satisfaction the repeated statements of Sir Edward Grey that the assurance which is under contemplation to be exchanged between the British and the German Governments would not conflict in any way with the Anglo-Japanese Alliance, and while placing an entire confidence on [*sic*] his expressions, it appears to me that there is a room for the following remark in regard to the wording of the proposed assurance.

From the same wording it may result that England would never attack Germany unless she was provoked by the latter. But supposing that Japan went into war with Germany under the conditions stated in Art[icle] II of the Anglo-Japanese Alliance, it would become incumbent upon England, although she might have received herself no provocation from Germany, to come to the assistance of Japan, and to conduct the war in common, and in consequence England would stand in a position obliging her to attack Germany without provocation. Thus I am afraid there may be an inconsistency between the Anglo-Japanese Alliance and the proposed assurance.

It is needless to say that the existing friendly relations between Japan and Germany preclude any cause for real apprehension, and that the above hypothesis is set forth merely for the sake of theoretical consideration, but as the matter seems to have in principle an important bearing on the Alliance Treaty, the Imperial Government deem it necessary to ascertain the views of the British Government in the above respect.

No. 547.

Sir Edward Grey to Sir E. Goschen.

F.O. 12308/5569/12/18.
(No. 69.) Secret.
Sir, *Foreign Office, March 21, 1912.*
With ref[erence] to my desp[atch] No. 50 of the 6th ins[tant],(¹) I transmit to Y[our] E[xcellency] herewith a Memorandum on the Anglo-German negotiations as affected by Lord Haldane's visit to Berlin.(²)

I request that Y[our] E[xcellency] will communicate this paper to the Imperial Chancellor as the reply of H[is] M[ajesty's] G[overnment] to the statements in the Memo[randum] handed to me by Count Metternich on March 6 last,(³) which was forwarded to Y[our] E[xcellency] in my des[patch] referred to above.

[I am, &c.
E. GREY.]

Enclosure in No. 547.(⁴)

Memorandum.

His Majesty's Government received on the 6th instant a Memorandum which the Imperial German Government were so good as to communicate through the hands of Count Metternich. His Majesty's Government are in complete accordance with

(¹) [*v. supra*, pp. 707–8, No. 530.]
(²) [The memorandum in its final form was drafted by Lord Haldane. Previously Sir A. Nicolson had prepared a draft which was apparently seen by Lord Haldane before he wrote his own draft. The draft by Sir A. Nicolson is in the Carnock MSS., Vol. II of 1912.]
(³) [*v. supra*, pp. 704–6, No. 529.]
(⁴) [Printed, with annotations by the Emperor William, in *G.P.* XXXI, pp. 205–10.]

the desire of the Imperial German Government to continue the discussion of a basis for good relations between the two countries in a friendly spirit and with perfect frankness on both sides. They will therefore, with the intention of preventing any misapprehension of their own view of what has up till now taken place, make a few comments on certain phrases which occur in the Memorandum.

Lord Haldane proceeded to Berlin in response to an intimation through an unofficial channel that it would not be otherwise than agreeable if a British Minister were to come there, in the first instance for the purpose of a private and unofficial interchange of views. Although his visit was private, he was received with the greatest friendliness by high personages of the German Government, and the suggestion made by him that the conversations, just because they were to be informal, should take place with complete openness and freedom from reserve, was acted on without difficulty on either side. He began by stating that, while in Berlin with the full approval of the King and of his Colleagues in the Cabinet, and while, as he thought, he was pretty intimately acquainted with their feelings and intentions as regards the topics which might come under discussion, he had no authority to bind them or to make any agreement. His purpose was, if this should prove agreeable to the German Government, to explore the ground as completely as was possible at this stage, with a view to ascertaining what ideas and purposes were common to both Governments, and thus getting the conception of a possible basis for more formal and authoritative discussion. He would state in a very open fashion where he thought there were possibilities of differences as well as of agreement. The informal character of his visit rendered this the more easily possible, and his impressions he would take back to his Colleagues. As he was not come to bind them, all would be *ad referendum*, and similarly those with whom he was speaking would presumably feel no more bound than he should feel. On this footing the conversations, which were very free and unrestrained, and were conducted in the most agreeable spirit, proceeded. Nothing was excluded.

Lord Haldane indicated that the various questions which might arise could not be considered in isolation, but should be looked on as part of a general negotiation. His Colleagues would have to satisfy Parliament and the British public about the outcome of such a negotiation. There was an excellent spirit, of which his Government would gladly avail themselves; but he ought to say that he thought naval prospects would very materially affect the question of how much was practicable.

As to naval matters, Lord Haldane was only cognisant of the plans of the Imperial Government for a third squadron for training purposes, and for three new battleships. The latter, he said, seemed to him as a civilian to present more difficulty than the former. The desire of Germany to provide for the better training of her recruits was not a matter on which he should venture to make any observation. Broadly speaking, what would cause concern here would be any plan which would impose on England the necessity of further increasing her fleet, and the three new battleships would certainly do this to a substantial extent. But he said that the question was of too technical a character for him to discuss it in detail. The Imperial Government most courteously presented Lord Haldane, shortly before he left, with a full copy of the Novelle. It was not suggested that he should examine it on the spot. He had of course neither the expert knowledge nor the time requisite for such an examination, and it was not until his return and its examination by the Admiralty in London that the increases in " personnel " and in small craft, which the Novelle contemplated, were realised. As to the three battleships, however, he was fully informed, and it was this information which caused him to express at Berlin some apprehension of difficulty.

These observations are made because it is not quite clear from some phrases in the Memorandum communicated on March 6th that Lord Haldane's general attitude has been quite correctly defined in these phrases. Against the increase in " personnel " he is stated to have had no objection to make. He made no comment only because, through no fault either of his own or of those with whom he was conversing, he had no knowledge of its nature or extent. Again, he is said to have declared that the British Government were willing to support such plans for the acquisition of the Portuguese Colony of Angola, as well as of parts of the Congo State, as it might eventually be the policy of Germany to entertain. While expressing his opinion that the British Government would be glad, in the event of the Secret Agreement of 1898 becoming operative, to make arrangements under which Germany might obtain a part of Angola which was not marked out as hers under that Agreement, and also, if Belgium became willing to part with some of the Congo, portions of that State, Lord Haldane referred to the fact that the relations of England to Portugal and Belgium were friendly, and that England could put no pressure on Portugal or Belgium to part with anything if they were unwilling to do so. Moreover, he referred to the circumstance that France had certain rights of pre-emption as regards the Congo State. Again, he did not make an unconditional, or for that matter any, offer to cede Zanzibar and Pemba. What he intimated was that these appeared to be very suitable assets to be considered for the purposes of a general settlement extending over all the topics of conversation. He and the high personages with whom he was conversing were discussing all these topics in the most open and informal fashion, with a view to ascertaining their mutual views as to practical possibilities. The questions of the Bagdad Railway, the Island of Timor, the conceivable shapes of a political formula, and the possibilities of diminution of the naval programme on the part of both Governments were all treated in the same spirit, and Lord Haldane no more regarded the Imperial Government as making formal offers, or as actually negotiating a Treaty, than he so regarded himself. Both were in his view on a voyage of discovery, the field of which was to be surveyed as a whole, as a preliminary step to more formal negotiation. It may be pointed out in particular that, in discussing the practicability of a neutrality formula, Lord Haldane drew attention to the immense difficulties to both countries which would result from an unconditional formula. He understood that these difficulties were appreciated.

The British Government therefore hope that, in the light of what has been above stated, the Imperial German Government will see that there has been no desire to shift the basis on which the conversations were conducted at Berlin. They take the opportunity of repeating their assurance of good feeling and of desire for the best relations between the two countries. Finally, they reciprocate with pleasure the friendly expression with which the Memorandum communicated on March 6th concludes.

No. 548.

Sir Edward Grey to Sir E. Goschen.

F.O. 12528/5569/12/18.
(No. 71.) Secret.

Sir, *Foreign Office, March 22, 1912.*

Count Metternich told me to-day([1]) that he had reported our last conversation to the Chancellor, and had heard from him that the difficulty between us was not the question of the continuation of the confidential relations established by Lord Haldane in Berlin, for the Chancellor of course wished to continue these; the difficulty was the question of armaments and the naval budget. The Chancellor could deal with this difficulty only if there was an agreement about neutrality of a far-reaching character, and leaving no room for doubt. Such an agreement would not be simply a present from Germany to us: it would have equal advantages for both sides. The Chancellor said that the situation had not been made easier by Mr. Churchill's speech, but the Chancellor did not relinquish hope. Mr. Churchill

([1]) [*cp. G.P. XXXI p. 203.*]

had spoken of limiting only German armaments, while reserving freedom for England. In fact, Germany, though she was situated between France and Russia, which had an Alliance, was not to increase her Navy : even without getting a promise from England to remain neutral.

Count Metternich reminded me that he had, in previous conversations, told me that there were very important internal questions in Berlin, depending upon our answer.

He added, with reference to rumours, which he believed were current in French circles, to the effect that Germany meant to attack France in the Spring, that he could give me the most absolute assurance that there was no such intention, nor anything which could serve as a basis for such reports. He asked whether I had heard these reports.

I said that I had heard reports from several quarters that in Germany war was expected in the Spring, and I had heard that a similar rumour was current in French circles. In Germany, as far as I could make out, the rumour was in some cases based upon the belief that we intended to attack Germany as soon as she announced her intention to increase her naval expenditure. In French circles, on the other hand, it seemed to be feared that Germany intended to attack France. I had never believed that any of these things were likely to happen and we of course had no intention of making war.

I expressed satisfaction at the Chancellor's desire to maintain confidential relations with us. This desire gave one a feeling of comfort and pleasure.

I explained to Count Metternich that, as the Cabinet was very much occupied by the crisis in the Coal Trade, I could not at the moment say more than that Lord Haldane had already pointed out, when he was in Berlin, the difficulty which there was in the way of either Germany or ourselves promising to remain neutral under all circumstances. I observed that, when Count Metternich was speaking to me the other day about neutrality of a far-reaching character, he had said, in reply to remarks of mine, that though the word " absolute " was not used it represented in effect the sort of neutrality for which the Chancellor was asking.

Count Metternich again confirmed this.

[I am, &c.]
E. G[REY].

No. 549.

Sir E. Goschen to Sir A Nicolson.

Private.(¹)

My dear Nicolson,   Berlin, March 22, 1912.

Your letter of the 18th instant(²) was most interesting. I feel that there is something ' up ' which has rendered the Germans so feverishly anxious for their formula. I think I told you in a former letter—or was it in a despatch—that Kiderlen had spoken to me very strongly about the state of feeling in France which he said ' displeased ' him very much. " Celá me déplait " were his words, and he added, you may remember, that pinpricks were small things, but might, if persisted in, cause dangerous irritation. Again Russell tells me that in military circles they talk very freely—surprisingly so—about the chances of a war with France in the near future. This feeling among German military men may be not only because they would *like* a war with France, but also because they think that the contemplated additions to their present enormous military strength may upset French public opinion and render the relations between the two countries more inflammable than

(¹) [Carnock MSS., Vol. II of 1912.]

(²) [Not reproduced. It deals with the same subjects as Sir Edward Grey's despatch No. 60 of March 15, which is printed *supra*, pp. 714–5, No. 539. It refers also to Sir A. Nicolson's first draft of the Memorandum sent to Sir E. Goschen on March 21. *v. supra*, pp. 722–4, No. 547, and *encl.*, and *note* (²).]

ever. Putting two and two together it looks very much as if they were trying to square us in good time.

The most interesting question at the present moment is whether the peaceful Chancellor contemplates retirement or not. That something of the sort is in the air is evident from what Metternich said to Sir Edward Grey about a change in the 'Personnel' in Berlin.(³) I suppose it depends a good deal as to whether the 'formula' for a political understanding framed by His Majesty's Government(⁴) satisfied them here. It is certainly, I should think, as far as we can go, if we are to remain on intimate terms with France and Russia. I shall probably know the impression it has made when I see the Chancellor to present the memorandum. This just comes a day too late for the Emperor to see, as he left tonight for the South. By the way he has invited Bethmann Hollweg to pass some days with him at Corfu—probably as soon as the Reichstag adjourns for the Easter holidays. There has been a perfect epidemic of rumours here during the last few days. But I have written about them fully, too fully I am afraid, in an official despatch.(⁵) I had not time to boil the despatch down, as, as usual, all the rumours appeared just before messenger day.

It is curious that nearly all the people I have seen seem to think it by no means improbable that if the Chancellor goes he will be succeeded by Tirpitz. Personally I can hardly believe this. Tirpitz is an exceedingly clever man, at his own job particularly, but he is a dreamer and a faddist, and I can't see him as Chancellor. Moreover, outside the big Navy people and the Pan Germans generally he has no political following. . . . .(⁶)

Yours very sincerely,
W. E. GOSCHEN.

(³) [cp. supra, p. 715, No. 539, and p. 718, No. 544.]
(⁴) [v. supra, pp. 713–4, No. 537, encl.]
(⁵) [Not reproduced.]
(⁶) [This letter concludes by quoting Press comments on the rate of Naval construction as described in the *Novelle*.]

No. 550.

Sir Edward Grey to Sir F. Bertie.

F.O. 12529/5569/12/18.
(No. 148.) Secret.
Sir.
Foreign Office, March 22, 1912.

I told M. Cambon to-day that, while he had been in Paris, the German Government had informed me that the formula which we had suggested was insufficient, and that they must have a declaration of neutrality if there was to be any arrangement for the diminution of naval expenditure.(¹)

I had pointed out, as Lord Haldane had already done in Berlin, the difficulty there was in the way of either Germany or ourselves promising to remain neutral under all circumstances; and I had explained that even a promise of conditional neutrality might give the impression that we would under all circumstances stand aside. I had, however, said that we were prepared to amplify our formula by saying not only that we would not make but also that we would not join in any unprovoked attack upon Germany. But this was insufficient, in the view of the German Government, to justify their coming to a naval arrangement with us; and for the time being the matter was in suspense, though the question of exchanging a formula such as

(¹) [v. supra, pp. 719–21, No. 545.]

I had suggested, or the question of territorial arrangements in South Africa, might be revived at any time.

M. Cambon appeared quite satisfied with the information, which I told him was for himself and M. Poincaré, confidentially.

[I am, &c.]
E. G[REY].

No. 551.

Sir E. Goschen to Sir Edward Grey.

Berlin, March 25, 1912.
F.O. 12849/5569/12/18.   D. 6·55 P.M.
Tel. (No. 35.) Secret. K.   R. 8·15 P.M.

Your despatch, Secret, of 21st March.(¹)

Have read memorandum to Chancellor and left copy with him.

His Excellency said he would consider it, and send answer if necessary. He asked me to say that he much appreciated friendly tone.

(¹) [v. supra, pp. 722–4, No. 547, and encl.]

No. 552.

Minute by Sir A. Nicolson.

F.O. 12952/5569/12/18.
Sir Edward Grey,   Foreign Office, March 25, 1912.

Tewfik P[ash]a said to-day that there was a report which he hardly liked to mention to me as it was so foolish, and that was that Germany had asked us to cede Zanzibar in return for her giving us concessions in regard to the Bagdad Railway. I asked where he had heard the report. He said it had appeared in some newspaper. I told him he should attach no importance to newspaper rumours. He said that he did not, but he wished to remark that Germany had nothing(¹) to give in regard to the Bagdad Railway.

A. N.

MINUTE.

I have also pointed this out to Metternich.

E. G.

(¹) [Sir Edward Grey has here added : " (very little) ".]

No. 553.

Minutes by Sir A. Nicolson and Sir Edward Grey.

F.O. 13088/5569/12/18.
Sir Edward Grey,   Foreign Office, March 25, 1912.

M. Cambon informed me to-day that he had been instructed to express to you the sincere thanks of M. Poincaré personally and of the French Gov[ernmen]t for the information which you had communicated in respect to the " neutrality " formula.(¹)

(¹) [cp. supra, p. 716, No. 540, and pp. 726–7, No. 550.]

I gathered from a remark made by M. Cambon that he was under the impression that you had definitely informed C[oun]t Metternich that H[is] M[ajesty's] Gov[ernmen]t had declined to agree to the neutrality formula, as he observed that all " the scaffolding which the Germans had wished to raise in connection with Lord Haldane's visit had fallen down by their desire to ask for a formula impossible for the Gov[ernmen]t to accord."

I told him that I believed you had not yet formally submitted C[oun]t Metternich's proposal to the Cabinet and had not given a final reply to the latter. M. Cambon seemed a little disappointed. I told him I did not think he need be unhappy.

A. N.

I did of course after consideration by the Cabinet decline Count Metternich's conditional neutrality formula(²)—the Germans have now suggested absolute neutrality; it goes without saying that this must be declined but I must tell the Cabinet of it.

E. G.

(²) [v. supra, pp. 714–5, No. 539, encl., and pp. 718–9, No. 544.]

No. 554.

Sir Edward Grey to Sir E. Goschen.

F.O.13108/5569/12/18.
(No. 74.)   Secret.
Sir,
 Foreign Office, March 26, 1912.
Count Metternich spoke to me again to-day(¹) about the question of neutrality.

I said that he had at first suggested conditional neutrality, as to which we had given a reply to the effect that we would not join in any attack. Subsequently, he had suggested what was equivalent to absolute neutrality. I had promised to lay this before my Colleagues, but I did not anticipate that we could give any answer other than we had already given.

Count Metternich said that the neutrality would certainly have to be of a very far-reaching character; but he reminded me that he had previously given me a long formula sent by the Chancellor. (This is the formula printed as an enclosure in the despatch despatch [sic] to your Excellency of March 15.)(²) He told me that I might still take that as what the Chancellor would like.

[I am, &c.]
E. G[REY].

(¹) [cp. G.P. XXXI, p. 204.]
(²) [v. supra, pp. 714–5, No. 539, and encl.]

No. 555.

Memorandum by Sir Edward Grey.

Private.(¹)
 Foreign Office, March 26, 1912.
Count Metternich told me to-day that he had reason to suppose that a communication through the informal channel had reached one of my Colleagues, to the effect that in a very high quarter in Germany some thing in the nature of our Alliance with Japan was considered desirable or necessary in order to effect a reduction in German and British naval expenditure.

(¹) [Grey MSS., Vol. 55.]

Count Metternich asked that what reached me through him should be my only guide in forming an impression of what the wishes of the German Government were. Things which came through the informal channel might give rise to a spurious impression, as they might be the expression of a passing impulse or idea.

He asked me to treat this as very private and confidential.

26 *March* 1912.

No. 556.

Sir F. Bertie to Sir A. Nicolson.

Private.(¹)   *Paris, March* 28, 1912.
My dear Nicolson,

Sir Edward Grey's despatch No. 135 secret of March 15(²) says that M. Cambon read the words of the draft formula(³) and seemed satisfied with them. The words were " England will make no unprovoked attack upon Germany and pursue no aggressive policy towards her. Aggression upon Germany is not the subject and forms no part of any treaty understanding or combination to which England is now a party, nor will she become a party to anything that has such an object.''

The further despatch No. 148 secret of March 22(⁴) says that ''M. Cambon appeared quite satisfied with the information'' given to him by Sir Edward Grey which was that owing to the German Government insisting—as a condition for the diminution of naval expenditure—on a declaration of neutrality, the matter of the formula was in suspense though the question of a formula or the question of territorial arrangements in South Africa might be revived at any time.

I very much doubt M. Cambon's satisfaction at the formula but no doubt he was pleased at the German Government having knocked it on the head, at all events for the time being—after the manner of the Dutch by giving too little and asking too much.

The formula would tie our hands and consequently diminish our value to France.

Attack is very often the best means of self defence. If Russia were occupied in such matters as prevented her from rendering useful military aid to France and the German Government were pressing some question on the French Government a question which though not one of importance to England was vital to France, the German Government might make every military preparation for war move troops towards the frontier with the evident intention of attack if the German demands were not conceded. If in such circumstances the French Government convinced that France was about to be attacked gave the order for the French troops to cross the frontier so as to gain a military advantage so essential to success, given the French temperament, who would be the real aggressor France or Germany? I say Germany, but if we joined France in order to prevent her being wiped out it would have to be at the beginning of the contest, to be of good use, for it might be too late after one or two French defeats, and yet we should be considered as having been the aggressors on Germany and as having joined in an attack on her.

Yours ever,
FRANCIS BERTIE

(¹) [Carnock MSS., Vol. II of 1912.]
(²) [*v. supra*, p. 716, No. 540.]
(³) [*v. supra*, pp. 713–4, No. 537, *encl.*]
(⁴) [*v. supra*, pp. 726–7, No. 550.]

No. 557.

Sir Edward Grey to Sir E. Goschen.

F.O. 13595/5569/12/18.
(No. 76.) Secret.
Sir,

Foreign Office, March 29, 1912.

Count Metternich to-day(¹) spoke to me again on the subject of the formula.

I said that we had considered the matter, and it seemed to us that the suggestion made for varying or extending the formula contained ambiguities, and involved the risk of misconstruction or giving a wrong impression. We did not see, and would be glad to have explained to us, what it was that Germany wished to have beyond what was covered by the words which we had suggested. I then went into the formula sketched by the German Chancellor,(²) pointing out the ambiguities and difficulties contained in it, especially in Paragraphs 3 and 4.

Count Metternich reverted to his original suggestion that we should remain neutral when a war was forced upon Germany.

I remarked that, since this suggestion was made, something very like absolute neutrality had been asked for; and it seemed to me that nothing short of absolute neutrality would really have an effect on German naval expenditure.

Count Metternich admitted that there was no chance of the withdrawal of the Novelle, but said that it might be modified. He thought that it would be disappointing to the Chancellor if we did not go beyond the formula which we had suggested.

I said that I could understand that there would be disappointment if we were to say that the carrying out of the Novelle would put an end to negotiations and to better relations. But we were not saying this, and we hoped that the formula which we had suggested might be considered in connection with the discussion of territorial arrangements, even if it was not effective in preventing the increase of naval expenditure. If some arrangement could be come to between us, it would have a favourable, though indirect, effect upon naval expenditure as time went on; and it would have a favourable and direct effect upon public opinion in both countries.

[I am, &c.]
E. G[REY].

(¹) [*cp. G.P.* XXXI, pp. 210–3.]
(²) [*v. supra*, p. 715, No. 539, *encl.*]

No. 558.

Sir Edward Grey to Sir F. Bertie.

F.O. 13567/5569/12/18.
Tel. (No. 136.) Secret.

Foreign Office, March 29, 1912.
D. 5·55 P.M.

M. Cambon was told this afternoon that German Ambass[ado]r has been informed(¹) that an extension of or change in the formula proposed by H[is] M[ajesty's] Gov[ernment] would probably give rise to ambiguities and misconstructions, and that if the German Gov[ernmen]t were not content with the formula which had been communicated to them they should indicate what it is they want which is not covered by the terms of that formula.

(¹) [*v.* immediately preceding document.]

No. 559.

Sir Edward Grey to Sir F. Bertie.

F.O. 13566/5569/12/18.
(No. 160.) Secret.

Sir, *Foreign Office, March* 29, 1912.

M. Cambon told me to-day([1]) that he felt rather anxious, as he had been informed by Sir Arthur Nicolson that the Cabinet had not yet been consulted about the formula of neutrality proposed by Germany, and as he had heard to the same effect from you. If we were to promise Germany that we would remain neutral in the event of aggression against her, our hands might be tied when Germany was not really the victim of aggression. If, for instance, at a time when there was diplomatic tension between Germany and France, Germany concentrated troops upon Aix-la-Chapelle with the obvious intention of entering Belgium, France might be compelled to take the initiative. Germany was quite clever enough to make it appear that she was the victim, just as she was now making it appear that it was England who was intending to attack her, though it was absolutely true that neither England nor France was aggressive towards Germany, and their intentions were most pacific.

I explained to M. Cambon that the formula of conditional neutrality proposed by Germany had been brought before the Cabinet, and that after consultation there I had offered to Count Metternich the formula of which I had already given M. Cambon the text, adding to it words stating that we would not join in any unprovoked attack upon Germany. It was, therefore, not the case that the Cabinet had not been consulted. They had been consulted on the formula of conditional neutrality. A formula of a more far-reaching character had now been proposed, the words of which seemed to me still more difficult for us to accept; but as it had been proposed, I must consult the Cabinet about it.

[I am, &c.]
E. G[REY].

([1]) [According to M. Poincaré (*Au Service de la France*, Paris 1926, Vol. I, pp. 170–2), Sir F. Bertie visited him on March 27, and, asking him to forget for a moment that he was Ambassador, urged him to try to prevent the British Government from making a declaration of neutrality. M. Poincaré reported this conversation to M. Paul Cambon and instructed him at once to take up the subject with Sir Edward Grey, without referring to Sir F. Bertie. For the latter's report of the interview of March 27. *v. infra.* p. 737, No. 564.]

No. 560.

Sir E. Goschen to Sir A. Nicolson.

Private.([1])

My dear Nicolson, *Berlin, March* 29, 1912.

While reading our counter memorandum([2]) to the Chancellor the other day I noticed that he shook his head and grunted at the part about Pemba and Zanzibar, but when I had finished and gave him the copy he said nothing except 'what I recorded in the telegram,([3]) *i.e.,* nothing particular. Afterwards we 'got talking,' and preluding his remarks by saying that he was not talking as Chancellor to the British Ambassador but as Bethmann Hollweg with Goschen he said that he quite admitted that Haldane had observed that all his remarks were *ad referendum*. Nevertheless he had given him (the Chancellor) the impression that in what he said he was speaking the mind of the King and the Cabinet. Lord Haldane's words were, he continued, "We are ready (wir sind bereit) to hand you over Zanzibar and Pemba." The Chancellor added that he could not forget those words, as they had caused him such intense surprise, because never in his wildest dreams had he

([1]) [Carnock MSS., Vol. III of 1912.]
([2]) [*v. supra*, pp. 722–4, No. 547, *encl.*]
([3]) [*cp. supra*, p. 727, No. 551.]

expected such an offer. But he had certainly regarded the offer as definite.([4]) I said that he must remember that Haldane had said that he only came to explore the ground and that when he had mentioned Zanzibar and Pemba he could only have meant that those were points which might form part of the materials for an agreement. But Bethmann Hollweg only shook his head and said that Haldane's words had been "We are ready to give you Zanzibar and Pemba" and that such an explicit statement could only mean that His Majesty's Government had authorized him to make the offer.

He said that anyway he would study the memorandum and see if it required a reply.

He then asked me what the public thought in England of the Fleet ' Novelle.' I replied that as far as I knew there had not been much comment on it in the Press; the few papers I had read had not been particularly pleased with the [sic: it]. He said that neither had some of the German papers been pleased with Churchill's speech.([5]) I asked him what he himself thought about it. He said that he certainly did not regard it, as some of the German papers did, as provocative. Churchill had certainly not minced matters and had talked of Germany alone throughout his speech, but he didn't quarrel with him for that as he liked frankness, and now everyone knew the exact situation. As regards the German naval proposals they were so modest and moderate that he wondered that even any paper in England could find fault with them. Two ships in six years—why it was nothing! I said that there was to be a third sometime or other; and in any case if the proposals proved to be unpopular in England it would be because the British public would have to put their hands in their pockets and build accordingly. He said that he did'nt see why! I said that he knew that if they built ships outside the existing Fleet Law, which had already brought them up to us closer than many people thought pleasant, we had decided that we should have to lay down ships in what we considered the proper proportion. The three ships contained in the new proposals *were* outside the existing Fleet Law, and so I supposed we should carry out our plans. This would cost money, and our people would find it, but that would not prevent a grumble against those who forced them to find it. He said that he could'nt for the life of him see what necessity there was for us to lay down two keels to one or even one and a half to one; Germany would never rival England at sea, and had no intention of trying to do so. I said that I was glad to hear him say so, but that everyone in Germany did not agree with him, and I quoted an article from a Berlin morning paper which had pointed out that Germany was catching up England fast, and that it was a huge mistake to give England breathing time by not laying down the three ships provided for by the Novelle at the rate of one every year for the next three years. He laughed and said that that article could only have been written by a man in the shipbuilding trade. "Anyway," he said, "that is not my opinion, as you can see by the modesty of our proposals. No!" he added, "there is no reason for you to find it necessary to add to your navy because of them. After I had told him that the reason was to be found in the fact, pointed out by so many German professors, that we should die of inanition in six weeks if we lost command of the sea in time of war, and that therefore preponderating maritime strength was a matter of life and death to us, he said "Would you still take that view if you had an understanding with us?" I said that, speaking for myself, I certainly should. I certainly should not like to see our margin of safety at sea reduced even if we had ententes with all the world. I then asked him what he thought of our formula. He said that it did'nt go half far enough; he would simply be laughed at if he produced such a meagre little formula as a reason for reducing the demands of the Naval Party, or as the basis of an

([4]) [cp. *supra*, p. 683, No. 506, and Appendix III, p. 710, No. 532, and *infra*, p. 746, No. 572. It will be seen that Lord Haldane contradicts the German Chancellor's assertion about Zanzibar and Pemba.]

([5]) [cp. *Parl. Deb.*, 5th Ser., Vol. 35, pp. 1549–74.]

understanding. We must furnish something fuller (etwas mehr rund) than that. "Make no unprovoked attack"—why it is nothing! I said that Sir Edward Grey's last suggestion was "will neither make nor join in any unprovoked attack."(⁵) He said he had not heard of that suggestion, but that it did not make much difference; he wanted something more comprehensive.

He again asked me to recollect that all that he had said to me was not to be regarded as an utterance of the Chancellor but as purely private and unofficial conversation. Therefore I did'nt telegraph any of it, which made you naturally think he had not been very communicative.

I asked him, by the bye, what he thought of the present general political outlook in Europe, and he replied that it caused him no anxiety whatever. Very different from Cambon who thinks the general situation one of some gravity.

Herr von Roeder, the introducer of Ambassadors, came to see me yesterday and told me that the moderation of the German naval proposals was the work of himself and a group of his friends who had devoted themselves to securing an increase in the army proposals and to reducing those concerning the navy to a minimum. It represented, he told me, in fact a victory for the Chancellor against the Big Navy Party headed by Tirpitz. I said that I presumed this meant that the Chancellor had no idea of retiring. He replied that that was so, Admiral Tirpitz had made a strong bid for the Chancellorship, but had failed. Even if the Chancellor did for any reason retire, which was highly unlikely, his successor would not be Tirpitz. He seemed to know who the alternative to Bethmann Hollweg might be, but I could not get it out of him.

Thanking [you] very much for your last letter(⁶) which was full of interest, I remain,

Yours very sincerely,
W. E. GOSCHEN.

I forgot to say that the Chancellor spent some time in trying to prove to me that the 'Novelle' is well *inside* the existing Fleet Law!

(⁶) [v. supra, p. 718, No. 544.]

No. 561.

Sir E. Goschen to Sir A. Nicolson.

Private and Personal.(¹)

My dear Nico,   *Berlin, March 29, 1912.*

From what Grey wrote to me on the 22nd(²) it seems that Metternich has been trying to press an enlargement of our formula upon us by hinting that unless we give it a wider scope we shall lose a favourably disposed Chancellor. He told Grey, apparently, that if we didn't enlarge our formula the Chancellor couldn't meet us on the Naval question and that if he could not do this his position might be affected: according to Metternich the question really was whether the Chancellor or Tirpitz would gain the day. But the Chancellor without our enlarging our formula has got the upper hand as regards reducing the Novelle and his friends regard it as a triumph and look upon his position as quite secure. Therefore I don't understand Metternich hinting that unless we enlarge the formula the Chancellor will not be able to meet us on the Naval question and be forced to resign. What does

(¹) [Carnock MSS.. Vol. II of 1912.]
(²) [cp. pp. 724–5, No. 548.]

he mean by "meeting us on the Naval question"? The Naval proposals have been published by the Government and Bethmann-Hollweg is quite satisfied with them. Moreover I presume that they are now in the form in which they will be presented to the Reichstag. Is it Metternich's idea that if we give him the formula he wants the Chancellor will stand up in the Reichstag and say that in view of England's friendliness and his promise to be neutral in any row that may occur, he proposes to drop the 'Novelle' altogether? That, I suppose, would be meeting us on the Naval question—and there would be such a howl throughout Naval and Pan-German and Conservative circles, that it might certainly end in his resignation. But personally I don't think that in view of the criticisms on the proposals as they now stand it is at all likely, whatever we do, that they will be further reduced. Too much has been said about the absolute necessity of the three new battleships for purposes of defence and for 'securing the safety of the Empire.' Anyhow we are, I hope, not going to give them any neutrality formula—so we need not discuss what might happen. What we offer them is quite sufficient to show friendliness—and that should be quite enough for them if they have no designs upon other people. . . . .(3)

Yours very sincerely,
W. E. GOSCHEN.

(3) [The omitted paragraph refers to personal matters.]

No. 562.

Sir A. Nicolson to Sir E. Goschen.

Private.(1)

My dear Goschen,   *Foreign Office, April* 1, 1912.

Many thanks for your two letters of the 29th.(2) Your conversation with the Chancellor was most interesting and illuminating, and it is perfectly clear to me that they are endeavouring to entangle us in some engagement which would absolutely prevent us having full liberty of action in case of certain eventualities. That we should get anything in return from them is quite out of the question, and so it would be really a very one-sided arrangement, and it would, moreover, certainly impair and weaken our relations with France and Russia, which we have only quite recently assured those two countries we have no intention whatever of doing. It is equally clear to me that so long as we remain free to act as circumstances may require, there is a very good chance of peace being maintained; while on the other hand, if the Germans were certain that we would not intervene, I could not give many months for peace being maintained. However, I do not think—in fact I am almost sure—that the Cabinet would go so far as the Chancellor would like us, though as you know there are many elements in the Cabinet who would do anything to obtain the so-called goodwill of Germany. I think your arguments with the Chancellor were very much to the point, and I am driving them home here with as much energy as I am able.

France is still a little uneasy as to what may be the ultimate developments, as we keep Cambon fully informed of what passes. I think that the sooner we give a definite negative, the better it will be. By the last conversation which Grey had with Metternich(3) we seem to be still walking round the question without being able to come to a definite decision. The fact is the Cabinet are most unwilling to have the appearance of breaking off discussions. . . . .(4)

[A. NICOLSON.]

(1) [Carnock MSS., Vol. II of 1912.]
(2) [*v.* the two immediately preceding documents.]
(3) [*cp. supra*, p. 730, No. 557.]
(4) [The omitted paragraphs of this letter give details on the general European situation.]

No. 563.

Sir F. Bertie to Sir A. Nicolson.

Private.([1])

My dear Nicolson, *Paris, April 1, 1912.*

The German Government appear to expect from us not only a disclaimer of aggression against Germany, but a promise of "benevolent neutrality" in the event of Germany being at war and not the aggressor, and an undertaking not to enter into any agreements limiting our observance of such neutrality.

To begin with there is, juridically no such thing as "benevolent" neutrality. Whenever the attitude of a non-belligerent towards a belligerent becomes benevolent it ceases to be neutral. It becomes partisan.([2])

Long before the Russo-Japanese war, I cannot remember when, the German Government instigated Japan to attack Russia stating that the British Fleet would prevent France from interfering and Germany would observe a benevolent neutrality towards Japan. The Japanese Government sought the advice of the British Government. They were recommended to ask the German Government what was meant by "benevolent" neutrality. The German answer was "strict" neutrality.

The engagements which the German Government seek to obtain from us are of a lasting character and are the high price to be paid by us for the temporary advantage of a promise to restrict within certain limits and for a short term of years the production of German Warships. It is true that the engagements sought from us are to be reciprocal to us from Germany, but whereas an attack on France by Germany with or without provocation is not at all improbable and would jeopardize British interests, it is most improbable that either France or Russia alone or in combination with each other would make an unprovoked attack on Germany, and if such a contingency occurred the crushing of France would be a great danger to England and it would be detrimental to our interests to have our hands tied by a neutrality promise.([3]) It is not always he striking the first blow who is the real aggressor. We ought to have our hands entirely free so that if war come about we can there and then decide whether it is to our interest to take part in it, and when, and not be hampered by previous neutrality promises. Our aid to France might be too late unless forthcoming at the outbreak of the war, and her ill-fate would be ours later on.

I had an audience of the President of the Republic on the 28th ultimo in order to arrange for his receiving the Prince of Wales. He was rather nervous concerning our negotiations with Germany. He hoped that the lately bred Germanophile tendencies of certain circles in England would not cause any slackening of the Entente between England and France. I foresee that if we sign the formula sanctioned by the Cabinet it will be a surprise very disagreeable to and resented by the French public; and still more so a more comprehensive one as seems to be contemplated,([4]) for to ask the Germans what more they want is much like saying that we are prepared to accord more.

Lord Haldane appears to have gone to Berlin full of good intentions towards the Germans and expecting to bring back something valuable. He seems to have been cajoled by the want of good faith, not perhaps of the German Chancellor, but of others at Berlin. What he said has been misrepresented and turned into alleged far reaching offers of territory and of surrender of reversionary claims.

Mr. Harcourt after discussing exchanges of territory, some in possession and some only in reversion and now the property of other States, acted the part of the tempter by suggesting to the German Ambassador that Germany might have as a set-off to Timor the reversion of the San Thomé and Principe Islands in the Gulf

([1]) [Carnock MSS., Vol. IV of 1912.]

([2]) [Marginal comment by Sir Edward Grey : " This is one reason why we have rejected it. E. G."]

([3]) [Marginal comment by Sir Edward Grey : " We shall not tie them. E. G."]

([4]) [Marginal comment by Sir Edward Grey : " This is not contemplated by us. E. G."]

of Guinea, which, as also Madeira and the Azores are not covered by the Secret Treaty of 1898.(5) Count Metternich thereupon mentioned the Cape Verde Islands as being in the same position and therefore I conclude proper for allotment to Germany. The Colonial Secretary seems not only to be a willing seller but a generous giver of what might almost be considered stolen or filched goods.

As to a Neutrality Declaration I do not imagine that the Cabinet will consent to one, whether far-reaching or not, unless it is intended to loosen our ties with France and to substitute for them the bonds of an understanding with Germany which as soon as it had served the German purpose of causing disagreement between France and England would be observed by Germany only in so far and so long as it might suit her interests and convenience.

Yours ever,
FRANCIS BERTIE.

(5) [This refers to the interview with Count Metternich on March 9, upon which Mr. Harcourt wrote a memorandum. As stated *supra*, p. 709, No. 531, *note* (3), the memorandum will be printed in a later volume.]

No. 564.

Sir F. Bertie to Sir Edward Grey.

F.O. 14431/5569/12/18.

(No. 158.) Secret.

Sir,

Paris, D. *April* 3, 1912.
R. *April* 6, 1912.

In your despatch No. 160 Secret of the 29th ultimo (13566/12)(1) which I had the honour to receive last night it is stated "Monsieur Cambon told me to-day that he felt rather anxious as he had been informed by Sir Arthur Nicolson that the Cabinet had not yet been consulted about the formula of neutrality proposed by Germany and as he had heard to the same effect from you, etc."

You explained to Monsieur Cambon that the formula of conditional neutrality proposed by Germany had been brought before the Cabinet and that after consultation there you had offered to Count Metternich the formula of which you had already given Monsieur Cambon the text adding to it words stating that we would not join in any unprovoked attack upon Germany. It was therefore not the case that the Cabinet had not been consulted. They had been consulted on the formula of conditional neutrality. A formula of more far-reaching character had now been proposed, the words of which seemed to you still more difficult for His Majesty's Government to accept; but as it had been proposed you must consult the Cabinet about it.

I think that you must have misunderstood Monsieur Cambon in regard to the information as to the Cabinet consultation so far as I am concerned for I did not see or have any communication with Monsieur Cambon between March the 18th when he came to speak to me on the part of Monsieur Poincaré respecting the Casablanca works (see my despatch No. 45 of March 18th)(2) and yesterday, and the formula, not of neutrality but of non-aggression which you communicated to His Excellency on the 15th ultimo and was transmitted to me in your despatch No. 135 Secret of that day(3) reached me only on the 19th, so that when I saw him on the 18th I had no information of the existence of either of the two formulas.

The confusion probably arose from the following circumstances. When I saw M. Poincaré on the 20th ultimo he spoke to me about the Anglo-German negotiations in a manner which indicated some anxiety as to the issue. I told him that you had informed me (see your despatch No. 135 Secret of March 15th)(3) that Monsieur Cambon had seemed satisfied with the words of the formula of non-aggression but I said if the French Government did not in fact feel satisfied it would be advisable

(1) [*v. supra*, p. 731, No. 559.]
(2) [Not reproduced.]
(3) [*v. supra*, p. 716, No. 540.]

that they should so inform you, through M. Cambon. Monsieur Poincaré, who made some general observations on the difficulty of defining the real aggressor in a dispute between nations, said that he would communicate with Monsieur Cambon on the subject. When next I saw Monsieur Poincaré to have any conversation with him, viz., on the 27th ultimo,(4) I had received on the previous night your despatch No. 148 Secret (12529/12) of March the 22nd(5) and I was therefore then in possession of the information that the German Government considered the non-aggression formula insufficient and required also a declaration of neutrality and that you had so informed Monsieur Cambon who appeared quite satisfied with the information which you had given to him in regard to a neutrality declaration and your willingness to amplify the non-aggression formula by saying not only that we would not make but also that we would not join in any unprovoked attack upon Germany. Monsieur Poincaré on this occasion (March 27th) again spoke to me about your negotiations with Count Metternich and expressed relief at the improbability of a declaration of non-aggression owing to the German Government insisting, so he had learnt from Monsieur Cambon, on a neutrality declaration also which was not at all likely to be made by His Majesty's Government. I then gave to Monsieur Poincaré the account of the situation contained in your despatch of the 22nd ultimo (No. 148 Secret) and he made some observations much to the same effect as those of Monsieur Cambon to you as recorded in your despatch of the 29th ultimo (No. 160 Secret) which I received last night, and His Excellency stated that he had instructed the Ambassador to put them before you.

On the night of the 29th ultimo I received your secret telegram of that evening(6) stating that you had caused Monsieur Cambon to be informed that you had intimated to the German Ambassador that ambiguities and misconstructions would probably be caused by an extension or change in the formula proposed by His Majesty's Government and that if it did not satisfy the German Government in the form in which it had been communicated to them they should indicate what are their requirements which are not covered by its terms. I have not seen Monsieur Poincaré since receiving that information, but Monsieur Cambon paid me a visit yesterday morning, and from his conversation, and from some observations made to me on the 28th ultimo by the President of the Republic when I had an audience of him for the purpose of arranging the exchange of visits between the Prince of Wales and him, it is evident to me that Monsieur Fallières and Monsieur Cambon as well as Monsieur Poincaré are preoccupied as to whether the issue of the Anglo-German negotiations may not be a hampering of our freedom of action which may be very detrimental to the interests of France in the event of a dispute between Germany and France. I beg leave to warn His Majesty's Government that the non-aggression Declaration whether in the restricted or in the more amplified form contemplated by them would be a disagreeable surprise to the French Public as calculated, and by the German Government intended, to loosen the ties of friendship and confidence between France and England and to form, in the interest of Germany, bonds restricting the liberty of action of England in a manner detrimental to the interests of France and dangerous to the peace of Europe. Monsieur Hanotaux as the expounder of the sentiments of distrust of England still felt by a small party in France, and others, some for monetary reasons, would not be slow to take advantage of such a situation to point out that little reliance is to be placed on *perfide* Albion in an emergency and that it would be well for France to come to some terms with Germany regardless of British interests. I do not say that such a campaign would be successful with the present French Government. It would however create a good deal of distrust of British policy amongst the general public in France.

I have, &c.
FRANCIS BERTIE.

(4) [cp. supra, p. 731, No. 559, note (1).]
(5) [v. supra, pp. 726–7, No. 550.]
(6) [v. supra, p. 730, No. 558.]

MINUTES.

We have travelled rather far from the original position taken up by H[is] M[ajesty's] G[overnment], when these negotiations were begun, that they would enter into no political agreement without a naval one which would enable them to effect a serious reduction of expenditure on armaments. But even at a later stage, H[is] M[ajesty's] G[overnment] declared that no political formula would be acceptable that could not be subscribed and approved by France and Russia.

Sir F. Bertie and M. Cambon clearly apprehend that we are now receding from this position also.

This whole question of negotiations with Germany appears to be drifting altogether away from any clear political aim. The original object was to secure a reduction of expense on armaments. Everything else was to be subsidiary to this. That has now gone by the board.

What is the new object?—I understand it is the " establishment of better relations " with Germany.

Before devising appropriate means for bettering relations, it is essential to have a clear idea what these relations are.

They became strained last summer. Why? Only a correct diagnosis of German policy as revealed on that occasion can afford a true answer. And the answer is that Germany was trying to fasten on France such political conditions as would, if accepted, have either inflicted a deep national humiliation on her, or forced her to acknowledge a German leadership in shaping her foreign policy. In either case France would have ceased to count as an independent Power, and a German hegemony over France would have been established.

H[is] M[ajesty's] G[overnment] considered that the continued existence of a strong and independent France was of vital interest to this country, and the proposition is too well founded and too well understood to require to be laboured. Hence H[is] M[ajesty's] G[overnment] intimated that England would stand by France in any quarrel which Germany might endeavour to fasten upon her as arising out of the then situation. Germany gave in, and it has suited her to make England the scapegoat for her discomfiture before German public opinion. This was done deliberately and by the employment of all the resources at the disposal of the German government, with the necessary result that relations became worse.

How are these relations then to be bettered? Is any real betterment—as distinguished from a temporary lull—possible or conceivable so long as the aim and objects of German policy remain unaltered? Clearly not. Again, therefore, everything depends on a correct understanding of what Germany wants.

What view have H[is] M[ajesty's] G[overnment] formed of what German policy is? I am of course not in a position to know whether there exists a thought-out and considered statement of the Cabinet's views on this all-important point, but I venture with all due respect, to urge that in the absence of a precise and authoritative formulation of what Germany's policy is believed to be, a formulation which could be tested and critically examined by the light of every authentic source of information and historical truth, any negotiations with the German government are bound to be indecisive, vacillating and highly dangerous.

The evidence which is in the possession of this office can leave very little doubt as to what Germany's policy is : She wants to have an absolutely free hand in dealing with any problem of foreign policy without fear of meeting with the opposition of third parties. She wants to make herself so strong that she can dictate terms to every Power. She therefore is bent upon (1) increasing her own armed strength to the uttermost limit; (2) gaining the co-operation of as many as possible of the greater States; and (3) preventing any possible co-operation against herself on the part of the others.

With this view Germany will never agree to any serious restriction of her liberty to increase either her navy or her army. She will steadily continue to do both, sometimes simultaneously, and sometimes successively. She will impose her will whether by conciliation or by threats and bullying, on the minor Powers which are her neighbours. She will leave no stone unturned to drive apart if possible the Powers of the Dual Alliance and England, America, and Japan. Nor has Germany any scruples of any sort whatever as to the methods to be employed for political ends. Bismarck and his successors have recognized no standard of right and wrong in questions of foreign policy, or indeed in questions of internal policy either.

The above is, I believe, well known here to be Germany's aim. It is not maintained that this view must be absolutely right. It may be open to criticism, and a different view of German policy may, on due examination, be found to be the true one. But has such an alternative view been formed? And if so on what does it rest, and how is it explained in relation to the facts of history?

I would earnestly submit that this question of correctly understanding the political issue is so important that the merits or demerits of any line of negotiation with Germany cannot be judged except by reference to it.

At present it is exceedingly puzzling to understand what exactly H[is] M[ajesty's] G[overnment] are aiming at and why they consider that the kaleidoscopic nature of the constantly changing stages in the negotiations carried on through many divers channels at the same time may be expected to bring them nearer to the object so aimed at.

E. A. C.(⁷)
Ap. 6.

It is quite evident that the French are getting nervous at the possible result of these negotiations of which they do not understand the drift.

It is to be remembered that at a much earlier stage of the negotiations, H[is] M[ajesty's] G[overnment] considered themselves as precluded from signing any political arrangement to which France and Russia could not be asked themselves to subscribe.

Clearly the formula which raises such apprehensions in Paris is not of this kind.

E. A. C.
Ap. 6.

On a minor point I think there has been some confusion. What I told M. Cambon had not been submitted to the Cabinet was what he was informed, when he visited the Sec[retary] of State in the H[ouse] of Commons, C[oun]t Metternich had requested—i.e. if I mistake not more or less absolute neutrality—a request which M. Cambon characterized as " prodigious "— I may be wrong in my recollection—in any case the matter is of no moment.

As to the wider and really important question the passage I have marked(⁸) in Sir F. Bertie's desp[atch] summarizes the position. As M. de Fleuriau explained to me both M. Fallières and M. Poincaré are afraid of the following very possible contingency arising, and they have in view only the restricted original formula we communic[ate]d to France on March 14th—i.e. that " England will make no unprovoked attack on Germany." The French statesmen say " Supposing Germany and France are involved in hostilities over some question in which England has no direct concern—a frontier incident for instance—Germany falls on France or forces France to attack her, England by the formula would have to stand aside as were she to join in, she w[oul]d be making an " unprovoked attack " on Germany as the latter had not provoked her (England)." It is with such contingencies in view that they mistrust the formula (of course neutrality—conditional or absolute—formulas are open to grave misgivings)—and say that if we sign it a shock will be given to the relations between France and England. To my mind it would be wiser to drop formulas—they are always " trappy " and it would be disastrous were we for the sake of having a formula to run the risk of alienating France and thereby probably Russia also. I need not specify the consequences of such a result. We have a very simple policy, not to tie our hands in any way with anyone, to remain the sole judges of our action, to keep on the close and intimate terms we have hitherto maintained with France and Russia, and which have been the best guarantees of peace, while being perfectly friendly with Germany and ready to discuss amicably with her any pending questions.

I see no reason for any new departure.

A. N.

All this is true and not to be disregarded but on the other hand it has to be borne in mind that Russia and France both deal separately with Germany and that it is not reasonable that tension should be permanently greater between England and Germany than between Germany and France or Germany and Russia.

E. G.

(⁷) [This minute appears on a separate paper attached to the one containing Sir F. Bertie's despatch, and bearing the same F.O. number. It is followed immediately by Sir A. Nicolson's minute reproduced above. There is no evidence that it was sent to Sir E. Grey. A new and much shorter minute by Sir E. Crowe, also reproduced above, was written on a new paper. Sir A. Nicolson's minute was copied after it, and these were then sent to Sir Edward Grey, the Prime Minister and Lord Haldane. Sir E. Crowe's first minute has however been thought worth printing, as Sir A. Nicolson had it before him when writing his own.]

(⁸) [The passage marked is in the last paragraph of Sir F. Bertie's letter. It begins " I beg leave to warn " and ends " dangerous to the peace of Europe."]

No. 565.

Memorandum by Mr. Tyrrell.(¹)

Foreign Office, April 3, 1912.

Herr von Kühlmann came to see me today, to talk about current affairs. Towards the end of our conversation, he referred to the efforts which the two

(¹) [Grey MSS., Vol. 55.]

3 в 2

Governments were making to place their relations on a better footing. He prefaced his remarks on this subject by the statement that they were entirely personal.

He said that he did not attach much importance to a formula, but he thought that a formula might be useful if we had come to some agreement for an exchange of territory in Africa for the purpose of " shop-window dressing." He attached great importance to such an agreement, as it would be a most effective way of removing the widespread impression amongst Germans that we grudged them any and every place under the sun.

With regard to the inclusion of neutrality in a formula, he expressed the opinion that the draft formula which Sir E. Grey communicated to Count Metternich(²) did in substance insure the neutrality of this country for all legitimate purposes. He said that he quite understood our reluctance to use the word "neutrality" in such a formula, as it might cause legitimate apprehensions in the minds of other Powers with whom we wished to remain on friendly terms.

In connection with the agreement for an exchange of territory in Africa, it had occurred to him that France might be roped in with regard to negotiations respecting the Belgian Congo, and also with regard to her position on the West Coast bordering on Angola. He added that the Germans could, of course, not put forward this suggestion.

On my asking him whether, if we did put forward this suggestion, the Germans would raise objections, he gave as his personal opinion that they would not.

W. T.

3 *April*, 1912.

(²) [*v. supra*, pp. 713–4, No. 537, *encl.*]

No. 566.

Minute by Sir A. Nicolson.(¹)

Sir Edward Grey, *Foreign Office, April* 4, 1912.

M. de Fleuriau, the French Ch[argé] d'Aff[aires] called today, and read to me a letter which he had received from M. Cambon. I told him I would hardly trust my memory to retain all the important points raised in it, and he kindly left it with me. I enclose a copy.(²)

The letter, as I am sure you will agree, merits most serious consideration. It would seem that neither M. Faillères nor M. Poincaré·like even our proposed formula regarding not joining in an "unprovoked attack"; and that they are nervous lest we should accept some German amendments to it which would tie our hands. In short they fear we may be entangled into some engagement, which would reassure Germany that, in the event of her being able to say that she was attacked or that a war was forced on her, we should stand aside. It is a truism that in a war it is very difficult to say who was really the original aggressor, or who forced a war upon the other—and, as M. Cambon points out, that, while we were debating these points, the invaluable moment would have passed by, and Germany would very likely have gained a decided initial advantage.

I am afraid that we are rapidly arriving at a very critical moment in our future relations with France, and consequently indirectly with Russia. The French Gov[ernmen]t are uneasy, and unless we can unequivocally assure them that we retain our complete liberty of action in any possible eventualities, I fear that their confidence in us may wane even to the extent of seriously impairing our relations— and such a result would at once react on our relations with Russia. The ultimate consequences are not pleasant to contemplate. We have an easy exit from the position into which I fear we may drift. Germany has practically rejected our formula and requires more than we can prudently, or as I think rightly, give.

(¹) [Carnock MSS., Vol. III of 1912.]
(²) [*v.* immediately succeeding document, *encl.*]

We can then withdraw our formula—and by so doing there is no reason why we should not at the same time express our desire to remain on the most friendly terms with Germany and be in a position always to discuss with her in a most amicable manner any questions which may arise between us. Let us definitely abandon formulas, which are at best dangerous and embarrassing documents, and the signature of which would apparently, in present circumstances, affect our relations with France. Were we to continue to endeavour to find words which would satisfy Germany, we should gradually be led into signing a document restrictive of our liberty of action, and which would thereby remove, to my mind, one of the best guarantees of peace. So long as Germany cannot rely on our abstention or neutrality, so long will she not be disposed to disturb the peace. I have jotted down these few observations and would gladly talk more at length with you, as the communication from M. Cambon is I think of the highest importance.

A. N.

No. 567.

Sir A. Nicolson to Sir Edward Grey.

Private.([1])

My dear Grey, *Foreign Office, April 6, 1912.*

I have said nothing to M. de Fleuriau as I think it better that you should speak with M. Cambon, whenever the latter returns. Moreover the French are not disturbing themselves as to any neutrality formula, but as to the formula given on March 14—I enclose an English translation of Cambon's letter([2])—in case you would wish to communicate it to any quarter. A despatch from Bertie on this subject goes to you in this pouch.

Benckendorff, as you will see, has comm[unicate]d the fact of the Treaty between Servia and Bulgaria.

Yours sincerely,
A. NICOLSON.

Enclosure in No. 567.

M. Paul Cambon to M. Fleuriau.([3])

Mon cher ami, *146, Boulevard Haussmann, Avril 3, 1912.*

J'ai pu voir lundi M. Poincaré que ses fonctions de Président du Conseil absorbent pour mille détails et qu'il est assez difficile d'atteindre. Dimanche il était obligé d'aller aux jardins pour la cérémonie commémorative de Gambetta et tous les jours il a des obligations du même genre. Cependant il suffit à tout, et il suit attentivement nos affaires.

Il s'est montré très préoccupé des démarches allemandes à Londres. Il aurait cru comme moi que la réponse de Sir Edward Grey à la demande de dèclaration de neutralité formulée par Metternich était definitive, et il s'en était félicité, mais la décision du Cabinet sur cette réponse ne lui parait pas satisfaisant. On aurait pu approuver simplement la réponse de Grey, et l'on eut ainsi coupé court à des conversations qui n'ont d'autre but que d'amener le gouvernement anglais à quelques declarations écrites dont le Gouvernement de Berlin fera grand état, qu'il publiera et qui donnera raison aux adversaires de l'Entente cordiale. Ils semblent très peu nombreux chez nous, et jusqu'à présent il a été facile de répondre a leurs manifestations de mauvaise humeur. Vous les connaissez et si un fait précis leur permet d'affirmer que nous ne pouvons pas compter sur l'Angleterre vous voyez d'ici le parti

---

([1]) [Grey MSS., Vol. 55.]

([2]) [The text of the French original is given here instead of that of the translation. It is taken from a copy in the Carnock MSS., Vol. III of 1912.]

([3]) [As stated in the document immediately preceding, the text of this letter is a copy made in the Foreign Office. The wording has been reproduced exactly without any elimination of what were no doubt copyist's errors.]

qu'ils en tireront. Impuissants jusqu'ici ils pourraient exercer sur l'opinion une influence desastreuse et ils ont pour eux le talent et la notoriete. C'est à l'Academie Hanotaux et Fred Masson—dans la presse le 'Correspondant' et les journaux blancs.

Grey a été invité à demander à Metternich quelles modifications son Gouvernement propose à la declaration verbale du 12 Mars.([4]) C'est très dangereux—on peut demander de Berlin l'introduction de tel ou tel mot qui n'aura l'air de rien mais qui pourra paralyser l'action d'Angleterre à un moment donné. On peut aussi demander que cette declaration verbale soit transformée en une echange de notes constituant un *accord*. L'une et l'autre demande paraissent à M. Poincaré devoir être écartées.

Quant à la declaration du 14 Mars en elle-meme elle lui semble preter a l'ambiguité. Il parait que Sir Edward Grey avait eu l'impression que je m'en étais montré satisfait;([5]) ce n'est par tout-à-fait exacte—quand il m'en a remis le libellé, je l'ai remercié de sa communication et je lui ai dit que je la transmettrais a mon gouvernement, mais je n'ai rien ajouté, et je n'ai manifesté aucune impression. Il est peutêtre regrettable qu'aussitot saisi de cette communication M. Poincaré ne m'ait pas chargé de présenter immédiatement au Foreign Office ses observations sur un point qui lui donne du souci. Le retard de sa reponse s'explique pas [par] ses occupations parlementaires. En tout cas il est necessaire de presenter son objection à Sir Edward Grey ou à Sir A. Nicolson. La voici :—

Le déclaration verbale du 14 Mars dit—"England will make no unprovoked attack upon Germany and pursue no aggressive policy towards her." Que l'Angleterre déclare qu'elle ne poursuit aucune politique d'aggression et ne s'associera à aucune politique de ce genre, c'est bien : mais que signifie exactement de ne se livrer a aucune attaque *sans provocation?*

Si l'Allemagne se jette sur la France elle pourra dire qu'elle ne provoque pas l'Angleterre, et qu'elle règle par les armes ses affairs entre elle et nous, que l'Angleterre n'a rien à y voir. En admettant la meilleure volonté du monde chez le gouvernement britannique il peut y avoir discussion sur le point de savoir si oui ou non il est tenu de rester neutre; dans cette discussion les germanophiles anglais interviendront et troubleront l'opinion, en un mot il y aura du temps perdu et vous savez qu'au debut des hostilités le temps perdu c'est une chance d'insucces.

En outre la publication d'une déclaration de cette sorte permettra d'agiter l'opinion en France, et de soutenir que l'Angleterre s'est liée les mains vis-à-vis de l'Allemagne.

Voila l'objet des préoccupations de notre Président du Conseil. Il les a fait partagés par le Président de la Republique qui hier m'en a entretenu pendant deux heures. Elles ne semblent pas justifiées par ce que nous connaissons des sentiments du gouvernement anglais et du roi. Au moment où le Prince de Galles vient à Paris, où les flottes anglaises et francaises vont se reunir a Nice pour célébrer la mémoire de la reine Victoria et du roi Edouard, où l'opinion anglaise se montre de plus en plus decidée a maintenir la suprématie navale de l'Angleterre, on ne peut douter que l'Entente cordiale ne réponde aux aspirations nationales dans les deux pays, mais nous avons affaire a des gens très retors. Leur but, poursuivi depuis huit ans sans désemparer, est de créer entre nous une fissure qui s'elargira et amenera tôt ou tard une rupture. Donc chaque parole, chaque demarche doit etre pesée, chaque insinuation analysée, chaque proposition tournée et retournée sous toutes ses faces.

M. Poincaré m'a demande de soumettre toutes ces considérations a Sir Edward Grey le plus tôt possible. Il est inutile de songer a la rencontre pendant ces jours de vacance, et j'ai demandé à M. Poincaré la permission de m'absenter pendant une huitaine de jours mais Sir Arthur Nicolson est toujours là. Il peut être utilement informé et consulté. S'il partage nos sentiments il peut veiller à ce que rien de définitive ne se dise avant que nous n'ayons pu nous expliquer et provoquer des éclaircissements sur le sens exacte de la declaration du 14 Mars.

([4]) [This is apparently a mistake for "14 Mars" and refers to the draft formula printed *supra*, pp. 713–4, No. 537, *encl.*].

([5]) [*v. supra*, p. 716, No. 540, but *cp.* p. 729, No. 556.]

J'ai donc dit au Ministre que je vous ecrirai et que je vous prierai de faire part au Sous-Secretaire d'Etat de ses apprehensions. On ne peut nier quant on voit les choses du point de vue de Paris qu'elles ne soient justifiées.

Je compte partit demain matin pour la Bretagne, je serai de retours le jeudi onze au soir, ou le douze au matin.

Vous pourrez m'écrire poste restante a Brest ou je serai le jour de Paques.
. . . .([6])

Le Prince de Galles est installé chez Breteuil; on est très content de le voir ici et il fait à tout le monde une excellente impression.

PAUL CAMBON.

([6]) [Thus in original.]

No. 568.

Sir A. Nicolson to Sir E. Goschen.

Private.([1])

My dear Goschen :— *Foreign Office, April 9, 1912.*

Many thanks for your letter of the 5th.([2]) Since I last wrote to you there have been some further developments in regard to our discussions with the German Government, and this time they have come from the side of the French. From communications which we have received, both from Bertie and from Cambon,([3]) it seems that the French President as well as the President of the Council are rather perturbed as to what is proceeding between us and Germany. We have kept Cambon very fairly informed as to what has been passing, and we have given him the various formulas which have from time to time been drawn up. If you look into your papers you will see that the first formula was given on the 14th March,([4]) and which contained the engagement that England will make no unprovoked attack upon Germany and pursue no aggressive policy towards her. This, as you know, is not considered satisfactory by the German Government or sufficiently full. It is on this formula that the French Government have communicated to us their apprehensions and perturbations: I think I cannot do better than to give you, for your own private information, certain extracts from a private letter which Cambon, who is at present on leave, has written to his Chargé d'Affaires here, and which the latter was good enough to leave in my hands.([5]) What Cambon says has been amply confirmed by Bertie who recently saw Cambon and also had a conversation on the same subject with the French President. The objections which the French Government take to the formula of the 14th March are thus formulated. They quite admit that there is no harm in England stating that she will pursue no aggressive policy towards Germany and will join in no policy of that character, but they ask what exactly is meant " that she will make no unprovoked attack upon Germany "? They point out that complications, such as a frontier incident for example, might arise between Germany and France in which England would have no direct concern and in which the interests of England, so far as the merits of the incident itself were concerned, were not directly implicated. Germany might then find it necessary to resort to active measures against France or might place the latter in such a position as would necessitate her taking active measures on her side to anticipate an attack which she knew was imminent. Should England consider it necessary, on the broader and greater question whether she would allow France to be crushed or humiliated by her neighbour, to enter into the arena and to support France materially, Germany might say that we were making an unprovoked attack

([1]) [Carnock MSS., Vol. III of 1912.]
([2]) [Not reproduced.]
([3]) [*v. supra*, p. 731, No. 559, pp. 736–7, No. 564, and pp. 741–3, No. 567, and *encl.*]
([4]) [*v. supra*, pp. 713–4, No. 537, *encl.*]
([5]) [*v.* immediately preceding document.]

upon her as she had not provoked us in any way. The French further point out that, in the contingency to which I have referred, the British Government might be at the outset in doubt as to whether they ought or ought not to remain neutral and would be discussing among themselves as to whether they were justified in taking part in the quarrel, and a most essential time would thereby be lost and intervention might arrive too late. The French Government consider that by signing a formula similar to that of the 14th March we would undoubtedly be tying our hands and restricting our full liberty of action. They do not, I gather, wish that we should pledge ourselves to take any action on their behalf, but they do insist upon the wisdom of our keeping our hands perfectly free and not being pledged to any specific line of action or any specific abstention. What they fear is that should such a formula be signed by us the German Government would not hesitate to make it known, and both the French President and the President of the Council and Bertie also consider that a very great shock would be produced in France and that the elements in that country hostile to our understanding would find a very good reason for impressing on their public that we had deserted France in favour of Germany. Moreover, they also are not at all pleased by our having asked Metternich to indicate what Germany really requires. They consider this a very dangerous request as they think that Berlin may suggest the insertion of certain phraseology which on the surface may have a perfectly innocent air, but which in reality would paralyze the action of England on a given occasion. Cambon points out in his private letter that the English Government should not forget that they are dealing with people who are exceedingly adroit and shifty and who are pursuing the same aim which they have followed with great persistency during the last eight years, and that is, to create if they can a fissure between France and England which might develop sooner or later into a rupture. Therefore, as Cambon points out, we should carefully scrutinise each word and every suggestion made to us and that we should examine carefully from all sides any proposal which may be submitted to us from Berlin. I have pointed out to Grey—who has been away on Easter holidays—that I am afraid we are rapidly arriving at a very critical moment in our future relations with France and consequently indirectly with Russia. I pointed out that the French Government are uneasy and that were we unable to retain our complete liberty of action in any possible eventuality their confidence in us may wane, even to the extent of impairing our relations and that naturally such a result would at once react on our relations with Russia, and the ultimate consequences are by no means pleasant to contemplate. Germany has practically rejected our formula of the 14th March and requires more than we can rightly give. There is therefore no objection to our withdrawing our formula and dropping all further reference to these very dangerous and embarrassing documents. I have said that if we continue to endeavour to find words which would satisfy Germany we would probably be led into restricting our liberty of action, and this would thereby remove one of the best guarantees of peace. I am convinced that so long as Germany cannot rely on our abstention or on our neutrality so long she will not be disposed to disturb the peace. I consider these communications which we have received from Paris as highly significant and most important, and they should require the most careful consideration on the part of the Cabinet. I just write to inform you of them for your own private information. Cambon returns, I believe, at the end of this week and I shall be anxious to have a long talk with him upon the points which have been raised. I am quite sure that even Cambon at the bottom of his heart was disturbed as to what was passing. . . . .(⁶)

[A. NICOLSON.]

(⁶) [The last paragraph of this letter refers to the Balkan situation.]

No. 569.

Sir Edward Grey to Sir F. Bertie.

Foreign Office, April 9, 1912.
D. 4·25 P.M.

Tel. Private.(¹)

Your private letter of yesterday to Nicolson.(²)

There is no new development about the formula and nothing more to be said, unless the Germans make a new suggestion. I refused to put in the word neutrality because it would give the impression that our hands were tied. If Germany attacked and forced war upon an ally or friend of ours it would be provocation to us and therefore formula as we proposed it would not tie our hands. I shall see French Ambassador on his return and be ready to consider anything he has to say. You may inform French M[inister for] F[oreign] A[ffairs].

(¹) [Grey MSS., Vol. 14.]
(²) [This letter has not been found.]

No. 570.

Sir F. Bertie to Sir Edward Grey.

Paris, April 10, 1912.
D. 7·10 P.M.
R. 9 P.M.

Tel. Private.(¹) (K.)

I have spoken to M. Poincaré in the sense of your private telegram of yesterday.(²) He says that if a formula such as has been proposed be signed and published it will be a painful surprise to French public and will also be viewed with disappointment by some of his colleagues. The French Amb[assado]r will speak to you on the subject.

(¹) [Grey MSS., Vol. 14.]
(²) [*v.* immediately preceding document.]

No. 571.

Mr. Asquith to Sir Edward Grey.

Private.(¹)
My dear Grey,   10, *Downing Street, Whitehall, April* 10, 1912.

I agree that the French are somewhat unduly nervous.

But I confess I am becoming more and more doubtful as to the wisdom of prolonging these discussions with Germany about a formula. Nothing, I believe, will meet her purpose which falls short of a promise on our part of neutrality: a promise we cannot give.

And she makes no firm or solid offer, even in exchange for that.

Yours ever,
H. H. A[SQUITH].

(¹) [Grey MSS., Vol. 61.]

No. 572.

Minute by Lord Haldane.(¹)

War Office, Whitehall, S.W., April 10, 1912.

I can only account for the Chancellor's impression that I offered to hand over Zanzibar and Pemba by the possibility that I was at the moment speaking in English, and that he had not understood. But from the rest of the conversation—even if this were so—he must have gathered that I was merely discussing possible parts of a great all round bargain every part of which depended on the rest, and the whole on what the two Governments and the Parliaments and public might say when the entire scheme was brought before them.

Indeed he agreed with this view himself. He seems to have been rather argumentative in his talk with Sir E. Goschen.

H. of C.
10/4/12.

(¹) [Grey MSS., Vol. 23.]

No. 573.

Sir Edward Grey to Sir E. Goschen.

F.O. 15371/5569/12/18.
(No. 81.) Secret.
Sir,

Foreign Office, April 10, 1912.

The German Ambassador informed me to-day(¹) that, in consequence of his last conversation with me, he had received a long letter(²) from the German Chancellor.

The Chancellor said that, as the formula which we had offered was insufficient from his point of view, and as we could not agree to the larger formula for which he had asked, the Novelle must proceed in the German Parliament, and was now solely a question between the German Government and the Reichstag. I had observed that the formula for which the German Government asked was something of a more far-reaching character politically than anything which we had with any European country except Portugal. The Chancellor observed in reply to this that what Germany had offered to do in limiting her naval expenditure was a thing unprecedented in history. . . . .(³)

[I am, &c.]
E. G[REY].

(¹) [cp. *G.P.* XXXI, pp. 267–70.]
(²) [v. *G.P.* XXXI, pp. 264–7.]
(³) [The rest of this despatch relates to the question of the Portuguese colonies, and will be printed in a later volume.]

No. 574.

Sir Edward Grey to Sir R. Rodd.

F.O. 15822/5569/12/18.
(No. 73.) Secret.
Sir,

Foreign Office, April 12, 1912.

The Italian Ambassador told me to-day that, as he was about to go to Rome, he was anxious to be in possession of the latest information as to our negotiations with Germany.

I said that I did not think any definite agreement was on the eve of being signed, but the relations between the two Governments had very much improved, and we now discussed frankly and without friction everything which was of mutual interest.

[I am, &c.]
E. G[REY].

No. 575.

Sir A. Nicolson to Sir E. Goschen.

Private.([1])

My dear Goschen,   *Foreign Office, April* 15, 1912.

Many thanks for your letter received by last Bag.([2])   I am glad to tell you that since I wrote you Metternich came here and said that as the two Governments were apparently unable to come to an agreement as to a formula, the Chancellor intended to proceed with the Naval Novelle in Parliament, but that he was quite ready to discuss in a friendly manner any questions as to territorial exchanges in Africa.   I have informed the French Chargé d'Affaires of the above, and I trust that it means that the formula question has been definitely buried and that we shall hear no more about it. I was really uneasy lest we should be entrapped into signing some engagement which would offend the French and render them suspicious, for it would be fatal for us to take any measure which would in any way impair our relations with France.   It is also quite clear that were we to do so, an unfavourable effect would be produced on our relations with Russia and also we should have to reconsider entirely the distribution of our naval forces, as we should not, as it apparently is the intention at present, practically leave the care of the Mediterranean to the French Navy. I have always maintained, and I have impressed as far as I can on those dealing with these matters, that it would be far more disadvantageous to have an unfriendly France and unfriendly Russia than an unfriendly Germany. The latter, it is true, can give us plenty of annoyance, but it cannot really threaten any of our more important interests, while Russia especially could cause us extreme embarrassment, and, indeed, danger, in the Mid-East and on our Indian frontier, and it would be most unfortunate were we to revert to the state of things which existed before 1904 and 1907.   Moreover, I do think that our relations with Germany have cleared considerably, so there seems no reason why we should not remain on perfectly friendly terms with her and discuss in an amiable manner any questions which may arise between us.   I am not, myself, however, enamoured with these territorial exchanges or cessions in Africa. . . . .([3])

[A. NICOLSON.]

([1]) [Carnock MSS., Vol. III of 1912.]
([2]) [Not reproduced.]
([3]) [The rest of this long letter refers to the Balkan situation.]

No. 576.

Minute by Sir A. Nicolson.

Confidential.([1])

Lord Morley,   *Foreign Office, April* 15, 1912.

M. Cambon spoke to me to-day in regard to our relations with France.   He said that in 1905 when Germany was pressing France hard Lord Lansdowne had mentioned to him that H[is] M[ajesty's] Gov[ernmen]t would be disposed to strengthen and extend the understanding with France, and would be ready to

([1]) [Carnock MSS., Vol. III of 1912.]

discuss the matter. M. Cambon had conveyed this proposal to M. Delcassé, then Foreign Minister, who had replied by telegraph authorising M. Cambon to enter upon discussions. M. Cambon did not act on these instructions, and wrote to M. Delcassé explaining that he would prefer, before entering on discussions with Lord Lansdowne, to be assured that M. Rouvier, then President of the Council, agreed with M. Delcassé and desired to strengthen and extend the understanding. M. Delcassé thereupon brought the question before the French Cabinet, and M. Rouvier declared that he was opposed to any extension of the understanding.([2]) M. Delcassé, therefore, tendered his resignation.

M. Rouvier, at that time, was initiating his negotiations with Germany in regard to Morocco, and was unwilling to take any steps which might hamper these negotiations. Later M. Rouvier discovered that he had made a blunder, and that Germany was leading him into a position which would be detrimental to French interests and was indeed manoeuvring him into a situation which was humiliating and irksome, and from which France would have difficulty in extricating herself. He, therefore, changed his attitude, and expressed his willingness to enter into discussions with H[is] M[ajesty's] Gov[ernmen]t with a view of securing to France the assistance of G[rea]t Britain in the event of France being forced into hostilities with Germany. In the meantime the Conservative Gov[ernmen]t had resigned office, and on M. Cambon approaching Sir E. Grey with the object of opening discussions on the lines indicated by Lord Lansdowne, he ascertained that the new British Gov[ernmen]t were unwilling to go as far as M. Rouvier desired, and the matter was dropped. Now M. Poincaré was frequently being asked by men of standing and influence in France as to how far France could count upon British support in the event of any difficulties with Germany. Public opinion, M. Cambon continued, had been much aroused in France over the Agadir incident and subsequent developments, and there was a universal feeling in France, of a strength and extent which was surprising, that should Germany endeavour to place on France any affront the country must resent and repel it. In Germany too there was a strong chauvinistic feeling prevailing, of which the large increases in the German army and the active military preparations were symptomatic. The French Gov[ernmen]t were convinced that an opportunity would be seized, perhaps not this year, but possibly next year or the year after, by Germany to create some incident which would arouse public feeling on both sides of the frontier, and which would, viewing the temper in both countries, very probably lead to war.

The German Emperor and the German Chancellor were doubtless pacifically inclined, but they were not in reality the influential and deciding factors. The Pan-Germans, the Navy League, and other chauvinistic elements, the military etc. were the factors which had the greatest weight and influence. In these circumstances M. Poincaré considered that it was necessary to take stock of the position of France, and to see on what outside assistance she could rely when the moment arrived. It was evident that the attitude of England was a very important factor, and the recent endeavours of Germany to neutralize her clearly indicated that England was regarded as the Power which held largely the balance for or against peace. Were Germany assured that England would remain neutral her hands would be free for dealing with France, were she in doubt, she would hesitate—but it was of great importance to France also to be assured what would be the attitude of England and if she could count upon her. M. Poincaré was anxious to be clear in his mind on that point, and the very recent communications and assurances which he had received from H[is] M[ajesty's] Gov[ernmen]t had not been sufficiently clear and precise to thoroughly satisfy and enlighten him.

I told M. Cambon that in a question of such importance I naturally could only give him my personal opinion. I would tell him frankly that personally I was, as he knew, a warm adherent of the understanding with France and no-one

([2]) [The Anglo-French discussions of this period are recorded from the British side in *Gooch & Temperley*, Vol. III, pp. 72–87, ch. XVIII.]

would be better pleased than myself if it were strengthened—but there were certain facts which should be borne in mind. In the first place I doubted extremely if H[is] M[ajesty's] Gov[ernmen]t would be at all disposed to tie their hands in any way as to the line of action which they would adopt in any possible contingencies. They would, I feel sure, desire to preserve complete liberty of action. Moreover among large sections of the community of late there was a strong feeling, which was shared possibly by some members of the Gov[ernmen]t, that some "understanding" should be arrived at with Germany; there was no very clear conception as to what was meant by an understanding—but it was felt that we had perhaps been a little obstructive towards Germany, limiting her expansion and keeping her out of her "place in the sun." Personally I considered that these misgivings and self reproaches had no basis in fact, but they existed. Those who were well acquainted with recent history would hardly regard Germany as an injured innocent, but there were many here who did, and of late there had been a very active propaganda by financiers, pacifists, faddists and others, in favour of close relations with Germany, and this propaganda had made considerable headway. No one would wish not to maintain friendly relations with Germany so long as they could be secured with due regard to British interests. If at this moment France were to come forward with proposals so to reshape our understanding as to give it more or less the character of an alliance, I felt pretty sure that neither the Gov[ernmen]t as a whole nor large sections of British public opinion would be disposed to welcome such proposals, which would be regarded by many as offering umbrage and a challenge to Germany. It would be far wiser to leave matters as they were—and not to strain an understanding which was at present generally popular, and did not by itself afford the slightest reason to any other country to resent or demur to it.

A. N.

No. 577.

Sir A. Nicolson to Lord Morley.

Private.(¹)

Lord Morley, Foreign Office, April 16, 1912.

It seems to me that I should record my conversation with M. Cambon of yesterday.(²) If I might suggest I do not think it ought to go further than the Prime Minister.

A. N.

MINUTE.

The Prime Minister.

M.
16.4.12.

I entirely approve the language used by Sir A. Nicolson.

H. H. A.
18 Ap. '12.

(¹) [Carnock MSS., Vol. III of 1912.]
(²) [v. immediately preceding document.]

No. 578.

Sir F. Bertie to Sir Edward Grey.

F.O. 16319/5569/12/18.

(No. 177.) Confidential. Paris, D. April 18, 1912.

Sir, R. April 19, 1912.

I dined with the Prince of Monaco at the Palace at Monaco on the 13th instant. M. Poincaré as well as the French Ministers for War and Marine were also guests of His Serene Highness. The President of the Council inform d me just before dinner that he had received a telegram from the French Ambassador in London stating that the proposal for a Declaration between the British and German Governments had been dropped. M. Poincaré expressed great relief at this information, for a Declaration such as had been suggested would, he said, have been liable to misinterpretation and would have been very embarrassing. It would have been a shock to French public opinion particularly at a moment when there were such demonstrations of cordial friendship between England and France as had just taken place at Nice and Cannes.

Monsieur Poincaré also informed me that he learnt from Monsieur Cambon that the conversations between His Majesty's Goverment and the German Government in regard to territorial questions in Africa were to be continued.

You will remember that during the Morocco negotiations between the French and German Governments the French Government kept His Majesty's Government informed of such territorial cessions or exchanges as might in their opinion affect British interests. I have no doubt that the French Government will expect a like considerate treatment from His Majesty's Government in regard to any proposed cession to Germany which might affect French interests.

I have, &c.
FRANCIS BERTIE.

MINUTE.

The French gov[ernmen]t want to know more than this office can tell him. The negotiations are at present *in nebulis.*

E. A. C.
Ap. 19.
F. D. A.
A. N.
M.

No. 579.

Sir E. Goschen to Sir A. Nicolson.

Private and Personal.([1])

My dear Nico,   *Berlin, April* 20, 1912.

In your letter([2]) you told me that Metternich had said that "as the two Gov[ernmen]ts were unable to come to an agreement as to a formula, the Chancellor intended to proceed with the Naval Novelle in Parliament." Do you think that even with a neutrality formula the Naval Novelle would have been withdrawn? I scarcely think so, as they have been before the country too long, and so much has been written and said about their inadequacy for the needs of the German Navy. I need hardly tell you that I feel great relief at the idea that the Formula question is in the process of interment; it has always been my dream to be on cordial relations with Germany *without* any definite political under-standing, and if, as I hope, the recent conversations have that result no one will be more pleased than I. They have tried hard to bustle us into a hampering formula and I rejoice that they have failed. You have been foremost in this good work. I heartily agree with you also about the conversations which are now going on about cessions and exchanges in Africa: and it rather makes my blood run cold when we talk to Germany about the shortcomings of our Portuguese Allies. Is

---

([1]) [Carnock MSS., Vol. III of 1912.]
([2]) [*v. supra*, p. 747, No. 575.]

it *quite* playing the game? Of course it is quite true what we say about them—but is it quite right or even politic to say it to the Germans? . . . .(³)

Yours ever,

W. E. GOSCHEN.

(³) [The omitted paragraphs refer to the Balkan situation and to possible changes in the German Foreign Office.]

No. 580.

Sir Edward Grey to Sir A. Nicolson.

Private.(¹)

My dear Nicolson, *Rosehall, N.B., April 21, 1912.*

You could have taken no other line with Cambon except what you did take.(²) I shall have to say the same; I shall however impress upon him that although we cannot bind ourselves under all circumstances to go to war with France against Germany, we shall also certainly not bind ourselves to Germany not to assist France.

Cambon should be told how the German affair was left by my last conversation with Metternich.(³)

Yours sincerely,

E. GREY.

I shall probably be back on Monday 29th, and at latest on May 1st.

(¹) [Carnock MSS., Vol. III of 1912.]
(²) [*v. supra*, pp. 747–9, No. 576.]
(³) [*cp. supra*, p. 746, No. 573.]

No. 581.

Sir E. Goschen to Sir Edward Grey.

Berlin, May 2, 1912.

F.O. 18649/6333/12/18. D. 7·50 P.M.

Tel. (No. 41.) R. R. 8·30 P.M.

Secretary of State for Foreign Affairs told me to-day that in answer to question in Budget Committee he had stated that there could be no question of failure of Lord Haldane's mission, as English Minister had only come to explore ground and discuss situation. When asked as to how matters now stood in consequence of visit he had said that, as confidential conversations were still continuing, he could give no information. On being threatened with vote of the committee to make him answer question he said that whatever committee voted he must abide by his decision.

MINUTES.

It would be interesting to know what M. de Kiderlen had in his mind when he referred to " confidential conversations still continuing." We have no record of such.

E. A. C.
May 3.
A. N.

The territorial questions especially about Portuguese Colonies will be resumed in conversation when Count Metternich returns. I think my last conversation with him implied that.

E. G.

No. 582.

Sir Edward Grey to Sir F. Bertie.

F.O. 19274/5569/12/18.
(No. 218.) Secret.

Sir,
Foreign Office, May 3, 1912.

As I had heard that an answer given by the Prime Minister in the House of Commons,([1]) on the subject of an amicable understanding with Germany, had given M. Cambon reason to suppose that some agreement of a far-reaching character had already been concluded, I took an opportunity of telling him to-day that we were not now discussing the question of a formula at all. The only things that we were discussing at present were some territorial arrangements in South Africa, practically the Portuguese Colonies on the mainland of Africa. As was generally known, though I was bound to keep it secret, an arrangement had been made between this country and Germany in 1898 with regard to these Portuguese Colonies. The purport of the arrangement was to settle between Germany and Great Britain what parts of the Portuguese Colonies each should acquire if Portugal disposed of them. The Portuguese islands off the coast of Africa had not been included. We were now discussing some modifications of the arrangement.

M. Cambon remarked that the arrangement could have only an academic interest, as Portugal was not parting with her Colonies.

I said that, in a sense, this was true; but the arrangement might have some practical importance, even at present: for if Portugal wished to raise money on her Colonies, and British or German financiers came to their Governments for support, the action of the Governments would be guided by the Secret Agreement.

M. Cambon then told me that it was the case that Mr. Asquith's answer in the House of Commons had given him the impression of which I had heard.

I said that the answer had been given in reply to a question asking about an amicable understanding between Germany and ourselves. The Prime Minister had replied that the relations between the two Governments were such that they discussed in a frank and friendly way any questions which were of mutual interest. This correctly represented the state of affairs, for the two Governments now did discuss in this way anything of mutual interest that arose. For instance, we had discussed the question of the Dardanelles as easily with Germany as with any other country. This better understanding was a real gain, and was all to the good. As to the negotiations for an Agreement with Germany, I told M. Cambon that I had already explained to him, very confidentially of course, what the present position was; and I would keep him informed if there was any new development.

[I am, &c.]
E. G[REY].

([1]) [*cp. Parl. Deb.*, *5th Ser.*, House of Commons, Vol. 37, p. 1679.]

No. 583.

Sir Edward Grey to Sir C. MacDonald.

F.O. 19927/5569/12/18.
(No. 81.) Secret.

Sir,
Foreign Office, May 8, 1912.

The Japanese Ambassador asked me to-day about our negotiations with Germany.

I told him that, at present, nothing was being negotiated with regard to a formula or naval understanding. The negotiations were confined entirely to possible territorial arrangements or exchanges, mainly in South Africa. We had had transactions of that kind with Germany before, and if another took place now it would be evidence that there was no illwill between the two countries.

[I am, &c.]
E. G[REY]

No. 584.

Sir Edward Grey to Sir E. Goschen.

Private.(¹)

My dear Goschen,   London, May 13, 1912.

. . . .(²) As to what Jules Cambon said to you,(³) you will have seen that I have kept Cambon here informed, and have told him that, at present, the practical part of the negotiations relates to the future of the Portuguese Colonies, negotiations with regard to naval expenditure and a formula having ceased for the present. Jules Cambon ought to bear in mind that the French have more than once negotiated with the Germans. They came to a friendly agreement with them in 1909 about Morocco. Russia has done the same on occasion. We cannot keep Germany at arm's length, and hold no converse with her about subjects of mutual interest. So long as France is kept informed of anything of importance that takes place, and we do nothing with Germany that is really of detriment to France, and do not change our general policy, the French must not complain. What I desire is that France, Russia, and ourselves should all be on the best terms with Germany, without losing touch with each other or impairing the confidence which exists between us.

Metternich has not said anything to me about the appointment of Marschall here, except to ask for the "agrément." There has been no indication from the German Government that they intend anything special by sending Marschall, and you may tell Jules Cambon so if you like.

Yours sincerely,

E. GREY.

(¹) [Grey MSS., Vol. 23.]
(²) [The opening paragraphs of this letter refer to rumours in the Press about the positions of Baron von Marschall and Sir E. Goschen.]
(³) [In a letter to Sir A. Nicolson of May 9 (Carnock MSS., Vol. III of 1912), Sir E. Goschen described a visit from M. Jules Cambon. They had a long conversation about the Anglo-German negotiations, and especially about the alleged offer of Zanzibar.]

No. 585.

Sir F. Bertie to Sir Edward Grey.

F.O. 20940/20079/12/18.

(No. 211.)   Confidential.-   Paris, D. May 16, 1912.

Sir,   R. May 17, 1912.

Yesterday was Monsieur Poincaré's weekly reception day and I paid him a visit at the Quai d'Orsay. His Excellency spoke to me on the subject of the withdrawal of Count Metternich from London and the appointment of Baron Marschall von Bieberstein to be his successor as German Ambassador. Monsieur Poincaré was evidently much exercised at this appointment. His manner was very earnest and he expressed himself very seriously. He said that it could not be supposed that the transfer to London of an Ambassador who was so successful in making the influence of Germany paramount at Constantinople had not a very great object in view. What Monsieur Poincaré then proceeded to say was so important that I asked His Excellency to repeat his observations so that I might report them to you textually. They were that he felt "de sérieuses inquiétudes à la pensée que la nomination du Baron Marschall indique l'intention de reprendre les pourparlers en vue d'une déclaration ou une formule d'arrangement dont la publication, quelque innocente qu'elle puisse être dans les intentions du Gouvernement anglais, ne le serait certainement pas dans les intentions de l'Allemagne et produirait en France le plus désastreux effet. Il serait très difficile dans ces conditions au Gouvernement français de maintenir l'opinion publique et de conserver à l'entente cordiale toute son efficacité. Quant aux questions d'échanges de territoires elles ne regardent pas d'une manière directe le Gouvernement français, mais il ne peut cependant pas être indifférent à la question de Zanzibar à cause du voisinage des îles Comoros et Madagascar, et il aurait le désir d'être renseigné, le moment venu, sur les projets du Gouvernement anglais de même que le Gouvernement français a tenu le Gouvernement anglais au courant des propositions territoriales pendant les négotiations au sujet du Maroc.''

Monsieur Poincaré then made some remarks on the strange ignorance which Germans in general seemed to have of the characteristics of other races than their own. The German Government in their dealings with France had given proof of that ignorance and he hoped that the intended increase of the German Navy just announced, which was a strange way of approaching the British public with the view to friendly negotiations, would keep open their eyes to the real designs of Germany. The policy of the German Government was to separate England and France and Baron Marschall would make every endeavour to that end.

I beg leave to remind you that in a Despatch of the 3rd ultimo (No. 158 Secret)(1) I warned His Majesty's Government that an Anglo-German Declaration whether in the restricted or in the more amplified form then contemplated would be a disagreeable surprise to the French public as calculated, and by the German Government intended, to loosen the ties of friendship and confidence between France and England and to form in the interest of Germany bonds restricting the liberty of action of England in a manner detrimental to the interests of France and dangerous to the peace of Europe. A fortnight later at Monaco (see my despatch No. 177 Confidential of April 18)(2) Monsieur Poincaré when informing me that the proposal for a Declaration between the British and German Governments had been dropped expressed great relief thereat for a Declaration such as had been suggested would, he said, have been liable to misinterpretation and would have been very embarrassing. It would have been a shock to French public opinion particularly at a moment when there were such demonstrations of cordial friendship between England and France as had just taken place at Nice and Cannes.

I have, &c.
FRANCIS BERTIE.

(1) [v. supra, pp. 736–7, No. 564.]
(2) [v. supra, pp. 749–50, No. 578.]

No. 586.

Sir F. Bertie to Sir Edward Grey.

Private.(1)

My dear Grey,   Paris, May 16, 1912.

As you will see from a despatch of today's date(2) which I am sending to you Poincaré is perturbed at Marschall's appointment. In his opinion it means a renewed and more determined attempt to get us into an entanglement with Germany separating us from France. He hopes that German brutal methods of which Marschall is a past master and which made him a success at Constantinople will be repeated in London for he thinks that Englishmen will not stomach that sort of negotiator and that those of your colleagues who may have been inclined for an Anglo-German Declaration will realize its dangers and relent.

Yours sincerely,
FRANCIS BERTIE.

(1) [Grey MSS., Vol. 14.]
(2) [v. immediately preceding document.]

No. 587.

Sir Edward Grey to Sir F. Bertie.

Private.(¹)

My dear Bertie, *Foreign Office, May 17, 1912.*

We haven't had the faintest indication that the German means any thing by Marschall's appointment. My own view is that he wanted to get away from Constantinople; he very cleverly recovered the ground lost by the Turkish revolution, but when having achieved that the Italian war followed and again upset his policy he must have been very sick. He was outspoken at Constantinople in denouncing the Italians and advising the Turks to hold out. The Italians knew this, and the German Government knew that the Italians knew it. The appointment of Marschall was precipitated while the German Emperor was at Corfu, having seen the King of Italy on his way there. If Marschall was to move from Constantinople, London was the only place to which he could retreat with éclat.

No doubt as much is expected of his coming to London, some thing will be attempted, but one report is that his stay will not be long and that London is a stepping stone to the Chancellorship. At Marschall's age I rather doubt this.

If Marschall tries brutal methods, he will make our policy very simple and easy, but I imagine him to be much too clever to do this.

Yours sincerely,

E. GREY.

(¹) [Grey MSS., Vol. 14.]

No. 588.

Sir Edward Grey to Sir F. Bertie.

F.O. 22031/5569/12/18.

(No. 246.) Confidential.

Sir, *Foreign Office, May 21, 1912.*

When seeing M. Cambon to-day, I told him that M. Poincaré had spoken to you with anxiety, at least once, about Baron Marschall's appointment to London.(¹)

I said that, in my opinion, both Baron Marschall and the German Government wished that he should leave Constantinople, where he had been outspokenly very anti-Italian. London was the place to which he could most easily be moved. We had no indication whatever from the German Government that his arrival was to inaugurate any new departure. Our negotiations with Germany were at present entirely confined to certain South African questions, mainly in regard to Portuguese Colonies; and we were waiting to hear what the German Colonial Office thought of certain suggestions which had been made by the Secretary of State for the Colonies here.

[I am, &c.]

E. G[REY].

(¹) [*v. supra*, pp. 753–4, Nos. 585–6.]

No. 589

Sir Edward Grey to Sir F. Bertie.

F.O. 20940/5569/12/18.
(No. 262.) Secret.

Sir,
                                        Foreign Office, May 31, 1912.

I have received Y[our] E[xcellency]'s despatch No. 211 of the 16th inst[ant](¹) reporting the serious apprehensions of M. Poincaré in connection with the appointment of Baron Marschall as German Ambassador in London.

I should be glad if Y[our] E[xcellency] would take an opportunity to thank M. Poincaré for having expressed so frankly the misgivings which were perplexing him, and to assure him that H[is] M[ajesty's] G[overnmen]t are fully determined, as they have so frequently asserted, not to adopt any line of policy which would in any way impair the intimate and friendly relations which they desire to maintain with France. H[is] M[ajesty's] Gov[ernmen]t have no intention of entering into any political engagements with Germany which would have this effect. They wish to encourage friendly relations with Germany in such a way as to ensure that these relations shall also imply a friendly attitude on the part of Germany towards France and no lessening of the close relations between France and Great Britain. As a matter of fact no political understanding is at present under discussion, but only certain territorial arrangements or exchanges of territory in Africa south of the equator. In the event of the question of the surrender of Zanzibar to Germany becoming a practical question, H[is] M[ajesty's] Gov[ernmen]t will give timely notice to the French Gov[ernmen]t so that the latter may have the opportunity of presenting any observations which they may wish to be taken into account.

[I am, &c.]
E. G[REY].

(¹) [*v. supra*, pp. 753–4, No. 585.]

No. 590.

Sir E. Goschen to Sir A. Nicolson.

Private.(¹)

My dear Nicolson,
                                        Berlin, June 21, 1912.

. . . .(²) Marschall came to see me on Monday just before he started for London. He seemed delighted with his new Post, but said that he feared that he had a difficult job before him. I said that I hoped not: relations were better than they had been and I knew that he would find Sir Edward Grey most cordial and ready to co-operate with him in smoothing off any rough corners that might exist in our relations. He said that he was sure of that and he assured me that it was only the exaggerations of the Press as to what he was and what was expected of him, that had made him feel sometimes that he was not equal to a task of such magnitude as it had been represented to be. He talked about all the nonsense that had been written and said on both sides about the imminence of war last Autumn, not a word of which he had ever believed for a moment; he also alluded to the "terrible 17 days of silence" which ought never to have occurred and which he thought would not have occurred had he been in London at the time!(³) and criticised the length of the Morocco-Congo negotiations, which he said was entirely the fault

(¹) [Carnock MSS., Vol. V of 1912.]
(²) [The opening paragraphs of this letter give details about the Turco-Italian war.]
(³) [Reference will be made in *Gooch & Temperley*, Vol. VII, to the period in July 1911, variously described in this document and the next as the "17 days of silence" and the "21 days' silence."]

of Kiderlen! He also deplored the marked increase of Chauvinism in Germany—
a plant, he said, of recent growth and, as shown by the word, of Foreign, not German
origin.

His whole conversation gave me the impression that he wishes to be regarded
as going to England with an open mind, free from prejudices of any sort and ready
to discuss everything with engaging frankness. . . . .([4])

Yours sincerely,
W. E. GOSCHEN.

([4]) [The rest of this long letter describes the position and influence of Herr von Kiderlen-
Waechter.]

No. 591.

Sir Edward Grey to Sir E. Goschen.

F.O. 27914/27914/12/18.
(No. 158.)
Sir,   *Foreign Office, June 25, 1912.*

The German Ambassador came to see me to-day, and spoke of the general
situation. He began by saying that he had seen the Emperor, who had spoken in
the most emphatic way of his desire for friendly relations with us and whose feelings
for England were of the most friendly nature. It was natural this should be so
for the Emperor was always proud of being Queen Victoria's eldest grandson. The
Ambassador mentioned the difficulties which there had been with regard to Morocco,
referring in this connection to what he called the 21 days' silence, but said
that it was wrong to suppose that Germany was aggressive. She had nothing to
gain by taking further territory; war would be disastrous, because of the financial
complications which would follow; and where the whole population was in the Army
an aggressive war was impossible, for every family would feel it.

I said that the real danger of war generally was in the occurrence of some
incident which seemed to affect national honour. I agreed that, if there was a great
European war, it was not likely to profit anyone, for even the Power which was
successful in the war might, on being relieved from external pressure for a time,
suffer to the extent of revolution from internal pressure.

The Ambassador deprecated the suspicion entertained in some quarters in
England that the German Fleet was being built against England—indeed at a later
period of our conversation he remarked that it was the German Emperor's admiration
for England that had stimulated his desire to have a fleet.

I remarked that the naval expenditure was a great fact which could not be
ignored. If our Fleet were inferior to the German Fleet we should run a tremendous
risk: for the considerations which operated against military war were necessarily
not so strong against naval war, which did not involve the whole population; if
once we were defeated at sea the consequences would be most disastrous to us.

The Ambassador admitted that, for us, the Fleet was a more vital thing than
for Germany. He realised that both countries had certain agreements and engagements which must be kept; but, without impairing these, he thought that we ought
to have friendly relations.

I said that this was our view also. To speak quite frankly, our agreements
with France and Russia had, in the first instance, been made to put an end to the
constant quarrels, which often brought us to the brink of war. We must avoid
anything which would cause us to relapse into that uncomfortable state with those
Powers, and we must retain our cordial relations with them. But we were also
anxious to have the most friendly relations with Germany. Since Lord Haldane's
visit to Berlin and the disappearance of the question of Morocco, which I hoped

had disappeared for good, we had endeavoured, by a frank discussion of points as they arose, to prevent difficulties from arising.

The Ambassador remarked that our agreements with France and Russia had had their origin in points of difference between us. It was strange that, because there were no points of difference between us and Germany, there was difficulty in our making an agreement with her.

I said that we had been discussing a certain agreement as to Portuguese Colonies.

The Ambassador treated this as somewhat academic, asking me whether I had any reason to suppose that Portugal intended to part with her Colonies.

I said that I had no reason to suppose that, but her Colonies were now derelict, and I thought that, if Germany and we could come to an agreement, it might be communicated to the Portuguese Government, and there might be impressed upon them the truth : that the sovereignty of their Colonies would be best secured by having them developed; and that, if this could not be done without foreign capital and enterprise, it should be done by German or British capital as the case might be. I understood that the Foreign Office in Berlin were discussing the proposals which Mr. Harcourt had originated, and which he and I had conveyed to Count Metternich; and I supposed that we should presently hear the German view of these.

The Ambassador was evidently not prepared to pursue the subject further at present.

It was evident that the Ambassador either had no instructions to speak of anything in particular or did not intend at present to act upon them. Indeed the impression I received was that he had probably arranged with the German Emperor and the Chancellor to come without any special instructions, to spend a little time in forming his own opinion here and then very likely to return on leave to Berlin and advise his own Gov[ernmen]t what his instructions should be.

I decided therefore to mention to him such points as seemed to be of mutual interest to Germany and ourselves, giving him what information I could and my view upon them, as practical evidence of a desire to prevent difficulties and to keep in touch. What was said with regard to the Bagdad Railway and Chinese Loans is recorded separately.

[I am, &c.]
E. G[REY].

No. 592.

Sir Edward Grey to Sir E. Goschen.

Private.(¹)

My dear Goschen,   *London, June 27, 1912.*

As I thought that Marschall would like to begin making the acquaintance of some of my Colleagues, I asked him to lunch at my house yesterday with the Prime Minister and Haldane.

Marschall himself began to talk about the political situation, and said the same things as I have put in the official records of his conversation with me earlier this week.

Yesterday, he headed rather in the direction of the exchange of some formula with Germany. We expressed the opinion that to keep frankly in touch with Germany about each question as it arose was a more sure way of avoiding difficulties than the exchange of any formulae. When he instanced what he considered the

(¹) [Grey MSS., Vol. 23.]

exceedingly good relations between Russia and Germany as being perfectly compatible with the Franco-Russian Alliance, we pointed out that the Alliance had precedence of any agreement which Russia might make with Germany, that it necessarily remained definite and intact, and that Russia could therefore go further perhaps than we could go, for our relations with France were much more vague; and, if we entered into an agreement with Germany more definite than any which we had with France, the agreement with Germany would necessarily tend to supersede our good understanding with France.

Marschall assumed that, if Germany tried to crush France, we would probably help France; but he said that that need not prevent us from promising not to join in an aggressive attack upon Germany.

We replied that we had no intention of joining in such an attack.

Marschall deprecated the suspicion entertained in some quarters in this country that the German Fleet was directed against us.

We said that, in judging British public opinion, allowance must be made for the peculiar position of Germany: she had the largest and strongest Army in the world, and she now had the second strongest Fleet. This was an unprecedented situation. Admitting that Germany had nothing but good intentions towards us at the present moment, it was nevertheless natural for people to ask, not as regards this year or the immediate future, but as regards a few years hence, to what use might be put so much power, concentrated in the hands of one Government.

Marschall said again that he did not approve of the grouping of Powers, as it produced an unfavourable impression.

On this, we observed that the increase of armaments in Europe generally, both on land and sea, necessarily increased the reluctance of any one Power to be left alone in this armed camp.

All this is little more than I have already recorded officially. Indeed, what Marschall said was exactly the same, and I therefore condensed it very much here. But, as what was said on our side yesterday rather amplified what had been said by me alone in my previous conversation with Marschall in the Foreign Office, I have thought it worth while to send you this letter.

Yours sincerely,
E. GREY.

No. 593.

Sir Edward Grey to Sir E. Goschen.

Private.(¹)
My dear Goschen,   *London, July 4, 1912.*
Marschall has again broached, though quite informally and in general conversation, the question of a formula.

He said to-day that, in studying the papers which had passed, he saw how difficult it was for us to say anything about neutrality, or to exchange some thing formal with Articles and Paragraphs. But he thought that a simple monologue, saying that we had no aggressive designs, and desired to be friendly, ought not to excite any suspicion in France.

I observed that this sort of thing might be said at any time in Parliament.

He urged, however, that such a statement would not have quite the same effect as some thing which could be pointed to, and of which people could say "litera scripta manet."

(¹) [Grey MSS., Vol. 23.]

I said that this would be true of a reported speech. We did not pursue the subject further.

Of course, what Marschall said is quite true : an exchange of writing does mean more than a speech in Parliament. But it is precisely because it does mean more that it might give rise to suspicions. So I hope that we shall go on with the Portuguese Colonial business, rather than with the discussion of the possibility of a formula.

I ended by observing that, if we could revise our Portuguese Agreement, and keep in touch about the Bagdad Railway, the Loan to China, the Italian-Turkish war, and in fact every thing which arose from time to time and in which Germany and we were interested, the effect upon the political atmosphere would in the course of two or three years be very ameliorating.

Yours sincerely,
E. GREY.

No. 594.

Memorandum on conversations with Herr von Kiderlen-Waechter during three days in November last.(¹)

July 25, 1912.

.... My friend, on his way to England within the last ten days, had another long conversation with Kiderlen-Waechter, who invited him to lunch with him quite alone—to talk over old times passed together, and also exchange ideas with him about matters in the Balkans. In discussing the relations between England and Germany my friend said that he thought the naval competition was going to be disastrous to Germany. He pointed out that England would be bound to be victor in the competition, partly because of her great financial resources and partly because unless England possessed supremacy of the sea, she must sink into the position of a second-rate Power; and no one who knew England could imagine that its inhabitants would ever be content with this. He went on further to show that it was a most dangerous game for Germany to play, for a defeat meant disaster to the monarchy and a victory would result in a confederation of the other Powers against Germany. For, he said, Europe would never stand another Napoleon. But apart from the danger of a federation of nations against Germany, a victory would entail a considerable widening of political privileges which would destroy autocracy, and ultimately have a very disastrous effect upon the monarchy. As in 1871 the price of Union was universal suffrage, so in the case of victory in any way with England, further privileges would have to be granted which would be most distasteful to the traditions of the German Government.

On hearing this, Kiderlen-Waechter showed considerable interest and, banging the table with his fist, he said, " Three days ago I said exactly the same thing to Admiral von Tirpitz, but I am afraid without effect." The German Foreign Minister then went on to say that he endorsed every word said by my friend; that he and the Chancellor were entirely against a war, but that von Tirpitz was a very strong man, who had perfected an instrument which he believed was capable of doing the work for which it was intended. In his conversations with the Emperor, von Tirpitz keeps on reiterating that the German fleet need not wait for superiority, or even equality, of numbers, because it is his firm conviction that the German modern battleships are superior to the British, owing to their secondary armament of 6″ guns. The British ships, he says, are armed with 12″ and 13·5″ guns, which

---

(¹) [Grey MSS., Vol. 68. A covering letter from Mr. Gwynne, then Editor of the *Morning Post*, states that the conversation recorded here took place between Herr von Kiderlen-Waechter and M. Také Jonescu. The first part of the memorandum is concerned with the Agadir crisis and will be printed in *Gooch & Temperley*, Vol. VII.]

enable them to fight at ·great distances; but they will be obliged, in order to be effective, to keep at a long distance, out of effective range of the 6″ guns, and this will entail manoeuvres on the part of the British fleet which would be disheartening, because to the crews it would appear as a continuous retreat. Besides that, he said, in the North Sea, it is only once in 30 days that the weather ·conditions permit of a long range, 12″ gun combat. The ordinary battle could be fought at ranges where the superiority of the German 6″ guns would be so pronounced as to nullify the British big gun fire to a very great extent. He puts the proportion of strength of a German Dreadnought to a British Dreadnought at $1\frac{1}{2}$ to 1.

These arguments have no small effect upon the Emperor and Kiderlen-Waechter expressed his anxiety lest his influence over the Emperor, backed as it is by these technical arguments, should be strong enough to persuade the Emperor to take some rash step. Among other technical arguments used by von Tirpitz which my friend remembered was that he said that the British Admiralty have exactly half the number of torpedo boat destroyers that are necessary for a blockade, and the time has already passed for the blockade of German ports by an English fleet.

I tried to get from my friend the German view of the international situation as regards the Great Powers, but all Kiderlen-Waechter would say was that he was quite satisfied with the meeting at Reval.

H. A. G[WYNNE].

July 25th, 1912.

APPENDIX I.

[*ED. NOTE.*—The following despatches from Sir E. Monson describing King Edward's visit to Paris in 1903 were not found until after the publication of Volume II, to which they properly belong.]

(a.)

Sir E. Monson to the Marquess of Lansdowne.

F.O. General 2159.

(No. 218.)   *Paris, D. May* 5, 1903.

My Lord,   R. *May* 5, 1903.

I was unable sooner to furnish Your Lordship with a report upon the King's visit to Paris, because I had the honour of accompanying His Majesty on his departure, yesterday, to Cherbourg, whence I have only returned this evening. I now transmit to Your Lordship extracts from the French press containing descriptions of the principal incidents of His Majesty's stay, including his entry into the Capital on the 1st May, the military review at Vincennes on the following morning, the visit to the Hôtel de Ville, the Race Meeting at Longchamps, the State dinner at the Elysée, and the Gala performance at the Opera.

Of the reception given to the King by the population of Paris I am happy to be able to report that it was throughout satisfactory, and on numerous occasions highly gratifying. On the day of His Majesty's arrival, when he drove to the Embassy through the Avenue du Bois de Boulogne, and down the Champs Elysées, the attitude of the crowds which lined the roadway, without being marked by any great warmth, was respectful and friendly. But when His Majesty appeared in public on the following day it was easy to perceive a marked increase of cordiality in the greeting which met him. The King was loudly acclaimed by a dense mass of citizens who had assembled on the " Place " opposite to the Hotel de Ville, and the welcome given His Majesty at Longchamps races by an immense collection of people, fairly representative of the well-to-do Parisian classes, can only be described as genuinely enthusiastic. His Majesty was again loudly and heartily cheered as he drove back from the races; and on the whole the case is fairly stated by the " Temps " of the 4th instant, which says that never had a Sovereign paying a visit of courtesy to a nation of which he was not the ally, been received with greater enthusiasm and cordiality. Perhaps the most remarkable feature of the King's visit was the good reception given His Majesty on his way to and from Vincennes by spectators drawn from the lowest classes of the population of the Capital.

Your Lordship will have already received the text, forwarded yesterday, of the speeches delivered at the Hôtel de Ville and the State dinner at the Elysée. His Majesty's words, which were spoken *ex tempore*, produced the happiest impression by their graciousness and evident sincerity, and were highly appreciated, as I have reason to know, by his hearers. Your Lordship will find in the newspaper reports which I now have the honour to enclose,(¹) the text of the address presented to the King on the 1st instant by the British Chamber of Commerce and of His Majesty's reply; as also of the Message sent by the King to the President from Cherbourg.

The tone of the French press as a whole during the past four days has been most friendly and cordial. The outcries of a few violent Anglophobe papers of the class of the " Patrie " appear to have produced little impression, and any slight irritation shown by the more serious papers, Monarchical or otherwise, of Nationalist tendencies, was manifestly directed not against His Majesty or Great Britain, but the Government which, its opponents fear, will reap some political profit from the Royal visit. The " Gaulois " of today publishes a leading article signed by General Zurlinden, former Minister of War, which, coming from such a quarter, is so

(¹) [Not reproduced.]

remarkable for the reasonableness of its treatment of the Faschoda incident and other Anglo-French differences that I cannot refrain from including it in the other Press extracts sent to Your Lordship herewith.

The lateness of the hour of my return from Cherbourg must be my excuse for confining this report to a general sketch of the incidents of the King's visit. I hope, by the earliest opportunity, to be able to send to Your Lordship some more extended comments and appreciations of this most interesting and important event, and of its effect upon Anglo-French relations; only repeating now that from the moment of His Majesty's arrival at Dijon down to that when I quitted him last night on board the yacht at Cherbourg, his sojourn in France was marked by a never ceasing demonstration of warm and genuine cordiality.

I have, &c.

EDMUND MONSON.

(b.)

Sir E. Monson to the Marquess of Lansdowne.

F.O. General 2159.
(No. 223.)   *Paris,* D. *May* 8, 1903.
My Lord,   R. *May* 9, 1903.

The public press has so copiously reported all the details of the King's visit to Paris that in placing on record the following comprehensive sketch of the leading incidents of the days spent by His Majesty in France I cannot hope to submit to Your Lordship any point of interest which has not already been brought to your notice. I have moreover already forwarded in previous despatches all such extracts from the French newspapers as have appeared to me the most suitable for the illustration and elucidation of the salient occurrences during His Majesty's brief stay in this capital. To enter into a detailed chronicle of the proceedings of every day would render my report too cumbersome; and I trust that in attempting an epitome, in which nothing of real importance is omitted, I shall best be serving the interest of the narrative and fulfilling the duty incumbent upon me.

I met the King at Dijon at 10 o'clock on the morning of the 1st May. I was accompanied by the Military and Naval Attachés of the Embassy, and by Vice-Admiral Fournier, General de Lacroix, and Commandant Chabaud, and three officers delegated by the President to be in attendance on His Majesty during the visit. The station at Dijon had been decorated with flags and flowering shrubs etc. with great taste, and on the platform were assembled in full uniform all the military and civil authorities of the district; namely the General in command of the Division, the Prefect of the Department, and the Mayor and members of the town Council, and other municipal functionaries.

The King alighted from the train; all the officials were presented to His Majesty by a representative of the Protocol; His Majesty reviewed the guard of honour, passing down the line, and saluting the French flag; and after a stay of ten minutes the royal train proceeded on its way.

The arrival station at Paris was that of the Porte Dauphine, at the bottom of the Avenue du Bois de Boulogne; and was punctually reached at three o'clock; the President of the Republic, the Presidents of the Senate and the Chamber of Deputies, the Cabinet Ministers and the Prefect of the Seine and of police, the President of the Municipality, and all the highest officials, civil and military, of the Government and the Capital, received His Majesty. The usual presentations were made; and the cortège was at once formed and proceeded up the Avenue du Bois de

Boulogne and down the Champs Elysées to the Place de la Concorde; whence turning up the Rue Royale and into the Faubourg St Honoré, it reached the Embassy. The whole route was lined with troops, the respective bands playing "God save the King" and the "Marseillaise"; and the landau in which the King and the President sat side by side, and which was drawn by four horses ridden by postilions, was surrounded by a strong escort of cuirassiers.

As in company with the Premier I followed close upon the leading carriage, I was able to appreciate the cordiality of the reception given to the King. The Avenue du Bois was thronged, and the windows of the houses crowded with spectators, who gave His Majesty the warmest welcome. There could be no mistake as to the genuine and sponta[n]eous nature of the demonstration, which became more and more conspicuous as the cortège approached the Embassy. The Rue Royale and the Faubourg St Honoré up to the Embassy had been decorated with all the taste characteristic of the Parisians; and the same may be said of the principal streets such as the Rue Castiglione, the Rue de la Paix and also the Place Vendôme, the brilliant effects of which the King had at a later hour the opportunity of seeing.

The President having accompanied the King inside the Embassy took leave of His Majesty and returned to the Elysée, where at five o'clock he was visited by His Majesty who proceeded to the Palace in the Ambassadorial State Coach accompanied by the members of his suite, as well as by the personnel of the Embassy. The short distance between this house and the Elysée required only a few minutes to traverse; and àll along the crowded street the King was received with hearty cheering. The Faubourg was lined with troops, and the Royal carriage was surrounded with a numerous escort of cuirassiers.

The King was received at the Elysée by the Director of the Protocol and the Chiefs of the Military and Civil Households of the President, and conducted into the saloon where Monsieur Loubet was waiting to receive him; but His Majesty and the President passed at once into the private apartment, where they remained for half an hour, and where they were subsequently joined by Madame Loubet, whom His Majesty had expressed his desire to see.

On returning to the Embassy the King received the President and principal members of the British Chamber of Commerce, who presented an address, to which His Majesty made a gracious and very interesting reply; the immediate publication of which produced in the whole of Paris an excellent effect; testifying as it did to the King's personal friendship for France and to His Majesty's sentiments in regard to the value of a good understanding between the two countries. The King's expressed conviction that such an understanding was daily becoming more and more assured, and that all danger of its being interrupted was steadily fading out of sight, has profoundly impressed the public mind.

The King invited the members of the Embassy to dinner; and at half past eight the President called for His Majesty; who went, accompanied by the members of his suite, to the Théâtre Français, where at his desire the management gave the piece entitled "L'Autre danger," which has for some months been having a great success. The King returned to the Embassy at midnight.

On the morning of the 2nd May the President came to the Embassy at about a quarter past nine, and the King, in uniform, entered his carriage and accompanied Monsieur Loubet to Vincennes. The cortège of carriages traversed almost the whole breadth of the city; the streets being thronged with people, who everywhere gave His Majesty a very cordial greeting. It was noticed that this was the case as much in the "operative quarter" of the Capital as in the more fashionable and business parts of the town; and that the passage of His Majesty through the streets in which the working classes live and labour attracted as much interest and demonstration as it had done in those inhabited by the affluent and the shopkeepers.

The Review held at Vincennes was a picturesque spectacle, the military aspect and composition of which will have been reported on by Colonel Stuart Wortley. The return was characterised by a very important detail of the programme arranged, namely the visit of the King to the Hôtel de Ville, and his reception there by the President of the Municipality; and the Prefect of the Seine, who both addressed a short speech to His Majesty expressing the gratification caused to the people of Paris by his visit to the seat of the Municipal Government.

To these addresses the King replied in an allocution most happily improvised, of which, as I stood amongst the crowd, I heard on every side the most delighted praise. The King's readiness to seize upon the opportunity of expressing his pleasure in a few improvised sentences of eloquent appreciation, made immediately the most gratifying impression upon all who heard him; an impression which their publication in the Press has since only served to intensify and render more profound.

At the conclusion of his allocution the King and the President signed the Protocol recording their visit, and drank to the President of the Municipality, who in reply begged His Majesty to deign to preserve as a souvenir the beaker in which the champagne had been offered to him. The cortège then returned to the Embassy by a slight détour affording His Majesty the opportunity of witnessing the street decorations.

The Presiednt [sic] took leave of the King at the Embassy and his Majesty entertained at luncheon some of his personal friends, together with the members of his suite and of the Embassy staff, althogether more than fifty guests; after which he accompanied the President to the race course at Longchamps, where a special meeting had been arranged by the Jockey Club in His Majesty's honour. The five races were named after the most successful of His Majesty's racing stud; the principal race for the sum of a thousand pounds, and a magnificent cup presented to the King, being entitled the "Persimmon stakes."

The King witnessed the races partly from the President's own tribune, and partly from the Jockey Club stand, where His Majesty's presence among his old friends excited the highest enthusiasm.

This long and fatiguing day was terminated by a banquet of 128 guests at the Elysée, during which the President and the King exchanged toasts; and by a Gala performance at the Opera, where the King and the President sat side by side in the very centre of the grand tier of the house, where a large box had been arranged for their reception.

The King's entrance was the signal for "God save the King" during which His Majesty advanced to the front, the cynosure of thousands of enthusiastic spectators; and the sight was one never to be forgotten by those who had the good fortune to be present. The brilliance of a Court such as would have graced the occasion in the Capital of any other of the European Great Powers was of course absent; but the concourse invited by the President included all that is most distinguished in Paris in the world of literature, science and art, as well as the representatives of the Legislature, Judiciary, the Army and Navy, and the Civil Service. If it cannot but be matter of regret that the inheritors of historic names, the representatives of the old nobility of France, should continue to hold aloof from official life and participation in the duties and privileges of State employment or legislative responsibility, and should have upon this occasion abstained from availing themselves of the opportunity which they knew would be gladly given to them of identifying themselves, not necessarily with their political opponents, but with France herself offering her respectful welcome to the Majesty of Great Britain, it is consoling to recollect that in spite of their unfortunate persistence in remaining irreconcilable adversaries of the Republic, the great majority of them are as cordially devoted to the King of England, whom they knew so long as Prince of Wales, as those of their political adversaries who have long recognised the value of England's friendship and whose sentiments in this direction have become intensified by the personal attitude of their Royal visitor.

The Gala performance at the Opera was over at midnight; and the King returned to the Embassy through the brilliantly illuminated streets in which all the most recent inventions of electric lighting had been utilised with the most picturesque and dazzling effect. Aud thus after a long day, filled to the utmost with incidents demanding constant exertion physical and mental on the part of the King, His Majesty was at length able to seek repose.

At eleven o'clock on Sunday, May 3rd, The King went on foot from the Embassy to the English Church in the Rue d'Aguesseau, where divine Service was performed by Doctor Noyes, Honorary Chaplain to the Embassy, assisted by his curates. The edifice was crowded; but admission had been given only to the regular congregation, and by ticket. Entire order was preserved and no one moved from his place until the King had left the building.

At One o'clock His Majesty and suite drove to the Ministry for Foreign Affairs, where Monsieur Delcassé had invited more than 100 guests to meet His Majesty at luncheon. The Representatives of Foreign Powers were present, as well as many officials and personages of distinction, among them being Monsieur Waldeck Rousseau, whom, after luncheon, I presented to the King, and with whom His Majesty had a prolonged conversation.

On the King's return to the Embassy His Majesty was so good as to plant a tree, (pink chestnut) in the garden. This interesting ceremony was witnessed by the children of the British school, (who sang " God save the King " as His Majesty approached;) and by the aged inmates of the Victoria Home for Women. Among those present was an old man named Coleman, formerly field rider and interpreter to Lord Raglan in the Crimea, with whom His Majesty most graciously conversed, and to whom he subsequently sent a medal.

The King also received a visit from Their Royal Highnesses the Duke and Duchess de Chartres.

At half past eight the King gave a dinner to the President of the Republic and Madame Loubet, to which all the members of the Government and their wives, the Ambassadors and Ambassadresses, a large number of officials, and several painters known to His Majesty, in all over 80 persons had been invited. The dinner was followed by a concert, at which the principal celebrities of the Opera assisted, and at which a limited number of persons known to His Majesty were also present. Upon the occasion, as also upon the night of May 1st, the Embassy building, and the garden were brilliantly illuminated by electricity.

At a few minutes past eleven on the following morning, (Monday May 4th) the President came to the Embassy to accompany the King to the " Gare des Invalides," from whence the Royal train was to start for Cherbourg. The cortège, made up in the same manner as on the occasion of His Majesty's arrival, proceeded down the Faubourg St Honoré past the Elysée, turned down the Avenue Marigny; and crossing the Champs Elysée, traversed the Pont Alexandre III, thus giving the King the opportunity of witnessing on his departure the imposing group of buildings which remain as the heritage of the Great Exhibition of 1900. As the King left the Embassy the Royal Standard was hauled down from the arch above the entrance gate, and the sentinels who had guarded the precincts for four days, were withdrawn to barracks.

At the station there was so dense a crowd that passage for the party was not easily gained. The King descended the flight of stairs in company with the President. A few minutes were devoted to a cordial leave taking; the train moved slowly off into the darkness of the underground way to the strains of the national anthem; and the official visit of the King to the President was over.

His Majesty having been so good as to sanction my accompanying him to Cherbourg I had the gratification of seeing the courtesy and cordiality shown by the Civic Authorities, and by the Naval and Military Commanders and high officials at that port on the occasion of His Majesty's embarcation and final departure from France. The royal train entered the Arsenal station at six in the evening. The thunder of the salutes by the heavy guns unluckily brought down the rain, but a commodious and handsomely decorated pavilion had been erected under which the final courtesies took place. A group of distinguished officers and officials received the King; a few brief words of respectful salutation were offered to His Majesty, who most graciously responded. His Majesty accepted the invitation of the Admiral to use his barge for the short trip to the Royal Yacht; descended the steps to the water's edge, and enveloped in his cloak took his seat in the barge, and left the soil of France amidst the pelting of the rain, acknowledging to the last the respectful adieux of the official spectators.

All of these, to the number of some twenty were invited to dine that evening on board the Victoria and Albert. At dessert Admiral Fournier addressed to His Majesty a few appreciative words respecting his visit; to which the King replied with great cordiality. An hour was passed on deck from whence the illuminations of the town and of the French and English squadrons were seen with great effect. Then the King parted from his guests with gracious words of compliment, and upon taking leave of him I ventured to congratulate him upon the success of his visit to Paris.

That it has been a success more complete that the most sanguine optimist could have foreseen does not admit of doubt. In my conversations with the President and the Prime Minister anterior to Monsieur Loubet's departure for Algeria, I received their very positive assurances that the inhabitants of this capital would give the King a very cordial welcome, but since I held those conversations a small number of journalists, chiefly belonging to the Nationalist party, had inaugurated, and pushed with unscrupulous energy, a campaign against the royal visit, carried on with a temper and a violence of language which, it might have been apprehended, would have had some influence upon the attitude of certain elements of the opposition calculated to spoil the unanimity of the reception.

The virulence and shamelessness of the attacks however defeated the object of those who launched them. All the respectful portion of the nationalist party detached itself from the fraction of the outrageous and the irrational: and whereas not long ago it might have been difficult to organise at the Hôtel de Ville such a demonstration as that with which the King was greeted, it became not only a matter of course but one of insistence on the part of the Municipality, (a body by no means altogether in sympathy with the Government), that the King should be entreated to afford them the opportunity of testifying in the most unmistakable manner to the fact that, whatever the ordinary divergence of opinion between the executive Government and the Municipality, there was complete unanimity in sentiment as to the popularity of His Majesty and as to the value of friendliness with England.

The Personality of the King, and the indefatigable readiness with which he adapted himself to the requirements of an overcharged programme of functions, augmented the influence of the sentiments above referred to: while, in another direction, the re-appearance of the frequent visitor of former years, the well known and popular Prince of Wales coming back to his old friends as King of England; returning to the capital for which he had never concealed his predilection, aroused a feeling of gratification only equalled by the satisfaction of that large party of politicians who, from motives of reason, reflection and clear comprehension of this country's interests, have always systematically favoured the "entente cordiale."

The current of popular feeling has consequently during the days of the King's sojourn in Paris set faster and faster in his favour; and has completely drowned the puny remonstrances of the malcontents. I had the opportunity on the morrow of my return from Cherbourg of discussing with the President the incidents and results of His Majesty's visit, and of learning how thoroughly he agreed with me on every point. I told him that the King had wished me to lose no time in waiting upon him to reiterate His Majesty's thanks for the manner in which he had been received by Monsieur Loubet himself by the Government of the Republic, and by the citizens of Paris; and I congratulated him upon the influence which the happy success of the visit must have upon the relations between France and England. Monsieur Loubet said that he had never entertained any doubt of that success; and that no-one could, in a greater degree than himself, help being impressed with the importance of the event and its action upon the future.

I saw M. Delcassé the same day, and he used language of an exactly similar nature. In the "Figaro" of this morning, a copy of which is enclosed in another despatch, Your Lordship will find a leading article recording His Excellency's views; and at his request and with his sanction, I consented to make an exception to my general rule of refusing to be interviewed; and gave for publication my entire agreement with the sentiments expressed by M. Delcassé.

In concluding this summary of the events of the first four days of the present month of May I desire to congratulate His Majesty's Government upon the complete success of the King's foreign tour. At Lisbon and at Rome it was safe to anticipate a national demonstration of enthusiasm. But in the capital of France, among a people notoriously fickle in their relations to Royalty, there might be warrant for doubt as to the exact character of the reception. That it would be civil, without trace of discourtesy, was certain; for whether the Paris public is chivalrous or not, it is inspired with a certain dignity which on such an occasion as this would not risk a disagreeable comparison with the attitude of the capitals which had just received the King with every demonstration of pleasure. But Paris has now shown herself more than courteous; and has displayed a measure of gratification at the presence of the King, such as must satisfy every impartial observer that there is no lack of genuine good feeling on the part of the public towards the country which it has been unfortunately the tradition to call the "enemy." That their good feeling is reciprocated in London M. Loubet and the French nation may convince themselves if the President should ever be able to realise his intention of returning His Majesty's visit.

I have, &c.

EDMUND MONSON.

[*ED. NOTE.*—The private correspondence of Lord Lansdowne, which has now been made accessible to the Editors, shows that there were no private letters from Sir E. Monson between April 24 and May 8, 1903. Sir E. Monson's letter of May 8 deals with the technical arrangements connected with the King's visit. It describes the visit as " a complete success," and refers to the despatch quoted above as containing a full account of the Ambassador's personal impressions.]

APPENDIX II.

Sir F. Lascelles to Sir Edward Grey.

F.O. 371/257.
(No. 38.)   Secret and Confidential.

Sir,

Berlin, D. February 1, 1907.
R. *February 4, 1907.*

I have the honour to forward, herewith, a despatch, as marked in the margin, which I have received from Captain Philip Dumas, R.N., Naval Attaché to this Embassy, relating to the probable uses of the German fleet in the case of a war with England.

I have, &c.
FRANK C. LASCELLES.

Enclosure.

Captain Dumas, R.N., to Sir F. Lascelles.

Secret.

Your Excellency,

Berlin, January 29, 1907.

I have the honour to submit the following general considerations of the probable uses of the German sea power, and ours in consequence, in the case of a war with England, or with England and France combined.

I ought, perhaps, to commence by stating that I do not think that any such war is probable—at all events, if the making of it lies in German hands; but eventualities may occur of which no one has even dreamed, and personally, having now been in my post for a year, I do not think I should be doing my duty if I were not to forward a general statement of the views which that year's particular study have given rise to.

I would also point out that one year's study of such a vast subject does not in truth fit one to be in any way dogmatic. Against that, unless some such views are put forward, there is no chance of that criticism which alone can produce a well-settled plan of action, and it is in that hope that I venture to indicate some suggestions towards a general mode of procedure. I would first of all attempt to justify my original statement, that I do not believe that such a war is probable.

The German fleet is composed at present as follows :—

	Battle-ships.	Coast Defence Ships.	Armoured Cruisers.	Small Cruisers.	Torpedo-boats.
Fighting ...	20	—	6	16	56
Small Value ...	4	8	6	6	47
Building ...	6	—	3	7	13

Of which there are now serving abroad one armoured cruiser, three small cruisers, and three torpedo-boats.

Against which we could certainly bring at any moment—

Battle-ships ...	...	...	...	48
Armoured cruisers ...	...	...	...	30
Cruisers ...	...	...	...	48
Scouts ...	...	...	...	12
Destroyers ...	...	...	...	120
Torpedo-boats ...	...	...	...	30
Submarines ...	...	...	...	24

of which the half, at least, of the armoured cruisers are of equal fighting value with the half of the German battle-ships; while in every case we have the undoubted superiority both in speed and armament.

[17590]

3 D

Reckoning thus, very roughly, and allowing for the German fleet at its absolutely maximum value, we should compare :—

				England.	Germany.
Battle-ships	...	...	...	63	24
Armoured cruisers	...	...		15	12
Unarmoured cruisers	...	...		60	22
Torpedo craft	...	...	...	150	100

which shows an overwhelming preponderance on our side.

By the year 1917 the German fleet is to be brought up to—

Battle-ships	...	...	...	...	38
Armoured cruisers	...	...	...	...	20
Small cruisers	...	...	...	...	38
Torpedo craft	...	...	...	...	144

and these are to be disposed of as follows :—

				Home Fleet.	Reserve.	Foreign Service.
Battle-ships	...	...	...	34	4	—
Armoured cruisers		...	...	8 + 4	4	4
Small cruisers	...	...	...	24	4	10
Torpedo craft	...	...	...	96	48	—

And it is noteworthy that, unless steps are taken very shortly, these numbers cannot be greatly exceeded, except as regards small cruisers and torpedo-boats, before that time.

This statement I base on my general inspection of the great ship-building yards of Germany made during the past year, also on the comparatively limited output of Krupp, who very unwisely, as it seems to me, have been allowed by the German Government to obtain an absolute monopoly of the manufacture of big guns and armour within the dominions of the Empire.

As regards the capacity for ship-building, the following are the firms and establishments capable of constructing the largest ships, with their maximum output, as I judged it, in ships and time shown against them. In a second column I try to show the more probable output, having regard, firstly, to the lack of skilled ship-wrights that would arise if all the firms were building together; and, secondly, to the difficulty in manufacturing and supplying the guns. I do not speak of the armour, because I have not been able to obtain any satisfactory data, but, as there are many firms which hold a licence from Krupp for this manufacture, I do not think, in fact Krupp would be mad to allow, delay to arise from that cause :—

	Maximum.		Probable.	
	Ships.	Years	Ships.	Years.
Schichau, at Danzig ...	5	3·75	3	3
Vulkan, at Stettin ...	2	2·25	2	2·75
Imperial, at Kiel... ...	1	2·50	1	2·75
Germania, at Kiel ...	1	2	1	2·75
Blohm and Voss, at Hamburg	4	3·50	2	2·75
Vulkan, at Hamburg. Not yet ready for building.				
Weser, at Bremen ...	2	2·50	2	2·75
Imperial, at Wilhelmshaven	1	2·75	1	2·75
Total	16	2·75	12	2·75 [sic]

The above, therefore, gives us a total of twelve ships capable of being constructed in 2·75 years, but it would be well to realize that it is highly improbable that this output could be kept up indefinitely, on account of the congestion that must arise in the various yards owing to the lack of suitable wharfage for the completion of such deep-draught ships after they are launched.

Also, if ships were to be built at such a rate, Krupp must increase his works, or, which is more probable, the Government must start their own. At present, according to a statement made to me by M. Eccius, one of the Directors, they can turn out thirty-six 28-centim. guns every nine months, but this is working at fever heat, and leaving undone all work for foreign nations.

We may therefore take, I think, thirty-two per year, or eighty-eight in 2·75 years, as the more probable output until the works are increased, and this I compute limits the tale of construction of ships to something like seven or eight per every 2·75 years.

In this connection it is interesting to note that Messrs. Krupp do not obtain the whole of their ore locally. So far from that, indeed, is the truth that 1,200 tons of steel per day are made at Rheinhausen from ore imported from Bilbao and Sweden to Rotterdam, and brought up the river in especial barges of 1,700 tons capacity, and this importation, ships, mines, and lighters, all belonging to the firm, should automatically stop in time of war.

Moreover, Essen and Rheinhausen, lying on or close to the Rhine, and being about 85 miles only from the French frontier, are almost threatened in case of war, and certainly not in so safe a position as could be desired.

I have ventured to point this out, as a second manufactory in the country would materially alter the feeling of safety of the German Government, and seeing the enormous profits (860,000l. last year) made by the firm, it is almost incredible that the Imperial Government should not shortly set up a second manufactory of its own.

Now, according to the programme, as approved in the Fleet Bill of 1900, two battle-ships and an armoured cruiser must be laid down each year, and completed within a period of three years.

But, owing to the delays of the past year, they must now, if the programme is to be kept to, either build the ships approved last April in two years, which is wholly unlikely, or in the autumn of 1909 they will have eight battle-ships and four large cruisers under simultaneous construction, which, it seems to me, will temporarily exhaust the capacity for construction of Germany. We may therefore acknowledge, I think, that an increase over the present number of ships is not likely to occur.

Also, in the course of conversation with Admirals Tirpitz and Büchsel and various other officers, I have elicited more than once that it is considered that the British fleet bears to that of Germany a ratio of four to one.

Any such calculation must, however, be so empirical that I do not wish to press this point beyond calling attention to what a preponderance our fleet has, in the eyes of the highest and most responsible German officers, over their own.

Again, should Germany go to war with us, it would indubitably be a great advantage for her to hold the Belts and Sound and so the approaches to the Baltic, and this I have been told, on good authority, she proposes to do by deflecting 350,000 men to overrun and hold Denmark. Of late there have been rumours, which I confess I feel myself have probably some justification in fact, though I cannot lay a finger on a cause, that Germany has come to some sort of an agreement with Denmark whereby this penetration may be peacefully accomplished and a large number of this army saved.

If it is not so, however, with this army tied up in one direction, and a possible second army, of a greater number still, deflected to hold the Russian frontier and preserve the peace in Poland, it might happen that the German forces would be found to be in an actual minority as against those of France, and here is a second and most potential reason for not disturbing the present state of peace. As regards the above, I must apologize for introducing military matters, but they are so germane to my whole argument that I cannot well leave them out.

Again, the whole of the imports and exports of Germany in 1904 was 637,000,000*l*., and of this sum no less than 129,000,000*l*. was trade with England or her Colonies. That with England herself amounted to 69,000,000*l*.

Now, all this must practically stop in time of war—firstly, because it is simplicity itself to close the trade of the rivers, and, secondly, because, of the whole trade, 83 per cent. was carried in English or German ships.

Lastly, the number and value of the German mercantile marine was, in round numbers, 4,224 vessels, of 2,352,000 tons, and costing some 35,000,000*l*. Of this, at least a quarter must always be afloat, and it would be strange indeed if less than a half of this, or a value of 4,400,000*l*. considered at its replacement value, was not immediately captured, while the whole of the remainder must be sold at a considerable, or interned at a total temporary, loss.

I have dealt with all the above at great length, but I think I have pointed out various good reasons why Germany would not go to war without the strongest extraneous motives. Of course, there are numerous possible causes for war, but these lie within the region of high politics, and, as such, are not within my province to consider.

It would, however, be foolish not to recognize that there is a feeling afield that war might suddenly break out; so, without hazarding a guess as to the reasons, I will now go on to consider the steps which it is permissible to deduce that the German fleet propose to take at the outset.

And I must also premise that—to me, at all events—all their fleet manœuvres of the past two years plainly point out England as the expected enemy.

And, moreover, in all their manœuvres one portion of their fleet, plainly stated in the local papers of Hamburg, Kiel and Cuxhaven to be representing the navy of Germany, has at once assumed the defensive off the mouth of the Elbe; and, further, in each case the fleet representing Germany has made a forced and rapid passage of the Kiel Canal.

We may therefore, I think, fairly deduce the following :—

1. That the Germans expect the mouth of the Elbe to be attacked without warning by the forces of England or France.
2. By the coming through the canal they expect to have to assume the defensive from the outset. Now, on one occasion, at least, of these manœuvres, while the battle fleet has gone through the canal, the outlooking or cruiser squadron has gone round the Skaw. Also at the present moment the said squadron is carrying out manœuvres connected with the idea of searching for and clearing the Belts, &c., of torpedo craft.
3. This shows that they expect a portion of our torpedo craft division to take them in the flank in the Baltic. As far as possible of late the h.s. torpedo-boats have been attached to the battle-ships for manœuvres.
4. This again indicates a defensive condition of the battle-ships with possible counter-attacks of their own h.s. torpedo-boats on the blockading fleet or the destroyers of the enemy. The smaller torpedo-boats have been variously used as a defensive or an offensive force left behind in Kiel or Cuxhaven, as a mine-laying division or a mine-seeking division. In war time also I believe that these would be their various rôles, and they therefore indicate—
5. Some such attack as that spoken of at 3.
6. The general system of defence of the Kiel Canal protected by counter-attacks.
7. That they expect us to attempt to block the mouths of the Elbe, Jade, and Weser with mines.

Of course, numerous other deductions might be made, but at present all I want to arrive at is the condition of affairs we might expect to find at the commencement of such a war, and these are, I believe, as follows :—

(a) The battle fleet at or off the mouth of the Elbe.

(b) The cruiser squadron between the Belts and the Skaw.

(c) The mouths of the Elbe, Weser, Jade, Ems, and Kiel Harbour closed with mines.

(d) An attempt to temporarily mine the Belts and Sound at their narrowest portions.

(e) The coast defence iron-clads cruising as a fleet in the Baltic, probably off Fehmarn.

(f) The h.s. torpedo-boats with the battle fleet and a portion thrown forward, probably as far as Borkum.

(g) The mine-seeking division at Cuxhaven.

(h) The remainder of the torpedo-boats divided between the Baltic (in the Belts and off the Sound) and Brunsbüttel.

(j) The Brunsbüttel end of the canal closed with a treble series of booms.

Now all this is, it seems to me, based on the belief that it is the principal metier of our fleet to take the mouth of the Elbe and so hold Hamburg, the commercial soul of Germany. This, however, I believe to be utterly wrong, both in tactics and strategy, at the beginning of a war. Before such a close blockade is carried out the main body of the German fleet should have been badly shaken, if not destroyed, and certainly the majority of the German torpedo-boats put *hors de combat*. This, in view of the lack of torpedo-nets in the German ships and our immense superiority in torpedo-craft, should be done by means of those vessels, while our battle fleet should await the advance of that of Germany.

It is true that Hamburg lives on sea-borne trade, but that trade must come to it from one of two inlets, which are the Elbe and or by Lübeck; further, the approaches to the Elbe and Lübeck are the Straits of Dover on the one hand and the Skagerrack on the other, also for both the passage north of Scotland; and the same remark holds good, I submit, with regard to the Rhine, the Ems, Weser, Oder, and Vistula; and all the great German towns situated thereon, with the traffic in the Straits and the Skagerrack stopped, would immediately begin to feel the pinch of poverty and consequent starvation wages.

It is therefore plain, I think, that the blockade of these rivers should take place from a position so far distant that the blockading vessels may carry out their work in peace and safety.

In this connection, however, the following very difficult point arises as to the Rhine :—

The mouths of this great river lie in Belgium and Dutch territory, and by international law, as interpreted in England, the flag covering the cargo, even if its ulterior destination is one of the belligerents, cargo, if carried in Dutch or any other non-belligerent ships, could be unloaded as usual in Rotterdam or Antwerp and transported in barges up the Rhine, or the opposite could occur.

Consequently in time of war, provided that shipping can be engaged for the purpose, it is practically possible, that the Southern German and Westphalian trade should suffer no diminution whatever—indeed, in view of the fact that the actual German ports would be closed, it would probably show an increase.

Moreover, such an increase of prosperity must accrue, if I am correct, to Holland and Belgium that they would be likely to strain every nerve to facilitate the passage of trade, and, what is more important, it is to Germany's great interest to preserve their neutrality to enable them to do so.

Now, in a broad sense, England possesses so little chance of striking at Germany except through her commerce that the above condition of affairs would presently,

I believe, prove intolerable, and it becomes a serious question for us to consider how far in time of war we could afford to recognize such a very, in this case, one-sided international law.

A still further point to consider is that, despite a war, our own shipping would—indeed, almost must—be employed in this extra trade of these two great towns, and unless this law be more clearly defined, we might see the ludicrous spectacle of English shipping enabling Germany to continue fighting against England, and actually enriching a portion of the country in doing so.

Again, if we were to stop such trade, as we easily could, it would result in throwing·Holland into Germany's arms—the very last thing we wish to do.

I must, however, leave this question to be settled by others, and return to the question of the employment of the fleets.

I have produced, so far, the whole of the German battle fleet at or off Cuxhaven, and the main object of our own forces would now, I presume, be to lure them into more open waters. This, however, in view of the overwhelming numbers that we could oppose, is by no means likely, until or unless a growing poverty in Germany forced on action.

It may therefore be again stated as axiomatic that our first move must be to stop their trade.

Should their fleet then emerge, I am of opinion that lack of practice in what we know as battle tactics should give us a decided advantage at the commencement, in so far as we could, from our previous experience and greater speed, make our approach from the best direction with regard to sun and wind.

Moreover, such information as I have been able to gather leads me to suppose that on the whole our firing is more accurate than theirs, and, seeing that our ships are better supplied with the heaviest guns than those of Germany, we should therefore gain by opening fire at long ranges.

I am further of opinion that every effort should be directed against the ship bearing the flag of the German Commander-in-chief, as it is a continual source of grumbling, of which I have had personal experience, and again quite lately, on the part of the junior flag officers, that their seniors give them little or no chance of exercising their individuality in the handling of the whole or even a portion of the fleet, and if this is so a sudden change in the direction of affairs to a more or less inexperienced Admiral must result in a benefit to ourselves.

It should be recollected that the cruiser squadrons of Germany have constant practice in reconnoitring, and therefore it is likely that they will have at least as early information of our approach as we should have of their having emerged into open water.

In their manœuvres the practice of the torpedo-boats breaking through the line has frequently been exercised, and this is a point therefore which must be guarded against—best, I venture to surmise, by preserving a long range, though then it must also be borne in mind that battles, to be turned into decisive victories, must almost certainly be concluded at comparatively short ranges.

As regards torpedoes, I was once told that practice at sea at greater ranges than 2,000 metres was not considered practical. This I have had confirmed, and, generally speaking, that may be looked upon as the maximum range to expect.

From a conversation I once had, I do not believe that German officers have grasped the possibility of rapid loading and firing with torpedoes from submerged tubes.

It should be remembered that all modern German battle-ships have six submerged tubes, ahead, astern, and four on the broadside, which latter are fixed, I believe, at 17 degrees before the beam as regards the forward, and on the beam as regards the after ones, but my information on this point is not certain.

I now propose to turn to the torpedo-boat flotillas.

These consist, broadly speaking, of 56 large boats, with speeds of 24 to 28 knots, say, an average sea-going speed of 25 knots; 22 boats of 130 to 170 tons, with speed of about 23 knots; 25 boats, old, used for mine-laying, searching, and harbour protection generally.

With all these duties to perform, and allowing for the usual percentage of boats laid up and broken down, which is I am sure at least as great in Germany as with us, we find that the actual body of torpedo-boats for outlying use would amount to some seventy at a maximum.

This of course is a large number, but in view of the much greater number—some 150—we could bring against them, there is nothing to be greatly feared, and I believe by careful organization we should be able to contain them from the outset.

Against this the German boats are continually at work, and officers and men alike know their boats thoroughly, and are said to handle them well.

I·may say, however, that my own very short experience leads me to doubt that they are so very perfect. This statement I base on my observation of their station-keeping, which is poor, and the comparatively large number of accidents of a preventable type which occur during the manœuvres.

Judging by the results of their manœuvres in September last, when after three days the whole of the boats were considered as *hors de combat* and had to be resuscitated, they must be handled in the most foolhardy way in such exercises. Indeed, one reads of broad daylight frontal attacks, and so on, and though these may be very daring and impressive, they are not so as showing a careful appreciation of the value of such an arm, and must to some extent be discounted in consequence.

It is noteworthy that a division of boats frequently goes out for three or four days' manœuvres in the North Sea. This I fancy must be an exercise such as the possible descent on Harwich, the Medway, or the destruction of the Forth Bridge, and steps should be taken to guard against such a surprise attack at the opening of a war.

In view of the large stowage of mines provided for the two mining vessels "Nautilus" and "B," and their great speed, I imagine that these ships would accompany such a raid in war time, when if skillfully handled they might cause us an immense amount of annoyance.

Such a raid would probably start from Embden [*sic.* Emden] or Borkum, behind which there is a good sheltered anchorage for small craft, while they could complete with coal or water alongside at Embden itself.

Under any circumstances, one of our first duties in the case of such a war would be to block this channel leading to Embden, and, if possible, land a party on Borkum to destroy the signal station.

A sufficient body to hold Borkum would be rather of an undertaking, and not, perhaps, to be carried out in the earliest days of a war.

But another adjacent point of enormous value, which must be raided and destroyed is the wireless telegraphy tower lately put up at Norddeich, just opposite Borkum. This is the outlying station for communication over the whole North Sea, and passes on information to those at Heligoland, Cuxhaven, Wilhelmshaven, Kiel, and even to Nauen, close to Berlin. It should therefore be destroyed at all hazards.

As regards raids from Germany on England, one of which would certainly start from this point, I have lately written at considerable length. As therein stated I believe such a raid to be possible though not probable, but under any circumstances, with a cruiser squadron in the vicinity, the arc of search is not great, and so its departure should be rapidly discovered and reported.

In this connection it is noteworthy that a belief exists in Germany that we are making arrangements to raid their coasts in time of war, and how strong is that belief is shown by their doubling the Schleswig-Holstein coast lines last year, avowedly on account of such a landing.

Personally I am of opinion that the threat of a landing would have a greater effect than a landing itself, and a well convoyed body of large and swift merchantmen (there need be no troops in them) should keep the whole of the northern coast of Germany in a perpetual ferment, so long as they appeared at different points of the northern districts, and, moreover, lock up large bodies of troops in that portion of the country.

If, as I believe, it is true that Germany proposes to overrun and seize Denmark in time of war with us, then we have before us the real battle-ground, if we should decide to make use of our own land forces, and, so soon as the first sea engagement is happily ended, this country must be the objective of any expeditionary force we may embark.

As regards the mouths of the Elbe, Weser, and the Jade, the defences both of mines and forts are very formidable indeed. Should, however, a portion of a battle fleet once pass Kugelbake Point at Cuxhaven one-half of the forts can be taken in rear, while the water is too shallow for it to matter much if a ship should be sunk.

It is a matter of interest that the signal station at Cuxhaven is the information collecting bureau for the German sea power, and as such every effort should be made to destroy it. This might be accomplished by landing a small party to the westward of Dünen and marching across country to come on it from the rear, when one or two charges or specially-prepared bombs should suffice to disorganize if not destroy it.

Of course there is every inducement for us to make torpedo-boat attacks on vessels lying in or off Cuxhaven. Equally, of course, the risks would be very great, but in view of the fact that this is the expected condition of affairs in such an attack, and that German war-vessels have no torpedo-nets, nothing could excuse us, in my opinion, from making these as frequently, as early, and as determinedly, as possible. It is worth while noting that there is undoubtedly a passage to the north of the Medem Sands—not marked on the charts—probably where the deep-water passage existed some thirty to forty years ago. I believe, from accounts of torpedo-boat attacks published in the papers, moreover, that this passage is straight and simple to navigate without leading lights or other help.

As regards Wilhelmshaven, except for small craft, I do not think it will be made use of at all in time of war. It must be remembered that the water is very shallow, and heavy ships can only get in and out from the dockyard, I am told, for about an hour or two on either side of high water.

It might possibly be worth while to organize a torpedo-boat attack on one or more of the basin-entrances, thus greatly disorganizing the whole of the yard, and possibly wrecking shipping lying inside, but any such attack would run tremendous risks of the loss of the boats before they even got there; while, on arrival, they must pass through the mine-fields and run the gauntlet of many well-armed forts.

At Geestemünde, the defences of which are not of superlative strength, much damage might be done to the harbour works and the shipping therein by the destruction of the lock-gates. It is stated that the harbour is defended by mines and torpedo batteries, but the damage (commercially) caused by low water in the basins would be enormous, and the idea is worth consideration. At this place also is a wireless telegraph station. It is not perhaps of great value, but should of course be destroyed if opportunity should occur.

Heligoland, which is just about to be rearmed, is, like all fortresses, a source of weakness to the enemy so long as it is not attacked. It provides, it is true, some shelter for shipping, but it is off the direct track to the Elbe, and can, in fact, be left alone with a considerable body of men locked up in it. Under any circumstances it would be of but little value to us in the early days of a war, and, considering that it will shortly be really well armed, the taking of it would certainly cause us much loss. Consequently I would prefer to leave it alone, when its principal menace would be that it is a very valuable signal station of the enemy.

Except for a very hazardous torpedo-boat attack on the mouth of the Kiel Canal at Brunsbüttel, I am not of opinion that we could harm this great work except by carefully organized treachery, or until we have cleared the Baltic of torpedo-craft. It is just possible that a submarine boat might reach the entrance by night, but the mine-field would provide an almost certain destruction for the boat, and, even if she did get there, I believe there is a triple boom defence of baulks of timber and torpedo nets.

The passing of a fleet into the Baltic would have to be preceded by a most careful search of the Belts and a clearance of the passage against mines.

Once inside, a large fleet, which should I believe be again accompanied by a genuine or bogus expeditionary flotilla, to trouble the Baltic coasts of Germany, should I think be able to silence the forts outside Kiel. (The German battle fleet, consisting of some ten vessels, was considered to have achieved this in the last August manœuvres). This done, or even partly done, should enable the same fleet to destroy the mouth, and ruin the value of the Kiel Canal at Friedrichsort.

Such an accomplishment would probably prove the end of the war, and is, in my opinion, the ultimate aim of a sea fight with the German Empire.

Under any circumstances the loss to Germany that would occur from the destruction of the establishments at Kiel would be enormous, and, with the canal blocked, irreparable. Kiel is further, it should be remembered, the largest actual seaport town that Germany possesses.

Materiel.

Although I have dealt with this in a broad sense in an earlier portion of this letter, I should like to remark further that I believe that the ships are generally well found and sufficient.

As regards steaming power, as far as one can judge, practice in full speed runs is not carried out to anything like so great an extent as with us. This exercise is so important that we must thereby gain a very great advantage.

Fleet drills are also rather discountenanced among the Germans, and although these need not necessarily possess much fighting value, yet they undoubtedly serve to make the fittings everywhere work more easily, and the men more reliable and quick-witted in an emergency.

As regards the provision of stores, it is probable that the quantity is all that can be desired; but whether the facilities for obtaining them, in the absence, so far as I know, of special trials, are so good is I think very doubtful.

Coaling stores are plentiful, existing at Pillau, Danzig, Stettin, Kiel, Friedrichsort, Brunsbüttel, Cuxhaven, Bremerhaven, and Wilhelmshaven, and each contains some 20,000 tons. There are also many others for torpedo-boats. Arrangements for the rapid taking in of fuel also seem to be well thought out, and every mechanical help supplied.

Whether these have been tried under war conditions I take leave to doubt, as that is where the German character fails, and in this I mean to point out that in the delight and interest of elucidating the multitude of details the end is frequently forgotten.

As regards the replenishing of ammunition my information is meagre. So far as I know, this can only be done at Danzig, Kiel, and Wilhelmshaven; but especial stores are now being built at Cuxhaven, and in any case the distances from these centres are short.

Hospital arrangements are, I believe, exceedingly good, but again I have not heard of their trial under war conditions.

Personnel.

As a whole the personnel of the German navy is, I believe, very good indeed, specially under peace conditions—that is, officers and men alike are sober, hard-working, industrious, and zealous, and, moreover, well-drilled, educated, and trained.

Against this, owing to the system of education which is universally pursued in Germany, every one is taught to be a servant and no one a master.

This is to be seen everywhere, and old servants making bad masters, the officers are anything but popular with the men, and the same feeling obtains, which is sad, from the lowest to the highest among the officers themselves.

Thus a change of command during a fight would I believe have more effect in a German ship than with us.

There can be no doubt also that there exists among German officers a state of nerves which is practically unknown with us. I should hardly call it nervous, but they are strung up to that pitch which induces, in the moments when the greatest *sang-froid* is required, a state of ill-balanced excitement which cannot fail to be detrimental to success.

I must confess that I have seen but little of this myself, but I have been so frequently told by German officers' wives, who deplore that fact, that I cannot but believe that it is true, and certainly, from six months of inquiries that I have cautiously made, the evidence is always the same and overwhelming.

As regards the men, from my small amount of information, they would appear to be hardworking, efficient, and good.

In view, however, of the comparatively small number who are long-service men, and the reasonable supposition that, man for man, they show no greater capacity for technical learning than a similar class of Englishmen, I do not see on what grounds it can be considered that the crew of a German ship is likely to be so good as that of an English one.

If we further take into account the splendid and inspiriting records of the British Navy as against those of the German, which are practically speaking nil, it would be folly not to recognize that our personnel is likely to do better in war time than that of the Imperial German Navy.

In conclusion, I wish to acknowledge that I may be said to have depreciated a possible enemy.

Against that charge I can only state that for some time now I have been interested in the German character, and my year's residence in the country has constantly tended to convince me that I had judged it rightly, and it is through that character, or rather lack of stability of character, that the German should, or might, be beaten.

Broadly speaking, the German has enormous organizing powers, where they can be imitative, but he has little originality, powers of initiation, or independent thought. Also while things go well, and in a line to which he is accustomed, he is a very able and energetic man, but under failure, great stress or strain, I doubt his staying power, or the faculty to rapidly reorganize afresh.

Finally, it is clear to the poorest observer that the martial or military spirit is passing from the mass of the nation; and whereas in earlier days, though unable to lead, he rather desired to be led, now he wants to be able to pursue his trade in peace, and to that end is beginning to make his voice heard in the public press.

If this be allowed to develop (and the present great prosperity, the Social Democratic propaganda, and the desire for luxury provided by universal education, is helping it forward by leaps and bounds), the Germans will not, I think, be found a nation to fear in twenty years' time.

I would like to finish, as I began, by apologizing for the dogmatic tendency of some of my remarks, especially as regards character. My only excuse is that I do not believe that these facts are generally recognized, and that they should, I submit, be taken into account in devising a campaign against this country.

I have, &c.

PHILIP DUMAS,
Captain and Naval Attaché.

APPENDIX III.

Memorandum by Sir Edward Grey.([1])

Memorandum given to the King by Sir E. Grey for his guidance at interview at Cronberg.

Count Metternich has recently been speaking in very gloomy terms to several people about the lack of good feeling between England and Germany.

In a conversation which Mr. Lloyd-George and Sir Edward Grey had with him informally at luncheon a few days ago, it was urged upon him that the sure way to improve feeling between the two countries would be to come to some arrangement by which the increase of Naval expenditure could be averted.

If the Germans continue to execute their Naval programme at a rapid speed, we shall certainly have to ask Parliament to vote a considerable increase to our expenditure : no Government of either party could avoid doing so. The justification and necessity for this increase, which would have to be openly avowed, would be the German expenditure. We have to take into account not only the German Navy, but also the German Army. If the German Fleet ever becomes superior to ours, the German Army can conquer this country. There is no corresponding risk of this kind to Germany : for however superior our Fleet was, no Naval victory would bring us any nearer to Berlin.

It is certain that if we have to propose a greater Naval expenditure next year the effect on the Press here and on public feeling in both England and Germany will be adverse to good relations.

If, on the other hand, the Germans are willing to arrest the increase of their Naval expenditure, we should do the same. There need not even be any formal agreement between the two countries. If we could announce in Parliament that, as a matter of fact, German shipbuilding was not proceeding at a rate which required any increased expenditure on our part, the result would be to allay the apprehensions of those numerous persons, both in England and in Germany, who credit the other country with hostile intentions; and feeling generally would improve.

If it could be shown that, as a result of the interview between the two Sovereigns, a slackening of activity in the building programmes of the two Navies had ensued, there is no doubt that the state of unrest prevailing in Europe due to apprehensions in England and Germany would be greatly appeased, and this would be of more value to the peace of the world than any Entente based on the settlement of territorial or commercial questions. Were such a happy result to be attained, the King and the Emperor would be rightly hailed together as the Peacemakers of Europe.

It would be natural that the King should pay an official visit to Berlin next year. It is believed that the Emperor would like it, and it is not a thing to which His Majesty's Government would desire to offer any objection. On the contrary, it is a step which they would welcome, and which under favourable conditions might have a beneficial effect upon the relations between the two countries. But we cannot but feel that such a visit might be coldly received by public opinion here, if at the time heavy Naval expenditure was being forced upon us by the extent to which German shipbuilding was being carried. Possibly, objection might be taken to the visit, on the ground that it would appear to imply that the competition in shipbuilding was a matter of indifference to the good relations of the two countries : an impression which would be the direct contrary to the fact.

31st July, 1908.

([1]) [Hardinge MSS., Vol. IV of 1908. A duplicate of the memorandum was given to Sir C. Hardinge by Sir E. Grey.]

APPENDIX IV.

The Marquess of Salisbury to Mr. E. B. Iwan-Muller.([1])   *August 31, 1896.*
(Communicated to Sir C. Hardinge by Mr. Iwan-Muller, September 29, 1908.)

Confidential.   *Walmer Castle, Deal.*

. . . .([2]) I feel I ought not to decline the opening you have given me, but I am afraid I shall fail to tell you anything you do not know very well already.

There is no such thing as a fixed policy, because policy like all organic entities is always in the making. I do not know that I can sum up the present trend of English policy better than by saying we are engaged in slowly escaping from the dangerous errors of 1846–1856. Palmerston was a disciple of Canning, and with him believed that foreign policy should follow your political proclivities. France was Liberal, Russia and Austria despotic,—therefore, in his mind, it was our policy to shake off the Russian and Austrian alliance and cultivate that of France. Such a policy is obviously unsound,—similarity of political faith is no more indicative of a useful ally than similarity of religious faith would be.

Politics is a matter of business : our allies should be those who are most likely to help or not to hinder the interests of which we, as a Government, are the trustees. Now the interests of France clashed with ours on almost every coast; those of Russia only on the Afghan-Perso frontier, those of Austria nowhere. Therefore it was our policy to maintain the friendship with Russia and Austria which had existed during the first half of this century, and by its help to keep France within bounds.

· But Palmerston would be guided by common sympathies instead of by common interests. He made war with Russia; he insulted Austria; and he ostentatiously made friends with France. In order to baulk and baffle Russia he, and his school, set up as a political faith the independence and integrity of the Ottoman Empire.

Forty years have passed away, and look at the results. We have not kept France,—she is more our enemy than ever. But the feud with Russia remains. Austria has become of less importance, because out of the fragments of her dominions or her followings Germany and Italy have been created; and we have to find in the nominal alliance of these two last what consolation we can for the necessity of coping, practically alone, with the alliance of France and Russia. If we had only listened to the Emperor Nicholas when he spoke to Sir Hamilton Seymour, what a much pleasanter outlook would meet us when we contemplate the continent of Europe.

It is much easier to lament than to repair. It may not be possible for England and Russia to return to their old relations. But it is an object to be wished for and approached as opportunity offers. At all events efforts should be made to avoid needless aggravation of the feud between them which Governments and not the nations have made. The French and German *people* both hate us; the Russian people do not. It is not possible to stop the impulse which past mistakes have given. The generation whose political beliefs were moulded by the passions of the Crimean war is only now dying out. We may, without any fault of our own, find ourselves opposed to Russia on this question or that, in consequence of past commitments. All we can do is to try to narrow the chasm that separates us. It is the best chance for something like an equilibrium of Europe.

There is no reason why Germany, under steady guidance, should not go with us, but steadiness is not the note of its Government just now.

Ever yours very truly,
SALISBURY.

([1]) [Hardinge MSS., Vol. **II** of 1908.]   ([2]) [Thus in original.]

[*ED. NOTE.*—The Editors think that Lord Salisbury's views of Canning and Palmerston are based on tradition and might have been modified in the light of modern research. Canning was only a " liberal " and " constitutionalist " when that course accorded with British interests. Thus in 1827 he was allied with despotic Russia, as well as with constitutional France, and he

APPENDIX V.

[*ED. NOTE.*—The following extract from the Minutes of the Committee of Imperial Defence contains the address by Sir Edward Grey at the meeting of May 26, 1911, to which the Dominion delegates to the Imperial Conference were invited. Sir Edward Grey was invited by the Prime Minister " to preface its deliberations by an exposition. comprehensive and strictly confidential, of the international situation." (*v.* H. H. Asquith: *The Genesis of the War* (1923), p. 121.) Portions of the speech were printed in *The Genesis of the War*, pp. 121–7, and these passages are here enclosed within square brackets. The full text is now given, except a few passages of which the general tenour is indicated. Lord Grey, to whom the speech has been submitted, has informed the Editors that he himself never revised the proof at the time. He has therefore corrected a few errors of grammar and punctuation and added the two explanatory footnotes on pp. 786 and 788 which are marked with his name.]

Extract from Minutes of the Committee of Imperial Defence at a Meeting of May 26, 1911.

FOREIGN POLICY.

SIR E. GREY: [The starting point, I imagine, of the consultation which we are now going to have on Foreign Policy and the foreign situation, is really the creation and growing strength of separate Fleets and Forces in the Dominions, of which the Prime Minister has just given some account. It is possible to have separate Fleets in a united Empire, but it is not possible to have separate Fleets in a united Empire without having a common Foreign Policy which shall determine the action of the different Forces maintained in different parts of the Empire. If the action of the Forces in different parts of the Empire is determined by divergent views of Foreign Policy, it is obvious that there cannot be union, and that the Empire would not consent to share an unlimited liability the risks of which it cannot gauge, because this liability would be imposed upon it by different parts of the Empire having different policies. Therefore, the first point I want to make is this, that the creation of separate Fleets has made it essential that the Foreign Policy of the Empire should be a common policy. If it is to be a common policy, it is obviously one on which the Dominions must be taken into consultation, which they must know, which they must understand, and which they must approve; and it is in the hope and belief that the Foreign Policy of this country does command the assent and the approval, and is so reasonable that it must command the assent and approval of the Dominions, that we wish to have a consultation, and I wish to explain, as fully as I can, the present situation of Foreign Affairs], and what our views and prospects are. [That is much better done at the Committee of Imperial Defence than at the Conference itself, first of all because there must be absolute secrecy. For two reasons there must be absolute secrecy: our Foreign Policy really is anything but a Machiavellian one; it is most simple and straightforward, as I hope will appear in the course of what I have to say; but at the same time you cannot show the whole of your hand openly to the rest of the world, which is not showing its hand to you. That is one reason for having it absolutely secret. In the next place, you cannot deal with the Foreign Policy of this country without also discussing somewhat freely your opinion of the Foreign Policy and views of other countries, and they even more dislike having their Foreign Policy canvassed in public than we ourselves do.] So for those two reasons there must be absolute secrecy; and in the next place, it is appropriate to have

[Margin note: The creation of separate Dominion Navies necessitates a common Foreign Policy for the Empire.]

[Margin note: Necessity for secrecy.]

---

seems to have preferred the first to the second. His policy was not therefore " to follow your political proclivities." This remark would be truer, and yet not wholly true, of Palmerston. He was certainly not always " liberal " to small States like Greece, Servia or Japan, and he inherited, and did not invent, the dogma of the integrity of the Ottoman Empire. He was anti-French before 1846, and after 1859. These facts should not, of course, be held to derogate from Lord Salisbury's opinions.]

it at the Committee of Defence, because [I shall try to bring out—especially with regard to our European policy—that what really determines the Foreign Policy of this country is the question of sea power. It is the Naval question which underlies the whole of our European Foreign Policy, and more than the European Foreign Policy; but I will deal with the Foreign Policy in Europe first, and try to bring out that point.] Of course it is difficult to deal with Foreign Policy as a whole. It is not like something which can be put into a Bill, or even expressed in a Resolution. It must necessarily be rather vague, but I will try and make it as definite as I can. To explain what the present situation is as between ourselves and other Powers in Europe, I think I must go back a little into history, because we cannot understand the present situation without knowing how we came to arrive at it. I must go back rather an alarming way to the time when I first became Under-Secretary at the Foreign Office in 1892; but though it sounds rather alarming to go back as far as that, it will not take very long to explain what the situation was then, and then to jump from that to the present moment. In 1892 the situation then, and for some years previously, had been this: that the two restless Powers in Europe were France and Russia; that is, they were the two Powers from whom trouble to the peace of Europe was expected, if at all. The solid quiet group in Europe at that time was the Triple Alliance of Germany, Austria, and Italy. It had been the policy of Lord Salisbury before 1892, and it was the policy of Mr. Gladstone's Government of 1892, not to join the Triple Alliance or come under definite commitment to it, but generally in diplomacy to side with the Triple Alliance as being the stable Power in Europe, and the one which was securing the peace. Therefore, because the Triple Alliance was the stable Power while France and Russia were supposed to be the restless Powers, which might trouble the peace, the weight of British influence and diplomacy was thrown, when required, quietly and unostentatiously, and not aggressively, but decidedly into the scale on the side of the Triple Alliance. Soon after 1892 the situation began slowly to change. It was never, perhaps, a very agreeable situation. During the whole of that time we were not by any means on the best of terms with Germany. We were constantly having —though we were siding with the Triple Alliance—friction about African questions— friction about questions in China, but the situation was not in the least alarming —there was no question of a breach of the peace, or the rupture of diplomatic relations—but there was constant friction. It was not very comfortable, even so far as Germany was concerned; but as regards Russia and France, the situation was very much worse. The diplomatic atmosphere between ourselves and Russia and France in those years was such that the least incident in any part of the world, whether the Russian seizure of Port Arthur, the Russian action on the Pamirs on the Indian frontier, or French action in Siam—the least incident of that kind—at once excited the press of both countries, and there were rumours of wars more than once. I know it was thought at one time that we were on the verge of war with France over Siam; for instance in 1893—I do not think it was ever really true, but it was bad enough that it should ever be thought so, and everybody knows the scares there were of war with Russia from time to time. We wanted peace. We did not want that sort of thing to go on, and the late Government, I imagine —I was not of course a member of it—got tired of the situation, and said, "Now after all, what are these troubles with France? Egypt is an old story; Siam really not a matter which two great nations ought to quarrel about—all these things between us and France surely are things which, if the diplomatic atmosphere could be made better, would cause no trouble really to the Governments of the two countries."

After discussions lasting a long time, the result was the Anglo-French Agreement of 1904. This agreement at once removed all risk of a quarrel between the United Kingdom and France, and by removing that, brought the two nations very rapidly to realise that there were no causes of quarrel which ought to divide them, and that there was no reason why they should not be the best of friends. So far, again, that was all to the good. Then, since we have been in office, after the bitterness of the Russo-Japanese war had disappeared, the same policy was pursued with Russia. I do not really think that Russia ever had designs on the Indian frontier for the invasion of India. Some military people in Russia may have had their private opinion about that, but I do not believe the Russian Government ever seriously had designs for invading India. But in any case it was thought that she had. After the Russo-Japanese war it became possible to talk over some of those questions with Russia, especially the question of Persia, which I will come to later on, and both countries convinced themselves, we, that Russia would cease to prosecute railways and so forth towards the Indian frontier, which might be disturbing to us; while she became convinced that we would not undermine her position in the north of Persia, and would not work against her in diplomatic matters in Europe. So that cause of quarrel disappeared, and, consequently, we and Russia have now become very good friends in diplomacy. That was all to the good. But nothing in these affairs is entirely to the good. As our relations with Russia and France improved, it became apparent that our relations with Russia and France were better than our relations with Germany were. The press, both in Germany and here, began to pay more attention to the differences between Germany and us. I think there was considerable jealousy in public circles in Germany that we should have put ourselves on such good relations with Russia and France. Germany could never profit by any difference between us and them, as she had undoubtedly done in previous years, and the result was generally that the diplomatic atmosphere as regards Germany was not so good as it was before. At the present moment the German and British Governments are not having difficulties with each other. The questions which we have to discuss we discuss frankly, and the difficulties are not between the two Governments. [We are most anxious to keep on the best of terms with Germany. I believe she is also genuinely anxious to be on good terms with us, and we smooth over the matters which arise between us without difficulty.] There is, for instance, the question of war claims,—General Botha may be surprised to hear that Germany is still making claims upon us for compensation arising out of those unhappy days which have now passed so far away from us. Questions of that kind are going on, and the two Governments do smooth them over, [but we must make it a cardinal condition in all our negotiations with Germany that if we come to any understanding with Germany of a public kind which puts us on good relations with Germany it must be an understanding which must not put us back into the old bad relations with France and Russia. That means to say that if we publicly make friendship with Germany it must be a friendship in which we take our existing friends in Europe with us, and to which they become parties], so that if to the world at large it is demonstrated that it is quite clear there is as little chance of there being a disturbance of the peace between us and Germany as there is at the present moment of there being a disturbance of the peace between us and France, or us and Russia, [it must also be clear that, side by side with that, it will become equally apparent that there is no chance of a disturbance of the peace between Germany and France or Germany and Russia. That is what I mean by taking our friends with us into any new friendship into which which we may go.] Why I lay stress on that is this: [There is no danger, no appreciable danger, of our being involved in any considerable trouble in Europe, unless there is some Power, or group of Powers, in Europe which has the ambition of achieving what I would call the Napoleonic policy. That would be a policy on the part of the strongest Power in Europe, or of the strongest group of Powers in Europe, of first of all separating the other Powers outside their own group from each other, taking them in detail, crushing them singly if need be, and forcing each into the orbit of the policy of the strongest Power, or of the strongest group of Powers. Now, if any policy of that sort was pursued by any Power, it could only be pursued by the strongest Power, or the strongest group of Powers in Europe at the moment. The moment it was pursued, the moment the weakest Powers in Europe were assailed, either by diplomacy or by force, one by one they

Russia and India.

Improvement in relations with Russia.

Deterioration in relations with Germany.

Improvement in our relations with Germany must not be at the expense of others.

An attempt at European domination by a single Power or group the only serious danger of war.

would appeal to us to help them. I may say at once we are not committed by entanglements which tie our hands. Our hands are free, and I have nothing to disclose to our being bound by any alliances, which is not known to all the world at the present time. But I do feel this very strongly, that if such a situation should arise, and there was a risk of all the Powers, or a group of Powers, acquiring such a dominating position in Europe that on the Continent of Europe it would be the arbiter not only (of) peace and war, but of the diplomacy of all the other Powers of Europe, and if while that process was going on we were appealed to for help and sat by and looked on and did nothing, then people ought to realise that the result would be one great combination in Europe, outside which we should be left without a friend. If that was the result, then the naval situation would be this, that if we meant to keep the command of the sea we should have to estimate as a probable combination against us of fleets in Europe not two Powers but five Powers. Now, that is the situation, and that is why I say, though I do not think there is any prospect that one can reasonably see at the present moment of our being involved in serious trouble in Europe, it is possible that under such extreme conditions as I have named the question might arise as to whether we ought to take part by force in European affairs, and if we did it would be solely because Sea Power, and the necessity of keeping the command of the sea, was the underlying cause and motive of our action. So long as the maintenance of Sea Power and the maintenance and control of sea communication is the underlying motive of our policy in Europe, it is obvious how that is a common interest between us here at home and all the Dominions.] Each Representative of a Dominion here can very well work out for himself how, in the case of his own Dominion, problems would be altered if the command of the sea was lost and they were cut off from all communications with the world outside. It would be rather presumptuous for me to go into it in detail at all as regards each particular Dominion, because the Prime Ministers of the Governments of those Dominions can estimate the consequences so much better than I can. But I would just take, for instance, the case of South Africa. South Africa has a powerful neighbour in the German Colonies, but I believe the strength of South Africa is such that as long as the control of the sea is in the hands of the British Empire, whatever troubles might arise South Africa would be master of the situation in her own part of the world; but the problem would become a very different one for her if by a combination of European fleets the British fleet was defeated and the control of the sea communications passed into the hands of, we will say, Germany, or the group of Powers to which Germany belongs and Germany was in a position to pour into her colonies on either side of South Africa—into German East Africa and German South-West Africa—as much as she pleased of the greatest and most powerful army in the world. That of course is merely one instance. Then you come to Australia and New Zealand. I do not wish to be an alarmist as to what the consequences would be, or to say that if we lost the command of the sea any European Power would engage in an actual campaign of conquest, but the situation for them would be just as unpleasant as the Foreign Power, which had gained control of the sea, thought it worth while to make it. As regards British New Guinea and the islands outside New Zealand and Australia themselves, of course they could only be held at the will of the Power which had control of the sea. Obviously the communications with the rest of the world would depend upon the good-will of the Power which had the command of the sea. Canada, of course, I know, is in a special position, because in North America the sentiment and determination not only of Canada, but of the United States also is so strong against having any European interference under any circumstances on that side of the Atlantic or in the Pacific Ocean, that the consequences might be different. But still even there, there would be complete severance of the British connection; that connection could not possibly be maintained, and what the actual consequences would be politically as regards Canada, Sir Wilfrid Laurier and his Government can, of course, judge better than I. Certainly, if the control of the seas was lost, it

The consequence of non-intervention in such a case.

The maintenance of our Sea Power the basis of our Foreign Policy and a common Imperial interest.

Effect of its loss upon the Empire.

South Africa.

Australia and New Zealand.

Canada.

would not only be the end of the British Empire as far as we are concerned, but all the Dominions would be separated from us, never to be rejoined, because the control of the seas, once having passed to a Great European Power, would never be allowed to return again; and not only would the Dominions be parted from us, but they would also be separated entirely from one another. Believing, as I think we all do, that we have now arrived at a stage at which the development of the Dominions is to be increasingly quick and prosperous, it seems to me quite obvious that it is only by maintaining the control of the sea power that the free, unrestricted development of those Dominions, free from foreign aggression or foreign influence, can be maintained. And of this I can assure you that, as far as we are concerned *British policy non-aggressive.* in Europe, there will be no aggression on our part. If we are ever involved in trouble, it will not be for the sake of any ideas of aggrandisement or ambition, or any other vain, empty things of that kind. We do not need to pursue any policy of ambition in Europe. There is nothing that we want to attain there. If there is trouble in Europe in which we are engaged and in which we have to appeal to the Dominions, it will be solely because, if we do not take part in it, we shall see that the combination against us in Europe may be such that the command of the sea may be lost. As regards the European policy generally and the present situation, I can only say that we are on the best of terms with the Powers of France and Russia. With Austria our relations are quite good, though they are slight, *Relations with Austria.* because Austria's policy is limited to her own internal affairs and her own more immediate part of the world, so that we come little into contact with her; but the relations are quite good. Any cloud there may have been two or three years ago, when Austria annexed Bosnia and Herzegovina, has entirely passed away, and we have no trouble whatever with the Austrian Government at the present moment. With Italy our relations have always been exceedingly cordial, largely due to the *Italy.* sentiment which has always existed between the British people and the Italians, because of the great part that Great Britain played when Italy was struggling for freedom and unity—a feeling which still remains. As regards Germany, there was *Germany.* some little time ago some idea—not, I think, in the minds of the German Government, but in the mind of German public opinion—that our good relations with France and Russia were being formed with an intention of making an iron ring around Germany and bringing pressure to bear on her. Now, however, I really believe that that impression is passing away even from the minds of German public opinion, and [the cause of anxiety now in public opinion here as regards Germany arises entirely from the question of the German naval expenditure, which is very *German naval expenditure.* considerable, which may be increased, and which, if it is increased, will produce an impression on the world at large that the object of Germany is to build a fleet which shall be bigger than the British fleet, and, if people once get that impression, they will say that can only be done with one object, which is the object of eventually taking the command of the sea from us. Therefore it is on naval expenditure that *Attempts at mutual agreement to reduce naval expenditure.* we have been trying especially to come to some agreement, if we can, with the German Government; such an agreement will make it clear that there is no rivalry between the two nations. It is an exceedingly difficult matter to deal with, because Germany feels it due to herself to have a large navy, and no one can but feel that that is perfectly natural on her part; but we shall do our utmost to ensure that as far as we can it shall be made plain that, though we must build if Germany builds, we are quite ready to give every possible guarantee that can be given that we are building with no aggressive purpose, and, indeed, so far as Germany is concerned, we could not build a fleet with any aggressive purpose so long as we keep our army within its present small dimensions. Because Germany, with her powerful army, if she had a fleet bigger than the British fleet, obviously could not only defeat us at sea, but could be in London in a very short time with her army. But however much our fleet is superior to the German fleet, however much we defeat the German fleet, with the army which we have, we could never commit a serious aggression by ourselves upon German territory.]

3 E

Peaceful policy
of France and
Russia. As to the prospects of the future, France and Russia I know to be most peacefully disposed in Europe; Russia is bent on her internal development and the working out of her internal government, which is exceedingly difficult. France, too, is most peacefully disposed, and in all our relations with these two Powers we are continually making clear to them our view that we do not wish them to have a quarrel with Germany, or to give Germany any provocation; so that as far as we are concerned you need be under no apprehension that our relations with France and Russia will ever be made a cause of provocation in policy. If Germany is content with the great strength that she is getting to have, that strength which will make her so strong that there is no question of any Power or group of Powers in Europe provoking a quarrel with her, then everything will go well. If she was to use that strength, which I do not for a moment suppose she would, to obtain the dominating Napoleonic position in Europe, then I think there would be trouble.

Now I have explained, as clearly as I can, what the present situation in Europe is, and the bearings of that situation upon British foreign policy, and how sea power and the control of the sea must be the dominating motive in all our relations with European Powers and in any part which we may take in European
Subsidiary
Questions. affairs. Of course, there are a number of subsidiary matters, such as the Congo, and the State of the Christian populations in the Balkans, and the labour recruiting
The Congo.
The Balkans. in Portuguese Colonies, which occupy a great deal of attention of the House of Commons; but in those matters we engage purely from humanitarian and moral
Portuguese
labour. motives. They lie entirely outside the region of foreign policy, and the general course of foreign policy; indeed, they very often run counter to it, because sometimes the line we have to take causes friction, for instance, with Belgium, as regards the Congo, which we do not want; but as they lie outside foreign policy I need not go into those matters at all.

Extra-European
relations. Now I will take our relations with the other great civilised Powers in the world. The greatest civilised Power in the world, outside Europe, is the United States. Here I need say very little. The policy of the United States has been formulated under the name of the Monroe Doctrine. We have not the least idea, and, indeed, we should be very foolish if we had, of attempting to acquire fresh
United States
of America. territory on the American Continent. Canada and the United States practically divide, I think, Lower California is an exception(¹)—the whole of the North American Continent between them. As long as it is the policy of the United States as I believe it always will be not to disturb existing British possessions, she may be perfectly certain we are ready at any time to give her any amount of assurance that we shall certainly not try to disturb, not only her possessions, but the possessions of other independent countries in Central and South America. In South America it is an instruction to all our Diplomatists that they are to regard their work there as not entailing upon them taking a hand in the politics of South America or acquiring political influence; they are to regard the main part of their work there as upholding our commercial interest and promoting British trade, in which, of course, I include the trade of the British Empire as a whole, and we have kept, and shall keep, carefully clear of all entanglements in the politics, which are often very complicated, of the Central and South American Republics with each other, so we shall not come across the United States as regards our policy in South
Treaty of
Arbitration. America. I trust the conclusion of an Arbitration Treaty sooner or later will make it clear to the whole world how very sure, not only we, but the United States, are that there can be no serious cause of trouble between the British Empire and the United States.

Asia. Then I must come to Asia. I suppose I ought to say a word about the Baghdad
Baghdad
Railway. Railway, because it is so often discussed and takes such a prominent place in the newspapers. I will try and make it very short. We have only got two objects as regards the Baghdad Railway; one is to secure that when that railway is made British trade shall not be at a disadvantage in the rates which are levied on goods

(¹) [*Note by Lord Grey.*—This refers to Mexico.]

transported, by the railway; and we should like to have some say in the management of the line or some part of the line which would enable us to know exactly how the rates on goods were being fixed, so as to make sure that the rates fixed on British goods were not higher than the rates fixed on goods in which Germany was more interested than we were, and so forth. That is one object. The other object is that the situation in the Persian Gulf—the strategic situation—should not be Persian Gulf. altered in a way which would damage our prestige or damage our strategical position. I use the word "prestige," as regards the Persian Gulf, because there we have entered into certain engagements with various of the Chiefs in the Persian Gulf under which we have given them to understand that if they behave themselves well we would give them what support we could if anybody attempted to disturb them. We cannot abandon those people who have been looking to us for many years past without it being felt all over that part of Asia, and it would undoubtedly have a very great effect in India, and so forth, and that is why the word "prestige," as regards the Persian Gulf, which is often a wholly meaningless word, has really an importance in the Persian Gulf which we must bear in mind. I think we shall be able to arrange all those things, but what makes them acute at the present moment is this: Turkey wants an increase of the customs dues. That increase of dues will Turkey. fall on the trade, and, though it will eventually be paid by the Turkish consumers, it will fall in the first instance on trade in which we are more interested than any other Power. The increased duties cannot be imposed without our consent. Turkey asks for our consent, and when she has got the money she is going to use it directly or indirectly to make the Baghdad Railway, and we have said to her we will agree to this burden on trade if it is necessary to increase your revenue; but we cannot agree to it if the money is going to be used to make a railway in which we shall have no share, and which possibly may be found to be to the disadvantage of British trade. That is why the question is acute between us and Turkey at present, and why we are negotiating. She wants our consent to increase the Turkish customs dues, and we want to get from her terms which will satisfy British public opinion as to our trading interests on the Baghdad Railway. The Prime Minister suggests to me that I ought to explain that the Baghdad Railway is a Concession given by Turkey to German Germany. Turkey has come under obligations in that Concession to find the money interests. for the making of the railway which the German concessionnaires are going to carry out. She has at present great difficulty in finding the money and in providing the security necessary for the German concessionnaires to make the whole of the railway. She has found it for a great deal, and she wants increased revenue in order to have more money at her disposal. She is quite willing to say the increase of the customs dues shall not go to the German concessionnaires, but really, of course, she will give to the German concessionnaires other revenue which she could not spare unless she was getting the increased customs dues. That is why I say directly or indirectly the customs dues will go in that direction. She cannot help herself in regard to the Baghdad Railway, because under this imprudent Concession given under the old régime in Turkey to the German concessionnaires she has come under obligation to find the money for them.

SIR WILFRED LAURIER: Has not Turkey independent power to increase the customs dues?

SIR EDWARD GREY: No, she is pledged to come to all the other Powers and get their consent. That follows from the arrangements which still exist. Turkey is, like Japan was some time ago: without a free hand to deal with her own customs tariffs, and needs our consent. Of course Germany is interested in this matter, because Germany wants the German concessionnaires to get on with and to have the control of the railway, and she is therefore interested in seeing Turkey find the money. That is how Turkey and Germany both come into it.

With regard to Asia, I ought to say a word about Persia and the Anglo-Russian Persia: Anglo-Agreement. Persia is an illustration of how well the Anglo-Russian Agreement has Russian Agreement.

worked. Before that Agreement was made the situation in Persia was really very uncomfortable. Persia was in a weak, chaotic state, the misgovernment was more than one can express, and, being in that state, of course invited interference from her neighbours outside. The Russians believed that we should use the weakness of Persia to get concessions in Persia, and to increase our influence in a way which would be damaging to Russia, because Russia is the neighbour of Persia on the north, with a long boundary between herself and Persia, very much interested in what goes on in the north of Persia. Russia believed that of us. We believed, on the other hand, that Russia was going to take advantage of every opportunity of weakness in Persia to strengthen her influence at Tehran, and get from the Persian Government concessions for making railways, and so forth, which would gradually approach to the Indian frontier and damage our strategic position there. So there went on for years and years the most unpleasant, sordid squabbling, struggling, and rivalry between the British and Russian Legations at Tehran, each suspicious of the other, and each trying to work the Persians against the other, and so forth. Latterly, since Persia has been in a state of revolution, had there been no Anglo-Russian Agreement, and had the state of Anglo-Russian relations which I have described still existed, Russia would certainly have taken advantage of the situation to occupy the northern province, establish herself at Tehran, and practically annex the north of Persia. We should then have been confronted with the alternative either of going to war with Russia to keep her out of Persia or else of compensating(²) ourselves by doing the same sort of thing in the south of Persia, and establishing ourselves there. This would have been very undesirable, because by so doing we should have greatly extended our land frontier and so have added enormously to the expense of defending our Indian possessions. One other course was possible, namely, to sit still and do nothing. That would have involved our seeing the situation gradually used more and more against us in Persia, and the independence of Persia would, of course, have gone completely. Happily the Anglo-Russian Agreement was arrived at before the revolution in Persia, and all suspicion was removed. The result of the Anglo-Russian Agreement has been that though Persia has really been in a state of chaos, and Russia has sent troops into three places in the north of Persia, she has never sent any to Tehran. She retains troops at two of those places which are just over her own frontier, where, I think, they are really necessary for the security of that frontier; but instead of sending them to Tehran, she has actually withdrawn them from Kazvin, the place nearest to Tehran, which she had occupied within the last few months. That she would never have done if she had not trusted us not to use the situation in Persia against her.

This state of affairs is unquestionably very much better than it would have been had there been no Anglo-Russian Agreement. We, in turn, though we have had to land troops once or twice, where the custom-house was in danger in one of the southern ports of Persia, have been able to withdraw those troops, and at the present moment our main trouble is this, that owing to the chaos and brigandage which exists the southern trade routes are blocked; no trade can get through, and we at the Foreign Office are getting constant complaints, especially from Manchester trading firms, that this state of affairs ought not to be continued indefinitely. We are anxious to do as little as possible which would commit us to interference with Persian affairs. The situation is really very difficult because, with chaos in Persia, our trade interests suffer, and it is impossible to sit still and do nothing towards getting the routes cleared for British trade; at the same time the general situation is infinitely preferable to what it would have been, if, instead of having complications with the Persian Government, and complications in the south of Persia only, we had to have complications with the Russian Government as well. From these we are happily free. I believe the Anglo-Russian Agreement has been of enormous

(²) [*Note by Lord Grey.*—The idea was compensation. only in the sense of protection.]

relief to the Government of India; and, indeed, everybody who has followed public affairs must feel relieved, if they will turn their minds back to the Penjdeh incident in 1885, the Pamir scare in 1892 and 1893, and the Port Arthur scare later on. What a relief that has been for the last four or five years! As regards Russia, not only have we had nothing of that kind although the situation in Persia has been so disturbing, but people are coming to dismiss the prospect of anything of that kind happening again from their minds altogether. So much with regard to Persia.

With regard to the defence of the Indian frontier, that has been immensely simplified by the Anglo-Russian Agreement which has existed, and though there are troubles on the Indian frontier—it is not my province to speak of them with Lord Crewe present to explain—I think he will agree in my saying that they are not matters now which have a bearing upon foreign policy at all. *The North-West Frontier of India.*

EARL OF CREWE: That is quite true.

SIR E. GREY: They do come up in our connections with China, but China is at present in such a condition that she does not really come into large questions of foreign policy. *China.*

Now i come to the last point to which I should like to ask your attention —the alliance with Japan. We were not in office when the alliance with Japan was first made, and I imagine it was made originally because of the trouble there had been with Russia about Port Arthur—the fear of Russian designs in the Far East—the fear of Russian designs on Chinese territory; and it was an alliance in the first instance for security against Russia. Then followed the war between Russia and Japan. The result of that war has been that Russia and Japan have no thought of fighting with each other again. Japan wants peace with everybody for some time to come. Russia is attending to her own internal development, and has given up the idea of those projects in the Far East which she used to entertain before the war. In fact, Russia and Japan have actually made an agreement with each other which secures peace between them. It is indeed more than this, for now, when we come to deal with questions in Manchuria, and so forth, instead of it being Russia against Japan, we find that Russia and Japan are in close concert with each other, and the tendency is for them to act together. Therefore the Japanese Alliance is not in the least likely now to bring us into trouble with Russia, whatever might have been the case at the time of the Russo-Japanese war. I should like to say this about the alliance with Japan. The Japanese Goverment have been good allies; they have never strained that alliance; they have never come to us and asked for anything of any kind which was not well within the terms of the alliance. I was very much struck with this at the time of the Russo-Japanese war . . . .[3] The reason why we have sounded the Japanese Government now as to prolonging it[4] is this Arbitration Treaty with the United States. We feel that if we were to make a General Arbitration Treaty with the United States the people in the United States would at once say: "Yes, but there is an alliance with Japan which was made previous to the Arbitration Treaty with the United States which has precedence over it. Supposing the United States becomes involved in a war with Japan, Great Britain, under the alliance, would be bound to go to the Japanese assistance; the Japanese Alliance will have precedence, being prior to the American Arbitration Treaty, and the American Arbitration Treaty will go by the board." So that if a General Arbitration Treaty is made—I am putting the possible United States point of view—between the United States and ourselves while the Japanese Alliance exists, the United States Government at the present moment might perfectly well urge, and would urge, if the point was not met, that they would be bound under *Japan. Russo-Japanese Agreement. Anglo-Japanese Alliance. Bearing of the Alliance on our relations with the United States.*

(3) [The omitted passages deal with the Russo-Japanese war, and suggest the prolongation of the Anglo-Japanese Alliance until 1921.]

(4) [i.e., the Anglo-Japanese Alliance.]

no circumstances to go to war with us, but we should be bound to go to war with them if they became involved in a quarrel with Japan. I do not think there is the least chance of a quarrel with Japan, because I am quite convinced that the Japanese

Japanese policy as regards emigration.

policy—her whole arrangements with Canada show it, and I find it in every way—is to concentrate her people in Korea and Manchuria and the parts neighbouring to herself in the Far East, and she does not want to encourage them to go abroad, though she has some difficulty in preventing them. There will never be a quarrel between Japan and the United States out of any attempt of Japan to settle herself on the American side of the Pacific Ocean; that being so, I am quite sure there will not be trouble. But the United States Government is perfectly entitled to say that a general Arbitration Treaty would be one-sided if the alliance with Japan entailed upon us any obligation to break that Arbitration Treaty and go to war with the United States, even in the very improbable event of there being trouble between the United States and Japan. We have anticipated that point, and have proposed

Renewal of the Alliance to exclude obligation to go to war with a Power with whom a Treaty of General Arbitration exists.

to the Japanese Government that when the alliance with them is prolonged for another ten years—if it is prolonged—it should be modified so as to contain an article stating definitely that the alliance should not entail upon us or upon Japan any obligation to go to war with a Power with which either of us has a General Arbitration Treaty.(⁵) If that is done, and done simultaneously with the conclusion of an Arbitration Treaty with the United States, it will entirely meet the United States point, and will demonstrate that an alliance with Japan is no obstacle to the conclusion of an Arbitration Treaty. The Japanese are quite willing that that modification should be introduced, but I ought to tell you that they have suggested that the modification should be qualified to this extent: it should entail no obligation to go to war with a Power with which we have a General Arbitration Treaty unless that Power goes to war with Japan, not alone, but assisted by some other Power, or joins some other Power already at war with Japan. That is a point we have now to consider. It is a detail in the matter, but it would leave it perfectly clear, for instance, that if the United States and Japan were at war we should not be bound to interfere; but supposing, say, Russia was at war with Japan, or Germany was at war with Japan, and the United States then went to the assistance of Germany, and we had no general Arbitration Treaty with either Germany or Russia, then undoubtedly we should be bound to take part in the war. It is a very unlikely and remote contingency, but I mention it as a qualification, and I put the general suggestion before you, and I think, as regards Foreign Policy, perhaps that is the practical point on which I hope a decision may be reached in this Committee, that the Japanese Alliance should be extended for another ten years on the condition I have named with that qualification about arbitration, and on the understanding that the extension of it does not in any way affect the question of the freedom of the Dominions to deal with the question of immigration. . . . .(⁶)

(⁵) [Reference will be made in a later volume to the subject of a General Arbitration Treaty with the United States.]

(⁶) [Sir Edward Grey's speech ended here and a general discussion began.]

[*ED. NOTE.*—The following Memorandum is that to which reference is made, *supra*, p. 377, *Ed. note.*]

APPENDIX VI.

Memorandum communicated to Tewfik Pasha, September 23, 1909.

F.O. 34716/659/09/44.   *Foreign Office, September 23, 1909.*

The S[ecretary] of S[tate] for F[oreign] A[ffairs] has the honour to ack[nowled]ge the receipt of the Mem[orandu]m addressed to him by the Ottoman Amb[assado]r([1]) explaining the reasons which actuate the S[ublime] Porte in asking for the assent of the Powers to an increase of 4% in the Customs duty on merchandise imported into the Ottoman Empire, and the objects to which it is proposed to devote the proceeds of this surtax. An assurance is at the same time given that the revenues arising from the proposed increase of the Customs duties will not be allocated to enterprises already sanctioned by the Ottoman Gov[ernmen]t, notably the Bagdad Railway, and that as a result of the imposition of the surtax the S[ublime] Porte will in the course of a few years be able to realise their project of abolishing transit and export duties, a measure which should be of considerable advantage to foreign trade.

H[is] E[xcellency] Tewfik Pasha will no doubt remember that it was only in 1907 that H[is] M[ajesty's] G[overnment] consented to an increase of 3% in the Customs duty on merchandise imported into Turkey,([2]) after prolonged negotiations and with some hesitation owing to the heavy sacrifices which the surtax would impose on British trade with Turkey. The desire of H[is] M[ajesty's] G[overnment] for the success of the reforms in the Macedonian provinces and for a general improvement in the Customs administration of the Ottoman Empire was the chief inducement to H[is] M[ajesty's] G[overnment] in consenting to this sacrifice on the part of British Commerce. The present demand for a further increase of 4% in the Customs duty on imports, making an increase of 7% or nearly double the duty, within the last two years, will impose a still further burden upon British commerce to which, in the absence of any special advantages accruing to foreign trade in general, it is difficult for H[is] M[ajesty's] G[overnment] to give their assent lightly.

Nevertheless, H[is] M[ajesty's] G[overnment], in their desire to do all in their power to assist the Turkish Gov[ernmen]t in the development of their resources and in the improvement of their administration, are ready to instruct H[is] M[ajesty's] Amb[assado]r at Const[antino]ple to open negotiations with the S[ublime] Porte upon the question of Customs duties.

There are, however, certain considerations in connection with this question to which it would be as well that the serious attention of the S[ublime] Porte should be drawn.

The Ottoman Ambassador has shown in his memorandum the material advantages to be derived by the Ottoman Empire in general from the proposed increase in the Customs duty on imports. It is, in the opinion of H[is] M[ajesty's] G[overnment] desirable and equitable that Egypt, which forms an integral part of the Ottoman Empire, should likewise profit by the sacrifices which it is proposed to entail upon Powers trading with Turkey. The prosperity and material development of Egypt has been of late greatly impeded by the restriction of the powers of the Egyptian Gov[ernmen]t to borrow money for national reforms and enterprises, and so long as this restriction is maintained it will be impossible for the material development of Egypt to proceed on its full and natural course. The removal of the restriction would entail no material sacrifice whatever upon Turkey, while it would undoubtedly increase the prosperity of her vassal State. Under these circumstances H[is] M[ajesty's] G[overnment], who are as deeply interested in the welfare and prosperity of Egypt as of the Ottoman Empire as a whole, are of opinion that it

([1]) [*v. supra*, pp. 375–6, No. 273.]
([2]) [*v. Gooch & Temperley*, Vol. V, pp. 198–9, No. 155, and *encl.*]

would be difficult to accede to the request of the S[ublime] Porte for an increase of the Customs duty on imports without an analogous concession being made to Egypt by the removal of the restriction on the borrowing powers of the Egyptian Gov[ernmen]t. This point is regarded by H[is] M[ajesty's] G[overnment] as one of essential importance.

H[is] M[ajesty's] G[overnment] take note of the undertaking given by the Ottoman Gov[ernmen]t that, in the event of their assent being given to the levy of an additional 4% import duty on British trade, the proceeds of this surtax will not be devoted to the Bagdad Railway. They are, however, of opinion that, in order to render this pledge effective it will be necessary that the S[ublime] Porte should obtain from the German Gov[ernmen]t an assurance of their willingness to waive their right to any of the proceeds from the Customs increase for the sections of the Bagdad R[ailwa]y now in course of construction or to be constructed in the future. A confi[dentia]l communication to H[is] M[ajesty's] G[overnment] that an assurance in this sense had been given by the German Gov[ernmen]t would remove one of the principal objections of H[is] M[ajesty's] G[overnment] to the proposed increase, and make it clear that the political promise given by the Porte would not subsequently embarrass relations with Germany.

Allusion is made in Tewfik Pasha's mem[orandu]m to the prospect of raising a large loan, on the guarantee of the additional Customs revenues, for the purpose of the development of agriculture, construction of Public Works, and the improvement of the judicial system. In the event of this project being realised H[is] M[ajesty's] G[overnment] will expect, in view of the security offered being contributed in very large proportion by British trade, that at least one-third of the loan shall be offered for subscription in London, the conditions being equally favourable with those offered elsewhere.

H[is] E[xcellency] Tewfik Pasha is no doubt aware of the conditions asked by H[is] M[ajesty's] G[overnment] and accepted by the S[ublime] Porte before the increase of the 3% surtax in 1907 received the assent of H[is] M[ajesty's] G[overnment]. These conditions, as H[is] E[xcellency] is no doubt aware, have only been partly fulfilled. H[is] M[ajesty's] G[overnment] wish however to show their complete confidence in the intentions of the S[ublime] Porte to carry out to the full the promises made by the late Gov[ernmen]t for the amelioration of the Customs Houses, &c. by instructing the British Amb[assado]r to discuss the question of the new and additional 4% surtax even before the conditions of the previous surtax have been completely fulfilled.

In submitting the foregoing considerations to the Ottoman Ambassador, Sir Edward Grey is anxious to assure H[is] E[xcellency] of his sincere desire to meet the wishes of the S[ublime] Porte in this question, and of his earnest conviction that the Ottoman Gov[ernmen]t will fully realise the equity of the views of H[is] M[ajesty's] G[overnment] and will take them into favourable consideration.

APPENDIX VII.

The Gwinner Proposals for British participation in the Bagdad Railway.

Memorandum by Sir H. Babington Smith of his conversation with Dr. Gwinner in November 1909.[1]

F.O. 41730/2074/09/44.

Dr. Gwinner introduced the subject of British co-operation in the Bagdad Railway.

He traced the history of the previous negotiations on the subject, and said that while he was confident that the line would be finished in course of time without British co-operation, he believed that with British co-operation it would be completed at an earlier date. He was therefore still desirous to have that co-operation.

He said that he would be prepared now to agree that the section from Bagdad to the Persian Gulf, Koweit or elsewhere, should be under British control, and should be constructed by British agency and with British material, the other interests only taking a subordinate share. It would be necessary to obtain the assent of the Turks to such an arrangement, but he believed that there would be less difficulty about this under the present than under the old régime.

I asked what relation the British group would have to the rest of the line. He said that the arrangement for that had been made, and that he thought the simplest plan would be to divide the enterprise into two parts at Bagdad. He therefore proposed that the British group should have nothing to do with the line North of Bagdad.

I pointed out that in order to complete the line to Bagdad, a very large annual sum would be required as guarantee and that it appeared to me that it would be a very long time, if not an indefinite time, before the Turks would be able to assume this heavy burden.

Dr. Gwinner said that he looked to the increase in the customs duties to provide the money. He was aware that the British Government had declined to give their assent unless a pledge were given that the revenues should not be applied to the Bagdad Railway. The Germans, on the other hand, desired that they should be so applied.

The Grand Vizier had spoken to him of the dilemma in which they were placed, and he, Dr. Gwinner, had suggested to the Grand Vizier that a solution was to be found in British co-operation on the basis of British control of the Bagdad–Gulf section.

I then pointed out that the type of railway now being constructed was unnecessarily expensive, that if the gauge were reduced and a more economical type of construction adopted, the guarantee at present provided for four sections, (840 kilometres from Bulgourlou onwards), would suffice to take the railway to Bagdad.

Dr. Gwinner admitted that the type of Railway was unnecessarily costly, especially in the Taurus section. He had endeavoured to persuade the Turks under the old régime to accept more economical curves and gradients for this section. They had, however, declined, and he was unwilling to enter upon a new negotiation because it would give hostile interests an opportunity for opposition.

I pointed out that if an agreement were arrived at for co-operation, this reason would cease to exist. Dr. Gwinner assented, but while admitting that economies might be made on the Taurus section, he strongly objected to a change of gauge and anticipated that the Turks would object on military grounds. He added that England, while glad to have a railway from the Mediterranean to the Persian Gulf would, he supposed, prefer a change of gauge, which would be an obstacle to the use of the line for military purposes or troops coming from Europe.

[1] [This memorandum was sent to Sir Edward Grey by Mr. Marling with his despatch No. 893 of November 9, 1909. The despatch is printed *supra*, pp. 384–5, No. 282.]

He did not give any final answer as to the possibility of a cheaper type of line; and I explained that this suggestion was merely from myself, and that I was not in any way authorised to make or accept proposals of any kind. Dr. Gwinner added that any decision regarding the change of type would have to be taken in six weeks as he would be beginning actual construction after that.

As regards the finance of the railway, Dr. Gwinner said that, taking into account the reserve of £600,000 kept in hand from the Konia Bulgourlou section, he expected that they would be about square when they reached El Helif; this reserve and the profit on the three easy sections sufficing to pay for the costly Taurus section.

As regards the remainder of this line from El Helif to Basrah, (about 1155 kilometres), Dr. Gwinner anticipated a net saving of £2,000 per kilometre, or over $2\frac{1}{4}$ millions. With this sum he proposes to create a reserve fund to meet the loss which there will be on the working when the traffic increases. Under the contract the company undertakes to work all traffic up to Frs. 10,000 per kilometre for a fixed sum of Frs. 4,500 per kilometre. Traffic receipts above that sum are to be divided in the proportion of 40% to the company and 60% to the Government. As the railway cannot work at 40% or even 45% of the gross receipts, there will be an increasing loss as the traffic grows, for which it is necessary to provide.

I suggested that the contract might be modified in this respect. If the economy of £2,000 per kilometre became unnecessary for the purpose of creating a reserve fund, this, with the adoption of a cheaper type of line, would permit of a very large reduction in the guarantee, which would, no doubt, serve as an inducement to the Government to modify the division of the receipts.

I mentioned Sir W[illia]m Willcocks' proposal for a railway from Homs to Bagdad. Dr. Gwinner spoke with some contempt of this scheme, and said that in his opinion it was impracticable without a guarantee. Even if it paid ultimately, it would not pay for a number of years. I thought it well to say that this scheme had not been devised or put forward in any way as a means of opposing the Bagdad Railway. It was proposed by Sir W[illia]m Willcocks entirely on his own initiative and without any political object whatever.

H. BABINGTON SMITH.

[*ED. NOTE.*—The following report by Sir Edward Grey of his conversation with Count Metternich on November 26 is referred to *supra*, p. 98, *Ed. note*, and p. 358, *Ed. note*.]

APPENDIX VIII.

Sir Edward Grey to Count de Salis.

F.O. 371/340.
39271/12/07/44.
(No. 355.) Secret.
Sir, *Foreign Office, November 26, 1907.*

Count Metternich spoke to me to-day on the subject of the Bagdad Railway.

He understood it was our idea that there should be a preliminary discussion between the four Governments. But the respective interests of the four Powers in the Railway were not geographically or intrinsically the same. Our interest was in the Persian Gulf; the Russian interest was different; and the French interest was different again. It was, therefore, rather difficult to have any thing like a Conference of the four Powers. In such a Conference, it might be that Germany would find herself opposed by the other three.

For these reasons, he thought it might be better for the German Government to communicate with each of the three Governments separately. The three Governments might communicate between themselves if they liked.

I said I had not got so far as to suggest a formal Conference, though I thought that the Meeting of business men which had been referred to would have to represent all four Powers, because it might deal with questions that affected all, such as through-rates.

The political aspect of the question might be disposed of before the business men met. I did not know what the views of the French and Russian Governments might be and it was difficult for them to formulate views till the German Gov[ernmen]t approached them. We had stated to the German Government our view of our own interest; and I had let the French and Russian Governments know what we had said.

Count Metternich asked what opinion they had expressed.

I told him the French and Russian Ambassadors had expressed the opinion that what we had said was satisfactory. But I had not heard from their Governments; nor did I see how they could formulate their views until the German Government had initiated a discussion. As a matter of fact, we had not come to any agreement among ourselves as to what should be said if the question of the Bagdad Railway was raised during the Emperor's visit. We had told them that we were not irreconcilable to the Railway project, nor opposed to any participation on any conditions; and they had agreed with us that it was for all of us to wait till the German Government expressed willingness to discuss the matter.

Count Metternich went at some length into what our own particular interest could be in the Railway, both from the commercial and the strategical point of view. He did not see how either could be endangered. He suggested that our strategic interest might be safeguarded if the railway stopped short of the Persian Gulf, say for instance at Busrah. He emphasised the fact that Germany must keep the Railway as a German concession, and that she was no longer so disposed, as she once had been to admit participation in the control.

I told him that I could not at this moment formulate any proposals as to the particular methods by which our strategical interest might be safeguarded : that was rather a matter to be examined by experts. I thought Busrah was within reach of the sea. But I was desirous that an agreement should be come to between all four

Powers, as it would remove a possible cause of friction and make the·political path very smooth.

To this Count Metternich assented.

In the course of this conversation Count Metternich emphasized the readiness of Germany to guarantee that there should be no preferential rates and should be equal treatment for all trade.

[I am, &c.]
E. G[REY].

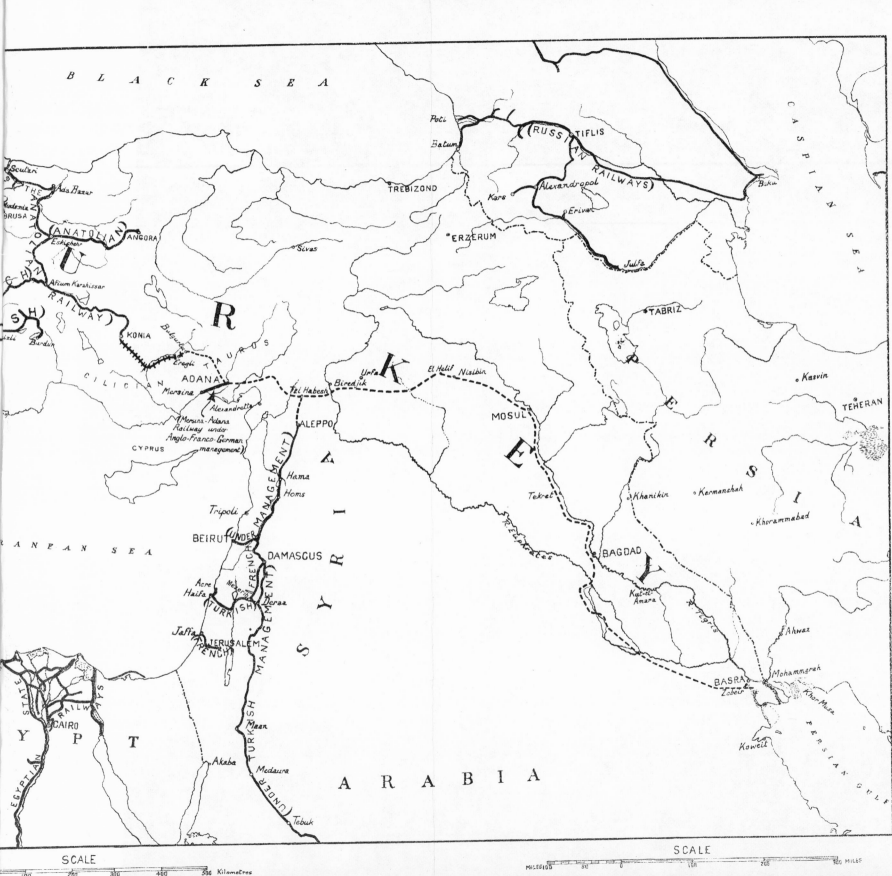

SKETCH MAP
SHOWING

RAILWAYS AND RAILWAY PROJEC[TS]
— IN —
ASIATIC TURKEY
AS IN THE YEAR 1907.

The Bagdad Railway
working in 1907 ++++++++++
in projection -----------
Other Railways ————————

BLACK SEA

Poti
Batum
TREBIZOND
(RUSSIAN TIFLIS
RAILWAYS)
Kars
Alexandropol
Erivan
Baku
CASPIAN SEA

Scutari
Ada Bazar
Mudania BRUSA
(ANATOLIAN
RAILWAY)
Eskishehr
ANGORA
Sivas
ERZERUM
Julfa
TABRIZ

Afium Karahissar
T U R K E Y
Kasvin
TEHERAN
P E R S I A

Ismidli
Burdur
KONIA
Bulgurlu
TAURUS
Eregli
CILICIAN
ADANA
Mersina
Alexandretta
Mersina-Adana
Railway under
Anglo-Franco-German
management)
CYPRUS

Tel Habesh
Biredjik
Urfa
El Helif Nisibin
MOSUL
Khanikin
Kermanshah
Khorrammabad

ALEPPO
Hama
Homs
Tripoli
BEIRUT
DAMASCUS
Tekret
BAGDAD
Kut-el-
Amara

MEDITERRANEAN SEA
Euphrates
Tigris

Acre
Haifa
Deraa
Jaffa
JERUSALEM
S Y R I A
Ahwaz

EGYPTIAN STATE RAILWAYS
CAIRO
Maan
Akaba
Medaura
Tebuk

A R A B I A

BASRA
Zobeir
Mohammgrah
Khor Musa
Koweit
PERSIAN GULF

SCALE
100 200 300 400 500 Kilometres

SCALE
MILES 100 50 0 100 200 300 MILES

INDEX OF PERSONS.

SHOWING WRITERS OF DESPATCHES, &C., AND OFFICIAL POSITIONS DURING
THIS PERIOD OF THE PRINCIPAL PERSONS MENTIONED IN THE TEXT.

ABDUL HAMID II, Sultan of Turkey, 1876–1909.
Interview with Mr. S. Whitman, May 1907, 37 (No. 21).

À COURT REPINGTON, LIEUT.-COL. CHARLES, British Military *Attaché* at Brussels and The Hague,
1899–1902; Military Correspondent of the *Times*, 1904–18.
And Naval co-operation with France, 168 (No. 106).
Letters by, to the *Times*, 594 (No. 442, *encl.*).

ACTON, RICHARD M. DALBERG-ACTON, SECOND BARON, 2nd (later 1st) Secretary at the British
Legation at The Hague, 1906–11; Lord in Waiting to King Edward VII, 1905, and to
King George V, 1910–5.
Conversation with Herr von Kühlmann, 703–4 (No. 528).
Private Letters—
To Sir Eyre Crowe, 703–4 (No. 528).

AEHRENTHAL ALOIS, BARON LEXA VON (COUNT from 1909), Austro-Hungarian Ambassador at
St. Petersburgh, 1899–1906; Minister for Foreign Affairs, 1906–12.
Conversation with Sir F. Cartwright, 233 (No. 147), 270 (No. 178).
Conversation with Sir C. Hardinge, 46–7 (No. 26), 48 (No. 28).
Conversation with M. Isvolski, 218 (No. 136).

AHLEFELD, Vice-Admiral in the German Navy.
125–6 (No. 81, *encl.*).

H.R.H. PRINCE ALBERT OF SCHLESWIG-HOLSTEIN.
Conversation with Sir F. Lascelles, 28 (No. 15).
And German Emperor, 45 (No. 25).

AMPTHILL, 1ST BARON (LORD ODO RUSSELL), British Ambassador at Berlin, 1871–84.
Prince Bismarck and, 56 (No. 35, *min.*).

ASQUITH, MR. H. H. (since 1925, 1ST EARL OF OXFORD AND ASQUITH), British Prime Minister
and First Lord of Treasury, 1908–16.
Minute by, 311 (No. 204), 368 (No. 267, *ed. note*), 369 (No. 267), 694 (No. 518), 749 (No. 577).
Private Letters—
To Sir E. Grey, 745 (No. 571).
Reply to question in House of Commons, on Anglo-German understanding, 752 (No. 582).
Speech by, at the Guildhall, November 1908, 165 (No. 105), 208–9 (No. 131), 217 (No. 135);
November 1909, 314 (No. 207); November 1910, 543 (No. 412).
Speech by, in House of Commons, March 16, 1909, 242–3 (No. 155), 245 (No. 156), 247
(No. 158), 320 (No. 210, *ed. note*).
Speech by, in House of Commons on Naval Estimates, July 1910, 495 (No. 380), 501 (No. 387).
Member of Cabinet Committee on political arrangement and reduction of naval armaments,
590 (No. 440).

AUBOYNEAU, M. G., Director-General of the Imperial Ottoman Bank in Constantinople.
339 (No. 223), 380 (No. 280).
Conversation with Dr. Zander, 352 (No. 245).

H.I.M. AUGUSTE VICTORIA, German Empress and Queen of Prussia.
162 (No. 102).

BAKER, MR. JOSEPH ALLEN, M.P. for Finsbury, East, 1905–18.
668 (No. 497).

BALFOUR, MR. A. J. (since 1922, 1ST EARL OF), British First Lord of the Treasury, 1895–1905;
Prime Minister, 1902–5.
Speech by, in House of Commons, April 1908, 145 (No. 93, *encl.*).

BALLIN, HERR ALBERT, General Director of the Hamburg-America Steamship Company.
283 (No. 186, *ed. note*).
And renewed Anglo-German negotiations, 1912, 666 (No. 493), 667 (No. 494), 672 (No. 502),
674 (No. 50?)

BARCLAY, MR. (since 1908, SIR) G. H., 2nd Secretary at British Embassy at Constantinople,
1898–1902; Secretary of Legation (later Councillor) at Tôkiô, 1902–6; Councillor of Embassy
at Constantinople, 1906–8 (sometimes *Chargé d'Affaires*); Minister at Tehran, 1908–12.
To Sir E. Grey, 359–60 (No. 255), 360–1 (No. 257), 363 (No. 259), 364 (No. 260), 364 (No. 261),
366 (No. 264).
Conversation with Ferid Pasha, 363 (No. 259), 365 (No. 263).

BARRÈRE, M. CAMILLE, French Ambassador at Rome, 1897–1924.
Conversation with Sir F. Bertie, 67 (No. 40).

BARRINGTON, SIR ERIC, Private Secretary to the Marquess of Lansdowne, 1900–5; Assistant
Under-Secretary of State for Foreign Affairs, 1906–7.
Minute by, 3 (No. 1), 13 (No. 2), 14 (No. 3, *ed. note*), 27 (No. 13), 33 (No. 17).

BARRY, MR., Director of the London Branch of the Imperial Ottoman Bank.
Conversation with Sir T. Sanderson, 329–30 (No. 213).

BASSERMANN, HERR E., Member of the Reichstag.
Speech by, 29 (No. 16).
Speech by, German Navy Bill, 1907, 78 (No. 43, *encl.*).

BAUDISSIN, VICE-ADMIRAL COUNT VON, Chief of the German Admiralty Staff, 1907–9.
125 (No. 81).

BAX-IRONSIDE, MR. (since 1911, SIR) H. G. O., British Minister at Berne, 1909–11; at Sofia, 1911–5.
To Sir E. Grey, 406 (No. 306), 435 (No. 326).

BEBEL, HERR AUGUST, Member of the Reichstag.
193 (No. 119).
Speech by, German Navy Bill, 1907, 78 (No. 43, *encl.*), 1908, 115–6 (No. 80, *encl.*).

BENCKENDORFF, ALEXANDER, COUNT, Russian Ambassador at London, 1903–17.
Conversation with Sir E. Grey, 101 (No. 68), 353–4 (No. 246), 717–8 (No. 543).
Conversation with Sir C. Hardinge, 412 (No. 310), 418 (No. 313).

BERESFORD, LORD CHARLES, Vice-Admiral of the British Navy.
234 (No. 149, *encl.*).

BERTEAUX, M., French Minister for War, 1911.
Conversation with Sir F. Bertie, 597 (No. 443).

BERTIE, SIR F. (since 1915, 1ST BARON; 1918, 1ST VISCOUNT), British Ambassador at Rome, 1903–4;
at Paris, 1905–18.
To Sir E. Grey, 25–7 (No. 13), 50 (No. 31), 55 (No. 35), 58–9 (No. 36), 67 (No. 40), 94–5 (No. 61),
100 (No. 67), 106–7 (Nos. 73–4), 110 (No. 76), 113–5 (No. 79), 219–20 (No. 137),
341 (No. 225), 349 (Nos. 239–40), 350 (No. 242), 391–2 (No. 291), 403–4 (No. 303),
424 (No. 319), 596–8 (No. 443), 617–20 (No. 460), 642–4 (No. 475), 699 (No. 525),
736–7 (No. 564), 749–50 (No. 578), 753–4 (No. 585).
Conversation with M. Barrère, 67 (No. 40).
Conversation with M. Berteaux, 597 (No. 443).
Conversation with M. Clemenceau, 22–3 (No. 9), 24 (No. 11), 25–7 (No. 13), 168–9 (No. 107),
349 (No. 239).
Conversation with M. Cruppi, 597 (No. 443).
Conversation with M. Delcassé, 113–5 (No. 79), 596–7 (No. 443).
Conversation with President Fallières, 735 (No. 563), 737 (No. 564).
Conversation with M. Henry, 341 (No. 225).
Conversation with M. Louis, 67 (No. 40).
Conversation with M. Monis, 597–8 (No. 443).
Conversation with M. Nelidov, 219 (No. 137).
Conversation with M. Pichon, 50 (No. 31), 100 (No. 67), 313–4 (No. 206), 349 (No. 239),
349 (No. 240), 350 (No. 242), 392 (No. 291), 403–4 (No. 303), 424–5 (No. 319),
439 (No. 331).
Conversation with M. Poincaré, 699 (No. 525), 731 (No. 559, *note*), 736–7 (No. 564),
745 (No. 570), 749–50 (No. 578), 753–4 (Nos. 585–6).
Conversation with Baron von Stumm, 686–7 (No. 508).
Annual Report for France, 1907, 361–2 (No. 258).
Private Letters—
To Sir E. Grey, 22–3 (No. 9), 24 (No. 11), 168–9 (No. 107), 313–4 (No. 206), 439 (No. 331),
440 (No. 333), 686–7 (No. 508), 745 (No. 570), 754 (No. 586).
To Mr. Mallet, 25 (No. 12).
To Sir A. Nicolson, 687–8 (No. 509), 729 (No. 556), 735–6 (No. 563).

CAMPBELL-BANNERMAN, SIR HENRY, British Prime Minister, December 5, 1905–April 4, 1908.
  Conversation with M. Clemenceau, 22–3 (No. 9), 23–4 (No. 10), 25–6 (No. 13).
  Article by, in *Nation* on disarmament, 15–6 (No. 5).

CAPRIVI, LEO VON, COUNT, Prussian General, Imperial Chancellor, 1890–4.
  152 (No. 96).
  Policy towards England, 155 (No. 98).

CARNEGIE, MR. L. D., Councillor of British Embassy at Vienna, 1907–8 (sometimes *Chargé d'Affaires*); at Paris, 1908–13 (sometimes *Chargé d'Affaires*).
  To Sir E. Grey, 222 (No. 139).

CARTWRIGHT, MR. (since 1908, SIR) FAIRFAX, Councillor of British Embassy at Madrid, 1905–6 (sometimes *Chargé d'Affaires*); Minister at Munich and Stuttgart, 1906–8; Ambassador at Vienna, 1908–13.
  To Sir E. Grey, 4–11 (No. 2), 15–7 (No. 5), 21–2 (No. 8), 29–32 (No. 16), 37–43 (Nos. 21–4), 51–4 (Nos. 32–3), 108 (*ed. note*), 110–1 (No. 77), 141–4 (No. 92), 150–3 (No. 96), 179–80 (No. 114), 190–2 (No. 118), 233 (No. 147), 270 (No. 178), 481–2 (No. 364), 495 (No. 380), 606–7 (No. 452).
  Conversation with Baron von Aehrenthal, 233 (No. 147), 270 (No. 178).
  Conversation with Count Seckendorff, 51–3 (No. 32).
  Conversation with M. Westmann, 151 (No. 96).
  And British Embassy at Berlin, 185 (No. 117).

CASSEL, SIR ERNEST, British Financier.
  To Sir C. Hardinge, 409–11 (No. 309).
  Conversation with Sir E. Goschen, 409 (No. 308).
  Conversation with Dr. Gwinner, 409–11 (No. 309, and *encl.*).
  Conversation with Sir C. Hardinge, 389–90 (No. 289), 411 (No. 309, *min.*).
  And Anglo-German negotiations for limitation of naval armaments, 283 (No. 186, *ed. note*), 666–7 (Nos. 492–4), 672 (No. 502), 674 (No. 504).
  And Bagdad Railway negotiations with Dr. Gwinner (*v. sub* Bagdad Railway (*Subject Index*)).
  Visit to Berlin, 1909, 316 (No. 208), 317–8 (No. 209).

CAWDOR, FREDERICK A. V. C., 3RD EARL, British First Lord of the Admiralty, 1905.
  Speech by, in House of Lords, March 1908, 145–6 (No. 93, *encl.* and *min.*).

CHAMBERLAIN, MR. J., British Secretary of State for the Colonies, 1895–1903.
  Speech by, 1901, 160 (No. 101).

CHIROL, MR. (later SIR) VALENTINE, Director of the Foreign Department of the *Times*, 1899–1912.
  Conversation with Herr von Holstein, 158–61 (No. 101).
  Memorandum by, 158–61 (No. 101).

CHURCHILL, MR. WINSTON L. S., British Under-Secretary of State for Colonies, 1906–8; President of Board of Trade, 1908–10; Secretary of State for Home Affairs, 1910–1; First Lord of Admiralty, 1911–5.
  Speech by, at Glasgow, February 9, 1912, 701 (No. 527, *note*).
  Speech by, at Swansea, August, 1908, 194 (No. 119).
  Speech by, in House of Commons, March 18, 1912, 720 (No. 545).
  And Bagdad Railway, 386 (No. 285).
  Visit to Berlin suggested, 666–7 (Nos. 492–3).
  Private Letters—
    To Sir E. Cassel, 666 (No. 492).
    To Sir E. Grey, 666–7 (No. 493).

CLARKE, SIR G. SYDENHAM.
  (*v. sub* SYDENHAM, 1ST BARON.)

CLEMENCEAU, M. GEORGES, French Minister of the Interior, 1906; Prime Minister and Minister of the Interior, 1906–9.
  Conversation with Sir F. Bertie, 22–3 (No. 9), 24 (No. 11), 25–7 (No. 13), 168–9 (No. 107), 349 (No. 239).
  Conversation with Sir H. Campbell-Bannerman, 22–3 (No. 9), 23–4 (No. 10), 25–6 (No. 13).
  Conversation with King Edward VII, 158 (No. 100, *min.*).
  Conversation with Sir E. Goschen, 157–8 (No. 100).

COCHIN, M. DENYS, French Deputy, 1904, 1905, 1907.
  114 (No. 79).

3 F

3 f 2

GORST, SIR ELDON, Financial Adviser to the Egyptian Government, 1898–1904; British Assistant Under-Secretary of State for Foreign Affairs, 1904–7; Agent and Consul-General in Egypt, 1907–11.

Minute by, 340 (No. 223), 347 (No. 235).

GOSCHEN, SIR W. E., British Ambassador at Vienna, 1905–8; at Berlin, 1908–14.

To Sir E. Grey, 36–7 (No. 20), 165–7 (No. 105), 169–71 (No. 108), 212–6 (No. 134), 220–1 (No. 138), 228–30 (Nos. 144–5), 232–3 (No. 146), 234–6 (No. 149), 246–53 (Nos. 157–62), 254–7 (Nos. 165–6), 260–1 (No. 169), 262 (No. 171), 265–7 (Nos. 174–5), 271–4 (Nos. 179–81), 276–8 (No. 183), 279–84 (Nos. 185–7), 289–91 (Nos. 196–7), 291–8 (Nos. 199–200), 304–9 (No. 204), 314–8 (Nos. 207–9), 319–24 (No. 210, ed. note), 434 (No. 325), 437–8 (No. 329), 441 (No. 335), 449–61 (Nos. 342–4), 488–9 (No. 373), 494–5 (No. 379), 499–501 (No. 386), 506–10 (No. 390), 511–2 (No. 393), 518–28 (Nos. 398–400), 530–3 (No. 403), 540–2 (Nos. 409–10), 555–60 (Nos. 416–7), 561–6 (Nos. 419–20), 567 (No. 422), 568–75 (No. 424), 581–3 (No. 430), 584 (Nos. 433–4), 585–7 (No. 436), 588–9 (No. 438), 591–5 (Nos. 441–2), 600–2 (Nos. 445–6), 604–6 (No. 451), 608 (No. 453), 610 (No. 455), 612–7 (Nos. 457–8), 621–2 (No. 462), 625–7 (No. 464), 638 (No. 470), 644–7 (Nos. 476–7), 653 (No. 483), 655–9 (No. 485), 661–3 (Nos. 488–9), 670–1 (No. 500), 727 (No. 551), 751 (No. 581).

Conversation with Herr von Bethmann Hollweg, 281–3 (Nos. 185–6), 293–8 (No. 200, and encl.), 301–2 (No. 201), 304–9 (No. 204, and encl.), 451 (No. 343), 454–7 (No. 344), 463 (No. 348), 494–5 (No. 379), 511–2 (No. 393), 512–3 (No. 395), 520–5 (Nos. 399–400), 528–9 (No. 401), 529–30 (No. 402), 549–54 (No. 414, encl.), 557–60 (No. 417), 568–70 (No. 424), 584–5 (Nos. 432–4), 600 (No. 445), 608–10 (No. 454), 621–2 (No. 462), 625–6 (No. 464), 647 (No. 477), 672 (No. 502), 674 (No. 504), 731–3 (No. 560).

Conversation with Prince von Bülow, 165–7 (No. 105), 169–71 (No. 108), 171–2 (No. 109), 218 (No. 136), 279–80 (No. 185).

Conversation with M. Jules Cambon, 472 (No. 353), 672 (No. 502).

Conversation with Sir E. Cassel, 409 (No. 308).

Conversation with M. Clemenceau, 157–8 (No. 100).

Conversation with King George V, 489 (No. 374).

Conversation with German Emperor, 233 (No. 146), 434 (No. 325), 437 (No. 328), 530–3 (No. 403), 600–2 (No. 446).

Conversation with Lord Haldane, 672 (No. 502).

Conversation with Herr von Kiderlen-Waechter, 265–6 (No. 174), 321–2 (No. 210, ed. note), 514 (No. 396), 542 (No. 410), 563–4 (No. 420), 610 (No. 455), 612–3 (No. 457), 662 (No. 489), 751 (No. 581).

Conversation with Baron von Marschall, 756–7 (No. 590).

Conversation with Count Metternich, 489–90 (No. 374).

Conversation with Signor Pansa, 489 (No. 374).

Conversation with Herr von Roeder, 733 (No. 560).

Conversation with Herr von Schoen, 251–2 (No. 161), 271 (No. 179), 276–8 (No. 183), 293–6 (No. 200), 296–8 (No. 200, encl.), 301–2 (No. 201), 304–7 (No. 204), 307–9 (No. 204, encl.), 314–5 (No. 207), 316 (No. 208), 321, 323, 324 (No. 210, ed. note), 408 (No. 308).

Conversation with Count Seckendorf, 171 (No. 109).

Conversation with Herr von Stemrich, 289–90 (No. 197), 449–50 (No. 342), 464 (No. 348).

Conversation with Herr von Stumm, 463–4 (No. 348), 562–3 (No. 420).

Annual Report on Germany, 1909, 319–24 (No. 210, ed. note).

Appointment as British Ambassador at Berlin, 162 (No. 102), 163–5 (No. 104), 184 (No. 117).

Memorandum by, communicated to Herr von Kiderlen-Waechter, 662–3 (No. 489, encl.).

Private Letters—

To Sir E. Grey, 157–8 (No. 100), 217–8 (No. 136), 261 (No. 170), 435–6 (No. 327), 510–1 (No. 391), 512–4 (Nos. 395–6), 528–9 (No. 401), 583–4 (No. 432), 608–10 (No. 454), 653–4 (No. 484).

To Sir C. Hardinge, 171–2 (No. 109), 287 (No. 192), 301–2 (No. 201), 408–9 (No. 308), 436–7 (No. 328), 463–5 (No. 348), 472–3 (No. 353), 489–90 (No. 374).

To Sir A. Nicolson, 529–30 (No. 402), 536–7 (No. 405), 539–40 (No. 408), 583 (No. 431), 587 (No. 437), 659–60 (No. 486), 672–3 (No. 502), 674–5 (No. 504), 716–7 (No. 541), 725–6 (No. 549), 731–4 (Nos. 560–1), 750–1 (No. 579), 756–7 (No. 590).

GRANDIN, French General, 1907.

Article by, in L'Europe Nouvelle, 54 (No. 33).

GRANVILLE, 2ND EARL, British Secretary of State for the Colonies, 1868–70; for Foreign Affairs, 1870–4 and 1880–5.

56 (No. 35, min.).

GRANVILLE, 3RD EARL, 2nd Secretary of British Embassy at Berlin, 1904–5; 1st Secretary at Berlin, 1905–8; at Brussels, 1908–11 (sometimes Chargé d'Affaires); at Berlin, 1911–3 (sometimes Chargé d'Affaires).

To Sir E. Grey, 47 (No. 27), 49–50 (No. 30), 700–2 (No. 527).

3 F 3

MACKAY, SIR JAMES LYLE (later VISCOUNT INCHCAPE OF STRATHNAVER), Member of the Council of India.
335 (No. 219).

McKENNA, RT. HON. R., British 1st Lord of the Admiralty, 1908–11; Secretary of State for Home Affairs, 1911–5.
Replies to questions in House of Commons, 1909 and 1911, compared by *Deutsche Tageszeitung*, 591–3 (No. 441, *encl.*).
Speech by, in House of Commons, March 1911, 605–6 (No. 451).
Speech by, in House of Commons, March 16, 1909, 242 (No. 155), 320 (No. 210, *ed. note*).
Speeches by, Herr von Bethmann Hollweg on, 558 (No. 417).

MAHMUD SHEFKET PASHA, Turkish Commander of Third Army Corps at Salonica, 1908–9; President of the Macedonian Financial Commission, 1908; Minister for War, 1910–2.
378 (No. 276).

MALLET, MR. (since 1912, SIR) LOUIS, Assistant Clerk, British Foreign Office, 1902–5; Private Secretary to Sir E. Grey, 1905–6; Senior Clerk, 1906–7; Assistant Under-Secretary of State for Foreign Affairs, 1907–13.
Minute by, 363 (No. 259), 364 (No. 261), 365 (No. 262), 368–9 (No. 267), 372 (No. 270), 404 (No. 303), 409 (No. 308), 450 (No. 342), 452–3 (No. 343), 456 (No. 344), 460 (No. 344, *encl.*), 466 (No. 349), 484 (No. 368).
Private Letters—
To Sir E. Grey, 286–7 (No. 191).

MANNEVILLE, COUNT DE, 1st Secretary at French Embassy at London, 1904–9 (sometimes *Chargé d'Affaires*); at Athens, 1909–10; at Brussels, 1910–2; Councillor at Berlin, 1912–4.
Conversation with Sir E. Grey, 194–5 (No. 120).

MARIE FEODOROVNA, Empress Dowager of Russia.
Visit to Queen Alexandra, 1907, 15 (No. 5).

MARLING, MR. (later SIR) C. M., Councillor of British Embassy at Tehran, 1906–8; at Constantinople, 1908–11 (sometimes *Chargé d'Affaires*); Minister at Tehran, 1911–9.
To Sir E. Grey, 380–1 (Nos. 278–80), 384–5 (No. 282), 396–7 (No. 295), 405 (No. 304), 407 (No. 307), 793–4 (*App.* VII).
Conversation with Sir A. Block, 396 (No. 295).
Conversation with Hussein Hilmi Pasha, 380 (No. 278).
Conversation with Baron von Marschall, 407 (No. 307).
Conversation with Mr. E. Whittall, 384 (No. 282).

MARSCHALL VON BIEBERSTEIN, ADOLF, BARON, German Secretary of State for Foreign Affairs, 1890–7; Ambassador at Constantinople, 1897–1912; at London, 1912.
Conversation with Sir E. Goschen, 756–7 (No. 590).
Conversation with Sir E. Grey, 757–60 (Nos. 591–3).
Conversation with Mr. Marling, 407 (No. 307).
Conversation with Sir H. Babington Smith, 447–9 (No. 341, and *encl.*).
And German Emperor's telegram to President Kruger, 159 (No. 101).
Appointment as Ambassador at London, 753 (No. 584), 754 (No. 586), 755 (No. 587), 756 (No. 589), 756–7 (No. 590).

MAXWELL, MR. R. P., Senior Clerk in British Foreign Office, 1902–13.
Minute by, 340 (No. 223), 528 (No. 400).

METTERNICH, COUNT PAUL VON WOLFF-, German Ambassador at London, 1901–12.
Conversation with Sir E. Goschen, 489–90 (No. 374).
Conversation with Sir E. Grey, 86 (No. 53), 89–90 (No. 58), 140–1 (No. 90), 154 (No. 97), 172–3 (No. 110), 206–9 (Nos. 130–1), 234 (No. 148), 237–46 (Nos. 151–6), 257–8 (No. 167), 275–6 (No. 182), 303 (No. 202), 312–3 (No. 205), 378–9 (No. 277), 393–4 (No. 293), 442 (No. 336), 479–80 (No. 362), 490–1 (No. 375), 496–7 (No. 382), 543 (No. 412), 544–5 (No. 413), 567–8 (No. 423), 575–6 (No. 425), 589–90 (No. 439), 598 (No. 444), 630 (No. 466), 650–1 (No. 480), 668–9 (Nos. 496–7), 688–9 (Nos. 510–1), 696–8 (Nos. 523–4), 707–9 (Nos. 530–1), 713–5 (Nos. 536–9), 718–21 (Nos. 544–5), 724–5 (No. 548), 728–9 (Nos. 554–5), 730 (No. 557), 746 (No. 573), 747 (No. 575), 795–6 (*App.* VIII).
Conversation with Lord Haldane, 710–1 (No. 533).
Conversation with Sir C. Hardinge, 367 (No. 266), 368 (No. 267), 484–5 (No. 369).
Memorandum by, Naval negotiations, March 1912, 704–6 (No. 529).
As Ambassador in London, Prince von Bülow and Sir C. Hardinge on, 45 (No. 25), 165–6 (No. 105).
German press attacks on, April 1907, 32 (No. 16).
Private Letters—
To Sir E. Grey, 254 (No. 164), 714 (No. 538).

Mévil, M. André, French Journalist.
Article by, in *The Times*, 206 (No. 129).

Meyer, M. Arthur, Editor of the *Gaulois*.
Article by, in *Gaulois*, 80 (No. 46).

Moltke, Count von, Prussian General, Chief of the General Staff, 1906–14.
198 (No. 124), 214 (No. 134, *encl.*).
And German Emperor, 8 (No. 2).

Monis, M., French Prime Minister and Minister for the Interior, 1911; Minister for Marine, 1913–4.
Conversation with Sir F. Bertie, 597–8 (No. 443).

Monson, Sir E. J., British Ambassador at Paris, 1896–1905.
To the Marquess of Lansdowne, 762–8 (*App.* I, (*a*), (*b*)).
Conversation with President Loubet, 767 (*App.* I, (*b*)).

Monts, Count, German Ambassador at Rome, 1902–9.
21 (No. 8).

Morenga, Hottentot Chief, 1907.
Incursion into German South-West Africa, 45–6 (No. 25), 47–8 (No. 28), 50 (No. 30), 90 (No. 58), 178 (No. 113, *min.*).

Morley, Mr. John (since 1908, Viscount Morley of Blackburn), British Secretary of State for India, 1905–10; Lord President of the Council, 1910–4.
Member of Cabinet Committee on political arrangement and reduction of naval armaments, 590 (No. 440).

Mühlberg, Dr. von, German Under-Secretary of State for Foreign Affairs, 1900–7; Minister to the Vatican, 1908–18.
Prince Bülow and, 62 (No. 38).

Müller, Admiral G. A. von, Chief of German Marine Cabinet, 1906–18.
126 (No. 81, *encl.*), 701 (No. 527, and *note*).
Conversation with Captain P. Dumas, 3 (No. 1, *encl.*), 83 (No. 49).

Müller, Herr, Member of the Reichstag.
On Count Metternich and British policy, 32 (No. 16).

Muraviev, Count Michael, Russian Minister for Foreign Affairs, 1897–1900.
And South African War, 205 (No. 129).

Musurus Pasha, Turkish Ambassador at London, 1903–8.
Conversation with Sir E. Grey, 49 (No. 29).

Nelidov, M., Russian Ambassador at Paris, 1903–10.
Conversation with Sir F. Bertie, 219 (No. 137).

H.I.M. Nicholas II, Emperor of Russia, 1894–1917.
Conversation with Sir A. Nicolson, 465–6 (No. 349).
Meeting with the German Emperor at Björkö, 1909, 276–7 (No. 183); at Swinemünde, 1907, 40 (No. 23).
Policy of, *re* intervention in South African War, 219 (No. 137).
Visit to England and France discussed, 150 (No. 95).

Nicolson, Sir Arthur (since 1916, 1st Baron Carnock), British Ambassador at Madrid, 1905–6; at St. Petersburgh, 1906–10; British Representative at Conference at Algeciras, 1906; Permanent Under-Secretary of State for Foreign Affairs, 1910–6.
To Sir E. Grey, 196 (No. 122), 202–3 (Nos. 126–7), 342 (No. 227), 344 (No. 231), 345 (No. 233), 346–7 (No. 235), 347 (No. 237), 357 (No. 251), 386–7 (Nos. 284–5), 388–9 (No. 288), 394–5 (No. 294), 398–402 (Nos. 298–300), 403 (No. 302), 412–7 (No. 311), 419 (No. 315), 444 (No. 338), 462–3 (No. 347), 465–6 (No. 349), 473 (No. 354), 473–4 (No. 356).
To M. Isvolski, 415–7 (No. 311, *encls.* 3–6).
Conversation with M. Bompard, 342 (No. 227), 344 (No. 231), 345 (No. 233).
Conversation with M. Paul Cambon, 693–4 (No. 518), 727–8 (No. 553), 747–9 (No. 576).
Conversation with M. de Fleuriau, 740–1 (No. 566).
Conversation with M. Isvolski, 202–3 (Nos. 126–7), 291 (No. 198), 342 (No. 227), 346–7 (No. 235), 347 (No. 237), 357 (No. 251), 386 (No. 284), 386–7 (No. 285), 388–9 (No. 288), 390–1 (No. 290), 394–5 (No. 294), 398–9 (No. 298), 400–1 (No. 299), 444 (No. 338).
Conversation with M. Louis, 402 (No. 300).
Conversation with Emperor Nicholas II, 465–6 (No. 349).
Conversation with M. Sazonov, 462–3 (No. 347), 473 (No. 354), 473–4 (No. 356).

WILLCOCKS, SIR WILLIAM, Adviser to Turkish Department of Public Works.
    Conversation with Sir C. Hardinge, 381–3 (No. 281).
    And Bagdad Railway and irrigation schemes (*v. sub* Bagdad Railway, and Great Britain
       (*Subject Index*)).

H.I.M. WILLIAM II, German Emperor, 1888–1918.
    To Prince von Bülow, 89 (No. 57).
    To King Edward VII, 88 (No. 56), 132 (No. 81, *note* (²)), 138 (No. 88).
    To Emperor Francis Joseph, 233 (No. 147).
    To Emperor Nicholas II, 184 (No. 117, *note*).
    To President Roosevelt, 278 (No. 184).
    To Admiral von Tirpitz, 197–8 (No. 124).
    To Queen Victoria, 215 (No. 134, *encl.*).
    Correspondence with Lord Tweedmouth, 132–3 (Nos. 82–3), 137–40 (Nos. 88–90), 143 (No. 92),
       176 (No. 112) (*v.* also *sub* Germany (*Subject Index*)).
    Telegram to President Krüger, 56 (No. 35, *min.*).
       Baron von Holstein's account of circumstances of its drafting and despatch, 158–9 (No. 101).
    Conversation with Herr von Bethman Hollweg, 281 (No. 185).
    Conversation with M. Jules Cambon, 659–60 (No. 486).
    Conversation with King Edward VII, 183 (No. 116), 184–5 (No. 117).
    Conversation with M. Étienne, 58–9 (No. 36), 113–5 (No. 79).
    Conversation with Archduke Franz Ferdinand, 160–1 (No. 101).
    Conversation with Sir E. Goschen, 233 (No. 146), 434 (No. 325), 437 (No. 328), 530–3
       (No. 403), 600–2 (No. 446).
    Conversation with Sir E. Grey, 92–3 (No. 60).
    Conversation with Mr. (later Lord), R. B. Haldane, 96–8 (No. 63), 99 (No. 65), 367 (No. 266),
       679–81 (No. 506).
    Conversation with Sir C. Hardinge, 46 (No. 25), 181–2 (No. 115), 183–4 (No. 116),
       184–90 (No. 117), 191 (No. 118), 199–200 (No. 124).
    Conversation with Captain H. L. Heath, 441 (No. 335, *encl.*), 488–9 (No. 373, *encl.*).
    Conversation with Sir F. Lascelles, 12 (No. 3), 14–5 (No. 4), 111–2 (No. 78), 133 (No. 84),
       135 (No. 85), 137–8 (No. 88), 162 (No. 102), 175–6 (No. 112), 181–2 (No. 115).
    Conversation with Count Osten-Sacken, 205 (No. 129).
    Conversation with M. Pichon, 488 (No. 372).
    Conversation with Mr. Cecil Rhodes, 93 (No. 60).
    Conversation with Lt.-Col. A. Russell, 594–5 (No. 442, *encl.*).
    Conversation with Count de Salis, 438 (No. 329).
    Conversation with M. Sazonov, 543 (No. 411).
    Conversation with Count von Szögyényi, 12 (No. 3).
    Conversation with Admiral von Tirpitz, 198 (No. 124).
    Conversation with Colonel F. Trench, 20–1 (No. 7, *encl.*), 109 (No. 75, *encl.*), 176–8
       (No. 113, *encl.*), 234–6 (No. 149, *encl.*), 252–3 (No. 162, *encl.*).
    Speech by, at Carlsruhe, 1904, 67 (No. 40).
    Speech by, at Guildhall, London, 1907, 175 (No. 112), 182 (No. 115), 190 (No. 117).
    Speech by, at Strassburg, 195–6 (No. 121).
    Speech by, at Windsor, 1907, 94 (No. 61).
    Speech by, to the Commanding Generals, January 1909, 228–30 (No. 145, *encl.*).
    Meeting with King Edward VII at Cronberg, 58 (No. 35, *min.*), 172–200 (Nos. 110–24).
    Meeting with King Edward VII at Wilhelmshöhe, 1907, 42 (No. 24), 43 (No. 25),
       58 (No. 35, *min.*), 92 (No. 59), 191 (No. 118).
    Meeting with President Fallières discussed, 39–40 (No. 22), 54 (No. 33).
    Meeting with M. Loubet, proposed, 1904, 67 (No. 40).
    Meeting with Emperor Nicholas II at Björko, 1909, 276–7 (No. 183).
    Meeting with Emperor Nicholas II at Swinemünde, 1907, 40 (No. 23).
    Visit to London, 1911, 631 (No. 467, *note*).
    Visit to Tangier, 1905, 159 (No. 101).
    Visit to Windsor (*v. sub* Germany (*Subject Index*), and Press, *German*).
    Visit to Queen Wilhelmina, announced, 85 (No. 52).
    And invasion of England, 117 (No. 80, *min.*), 186–7 (No. 117).
    And policy of the " open door," 93 (No. 60).
    And South African War (*v. sub* Africa, South, British (*Subject Index*)).
    Interview with, published in *Daily Telegraph*, 164 (No. 104), 165 (No. 105), 170 (No. 108),
       201–26 (Nos. 125–42) (*v.* also *sub* Germany (*Subject Index*)).
    Opinions of, on British and German armies, yellow and white races, 234–6 (No. 149, *encl.*).
    Relations with King Edward VII, 46 (No. 26); Herr von Holstein on, 159 (No. 101);
       improved relations, 179 (No. 114).
    Relations with King George V, 489 (No. 374).
    And Prince Albert of Schleswig-Holstein, 45 (No. 25).
    And Lord Lonsdale, 45 (No. 25).

SUBJECT INDEX.

3 G 4

discussed by Sir E. Goschen and Herr von Bethmann Hollweg, agreement as to data to be communicated and visits of *Attachés* to building yards, 586–7 (No. 436); German Emperor states that exchange of naval information is useless, 594 (No. 442, *encl.*); British comments on, 595–6 (No. 442, *min.*); Great Britain ready to proceed with the proposals, 598 (No. 444, *encl.*); Herr von Bethmann Hollweg's regret at delay in reply, 600 (No. 445); Sir A. Nicolson on, 603 (No. 449); Austro-Hungarian press comments on the proposal for exchange, 607 (No. 452); German reply to British proposals promised, 608 (No. 453); Herr von Bethmann Hollweg communicates reply to Sir E. Goschen, 608–9 (No. 454); Germany accepts British suggestions as to data to be exchanged, but suggests that the information be exchanged simultaneously, 608–9 (No. 454), 612–3 (No. 457); Sir E. Goschen on effect of the proviso, 609 (No. 454), *Text* of German reply, 610 (No. 455); discussed by Sir E. Goschen and Herr von Kiderlen-Waechter, 612–3 (No. 457); British comments on omissions of, 611 (No. 455, *min.*); Sir A. Nicolson on German attitude to limitation of naval armaments, 611 (No. 456); Captain Watson on German reply, question of exchange of information in relation to limitation of armaments, 613–4 (No. 457, *encl.* 2), British comments on, 614–5 (No. 457, *min.*); opinion of British Admiralty requested, April, 617 (No. 459); reply of Admiralty, acceptance of principle of simultaneous exchange of information, but demur to extending the arrangement to be of a binding character, 629–30 (No. 465); summary of negotiations, 636 (No. 468); British Memo. for communication to Germany as basis for an agreement, June, 636–7 (No. 469); German reply agreeing to main points, but suggesting that date of communication and technical details should be left to respective naval authorities, 640 (No. 472, *encl.*); British comments on, all essential matters should be in the agreement, 640–1 (No. 472, *min.*); communicated to British Admiralty, 641 (No. 473); Admiralty reply, in general agreement, but would

reserve date for exchange of technical information until the next year's programme is communicated, 642 (No. 474); date of German naval estimates to be altered from November to March, Captain Watson on effects of this change, September, 644–5 (No. 476, *encl.*), Sir Eyre Crowe on, 646–7 (No. 476, *min.*); Herr von Bethmann Hollweg on British interruption of negotiations, November, 647 (No. 477); British Admiralty's review of the question and proposals, December, 647–9 (No. 478); a full and final statement, 652 (No. 481), forwarded to Sir E. Goschen with instructions to offer his view as to advisability of reopening the discussion, 652 (No. 482); Sir E. Goschen on question of resumption of negotiations, 653–4 (No. 484); that the proposals be submitted as soon as elections are completed, January 1912, 655–6 (No. 485); Captain H. Watson suggests that Senior Naval Officers would welcome a better understanding and that the time is favourable for presenting proposals, 656–9 (No. 485, *encl.*); that German opinion is extending that a limit to Naval expansion is nearing, 658 (No. 485, *encl.*); Sir E. Goschen instructed to present British proposals, 661 (No. 487); proposals presented, *Text*, 662–3 (No. 489, *encl.*).

Italy,
Suggestion that navy might be placed at disposal of Germany, 267 (No. 175); Italian building, 269 (No. 177, *encl.*), 270 (No. 178), 276 (No. 182); Signor Luzzatti on good condition of navy, January 1911, and that Great Britain can always count on Italian Navy, 578 (No. 426); Italy arming against Austria-Hungary, Sir Eyre Crowe on, 578–9 (No. 426, *min.*).

Japan,
Naval position, March 1907, 18–9 (No. 6, *encl.*).

United States of America,
Naval position, March 1907, 19 (No. 6, *encl.*); omission of in British calculations, 276 (No. 182); President invited to propose a reduction in armaments of Great Powers, July 1909, 278 (No. 184).

AUSTRIA-HUNGARY.
Desire for continued union of Austro-Hungarian Empire, August 1907, 41 (No. 23); German and Italian view, 41 (No. 23); Russian influence, 41 (No. 23).

3 H

BAGDAD RAILWAY—(*continued*).

British participation in—(*continued*).

(b) *The Gwinner–Cassel negotiations, 1909–10*—(continued).

Britain will only negotiate à quatre, 386 (No. 284), 387 (No. 285); Sir E. Grey understands that Germany might waive her rights in British favour for construction of line south of Bagdad; Great Britain to arrange with Turkey for Bagdad-Gulf line, 388 (No. 287), 414–5 (No. 311, *encl.* 2); Great Britain would then unconditionally agree to increase of Turkish customs dues, 388 (No. 287), 414 (No. 311, *encl.* 2); M. Isvolski on the Anglo-German proposed division and abandonment of conversation à quatre, 389 (No. 288); Sir A. Nicolson on M. Isvolski's attitude, 390–1 (No. 290), and views on the German offer, 390–1 (No. 290); Sir E. Cassel's comparison between Bagdad-Gulf and Hit railways, 389 (No. 289); comments on Sir W. Willcocks's scheme, 389–90 (No. 289); Sir E. Grey on, 394 (No. 293); the German offer communicated by Sir F. Bertie to M. Pichon, 392 (No. 291); Sir E. Grey explains British attitude for M. Isvolski, 392–3 (No. 292), 398 (No. 297): and to M. Paul Cambon, 393–4 (No. 293); M. Isvolski on British policy with regard to German offer, 394–5 (No. 294); British anxiety to ascertain Russian conditions of participation, 395 (No. 294), 399 (No. 298, *min.*), 415–6 (No. 311), *encl.* 4); M. Isvolski will examine the question, 399 (No. 298); question of Great Britain abandoning interests to north of Bagdad, 399 (No. 298, *min.*), 415–6 (No. 311, versations à deux with Germany, 399 (No. 298); Mr. A. Parker on, 399–400 (No. 298, *min.*); difference between proposals of Dr. Gwinner and Sir H. Babington Smith and Mr. E. Whittall's reports, 399 (No. 298, *min.*); Sir A. Nicolson's summary of Russian attitude, and conversations, 400–1 (No. 299); Bagdad to Khanikin branch line, suggested; British Group would like a concession for, November 1909, 398 (No. 297), 416 (No. 311, *encl.* 5); German company already have a concession, 398–9 (No. 298), 401 (No. 299); Sir C. Hardinge on Russian policy, December 1909, 412 (No. 310); no negotiations taking place with Germany, Dr. Gwinner has opened communication with English financiers, any agreement will be à quatre, 402 (No. 301), 415

BAGDAD RAILWAY—(*continued*).

British participation in—(*continued*).

(b) *The Gwinner–Cassel negotiations, 1909–10*—(continued).

(No. 311, *encl.* 4), 417 (No. 311, *encl.* 6); M. Pichon on British policy, December 1909, 403–4 (No. 303); negotiations to be continued at Berlin between Sir E. Cassel and Dr. Gwinner, 405–6 (No. 305); Mr. Marling on the negotiations between Mr. Whittall, Dr. Gwinner, Sir E. Cassel, Sir H. Babington Smith, December 1909, 407 (No. 307); Baron von Marschall hopes for some result, 407 (No. 307), and on Sir W. Willcocks's scheme, 407 (No. 307); Herr von Schoen on the Gwinner–Cassel discussions, Germany would look for some return for this concession, 408 (No. 308), and suggests future discussions for Anglo-German political understanding, 408 (No. 308); Sir E. Goschen on, 408–9 (No. 308); Sir E. Grey suggests that British *quid pro quo* is consent to 4% increase of customs dues, 409 (No. 308, *min.*); Mr. L. Mallet on advantages equally shared by England and Germany, 409 (No. 308, *min.*); Memo. of conversations between Dr. Gwinner and Sir E. Cassel, 410–1 (No. 309, *encl.*); formation of a new company to construct line Bagdad–Persian Gulf, proportion of British control; stipulation for construction of whole line from Helif to the Gulf; financial considerations, 410–1 (No. 309, *encl.*); conditions to which Dr. Gwinner will assent, communicated to Sir H. Babington Smith, 414 (No. 311, *encl.* 2); British consistent demand for control and construction of line south of Bagdad, 415–6 (No. 311, *encl.* 4); Great Britain would be ready to waive interests in railway north of Bagdad, 416 (No. 311, *encl.* 5); Sir E. Grey explains British policy and present stage of negotiations to France and Russia, December 1909, 417 (No. 312); no agreement yet between Dr. Gwinner and Sir E. Cassel, December 1909, 418 (No. 313); Sir C. Hardinge on probable procedure if agreement were reached; German proposals, consultation with France and Russia and necessity of acceptance by Turkey, 418, (No. 313); Sir E. Grey on procedure, 418 (No. 314); Sir C. Hardinge sceptical as to result of the negotiations, January 1910, 419–20 (No. 316); Sir E. Grey on British policy

BAGDAD RAILWAY—*(continued)*.
German participation—*(continued)*.
Germany renounces idea, &c.—*(continued)*.
min.); Sir E. Grey disinclined to negotiate further at present, July 1908, 369 (No. 267, *min.*).
Rumoured Anglo-Franco-German combination for last section of railway, November 1909, 386 (Nó. 284), 386–7 (No. 285).
Attitude of opposition to Gwinner–Cassel negotiations upon Bagdad Railway, January 1910, 419–20 (No. 316); Sir E. Grey on, 420–1 (No. 317); any Anglo-German agreement would require discussion by France and Russia, 421 (No. 317); Sir H. Babington Smith on German position, February 1910, 427 (No. 322); Sir C. Hardinge on, 430 (No. 323); attitude towards British co-operation, 427 (No. 322).
Anglo-German negotiations, 1910 (*v. sub* Bagdad Railway, British participation).
Russian participation,
Opposition to on commercial grounds, 336 (No. 222); Sir E. Grey and M. Paul Cambon on Russian attitude, 336–7 (No. 222); Sir N. O'Conor suggests Russian disfavour at an Anglo-French combination, April 1906, 339 (No. 223); M. Bourgeois infers Russian objections to the scheme, 341 (No. 225); M. Isvolski in favour of Russian participation, 342 (No. 227); Sir C. Hardinge and Sir E. Grey on importance of Russian attitude, 342 (No. 227, *min.*), and participation of, 342 (No. 228), 343 (No. 229), 344 (No. 232); Sir E. Grey not desirous of creating friction with Russia, 343 (No. 230): French desire for Russian participation, 344 (No. 231); M. Paul Cambon to obtain views of Russian Government, 346 (No. 234, *min.*); Herr von Schoen and M. Isvolski's discussions on, 1906, 97 (No. 63), 98 (No. 64), 99 (No. 65), 104 (No. 71); Count Benckendorf and, 101 (No. 68); M. Isvolski on Russian position, 101 (No. 68, *ed. note*); M. Isvolski agrees that last section should be international and would discuss with Great Britain, November 1906, 347 (No. 235), 348 (No. 238); form of proposals, 347 (No. 236), M. Isvolski and Sir A. Nicolson on, 347 (No. 237), Sir C. Hardinge on, 348 (No. 237, *min.*); Sir E. Grey on Russia no longer regards the railway as to be opposed, 353 (No. 245); statement of British attitude communicated to France and Russia, June 1907, 355–6 (No. 250); M. Isvolski thinks the statement may not be pleasing to Germany, 357 (No. 251); German Emperor agrees to include Russia in

BAGDAD RAILWAY—*(continued)*.
Russian participation—*(continued)*.
discussing rights, November 1907, 97–8 (No. 63), 104–5 (No. 71); Sir E. Grey on Russian attitude, October 1908, 379 (No. 277); Russo-German negotiations, Russian refusal to build a branch line into Persia, February 1908, 358 (No. 253); attitude towards German offer to Great Britain to waive rights for construction of railway South of Bagdad, 389 (No. 288), 390 (No. 290), 392 (No. 291); Sir E. Grey explains British attitude, 392–3 (No. 292), 398 (No. 297); M. Isvolski on British policy with regard to the German offer, 394–5 (No. 294); Sir C. Hardinge on M. Isvolski's attitude, 397 (No. 296); Sir E. Grey on Russian interests in Persia, and no British objections to Russo-German negotiations as to participation in line north of Bagdad, 398 (No. 297), 416 (No. 311, *encl.* 5); if Great Britain commence negotiations upon Herr Gwinner's proposals, Russia would have to negotiate with Germany on her own behalf, 399 (No. 298); Mr. A. Parker on, 399–400 (No. 298, *min.*); Sir A. Nicolson's summary of Russian attitude and conversations, 400–1 (No. 299); M. Isvolski perplexed as to basis of approach to Germany, 402 (No. 300); possible railway concessions in Persia, 402 (No. 300), 412 (No. 310); M. Pichon on M. Isvolski's attitude, December 1909, 404 (No. 303), his policy, 412 (No. 310), Sir C. Hardinge on, 405 (No. 305); M. Isvolski's reply to British communications giving observations on Russian views, 413–4 (No. 311, *encl.* 1); will keep Great Britain informed of course of any negotiations with Germany, January 1910, 419 (No. 315); Sir E. Grey invites exchange of views, April 1910, 461 (No. 345); informs Russia of British application for separate concession in Tigris Valley, 473 (No. 355).

Turkey and,
Customs duties, increase of, as guarantees for construction of, 326 (*ed. note*); German dependence on increase of, as kilometric guarantees, December 1906, 350 (No. 242); Turkish loan with Anglo-French Ottoman Bank, and effect on construction of railway, May 1907, 38 (No. 21); pressure for prolongation of line on security of surplus ceded revenues, April 1908, 359–60 (No. 255), 360 (No. 257), 364 (No. 260); Sir E. Grey on possible withdrawal of consent to increase unless Macedonian deficit were paid, 360 (No. 256), Mr. L. Mallet on, 363

GERMANY—(continued).
  and Great Britain—(continued).
    General relations with, 1907—(continued).
      of the German Emperor, 51 (No.
      32); popular alarm at English
      diplomacy, 51–2 (No. 32); Baron
      Holstein as an Anglophobe, 160
      (No. 101); M. Etienne's article on
      Anglo-German relations; not to be
      regarded as irreconcilable enemies,
      September 1907, 55–8 (No. 35);
      Mr. G. S. Spicer's analysis and
      comments on, 56–8 (No. 35, min.);
      that Germany has been consistently
      unfriendly to British interests, 56
      (No. 35, min.); Prince Bismarck's
      policy, 56 (No. 35, min.); did not
      desire a war between, 56 (No. 35,
      min.); German Emperor and visits
      of British Ministers, 20 (No. 7,
      encl.), 189 (No. 117), Sir C.
      Hardinge on, 21 (No. 7, min.),
      Sir E. Grey makes no foreign
      visits, 21 (No. 7, min.); desire for
      downfall of England existent in
      Germany, 1907, Captain P. Dumas
      on, 122 (No. 81, encl.); Sir Eyre
      Crowe on German hatred of
      England, 131–2 (No. 81, min.);
      German feeling of humiliation over
      Algeciras Conference, 118–9 (No.
      81, encl.), and over Hague Con-
      ference, 118 (No. 81, encl.), fear
      of England and demand for a great
      navy, 119 (No. 81, encl.); Captain
      P. Dumas asserts German public
      opinion adverse to war, 119 (No. 81,
      encl.); Mr. Eyre Crowe denies, 131
      (No. 81, min.); but determined to
      possess a fleet, 119 (No. 81,
      encl.); Naval authorities fear British
      power and aims, 121 (No. 81,
      encl.); Anglo-German relations,
      Temps comment on Sir E. Grey's
      speech, December 1907, 106–7 (No.
      74); France no objection to evolu-
      tion of, 106 (No. 74); Sir F.
      Lascelles on greatly improved rela-
      tions of 1906–7, 112 (No. 78);
      German Emperor on 1905 as a
      terrible year, 112 (No. 78).

    General relations with, 1908,
      Prince Bülow's utterances respecting
      Germany's good relations with
      England, March 1908, 141–2 (No.
      92); Prof. Schiemann on Reichstag
      desire for good relations, 142–3
      (No. 92); Count Reventlow on
      Anglo-German Naval situation,
      144–6 (No. 93, encl.); suggested
      uneasiness in Germany upon
      possible British action, April 1908,
      144–6 (No. 93, encl.); Prince Bülow
      and Mr. Saunders' discussion on
      relations of last twenty years, June
      1908, 154–6 (No. 98); Prince
      Bülow says relations have grown
      less cordial, Mr. Saunders on

GERMANY—(continued).
  and Great Britain—(continued).
    General relations with, 1908—(continued).
      causes of the change, 154–5 (No.
      98); M. Clemenceau nervous about
      situation and fears that any
      incident may cause a rupture,
      August 1908, 157 (No. 100); Sir E.
      Goschen on no outstanding ques-
      tions, 157 (No. 100); but M.
      Clemenceau suggests Naval Arma-
      ments question, 158 (No. 100);
      King Edward VII on, 158 (No. 100,
      min.); Herr von Holstein and
      Mr. V. Chirol's discussion on
      various stages of differences
      between, October 1908, 158–61
      (No. 101).

    Captain P. Dumas on strategical questions
      which would maintain peace for next
      three or four years, 124–5 (No. 81,
      encl.), Mr. Eyre Crowe on, 132
      (No. 81, min.); Sir C. Hardinge
      and Sir E. Grey on, 132 (No. 81,
      min.); German Emperor suggests
      that no one in England would
      seriously believe in a German
      attack, February 1908, 138 (No. 88).

    Rapprochement, 1908, German efforts
      for, Mr. Cartwright suggests that
      they denote a design of gaining
      time for necessary preparations
      against England, 108 (ed. note);
      Sir E. Crowe on German anti-
      English policy and efforts to win
      England's friendship temporarily,
      108 (ed. note); Mr. W. Langley
      and Sir E. Grey on German Naval
      programme, 108 (ed. note).

    Present and future relations, 1908,
      Sir E. Grey on; anxiety as to pro-
      bable future relations founded upon
      rival naval expenditure, 173–4
      (No. 111); German Emperor com-
      plains of British suspicious atti-
      tude, August 1908, 175 (No. 112),
      181 (No. 115); and affirms his
      pacific intentions, 175 (No. 112),
      181 (No. 115), 186 (No. 117);
      result of a war would be mutual
      ruin to the benefit of America,
      181 (No. 115).

    Sir F. Lascelles terminates his appoint-
      ment as British Ambassador, 162
      (No. 102); appointment of Sir E.
      Goschen, 162 (No. 102); Sir E.
      Grey reviews the situation for
      Sir E. Goschen, 163–5 (No. 104).

    General relations with, 1909,
      Good effect of Franco-German Morocco
      Agreement and Sir E. Grey's
      friendly message, February 1909,
      230 (No. 145, ed. note), 234 (No.
      148); German press indicate
      possibility of an understanding
      with England, March 1909, 247–8
      (No. 158, and min.); Prince Bülow

GERMANY—*(continued)*.

and Great Britain—*(continued)*.

General relations with, 1909—(continued).

on furtherance of friendship between, 257 (No. 166); Mr. Findlay on moderate and courteous attitude of German press, 258–9 (No. 168); Mr. G. H. Villiers, Sir Eyre Crowe, Mr. Langley and Sir C. Hardinge on, 259–60 (No. 168, *min.*); Professor Schiemann suggests an Anglo-German-Austro-Hungarian Alliance, April 1909, 260 (No. 169); British views of, 260–1 (No. 169, *min.*); suggestions of German press and Herr von Kiderlen-Waechter for Anglo-German political *entente* or a naval convention, April 1909, 265–6 (No. 174); British views on motives for and undesirability of, 266 (No. 174, *min.*), 267 (No. 175, *min.*); Herr von Schoen suggests an understanding upon Colonial Affairs, May 1909, 271 (No. 179); British views on, 271–2 (No. 179, *min.*); article by Herr F. Dernburg advocating a better Anglo-German understanding, 272–3 (No. 180); Sir E. Grey's conversation with Count Metternich on Anglo-German relations, June 1909, 275–6 (No. 182); Herr von Schoen on necessity for an understanding of some sort, June 1909, 277–8 (No. 183); Naval question dominates the situation, 277–8 (No. 183, and *min.*); Prince Bülow's conversation with Sir E. Goschen, July 1909, 279–82 (No. 185); Prince Bülow on consequences of a war, 280 (No. 185); Herr von Schoen's conversation with Sir E. Goschen on Anglo-German relations, July 1909, 280–1 (No. 185); Herr von Bethmann Hollweg's declaration of friendly feelings, 281 (No. 185); and readiness to exchange views on Anglo-German relations, 283 (No. 186); and suggests the lines of an understanding, 284 (No. 187); Mr. Langley on difficulty of finding a formula, 284 (No. 187, *min.*); Sir E. Grey would welcome proposals, 284 (No. 187, *min.*), 285 (No. 188), 288 (No. 193), 288 (No. 194); Sir E. Grey on a general political understanding, 284 (No. 187, *min.*); Sir C. Hardinge on the proposals, 285 (No. 189); suggests a declaration of general policy, 286 (No. 190); Mr. L. Mallet on the proposals, Russia should be informed, 286–7 (No. 191); Sir E. Goschen on effect upon French and Russian relations, 287 (No. 192); Sir E. Grey on effect with France and Russia and desirability of

GERMANY—*(continued)*.

and Great Britain—*(continued)*.

General relations with, 1909—(continued).

enlarging to include, 288 (No. 194), 289 (No. 195).

(For a continuance of these proposals as regards naval affairs, *v. sub* Armaments, Naval.)

German delay in negotiations until October 1909, 289 (No. 196), 290 (No. 197); Herr Stemrich on possibility of opposition, 290 (No. 197); German view that a declaration should precede the suggested naval arrangement, 290 (No. 197); King Edward VII on, 291 (No. 197, *min.*); Sir A. Nicolson and M. Isvolski on the suggested understanding, September 1909, 291 (No. 198); conversation between Herr von Bethmann Hollweg, Herr von Schoen and Sir E. Goschen, October 1909 : suggested exchange of pacific assurances; to precede naval arrangement, 293–300 (No. 200, and *encl.*); Herr von Schoen suggests an agreement on the lines of the Baltic Agreement, 295 (No. 200); existing friendships of Great Britain with other Powers not to be disturbed, 293, 297 (No. 200, and *encl.*); desire for secrecy concerning negotiations, 297 (No. 200, *encl.*); Great Britain could not grant Germany more than to existing *Entente* Powers, 294, 297 (No. 200, and *encl.*), 305–6 (No. 204), 308 (No. 204, *encl.*); outlines of a general declaration of friendship, 294, 297 (No. 200, and *encl.*); non-intervention in case of attack upon other Power, 305–6 (No. 204); Sir Eyre Crowe on the vagueness of German proposals and considerations arising therefrom, 298–9 (No. 200, *min.*); Mr. Langley on, 299 (No. 200, *min.*); Sir C. Hardinge on basis of Baltic Agreement as unacceptable, and a suggested reply to German Chancellor, 299–300 (No. 200, *min.*); Sir E. Goschen's account of the conversations, 301–2 (No. 201); Sir E. Grey would be ready to proceed with the negotiations, no difficulty in giving pacific assurances, a general understanding of no benefit if naval expenditure remained undiminished, 303–4 (No. 202); is ready to receive proposals, 304 (No. 203); conversations continued, November 1909, 304–12 (No. 204); German suggestion that a naval arrangement and political assurances should be simultaneous, 305, 307 (No. 204, *encl.*), 313 (No. 205); question of an unprovoked attack, 305–6 (No. 204), 308 (No. 204, *encl.*); Sir E.

3 K 4

RUSSIA—(continued).
and Germany—(continued).
likelihood of German complaisancy towards Russia for next few years, 125 (No. 81, encl.); meeting of German and Russian Emperor's at Björkö, June 1909 : no arrangements concluded, 276–7 (No. 183); General Foch on German policy towards Russia, April 1911, 618 (No. 460, encl.); German press on, 653 (No. 483).

and Great Britain,
Anglo-French-Russian Triple Alliance suggested, May 1908, 150 (No. 95); visit of King Edward VII to Reval, 150 (No. 95); possible grave effect with Germany, 151 (No. 96); Sir E. Grey on no reason for apprehension, no new agreement proposed, 154 (No. 97); Prince Bülow and M. Isvolski on close understanding between, November 1908, 203 (No. 127); Count Metternich and Sir E. Grey on Anglo-Russian friendship, 275–6 (No. 182).

German press foreshadows an understanding, 16 (No. 5); Sir E. Grey on general relations with, 1911, 782–3, 785, 787–8 (App. V).

Negotiations, re Indian Frontier, March 1907, 354 (No. 247).

Scope of Anglo-German discussions communicated to Count Benckendorff, March 1911, 603 (No. 448); as also Lord Haldane's conversations with Herr von Bethmann Hollweg, February 1912, 692 (No. 515); Russian attitude towards conversations and enquiry re South Persia, 694 (No. 519); Sir E. Grey on main object of conversations to remove suspicions and misapprehensions : Great Britain considering steps for re-establishment of order in South Persia, 695 (No. 520); Russian attitude towards Lord Haldane's visit, 696 (No. 522); draft formula communicated to Russia, March 1912, 717–8 (No. 543).

Visit of King Edward VII to Cronberg and Ischl, 1908; Russian Minister informed of conversations, 196 (No. 123).

and Persia (v. sub Persia).
and South African War (v. sub Africa, South, British).

ST. LUCIA BAY.
German raids on, 56 (No. 35, min.).

SAMOA.
Anglo-German agreements re, 57 (No. 35, min.); Mr. C. Rhodes and difficulties in, 93 (No. 60).

SERVIA.
Alleged British financial assistance to, 253 (No. 162, and min.).

SPAIN.
and Germany, general relations, April 1907, 30 (No. 16).

SWEDEN.
Attitude towards arbitration and disarmament, Count Taube on, 624 (No. 463).

SYRIAN RAILWAYS.
and Bagdad Railway, 352 (No. 245), 404 (No. 303).

TABAH INCIDENT.
German influence and, 58 (No. 35, min.).

TIMOR, ISLAND OF.
Anglo-German discussions re, 679 (No. 506), 684 (No. 506), 697 (No. 523), 697–8 (No. 524), 706 (No. 529, min.), 710 (No. 532), 724 (No. 547, encl.).

TREATIES, AGREEMENTS, ALLIANCES, &c.
i. Agreements, &c.
Anglo-French Agreements, 8 April, 1904, (for views on the Anglo-French entente, and effects of v. sub France, and Great Britain).
Anglo-German Arbitration Treaty, 57 (No. 35, min.).
Anglo-German Secret Convention, 30 August, 1898, re Portuguese Colonies in Africa,
Anglo-German discussions, 1912, and, 651 (No. 480), 703 (No. 528), 724 (No. 547, encl.) (v. also sub Africa, Portuguese Colonies).
Anglo-Japanese Alliance, 30 January, 1902, Sir E. Grey on its origin and renewal, 789 (App. V).
Anglo-Russian Convention, 31 August, 1907, commented on by Frankfort Gazette, March 1907, 16 (No. 5); Prince Bülow welcomes the Agreement, August 1907, 43–4 (No. 25), 48 (No. 28); German interests not infringed by, 91 (No. 59); suggested Russian concessions in Persia and, 401 (No. 299); Sir E. Grey's review of the agreement for the Committee of Imperial Defence, 787–9 (App. V).
Baltic Agreement, Denmark, Germany, Russia and Sweden, 23 April, 1908, 295, 298 (No. 200, and min.).
Dreikaiserbund (v. supra, Alliance, Austria-Hungary, Germany, Russia).
Egypt, Khedivial Decrees, 1904, German adhesion to, 57 (No. 35, min.).
Franco-German Agreement relating to Morocco, 9 February, 1909, 230 (No. 145, ed. note), 234 (No. 148).
Franco-German Commercial Treaty suggested, August 1907, 49 (No. 30).